MEDITERRANEAN SEA

Siwa Oasis

WESTERN DESERT

Bahariya Oasis

Dakhla Oasis

Kharga Oasis

FAIYUM BASIN

Medinet el-Fayum

Hawara

Oxyrhynchus

Hermopolis Magna
el-Ashmunein

Tuna el-Gebel

Meir

Asyut

Cusae

Hatnub

Bersheh

Antinoöpolis

Beni Hasan

Zawyet el-Amwat

el-Amarna

Badari

Antaeopolis

Abydos

Akhmim

Diospolis Parva

Gebelein

Hierakonpolis

Esna

Edfu

Elkab

Mo'alla

Armant

Naqada

Coptos

Dendera

Thebes (Luxor)

Valley of
the Kings

Gebel es-Silsila

UPPER EGYPT

EASTERN DESERT

LOWER EGYPT

Memphis

el-Lisht

Illahun

Herakleopolis

Meidum

Gulf of Suez

SINAI

Wadi Mughara

ARABIA

Gulf of Aqaba

RED SEA

PALESTINE

Gaza

Joppa

Jerusalem

Dead Sea

THE OXFORD ENCYCLOPEDIA OF ANCIENT EGYPT

G

GAMES. The ancient Egyptians possessed many types of games, both athletic and sedentary, which became known from illustrations on tomb and temple walls, from text references, and from surviving game equipment. Some games were enjoyed exclusively by the royalty and nobility; some transcended class; some were played only by children; many had religious significance. Like those of the ancient Greek, Egyptian athletic games had been derived from competitive manly pursuits: running, hunting, fighting, throwing, and so on. The Egyptian national attitude toward them was, however, entirely different from that of the Greek. Whereas the Greeks extolled the individual champion, the Egyptians could accept no champion other than the king. For this reason, we know little about organized Egyptian sports and even less about the nonroyal competitors.

Sports played an important role in ancient Egyptian kingship ideology. Since the strength of the state was identified with the king's strength, the king periodically had to prove his fitness and to renew it magically. Part of his *sed*-festival, a jubilee that was held after thirty years of rule, involved a foot race around a course in which the king was the only runner and in which his only competitor was infirmity. The third dynasty's Djoser complex at Saqqara preserves such a race course; it has been called "the world's oldest surviving sports facility."

In Egypt, from earliest times, much emphasis was placed on running. The kings performed their ritual runs at the coronation and at the *sed*-festival; there, too, soldiers were awarded the title of "swift runner" and royal guards ran beside the king's chariot. No evidence exists for competitive running, however, until the Dahshur stela of Taharqa (c.684 BCE), which records a royally sponsored footrace, from Memphis to the Faiyum and back, by units of the army. While the winners and runners-up received prizes, the king interpreted the excellent overall performance of his troops as a confirmation of his own superiority.

The mastery of horses and chariots and the use of the composite bow were activities introduced into Egypt by the Near Eastern conquerors known as the Hyksos (who ruled Egypt during the fifteenth and sixteenth dynasties), and by the early eighteenth dynasty, these had been adopted by the Egyptian elite and were combined to create a new royal sporting tradition. Although target archery is known from the fourth dynasty, the introduction of the costly and powerful composite bow—which combined hard and soft woods, horn, and animal sinews—made archery a favorite sport of kings, performed either on foot or from a moving chariot. On his Armant Stela, Thutmose III (of the eighteenth dynasty) recorded shooting and piercing copper ingots, a boast perpetuated by most later kings to Ramesses II (of the nineteenth dynasty). Amenhotpe II (of the eighteenth dynasty), trained in archery from childhood, bragged of shooting arrows through copper ingots in series while driving his own chariot, reins around his waist; his Medamud Stela records a challenge he made to his courtiers to better his shots, offering the only hint of competition between king and commoners. Ordinary mortals could never officially surpass the performance of kings, but kings could surpass their own records and those of earlier kings.

Wrestling appears in Egyptian art as early as the first dynasty. Wrestling pairs are known among Old Kingdom servant figurines, and naked boys wrestle in the fifth dynasty tomb of Ptahhotep at Saqqara. In the twelfth dynasty tombs at Beni Hasan, there are some two hundred depictions of wrestlers. At Bersheh, wrestlers even appear with a referee. Wrestling became a part of royal ceremonial during the New Kingdom, where the contestants were portrayed as soldiers of Nubian origin. The Theban tomb of Tjanuni (tomb 74) has a scene with a group of Nubian wrestlers carrying a standard, suggesting that they belonged to a special wrestling unit. At the sites of Tell el-Amarna and Medinet Habu, Egyptian wrestlers and foreign opponents were represented fighting each other before the king. Presumably, the Egyptian in each pair had to win in order to ensure that the king would dominate foreign nations.

Stick fighting sometimes accompanied ritual wrestling. The contestants often used boardlike shields that were fastened to their left forearms. They wore protective padding for their faces. Some examples of their cudgels have survived from the tomb of Tutankhamun (of the eighteenth dynasty). Boxing has appeared only once, in the Theban tomb of Kheruef (tomb 192), where it was shown with stick fighting in connection with the ritual of raising the Djed pillar.

The ancient Egyptians enjoyed many types of water sports. The biography of Kheti (of the eleventh dynasty)

GAMES. *Gameboard and playing pieces for the game* senet, *eighteenth dynasty, reign of Thutmose III.* It is made of wood, inlaid with panels of faience. (The Metropolitan Museum of Art, Gift of Egypt Exploration Fund, 1901. [01.4.1A-P])

reveals that children were taught to swim. Frequently illustrated on tomb walls were family outings on papyrus rafts in the Nile marshes, undertaken for the pleasure of fishing or for hunting birds with throwsticks. Some tombs of the Old and Middle Kingdoms have scenes of a water sport in which teams of men on papyrus rafts attempted to push each other with poles into the water or to overturn their boats. Although there is no evidence for boat races, they must have been held. Amenhotpe II recorded working the rowers of his ship to exhaustion while he held the helm over a course of three *iteru* (*itrw;* about 31 kilometers/20 miles).

In some twelfth dynasty tombs, women were depicted catching and juggling balls, sometimes while sitting upon the shoulders of others. Many original Egyptian balls survive, made either of leather (sewn around a core of straw, hair, or yarn) or of wood, clay, papyrus, or palm leaves. A royal ritual game called "hitting the ball" has been represented abundantly between the eighteenth dynasty and Ptolemaic times; there, the king hit a ball with a bat in a symbolic act thought to damage the eye of the demon Apophis. In the Edifice of Taharqa at Karnak, the king was shown ceremonially, throwing four balls, toward the four cardinal points of the compass.

Children's games, illustrated in five tombs of the Old and Middle Kingdoms, included jumping contests, contortionist competitions, games in which boys were carried on the arms or backs of others, tugs of war, whirling games designed to induce dizziness, guessing games, games with hoops and sticks, and others.

The Egyptians had at least four board games. Three can be documented from the first dynasty; they also were found as complete sets in a third dynasty painting in the tomb of Hesy-Re at Saqqara. Their names occur in a fourth dynasty offering list in the tomb of Rahotep at Meidum. The fourth game seems to have entered Egypt as an import from the Near East during the seventeenth dynasty. The most popular of the original three was *senet* (*znt;* "passing"), which can be documented from Predynastic to Roman times. Its longevity was due to its role as an allegory about the struggle of the dead to attain the happy afterlife. It thus became standard funerary equipment and was even depicted regularly in the *Book of Going Forth by Day* (*Book of the Dead*), in chapter 17. It was a game for two, played on a rectangular board of thirty squares (10 × 3). Each player used seven pieces and controlled the moves by means of flat two-sided dice sticks. By blocking and by leaping the opponent's pieces, a player attempted to remove all his or her pieces from the board first, which became a symbol of resurrection.

The second game, *men* (*mn;* "endurance"), was also a game for two, played on a long narrow board that was ruled into thirteen or more sections. Each player used five pieces and moved them probably by means of stick dice. Actual remains of this game are rare, but it appears to have been a race game. In its original form the game disappeared even before the Old Kingdom, but a very similar game, played with carved pegs on boards with two tracks of thirty holes each, made an appearance in the First Intermediate Period and continued to be shown well into the Late period. Numerous examples were found in the Near East, but it is unclear whether the original Egyptian *men* game was redesigned as a peg game in Egypt and exported or whether it was replaced by the peg game as a more entertaining foreign import.

The third game was *mehen* (*mhn;* "serpent"). It was played on a round slotted board, in the form of a coiled snake. In Hesy-Re's painting, the board is accompanied by a box divided into six compartments, each containing six marbles of one color and a lion-shaped piece, suggesting that up to six could play the game. In the fifth dynasty tomb of Rashepses at Saqqara, four are shown playing. Like *senet*, the game seems to have acquired early funerary significance, but it disappeared entirely after the First Intermediate Period. The reason has been attributed to the sudden prominence of the serpent god Mehen, a protector of the sun god Re. Since the snake of the game board was slotted, and since slotting or cutting was tantamount to killing the snake, the making of *mehen* boards may have been discontinued for fear of magically injuring the god of the same name. A variant of the game, however, seems to have survived in the Sudan.

A fourth board game, called "Twenty Squares," appeared in Egypt during the seventeenth dynasty, a probable Hyksos import. From that time onward, it appeared on one side of the boxes on which *senet* was played. It was a game for two; the players used five pieces each. The board was divided into twenty squares (4 + 12 + 4). Every fourth square was marked with a rosette. Many Near Eastern parallels for the game are known, even as early as the third millennium BCE; it has been theorized that this game was the ancestral form of the Indian game called in Hindi *pachisi* (now "Parcheesi" in English).

[*See also* Sports.]

BIBLIOGRAPHY

Decker, Wolfgang. *Sports and Games of Ancient Egypt.* New Haven, 1992. Full documentation and discussion of ancient Egyptian games.

Finkel, Irving, ed. *Board Games in Perspective.* London, 1998. Contains articles with full documentation and discussion of the Egyptian board games.

TIMOTHY KENDALL

GARDENS. In ancient Egypt, gardens had two functions: economic and religious. The kitchen gardens attached to houses served to supply households with fresh vegetables and fruit. Since they were tended beyond the area that the Nile flooded annually, they needed to be watered. Until the eighteenth dynasty, this was accomplished with the help of a pair of ceramic jugs that workers carried on a yoke. From the Amarna period (late eighteenth dynasty) onward, they also used the *shaduf,* a long pivot pole with a bucket on one end and a counterweight at the other. With this, larger areas were watered. In Egyptian, "gardeners" were called *kȝmw, kȝnj,* or *kȝrj.*

As yet, no traces of kitchen gardens have been found during the excavation of settlements, so establishing the plants that were cultivated has been based on representations in tomb paintings. For example, small plots of land divided by raised mud paths can be seen in a few Old Kingdom tomb scenes. An optimal use of the laborously transported water would be cultivation of garden plants. From the tomb scenes, only lettuce (*Lactuca sativa*) and onions (*Allium cepa*) are recognizable; assumedly, in such plots, Egyptians also grew other allium varieties, such as garlic and leek, as well as pulses and melons. Medicinal plants and herbs were almost surely grown as well, among them coriander (*Coriandrum sativum*), caraway (*Trachyspermum ammi*), dill (*Anethum graveolens*), and cumin (*Cuminum cyminum*), known from finds that were dated to the New Kingdom. Presumably, medical practitioners had very special gardens, since the majority of the remedies known from the medical papyri have a vegetable base.

As well as foods and herbs, Egyptians planted flowers in the kitchen gardens, to make the floral bouquets needed for banquets, the stick bouquets needed for offerings to the gods, and the garlands that decorated the mummy at a funeral. In addition to indigenous flowers, others were also grown; most had been adopted from the Palestine region during the eighteenth dynasty—above all, the blue cornflower (*Centaurea depressa*) and the red poppy (*Papaver rhoeas*). There were special garden enclosures for fruit trees and bushes (*kȝmw*). These were either cultivated in monoculture, such as the date palm and the grapevine, or various types were grown together in one garden. In Thebes, at the tomb of Ineni (tomb 81, eighteenth), a rare record has been preserved, which provides information about the planting of a mixed orchard. A list cites twenty types of trees and more than four hundred seventy specimens growing in Ineni's garden. One illustration shows the garden with trees planted in rows. The most commonly cited trees in the list are the date palm (*Phoenix dactylifera*), Egyptian *bnrt;* the dom palm (*Hyphaene thebaica*), Egyptian *mȝmȝ;* the persea tree (*Mimusops laurifolia*), Egyptian *šwȝb;* the sycomore fig (*Ficus sycomorus*), Egyptian *nht;* and the carob tree (*Ceratonia siliqua*), Egyptian *nḏm*. There were also the grapevine (*Vitis vinifera*), Egyptian *iȝrrt;* the fig (*Ficus carica*), Egyptian *nht nt dȝb;* the pomegranate tree (*Punica granatum*), Egyptian *inhm;* the Christ's-thorn tree (*Zizyphus spina christi*), Egyptian *nbs;* the moringa tree (*Moringa peregrina*), Egyptian *ḳb-bȝḳ;* the willow (*Salix subserrata*), Egyptian *ṯrt;* and the tamarisk (*Tamarix* sp.), Egyptian *isr;* as well as the argun palm (*Medemia argun*), Egyptian *mȝmȝ n ḫȝnnt*. A few other of the trees mentioned in Ineni's list have not yet been identified.

The gardens belonging to the larger houses and properties did not have an exclusively economic purpose. Some may be described as pleasure gardens, which were laid out for leisure and relaxation. Their size would also reflect the social status of the owners. A large part of daily life took place in those pleasure gardens. The confinement pavilion, where the ladies of the house would give birth to their children, was situated there. Texts with an erotic background also describe lovers meeting in the garden. Information about the architectural layout of the pleasure gardens and their plants has been provided by some representations in the private tombs of the eighteenth dynasty and the nineteenth, as well as by wall and floor paintings from the palace grounds at Tell el-Amarna. The centerpiece of the gardens was an artificial pool, usually square or T-shaped; in it grew blue and white lotus (*Nymphaea coerulea* and *N. lotus*), and many types of fish and water birds lived in it. At the same time, the pool served as a water reservoir for the watering of the garden plants. In Thebes, at the tomb of Ipui (tomb 217, nineteenth dynasty) gardeners can be seen scooping water out of a pool with the help of a *shaduf*. In a few instances, the pool was so large that it was possible to sail a boat on it.

At the edges of the pool grew papyrus, rushes, cornflowers, poppies, and usually a plant with large, elongated leaves and yellow oval or spherical fruit. This may be the mandrake (*Mandragora officinalis*), imported from Palestine, of which no substantial remains have as yet been found from pharaonic times. Behind the flowers, shrubs and small trees were planted, among which the grapevine, the fig, the sycomore fig, and the willow can be identified in depictions. Larger trees, such as the palm, grew at the very edge of the garden, which was surrounded by a wall.

In the garden, kiosks and pavilions provided shade and served as resting places for the occupants of the house. Excavations in the palace precincts at Tell el-Amarna have shown that a part of the garden could also be directly integrated into the building complex; thus a garden area was found there, in an inner courtyard, surrounded by living quarters.

The architectural layout of an Egyptian garden was chiefly determined by religious standpoints. Its formal, strictly ordered and often symmetrical arrangement was meant to represent a *microcosmos*, a perfect world in miniature. The pool with its lush plant growth and animal life symbolized the primeval ocean Nun, from which all life once arose. Numerous plants were associated with certain gods. The lotus was the sun god in his early morning form, Nefertem; papyrus was the goddess Hathor; sycomore and acacia trees were the goddesses Nut, Hathor, and Isis. The date palm was regarded as the symbol of the sun god Re and the doum palm that of the god Thoth. For Egyptians, the entire vegetation of the garden—some with perennial stability and some with an annual dying off and reawakening—represented symbolic life and regeneration. Since people hoped to awaken to new life in the hereafter, in the realm of the hereafter, there was a garden with lush vegetation.

The garden sometimes played a role in the burial ritual. In some wall paintings, a boat with a mummy on a bier can be seen sailing across a pool in a garden. Egyptians also wanted a garden immediately in front of the tomb, so that the soul, in the form of the *ba*-bird, could refresh itself with cool water in the shade of a tree. In the entrance areas to some tombs, planting holes with the remains of trees have been found, usually the date palm; however, in most cases these tomb gardens must have been very small, because of the restricted nature of the cemetery area. Much more extensive were the gardens attached to the royal mortuary temples. Evidence of tree planting has been found in the temple precinct of the fourth dynasty pyramid of Sneferu at Dahshur. Avenues of sycomore figs led to the eleventh dynasty mortuary temple of Montuhotep II, and persea trees to that of Hatshepsut, which were also planted on the terraces of her eighteenth dynasty temple at Deir el-Bahri. Only one private individual—Amenhotep, son of Hapu—earned the privilege of having his own mortuary temple. His eighteenth dynasty complex included a pool, at whose edges grew twenty sycomore fig trees.

On the desert edges of Western Thebes, where the royal mortuary temples were built, a great effort was needed to plant trees in avenues and to keep them growing. First, a very large planting hole was dug out, which was partly surrounded by a wall. It was then filled with a mixture of Nile silt and sand and the young tree. Finally, a permanent watering system had to be established. In addition to arbors, royal mortuary temple precincts might also have fairly large gardens, with flowers, fruit trees, and vines, as is known from Medinet Habu, Ramesses III's twentieth dynasty mortuary complex. Avenues of trees were also planted to lead to the entrances of the great temples to the gods. The tree plantings at the Aten temple in Amarna were even continued into the interior of the temple. In a few instances, a divine grove was also associated with a temple.

GARDENS. *Funeral ceremony in a temple garden with pool, eighteenth dynasty, reign of Thutmose III.* The copy (by Charles K. Wilkinson) is of a painting in the tomb of Minnakhte at Thebes. (The Metropolitan Museum of Art, 30.4.56)

In the building complexes of large temples, such as at Karnak, several gardens were usually laid out, always including a pool. A peculiarity of Karnak is the so-called Botanical Garden, set up by Thutmose III; animals and plants were depicted there in relief, including a few exotic plants previously unknown in Egypt: the dragonwort (*Dracunculus vulgaris*), the arum (*Arum italicum*), and a type of iris (perhaps *Iris albicans*). Because those plants were drawn realistically, they must have been growing in the temple garden at that time; they are not known in ancient Egypt from other representations of gardens. Many of the flowers grown in the temple gardens were turned into stick bouquets or other wreaths, which were then offered to the gods. They also supplied the fruit almost always seen in the representations of offering tables and offering goods. Above all, for the Egyptians, the temple garden—with its formal, strictly ordered arrangement, like that of the private gardens—was a symbol of perfect world order. As such, it was an important part of the temple grounds.

BIBLIOGRAPHY

Dittmar, Johanna. *Blumen and Blumensträuße als Opfergabe im alten Ägypten.* Münchner Ägyptologische Studien, 43, Berlin, 1986.

Germer, Renate. *Flora des pharaonischen Ägypten.* Sonderschrift des Deutschen Archäologisches Institut. Abteilung Kairo, 14. Mainz, 1985.

Germer, Renate, *Katalog der altägyptischen Pflanzenreste der Berliner Museen.* Ägyptologische Abhandlungen, 47. Wiesbaden, 1988.

Germer, Renate. *Die Pflanzenmaterialien aus dem Grab des Tutanchamun.* Hildesheimer Ägyptologische Beiträge, 28. Hildesheim 1989.

Germer, Renate. "Die Blutenhalskragen aus RT 54," *Miscellanea Aegyptologica, Wolfgang Helck Zum 75. Geburstag,* edited by Hartwig Altenmüller and Renate Germer. Hamburg, 1989.

Hepper, Nigel F. *Pharaoh's Flowers: The Botanical Treasures of Tuboukhamun.* London, 1990.

Keimer, Ludwig, *Die Gartenpflanzen im Alten Ägypten: Ägyptologische Studien.* Vol. 1. Hamburg, 1924.

Keimer, Ludwig. *Die Gartenpflanzen im Alten Ägypten: Ägyptologische Studien.* Edited by Renate Germer, Vol. 2. Sonderschrift des Deutsches Archäologisches Institut, Abteilung Kairo, 13. Mainz, 1984.

Manniche, Lise. *An Ancient Egyptian Herbal.* London, 1989.

RENATE GERMER

Translated from German by Julia Harvey and Martha Goldstein

GAZA, present-day Tell Ḥarube, a large site on the southern coastal plain of Palestine, about 5 kilometers (3 miles) inland from the Mediterranean coast. The tell, which is within the confines of Gaza City, covers an area of about 55 hectares. The ancient town (called *Gḏt* in Egyptian, and *Ḥazzatu* or *Azzatu* in Akkadian) lies along the principal military and commercial route that connected Egypt and the Near East in antiquity.

Archaeology provides only limited evidence for the site's history, since virtually continuous occupation of the area from ancient times to the present day, combined with the unsettled political and military situation in the region for most of the twentieth century, has prevented its extensive excavation. W. J. Phythian-Adams cut several trenches through the mound's Late Bronze Age and Iron Age strata in 1922 on behalf of the Palestine Exploration Fund, but none of his finds can be linked to Egyptian activity at the site. More recent excavations have been conducted primarily near the coast, in the vicinity of Gaza's ancient harbor, and have focused on the city's abundant Roman and Byzantine remains.

Although Gaza is not mentioned in Egyptian texts before the New Kingdom, other sites in the vicinity have yielded evidence for Egyptian activity as early as the late Predynastic period. For example, excavations at Taur Ikhbeineh, a site on the Wadi Gaza about 8 kilometers (5 miles) south of Gaza, have uncovered both imported and locally made Egyptian pottery of the Naqada II horizon in association with Canaanite ceramics of the Early Bronze IA period (c.3500–3300 BCE). Such discoveries indicate that future excavations at Gaza should produce similar results.

Gaza first appears in Egyptian inscriptions in the fifteenth century BCE. In the *Annals* of Thutmose III, the king reports that he reached the town, "That-Which-the-Ruler-Had-Taken, *Gḏt*," during his first Near Eastern campaign, after a ten-day march across the Sinai from Sile in the eastern Nile Delta. The appellation preceding the name "Gaza" suggests that the town had already come under Egyptian control at some point prior to Thutmose III's reign. For more than three hundred years thereafter, Gaza was the administrative center for the Egyptian province of southern Canaan and the staging point for Egypt's military campaigns in the Levant. The town's importance as an Egyptian administrative and military center is clear from its mention in a cuneiform tablet found at Taanach in the Jezreel Valley, which dates to the fifteenth century BCE, as well as from Amarna Letters 289 and 296 from the period of Amenhotpe IV (Akhenaten).

Gaza next shows up in Egyptian texts of the Ramessid period, when it is sometimes called "(the town of) the Canaan." This term emphasized Gaza's important status for Egypt's control of the southern Levant. It first appears in a relief of Sety I in the hypostyle hall at Karnak, where the king reports on his storming of "the Canaan." Two other nineteenth dynasty texts in which the town is mentioned are Papyrus Anastasi I and III. In the former document, which dates to the reign of Ramesses II, the town appears at the end of a recitation of the various way stations on the "Ways of Horus," the Egyptian route across the northern Sinai. In an extract from Papyrus Anastasi III, which dates to regnal Year 3 of Merenptah and is often known as the *Journal of a Border Official*, several minor functionaries of the Egyptian administration at Gaza are named. Fragments of two architectural blocks inscribed with the names of Ramesses II were found in the 1970s, during road construction south of Gaza; they probably come from one of the fortified Egyptian sites near the northern terminus of the "Ways of Horus."

Papyrus Harris I of the twentieth dynasty includes a reference to a temple of Amun called "The House of Ramesses-Ruler-of-Heliopolis," built by Ramesses III in "the Canaan" in the land of Djahy. The invasion of Palestine by the Sea Peoples in that same king's reign resulted in Egypt's loss of Gaza and the rest of the southern coastal plain. The *Onomasticon of Amenemope* from later in the dynasty mentions Gaza, once again called *Gḏt*, in a part of the document that also names various southern Palestinian towns and groups of Sea Peoples. Gaza was the southernmost of the five cities of the Philistine Pentapolis, and it remained a Philistine urban center for nearly half a millennium.

The name of the town is probably intended in a partially preserved entry of the topographical list carved by Sheshonq I (r. 931–910 BCE) at Karnak to commemorate his invasion of Palestine at the beginning of the twenty-second dynasty. The town became an Assyrian vassal in the late eighth century BCE. Gaza was briefly occupied by Necho II in 609 BCE, during the course of his campaign to support the Assyrians against the Babylonians. The Egyptians apparently recaptured Gaza in 600 BCE for a short time, after they defeated the Babylonians in a battle on Egypt's eastern border. The town was incorporated into the Persian Empire during the twenty-seventh dynasty and was held by a Persian governor. The Egyptians briefly retook Gaza in the thirtieth dynasty, during a rebellion against the Persians. Alexander the Great besieged and destroyed Gaza on his way to Egypt in 332 BCE, and the town subsequently came under Ptolemaic rule in the late fourth century BCE.

BIBLIOGRAPHY

Gardiner, Alan H. "The Ancient Military Road between Egypt and Palestine." *Journal of Egyptian Archaeology* 6 (1920), 99–116. The classic article on Egypt's military route across the northern Sinai during the New Kingdom.

Giveon, Raphael. "Two Inscriptions of Ramesses II." *Israel Exploration Journal* 25 (1975), 247–249. Publishes the architectural blocks of Ramesses II found south of Gaza.

Katzenstein, H. Jacob. "Gaza in the Egyptian Texts of the New Kingdom." *Journal of the American Oriental Society* 102 (1982), 111–113. Surveys the textual sources for the history and name of the city during the New Kingdom.

Katzenstein, H. Jacob. "'Before Pharaoh Conquered Gaza' (Jeremiah

XLVII 1)." *Vetus Testamentum* 33 (1983), 249–251. Attributes this biblical phrase to an event of 600 BCE.

Katzenstein, H. Jacob. "Gaza: Prehellenistic Gaza." In *The Anchor Bible Dictionary*, edited by David Noel Freedman, vol. 2, pp. 912–915. New York, 1992. A history of Gaza, based on textual sources, up to the city's conquest by Alexander the Great.

Ovadiah, Asher. "Gaza." In *The New Encyclopedia of Archaeological Excavations in the Holy Land*, edited by Ephraim Stern, vol. 2, pp. 464–467. New York, 1993. Focuses on the history and excavations of Gaza.

Phythian-Adams, W. J. "Second Report on Soundings at Gaza." *Palestine Exploration Fund Quarterly Statement*, 1923, pp. 18–30. Phythian-Adams' report on his excavations at Gaza in 1922.

JAMES M. WEINSTEIN

GEB. As god of the Earth, Geb plays a crucial role in the Egyptian cosmogony; he is the planet personified. On his back, which forms the globe, vegetation is cultivated. He has been likened to the god Chronus in classical mythology.

Geb is the product of the divine alliance of Shu, the god of the air, and Tefnut, the goddess of moisture; both were created by the sun god Atum-Re. Geb has been referred to as the "father of the gods"; his union with his twin sister, Nut, goddess of the sky, spawned some of the most prominent deities in Egyptian mythology—Osiris, Isis, Seth, and Nephthys. He is a member of the Ennead of Heliopolis, a group composed of the nine most important divinities venerated by the priests of the city. The others are his four sons, as well as Nut, Tefnut, Shu, and Atum-Re. This cult was closely connected to the religious interests of the pharaoh.

Geb's father, Shu, disapproved of Geb's relationship with Nut. He set out to split the two. Geb was deeply saddened by this loss and his many tears formed the oceans. Above the earth, there was the sky, and below, the underworld. This is represented by a figural composition in which Shu (the air, the void) is supported by the goddess Nut (the sky) and beneath her lies Geb, the earth.

Geb's two sons Osiris, the god of order, and Seth, the god of chaos—are involved in the greatest Egyptian mythological conflict: the power-hungry Seth brutally murders Osiris. Their father judges the case when it is tried before the Heliopolitan gods. Geb's mythological rule was fraught with other problems. A tale involving the god Re illustrates these troubles. Geb finds a gilded chest containing the uraeus of Re, which has been placed with Re's hair and staff at the country's border to ward off evil forces. When the case is opened, a snake lunges out. Its breath kills all Geb's friends. Although Geb survives, he is seriously harmed. His injuries can only be repaired by the magic strands of Re's hair—so powerful that they cure him on contact. Upon recovery, the god of the earth is again a prudent ruler and administrator.

Geb is involved in the cult of the dead. He is said to travel through the sky with Atum-Re as a member of the crew in his solar boat. In representations, Geb wears the crown of Lower Egypt. He is also seen with a goose on his head. He is sometimes referred to as "the Great Cackler"; according to myth, he laid the egg that hatched into the Sun. As a "divine pharaoh," Geb was succeeded by his son, Osiris, and then by Horus. All the mortal rulers of dynastic Egypt viewed him as their noble ancestor. His image appears on the walls of the third dynasty temple of the pharaoh Djoser in Heliopolis, among others.

BIBLIOGRAPHY

Allen, James. *Genesis in Egypt.* New Haven, 1988.

Ames, Delano. *Egyptian Mythology.* London, 1965.

Clark, R. T. Rundle. *Myth and Symbol in Ancient Egypt.* London, 1991.

David, A. Rosalie. *The Ancient Egyptians.* London, 1982.

Gardiner, Alan. *Egypt of the Pharaohs.* Oxford, 1961.

Goff, Beatrice L. *Symbols of Ancient Egypt in the Late Period.* The Hague, 1979.

Griffiths, J. Gwyn. *The Conflict of Horus and Seth.* Liverpool, 1960.

Lurker, Manfred. *The Gods and Symbols of Ancient Egypt.* New York, 1974.

Quirke, Stephen. *Ancient Egyptian Religion.* London, 1992.

Te Velde, H. "Geb." In *Lexikon der Ägyptologie* 2:427–429.

Watterson, Barbara. *Gods of Ancient Egypt.* Gloucestershire, 1996.

CATHERINE SIMON

GEBEL BARKAL. *See* Napata.

GEBELEIN, a site 32 kilometers (20 miles) south of Thebes, on the western bank of the Nile, in the third Upper Egyptian nome (25°29′N, 32°29′E). The two hills that form it are the source of its Arabic name, Gebelein, and its ancient Egyptian name, *Inr-ti* ("two rocks"); the southern hill is long and narrow, falling sheerly to the Nile. The site was also known by the Greek names Aphroditopolis and Pathyris, from Old Egyptian *Per-Hathor* (*pr ḥwt-ḥr*).

A temple to the goddess Hathor was built at this site, and during the Late period it was surrounded by a fortified wall of mud brick. On the western slope and the northern plain stood the ancient town, now partially covered by a modern village. In the wall that juts out over the Nile, there is a grotto dedicated to Hathor, a T-shaped vestibule and shrine. The northern hill, wider and more irregular in outline, is the site of a necropolis that has been incompletely investigated.

Although this site was known to the authors of the *Déscription de l'Egypte* (1804), it was not explored until 1884, after clandestine excavation indicated its importance. Investigations were then carried out by E. Grébaut and G. Daressy (1891), J. Morgan and G. Foucart (1893), G. W. Fraser and M. W. Blackden for the Egyptian Exploration Fund (1893), and H. de Morgan, L. Lortet, and C. Gaillard

GEBELEIN. *View of Gebelein.* (Courtesy Donald B. Redford)

(1908–1909). The objects found by the first phase of exploration are now kept in Cairo, Berlin, and Lyon. The Guimet Museum in Lyon holds two extremely important prehistoric statuettes. The Egyptian Museum of Turin, then directed by Ernesto Schiaparelli, began its excavations in 1910, continuing in 1911, 1914, and 1920; Schiaparelli's successor, Giulio Farina, worked there in 1930, 1935, and 1937. The Turin Museum renewed explorations and excavation since 1990 in order to draw an archaeological map of the site.

The excavations in the area of the temple, on top of the first hill, unearthed the remains of the temple of Hathor within a fortified wall of mud bricks, on which the cartouche of the high priest Menkheperre, son of Pinudjem, is carved. Objects found include a royal stela from the second or third dynasty; many fragments of wall reliefs from the reign of Nebhepetre Montuhotep I (eleventh dynasty) and from the thirteenth and fifteenth dynasties; a foundation deposit from the time of Thutmose III; stelae and some stela fragments from the New Kingdom; and some Ptolemaic reliefs.

From the area of the town have come several collections. Together with papyri, there are probably more than four hundred Demotic and Greek ostraca, discovered by Schiaparelli, which reflect the life of the mercenary garrison quartered there from 150 to 88 BCE. Other Greek and Coptic texts on sheets of leather, dating from the late fifth and early sixth centuries CE, constitute evidence of the presence of the Blemmyes at Gebelein or on the island facing it.

The necropolis extends along the eastern slopes of the northern hill and onto the northern plain. It yielded evidence from the Predynastic period to the end of the Middle Kingdom. Among the most important discoveries were a Naqada II painted sheet, showing boats and funerary dancers; some Predynastic tombs with black-topped pottery; and a series of administrative papyri from the end of the fourth dynasty, which show great similarity to slightly later papyri discovered at the pyramid of Neferirkare at Abusir. Notable features of the necropolis included an intact tomb from the fifth dynasty, containing three burials with rich furniture; a tomb with equipment from the end of the sixth dynasty; a tenth dynasty tomb (now reconstructed at the Turin Museum) with unique stylistic characteristics, belonging to Ini, nomarch and high priest of the temple of Sobek, Lord of Sumenu. The porticoed tomb of another Ini, a general and treasurer of the eleventh dynasty, was decorated with a series of paintings of ceremonial scenes (in the chapel) and images of daily life (on the pillars and the walls of the portico); these paintings are of extraordinary interest because they combined Egypt's classical style with novel and lively elements, typical of provincial culture. The end of the twelfth dynasty is attested by some inscriptions of Coffin Texts and by the remains of the rich equipment of Iqer that was devastated by thieves and termites.

Stelae of Nubian mercenaries of the First and Second Intermediate Periods display a rough, vigorous style. These are now in various collections, including the Turin Museum, along with objects from the C-Group and Pan-Grave cultures that displayed both provincial elements and some Nubian influence.

The earliest tombs are simple ovals or rectangles. From the third to fourth dynasty the types vary: some consist of one or more rooms dug into the mountain, apparently without a façade; others are shaped like large, small, or even minute *mastaba*s. By the eleventh or twelfth dynasty, as in the area of Thebes, there appear *saff*-tombs; these are constructed with porticoes of mud brick and a vaulted corridor, and at least one has paintings. To date, little is known about tomb types of the New Kingdom and the Late period; from the Schiaparelli excavations, only some skeletons of secondary burials are known—probably from the Ptolemaic period—found in a twelfth dynasty tomb.

BIBLIOGRAPHY

Bingen, J. "Vente de terre par Pétéharsemtheus (Pathyris, 100 av. J. Ch.)." *Chronique d'Égypte: Bulletin périodique de la Foundation égyptologique Reine Elisabeth* 64 (1989), 235–244.

Curto, S. "Nota su un rilievo proveniente da Gebelèn nel Museo Egizio di Torino." *Aegyptus* 33 (1953), 105–124.

Curto, S. "Gebelein: prospettive di ricerca." In *Mélanges Gamal Eddin Mokhtar*, edited by Paule Posener-Kriéger, pp. 168–175. Bibliothèque d'étude, 97. Cairo, 1985.

Donadoni Roveri, A. M., E. D'Amicone, and E. Leospo. *Gebelein: Il villaggio e la necropoli.* Torino, 1994.

Fischer, H. G. "The Nubian Mercenaries of Gebelein during the First Intermediate Period." *Kush* 9 (1961), 44–80.

Hägg, T. "Blemmyyan Greek and the Letter of the Phonen." *Nubische Studien: Tagunsakten der 5 Internationalen Konferenz der International Society for Nubian Studies, Heidelberg 22–25 September 1982,* edited by M. Krause, pp. 281–285. Mainz, 1986.

Kaplony-Heckel, U. "Pathyris: Demotische Kurz-Texte in Kairo." *Enchoria: Zeitschrift für Demotistik und Koptologie* 19–20 (1992–1993), 45–86; 21 (1994), 23–62; 22 (1995), 40–122.

Krall, J. Beiträge zur Geschichte der Blemyer und Nubier, pp. 1–26. *Denkschriften der Kaiserlichen Akademie der Wissenschaften in Wien, Phil.-hist. Klasse* 46.1. Vienna, 1898.

Pestman, P. W. "Les archives privées de Pathyris à l'époque ptolémaique." *Papyrologica Lugduno-Batava* (1965), 47–105.

Porter, Bertha, and Rosalind L. B. Moss. *Topographical Bibliography of Ancient Egyptian Hieroglyphic Texts, Reliefs, and Paintings,* vol. 5: *Upper Egypt: Sites,* pp. 162–164. Oxford, 1937.

Posener-Kriéger, Paule. "Les papyrus de Gebelein: Remarques préliminaires." *Revue d'égyptologie* 27 (1973), 211–221.

Posener-Kriéger, Paule. "Le coffret de Gebelein." *Hommages à Jean Leclant,* edited by Catherine Berger, et al., vol. 1, pp. 315–326. Bibliothèque d'étude, 106. Cairo, 1994.

Robins, Gay, ed. *Beyond the Pyramids: Egyptian Regional Art from the Museo Egizio, Turin.* Atlanta, 1990.

Roccati, A. "Gebelein nelle lotte feudali." *Rivista degli Studi Orientali* 42 (1967), 65–74.

Wildung, Dietrich. "Gebelein." In *Lexikon der Ägyptologie,* 2: 447–449. Wiesbaden, 1987.

ANNA MARIA DONADONI ROVERI

GEBEL ES-SILSILA. *See* Quarries and Mines.

GEMS. From at least as early as 4500 BCE, in the Badarean phase of the Predynastic period, the Egyptians were using gemstones for jewelry. Several chapters of the *Book of Going Forth by Day* (*Book of the Dead*) mention particular gems as the ideal materials for specific types of funerary amulets. When imitation gems began to be manufactured from glass, from the eighteenth dynasty onward, it became more common to add the word *m3ˁ* ("true") after the terms for such stones as turquoise, lapis lazuli, and amazonite, presumably to indicate their authenticity.

During pharaonic times, the Egyptians were carving and piercing a wide variety of stones, including malachite, garnet, hematite, mica, serpentinite, lapis lazuli, olivine, fluorspar, turquoise, and microline (amazonite, a green feldspar), as well as many varieties of quartz, such as amethyst and rock crystal. By the Ptolemaic period, they were also using emerald.

The earliest Egyptian beadmakers probably carved and pierced gems with flint or chert tools, but by the Naqada phase (4000–3100 BCE) of the Predynastic period copper drills were being used with abrasives—quartz sand and emery (7 and 9, respectively, on the Mohs Scale of Hardness)—to perforate the stone. The copper wires that were used to cut small gems from the Predynastic period onward sometimes left behind distinctive serration marks on the beads. By the New Kingdom, jewel makers were employing sophisticated bow-drilling equipment to drive the drills. This technological development is indicated by the fact that six Theban tombs, dating to the eighteenth and nineteenth dynasties, contain scenes showing the drilling of stone beads. The wall paintings in the tomb of the eighteenth dynasty vizier Rekhmire include scenes of temple workshops in which all kinds of objects, from royal statuary to jewelry, were being produced. In the gem-processing scene, one workman is shown drilling three beads simultaneously.

The British Egyptologist Denys Stocks (1989) has undertaken innovative studies of Egyptian gemstone working, by means of a series of reconstructions and experiments based on the surviving artifactual and artistic evidence. Although no New Kingdom multiple drills are known from the archaeological record, Stocks hypothesized that the bow shaft was probably made from some kind of bamboolike reed, such as *Arundo donax*. He was then able to use the evidence from the Theban tomb scenes to create a replica of the ancient multiple drill and bow. The bows depicted in the tomb of Rekhmire were longer than those represented in other tombs (at about 120 centimeters/47 inches in length), and Stocks noted that the operators of the drills had their fingers entwined in the bowstrings at the far end (a technique which his experimental work showed to be essential for multiple drilling).

Turquoise. Highly prized by the Egyptians was turquoise, an opaque blue-green or pale sky-blue gemstone, the greener form of which was considered special. Many of the Egyptian inscriptions in the turquoise mines at Wadi Mughara and at Serabit el-Khadim in the Sinai Peninsula refer to the procurement of a substance called *mfk3t*. This word was once translated as "malachite," but it is now taken to mean "turquoise." By the Late period, the word *mfk3t* had become a synonym for "joy," presumably indicating the auspicious nature of the material, which, like other green materials, served as a metaphor for fertility and rebirth. Turquoise was used primarily for jewelry from the Predynastic to Greco-Roman times. The earliest significant piece of jewelry incorporating turquoise gems is a bracelet from c.3000 BCE, consisting of thirteen gold and fourteen turquoise *serekh*-plaques, each crowned by a falcon, excavated from the first dynasty tomb of King Djer at Umm el-Ga'ab, Abydos.

Lapis Lazuli. Known to the Egyptians as *ḥsbd* (*m3ʿ*) or *tfrr*, lapis lazuli was used for beads and inlay at least as early as 3500 BCE, the Naqada phase of the Predynastic. The deep blue color of *ḥsbd* meant that it was identified with the night sky. From the later Predynastic period onward, it was also carved into amulets and scarabs. It was carved into vessels only between the Naqada III period and the Early Dynastic period (apart from one Middle Kingdom example). A temporary cessation in its use occured during the second and third dynasties, and this two-century gap may correspond to a roughly synchronous dearth of lapis lazuli in Mesopotamia, perhaps caused by a loss of commercial contact with the mines at Badakhshan (in Afghanistan), the only ancient source so far identified.

The cache of twelfth dynasty treasure found at Tod comprised a set of four bronze chests containing numerous gold and silver items, several lapis lazuli cylinder seals from Mesopotamia, which were presumably intended to be recycled by Egyptian craftsmen, as well as beads, unworked fragments, and large blocks of stone. Lapis lazuli was used frequently in jewelry until the Third Intermediate Period and was featured in the jewelry placed in the tomb of Tutankhamun and in the tombs of

the rulers buried at Tanis, but thereafter it became a less common element in personal ornamentation. In the Late period, it was one of the most popular materials for very small amulets.

Quartz. Among the hardest of the materials worked by the ancient Egyptians were the varieties of quartz (7 on the Mohs Scale of Hardness). Both milky quartz and rock crystal seem to have been known to the Egyptians as *mnw ḥd* ("white quartz"). Milky quartz is a cloudy, white stone that, from the late Predynastic until the end of the Early Dynastic period, was frequently carved into pendants and funerary vessels (numerous examples survive in the elite tombs at Abydos and Saqqara). In the Old Kingdom, it was also used for the model vessels forming part of the funerary ceremony of the Opening of the Mouth, later becoming a popular material for inlay and beads during the Middle Kingdom.

From the Predynastic period onward, rock crystal (the colorless, translucent form of quartz) was used for beads and small vessels. During the New Kingdom, it was often used for inlay and as a decorative element in prestige goods, such as weaponry (e.g., the pommel of Tutankhamun's iron dagger) or funerary equipment. Many of the red inlays in the jewelry of Tutankhamun's tomb consisted of rock crystal or milky quartz placed over a bed of red cement, to achieve the effect of carnelian or red glass. Prase, a green form of quartz (which the Egyptians perhaps called *prḏn*), was also sometimes used for beads during pharaonic times.

Amethyst is a translucent, violet form of quartz, the Old Egyptian word for which was probably *ḥsmn*. Although in a few instances, amethyst was used for beads, amulets, and small vessels from the late Predynastic period to the end of the Old Kingdom, it was restricted to items of jewelry that date either to the Middle Kingdom or to the Roman era. The most successful uses of amethyst in Egyptian jewelry tend to be necklaces or bracelets comprising simple alternations of gold and amethyst amulets, as in the case of the twelfth dynasty girdle of Sithathoriunet from Illahun. There is some evidence for the trading of amethyst with Crete from at least the Middle Kingdom onward (perhaps in exchange for such products as animal horns, oils, and lichen).

Chalcedony. The term *chalcedony* has been used to refer to a number of types of gemstones, including yellow-red carnelian and brownish-red sard. The Egyptians appear to have used the terms *ḥrst* and *ḥrst dšrt* ("red *ḥrst*") to refer to carnelian and sard, respectively. Carnelian was one of the earliest gemstones to be used by the Egyptians. At first, in the Predynastic period, only the red and brown forms of carnelian and sard were used for beads and amulets (sometimes covered in glaze), but a yellowish form began to be used during the Middle and New Kingdoms.

In pharaonic times, carnelians were used for inlay on jewelry, furniture, and numerous items of funerary equipment (such as coffins), as well as for rings, scarabs, amulets, and even small vessels. During the New Kingdom, when most inlay had begun to be made from colored glass, carnelian was one of the few gemstones still frequently used, although it was sometimes imitated by placing rock crystal or milky quartz on red-painted cement.

The Egyptians may have used the terms k_3 hd and k_3 km to refer to two other forms of chalcedony: agate (usually banded with several colors) and onyx (usually black), which were used in jewelry in the form of unworked pebbles, beads, and drop pendants. In pharaonic times, its use in jewelry was comparatively infrequent, although it was sometimes used for amulets. It was employed for small vessels in the twenty-fifth and twenty-seventh dynasties, as well as in the Roman era. Onyx was used for beads from the Predynastic period onward, but it was not until after the twenty-first dynasty that onyx and sardonyx became popular; they were most commonly used in Ptolemaic and Roman times (particularly for cameos, intaglios, and ring settings). Chrysoprase (perhaps identified by the Egyptian term $prdn$) is a yellowish-green form of chalcedony, used occasionally for beads, amulets, and pendants from the Predynastic period to Roman times.

Jasper. The gemstones known as jasper are a group of brightly colored forms of chert (an opaque form of quartz or chalcedony). Jasper can be opaque red, green, yellow, or brown. Red jasper was probably the color most commonly used by the Egyptians; the green and brown jaspers are easily confused, visually, with other stones. The Egyptian term $hnmt$ (or $mhnmt$) was applied to red and yellow jasper, while the green jasper may have been known as *nemehef*. Chapter 156 of the *Book of Going Forth by Day* recommends $hnmt$ for the "girdle of Isis" amulet (the *tit*), while Chapter 30 suggests *nehemef* (perhaps "green jasper") as the most effective material for heart scarabs. Both red and green jasper were used for beads from the Badarian period onward, with red jasper being particularly popular for New Kingdom earrings and hair-rings. During pharaonic times, red jasper was used for amulets, jewelry inlay, scarabs, small vessels, and parts of composite statues (such as a foot from a composite statue at Tell el-Amarna). A large fragment of unworked red jasper was found in a foundation deposit for Ramesses IV at Deir el-Bahri.

Yellow jasper was used in Egypt for sculpture from the eighteenth dynasty onward, but it was not used for jewelry until Roman times. Brownish jasper seems to have been used only in the Middle Kingdom, primarily for scarabs. The Minoans may have obtained their jasper from trade connections with Egypt, since it does not seem to have been otherwise used by the Greeks.

Garnet. Occurring in all colors except blue, garnets are common and widespread in Egypt, including the Aswan region, the Eastern Desert, and the Sinai Peninsula. Almandine and pyrope garnets are fairly common in Egypt, but their quality is often poor. The color of garnet most frequently used by the Egyptians was the dark-red or the reddish-brown, and the term used to refer to the stone was probably hm_3gt. No ancient quarries have been found, presumably because of the stone's widespread availability. Lumps of a red substance identified as hm_3gt were shown as items of Nubian tribute in the eighteenth dynasty tomb of Rekhmire at Thebes.

From the Badarian period until the end of the New Kingdom, garnets were used for beads and—primarily during the Middle Kingdom—inlays. In general, however, the Egyptians seem to have used comparatively few garnets, presumably because the stones tend to be fairly small, with poor color, compared to other gems. Yet the importance of Egypt as a source of garnets during pharaonic and Ptolemaic times should not be underrated: the garnets in Mycenaean jewelry may well derive from commercial links with Egypt, rather than being European in origin, and only gemological analysis may settle their derivation.

Hematite. The gem quality iron-rich stone called hematite was known by the same Egyptian name as iron (bi_3). It was used for beads, for amulets (particularly the plummet, carpenter's square, and headrest amulets) and for small vessels, and was especially popular for kohl sticks (and sometimes also kohl vessels) during the Middle Kingdom and Second Intermediate Period. The type of hematite favored during the pharaonic period was black in color, with a metallic luster, the precise source of which has not yet been found.

Jade. The term *jade* is commonly used to refer to two different minerals: jadeite and nephrite. Jadeite can be white, green, brown, orange, and even (rarely) lilac. Nephrite, more common than jadeite, usually ranges from green to creamy white. No scientifically confirmed examples of either were found in materials from ancient Egypt, apart from a single funerary amulet in a New York private collection, which has ben identified as jade by X-ray diffraction analysis. Another possible example is a double-bezel ring from the tomb of Tutankhamun, which was identified by Alfred Lucas (1962) as nephrite. The New Kingdom heart scarab described by W. M. Flinders Petrie (1917, p. 48) as "true jade," has been revealed as a mix of quartz, magnesite, and dolomite.

Amazonite. The green to bluish-green amazonite is a variety of microcline (green feldspar), found mainly in the Eastern Desert, in the area of Wadi Higelig and Gebel Migif. Known to the Egyptians as *nšmt (m3ʿ)*, it was listed as one of their six most precious stones; inscriptions during pharaonic times often associate it with turquoise and lapis lazuli. It was carved into small beads from the Predynastic period onward, with a particular peak of popularity in the jewelry of the Middle Kingdom. It was also used for New Kingdom amulets, inlay, and small vessels.

Olivine. From the Predynastic onward, olivine, a yellow-green stone was used for jewelry (beads, pendants, and amulets); but peridot, the transparent light green gem variety, is not known to be used until Ptolemaic times, when it became a popular material for intaglios and cabochons. It was perhaps known to the Egyptians as *prdn* and was obtained only from the island of Zabargad (Saint John's Island) in the Red Sea, about 80 kilometers (50 miles) southeast of ancient Berenice.

Emerald. The ancient Egyptians did not use emerald (gem-quality green beryl) until Ptolemaic times, at the earliest. The Egyptian mines, worked from at least 332 BCE, the beginning of the Ptolemaic period, are widely believed to have been the only known source of emeralds for Europe, Asia, and Africa in the Hellenistic period. Although an uncut emerald has been identified in a necklace from the Predynastic site of Kubanniya, immediately to the north of Aswan, such gem-quality beryls do not appear regularly in Egyptian jewelry until Ptolemaic times, when techniques for polishing such stones were probably introduced. Egyptian emeralds continued to be used in jewelry until at least the Middle Ages, when Arab writers documented the appearance of the larger, heavier emeralds from the Indian subcontinent.

[*See also* Color Symbolism; *and* Jewelry.]

BIBLIOGRAPHY

Andrews, C. A. *Ancient Egyptian Jewellery*. London, 1990.
Aston, B. G., J. Harrell, and I. Shaw. "Stone." In *Ancient Egyptian Materials and Technology*, edited by P. T. Nicholson and I. Shaw. Cambridge, 1999.
Aufrère, S. *L'univers minéral dans la pensée égyptienne*. 2 vols. Cairo, 1991.
Bavay, L. "Matière première et commerce à longue distance: le lapis-lazuli et l'Egypte prédynastique." *Archéo-Nil* 7 (1997), 65–79.
Chartier-Raymond, M., B. Gratien, C. Traunecker, and J.-M. Vinçon. "Les sites miniers pharaoniques du Sud-Sinaï: quelques notes et observations de terrain." *Cahiers de Recherches de l'Institut de Papyrologie et d'Egyptologie de Lille* 16 (1994), 31–80.
Drenkhahn, R. "Artisans and Artists in Pharaonic Egypt." In *Civilizations of the Ancient Near East*, edited by J. Sasson, vol. 1, pp. 331–43. New York, 1995.
Grubessi, O., C. Aurisicchio, and A. Castiglioni. "The Pharaohs' Forgotten Emerald Mines." *Journal of Gemmology* 223 (1990), 164–177.
Herrmann, G. "Lapis Lazuli: The Early Phases of Its Trade." *Iraq* 30 (1968), 21–57.
Klemm, R., and D. D. Klemm. *Steine und Steinbrüche im Alten Ägypten*. Berlin, 1993.
Kulke, H. "Die lapislazuli-lagerstätte Sare Sang (Badakshan): Geologie, Entstehung, Kulturgeschichte und Bergbau." *Afghanistan Journal* 32 (1976), 1–16.
Lucas, A. *Ancient Egyptian Materials and Industries*. 4th ed., rev. by J. R. Harris. London, 1962.
Ogden, J. *Jewellery of the Ancient World*. London, 1982.
Petrie, W. M. Flinders. *Scarabs and Cylinders with Names*. London, 1917.
Shaw, I. "Exploiting the Desert Frontier: The Logistics and Politics of Ancient Egyptian Mining Expeditions." In *Social Approaches to an Industrial Past: The Archaeology and Anthropology of Mining*, edited by B. Knapp, pp. 242–258. London, 1998.
Shaw, I., and R. Jameson. "Amethyst Mining in the Eastern Desert: A Preliminary Survey at Wadi el-Hudi." *Journal of Egyptian Archaeology* 79 (1993), 81–97.
Shaw, I., J. Burbury, and R. Jameson. "Emerald Mining in Roman and Byzantine Egypt." *Journal of Roman Archaeology* 12 (1999), 1–13.
Stocks, Denys A. "Ancient Factory Mass-Production Techniques: Indications of Large-Scale Stone Bead Manufacturing during the Egyptian New Kingdom Period." *Antiquity* 63 (1989), 526–531.
Wilkinson, R. H. *Symbol and Magic in Egyptian Art*. London, 1994.
Yoyotte, J., ed. *Tanis, l'or des pharaons*. Paris, 1987.

IAN SHAW

GENDER ROLES. Within cultural constructs, gender is used to assign certain social characteristics, such as modes of behavior, types of activity, employment, and ways of dressing. Gender is based on the distinction between male and female biological sex, yet sexual distinction may also be constructed, to some extent, since the few children born with indeterminate genitalia are usually assigned to a sex. The construction and even the number of genders vary from one society to another. In ancient Egypt, two genders were recognized, corresponding to the male and female biological sexes. Different social and ritual roles were then considered appropriate to Egyptian men and women, and a number of strategies were incorporated into the social life, by which the two genders were differentiated.

In ancient Egypt, the gender roles did not remain unchanging during three thousand years of culture history. One constant, however, was the male role of king; so the few women who ruled were female kings, not queens. Royal succession normally passed from father to son, however, so kings needed royal women to produce their heirs. Kings' mothers and kings' wives, in addition to their reproductive duties, played a ritual role in relation to the king; in it, they were bearers of divine queenship, complementing the divine aspect of kingship.

A second gender role constant was the male character of the bureaucracy. Only men could become government officials, for which the basic qualification was literacy. Boys from elite families were taught to read and write by their fathers, by tutors, or in school. Some elite women may have been literate, but the skill was not fundamental to their identity and could not gain them government office. During the Old Kingdom, some elite women had administrative titles, but they seem to have been in the service of high-ranking women, not part of the state bureaucracy. By the Middle Kingdom, the number of female administrative titles, which had never been large, was much reduced. Throughout Egyptian history, women were responsible for managing the household and, from the Middle Kingdom onward, were given the title *nbt pr* ("mistress of the house"). One of the most important female duties was bearing and rearing children. Related to this biological role was the position of royal wetnurse, held by a number of elite women during the New Kingdom's eighteenth dynasty. Some elite men were appointed tutors to the royal children.

Evidence for nonelite occupations in ancient Egypt comes from elite textual and representational sources. Household servants were both male and female, although certain tasks, such as grinding grain and baking, were associated with women; brewing, butchery, and the preparation and cooking of meat were usually depicted as being carried out by men. Musicians and dancers seem to have been exclusively female during much of the Old Kingdom, but by the end of that period male singers and musicians were portrayed. In eighteenth dynasty tomb chapels, musical performers were a regular feature of banquet scenes that represent the meal with the deceased at the annual Festival of the Valley. In the scenes, the groups may be all male, all female, or mixed.

Known from tomb-chapel decoration, where the personnel are shown as male, are the royal and temple workshops for the production of goods, such as sculpture, jewelry and metal items, furniture, and leather goods. Only in textile production were large numbers of women involved, exclusively so in the Old and Middle Kingdoms. By the New Kingdom's eighteenth dynasty, scenes of male weavers working the newly introduced vertical loom occur, but women continue to be involved, and there is evidence that the households of some royal women were centers of cloth production.

In tomb-chapel scenes, the outdoor laborers working in the fields and marshes were overwhelmingly male. Female labor was mostly associated with the harvest. During the Old Kingdom, women were shown as winnowers; from the end of that period and onward, they were depicted following the male reapers and gathering the ears of grain that fell to the ground. In the eighteenth dynasty, both men and women harvested flax, which was pulled up by the roots, not cut. Those scenes all depict the large estates belonging to the king, temples, and officials, so they probably represent the elite ideal of male and female roles. Possibly gender roles were not so neatly divided on smaller plots of land owned or rented by individuals, whether male or female, and worked with the help of their families.

During the Old and Middle Kingdoms, priests were overwhelmingly male in every cult, except in the cult of Hathor, where only women served that goddess. Women were, less often, priestesses of other goddesses and even,

but rarely, served in the cult of a god. The title of "priestess" (*ḥmt nṯr*) of Hathor marked the bearer as belonging to the upper ranks of the elite. By the New Kingdom, serving in the priesthood had become a full-time occupation as a branch of the bureaucracy. As a result, priests in all cults were almost exclusively male. Female members of elite families frequently held the title of "musician" (*šmꜣyt*) in the cult of a particular deity, male or female, where they served as part of the temple's musical troupe, which provided musical accompaniment to ritual. Each musical troupe was headed by a superior who was a high-ranking woman, often married to a senior priest of the cult in which she served. Male musicians were sometimes shown alongside the female, but the title "musician" was not carried by officials, suggesting that the role of male musician lacked status.

Traditionally, the eldest son was supposed to carry out the funerary ritual for his parents, but the ritual could be performed by other family members and paid priests. During the Old Kingdom, both male and female funerary priests are known. During the New Kingdom, funerary stelae depict funerary rituals being performed before the deceased by both male and female relatives; at the funeral itself, in the rites before the tomb, the priests performing the rituals on the mummy are shown as male. The mourners, relatives of the deceased and hired professionals, are shown as predominantly female, and two women enacted the roles of the archetypal mourners, the goddesses Isis and Nephthys.

Traditional gender roles to some extent affected the economic and legal standing of men and women, although this would also have depended on social status. Among the elite, the chief economic disparity was that male officials received a government income to support themselves and their families. Most men were therefore likely to be wealthier than women of a comparable social level. In private economic and legal matters, however, women were, in theory, on an equal footing with men. Both men and women freely engaged in business transactions, owned land and goods, managed estates, rented land, inherited and handed on wealth, owned slaves and rented them out, adopted heirs, and appeared in court as plaintiff, defendant and witness. Although there is evidence that some elite women were very wealthy in their own right, there are also signs that other women were often less well off than men. Little evidence exists as to the legal and economic status of the nonelite, male or female.

Although elite men and women were believed to share the same afterlife and to need the same burial rites and funerary cult performed for them, there are often disparities between the burials of men and women of the same socioeconomic status; whether those are due simply to economic factors is unclear. The vast majority of tomb chapels were made for men. Only relatively high-ranking officials possessed such chapels, which were probably the most costly single item of funerary equipment. One might have expected at least some women with large incomes in their own right to have commissioned tomb chapels for themselves, if it were simply a matter of wealth. More likely, such monuments were linked in some way to the holding of a particular level of office.

In eighteenth dynasty burials, the husband normally had a richer set of equipment than the wife did, which often included an extra coffin. Some items, such as the *Book of Going Forth by Day* (*Book of the Dead*), are shared, with the husband as the primary owner. Although economic factors may sometimes have played a role, the same disparity was found in the burials of Yuya and Tjuyu, the parents of Tey, principal wife of Amenhotpe III.

Elite views of gender roles and gender differences were encapsulated in the portrayals of men and women as depicted in art. The major difference was the skin color, with men given reddish skin and women yellow. Although the precise color tones used varied from monument to monument, as a general rule male skin was darker than female. The distinction might have related, in part, to male and female roles, since women tended to be indoors more often, spending less time in the sun than did men. There was almost certainly a deeper significance, however, since the color distinction was frequently maintained both for male and female household servants and for men and women working together outdoors at the harvest. Red and yellow were both regarded as warm colors, relating to the sun. Red was also connected to blood and fire, both of which, being life-giving and life-destroying, held great power. Yellow symbolized gold, a metal closely linked to the sun and also to the goddess Hathor (so maybe in this association connected to an ideal of female beauty). Although there were occasions—most notably during the Amarna period—when women were given the same skin color as men, the color distinction was generally maintained from the Old Kingdom through Greco-Roman times, as applied to divine, royal, elite, and nonelite figures. Whatever the significance of the two colors, most likely they encoded for ancient Egyptians a fundamental distinction between men and women. [*See* Color Symbolism.]

Gender differences also occur in the poses portrayed for royal and elite male and female figures. Male figures, in both two and three dimensions, stand in an active pose with their feet apart, one well in advance of the other. Women normally stand more passively, with their feet together or with one foot slightly advanced, but with no clear space between the two feet. In addition, male figures are often carrying a staff, symbolizing authority, or they are performing some action. Women rarely carry a staff and often, although by no means always, stand passively

with their arms at their sides. Although sitting was basically a passive pose for both men and women, men tend to clench one or both fists, whereas women usually rest their hands palm down on their thighs; a similar distinction between clenched and open hands is found on male and female coffins when the hands are shown. Nonelite figures show a much wider variety of poses than those of the elite, and the women are often as active as the men when engaged in the same occupations.

The relative social importance of human figures was encoded by Egyptian artists in a number of ways—by scale, pose, or compositional position, and by the texts used for identification. Depictions of elite couples, such as an official and his wife (or, less often, his mother) reflected the relative status of each partner. In many cases, the couple are on the same scale or the man is somewhat larger than the woman, as might occur in nature. Although there are likely to have been couples where the man was shorter than the woman, such a possibility was not represented. During the Old Kingdom, in both two and three dimensions, the woman was often portrayed on a miniature scale in relation to the man, but the woman was never found as the dominant figure with her husband in miniature. During the Old and Middle Kingdoms, the man was often shown in the superior pose of sitting while the woman stood, but rarely were they shown with the woman as superior. In scenes from the Old Kingdom onward that show couples, the man was almost always placed in a dominant compositional position. If the couple are in the same register, he was placed in front of the woman nearer the center of the scene and the action. If they are in different registers, the man was placed above the woman. In the majority of New Kingdom statues, the man was placed in the dominant position on the woman's right. The texts on monuments most commonly identify men by their official titles and women by their relationship to the man they accompany. Further, the man's position as a government official was frequently reflected by a string of titles, whereas women had few titles available to them, so their identifying text was usually shorter. The texts on the two sides of the seat of New Kingdom pair statues often displayed an imbalance, with the man's side referring to the man alone and the woman's side referring to both partners, with the man's name first.

Although in different periods the elite couples were represented in different ways vis-à-vis each other, in the majority of cases one or more strategies were employed to mark the primary status of the man and to subordinate the woman. By contrast, nonelite couples were not identified. Although one may speculate that some form of gender hierarchy extended into the lower echelons of society, there is no representational proof.

Differences in male and female roles were reflected in

the idealizing images that represented the elite. The two images used for men related to different stages of their lives. One showed the man as youthful, in peak physical condition; the other as mature, often with a thicker body or rolls of fat on the chest and, in some periods, an older face. Women were overwhelmingly depicted with a youthful image that stressed the contours of the body, including the stomach, hips, and pubic area. The mature male image seems to represent the successful official who eats well and leads a sedentary lifestyle in the office all day. By contrast, since women could not be government officials, one of their most important functions was to bear children; thus it seems that the ideal female image needed to incorporate a woman's childbearing potential. A mature female image, one that might suggest a woman past her most fertile years, would have been inappropriate.

Images of the nonelite have a wider range of variation than those of the elite. Although most are generic and rarely represent named individuals, they did not need to be idealized and often included deformed, diseased, and aged figures. Such "nonidealizing" images are found for many more male than female figures, possibly because more nonelite figures represented men.

The costume of the elite and nonelite, as depicted in all periods of Egyptian art, displays gender differences. For the elite male, the basic garment was a knee-length kilt that left the chest, arms and lower legs uncovered. In mature figures of the Old and Middle Kingdoms, the kilt was usually lengthened to mid-calf level. From the Middle Kingdom onward, the kilt was often worn with a semitransparent bag tunic that covered the torso and fell to mid-calf level. Male garments became increasingly elaborate through time, with a trend that included more layers of material and more covering of the body; jewelry—collars, bracelets, and armlets—was worn, but not anklets and only very rarely earrings. The basic female garment, as represented from the Old Kingdom to the New Kingdom's mid-eighteenth dynasty, was the so-called sheath dress (which fell from just below the breasts to just above the ankles, with straps covering the breasts). From the mid-eighteenth dynasty, female figures wore a loose garment that covered one or both shoulders and fell to the feet, often with a large shawl worn over it. The outline and details of the female body were frequently drawn in, as though seen through sheer linen. In addition to the collars, bracelets, and armlets that were also worn by male figures, female figures wearing the sheath dress were shown with anklets. Earrings were introduced in the late Middle Kingdom and were thereafter commonly worn by elite women. [*See* Jewelry.]

Although hairstyles varied from period to period—some being more enduring than others—they were usually differentiated by gender. In general, male styles tended to be shorter than female styles, with men's hair or wigs being shoulder length or shorter, but women's longer than shoulder length. There were exceptions, however, for example, during the Old Kingdom and much later in the Third Intermediate Period, some female hairstyles were short, whereas from the late eighteenth dynasty through the end of the New Kingdom, the front lappets of male wigs lengthened to fall below the shoulders onto the chest. During the Old and Middle Kingdoms men were often shown with their hair cut into a short cap style, one especially associated with the image of the mature official. From the eighteenth dynasty onward, the short cap of hair was replaced by the image of a completely shaven head, which is particularly linked to priestly office. During the Old Kingdom, some elite women, including wives of tomb-chapel owners, were shown with a short cap of hair (similar to the male style, instead of the more usual long tripartite wig), but the significance remains unclear. Women are not shown with shaven heads. Images in art are often difficult to link with actual practice, but evidence from mummies shows female hair tending to be kept longer than male hair. Texts suggest that a woman's hair and her sexuality were connected, and that may account for the generally longer female hairstyles and the lack of shaven heads on female figures. By contrast, no evidence suggests that male sexuality and hair were linked. [*See* Hairstyles.]

The costume and hairstyles of nonelite figures were much less elaborate than those of the elite, but gender distinctions were maintained. Male household servants and musicians generally wore the simple knee-length kilt without any jewelry. During the Old and Middle Kingdoms, their hair was cut short; in the eighteenth dynasty it was shaved. Workshop personnel and outdoor laborers were sometimes depicted in kilts. During the Old and Middle Kingdoms, and occasionally in the early eighteenth dynasty, laborers—especially those working in the marshes—might be shown nude or wearing waist sashes or brief garments that leave the genitals visible. In the eighteenth dynasty, laborers were very often shown wearing nothing but a loincloth; the hair of Old Kingdom and eighteenth dynasty workshop personnel was sometimes shown in a style similar to the elite round wig, arranged in rows of curls. Whether the art actually shows a wig, the natural hair cut in layers, or has some other significance remains unclear. Some figures were shown with caps of short hair during the Old and Middle Kingdoms, or with shaven heads in the eighteenth dynasty; others were depicted with receding hair or with bald patches, with the remaining hair cut short but often rather unkempt. Straggly beards and stubble were sometimes shown and, occasionally, chest and pubic hair. [*See* Clothing and Personal Adornment.]

Female household servants usually wore the sheath dress, except when performing strenuous duties, such as grinding grain, when they were often shown in a tight, wraparound knee-length skirt that left the torso bare. During the Old and Middle Kingdoms, they often wore a short cap of hair. In banquet scenes of the eighteenth dynasty, older female servants waiting on guests frequently wore the tripartite hairstyle that was similar to the style worn by elite women. Few nonelite figures had jewelry, the exception being female dancers. During the Old Kingdom, dancers often wore knee-length kilts with an elaborate arrangement of straps wrapped around the torso, as well as collars, bracelets, and anklets. Their hair was cut into a short cap, sometimes with a long weighted braid falling down the back, which would swing with the dancers' movements. During the eighteenth dynasty, young dancers were often shown nude except for elaborate jewelry. Women shown working in the fields wore either the sheath dress or the wraparound skirt; their hair was not arranged elaborately and, unlike men in the fields, they were seldom shown nude.

[*See also* Family; Marriage and Divorce; Social Stratification; *and* Women.]

BIBLIOGRAPHY

Barber, Elizabeth Wayland. *Women's Work: The First 20,000 Years. Women, Cloth and Society in Early Times.* New York, 1994. Includes information on women and textile production in ancient Egypt.

Bryan, Betsy M. "In Women Good and Bad Fortune Are on Earth: Status and Roles of Women in Egyptian Culture." In *Mistress of the House, Mistress of Heaven: Women in Ancient Egypt,* edited by Anne K. Capel and Glenn E. Markoe, pp. 25–46. New York, 1996.

Derchain, Philippe. "Symbols and Metaphors in Literature and Representations of Private Life." *Royal Anthropological Institute News* 15 (August, 1976), 7–10. Discusses hair as a symbol of female sexuality.

Fischer, Henry G. "Priesterin." In *Lexikon der Ägyptologie,* 4:1100–1105. Wiesbaden, 1984. Important English-language article on the role of women as priestesses.

Robins, Gay. "While the Woman Looks On: Gender Inequality in New Kingdom Egypt." *K.M.T.: A Modern Journal of Ancient Egypt* 1.3 (1990), 18–21, 64–65.

Robins, Gay. *Women in Ancient Egypt.* London and Cambridge, Mass., 1993. Studies women in the context of ancient Egyptian society and discusses elite and nonelite gender roles.

Robins, Gay. "Some Principles of Compositional Dominance and Gender Hierarchy in Egyptian Art." *Journal of the American Research Center in Egypt* 31 (1994), 33–40. Discusses the dominance of husbands over wives within compositions in ancient Egyptian art.

Roehrig, Catharine H. "Woman's Work: Some Occupations of Nonroyal Women as Depicted in Ancient Egyptian Art." In *Mistress of the House, Mistress of Heaven: Women in Ancient Egypt,* edited by Anne K. Capel and Glenn E. Markoe, pp. 13–24. New York, 1996.

Smith, Stuart Tyson. "Intact Tombs of the Seventeenth and Eighteenth Dynasties from Thebes and the New Kingdom Burial System." *Mitteilungen des Deutschen Archäologischen Instituts Abteilung Kairo* 48 (1992), 193–231. Shows tendency for husbands to have slightly wealthier burials than their wives.

Sweeney, Deborah. "Women's Correspondence from Deir el-Medineh." In *Sesto Congresso Internazionale di Egittologia: Atti,* Proceedings of the International Congress of Egyptology, Turin, Italy, 1–8 September 1992, vol. 2, pp. 523–529. Turin, 1993. Discusses the possibility of female literacy in relation to material from Deir el-Medina.

Troy, Lana. *Patterns of Queenship in Ancient Egyptian Myth and History.* Uppsala, 1986. Explores the female role of queenship as the complement to male kingship.

Vogelsang-Eastwood, Gillian. *Pharaonic Egyptian Clothing.* Studies in Textile and Costume History, 2. Leiden, 1993. Describes male and female dress in ancient Egypt.

GAY ROBINS

GEOGRAPHY. Egypt has been both a land and an idea. As a modern nation-state, Egypt has clear and well-defined borders; this is a feature of modern states, the strict definition of borders as a means of delineating their domain of sovereignty and authority over political, civic, and economic matters. Although borders were recognized in antiquity, their definition was not as clear as that of modern nation-states. Egypt became a nation after its unification, about 3000 BCE. It was not a nation unified either by its people or by territory; different groups had inhabited the same territory historically. It was also not a nation because its people were homogeneous (a "race" in the biological sense), or claiming descent from a common ancestor. The Egyptians exhibit a variety of physical types, having assimilated peoples from Nubia, Libya, and the Levant. Egypt became a nation by virtue of their union under the sovereignty of a single monarch; this pharaoh not only unified disparate ethnic groups but also provided the ideological basis for the territorial integration of the Nile Valley lands from Elephantine, an island in the Nile River, in the South to the marshlands of the Delta in the North.

From the inception of the first dynasty, the Egyptians viewed their country as consisting of two parts, Lower Egypt (the North) and Upper Egypt (the South), perhaps in part because these regions represented two distinct cultural areas in mid-Predynastic times (c.3600 BCE) but also because the Egyptian cognitive reality favored complementary dualities. Lower Egypt included the lower reaches of the Nile—the Delta region with its frontier towns and agricultural villages—and a zone immediately south of the Delta's apex, at times extending into what is sometimes called Middle Egypt (which could include the zone north of the Faiyum Depression entrance or even as far south as Asyut). The Delta was generally perceived as two halves, perhaps because of the duality principle or because the eastern region was characterized by cultural traits that differentiated it from the western. The area between the two main branches of the Nile was at times distinguished as a "Central Island."

On a national level, Egypt consisted of the "Two Lands," so the king's crown was, therefore, the Double Crown of Upper and Lower Egypt. The Two Lands were associated with deities—Nekhbet in Upper Egypt, a vulture goddess from Nekhen (Elkab, opposite the Predynastic site at Hierakonpolis) and Wadjet in the northwestern part of the Delta, the *uraeus* serpent of Buto (Tell el-Fara'in). The king was also identified with the god Horus, represented by a falcon and primarily associated with Hierakonpolis (Elkom el-Ahmar) in Upper Egypt, as well as later, with Behdet (Tell el-Balamoun) in the marshlands of the northeastern Delta. Lower Egypt was identified by the green papyrus plant, whereas Upper Egypt was represented by a sedge. In addition, the Red Crown of Lower Egypt was worn by Neith, a goddess of Sais (Sa el-Hagar), in the northwestern-Delta vicinity of Buto. The earliest representation of Nekhbet is on a stone vase from the second dynasty that carried the name of King Khasekhemwy (c.2700 BCE). In Predynastic times, Hierakonpolis, Sais, and Buto were cult centers and prominent towns. A unified Egypt thus extended in royal cosmography from the political domain of Hierakonpolis (Nekhen) in the South to that of Sais and Buto in the northwestern Delta. Lower Egypt was also symbolized by the bee (*bit*), which was associated with Neith of Sais. The king's titulary "He of the Sedge and the Bee" (*nsw-bit*) was bound with the name of the Red Crown as *bit*. The cosmogonic ideology of kingship also included the god Atum, Lord of Heliopolis (Eg., *iwnw;* the biblical site of On) in the eastern Delta, as well as the sun god Re from the same locality. During the Middle Kingdom, some pharaohs incorporated Amun in their names, and his cult was celebrated in many sanctuaries in Thebes. Regarded as the supreme god of the Egyptian pantheon, Amun was depicted anthropomorphically as a pharaoh seated on a throne with two plumes surmounting his crown.

The king of Egypt was the "Lord of the Two Lands." He was also regarded as the "Lord of the Black-land" (*kmt*), which referred to the fertile land of the Nile Valley, the Delta, and the adjacent deserts. If the floodplain of the valley and the Delta provided the farming land and pasture that supported the majority of Egypt's population, the deserts—to the east of the Nile (the Eastern Desert) and to the west (the Western Desert, including the Sahara), as well as the Sinai to the northeast and the Nubian desert to the southeast—were rich in rock and mineral resources. In addition to stones for building and for other industries, the Sinai, the Eastern Desert, and the Nubian desert proved key sources of gold and copper, minerals of special significance within the religious ideology of Egyptian kingship. The boundaries of Egypt, therefore, were never restricted to the narrow strip of the Nile Valley but were extended to the surrounding deserts, as far as possible, and even to the Red Sea. In reality, the borders varied according to the ability of Egyptian kings to defend or control useful outlying territories from neighboring powers; such powers belonged to nomadic tribes and tribal chiefdoms, as well as to mighty empires.

In one of his titles, the king claimed to be the "Sovereign of the Nine Bows" (originally they were seven in the Pyramid Texts), a confederation of lands and peoples under his authority. In addition to Upper and Lower Egypt—the core domain of the king—the lands included the Iuntiu of Ta-sety, south of Aswan (or Nubia, a word probably derived from the Old Egyptian for "gold" [*nbw*]); the Land of Shat farther to the south; the people of Ta-shu (the "empty quarter") and the Tjehenu in the area west of the Delta; and the Tjemehu, the oasis dwellers of the Western Desert. The Mediterranean settlers included in the list were referred to as Hau-nebu, which may mean the Greeks. In the fifth dynasty temple of Sahure, the gods were shown leading bound conquered peoples to the king. The Egyptians also spoke of Keftiu, a term identified with the Canaanite island of Kaptara, or Crete. The Egyptians recognized the "East" or the "Northern Lands" (the Near East) as Setjet.

Regardless of the varying size of the peripheral territory, the Nile Valley and the Delta formed the core of the Egyptian state, the area of the greatest demographic, economic, and social interactions. Regardless of a certain degree of geographically and socially induced clusters and gradational differences, the Two Lands had been the crucible of Egyptian nationhood. Its people were, however, in Predynastic times a mix of breeding populations that included inhabitants of the Valley and the Delta, newcomers from the adjacent deserts, and settlers from the Nubia lands. In dynastic times, peoples from the Mediterranean lands and as far as the Maghreb (North Africa) Mauritania, Yemen, Afghanistan, the Caucauses, the Anatolian Plateau, and the Balkan Peninsula were assimilated. Throughout pharaonic times, there were additions to Egypt's population, as a result of trade, immigration, and warfare (settlers, captives, invaders). Depending on the source of the newcomers, as well as the differences generated by geographic and social distances, regional differences prevailed in both dialects and appearances. Dialectal differences still exist in the Arabic spoken in Upper Egypt, as distinct from the Delta. Qena and Aswan were long regarded as an exile area to inhabitants of Cairo and the Delta (Ar., Wagh Bahari). The inhabitants of southern Egypt (Ar., Wagh Gibli) distinguish themselves as Sa'iyda (the Arabic singular is Sa'idi) from the Baharawiya (the Arabic singular is Bahrawi) of northern Egypt.) Upper Egypt is also subdivided into an inner part (Ar., Sa'id Gwanni), south of Qena, and an outer part (Ar., Sa'id Barani), farther to the north. The Nubians (Ar., Al-Nubiyeen,

Nubi is the singular) are regarded as a distinct group. During the New Kingdom, in the reign of Sety I, in contradistinction with the Egyptians, the Nubians were joined with other ethnic groups such as the "Asiatics" (Near Easterners) and the "Libyans" (North Africans). Iconography reveals not only perceptions of differences in anatomic features but also differences in attire and body treatment. The Egyptians, as did many other groups, called themselves "the people" (*rmṯ*).

The land of Egypt was not primarily a tract of land, but within the conceptions of Egyptian kingship, a sacred territory in which order and stability prevailed. The king was responsible for maintaining that order. In the process he had both to defend Egypt against invaders and to maintain internal cohesion and stability. Divine kingship in Egypt, in addition, was intertwined with an ideology that included mortuary cults, requiring mineral resources from outside Egypt; the pharaohs were thus compelled to maintain the production and flow of incense, gold, copper, and copper minerals, as well as other temple and mortuary materials. From earliest dynastic times, therefore, Egypt came into contact, and sometimes conflict, with the peoples of the adjacent regions.

Geomorphic Divisions. The fertile floodplain of the Nile Valley and the Delta made the economics of ancient Egypt possible. Physiographically, the Nile flows in a canyon that had split that eastern rim of the Great Sahara of North Africa into an Eastern Desert, dominated by a range of hills and elevated plateaus, and a Western Desert of plateaus, depressions, sand sheets, and hospitable oases. The Sinai, to the northeast of the Delta, is separated from the northern part of the Eastern Desert by the Gulf of Suez.

The Nile Valley constitutes the northernmost alluvial floodplain of the Nile River. Originating in Ethiopia and eastern equatorial Africa, to the north of the confluence of the White Nile and the Blue Nile, the river runs with no significant contributions from its local surroundings. Cascading over a series of cataracts, it reaches the northernmost, the First Cataract, just to the south of Aswan. The construction of Egypt's new Aswan High Dam in the 1960s and 1970s has created a huge lake, which covers some 6,000 square kilometers. The Nile flows northward toward the Mediterranean, following the gradient of the land for some 1,200 kilometers (725 miles), with an average width of 0.75 kilometer (0.5 mile). The floodplain is about 10 kilometers (6.2 miles) wide, on average, and covers approximately 10,000 square kilometers. A branch of the Nile used to flow along the course of the canal known today as Bahr Yusef; with an inlet near Dairut, the branch flowed northward, paralleling the main channel, then into the Faiyum Depression, forming a great lake. The lake has long since dried up, and only a relatively small part of the depression is occupied by a brackish lake, the Birket

Qarun, of 200 square kilometers. The Nile tends to run through the eastern part of the north–south valley, except near Qena where the channel makes a great bend bounded by impressive limestone cliffs. South of Isna, the surrounding plateau is sandstone. Granitic islands, the oldest rock in the Nile Valley, dot the course of the river near Aswan.

Nile delta. Today, the Nile bifurcates into two branches some 20 kilometers (13 miles) north of Cairo, marking the apex of a Delta that covers a total area of approximately 22,000 square kilometers. In classical antiquity, the Delta was documented with seven branches: the Pelusiac, the Tanitic, the Mendesian, the Phanitic, the Sebennytic, the Bolbitic, and the Canopic. The Pelusiac branch extended in a northeastern direction to the northwestern corner of the Sinai Peninsula. Yet another branch, which flowed in prehistoric times, is today's Wadi Tumeilat which traverses the desert east of the Delta to the depressions north of Suez; the Suez desert contains low sand terraces of old Nile sediments and even older geologic formations. Relics of old Nile deposits called sand islands dot the central and eastern part of the Delta. West of the Delta, the Wadi el-Natrun—a series of small depressions in a desert plain of old Nile and even older fluviomarine deposits—is fed by seepage from the Nile's floodwaters. The northern rim of the Delta has a series of lakes and the lagoons and marshy wetlands that meet the Mediterranean Sea.

The area west of the Delta consists of an immense limestone plateau—the Diffa of the Marmarica Plateau—overlooking the Mediterranean. The plateau is marked by the Qattara Depression, an area of approximately 20,000 square kilometers; its lowest point is 135 meters (400 feet) below sea level. Several oases occupy depressions south of Qattara, including the oases of Siwa, Bahrein, el-Arag, Sitra, and Numeisa. North of Qattara, the plateau slopes gently to the sea and forms a low-relief plain of wadi, coastal, and lagoonal deposits. The coast is marked by several inlets and spits; west of Alexandria, for example, the Al-A'rab Gulf is a prominent bay. South of the coast, several high ridges run parallel to it, creating a demarcated, coastal desert zone.

Western Desert. Most of the desert west of the Nile (the Western Desert, also known as the Libyan Desert, the Eastern Sahara, and the Egyptian Sahara) consists of a vast limestone plateau of 200 to 300 meters (600 to 925 feet) in elevation above sea level. The plateau, consisting of a stony surface, is covered in places—especially along its western margin—by extensive sand sheets. It is traversed by sand dunes and is broken by a number of depressions, which are marked by a series of pediments and escarpments having relics of endoreic (internal) drainage. The depressions support a series of oases—from north to south, the Baharia, Farafra, Dakhla, and Kharga oases.

South of the limestone plateau, marked by a promi-

GEOGRAPHY. *Engraving (c.1890) of Asyut during the Nile inundation.*

nent escarpment, is Sin el-Kidab, to the southwest of As-wan. Two small oases, Kurkur and Dungul, are nested in the southernmost edge of the plateau. The desert south and southwest of Sin el-Kidab consists of a sandy plain with relict sandstone hills and dispersed outcrops of base-ment granites, diorites and gneiss. It is traversed by the Araba'in desert track, which runs from Al-Fashir and El-Ubayyad in Sudan to Asyut. The area is covered by de-flated residual desert gravel, sand sheets, and dune forma-tions. In several places within the desert depressions there are remnants of Holocene (10,000 years ago to the pres-ent) sediments, ephemeral lakes, and playas. Topographic lows in the Arba'in desert contain playas that have yielded important terminal Paleolithic and Neolithic remains, as at Nabta and Bir Kisseiba. The most spectacular feature of the southwestern area of the Eastern Sahara is the mountain massif of Gebel Uweinat, with an elevation of 1,900 meters (6,000 feet) above sea level, and the Gilf el-Kebir, a plateau that rises from 600 to 1,000 meters (1,800 to 3,000 feet).

Eastern Desert. Between the Nile Valley and the Red Sea, the Eastern Desert is marked by prominent moun-tains from latitude 28°30′N to Sudan. That mountain range, of igneous and metamorphic basement rocks, rich in mineral resources, is crossed by wadis. In the northern part of the desert, Wadi Qena separates the coastal hills from the extensive Ma'aza limestone plateau. Mount Elba is in the Halaib-Shalatin southern area and the Gebel Shayeb is in the central range. To the south of Qena, sand-stone replaces limestone as the predominant sedimentary cover. Broad valleys and wadis connect the Nile Valley with the Red Sea Coast, as, for example, the Wadi Ha-mammat. Other Wadis served, during Africa's rainy Pleis-tocene periods (the pluvials) as tributaries to the Nile: the Wadi Shait, Wadi Kharit, and Wadi Alaqi.

Sinai desert. Continuous with Southwestern Asia, the Sinai fronts the Mediterranean in the north and has mountains in the south, with Mount Katherina at 2,641 meters (8,452 feet). The mountainous core of igneous and metamorphic rock, exposed in the south, is mantled in the north by the limestone beds of the Tih Plateau. To the east, the Tih escarpment overlooks Wadi Arabah. The landscape in northern Sinai is characterized by hills and depressions; these are covered by sand dunes to the south of the Mediterranean. The Wadi Al-Arish, in northern Si-nai, is a broad valley with a large catchment area.

Borders and Administrative Districts. The Nile Val-ley south of the Delta to Aswan was the heartland of Egypt. The First Cataract, south of Aswan, marked the general southern boundary. It was later extended to the south to include parts of Nubia (now in Sudan), but it also was shifted northward at times. During the Middle

Kingdom, the Egyptians established forts at the First Cataract to control that border. West of the Nile, the oases formed a favorable location for Egyptian settlements that extended along the line of what is now called the "New Valley" (from Kharga to Siwa). Along the Mediterranean coast, a series of forts were established during the New Kingdom, by Ramesses II, as far west as Zawyet Umm el-Rakham; the inhabitants of that region were called "Libyans."

Egypt was divided into administrative units, each a *sepat* (*sp3t;* "nome" in Greek). The sign for *sepat* was a piece of land divided by canals. The nomes were clearly demarcated by the fifth dynasty, as indicated by a list of Upper Egyptian nomes in the Kiosk of Senowsret I at Karnak. The number and boundaries of the nomes varied in time, but the variations were not dramatically significant. Under the Old Kingdom, the total number of nomes was thirty-eight or thirty-nine. In the Late period, the nomes numbered forty-two, including twenty-two in Upper Egypt and twenty in the Delta, as indicated by lists in the temple of Edfu and at Dendera. (The judges of the dead numbered forty-two and were sacred.) Each nome was depicted by an ensign, associated with a deity, and had a capital city.

[*See also* Nile; *and articles on specific geographical divisions.*]

BIBLIOGRAPHY

Baines, J., and J. Malek. *Atlas of Ancient Egypt.* Oxford, 1984.
Butzer, Karl W. *Early Hydraulic Civilization in Egypt, A Study in Cultural Ecology.* Chicago, 1976. Includes an informative description of the hydrography and geomorphology of the Nile floodplain.
Kees, Herman. *Ancient Egypt, A Cultural Topography.* Chicago, 1961. A classic description of the Egyptian landscape from historical and cultural perspctives.
Silverman, D. P., ed. *Ancient Egypt.* London, 1997. Includes chapters on the cultural geography of Egypt, with a section on the cosmic geography of the Egyptian landscape.
Trigger, B. G., B. J. Kemp, D. O'Connor, and A. B. Lloyd. *Ancient Egypt, A Social History.* Cambridge, 1983. Essential for a full understanding of the changing dynamics of Egyptian borders and the human impact on the Egyptian landscape.

FEKRI HASSAN

GEOLOGY. *See* Land and Soil; *and* Minerals.

GERZEAN PERIOD. *See* Predynastic Period.

GESTURE. Widely utilized to accompany, supplement, or replace verbal communication in many cultures, gesture in both ritual and nonritual contexts was particularly important in ancient Egypt. The depiction of gestures (in-

cluding poses of the whole body as well as gestures of the fingers, hands, and arms) in all types of figural representation and in all periods indicates that gesture symbolism represented an important nonverbal vocabulary for many aspects of ancient Egyptian life and culture. Certainly no other aspect of iconographic symbolism is as widespread in Egyptian art as the use of gestures to connote specific contextual meaning and significance. The detailed pictographic nature of the Egyptian hieroglyphic script also meant that special attention was paid to gestures in many determinative signs that dealt with human activities. This widespread representation of gestures in art and writing may well have perpetuated the form and function of many gestures in life.

Chronology and Evidence. The representation of gestures was an important part of Egyptian art from the beginnings of formalized representation. Gestures of dominance and submission appear in early dynastic works along with other formalizing aspects, such as a defined ground line and temporal register division; the Narmer Palette provides a clear example. Although an established protocol of gesture symbolism is clearly present and probably continues unbroken from this early time, our knowledge of the situation is less extensive for some periods than for others, owing to the nature of extant representational material. Evidence for the Old Kingdom and Middle Kingdom comes primarily from private tombs and consists mainly of parietal painting and relief, which show a wide repertoire of gestures in use by servants, workmen, farmhands, boatmen, herders, and others in the course of everyday activities—as well as gestures depicted in representations of the tomb-owner. Sculpture of these periods, however, utilizes relatively static poses with few explicit gestures.

Conversely, two-dimensional mortuary depictions of the New Kingdom and later periods provide fewer examples of everyday gesture, the body of evidence enriched by temple representations showing formalized gestures of gods, kings, and priests in various genre scenes and involved in the ritual activities of the cult. New Kingdom and later statuary also shows a wider range of gestural expression that considerably expands the corpus of evidence.

Analysis and Interpretation. Successful analysis and interpretation of the evidence for Egyptian gesture symbolism and meaning is complicated by a number of factors. As in life, gestures may or may not be accompanied by spoken words: the representations may or may not have associated texts that help to explain their context and meaning. Sometimes analysis is complicated by the conventions of Egyptian figural representation, in that it is not always entirely clear whether an actual gesture is being performed or whether figures are simply represented in a manner consistent with artistic conventions of the time or with individual artistic idiosyncrasies.

Even when it seems clear that actual gestures are involved, it must be remembered that in order to facilitate recognition in representations, gestural movement was usually "frozen" at its most characteristic point (usually the midpoint of an action—the raised arm about to strike, etc.). Thus, it is not always clear if what appear to be depictions of different gestures with potentially different meanings are the result of variations in representational styles, or if they represent different parts of the same gesture, or yet again, if they are discrete gestures with the same range of meaning.

Sometimes the same gestures are used with widely different meanings, and only text or context can differentiate them, as in the case of poses such as those with the arms held high above shoulder level in scenes of rejoicing and sorrow alike. Even slight differences in the expression of the gesture itself may indicate totally different meanings. While arms slightly outstretched before the body with palms facing down represent a gesture of respect or submission, the same gesture with palms upward represents giving, as when deities proffer the hieroglyphic water sign in scenes of the purification and welcoming of the deceased into the afterlife. Both the *orientation* of the hand (for example, with palm facing outward toward the recipient of the gesture, or palm facing inward toward the gesturer) and the *angle* of the hand (in its alignment relative to both the horizontal and the vertical) may affect gestural meaning specifically.

The most common difficulty associated with interpretation, however, is simply the level of uncertainty involved in gestures that neither text nor context clearly define and that are susceptible to two or more equally plausible interpretations. An example is seen in Old Kingdom tomb paintings in which boatmen stretch out an arm with extended forefinger toward the far riverbank or toward a crocodile lurking in the river's depths, and scenes in which handlers point dogs to game, children point to animals or birds, or supervisors point to cattle at birth. In the absence of textual indicators, it is sometimes unclear whether these gestures are simply indicative or directive, or whether a protective meaning is involved—as often seems to be the case.

Areas of Gesture Usage. Despite the difficulties inherent in the analysis of certain representations, various categories are commonly used which subsume the majority of the gestures and poses depicted in Egyptian art. Most of these categories are based on classification according to the role played by a given gesture—that is, the area of usage in which it is found—and these areas usually cut across ritual and nonritual, formal and informal contexts, though some categories contain gestures found mainly in the representation of the human sphere and others are utilized mainly in the divine sphere. The most frequently cited of these categories (and of the Egyptian words commonly associated with representations of the gestures found in each) include the following:

1. Greeting: salutation, welcome (*nyny, nḏwt-r, nḏ-ḥrt*)
2. Status: dominance, submission, respect (*ḫrḫr, ksi, iȝw*)
3. Asking: requesting, pleading, praying (*dbḥ, snm*)
4. Praising: reverence, worship (*dwȝ, ḥknw, hnw*)
5. Offering: giving of offerings, libations, gifts (*drp, ḥnk*)
6. Speaking: address, oration, recitation (*nis, šdi*)
7. Indicating: pointing, drawing attention to (*mȝꜥ, ḏbꜥ*)
8. Commanding: directing, signaling (*wḏ, wḏ-mdw*)
9. Counting: indicating numbers on the hands (*ḥsb, ip*)
10. Music: guidance of musicians (*ḥsi, šmꜥ*)
11. Dance: ritual dance, mime (*rwi, ḫbi*)
12. Rejoicing: celebration, victory (*ḥꜥi, rnn*)
13. Sorrow: sadness, bereavement, mourning (*ḫȝi, kmȝ*)
14. Magic: apotropaic protection, defense, offense (*ḥkȝw*)
15. Support: sustaining, strengthening, bestowing of power (*twȝ, fȝi*)

It will be seen that a good deal of overlapping exists among these categories. For example, gestures of greeting (1) may also be gestures expressing dominance or submission (2); signaling may be a function of indicating a fact (6) or conveying a command (7); and the gestures used in musical performance (9) are clearly directive (7). In a general way, these categories represent areas of actual gesture usage and are useful for descriptive and comparative purposes. Yet, such categories usually tell us little more than the context in which a given gesture appears, and it is often more profitable to consider gestures and poses from various analytical perspectives—in terms of aspects of their usage.

Aspects of Gesture Usage. Some of the more important types of gestures, in terms of aspects of usage, include categories defined by gestural origin, mechanics, extent, interaction, specificity, and decorum.

Origin. Natural gestures are developed in the normal course of life without instruction or conscious attempts at learning or employment. The category includes gestures such as pointing and shielding oneself from threat, as well as a number of gestural expressions of emotion in mourning ("[to place] the head on the knees"), rejoicing ("to raise the arms"), and so on.

Formalized gestures are often quite complex and include gestures and poses that must be consciously learned as part of ritual behavior. Formal gestures of offering presentation and the complex *hnw* sequence of praise and jubilation are examples of this type.

Mimetic gestures, although similar to formal gestures in being consciously learned and employed, mimic natural behavior in some way. Examples include the mimetic gestures of mourners that depict the crossing of the arms on the chest of the mummified deceased, or the mythic enfolding of the deceased in the arms of protective goddesses. Many gestures of this type are natural gestures formally utilized, such as the childlike holding of the finger to the mouth sometimes shown in adult figures depicted as children.

Mechanics. *Hand gestures* normally involve the use of only the fingers and hands, or the arms inasmuch as the latter are necessary to position the hands. While some hand gestures are performed only in conjunction with related bodily gestures, others (such as counting on the hands) may be performed independently in any position.

Bodily gestures or poses involve the positioning of the upper, lower, or whole body, or the head. They may add to or strengthen the implication of associated hand gestures (as in certain gestures of respect) or may exist as gestures with independent meaning, as in the prostration of the body in the performance of proskenysis.

Extent. *Independent or simple gestures* are individual, static gestures or poses affected briefly and in isolation; they have complete meaning in and of themselves, without reference to any other gesture, action, or context. Most natural and mimetic gestures are of this type.

Sequential or complex gestures are gestures or poses that exist in sequences of continuous action or as part of a dynamic behavioral pattern such as a dance or religious ritual. Many formalized gestures of offering, praise, and so on, are of this type.

Interaction. *Noninteractive gestures*, such as many gestures of praise before deities, are often made by individuals without any response or reciprocal gesture being involved, although such gestures may be performed individually or collectively. Noninteractive gestures often imply a difference in status between the performer of the gesture and its recipient.

Interactive gestures, which involve gestural reciprocation between two or more individuals (such as some ges-

GESTURE. *Examples of types of gesture, classified according to origin:* (top) *a natural gesture—pointing;* (middle) *a formalized gesture—the complex hnw sequence of praise and jubilation;* (bottom) *a mimetic gesture—the childlike holding of the finger to the mouth.* (Courtesy Richard W. Wilkinson)

tures of greeting), tend to be formulaic and dictated by status. However, the protocol of interactive gestures between Egyptian deities and kings (see "Decorum" below) is especially interesting in that a wide range of expression is evident in certain time periods and even in monuments of the same reign. Depending on context, representations of the same monarch may include scenes where the king and deity are spatially separated with little if any interaction (as in many temple scenes), and others (such as mortuary scenes) showing gestures of close physical contact and demonstrating divine acceptance and affection for the king.

Specificity. *Nondirective gestures* express inner attitudes or emotions but have no specific content signaling commands or directions. Such gestures are found across a broad range of gesture categories, from rejoicing to mourning.

Directive gestures may be general or very specific, as in the case of gestures used in the navigation of river craft or in the performance of music. It is believed that the Egyptians invented chironomy, the use of hand gestures to guide musicians; and a number of representational works show vocalists or others leading instrumentalists with such gestures, which must have had specific meaning content.

Decorum. *Divine/royal usage of gestures* is normally found only in representations of deities and kings (and sometimes queens), because decorum necessitated that certain gestures be held the prerogatives of divine or royal subjects. Gestures of embrace between gods and kings provide obvious examples of this type.

Human/nonroyal usage of gestures, conversely, is usually found only in scenes depicting nonroyal humans, or those of kings which include servants, subjects, or prisoners. However, gestures of worship, respect, and praise form an interesting interface between these two categories. Not only do commoners make the same gestures of worship and praise before kings and gods as kings use before the gods, but certain gestures in use by commoners are also occasionally utilized by royalty.

Gestural Variants. Although a number of very similar or even identical gestures may be found to have different meanings dependent upon context, it is more common to find a variety of different gestures within a given category of expression. We might thus speak of a gesture "range" or a "complex" of meaning-related gestures as opposed to the different parts of a single sequential gesture. There are, for example, literally dozens of discrete gestures conveying respect. These gestures of respect include a large number of variations of placing one or both hands—flat or clenched—on the knees, arms, or shoulders, or on or across the chest. A number of other variants exist in this complex, and most of the gestures shown could be per-

formed in reverse by utilizing the opposite hands in each case. Therefore, the effective number of possible variations for this one gesture group could be more than double the number depicted. Although the number of variants in this one gestural complex is thus quite large, they are all subsumed in the two basic forms of displaying the hands pressed either on the knees or on some part of the upper torso. From the perspective of gestural mechanics, it should be noted that the gesturer's hands are also placed palm toward the body in all these examples. Although most gestural categories utilize such complexes, a greater range of variants is often found for independent gestures than for sequential gestures, which are usually more formally controlled in expression and usage.

Combination of Gestures. It is also important to realize that two or more different gestures might be performed by the same subject at the same time. Not only do bodily gestures frequently supplement hand gestures, but most gestures utilizing two hands could also be effected with one hand, as may be seen in many representations of individuals engaged in offering, rejoicing, praising, mourning, or jubilation. Worshipers before a deity, for example, are commonly depicted presenting offerings with one arm while lifting the other arm in praise, or some other gesture such as protection, as shown by the offering text, "I give you Maat with my left hand, my right hand protecting her." In mourning, too, mourners may be depicted placing one hand on the face or hair while utilizing the other hand to make one of the gestures of respect.

In many representations from the New Kingdom on of the deities Isis, Nephthys, Horus, or Anubis standing behind the figure of the god Osiris, whether the deity actually touches Osiris or simply raises an arm behind him, both gestures are often described as a gesture of support. It is more probable, however, that two separate gestures are actually involved. In scenes that clearly indicate support, as is occasionally explained in descriptive labels, both hands are placed on Osiris—usually one on the shoulder and the other on the lower torso or arm. In other scenes, where one hand rests on the god and the other hand is raised behind him, a combination of support and praise is probably intended.

Diffusion of Gestures through Space and Time. A basic comparative approach to the corpus of gestures found in Egyptian art indicates that while most gestures may be culture-specific, a number of these gestures and poses can also be found in the art of other cultures of the ancient Near East. It seems fair to conclude that at least a limited number of gestures were "shared" in the sense that, having been spread through trade, diplomacy, or warfare, they were understandable to people of different cultural and linguistic backgrounds. For example, the appearance of the raised-arm gesture—in which one hand is held above shoulder height as if about to smite or protect—in many ancient Near Eastern magical figurines shows that this was a widely understood apotropaic gesture. While some natural gestures of this type could have developed independently, other shared gestures are clearly formal in nature and quite specific in meaning, like the turned bow.

Many representations from Egypt and other ancient Near Eastern cultures show the bow being held backward by gods and kings in a symbolic gesture in which the bowstring is held toward subjects of lesser status. This appears to represent a formal gesture of dominance: a god might hold a bow in this way before a king, a king before subjects or prisoners, or occasionally even a nondivine or nonroyal superior before subordinates. But the reverse is never true, and the "turned bow" is never directed toward a god by a king, a king by a subject, or an Egyptian by an enemy. In Egypt the gesture is commonly represented, as might be expected, in New Kingdom scenes of the king confronting enemies on the battlefield or in the symbolic slaying of captives. An interesting variant of this widespread gesture is also found in New Kingdom battle reliefs, where enemy soldiers hold the turned bow above themselves in the presence of the Egyptian king as a gesture of abject surrender. The "turned bow" appears in similar representations in the art of Egypt, Mesopotamia, and Iran; it was not only clearly understood as a gesture of dominance in all of these cultures, but it also appears even in the derivative art of later cultures of the Hellenistic period.

Gestures of many other types were used throughout long periods of Egyptian history and continue in the gesture protocols of other cultures and areas influenced by the Egyptians, in some cases surviving even to the present day. In the Islamic performance of *salat* (the ritual of prayer), for example, the gestural forms of *ruku* (the position in which the believer stands with body bent forward at the waist and hands on knees) and *sujud* (the position in which the believer prostrates himself with hands, knees, feet, and face touching the ground) can both be exactly paralleled in representations of ancient Egyptian worship and doubtless continue ancient gestural forms.

[*See also* Symbols.]

BIBLIOGRAPHY

Brunner-Traut, Emma. "Gesten." In *Lexikon der Ägyptologie*, 2:573–585. Wiesbaden, 1977. Thematic overview of gesture, with many examples drawn from a number of categories.

Dominicus, Brigitte. *Gesten und Gebärden in Darstellungen des Alten und Mittleren Reiches.* Studien zur Archäologie und Geschichte Altägyptens, 10. Heidelberg, 1993. Detailed discussion of mainly nonroyal evidence of the Old and Middle Kingdoms.

Grapow, Herman. "Wie die Alten Ägypter sich anredeten, wie sie sich grüssten und wie sie miteinander sprachen." *Abhandlungen der Preussischen Akademie der Wissenschaften.* Berlin, 1939–1942. Early analysis of gesture communication in Egyptian society and art.

Gruber, Mayer I. *Aspects of Nonverbal Communication in the Ancient Near East.* Rome, 1980. Examines gesture symbolism in the broader context of nonverbal communication.

Muller, H. "Darstellungen von Gebärden auf Denkmalern des Alten Reiches." *Mitteilungen des Deutschen Archäologischen Instituts, Abteilung Kairo* 7 (1937), 57–118. Early study of gestures and poses depicted in Old Kingdom monuments.

Ogdon, Jorge R. "Observations on a Ritual Gesture, after Some Old Kingdom Reliefs." *Journal of the Society for the Study of Egyptian Antiquities* 10.1 (1979), 71–76. Discussion of the *hnw* ritual provides a clear example of a sequential gesture complex.

Sourdive, Claude. *La main dans l'Égypte pharaonique: Recherches de morphologie structurale sur les objets égyptiens comportant une main.* Bern and New York, 1984. Study of the hand in ancient Egyptian culture, showing its symbolic importance and use.

Teeter, Emily. *The Presentation of Maat: Ritual and Legitimacy in Ancient Egypt.* Studies in Ancient Oriental Civilizations, 57. Chicago, 1997. Contains detailed analyses of offering gestures.

Wilkinson, Richard H. "The Turned Bow in Egyptian Iconography." *Varia Aegyptiaca* 4.2 (1988), 181–187. Analyzes a specific gesture of dominance.

Wilkinson, Richard H. "The Turned Bow as a Gesture of Surrender in Egyptian Art." *Journal of the Society for the Study of Egyptian Antiquities* 17.3 (1991), 128–133. The inverse of a gesture of dominance providing a gesture of submission.

Wilkinson, Richard H. "Ancient Near Eastern Raised-Arm Figures and the Iconography of the Egyptian God Min." *Bulletin of the Egyptological Seminar* 11 (1991/1992), 109–118. Study of a shared gesture found in a number of ancient Near Eastern cultures.

Wilkinson, Richard H. *Symbol and Magic in Egyptian Art.* London, 1994. Overview of symbolism in Egyptian art, with a number of illustrated examples of gesture types in chapter 9, "The Language of the Body."

RICHARD H. WILKINSON

GIRAFFES. About 3000 BCE, an ecological event occurred that affected the natural range of the giraffe (*Giraffa camelopardalis*). At the end of the Neolithic pluvial (a geological wet, or rainy, phase), which lasted until about 2500 BCE, what had been savanna dried up; many of the trees, on whose leaves giraffes fed, disappeared and desert conditions prevailed in northern Africa. Thus, while prehistoric rock drawings around the Nile Valley had teemed with giraffes, they were portrayed only occasionally thereafter, as in the hunting scenes in the tomb of Weh-hetep at Meir or in the New Kingdom tombs of Huy and Rekhmire, where Nubians and Puntites were shown bringing giraffes to Egypt. In the tomb of Rekhmire, a small green monkey was portrayed climbing up the neck of a giraffe as it would a tree. Those giraffe were not native to Punt but were brought there from the sub-Saharan interior to be shipped to Egypt. In the Puntite village scene preserved on Queen Hatshepsut's temple at Deir el-Bahri, a giraffe was depicted.

The Egyptians valued giraffes first and foremost as denizens of their zoological gardens. In addition, their spotted skins were used to make coverings. Giraffe tails were brought via the southern lands to Egypt as tribute. From the fine, long black hair of the tail, the Egyptians made wigs, long ribbons such as the one the king wore over his shoulder during hippopotamus hunts, and woven armbands.

While the giraffe seems to have had no sacred qualities attributed to it, some Egyptologists have sought to identify the animal associated with the god Seth—a creature difficult to identify zoologically—as a giraffe and to see its head as the model for the royal *was*-scepter. Indisputably, the giraffe has made contributions to Old Egyptian in the word *sr,* meaning "to announce," "to foretell," "to proclaim," or "to prophesy." Those verbal associations were based on its 2 to 3 meter (6 to 10 foot) neck.

BIBLIOGRAPHY

Drenkhahn, Rosemarie. *Darstellungen von Negern in Ägypten.* Hamburg, 1967.
Reisner, George A. *Excavations at Kerma.* Harvard African Studies, 6. Cambridge, 1923.
Säve-Söderbergh, Torgny. *Ägypten und Nubien: ein Beitrag zur Geschichte altagyptischer Aussenpolitik.* Lund, 1941.

EMMA BRUNNER-TRAUT
Translated from German by Julia Harvey

GIZA, a pyramid plateau group (30° N, 31°20′E). When Sneferu, first king of the fourth dynasty (r. 2649–2609 BCE) died at Dahshur and was buried in his recently completed third pyramid there, his son Khufu (better known under his Greek name Cheops) succeeded. No convenient place remained at Dahshur for his planned Great Pyramid, so Khufu moved his court and residence farther north, where his prospectors had located a commanding rock cliff (overlooking present-day Giza) appropriate for a towering pyramid; this rock cliff was in the northernmost part of the first Lower Egyptian nome, Ineb-hedj ("the white fortress"), which later became the capital city of Memphis. According to a treatise on the geology of the pyramid plateau by Thomas Aigner, it is part of the Middle Eocene Mokattam Formation, which dips slightly southeast, comprising limestones and dolomites. To the south, the Mokattam and dolomitic limestones are overlain by the marly limestones and sandy marls of the Upper Eocene Maadi Formation. To the north and east, the Mokattam Formation is characterized by two steep escarpments about 30 meters (92 feet) high. It continues to the Great Sphinx ditch, which must at one time have formed a high peak. From there, stonemasons cut the core blocks for the Great Pyramid.

The older pyramids of the third and early fourth dynasties were built on thick layers of marl and slate. These marl layers were easier to dig than limestone, so excavation of the large shafts that extend as much as 30 meters

beneath the step pyramids was accomplished in a reasonable time. Yet there was a serious disadvantage: as the pyramids were built, the marl layers could not support their weight. The underlayer gave way, and the constructions became unstable. This happened with the South Pyramid at Dahshur, where cracks and serious damage appeared in the corridor system and in the chambers, so that pyramid had to be abandoned.

When Khufu (r. 2609–2584 BCE) planned his own ambitious pyramid, which was to reach an unrivaled height of nearly three hundred Old Egyptian cubits, he was looking for a solid rock base, nearby quarries, and a dominating position overlooking the Nile Valley. This he found at Giza, the nearest place combining these features. The high plateau of Giza was not virgin ground; it was occupied by a necropolis, with large *mastaba* tombs of princes and high officials lining the high cliffs. Those in the north and east were cleared away, their shafts filled or even totally destroyed during the quarrying for Khufu's pyramid. Only those on the hills to the far south were left undisturbed.

The large pyramid precinct was named Akhet-Khufu ("the Western Horizon of Khufu"). Besides the pyramid and the temples, it included the royal palace, administrative buildings, and the pyramid city (with the mansions of the royal princes and highest officials, and the houses of priests, artists, and architects). The royal palace and the pyramid city are probably hidden under several meters of Nile deposits, beneath the present-day village of Nazlet es-Sissi, much farther to the east than has been assumed. The workmen lived far from the exclusive residential city, in barracks to the south.

In Giza, the development of the pyramid complex—with a monumental pyramid and its temples and causeway—reached its apogee. Since the time of the early step pyramids, the alignment of pyramids to the cardinal points had been an important concern. Khufu's pyramid is oriented almost exactly to truth north, with a minor deviation of only 5 minutes. The pyramids of Khafre and Menkaure seem to be aligned by a diagonal that touches the corners of all three pyramids. (The other purported alignments among the three pyramids and the temples are merely the fantasy of pyramid enthusiasts. This is also undoubtedly the case in regard to theories of a celestial origin for the layout of the Giza pyramids—claiming that it reproduces the orientation of the belt stars in the Orion constellation—but in the Pyramid Texts this was identified with the deity Osiris.

The technical perfection of Khufu's pyramid compels our highest admiration: the accurate orientation toward the north; the leveling of the corners, which does not differ more than 2.1 centimeters (less than an inch); the minute difference in the lengths of the sides, only 4.4 centimeters (1.75 inches); and the variation of the angles, only

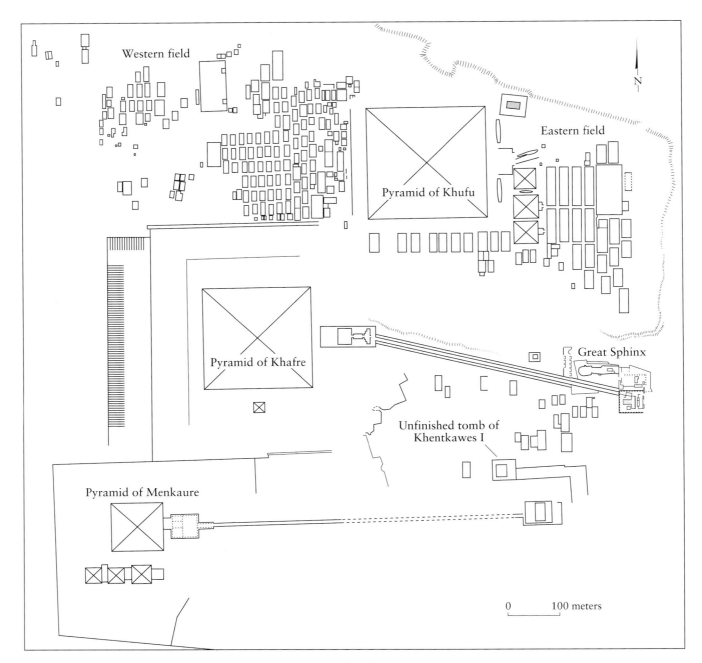

GIZA. *Plan of Giza.*

2°48′. All this seems incredible, considering the simple tools available to the builders. In contrast to the low 45° angle of slope of Sneferu's last pyramid, the builders dared to construct Khufu's pyramid at 51°50′40″. With a side of 440 cubits, or 230.37 meters (700 feet), it originally attained a height of 280 cubits (146.59 meters/450 feet), close to their ideal height of 300 cubits. Today, with the fortunes of time, the pyramid still reaches 138.75 meters

(420 feet). The arrangement of the corridor-and-chamber system within the pyramid is as perfect as the surveying and workmanship of the superstructure. In a purely positivist and rather superficial interpretation, the presence of three burial chambers within the pyramid has hitherto been attributed to successive changes of plan; this, however, does not do justice to the builders who created this unique monument with such precision. We cannot as-

sume that they did not have a plan for the pyramid's irreducible feature, the system of burial chambers that was the occasion and goal of the undertaking. Moreover, the external construction and its measurements fit completely with the design of the chamber system. The identification of the three-chamber principle in royal tombs provides further evidence for the unified planning of the pyramid. (It also refutes the "pyramid mysticism," which has assumed epidemic proportions in the West in recent years, with its assertions that the chamber system of Khufu's pyramid conceals arcane knowledge or additional treasure chambers called "chambers of knowledge.")

The only external part of the pyramid complex was the funerary temple, today reduced to its basalt pavement and the recently discovered south tomb near the southeastern corner of the pyramid. Traces in the pavement show that the temple consisted principally of a broad pillared courtyard and a chapel for sacrifices. Fragments of statues in many different hard stones, and of limestone reliefs carved in an austere style, provide evidence that it was once richly decorated. The causeway has been completely destroyed. Heredotus, the fifth-century BCE Greek historian, described it as another wonder, rising more than 40 meters (122 feet) above ground, with walls, for the first time, decorated with carved reliefs. Blocks of this causeway and basalt blocks of the valley temple's pavement, together with a large enclosure wall, have been discovered during construction work more than a kilometer (a half mile) east of the plateau. This new find suggests an enormous pyramid precinct extending more than a kilometer from east to west, and this makes it reasonable to suppose that the cyclopean stone wall to the south of the main wadi was built by Khufu as the southern boundary of his pyramid complex. Moreover, the Great Sphinx, almost certainly a monument of Khufu, is situated in his greater pyramid precinct and depicts a majestic image of the greatest of the Giza kings.

The necropolis was as thoroughly and strictly planned as the pyramid complex. Five large rock-cut pits to the east and south of the pyramid once contained Khufu's funerary boats—which are not solar barks, as was once maintained. On the eastern side of the pyramid are three smaller pyramid tombs—of the king's mother, Hetepheres, and of his two principal queens, Meritites and Henutsen, the mothers of Khufu's sons and successors, Djedefre and Khafre. Khufu's sons and daughters received enormous solid stone double *mastaba*s to the east, apportioned strictly according to their ages. The high dignitaries of the court and the pyramid's master builders—including Prince Hemiunu, the king's nephew and the son of his older brother Nefermaat—were assigned positions in the western cemetery. Never before or after in Egyptian history were the claims of divine kingship so thoroughly

considered and so perfectly displayed. The king intervened even in the plan and decoration of the tomb chapels, which uniformly contained only the most important offering scenes. At Giza, large-scale sculpture of notables was deliberately restricted to a few exceptional individuals, such as the powerful overseer of buildings and works and Prince Hemiunu. Even the highest of the other dignitaries had to be content with portrait heads, the so-called reserve heads, in their burial chambers. For the first and only time, all of state and society were integrated into the strict order of the royal necropolis and into the conception of the king's destiny in the hereafter—so that they would be available to serve him eternally. By this means they were assured of receiving royal favor and offerings in perpetuity from the king's central funerary temple.

Khufu's son and first successor, Djedefre (r.2584–2576 BCE), abandoned Giza and chose the nearby prominent cliff at Abu Roash to build his steep, high pyramid. In Giza, however, he completed his father's funeral ceremony, closing the pyramid and the shafts of the funerary boats which bear his name and seal.

After Djedefre's early death, another son of Khufu, Khafkhufu, ascended to the throne; he modified his name to Khafre (Khephren; r. 2576–2551 BCE). His pyramid is the only one built by a successor of Khufu that was truly completed; it was intended to match his father's in height or even to outdo it. To economize on construction, Khafre reduced the length of the sides of the base but chose a slightly higher site and a steeper angle of slope. Thus, although the pyramid's mass was smaller than that of Khufu, its height seemed greater—which was apparently the desired effect—and Khafre could name his pyramid "Khafre is the Greatest." At the top of this pyramid, the original casing is still preserved. Inside the pyramid, the arrangement of the funerary apartments is strikingly simple. In contrast, the architecture of his funerary and valley temples is of a type not found again until the fifth dynasty. The rooms are surrounded by massive cyclopean stone walls, creating the impression that the temple was either enclosed in a solid cliff or that it was carved out of the heart of the pyramid and set down outside it. More than seventy majestic hard-stone statues that once decorated the funerary and valley temples contribute to this effect by depicting the king as the visible image of the gods. Excavations in front of the valley temple have yielded important cult installations, connected with the cult of Sokar. This was certainly part of Rosetau—perhaps the first stage of this famous cult location, which was reported from the fourth dynasty until Roman times. To the south of the main pyramid, the outline and some casing blocks of the South Pyramid are still in place. The subterranean corridor and chamber are an exact copy of the newly discovered one of Khufu. In a separate shaft slightly to the

GIZA. *Pyramids and the Great Sphinx.* (Courtesy Dieter Arnold)

west of this pyramid, a wooden box was hidden, which contained an enigmatic scaffolding, probably a carrying shrine for the *ka*-statue buried in the South Pyramid.

The third pyramid at Giza, the pyramid of Menkaure, is remarkably small, although it had a casing of sixteen courses of red Aswan granite. Menkaure (r. 2551–2523 BCE) had a long and peaceful reign and there is no evidence of an economic crisis during it, so the reasons for the reduction of the height and mass of his pyramid must be sought elsewhere. To understand this, it is necessary to view the pyramids not just as royal monuments representing power but also as religious monuments, comparable to European cathedrals of the Middle Ages and Renaissance. The importance of a pyramid is not determined solely by its size but also by its religious significance. In contrast to its small size, the system of corridors and funerary apartments in the pyramid of Menkaure is characterized by an extraordinary succession of rooms, comparable only with those of Khufu's pyramid, except that those of Menkaure lead down into the rock whereas those of Khufu ascend. Certainly the difference in this design was not the result of secondary architectural corrections; it may attest to a new concept of the underworld god Osiris. Menkaure's funerary temple is more like that of Khufu, consisting of a broad, open courtyard with a large,

deep offering chapel. Within the temple and the valley temple a large number of statues have been discovered. The last royal monument constructed at Giza is the monumental tomb of Queen Khentkawes, mother of at least two and perhaps three kings of the fifth dynasty. Often pronounced the "fourth pyramid," this is in reality an enormous stepped-stone *mastaba* of Early Dynastic style.

Around the pyramids of their kings, the members of the royal families and the high officials and attendants were given their tombs. During the reign of Khufu, the distribution of tombs and their location were strictly regulated, but in the reign of Khafre this strict regulation was relaxed. Family members and attendants built their tombs against and between the existing *mastaba*s. New cemeteries were created south of Khafre's causeway, and the rock façades of the ancient quarries were cut and hollowed out. Thus, a new type of representative tomb was invented: the rock-cut tomb. Throughout the Old Kingdom the cemetery of Giza remained the most prominent, even when the kings resided again in Southern Saqqara. Such important officials as the architects of the 'Inti family, who constructed the pyramids of the fifth and sixth dynasties, lived in the pyramid town of Khufu and had their family tombs at Giza. In the late sixth dynasty, the decoration and painting of the subterranean chambers in

Giza was much more progressive than in the residential cemeteries of Saqqara.

During the First Intermediate Period, the pyramid town of Khufu and the cemetery of Giza were abandoned, and they remained so during the Middle Kingdom. The pyramids were forcefully opened and plundered, and the private tombs also suffered from such barbarous acts. Since the causeways and temples were used as quarries by the architects of the kings of the twelfth dynasty, no important tomb or cult installation of that period is attested. This changed completely during the New Kingdom. The kings of the eighteenth dynasty showed deep respect for the pyramids as the monuments of their ancestors at Giza. Giza also regained considerable religious significance as the center of royal worship to the Great Sphinx, "Lord of Setpet, the Chosen Place." Princes and kings of the eighteenth and nineteenth dynasties erected stelae between the paws of the Sphinx; and the Sphinx was no longer seen as a royal statue but instead was adored as an image of the sun god Harmachis, "Horus in his Western Horizon," which was a reference to the "Horizon of Khufu." Amenhotpe II dedicated a small temple to Harmachis to the northeast of the Sphinx. On foundation tablets of that temple, the Sphinx is also named Harmachis-Hauron. Hauron is the name of a Syrian-Palestinian god of the netherworld that a community of Syrian-Palestinians living near the Great Sphinx identified with his image, dedicating stelae and offerings to him. Then Ramesses II installed a sanctuary within the forepaws. The famous group of the monumental falcon god Hauron protecting Ramesses II as a child may originally have been dedicated by Ramesses to this sanctuary. Officials and private persons joined this cult community.

In the Late period, Osiris became the dominant god of the area, taking over the cult locations of Rostau from Sokar and installing his cult in the Sphinx. Also, high, massive pedestals were added to the body of the Sphinx, on which chapels of Osiris and probably Isis stood. Isis became known as the "Lady of the Pyramids." Greek travelers from the sixth century BCE onward admired those enormous monuments but did not understand their religious meaning. When Herodotus saw the pyramids in the fifth century BCE, he could only reject the buildings as works of hubris. Later visitors were more admiring: a Greek poet of the second century BCE included the pyramids of Giza within the Seven Wonders of the World. They are the only one of the original seven that have survived to the present. During the Arab-dominated Middle Ages in Egypt, the pyramids were the object of continuous plundering. Under order of Sultan Saladin (r. 1174–1193), the casing of the pyramids and the temples was stripped, to be reused in the construction of the Citadel and the bridges of Cairo. Then the Ottoman caliphs and sultans

and the Mamluk beys sent parties to search the burial chambers and break the sarcophagi in the vain hope of finding treasure. Christian pilgrims, ambassadors, and heads of Western missions also showed an interest in the pyramids. At the end of the fifteenth century, a German traveler, Bernhard von Breydenbach, was the first to doubt the medieval theory that the pyramids were Joseph's granaries; knowing the classical authors, he rightly attributed the pyramids to the kings of the fourth dynasty. The first outstanding research and publication on Giza was accomplished by John Greaves, professor of astronomy at Oxford, in his *Pyramidographia*. Travelers like the Englishman Richard Pococke and the Danish marine officer Frederic Norden, with their elegant engravings in folio publications, opened the way to European enlightenment about Egypt.

Serious study of the pyramids began with the scholars of Napoleon's 1798 expedition, who drew the first maps and who cleaned and measured the upper chambers of the Great Pyramid and the head of the Sphinx. In the early nineteenth century, a ship's captain from Genoa, Giovanni Battista Caviglia, descended the so-called well in the Great Pyramid and reached the subterranean rock chamber; he then turned his activities to the Sphinx and excavated between the forepaws, where he discovered the famous Dream Stela of Thutmose IV. He was rivaled by another Italian adventurer, Giovanni Battista Belzoni, who forced his way through the rubble on the eastern side of Khafre's pyramid and reached the burial chamber. A British colonel, Howard Vyse, employed Caviglia briefly in excavations at Giza but finally found a more trustworthy assistant in John Shae Perring, an engineer, who produced maps, plans, and profiles not just of the Giza pyramids but of all pyramids from Abu Roash to Dahshur, publishing his results in three folio volumes. Vyse had no qualms about blasting his way through obstacles with dynamite; this he did in the Great Pyramid, blasting and forcing a passage from Davison's chamber, the lower relief chamber above the king's burial chamber, up to the four additional stress-relieving chambers; on the southern side of the pyramid, he blasted a deep hole into the mass of the core, hoping to find another entrance. Vyse also opened Menkaure's pyramid, where he discovered the extravagantly decorated but empty basalt sarcophagus of the king; he intended to bring it to London, but the ship bearing it sank during a storm in the Mediterranean, off Cartagena. In 1842, Richard Lepsius and the artists of the Prussian Expedition spent weeks in Giza, surveying the pyramids and copying the decorations of the tombs. His publication, twelve volumes of meticulous recording and engravings, is still standard and fundamental. Auguste Mariette, a French archaeologist and the founder of the National Egyptian Antiquities Service, worked in 1853 at the valley temple of Khafre, where he discovered the diorite statue of that king. He also began the reexcavation of the Great Sphinx. His work was continued and completed by Gaston Maspero and Emile Baraize in the early twentieth century.

The nineteenth-century publications of the French and Prussian expeditions sparked the rise of pyramid mysticism—the belief that the Great Pyramid was constructed with a special unit of measurement, and that from its measurements the secrets of faith, the past, and the future could be derived. The main proponent of this theory was Piazzi Smyth, an astronomer, who acquired many fervent adherents; even the young William Matthew Flinders Petrie was, when he arrived in Egypt at the end of that century, an admirer of Smyth's ideas. Petrie's own meticulous measurements of the pyramids soon disproved scientifically all the mystical notions about them.

A great period of excavation at Giza began in the early twentieth century, when the pyramid plateau was divided into three larger excavation zones: a German zone under Georg Steindorf, Uvo Hölscher, and Hermann Junker; an American zone under George Reisner; and an Italian zone under Ernesto Schiaparelli, who eventually gave his portion to Reisner. The Antiquities Service continued work at the Sphinx. Cairo University was also granted a site; its excavations were directed by Selim Hassan and later by Abu Bakr. The newest excavations, under Zahi Hawass, encompass the whole plateau and even the southern plain of Giza, including the successful restoration of the Great Sphinx.

BIBLIOGRAPHY

Edwards, I. E. S. *The Pyramids of Egypt.* London, 1985.
Lauer, J. P. *Le Mystère des Pyramides.* Paris, 1988.
Lehner, M. *The Complete Pyramids.* London, 1997.
Stadelmann, R. *Die Grossen Pyramiden von Giza.* Munich, 1990.

RAINER STADELMANN

GLASS. The first glass used by prehistoric people was obsidian, a natural glass of volcanic origin. It was considered a stone and was worked into artifacts by the Egyptians from the Predynastic period onward. (The Libyan Desert glass that had been formed by the heat of meteoritic impact was not exploited in antiquity.) From Neolithic times onward, craftsmen worked with controlled fire and pyrotechnological processes, experimenting with a variety of materials and also the basic materials that were later to be used in glassmaking: these included quartz sands, containing powdered mollusk shells (which became slaked lime with heat); sea-plant ashes that had high contents of soda and/or impure soda (used as flux to lower the melting temperature); and metallic ingredients that became coloring agents. Processing various proportions of the ingredients resulted in glaze, Egyptian faience, Egyptian blue, Egyptian green, frit, glassy faience, and many intermediate vitreous products (some of them used as pigments).

The first artificial glass that occurred in the ancient Near East was a glaze. It perhaps accidentally resulted as a byproduct of metallurgy—like vitreous slags and layers on interior walls of prehistoric metalworking installations. In the mid-sixteenth-century BCE, glass was produced as a material in its own right and was soon worked into artifacts. Where the various glass and glasslike materials were first made is, as yet, uncertain, although the Near East is the favored locale. Investigations by Christine Lilyquist and Robert Brill in *Studies in Early Egyptian Glass* (The Metropolitan Museum of Art, New York, 1993) indicate that almost no examples of pre-sixteenth-century BCE glass exists in Egypt.

Glassmaking. The melting of basic ingredients to make raw glass was certainly at first confined to specialized centers with sufficient nearby fuel. They made uncolored glass and exported it as chunks or ingots, which would be used in glassworking (see below). Ancient glass may have been made in a one-stage or a two-stage heating process. For the two-stage process, the crushed ingredients were heated for a long time, at about 850°C to produce a frit; then the cooled frit was ground to a powder and melted at about 900° to 1100°C, to become a refined glass. The melting process for glass depends on the ingredients, temperature, and time. Long heating can lower the melting temperature, as low as 900°C. Ancient raw glass is translucent and has tints of blue, green, or yellow, resulting from trace metal elements included in the quartz sand. Clear glass was rarely known in Egypt before Ptolemaic times, since traces of metallic inclusions were not yet being carefully controlled. Glass was generally made transparent to opaque and mostly colored in bright shades of dark blue, turquoise blue, violet-purple, yellow, white, and red—to often imitate precious stones.

In the cuneiform texts called the Amarna Letters, written in the Hurrian and Akkadian languages, "glass" is termed *ehlipakku* and *mekku*. The Egyptians never developed a name for it but called it "the stone that floats," "molten turquoise," as well as "artificial" or "molten lapis lazuli."

Glassworking and Glassware. The manufacture of glass objects was possible wherever glass chunks or ingots and a forced fire were available. No evidence exists for glass furnaces dating from pre-Roman times. When Egyptian rulers in the sixteenth century BCE had freed Egypt from the Hyksos (invaders from the Near East), the first securely dated glass artifacts appear in Egypt; for example, beads of uncolored, translucent glass that are engraved with the royal names of the early eighteenth dynasty. According to his Annals at the temple of Karnak, Thutmose III (1504–1452 BCE) imported chunks of raw glass from his Near Eastern military campaigns. Captive glassworkers, perhaps from northern Syria and the Mitanni region seem to have been involved in the development of a variety of glassworking techniques for Egypt's young glass industry. Outstanding pieces were glass vessels, a *persea* fruit, and a *shawabti* figure, all inscribed with the king's name, as well as a miniature sarcophagus and multicolored jewel inlays.

Beads were formed around a rod, and inlays were cut from flat plaques or made in open molds. Solid monochrome objects could be molded and retouched, as were the rare small glass sculptures—made mostly for the court. Vessels were shaped around a preformed core that was fastened at the end of a rod. The core, corresponding to the interior of the vessel, was apparently covered with crushed glass and heated above a fire, which melted the glass and created a layer of glaze. This procedure was repeated until the glass wall had the required thickness. The layers smoothed—as did the later applied threads—because of the surface tension of the hot glass. The thread decoration of Egyptian glass vessels was achieved by holding them above a fierce fire; prefabricated glass canes were thereby softened, and wound around the vessel, dragging them into patterns. This technique was confirmed in 1994, by B. Schagemann's experiments as director of the Lehr- und Versuchsglashütte des Staatlichen Berufsbildungszentrums für Glas in Zwiesel, Germany. The core's coating was neither made by dipping (the molten glass was too viscous) nor by trailing a coil of glass around the core as William Matthew Flinders Petrie had suggested in his 1894 monograph *Tell el Amarna*. No evidence of spiral coiling of early glass vessels exists; however, coiling was a characteristic technique only after core-forming was revived in the first millennium BCE. The finished vessels—the early as well as the late ones—were cooled in hot ashes, the rods were removed, and the cores scraped out, leaving sandy-looking remains on inner surfaces, which added to the opacity.

Many glass artifacts were recovered from the tomb of Amenhotpe II (r. 1454–1419 BCE), whose campaigns to the Near East are well documented. Among them are fragments of more than seventy glass vessels; some are inscribed with his name, including Egypt's tallest, 40 centimeters (about 16 inches) high; some revealing Near Eastern influences. Ornaments and first inlays on coffins have also been identified from this time. Two *shawabti* figures of the king's officials and engraved heads, probably representing Amenhotpe II, are master sculptures.

These early glass artifacts in Egypt include the largest known until Roman times. They also show an array of glassworking techniques never surpassed until the fifth century BCE, which include the following: rod-and-core forming, molding, twisting canes, fusing-on chips, prefabrication of appliqués and inlays, enameling, reverse painting on translucent glass, the assembling and fusing of glass mosaics, engraving, and grinding.

Glass objects from the tomb of Amenhotpe's successor Thutmose IV (r. 1419–1410 BCE) are smaller than the early pieces and of typical Egyptian shape. During peace with the Asian provinces, Amenhotpe III (r. 1410–1372 BCE) installed Egypt's earliest known glassworking site, in typical proximity to faience production, at his royal residence, Malqata, at Thebes. Finds there included an uncolored chunk of raw glass, glass canes, parts of crucibles, and coloring agents. Malqata's glassworkers went with Akhenaten (r. 1372–1355 BCE) to Tell el-Amarna (ancient Akhetaten), a town with many glass finds including jewels and amulets. There, workers had quarters in which the different crafts shared materials, equipment, and knowledge. Quantities of glassworking remains and the excavations directed by Paul T. Nicholson revealed evidence for at least an experimental phase of glassmaking in Egypt.

Some one hundred and seventy, mostly blue, glass ingots, the complete ones weighing about 2.5 kilograms (5.5 pounds) each, were found in the late Bronze Age shipwreck discovered at Ulu Burun, off the south coast of Turkey. Those ingots would fit roughly into the cylindrical crucibles at Amarna. Their glass is reported as similar to contemporary Egyptian and Mycenaean glass. Ulu Burun glass might have been sold to Egypt for scrap gold, including the Nefertiti scarab found in the wreck. If the secret of making glass from Amarna's sand and other nearby ingredients was already known, why would the king ask, in the Amarna Letters, for glass from his vassals in Palestine? It is certain that, for instance, yellow glass was not made in Egypt.

Tutankhamun's (r. 1355–1346 BCE) tomb yielded masterpieces of turquoise glass, such as two headrests and the writing set. Yet the king's purplish-blue glass figurine, perhaps made by the lost-wax technique, and the glass vessels show poor workmanship. Tutankhamun's burial equipment was lavishly embellished with glass inlays, including his coffins, his gold mask, and his throne. While inlays were used in the early eighteenth dynasty, they have extensively adorned sarcophagi, shrines, and furniture only since the reigns of Amenhotpe III and IV, where figures with fine relief faces decorated coffins discovered at Saqqara. From the fourteenth to the twelfth century BCE, great quantities of glass were worked; reliefs on palaces and on temple walls were even highlighted with faience and glass inlays.

A spectacular central production site for red glass has been dated to the reign of Ramesses II (r. 1304–1237 BCE). It was integrated into an area of multifunctional work-

GLASS. *Two polychrome vases from the eighteenth dynasty.* Their decorative effect derives especially from the combination of colors: turquoise, dark blue, yellow, and white. (The Metropolitan Museum of Art, Carnavon Collection, Gift of Edward S. Harkness, 1926 [26.7.1176]; The Metropolitan Museum of Art, Gift of Theodore M. Davis, 1917 [30.8.170])

shops and a huge bronze-working industry at Piramesse, in the eastern Nile Delta. There, a red ingot and the remains of forty crucibles for melting one hundred kilograms of glass are comparable in shape to Ulu Burun's ingots and Amarna's cylindrical vessels. New excavations by Edgar B. Pusch (1997) demonstrate the first securely dated making of uncolored raw glass in Egypt. As no artifacts were excavated, the site has been interpreted as a specialized center for making and coloring glass for distribution.

At the entrance to the Faiyum, near el-Lisht, glassworking materials were found in a village house, used mostly in the thirteenth century BCE. A huge lump of translucent blue glass was also found. While Malqata and Amarna glass were colored blue with imported cobalt ore, the nonroyal Ramessid el-Lisht workshop used only cop-

per. Glassworking is also assumed at Medinet el-Ghurab, Menshiya, and Tell el-Yahudiyya.

Glass vessel manufacturing ceased after the end of the New Kingdom, around 1081 BCE. Beads, amulets, and inlays continued to be made, on a small scale, until their production was increased in the sixth century BCE, when elaborate figural and hieroglyphic inlays were employed to decorate numerous wooden shrines. From the fifth century BCE to early Roman times, inlays also embellished coffins of wood, cartonnage, plaster, or gesso. The latest coffin is dated around the second century CE. Most ancient Egyptian inlays were monochromatic. In Aper-El's burial in the fourteenth century BCE, inlays were made by fusing different colored pieces of glass. Increasingly developed for inlays of coffins and furniture, this technique resulted in Egypt's true mosaic technique. The earliest examples were discovered at the Kharga Oasis in a fifth-century BCE temple complex and identified by Marie-Dominique Nenna.

The minute designs of such mosaic inlays were fabricated by bundling cold, colored-glass canes into the desired pattern, then fusing them to a bar. To miniaturize the pattern, the bar was lengthened by pulling. Thereafter, mosaic slices were cut from the bar, ground, and polished. Both monochromatic and mosaic inlays were excavated from temporarily erected temple-decoration workshops of Ptolemaic and early Roman times in Gumaiyima near Tanis, and in Tebtynis at the Faiyum. The mosaic technique was mastered when Alexander the Great founded the port city of Alexandria in 332–331 BCE. According to ancient authors, Alexandria was famous for her luxurious glasses. Alexandrian glassworkers probably developed mosaic glass bowls. Alexandrian mosaic inlays with Egyptian and Greek designs were found at many Egyptian sites; some were exported even to the kingdom of Meroë (in modern Sudan) until the first century CE.

The manufacture of core-formed vessels had a renaissance in the Near East and the Mediterranean during the first millennium BCE. They were made in a new technique by coiling a hot glass thread around a prefabricated core. The few vessels of this era excavated in Egypt may have been made in Alexandria. Since glass finds have been scarce in Alexandria and environs, it can only be assumed that Alexandrian workshops produced luxurious vessels, such as cameo, overlay and gold glass vessels: all were made of hot glass on the turning wheel. Certain types of glass vessels and artifacts found in the kingdom of Meroë among glasses imported from the Hellenistic world and the Roman Empire—once ascribed to Alexandrian glass houses—are now assigned to Meroitic glass workshops.

In Egypt, only gold and silver were more highly prized than glass, which equaled the precious lapis lazuli and turquoise in value during the eighteenth dynasty. Consequently, glass manufacture was long under royal control. Comparing the Annales of Thutmose III to the Harris Papyrus of Ramesses III, in enumerating presents to the gods and their temples, the value of glass fell slightly. Although the number of royal names on glass artifacts decreased during the New Kingdom, glass remained precious throughout Egyptian history. Valuable coffins, royal furniture, and the shrines of deities were embellished with glass until early Roman times. Glass vessels, the most ambitious glass artifacts beside sculpture, served as fine tableware or containers for valuable unguents, oils, and cosmetics. They were donated as royal gifts to privileged persons and to temples in Egypt and abroad. Excavated from wealthy tombs and temples on eastern Mediterranean islands, such as Cyprus, or in the Syria-Palestine region, their export quantity increased from the reign of Thutmose IV (1419–1410 BCE) to the Ramessid period.

When glass blowing was invented in the first century BCE, glass became available for nonroyalty. A vast glass industry was settled on the hills near the salt lakes of the Wadi Natrun, where innumerable and as yet insufficiently studied relics provide evidence of an enormous growth in glass manufacture.

BIBLIOGRAPHY

Bass, George F. "Oldest Known Shipwreck Reveals Splendors of the Bronze Age." *National Geographic* 172 (December 1987), 716–718, 732. Concerning the largest find of ancient glass ingots.

Bianchi, Robert S. "Those Ubiquitous Glass Inlays from Pharaonic Egypt: Suggestions about Their Functions and Dates." *Journal of Glass Studies* 25 (1983), 29–35. First comprehensive study on Egyptian glass inlays.

Cool, H. E. M. "Sedeinga and the Glass Vessels of the Kingdom of Meroe." *Annales du 13ᵉ congrès de l'Association Internationale pour l'Histoire du Verre*, pp. 201–212. Lochem, 1996. On Nubian glass manufacture in Meroitic times.

Cooney, John D. *Glass*, British Museum, 4. London, 1976. Catalog of one of the major collections of Egyptian glass, with examples of almost all kinds of artifacts and techniques.

Cooney, John D. "Glass Sculpture in Ancient Egypt." *Journal of Glass Studies* 2 (1960), 11–43. The most comprehensive study on glass sculpture.

El Goresy, Ahmed, Fuad Tera, Birgit Schlick-Nolte, and E. Pernicka. Chemistry and Lead Isotopic Compositions of Glass from a Ramesside Workshop at Lisht and Egyptian Lead Ores: A Test for a Genetic Link and for the Source of Glass." *Seventh International Congress of Egyptologists, Cambridge, 3–9 September 1995*, pp. 471–481. Leuven, 1998. On the import of lead ores and yellow glass to Egypt.

El Goresy, Ahmed. "Polychromatic Wall Painting Decorations in Monuments of Pharaonic Egypt: Compositions, Chronology, and Painting Techniques." *Proceedings of The First International Symposium on the Wall Paintings of Thera. August 30th through September 4th, 1997*. Santorini, Greece. Half of the contribution is devoted to the vitreous pigments used.

Goldstein, Sidney M. *Pre-Roman and Early Roman Glass in the Corning Museum of Glass*. Corning, N. Y., 1979. Illustrates the full history of early glass with examples from the collection.

Grose, David F. *Early Ancient Glass*. New York, 1989. Offers a good catalog from The Toledo Museum of Art, of early glass until the first century CE; includes modern imitations.

Keller, Cathleen A. "Problems of Dating Glass Industries of the Egyptian New Kingdom: Examples from Malkata and Lisht." *Journal of Glass Studies* 25 (1983), 19–28. Presents unpublished glass remains from two main glassworking sites.

Lierke, Rosemarie. "Early History of Lampwork—Some Facts, Findings and Theories. Part 2 Fire or Flame? Lampworking Techniques in Antiquity." *Glastechnische Berichte* 65.12 (1992), 347. Demonstrates that an open fire must have been used in ancient glassworking.

Lierke, Rosemarie. "Glass Vessels Made on a Turning Wheel in Roman Times (survey), Also Glass Vessels Made on a Turning Wheel. Cameo Glass." *Annales du 13ᵉ congrès de l'Association Internationale pour l'Histoire du Verre*, pp. 55–76. Lochem, 1996. (Footnote 11 on page 71 concerns core-formed vessels of the first millennium BCE). The author rediscovered, by her own experiments, the ancient secret of working hot glass on a turning wheel in manyfold techniques.

Nicholson, Paul T. *Egyptian Faience and Glass*. Aylesbury, 1993. Short introduction to the history and technique of vitreous materials.

Nicholson, Paul T. "New Evidence for Glass and Glazing at Tell el-Amarna (Egypt)." *Annales du 13ᵉ congrès de l'Association Internationale pour l'Histoire du Verre*, pp. 11–19. Lochem, 1996. Promising results of excavating furnace and glass remains at Amarna.

Nenna, Marie-Dominique. "Eléments d'incrustation en verre des nécroples alexandrines." *Annales du 12ᵉ congrès de l'Association Internationale pour l'Histoire du Verre*, pp. 45–52, Amsterdam, 1993. Presents new evidence for dating monochromatic and mosaic glass inlays from Alexandrian sites.

Nolte, Birgit. *Die Glasgefässe im alten Agypten*. Münchner Ägyptologische Studien, 14, Berdini 1968. Comprehensive study of the glass vessels from New Kingdom times.

Rehren, Thilo, and Edgar B. Pusch. "New Kingdom Glass Melting Crucibles from Qantir–Piramesses." *Journal of Egyptian Archaeology* 83 (1997), 127–142. Important excavations of a huge glass-melting center.

Schlick-Nolte, Birgit. "Kostbare Glasgefässe aus dem 'Schatzhaus.' " In *Kamid el-Loz 12. 'Schatzhaus'-Studien*, edited by R. Hachmann, pp. 183–202, pl. 34–36. Saarbrücker Beiträge zur Altertumskunde, 48. Bonn, 1996. For the value and the export of glass vessels to the Mediterranian and the Near East.

Schlick-Nolte, Birgit, and Rosemarie Lierke. "From Silica to Glass: On the Track of the Ancient Glass Artisans." In *Miracles of Glass*. Jerusalem, 2000. From the ingredients and objects of glass to the techniques before glassblowing.

Simpson, Philip. "Egyptian Core Glass Vessels from Sinai." *The Journal of Egyptian Archaeology* 76 (1990), 185–186. Report about almost one thousand core-glass vessel fragments—the probable remains of donations to the temple of Hathor.

Stern, E. Marianne, and Birgit Schlick-Nolte. *Early Glass of the Ancient World. 1600 B.C.–A.D. 50: Ernesto Wolf Collection*. Ostifildern, 1994. Technical considerations on glassmaking and glassworking, including the working properties of glass, the pyrotechnological facilities, and the various manufacturing techniques demonstrated on artifacts from the Near East, Egypt, and the Mediterranean in a catalog of fine-quality ancient glass.

Wuttmann, Michel, et al. "Premier rapport préliminaire des travaux sur le site de 'Ayn Manawir, oasis de Kharga." *Bulletin de l'Institut*

Français d'Archéologie Orientale 96 (1996), 385–451. Mosaic inlays, identified recently by M.-D. Nenna, and monochrome glass inlays from a fifth-century BCE temple complex.

BIRGIT SCHLICK-NOLTE

GLASSWORKING. *See* Glass.

GNOSTIC TEXTS. *See* Nag Hammadi Codices and Related Texts; *and* Manichaean Texts.

GOATS. *See* Sheep and Goats.

GOLD. The words used by Egyptologist Howard Carter, "gold—everywhere the glint of gold," described his initial glimpse of the treasure of the young king, Tutankhamen, whose tomb he and Lord Carnavon discovered in 1922. This find, which included a wide range of funerary objects, was reduced by the famed archaeologist to "gold," which was then the most dazzling, desired, and culturally meaningful of the known chemical elements. Carter's response to the three-thousand-year-old entombed treasure demonstrates the timeless allure of this metal. Its importance—originally linked to its color and sun-like brilliance, its resistance to corrosion, and its malleability—was enhanced by its rarity. For the ancient Egyptians, gold had profound implications for the afterlife. Upon completion of the embalming process, the newly deceased was ideally encased in gold. Masks, caps for vulnerable fingers and toes, and occasionally entire coffins were crafted from gold sheet. Considered "the flesh of the gods," this immutable (nontarnishing) metal was used as a means of attaining immortality.

One reason for Egypt's ascendancy in the ancient world was its trade policy; gold was exported to obtain raw materials such as copper, tin, and silver from the Near East. Requests for gold appear in second-millennium BCE letters from kings who enviously described the gold of Egypt as literally lining the streets. A letter from Tushratta, king of Mitanni, to Queen Tiye, wife of the eighteenth dynasty ruler Amenhotep III reads, "My brother, pray send gold in very great quantities . . . in the land of my brother is not gold as the dust upon the ground?" In antiquity, the Nile Valley—that fertile ribbon of land extending from the Delta in the North to Khartoum in the South—was host to the two great civilizations of Egypt and Nubia (Sudan). Those lands were rich in both alluvial gold and gold ore.

The word *Nubia* may, in fact, derive from the ancient Egyptian word *nbw*, which means "gold" and is represented hieroglyphically by a golden collar with pendants.

Gold from the Nile Valley varies considerably in purity; it ranges from 80 to 99 percent pure. Samples of placer deposits indicate that it is naturally alloyed with silver, which may account for as much as 20 percent of any given sample. Silver-rich gold (electrum) is pale in color and darkens as the silver oxydizes. Small amounts of copper, between 0.5 and 2 percent, may be included in gold, while platinum is included less frequently. Ancient goldwork is notable for the occasional presence of minute inclusions of platinum on the surface, since the working temperatures of ancient metalsmiths did not reach the melting point of platinum.

Egypt's gold-bearing region was situated in the South, along a quartz-bearing plateau in the Eastern Desert adjacent to the Red Sea. South of Aswan, in Nubia, gold fields flanked the Nile in areas of exposed quartzite; larger gold deposits were to the southeast of the Second Cataract. In describing gold, the ancient Egyptians often referred to its geographic source. From southeastern Egypt, including the hill region that paralleled the Red Sea along the Wadi Hammamat and Wadi Abbad, came the "gold of Coptos," while Lower Nubia supplied the "gold of Wawat." Wawat included the rich mines of the Wadi Allaqi and Wadi Cagbaba. The "gold of Kush" was derived from the region south of the Second Cataract, which included riverine alluvial deposits as well as desert lands that stretched to the Red Sea. These gold-bearing areas were extensively worked in antiquity by shallow surface mining.

The oldest Egyptian geological map is today in the Egyptian Museum in Turin; it dates to the New Kingdom reign of Ramesses IV. Drawn on papyrus, it details a mountainous route, bearing eastward from the Nile, along the Wadi Hammamat, toward the Red Sea. The gold-bearing zones, identified in Hieratic script as "mountains of gold," are designated at various points throughout this mineral-rich region. Houses and work stations, where final cleaning and preparation for transport took place, are situated near a sizable well. For several centuries, expeditions went to this important gold source, often involving thousands of workmen. In this region, a well-preserved cistern of Roman date indicates that the gold far outlasted pharaonic rule. The simplest form of gold recovery is panning in streams and wadis for placer deposits. Once those finds are depleted, it is necessary to follow the gold to its source. While Egyptian texts do not provide information on the means of removing gold from quartz ores, a description by Agatharchides, a second-century BCE Greek, has provided insight into Ptolemaic

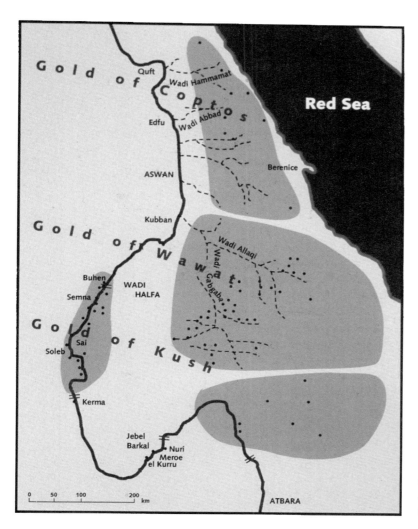

GOLD. *Map of the goldmining regions of ancient Egypt and Nubia.* (Graphic by Yvonne Markowitz and Peter der Manuelian)

working conditions of miners and their methods of extraction; his account describes a harsh work environment, with criminals, slaves, and captives performing the dangerous hammering of rock with picks, often following promising veins deep into hillsides through dark, narrow tunnels. There is some evidence that fire was used to create fissures in the stone, to aid in the removal of large chunks of quartz; the pieces were then transported to the open air where another team pounded the stones into smaller bits. The small fragments were ground into a gritty powder by older men and women, and the product was washed over a sloping table to separate the quartz from the gold. The gold dust was then ready to melt into ingots, thick, heavy strips that were sometimes made into rings. This technique of mining is undoubtedly of considerable antiquity, and the discovery of two Meroitic gold-washing stations at Faras East in Nubia by J. Vercoutter (1955) provides material support. Vercoutter also outlined the division of labor in mining operations, based on Classical-era texts. They include artificers (who locate gold veins), diggers, pounders, grinders (mostly women), and washers. Egyptian sources provide a few titles, too: miner, gold washer, and staff of gold washers. Great emphasis was accorded officials and workers who were directly or indirectly involved in goldworking—no doubt a reflection of their high status in the community. Among the titled officials were the "Scribe-Reckoner of Gold" (in charge of weighing the gold), "Overseer of the Gold Lands" (a high official in charge of the gold regions), "Captain of the Archers of Gold" (a supervisor of the gold washers), "Overseer of the Treasury" (in charge of gold mining in Upper Nubia), and "Scribe of the Treasury" (in charge of inspecting and supervising the mines). The craftsmen who processed the gold into objects were known as *nby* ("goldworkers"), and the "Overseer of Gold Workers" supervised their activity in the workshop.

Ancient Egypt's mining, supply, and distribution of gold was controlled by the state, so gold was largely worked either in workshops attached to the royal palace or within temple precincts. The New Kingdom scenes of craftsmen in the Theban tomb of the vizier Rekhmire illustrate the typical temple workshop; in them, men weigh, record, and work gold into stands and vessels. The number of people employed, the division of labor, and the splendor of the items are consistent with goods destined for use by the state or the elite. Little is known about the merchant-jeweler, who crafted and bartered trinkets of a modest type. Records relating to tomb robberies of the Ramessid period provide evidence of the universal practice of recycling precious metals, so it is likely that some of the stolen metal found its way to independent craftsmen, some of whom were temple metalsmiths working surreptitiously for private clientele. At the New Kingdom city of Amarna, domestic craft industries were spread throughout the suburbs; metalsmiths were probably included in their ranks. Such metalworkers would have supplied the gold beads and amulets that were common among average Egyptians' burial goods.

Despite the abundance of Egyptian gold fields and the intense efforts to maximize retrieval from alluvial deposits, by the New Kingdom demand exceeded supply—a crisis that led to the development of tunneling techniques. Gold may also have been the incentive for the series of forts built along the Second Cataract of the Nile early in the second millennium BCE. The forts functioned as trading posts, and there Nubians exchanged cattle and luxury items—ivory, ebony and gold—for Egyptian staples such as grain and wine. The fort at Kubban, in close proximity to the Wadi Allaqi, was built to control the copper and gold traffic along that metal-rich desert watercourse. Gold was an important commodity at those outposts, as evidenced by a find of several scales and stone goldweights. Much of Nubia came under Egyptian control about 1450 BCE, and gold was paid to the pharaohs as tribute. Nubians presenting gold dust and circular ingots were painted into Theban wall scenes of the eighteenth dynasty. The quantities of gold recorded on monuments do not seem to be excessive, so it is likely that such tribute scenes were meant to record, define, and enhance the role of Egypt's king as a mighty ruler.

Early in the first millennium BCE, an Upper Nubian elite established a powerful state with a capital at Napata, near the Fourth Cataract. Egypt, in a period of fragmentation and decline, was overtaken by those forceful Nubian rulers, who unified both lands and presided over them. The Nubian kings—the twenty-fifth, or Kushite, dynasty—adopted and then incorporated many Egyptian ideas and customs into Nubian culture. In southern Nubia, by the Napatan period (c.750–270 BCE), gold had an elevated status that can be viewed as the result of several factors: its ubiquitous presence in the Nubian landscape; its importance in the state economy; and its identification—as a dazzling, sun-like metal—with the sun god Amun. If Egyptians characterized gold as "the flesh of the gods," an enduring substance that could be beaten into thin sheets and adapted as a "skin" to vulnerable surfaces of the body, Nubians saw in it a divine significance. Their attitude toward even the raw material explains the presence of nugget-jewels in a land with skilled metalsmiths and jewelers. The earliest known nugget-jewel belonged to an ancestor of Piye, the first Kushite king (mid-ninth century BCE). This chieftain was buried in a pit grave, under a circular gravel mound, at el-Kurru, an early Kushite cemetery near the Fourth Cataract. Although the grave was partially plundered in antiquity, several items of jewelry were found *in situ* around the head, chest, and left hand. They include a gold lunate earring, a plain gold finger ring, and two necklaces. One of the necklaces (now in the Sudan National Museum in Khartoum) consists of sixteen biconical beads of gold sheet, an alluvial nugget, and a hollow gold Ptahtek amulet. The nugget is pierced for suspension, inscribed with a dedication to the deity Amun, and measures 30 millimeters (0.12 inches) by 17 millimeters (0.07 inches). A suspension boring was artfully situated by the ancient metalsmith in an elongated outgrowth that simulates a ball. The surface was planed flat for the inscription: "The Lord [god] Amun, may he give the perfect life." This dedication establishes a relationship between an earthly material (gold) and the divine or magical. Its inclusion in a royal burial also marks the nugget as a prestige or status item. In fact, two of the thirteen nugget-pendants excavated from Napatan tombs by the Harvard-Museum Expedition in 1923 at nearby Nuri and Meroë come from royal burials; these later nuggets, smaller and uninscribed, were found among the plundered remains of two queens who were buried nearly a century apart. In the case of Queen Madiken, buried at Nuri around 500 BCE, a 12-millimeter (0.05-inch) nugget was found on a gold wire necklet. It appears that gold, in its native or unworked state, had assumed the role of a powerful amulet.

Goldworking. One of gold's properties is that of malleability (able to be hammered or pressed without breaking), a characteristic that permits the artisan to work the metal in its native state, called cold-working. A common cold-working technique in antiquity was that of hammering, so that the metal was pounded into sheets of varying thickness, which could then be used in crafting jewelry, *objets d'art,* and funerary items. To prevent marring and damage from the hand-held stone beaters during the pounding, the metal was placed between layers of leather or papyrus resting on a stone anvil. If the metal became hard or brittle, it could be annealed, softened through repeat heatings. Thick or heavy-gauged sheet could be used in the forming of vessels that were raised by rotating and hammering a gold disk. Thinner sheet, known either as foil (0.17–0.54 millimeters thick) or leaf (0.013–0.001 millimeters thick) were used for decorating surfaces, such as wood or cartonnage.

Perhaps the most common use of gold sheet was in jewelry making. The typical Egyptian ornament is an assemblage of parts made from metal sheet that was cut, shaped, and soldered together. The cutting was done with a metal chisel or knife, and the metal was pressed into molds or wrapped around a core to create shapes. Many of the gold-sheet amulets that accompanied the deceased were crafted by that simple process. Greater skill was needed if soldering was required, and solder, used for fusing the joint between metal parts, was of the hard variety in Egypt, usually made by adding a small amount of copper to the gold specimen; the ingredients were heated in a crucible, creating an alloy with a lower melting point than the metal being fused. The alloy or solder could then be used to join the separate parts without damaging the ornament. Although gold was first worked cold, it was soon worked hot, melted and poured into molds. An important task of the ancient goldsmith was that of melting the precious metal. A measured amount of the material was placed in one or more crucibles and heated over an open charcoal-fired hearth. To raise the temperature above gold's melting point (1063°C), it was necessary to fan the fire. Several goldworking scenes from Old Kingdom tombs indicate that this was done by means of reed blowpipes with clay nozzles. By the Middle Kingdom the animal-hide bellows was in use. The blowpipe plus dish bellows was a New Kingdom innovation that permitted the melting of large amounts of metal.

Once gold has been melted, it can be poured into hollow molds of varying shapes. Molds were typically of hand-carved steatite (soapstone) or limestone, and they could be open or closed types. Gold items were also crafted by the lost-wax method (*cire perdue*), in which a wax model of the desired object is formed, encased in clay, and then heated so that the wax melts and exits through a hole in clay. The hole then serves as the entry into which the molten gold is poured. Once cooled, the clay is removed, and the gold object is ready for hand-finishing and polishing. Complex or large gold items were made by casting several parts, which were soldered. Since

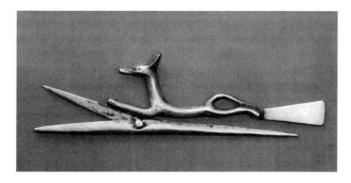

GOLD. *Scissors with representation of a running dog, early New Kingdom.* Length: 8.6 centimeters (3.4 inches). (The Metropolitan Museum of Art, Lila Acheson Wallace Fund, Inc., Gift, 1977. [1977.169])

cast objects used relatively large quantities of precious metal, as compared to those made by sheet metal assemblage, casting was reserved for the finest goods.

The enhancement and decoration of gold surfaces was accomplished through several methods: (1) *chasing* involved the formation of patterns by indenting into the front surface with a wooden or metal tool, (2) *repoussée* involved hammering the metal from the inside surface to create a relief pattern on the front; (3) *wirework* involved the fabrication of slender rods from strips of metal that were cut and rolled between two hard surfaces; (4) *granulation* was a labor-intensive Middle Kingdom innovation, whereby tiny gold granules were soldered onto a sheet gold base; (5) *plating* of copper and silver involved overlays of gold; (6) gold-sheet *inlaying* embellished wood and bronze; (7) gold *pins* and *rivets* were used as fasteners; (8) *engraving*, a process sometimes confused with chasing, involves the removal of metal with a graver. Engraving was infrequent in the Nile Valley before Greco-Roman times, as was gold refining, a technology discovered in the Near East and introduced with coinage into Egypt during Ptolemaic times.

Throughout the course of Egyptian history, gold remained a substance of supreme value—a symbol of the gods, a guarantee of immortality, an emblem of prestige, a key to power, and an enhancer of beauty. Revered, traded, gifted, stolen, recycled, and demanded as tribute, gold was a cultural obsession—a preoccupation that continues to influence our own attitudes toward the land of the Nile.

[*See also* Jewelry; *and* Quarries and Mines.]

BIBLIOGRAPHY

Gnädinger, Louise. "Six Thousand Years of Gold Mining." In *Gold,* edited by N. Flüeler and S. Speich, pp. 10–15. Lucerne, 1975.

Harris, Lucas A., and J. R. Harris. *Ancient Egyptian Materials and Industries.* London, 1989. An excellent in-depth survey of material and methods in ancient Egypt.

Ogden, Jack. *Jewels of the Ancient World.* London, 1982.

Scheel, Bernd. *Egyptian Metalworking and Tools.* Aylesbury, 1989. An excellent illustrated introduction to the subject is included in this small volume.

Vercoutter, J. "The Gold of Kush." *Kush* 7 (1959), 120–153.

YVONNE J. MARKOWITZ
AND PETER LACOVARA

GRAFFITI. The Italian word *graffiti* (sing. *graffito*) is used today for a great variety of inscriptions or pictures that were scratched, hammered, picked, painted (or sprayed) on a hard surface, such as stone. One factor for such expression is that, in many cases, it was not intended for eternity—it was just a certain momentary idea or inspiration. That basic intention changed in the course of time and, perhaps, ancient Egyptian elite culture was the first to leave graffiti for eternity, to perpetuate individual achievements and names, and to communicate with future generations. Predynastic examples include Egyptian "royal" names, with the falcon of the god Horus mounted on the façade of a palace; they are found as far south as Gebel Sheikh Suleiman at the Second Cataract of the Nile. The name of King Wadji ("snake") of the first dynasty was found at Wadi Abbad, but it is very doubtful that the king himself was present on the spot. Longer hieroglyphic inscriptions are not found before the third dynasty at Wadi Maghara in the Sinai, with the names of the pharaohs Sekhemkhet and Zanakht.

In prehistoric times, humans hammered or picked out pictures with a hard pebble—for example, of the game they were hunting. Upper Paleolithic people in Europe and the Aborigines in Australia created paints for their pictures, in bright colors. In Egypt, countless hammered, scratched, and ink-drawn graffiti were left by people moving through the deserts, from the time of prehistoric hunter-gatherers until today. A good collection was recorded by Hans Winckler in his *Rock-Drawings of Southern Upper Egypt* (London, 1938–1939). The deserts were never inaccessible empty spots but were busily trodden by both small groups and huge caravans, at least in certain eras. Prehistoric rock pictures are found beneath graffiti in hieroglyphic, Hieratic, Demotic, Greek, Coptic, Latin, Arabic, English, and French—often accompanied by pictures. Countless suitable rock surfaces were used, usually at ancient, traditional resting places, at panorama points or hills, and on remarkable single rocks—forming a living and unbroken tradition. How many graffiti were destroyed in the course of time, and how many still await discovery can hardly be imagined. Only a minority of these pictures and inscriptions are pharaonic Egyptian. Even fewer are dated or datable by chance. The youngest dated hieroglyphic graffito is from 394 CE; the youngest

Demotic graffito is from 452 CE, both from the temple at Philae. About three hundred graffiti and rock inscriptions have been published from Old Kingdom times, more than three hundred from the Middle Kingdom, and another three hundred from the New Kingdom (without hundreds known from the region of the First Cataract).

Hieroglyphic and Hieratic inscriptions far from the Nile Valley are some of the most informative texts that were left by Egyptian civilization. Nonetheless, similarly informative Nile Valley graffiti can be found in quarry regions or at ancient resting places. They show a great variety in writing—in hieroglyphic, Hieratic, and Demotic—providing fascinating style, content, and quality. Some contain only a crudely scratched name: the scribble of a nearly illiterate donkey boy, perhaps. Some are twenty lines long or more, and some are accompanied by carefully incised reliefs that were authorized by a vizier, high-steward, chief treasurer, or even by the pharaoh. Many do not differ in quality and content from inscriptions on stelae, in temples, or in tombs—the only difference being the surface or venue. Some display an offering formula for the benefit of the author (who is often represented in an accompanying picture), with an appeal to future visitors to recite it aloud; not only was this a proof of his presence but also the medium for the immortalization of his name and person.

Some examples: graffiti of a twelfth dynasty official on the rocks near the Nubian fortress of Kumma have an identical appeal: "As to everyone who shall pass by this stela (the texts are in fact graffiti), and who may reach his home [Egypt] in good condition, his wife being in joy, and who may embrace his kindred, may he say [the offering formula]. . . ." Some graffiti like the following from Hatnub offer promises: "As for every traveler who may raise his arm [in prayer] for this picture (the graffito is modeled after a stela): he shall reach his home in safety after he has accomplished that for which he came here!" Others close with the threat of harsh sanctions: "Who will damage this picture: the gods of the nome will punish him!"

A special type of text, long in use by ancient Egyptians, is visitors' graffiti. They were left—as they are today—by people who visited a building, tomb, pyramid, or other interesting or holy place, just to tell future visitors, "I was here!" This is also the intent of many graffiti in the mining areas. Some give just the name and an often standardized remark on the quality of the building visited: "The scribe X came to see the building of. . . . He found it like heaven in its interior." Other remarks have a votive character and appeal to the gods, such as those on pavements and the roofs of temples, and are often accompanied by a scratched sketch of the feet of the devotee. The main period for visitors' graffiti in both hieroglyphic and Hieratic script was the New Kingdom, especially the Ramessid period, when elite visitors went to see their ancient monuments in a spirit of admiration. (Not considered here are the innumerable graffiti left by foreign mercenaries, such as Cariens, Cypriots, Phoenicians, and Aramaeans or by Greek, Roman, and more recent tourists.)

Beyond the Nile Valley, graffiti (and comparable texts on stelae) are clustered in those regions that were of economic interest to the Egyptians. Some sites developed a special tradition of texts with high literary quality, the so-called Expedition Texts, or reports on an enterprise's successful accomplishment: in the Sinai, and at Hatnub, Wadi Hammamat, and Wadi el-Hudi. Other sites of equal or greater economic importance lack these: for example, no graffiti (except some laconic stelae) are known from Gebel Zeit (galena mines) or Timna (copper mines).

The Egyptians came to the Sinai for copper, malachite, and turquoise. At Serabit el-Khadim, a sanctuary to Hathor, "the Mistress of Turquoise," was developed and enlarged until the Ramessid era. Published inscriptions from this site include about twenty-six inscriptions from the Old Kingdom, about one hundred six inscriptions from the Middle Kingdom, and eighty-five from the New Kingdom. The Old Kingdom inscriptions were scratched or hammered on the rock surface and often contain only a date and the titles and names of the expedition's staff. A local tradition is the icon of the king smiting his enemies, sometimes helped by a deity (Thoth, Sopdu, or Hathor). The Middle Kingdom inscriptions are mostly composed on single-, double-, or even four-sided stelae erected in Hathor's temple at Serabit el-Khadim. Many were authorized by supervisors of the thirty or so expeditions organized in the reign of Amenemhet III. They display the winged sun disk in a lunette, a date, names of the king, and a short self-praising sequence of epithets and titles of the official responsible for the stela, augmented by a statement that he came there on the king's order, a report on the successful enterprise, an appeal to future visitors, and a list of the staff and their provisions. The expedition's success is attributed to the gods of the earth, acting for the benefit of the pharaoh: they only give him what already belongs to him. A standard formula is, "His [the king's] father Geb gave it [the minerals] to him, Tatenen offers what is in him," or "The mountains are offering to him what is in them, they bring to light what was hidden in them." This view is similarly expressed in inscriptions from Wadi el-Hudi and Wadi Gawasis. Accordingly, many texts contain praise of the king and his power.

Inscriptions dated to the third dynasty are found only in Sinai, and there are not many inscriptions from the fourth and fifth dynasties at well-known sites. The sixth dynasty, however, is an important time for inscriptions naming the staff of officials on expedition in the Sinai, Wadi Hammamat, and numerous other places—some-

times very remote—in the Eastern and Western deserts. A large group of inscriptions was found in the Eastern Desert in the region of Wadi Dungash and Wadi Muweilha, which was once reached by leaving the Nile Valley near Kom Ombo or opposite Edfu and passing through Wadi Abbad and Wadi Barramiya. A scribe of the time of Pepy II boasts of digging a well for the troops' water supply with the formula, "I gave water to the thirsty and food to the hungry." Typically enough, the purpose of the enterprise is not mentioned, but it might have been a search for minerals, such as copper and gold.

The quarrying and mining region of the Wadi Hammamat was reached by leaving the Nile Valley at Coptos—and there the greatest amount of graffiti is on display: more than four hundred hieroglyphic and Hieratic, forty Demotic, and one hundred Greek graffiti from Ptolemaic and Roman times have been published to date. There are about ninety-five graffiti from the time of Djedefre until the end of the Old Kingdom. In contrast to the Old Kingdom rock inscriptions from Sinai, only few texts were authorized by kings; this practice changed in the eleventh dynasty, from which the most spectacular texts were recorded: two "wonder stories" that happened during the reign of Montuhotep III, during an expedition led by his vizier, Amenemhet (who probably later became pharaoh). The lucky finding of a well, and the marvelous event of a gazelle giving birth on a stone then found suitable for the king's sarcophagus, were interpreted as manifestations of the power of the god Min on behalf of the king. Another inscription, authorized by the royal steward Henenu in the time of Montuhotep II, records an expedition of three thousand men leaving from Coptos to the Red Sea coast, where they constructed ships heading for the "gods' land," perhaps the country called Punt. Among the approximately sixty texts from the First Intermediate Period and Middle Kingdom are many dated or datable to the reigns of Senwosret I and Amenemhet III. In the reign of Senwosret I, the highest number of participants on an expedition is recorded: seventeen thousand men. All had to be provisioned for thirty days with their due portions of bread, beer, and meat, according to their rank, by very effective logistics: the expedition's head got two hundred loaves and five beers each day, while the modest forced laborer got only ten loaves and one-third portion of beer. The troops were accompanied by twenty brewers, twenty millers, and twenty bakers. The outcome of all their efforts was stones for one hundred fifty statues and sixty sphinxes. Not until the reign of Ramesses IV did another expedition of comparable size go there; the texts speak of more than eighty-three hundred men. The hardships of the enterprise are readily conceivable, and the text duly records the death of nine hundred men.

In the alabaster (calcite) quarries of Hatnub, the oldest

inscriptions are from the time of Khufu. Later, Hatnub is known for a group of famous texts of the eleventh and twelfth dynasty families of governors of the Hare nome, who were buried at Bersheh. Inscriptions found in the Wadi el-Hudi have been dated as far back as the eleventh dynasty, but the search for amethyst ceased there after about fifteen expeditions (and more than eighty texts) in the thirteenth dynasty (Sobekhotpe IV). A few preserved royal inscriptions in the limestone quarries of Tura, south of Cairo, date to the Middle and New Kingdom; they use a standardized formula commemorating the reopening of the quarry (Amenemhet III, Ahmose, Amenophis II, Amenophis III).

During the Middle Kingdom, immortalization by rock inscription became very popular, at least among the elite and officials on tour. The twelfth dynasty was also the main period for graffiti in the Nile Valley. Hundreds of graffiti can still be seen in the region of the huge granite monoliths around Elephantine Island in the Nile and the First Cataract. A favored spot for graffiti since the Old Kingdom was the island of Sehel, where the goddess Anuket was worshiped. Many consist simply of an offering formula and long lists of names of the authors' relatives, often accompanied by sketched figures of the named people.

During the military expeditions led by Amenemhet I and Senwosret I to conquer the Sudan, about seventy inscriptions were cut into the rocks of Gebel el-Girgawi near Korosko. They commemorate participation in those expeditions by high officials and modest rank-and-file soldiers. Some were modeled after tomb inscriptions, such as the above-mentioned graffiti from Hatnub, ending with a threat formula. One example reads: "I am a man of the troops, who attacks the fighter, and who loves life and hates death. For him who shall erase this graffito, death shall be found for him." Many later graffiti were found in the surroundings of the Nubian fortresses, left by garrison members and priests. A special feature from the times of Amenemhet III, Amenemhet IV, and Queen Sobekneferu are the incised levels of the Nile's inundation heights at Semna and Kumma.

The mouth of the Wadi es-Shatt er-Rigale north of Gebel es-Silsila offered a suitable resting place for people coming by ship from Thebes, Edfu, or Elephantine. They used the time to immortalize themselves on the spot, and even kings left their marks on the rocks. Well known is the huge tableau of Nebhepetre Montuhotep I with his mother Iakh ("moon") and his father Antef ("son of the sun [Re]"), accompanied by the chancelor Khety. Another typical resting place used for graffiti was atop the high cliffs at Deir el-Bahri in Western Thebes. Priests of the temples below sat there awaiting the solemn processions of Amun, spending their time scratching their names and

offering formulas for their own benefit on the rock: "Giving praise to Amun, and kissing the earth for the lord of the gods, at his festival days in summer, when he dawns, at the day of the procession to the valley of Nebhepetre, by the priest of Amun Nefer-abed." A comparable spot for graffiti is the "Vulture Rock" in the desert of the delta of Wadi Hellal east of Elkab, where priests immortalized their names, long genealogies, and their participation in the feasts of the goddess of the valley.

Of more economic and strategic importance was a system of ancient roads that began at Western Thebes, passed the so-called Mountain of Thoth, with its mountain temple of Montuhotep I, and leading across the desert heights to shorten the Qena bend of the Nile to Hiw (Diospolis Parva) near present-day Nag Hammadi. This road significantly reduced the traveling time between Thebes or Armant and Abydos or Thinis. Control of movements on these roads was very important in the First and Second Intermediate Periods, so among hundreds of other inscriptions, there are remarkable inscriptions of Second Intermediate Period kings at a significant resting place, Wadi el-Hol, at the midpoint of the "Farshut road"; at another site is an inscription by the eighth to ninth dynasty nomarch of the Coptite nome, Tjauti.

Very few graffiti are known from the Libyan or the Western Desert, owing to different geophysical conditions. There are caravan routes that have been used since ancient times to the oases of Bahrija and Kharga and farther south, via Dungul into Sudan and Darfur; in the Dakhla Oasis, a proper settlement administered by the Egyptians developed in the sixth dynasty. There are some hints that, at least during the Old Kingdom, the Egyptians surveyed the Western Desert, perhaps in search of minerals: in 1917, about 200 kilometers (125 miles) southwest of the village of Mut, going from Dakhla Oasis to Gebel Uweinat, a large cache of Old Kingdom water pots was discovered (at Abu Ballas or "Pottery Hill."). Somewhere in that area, a steward named Mery left a graffito; he came there "in search of the oasis people," in the twenty-third year of the reign of an unknown twelfth dynasty pharaoh. Most of the travelers on the caravan routes, however, seem not to have thought their experiences worth recording.

Finally, one must mention builders' and setting marks, team marks, and control notes that were left on building stones or in tombs for technical and administrative reasons. Setting marks, painted in ink in burial chambers, often consist of single signs in a special builder's code, meaning for example "south, top," or they display the numbering of blocks, perhaps with a simple *nfr*-sign. Generally they were removed after reassembling the precut chamber, and so they are found only in unfinished tombs. Team marks were special signs, mostly single hieroglyphs chiseled out or painted in red ink on blocks, that were often used in connection with noting the home town of the laborers. Core blocks from the pyramid of Senwosret I carry notes, painted in red ink during transportation, such as "Year 12, second month of winter, day X. Brought from the quarry by [the gang of] the third district of Heliopolis."

The modern recording and publication of a pharaonic site or monument should include all visitors' graffiti, both ancient and modern.

BIBLIOGRAPHY

Arnold, Felix. *The Control Notes and Team Marks: The South Cemeteries of Lisht.* New York, 1990. With introduction and further literature on the topic.

Bernand, André. *De Koptos à Kosseir.* London, 1972. Includes publication of the graffiti in Greek script from Wadi Hammamat.

Blumenthal, Elke. "Expeditionsberichte"; "Expeditionsinschriften." In *Lexikon der Ägyptologie,* 2:59–62. Wiesbaden, 1987.

Černý, Jaroslav. *Graffiti hiéroglyphiques et hiératiques de la nécropole thébaine.* DFIFAO, 9. Cairo, 1956.

Černý, Jaroslav, and A. A. Sadek. *Graffiti de la montagne thébaine.* Cairo, 1969–1972.

Černý, Jaroslav, A. H. Gardiner, and T. E. Peet. *The Inscriptions of Sinai.* London, 1952–1955.

Darnell, Deborah, and John Darnell. "Exploring the 'Narrow Doors' of the Theban Desert." *Egyptian Archaeology* 10 (1997), 24–26. Report on the survey of the Theban desert roads and its sensational results.

Desroches-Noblecourt, Christiane. "La quête des graffiti." In *Textes et langages de l'Égypte pharaonique.* Bibliothèque d'Étude 64.2 (1972–1974), 151–183. Includes full bibliography.

Dunham, Dows. *Second Cataract Forts,* vol. 1: *Semna, Kumma.* Boston, 1960.

Dunham, Dows. *Second Cataract Forts,* vol. 2: *Uronarti, Shalfak, Mirgissa.* Boston, 1967.

Goyon, Georges. "Les inscriptions des carrières et des mines." In *Textes et langages de l'Égypte pharaonique.* Bibliothèque d'Étude 64.2 (1972–1974), 193–205. Includes most of the relevant editions of inscriptions.

Goyon, Georges. *Nouvelles Inscriptions rupestres du Wadi Hammamat.* Paris, 1957.

Griffith, Francis Ll. *Catalogue of the Demotic Graffiti of the Dodecaschoenus.* Oxford, 1937.

Hintze, Fritz, et al. *Felsinschriften aus dem sudanesischen Nubien.* Berlin, 1989. Graffiti from Faras, Serra, Abusir, Mirgissa, Shelfak, Uronarti, Kumma, Semna, and more.

Lopez, Jésus. "Felsinschriften." In *Lexikon der Ägyptologie,* edited by Wolfgang Helck and Wolfhart Westendorf, vol. 2, cols. 159–161. Wiesbaden, 1987.

Marciniak, Marek. *Les inscriptions hiératiques du temple de Thoutmosis III. Deir el-Bahari, Vol. 1.* Warsaw, 1974. Publication of New Kingdom graffiti from a Deir el-Bahri temple, with an introduction on graffiti.

Rothe, Russel D., G. Rapp, Jr., and W. Miller. "New Hieroglyphic Evidence for Pharaonic Activity in the Eastern Desert of Egypt." *Journal of the American Research Center in Egypt* 33 (1996), 77–104. Publication of forty-three graffiti from the region southeast of Edfu.

Sadek, Ashraf I. *The Amethyst Mining Inscriptions from Wadi el-Hudi.* 2 vols. Warminster, 1980–1985.

Seyfried, Karl-Joachim. *Beiträge zu den Expeditionen des Mittleren Reiches in die Ost-Wüste.* Hildesheimer ägyptologische Beiträge, 15. Hildesheim, 1981. Collection and interpretation of texts at Wadi el-Hudi, Sinai, and Wadi Hammamat, with special weight on the number and organization of expeditions, and the formulaic corpus of the texts.

Thissen, Heinz-Josef. "Graffiti." In *Lexikon der Ägyptologie,* 3:880–882. Wiesbaden, 1977.

Thissen, Heinz-Josef. "Demotische Graffiti des Paneion im Wadi Hammamat." *Enchoria* 9 (1979), 63–92.

Winlock, Herbert E. "Graffiti of the Priesthood of the Eleventh Dynasty Temples at Thebes." *American Journal of Semitic Languages and Literatures* 58 (1941), 146–.

Zába, Zbigniew. *The Rock Inscriptions of Lower Nubia. Czechoslovak Concession.* Prague, 1974. Publication of the graffiti at Gebel el-Girgawi (Korosko).

DETLEF FRANKE

GRAMMAR. [*This entry surveys the chronological development of Egyptian grammar, distinguishing between grammars of literary and non-literary texts, and giving important examples of each. It also discusses significant developments in orthography. It comprises six articles:*

An Overview
Old Egyptian
Middle Egyptian
Late Egyptian
Demotic
Coptic

For related discussions, see Language *and the composite article* Scripts.]

An Overview

Egyptian is a dead language. Even Coptic, its last stage, became extinct as a spoken idiom in the seventeenth century CE at the latest, though it survives, little understood, as the liturgical language of the modern Egyptian Christian church. As a result, the grammar of Egyptian—the systematic analysis of the structure of the language, as used by a native speaker—is now accessible only through written realizations. In linguistic terms, what is within the reach of the Egyptologist is called a "corpus" (or "performance") grammar, because it is based on a finite body of texts. The native speaker whose mastery is to be explained is the unknown author of the text, and the text reflects his education, his skill in composition, and his adherence to writing conventions. A grammatical rule cannot be verified by proposing an utterance produced according to it to a native speaker; only other Egyptologists can evaluate such rules. For the past century and a half, the study of Egyptian grammar was aimed mainly at producing philological competence, or the capacity to read texts and to use their linguistic features in historical analysis. Only for the past few decades have efforts been made to process the grammatical material under the terms of modern linguistics. Nonetheless, the Egyptologist of today can confidently assert his or her ability to enter into written communication with ancient Egyptians, should the need arise.

Major grammars and grammatical studies devoted to Old Egyptian include works by E. Edel (*Altägyptische Grammatik*, Analecta Orientalia 34–39, Rome, 1955–1964) and J. P. Allen (*The Inflection of the Verb in the Pyramid Texts*, Bibliotheca Aegyptia II. Malibu, 1984); for Middle Egyptian, see Gardiner (1957) and others in most European languages; for Late Egyptian, see Černý and Groll (1975); Demotic, Wilhelm Spiegelberg (*Demotische Grammatik*, Heidelberg, 1925) and Johnson (1976, 1991).

Egyptian is documented in texts from around 2600 BCE (there are notes and labels as old as c.3000 BCE) up to the Middle Ages, so Egyptian grammar has had a very long productive history. Scholars have divided this long continuum into stages roughly linked to the periods of Egyptian history. These stages were treated as synchronic cuts—that is, points at which the language is studied as it existed then, disregarding any ongoing changes—and they were described more or less systematically in philological grammars. Traditionally, Old Egyptian, Middle Egyptian, Late Egyptian, Demotic, and Coptic were considered to constitute such stages (for a more refined classification, see the article on "Language"). In addition, there is an obvious typological line that separates Old and Middle Egyptian from Late Egyptian, Demotic, and Coptic.

Graphemics and Phonology. The Egyptian hieroglyphs, the writing symbols used primarily on monuments, are stylized pictures of living beings, objects, or parts of these. It is misleading, however, to call them "pictographs" or "ideographs." Hieroglyphs are not the symbol writing they were thought to be for more than a millennium after the end of the Egyptian civilization. Instead, the signs are members of a conventionalized set: the set may comprise about 750 to 1,000 signs, but only 200 or 300 were in frequent use. In Ptolemaic times the sign-producing process was revived and the number of signs in use multiplied to several thousand, thereby restricting the ability to read hieroglyphs to a few specialists, both in antiquity and among modern scholars.

The hieroglyphs primarily represent sequences of one to three sounds, originally based on the name of the object represented but extended to words with similar sound sequences by means of the "rebus" principle. In this way, abstract words could be represented; for example, the sequence *ḫt* ("wood") could also be used for *ḫt* "after." In a secondary and more complex process, hieroglyphs can be used iconically, either to classify words according to their semantic field or to represent the actual entity they depict. For instance, the conventionalized symbol of a simple hut's stylized ground plan may represent three kinds of referents: first, it may signify the Egyptian word **pāruw* ("house"; the asterisk is the linguistic convention indicating a reconstructed form), in which case the hieroglyph is called a "logogram"; second, it may indicate the sequence of phonemes (sounds that differentiate meaning) *p–r* in, for example, the word **pirjit* ("come out"), an example of a "phonogram"; and third, it may classify buildings and architectural elements, serving as an iconic index to some other phonogram, in which case it is called a "semogram" or "determinative."

The Egyptians developed two sets of cursive abbreviations of the hieroglyphic signs: Hieratic, and the even more simplified Demotic. In these systems the signs have lost their pictorial appearance, but as graphemes (written units) they follow the same functional principles. Scholars customarily transcribe Hieratic texts into hieroglyphs, but they refrain from doing this with Demotic texts because the result is not useful in understanding the text. The orthography of words and phrases may differ considerably between the same text rendered in hieroglyphic and Hieratic, a difference made obvious by this kind of transcription.

In principle, the Egyptian writing system can be characterized as phonematic. The conventional writing symbols, or graphemes, tend to represent three classes of speech elements that carry meaning: first, the consonants, the most auditorily distinct segments of speech (distinct because they are produced by an obstruction of the airflow, while vowels are analog segments of a continuous airflow); second, the phonemes, the set of consonantal segments that differentiate lexically distinct items of this particular language; and third, the morphemes, those combinations of phonemes that have meaning or grammatical function as parts of words. There are elementary graphemes for the entire set of phonemes. However, these are not used like an alphabet, but rather as complementizers of the multiliteral graphemes. The phonematic inventory is complemented by the semograms, or graphemes that assign the phoneme group representing a morpheme to a class of meaning, thus completing the representation. For example, an utterance like **san manuwat* ("the brother is in town") is written *s-n*[man] *m n-(w)-t*[town]. For scholarly use, these consonantal skeletons have been assigned a conventional pronunciation.

The Egyptian writing system differs from alphabetic systems only in a slight shift in information redundancy. An alphabetic rendering gives exclusively phonemic information, but it gives more than a literate native speaker really needs to recognize the linguistic units. Thus, a native speaker of English has no difficulty reading the following compressed sentence (the sign ' represents the glottal stop introducing a word-initial vowel): "Ths rmns 'ndrstndbl, 'vn whn n vwls 'r wrttn." In the Egyptian system, by contrast, the linguistic units may be incompletely coded in phonemic terms, but they are provided with direct semantic information. As an encoding device for language, it achieves about the same ends as an alphabet, but this holds true only for the competent—native—speaker, who needs only a certain level of information to recognize the phenomena of his language. The scholar, a less competent speaker, has no direct access to those bits of information that the script systematically fails to disclose, such as all grammatical features represented by vowels, or internal vocalic modifications of the type seen in English "foot, feet." Nor can the scholar easily guess at information the writer did not think was worth noting.

To a certain extent, linguists can counterbalance this deficiency by using indirect evidence obtained through comparative reconstruction. We can compare the same words as they are written in Egyptian and in contemporary Akkadian, Canaanitic, or Greek documents; for example, the royal name *Rˁ-ms-sw* appears in Middle Babylonian as *ri-a-ma-še-ša*, and in Greek as *Ramses*. We can also apply the laws of phonological evolution that led to Coptic. The resulting reconstructions of the phonological system, and parts of the morphology, thus necessarily involve a fair amount of hypothesis.

The following account of the phonological system of the earlier stages of Egyptian is based on an unpublished essay, "The Sounds of a Dead Language," by F. Kammerzell; for details, see the works by Kammerzell, Loprieno, and Schenkel cited in the bibliography.

The phonological system of the earlier group uses an inventory of twenty-four to twenty-six consonantal and semiconsonantal phonemes, as follows:

- Semiconsonantal glides: /j/ /w/
- Sonorants and sibilants: *h, w, s, m, n, l* (in the Egyptological tradition rendered as *r*), *r* (traditionally rendered *ꜣ*)
- Plosive and fricative obstruents in ternary opposition:
  - "voiceless": *p, t, z* (/ts/), *t* (/c/), *š* (/ç/), *k, ḫ* (/x/)
  - "emphatic": *f, ḏ* (/ṭ/), *ḏ* /č̣/), *q* (also written *ḳ*), *ḥ*
  - "voiced": *j* (traditionally *i* or *y*), *b, d* (traditionally *ꜥ*!), *g, ḫ* (/γ/)

Although the traditional transliteration signs of these phonemes are of little denotative value (and moreover differ among anglophone, francophone, and germanophone Egyptology), they can be retained for most practical purposes, provided that one keeps in mind that they are scholarly conventions.

For both long and short stressed syllables, three vowels can be reconstructed: /i/, /a/, and /u/. We can reconstruct such pronunciations as *nṯr* ("god"), pronounced /nácar/,

since we have Coptic *nūte*, and we know that /na/ developed into /nu/; similarly, the participle *ḥtp* was /ḫātip/, with a structure and vocalism comparable to that found in Arabic.

Historical sound changes led to modifications in the components of the system in the later stages of Egyptian. In certain cases the oppositions between voiced and voiceless phonemes tend to become neutralized in Late Egyptian. Some graphemes for voiced phonemes become allographs (alternate symbols) for voiceless phonemes, and ˁ is weakened to the value "ˁayn," as it is known in the Egyptological tradition. At the end of a stressed syllable, the phonemes *t, n, r, j,* and *w* can be dropped, or weakened into a glottal stop (' or *ꜣ, i*). The vowels undergo major changes: long /a/ and /u/ become long /e/ and /o/; short /u/ becomes /a/, and the other short vowels become *shwa* (the sound of *er* in English "other" or the *a* in "ago").

Despite these developments, the notation principles did not change very much; however, a few signs that are outwardly identical to Middle Egyptian signs acquired new values. Thus, the graphemes for *t, r, j* now represented *ꜣ*, while *d* represented both *d* and *t*. Sound changes can be concealed underneath familiar traditional forms, or they can appear written a new way: for instance, the personal pronoun *sw* was reduced in Late Egyptian to *s'*, but in writing it may be encountered both as *sw* and simple *s*. Although the traditional writing system was still in use, it had to acquire new allographs and graphemes, which emerged from the traditional phonograms through sound change; the former conventional relationship between sign and signified—between grapheme and phoneme—thus gradually loosened. This is a familiar phenomenon in European languages and is particularly evident in English. If a writing system is almost never adjusted to account for phonetic changes in the spoken language, the sign inventory will always reflect an earlier stage, even though used to represent a later one: the languages of phonemes and graphemes are destined to go separate ways. Nonetheless, the Egyptian writers sometimes required an unambiguous notation for a word, so they compensated for the devaluation of the unilateral graphemes by using a set of so-called group writing signs as elementary graphemes (e.g., *ˁꜣ* for *ˁ*, *pꜣ* for *p*, *rw* for *r*). Demotic script would use these signs throughout its history, though again with the marks of subsequent devaluation by ongoing sound change.

The Coptic phonological system has lost most of the voiced plosives (*d, g,* and *z* are present only in Greek loan words), with the exception of *b*. ˁ merged with the glottal stop, which was present but no longer represented in writing. Owing to the use of the Greek alphabet, the vocalic system was now explicitly represented; it displays the further consequences of Late Egyptian and Demotic sound change, but it also reveals context-sensitive developments and morphological features of Egyptian that were concealed by the older scripts.

Morphology and Syntax

The earlier group—Old and Middle Egyptian. Egyptian words are structurally based on a lexical root of one to four consonants. Most roots are biconsonantal (termed "biradical" or "2-rad."; e.g., *ḏd* "say") or triconsonantal ("3-rad."; e.g., *sḏm* "hear"), or they display a semiconsonantal final root consonant or radical (e.g., III.inf. *mri* "love"). The descriptive terms in parentheses were introduced by traditional linguists working with Afro-Asian and Semitic but also schooled in Latin; thus "III.inf." means *verba tertiae radicalis infirmae,* "verbs of weak third root radical." Roots are commonly modified by reduplication of the entire root or parts of it, or by gemination of one radical. The functional form—the stem—is derived from the lexical root through affixes, superimposition of a vocalic pattern, or both in combination. The stem in turn is extended by affixes to become the actual occurring word.

Words can have one or more syllables. Each syllable begins with a consonant (or semiconsonant) and contains a long or short vowel; it may or may not end with a consonant. If a syllable ends without a consonant, the syllable is usually open with a long vowel, and another syllable must follow—e.g., the first syllable in *nācar* (*nṯr*) "god." If it ends with a consonant, the syllable is closed and the vowel is usually short, e.g., *zăḫ-ȝaw* (*zš*) "scribe." The stress falls on either the last (ultimate) or next to last (penultimate) syllable of the word; when grammatical endings and suffixes increase the number of syllables, the stress is shifted. Unstressed syllables can be severely shortened.

Egyptian words, like Indo-European and Semitic words, can be functionally categorized in terms of parts of speech: noun/pronoun, adjective, verb, adverb, determiner, preposition, and interjection. Nouns and verbs are the largest classes by far; there is only a small number of original adverbs (adverbials are mostly prepositional phrases, i.e., preposition-noun syntagmas), and there are no original adjectives. Words describing nouns are derived either from nouns or from prepositional phrases by means of a suffix *-y* (*nṯr.y* "divine" from *nṯr* "god"; *im.y pr.w* "being in the house" from *m pr.w* "in the house"; cf. the Semitic *nisba*-adjectives), or from participles of the so-called adjective-verbs (e.g., *nāḏim* "sweet" from *nāḏam* "to be sweet").

Nouns are often verbal derivatives (Nomen Agentis, Nomen Actionis, etc.). They are divided into two gender classes, masculine and feminine; the feminine is marked by a suffix *-.t,* realized as *-at, -it,* or *-ut* (e.g., *sn* "brother," *sn.t* "sister"). Nouns exhibit the grammatical numbers singular, dual (productive in Old Egyptian, but later lexi- calized and restricted to entites that naturally occur in pairs), and plural; the plural suffix is often *-.w,* fem. *-.(w)t* (e.g., *sn.w* "brothers," *sn.(w)t* "sisters"), and the vocalic patterns of plurals can be rather complex. Nouns are the nuclei of noun phrases built by means of postposed attributive nouns (e.g., *nzw* "king," *zḥ3.w nzw* "secretary of the king"—the so-called direct genitive, but note that there are no cases attested during the historic period), by determiners, by relative phrases or adjectives (e.g., *zḥ3.w pn iqr* "this excellent scribe"), or by adnominal adverbial phrases. The opposition definite/indefinite remains unexpressed on the surface; there are no articles. Noun phrases are important structural elements as members of prepositional phrases and verbal phrases, and as immediate constituents of sentences.

There are three sets of personal pronouns which substitute nouns and noun phrases according to their syntactic function. Dependent nouns in noun phrases and prepositional phrases, as well as the agent/subject roles of verbs, are substituted by an affixed pronoun termed a "suffix pronoun" (e.g., *=f* in *zḥ3.w-f* "his scribe"). Nouns in the subject role of adverbial sentences (see below) and in the object role of verbs are substituted by an enclitic pronoun: *sw* "he" or *si* "she." Finally, nouns as immediate constituents are substituted by non-enclitic pronouns: *ntf* "he" or *nts* "she."

Verbs display a variety of morphological patterns that depend on the class they belong to (i.e., the root classes 3-rad., II.gem, III.inf., etc., discussed above). There are conjugated, finite, and non-finite forms, including infinitives and participles (e.g., *sḏm* "listening," *mry* "beloved"); both perform important roles in the construction of the sentence. The basic conjugation pattern is composed of the verbal stem—the lexical root with the addition of affixes—followed by the agent/subject expression: for example, *sḏm z.t* "when the woman listens," *sḏm=f* "when he listens," *sḏm.n=s* "when she listened." This example shows the so-called suffix or *sḏm=f* (conventionally pronounced *seḏemef*) conjugation, *sḏm* having been chosen as the paradigm verb by Egyptologists. This pattern carries various markers of verbal categories—voice, tense, aspect, and mood—and it has a broad range of syntactic uses, for example as circumstantial clauses or noun clauses; as relative clauses, the verbal forms are called participles and relative forms. Semantic categories and syntactic functions are conveyed by affixes, or through internal modifications in vowel and stress patterns, which are concealed by the writing system (cf. *săḏmăf* "when he listens" vs. *sāḏmăf* "that he listens"). The *sḏm=f* conjugation is the nucleus of a verbal phrase that contains one or two noun phrases (the agent/subject phrase and, in the case of transitive verbs, the object phrase), and very often a prepositional phrase that is closely linked with the verb and modifies its lexical meaning (much as in English verbal semantics). Verbal phrases of this type are very frequent in a variety of syntactic contexts: as noun clauses, which are of particular synchronic and diachronic interest (subjunctive *sḏm=f;* as object clause of the verb *ḏi* "give, cause," *ḏi sḏm=f* "to cause that he listens, to make him listen"); as subject clauses of sentences and verbs; and as noun clauses after prepositions, which then function as conjunctions (*m sḏm=f* "when he listened").

In addition to the forms of the *sḏm=f* pattern, there is a verbal pattern with different suffix endings that is an authentic cognate of the Semitic suffix conjugation. These endings change the verb from fientic (event-reproducing) to a word denoting a state, condition, or quality; for example, "to come" becomes "arrived," and "to do" becomes "done." Such a verbal form requires a preceding subject with which its suffixes are in concord: *z.t šm.ti* "the woman is gone." Syntactically, such a form shows features of an adverbial phrase. It has been given a number of labels that attempt to denote its different functions: old perfective, stative, pseudoparticiple, and qualitative (the last is used for the corresponding Coptic form).

Adverbial phrases comprise a few original adverbs and a large number of prepositional phrases (preposition + noun phrase); they express local, temporal, modal, causal, or other logical conditions and circumstances. A very important subgroup is the so-called pseudoverbal construction, which uses the prepositions *ḥr, m,* and *r* followed by the infinitive as the noun phrase; these express progressive or future action (e.g., *z.t ḥr sḏm zḫ3.w* "the woman is/was interrogating the scribe," *z.t r sḏm* "the woman shall listen"), and they are functional and semantic counterparts of the old perfective. No less important are the uses of the *sḏm=f* conjugation as adverbials of superordinated sentences, unless these are not "circumstantially adverbial," as Collier (1991) puts it. As adverbial adjuncts, adverbial phrases are a means to extend sentences syntactically and semantically.

Egyptian sentence formation (like that of English) is first of all dominated by word order: a word's function depends on its position. Not just verb phrases, but also noun and adverbial phrases, take part in predicate-building—not unlike Egyptian's Afro-Asiatic language family relatives, but unlike Indo-European. The non-verbal sentences are characterized by the absence of a copula or copula verb (i.e., an equivalent of "to be"); they appear in two basic patterns, called "nominal sentences" and "adverbial sentences." In its pure form, as a sentence with one noun phrase functioning as subject and another as predicate, the nominal sentence is rarely used in Old and Middle Egyptian outside religious texts, but it does occur: *pḥ.ti=f pḥ.ti stš,* "his strength [is] the strength of Seth." The nominal sentence pattern is realized mainly in

three subtypes: (1) the sentence type with the demonstrative *pw* in second noun position, both in minimal form (*tzm pw,* "dog this" = "it is a dog"), and in elaborated versions widely used in explanatory or commentary passages; (2) the adjective sentence, in which the first noun is a nominalized participle of an adjective-verb (*nfr sw,* "perfect he" = "he is perfect"), a sentence that expresses a permanent quality; and (3) the cleft sentence, with a first noun introduced by a particle and, in second noun position, a nominalized participle without concord (*in z.t irr st,* "it is the woman who does it")—a focusing construction, like its English counterpart.

The other large sentence category, the adverbial sentence, is the most versatile of the Egyptian sentence patterns and is widespread in texts of all kinds. In its basic pattern, a nominal or pronominal subject, either bare or preceded by a particle, is followed by an adverbial phrase as predicate: *zḫ3.w ʿ3,* "the scribe is here"; *zḫ3.w m prw=f,* "the scribe is in his house." If the subject is pronominal, an introducing particle is mandatory: *mk tw ʿ3,* "Look, you are here." The adverbials that may function as predicates range from adverbs proper and prepositional phrases of all types, to the pseudoverbal construction with its temporal and aspectual features, and they may include the *sḏm=f* forms (this question will be treated below). The sentential meaning of the adverbial sentence as a whole is the plain presentation of real or fictive facts. This meaning is changed to an overt assertion of truth on the part of the speaker by the introductory element *iw,* and to narrative sequence by *ʿḥ.n* and *wn.in.* In the case of a pronominal subject, all these "compound tenses" use the suffix pronouns.

Although basically simple in structure, the adverbial sentence is elaborated in proportion to the elaboration of the noun phrases involved. The highest degree of complexity is obtained through the use of subject clauses, as analyzed by Polotsky (1976). In complex adverbial sentences, the noun in subject or theme function is substituted by specific forms of the *sḏm=f* that show gemination in the "weak" verbal classes (II.gem., III.inf., some of IV.gem.); this apparently produces an effect of focalization of the adverbial predicate (*irr=t p3 ib ḥr-m* "that you make this emotion is why?" = "why are you in this mood?"). These forms had been termed "emphatic" since Erman's time; Polotsky (1965) reinterpreted them as conveying the focalization effect, and later (1976) introduced the now current term "substantival forms of the *sḏm=f* conjugation."

Egyptological grammarians are at variance in the description of verbal sentences, depending on which notion of the Middle Egyptian sentence they prefer. If one favors a stringent, abstract notion of the sentence along Polotsky's line and entertains a nominalistic approach to verbal sentences, as I do, one can explain the use of verbal phrases within the frame of the adverbial sentence. Verbal sentences are then those adverbial sentences that use *sḏm=f* phrases in predicate position and hence have a Subject-Verb-Object (SVO) structure: *z.t sḏm=s zḫ3.w* "the woman interrogates the scribe," *iw=s sḏm=s st* "she does it habitually." Verbal phrases are marked for subordination and need higher units in which to function. If, however, one prefers a pragmatic notion of the sentence and an essentialistic (or Platonic) approach, the *sḏm=f* phrases may as well be explained as verbal non-initial main clauses/sentences—forms that appear only in second position after initial sentence forms—which are initialized by the particles *mk, iw*, etc. Verbal phrases are marked for independence and hence are embedded into subordination functions in higher units; they do not enter into substitution relations with adverbials, but rather with bare adverbial or pseudoverbal sentences. They have a VSO structure; preceding nouns are topics of the verbal sentence (i.e., *z.t, sḏm=s zḫ3.w*, "the woman, she interrogates the scribe"); and "emphatic" forms are thematized or topicalized predicates, that is, predicative forms that are made the theme of an utterance or that foreground what is in the speaker's interest. The latter explanatory framework has been proposed and elaborated by Collier and extended by Loprieno.

The verbal sentence is also realized in forms with specific affixes, the contingent tenses *sḏm.in=f, sḏm.ḥr=f, sḏm.k3=f*; the sequence depends on previous circumstances. Finally, there are the request sentences, expressed by imperatives or initial "prospective" *sḏm=f* ("subjunctive" in Old Egyptian).

The later group—Late Egyptian, Demotic, and Coptic.
On the surface, Late Egyptian appears to be a closely related continuation of Middle Egyptian. However, its grammatical system represents the first step of a rather radical change, which will become more obvious in Demotic and Coptic.

Many Late Egyptian morphological and syntactic variations can be subsumed under the expression "analytic tendency." This tendency frequently dominates linguistic evolution in general, for example in the tendency to distribute individual functions to several individual morphemes in order to preclude ambiguity (e.g., Latin *legi* > *habeo lectum* > Italian *ho letto*, "I have read"). German and Latin are languages of the synthetic type, while Italian, French, and English are analytic. Middle Egyptian constructions and phrases are generally characterized by syntactic thickness, but the speakers of the New Kingdom tend to dissolve this thickness. Thus, the Middle Egyptian sentence *gmi.n=i zi sḏr.w* "and I found the man sleeping," appears in Late Egyptian as *iw=i gm p3 zi iw=f sḏr* (or, etymologizing, *iw=i ḥr gm.t p3 zi iw=f sḏr.w*). Grammatical and semantic features that were formerly expressed with one or a few morphemes are now distributed among a larger number of morphemes. This is accompanied by a tendency to exchange the positions of the linguistic item defined and the item defining it—that is, to place the defining expression in the nucleus position of a syntagma or group of expressions. These principles can be illustrated as follows.

Middle Egyptian *sḏm.n=f* is synthetically constructed from the root morpheme {*sḏm*}, meaning "hear," to which the dependent morpheme {.*n*} is joined to give the meaning "have heard." When the suffix pronoun {=*f*} is attached to the stem, {*sḏm.n*} carries both meaning and conjugation. Its conjugation form (*sḏm=f*) distinguishes it from the other conjugations. In Late Egyptian, such a form is "analyzed" into the conjugation base {*iri*} (with reference to tense "past"), the agent expression {=*f*}, and the meaning expression {*sḏm*}, giving *iri=f sḏm*. The development toward this perfectly "periphrastic" conjugation was not complete until the Late Demotic stage; for a while, in Late Egyptian, *sḏm=f* took over the function of Middle Egyptian *sḏm.n=f*.

Noun phrases underwent a comparable evolution. Middle Egyptian *prw=n* ("our house") became Late Egyptian *p3y=n pr* when the marking of grammatical gender, specification (definite/indefinite, known/unknown), and possession were removed from the meaning expression ("house") and transferred to the so-called possessive article. In Egyptian, the constituent in second position is usually dependent on that in the first: in the Middle Egyptian noun phrase, *prw* is the pivot, or nucleus, of *prw=n*, and the dependent suffix =*n* is its satellite; in Late Egyptian *p3y=n pr*, by contrast, the article form *p3y=n* becomes the nucleus of the phrase, with *pr* as its satellite. This transfer of a specifying linguistic feature from the position of satellite to nucleus, or vice versa, is termed "conversion," and it is another indication of the analytic tendency of Late Egyptian.

The other main evolutionary tendencies of this stage may be called "morphologization" and "paradigmatization." Middle Egyptian was characterized by a wide variety of adverbial phrases with a correspondingly large spectrum of uses. They played a significant role in sentence structure itself, and, as adverbial adjuncts or sentence adverbials, they modified and enhanced sentences. In Late Egyptian, the entire range of adverbial phrases is still present—adverbs, prepositions with nouns and infinitives, and old perfectives. All these except the prepositional phrases (which do double duty as adverbial adjuncts) now become essentially restricted to the predicate position of the initial or non-initial adverbial sentence, now called the "first present." The sentence constructions of the Middle Egyptian type have become morphologically invariable, and each has a fixed role in the field of Egyptian sentential semantics. The syntactic status of those sentence types of Late Egyptian, Demotic, and Coptic that use verbal formations is described under the notions "sentence conjugation" and "clause conjugation" (adopted from Polotsky 1960 and transferred to Late Egyptian by Frandsen 1974, and to Demotic by Johnson 1976). In the first case, they are the minimal form of an independent sentence; in the second, they perform the functions of parts of speech as subject, object, or adverbial, in their superordinated sentence conjugation, the independent sentence. Morphological development from Late Egyptian to Coptic is fairly straightforward, though often concealed by the different writing systems; the latter group tends to be more tense-oriented than the former.

The adverbial sentence or first present has remained basically the same as in Middle Egyptian, but there are already a few morphological traits that presage the eventual form of the pattern in Coptic: a new type of subject pronoun in initial position (*tw=i* "I"/ *sw* "he"); and the gradual loss of the preposition *ḥr* in writing (completed during the twentieth dynasty), and of the formatives of the old perfective. The earlier form referred to present or relative present time; still in Coptic, infinitive and qualitative (lexicalized since Demotic times) are in substitutional relations to adverbs and prepositional phrases, as they were in Middle Egyptian (*mk wi ḥr sḏm* > Late Egyptian and Demotic *tw=i sḏm* > Coptic ϯⲥⲱⲧⲛ̄ "I listen").

In Late Egyptian and Demotic the preterite tense is expressed by *sḏm=f* (the functional heir of Middle Egyptian *sḏm.n=f*—more exactly, *iw sḏm.n=f*). Not until the Late Demotic (Roman) period did the periphrastic form (*iri=f stm*), the precursor of the Coptic preterite (ⲁϥⲥⲱⲧⲛ̄ "I listened"), come into use. Future tense is expressed by the *iw*-sentence of old with *r* + infinitive, now called "third future" (*iw=f r sḏm* > *iw=f stm* > ⲉϥⲉⲥⲱⲧⲛ̄ "he shall listen"). Sentences with imperatives (now with a prefix, *i.sḏm* "listen!") or with the initial and independent prospective *sḏm=f* express requests and wishes; the *sḏm=f* as noun clause following the imperative of the verb "give, cause" has been widely used during all times, but now the construction becomes morphologized as the precursor of the Coptic causative imperative/jussive (*im sḏm=f* "make him listen!" > Demotic *mi ir=f stm* > Coptic ⲙⲁⲣⲉϥⲥⲱⲧⲛ̄); its subordinate equivalent is morphologized as clause conjugation, the Coptic finalis (*di=i sḏm=f* > Demotic *di=i ir=f stm* > Coptic ⲧⲁⲣⲉϥⲥⲱⲧⲛ̄ "so that I make him listen"). The noun clauses in the subject/theme position of the adverbial sentence ("emphatic" *sḏm=f*) appear in a single periphrastic form in Late Egyptian (as a *sḏm=f* form of *iri* "to do" with prefix *i.-*, *i.ir=f sḏm*); as a further linguistic development, the construction will evolve into a "converter."

Since the Demotic stage there existed a special morphologized form for the expression of general truths, as the English present tense does (*ḥr sḏm=f/ ḥr ir=f stm* > ϣⲁϥⲥⲱⲧⲛ̄; historically, it is a derivation of Middle Egyptian *sḏm.ḥr=f*).

All the constructions listed are negated either by the negation particles *bn/bw* (which are graphematic variants of Old and Middle Egyptian *nn/n;* Coptic again ⲛ̄ or ⲙ), or by corresponding negative conjugation patterns.

Besides the sentence conjugations as forms of the independent sentence, there are diachronically adjusted forms of the non-verbal sentences, cleft sentence, "pure" nominal sentence, adjectival sentence, and the sentence with demonstrative *pȝy* (< Middle Egyptian *pw*); most of them survive, slightly modified, into Coptic.

While the sentence conjugations were thus becoming morphosyntactically fixed, so were a number of constructions that logically subordinate: the clause conjugations. The former group of adverbial phrase constructions made of verbal phrases was restricted primarily to prepositional phrases, which in turn became morphologized constructions formed by conjunctions and specific forms of the verb: the infinitive, subjunctive *sḏm=f*, and the *sḏm.t=f.* These can be etymologically recognized only as forms of former prepositional phrases: (1) the "temporal" (*m-ḏr sḏm=f* > Demotic *n-ḏ ir=f stm* >ⲛ̄ⲧⲉⲣⲉϥⲥⲱⲧⲛ̄ "when he listened") and a few other constructions of this type; (2) the "terminative" (*r-ir.t=f-sḏm/ šȝ'-i.ir.r=f-sḏm* > Demotic *š'(m)tw=f stm* > ϣⲁ(ⲛ)ⲧ̄ϥⲥⲱⲧⲛ̄ "until he listened"); and (c) the "conjunctive" (*mtw=f-sḏm,* out of the earlier *ḥn'-sḏm, ḥn'-ntf-sḏm;* Demotic has the same form, Coptic ⲛ̄ϥⲥⲱⲧⲛ̄ "and he shall listen"). The forms are negated by using *tm,* the negative verb.

Aside from the clause conjugations thus constituted, quite different forms of sentence extension appear in place of the adverbial phrases. It is now the sentence itself that becomes the means of sentence extension by being subordinated with conjunctions, termed "converters" in Egyptology. The most important converter in Late Egyptian and Demotic is *iw* (Coptic ⲉ-). *iw* converts sentence conjugations into clauses, various kinds of adverbial or circumstantial clauses, and occasionally even noun clauses and so-called content clauses. Syntactically important also is the relative converter *nty* (Coptic ⲉⲧ(ⲉ) ⲉⲛⲧ), which subordinates independent sentences as relative clauses. Especially in Late Egyptian, but less so in Demotic, *nty*-relative clauses are still in complementary use with participles and relative forms, which have disappeared in Coptic. The "emphatic" *sḏm=f/i.ir=f sḏm* of old is reduced to another converter in Demotic, *i.ir* (Coptic ⲉ-/ ⲉⲧⲉ-/ ⲛ̄ⲧ-), which more and more tends to be used with the whole set of sentence conjugations; Coptic displays a full-fledged system of "second tenses" thus constructed.

The complete change in the grammatical character of *iw* has always been felt to be a major obstacle in accepting a historical continuity in linguistic evolution from the earlier to the later group. In Middle Egyptian, *iw* was employed primarily to begin independent sentences, while in Late Egyptian, it has become a characteristic feature of subordination.

The manner in which the Late Egyptian forms were derived from the Middle Egyptian forms can best be seen in the adverbial sentence. In a Middle Egyptian adverbial sentence like *z.t im* ("the woman is there"), the constructive boundary is between the nominal and the adverbial phrase; that is, the relationship between the noun *z.t* and the adverb *im* is the same as the relationship of *iw z.t* and *im* in the *iw*-sentence, *iw z.t im* ("it is the woman there"). In Late Egyptian, the internal relationship of a *iw*-sentence of the *iw z.t im* type has been changed by the principles of boundary shift. This shifting eventually established a boundary between the modifier and the clauses that follow it. This meant, in principle, that [*iw* + noun] and [preposition + noun] became [*iw*] and [noun + preposition + noun]. Apparently it is the sentence conjugation *z.t im* (first present/adverbial sentence) itself that follows *iw*; it thus would appear that the adverbial sentence itself has been "subordinated" to *iw*. The clause following *iw* is thus understood as a dependent form of an independent sentence, made dependent by *iw*. The same holds true for the entire set of Middle Egyptian *iw*-sentences (only in the form of the third future does *iw* retain its previous role). The Late Egyptian sentence conjugation forms are derived from the Middle Egyptian *iw*-sentence, and this origin likewise explains the functional shift of *iw*, which has become the marker indicating the dependency of the following clause.

[*See also* Language.]

BIBLIOGRAPHY

Černý, Jaroslav, and Sarah I. Groll. *A Late Egyptian Grammar*. 4th ed. Studia Pohl: series maior, 4. Rome, 1975. An exhaustive structuralist description of the grammar of the everyday texts of the twentieth dynasty; reference grammar.

Collier, Mark. "Circumstantially adverbial? The circumstantial sḏm (.f) / sḏm.n (.f) reconsidered." In *Middle Kingdom Studies*, edited by Stephen Quirke, pp. 21–50. London, 1991. One of three articles (the others: "The Circumstantial *sḏm (.f) / sḏm.n (.f)* as verbal verb-forms in Middle Egyptian," *Journal of Egyptian Archaeology* 76, 1990, pp. 73–86; "Predication and the Circumstantial *sḏm (.f) / sḏm.n(.f)*," *Lingua Aegyptia* 2, 1992, pp. 17–65), the author spent on the revision parts of the linguistic concept of Polotsky and Junge: verbal phrases are not adverbials but non-initial main sentences.

Frandsen, Paul J. *An Outline of the Late Egyptian Verbal System*. Copenhagen, 1974. The fundamental study of all types of Late Egyptian verbal phrases and sentences; exemplary discussions of synchronic and diachronic features and useful indices that help to find the occurences of their grammatical analysis.

Gardiner, Alan H. *Egyptian Grammar: Being an Introduction to the Study of Hieroglyphs*. 3d rev. ed. London, 1957. Still the standard introductory grammar for anglophone students combined with a nearly complete philological description of Middle Egyptian; a magistral work which has come into years in terms of descriptive adequacy but which is still most useful as reference grammar.

Groll, Sarah I. *Non-Verbal Sentence Patterns in Late Egyptian*. London, 1967. Classificatory study of all non-verbal and nominal sentences.

Groll, Sarah I. *The Negative Verbal System of Late Egyptian*. London, 1970. Classificatory study of all methods and forms of negation of verbal phrases and sentences.

Johnson, Janet. *The Demotic Verbal System*. Studies in Ancient Oriental Civilization, 38. Chicago, 1976. The fundamental description of the Demotic verbal forms and sentences with detailed account and discussion of the diachronic features of the forms in question.

Johnson, Janet. *Thus Wrote 'Onchsheshongy: An Introductory Grammar of Demotic*. 2d rev. ed. Studies in Ancient Oriental Civilization, 45. Chicago, 1991. Short comprehensive teaching aid for academic instruction in Demotic script and grammar.

Junge, Friedrich. *"Emphasis" and sentential meaning in Middle Egyptian*. Göttinger Orientforschungen IV, 20. Wiesbaden, 1989. A study of the meaningful speech units of the sentence: subject and predicate, theme and rheme, focus and topicalization, sentence patterning and pragmatics.

Junge, Friedrich. *Einführung in die Grammatik des Neuägyptischen*. Wiesbaden, 1996. Detailed introductory grammar and latest description of the entire system of Late Egyptian grammar. English edition in preparation.

Kammerzell, Frank. "Zum Umschreibung und Lautung des Ägyptischen." In *Grosses Handwörterbuch Ägyptisch-Deutsch*, edited by Rainer Hannig, pp. 23–59. Kulturgeschichte der antiken Welt, 64. Mainz, 1995. Latest and most modern account of the state of the art in Egyptian phonematics.

Kammerzell, Frank. "The Sounds of a Dead Language. Reconstructing Egyptian Phonology." *Göttingen Betrage zur Sprachwissenschaft* 7(1998), 21ff.

Lambdin, Thomas O. *Introduction to Sahidic Coptic*. Macon, Ga., 1983. The standard English handbook for teaching classical Coptic.

Loprieno, Antonio. *Ancient Egyptian: A Linguistic Introduction*. New York, 1995. The first and latest comprehensive treatment of Egyptian through all stages. If offers a detailed study of phonology, the first for English readers, discusses historical morphology and analyzes the syntax along the lines of functional sentence perspective combining synchronic and diachronic approaches.

Polotsky, Hans Jakob. "The Coptic Conjugation System." *Orientalia*, n. s., 29 (1960), 392ff. (See also his *Collected Papers*, Jerusalem 1971, 238ff.) This paper organized Coptic Syntax anew in a way that proved to be highly productive f or the grammatical description of Late Egyptian and Demotic, as well.

Polotsky, Hans Jakob. *Egyptian Tenses*. Jerusalem, 1965. Widely known and influential study of Egyptian verbal forms. Complementary to the "emphatic forms" that have been elaborated in his *Études de syntaxe copte*, Cairo, 1944, the substitutional features of the *sḏm=f* forms as adverbial phrases/circumstantials were put forward for the first time.

Polotsky, Hans Jakob. *Les transpositions du verbe en égyptien classique*. Israel Oriental Studies, 6. Jerusalem, 1976. Influential elaboration and systemization of his *Egyptian Tenses*.

Schenkel, Wolfgang. *Einführung in die altägyptische Sprachwissenschaft*. Orientalistiche Einführungen. Darmstadt, 1990. An account of the state of the art in traditional Egyptological linguistics with the most comprehensive study of Egyptian phonology at hand.

Sisha-Halevy, Ariel. *Coptic Grammatical Categories*. Analecta Orientalia, 53. Rome, 1986. Offers an exhaustive, corpus-based grammatical description at the highest level for the absolute expert of Coptic; no translations of source material.

Vernus, Pascal. *Future at Issue: Tense, Mood, and Aspect in Middle Egyptian: Studies in Syntax and Semantics.* Yale Egyptological Studies, 4. New Haven, 1990. Systematic treatment of these notions the existence of which is in part still disputed, and the forms considered to express them.

Winand, Jean. *Études de néo-égyptien, 1: La morphologie verbale.* Aegyptiaca Leodiensia, 2. Liège, 1992. The most recent study—and the first after a very long time—that treats morphology and graphematics of the Late Egyptian verb.

FRIEDRICH JUNGE

WITH HEIKE BEHLMER

Old Egyptian

The name given to the first attested stage of the ancient Egyptian language is Old Egyptian. It can be subdivided historically into several phases. The first hieroglyphic inscriptions, from the Predynastic and Early Dynastic period (c.3050–2687 BCE), consist mostly of labels in a developing form of hieroglyphic writing; they reveal little about the grammar of the language other than the identity of some of its words. Texts from the Old Kingdom (third through sixth dynasties, c.2687–2191 BCE) represent the classical phase of Old Egyptian—the phase to which the term *Old Egyptian* normally refers. Inscriptions from the First Intermediate Period (eighth through eleventh dynasties, c.2190–1998 BCE) reflect the final phase of Old Egyptian. Most of these are written in a form of the language that is transitional between Old Egyptian and the next major phase, known as Middle Egyptian. Factors such as dialectal differences and the conservative nature of some texts, as well as the gradual nature of language change, make it impossible to determine a point at which Old Egyptian ended and Middle Egyptian began.

Texts. The first texts to reveal major grammatical features of the language appeared at the beginning of the Old Kingdom, contemporary with the standardization of hieroglyphic signs and orthography. The earliest inscriptions that consist of more than mere labels are the speeches of various divinities on a shrine of Djoser, first pharaoh of the third dynasty (r. 2687–2668 BCE), and the tomb biography of an official named Metjen, whose career spanned the end of the third dynasty and the beginning of the fourth (c.2630 BCE). These two sources also represent the two major genres of Old Egyptian texts, religious and secular.

The genre of Old Egyptian religious texts is represented primarily by the Pyramid Texts, a collection of funerary rituals and spells inscribed on the sarcophagi and subterranean walls of royal tombs from the end of the fifth dynasty through the eighth dynasty. The language of these texts is largely homogenous and, given the generally conservative nature of religious inscriptions, probably represents the earliest form of Old Egyptian, despite the relatively late date of the tombs in which they were in-

scribed. During the First Intermediate Period, Pyramid Texts were also inscribed on the walls of nonroyal tombs, sarcophagi, and coffins. At the same time, the older texts were often re-edited and expanded with additional spells. Some of these newer texts, known as Coffin Texts, are written in the Old Egyptian of the Pyramid Texts and may have been a part of the older genre that was not inscribed in the Old Kingdom royal tombs. Others reflect a late form of Old Egyptian (or an early form of Middle Egyptian), and were probably composed during the First Intermediate Period. Like the transition between Old Egyptian and Middle Egyptian, the evolution of Pyramid Texts to Coffin Texts cannot be dated precisely, and it is not always possible to separate the two bodies of texts on the basis of language alone.

The genre of religious texts also includes inscriptions from the mortuary temples and chapels of royal and nonroyal tombs. Such inscriptions normally accompany scenes of daily life or offering bearers carved on the walls of these buildings, and are often no more than extended labels describing the scenes and their participants. In a few cases, however, the scenes depict religious rituals, and their texts record parts of the liturgy of these rites. Notable examples are the *sed*-festival reliefs of Newoserre Any (fifth dynasty, r. 2474–2444 BCE), which recorded the rituals that commemorated this pharaoh's thirtieth year of reign, the scenes of funerary rites, and the postmortem pilgrimage to Abydos on the walls of some nonroyal tomb-chapels. Although nonroyal tombs of the Old Kingdom were not inscribed with Pyramid Texts, they do contain a table of ones, which reflects in its contents and order the same ones recorded in the spells of the Offering Ritual from the Pyramid Texts.

The genre of Old Egyptian secular texts is more varied. Beginning with the inscriptions of Metjen, it is represented primarily by the biographies inscribed in the tombs and on the stelae of officials from the fourth dynasty into the First Intermediate Period. These texts were intended to demonstrate the exemplary character of their authors, a prerequisite for the privilege of a mortuary cult. Such texts often relate notable deeds that the deceased performed in the service of the king. As such, they constitute a major source for historical events of the Old Kingdom. A prime example is the biography of the official Weni, who served as military commander in the Near East, governor of Upper Egypt, and judge of a harem trial in the royal residence during the sixth dynasty (c.2360–2300 BCE). This text, the longest of its type, was considered by later generations of Egyptians as a model of the genre. Secular texts also include several royal decrees made on behalf of Egyptian temples and an archive of priestly service in the mortuary temple of the fifth dynasty pharaoh Neferirkare Kakai at Abusir during the late fifth and early sixth dynasties (c.2430–2330 BCE).

During the reign of Izezi (fifth dynasty, r. 2436–2404 BCE), the genre of letters first appears in Egyptian texts. The earliest recorded examples are communications from Izezi to his viziers Rashepses and Senedjemib, recorded as part of their tomb biographies. One of the more famous Old Egyptian texts is a letter from the young pharaoh Pepy II (sixth dynasty, r. 2300–2206 BCE) to the official Harkhuf, recorded in the latter's autobiography, in which the king eagerly instructs Harkhuf in the handling of a dwarf that Harkhuf was bringing back from an expedition to the Sudan, "for My Majesty wants to see this dwarf more than the products of Sinai or Punt." Private correspondence as such has not been preserved. Its closest representatives are a number of letters to the dead, written on objects placed in private tomb-chapels, and a letter of complaint from a quarry chief to the vizier; all of these date to the late sixth dynasty and the First Intermediate Period.

Old Egyptian is not represented in some of the more "literary" genres of later stages of the language, such as stories and wisdom literature. This may be an accident of preservation, but there is evidence that these genres may not have existed until after the Old Kingdom ended. This is particularly true for wisdom literature: although a number of such texts, such as the *Instruction of Ptahhotep* and *Instructions of Kagemni*, were assigned to the authorship of Old Kingdom officials, their preserved copies are written in Middle Egyptian or, at the earliest, in the latest form of Old Egyptian. This is also true of medical texts whose origin has been placed in the Old Kingdom, such as the Edwin Smith Papyrus. The theological treatise known as the Memphite Theology, which is preserved in a twenty-fifth dynasty copy, has long been dated to the Old Kingdom, but more recent research indicates that it was composed, at the earliest, during the nineteenth dynasty.

Most of the extant Old Egyptian textual sources are inscribed in hieroglyphs. Documents composed in the handwritten script known as Hieratic are limited to a few archives and nonroyal letters. The Pyramid Texts, however, show signs of an original written in cursive hieroglyphs; this script, as well as Hieratic, is also employed in some copies of the Pyramid Texts and Coffin Texts from the First Intermediate Period.

The formal nature of most Old Egyptian texts constrains the degree to which they represent the contemporary spoken language. As a rule, religious texts can be considered more archaic in this respect than those of the secular genre. The composition of most Pyramid Texts can be dated, at the latest, to the mid–fifth dynasty by comparing their verbal system with that of the tomb biographies. The theology of these texts, and the architecture of the pyramid substructures reflected in them, suggest that they originated in the late fourth dynasty at the earli-est. Colloquial Old Egyptian is best represented by the speech of laborers recorded as an adjunct to certain tomb scenes. These texts show verbal features of later Old Egyptian and Middle Egyptian as well as certain elements that did not become a regular part of the written language until Late Egyptian—in particular, the use of the demonstrative *pȝ* as the definite article.

Orthography. Two major orthographic features distinguish Old Egyptian texts: the reliance on ideograms and phonograms, and the spelling of the dual and plural. Old Egyptian spells most words either with ideograms (single hieroglyphs representing words, such as the picture of a leg for *rd*, "leg") or phonograms (hieroglyphs representing sounds, such as the image of a mouth, *r*, and hand, *d*, for *rd*, "leg"), whereas later texts frequently add one or more ideograms as "determinatives" at the end of a word spelled with phonograms (such as MOUTH plus HAND plus LEG as determinative, for *rd*, "leg"). Old Egyptian regularly spells the dual and plural of nouns by repeating ideograms, determinatives, or entire words (e.g., LEG–LEG for *rdwj*, "two legs"; MOUTH–HAND–LEG–LEG–LEG or MOUTH–HAND–LEG repeated three times for *rdw*, "legs"), while later texts normally add two or three short strokes or dots to the singular for the same purpose.

These features reflect the historical position of Old Egyptian at the beginning of Egyptian writing. The use of strokes (or dots) to indicate the dual and plural is clearly a simplification of the earlier convention. The addition of determinatives may have begun as a feature of handwritten texts in cursive hieroglyphs or Hieratic, whose simplified signs require less effort to make than those of carved inscriptions. The older conventions are most often found in religious texts, in line with their more conservative nature.

Phonology. Old Egyptian has twenty-two phonemes (distinctive sounds), most of which are identical to those found in later stages of the language. The sounds transcribed as *z* (perhaps a *th* sound, as in English *think*) and *s* are distinct in Old Egyptian, though by Middle Egyptian they had coalesced into a single phoneme, *s*. The sound represented by *ẖ* (probably a palatalized *kh*, as in German *ich*) seems to have evolved during the course of the Old Kingdom: Old Egyptian texts use *š* (*sh*, as in English *shoe*) as well as *ẖ* to spell words later written with *ẖ* alone, indicating that this sound was not part of the original phonemic inventory.

The Pyramid Texts contain evidence of the development of phonemic *ṯ* (a palatalized *t*, as in British *tune*) from *k* (e.g., *kw* > *ṯw*, "you"), both of which occur in these texts. Old Egyptian also shows the beginning of several sound changes that are better attested in Middle Egyptian: the change of *ȝ* (perhaps an original *l*) to ʾ and *r* to ʾ in syllable-final or word-final position, as well as *ṯ* to *t* in some words; the coalescence of *z* and *s* into *s;* and the loss of the feminine ending *t* in word-final position.

Old Egyptian often has the phoneme *i* (probably a vowel marker or glottal stop) in forms where Middle Egyptian has *w*. This includes the demonstrative *pi* (found in older Pyramid Texts) for *pw*, the impersonal/passive suffix *ti* (Middle Egyptian *tw*), and third person masculine singular stative suffix *i* (Middle Egyptian *w*). The double reed-leaf usually represents *ii* (deriving from *i* + *i*, *i* + *w*, or *w* + *i*) in Old Egyptian, but by Middle Egyptian it has become a separate phoneme *y*.

Grammar. The history of the Egyptian language shows an overall development from synthetic to analytic forms: that is, from signaling differences in meaning by changes in the form of a word (e.g., English *bring* versus *brought*) to indicating them by combining words (e.g., English *bring* versus *will bring*). Old Egyptian stands at the beginning of this development, and is, therefore, the most synthetic phase of the language. This feature is most visible in the verbal system, but can be seen in other grammatical classes as well.

The major grammatical differences between Old and Middle Egyptian can be summarized as follows:

- use of a productive dual, not only in nouns but also in pronouns, adjectives, and verb forms. By Middle Egyptian the dual exists primarily in nouns alone; and then mostly for things that can be paired, such as *irti*, "eyes."
- full agreement in gender and number between nouns and their modifiers. In Middle Egyptian, modifiers are usually either masculine singular, masculine plural, or feminine.
- demonstrative pronouns fully declined for differences in gender and number. Middle Egyptian has only three declined demonstratives: masculine singular, feminine singular, and generic.
- second and third person singular independent pronouns based on the dependent forms (*twt* and *tmt*, "you"; *swt*, "he"; *stt*, "she"). In Middle Egyptian these are replaced by forms constructed from the base *nt* plus the suffix pronouns (*ntk* and *ntt*, "you"; *ntf*, "he"; *nts*, "she"). The newer form *ntf* first appears in a Pyramid Text of Pepy II.
- productive use of the relative pronoun *iwti* as the negative counterpart of *nty* "who, which, that." In Middle Egyptian *iwti* is usually replaced by the analytic construction of *nty* plus a negative word.
- regular use of the bipartite nominal-predicate pattern A B ("A is B" or "B is A"). In Middle Egyptian this pattern is more limited in use.
- agreement in gender and number between the "copula" and A in the nominal-predicate patterns A *pw* ("It

is A") and A *pw* B ("B is A" or "A is B"). Middle Egyptian uses only invariable *pw* in this construction.
- frequent use of the prefix *j* in many verb forms. This is primarily a feature of religious texts, and is less common in secular inscriptions. The prefix in Middle Egyptian is limited to the imperative of a few verbs.
- regular use of the simple transitive perfective (or "indicative") *sḏm.f* and the transitive and intransitive stative as independent past tense verb forms. In Middle Egyptian these forms are supplanted by the perfect (*sḏm.n.f*) of transitive verbs and the stative of intransitive verbs, normally as the second element of a compound construction. This change is first attested in secular texts of the later Old Kingdom.
- productive use of a synthetic future tense, the prospective (or "*sḏmw.f*") and its passive (*sḏmm.f*). By Middle Egyptian the prospective survives only in a few constructions and is otherwise replaced by the subjunctive (*sḏm.f*) or the analytic "pseudoverbal" future construction (*iw.f r sḏm.*) The change from prospective to subjunctive is documented in the Pyramid Texts, and secular texts show the analytic construction already in the mid-fifth dynasty.
- use of the analytic construction SUBJECT *sḏm.f* to express the imperfect. Middle Egyptian regularly uses the "pseudoverbal" construction SUBJECT *ḥr sḏm* for this purpose, as do secular texts beginning in the fifth dynasty.
- use of the particle *iw* primarily in main clauses. In Middle Egyptian this particle also occurs in circumstantial clauses, for which Old Egyptian texts regularly use *sk*.
- a single negative particle *ni* in place of the Middle Egyptian negatives *ni* and *nn*.
- the negative particles *nii* and *w*, for which Middle Egyptian uses *ni is* and *nn*, respectively.
- use of the negative verb *imi* in the negation of purpose clauses. Middle Egyptian texts generally show the negative verb *tm* in this use.

The grammar of Old Egyptian, even in its "classical" stage, is far from uniform. For the most part it reflects the slow evolution of the language throughout the seven hundred years that Old Egyptian is attested. As already noted, the Pyramid Texts seem to represent the earliest stage of the language, which is also that of secular texts until the mid-fifth dynasty. Differences between the language of two genres during this time lie more in orthographic conventions and the varying requirements of their subject matter than in grammar. The Pyramid Texts are generally more liberal in writing "weak" verbal elements, such as the phoneme *i* as a prefix or ending, while narrative forms and constructions are attested primarily in the tomb biographies and not in the ritual spells of the Pyramid Texts.

In the middle of the fifth dynasty, however, secular texts begin to show changes in the language that are not reflected, at least not to the same extent, in the more conservative religious texts. The most important of these are the gradual loss of the synthetic future forms (also reflected in the Pyramid Texts) and the introduction of the "pseudoverbal" constructions (which do not appear in the Pyramid Texts). It is for this reason that the secular texts can be considered more representative of the contemporary language than those of the religious genre. A number of important changes in the verbal system also have to do with narrative forms, which are by and large absent from religious texts: in particular, the replacement of the perfective (*sḏm.f*) by the perfect (*sḏm.n.f*) for the narration of past action—a development that is paralleled in the history of modern French and German, where the perfect (*il a fait, er hat getan*) has also largely replaced the simple past tense (*il fit, er tat*).

Many of the distinctions between Old Egyptian and Middle Egyptian are evidently the result of such grammatical changes over the course of time. Of the fifteen major differences listed above, eleven can be traced to diachronic evolution: features that change or disappear in Middle Egyptian and do not revert or reappear in the history of the language. In four cases, however, Old Egyptian features that disappear in Middle Egyptian reappear in Late Egyptian: regular use of the A B nominal-predicate pattern, "copula" agreement in the A *pw* pattern, use of the prefix, and use of the *sḏm.f* as a narrative past tense. Although the last of these has been explained as a development from the Middle Egyptian perfect (*sḏm.n.f*), the remaining three suggest that Old and Late Egyptian represent one dialect and Middle Egyptian another. Historical and linguistic considerations point to a northern origin for Old and Late Egyptian; the origin of Middle Egyptian has not been identified.

[*See also* Scripts, *article on* Hieroglyphs.]

BIBLIOGRAPHY

Allen, James P. *The Inflection of the Verb in the Pyramid Texts.* Bibliotheca Aegyptia, 2.1–2. Malibu, 1984. Comprehensive study of the verbal system of the Pyramid Texts.

Doret, Eric. *The Narrative Verbal System of Old and Middle Egyptian.* Cahiers d'Orientalisme, 12. Geneva, 1986. Particularly informative for differences between the two language stages.

Edel, Elmar. *Altägyptische Grammatik.* Analecta Orientalia, 34 and 39. Rome, 1955–1964. Primary reference work for Old Egyptian grammar.

Edgerton, William F. "Early Egyptian Dialect Interrelationships." *Bulletin of the American Schools of Oriental Research* 122 (April, 1951), 9–12. Evidence for the dialectical relationship between Old and Late Egyptian.

Faulkner, Raymond O. *The Ancient Egyptian Pyramid Texts.* Oxford, 1969. Complete translation of the Pyramid Texts.

Lichtheim, Miriam. *Ancient Egyptian Literature*, vol. 1: *The Old and Middle Kingdoms.* Berkeley, 1973. Includes translation of some of the major Old Egyptian texts.

Loprieno, Antonio. *Ancient Egyptian, a Linguistic Introduction.* Cambridge and New York, 1995. General introduction to the features of Egyptian grammar for all stages of the language.

JAMES P. ALLEN

Middle Egyptian

The written language of the Middle Kingdom (c.2040–1665 BCE) is Middle Egyptian. An early form of Middle Egyptian appears in texts from the First Intermediate Period (c.2165–2040 BCE), and a late form of it in texts from the Second Intermediate Period (c.1665–1569 BCE) and the early New Kingdom (c.1569–1502 BCE). The use of Middle Egyptian in later times is discussed at the end of the article's bibliography. Although Middle Egyptian differs in minor points from earlier Old Egyptian, the language of the Old Kingdom, they resemble each other closely. For this reason, Middle Egyptian is often classified together with Old Egyptian as Earlier or Older Egyptian.

There is a greater difference, and to a certain extent a fundamental one, between Middle Egyptian and Late Egyptian, the language of the New Kingdom. Late Egyptian and all following language phases of Egyptian and its successor Coptic have been conjointly named Later Egyptian (-Coptic). The most important difference between Middle Egyptian (or Earlier Egyptian as a whole) and Late Egyptian (or Later Egyptian [-Coptic] as a whole) is that the former is more synthetic and the latter more analytic. An example of the general tendency for the synthetic Middle Egyptian language to develop into an analytic language can be seen in the development of specification of noun gender. The older, synthetic type of language identifies gender with a suffix that is a firm part of the noun: Middle Egyptian, or Early Egyptian, feminine nouns have the ending *t*, while masculine nouns do not—e.g., *sn* "(the) brother," *snt* "(the) sister." In the analytic language that followed, gender could be indicated by an article, a separate word preceding the noun, which made redundant the *t* at the end of the noun: *p3 sn* "the brother," *t3 sn(t)* "the sister."

Sources. Middle Egyptian was the standard language of the Middle Kingdom and served as an acrolect (elite language) thereafter. During the Middle Kingdom, Middle Egyptian was used in monumental inscriptions and literature as well as in vernacular communication, especially in correspondence. The stylistic viability of the tradition of the late Old Kingdom's Pyramid Texts is evident in many religious texts, which thus resemble Old Egyptian texts in their language. Some learned writings (e.g., medical and mathematical texts) continue to use antiquated language. Middle Egyptian inscriptions in monumental hieroglyphs were placed on the walls of temples, royal stelae (e.g., border stelae), the walls of tombs and memorial chapels, and statues.

Middle Egyptian literature can be divided into several genres: instructions, such as the *Instruction of Ptahhotep*, the *Instructions for Merikare*, the *Instructions of Amenemhet* (for his son Senwosret I), or the *Instructions of Khety*; tales, such as the *Story of Sinuhe*, the *Story of the Shipwrecked Sailor*, or the *Story of King Khufu's Court*; and hymns, such as the *Hymn to the Nile* and a cycle of hymns to Senwosret III. Other Middle Egyptian texts, which can be given a generic term only with some difficulty, are the *Prophecies of Neferti*, the *Complaints of Khakheperre-sonb*, the *Admonitions of Ipuwer*, the *Dialogue of a Man and his Ba*, and the *Satire of Trades*. A considerable portion of the typologically varied Coffin Texts, which were carved on the insides of coffins, are composed in Middle Egyptian, although many of these religious texts continue in the Old Egyptian tradition.

Among the nonliterary texts in Middle Egyptian, correspondence features prominently. The Kahun Papyri, the archives of the town adjacent to the pyramid of Senwosret II near Illahun, including administrative documents; letters addressed to the dead, pleading for intercession on behalf of the living writers of the letters; and the private correspondence of the traveling businessman Hekanakhte, in which he attempts to organize all aspects of his family's life, at times in a very emotional manner.

As a result of its position as the language of literature during the Middle Kingdom, Middle Egyptian rose in status to become the classical standard language. It remained an ideal for assorted areas of practical language use until the end of hieroglyphic creative tradition. Middle Egyptian is consequently also known as Classical Egyptian. Although the Middle Egyptian of the New Kingdom has not been given a specific name that is generally accepted, the Middle Egyptian that was more intensively cultivated from the Third Intermediate Period on is generally known as Late Middle Egyptian or Neo-Middle Egyptian. A comprehensive name for the entire later use of Classical Egyptian has been achieved in the French expression *égyptien de tradition*.

Linguistic Aspects. An impression of the linguistic nature of texts in Middle Egyptian can be obtained by examining aspects of morphology, syntax, and pragmatics. An excerpt from the Middle Egyptian verbal paradigm follows to illustrate morphology; this is followed by a sketch of its syntax and pragmatics, on which the grammar of Middle Egyptian is based and which constitute a major research area of linguistic Egyptology. The linguistic contrasts of literary and nonliterary everyday texts are then outlined.

Morphology. Verbal forms are predominently synthetic; some analytic forms also exist. Synthetic verbal forms combine lexemes and inflectional elements in a single word form. This form is taken by verbs in the suffix conjugation (so called because of the final pronominal subject added directly to the verbal form). For example:

1. *ḥtp.k*
   may-be-gracious.you
   "may you be gracious"

2. *ḥtp.n nṯr(w)*
   when/that-gracious.were (the) gods
   "when/that the gods were gracious"

Apart from the suffix conjugation, peculiar to Egyptian, Middle Egyptian uses another synthetic verbal form that is inflected differently: the pseudoparticiple also called the old perfective, or stative. (This is related to the Akkadian stative and the West Semitic perfect form):

3. *ḥtp(w)*
   he-is-gracious
   "he is gracious"

Analytic verbal forms consist of the infinitive preceded by one of the prepositions *ḥr* "on", *m* "in," and *r* "to":

4. *t3 ḥr mnmn*
   (the) earth (is) on trembling
   "the earth trembles"

5. *t3 r mnmn*
   (the) earth (is) to tremble
   "the earth will tremble"

It is controversial to what extent particular series of verbal forms exist for different syntactic slots. Strictly speaking, the so-called standard theory of Egyptian verbal syntax prescribes two morphologically distinct verbal forms for series such as the two presented here; one stands syntactically in nominal slots, and the other in adverbial slots, as in this example:

6. *šm.n.ṯ, ʿnḫ.ti*
   (that) depart.ed.you (is), being-alive.you
   "you departed alive"

The first verbal form, "that you departed," is nominal because it is syntactically equivalent to the noun phrase "your departure." The second is adverbial because "being alive" is equivalent to the prepositional phrase "in life."

Current opinion favors the existence of two series: one is nominal, as the standard theory presupposes ("that you departed"); the other, however, is not adverbial ("being alive") but rather verbal ("you live"). The translation "being" for the latter arises from the embedding of a verbal form in an adverbial slot, but not from the verbal form itself. On the other hand, it is legitimate to argue that all verbal forms are to be interpreted verbally—that verbal forms make up a single series morphologically, but that different parts of this series are used in different syntactic slots.

Syntax and pragmatics. Sentence word order is strictly prescribed. The details of the rules are complex because word order depends on numerous syntactic factors, such as the type of predicate. The order in which subject, predicate, object, and adverbial phrases follow each other is, however, straightforward in virtually every case. This has led to the mistaken belief that Middle Egyptian is relatively inexpressive. On the contrary, it has a wide range of methods of expression at its disposal, which grants the language ample expressionistic flexibility.

The first source of this flexibility is the fact that a sentence can begin with a situational particle, a topic, background information, or a particle of presentation:

7. Situational particle *iw:*
   iw: in.n.i Ḏdi
   it-is-the-case: brought.have.I Djedi
   "I have brought (the man called) Djedi"

8. Nominal topic:
   ḥḳȝ pf: nḏnḏ.f ḥnʿ.i
   ruler that: conferred.he with.me
   "that ruler conferred with me"

9. Verbal background information:
   ḫpr.n.i: ḫpr.n ḫprt
   come-into-existence.have.I: come-into-existence.have existing-things
   "as soon as I came into existence, being came into existence"

10. Particle of presentation *mk:*
    mk: pḥ.n.n ḫnw
    look: reached.have.we home
    "look, we have reached home"

Furthermore, various sorts of sentence construction permit the author to focus on certain parts of a sentence. Some of these are irregular with respect to basic sentence construction. The following example of a focalizing construction stresses the adverbial phrase:

11. *gm.n sw ipwtiw: ḥr wȝt*
    (that-)found.have him (the) messengers: on (the) road
    "on the road the messengers found him"

This particular type of sentence is of special importance in the history of Egyptological linguistics. It was this pioneering discovery of Hans Jakob Polotsky that led to formulation of the standard theory of Egyptian verbal

syntax. Nevertheless, extension of this theory became problematic, and it is not fully, or not at all, accepted by most grammarians today.

Stylistic Differences. Nonliterary texts such as correspondence diverge from inscriptions and literary texts principally in diction, not in grammar. Nonliterary texts are primarily illocutive, addressing the reader himself, and literary texts are predominently delocutive, simply describing states of affairs. The illocutive nonliterary texts seek to seize the attention of the addressee and employ particles of presentation, such as the presentational *mk* "look," to this end:

12. *mk grt: pȝ.k pr, mk: sw rḏ(w) n pȝ wʿb Nḫt*
    look now: that-of.you house—look: it is-given to the priest Nakht
    "look now, your house—look, it is sold to the priest Nakht"

Example 12 also demonstrates the gradual completion of thought typical during speech. The message opens with an illocutive *mk* "look" and the establishment of a topic ("your house, it is") and reopens with a further illocutive *mk* "look." Anacolutha—changes from one grammatical construction to another within a single sentence—also follow this pattern.

Literary texts, by contrast, are so strongly structured that they sometimes border on becoming schematic. This occurs to varying degrees. Most commonly, a type of prose poetry results, consisting of verse group formation, thought couplets, triplets, and quatrains, frequently connected by the stylistic device of parallelism of members. The verses in literature used in schools are often separated from each other by versification dots also called verse points, a method of punctuation (indicated hereafter by °; a slash indicates the end of a verse without versification dots, and verse groups end with a double slash).

The *Story of Sinuhe* presents the initial state of affairs in the following words:

13. *iw: ḫnw m sgr, ibw m gmw °*
    rwti wrti ḫtm(w) °//
    šnyt m tp-ḥr-mȝst °
    pʿwt m imw °//

    It-is-the-case: (the) residence (was) in silence, (and) hearts (were) in mourning. °
    (The) two-portals, (the) two-great-ones, were-shut. °//
    (The) entourage (was) in head-upon-(the-)knee. °
    (The) subjects (were) in grief. °//

    "The residence was in silence, hearts were in mourning. °
    The two portals were shut. °//
    The entourage was bowed down. °
    The subjects were in grief." °//

The first two lines present the situation at the residence in two statements (the use of "the two great portals" is metonymic for "residence"). The first line, again, is conventionally divided into two parts ("silence" parallel to "mourning"). The last two lines separate the people involved into two complementary groups, "the entourage" and "the subjects," whose respective characteristics are "bowed down" and "in mourning."

A sequence of events can also be structured in this manner, as the following passage does for the flight of the story's hero, Sinuhe, from the Libyan camp of the royal army into foreign lands of the Near East:

14. *nmi.n.i Mꜣʿti m hꜣw Nḫt* °
smꜣ.n.i m ʿIw-Snfrw °//
wrš.n.i m ʿd n sḫt °
wḏ.n.i wn hrw °//

Come-across.have.I (lake) Maati: in (the) region (of) (village) Sycomore. °
Come.have.I: to (village) Isle-(of-)Snofru. °//
Passed-a-time.have.I: on (the) edge of (a) field. °/
Started.have.I: (it) being daylight. °//

"I went across Lake Maati *in the region of Sycomore Village.* °/
I came *to Isle of Snofru Village.* °//
I passed a time *at the edge of a field.* °/
I started, *when it was daylight.*" °//

Both of these pairs of sentences are constructed in the same syntactic pattern: in each sentence an adverbial phrase (shown in italics) is stressed. Although the first thought couplet is held together by the names of certain places and the second by expressions of time, albeit of different types, the two pairs of lines are not really separated from each other. The first line of the second thought couplet focuses on a place, as do both lines of the first thought couplet. One could consider adding the third line to the two preceding it to make a triplet, leaving the fourth as the beginning of what comes next. This possibility cannot be resolved here; it must suffice to appreciate that the narrative is made up of a sequence of syntactically more or less similar verse elements loosely or closely connected by parallelisms of style or content.

Linguistically progressive language elements such as the article or the possessive article occur occasionally in both nonliterary texts and the more recent stylistically vernacular tales of Papyrus Westcar: for example, *pꜣ wʿb* "the priest" instead of *wʿb* "(the) priest"; *pꜣ.k pr* "that-of.you house" instead of *pr.k* "house. of.you." Although these nonliterary examples feature common linguistic elements which become evident very quickly, their grammatical system on the whole corresponds to that of the literary texts.

Conversely, literary and particularly religious texts sometimes contain expressions reminiscent of the Old Kingdom. Such archaic elements are, however, limited in number. Surprisingly, retention of the language of the Old Kingdom is apparent in the letters of Hekanakhte, which are minimally stylized and very close to colloquial speech. In this case, however, it is important to remember that the texts were possibly not written in archaic language, but in a dialect that is closer to the literary language of the Old Kingdom than to that of the Middle Kingdom. Just as in the rest of the world, we must assume the existence of dialects in pharaonic Egypt. Changes in the location of the royal residence and changes in the origin of the elite no doubt allowed various dialects to influence the character of written language at different times.

Writing Systems. The Middle Egyptian texts are written in monumental hieroglyphs or in cursive Hieratic. Inscriptions in stone are generally written in monumental hieroglyphs. Examples of this style are inscriptions on the walls of temples or on royal stelae and in the funerary texts of the elite. The majority of the literary and everyday texts are generally written in Hieratic script on papyrus.

Although the great wealth of Egyptian writing signs and the ease with which they can be combined gave the writer a generous choice of ways to form words and their inflections, only a small subset of the possible combinations was actually used. The variety of accepted ways of writing is not unlimited, but no orthographic norms exist either; for individual words and their inflections, certain forms were considered eugraphic, or "good."

The manner in which signs were combined in hieroglyphic inscriptions in stone and in cursive Hieratic texts is not identical. Short, concise alternatives that minimize labor and space predominate in hieroglyphic inscriptions. They maintain their clarity in this form, for the most part. Hieratic texts in general are written with more signs. The far lower cost of the papyrus on which they were written allowed it to be used more freely, but cursive writing lacked the clarity and unambiguity of monumental hieroglyphs in stone. This in turn made it necessary to add clarifying signs on papyrus. In the Hieratic script, biconsonantal signs are regularly complemented by repetition of one or both of the component consonants. The biconsonantal sign *mn*, for instance, is regularly complemented by the monoconsonantal sign *n*, so that *mn* seems to be written *mn+n*. Monumental hieroglyphs use such complements less often than do cursive Hieratic texts.

A eugraphy (spelling convention) which can be termed "classical" became established at the onset of the twelfth dynasty. In addition to a general tendency toward regularity, the eugraphy reform affected primarily the determinatives, the signs added to a word or its inflection to clarify its semantic content. At this time, individual determinatives that had been associated with only one or very few words began to be replaced by classifying determinatives of a more general nature. For example, instead of complementing the name of each bird with an image of that bird, all bird names were complemented by a picture of a goose, the Egyptian bird *par excellence*. Again, the word for "livestock" is no longer classified by any one of a variety of determinatives for the common livestock—cattle, donkeys, and goats—but solely by the symbol for cattle, the most highly valued livestock. The ability to write with fewer specifying signs to which standardization gave rise was especially advantageous for writing in cursive Hieratic signs, which were not able to reproduce graphic details as well as were the more pictorial monumental hieroglyphs.

After the Ramessid period (c.1321–1076 BCE), the determinatives and logograms tend to regain their pictorial character, and their detail increases. In the Greco-Roman period (from 332 BCE on), the temple inscriptions become showcases for the celebration of pictorial intricacy and diversity. The distinctions of old pictographs are refined individually to the utmost and extended with the addition of further individual details. Ultimately, this pursuit of singularity resulted in the creation of completely new pictographs, unique in every way.

[*See also* Scripts, *articles on* Hieroglyphs *and* Hieratic Script.]

BIBLIOGRAPHY

Works on the Language of the Middle Kingdom
Allen, James P. "Colloquial Middle Egyptian: Some Observations on the Language of Heqanakht." *Lingua Aegyptia* 4 (1994), 1–12. Classifies the language of the *Hekanakhte Letters* typologically as Late Old Egyptian.
Borghouts, Joris F. *Egyptisch: Een inleiding in taal en schrift van het Middenrijk* [Introduction to the Language and Writing of the Middle Kingdom]. Leiden and Leuven, 1993. An excellent, theoretically and philologically well-grounded modern introduction.
Depuydt, Leo. *Catalogue of Coordinates and Satellites of the Middle Egyptian Verb.* Leuven, 1996. A very clear, systematic presentation of verbal forms based on the Standard Theory.
Eyre, Christopher J. "Was Ancient Egyptian Really a Primitive Language?" *Lingua Aegyptia* 1 (1991), 97–123. Describes Classical Egyptian as an artificial "poetic" dialect, a type of Egyptian "Homeric." The language of the *Hekanakhte Letters* is considered a spoken language.
Gardiner, Alan. *Egyptian Grammar, Being an Introduction to the Study of Hieroglyphs.* 3d rev. ed. London, 1957 (and later printings). Although outdated in certain vital points because it was first published in 1927 and only slightly revised in 1950, this is still the standard reference grammar for Middle Egyptian, and the best basic book in English for learning Egyptian.
Ockinga, Boyo. *A Concise Grammar of Middle Egyptian.* [Basic Middle Egyptian Grammar. Revised edition of *An Outline of Middle Egyptian Grammar* by H. Brunner]. Mainz, 1998. Introduction to language and writing based on latest research; much more detailed than the *Outline* by Brunner on which it is based.
Schenkel, Wolfgang. *Tübinger Einführung in die klassisch-ägyptische Sprache und Schrift* [Tübingen Introduction to Classical Egyptian Language and Writing]. Tübingen, 1997. Instruction book based on current research, textbook for university lectures. Available from the author, Ägyptologisches Institut, Schloss, D–72070 Tübingen.

Works on the Literature of the Middle Kingdom
Lichtheim, Miriam. *Ancient Egyptian Literature.* Vol. 1, *The Old and Middle Kingdoms.* Berkeley, Los Angeles, and London, 1975. Representative anthology of translations with introduction and commentary.
Parkinson, R. B. *Voices from Ancient Egypt. An Anthology of Middle Kingdom Writings.* London, 1991. Thematic compilation of literary and nonliterary texts of all types, with partial translations, introductory remarks, commentary, and illustrations.
Parkinson, R. B. *The Tale of Sinuhe and Other Ancient Egyptian Poems 1940–1640* BCE. Oxford, 1997. Anthology of classical literature in translation, with introduction and commentary.

Works on the Later Use of Middle Egyptian and on Diglossia
Jansen–Winkeln, Karl. *Text und Sprache in der 3. Zwischenzeit* [Text and Language of the Third Intermediate Period]. Wiesbaden, 1994. Describes types of text and shows which texts were written in Middle Egyptian, in Late Egyptian, or in a combination of both.
Jansen-Winkeln, Karl. "Diglossie und Zweisprachigkeit im alten Ägypten" [Diglossia and Bilingualism in Ancient Egypt]. *Zeitschrift für die Kunde des Morgenlandes* 85 (1995), 85–115. Describes the parallel use of Earlier Egyptian and Later Egyptian with reference to texts.
Jansen-Winkeln, Karl. *Spätmittelägyptische Grammatik der Texte der 3. Zwischenzeit* [Late Middle Egyptian Grammar of the Texts of the Third Intermediate Period]. Wiesbaden, 1996. Detailed referential grammar.
Manuelian, Peter Der. *Living in the Past: Studies in Archaism of the Egyptian Twenty–Sixth Dynasty.* London and New York, 1994. On the integration of the Late period into intellectual history and on the grammar of Late Middle Egyptian.

Works of Reference
Faulkner, Raymond O. *A Concise Dictionary of Middle Egyptian.* Oxford, 1962 (and later printings). Very useful, but no longer completely up to date.
Hannig, Rainer. *Die Sprache der Pharaonen: Grosses Handwörterbuch Ägyptisch-Deutsch (2800–950 v. Chr.)* [The Language of the Pharaohs: Large, Concise Egyptian-German Dictionary 2800–950 BCE]. Mainz, 1995. Most recent compilation of current lexical knowledge, but unfortunately lacking references and including much questionable material.

WOLFGANG SCHENKEL

Late Egyptian

Late Egyptian is generally considered to be that phase of the Egyptian language employed in writing manuscript documents of the nineteenth through the twenty-first dynasties, although there are also examples of monumental hieroglyphic inscriptions composed in Late Egyptian. Monumental texts from the reign of Akhenaten are, in fact, the first to display broad usage of Late Egyptian as a literary language. It is, however, incorrect to regard Late Egyptian as a creation of the Amarna period, because Late Egyptian elements can be found in earlier texts. New Kingdom monumental inscriptions prior to the Amarna period are composed in a brand of Middle Egyptian with occasional intrusions of Late Egyptian. The degree to which isolated Late Egyptian features are revealed in pre-Amarna inscriptions depends on the nature of the document. The annals of Thutmose III, for example, contain more Late Egyptianisms than do some of the more formal documents of his reign. Some inscriptions of the Theban seventeenth dynasty actually possess more Late Egyptian elements than do many eighteenth dynasty monumental texts, which were consciously crafted in classical Middle Egyptian.

During the course of the New Kingdom, the spoken language experienced change. The documents that provide the closest approximation to the colloquial language are written in the Hieratic script on papyri and ostraca. For the eighteenth dynasty such sources remain limited; the Ramessid nineteenth and twentieth dynasties are much better represented by manuscript documents. In particular, the area of Deir el-Medina, where the artisans and laborers who excavated and decorated the royal tombs in western Thebes lived and worked, has been the source of thousands of ostraca and numerous papyri. With the additional Tomb Robberies Papyri, which record the depositions of witnesses in the late twentieth dynasty, and the corpus of Late Ramessid Letters, the twentieth dynasty is especially well represented. Although some grammars of Late Egyptian have been broad in scope, using both nonliterary and literary texts beginning with the Amarna period, this diachronic approach to the study of Late Egyptian has more recently yielded to a synchronic one that focuses on the nonliterary documents of a restricted period of time. The currently standard grammar of Late Egyptian (Černý and Groll 1984) is essentially one of nonliterary Late Egyptian of the twentieth and twenty-first dynasties, with only occasional citations from earlier inscriptions, supplemented by a small section on literary Late Egyptian. Nonetheless, the broader approach to Late Egyptian still has considerable value, especially because literary texts occasionally contain good examples of colloquial Late Egyptian usage that have not yet been discovered in the corpus of nonliterary Late Egyptian documents.

It has been noticed that there are several phenomena that Late Egyptian shares with Old Egyptian of the Pyramid Texts, but not with Middle Egyptian: the prothetic syllable of certain verb forms; sentences consisting of two nouns without copula; and differentiation of gender and number of the demonstrative pronoun subject following a noun or pronoun predicate. If Late Egyptian was primarily an Upper Egyptian dialect, as is generally believed because of the abundance of documents of Theban provenience, then it appears that certain dialectal features of the oldest Egyptian were preserved in the south but lost in the more northerly-influenced Middle Egyptian.

From the testimony of literary texts, we know that dialects existed in the New Kingdom, such that a man of the Nile Delta might have some difficulty conversing with a man from Elephantine in the south of Egypt. The extent to which Late Egyptian texts reflect dialect diversity is not as readily apparent as in Coptic, where vowels were clearly indicated in its alphabetic writing system. Although Sarah Groll (1984) believes to have discerned a regional dialect in a late twentieth dynasty text from Middle Egypt, on the whole there is remarkable homogeneity in the language of nonliterary documents written contemporaneously in various parts of Egypt. Given the centralized nature of the Egyptian government and the administration of vast temple holdings throughout the land, which required extensive travel and communication by officials and scribes, it is unlikely that dialect variation greatly intruded on the written language. Particularly in administrative documents and letters, often sent over considerable distances, the written language must have been a standardized form of the Theban dialect of Late Egyptian that had become universal and could be understood by any literate person. A common core of texts, copied in the schools of both Upper and Lower Egypt, contributed to maintaining consistency in written communication. As a result, dialect nuances were not much reflected in the written documents, as officials constantly communicated in writing from one end of Egypt to the other.

Orthography. Because of the conservative nature of the Egyptian writing system, many words in Late Egyptian preserve the traditional orthography in which they had been written in Middle Egyptian. Old orthographies were even retained for words that had undergone phonetic change. For example, although by the Ramessid period the word for "star," *sb3*, had lost the medial *b* and was pronounced something like *siou*, scribes continued to include the *b*-hieroglyph in spelling the word. The word for "day," *hrw*, often continued to be written with the medial *r*-hieroglyph, but variant spellings indicate that the pronunciation was actually similar to Coptic *hoou*. Similarly, the weak consonants (*3, i,* and *w*) were still written in words where they had probably disappeared from pronunciation. Such a situation suggests that in penning a Hieratic text, the Late Egyptian scribe was thinking logographically rather than spelling out words analytically consonant by consonant: he considered the entire word in its conservative spelling as a kind of logogram. In Late Egyptian the consonant *r* at the end of words had become vocalic *e*. Feminine nouns in the absolute state lost their consonantal *t*-suffix, which, however, was preserved as a consonant in the pronominal state, as shown by the occurrence of either *tw* or *ti* before the suffixed pronoun. Several consonants had also begun to coalesce, as indicated by occasional variant spellings, of the same word.

It is especially in the spelling of foreign—chiefly Semitic—loan words, which entered the lexicon during the Empire period; that the so-called syllabic orthography is encountered. Sometimes referred to as "group writing," this system is characterized by sign-groups containing the weak consonants, which probably, in a rudimentary way, represented the vowels *a*, *i*, and *u*; however, the degree to which the vowels of loan words were systematically indicated in syllabic writing has been a matter of debate. The principles of group writing seem to be less precisely operative in Late Egyptian than in older Egyptian.

In Late Egyptian one frequently encounters spellings with redundant determinatives and extraneous signs, often merely strokes of the reed brush toward the end of a word, which the reader must gloss over. In general, the orthography of Late Egyptian is not as strict as in earlier phases of the language, so that the modern scholar approaches the reading of a Late Egyptian text with a degree of flexibility, whereas reading earlier Egyptian texts requires a more thorough accounting for each written sign.

Another feature of Late Egyptian is the occasional omission in writing of certain common prepositions in adverbial phrases containing a noun. Somewhat different from this phenomenon is the omission of the prepositions *ḥr* before the infinitive in pseudo-verbal constructions. The term "pseudo-verbal" refers to a verbal sentence pattern that conforms to that of a sentence with simple adverbial predicate. Here one witnesses the gradual falling away of the preposition *ḥr*, so that by the twentieth dynasty it must have been lost in speech as well as writing. The omission in writing of the preposition *r* before the infinitive in the future tense also became regular by the twentieth dynasty, but as we know from Coptic, it still must have been present as a vowel *e*.

Grammatical Characteristics. A development that is discernible in the history of the Egyptian language is the shift from synthetic verbal forms to analytic constructions. In Old and Middle Egyptian, the preponderant synthetic forms had the verb first followed by the subject (e.g., *stp.f*, where *stp* is the verb and *f* is the pronominal subject). In such synthetic forms, verbal nuances were conveyed by variations in internal vocalization. Although five distinct *stp.f*-forms existed in older phases of the language, the number of *stp.f*-forms was reduced in nonliterary Late Egyptian. The prospective *stp.f* is still frequently encountered as an optative or jussive in main clauses, as well as in purpose clauses and subordinate clauses after the verb "cause," while the indicative *stp.f* survives in colloquial Late Egyptian only after the negative word *bw*, principally in the common phrase "He does not know."

In Late Egyptian there existed a perfect *stp.f*-form that was commonly employed with transitive verbs as a present perfect tense in independent clauses or as a preterit at the beginning of a narrative. Although this Late Egyptian form superficially resembles the older indicative *stp.f*, it actually derived from Middle Egyptian *iw stp.n.f*, with loss of the past formative element *n* and disappearance of the particle *iw*, which in Late Egyptian has become a subordinating particle.

With the reduction in synthetic verbal forms, Late Egyptian has recourse to analytic constructions involving the infinitive. Thus, pseudo-verbal constructions that make use of a preposition (*ḥr*, *m*, or *r*) before the infinitive form of the verb became more prominent. The present and future tenses in Late Egyptian both employ pseudo-verbal constructions; especially characteristic of Late Egyptian is the non-initial pseudo-verbal construction that continues a past narrative initiated either by a perfect *stp.f* of a transitive verb or, in the case of intransitive verbs of motion, by a pseudo-verbal construction containing an adverbial form of the verb known as the old perfective or stative, which expresses the result of the process of movement. By using analytic pseudo-verbal constructions that conform to the pattern of sentences with simple adverbial predicate, Late Egyptian tends toward placing the subject before the verb rather than after it, as in older synthetic forms. This word order is also characteristic of periphrastic constructions that use an auxiliary verb or particle before the subject and the main verb that follows.

Just as Late Egyptian employs a pseudo-verbal construction to continue a past narrative, similarly a new conjunctive tense serves to continue an imperative, a future tense, or occasionally past habitual action. Middle Egyptian forerunners of this construction indicate that the original literal meaning was "together with (= and) choosing on his part." Both the past narrative continuative and the conjunctive are analytical constructions in which the infinitive follows the conjugation prefix and specification of the subject.

To compensate for the reduction in synthetic verbal forms and their attendant individual nuances, Late Egyptian in its analytic approach systematically employs words called "clause converters," which are positioned before forms and constructions that would otherwise be independent. Thus, there is a circumstantial converter *iw*, a preterit converter *wn*, and a relative adjective *nty*. The relative adjective *nty* is employed only after defined antecedents, whereas a relative clause modifying an undefined antecedent is formed along the lines of a circumstantial clause by using the subordinating converter *iw*. Similarly, participles and the related relative forms, which in Late Egyptian are almost exclusively past in tense, appear only after defined antecedents.

A peculiar feature of the Egyptian language was its capacity to emphasize adverbial adjuncts after a verb so that the verb was no longer simply predicative. In older phases of Egyptian, synthetic nominal forms of the verb served to emphasize a following adverbial phrase or subordinate clause. Nonliterary Late Egyptian, however, has developed a periphrastic construction involving the verb *iri.* "make, do," as an auxiliary, followed by the subject and then the main verb as an infinitive object of the auxiliary (*iir.f stp*). In essence, the lexical meaning of the auxiliary is lost so that it becomes merely a conjugation element. Although this formation is not restricted as to tense, there also exists—for verbs of less than three radicals—a special form with a prefixed prothetic element that is generally restricted to emphasizing an adverbial adjunct when the tense is future. In a similar vein, Late Egyptian possesses a complex system of nominal sentence patterns whereby various elements of a sentence, such as the subject or object, could be emphasized.

Characteristic of Late Egyptian is a set of pronouns that stand independently as the subjects of sentences with adverbial predicates, including pseudo-verbal constructions; in Middle Egyptian, pronoun subjects of such sentences must be preceded by some sort of particle. It is customary to refer to these new pronouns, the earliest examples of which appear in the seventeenth dynasty, as "pronominal preformatives of the first present."

In contrast to older Egyptian, the definition of a noun is now more consistently marked through the use of definite or indefinite articles placed before the noun. A much wider application of possessive articles, also positioned before the noun, appears in Late Egyptian, leaving the suffix pronoun, which was appended to the noun, to express possession only after certain nouns such as body parts. The nominalization of the infinitive allows for the distinction between a tenseless infinitive ("his choosing") and one clearly marked as past through periphrasis with the verb *iri* ("his having chosen," literally "the choosing which he did").

In Late Egyptian there are two negative particles, written *bw* and *bn.* Although there are isolated Middle Kingdom occurrences of *bw* in personal names, this negative word in Late Egyptian corresponds in function to the Middle Egyptian negative *n*, but it may have derived from the old negative *im. Bw* negates only verbal sentences. In nonliterary Late Egyptian, *bw* serves mainly as a negation of the past or perfect in the periphrastic construction: "He did not do in the past a choosing." In literary Late Egyptian, however, *bw* has more expanded usage. The negative *bn*, functionally equivalent to the Middle Egyptian negative *nn*, is employed to negate non-verbal and verbal sentences in a variety of constructions. The tense is usually either present or future. Besides these two negative words, the negative verb *tm* served to negate the prospective *stp.f* in final clauses, infinitives (including those in non-initial pseudo-verbal constructions), and participles.

In translating Late Egyptian nonliterary texts, one senses that with the trend toward analytical constructions, greater precision is achieved in respect to tense at the expense of aspectual nuances. Nonetheless, tense is still not as clearly defined as in Coptic.

Literary and Monumental Late Egyptian. Literary texts in Late Egyptian vary in the degree to which they reflect colloquial Late Egyptian. The Late Egyptian stories retain some of the narrative verbal constructions of Middle Egyptian, the earlier stories more so than the later ones. In considering the grammar of the Late Egyptian stories, a valid distinction can be made between the narrative portions and non-narrative sections; the latter consist of recorded speech and are generally closer to colloquial Late Egyptian. In the Late Egyptian Miscellanies there are examples of quite good Late Egyptian, particular in those texts that were probably drawn from original letters, but the Miscellanies also contain texts that diverge considerably from the nonliterary idiom. In particular, the texts that are of gnomic nature—describing, for example, the hardships of the soldier's life—make frequent use of non-periphrastic forms of the verb. Here the writer often uses a sequence of *stp.f*-forms that can be translated as a present. It is likely that this *stp.f*-form is identical with the Late Egyptian perfect *stp.f*, employed to express completed action that is gnomically valid. The negative *bw stp.f* occurs quite frequently in the Miscellanies to express a gnomic negative, translatable as a present.

Similarly, Ramessid monumental inscriptions vary considerably in the degree to which they reflect colloquial Late Egyptian. The decree portion of Sety I's Nauri Decree and the Kadesh Bulletin of Ramesses II resemble nonliterary Late Egyptian more closely than do the long narrative texts of Ramesses III at Medinet Habu, which avoid using the typically Late Egyptian past narrative continuative. The narrative at Medinet Habu comprises a sequence of perfect *stp.f*-forms, such as are used only to initiate narratives in nonliterary Late Egyptian texts. These monumental inscriptions, together with the Late Egyptian Miscellanies, can be considered as being composed in an intermediate phase of literary Egyptian which was transitional between classical Middle Egyptian and colloquial Late Egyptian. It is doubtful, however, that the language of these texts was ever the spoken language of the elite officials; however, highly placed bureaucrats were certainly able to compose texts in this elevated style, and educated scribes were able to read them. The contribution of monumental and literary texts to the study of Late Egyptian is primarily on the level of morphology and individual sentences rather than in the area of clause consecution and relationships, which are best revealed in nonliterary documents.

[*See also* Scripts, *article on* Hieratic Script.]

BIBLIOGRAPHY

Behnk, Frida. *Grammatik der Texte aus El Amarna*. Paris, 1930. This out-of-print work is still useful in its presentation of Late Egyptian features in texts of the reign of Akhenaten.

Černý, Jaroslav, and Sarah Israelit-Groll, assisted by Christopher Eyre. *A Late Egyptian Grammar*, 3d rev. ed. Rome, 1984. Currently the standard grammar of Late Egyptian as revealed in nonliterary texts of the twentieth and twenty-first dynasties. The analysis is synchronic rather than diachronic.

Depuydt, Leo. *Conjunction, Contiguity, Contingency: On Relationships between Events in the Egyptian and Coptic Verbal Systems*. New York, 1993. Contains important obervations on sequential sentences in Egyptian, especially the conjunctive tense in Late Egyptian.

Depuydt, Leo. "Four Thousand Years of Evolution: On a Law of Historical Change in Ancient Egyptian." *Journal of Near Eastern Studies* 56 (1997), 21–35. Discusses the gradual transition from synthetic verb forms to analytic constructions in ancient Egyptian.

Edgerton, William F. "Egyptian Phonetic Writing, from its Invention to the Close of the Nineteenth Dynasty." *Journal of the American Oriental Society* 60.4 (December 1940), 473–506. Presents a negative position regarding the syllabic theory of group-writing.

Edgerton, William F. "Early Egyptian Dialect Interrelationships." *Bulletin of the American Schools of Oriental Research* 122 (April 1951), 9–12. Argues that Old and Late Egyptian share dialectical features not present in Middle Egyptian.

Erman, Adolf. *Neuägyptische Grammatik*, 2d rev. ed. Leipzig, 1933. For many years the standard grammar of Late Egyptian as revealed in nonliterary and literary texts, including monumental inscriptions beginning with the Amarna period.

Frandsen, Paul John. *An Outline of the Late Egyptian Verbal System*. Copenhagen, 1974. A lucidly argued study of the verbal system in Late Egyptian, based primarily on nonliterary texts.

Groll, Sarah Israelit-. "Late Egyptian of Non-Literary Texts of the 19th Dynasty." In *Orient and Occident: Essays Presented to Cyrus H. Gordon on the Occasion of his Sixty-fifth Birthday*, edited by Harry A. Hoffner, Jr., pp. 67–70. Alter Orient und Altes Testament, 22. Neukirchen-Vluyn, 1973. Highlights some of the differences between nineteenth and twentieth dynasty nonliterary Late Egyptian.

Groll, Sarah Israelit-. "A Literary Late Egyptian *stp.f* Formation Indicating the Present Simple Tense." *Israel Oriental Studies* 4 (1974), 12–13.

Groll, Sarah Israelit-. "Diachronic Grammar as a Means of Dating Undated Tests." In *Egyptological Studies*, edited by Sarah Israelit-Groll, pp. 11–104. Scripta Hierosolymitana, 28. Jerusalem, 1982. Concentrates on the presence and absence of prepositions in pseudo-verbal constructions as a means of dating texts.

Groll, Sarah Israelit-. "A Short Grammar of the Spermeru Dialect." In *Studien zu Sprache und Religion Ägyptens: Zu Ehren von Wolfhart Westendorf*, vol. 1: *Sprache*, edited by Friedrich Junge, pp. 41–61. Göttingen, 1984.

Hintze, Fritz. *Untersuchungen zu Stil und Sprache neuägyptischer Erzählungen*. Berlin, 1950–1952. Although out of print, this work is a thorough study of the grammar of the Late Egyptian stories.

Hoch, James E. *Semitic Words in Egyptian Texts of the New Kingdom and Third Intermediate Period*. Princeton, 1994. Discusses the principles involved in syllabic orthography.

Korostovtsev, M. A. *Grammaire du Neo-Égyptien*. Moscow, 1973. A comprehensive grammar of Late Egyptian, making use of both literary and nonliterary texts, many of which have been published since Erman's grammar.

Kroeber, Burkhart. "Die Neuägyptizismen vor der Amarnazeit: Studien zur Entwicklung der ägyptischen Sprache vom Mittleren zum Neuen Reich." Ph.D. diss., Tübingen, 1970. Although difficult to obtain, this study is a fundamental contribution to Late Egyptian features that appear in texts prior to the Amarna period.

Lesko, Leonard H., ed. *A Dictionary of Late Egyptian*. 5 vols. Berkeley, 1982–1990. Useful as a means of surveying the orthography of words in both nonliterary and literary Late Egyptian texts.

Loprieno, Antonio. "Methodologische Anmerkungen zur Rolle der Dialekte in der Ägyptischen Sprachentwicklung." *Göttinger Miszellen* 53 (1982), 75–95. Presents a forceful argument against the discernment of dialects in written texts.

Spalinger, Anthony. "A Sequence System." *Revue d'Égyptologie* 39 (1988), 107–129. Examines narrative sequence patterns in various monumental texts.

Winand, Jean. *Études de néo-égyptien, I: la morphologie verbale*. (Aegyptiaca Leodiensia 2) Liege, 1992. This study of the Egyptian verb and verbal constructions is largely diachronic in nature, including literary and nonliterary inscriptions from the eighteenth to the twenty-fifth dynasty; contains useful bibliography.

EDWARD F. WENTE

Demotic

Demotic grammar shares general features of Egyptian that have been identified in all stages of that language: a basically tripartite root system; strict rules of word order; and apparent Verb-Subject-Object (VSO) word order, with adverbials, including subordinate clauses (except temporal and conditional clauses), following this sentence core. It forms part of, and reflects the development of, "Later" Egyptian (Late Egyptian into Coptic), in contrast to the "Earlier" group (Old and Middle Egyptian), sharing in Later characteristics such as overt expression of the definite article and use of the possessive article rather than the suffix pronoun to indicate possession. Demotic displays some changes through its history of more than a millennium—for example, the increased use of periphrastic constructions, frequently corresponding to the increasing replacement of synthetic forms with analytic ones. The extent to which Demotic ever represented the contemporary spoken language, and its "artificiality" to the extent that it did not, have been discussed extensively, most fruitfully in the context of the synchronic and diachronic relations of all stages of Egyptian.

Traditionally Egyptian, including Demotic, has been analyzed using the categories and the terminology applied to modern European languages. This works well for many categories (e.g., nouns, pronouns, verbs, adverbs, prepositions), but less well for other categories (e.g., adjectives). Thus, Egyptian, including Demotic, has what are called "adjective verbs," and the participles derived from these could serve as the equivalent of the "adjectives" of most modern European languages. In addition, Demotic has a series of articles (see below) and other "determiners" (especially *nb* "all, every") that correspond to adjectives in modern European languages but that do not derive from adjective verbs. But Egyptian, including Demotic, also has significant categories that are not an important part of modern European languages, notably the particles; especially important in Demotic are "sentence markers" (optional particles that affect the meaning or the syntactical status of the entire following clause), negative particles, and particles used in forming certain conjugation patterns (e.g., aorist, conditional).

The interrelationship of what are frequently considered distinct parts of speech is exemplified by the verb, which has not only "true" verbal forms (the conjugated *sḏm=f* and the imperative), but also a nominal form (the infinitive) and a form that was historically an adverb (the stative, also called the "qualitative" or "old perfective"). Little work has been done on Demotic semantics. Aside from a small amount of work on the functioning of nouns and articles in generic statements, little attention has been paid to the importance of categories such as count nouns, collective nouns, and mass nouns (including abstract nouns). With regard to verbs, it is clear that categories such as "adjective verb" are still viable; in addition, there are several individual verbs that behave distinctively (e.g., *mr* "to love," *msḏ* "to hate," *rḫ* "to know," and *iy/iw* "to come").

Basic Synopsis of Grammar. *Verbs* are transitive (can take a direct object) or intransitive (including adjective verbs and verbs of motion). Final weak radicals are rarely written and had, presumably, disappeared from most forms; the final /e/ found on many verbs and in many forms sometimes, but not consistently, corresponds to a final short vowel in Coptic. There are probably three distinct forms of the conjugated *sḏm=f:* the indicative, used in main clause, past tense; the prospective/subjunctive, in main or subordinate clause, future tense; and the *sḏm=f* combined with preceding particle *ḫr* to form the aorist. However, these were seldom distinguished in writing (rare examples include *rḫ=f* versus *ir-rḫ=f* from the verb *rḫ* "to know" and the presence or absence of *n₃* at the beginning of the *sḏm=f* of adjective verbs). All are active; the passive is indicated by using a third person plural pronoun with an active form. A small number of verbs have separate imperative forms; others use the infinitive as the imperative.

There is evidence that the three forms of the *infinitive* identifiable in Coptic with transitive verbs were also distinguished in Demotic. These are the pronominal used before an immediately following suffix pronoun direct object, the construct used before an immediately following noun or noun phrase direct object, and the absolute. The pronominal infinitive of final weak verbs is regularly written with a *ṯ* after the infinitive, before the suffix pronoun; although there is no consistent graphic evidence for a distinction between the absolute and construct forms of the

infinitive of transitive verbs, the implementation of the Jemstedt rule (use of an oblique object in the present tense except when the direct object is an undetermined noun) implies a distinction between the two. As noted above, the infinitive is a nominal form of the verb. Although it can be used anywhere that a noun can be used (subject or object of a verb, object of a preposition, or element of a nominal sentence), it is most frequently used where it serves, at least historically, as object of a preposition, including examples where it forms the apparent predicate in so-called sentences with adverbial predicates—e.g., present tense *tw=y (ḥr) sḏm*, future *iw=f (r) sḏm;* for Demotic sentence types, see below.

The *stative* was, historically, an adverbial form of the verb, indicating the state resulting from the action; it is frequently translated as a passive. The stative endings, which originally agreed in number and gender with the subject of the stative, lost this association to the subject and, by the Ptolemaic period, when they are used at all, they merely serve as graphic indicators of the stative form. The stative is used only as the apparent adverbial predicate in a sentence with adverbial predicate. Although clear graphic distinctions among the infinitival or *sḏm=f* forms of verbs are rarely made by Demotic scribes, there are several verbs for which the standard writing of the infinitive differs consistently from the writing of the stative and *sḏm=f*.

Nouns are either masculine or feminine; the feminine .t ending is frequently written in Demotic (after the determinative), but it was not pronounced. Plural nouns are indicated by writing the plural mark (.w) after the determinative, and using the plural form of the article, as appropriate. Nouns could be modified by "determiners"— adjectives, articles (definite, indefinite, demonstrative, or possessive), direct genitive, or *nb* "all, every"—indirect genitives, numbers, and/or prepositional phrases. A few nouns, basically ones denoting body parts, can take a suffix pronoun possessive; the pronominal forms of those that end in a feminine .t or final (pronounced) root t often have a *ṯ* added to or replacing the feminine .t, after the determinative. Indefinite nouns cannot be followed by relative clauses, but only by circumstantial clauses serving as "virtual relative clauses"; when an indefinite noun serves as subject in a present tense sentence this forces the retention of the verb "to be" (see below). Nouns and *pronouns*—the latter comprising independent, dependent, suffix, interrogative, demonstrative, possessive, and proclitic (the pronoun series used to indicate the subject in a present tense sentence with adverbial predicate)— were used much as in other stages of Egyptian. *Adverbs* of quality, place, and time are attested. Both simple and compound *prepositions* are attested; the latter is a simple preposition followed by and combined with a noun, frequently a noun denoting a body part; when the noun has a separate pronominal form, so does the compound preposition. Some prepositions have distinctive pronominal forms.

Demotic is a *tense-based* language, distinguishing both a positive and a negative form of the perfect, past, present, future, and "aorist" (an "extratemporal" form that frequently indicated customary action and that can be translated into English by using the simple present or an adverb such as "always, regularly, normally"). Thus Demotic, like Coptic but unlike Late Egyptian, does not need to rely on particles and adverbs to distinguish between, for instance, immediate present and simple present or aorist. The negative forms use the negative particles *bw* and *bn*.

There are two basic *sentence* types. Nominal sentences establish a relationship—frequently identity—between two nominal elements; and verbal sentences consist of, at minimum, a verb and its following nominal subject (except in the imperative, where the subject is not expressed); most verbal sentences also contain a nominal direct object and/or adverbials. The rules of word order for nominal sentences take into consideration whether one or both elements is pronominal, and if so, whether first, second, or third person; in a tripartite nominal sentence, the copula pronoun, if used, immediately follows the "predicate" or "comment" but agrees in number or gender with the other nominal. What has been analyzed traditionally as a third sentence type, the sentence with adverbial predicate, follows all the rules for verbal sentences and can be understood as a present tense verbal sentence from which the verb "to be" is normally omitted. This verb "to be" is actually preserved in such sentences in specific syntactic positions (i.e., present tense sentences with an indefinite subject and past tense sentences); when, in earlier stages of Egyptian, a sentences with adverbial predicate was embedded in another sentence as a subordinate nominal or adverbial clause, the verb "to be" was also retained. Such present tense sentences can have as their apparent adverbial predicate an adverb(ial) (including prepositional phrases), a qualitative, or an absolute infinitive. Historically, this infinitive was the object of a preposition, and the two together formed a prepositional phrase; for the restrictions against the use of the construct and pronominal infinitives in the present tense, see above.

As in other stages of Egyptian, strict rules of word order preclude simply moving an element in a sentence to put stress or focus on it. Occasionally, an adverb(ial) or nominal may be lifted from a sentence (and replaced by the appropriate pronoun, in the case of a noun or noun phrase), and juxtaposed to the sentence, usually by placing it in front of the sentence. More formal indications of stress or focus involve various transformations of a verbal sentence: into a cleft sentence, to stress a noun or noun phrase; or into a noun clause ("second tense"), to stress an adverbial—the "second tense" noun clause served grammatically as the subject of the stressed adverbial, using the form of the sentence with adverbial predicate.

Main clause constructions can be "converted" to subordinate adverbial (i.e., circumstantial), nominal ("second tense"), or adjectival (relative) clauses by prefixing the appropriate "converter": *ỉw* for the circumstantial, *ỉir* for the second tense, or *nt* (< *nty*) for the relative, except in the past tense, where the past participle and relative forms are preserved. Similarly, the tense of any sentence can be set one step in the past by prefixing the "imperfect converter," historically the past tense of the verb *wn* "to be." There were also a number of "clause conjugations," constructions that formed subordinate clauses rather than complete sentences. Among the more common of these are temporal, conditional, and purpose clauses, and the conjunctive. Such forms are negated by using the negative verb *tm*, which is also used to negate the infinitive. Both direct and indirect quotes are introduced by *ḏ* (< *ḏd* "to say"), which is also used in many grammatical situations to introduce a clause serving as direct object. Questions for specification use interrogative pronouns or adverbs; yes-or-no questions may be unmarked or introduced by the question particle *in*.

A suggested scheme for the diachronic relations between verbal systems from Late Egyptian through Demotic into Coptic is presented in Table 1. The switch from synthetic to analytic verb forms had already begun with Late Egyptian (where Middle Egyptian present-tense conjugated verb forms were replaced by constructions involving an auxiliary and nonconjugated forms of the verb) and came to almost total dominance in Coptic, but it is not reflected in Demotic until quite late, when a series of periphrastic forms that are the immediate ancestors of the Coptic forms appear. Synchronically, Demotic grammar is normally found only in texts written in Demotic script. The Demotic versions of the synodal decrees issued under the middle Ptolemies differed from the hieroglyphic versions not only in script and grammar but also in lexicon. However, there are a few early texts (e.g., Papyrus Vandier) that employ what is basically Demotic grammar even though they are written in Hieratic. A few early stelae from Saqqara inscribed in hieroglyphs or Hieratic appear to be translations from Demotic originals; it has been suggested that this practice was common and that it may even underlie some Roman period temple hieroglyphic inscriptions, but it can be recognized only in cases where the translation was not well done. Literary, and especially religious, texts frequently used more archaic grammar than documentary texts, sometimes reflecting

GRAMMAR: DEMOTIC. TABLE 1. *Historical Development of the Egyptian Verbal System.*

Meaning	Late Egyptian	Demotic	Coptic
Present	*tw=y (ḥr) sḏm*	*tw=y sḏm*	ϯⲥⲱⲧⲙ̄
Circumstantial Present	*iw=y rdi.k*	*iw=y sḏm*	ⲉϥⲥⲱⲧⲙ̄
Relative Present	*nty tw=y sḏm*	*nt iw=y sḏm*	ⲉϯⲥⲱⲧⲙ̄
Second Present	*iir=f sḏm*	*iir=f sḏm*	ⲉϥⲥⲱⲧⲙ̄
Negative Present	*bn tw=y (ḥr) sḏm (iwn₃)*	*bn tw=y sḏm in*	(ⲛ̄)ϯⲥⲱⲧⲙ̄ . . . ⲁⲛ
Circumstantial Negative Present	*iw bn tw=y (ḥr) sḏm (iwn₃)*	*iw bn tw=y sḏm in*	ⲉⲛϯⲥⲱⲧⲙ̄ . . . ⲁⲛ
Progressive	*tw=y m nꜥy r sḏm*	*tw=y n₃ sḏm*	ϯⲛⲁⲥⲱⲧⲙ̄
Aorist	*ḥr sḏm=f*	*ḥr sḏm=f*	
		ḥr ir=f sḏm	ϣⲁϥⲥⲱⲧⲙ̄
Negative Aorist	*bw ir=f sḏm*	*bw ir=f sḏm*	ⲙⲉϥⲥⲱⲧⲙ̄
Future	*iw=f r sḏm*	*iw=f (r) sḏm*	ⲉϥⲉⲥⲱⲧⲙ̄
	sḏm=f	*sḏm=f*	
Negative Future	*bn iw=f (r) sḏm*	*bn iw=f sḏm*	ⲛ̄ⲛⲉϥⲥⲱⲧⲙ̄
Past	*sḏm=f*	*sḏm=f*	
		ir=f sḏm	ⲁϥⲥⲱⲧⲙ̄
Second Past	*iir=f sḏm*	*iir=f sḏm*	ⲛ̄ⲧⲁϥⲥⲱⲧⲙ̄
Negative Past	*bw-pw=f sḏm*	*bn-pw=f sḏm*	ⲙⲡⲉϥⲥⲱⲧⲙ̄
Perfect	*sḏm=f*	*wꜣḥ=f sḏm*	ⲁϥⲥⲱⲧⲙ̄
			early ϩⲁϥⲥⲱⲧⲙ̄
Negative Perfect	*bw-irt=f sḏm*	*bw-ir-tw=f sḏm*	ⲙ̄ⲡⲁⲧϥ̄ⲥⲱⲧⲙ̄
Optative	*imi sḏm=f*	(my) *sḏm=f*	
		my ir=f sḏm	ⲙⲁⲣⲉϥⲥⲱⲧⲙ̄
Negative Optative	*m-dyt sḏm=f*	*m-ir ti sḏm=f*	
		m-ir ti ir=f sḏm	ⲙ̄ⲡⲣ̄ⲧⲣⲉϥⲥⲱⲧⲙ̄
Terminative	*šꜥ₃ iirt=f sḏm*	*šꜥ-(m)tw=f sḏm*	ϣⲁ(ⲛ)ⲧϥ̄ⲥⲱⲧⲙ̄
Temporal	*m-ḏr sḏm=f*	*(n-)ḏr.(t) sḏm=f*	ⲛ̄ⲧⲉⲣⲉϥⲥⲱⲧⲙ̄
Conditional	*ir iw=f ḥr sḏm*	*iw=f sḏm*	ⲉϣⲱⲁⲛⲥⲱⲧⲙ̄
		in-n₃ Noun sḏm	
Negative Conditional	*ir iw=f ḥr tm sḏm*	*iw=f tm sḏm*	ⲉϥⲧⲙ̄ⲥⲱⲧⲙ̄
Irrealis	*h(₃)n(₃) wn*	*hwn-n₃w*	ⲉⲛⲉ
Causative Infinitive	*di sḏm=f*	*ti sḏm=f*	
		ti ir=f sḏm	ⲧⲣⲉϥⲥⲱⲧⲙ̄
Finalis		*ti=y sḏm=f*	
		ti=y ir=f sḏm	ⲧⲁⲣⲉϥⲥⲱⲧⲙ̄
Conjunctive	*mtw=f sḏm*	*mtw=f sḏm*	ⲛϥ̄ⲥⲱⲧⲙ̄
Purpose Clause	*r* + infinitive (subjunctive)	*r* + infinitive (subjunctive)	ⲉ + infinitive
	sḏm=f	*sḏm=f*	

translation from an original composed much earlier. A small number of texts have been preserved that are written in Demotic script although their grammar is archaic "Classical Egyptian" (e.g., the Hymn to Amun-Re preserved in Ostracon Naville).

There is a small amount of evidence in Demotic of regional dialects, and some work has been done trying to correlate such evidence with identifiable Coptic dialects. The most noticeable differences among Coptic dialects are phonetic, especially vocalic. Phonetic differences have been identified in some Demotic texts of the Roman period, when more alphabetic signs are used in writing Demotic vocabulary; especially clear are texts that, like the Faiyumic dialect of Coptic, fail to distinguish between *r* and *l*. Words written in "alphabetic Demotic," especially foreign words transcribed into Demotic or words also glossed in Old Coptic, have also provided evidence for re-

gional pronunciations. Egyptian words, especially personal names, transcribed into Greek in texts written in different parts of the country also provide some evidence of regional pronunciations. Slight differences in grammatical and lexical inventories may also reflect regional differences in Demotic, as in Coptic. However, to the extent that Demotic was an official language, scribes might consciously have adhered to set standards, filtering out differences owed to regional dialects as well as changes through time.

[*See also* Scripts, *article on* Demotic Script.]

BIBLIOGRAPHY

Depauw, Mark. *A Companion to Demotic Studies*, Papyrologica Bruxellensia, 28. Fondation Égyptologique Reine Élisabeth. Brussels, 1997.

JANET H. JOHNSON

Coptic

Coptic is one of the languages spoken in Egypt, mainly by the Christians during the third through eleventh centuries CE, the others being Greek (first to seventh centuries, when Aramaic was also extensively spoken) and Arabic (seventh century onward). The coexistence of two or more languages produced widespread bilingualism among the more cultivated part of the population, with consequently some peculiar features in their literary production.

Coptic was probably born as an artificial literary language, with the aim of recapturing in a Christian environment what was possible of the ancient Egyptian culture. Coptic was built on the structure of the surviving Egyptian language, which by that time had lost most of its literary potential and therefore was enriched with the introduction of Greek words; this was possible because the writers and speakers of Coptic were mostly bilingual, with more or less equal mastery of Egyptian and Greek. Greek also had a strong influence on the syntactic patterns of Coptic, because of the difficulty of using Egyptian syntax in the translation of such abstract Greek works as the Epistles of Paul or gnosticizing, semi-philosophical tractates.

We do not know of any description of the Coptic language written by the Copts themselves before the invasion of the Arabs in 632 CE. When Arabic began to be widely used alongside Coptic (tenth century CE), tools were produced to facilitate the translation of texts and the learning of Coptic, presumably by Arabic-speaking Copts. These so-called Scalae were also used by the first European scholars confronted with Coptic manuscripts (after 1415; mainly in the sixteenth century), who in their turn produced Coptic grammars shaped according to the criteria of the classical languages, and therefore utilizing classical terminology. When the grammar of Egyptian began to be understood in the early nineteenth century, some new descriptions were produced (notably by Ludwig Stern, then Georg Steindorff, Walter Till, and others), on the basis of a compromise between Classical terminology and some new terms taken from Egyptian grammar. A revolutionary arrangement produced by Hans Jakob Polotsky in 1950 is still the most reasonable formulation; more recent efforts to come to terms with modern linguistic criteria (Polotsky himself in his last essays; Ariel Shisha-Halevy; Bentley Layton) are excellent but have not yet reached a standard. The formal and possibly objective description which follows is independent from the traditional descriptive criteria of the classical languages. For brevity, the Sahidic forms will be used (see below on dialects).

Coptic sentences are formed around a verbal nucleus that is obtained through the arrangement, in a certain order, of words and phrases, themselves lacking a "conjuga-tion." Other "complementary" phrases are likewise obtained through the ordered arrangement of words that may be labeled "prepositions" and "substantives." Adjectives and adverbs (which do not exist in Coptic as independent categories, or parts of speech) are also constructed through appropriate ordering and the use of particles. A verbal nucleus consists of one of two kinds of phrases, called respectively the "bipartite" and "tripartite" patterns.

The bipartite pattern has two possible forms, adverbial and nominal. In the adverbial bipartite pattern, the first slot is filled by a pronominal particle or by a noun phrase, and the second by a particular class of substantives (called "verbal substantives"), or by a "qualitative" (a class of words which comes from one form of the old Egyptian conjugation), or by an adverbial phrase. In the nominal bipartite pattern, two forms are distinguished: that for the 1st and 2nd person comprises a first part of the personal pronoun in nominal form, and a second part of the noun phrase); and that for the 3rd person, where the first part is a noun phrase, and the second part is one of the three pronouns *pe, te, ne*.

The tripartite pattern is formed by the conjunction of three elements: (a) a verbal particle (the last remnant of the Egyptian conjugation); (b) a pronominal particle or a noun phrase; and (c) a verbal substantive (see above). Some of the verbal particles have both a positive form and a negative one; others are negativized by means of the particle *tm*.

Certain particles may be prefixed to the bipartite and tripartite patterns, to transform their meaning into past imperfect (*ne, nere*), circumstantial clause (*e, ere*), relative clause (*e, et, etere, nt,* etc.). There is also a special pattern which is not yet well understood (*e, ere, ent*), the so-called second tenses.

Noun phrases are comprised of articles (definite and indefinite), substantives, and a special particle *n*. Two nouns may form a noun phrase when the first is in nominal form; otherwise, they may be joined by means of the particle *n*, with different meaning depending on whether the second substantive is determined or not.

There exists (as in the classical languages) a class of prepositions, which in conjunction with pronominal particles or noun phrases form the complements. In some cases the resulting phrases are so lexicalized as to be considered adverbs (*ehrai, ebol, hnouypnyop*).

Sentence structure is rather consistent: the verbal structure (including the subject) is in first position, followed by the object, then by the circumstantial determinations or complements. The syntax is modeled on Greek because Coptic arose in a strongly Hellenized environment, and initially Coptic texts were translations from Greek. Most of its conjunctions come from Greek. Nonetheless, Coptic syntax deserves to be studied extensively, particularly in relation to Coptic style, a study that has not yet been undertaken.

The Coptic vocabulary is an almost unique example of a blend of two preexisting ones: Egyptian and Greek. Late Egyptian words are its main component, but the very numerous Greek words cannot properly be considered loan words. On the contrary, Coptic authors (including translators) were free to use any Greek word they deemed fit for the circumstance, according to their personal taste, as well as to traditional conventions derived from the secular contact of the two languages. Greek nouns were used indeclined, mainly in the nominative case, as were adjectives, which otherwise were treated as substantives; Greek verbs assumed a simplified shape of the infinitive form; the other categories (prepositions, adverbs, conjunctions) conserved their original forms.

Since the Coptic language first became known in Europe, scholars understood that it presented variations, mainly in orthography but also in some morphological and syntactic forms, that could be interpreted as representing different dialects. Already in the eighteenth century three main dialects were distinguished: Bohairic, belonging to the Nile Delta; Sahidic, belonging to the southern regions; and Faiyumic, belonging to the Faiyum oasis in Middle Egypt. Documents discovered later showed that in reality the dialect situation was much more complex, and other dialects were proposed: Achmimic, Subachmimic, Oxyrhinchyte (or Middle Egyptian), etc. It is, however, doubtful in what sense we can properly speak of Coptic dialects, because we do not know exactly which sounds were represented by the different graphemes in different manuscripts; we do not know to which regional reality the texts we have were bound, if any; and no Egyptian text, whether in Coptic or in Greek, offers ancient statements concerning Coptic dialects. Interpreters between Greek-speaking and Coptic-speaking people are often mentioned, but never interpreters between different Coptic dialects. Therefore, scholars are able to describe in detail the different orthographic and morphological features of the texts, but their relation to the spoken language is a matter of conjecture.

In fact, it is almost certain that Sahidic was much more than a dialect; it was the standard literary language between the fourth and ninth centuries, and therefore the true medium for literary texts during the time Coptic was a living language, when (especially after the fifth century) original texts were produced. Such a role for Sahidic was due in part to the fact that it derives from a common late "high" Egyptian language, but above all to the influence of the fourth-to-fifth century abbot Shenoute and his White Monastery scriptorium, where Sahidic was employed. During the ninth century, Sahidic was superseded by Bo-

hairic, which until then was itself a distinct dialect, attested as such from the fourth century. But Bohairic was scarcely productive as a language, outside liturgy. Other dialectal corpora, used only for translations, are found for Fayyumic, Akhmimic, Oxyrhinchite (or Middle Egyptian, or Mesokemic), and Subakhmimic (or Lycopolitan).

In discussing dialectal variation in grammar, only the morphological variations will be outlined, because the phonetic/graphematic variations are probably less meaningful (see discussion above). As Funk notes in the *Coptic Encyclopedia*, "The majority of formal grammatical devices used in given paradigms and/or for given purposes are either phonemically and graphemically invariable . . . or their varying phonemic/graphemic representations are conditioned by general phonological rules" (vol. VIII, p. 102). The main variations are as follows: the presence of a special element *er* incorporating the joint relative and perfect particles in Oxyrhynchite, which is absent in the other dialects; the presence of the temporal tripartite *ntere, ntare* in Sahidic, Achmimic, and Subachmimic, versus its absence in Bohairic, Fayyumic, and Oxyrhynchite; and the presence of the prefix *(e)r* before verbal substantives from Greek in Achmimic, Bohairic, and Fayyumic, versus absence in Sahidic and Oxyrhynchite.

In dealing with the Coptic alphabet(s), one should be careful to distinguish the spoken from the written sounds. As stated above, the phonetic situation of the language does not permit a satisfactory description (although much can be said; see the article "Phonology," by Rodolphe Kasser, in the *Coptic Encyclopedia* [1991]), so only the written alphabets will be described here.

The birth of the Coptic alphabet was bound to the idea of writing in Greek script instead of the Egyptian scripts still in use, though to different extents and for different purposes: hieroglyphic, Hieratic, and Demotic. This idea is apparent at least by the second century BCE and resulted in some documents, mainly of "magic" character, in what is conventionally called Old Coptic. A formally consistent and widely used writing system was conceived around the second century CE in a Christian environment, together with the idea of producing a Coptic literature. The entire Greek alphabet was used, probably with the same phonetic correspondences as in contemporary Greek pronunciation, though there is some reason to suppose that originally the sounds of the vowels *eta, iota, upsilon,* and the others were distinctive and not iotacistic. Some further letters were derived from the Demotic script, where the phonemes *shai, fai, hai, hori, janja, cima* could be reduced to a Greek letter. It is interesting to note that the forms of such graphemes were slightly changed to match the general appearance of the Greek script.

The scribal style adopted was initially that of biblical majuscule, where single letters tend to be inscribed in a square. Variation in style was obtained through differentiation in thick and thin strokes to compose letters, versus uniform strokes, and sometimes by varying the slope of letters. In the ninth century a new style developed, with strong differentiation between large-bodied letters (*p, k, sh, eta, f, t,* etc.) and thin letters (*e, o, a,* etc.).

Breathings and apostrophes were not included in Coptic writing, except in special cases, and were soon altogether abondoned; accents were no more widely used even in Greek. Nevertheless, some signs were added to help reading, and thence to separate words, since in the manuscripts words were written without spaces. Note especially the superlinear stroke (to indicate a syllable, in various ways), the hyphen (also to separate syllables, but especially the end of some words), the trema (on vocalic *i,* and sometimes *u*). Also, the comma was used, as a word separator (especially after word-final *e* and *s*) rather than as a punctuation mark.

Discourse units (paragraphs) were signaled by means of final punctuation, as in the contemporary Greek manuscripts of the third and fourth centuries: a simple stop, generally in the middle of the line. In the course of time, from the fifth century on, Coptic developed, independently from Greek, a fuller system of punctuation. The simple stop was used inside a paragraph, to mark individual parts of a sentence; at the end was placed a stop followed by a stroke. Later, capital letters were also used to mark the beginning of paragraphs.

The passage from classical Egyptian to Coptic was a very long process, during which the various components of the language—phonetics, script, and grammar—evolved at differing rates and for different reasons. Around the second century CE, the Demotic script was in use, although some tentative essays of transcription in the Greek alphabet are documented; their phonetics and grammar are more or less those we know through the Coptic texts. Yet it is likely that the formal arrangement of the language known from the true Coptic texts was produced over a very brief span in the second and third centuries CE by groups of determined Christian scholars. Coptic remained for some time one of several of the cultural media of the Christian community, in which are included the gnosticizing groups. Outside it, only the Manichaeans adopted the same standard, producing extensive literary works translated from Greek and Syriac.

By the time of the seventh-century Arab invasion of Egypt, Coptic was the vernacular language, and Greek was used mainly in political administration and in higher education (both Christian and non-Christian). It took about three centuries for Arabic and Coptic to become equally widely spoken in Egypt, and another three centuries for it to supersede Coptic, resulting in the translation into Arabic even of liturgical books. By the sixteenth century, Coptic was probably spoken only in peripheral territories; soon it was not spoken at all, but only studied by the clergy for liturgical reasons. In the nineteenth century, when the Coptic church knew a period of renaissance, efforts were begun to reinstate Coptic as a spoken idiom, and these efforts continue today, though without much effect. In addition, they are based on somewhat incorrect assumptions, because the language chosen is the late Bohairic of the liturgy, and the pronunciation is largely affected by Arabic phonology.

[*See also* Scripts, *article on* Coptic Script.]

BIBLIOGRAPHY

General Works

Atiya, Aziz, S., ed. *The Coptic Encyclopedia.* 8 vols. New York, 1991. Volume 8 is dedicated to problems of the Coptic language, but there is no general description of the grammar.

Camplani, Alberto, ed. *L'Egitto cristiano: Aspetti e problemi in et à tardo-antica.* Rome, 1997.

Orlandi, Tito. *Coptic Bibliography.* 12th ed. 4 vols. Rome, 1995.

Grammars

Callender, John Bryan. *Studies in the Nominal Sentence in Egyptian and Coptic.* Near Eastern Studies, 24. Berkeley, 1985.

Emmel, Stephen. "Coptic Language." In *The Anchor Bible Dictionary,* vol. 4, pp. 180–188. New York, 1992.

Lambdin, Thomas O. *Introduction to Sahidic Coptic.* Macon, Ga. 1983.

Mallon, Alexis. *Grammaire copte.* Beirut, 1904. On Bohairic.

Orlandi, Tito. *Elementi di lingua e letteratura copta.* Milan, 1970.

Plumley, J. Martin. *An Introducory Coptic Grammar.* London, 1948.

Polotsky, Hans-Jakob. *Grundlagen des koptischen Satzbaus.* 2 vols. Atlanta, Ga., 1987, 1990.

Shisha-Halevy, Ariel. *Coptic Grammatical Categories: Structural Studies in the Syntax of Shenoutean Sahidic.* Analecta Orientalia, 53. Rome, 1986.

Shisha-Halevy, Ariel. *Coptic Grammatical Chrestomathy: A Course for Academic and Private Study.* Louvain, 1988.

Vergote, Jozef. *Grammaire copte.* 2 vols. Louvain, 1973, 1983.

Dialects

Funk, Wolf-Peter. "Dialects Wanting a Home: A Numerical Approach to the Early Varieties of Coptic." In *Historical Dialectology, Regional and Social,* edited by Jacek Fisiak, pp. 149–192. Berlin, 1988.

Funk, Wolf-Peter. "L'apport de la dialectologie à l'étude des documents littéraires coptes." *Annuaire, École pratique des Hautes Études* 99 (1990–1991), 321–324.

Kasser, Rodolphe. "Prolegomènes à un essai de classification systématique des dialectes et subdialectes coptes selon les critères de la phonétique." *Le Muséon* 93 (1980), 53–112, 237–298; 94 (1981), 91–152.

Kasser, Rodolphe. "Le grand-groupe dialectal copte de Haute-Egypte." *Bulletin de la Société d'Égyptologie Genève* 7 (1982), 47–72.

Kasser, Rodolphe. "Le grand-groupe dialectal copte de Basse-Égypte et son extension véhiculaire panégyptienne." *Bulletin de la Société d'Égyptologie Genève* 13 (1989), 73–82.

Kasser, Rodolphe. "A Standard System of Sigla for Referring to the Dialects of Coptic." *Journal of Coptic Studies* 1 (1990), 141–151.

TITO ORLANDI

GRANITE. *Lower level of the Pyramid of Menkaure at Giza, fourth dynasty.* (Courtesy Dieter Arnold)

GRANITE. The term *granite* includes several rocks. Geologically, granite is a hard, igneous stone, with 10 to 50 percent quartz, 65 to 90 percent alkali feldspar, and small percentages of dark ferromagnesium grains (6–7 on the Mohs Scale of Hardness). Rocks with these compositions are reddish, orange, or brown. The Egyptology literature is, however, filled with references to "gray granite" (generally diorite and similar stones), "gray-to-pink granites" (often gneissic granites), and "black granite" (generally granodiorite or gabbro). Such rocks are low in quartz, have little or no alkali feldspar, and are thus chemically very different from true granites.

Important quarries for true granites are located near Aswan, with many sites between Aswan and Shellal, as well as on the eastern bank of the Nile River and the islands in the Nile's Tumbos area, at the south end of the Third Cataract. The Third Cataract site is a source for the pink-to-gray granites. Major sources of granites are in Upper Egypt, while construction sites are usually in Middle and Lower Egypt, thus necessitating transport for often large and heavy stone masses. Granite was often chosen for statues, probably for the high stone polish achievable, the beauty of the coarsely crystalline rock, and perhaps because of its relative rarity. "Black granites" (granodiorites) were associated with Egypt's sense of *kmt* (the "black land"), while reddish varieties may have been linked to solar worship.

Large masses of granite were often quarried and transported by ancient Egyptians. Thutmose III had a pair of 32.5-meter (99.5-foot; 350-ton) obelisks quarried and transported from Aswan to Luxor in seven months. Even more impressive is the fallen 17-meter (52-foot; approximately 1,000-ton) monolithic statue of Ramesses II at the Ramesseum near Luxor; it may be the largest single block of granite ever quarried.

Granite was used less often in building construction than for monuments. The base of Menkaure's pyramid at Giza was partially sheathed in granite, the valley temple of Khafre beside the Great Sphinx has huge granite columns and roofing beams, while there are floor slabs and burial-chamber linings in some of the pyramids. Granite is not significantly stronger than properly engineered sandstone or limestone slabs, so the greater difficulty in obtaining, shipping, smoothing, and lifting did not justify granite use in any but extraordinary structures. A good example is the use of huge granite beams in the "relieving chambers," above the upper burial chamber, in Khufu's pyramid.

Granite is known from ancient sources under a number of names. Ordinary granite (no color designated) is *mȝt* and *inr-n-mȝt*. Red granite is *mȝt*, *inr-nfr-n-mȝt*, *inr-n-ȝbw*, and *mȝt-rwḏt*. Black granite (probably better termed granodiorite) is *mȝt-kmt*, *inr-km*, and *inr-km-n-mȝt*.

BIBLIOGRAPHY
Arnold, Dieter. *Building in Egypt. Pharaonic Stone Masonry.* Cambridge, 1991.

Faulkner, Raymond O. *A Concise Dictionary of Middle Egyptian.* Oxford, 1962.

Gardiner, Alan. *Egyptian Grammar—Being an Introduction to the Study of Hieroglyphs.* 3d ed. rev. Oxford, 1982.

Harrell, James A. "An Inventory of Ancient Egyptian Quarries." *Newsletter of the American Research Center in Egypt* 146 (1989), 1–7, plus cover photo.

Harris, J. R. *Lexicographical Studies in Ancient Egyptian Minerals.* Deutsche Akademie der Wissenschaften zu Berlin Institut für Orientforschung, 54. Berlin, 1961.

Kozloff, Arielle P., and Betsy M. Bryan. *Egypt's Dazzling Sun. Amenhotep III and His World.* Bloomington, Ind., 1992.

Lesko, Leonard H., and Barbara Switalski, eds. *A Dictionary of Late Egyptian.* 4 vols. Berkeley, 1982.

CLAIR R. OSSIAN

GRID SYSTEMS. From the early Middle Kingdom onward, artists often laid out sketches of divine, royal, and human figures on squared grids. No evidence for grids used in this way has been found from the Old Kingdom, although grids were used for other purposes. Instead, from the fifth dynasty of the Old Kingdom through the Theban eleventh dynasty of the First Intermediate Period, a simple system, using horizontal and vertical guide lines, laid out standing human figures, especially those in rows.

Guide lines and grid lines were usually made by dipping a length of string in red paint, stretching it taut, and snapping it against the drawing surface at the desired level. This method often left small splatters. Alternatively, the lines could be ruled against a straight edge, creating a crisp, more even result.

Grids were used for two-dimensional decoration in tomb chapels, royal tombs and temples, and occasionally for stelae. Evidence suggests that grids were also employed in the initial stage of stone statue production: front, back, and both side views of the statue were sketched on a grid that went over the front, back, and sides of the rectangular stone block. A single uniform grid would help the sculptors line up the sketches of all four sides. Both the grids and the sketches would be cut away as work proceeded, so little evidence has survived concerning the use of grids on statues. Although grids on two-dimensional works were also never meant to be seen when the work was completed, in fact a lot of evidence

remains concerning their use, because many tomb chapels were never finished and the initial artists' grids and sketches remain visible. Further, in tomb chapels that were painted as opposed to being cut into relief, the grids and sketches were not removed but merely covered by the paint of the finished scene. Often, the paint has fallen off to reveal the grids and sketches beneath. Thus we have a good idea about the way guide lines and grids were used.

During the Old Kingdom and First Intermediate Period, the guide line system had up to eight horizontal lines in addition to the baseline on which a human figure stood; a single vertical line ran through the ear, to roughly bisect the figure. The horizontals marked the top of the head; the hairline at which the hair and forehead meet; the junction of the neck and shoulders; the armpits; the elbow of the hanging arm; the lower border of the buttocks; the top of the knee; and the middle of the calf. Not all lines were present on every figure. It was, for example, unusual for both the line at the top of the head and the hairline to appear; of the two, the hairline was more commonly marked. The calf line was only introduced in the sixth dynasty. The knee line and the elbow line divided the hairline height of the figure into thirds, and the line at the lower border of the buttocks divided it in half. When measured upward from the soles of the feet, the junction of the neck and shoulder line was at eight-ninths of the hairline height, and the armpit line was at four-fifths.

Probably in the Middle Kingdom, by the late eleventh dynasty and certainly by the twelfth, the system of guide lines was developed into a squared grid system, in which standing figures comprised eighteen squares between the hairline and the soles of the feet. Thus the old hairline became horizontal 18, the junction of the neck and shoulder line became horizontal 16, the elbow line became horizontal 12, the lower border of the buttocks line became horizontal 9, the knee line became horizontal 6, and the calf line became horizontal 3. The old axial vertical was incorporated as a grid vertical. Neither the line at the top of the head nor the armpit line corresponded to a grid horizontal, and these levels were left unmarked.

By the eighteenth dynasty of the New Kingdom, the top of the head was raised to coincide with horizontal 19. Not all the grid horizontals marked salient points of the body, but horizontal 17 normally passed beneath the nose, and horizontal 14 through or near the nipple. Like the guide line system, the grid system was used for both male and female human figures. The proportions of the figures were not static; they varied from period to period. Early twelfth dynasty figures that had been modeled on Old Kingdom figures of the fifth and early sixth dynasty, had broad shoulders approximately six squares wide, with the armpits about four squares apart. The small of the back was placed on or near horizontal 11. Female figures were

GRID SYSTEMS. *A copy (by Lancelot Crane) of an unfinished painting of Nakht and his wife, eighteenth dynasty.* Its incomplete state allows us to see the preliminary drawing and the grid lines (in the upper left corner) used in setting up the picture. In the tomb of Nakht at Sheikh Abd el-Qurna. (The Metropolitan Museum of Art, 15.5.19f)

narrower across the shoulders, roughly four to fives squares wide, and they had a higher small of the back, which was at or near horizontal 12. Similar proportions were also used at the beginning of the eighteenth dynasty. In the intervening period, however, different proportions were used. Male figures were given shoulders of less than six squares wide and the small of the back was raised to horizontal 12, thus reducing the size of the upper torso; female figures also became more slender. From the mid-eighteenth dynasty, proportions changed again; the small of the back was raised to horizontal 12, and the lower border of the buttocks to horizontal 10.

In the post-Amarna period through the New Kingdom's nineteenth and twentieth dynasties, nonroyal male figures become increasingly slender, and the small of the back was placed as high as horizontal 13. Royal and divine figures were affected less in the change of proportions, yet the lower leg was often lengthened so that it was the lower border of the kneecap or even the tibial tubercle below that rested on horizontal 6. As the male figures were changed, so also were the female, to maintain their gender differences. The use of the eighteen-square grid system did not, therefore, impose a single set of proportions on figures.

In the Middle and New Kingdom system, seated figures normally comprised fourteen squares between the hairline and baseline, consisting of the distance between the hairline and the lower border of the buttocks together with the height of the seat. Kneeling figures, in which the buttocks rest on the heel of the vertical foot, comprised eleven or twelve squares, depending on whether the foot was two or three squares high. The smaller foot seems to have been used until the middle of the eighteenth dynasty, and the larger foot was used in the later eighteenth dynasty, as well as the nineteenth and twentieth dynasties.

During the Amarna period in the late eighteenth dynasty, the grid system was modified, presumably to incorporate new proportions used for male and female figures, so that twenty squares ran between the hairline and the soles of the feet. The knee was still on horizontal 6, and the lower border of the buttocks was still on horizontal 10 in the early style, but often it was lowered to horizontal 9 in the later style. The nipple was frequently related to horizontal 15, not 14, showing that an extra square had been added between the two points. The distance between the junction of the neck and shoulder on horizontal 17 (not 16, because of the extra square in the torso) and the hairline on horizontal 20 was three squares, not two as in the traditional figure, showing that an extra square had been added in the face. One of the effects of that change was to reduce the length of the lower leg in relation to the hairline height. Although few grid traces have survived from the Amarna period, the proportions of the figures of

Nefertiti and nonroyal individuals also relate to a twenty-square grid, although many figures, particularly the nonroyal, may have been drawn freehand.

With the return to orthodoxy, the traditional eighteen-square grid was used once again. Evidence from the Late period's twenty-fifth dynasty shows a new grid system to have come into use, and it continued to be employed through Greco-Roman times. Lack of evidence from the twentieth dynasty and the following Third Intermediate Period makes it hard to determine when the change took place, although it has been argued from evidence in the tomb of Montuemhat (Theban tomb 34) that it occurred during the twenty-fifth dynasty.

In the Late period grid system, standing figures comprised twenty-one squares between the upper eyelid or root of the nose and the baseline. Horizontal 20 ran through the mouth, horizontal 19 through the junction of the neck and shoulders, 13 through the small of the back, 11 through the lower border of the buttocks; 7 was at the top of the knee, and 6 was at the bottom of the tibial tubercle. A vertical ran through the ear, dividing the male torso across the shoulders into approximately three-and-a-half squares on each side. Female figures were also more slender, and they usually had a higher small of the back. Male and female seated figures normally comprised seventeen squares between the upper eyelid and the baseline.

Unlike the Amarna grid system, which was developed to accommodate the changed proportions of that period, the Late period grid system did not significantly change proportions. In the twenty-fifth dynasty and the twenty-sixth, proportions were modeled on those of the fifth and sixth dynasties, which later were also current in the early Middle Kingdom and the early New Kingdom. In the Late period system, the grid squares became only five-sixths the size of the old grid squares, bringing the level of the hairline to 21 and 3/5 squares above the baseline. Because the hairline no longer fell on a grid horizontal, it ceased to be used as the upper point of a figure; instead, the upper eyelid or root of the nose, which coincided with horizontal 21, was used. Other salient points of the body that had been marked in the old grid system were slightly adjusted to coincide with new horizontals: the knee to line 7, from 7 and 1/5 squares; the lower border of the buttocks to 11, from 10 and 4/5 squares; the small of the back to 13, from 13 and 1/5 squares; and the junction of the neck and shoulders to 19, from 19 and 1/5 squares. The reason for this change in the grid system is not yet known.

During the different periods, the way that grids were used varied. For example, in eighteenth dynasty tomb chapels dated to the reigns of Thutmose III and Amenhotpe II, there was a tendency to employ grids far more extensively than in the chapels of the reigns that followed.

They were not used at all in Ramessid chapels, owing to a change in technique whereby artists painted directly on a thin white or yellow ground that was not subsequently repainted.

On monuments for which grids were used, artists had a choice about how to deploy them. They could place a single grid appropriate to the major figure over a complete scene, then add other figures freehand, or they could use a series of grids with different square sizes appropriate to the different sized figures in the scene. Sometimes the two methods were employed in the same tomb chapel. Grids could also influence the layout of scenes, including the placement of various objects and hieroglyphic inscriptions, although the extent to which they did so varied according to a number of factors, including period. When figures in different poses occurred in the same scene—such as, when a standing king makes an offering to a seated deity—the figures could be drawn on the same scale, and so fit the same grid, or they could be drawn with slightly different scales, in which case the same grid would not fit both figures. The first method was widely employed in the eighteenth dynasty and in Greco-Roman times, while the second was more common in the nineteenth to twentieth dynasty.

In ancient Egypt, squared grids functioned as artists' tools for roughly two thousand years. They helped artists achieve acceptable proportions and the proper layout of whole scenes. The extent to which artists used grids varied, as draftsmen were quite capable of drawing freehand. Not enough evidence exists to say whether grids were used for squaring up (in size) from smaller sketches. Grids were helpful to artists working in cramped spaces or from scaffolding high up on temple walls, since they could not step back to gauge the proportions of the complete figure.

[*See also* Painting; Relief Sculpture; *and* Sculpture: An Overview.]

BIBLIOGRAPHY

Baud, Marcelle. "Les dessins ébauchés de la nécropole théebaine (au temps du nouvel empire)." *Bulletin de l'Institut français d'archéologie orientale*, 63. Cairo, 1935. Although the author does not discuss grid systems in any detail, she illustrates a large number of unfinished scenes with surviving grids.

Blackman, Aylward M. *The Rock Tombs of Meir.* vol. 2. *The Tomb-Chapel of Senbi's son Ukh-hotp (B, No. 2).* London, 1915. Publishes line drawings of the decoration of a Middle Kingdom tomb chapel with extensive surviving grids.

Edgar, Campbell C. "Remarks on Egyptian 'Sculptors' Models'." *Recueil de travaux rélatifs à la philologie et à l'archéologie égyptiennes et assyriennes* 27 (1905), 137–150. Discusses the so-called sculptors' trial pieces, with incised grid lines, from the Ptolemaic period.

Edgar, Campbell C. *Sculptors' Studies and Unfinished Works.* Cairo, 1906. Includes two- and three-dimensional examples of so-called sculptor's trial pieces, with incised grid lines, from the Ptolemaic period in the collection of the Egyptian Museum, Cairo.

Mackay, Ernest. "Proportion Squares on Tomb Walls in the Theban Necropolis." *Journal of Egyptian Archaeology* 4 (1917), 74–85. Discusses and illustrates with line drawings a number of scenes having surviving grids, as found in eighteenth dynasty Theban tomb-chapels.

Robins, Gay. *Proportion and Style in Ancient Egyptian Art.* Austin, 1994. The most recent study devoted specifically to the use of guide lines and squared grids in ancient Egyptian art.

Robins, Gay. "Abbreviated Grids on Two Scenes in a Graeco-Roman Tomb at Abydos." In *Studies in Honor of William Kelly Simpson*, edited by Peter Der Manuelian, vol. 2, pp. 689–695. Boston, 1996.

Robins, Gay. "The Use of the Squared Grid as a Technical Aid for Artists in Eighteenth Dynasty Painted Theban Tombs." In *Colour and Painting in Ancient Egypt*, edited by W. V. Davies. London, forthcoming.

Romano, James F., and Gay Robins. "A Painted Fragment from the Tomb of *D'w* at Deir el Gebrawi." *Journal of the American Research Center in Egypt* 31 (1994), 21–32. Discusses the guide lines visible on a painted fragment from an Old Kingdom tomb chapel at Deir el-Gebrawi.

GAY ROBINS

H

HAIRSTYLES. In ancient Egypt, hairstyles changed through time, although deities and occasionally kings and queens were shown with archaic coiffures. Hair was worn at varying lengths and in various styles during the same time period, reflecting changes in fashion as well as differences in sex, age, and social status. In the past, the chief sources of information on hair have been artistic, although some archaeological evidence has been utilized. The hair of mummies, which provides the most immediate source of information on ancient coiffures, has now been studied by the scholar Joanne Fletcher.

The large number of items relating to hairdressing that have been excavated in tombs and at other sites reflects the importance of a well-kept head of hair in ancient Egyptian society. These artifacts include bone, ivory, or metal hairpins, combs, and scissor-shaped metal implements used either for curling or braiding the hair. Upperclass persons would have worn wigs of human hair; occasionally the wigs were padded with vegetable fibers. A New Kingdom nobleman's wig (now in the British Museum) consists of a mesh covered with tightly braided tresses that were attached with beeswax and resin and by looping the strands over the matrix. A portion of the braided tress was then wrapped around this loop. Judging by reliefs on the Middle Kingdom sarcophagi of the wives of Montuhotep I, artificial curls could be added singly, serving to augment fullness in the coiffure, although for one queen they were necessary to cover up a bald spot. Individual braids of human hair have been found at el-Lisht (presently in The Metropolitan Museum of Art, New York). It has been suggested that the mysterious scissorlike toilet implements might have been used to weave those locks into the hair. The implements, which are included in burials from the end of the Old Kingdom to the Late period, consist of two elements: the upper blade was often decoratively shaped and ended in a papyriform element; the lower blade was straight, with a point at one end and a slot at the other.

Jars of beeswax and resin, which the scholar Lise Manniche suggests could have been used as setting lotion, have also been excavated. Depictions of gray hair are almost unknown, except for a few representations in a funerary context. According to surviving recipes, graying hair could be concealed by coloring it with a paste made of juniper berries and other plants. Dye from the henna plant is not mentioned in the recipes. From the eighteenth dynasty onward, cone-shaped objects were depicted resting atop the coiffures of both male and female party-goers in tomb reliefs and paintings. These objects, often called "cosmetic cones," were impregnated with perfume of myrrh. Although scholars have suggested that these were made of wax, they were probably made of tallow or other fat, and could have been used to condition wigs or natural hair, both of which no doubt suffered from dryness caused by the arid climate and the sun.

Priests often shaved (or otherwise depilated) their heads, and probably their entire bodies, as a part of their ritual purification. Numerous razors and tweezers have been found in archaeological contents and texts preserve several recipes for concoctions which were supposed to remove hair. Razors came in a variety of shapes: the two most common were the symmetrical blade with a cutting edge at the end and a slender blade-like variety with a cutting edge that curves into the handle to form a hook. Other ancient Egyptians may have cropped their hair short for coolness or to fit under a wig. Another reason for cropped hair might have been to get rid of lice, the eggs and adults of which have been found in the hair of mummies. Lice may have been the reason that children were also often (but not always) depicted with shaved heads. Sometimes a single thick tress of hair, the "sidelock of youth," was left uncut near one temple in depictions of young children. This braided and curled lock of hair came to have symbolic significance, as a reference to youthful gods, such as Khonsu, and to the reborn and rejuvenated pharaoh. Amulets and other small representations of a crouching figure wearing a sidelock have survived from the Amarna period.

Among the amulets or ornaments depicted in the hair are fish pendants and ball-shaped attachments worn by female dancers. In the Middle Kingdom, small fish-shaped ornaments were occasionally shown attached to a girl's plait of hair. It is believed by scholars that these were amulets against drowning, as indicated by their mention in the story of King Snefru's girl sailors in Papyrus Westcar, rather than purely decorative elements. A number of other hair ornaments have been dated to the Middle Kingdom. These include small gold tubes that fit over plaits of hair, and small cornflowers of gold foil that were also apparently attached to the hair. The single, thick tress of the sidelock worn by preadolescents was also held in place by a clasp or ring. From the Old Kingdom forward, female dancers were shown with their hair pulled back in a long tail, that terminated in a ball-shaped element. Dancers with this hairstyle were characteristically shown performing energetic dances and wearing only brief garments around the hips. A Middle Kingdom relief from the tomb of Queen Neferu depicts performers with a single string of ornaments in their hair; according to the scholar, Cyril Aldred, these were large silver disks. By analogy with other African hairstyles, however, the ornaments might be strands of large beads that were woven into a braid of hair. During the New Kingdom, frontal bands woven from leaves and flower petals were often shown in party scenes, along with cosmetic cones. In addition, men and women were depicted with strips of cloth tied around their heads, especially in the context of funerals. Fillets of flowers, or their imitations in precious metals, were depicted in art from the Old Kingdom forward. Both dancers and boatmen were shown with lotus blossom fillets in festival scenes from Old Kingdom tombs. An Old Kingdom burial from Giza contained a plaster and copper imitation of such a fillet. Later burials of queens and princesses occasionally included circlets that owe their inspiration to the floral headgear. Excavation of the twelfth dynasty burial of the king's daughter Khnumet revealed delicate and beautiful golden circlets utilizing the floral forms of cornflowers and papyrus. Headcloths or wig-covers figure prominently in the headgear of mortals and gods, from the kingly *nemes*-headcloth to the *khat* or *afnet* (also known as the bag-wig) that derives from the kerchiefs covering the heads of winnowers.

In ancient Egypt, most men were shown clean-shaven, but noblemen occasionally grew a short goatee; kings and male deities were depicted with false beards; the straps that hold on the beard were often represented along the side of the face, passing over the ears. In the case of living pharaohs the beards are long and cut straight across at the end. Anthropomorphic gods and deceased pharaohs wore false beards that were braided and curled up at the ends. Eventually this type of beard would be represented on the coffins of many ordinary Egyptians, indicating that those deceased citizens had attained immortality. Amulets in the shape of the divine beard have been found in jewelry from some burials, but their exact significance is difficult to determine. (It has also been suggested that the amulets represent the "sidelock of youth" and they are a reference to rejuvenation, but a list of amulets in the Mac-Gregor Papyrus makes it clear that beard amulets did exist.)

Hairdressers and cosmeticians in ancient Egypt were of both sexes although few examples exist from extant re-

cords. The army, temples, wealthy households, and the king's entourage contained men known as "shavers." Among the most famous depictions of hairdressing are those from the sarcophagi belonging to the two minor wives of Montuhotep I. In both examples, the hairdresser is shown attaching a false curl to the hair of the deceased. The coiffeuses typically stand behind their clients, who are often depicted looking into a mirror. Interestingly, combs are not shown in use by hairdressers; they seem to use hairpins exclusively. Those were made of many materials and often terminated in tiny decorative sculptures of animals.

The typical wigs of Old Kingdom noblemen were thick, straight, and shoulder-length. In three-dimensional representations, they typically were swept back in wing shapes. It was not uncommon, however, for elite men of that period to be shown with their natural, short-cropped hair exposed. During the Old Kingdom, small, closely-clipped moustaches and chinbeards were also popular. Middle Kingdom men's wigs were similar to those of the preceding period, but were often longer and were worn pushed behind the ears. Men were less likely to be shown with facial hair; elite men were rarely depicted with their natural hair exposed. Judging by the wigs for both sexes, which tend to come far down on the brow, a low forehead may have been a mark of attractiveness at this time. In the Archaic period, and until the end of the fourth dynasty, women were often shown with very thick, long hairstyles that consisted of heavy ringlets and braids of hair. During that time, the most popular wigs for women were shoulder-length or longer, although short hairstyles were also worn. For example, the mother of Djoser was represented with a short-cropped hairstyle; in the fourth dynasty women of the royal family were also often represented with this cropped hairstyle. A very popular coiffure among women of the upper classes was a very thick wig that touched the shoulders. A few locks of the woman's real hair may sometimes be seen underneath. The most popular type of long wig was often depicted with straight hair and divided into three sections; it is designated by modern scholars as *tripartite*. It is impossible to say that any one hairstyle worn by women was characteristic of only one class of women at that time, although by the New Kingdom the long, straight wig was often shown on goddesses.

During the Middle Kingdom, short, curled wigs or hairstyles were also worn by women. A wig similar to the tripartite wig of the Old Kingdom was developed for use by royal women. It consisted of thick and wavy hair that came forward over their shoulders in two curled tresses, but that allowed their real hair to be seen in back. The curled tresses often terminated in ball-like elements. This coiffure, called the *Hathoric* wig, was often seen on that goddess. It was worn by a few queens of the Middle Kingdom and the early eighteenth dynasty, together with the vulture cap. This hairstyle, which was so intimately connected with a goddess, is, in fact, absent from most two- and three-dimensional images of Hathor. This goddess was often represented in much the same coiffure and clothing as other female deities, with the eponymous hairstyle shown only in certain full-face representations of her, such as those on the pillars of the temple at Dendera.

The long, straight wig for women was often depicted in the New Kingdom and later, although by that time it was an archaic coiffure worn by queens and goddesses. Although it was often represented in painting and relief without indications of curl or braid, it is apparent from other reliefs and sculptures that this hairstyle could be arranged in vertical rows of short ringlets. These elaborations, however, are rarely seen when the wig was shown on deities such as Isis or Hathor. Ordinary upper-class women wore massive wigs of human hair, elaborately braided, curled, and frizzed. These wigs, which generally cover the wearer as far as her shoulder blades, have been dubbed *enveloping* wigs because they are shown without divisions and with the ears covered. This distinguishes the coiffure from the Hathoric and tripartite wigs that are pushed behind the ears.

During the latter half of the eighteenth dynasty, the distinction between male and female hairstyles blurred when coiffures such the Nubian wig became popular. This hairstyle consisted of tapering rows of tightly rolled ringlets in successive layers. Similar hairstyles are worn in sub-Saharan Africa today; the pharaonic hairstyle is believed to have been influenced by contemporaneous Nubian styles. Another hairstyle worn by both sexes, and influenced by Nubian styles consisted of a rounded wig that reached to the nape of the neck and was often set in ringlets. By the late eighteenth dynasty, men of the upper classes often wore shoulder-length wigs cut in two layers; the bottom layer was be arranged in overlapping ringlets or in loose, flowing hair.

These coiffures were worn both by private individuals and by the king and queen. Often, the only distinguishing factor was the complexity of the arrangement of curls in the wig. For example, on the back of the throne of Tutankhamun, he is represented in a "round" wig with three descending layers of overlapping curls at the bottom. His queen is shown in a multilayered Nubian wig. By contrast, the lesser women and men of the court at Amarna were often depicted without indications of this elaborate layering. Young women, including princesses, were sometimes shown wearing wigs similar to the Nubian type, but cut straight across the bottom, with the addition of an

elaborately braided sidelock that hung down as far as the shoulder. The added hairpiece may have been intended to imitate the curled "sidelock of youth" traditionally worn by children. At the end of the dynasty, representations of elderly male courtiers showed a wig of loose, wavy hair flowing over both shoulder blades, unlike the intricately curled hairstyles of younger men.

In the nineteenth and twentieth dynasties the "unisex" coiffures of the Amarna period went out of use and both men and women were shown in very long wigs. Among upper-class women the wigs sometimes reached to their waists, falling in three locks over the shoulders and down their backs. The hairstyles of men were often more than shoulder-length. The divided wigs of the late eighteenth dynasty were still in evidence during the reigns of Sety I and Ramesses II, but the men at the artists' village of Deir el-Medina were shown with hair (wigs) to their shoulder blades. At Deir el-Medina, young children of both sexes were depicted with their heads partially shaved. The daughters of Sennedjem, for example, appeared with several small locks of hair on their otherwise clean-shaven heads. Elsewhere in the tomb, another daughter, depicted wearing a long gown, was represented with a long, thick, braided sidelock of hair on the right side of her shaven skull. The long dress, and probably the long sidelock, are indicators that she was to be regarded as an adult.

In the twenty-fifth dynasty and later, when Nubian influence was once again strong, men and women were shown in short, tightly-curled hairstyles; the "round" wig returned for women as well. The extreme stylization of details of personal appearance in Egyptian art at any time, and the tendency to archaize during this period, make it difficult to say what fashions in hairstyle actually were.

Throughout Egyptian history, menials of both sexes and all types were represented with hairstyles not seen elsewhere. For example, male pattern baldness was primarily depicted on herdsmen and other low-status workers. The young girls who are used as models for the handles of mirrors and cosmetic spoons, however, were shown with thick, elaborate wigs, probably because of the erotic connotations of hair and wigs in ancient Egypt. Certain stories, such as the *Story of the Two Brothers*, which dates to the late eighteenth dynasty, refer to the role of hair in sexual attraction. A lock of hair from a beautiful woman becomes entangled in pharaoh's laundry, and its scent—perhaps suggestive to the ancient Egyptian audience of the myrrh fragrance of the cosmetic cones—fills him with such desire that he is willing to kill her husband in order to possess her. It is the unique perfume of her hair, reminiscent of the special scent that signals the presence of gods that attracts the king (Hollis

1990). In art, hair, in the form of the "sidelock of youth," is one of the significations of childhood. It can also be a method of indicating wealth and status, of signaling erotic potential, and of connecting a person with a particular role or profession.

BIBLIOGRAPHY

Aldred, Cyril. *Jewels of the Pharaohs.* New York, 1971.

Boston Museum of Fine Arts. *Egypt's Golden Age: the Art of Living in the New Kingdom, 1558–1085 B.C.* A Catalogue of the Exhibition held 3/2–5/2/82. Boston, 1982. This exhibition catalog includes several sections on Egyptian clothing and personal adornment; they are "Mirrors," "Razors," "Toilette Implements," "Wigs and Hair Accessories," and "Cosmetic Arts."

Capel, Anne K., and Glenn E. Markoe, eds. *Mistress of the House, Mistress of Heaven: Women in Ancient Egypt.* New York, 1996; Hudson Hills Press, New York, in association with the Cincinnati Art Museum. Another exhibition catalog which includes a number of items relating to personal adornment.

Cox, J. Stevens. "The Construction of an Ancient Egyptian (c,1400 B.C.) Wig in the British Museum," *Journal of Egyptian Archaeology* 63 (1977), 67–70.

Fletcher, Joanne. "Cosmetics and Bodycare." In *Clothing of the Pharaohs,* edited by Gillian Vogelsang-Eastwood. Leiden, 1994.

Fletcher, Joanne. "A Tale of Hair, Wigs and Lice," *Egyptian Archaeology: Bulletin of the Egypt Exploration Society,* no. 5 (1994), 31–33.

Hollis, S. *The Ancient Egyptian Tale of Two Brothers,* Norman, Okla., and London, 1990.

Vandier, Jacques. *Manuel d'archéologie égyptienne,* vol. 3: *Les Grandes Époques: La Statuaire.* Paris, 1958. See "Coiffure, Costume et parure" (Ancien empire), pp. 106–115; "Costumes et Coiffures" (Moyen empire), pp. 248–250, 252–253; (Nouvel Empire) 347–352, 408–413, 493–500.

LYN GREEN

HAMMAMAT, WADI. *See* Eastern Desert and Red Sea.

HAPY. *See* Four Sons of Horus.

HARDEDEF. *See* Hordjedef.

HAREM. The Turkish word *harim* (Arab., "forbidden, inviolable") refers to the part of a palace where the women and their resident personnel lived in seclusion. They were under the authority of the ruler, but within the harem existed a hierarchical order, the top of which was the sultan's mother. A woman treasurer was responsible for the management of the harem. At the next rank are the sultan's favorite, then his sisters and daughters. The favorite who bore the first son to the sultan became his first spouse; he could have four. Women slaves assumed higher rank if they bore the sultan's children. Women enjoying privileged status had their own household and income; the highest in rank owned palaces within the domain of the harem. Within the harem itself, the crown prince had his own harem. The work was done by numerous ordinary slaves and servants, watched over by eunuchs. The struggle for position was carried out through intrigue, and succession was often linked to murder.

Judging from administrative titles and texts, it seems that the institution of the harem in ancient Egypt was structured in a similar way. The Egyptian harem residents, however, were not cut off from public life, and there is no evidence for the presence of eunuchs in the royal harem or private household.

In the Old Kingdom, several queens of the kings Khufu, Pepy II, and Teti possessed smaller subsidiary pyramids. These are depicted in the cult areas of the kings' pyramids. In the Middle Kingdom, shaft tombs were built for certain queens and princesses. Behind the tomb-temple of Montuhotep I in Deir el-Bahri are burials of six young royal women who bore the titles "king's wife," "sole royal ornament," and "priestess of Hathor"—titles that tie them to the cult of the king as living god (Min), as Sabbahy (1997) discusses. Nearby are the tombs of Queen Tem, mother of Montuhotep II, and his sister and queen Neferu.

Near the pyramid of Amenemhet I in Faiyum are nine small pyramids for the royal ladies, the pyramid of the queen being larger than the others. After the beginning of the eighteenth dynasty, the queens and princes of the New Kingdom, as well as the princesses and favorites, were buried in the Valley of the Queens. They had their own area, separate from the king, who was buried in the Valley of the Kings. However, the queens could participate in the cult for the dead in the mortuary temple of the king. An exception is the huge family mausoleum for the fifty-two sons of Ramesses II in the Valley of the Kings, not far from his own tomb.

The costly maintenance of a harem was possible only for a king, but well-to-do private persons might have more than one wife, or several concubines, as we see in representations in private tombs of the Middle and New Kingdom. Simpson (1974) gives several examples that document polygamy in Egypt. In the wall paintings of the tomb of the nomarch Khnumhotep II (nineteenth century BCE), in Beni Hasan in Middle Egypt, two wives are represented, but only one, Kheti, bears the titles "mistress of the house" and "his beloved wife" and is depicted the same size as Khnumhotep. The second wife is the same size as the children and is not featured in such a prominent position as Kheti. The first of the boats on the "journey to Abydos" is occupied by the sons of the monarch; female persons sit in the cabin of the second boat, labeled by the inscriptions as the mistress of the house Kheti, the (female) children of the nomarch, and women—one of them his second wife—who also bore him children. Neither the spouse nor any concubines of a private person had property that would require administration.

The oldest Egyptian term that is usually translated "harem" is *ipt*, found on imprints of a cylinder seal from the first dynasty in the tomb of King Semerkhet, which mentions the "cellar of the weaving workshop of the *ipt*."

One must keep in mind that "harem" does not mean simply concubines, but the community of women and children who belong to the royal household but live in separate apartments or buildings, having their own income, as we can see in administrative documents from the New Kingdom.

The term *ipt nswt*, which first appears in Old Kingdom inscriptions, according to Del Nord seems "to denote the private quarters of the [king's] palace in which lived the queen(s?), the royal children and certain favored nonroyal children" (1975), but this does not imply a harem.

From archaic times up to the Middle Kingdom, we see the word *ipt* written only as a phonogram, with rare examples of the phonetic complement found in writings of the New Kingdom. The hieroglyph seems to depict a kind of a simple vaulted building, or sometimes a carrying chair of similar appearance. David Lorton (*Journal of the American Research Center in Egypt* 11, 1974: 98–101) tries to find evidence that *ipt* means "counting-house," and *ipt nswt*, "royal counting-house." This view is shared by William A. Ward (1986), but he admits that "royal counting-house" does not always make sense in the given contexts, and that "royal apartment" or sometimes "royal granary" would be more suitable.

From the Old Kingdom, the term *ḫnr* stands for a group of women formerly defined as "the harem and its inhabitants"; it is etymologically derived from "restrain, confine." There are various spellings: the earliest form in the Old Kingdom is *ḫn(i)* without phonetic complement for the ending, but from the sixth dynasty on it is written *ḫnr*. Bryan (1982) therefore prefers a connection to the older form *ḫni* "to keep rhythm" and *ḫnw/i(t)* "musician." These women are headed by the *imjt r3 ḫnr* "(female) overseer of the *ḫnr*," a title that is also held by royal women. From inscriptions of the Old and Middle Kingdoms, we know about their activities as dancers and singers, mostly in connection with the funerary estate and religious performances in temples for Bat, Hathor, Horus, Onuris, and Min. Therefore the translation "musical performers" has been suggested by Nord (1981), and "troupe of singers and dancers" by Ward (1986) for the Old to Middle Kingdoms. The latter would like to have it understood exclusively in this sense, as he denies the existence of harem women in earlier periods.

The female title *ḫkrt nswt* ("ornament of the king") or *ḫkrt nswt wʿtt* ("sole ornament of the king") is attested already for the fifth dynasty and was commonly used beginning in the Herakleopolitan period. It is a title of honor used for princesses and for women of high social status, often those married to courtiers and priests. Ward defines these women as "ladies-in-waiting" who could also belong to the queen's household. Their actual origin is in most cases not indicated, and perhaps we may assume that they came from a lower social class and were chosen because of their beauty or outstanding talents like singing and dancing to be educated for the king's court. Their esteem at court made them suitable for marriage to distinguished men, who were thus bound more closely to the king's court and hence could further their careers. Their descendants also had better chances for a career at court. The women were by no means just concubines of the king. Wall paintings in private tombs of the New Kingdom in Thebes depict them as graceful girls with magnificent diadems. Some of these "ornaments of the king" were accorded burial by the king, even in the Valley of the Queens.

Another word for female is *nfrwt* ("the beautiful ones"). Like the *ḫkrt nswt*, they have been associated with the cult of Hathor. "The beautiful ones" is a term used for young girls who have not given birth yet, according to Papyrus Westcar. Lana Troy (1986, p. 78) explains the difference between *ḫkrt nswt* and *nfrwt* as a distinction between age groups. One could consider the *nfrwt* as novices. This would make sense in the title *imj r3 ḫnrwt n nfrwt* ("overseer of the *ḫnr* of the beautiful ones"), which once belonged to Khesu the Elder from Kom el-Hisn, a priest of the Hathor temple in the twelfth dynasty. He also bore the titles *imj r3 ḫnrwt* and *ḫri tp nfrwt* ("chief of the beautiful ones"); *ḫnrwt* is the group of women, and *nfrwt* the specification.

Boys as well as girls were educated together with the royal children at the king's court, in the harem. They held the title *ḫrdw n kp* ("children of the *kap*" or "pages"). *Kap* is a part of the palace—a school or nursery. During the eighteenth dynasty, a great number of officials connected with the king's court were educated there. At the time of the Ramessids, the title "children of the *kap*" was no longer in use.

During their first years, royal children were kept in the care of the wet-nurse, royal nurse, and chief royal nurse. The nurses were held in high regard. Several of these ladies were wives or mothers of high officials. The royal ornament, chief royal nurse, and wet-nurse of Queen Nefertiti became the wife of the vizier and later king, Ay. In the Middle Kingdom even men could bear this title, indicating that it does not designate only the feeding and rearing of babies but also education and teaching.

In the New Kingdom, the importance of the harem increased. Women and children of high rank who were

HAREM. *Ramesses III depicted with women of his harem, twentieth dynasty.* This is a copy of a relief from the Eastern Gate of the temple of Medinet Habu.

taken as spoils of war and brought to Egypt also lived in the harem. Diplomatic marriages between Egyptian kings—such as Amenhotpe III and Ramesses II—and foreign princesses were frequently arranged to guarantee peace. These women became secondary queens and brought along with them rich dowries and their own retinues. The Mitanni princess Giluchepa, who was sent to Amenhotpe III, came with 317 women, the "chief women of the *ḫnrw*." In this period, harem women were also bequeathed: after the death of Amenhotpe III, the Mitanni princess Taduchepa was passed on to the harem of his successor, Amenhotpe IV.

The royal harem was an autonomous institution with its own administration. Like the royal household and temples, it received regular revenue from taxes of the city in which its permanent residence was situated. When the harem was traveling, supplies were provided by the local mayors in cities it passed through. The harem owned agricultural land, cattle, and manufacturing workshops such as mills and weaving centers. The mills ground grain for the households of the king and the queen. It is likely that fabrics for the entire royal household were produced in the weaving workshops of the harem—above all, the finer textiles such as royal linen. Foreign women also worked there, especially Syrians, whose weaving was in great demand on account of its magnificent colors and patterns.

Beginning in the New Kingdom we find the term *pr ḫnrt* or *pr ḫnty*—a variation derived from the confusion of two similar Hieratic signs—which appears to mean "household of the harem" as an administrative unit; compare *pr*, "household" of the king, queen, princes, and royal children. The highest administrative official was the *imi r₃ ipt nswt* "overseer of the royal harem," a title attested as early as the fourth dynasty from private tombs in Giza. He held a position of exceptional trust, as demonstrated by additional titles that indicate special proximity to the king: "master of the secrets," "sealbearer of the king,"

"sole companion." In the Middle and New Kingdoms, the title "tutor of the royal children" is sometimes added. He had access to the harem and may also have been an overseer of the queen's household. His sphere of activity is sometimes indicated by the title "overseer of the royal harem of the household of the harem of Memphis," "of the household of the harem of Ghurob," or "of the household of the harem in the suite." Among the accused persons listed in the Turin Judicial Papyrus, besides the "overseer of the royal harem," are several other officials of the household of the harem *ḥr šmsw* ("in the suite"). This was the harem that accompanied the pharaoh on his journeys, a small group of carefully selected persons along with their staff.

Next in rank was the *idnw n pr ḫnr* or *idnw n pr ḫnrt* ("deputy of the household of the harem"), likewise specified as located in Memphis, Ghurob, or with the suite. Actively engaged in administration were the "scribes of the royal harem," "royal scribes of the household of the harem," and "scribes of the treasury of the household of the harem." A frequent title in the New Kingdom is *rwḏ n pr ḫnrt* ("inspector of the harem"). Persons bearing this title were also associated with the harem in the suite; together with the *sš wḏḥw* ("scribe of the table"), they were responsible for the purveyance of food.

The gates of the harem quarters were guarded by the *rmṯ p₃ sb₃ n pr ipt* or *s₃w n ipt nswt* ("doorkeepers of the king's harem"). The term *s'š₃* seems to indicate a kind of palace guard distinguished by the flat club made of leather which he held in his hand. Fischer (1978) gives a plausible explanation for the shape and material of this special club, based on various representations in New Kingdom tombs of high officials and on temple walls. These guards were monitors who ran ahead of the king and queen at public appearances. Their special task was to clear the way and keep the crowd at a proper distance.

The *talatat* blocks from the temple of Amenhotpe IV (Akhenaten) in Karnak offer a good illustration of the public appearance of the king with his family and retinue. We always see the same order: king, queen, and children of the king. The officials who are seen bowing next to the palanquins, carrying the children of the king, or near ladies holding fans in their hands are, as the inscriptions indicate, the overseer of the king's harem, inspectors of the harem, and the sʿšȝ (guards or police).

As we know from a few archeological finds, the king's harem, though considered a part of his palace-household, was housed in a building of its own. Papyri from the times of Amenemhet III and Senwosret III, found in Illahun, mention several persons connected with the harem and thus prove the existence of a harem in the neighborhood of this town, the capital of that period. A large palace enclosure near Illahun, discovered by Flinders Petrie before 1890, indicated that the oasis of Faiyum was later a popular place of residence for the royal family. There are the remains of a small city and a small temple from the time of Thutmose III (1490–1439 BCE) within an enclosure wall. Two large rectangular complexes are situated lengthwise, parallel to each other. Both are divided by corridors into two parts. The northern part, with its column bases and doors partially cased with stone, is the more stately building. This corridor may have separated the chambers of the queen and her court from the rest of the harem. The parallel southern building, which has the same partition, contained the harem's housekeeping areas. Artifacts such as jewelry, cosmetic articles, children's toys, tools from the weavers' workshops, a statuette of the chief of weavers Lady Teye, pottery, fragments of furniture, and rings inscribed with royal names (one with the bezel in the shape of a cartouche with the prenomen of Sety II), confirm that these buildings were inhabited at least up to the nineteenth dynasty, and to some extent up to the time of Ramesses III (twelfth century BCE). Kemp (1978) gives a list of objects bearing names and titles of officials from the royal harem at Medinet el-Ghurob. Tombs of male and female residents were found in the vicinity, among them a large one belonging to Ramessu-nebweben, a Ramessid prince.

The great residential area of Amenhotpe III (r. 1410–1372 BCE) in Malqata on the west side of Thebes, with its huge artificial lake, exhibits several residential palaces. The center of the king's palace is a large columned hall with a throne and several apartments, the latter probably designated for the most important concubines. The queen had her own palace next to the king's and arranged in similar fashion, but smaller. Remains of wall paintings were also found there. Additional palaces and villas were designated for the successor to the throne, Akhenaten, for princes and princesses, and for foreign princesses and their households; it is likely that his parents-in-law Yuya and Tuya were also quartered there.

In Tell el-Amarna, the residence of King Akhenaten (r. 1372–1355 BCE) in Middle Egypt, we also find public quarters and living quarters with a private palace for the king, as well as palaces for the royal family and for their entourage. The so-called north palace may well have been the main residence of Akhenaten's oldest daughter Meritaten, who became the "great royal wife" after the death of Nefertiti. The women's wing is divided into the southern and northern harems, furnished with gardens and ponds. Walls and pavements were painted, depicting flowers, fruit stands, pools surrounded by vegetation, and animals. Bound enemies were painted on the pathways of the halls. In addition, the walls and columns were decorated with colorful faience inlay.

Outside the capital, the kings also had palaces in other towns, which surely included a private palace and a harem. The small palaces near the mortuary temples in western Thebes may serve as a model. These are situated at the first court of the temple and have a "window of appearance" for ceremonial presentation. On the topmost levels of the High Gate of Medinet Habu, the towerlike structures of the front entrance in the enclosure wall of the mortuary temple of Ramesses III, private rooms were decorated with reliefs and paintings depicting the king surrounded by girls and princesses.

Through a few texts preserved from the Old, Middle, and New Kingdoms, we may learn directly or indirectly about intrigues within the royal harem in connection with the succession to the throne. Since it is known that the kings often had several wives, conflicts readily arose if the crown prince was not officially designated by the ruling king. For the Old Kingdom, there is a hint of a plot against Pepy I, planned by Queen Weret-imtes. Weni, who made his career under the kings Teti, Pepy I, and Antyemsaf, informs us in an autobiographic inscription in his tomb at Abydos about a secret investigation in the royal harem against the queen. He points out that he was the confidant of the king, the only one to enter the harem and to "hear the secrets of the royal harem."

Amenemhet I, the first king of the twelfth dynasty, who ruled for almost thirty years, appointed the crown prince, Senwosret, as coregent in his twentieth year of rule. Based on the *Instructions of Amenemhet* and the *Story of Sinuhe*, it is assumed that the king was murdered as a result of a harem plot (see Volten 1945). Assassination is mentioned in the *Instructions of Amenemhet*, but this is a propaganda text that was written at the time when Senwosret I was already the absolute ruler, undoubtedly to justify his coregency.

Likewise considered to be propaganda texts are papyri that tell about the trial of persons who planned the murder of Ramesses III. The principal defendant was the secondary queen Tiy, who wanted to place her son Pentewere on the throne. At the same time, a revolt was supposed to take place outside of the palace. Ramesses IV, the successor to the throne, conducted the investigation. The jury was composed of fourteen officials. Twenty-eight persons were sentenced to death, and others were allowed to die by their own hand, among them Pentewere. A few of the investigating judges, who had connections to the persons accused, were punished by having their noses and ears cut off. Ramesses III died during the trial at an age of sixty-five in his thirty-second year of rule, but not as a result of this harem plot. There were no injuries found on his mummy—just a high degree of arteriosclerosis, which probably led to his death.

The propaganda text, which was written during or before the accession of Ramesses IV to the throne and was posted publicly in the temple area of Medinet Habu, was supposed to confirm that Ramesses III had designated his son Ramesses to be his successor.

BIBLIOGRAPHY

Aldred, Cyril. *Akhenaten King of Egypt.* London, 1988.

Bryan, Betsy M. "The etymology of ḫnr 'group of musical performers'." *Bulletin of the Egyptological Seminar* 4 (1982), 35–54.

Clayton, Peter A. *Chronicle of the Pharaohs: The Reign-by-Reign Record of the Rulers and Dynasties of Ancient Egypt.* London, 1994.

Fischer, Henry George. "Notes on Sticks and Staves in Ancient Egypt." *Metropolitan Museum Journal* 13 (1978), 20.

Fischer, Henry George. *Egyptian Women of the Old Kingdom and of the Heracleopolitan Period.* New York, 1989. Comments on the term ḫnr for a group of women and the role they played in various cults.

Jánosy, Peter. *Die Pyramidenanlagen der Königinnen. Untersuchungen zu einem Grabtyp des Alten und des Mittleren Reiches.* Österreichische Akademie der Wissenschaften, Denkschrift 13, Zweigstelle Kairo. Vienna, 1996.

Janssen, Rosalind M., and Jac J. Janssen. *Growing up in Ancient Egypt.* London, 1990. Special attention is paid to royal children and their playmates, nurses, and tutors.

Kemp, Barry J. "The Harem-Palace at Medinet el-Ghurab." *Zeitschrift für Ägyptische Sprache und Altertumskunde* 105 (1978), 131.

Kemp, Barry J. *Ancient Egypt: Anatomy of a Civilization.* London and New York, 1989. Emphasizes archeological evidence of New Kingdom towns, their inhabitants and organization, and royal palaces.

Kitchen, K. A. *Pharaoh Triumphant: The Life and Times of Ramesses II.* Warminster, 1982.

Lacovara, Peter. *The New Kingdom Royal City.* London and New York, 1997.

Nord, Del. "The Term ḫnr: 'Harem' or 'Musical Performers'?" *Studies in Ancient Egypt, the Aegean and the Sudan* (1981), 137–145.

Reiser, Elfriede. *Der königliche Harim im Alten Ägypten und seine Verwaltung.* Vienna, 1972.

Robins, Gay. *Women in Ancient Egypt.* Cambridge, Mass., 1993.

Sabbahy, Lisa K. "The Titulary of the Harem of Nebhepetre Mentuhotpe, Once Again." *Journal of the American Research Center in Egypt* 34 (1997), 163–166.

Simpson, William Kelly. *Journal of Egyptian Archaeology* 60 (1974), 100–105.

Smith, Ray Winfield, and Donald B. Redford. *The Akhenaten Temple Project I: Initial Discoveries.* Warminster, 1976. Reliefs represent the pharaoh, his family, the entourage, and officials of the royal household.

Smith, W. Stevenson. *The Art and Architecture of Ancient Egypt.* 2d rev. ed., edited by William Kelly Simpson. New Haven and London, 1981. Plans of towns and palaces, with photos of wall paintings and other decorations, especially of the palaces of Amenhotpe III at Malqata and of Akhenaten at Tell el-Amarna.

Troy, L. *Patterns of Queenship in Ancient Egyptian Myth and History.* Uppsala, 1986.

Tyldesley, Joyce. *Daughters of Isis: Women of Ancient Egypt.* London, 1994.

Volten, Axel. *Zwei altägyptische politische Schriften: Die Lehre für König Merikarê (Pap. Carlsberg VI) und Die Lehre des Königs Amenemhet.* Analecta Aegyptiaca, 4. Copenhagen, 1945.

Ward, William. A. *Essays on Feminine Titles of the Middle Kingdom and Related Subjects.* Beirut, 1986. Social status of nonroyal women during the Middle Kingdom, interpreted by their titles and those of their husbands. Special chapters concisely discuss words and titles that were translated as "harem" or thought to be connected with the harem, with the conclusion that harems or concubines did not exist in the Middle Kingdom, at least as recognized institutions.

Whale, Sheila. *The Family in the Eighteenth Dynasty of Egypt: A Study of the Representation of the Family in Private Tombs.* Sydney, 1989. Families of the upper classes as represented in the private tombs; the question of concubines and polygamy is considered.

ELFRIEDE HASLAUER
Translated from German by James Goff

HARES. The Cape hare (*Lepus capensis*) routinely appears in ancient Egyptian art and in hieroglyphs. It was always rendered in a couchant position. Immediately recognizable by its distinctive large ears and short tail, Egyptian artisans created highly accurate and appealing representations of this small desert mammal, which was called *sḫ't*. As a standard hieroglyphic sign, the hare had the phonetic value *wn*. The Cape hare remains a relatively common and wide-ranging resident. The domestic rabbit (*Oryctolagus cuniculus*) first arrived in the Nile Valley during late Roman to Coptic times, and was therefore unknown in pharaonic times.

One of the earliest occurrences of the hare in Egyptian iconography is preserved on the Hunters' Palette, from the Late Predynastic period (Naqada III), portrayed amid a group of chased game. From that time onward, it was depicted in countless desert hunting compositions on private tomb-chapel walls and elsewhere. Hares characteristically appeared in those works either fleeing at top speed, attempting to escape the hunter's rain of arrows and pack of dogs, or crouching behind a tree or bush, hoping to go unnoticed. They were bagged, however, so hares occasionally appeared in small cages among the fruits of the field and harvest delivered by bearers in offering processions. In several New Kingdom vignettes of Theban tomb-chapels, they are shown being carried by their long ears; these were probably intended to be enjoyed as table fare in the afterlife. The hare was also sometimes considered desirable quarry for sporting kings. For example, a pas-

HARES. *Amulet in the form of a hare, of light blue faience, twenty-sixth dynasty.* (The Metropolitan Museum of Art, Rogers Fund, 1944. [44.4.25])

sage of an eighteenth dynasty text, from the time of Amenhotpe II, mentions that the king hunted hares near the city of Kadesh while on a military campaign. An ornate bow case, discovered in the tomb of Tutankhamun (tomb 62) in the Valley of the Kings, was decorated with a scene of the young pharaoh in a chariot, pursuing a variety of desert animals with bow and arrow, including a hare.

The hare was the ensign of the fifteenth Upper Egyptian nome, including the important city of Hermopolis Magna as its capital. It was also the emblem of the local goddess Unas ("The Swift One"). Although amulets in the shape of hares had been in use since the late Old Kingdom, it was during the Late period that they were most abundantly produced; these are invariably made of light-green faience (and are very popular with collectors today). The significance of these amulets is not precisely understood. Several leading Egyptologists have suggested that they were connected with the domain of regeneration. In any case, the hare's legendary fecundity and well-known, fleet-footed abilities were likely to be some of the desirable attributes that their wearers wished to assimilate; Classical-era writers did refer to these and other supposed traits of the hare as accountable for its esteemed place in Egyptian thought. Then too, a demon who inhabited the netherworld, as illustrated on the walls of some late New Kingdom royal tombs in the Valley of the Kings and on mythological papyri also took the form of a hare. From the Ptolemaic period comes an unusual bronze figure of a hare (now in the Ägyptisches Museum, Berlin), which may have functioned as a votive object.

BIBLIOGRAPHY

Andrews, Carol. *Amulets of Ancient Egypt.* Austin, 1994. Excellent illustrated survey of amulets in pharaonic Egypt, based chiefly on those in the collections of the British Museum, London.

Boessneck, Joachim. *Die Tierwelt des alten Ägypten: Untersucht anhand kulturgeschichtlicher und zoologischer Quellen.* Munich, 1988. Provides an authoritative discussion on wildlife in ancient Egypt, including the Cape hare.

Hornung, Erik, and Elisabeth Staehelin, eds. *Skarabäen und andere Siegelamulette aus Basler Sammlungen.* Mainz, 1976. Discusses hares as scaraboids and amulets; the authors present a valuable overview of hares in ancient Egypt, with many references.

Houlihan, Patrick F. *The Animal World of the Pharaohs.* London and New York, 1996. Aimed at a general audience; surveys the ancient Egyptian animal world and contains several fine illustrations of hares; extensive bibliography.

Osborn, Dale J., and Ibrahim Helmy. *The Contemporary Land Mammals of Egypt (Including Sinai).* Fieldiana Zoology, n.s., 5. Chicago, 1980. The standard text on the land mammals of modern Egypt; includes much information on the Cape hare.

PATRICK F. HOULIHAN

HARKHUF. *See* Horkhuf.

HARPOKRATES. *See* Horus.

HARWA, one of the principal dignitaries of the Kushite dynasty (twenty-fifth dynasty, 710–c.650 BCE), whose vast tomb was dug into the Asasif (western bank of Thebes). He was the grandson of a certain Ankhefenamen; his father was Pedimont, a member of the Theban clergy, and his mother's name was Nestwereret. His family was allied to the Ethiopian dynasty. As "Director of All Divine Functions," he was the great major-domo of the two Divine Adoratrices—Amenirdis I, whom he outlived, and Shepenupet, daughter of King Piya. Apart from his tomb at Thebes (tomb 37), we know of Harwa through some beautiful statues, an offering table found at Deir el-Medina, and some small funeral statuettes (*shawabti*s).

BIBLIOGRAPHY

Aubert, J. F., and L. Aubert. *Statuettes égyptiennes.* Paris, 1974.

De Meulenaëre, H. "Harwa." In *Lexikon der Ägyptologie,* 2:1021–1022. Wiesbaden, 1977.

von Droste, V., and Birgit Schlick-Nolte. *Liebighaus, Ägyptische Bildwerke.* Vol. 2, 1991.

JEAN LECLANT
Translated from French by Susan Romanosky

HATHOR. The goddess Hathor was one of the most important and popular members of the Egyptian pantheon. She was most commonly represented as a cow goddess. Her manifestations and associated activities were numerous and diverse, and complementary aspects such as love and hate, or creation and destruction, characterized her from the earliest stages of her worship. Because she was a prehistoric goddess, the origins of her nature and her cult are difficult to discern, but her existence is evident from prehistoric times continuously through the period of Roman domination. Her aspects incorporated animals, vegetation, the sky, the sun, trees, and minerals, and she governed over the realms of love, sex, and fertility, while also maintaining a vengeful aspect capable of the destruction of humanity.

Hathor's name in Egyptian, *Ḥwt Ḥr*, means "House of Horus" and is written in hieroglyphs with the rectangular sign for a building, with the falcon symbol of Horus inside. The imagery of Hathor emphasizes her primary manifestation as a cow goddess. She most often appears as a female figure wearing a headdress comprised of a sun disk with an appended *uraeus* set between two tall cows' horns. In later times this headdress often incorporates two tall feathers standing between the horns; or she may wear a vulture cap or the hieroglyph for "west," depending on the context of her depiction. She very often wears a *menat*, a necklace made of many strings of beads counterbalanced by a heavy pendant at the back. Hathor is also frequently depicted as a cow; the Hathor cow usually bears the sun disk between its horns and wears the menat necklace. A third type of image of Hathor is a female face seen from the front, with the ears of a cow and a curling or tripartite wig. This face appears on certain types of votive objects and can form the capitals of columns in temples to the goddess. The back-to-back version may have originated from the cult object of another cow goddess, Bat, whose similar iconography was absorbed by Hathor by the eleventh dynasty.

The roots of Hathor's cult may be found in the predynastic cow cults, in which wild cows were venerated as embodiments of nature and fertility. Even in early images of her, the multiplicity of Hathor's aspects is apparent. For example, the rim of a stone urn from Hierakonpolis, dated to the first dynasty, is decorated with the face of a cow goddess with stars at the tips of its horns and ears, a reference to her role (or that of Bat) as a sky-goddess (compare also the Narmer Palette). This role may be linked to her relationship to Horus: since he was a sun and sky god, she, as his "house," resided in the sky as well. Evidence for this belief appears in the funerary texts: as early as the Pyramid Texts, the pharaoh is said to ascend to Hathor in the sky, and later, in the Coffin Texts, the nonroyal deceased also engage her there.

An ivory engraving from the first dynasty shows a recumbent cow and is inscribed "Hathor in the Marshes of King Djer's city of Dep (Buto)," reflecting Hathor's association with the papyrus marsh and vegetation in general. Hathor was also a tree goddess, and from the Old Kingdom was called "Mistress of the Sycamore." Her role as tree goddess complemented her aspect as cow goddess, allowing her to embody all the creative and fertile qualities of the natural world. The tree goddess was also important to the deceased, to whom she offered shade and a drink from her branches. Hathor's aspect as tree goddess originated in the Nile Delta, and in this role she had a close relationship with Ptah, a creator god from Memphis. A procession in the New Kingdom brought Ptah to visit Hathor, then referred to as his daughter.

Hathor was also a goddess associated with love, sex, and fertility. On another ivory engraving from the first dynasty, a front-facing Hathor is flanked by signs for the god Min, a god identified with fertility, indicating their affiliation. The Greeks likened her to Aphrodite, their own goddess of love and beauty. Numerous hymns praise her and the joy and love for which she was responsible, and in these she is often addressed as *Nb.(t).* "the Golden One," a name whose origins and intent are uncertain. Throughout the history of her cult, Hathor received as offerings a variety of fertility figurines, as well as votive phalli, and she was viewed as a source of assistance in conception and birth. One of her epithets was "Lady of the Vulva," and she appears in medical texts as well as prayers in relation to pregnancy and childbirth.

Hathor was an important funerary goddess. In Thebes she was called "Mistress of the West" or the "Western Mountain," referring to the mortuary area on the west bank of the Nile. Her prominent role in funerary imagery and ritual was strongly connected with her role in promoting fertility. It was believed that Hathor, as the night sky, received Re each night on the western horizon and protected him within her body so that he could be safely reborn each morning. Based on this divine paradigm, Hathor was seen as a source for rebirth and regeneration of all the deceased, royal and nonroyal, and they all hoped for similar protection from her.

Hathor was also associated with the mountains in the Sinai, where the Egyptians mined for turquoise and copper. The "cave of Hathor" formed the core of her temple at Serabit el-Khadim, where she was worshipped as "Mistress of Turquoise." She was also worshipped at the copper mines at Timna, a site on the eastern edge of the Sinai Peninsula. Hathor's popularity extended out of Egypt to foreign cities; she was worshipped as "Mistress of Byblos" at that city on the eastern coast of the Mediterranean Sea.

Because the prehistoric cow cults from which Hathor's cult emerged existed throughout the country, her original

HATHOR. *Small Hathor-capital from Deir el-Bahri, of painted limestone, eighteenth dynasty.* (University of Pennsylvania Museum, Philadelphia. Neg. # S8–72100)

cult center is difficult to determine. Her cult may have originated in the Delta region, where her son Horus also had an important role, and she is known from the site of Kom el-Hisn. Dendera in Upper Egypt was an important early site of Hathor, where she was worshipped as "Mistress of Dendera (*Iwnt*)." Meir and Kusae were also important cult sites from the Old Kingdom and later. Based on the distribution of titles within her cult, it appears that the Giza–Saqqara area was the focus of the cult in the Old Kingdom. By the First Intermediate Period, however, that

focus had shifted southward, and from then on Dendera served as the cult center of Hathor. Evidence indicates that a temple existed there from the Old Kingdom, and a temple structure of some sort was maintained continuously through the time of the major Greco-Roman temple that still stands today. At Dendera, Hathor had a close relationship with Horus of Edfu, a nearby site. In this case she was not mother but consort to Horus, and had with him two children, Ihy and Harsomtus.

Deir el-Bahri, on the western bank of Thebes, was also

an important cult site of Hathor. The area was the site of a popular cow cult prior to the Middle Kingdom. This cow goddess was specified as Hathor in the eleventh dynasty when the pharaoh Nebheptre-Montuhotpe built his mortuary temple there. He closely identified himself with the falcon god Horus and took the title "Son of Hathor, Lady of Dendera"; he also built temples to Hathor at Dendera and Gebelein. In the New Kingdom, both Hatshepsut and Thutmose III built their mortuary temples at Deir el-Bahri, and both temples incorporated Hathor shrines. Hathor was worshipped as a cow at this site, and the mortuary temples were decorated with reliefs of the king being suckled by Hathor as a cow.

Hathor's appearances in narrative mythology equally reflect her varied and often obscure nature. One unusual myth, the meaning of which is uncertain, nonetheless clearly implies her sexual aspect. In the *Contendings of Horus and Seth*, a troubled Re is approached by Hathor, who then exposes her self to him, causing the god to laugh. Two more fully understood myths that involve Hathor and Re reveal the duality of Hathor's nature, veering between joyful and destructive. In the *Destruction of Humanity*, the elderly Re, ruling on Earth, sends Hathor as his eye to punish his wayward subjects. Upon witnessing the destruction wreaked by Hathor, Re repents his decision, and to stop her from continuing, floods the land with beer dyed to resemble blood, to which Hathor is drawn. She becomes harmlessly drunk, and the people are saved. Based on this myth, Hathor was also worshipped as the goddess of drunkenness. In a second myth, Hathor is described as a lioness in the Nubian desert. Re sends Thoth to bring her to him for protection and companionship. On their return, Thoth immerses the lioness in the cool waters of the Nile in order to quell her fierceness, rendering her calm and joyful. These myths illustrate the aggressive and destructive aspects of Hathor which were integral to her complete character. In this mode she was linked to Sakhmet, the destructive lioness, and Tefnet, the angry lioness in the Nubian desert. This transformation of the goddess from a destructive aspect to a calm and joyful one was essential for the Egyptians in the maintenance of their cosmos, and thus festivals devoted to Hathor incorporated excessive drinking along with music and dance with the intent of pacifying the great goddess.

These myths also illustrate Hathor's complicated relationship with Re. In the myth in which Hathor is the eye of Re, she is interpreted as his daughter, as is also the case in the *Contendings of Horus and Seth*. Yet Hathor is commonly perceived as the mother of Re, based on several factors. Hathor was understood to be the mother of Horus, based on a metaphorical reading of *Ḥwt* as "womb," and as Re overtook Horus in the mythology, especially as related to kingship, Hathor was described as

HATHOR. *Diorite head of a statue of Hathor, depicted with a cow head, eighteenth dynasty, reign of Amenhotpe III*. Between her horns is the sun disk (which may refer to her roles as both the daughter and the eyes of the sun god Re). (The Metropolitan Museum of Art, Rogers Fund, 1919. [19.2.5])

the mother of Re as well. She also absorbed this role from another cow goddess, *Mḥt Wrt*, the great flood, who in the creation myth was the mother of Re; she gave birth to the sun god and carried him between her horns, an iconographical element later adopted by, and essential to, Hathor. Hathor's role as Re's mode of successful rebirth each day made her both wife (whom he impregnates with himself) and mother (who gives birth to him on the eastern horizon).

In her role as mother, Hathor's importance in the institution of kingship was established from its earliest stages. Because Horus was the first royal god, Hathor became symbolically the divine mother of the pharaoh. She is often depicted in this role as a cow, linked to a myth in which the infant Horus is hidden from his murderous uncle Seth in the marshes of Chemmis, and there suckled by the divine cow. The image of Hathor as a cow suckling the pharaoh is common from the New Kingdom, emphasizing the divine aspect of the king, and it was as a cow that Hathor was worshipped at Deir el-Bahri, site of several royal mortuary complexes. The cow goddess is integral to the concept of kingship from its first appearance, exemplified on the Narmer Palette, which depicts the original unification of Egypt and presents the canonical image of the Egyptian king. The top of the palette shows the name of the king flanked by two cow heads—perhaps of Bat, in this case, but because of Bat's close relationship and eventual submission to Hathor, this can be seen as basic to Hathor's character as well.

Hathor also appears in relation to the king in the Pyramid Texts, in which the king is said to perform ritual dancing and shaking in the Hathor cult. Sculptures of the king with Hathor appear as early as the reign of Menkaure and are common through the late periods. In addition, Hathor played a significant part in the *sed*-festival, the royal ritual devoted to the symbolic rebirth of the king, as is illustrated by the reliefs in the tomb of Kheruef depicting the *sed*-festival of Amenhotpe III.

Rituals in Hathor's honor often incorporated music and dance. Beginning in the Old Kingdom, we find numerous tomb scenes showing dancers performing with musicians in her honor. In Thebes, the music and dancing integral to the Valley Festival, a celebration that brought relatives to the tombs of their deceased family members on the western bank, were performed under the patronage of Hathor. The two objects most characteristic of and sacred to Hathor were the sistrum, a type of rattle, and the *menat* necklace, which could be shaken like the sistrum; both were utilized in these dance and music rituals. A related ritual was the *zšš wȝd*, or Shaking of the Papyrus, which is said to be performed by the king in the Pyramid Texts and is portrayed in the tombs of many private individuals as well. The shaking of the papyrus plants sacred to Hathor is linked to the shaking of the sistrum, which in its earliest form was called *zššt* ("shaker"). The king also danced for Hathor during his *sed*-festival, as written in the reliefs from the tomb of Kheruef.

The calendar in the temple at Dendera lists more than twenty-five festivals in which Hathor was celebrated. Many occurred only under her aegis, while others were specifically celebrated for her. On New Year's Day her cult statue was brought to the roof of her temple so that she could be united with Re in the form of the sun rays, an act which occurred on other festival days as well. On the twentieth day of the first month, the Egyptians celebrated the Festival of Drunkenness in her honor, and in the

spring there was another festival in her honor that related to the myth of her return from the Nubian desert. The most prominent and elaborate festival of Hathor was her sacred marriage as Mistress of Dendera to Horus of Edfu. In this summer festival, Hathor's cult statue was taken by boat from Dendera to Edfu, stopping along the way at several cult sites and arriving at Edfu at the new moon. She stayed at Edfu with Horus for thirteen days before returning to her temple. This union produced two sons, Ihy and Horus-Sematawy.

Hathor was one of the most complex and mysterious of the Egyptian gods, and also one of the most enduring. Her status as a prehistoric goddess makes determining her origins nearly impossible, and it is also difficult to untangle the myriad aspects and myths which together form her character. Nonetheless, it is clear that she played a vital role in Egyptian society from its highest levels to its lowest, essential to the identity and characterization of the king and a favorite goddess of the general population, who flooded her local cults with offerings and prayers.

BIBLIOGRAPHY

Allam, Schafik. *Beitrage zum Hathorkult (bis zum Ende des mittleren Reiches)*. Berlin, 1963.

Bleeker, C. J. *Hathor and Thoth: Two Key Figures of the Ancient Egyptian Religion*. Leiden, 1973. An overview of Hathor, in English.

Galvin, Marianne. "The Priestesses of Hathor in the Old Kingdom and the First Intermediate Period." Ph.D. diss. Brandeis University, 1981. A systematic study of the distribution and relationships of titles in the Hathor cult.

Pinch, Geraldine. *Votive Offerings to Hathor*. Oxford, 1993.

Roberts, Alison. *Hathor Rising: The Power of the Goddess in Ancient Egypt*. Rochester, Vt., 1997. An interpretive study focusing on the serpent aspect of Hathor.

Troy, Lana. *Patterns of Queenship*. Uppsala, 1986. An investigation of the mythology and character of Hathor and how it defines the structure of royalty and ritual, especially of women.

Wente, Edward F. "Hathor at the Jubilee." In *Studies in Honor of John A. Wilson*. Chicago, 1969.

DEBORAH VISCHAK

HATNUB. *See* Bersheh.

HATSHEPSUT (r. 1502–1482 BCE), fifth king of the eighteenth dynasty, New Kingdom. The daughter of Thutmose I and Queen Ahmose, Hatshepsut married her half brother, the future Thutmose II and produced one child, Neferure. After the premature death of Thutmose II, his son from a union with another woman, Isis, was crowned as Thutmose III, who possibly married Neferure to gain legitimacy. Since Thutmose III and Neferure were both children at Thutmose II's death, the king's "Great Wife" Hatshepsut ruled Egypt as regent. From two to seven

HATSHEPSUT. *Head of a red granite statue of Hatshepsut, from her Valley Temple at Deir-el-Bahri, eighteenth dynasty.* (The Metropolitan Museum of Art, Rogers Fund and Edward S. Harkness Gift, 1929. [29.3.3])

years later, she assumed full power and crowned herself "king," using all royal titles. To vindicate her claim to the throne, the priests made use of a story of divine birth: the god Amun visited Queen Ahmose in the guise of her husband and begot Hatshepsut. She acted as king and frequently posed and dressed as a man. Though Hatshepsut counted the beginning of her reign from the coronation of Thutmose III, his role as ruler was downplayed. She appeared in written sources for the last time in the twentieth year of Thutmose III's reign, the same year in which he was represented with her as an equal for the first time. Previously, she always took precedence over her stepson, leaving no doubt concerning her role as senior pharaoh.

Hatshepsut sent military expeditions to Nubia and Syria-Palestine, yet her reign is better remembered for the high quality of its architecture and art. She was devoted to building temples and presented herself as the restorer of what "had been dismembered." Her building program affected Thebes, provincial towns, and localities outside Egyptian territory, such as Buhen in Nubia and the Wadi Mughara in the Sinai. Her most important edifices are located in central Karnak where she erected two groups of chambers and the sanctuary now called the Red Chapel, in ancient times known as the Palace of Maat, which referred to the concept of truth and justice basic to Egyptian religion. The Red Chapel represented a real architectural achievement; it was constructed of regularly shaped quartzite blocks with exact vertical and horizontal joints. The block's size corresponded to the scenes carved on them. Hatshepsut transformed the existing hall between the fourth and fifth pylons by placing two obelisks there. A second pair of obelisks was erected in eastern Karnak. She built the eighth pylon and the bark-shrines on the processional avenue from Karnak to Luxor, which ran through it. The best-known building completed during Hatshepsut's reign is her mortuary temple at Deir el-Bahri, bearing a series of wall reliefs representing the most important achievements of her reign: the expedition to Punt undertaken in Year 9 under the treasurer Nehesi that depicts the return with exotic goods, and the quarrying, transport, and erection of a pair of obelisks in Year 16. In Medinet Habu, she built a small temple for Amun; while on the island of Elephantine she founded two temples for local gods.

Many of the temples built in the provinces under the rule of Hatshepsut disappeared completely in antiquity and are known only from textual references. Yet the few structures that remain show that her architects were exceptionally creative. For example, the Speos Artemidos in the vicinity of Beni Hasan was the first rock-cut temple in Egypt. The temple at Deir el-Bahri, though not original in general layout, was a harmonious and imposing creation.

Hatshepsut built two tombs during her reign. The first, left unfinished, was prepared when she was still Thutmose I's "Great Wife." The second tomb—the longest and deepest in Egypt—was probably first begun in the Valley of the Kings for Thutmose I (tomb 20 in the Valley of the Kings). Two quartzite sarcophagi were found there; both were made for Hatshepsut, although one was altered for Thutmose I.

The many splendid tombs in the Theban necropolis that date to Hatshepsut's reign preserve records of many of her high officials. The most influential was the steward of Amun Senenmut. He was responsible for building the most important monuments of the queen. Senenmut, the treasurer Nehesi, and the administrator of the royal estate Amenhotep, were in disfavor with Hatshepsut circa Year 16 of the reign; the reason for this is not clear.

After Hatshepsut's death, Thutmose III, already a grown man, continued her building program. He enlarged and decorated many of her monuments, though he replaced some with his own buildings. After Year 42 of his reign, for unknown reasons, the name of Hatshepsut was erased from all monuments and her memory obliterated: her statues were smashed, her representations in wall reliefs were destroyed, and screen walls were built around her obelisks between the fourth and fifth pylons in Karnak. The names of three Thutmoside kings replaced Hatshepsut's. In the later king lists the queen was omitted,

and only long and painstaking Egyptological research revealed her existence and accomplishments.

[*See also* Queens.]

BIBLIOGRAPHY

Dorman, P. F. *The Monuments of Senenmut.* London, 1988.
Forbes, Dennis C., ed. "Hatshepsut Special." *K.M.T.: A Modern Journal of Ancient Egypt* 1.1 (Spring, 1990), 4–33.
Ratié, S. *La reine Hatchepsout: sources et problèmes.* Leiden, 1979.
Seipel, Wilfried. "Hatschepsut." In *Lexikon der Ägyptologie* 2: 1045–1051. Wiesbaden, 1975.
Tyldesley, J. *Hatshepsut, the Female Pharaoh.* London, 1998.
Yoyotte, Jean, et al. "Hatshepsout, femme Pharaon." *Dossiers d'Archeologie* 187 (November, 1993).

JADWIGA LIPINSKA

HAWAWISH. *See* Akhmim.

HEALING. *See* Medicine; Magic, *article on* Magic in Medicine; *and* Disease.

HEDGEHOGS. Egyptologists have long maintained that from pharaonic monuments and representations in the round, two species of hedgehogs are identifiable—the long-eared hedgehog (*Hemiechinus auritus*) and the desert hedgehog (*Paraechinus aethiopicus*). Among the multitude of their portrayals, a sharp distinction is seldom clearly indicated. Also, the Old Egyptian name for "hedgehog" is not certain; it may have been *hnty* or *hnt₃*, but this term might have also referred to the North African porcupine (*Hystrix cristata*). Possibly, this designation applied to all hedgehogs, since they possess a coat of prickly spines. Hedgehogs still live in the region.

In the Gerzean period (Naqada II, 3500–3000 BCE), images of the hedgehog were included in human burials, notably in the form of ceramic vessels. Thereafter, the hedgehog was an important and recurring decorative motif. In tomb-chapel scenes of the Old and Middle Kingdoms, hedgehogs are sometimes on the prows of Nile ships as figureheads, looking backward; mostly, they occur in hunting scenes, scurrying along the sparsely vegetated desert margin, mating or about to vanish into the safety of their burrows. Occasionally, they can be seen snapping up a grasshopper. The ancient Egyptians also seem to have enjoyed eating hedgehogs; in offering processions, they are transported in small cages as spoils of the chase, presumably destined for the table of the deceased in the beyond.

During the Middle Kingdom, faience hedgehog statuettes were sometimes placed in tombs. By the New Kingdom, miniature hedgehogs, fashioned as scaraboids and amulets, were popular. Containers for eye-paint fashioned in their plump likeness are known from the Late period. The hedgehog was not associated with a specific deity in the pharaonic pantheon, but its repeated use indicates that its image bore a magical, protective significance; this is almost certainly linked with the hedgehog's characteristic defensive posture—rolling itself into a ball and covering the vulnerable parts of its body with its impenetrable mat of bristling spines—and its ability to resist venomous bites and stings. Some scholars have suggested that the hedgehog was also a symbol of regeneration. In the Ebers Papyrus, Spells 464–474, the animal's spines are mentioned in a remedy for curing baldness but a porcupine may be meant instead of a hedgehog there.

BIBLIOGRAPHY

Andrews, Carol. *Amulets of Ancient Egypt.* Austin, 1994. Excellent illustrated survey of amulets in pharaonic Egypt, including those of hedgehogs.

Boessneck, Joachim. *Die Tierwelt des alten Ägypten: Untersucht anhand kulturgeschichtlicher und zoologischer Quellen.* Munich, 1988. Provides an authoritative discussion on wildlife in ancient Egypt, including the hedgehog.

Droste zu Hülshoff, Vera von. *Der Igel im alten Ägypten.* Hildesheimer Ägyptologische Beiträge, 11. Hildesheim, 1980. This book will remain the definitive study on the hedgehog in ancient Egypt for the foreseeable future; however, a few of the interpretations offered for its symbolic role in antiquity seem speculative.

Houlihan, Patrick F. *The Animal World of the Pharaohs.* London and New York, 1996. Aimed at a general audience; surveys the ancient Egyptian animal world and contains several fine illustrations of hedgehogs; extensive bibliography.

Osborn, Dale J., and Ibrahim Helmy. *The Contemporary Land Mammals of Egypt (Including Sinai).* Fieldiana Zoology, n.s., 5. Chicago, 1980. Now the standard text on the land mammals of modern Egypt; includes much information on hedgehogs.

PATRICK F. HOULIHAN

HELIOPOLIS, one of the three major cities of ancient Egypt, along with Memphis and Thebes, located northeast of present-day Cairo (30°05′N, 31°20′E). Today the site is largely covered by the suburban Cairo settlements of el-Matariya and Tell Hisn. Unlike most ancient Egyptian sites, Heliopolis was situated not on the Nile River but inland, to the west of the river, to which it was connected by an ancient canal.

The ancient Egyptian name of the city was Iunu (*iwnw*; "pillar"), preserved also in Akkadian cuneiform, *a-na*, and in Biblical Hebrew, *on* (*Gn.* 41.45). The Greek name Heliopolis ("city of the sun") occurs in classical sources from Herodotus (c.450 BCE) onward, reflecting the city's association with solar theology.

Most of what is known about Heliopolis comes from textual sources rather than from archaeology. By the time of the Old Kingdom, the city was established as a center of astronomy, as reflected in the title of its high priest, "Chief of Observers." The city also had a reputation for learning and theological speculation, which it retained into Greco-Roman times; much of that was centered on the role of the sun in the creation and maintenance of the world and in the persons of the gods Atum and Re-Horakhty. Heliopolitan theology was summarized in the concept of the Ennead, the group of nine gods that embodied the creative source and chief forces of the universe. By the beginning of the Old Kingdom, that system had already been formulated into a coherent philosophy, and it continued to dominate Egyptian thought for the next three thousand years. [*See* Re and ReHorakhty.]

Despite the intellectual prominence of Heliopolis, little is known about the city itself. Its principal feature was a temple devoted to Atum and Re-Horakhty, the precise location and shape of which is uncertain. Today, the only standing monument is a large, twelfth dynasty obelisk, dedicated by Senwosret I. Earlier structures include the third dynasty fragmentary shrine of King Djoser, part of a sixth dynasty obelisk of King Tety, and several Old Kingdom tombs of high priests. A stela of Thutmose III, from the eighteenth dynasty, commemorates a wall that encloses the solar temple. Excavations have revealed some Ramessid construction—several temples and a cemetery for the Mnevis bulls (considered incarnations of the sun god). [*See* Bull Gods.]

Twentieth dynasty donation lists from the time of Ramesses III indicate that the temples at Heliopolis were second only to those of Amun at Thebes. After the Ramessid era, however, the fortunes of Heliopolis began to decline. Later building activity is known primarily from a few twenty-sixth dynasty Saite tombs and some circumvallations. The city was largely destroyed during the Persian invasions of 525 BCE and 343 BCE, although enough of its structures and reputation remained to attract tourists in Greco-Roman times, such as Herodotus. When Strabo visited the site in the late first century BCE, he found it partly abandoned. By the first century CE, most of its statuary and obelisks had been moved to Alexandria and Rome; its remaining structures then served as a quarry for the building of medieval Cairo. Today, apart from the standing obelisk of Senwosret I, the ancient site is commemorated only in the name "Heliopolis," which is still used to designate what has become the northeastern suburb of Cairo.

[*See also* Myths, *article on* Creation Myths.]

BIBLIOGRAPHY

Kákosy, Láslo. "Heliopolis." In *Lexikon der Ägyptologie,* 2: 1111–1113. Wiesbaden, 1977. A recent summary, intended as a basic reference for Egyptologists.

Kees, Hermann. *Ancient Egypt, a Cultural Topography.* Chicago, 1961. The most accessible summary of the history, archaeology, and significance of the site.

Petrie, William Matthew Flinders. *Heliopolis, Kafr Ammar and Shur-*

afa. Publications of the Egyptian Research Account and the British School of Archaeology in Egypt, vol. 24. London, 1915. Report of the only archaeological excavation of the site so far published in detail.

Porter, Bertha, and Rosalind L. B. Moss, *Topographical Bibliography of Ancient Egyptian Hieroglyphic Texts, Reliefs and Paintings,* vol. 4: *Lower and Middle Egypt.* Oxford, 1934. A list of all monuments from the site known at the time of publication, with summary bibliography.

JAMES P. ALLEN

HELIOPOLITAN COSMOGONY. *See* Myths, *article on* Creation Myths.

HELL. The principal sources for our knowledge of the Egyptian conception of hell are the so-called Books of the Underworld which are found inscribed on the walls of the royal tombs of the New Kingdom (eighteenth to twentieth dynasties) in the Valley of the Kings at Thebes, then later also on papyri and other funerary objects belonging to nonroyal persons. The chief subject of these richly illustrated books—the most important of which are the *Book of That Which Is in the Underworld* (*Book of the Hidden Room,* commonly known as the *Amduat*), the *Book of Gates,* and the *Book of Caverns*—is the nightly voyage of the sun god Re through the underworld. During this journey the sun god temporarily unites with the body of Osiris, the god of the dead, which is resting there, and this enables him to regenerate and to be reborn in the morning. Since the underworld also harbors the abode where the damned are punished and annihilated, these books contain vivid descriptions and depictions of this terrifying place.

The nocturnal journey of the sun god through the underworld is not yet a prominent theme in the oldest corpus of royal mortuary literature, the Pyramid Texts, and descriptions of hell are therefore absent from these spells. By contrast, the picture that emerges from the Books of the Underworld is reflected in the nonroyal funerary spells found in the Coffin Texts and the *Book of Going Forth by Day* (the *Book of the Dead*), even though these do not contain elaborate descriptions of hell either. This is not surprising, as these spells take it for granted that their owners have successfully passed the judgment of the dead and are therefore numbered among the blessed who follow the sun god Re on his eternal journey along the sky and through the underworld. Spells mentioning the dangers of the world of the damned which the blessed dead pass on this journey are plentiful, but these spells are aimed principally at steering clear of such dangers, and the subject of the fate of the damned is therefore usually avoided as well. The role of the divine pharaoh is different, however. During his life he had been the earthly in-carnation and representative of the sun god; his principal task had been to maintain the cosmic and social order (*maat*) established by the god at creation and to repel the forces of chaos which constantly threaten the ordered world. This he did either symbolically, by means of the daily temple ritual, or more literally, for example by hunting dangerous animals in the desert or fighting battles against Egypt's enemies, or by administering justice and punishing criminals. After his death the king "unites with the sun disk and his divine body merges with him who made him"; that is, he is identified with the sun god, and in this new existence he continues to perform the task of subduing the powers of chaos. This active role of king and sun god necessitates a detailed description of the punishment of the damned, who represent the forces of evil. Their fate is therefore described in terms similar to those used for earthly adversaries of the king and of Egypt: they are "enemies" who are "reckoned with," "overthrown," "repelled," "felled"; they are "under the feet of" the king or the god. The exact nature of their misdeeds is never spelled out, nor is there a direct relationship between their punishment and the crime they committed. There are no separate areas in hell for different categories of evildoers, nor is there any sort of Purgatory, where sinners can repent so that they can be admitted to the company of the followers of Re at a later stage. The crimes of those who are condemned to hell consist of nothing more and nothing less than having acted against the divine world order (*maat*) established at the beginning of creation; by doing so they have excluded themselves from *maat* and revealed themselves as representatives of chaos. After death they are forever reduced to the state of "non-being"—the chaotic state of the world before creation, for which they have shown themselves to be predestined by their behavior in life. For them there is no renewal of life, but only a second, definitive death. In mythological terms, they are the "gang of Seth," the god who brought death into the world by murdering Osiris, or the "children of Nut" (the mother of Seth), the first generation of mankind, who rebelled against Re.

The fate of the damned is in every respect the opposite of that of the blessed (*ꜣḫw*). When the righteous die and are mummified and buried with the proper rites, they successfully pass the judgment of the dead and start a new life in the company of Re and Osiris. Their limbs are "tied together" again, and the ritual of the Opening of the Mouth ensures that they regain control over their senses. Their bodies rest in their tombs, and at sunrise, when Re is reborn from the underworld in the east, their *ba*-souls leave the tomb unhindered and join the sun god. They spend a happy time in the Fields of Rushes (paradise), where they have plenty of cool air, food, drink, and sexual pleasures. At night, when Re once more enters the underworld in the west and unites with Osiris, they too return to their mummified bodies. When the damned (*mtw*) end their earthly lives, however, demons tear away their mummy wrappings and uncover their bodies, which are left to decompose. In the place to which they are condemned, the normal order of things is reversed, even to the extent that the damned have to walk upside down, eat their own excrement, and drink their own urine. Their hands are tied behind their backs, often around stakes; their heads and limbs are severed from their bodies and their flesh is cut off their bones; their hearts are taken out; their *ba*-souls are separated from their bodies, forever unable to return to them; and even their shadows are wiped out. They have no air and suffer from hunger and thirst, for they receive no funerary offerings. Worst of all, they are denied the revivifying light of the sun god, who ignores them, even though they cry out loud and wail when he passes them in the underworld at night. Thus, they are excluded from the eternal cosmic cycle of the renewal of life. Instead, they are assigned to the "outer darkness" (*kkw sm3w*), the primeval darkness of the chaotic world before creation, which is situated in the deepest recesses of the underworld, outside the created world. There they are punished by demons, the representatives of chaos, who are often recruited from the ranks of the damned dead (*mtw*) themselves, so that they torture and kill one another. They are subjected to knives and swords and to the fire of hell, often kindled by fire-spitting snakes.

These terrible punishments are carried out in the "slaughtering place" (*nmt*) or "place of destruction" (*ḥtmyt*), presided over by the fierce goddess Sakhmet, whose butchers (*nmtyw*) hack their victims to pieces and burn them with inextinguishable fire, sometimes in deep pits (*ḥ3dw*) or in cauldrons (*wḥ3wt*) in which they are scorched, cooked, and reduced to ashes; demons feed on their entrails and drink their blood. Another location is the Lake of Fire (*š n sḏt*), which is already mentioned in the so-called *Book of Two Ways* in the Coffin Texts (Spell 1054/1166) and illustrated in the *Book of Going Forth by Day* (chapter 126). Like the "outer darkness," it is a place of regeneration for the sun god and his blessed followers, to whom it provides nourishment and cool water, but a place of destruction for the damned. Birds fly away from it when they see its burning, bloody water and smell the stench of putrefaction which rises up from it. In the vignette of chapter 126, its shores are guarded by "the four baboons who sit at the bow of the bark of Re," and who are usually associated with sunrise. Here they figure as the judges of the divine tribunal "who judge the poor as well as the rich" and who decide who is going to be granted access through "the secret portals of the West" and who will be delivered to the hellhound, who, according to another spell (CT 335 BD 17), is in charge of this place, the "Swallower of Millions" who "devours

corpses (or shadows), snatches hearts and inflicts injury without being seen."

At the end of the eighteenth dynasty, a similar monster appears in the well-known vignette of chapter 125 of the *Book of Going Forth by Day* that shows the judgment of the deceased before the divine tribunal. In this scene, the heart of the deceased is weighed in the balance against a feather, the symbol of *maat*. In many cases, the Lake of Fire of chapter 126 is also shown in this vignette. A late (Demotic) text explains that "if his evil deeds outnumber his good deeds he is delivered to the Swallower . . . ; his soul as well as his body are destroyed and never will he breathe again." In the vignette this monster is called "Swallower of the Damned" ('*mt mtw*); she is depicted with the head of a crocodile, the forelegs and body of a lion, and the hindquarters of a hippopotamus. Another name for her is *š3yt* ("beast of destiny"). She is usually sitting close to the balance, ready to devour her victim, but since the owner of the *Book of Going Forth by Day* in question is naturally supposed to survive the judgment, the Swallower is almost never shown grabbing her prey. Only a few very late instances dating to Roman times depict this; in one case, the monster is sitting beside a fiery cauldron into which the emaciated bodies of the damned, stripped of their mummy wrappings, are thrown.

In these late times, Egyptian conceptions began to be influenced by images from elsewhere in the Hellenistic world, as is shown by a representation of the Swallower that is very reminiscent of the Greek Sphinx, who was also a demon of fate and death. In their turn, later Egyptian representations of the Christian Hell, from Coptic and other early Christian texts, may well have influenced medieval European descriptions and depictions of the Inferno.

[*See also* Afterlife; Book of Going Forth by Day; Book of That Which Is in the Underworld; Demons; Ethics and Morality; Judgment of the Dead; *and* Paradise.]

BIBLIOGRAPHY

Hornung, Erik, *Ägyptische Unterweltsbücher*. Zürich and Munich, 1972; 2d edn., 1984. Offers complete and reliable translations of the *Amduat*, *Book of Gates*, *Book of Caverns*, and *Book of the Earth*, and excerpts from related compositions such as the *Litany of Re* and the *Books of Day and Night*. With introduction, notes and bibliography.

Hornung, Erik. *Altägyptische Höllenvorstellungen*. Abhandlungen der Sächsischen Akademie der Wissenschaften zu Leipzig, Philologisch-historische Klasse, 59:3. Berlin, 1968. An authoritative account of the Egyptian conceptions of Hell, the only monograph on the subject.

Piankoff, Alexandre, and N. Rambova. *The Tomb of Ramesses VI*. Bollingen Series, 40.1. New York, 1954. Vol. 1 contains English translations of all of the Books of the Underworld represented on the walls of this magnificent royal tomb, including the *Amduat*, *Book of Gates*, *Book of Caverns*, etc. Vol. 2 is a complete photographic record of the tomb and its decoration.

Seeber, Christine. *Untersuchungen zur Darstellung des Totengerichts im Alten Ägypten.* Münchner Ägyptologische Studien, 35. Munich and Berlin, 1976. Detailed study of the depictions of the Judgment of the Dead in papyri and on tomb walls, sarcophagi, etc., from the eighteenth dynasty down to Roman times. Also contains thorough discussions of the hybrid monster who devours the damned and of the Lake of Fire.

Velde, Herman te. "Dämonen." In *Lexikon der Ägyptologie,* 1: 980–984. Short but very informative article (in English) on demons, who are defined as representatives of chaos.

Zandee, Jan. *Death as an Enemy According to Ancient Egyptian Conceptions.* Leiden, 1960. This book deals with the negative aspects of death; it provides a detailed catalogue of the dangers which face the deceased in the hereafter and of the rich vocabulary used to describe these dangers. The material is drawn from the Pyramid Texts, Coffin Texts, *Book of Going Forth by Day,* and later funerary compositions, as well as the various Books of the Underworld. Separate chapters deal with representations of the netherworld in Demotic literature and punishments in the hereafter according to Coptic texts.

JACOBUS VAN DIJK

HEMATITE. *See* Gems.

HEMEROLOGIES. *See* Horoscopes.

HERAKLEOPOLIS, the capital of the twentieth Upper Egyptian nome (province), at the entrance to the Faiyum. The exact location of Herakleopolis is unclear, and the name is a general designation for an area encompassing the present-day villages of Ihnasiya, Kom el Aqarib, and Sedment, which are in close proximity (29°5′N, 30°56′E). To the southwest of Ihnasiya are the remains of a temple to the ram-headed deity Heryshef, who was known to the Greeks as Harsaphes and equated by them with Herakles, after whom the city was named in the Classical period. The earliest occupation of Herakleopolis is not known. The first phases of the temple date to the twelfth dynasty, and it remained in use throughout the Late period. The other important archaeological remains are the cemeteries that date from the First Intermediate Period through the Roman occupation.

Until the Late period, the city was known in Egyptian as *Nn(w)-nswt.* Many variant spellings existed, the most important of which was *Ḥnn-nswt.* In the Late period, that alternative spelling was reinterpreted as *Ḥwt-nn-nswt,* which became Hnes in Coptic and then Ahnas or Ihnasiya in Arabic. The full designation for the current village Ihnasiya is Ihnasiya el-Medina.

HAERAKLEOPOLIS. *Portal and columns.* The portal is probably a Ptolemaic period gate leading into the *temenos* of the local god. The columns are from the city's agora. (Courtesy Donald B. Redford)

HERAKLEOPOLIS. *Inscribed Ramessid-era blocks.* (Courtesy Donald B. Redford)

Herakleopolis was the capital not only of its nome but also of Egypt's northern kingdom during the time of intermittent civil strife known as the First Intermediate Period. Almost nothing is known of the Herakleopolitan kings, some of whom were named Kheti. The most famous king was Merikare, who was the addressee of a Middle Egyptian treatise on kingship, *Instructions for Merikare.* The Herakleopolitan kings were buried at Saqqara and perhaps elsewhere; no royal burials have been found at Herakleopolis itself. Toward the end of the twentieth dynasty, Libyan groups moved east into Egypt and settled in and around Herakleopolis. One of their descendants came to the throne in the twenty-second dynasty as Sheshonq I. Still another Libyan king, Peftjau(em)awybastet, ruled from Herakleopolis during the Third Intermediate Period, but his exact chronological position is not certain because he ruled concurrently with other rival pharaohs in other parts of Egypt. During the Late period, the city was home to a family of important shipping magnates.

Herakleopolis was first explored in 1891 by the Swiss archaeologist Edouard Naville on behalf of the Egypt Exploration Fund (now Society) in London. Naville's most important finds were "Coptic" reliefs distinguished by their angular and deep carving. Herakleopolis is the type site for works in this renowned style. Whether all the reliefs found at the site were made there or in other areas is not certain. Although these reliefs are most often termed "Coptic," the predominance of scenes from classical mythology has been cited often to indicate the problems of identifying Coptic art as Christian. In 1904, the British archaeologist William Matthew Flinders Petrie excavated at the temple. Among Petrie's many finds was a large quantity of ceramic oil lamps and molds. The lamps, now in the Petrie Museum of Egyptology, University College London, became an important dating tool. However, the most important campaign did not begin until 1966, when a Spanish mission explored the First Intermediate Period cemetery. A group of coffins and niche stelae was then discovered, whose epigraphy has done much toward the development of criteria for distinguishing between monuments of the Herakleopolitan period and the later, similar works of the Middle Kingdom. The Spanish excavations have continued sporadically, and the finds have been divided between the Egyptian Museum, Cairo, and the National Archaeological Museum, Madrid.

BIBLIOGRAPHY

del Carmen Perez-Die, María. "La réutilisation de la nécropole de la Troisième Période Intermédiaire début de l'Époque Saïte à Êhnasya Medina (Hěrakléopolis Magna)." In *Stationen: Beiträge zur Kulturgeschichte Ägyptens. Rainer Stadelmann gewidmet,* edited by Heike Guksch and Daniel Polz, pp. 473–483. Mainz, 1998.

del Carmen Perez-Die, María, and Pascal Vernus. *Excavaciones en Eh-*

nasya el Medina (Hĕracleópolis Magna). Madrid, 1992. Contains important summary of work at Herakleopolis and extensive bibliography.

Gomaà, Farouk. "Herakleopolis Magna." In Lexikon der Ägyptologie, 2: 1124–1128. Wiesbaden, 1971.

Lopez, Jesús. "Rapport préliminaire sur les fouilles d'Héracléopolis." Oriens Antiquus 13 (1974), 299–316; 14 (1975), 57–78.

Mokhtar, Gamal. Ihnâsya el Medina (Herakleopolis Magna). Bibliothèque d'Ètude, 40. Cairo, 1983.

Monneret de Villard, Ugo. La scultura ad Ahnâs. Note sull'origine dell'arte copta. Milan, 1923.

Naville, Edouard. Ahnas el Medineh. London, 1894.

Roccati, Alessandro. "I testi dei sarcofagi di Eracleopoli." Oriens Antiquus 13 (1974), 161–197.

DONALD B. SPANEL

HERIHOR, a general and high priest of Amun, who flourished about 1087 BCE. On the confused stage of late Ramessid history, in the nineteenth year of rule of Ramesses XI, the last pharaoh of the twentieth dynasty, Herihor ("Horus-is-chief") was apparently delegated to restore order over the Southern half of Egypt, particularly the Theban region. Before then, virtually nothing is known about him, but his titulary indicates that he had become the highest military official in the land, by which time he likely was fairly advanced in age. Information about Herihor's family background is rather tenuous, except for indications that he may have been related by blood or by marriage to the royal family and that Smendes, his Northern counterpart, may have been his (eldest?) son by his wife Nodjmet. Since Herihor had at least nineteen sons, he must have had another wife later in his life. Judging from the names of some of his sons in a relief in the Khonsu temple at Karnak, Herihor may have been of Libyan extraction—hardly surprising for the late Ramessid era.

Herihor's sudden promotion was certainly connected with the institution of the wḥmśwt ("Renaissance," lit., "repeating-of-births") era in the Theban region. For the next seven years or so, official notices in the South were dated according to the Renaissance rather than the king's regnal years. Herihor's sudden ascendancy is most likely connected with the inability of Panehsy, the viceroy of Nubia, to pacify southern Egypt in the aftermath of the obscure "War of the High Priest," during which the high priest of Amun, Amenhotep, had been "suppressed" and replaced by Ramesses-nakhte (II). The heavy preponderance of army-related offices that Herihor held shows that he was primarily a military governor. The division of power between Herihor, effectively the ruler of the South, and Smendes, his counterpart at Tanis in the North, set a pattern for Egypt's governance that was to carry over into the early part of the Third Intermediate Period, following Ramesses XI's death.

After this appointment, Herihor styled himself "High Priest of Amun, the Generalissimo (Great Overseer) of the Army, Army-Chief, and Captain at the Forefront of the Army of the Entirety of Egypt," an unprecedented combination of religious and military offices. His activities were certainly wide-ranging. Those who had robbed the royal tombs and temples were quickly tried and punished. Once the trials were completed, Herihor may have initiated the removal of the royal corpses and their equipment from their tombs. He appears to have replaced Panehsy as King's Son of Kush, and then to have conducted a campaign against him in Nubia.

Herihor eventually assumed the role of vizier, thereby concentrating the supreme civil and religious offices in the South under his control. In the fifth year of the Renaissance, he dispatched Wenamun, an official of the Karnak temple, to Lebanon for timber in order to refurbish the Userhet bark of Amun, a mission that also needed Smendes's approval. In a group of scenes and inscriptions within the Khonsu temple at Karnak, Herihor assumes the royal prerogative of writing his name in a fivefold titulary, with his title as high priest and his last name enclosed in cartouches. His "kingship," however, appears only here and on his burial equipment. Herihor seems to have died shortly thereafter, during the seventh year of the Renaissance. He was succeeded in most of his offices by a certain Piankh, who was not his son, as has previously been thought. After Year 10, no further dates in the Renaissance are attested, and dating according to the year of Ramesses XI was resumed for the rest of his reign.

BIBLIOGRAPHY

Beckerath, J. von. "Zur Chronologie der XXI. Dynastie." In Gedenkschrift für Winfried Barta, edited by D. Kessler and R. Schulz, pp. 49–55. Frankfurt am Main, 1995. A detailed refutation of key aspects of Jansen-Winkeln's proposals for a revision of late twentieth dynasty history.

Cerný, J. "Egypt: From the Death of Ramesses III to the End of the Twenty-first Dynasty." In Cambridge Ancient History, vol. 2, pp. 606–657. Cambridge, 1975. Somewhat out of date, but reliable on most of its major points.

Goelet, O. "A New 'Robbery' Papyrus: Rochester MAG 51.346.1." Journal of Egyptian Archaeology 82 (1996), 107–127. Publication of a recent papyrus find, revealing thefts at the Karnak temple, which probably would have led to the discrediting of the Theban hierarchy and the subsequent installation of Herihor at the beginning of the Renaissance.

Jansen-Winkeln, K. "Das Ende des Neuen Reiches." Zeitschrift für Ägyptische Sprache und Altertumskunde 119 (1992), 22–37. A controversial study of the events and personalities at the end of the twentieth dynasty.

Kitchen, K. A. The Third Intermediate Period in Egypt (1100–650 BC). 2d ed., with supplement and preface. Warminster, 1995. Recently updated, and still by far the most comprehensive and accurate source for the history, genealogies, and dating systems of the late twentieth dynasty.

OGDEN GOELET

HERMOPOLIS. The site of the ruins of the ancient city of Hermopolis (Magna) lies to the northwest of the city of Mallawi in the governorate of el-Minia in Middle Egypt. The southern side of the ancient hill (or *tell*) is covered by the large village of el-Ashmunein, while today the village of el-Idara is situated on the northern side. Sandy mounds, which were swept up by an ancient arm of the Nile in the middle of the cultivation area, formed the foundation for a settlement, which is attested only from the time of the fourth dynasty by inscriptions from its cemetery near Bersheh, but may well be older. From an early date, the place was called Khemenu ("the City of the Eight")—that is, the city of the eight primeval gods of the so-called Hermopolitan creation of the world. Another name was Wenu ("the City of Hares"), probably derived from the name of the fifteenth Upper Egyptian district, which had as its emblem the royal hare standard, and its administrative center in Hermopolis. The present-day name el-Ashmunein was derived from Khemenu by way of the Coptic place-name Shmun. The chief god of the place was the god of the moon and administration, Thoth, whom the Greeks identified with Hermes, hence their name Hermopolis ("the City of Hermes"). During the Greco-Roman period, Hermopolis was the metropolis of the district (Gr., *nomos*) of Hermapolites, which belonged to the larger unit of the Upper Egyptian region Thebais.

From 1673, reports from European travelers about the ruins of Ashmunein began to appear. The first archaeological map with a detailed description of Hermopolis is found in the French *Description de l'Égypte* by Jomard, a member of Napoleon's Egyptian Expedition in 1798–1799. The hall of columns (portico) of the temple of Thoth, which was still standing at that time, was destroyed in about 1825. In the nineteenth century, the cultivation fields of the ancient city were given over, with official sanction, to the surface extraction of organic fertilizers; in the most recent period, trains were used to transport the material. The numerous small objects that were found led to a lively trade in antiques, which continues even today.

Toward the turn of the twentieth century, papyri, most of them in Greek, were uncovered in the ruins of houses from the Roman period by official investigators—Germans (Rubenssohn and others) and Italians (Breccia and others) between 1902 and 1904 or 1905. Between 1929 and 1939, the central part of the hill, the area south of the temple of Thoth itself, was explored by a Hildesheim expedition under the leadership of Günther Roeder. Among the areas unearthed were the hypostyle hall of the temple of Thoth, the southern sacred complex at el-Ashmunein, and the area of the central basilica of Ptolemy III, which was transformed into a church in the fifth century CE. Under the direction of A. Spencer, the British

Museum resumed the excavations in the central area between 1980 and 1990. As a result, burial sites of the First Intermediate Period were uncovered north of the Ramessid Amun temple. In the northwestern sector, houses from the Third Intermediate Period and from the beginning of the twenty-sixth dynasty were uncovered. In the context of a joint Polish-Egyptian project, the area of the Ptolemaic basilica was recently reexcavated and restored. Most recently, P. Grossman did research on a church complex from the late Roman period for the Deutsche Archäologische Institut in the southern sector.

Up to the present time, population pressure has been the cause of a large number of smaller excavations by the Egyptian Archaeological Service. The modern excavations run into two obstacles. The first is that the oldest layers are located below the water table, which is presently high. The other is that the excavations of the settlement hill have left behind a fragmented and irregular surface contour. Thus, especially underneath the modern village of el-Ashmunein and in the eastern sector, there are still parts of the city left standing (including a water tower) that date from the late Greco-Roman and early Arabian period. Elsewhere, broad areas with their more ancient layers have been completely destroyed.

Hermopolis was always an important administrative city and also, because of its temple of Thoth, a significant religious center. It was surrounded by fertile farmland. From the time of the New Kingdom, a wide elevated canal connected the city with the Nile, and a westerly route to Tuna el-Gebel led on to the Bahariya Oasis. The royal administrators of the District of the Hare had themselves buried in the necropolises of Sheikh Said and Bersheh. Beginning in the New Kingdom, they were buried to the west near Tuna el-Gebel, while the mass of the population often merely sought out free spots within the city itself. The nomarch of Hermopolis, who was often also the high priest and thus controlled the temple of Thoth, must certainly have played a decisive role in the unification of the kingdom of Thebes under Montuhotep I, and again later in the unrest that occurred when Amenemhet I was removed from the throne. For a long time he was able to enjoy a largely independent status. Under his control were the calcite (Egyptian alabaster) mining areas in the east, which were important for the pharaoh from the time of the Old Kingdom, particularly the quarry of Hatnub. From the Middle Kingdom, a structure from the temple of Amun dated to Amenemhet II has been preserved. As early as the end of the Middle Kingdom, after the breakup of the districts of the Old Kingdom, Hermopolis—together with the northern fortification and temple cities of Herwer and Neferusi—was the center of a large territory characterized largely by farming, which extended from Tuna el-Gebel in the north to Gebel Abu el-Foda to the

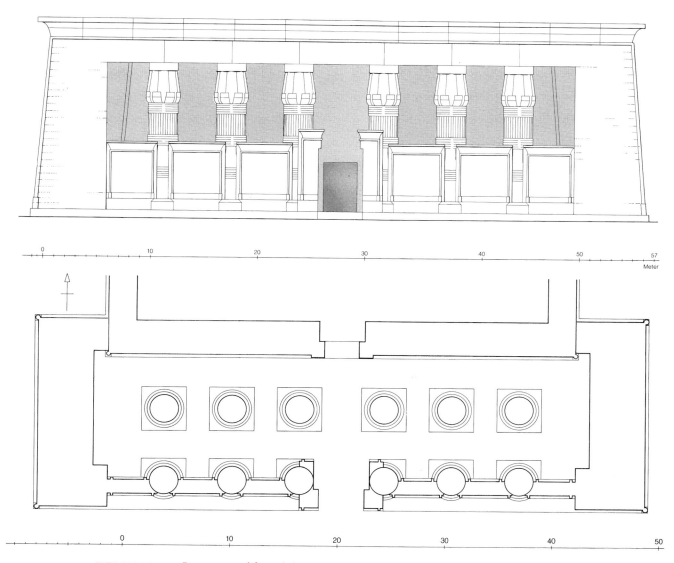

HERMOPOLIS. *Reconstructed frontal elevation and plan of the pronaos of Nektanebo I, thirtieth dynasty.* (From: Dieter Arnold, *Temples of the Last Pharaohs.* New York, 1999.)

north of Asyut. Officially, at that time, Hermopolis was in the region of Neferusi. Under the New Kingdom, the temple of Thoth of Hermopolis was constantly rebuilt and expanded. An altar of Amenhotpe II stood near the entrance at the Dromos. In the foundations of the temple of Thoth of the thirtieth dynasty were found pieces of colossal baboons made of quartzite, dating from the time of Amenhotpe III: they have since been erected in the northern sector. Horemheb erected a new southern entrance pylon for the temple of Thoth. Nearby Tell el-Amarna, with the easily accessible blocks of the ancient residence of Akhenaten, provided the material for the numerous new buildings erected under Ramesses II. In the area of the temple

of Thoth, Ramesses II erected an entrance pylon, cobbled the court to the south of the Horemheb pylon, and rededicated the cult to Amun by means of a temple that was oriented on an east–west line. Further decoration was subsequently added by Merenptah and Sethos II. The temple took into consideration the cemetery of the First Intermediate Period, which had long existed. Possibly this slightly elevated spot was seen as the place of the primeval hill in the Hermopolitan myth of creation. The location of the sacred lake is unknown; it must have corresponded to the Lake of Fire or the Island of the Hermopolitan Creation. Another sacred complex, dating from the time of Ramesses III, was situated in the southern part of the

HERMOPOLIS. *Roman ruins.* (Courtesy David P. Silverman)

temple of Thoth. Here there were possibly chapels of various gods; in any case, the texts refer to numerous buildings in Hermopolis in honor of Osiris, Ptah, Horus, Hathor, Mut, and the southern Thoth, and also statues of the protector gods of the city in the shape of baboon and ibis which stood in the courts. As yet it has been impossible to locate most of the chapel, or the very ancient "house of the (bird) net."

In the Libyan period, Osorkon III established numerous new productive estates for the temple of Thoth. As Libyan central control became weaker, the Libyan military leader of Hermopolis was able to claim for himself the title of pharaoh. A certain Namlot became the founder of his own Hermopolitan royal dynasty. It is suspected that his palace was in the western part of the temple area and separated off by a wall. When the Kushite Piya of Thebes pushed northward (twenty-fifth dynasty), he met resistance from another Namlot, who had entered into an alliance against Herakleopolis with the ruler of Sais and Memphis. Finally, after a prolonged siege by the fleet of Piya he was subverted to Kushite hegemony and was obliged to supply horses; however, he was able to retain the title of king. His successors maintained friendly relations with Thebes. It was only Psamtik I who managed to put an end to the city's autonomy.

A subsequent renovation of the central part of the temple of Thoth took place under Nektanebo I and Nektanebo II, and the temple was further expanded under Philip Arrhidaeus. The sacred precinct was surrounded by a thick quadrilateral wall made of mud brick. The southern access to the temple (later called the Dromos of Hermes), at the pylon of Ramesses II, was the so-called Gate of the Sphinx. The Antinoitic Road, running along the southern wall of the temple, led to Tuna el-Gebel in the west and to Antinoöpolis in the east, and divided the city into a northern and a southern half. To the east of the temple of Thoth there was a temple built under the Roman emperor Domitian, probably dedicated to the goddess consort of Thoth, Nehmetaway. Under Nero, the southern temple of Ramesses II was expanded. In Roman times, Hermopolis increasingly evolved into a major regional center. Its main harbor was situated on the eastern bank of the Nile near the later city of Antinoöpolis. Greek and Roman soldiers were served by religious and social institutions such as the Komasterion, several Serapis shrines, and a Mithras shrine.

BIBLIOGRAPHY

Arnold, D. "Zur Rekonstruktion des Pronaos von Hermopolis." *Mitteilungen des Deutschen Archäologischen Instituts* 50 (1994).

Hanke, Ranier. "Amarna-Reliefs aus Hermopolis." In *Hildesheimer Ägyptische Beiträge*, 2. Hildesheim, 1978.

Mysliwiec, K. "Der Kopf einer Statue Nektanebos I aus Hermopolis

Magna." *Mitteilungen des Deutschen Archäologischen Instituts* 47 (1991), 263–268.

Polish-Egyptian Archaeological and Preservation Mission at el-Ashmunein. *Reports from Ashmunein*. 2 vols. Warsaw, 1989, 1992.

Roeder, Günther. *Hermopolis 1929–1939: Ausgrabungen der Deutschen Hermopolisexpedition in Hermopolis, Ober-Ägypten*. Hildesheim, 1959. Summary of earlier expeditions, also described in detailed preliminary reports of the German Archaeological Institute, 1931–1939.

Roeder, Günther. "Zwei hieroglyphische Inschriften aus Hermopolis." *Annales du Service des Antiquités Égyptiennes* 29 (1939), 315–442.

Roeder, Günther. *Amarna Reliefs aus Hermopolis: Ausgrabungen der Deutschen Hermopolis-Expedition in Hermopolis 1929–1939*. Vol. 2. Hildesheim, 1969.

Spencer, A. J. *Excavations at el-Ashmunein, British Expedition to Middle Egypt*. 4 vols. London. Vol. 1 covers site topography; vol. 2, the temple area; vol. 3, the town; and vol. 4, Hermopolis Magna (buildings of Ashmunein).

Wace, A.J.B., et al. *Hermopolis Magna, Ashmunein: The Ptolemaic Sanctuary and the Basilica*. Alexandria, 1959.

DIETER KESSLER
Translated from German by Robert E. Shillenn

HERMOPOLITAN COSMOGONY. *See* Myths, *article on* Creation Myths.

HERODOTUS. Greek historian (c.484–c.420 BCE). Born in Halicarnassus (present-day Bodrum) in southwestern Asia Minor, he was related to the epic poet Panyassis, and the family was active in city politics, a situation which led to Herodotus's departure (probably to exile) in the 450s. He traveled widely, though in what capacity we do not know, and eventually settled in Thurii in southern Italy, where he probably died. His only extant work is the *History*, a nine-book exploration of the conflict between the Greek states and the Persian Empire from the sixth century to 478. The early books describe the preliminaries to the invasions of Greece by the Persian emperors Darius and Xerxes and are used to define the religious, cultural, and moral issues as seen from a Greek perspective. Therefore, they serve not only to outline the expansion of the Persian Empire but also to characterize both the Greek states and the peoples brought under Persian control, building a picture of the resources of the empire and creating a dynamic sense of approaching menace, which ends with the crescendo of the great assaults on Greece in 490 and 480. Within this context, Egypt—a major part of the Persian Empire—receives fuller treatment than any other state. The whole of book II is devoted to it, as well as the early section of book III though references to things Egyptian also occur elsewhere in the work.

Herodotus's sources for Egypt are easily identified. He is much given to emphasizing his autonomy in acquiring information, describing his entire work as a "(personal) enquiry," and he claims to have traveled throughout the country himself, a claim which is generally, though not universally, conceded. (The date of this visit is probably between 449 and 430.) For the first ninety-eight chapters, he insists on his use of *autopsy*, or personal analysis and oral inquiry (II,99,1). Subsequently he continues to employ *autopsy* but also draws on Egyptian tradition, gleaned particularly from priests but also from Egyptians in general, local sources, and once an interpreter. From the point of book II,147,1, non-Egyptian traditions assume major importance. These would have been overwhelmingly Greeks and Carians, but Libyans and Colchians also feature. Nevertheless, Herodotus did have his precursors in writing on Egypt. Homer spoke of it and played a significant, if unobvious, role in setting the agenda for discourse on that mysterious land, and other epic writers as well as Greek dramatists made significant contributions to the body of data, opinion, and attitude on which Herodotus drew. The major written sources that either fed him or provided points of departure or reaction were Anaximander for geography, geology, and meteorology and Hecataeus for cartography, geography, ethnography, botany, mythology, and legends; neither, however, is explicitly acknowledged as a quarry of information, and much research has been expended in trying to determine the extent of his indebtedness to these two authors.

Herodotus's account of Egypt is all-embracing: at book II,1, he gives the justification for his discussion—the incorporation of Egypt into the Persian Empire—and then proceeds to investigate the antiquity of Egyptian civilization (2–4), the geography of Egypt (6–18), the Nile and its behavior (19–34), and Egyptian manners and customs, with particular emphasis on things religious (35–98). The geographical section is developed against the background of contemporary debates on the origins and structure of land masses. In the ethnographic excursus, the perspective is determined by a concern with differences between Egyptians and Greeks; the unwritten agenda is to define Greek ethnicity as well as that of the Egyptians. Not surprisingly, therefore, his attention is arrested by anything *thomasion* ("astonishing, marvelous") in Egyptian behavior. At the same time, he shows a remarkable willingness to admit Egyptian cultural priority in many areas, and there is a pervasive conviction that numerous elements in Greek civilization derived from Egypt, particularly in the sphere of religion. This conviction is based on little more than the operation of the *post hoc ergo propter hoc* fallacy: that is, if something in Egypt resembles something in Greece, it is argued that it must have come from Egypt because Egyptian civilization is so much older. The result is that many erroneous claims are made, but this has not prevented Herodotus's assertions and those of later and frequently derivative classical writers from being used to support highly dubious Afrocentric theories of cultural diffusion. The cultural picture is further distorted by a marked tendency to oversimplification, which leads him to convert trends into hard-and-fast rules.

At book II,99, Herodotus moves on to history, which he discusses in two sections: chapters 99–146 cover events from the beginning of Egyptian history to the seventh century, and chapters 147ff. study the Saite period and the Persian conquest. The history of Egypt, like that of all non-Greek peoples, is presented within a thoroughly Greek framework. It also shows a common Herodotean trait in its predilection for digression into excurses on matters that particularly interested him. However, the two historical sections differ considerably in character. The first is chronologically confused and consists largely of oral tradition customized to a greater or lesser extent for Greek consumption; its value as evidence lies in the insight it offers into the nature of Egyptian oral tradition on early history. Once Herodotus gets to the seventh century, things improve greatly. His account of the Saite dynasty and the Persian conquest is the earliest consecutive account that we have from any source, and it largely defined the parameters of the subject for later writers. Its points of emphasis are those of interest to Greeks, and the account is subject to Greek and Egyptian propaganda.

Caution is always required when dealing with Herodotus's data, but much valuable information is conveyed not only on historical events but also on Late period culture. The surprise is not that things sometimes go wrong, but that so much goes right.

BIBLIOGRAPHY

Armayor, O. Kimball. *Herodotus' Autopsy of the Fayoum: Lake Moeris and the Labyrinth of Egypt*. Amsterdam, 1985. A good example of the work of the liar-school which examines closely the section of Book II dealing with two features of Middle Egypt.

Fehling, D. *Herodotus and His "Sources."* 1989. A critique of Herodotus's veracity, well assessed by J. P. A. Gould: "There are problems, certainly, about believing everything that Herodotus says he saw or was told but they are not so great as the problem of recognizing Fehling's Herodotus in the text that we have."

Godley, A. D. *Herodotus*. Loeb Classical Library. 4 vols. London and New York, 1920–1924. A reliable translation with facing Greek text and some notes.

Gould, John. *Herodotus*. London, 1989. Probably the best discussion of Herodotus in English.

Hall, E. *Inventing the Barbarian: Greek Self-definition through Tragedy*. A brilliant exploration of Greek perceptions of ethnicity. Its position is exaggerated, but it is required reading.

Hartog, F. *The Mirror of Herodotus: The Representation of the Other in the Writing of History*. Berkeley and London, 1988. A penetrating and thought-provoking attempt to define Herodotus's conceptual world. Unmissable.

Hunter, Virginia. *Past and Process in Herodotus and Thucydides*. Princeton, 1982. Essential reading on the nature of fifth-century Greek historical thought.

Lloyd, Alan B. *Herodotus Book II*. Études préliminaires aux religions orientales dans l'empire romain, 43. 3 vols. Leiden, 1975–1993. The introduction contains a detailed discussion of the pre-Herodotean tradition and Herodotus's sources and methods. The commentary addresses all aspects of Herodotus's discussion of Egypt.

Lloyd, Alan B. "Herodotus on Egyptian Buildings: A Test Case." In *The Greek World*, edited by Anton Powell, pp. 273–300. London and New York, 1995. An evaluation of Herodotus's capacity for accuracy against the evidence of buildings which still survive.

Pritchett, W. Kendrick. *The Liar School of Herodotus*. Amsterdam, 1993. Polemic against the position of Armayor and Fehling.

ALAN B. LLOYD

HIERAKONPOLIS, site known in ancient Egyptian as *Nekhen*, located on the western bank of the Nile in Upper Egypt (25°06′N, 32°46′E). The site is intimately associated with kingship and the formation of the unified Egyptian state. The city was the major cult center of the god Horus, to whom every king of Egypt was assimilated and whose sacred bird figured in its later Greek name, Hierakonpolis ("city of the falcon"). Currently, the site is known in Arabic as *Kom el-Ahmar* ("the red mound"), after the potsherds heaped at the entrance to the low desert; but this descriptive name well suits the entire expanse of the vast site. The enormous growth of the settlement in late predynastic times (c.3500 BCE) testifies to the importance of Hierakonpolis as a regional center of power, possibly as the capital of an early, pre-unification kingdom.

Today, Hierakonpolis appears as two separate archaeological zones. One zone is the low mound located in the floodplain, constituting the remains of the town and the temple mound of the dynastic period site of Nekhen. The other zone has a group of interrelated sites, stretching for 3.5 kilometers (more than 2 miles) across the low desert and extending westward for 2 kilometers (about 1.5 miles) into a wadi of the Western Desert. These desert sites represent the largest Predynastic town still extant and accessible.

The first scientific exploration of Hierakonpolis was conducted from 1897 to 1899, by the British Egyptologists James E. Quibell and Fredrick W. Green. Within their first week of excavation on the town mound of Nekhen, they discovered the gold-headed cult statue of the falcon god Horus, as well as the life-sized copper statue of King Pepy I of the sixth dynasty and a smaller version, the earliest large-scale metal statuary known from antiquity. They were found beneath the floor of a mud-brick temple replacing an earlier shrine that once stood on a mound of clean, white sand supported by an oval stone wall. Presumably at this early shrine, the famous caches of discarded temple furnishings and votive offerings, known collectively as the "Main Deposit," were originally dedicated. Among the hundreds of ivory, stone, and faience objects were some of the most important documents of the Early Dynastic period, among others, the large ceremonial mace heads of King "Scorpion" and Narmer, as well as the Narmer Palette. The discoveries support the ancient traditions about the importance of Hierakonpolis.

Although the site was subsequently investigated by a number of scholars, not until the ongoing expedition (led first by Walter Fairservis of Vassar College and later by Michael Hoffman of the University of South Carolina) began in 1967 did the Predynastic underpinnings of these traditions become evident. As a result of their work, a full picture of the city emerged and, with it, a better understanding of the developments that led to the rise of the world's first nation-state, at about 3100 BCE.

Intensive surveys and excavations have identified several functional zones within the vast desert town, and these include cemeteries, residential quarters, pottery kilns, breweries, ceremonial centers, petroglyph stations, and stone-built structures that were perhaps for administrative uses. The early complexity of Predynastic society was deduced from a series of kilns excavated in the wadi, which specialized in the production of fine black-topped pottery to be used for grave goods. Within the town, several potters were responsible for supplying utilitarian wares. Clearly, by 3500 BCE, craft specialization had been well developed.

Beer was another specialized product. At the desert's edge, there was an installation of huge pottery vats for brewing wheat-based beer; nearby, there was a kiln that manufactured standard-sized jars in which to package it. Egypt's earliest brewery has been estimated to produce about three hundred gallons of beer per day. At that rate, the brewery could supply a daily ration for more than two hundred people. So far, only a small fraction of that brewing quarter has been investigated. Thus, much of Hierakonpolis's greatness may stem from the organization of a Predynastic, redistributive economy. [See Beer.]

The growing social distinctions in Predynastic society were emphasized by separate cemeteries for the elite, the middle class, and the lower class. One elite cemetery is the site of the only known decorated, Predynastic tomb (about 1 kilometer to the south of the town). Renowned as the "Painted Tomb," its paint-on-plaster walls provide the earliest examples of design motifs that would designate Egyptian kingship for the next three thousand years, including scenes of animal taming, the smiting of enemies, and the funerary flotilla. The owner of this tomb must have been a king and as such may have been crowned in Egypt's earliest religious complex. The religious complex was discovered in 1987, in the midst of the desert town. The complex included a tripartite shrine made out of mats and poles, fronted by four huge posts that faced onto a fenced, oval courtyard. The remains are similar to the Early Dynastic representations of the archetypal shrine of Upper Egypt, known as the *pr-wr* ("great

house"). The home of this great shrine has long been thought to be at Hierakonpolis and it is possible that the recently uncovered remnants may be this very structure, later recreated in stone at the Saqqara Step Pyramid complex. When, owing to factors not yet understood, the desert town was abandoned and the population moved onto the floodplain, this complex was also abandoned for the new temple within the walls of Nekhen.

At Nekhen, a palace was found to the east of the temple in 1969; it had been used throughout the first two Egyptian dynasties. It is the only known example of niched-brick architecture in a nonmortuary context. In contrast, there is the large rectangular mortuary enclosure standing at the desert's edge, built by Khasekhemwy, the last king of the second dynasty. The oldest standing mud-brick building in the world, its once white-plastered, niched walls rise to a height of 11 meters (34 feet) and are about 5 meters (15 feet) thick. This king was buried at Abydos, so why he built this commanding structure at Hierakonpolis remains unknown—but it may be his cenotaph.

After the Early Dynastic period, Hierakonpolis declined from a national to only a provincial center. The continued royal concern with its patron deity Horus, however, is clear from finds on the temple mound and from the tomb stela of the local official Horemkhawef, who boasted that he was commissioned to fetch a new cult image by a thirteenth dynasty king. In the eighteenth dynasty, Hatshepsut and Thutmose III built Horus a new temple. Later refurbished by Ramesses XI, the last king of the twentieth dynasty, it is illustrated in great detail on the walls of the local tomb of the priest Hormose.

A combination of changing environmental factors and the changing political map of Egypt led to the diminution of Hierakonpolis; it was reduced to the status of an ancestral shrine. Even so, throughout the millennia its early significance was not forgotten by the ancient Egyptians. Still preserved in its soil remain some of the earliest evidence for the artistic and architectural forms of pharaonic times, as well as some of the social and economic concepts that propelled Egypt into its development as one of the great nations of antiquity.

[See also Early Dynastic Period.]

BIBLIOGRAPHY

Adams, Barbara. *Ancient Nekhen: Garstang in the City of Hierakonpolis.* New Malden, 1995. Recommended overview of research in the context of the rise and fall of the city forms two important chapters; with full bibliography.

Friedman, Renée F. "The Ceremonial Centre at Hierakonpolis Locality HK29A." In *Aspects of Early Egypt,* edited by Jeffrey Spencer, pp. 16–35. London, 1996. Discussion of the Predynastic ceremonial complex within the desert town.

Friedman, Renée F., and Barbara Adams, eds. *The Followers of Horus: Studies Dedicated to Michael Allen Hoffman 1944–1990.* Oxford, 1992. Many contributions cover site discoveries since 1982; includes other topics related to the site and objects found there.

Hoffman, Michael A. *Egypt before the Pharaohs.* 2d rev. ed. Austin, 1991. Although the rate of new discoveries renders it out of date, provides a semipopular discussion of the entire Predynastic and Early Dynastic, with Hierakonpolis as its focus.

Hoffman, Michael A., et al. *The Predynastic of Hierakonpolis: An Interim Report.* Cairo and Macomb, Ill., 1982. Preliminary reports on excavations in the Predynastic town, as undertaken between 1978 and 1980.

Kemp, Barry J. *Ancient Egypt: Anatomy of a Civilization.* London, 1989. Various aspects of the site and objects found within it are cogently discussed.

Quibell, John, E. *Hierakonpolis,* vol. 1. London, 1900. Reprinted in 1989. Mainly photographs and line drawings of the artifacts from the "Main Deposit."

Quibell, John E., and Fredrick W. Green. *Hierakonpolis,* vol. 2. London, 1902. Reprinted in 1989. Account of the discoveries from 1897 to 1899.

RENÉE F. FRIEDMAN

HIPPOPOTAMI. The largest animal indigenous to Egypt was the hippopotamus (*Hippopotamus amphibius,* Egyptian *db* or *ḥȝb*). Numerous representations of this heavily built mammal, with its plump features and enormous mouth, indicate that it had been familiar to the inhabitants of Egypt since Predynastic times. For ages, the species dwelt in the marshes of the Nile Delta and along the banks of the Nile. Over the course of history, the population of hippopotami was gradually reduced to a few groups living in restricted areas in the Delta only. Hunting and the growing need for land for cultivation (which steadily diminished the environment suitable for wildlife) finally resulted in the complete extinction of the hippopotamus in Egypt in the early nineteenth century. Before this, the crocodile was the principal enemy of the hippopotamus in the animal world.

Although the hippopotamus is generally known to be peaceable by nature, it was regarded as an enemy by the Egyptian people. As herbivores, hippopotami do not generally attack people—leaving aside Manetho's dubious report that King Menes was carried off by a hippopotamus—unless forced to defend their lives, young, or territories from danger. If threatened or in agony (most often caused by humans), the animal might turn into an aggressive colossus whose fierce attacks and grim tenacity endangered everyone around. The hippopotamus was feared and despised not just because of its ferocity when threatened or its awesome appearance but also because its massiveness (a mature hippo can weigh more than three tons) and its voracious appetite, which seriously damaged

HIPPOPOTAMI. *Blue faience statuette from the twelfth dynasty, found in the tomb of Senbi at Meir.* The body of the hippopotamus is decorated with figures of lotus flowers, buds, and leaves. The statuette was presumably associated with fertility and the regenerative power of the Nile. (The Metropolitan Museum of Art, Gift of Edward S. Harkness, 1917. [17.9.1])

farmland. Whenever a shortage of preferred food, principally water plants, led the hungry animals to set foot on the land to replenish their vegetarian diet with readily available crops, they left a trail of devastation.

Prehistoric sketches, Early Dynastic decorated pottery, and wall paintings and reliefs in Old Kingdom *mastabas* and in Middle and New Kingdom tombs frequently depict hippopotamus hunting. According to depictions and texts ranging from the Old Kingdom (tomb of Sesh-seshet, sixth dynasty) to Ptolemaic times (primarily at Edfu), the usual method was to harpoon the animal and drag it ashore with the attached ropes. Occasionally, some of these animals may have been kept alive in enclosures, but there are no indications of attempts at domestication. Anyone—god, king, or man—who was able to kill a hippopotamus was considered a hero.

The hippopotamus was valuable game. Although it is not mentioned in food-offering lists, archaeological finds suggest that the meat was used for human consumption. In some parts of Africa today, hippopotamus meat is considered a delicacy. The enormous teeth provided good-quality ivory, while bones, tails, skin, and fat served various purposes, including as ingredients in medicines.

Great amounts of artifacts from all periods, such as domestic utensils, amulets, and apotropaic objects have been found throughout Egypt, including numerous small blue faience statuettes of hippopotami, grave gifts that are often decorated with floral elements. These figurines probably refer to the desirability of the hippopotamus as game and not, as is often suggested, to its religious association with the deities Taweret and Seth. The goddess Taweret ("the Great One," Greek Thoeris) is the most famous of the many "hippopotamus goddesses" known since Predynastic times. As the protector of women and their newborn babies, Taweret was concerned with the vulnerable period of pregnancy and childbirth. She is a composite: standing upright on her hind legs, she has the head of a hippopotamus, a crocodile's back, and a lion's paws, her pregnant belly may be that of a woman. Although Taweret was always popular, she enjoyed an official cult with a temple dedicated to her only in Karnak during the Ptolemaic period. The connection of this remarkable figure with helpless infants obviously originates from its monstrosity, a feature expected to scare off dangers and demons. Indeed, she sometimes brandishes a knife. It is likely that Taweret's hippopotamus aspect refers to the animal's tendency to rampage when confronted with danger.

The sheer power and roaring rage of the hippopotamus were also related to Seth, the god of the wilderness. Since the Osirian theology had become the dominant religious doctrine by the end of the Old Kingdom, Seth was accordingly considered the embodiment of anger and evil, the enemy of Horus, and was sometimes pictured as a hippopotamus. It is questionable whether it is always correct to give a symbolic interpretation to scenes of hippopotamus hunting (wherein harpooning the wild animal means slaying Seth, in the same way that later images showing the killing of the serpent Apophis can be explained as the destroying of evil). In the religious constellation, Seth was not always regarded as the manifestation of evil; his religious ambivalence reflects both negative and positive elements.

BIBLIOGRAPHY

Behrmann, Almuth. *Das Nilpferd in Vorstellungswelt der Alten Ägypter.* Vol. 1: *Katalog.* Frankfurt am Main, 1989; Vol. 2: *Textband.* Frankfurt am Main, 1996. A comprehensive description of collected materials and textual evidence; general survey of problematic issues and recent discussions on the subject.

Säve-Söderbergh, Torgny. *On Egyptian Representations of Hippopotamus Hunting as a Religious Motive.* Horae Soederblomianae, 3. Uppsala, 1953.

Störk, Lothar "Nilpferd." In *Lexikon der Ägyptologie,* 4: 501–506. Wiesbaden, 1979.

Wildung, Dietrich. *Nilpferd und Krokodil: Das Tier in der Kunst des Alten Ägypten.* Munich, 1987.

ALEID DE JONG

HISTORICAL SOURCES. [*This entry surveys the sources used in the writing of various "histories" of ancient Egypt (i.e., general, social, economic, art history, religious, military, etc.), and discusses problems inherent in interpreting this evidence. It comprises two articles:*
    Archaeological and Artistic Evidence
    Textual Evidence
For related discussions, see Interpretation of Evidence.]

Archaeological and Artistic Evidence

The evidence used to construct a history of ancient Egypt consists of three types. The first and most immediate source is the inscriptional record of the Egyptian language; this only became accessible in the early nineteenth century when the translation of hieroglyphs became possible. The works of ancient Greek and Roman historians, as well as records and correspondence in various Near Eastern languages, supply considerable information and form a secondary textual source, although those sources usually contain an inherent cultural bias. The third source is nontextual evidence derived from the material remains and analyses of archeological excavation, supplemented by the graphic representations on tomb and temple walls. Artifacts and symbolic images provide resources for the study of Egyptian history even when they are not accompanied or amplified by written record.

Archaeological Evidence. The archeological evidence that contributes to a history of ancient Egypt consists of standing monuments, many never completely lost, and the material remains from excavations of the eighteenth and nineteenth centuries. From prehistoric sites, the physical evidence has been essentially in the form of Paleolithic stone tools. Later graves from the Predynastic period, along with the material preserved in them, give some indication of material wealth, the level of artistic crafts and their specialized development, population concentration, relative rank in society, and the appearance of a belief in an afterlife for which preparation had to be made. Early excavations were limited to graves and cemeteries; during the late twentieth century, scientific excavations of a limited number of settlements or villages have made it possible to postulate differing ranks and social classes, as well as the beginnings of a more complex and organized society that had rulers who were differentiated from those they ruled. Sophisticated scientific techniques have made it possible to identify the frequency and distribution of plant and animal components of the diet. Interpretation of the religious iconography frequently encountered from the Predynastic period is speculative and based on the design elements on pottery, as well as the physical appearance of clay figurines and other devices that may have been amuletic.

One of the difficulties encountered by archaeologists who study the remains of the historic period in ancient Egypt is the paucity of domestic architecture recovered by excavation. Tombs and temples were generally constructed of stone or cut into stone hillsides, whereas domestic architecture for both palaces and ordinary houses was usually made of unbaked mud bricks that have not survived in the archeological record. The Spanish word *adobe,* used to designate the building style in the American Southwest, is actually based on the word *ṭube,* Arabic for brick (Coptic, *tōbe;* ancient Egyptian, *ḏbt*), suggesting the use of similar architectural material. In the Early Dynastic period, funerary architecture was not always made of stone, however. In the first and second dynasties, archeological evidence includes royal or noble tombs that were also constructed of mud brick. The articulation and decoration of these structures for the protection of the burial suggest that their designs were based on houses or palaces for the living. The tomb goods included in these early burials of important people attest to well-developed standards of craftsmanship, particularly in the manufacture of a multitude of stone vessels of various types, but also in the manufacture of pottery, metalworking, ivory carving, and decorative glazing. Some few remains of furniture fragments also have been found.

The archeological material from the Old Kingdom is more extensive and contributes to a picture of the daily life of the ancient Egyptians of several classes. The necropolis (Gr., "city of the dead") for the nobility was laid out in a regular pattern, suggesting the beginnings of organized city planning. Rare examples of royal furniture found there have been reconstructed from decayed remnants of wood and decorative elements of gold and other materials. The developing complexity of the funerary cult included objects of daily use supplemented with limestone statues that represented specialized workmen and women. The importance of these figures for the historical information they provide lies in the various craft activities portrayed in detail, such as the grinding of grain for bread and the straining of mash to make beer. Cooking, pottery making, and a variety of other crafts were regularly represented. These statues of working people portray ordinary persons carrying out the mundane tasks necessary to life in this world, although they were intended to provide for the good of a spirit in the next.

Although it may be attributed to accidental situations of preservation, burials of the Middle Kingdom contain an increasingly representative range of artifacts. Complete examples of furniture of many types have been preserved. Elaborate jewelry of gold and semiprecious stones attests not only to an elite class but also to the highly skilled craftsmen who could produce such luxury goods in a society of highly specialized occupations. Besides the necessities of pottery and furniture, actual examples of tools, weapons, musical instruments, games, and clothing have been preserved. In the Middle Kingdom, the custom of including models of activities in the tomb furniture became more elaborate. Rather than limestone figures of single workers, complex representations made of plastered and painted wood serve to record many details of crafts and other activities.

The tomb of the nobleman Meketra and its contents, found in the Theban necropolis, serve as an excellent example of this tradition. Twenty-four models were found in this tomb. Of these, three were representations of offering bearers meant to serve as a part of the funeral preparations, and thus cannot be considered examples of daily life. An elaborate and detailed model depicting the master of the house counting his cattle was supplemented by one of the barn where the animals were tended and fed. A model butcher shop was found that showed where meat was prepared. A granary illustrated the storage of grain, and a brewing and baking establishment depicted its products. The finely detailed weaving and carpentry workshops furnish considerable information on the tools and procedures of both crafts. There were also two gardens, complete with water pools and model trees. The flotilla of model boats in this burial included large and small pleasure craft, separate kitchen craft, and specialized fishing boats. As a general observation, these miniature representations of daily life are fascinating for their detail, but their importance lies in the information they provide on aspects of daily life that would not have been included in any formal, written history.

From the Middle Kingdom onward, excavations have also provided information on some aspects of urban architecture and community organization, based on a limited number of preserved examples of villages, as well as fortifications. [See Illahun.]

By the New Kingdom, the amount and kinds of material included in a burial had become so large and diverse that it is difficult to itemize all funerary goods. It is only necessary to recall the wealth of grave goods included in the tomb of Tutankhamun, a relatively minor ruler, to realize the importance of this aspect of the preparation necessary for the afterlife. From that tomb scholars can examine not only the wealth of decorative objects of gold, calcite (Egyptian alabaster) and other materials but also the king's actual clothing and footwear, his childhood and adult furniture, his toys, games, and weapons, wine jars, and food containers. While this material does not explain the causes for the social and political decline of the eighteenth dynasty, it provides invaluable evidence for the high level of material culture of that time.

The archaeological evidence from ancient Egypt is supplemented by material interred with the dead, but dating to the New Kingdom there are also preserved examples of palaces, towns, and cities (Malqata, Deir el-Medina, Tell el-Amarna) that have provided considerable information on social organization, lifestyle, personal religion, and various crafts.

Although the evidence for thirty centuries of dynastic Egyptian history derived from archaeological excavation and examination is uneven and might even be described as somewhat misleading because of the accidents of preservation, there is considerable physical evidence attesting to many aspects of ancient Egyptian life. It is also possible to deduce the basic outline of the way urban civilization developed, to have solid information about what people ate and wore, to understand how craftsmen worked and craftsmanship evolved, and to learn about other details.

Artistic Evidence. To augment the archaeological evidence, considerable information can be derived from the decoration of monuments, primarily temples, and tombs, once the formalist nature of Egyptian representation is understood. Since Egyptian artistic practice was of symbolic intent, the interpretation of some of the reliefs and paintings is not a simple matter since scale, color, and position were all considered from a symbolic point of view, not as a realistic rendering of nature. With that understanding in mind, it is possible to derive a great amount of information from the two-dimensional designs concerning a wide variety of subjects. The decoration on temple walls, even without the aid of the written texts that explain or identify them, can convey information con-

cerning aspects of ancient life, such as the appearance of religious ritual, foreign tribute or trade, costume, armament, transportation, and even provides information on some types of architecture, such as palace complexes, temples, and foreign fortifications.

The decoration of tombs informs scholars about fundamental funerary practices through illustrations of the rituals carried out, including the funeral procession, the presence of organized mourners, the material goods brought to furnish the tomb, the funerary banquet with relatives and mourners in attendance, the ritual carried out at the entrance of the tomb, as well as representations of the tomb entrance itself. Beyond the representations directly concerned with funerary practices, the depictions of daily life provide a veritable encyclopedia of crafts, agriculture, entertainment, and hunting. A mine of information is encoded in the wall designs of tombs—material that would not have been considered important enough to chronicle in any formal history or personal biography. This is one of the important legacies preserved in the tombs, not from any sense of preservation of history as it is now understood, but as a result of a belief in an afterlife for which preparation had to be made. From the New Kingdom, in the tomb of Rekmire, mayor of Thebes early in the eighteenth dynasty, a large number of crafts carried out in temple workshops are depicted. Of the many shown there, the production of a range of materials and objects, including sculpture, furniture, jewelry, leather goods, cordage, metal wares, and even mud brick is depicted; one specific example, the production of bronze doors is shown in some detail. From the smelting of the ores with the use of hide-covered pot-bellows to the pouring of the molten metal and the finished objects, the craft is visually explained on the walls of the tomb. This might be favorably compared to the sixteenth-century sculptor Benvenuto Cellini's detailed written description of the casting of his bronze statue of Perseus but for the difference in intention. From tombs of all periods, representations of activities provide a window on the world of ancient Egyptian life, preserved as they were through a belief in an afterlife.

Other artistic examples from ancient Egypt include the representation of exotic materials and animals (bears are one example not native to Egypt) on Old Kingdom temple walls, the depiction of the moving of a colossal statue in a tomb of the Middle Kingdom, the rewarding of nobles and military officers by the king on stelae and on tomb walls, and the bringing of exotic tribute (or trade) including ivory, gold, elephants, and ebony wood. The many representations of fauna in Egyptian art provide scholars with a vivid catalog of the animal life during ancient times, both foreign and domestic. The propagandistic displays on the walls of temples tend to concentrate on the deeds, real or alleged, of the king. Scenes of battle and conquest provide considerable detail concerning dress, armament, and transportation, both Egyptian and foreign. Tribute to the king, certain religious rituals for special feasts, and the role of the king in making offerings to the gods are all illustrated, but these often require a knowledge of the texts that accompany them to make them completely understandable.

Whereas written texts in the ancient Egyptian language provide an overall framework for the construction of history as well as many insights into political and social matters, it is the archaeological and artistic evidence that makes it possible to further an understanding of some aspects of the ancient culture never treated in the inscriptional material. In general, those aspects of daily life, represented in tombs, would never have merited inclusion in any kind of formal inscription. No inscription would explain the development of town or settlement layout and organization. The archaeological remains, the artistic representations, and the written texts serve to supplement one another. All three types of information are vital to a reconstruction of Egyptian history.

[*See also* Archaeology; *and* Interpretation of Evidence.]

BIBLIOGRAPHY

The Archaeology, Geography and History of the Egyptian Delta in Pharaonic Lives. Oxford, 1989.
Assmann, J., G. Burkhard, and V. Davies, eds. *Problems and Priorities in Egyptian Archaeology.* London, 1987.
Bard, K. A. *Encyclopedia of the Archaeology of Ancient Egypt,* London and New York, 1999.
Grimal, Nicolas. *A History of Ancient Egypt,* translated by Ian Shaw. Oxford, 1992.
Kemp, Barry J. *Ancient Egypt: Anatomy of a Civilization.* London, 1989.
Schäfer, Heinrich. *Principles of Egyptian Art,* translated and edited by John Baines. Oxford, 1986.

WILLIAM H. PECK

Textual Evidence

This entry will address textual evidence deemed of use to the modern historian, rather than any category viewed as historiographical by the ancients.

The Egyptian script, enumeration system, and celebratory art came into being toward the end of the fourth millennium BCE to serve the needs of the incipient civil service that constituted the new phenomenon of a nation-state government, centered on the equally new phenomenon of a divine ruler on earth. The visible recording of events in sequence derived only minimally (if at all) from any sense of historical process: rather, it provided the state with an extended and recorded memory, reaching back over generations—a prime concern for bureaucrats interested in statistical assessment, revenues, and long-

term social trends. Taxes could be reckoned, commodities noted, and individuals identified at long range, even if the secretary had never laid eyes on either object or person. Out of these practical concerns grew the "document archive" (*pr mdɜt*) at the royal residence at Memphis.

The contents of this document archive, although no longer extant, constitute the ultimate derivation for a number of surviving texts. A set of ongoing annals (*gnwt*), which combined a graphic record of salient events for the year with inundation data, was the backbone of the archive. Reflections of this sequencing of years survive in the wooden and ivory labels or jar-inscriptions—from Saqqara, Abydos, Naqada, and elsewhere—used to identify and date the contents of storerooms. Toward the close of the Old Kingdom, the total list of such annals, or "year-rectangles" (indicative of the format), was "published" on stone as a pious act, but only fragments survive (Palermo Stone, Memphite, University College fragments). Another ongoing series was the "count records" (*tnwt*), the results of the biennial cattle census taken throughout the realm. Royal decisions were immediately committed to writing and sealed in the king's presence. These royal decrees (*wd-nsw*, often granting immunity from forms of government interference) and rescripts are occasionally preserved on stelae set up in temples benefiting from the exemption. Work-orders (*wpt-nsw*) and orders for conscription (*srw*) are often reproduced in the form of rock inscriptions by expedition leaders at the quarries and mines to which they were sent. These sometimes take the form of relief tableaux showing the king subduing the foreign lands. The royal archives also contained records of taxation, copies of all royal charters and "empowering"-documents ('*-nsw*), and all property transfers (*imyt-pr*) made throughout the country. Presumably, documents relating to the complex system of offering-reversion and quasi-scientific treatises (medical, pharmacopeic, and engineering) also found a place in this amazing library.

Royal stelae or inscriptions promoting the king, recording events, or enjoining loyalty are notably absent from the Old Kingdom. There is some indication that the walls of some parts of the pyramid complex (e.g., the causeway) were once inscribed with texts and reliefs recording specific events, but very little has survived.

Better preserved are private inscriptions from the Old Kingdom. The urge of self-promotion for the practical purpose of the survival of one's life-force and memory led at an early date to the inscribing of the deceased person's names and titles on a name stone or slab stela placed at the burial site. With the expansion of the private *mastaba*-tomb, mortuary formulae were added, and sometimes the contract with the mortuary priest(s) was inscribed on the walls for permanence. In order to influence the passerby to honor and intercede for the deceased, an address to the living came to be added, involving an argument as to why the living should make offering or repeat the formula. In this rhetorical exercise the deceased often presented his offices (*iȝwt-ḥrt-nṯr*) and the salient events of his life with the clear intent of creating a favorable impression on posterity. Such statements, whether at the Residence or in the provinces, provide the greatest source for the historian interested in political and social events of the Old Kingdom.

It is a moot point whether we should conjure up a distinction between a *royal* archive and a *temple* library, but collections of what appear to be religious writings did exist. These encompass the categories of "beatifications" (*sȝḫw*), "magic spells" (*ḥkȝw*), and "ritual-books" (*ḥbw*), all reflected in the secondary transfer as "Pyramid Texts" of this material to the walls of the corridors and burial chambers of the Old Kingdom kings from Unas to the ephemeral monarchs of the eighth dynasty. What the accounts and administrative records of a large institution of the Old Kingdom must have looked like is vouchsafed for us by the Abusir papyri, the "waste basket" of a scribe belonging to the temple of King Neferirkare Kakai of the fifth dynasty. Here are preserved such genres as "duty-table" (*sšm-iȝt*), "service regulation book" (*sšm r imy-st-ꜥ*), salary sheets (a variety of terms), "(written) receipts" (*sšp-ȝwt*), "grain-distribution records" (*sšm n swt*), and "gift-receipt documents" (*sš n nḏt-ḥr*).

These rich archives were swept away and destroyed in the collapse of the Old Kingdom; what replaced them is difficult to ascertain. Presumably royal decrees continued to be issued, draft-lists and work-orders written up, and property transfers registered as far as possible. But the almost total absence of written sources from the Herakleopolitan regime prevents any certainty on this point.

Ironically, what does proliferate during the centuries of anarchy and illiteracy following the sixth dynasty is the biographical statement. Slab stelae, tomb inscriptions, and graffiti in quarries and along transit corridors broadcast the acceptable character of the time (self-reliant, skilled in rhetoric) and not infrequently record in passing a historical event. Since the latter are most often recounted from a personal or parochial point of view, their evidential value in reconstructing the broader picture often depends on shrewd guesswork. When inscriptions of royal authorship first make their appearance in the eleventh dynasty, they are set in a continuum of biographical statements stretching back to a point before the family seized the cartouche. In the same vein as the stelae of commoners, they dwell on the king's self-reliance, his ability to speak with his mouth and act with his arm, and his piety. By the twelfth dynasty, the type has developed into an important historical source, the formal "royal séance" (*ḥmst-nsw*) at which the king delivers a speech (biography, apologia, or anouncement) to his court; these survive in numerous stelae, with or without the identifying genre label. One of the important innovations of the Middle Kingdom was the "day-book" (*hrwyt*), a calendrically arranged journal noting receipts and disbursements, arrivals and departures, and other events of immediate interest. Large institutions like the king's house, the courts of law, government departments, the temples, and presumably the army kept such journals, and from them derives much of the material found in embellished form on stelae.

The New Kingdom carried on and developed many of the document types and recording techniques devised by the twelfth dynasty. The royal archive (*ḫȝ n sšw*) of the eighteenth and nineteenth dynasties was a repository for decrees, speeches at séances, "ex cathedra" palace orders (*ḏdt m ḥm n stp-sȝ*), communiqués (*wsty*), royal encyclicals (*wstn*), the journal of the king's house, inventories and inspectors' reports (*sipty*), work assignments and regulations (*sḫnt*), memoranda (*sḫȝ*) and the like. The vizier's archives (*ḫȝ n sšw n ṯȝty*) undoubtedly would have overlapped with and duplicated much that was in the king's library, but they also contained property transfers, transcripts of trials (*smtr*), depositions (*ꜥwt ḏdt.n N*), the criminal register (*šfdw n ḫbnty*), petitions, provincial reports, census lists, and nome records (*sš n spȝt*). Royal correspondence was written out and (presumably) copies were kept in "the office of the letters of pharaoh" (*st nȝ šꜥwt pr-ꜥȝ*). Related institutions kept documentation pertinent to their spheres of interest: the treasury archives held treasury records of imposts, quotas, and other forms of taxation (*sšw n pr-ḥd*), inventories (*ipw*), lists of taxable individuals, and the land-cadaster of Egypt (*dnyt nt Kmt*); the "office of the granaries of pharaoh" kept grain assessments and tax assessors' journals (*sšw n tȝ šnwt*), inventories, registers of grain receipts (*ꜥwty n šsp it*), and conscription records of cultivators (*ꜥwty mrt*); the army kept draft lists and other documentation relating to equipment and personnel (*sšw n pȝ mšꜥ*).

While the rich contents of these repositories survive only spottily in papyrus form in the original format, they provided the source material for large numbers of "historical" stelae. Often the genre title occurs in the text. Thus "royal decrees," promulgated much as in the Old Kingdom, and speeches at "royal sittings" with or without dated introductions, found their way into stelae of the same name. Military extracts from the day-books, quoted verbatim (as often in Thutmose III's "annals"), or embellished (Amenophis II, Thutmose IV), provide the factual grist or sometimes simply the inspiration for the "victory stela" (*wḏ n nḫtw*) or simply "victories" (*nḫtw*), a freewheeling textual treatment, often lyrical and metrically arranged, bombastically celebrating the mighty deeds of the king in peace and war. Also subsumed under the broad rubric "victory stela" are several topoi, smacking of artificiality, within which a dated historical event is treated expansively: the arrival of the messenger with bad news, the king brooding far into the night over the state of the land, the council of state advising the sovereign badly, the dream of pharaoh, god's benediction and blessing.

These topoi, all infelicitously grouped by modern scholars under the term *Königsnovelle* (a genre that does not exist), in their singular preoccupation with adulating the monarch conjure up the stilted atmosphere of a court orality. The latter gave rise early in the eighteenth dynasty to a species of text dubbed by the ancients "the collection of deeds" (*sḥwy n spw*), in which the accomplishments of pharaoh (often historically verifiable) are passed in review by an unidentified speaker who addresses the reader in a chatty manner (cf. the Armant Stela [Thutmose III] and the sphinx stelae [Amenophis II]). In the nineteenth dynasty the adulatory function is served by the so-called Rhetorical Stelae, songs to be sung to the accompaniment of the harp, in which the metrically arranged stanzas each end in the cartouches of the reigning pharaoh. The content is high-flown, laden with strained figures of speech, and largely divorced from historical reality. Possibly emanating from the same circle of oral or written composition within a court context are such genres as dated adulation of the king, the god's address to the king, the king's apologia to the god, and the widespread "adoration" (*dwꜣ*), a hymn of praise to god or king.

A special type of royal text with a long history is the dedicatory inscription. These almost always begin with the phrase "He made it as his monument for god X, making for him a . . . ," followed by the name of the object, or building, or sometimes the deed that the king has performed. Such texts can be brief and formulaic, or lengthy and highly embellished.

A New Kingdom innovation is the elaborate textual "gloss" designed to accompany relief scenes commemorating and celebrating military victories. These were almost always confined to the exterior walls of temples for the edification and admonition of the laity, who were not allowed to enter the sacred precincts. The combined scene and text undergoes an evolution during the eighteenth through twentieth dynasties: an increasing degree of complexity and an enlarged sequence of scenes are introduced, tracing in cartoon fashion the various steps in a campaign. Associated with such scenes are toponym lists that purport to record all the settlements conquered by the contemporary pharaoh.

Of sources preserved (or reflecting originals) on papyrus, letters are the most numerous. These range from letters of royal authorship to those of the barely literate, and they are germane to political, social, and economic history. Of particular importance for international relations during the fourteenth and thirteenth centuries are the collections of royal correspondence and treaties comprising

the Amarna Letters (Amenophis III, Akhenaten), the Boghaz Keui cache (Ramesses II and his family and court), and occasional letters from Ugarit (Merenptah and Beya). Model letters and miscellanies, designed to inculcate penmanship, style, and vocabulary, yield circumstantial evidence on administration and society. The economic historian is well served by the fortunate preservation, especially from the twentieth dynasty, of half a dozen papyri and hundreds of fragments and ostraca bearing on the assessment of revenues (Papyrus Wilbour, Papyrus Prachow, Papyrus Rheinhardt), grain receipts (Papyrus Amiens, the Turin "Taxation" Papyrus), and lists of imposts (Turin Canon, *recto*). The ostraca from the workmen's village at Deir el-Medina, which span seven or eight generations, are of very great value for socio-economic history as well as for the light they shed on the political vicissitudes of the time. Trial transcripts bearing on cases of treason (the attempt on the life of Ramesses III) and tomb robberies and the like (Papyrus Abbott and related documents), as well as indictments and official reports (the Turin "strike" Papyrus and "pseudo-reports" such as Wenamun and the Moscow Letter), provide vivid if circumstantial evidence regarding the stressful times preceding the end of the New Kingdom.

With the abandonment of Thebes as a district headquarters of the central government at the beginning of the twenty-first dynasty, the temple of Amun and its satellite shrines ceased to be a center for the celebration of events in relief and stela. The so-called Third Intermediate Period (c.1070–711 BCE), with the advent of Libyan dynasties, witnessed an abeyance in the committing of the mighty acts of king (or god) to publication in stela form. In the absence of stelae, the historian is thrown back on a type of document that, though not unknown in the New Kingdom, comes into its own in the twenty-first and twenty-second dynasties—the statue inscription. These, being of private authorship, show a rather narrow focus in that they highlight the lineage and occasionally the accomplishments of their owners, without much regard to a broader, national picture of history. The historian complements their meager offerings with such equally sparse sources as the quai inscriptions (records of inundations) at Thebes, a smattering of formulaic inscriptions from Tanis and Bubastis, and the stelae from the Memphite Serapeum, which provide a loose continuum from the New Kingdom into the Late period.

The Kushite–Saite revival (twenty-fifth and twenty-sixth dynasties, c.711–525 BCE) looked to the past for models but failed to revive its salient spirit. There is a marginal increase during this period in "historical" stelae, but the motivation for their inscripturation is piety rather than an intent to make facts public. Some were erected in temple contexts, but others are in desert areas (Dahshur stelae of Taharqa and Psamtik I), sparsely frequented frontiers (Aswan, Psamtik II), or funerary contexts (the Serapeum).

Of greater importance to the historian of the eighth through sixth centuries BCE are private biographical statements, Demotic papyri, sources in Akkadian (Assyrian records) and Hebrew (the Bible and sundry ostraca from Samaria, Lachish, Arad, etc.), and Greek sources. Biographical texts dwell on internal matters and their owners' personal contributions to the life of the community, while Demotic texts provide evidence on society and economics. (The principal exception is the Demotic text Papyrus Rylands IX, a legal deposition that chronicles a single family's history from c.664 to 510 BCE). Akkadian and Hebrew texts provide a refreshing "outsiders" look at the true state of affairs in the Nile Valley, and often provide the sole source for major events in which Egypt participated. Beginning with the seventh century BCE, such Greek writers as Hecataeus, Herodotus, Solon, and Bacchylides begin to show a certain degree of reliability in the collective historical memory of things Egyptian.

For the period of Persian occupation (525–332 BCE), while Akkadian and biblical references are almost wholly lacking, private biography and demotica abound; Greek sources are on the increase, and Aramaic records put in their first appearance. Biographies are little changed in intent, format, and content. As before, their provenance is the temple ambulatory or the tomb, and they often link the owner's piety with real historical situations. Demotic business documents begin to shed considerable light on commercial practice, law, and social history; while the Aramaic papyri from Elephantine illumine such things as trade, race relations, administration, and social conditions during the fifth century BCE.

A king list had taken shape at least as early as the beginning of the second millennium BCE. Not only were royal names entered in sequence with lengths of reign, but annalistic and folkloric material was also occasionally inserted at appropriate points. The one pharaonic exemplar that survives (the Turin Canon of kings, c. 1250 BCE) shows rudimentary attempts to group kings into broad "houses" with summations of years. The king-list tradition informed other lists that were cultic (daily liturgy in the temple of Amun-Re), offertory (Abydos lists, Saqqara list), or celebratory (statue "parade" at the Min festival). The most complete (albeit garbled) king list now known is that preserved in the versions of the Epitome made of Manetho's *Aegyptiaca* (first quarter of the third century BCE). Close examination of the Epitome reveals that Manetho made use, somewhat uncritically, of a sizable body of folktales that had achieved acceptance in the temple libraries of his day, while ignoring the more sober and contemporary records that must still have stood on stelae throughout Egypt. Such folk interest in kings of the past had long since spawned a "literature" that existed both

in writing and orality. The Middle Kingdom told yarns of Nebka, Djoser, Sneferu, Khufu, Pepy II, and the Akhtoys; the New Kingdom spun adventure tales highlighting the conquests of Thutmose III and Sesy-re (Ramesses II). The latter underwent a transmogrification in the Late period into Sesostris, a legendary conqueror who combines the exploits of twelfth, eighteenth, and nineteenth dynasty kings.

Problems relating to interpretation of textual sources place an unusually heavy burden on historians of ancient Egypt. Not only must they be completely conversant with the language(s) in which the material is written, but they must also have epigraphic skills and knowledge of cursive. Even so, in view of the fact that Egyptian grammar and syntax have been reconstructed inductively, getting the translation right often occupies more of a scholar's time than it would in classical or medieval history. Identifying genre, *Sitz im Leben*, and intended audience often demands introducing literary theory, form criticism, and orality theory into the discussion. Most, if not all, of the inscriptional evidence placed on view for public consumption lent itself to, and indeed was intended for, oral recitation; it was thus lyrical in formulation and displays all the earmarks of metrical and oral formulaic composition. The weight of texts *not* intended immediately for a public dissemination—contents of archives, business documents, letters, and so on—is often easier to control; but in light of the haphazardness of preservation, it is rare that scholars can use their data in statistical analyses. Since in many cases the contents of biographical statements and royal stelae originated in personal perorations, historians must also address matters of style and idiolect.

[*See also* Ancient Historians; Annals; Biographies; Herodotus; Historiography; Interpretation of Evidence; King Lists; Manetho; *and* Plutarch.]

BIBLIOGRAPHY

Assmann, J. *Zeit und Ewigkeit im alten Ægypten.* Heidelberg, 1975.

Assmann, J. *Das kulturelle Gedächtnis: Schrift, Erinnerung und politische Identität in frühen Hochkulturen.* Munich, 1992.

Bjorkman, G. "Egyptology and Historical Method." *Orientalia Suecana* 13 (1964), 9–33.

Bleiberg, E. "Historical Texts as Political Propaganda during the New Kingdom." *Bulletin of the Egyptological Seminar* 7 (1985–1986), 5–15.

Breasted, J. H. *Ancient Records of Egypt.* 5 vols. Chicago, 1905.

Cumming, B., and B. G. Davies. *Egyptian Historical Records of the later Eighteenth Dynasty.* Warminster, 1984–1995.

Donadoni, S., ed., *Le Fonti indiretti della storia egiziana.* Rome, 1963.

Goedicke, H. *Kœnigliche Dokumente aus den alten Reich.* Wiesbaden, 1967.

Helck, W. *Manetho und die altægyptischen Kœnigslisten.* Berlin, 1956.

Helck, W. *Altægyptische Aktenkunde des 3. und 2. Jahrtausends vor Christus.* Munich and Berlin, 1974.

Hoffmeier, J. K. "The Problem of 'History' in Egyptian Royal Inscriptions." In *VI Congresso internazionale di egittologia, Atti I,* pp. 291–299. Turin, 1992.

Jansen-Winkeln, K. *Ægyptische Biographien der 22. und 23. Dynastie.* Wiesbaden, 1985.

Johnson, J. "The Demotic Chronicle as an Historical Source." *Enchoria* 4 (1974), 1–18.

Kitchen, K. A. *Ramesside Inscriptions.* Oxford, 1969–.

Lichtheim, M. *Ancient Egyptian Autobiographies, Chiefly of the Middle Kingdom: A Study and an Anthology.* Fribourg, 1988.

Lloyd, A. B. *Herodotus, Book II. A Commentary.* 3 vols. Leiden, 1988.

Loprieno, A. *Topos und Mimesis.* Wiesbaden, 1988.

Loprieno, A., ed. *Ancient Egyptian Literature: History and Form.* Leiden, 1996.

Malinine, M., G. Posener, and J. Vercoutter. *Catalogue des stèles du Serapéum de Memphis.* Paris, 1968.

Otto, E. "Geschichtsbild und Geschichtsschreibung in Ægypten." *Welt des Orient* 3 (1966), 161–176.

Redford, D. B. *Pharaonic Kinglists, Annals and Daybooks.* Mississauga, Ont., 1986.

Roccati, A. *La littérature historique sous l'ancien empire égyptien.* Paris, 1982.

Sethe, K. *Urkunden des Alten Reichs.* Leipzig, 1933.

Sethe, K., and W. Helck. *Urkunden des 18. Dynastie.* Leipzig and Berlin, 1927–1961.

Spalinger, A. J. *Aspects of the Military Documents of the Ancient Egyptians.* New Haven, 1982.

Vercoutter, J. *Textes biographiques du Serapéum de Memphis.* Paris, 1962.

Wildung, D. *Die Rolle ægyptischer Kœnige im Bewüsstsein ihrer Nachwelt.* Vol. 1. Munich, 1969.

DONALD B. REDFORD

HISTORIOGRAPHY. Modern historians of pharaonic Egypt have usually followed a sequential periodization based on the idea of the centrality of the monarchy to Egypt's history. Thus, Egyptologists have generally written of thirty (or thirty-one) dynasties—i. e., "families" of rulers—and have clustered them into a broad schema the Early Dynastic (or Archaic) period (dynasties 1–2), the Old Kingdom (dynasties 3–6), First Intermediate Period (dynasty 7–mid-dynasty 11), Middle Kingdom (mid-dynasty 11–dynasty 13), Second Intermediate Period (dynasties 14–17), New Kingdom (dynasties 18–20), Third Intermediate Period (dynasties 21–25), and, the catch-all label for the last centuries of pharaonic history just prior to the conquest by Alexander the Great, the Late period (dynasties 26–30 [or 31]). Recently, recognizing that the unification of Egypt around the end of the fourth millennium BCE proceeded over some period of time rather than being the work of a single conquering ruler, some scholars have employed the device of a Dynasty "0" to incorporate this reality into the traditional dynastic sequence.

To a surprising extent, this broad outline owes its main features to the Egyptians' own sense of their country's past. If time in general began with the ordering of the universe by a primordial creator-god, ushering in the "time of the gods," then "historical" time began with the emergence of the unitary monarchy over Upper and Lower Egypt that came to represent the embodiment of the moral, social, and political order (*maat*) of this world, the reflection on earth of the cosmic order embedded in the created universe. Although the names for the various kingdoms and intermediate periods are modern, the basic notion that there was some sort of periodization is clearly ancient. In his funerary cult temple across the Nile from Thebes, the image of Ramesses II views a series of statues of former kings. Following his own image are the named statues of eleven predecessors—Queen Hatshepsut and the Amarna pharaohs have become "nonpersons"—going back to Ahmose I, founder of the eighteenth dynasty and the New Kingdom. Only two royal figures precede these monarchs: Menes, the traditional founder of the united kingship of Upper and Lower Egypt, and Nebhepetre Montuhotep I, regarded as the restorer of unity that ended the First Intermediate Period. This is the ancient prototype for the notion of three great eras in Egyptian history, as seen from the vantage point of the nineteenth dynasty. It stands in contrast to the list of kings in the temple begun by Ramesses I's father, Sety I, at Abydos; there father and son review the cartouches (royal name rings) of a large, but edited and therefore incomplete, list of kings going back to Menes, but without any indication of periodization, no matter how broad. The modern use of intermediate periods is likewise a reflection of the ancient view that, because they lacked a strong central monarchy, the periods separating the Old and Middle Kingdoms and the Middle and New Kingdoms were eras of disruption, civil unrest, and foreign invasion—in short, a kind of anarchy. (It is not unusual to find modern Egyptologists still echoing this vision as though it were literally, historically true rather than an ancient ideological vision.) The most unusual example of the ancient Egyptian sense of periodization comes in the great Harris Papyrus from the time of Ramesses III, the second king of the twentieth dynasty, which describes the various stages that separated the end of the nineteenth dynasty and his father's usurpation of power: "The land of Egypt had been cast adrift, each man his own standard. They were without a chief for many years, from the former period [*h3w* = a block of time, normally the regnal period of a king] to the next, the land consisting of great ones and mayors of towns." He characterizes this period as one of lawlessness. Then he reports: "Another period (*h3w*) ensued, consisting of 'empty' years (i.e., of no consequence); a Syrian named I-ir-sw ('a self-made man') was there as prince and made the land tributary to himself." Then the gods designated Sethnakhte, Ramesses' father, to set things right, and a new, unified, orderly period began, and is continued by Ramesses III himself.

We owe the modern schema of dynasties to a third-century BCE Egyptian priest named Manetho who, under royal Ptolemaic commission, wrote in Greek a "history" of his country organized along a sequential dynastic framework. This work, the *Aegyptiaca*, followed an annalistic tradition giving key events in each royal reign, thereby characterizing the particular monarch. It is likely that Manetho drew upon some document like the well-known Turin Canon of the nineteenth dynasty (see below). It is clear that whatever source(s) Manetho had before him, he did not always understand the notations or arrangements of columns, and, in the absence of a more critical turn of mind, this sometimes led him to erroneous attributions of regnal time spans. Even more problematic is the fact that Manetho was a victim of his sense—perhaps likewise derived from the annalistic documents—that the dynasties followed one after the other, thus he produced a "long" chronology which, to give but one example, did not reflect the fact that the eleventh dynasty was essentially coeval with the ninth and tenth, rather than their successor. His dynastic schema is essentially his interpretation of the columns of royal names in the prototype(s) he used, and it incorporates the Egyptian idea that each king succeeded his predecessor, just as Horus succeeded his father Osiris in the most enduring myth underpinning the ideology of the Egyptian monarchy. Manetho defines his dynasties in terms of place of origin within Egypt, as well as by kinship. In the Egyptian view, then, we see two seemingly incompatible ideas operating side by side, each king is a manifestation of Osiris or Horus—i.e., part of an eternal cycle—and, at the same time, each monarch is a discrete historical entity eager to be seen by posterity as an achiever of unique deeds, surpassing his predecessors in extending Egypt's frontiers, in displays of piety toward the gods, or in monumental building projects. Ptolemy's interest in this history was no doubt the same as that of his pharaonic predecessors: the legitimization of his succession to the throne of the pharaohs and his place in the maintenance of the cosmic and social order.

The idea of an unbroken succession of kings was very old in Egypt. The fragments of a later Old Kingdom annalistic inscription, the so-called Palermo Stone, contain year-lists for the kings from Menes to the mid-fifth dynasty. Each year of a particular king is distinguished by reference to one or more events particular to that year, as well as a notation of the height of the Nile inundation for that year. Although the regnal years are not sequentially numbered in the inscription, reigns were in fact summarized in years, months, and days. The year in which a given ruler died is divided realistically between the portion of the last year of the deceased king and the fragment of a year his successor reigned, in short, such a year of transition amounts to no more than one year in the civil calendar. This nicety is a reflection of one important concept of time in the formulation and use of the papyrus documents that lay behind the inscription; it was necessary to keep an accurate sequence of years for such purposes as wills, contracts, rentals, and work agreements, which relied on the ability to make accurate determinations of the passage of years, months, and days in order that they would be effective legally and economically. Maintenance of the integrity of the historical timeline was essential. Early in the nineteenth dynasty, a certain legal case whose roots went back some time into the pre-Amarna eighteenth dynasty required that the sequence of years from the original eighteenth dynasty agreements down to the time of the dispute had to be unbroken, thus, although no direct mention of Akhenaten and his immediate Amarna successors would be tolerated, a terminological subterfuge—"Year X of that Criminal of Akhetaten," for instance—allowed for a precise reckoning of the intervening years. In the case of Queen Hatshepsut, no such device was needed, since her twenty-one-year reign, no longer recognized as legitimate in later times, fell entirely within the fifty-four-year reign of her coregent, Thutmose III, and so there were no lost years to be dealt with. The Palermo Stone, interestingly enough, includes a group of unnamed rulers of the era before Menes, regarding them somewhat vaguely as "spirits," presumably including those real kings now regarded as comprising Dynasty "0," but generally reflecting a notion of a golden age.

It should be noted that the Egyptians never devised a continuous dating system such as ours; they were therefore dependent on a complete list of regnal years, rather like the archon lists of Athens or the consular fasti of Rome, to make possible such basic temporal or historical operations as locating an event or lifetime in the past, calculating the duration of some activity or process, or determining the interval between events. Such a list is the Turin Canon (Turin 1874), a badly tattered remnant of a list of the names and regnal year totals of many kings, from Menes down to the Ramessid era, likely based on a more complete prototype. Nonroyal individuals located their birthdays and lifetimes by reference to the era of a certain king ("I was born in year X of King N," or, "I was born in the time [literally, 'temporal vicinity'] of King N"); only occasionally do we read a reference to someone being praised or rewarded by "the king of my time." In his biographical inscription, the Old Kingdom official Ptahshepses periodizes the stages of his lifetime and career from his birth in the reign of King Menkaure of the fourth dynasty through the reigns of subsequent rulers down to the time of King Newoserre Any of the fifth dynasty, the reigning monarch when his tomb was being decorated. Sometimes the reference to past circumstances of a more mundane sort requires a clear sense of the passage of time; thus, in the Tomb Robbery Papyri, one of the robbers notes "Now when Year 13 of Pharaoh had begun, four years ago." A considerable array of daily documents was dated according to the regnal year, season, month, and day. The Egyptian civil calendar consisted of three seasons: Akhet (Inundation), Peret (Growing), and Shemu (Dearth of Water[?]); each season consisted of four thirty-day months. The 365-day calendar was completed by the addition of five epagomenal days ("the days beyond the year"). A typical date formula might read: "Year X under the majesty of King N, 3rd month of Peret, day 23." Some documents of short-term value or meant to be entered under a year heading in a journal, ledger, or daybook lack a regnal year designation or the name of the king in question.

Although the Egyptians appear never to have envisioned or written the sort of interpretative history that had its beginnings in the Western tradition with Herodotus and Thucydides and is well known in Asia at least as early as Han China (e.g., the work of Ssu-ma Ch'ien, c.145–c.90 BCE), they nonetheless had a profound interest in the past. First and foremost, the Egyptians regarded the past as the repository of all knowledge and wisdom. The basic forms and models were thought to go back to the primordial era ("the First Time"), or at least to some very early time. Thus, a number of medical texts, treasured for their alleged efficacy, were said to have been set down in the very early dynasties. This knowledge was obtainable by investigation in the ancient books and was thought to be useful. The Ramessid author of Papyrus Chester Beatty IV laments the transitoriness of such things as tombs, but reminds his reader that knowledge and tradition are made permanent in books, that it is books that preserve the names and works of the famous sages of the past. The author mentions a group of ancient learned men, mostly known to us today, whose learning allowed them to foretell the future accurately, which attests to the worth of their words and to their great value as teachers of the young. A certain Djehuty claims that his investigations of "yesterday" enabled him to foretell what would happen in the future. The prediction of the future as an attribute of knowledgeable men became a literary motif. One Middle Kingdom tale set in the time of King Khufu (fourth dynasty) has a sage predict for that ruler the future transition from his descendants (i. e., dynasty) to the rulers of the fifth dynasty; in another such story, a knowledgeable priest goes into a trance and predicts for King Sneferu (fourth dynasty) that down the road, after a period of lawlessness and social disruption, a king will come (clearly Amenemhet I of the twelfth dynasty) to restore *maat*. The authors of both narratives have the benefit of historical hindsight, but subordinate what might have been written as history to the far more potent technique of placing predictions of the future into remote historical periods. The first prediction tale also reflects

some notion of dynasty, a concept that appears to have informed, at least in part, some features of the Turin Canon, in which the entries for certain rulers—Djoser of the third dynasty being the clearest example—are marked in red.

While "objective" interpretation of the past is absent from our Egyptian sources, they were nonetheless interested in explanation of certain kinds of events. Military victories were attributable to the divinity of the king and to his divine father (Amun-Re, etc.). The breakdown of civic order described above by Ramesses III was due to the gods' having turned away from Egypt, and the restoration to the return of divine favor.

The investigation of the past, either out of the desire to learn or for practical reasons, was a fairly common activity. Khaemwaset, one of the sons of Ramesses II, was said to have wandered through the tombs to learn what their owners might report about the past. King Neferhotpe I of the thirteenth dynasty consulted the records in the temple of Osiris at Abydos in order to learn the proper procedures for fashioning a new statue of the god. Hatshepsut compared her own achievements with those of her predecessors and concluded that such deeds as hers had "not been seen in the records of the ancestors"; her steward Senmut claims to have delved into the records of the priests and to have learned everything that happened since "the first time." The Middle Kingdom writer Khakheperreseneb claims to have arrived at his views of life from what he had seen (presumably in the records) from the first generation of men down to his own times. (His claim to our attention depends also on his somewhat unusual desire to say something new.) The Nubian pharaoh Shabaqa (eighth century BCE) claims to have found an old, worm-eaten text in the priestly library and, as an act of piety, had it copied—with the lacunae—onto a piece of stone (the famous Memphite Theology). This may be a kind of conceit to give the work the veneer of antiquity, since great effort was taken to make the text appear to date to the Old Kingdom. It does not matter whether these claims are factual or not; the point is that the past was real and there were important things to be learned there. Knowledge is once again validated by reference to its antiquity.

Modern approaches to the writing of ancient Egyptian history have run the gamut of the interests and intellectual currents of the past century and a half. Perhaps the most persistent point of departure was the desire to link Egyptian history with the Bible, largely to support the historicity of the latter. Broad one-volume histories have tended to emphasize the great epochs of Egyptian history primarily from a political or cultural point of view; only recently have the gaps between these periods been given more attention. Attempts to write economic history have been few and largely limited by the quantity, quality, and distribution of the sources. Much of the historical writing on ancient Egypt has been dominated by the sense of the primary importance of religion, while some works still proceed from the premise that royal reigns should form the backbone of any attempt at interpretation. An early emphasis on the archeological survivals has given way to greater reliance on the full range of surviving documents, although the process of developing a historically based source criticism lagged for some time. It is true, however, that the early tendency to take the sources more or less at face value has given way to more sophisticated appreciation of the difficulties attendant on the written record. Comprehensive, wide-ranging interpretations based on a broad spectrum of disciplinary approaches have been lacking, partly because most Egyptologists tend to think of themselves primarily as philologists, or archaeologists, art historians, students of religion, and so on. Even though some Egyptologists claim to be historians, few have been formally trained as such. Most lack the integrative point of view, or use it but haphazardly. More successful have been some recent attempts to deal historically with more broadly thematic issues; such works form a prolegomenon to a future comprehensive history of ancient Egypt.

[See also Biography; Calendars; Chronology and Periodization; Historical Sources; Interpretation of Evidence; King Lists; Manetho; and Time.]

BIBLIOGRAPHY

Altenmüller, H., and A. Moussa. "Die Inschrift Amenemhets II. aus dem Ptahtempel von Memphis Ein Vorbericht." Studien zur Altägyptischen Kultur 18 (1991), 1–48.

Assmann, J. Ägypten. Eine Sinngeschichte. Munich, 1996.

Baines, J. "Ancient Egyptian Concepts and Uses of the Past 3rd to 2nd Millennium BC Evidence." In Who Needs the Past: Indigenous Values and Archaeology, edited by R. Layton, pp. 131–149. One World Archaeology, 5. London, 1989.

Breasted, J. H. A History of Egypt. New York, 1905.

Drioton, E., and J. Vandier. L'Égypte. Des origines à la conquête d'Alexandre. 4th ed. Paris, 1962.

Eyre, C. J. "Is Egyptian Historical Literature 'Historical' or 'Literary'?" In Ancient Egyptian Literature. History and Forms, edited by A. Loprieno, pp. 415–433. Leiden, 1996. The Loprieno volume has an extensive bibliography relevant to this topic.

Gardiner, Alan H. Egypt of the Pharaohs. Oxford, 1961.

Gnirs, A. "Die ägyptische Autobiographie." In Loprieno (1996), pp. 191–241.

Grimal, N. A History of Ancient Egypt. Translated by Ian Shaw. Oxford, 1992.

Helck, W. Wirtschaftsgeschichte des Alten Ägypten in 3. und 2. Jahrtausend. Leiden, 1975.

Hornung, E. "Zur geschichtlichen Rolle des Königs in der 18 Dynastie." Mitteilungen des Deutsches Archäologisches Institut, Abteilung Kairo 15 (1957), 120–133.

Hornung, E. Geschichte als Fest. Darmstadt, 1966.

Hornung, E. "Zum altägyptischen Geschichtsbewusstsein." In Archäologie und Geschichtsbewusstsein, edited by H. Müller-Karpe, pp. 13–29. Munich, 1982.

Hornung, E. History of Ancient Egypt: An Introduction. Translated by David Lorton. Ithaca, 1999.

Kemp, B. J. Ancient Egypt: Anatomy of a Civilization. London, 1991.

Lichtheim, M. Ancient Egyptian Literature. 3 vols. Berkeley, 1973–1980.

Loprieno, A. "The 'King's Novel'." In his Ancient Egyptian Literature: History and Forms, pp. 277–295. Leiden, 1996.

McDowell, A. "Awareness of the Past in Deir el-Medina." In Village Voices, edited by R. Demarée and A. Egberts, pp. 95–109. Centre national de la recherche scientifique publications, 13. Leiden, 1992.

Málek, J. "The Original Version of the Royal Canon of Turin." Journal of Egyptian Archaeology 68 (1982), 93–106.

Málek, J. "The Annals of Amenemhet II." Egyptian Archaeology 2 (1992), 16.

Redford, D. B. "The Historiography of Ancient Egypt." In Egyptology and the Social Sciences, edited by K. Weeks, pp. 3–19. Cairo, 1979.

Redford, D. B. Pharaonic King-Lists, Annals and Day-Books. Society for the Study of Egyptian Antiquities Publications, 4. Mississauga, Ont., 1986.

Simpson, W. K. "Belles Lettres and Propaganda." In Loprieno (1996), pp. 435–443.

Trigger, B. G, et al. Ancient Egypt: A Social History. Cambridge, 1983.

Velde, H. te. "Commemoration in Ancient Egypt." In Visible Religion, edited by H. G. Kippenberg et al., vol. I, pp. 135–153. Leiden, 1982.

Vernus, P. Essai sur la conscience de l'histoire dans l'Égypte pharaonique. Paris, 1995.

Wilson, John A. The Burden of Egypt. Chicago, 1951.

GERALD E. KADISH

HITTITES. Egyptians and Hittites were in contact since the early days of the Hittite Old Kingdom, established by Hattushili I (c.1700 BCE). There, in the new capital city, Hattusas, on the central plateau of Anatolia (present-day Turkey), a vase fragment inscribed with the name of the Hyksos king Khyan was found by German excavators in the twentieth century. It was an indicator that Egypt and the Hittites were in at least indirect contact by the time of Egypt's Second Intermediate Period. For some five hundred years, from the seventeenth through the twelfth centuries BCE, their contact was more usually hostile than peaceful, but trade and exchange did take place.

Few Hittite artifacts have been recognized and reported from Egypt, however, apart from a silver Hittite figurine of a child that was found at Amarna; this is perhaps not surprising, because Hittite objects are notoriously difficult to recognize. Only a few have been reported from elsewhere in the Eastern Mediterranean or Aegean areas. To judge from their texts, the Hittites seem to have primarily imported and exported perishable goods—grain, horses, metals (both raw and finished objects), jewels, furniture, and fabrics; for the second millennium BCE, this is true for their dealings with Egypt as well as with other polities. Thus, recognizable Egyptian goods in the Hittite homelands, while more numerous than Hittite objects in Egypt, are also relatively rare; in addition to the above-mentioned vase fragment of Khyan, extant objects include only some ceramics and stone vessels, plus occasional scarabs and pieces of small statuary.

The first Egyptian textual mention of "Hatti" (*Ḫ-t-ꜣ*; alt., *Ḫt*), as Hittite Anatolia was known during the second millennium BCE, appears during the time of Thutmose III. References to "Hatti" do not consistently appear in Egypt until the reign of Amenhotpe III, when it is found five times in four geographical lists—at Kom el-Hetan, Soleb, and Karnak (twice)—and is mentioned in Amarna Letter EA 31; Amarna Letter EA 45 may also mention the "King of Hatti." Additional letters in the Amarna archive (EA 41–44) are important, clearly the remnants of actual, direct correspondence between the Hittite and Egyptian courts around the time of Akhenaten or later.

During the second millennium BCE, there are also New Kingdom Egyptian references to, and interactions with, other inhabitants or political entities in Anatolia besides the Hittites. The Hittite "Aššuwa" (Eg., *I-s-y*, better known as Isy) was recorded a number of times during the reign of Thutmose III: once on his Poetic Stele, in the company of "Keftiu" (Crete), and three times in his Annals, in which he reports that *inu* (frequently translated from Egyptian as "tribute" but perhaps better understood as "supplies" or "gifts") were received, including blocks of pure copper and lead, lapis lazuli, ivory tusks, wood, and horses. Some later New Kingdom references to "Isy" are in lists of Sety I, Ramesses II, and Ramesses III (but these lists are considered to be historically inaccurate and untrustworthy).

A Bronze Age kingdom located in southwestern Anatolia, "Arzawa" (*I-r-t-[w]*; alt., *ꜥrt[w]*), appears twice in Amenhotpe III's geographical lists at Kom el-Hetan and Soleb. It is the actual destination and origin, respectively, of two Amarna Letters (EA 31 and 32), which are concerned with the marriage of Amenhotpe III to the daughter of the Arzawan king Tarkhundaradu. Amarna Letter EA 31 also mentions the fourth Anatolian group known to the New Kingdom Egyptians, the "Kashka" (KUR*Ga-ash-ga*). They were a neighboring group, located to the northeast of the Hittite capital of Hattusas, and frequently at war with the Hittites. They sacked that Hittite capital on at least one occasion. The term *ꜥ-r-w-i-šꜣ-n*, which appears once in a New Kingdom geographical list at Soleb, has been tentatively identified as the Hittite state of Arushna, perhaps located in southwestern Anatolia.

Relations between Egypt and Hatti truly began to deteriorate during the reigns of the Egyptian pharaohs Amenhotpe III and Akhenaten and the Hittite king Shuppiluliuma I. In large part this was caused by Hittite territorial expansion during their New Empire period, under the leadership of Shuppiluliuma I (c.1400 BCE). They quickly came into contact and conflict with the New Kingdom Egyptians in the region of North Syria, an area which had been under Egyptian domination and influence since the days of Thutmose III (c.1450 BCE). There are indications in the Amarna Letters that an Egyptian–Hittite peace treaty was eventually signed between Shuppiluliuma I and Amenhotpe III in the early fourteenth century BCE; this is possibly the famous Kurushtama Treaty, which is known to have been ratified by these two major second-millennium BCE powers. More certain is a treaty signed between Shuppiluliuma and Akhenaten several decades later, perhaps after actual fighting between the two forces. Ironically, Shuppiluliuma I and his eldest son eventually fell victim to, and died from, a plague brought to the Hatti homelands in Anatolia by Egyptian prisoners who had been captured by Hittite forces in North Syria during one of those intermittent conflicts.

One of the most interesting, and certainly bizarre, interactions between the Egyptians and the Hittites at that time was the unexpected proposal by a widowed eighteenth dynasty Egyptian queen (possibly Nefertiti, widow of Akhenaten, but more likely Ankhesenamen, widow of Tutankhamun) that Shuppiluliuma I send one of his sons to her in a royal marriage, to help her rule over Egypt:

> My husband has died and I have no son, but of you it is said that you have many sons. If you would send me one of your sons, he could become my husband. I will on no account take one of my subjects and make him my husband. I am very much afraid. (Translation following Oliver R. Gurney, *The Hittites*. New York, 1990, p. 24)

After the exchange of several letters, in which Shuppiluliuma I initially expressed his disbelief and the Egyptian queen reiterated her request, the Hittite prince Zinanza made his way to Egypt. He was murdered *en route* by assassins, possibly hired by Ay, who later became king of Egypt. The assassination of the Hittite prince nearly led to renewed war between the two powers, ending any hope of an Egyptian–Hittite alliance at that time.

Although there were a number of additional attempts by Egyptian forces to regain control of North Syria, as for example during the reign of Sety I in the early nineteenth dynasty, Egyptian influence was primarily limited to the region south of the city of Kadesh in Syria. The discovery of both Egyptian and Hittite artifacts at the site of Ugarit/Ras Shamra, however, reveals that this thriving North Syrian port city was allowed to remain an international entrepôt even after the Hittites had wrested the area from Egyptian control.

The most famous conflict between the Egyptians and the Hittites was fought in Year 5 of the reign of Ramesses II, at the Battle of Kadesh, by the Orontes River in Syria. There are two Egyptian accounts of that battle, known as the *Bulletin* (or *Record*) and the *Poem*; these are supplemented by pictorial reliefs (wall scenes) with explanatory captions. The narratives were inscribed on the walls of temples at various locations in Egypt, including Abydos, Luxor, Karnak, Abu Simbel, and the Ramesseum.

The Hittites, under the command of King Muwatalli, were encamped by the city of Kadesh, at the southern end of their sphere of influence. They sent out two spies—who had false information that the Hittite army had moved north again and was located some 200 kilometers (120 miles) away in the vicinity of Aleppo—and deliberately allowed them to be captured by the Egyptians. The Egyptian forces, four divisions under the command of Ramesses II, headed toward Kadesh upon learning this misinformation. The four divisions, each composed of infantry and chariotry, were named after great Egyptian gods: Amun, Re (or Pre), Ptah, and Seth.

The Hittite forces, concealed on the far side of the city, allowed the first Egyptian division (Amun) to pass by and then fell upon the second division (Re), cutting it to pieces, while the third division (Ptah) was still crossing the Orontes River and the fourth division (Seth) was even farther behind:

Now the vile Foe from Khatti and the many foreign countries with him stood concealed and ready to the northeast of the town of Qadesh, while His Majesty was alone by himself with his attendants, the army of Amun marching behind him, the army of Re crossing the ford in the neighborhood south of the town of Shabtuna at a distance of one *iter* from where His Majesty was, the army of Ptah being south of the town of Ironama, and the army of Seth marching on the road. And His Majesty had made a first battle force from the best of his army, and it was on the shore of the land of Amor. Now the vile Chief of Khatti stood in the midst of the army that was with him . . . and they had been made to stand concealed behind the town of Qadesh.

Then they came forth from the south side of Qadesh and attacked the army of Re in its middle, as they were marching unaware and not prepared to fight. Then the infantry and chariotry of His Majesty weakened before them, while His Majesty was stationed to the north of the town of Qadesh, on the west bank of the Orontes. . . . Then His Majesty drove at a gallop and charged the forces of the Foe from Khatti, being alone by himself, none other with him. His Majesty proceeded to look about him and found 2,500 chariots ringing him on his way out, of all the first troops of the Foe from Khatti and the many countries with him. (Translation following Miriam Lichtheim, *Ancient Egyptian Literature*, vol. II: *The New Kingdom*. Berkeley, 1976, p. 64)

In a premature anticipation of complete victory over the Egyptian forces, the Hittite troops began looting the equipment and belongings of the dead Egyptians from the Re division, thus allowing the remaining Egyptian divisions time to approach and fall upon the Hittites, decimating their forces in turn. Although both sides had suffered defeat, and the battle ended in stalemate, both the Egyptians and the Hittites claimed victory upon their respective return home.

A treaty between the two powers was ultimately signed

some years later, which still exists in two copies: an Egyptian version inscribed twice at the Temple of Karnak and at the Ramesseum in Egypt (said to have been copied from the original text that was reportedly engraved on a silver tablet), and a version in Akkadian on a cuneiform clay tablet found at the Hittite capital city of Hattusas. To further cement the new peaceful relations between the Hittites and the Egyptians, Ramesses II later married a Hittite princess in an effort to establish familial bonds between the two powers. There are indications that the Hittite crown prince (later king) Tudhaliya IV, and then the king himself, Hattushili III, subsequently visited Egypt as royal guests, during Ramesses II's thirty-sixth and fortieth years of rule. Then, in Ramesses II's Year 44, he married a second Hittite princess, and it was said:

The daughter of the king of Hatti arrived in the land of Egypt, and two great countries became a single county. . . . In that day two great countries became a single country, and two great kings became a single brotherhood. (Translation following Mario Liverani, *Prestige and Interest*. Padova, 1990, p. 282)

An era of peaceful relations followed, exemplified by the pharaoh Merenptah's efforts to send a shipment of grain to the Hittites during a time of need in the late thirteenth century BCE. The peaceful times were not destined to last long, however, for the Hittite Empire was destroyed about 1200 BCE, by either the Sea Peoples, who were roving the Aegean at that time, or the Kashka, those quarrelsome neighbors of the Hittites located to the northeast of Hattusas. Soon, Egypt was also fighting for her very survival, against the same Sea Peoples, who had proceeded south from Anatolia, past Cyprus and Syria-Palestine, to the Nile Delta. Ironically, one of the last Egyptian mentions of the Hittites is in the records of Ramesses III, in which Hittite mercenaries were depicted fighting on the side of the Sea Peoples—perhaps renegade remnants of the once-powerful Hittite Empire, which by that time lay in ruins.

[*See also* Battle of Kadesh; *and* Mediterranean Area.]

BIBLIOGRAPHY

Cline, Eric H. *Sailing the Wine-Dark Sea: International Trade and the Late Bronze Age Aegean*. Oxford, 1994. An overview of the international trade in the Mediterranean during the second millennium BCE; chapters on Anatolia and on trade goods are particularly relevant.

Grimal, Nicholas. *A History of Ancient Egypt*. Oxford, 1992. A good overall view of the history of ancient Egypt.

Gurney, Oliver R. *The Hittites*. 3d ed. New York, 1990. Good introductory survey of the Hittites, from their origin to their fall.

Helck, Wolfgang. *Die Beziehungen Ägyptens zu Vorderasien im 3. und 2. Jahrtausend v. Chr.* Darmstadt, 1971. Detailed and scholarly presentation and discussion of Egyptian international contacts during the third and second millennia BCE, including those with the Hittites and other inhabitants of Anatolia.

Macqueen, James G. *The Hittites and Their Contemporaries in Asia*

Minor. London, 1986. Another good introductory discussion of the Hittites, their neighbors in Anatolia, and their international contacts in the second millennium BCE.

Moran, William L. *The Amarna Letters.* Baltimore, 1992. Recent translation into English of the Amarna Letters of Amenhotpe III and Akhenaten, including letters to and from the Hittites and other polities in Anatolia.

Schulman, Alan R. "Hittites, Helmets and Amarna: Akhenaten's First Hittite War." In *The Akhenaten Temple Project,* vol. 2: *Rwd-Mnw, Foreigners and Inscriptions,* edited by Donald B. Redford, pp. 54–79. Toronto, 1988 A hypothetical reconstruction of a possible war fought between Akhenaten and the Hittites.

ERIC H. CLINE

HONEY. *See* Bees and Honey.

HORDJEDEF, son of the fourth dynasty king Khufu. Hordjedef's (or Djedefhor's) titles include "Overseer of the King's Works." He was buried in Giza (mastaba 7210/20), east of his father's Great Pyramid. The tomb is unfinished and shows signs of desecration, leading some scholars to suggest a power struggle among Khufu's princes after his death. Hordjedef did not accede to the throne, despite being named as a king in a later Middle Kingdom graffito in the Wadi Fawakhir. This royal status probably can be attributed to his fame as a cult hero at that time. There are signs of reverence at his tomb dating to the later Old Kingdom, despite the desecration.

His later fame is attested by a Teaching attributed to him pseudonymously, in which his name and title are given as The King's Son Hordedef. The Teaching is incompletely preserved in Ramessid and later manuscripts, and the date of composition is very uncertain, possibly in the early twelfth dynasty.

The prince is featured in the late Middle Kingdom *Story of King Khufu's Court* (Papyrus Westcar), in which he is portrayed in a sympathetic manner, and seems to be presented as the most important of Khufu's princes.

Hordjedef's reputation as a wise man was further attested in the early New Kingdom, when several spells in the *Book of Going Forth by Day* (*Book of the Dead*) refer to him as having discovered them in the Temple of Thoth in Hermopolis, an event ascribed to the reign of Menkaure. His words of wisdom (presumably his Teaching) are mentioned in several New Kingdom literary texts: the Harpist's Song from the Chapel of Antef, which is first attested in the late eighteenth dynasty, the Ramessid Satirical Letter of Papyrus Anastasi I, and the list of classic authors in the Ramessid Eulogy of Dead Writers of Papyrus Chester Beatty IV.

BIBLIOGRAPHY

Beckerath, Jürgen von. "Djedefhor." In *Lexikon der Ägyptologie,* 1: 1099. Wiesbaden, 1975.

Helck, Wolfgang. *Die Lehre des Djedefhor und die Lehre eines Vaters an seinem Sohn:* 1–24. Kleine Ägyptische Texte. Wiesbaden, 1984. Edition of the teaching attributed to Djedefhor.

Posener, Georges. "Lehre des Djedefhor." In *Lexikon der Ägyptologie,* 3: 978–980. Wiesbaden, 1980.

Wildung, Dietrich. *Die Rölle ägyptische Könige im Bewußtsein ihrer Nachwelt,* vol. 1, pp. 217–221. Münchner Ägyptologische Studien 17. Berlin, 1969. Study of Djedefhor in later tradition.

R. B. PARKINSON

HOREMHEB (r. 1343–1315 BCE), last ruler of the eighteenth dynasty, New Kingdom, Djeserkheprure Horemheb was not of royal blood—names of his parents are unknown. He was probably born and raised in Hut-Nesut, in Middle Egypt. His special relationship with Horus, the local god of his birthplace, is apparent in his name which means "Horus-is-in festival."

It is possible that Horemheb assumed his first official duties under Akhenaten (r. 1372–1355). In Akhetaten (Tell el-Amarna), Akhenaten's new residential city, Horemheb probably made his first acquaintance with both friends and enemies who were destined to play a key role in his career: prince Tutankhaten, princess Ankhesenpaaten, the priest and tutor of the royal children Ay, and possibly also Ay's son, the officer Nakhtmin from their first meeting. Maya, who acted as Director of the Treasury under both Tutankhamun and Horemheb, became a close companion.

Following the disappearance of Akhenaten, Tutankhaten ascended the throne and order was restored. The young king changed his name to Tutankhamun, while his wife became Ankhesenamun. The royal court was transferred to Thebes, then to Memphis, and the cults for all the gods were restored. The boy king Tutankhamun was only the titulary leader of Egypt; Horemheb, who by then was Tutankhamun's commander-in-chief of the Egyptian armies actually led the country. From various sources, which corroborate each other, we know that the young king had nominated Horemheb as *iry-pʿt* ("crown prince") and had designated him as his *idnw* ("deputy"), which in fact meant that he would have the right to succeed Tutankhamun if there was no heir to the throne.

The earliest information about Horemheb's relationship to Tutankhamun has been dated to the earliest years of Tutankhamun's rule. Textual evidence can be found in the impressive tomb Horemheb had begun to build in the Memphite necropolis on the desert plateau of Saqqara. The so-called General's Tomb of Horemheb was rediscovered in 1975 by a joint-expedition of the British Egypt Exploration Society and the National Museum of Antiquities in Leiden. Reliefs in this tomb commemorate the presentation of captives from Syria and Nubia to Tutankhamun by Horemheb. In one of the inscriptions on the walls the generalissimo boasts that "his name was famous in the land of the Hittites, as he was traveling to the north."

During his reign Horemheb decreed measures to protect individual property, ordered the restoration of the judicial and military administration of Egypt, and engaged in building projects. To the Amun temple complex at Karnak, Horemheb added the ninth, tenth, and second pylons. For this, he reused *talatat* blocks made for the Aten temples built by Akhenaten. He usurped and enlarged the funerary temple of Ay, eliminating the names of his predecessors and substituting his own. Since the restoration of the country under Tutankhamun was in fact his work, he also placed his name on Tutankhamun's Restoration Stela. Although he left Tutankhamun's tomb intact, he usurped several of his statues. He took revenge, however, on Ay and Nakhtmin by destroying their monuments. Queen Ankhesenamun also fell victim to this—her image was erased from the Restoration Stela. This act may indicate that Ankhesenamun backed Ay's coup and was considered an enemy by Horemheb.

Inscriptions and archaeological evidence prove that Horemheb married twice and that his spouses were both buried in his General's Tomb at Saqqara. The interment of his first wife, Amenia, the "Songstress of Amun," took place in the first year of Tutankhamun's reign, whereas his second wife and queen, Mutnodjemet, was entombed in Year 13 of her husband's reign. Once king, the royal *uraeus* was added to Horemheb's brow on his images in the Saqqara tomb. Horemheb was buried in the Valley of the Kings (tomb 57). Both the architecture and decoration of his tomb were innovative: it was the first royal tomb to have corridors and chambers arranged in a single row. It has painted reliefs and contains the earliest example of the so-called *Book of Gates*.

The length of Horemheb's reign is still a subject of debate. Year 59, the latest date known, was mentioned in a document from the reign of Ramesses II, but this could have been an act of deliberate falsification. The Amarna kings, who were considered by the Ramessid rulers as heretics, were simply struck from the records, and their regnal years, totalling thirty-five, could have been added to Horemheb's. This reassessment would reduce Horemheb's reign to twenty-four or twenty-five years. In the tomb of Amenmose, overseer of the harem under Ramesses I, in which several kings are shown, Horemheb, indeed, is represented between Amenhotpe III and Ramesses I, his successor.

Ramesses I was a vizier and officer whom Horemheb had elected as his crown prince. Thus, Horemheb became, in effect, the founder of the nineteenth dynasty. As the initiator of a new era, his memory was held in great esteem. It is possible that he was venerated as a god during his own lifetime. A cult for Horemheb-the-god was celebrated in his General's Tomb at Saqqara, which became a favorite burial place for members of the Ramessid royal family. The deified Horemheb is represented on the

HOREMHEB. *Horemheb as a scribe, eighteenth dynasty.* According to its inscriptions, this gray granite sculpture was dedicated to the gods Thoth and Ptah. It was presumably found in the temple of Ptah at Memphis. (The Metropolitan Museum of Art, Gift of Mr. And Mrs. V. Everit Macy, 1923. [23.10.1])

From this we may infer that he led several military operations during the reign of Tutankhamun, in an attempt to reestablish Egypt's prestige abroad.

At the death of Tutankhamun, the aged priest Ay became the new king rather than his heir apparent, Horemheb. Probably a victim of a coup led by Ay, he was eclipsed by general Nakhtmin, who was appointed as the new crown prince. After Ay's death, however, it was not Nakhtmin, but Horemheb who was crowned king. The events of his election by his patron-god Horus of Hut-Nesut and his coronation by Amun are related in his so-called Coronation Decree, which is inscribed on a pair-statue from Thebes (now in the Turin Museum) that depicts Horemheb with his queen.

HORKHUF. *Relief from the tomb of Horkhuf at Aswan.* (Courtesy of David P. Silverman)

coffin of Khonsuhotep (now in the Leiden Museum), who was an employee of the temple of King Horemheb during the twenty-first dynasty. The last evidence we have for the cult can be found on the *shawabti*s of the general Wahibre from the thirtieth dynasty, who was also a "prophet of Horemheb." As all other priestly titles of this man are linked with Bubastis in the Delta, it can be assumed that the last cult of the deified king Horemheb was located there.

BIBLIOGRAPHY

Martin, G. T. *The Memphite Tomb of Horemheb, Commander-in-Chief of Tut'ankhamūn* I. *The Reliefs, Inscriptions and Commentary.* London, 1989.
Schneider, H. D. *The Memphite Tomb of Horemheb, Comander-in-Chief of Tut'ankhamūn,* vol. 2: *A Catalogue of the Finds.* Leiden and London, 1996.
van Dijk, J. *The New Kingdom Necropolis of Memphis, Historical and Iconographical Studies.* Groningen, 1993.
Vandersleyen, Claude. *l'Egypte et la vallée du Nil.* Vol. 2. Paris, 1995.

HANS D. SCHNEIDER

HORKHUF, an important sixth dynasty official from Elephantine, responsible for Egyptian interests in Nubia. According to his "autobiographical" inscription on his tomb at Qubbet el-Hawa (Aswan), Horkhuf began his career under King Merenre Antyemsaf as understudy to his own father, Iri, charged with the maintenance of trade and with trade access to the South; their trip to the distant land of Yam took seven months. Two more trips were undertaken at the behest of the king, Horkhuf's first independent venture, lasting some eight months. The third trip is of particular historical interest; Horkhuf followed the ruler of Yam, who had gone off to do battle with some Tjemehu-Libyans, and he persuaded him to desist. In addition, Horkhuf reported that a Lower Nubian chief had consolidated his control over much of that area and was inclined to hinder the return journey, presumably to extort some sort of payment when he saw the three hundred fully laden donkeys. Horkhuf had recruited some Yamite mercenaries, and these, together with his Egyptian contingent, proved adequate to secure safe passage. This account probably reflects the growing presence in Lower Nubia of a new and more aggressive population (referred to as the C-Group). [*See* C-Group.]

Horkhuf made a fourth trip to Yam early in the reign of Pepy II. On the façade of Horkhuf's tomb is a copy of a letter from the very young king, excited by the news that Horkhuf was bringing a pygmy back with him. Additional historical interest is provided by the king's letter, which refers to a pygmy that had been brought from Punt on a previously unknown expedition there a century earlier, by an official of the fifth dynasty King Izezi.

Like many Old Kingdom officials, Horkhuf held a variety of functional titles and rank indicators. He was, in addition to being "Overseer of Foreigners," a lector-priest and "Overseer of Upper Egypt." His biography and his burial in his home district probably reflect the growing self-assurance of such provincial officials.

BIBLIOGRAPHY

Lichtheim, M. *Ancient Egyptian Literature.* Berkeley, 1973.
Zibelius-Chen, K. *Die ägyptische Expansion nach Nubien.* Wiesbaden, 1988.

GERALD E. KADISH

HOROSCOPES. There is a body of Egyptian texts, spanning in time from the Middle Kingdom to the late Greco-Roman period, that treat, in part, the fate of an individual as a prediction or prognostication dependent on the day of his or her birth. Only a few texts, primarily on ostraca from the latter era, can be regarded as "horoscopes" in the truest sense of the word: the positions of the sun, moon, and planets with respect to background constellations, given for the hour of birth, which govern that person's destiny. The connection of fates or omens with positional astronomy, however, is of Babylonian and Greek origin, not Egyptian. In fact, the omens on the extant late Egyptian documents are very fragmentary. It is possible that the earlier Egyptian texts of this genre may have developed their own strictly Egyptian positional astronomical relationships, as elucidated below. These earlier texts are usually referred to as the Calendars of Lucky and Unlucky Days.

The source material for the Calendars of Lucky and Unlucky Days (see Troy 1989, Appendix I, for a list of documents) ranges in time from about the twelfth to the twentieth dynasty and covers broader social topics than merely the fate of individuals born on certain days. The principal focus of this material is religious, concerning the relationships and interactions among Egyptian gods and goddesses. The documents tally the days on which certain favorable or unfavorable events occurred among various deities and how these might affect humankind—hence the appellation, Calendars of Lucky and Unlucky Days. They also give explanations for the manner in which these deeds govern divine influences on society, and they provide formulae or spells for warding off evil actions or for placing an individual in the most propitious position to benefit from a desirable influence.

Some of these documents also provide the life destiny of an individual born on a particular lucky or unlucky day. These predictions take the form: "The one born on X will die of old age," ". . . will die by crocodile," ". . . will die of blindness," or of various other ills and conditions that can befall humankind, including death in copulation and death by drunkenness. A given ill, of course, is the result of something that befell a deity on that specific day. Favorable predictions also occur in the form, "The one born on X will lead the life of a nobleman," and so on. Although corresponding positions of astronomical bodies on these specific days are lacking, these prognostications are the closest purely Egyptian sources comparable to the term "horoscopes."

These fates for an individual according to day of birth should probably be considered a subset of broader, more general predictions for the population as a whole. On certain days of the month when all the gods are in harmony, a holiday can be proclaimed for the entire land; and conversely, there are days when strife among the gods is so pervasive that people are advised to stay home all or part of the day. There are many admonitions of this nature: do not eat or drink this food on this day of the month; do not kill this animal; do not travel on the river on this day; do not allow a bull to pass you; do not work at this occupation on this day; no construction of houses or boats on this day. All these warnings are related in the texts to divine governing factors.

From the lengthy enumeration of prohibitions and influences imposed by these Calendar Days, given by Troy (1989) and discussed by Bács (1987, 1990), one might conclude that ancient Egypt had a very anxiety-ridden society. As Troy points out, however, the provenance of all the source material for the Calendars is the various temples where they were originally excavated; that is, they were compiled by priests. There is no documentation that would indicate how deeply into Egyptian society the use of these Calendars and their warnings permeated. They may simply reflect religious doctrine compiled by a particular body of priests and not practiced by the public at large; or they may have formed a necessary and essential aspect of the daily life of the average citizen. Both views have been expressed (Drenkhahn, 1972; Brunner-Traut, 1981). Given that small altars and wall niches for religious statuary have been uncovered in excavations of private houses, and that amulets and charms with iconography related to the myths associated with the Calendars were frequently worn at all levels of society, it is likely that the superstitions related to the spells in the Calendars had some effect, though possibly not the extremes cited above.

The temple provenance of the Calendars poses an interesting question: Why were the positions of astronomical bodies associated with the gods on particular days not tabulated with the various admonitions, spells, and influences, as they were in the later Greco-Roman horoscopes? An important priestly caste was the *imyw-wnwt*, the Overseers of the Hours, whose duties involved marking the hours at night and keeping the lunar calendar regulated, a practice that can be traced back to the earliest Predynastic times. They were certainly well versed in both mythology and positional astronomy, since the two developed concomitantly.

The answer may be related in part to the fact that there are admonitions for every day of the year, but there are many fewer astronomical events that are uniquely correlatable. For example, specific phases of the moon occur every month. A given lucky or unlucky day may have been associated with a specific phase—but in which month? Or perhaps the association might have been for every month. Indeed, the earliest extant document from the Illahun collection of papyri contains a list of thirty unnumbered days, each identified as "good" or "bad." That might be construed as applying to each month (Spalinger, 1991, p. 215).

Every month contained religious festivals, and it is conceivable that the most important of these might have been associated with specific astronomical events in addition to the obvious *Prt Spdt* or *Mswt Rʿ*. Although there are no written instances of the association of a festival with such an event, there could nevertheless have been an oral tradition that was common knowledge in the priesthood and thus required no writing down (much as the modern religious observance of Easter always occurs on the first Sunday after the first full moon after the spring equinox). One might then speculate that this difference between the purely Egyptian Calendars of Lucky and Unlucky Days and the later Greco-Roman horoscopes results simply from foreign intrusion of the latter.

Analysis of the feasts celebrated in the Egyptian calendar is an important area of study. Their order of occurrence in a given month and throughout the year provides a relative dating scheme into which the Lucky and Un-

lucky Days can be tied. The matter is highly complicated because there are feasts in both the Egyptian lunar and civil calendars, there are variable differential shifts between the two calendar systems, and there is no reliable single datable anchor point on which to hang the framework.

[*See also* Astrology; *and* Festival Calendars.]

BIBLIOGRAPHY

Bács, T. A. "Prolegomena to the Study of Calendars of Lucky and Unlucky Days." In *La magia in Egitto ai tempo dei faraoni*, edited by A. Rocatti, and Silotti, pp. 245–256. Modena, 1987. A good introduction in English.

Bács, T. A. "Two Calendars of Lucky and Unlucky Days." *Studien zur Altägyptischen Kultur* 17 (1990), 41–61.

Brunner-Traut, E. "Mythos im Alltag." In *Gelebte Mythen*, pp. 18–33. Darmstadt, 1981. Proposes the observance of the superstitions as a necessary ingredient of everyday life, p. 31.

Chabas, F. J. "Le Calendrier des jours fastes et néfastes de l'année égyptienne." *Bibliothèque Égyptologique* 12 (1905), 127–235. An early detailed treatment of the subject which is a classic in the field.

Drenkhahn, R. "Zur Anwendung der Tagewählkalendar." *Mitteilungen des Deutschen Instituts für Ägyptischen Altertumskunde in Kairo* 28 (1972), 85–94. Poses a contrary view that the Calendars' divine relationships and influences were products of the elite priesthood as religious expositions, because the source documents are from temple archives.

Harrison, G. "The Position of the Day *grḥ nḫnw m sš.f* 'the Night the Child Is in his Nest' within the Epagomenal Period." *Göttinger Miszellen* 143 (1994), 77–79. A short argument on the location of one of the named epagomenal days, the group of five days added to the civil year, considered very unlucky because they were a buffer between one year and the next.

Krauss, R. "Vorläufige Bemerkungen zu Seth und Horus/Horusauge im Kairener Tagewählkalender nebst Notizen zum Anfang des Kalendartages." *Bulletin de la Société d'Egyptologie Genève* 14 (1990), 49–56. A treatment of the Seth-Horus legend and the search and recovery of the Eye of Horus in relation to admonitions in the Calendars.

Leitz, C. *Das Buch ḥ3t nḥḥ pḥwy ḏt und verwandte Texte*. Wiesbaden, 1994. Contains a comprehensive tabulation of source material and references invaluable for study on the subject.

Neugebauer, O., and R. A. Parker. "Two Demotic Horoscopes." *Journal of Egyptian Archaeology* 53 (1968), 231–235. An excellent demonstration of the dating of a document by positions of the astronomical bodies mentioned in text, although the omens are mostly missing.

Neugebauer, O., and R. A. Parker. *Egyptian Astronomical Texts*, vol. 3: *Decans, Planets, Constellations and Zodiacs*. Providence, R. I., 1969. A full discussion on zodiacs in Egypt and a treatment of some Greco-Roman horoscopes.

Posener, G. "Ostraca inédits du Musée de Turin (Recherches Littéraires III)." *Revue d'Egyptologie* 8 (1951), 171–189. An important French contribution to the subject.

Spalinger, A. "An Unexpected Source in a Festival Calendar." *Revue d'Egyptologie* 42 (1991), 209–222. An excellent technical treatment of the subject, with discussion in lengthy footnotes on the historical development of the study of the Calendars of Lucky and Unlucky Days.

Troy, L. "Have a Nice Day! Some Reflections on the Calendars of Good and Bad Days." In *The Religion of the Ancient Egyptians—Cognitive Structures and Popular Expressions: Proceedings of Symposia in Upp-

sala and Bergen, 1987 and 1988, edited by G. Englund, pp. 127–147. Uppsala, 1989. Readers who wish a more detailed structure of the contents of the Calendars will find it in this highly recommended account of the subject, although the caveat in Spalinger's (1991) footnote 7 should be noted.

RONALD A. WELLS

HORSES. *See* Equines.

HORUS, the name of the deity generally written with the falcon hieroglyph and transliterated fully *Ḥrw,* commonly *Ḥr.* The generally accepted etymology is "the distant one," which seems to be supported by Pyramid Text orthographies, as well as an implied pun in the Coffin Texts, Section 148. The ancient Egyptians also seem to have connected it to *ḥry* ("one who is above/over"). The name occurs in many compounds, notably *Ḥr-sm₃-t₃wy* (Gk., Harsomtus, "Horus Uniter of the Two Lands"). The name of Horus has been widespread in theophorous personal names throughout Egyptian history. As a personal name, Hor has outlived the native Egyptian religious tradition, often the case with theophores (e.g., Thor, Isadora, Onnofrio, Diana, etc.).

The roles, local cult foundations, and titles or epithets of Horus are sometimes correlated with distinct or preferred forms in iconography; for example, the falcon, the falcon-headed man, the winged disk, and the child with a sidelock (sometimes in his mother's arms). Egyptologists therefore often speak of distinct, sometimes originally distinct, Horuses or Horus-gods. Combinations, identifications, and differentiations were, however, possible for Horus, and they are complementary rather than antithetical. A judicious examination of the various Horuses and the sources relating to them supports the possibility that the roles in question are closely interrelated, and so they may be understood as different aspects, or facets, of the same divine persona.

Horus is one of the earliest attested of the major ancient Egyptian deities, becoming known to us at least as early as the late Predynastic period (Naqada III/Dynasty 0); he was still prominent in the latest temples of the Greco-Roman period, especially at Philae and Edfu, as well as in the Old Coptic and Greco-Egyptian ritual-power, or magical, texts. The earliest documented chapter in the career of Horus was as Horus the falcon, god of Nekhen (Hierakonpolis) in southern Upper Egypt. In this capacity, Horus was the patron deity of the Hierakonpolis monarchy that grew into the historical pharaonic state, hence the first known national god, the god of kingship. Both his sponsorship of the monarchy and, probably, his identification with the king were shown on early decorated

HORUS. *Basalt statue of Horus in the form of a hawk, from Heliopolis, thirtieth dynasty.* The god is shown protecting Nektanebo II, the last native king of Egypt. (The Metropolitan Museum of Art, Rogers Fund, 1934. [34.2.1])

monuments from Hierakonpolis and by his appearance in the king's Horus-name, which came from the same period. Horus became the patron of several Egyptian military colonies in Nubia, Buhen, Miam (Aniba), and Baki (Kuban).

With the rise of the full-blown Horus-Osiris-Isis mythological complex (visible in the Pyramid Texts during the late Old Kingdom), the living king was identified as an earthly Horus and the dead king (his father/predecessor) as Osiris. When the king died, he became Osiris (or, as I have suggested, joined the sphere of identity of Osiris, in *NAOS, Notes and Materials for the Linguistic Study of the Sacred* 12.1–3 [1996], pp. 2–5). Horus is the royal heir/

successor *par excellence*, the epitome of legitimate succession. In the expanded Osiris mythological complex, Horus vindicates and avenges his father Osiris, thus bringing us to a consideration of the vital relationship between Horus and the god Seth.

Seth, the embodiment of disorder, was predominantly seen as a rival of Horus, a would-be usurper who assassinated Osiris and was defeated; Seth was also portrayed in a balanced complementarity with Horus, so that the pair of them represented a bipolar, balanced embodiment of kingship. Thus, on the side of the throne, Horus and Seth—symmetrical and equal—tie the papyrus and lotus around the *sema*-sign (*sm3;* "unity"): see also, the end of the Thutmose III Poetical Stela. When the full Osiris complex became visible, Seth appeared as the murderer of Osiris and the would-be killer of the child Horus. Since about the turn of the twentieth century in Egyptological research, much debate has ensued about whether the struggle of Horus and Seth was primarily historical/geopolitical or cosmic/symbolic; the answer depends partially on the researcher's choice of myth interpretation theories. In addition, this question has been complicated by the ambivalent geographical polarities of the two gods' cult centers. For Horus, Hierakonpolis (Nekhen) and Edfu (Djeba, Mesen) in Upper Egypt are complemented by Hermopolis Parva I, Letopolis (Khem, Ausim) and Behdet (Tell el-Balamun?) in the Nile Delta (Behdet is also identified with Edfu). Another Delta site important in connection with Horus is Khemmis (Akhbit), regarded as his birthplace. For Seth, Ombos (Nubt, near Naqada), in Upper Egypt, was balanced by his center in the Sethroite nome of the Delta, ostensibly established by the Hyksos at Avaris. Other relevant deities also show both Southern and Northern centers, for example, Osiris at Abydos and at Busiris/Djedu. A crucial observation is that Ombos, although in Upper Egypt, is north of Hierakonpolis and that the so-called Lower Egyptian Red Crown was first attested on a sherd from Naqada. This suggests the possibility that one source at least of the conflict is in the early expansion of the proto-kingdom of Hierakonpolis and its absorption of the proto-kingdom of Naqada.

A Horus–Seth conflict occurred in the second dynasty and was resolved under Khasekhemwy, presumably setting the stage for the subsequent equilibrium. The nature of this conflict is not entirely clear, but it was reflected in the following: the use of a Seth-name instead of the usual Horus-name by King Peribsen; the combining of Horus and Seth above the *serekh* (*srḥj;* palace-façade design) of Khasekhemwy; and the indications of warfare, as well as some limited geographical ranges, for some rulers. During the Old Kingdom, the Horus-name was joined in the royal titulary by the so-called name of "Golden Horus" or "Horus of Gold" (the interpretation of which is highly de-

bated). Some regard it as signifying "Horus and the Ombite (Seth)" or "Horus over the Ombite," the latter allegedly supported by both the Demotic and Greek translations: "He who is over his enemy/superior to his foes."

The most common genealogy of Horus is as the son of Osiris and Isis, making a tenth on the family tree of the Heliopolitan Ennead. The full picture is more complex: Hathor (herself identified with Isis) also appears as the mother of Horus; Horus the Elder (Haroeris) can appear in the Heliopolitan family tree as a brother of Osiris and son of Geb and Nut, thus an uncle of Horus in his more usual manifestations; Osiris can also be equated with Haroeris, who in that scenario is the murdered victim of Seth. Analogously, at Edfu, Horus appears as the consort of Hathor and the father of another form of himself, Harsomtus ("Horus Uniter of the Two Lands"). Horus and Seth are sometimes described as nephew and uncle, sometimes as brothers.

Horus the falcon was predominantly a sky god and a sun god; as the former, his eyes are the sun and moon; as the latter, he has a sun disk on his head and is syncretized with the deity Re, most often as Re-Harakhty. He also appeared frequently as a hawk-headed man. Horus of Behdet/the Behdetite was normally shown as a winged disk with pendant *uraei* (snakes) and, as such, often appeared on the upper border or lunette of stelae. Horus the falcon/disk had the epithets *nṯr ʿ3 nb pt s3b šwt*, "Great God, Lord of Heaven, Dappled of Plumage." Horus the child/Horus son of Isis and Osiris was often portrayed as a boy wearing the sidelock and frequently appeared in the arms of his mother Isis. Bronzes representing him, with or without Isis, were ubiquitous in Late and Greco-Roman times. Horus as a boy with the sidelock also appears dominating crocodiles, serpents, and other noxious animals on *cippi* of Horus or apotropaic stelae of "Horus-on-the-Crocodiles," which were the common manifestation of the importance of Horus in healing ritual and popular ritual practice. Horus the successor was also referred to as Iunmutef ("Pillar of His Mother"), which was used as a funerary priestly title (often the deceased's eldest son). The Great Sphinx at Giza was identified during the New Kingdom as Harmakhis (*Ḥr-m-3ht;* "Horus in the Horizon"). In the person of the Sphinx and elsewhere, Horus was identified in the New Kingdom with the Syrian-Canaanite deity Hauron (an identification regarded by some as contributing to the choice of the Arabic name of the Sphinx, Abu-ʾl-Hul, "Father of Terror"). Aside from the sun disk already mentioned, Horus in various forms often wore the Double Crown, as befitted his status as king of Egypt; the *atef* (*3tf;* a type of crown), triple *atef*, and disk with two plumes were also used. On *cippi*, the head of the child Horus was often surmounted by a full-faced Bes-head (or mask?).

HORUS. *Statuette of Horus, with a hawk head and a human body, making a libation, twenty-second dynasty.* This statuette is now in the Louvre Museum in Paris. (Giraudon / Art Resource, NY)

The iconography of Horus either influenced or was appropriated in early Christian art. Isis and the baby Horus may often be seen as the precursor for Mary and the infant Jesus; Horus dominating the beasts may have a counterpart in Christ Pantokrator doing the same; and Horus spearing a serpent may survive in the iconography of Saint George defeating the dragon.

The textual and mythological materials relating to Horus are extremely rich, comprising hymns, mortuary texts, ritual texts, dramatic/theological texts, stories, the Old Coptic and Greek so-called magical papyri, and the most complete ancient exposition of the Osiris narrative, Plutarch's *De Iside et Osiride* (in Latin translation). In characteristic Egyptian fashion, many of the hymns and the mortuary and ritual texts incorporated substantial narrative material or were taken from narrative, though they are not comprehensive, consecutive myths *per se*. In addition to Plutarch's account in Greek, the most substantive sources for the Osiris-Isis-Horus cycle include the following: the Memphite Theology or Shabaqo Stone (now generally placed at least as late as the New Kingdom); the *Mystery Play of the Succession;* Coffin Texts, Spell 148; the "Great" Osiris hymn in the Louvre; the Late Egyptian *Contendings of Horus and Seth* (and perhaps, in allegorical form, *Truth and Falsehood*); the Metternich Stela and other *cippus* texts; and the Ptolemaic *Myth of Horus at Edfu* (also known as the *Triumph of Horus*). These texts take the reader or audience, with a number of variations and contrasting perspectives, from the conception and birth of Horus, through his childhood hidden in the marshes, his protection by Isis, his conflict with Seth and his followers, and his succession as legitimate king. The healing of Horus from scorpion stings by Isis provided the reason for the production of the *cippi* of Horus and his role in healing. The blinding of one of Horus' eyes by Seth and its restoration by Thoth was the mythological basis for the popularity of the Eye of Horus (the *wḏꜣt* or "whole or sound [eye]") amulet and its significance in offerings and sacrifice (as found in Pyramid Texts offering liturgies). The roles of Horus and Seth are interesting for folkloric analysis. Seth is often considered the "trickster" figure of ancient Egyptian religion, but it has been noted that in the *Contendings of Horus and Seth,* Horus had elements of the "trickster" and Seth acted the fool.

Horus was combined, syncretized, and closely associated with deities other than the sun god Re, notably (but not exclusively) Min, Sopdu, Khonsu, and Montu. The Greeks' association of Horus with Apollo gave rise to the name of the author of the *Hieroglyphica,* Horapollo. The deities of the canopic jars, protectors of the four internal organs removed during mummification, were known as the "Four Sons of Horus." Throughout the Roman Empire, Horus became popular, along with his fellow deities of the Osirian family and others, such as Anubis. That and his prominence in the Isis temple of Philae, the last functioning center of the traditional Egyptian religion, made Horus one of the ancient Egyptian deities who survived longest, as Christianity slowly gained its ascendancy over the Roman world.

[*See also* Contendings of Horus and Seth; Cults, *articles on* Royal Cults *and* Divine Cults; Dieties; Myths, *articles on* Osiris Cycle *and* Solar Cycle; *and* Seth.]

BIBLIOGRAPHY

Allen, Thomas George. *Horus in the Pyramid Texts.* Chicago, 1915.
Blackman, Aylward M., and H. W. Fairman. "The Myth of Horus at Edfu (II)." *Journal of Egyptian Archaeology* 28 (1942), 32–38; 29 (1943), 2–36; 30 (1944), 5–22.
Bonnet, Hans. "Horus." In *Reallexikon der Ägyptischen Religionsgeschichte,* pp. 307–314. Berlin, 1952; reprint Berlin and New York, 1971. Though old, still one of the most useful reference works on Egyptian religion.
Fairman, H. W. "The Myth of Horus at Edfu (I)." *Journal of Egyptian Archaeology* 21 (1935), 26–36.
Fairman, H. W. *The Triumph of Horus: The Oldest Play in the World.*
London, 1974. A dramatic account from the Ptolemaic temple of Edfu, and how the play was staged under the author's direction.
Gardiner, Alan H. "Horus the Behdetite." *Journal of Egyptian Archaeology* 30 (1944), 23–60.
Griffiths, J. Gwyn. *The Conflict of Horus and Seth. From Egyptian and Classical Sources: A Study in Ancient Mythology.* Liverpool, 1960. A comprehensive but somewhat outdated discussion of the rivalry of these deities and its possible historical background.
Hornung, Erik. *Conceptions of God in Ancient Egypt: The One and the Many.* Translated from German by John Baines. Ithaca, 1982. First published as *Der Eine und die Vielen,* Darmstadt, 1971. A sensitive and profound exploration, showing the necessity of both "one" and "many" in Egyptian ontology and proposing "many-valued logic" as an approach to that worldview.
Kemp, Barry J. *Ancient Egypt: Anatomy of a Civilization.* London and New York, 1989. A masterful study of the workings and development of Egyptian society, with detailed and insightful discussion of the rise of the state and the monarchy.
Lichtheim, Miriam. *Ancient Egyptian Literature: A Book of Readings.* 3 vols. Berkeley, 1973–1980. The most chronologically and generically inclusive anthology of ancient Egyptian texts in English, including a number of important selections that pertain to Horus.
Meeks, Dimitri, and Christine Favard-Meeks. *Daily Life of the Egyptian Gods.* Translated from French by G. M. Goshgarian. Ithaca, 1996. First published as *La vie quotidienne des dieux égyptiens,* Paris, 1993. An excellent complement to Hornung (1982), expanding on the deities, their histories, and the cults from which they interface with the human world.
Mercer, Samuel A. B. *Horus: Royal God of Egypt.* Grafton, 1942. Not only outdated but full of errors and idiosyncratic ideas, some of which are listed in J. Janssen's review in *Bibliotheca Orientalis* 3. 4 (1946), 82–85.
Schenkel, W. "Horus." In *Lexikon der Ägyptologie,* 3: 14–25. Wiesbaden, 1980. An encyclopedic treatment for Egyptologists.
te Velde, Herman. *Seth, God of Confusion.* 2d ed. *Probleme der Ägyptologie,* 6. Leiden, 1977. While focusing on Seth and his role, this work also sheds much light on Horus.

EDMUND S. MELTZER

HOUSES. Every culture develops its own social and architectural definition of the house. Socially, the ancient Egyptian house was defined by a set number of often closely related individuals (a household), who lived and worked together. Unlike Arab culture, Egyptian culture attached little genealogical significance to the house.

Architecturally, the definition of the house usually implies the differentiation of an "inside" from an "outside." Owing to the hot climate, the division between the inside and the outside was particularly emphasized in Egyptian houses. While the outer appearance of the house was fortresslike, the interior was organized around a central hall or courtyard. In studying ancient Egyptian houses spatially, a distinction between three overlaying spatial definitions of houses proves helpful: (1) a house is the entire space used by the household (a functional definition); (2) a house is a piece of land delineated by an enclosure wall (implying a legal definition); (3) a house is a building comprising a set of rooms serving a set number of individuals as living space.

The ordinary word designating a "house" in Egyptian was *pr,* a term that focuses on the house as something from which its inhabitants "come forth" (*pri*). The word's range of meaning was extended both in content and in spatial terms to designate, for example, someone's property. More restricted to the architectural aspect of a house may have been *ʿ.t* ("element" or "limb"). Domestic architecture was for a long time neglected by Egyptology in favor of monumental and religious architecture, despite two early excavations that had uncovered significant remains of domestic architecture: at Kahun (now called Illahun) by William M. Flinders Petrie from 1889 to 1891 and Tell el-Amarna by Ludwig Borchardt from 1913 to 1916. For a long time, Herbert Ricke's *Der Grundriß des Amarna-Wohnhauses* remained the only thorough investigation of the subject. Scientific exploration of town sites was initiated in the 1960s particularly by Manfred Bietak at Tell ed-Dabʿa and by Werner Kaiser at Elephantine. Especially in the 1980s, such studies predominated, but in contrast to the architectural approach followed by Ricke, they have focused largely on social and functional aspects.

Prehistory. Evidence for the origins of Egyptian architecture is still scanty. Structures found at settlement sites of the fifth millennium BCE (at Merimde, el-Hammamiya, Omari, and Maadi) include semisubterranean, oval shelters constructed of mud. The earliest rectangular buildings, the Naqada I period at Hierakonpolis and Maadi, were single-roomed structures, that measured about 3 by 4 to 5 meters (10 by 13 to 16 feet). Later sources have suggested that a variety of other building types, constructed both of bricks and of organic materials, existed during Predynastic times.

Old Kingdom. The domestic architecture of the Old Kingdom has been little studied. At town sites (such as at Elephantine or Hierakonpolis) and in most of the priests' settlements (near the pyramids of Sneferu at Dahshur, Menkaure at Giza, Neferirkare Kakai at Abusir, and Pepy II at Saqqara and near the sun temple of Userkaf at Abusir), only small dwellings have been recorded. Typical were houses with a large room (the hall or court) in the back of the house and two smaller rooms in the front, one serving as an antechamber, the other as a private room accessible only from the back room. Staircases were sometimes found in the antechamber.

Larger, more complex houses have been found only at the funerary complex of Khentkawes at Giza. Characteristic is an elongated central chamber whose southern end is partitioned by pilasters. Located in a public section of the house, the room is likely to have served the master of the house as one in which to present himself to guests. One of the more private chambers possesses a niche for a bed along one end of the side walls. Winding entrance corridors isolate the interior of the house from the outside.

Houses comparable neither to examples of the Old Kingdom mentioned above nor to any type familiar from the Middle Kingdom have been found in rural Egypt (at Kom el-Hisn, at Abu Ghalib, and at Tell ed-Dabʿa, stratum e).

Middle Kingdom. In the 1980s, the most progress was made in the study of the domestic architecture of the Middle Kingdom. At least four contemporary house types may now be differentiated. Most of the evidence still derives from settlements founded by the state (such as the pyramid cities at Illahun and Dahshur, the temple complexes at Abydos and Medamud, the settlement at Kasr el-Sagha, and the fortresses in Nubia: Buhen, Mirgissa, Askut, Shalfak, Uronarti, Semna, and Kumma); all therefore reflect the architecture designed and employed by the state.

One type of house attested at those sites is characterized by identical, extremely elongated, vaulted chambers placed one next to the other. Two, four, or five such chambers were each entered separately from a front court, which united the rooms to constitute a house unit. The crucial difference in houses of the second type are connecting doorways within the elongated chambers. Their ground plans also are more differentiated than examples of the first type. Such houses have either two or three chambers, with only the central one (usually wider than the others) being directly accessible from the front court. One of the neighboring chambers sometimes has a niche at the back end, possibly for a bed. Frequently, some smaller, square rooms are added behind the chambers. A special status symbol was a portico, constructed against the house and along the entire width of the courtyard, to shade and protect the entrance to the central chamber. An antechamber—often found in combination with an entrance corridor—ensured the privacy of the house.

At many sites, the smaller houses can be attributed to the first type and the larger houses, usually the residence of the official in charge, to the second type. At Illahun, however, houses of all sizes were derived from the second type. In examples of small size, built to house workmen or low-ranking officials, only one or two chambers were found, the court being reduced to a broad antechamber. An additional annex (serving as a separate living unit or as a work area?) was commonly in evidence. High officials of the settlement were accommodated in large complexes, in which three houses of different sizes were combined with various storage facilities and workshops.

At settlements not constructed by the state, there was a range of house types. At el-Lisht, the architecture of the state had great influence on the design of houses, with some resembling closely the houses of the second type.

The type found most frequently at Tell ed-Dabʿa, though, resembling the small examples at Illahun, is different enough in character to constitute a distinct type of house. This third type usually has only two interconnected, elongated rooms, constructed within an enclosed yard; the rooms are more spacious than those in houses of comparative size at Illahun and, in contrast, were not vaulted.

A fourth, entirely unrelated type of house is being excavated at Elephantine. The dominant feature within them is a large central space (a columned hall or courtyard)—usually, but not always, occupying the entire width of the building. Among the other, smaller rooms surrounding the central space are an antechamber at the entrance to the house, a room with an oven or fireplace for cooking, and a room with a central column. Similar houses have been discovered at Deir el-Ballas.

Additional evidence for the domestic architecture of the Middle Kingdom has been supplied by models of houses to be deposited in tombs, made of pottery (from Rifeh) or wood (from Meketra). While undoubtedly reproducing the general character of contemporary architecture, the models are primarily of a symbolic nature; therefore, the reliability of the models as a source of information on contemporary houses is controversial.

New Kingdom. The house of the New Kingdom as known from Tell el-Amarna is the best documented of all Egyptian house types. Herbert Ricke's *Der Grundriß des Amarna-Wohnhauses* remains the fundamental study on the subject, despite the fact that the evidence on which his study was based has since been complemented by work both at Amarna and at many other sites (Elephantine, Deir el-Medina, Malqata, Medinet Habu, Sesebi, Tell ed-Dabʿa, and el-Lisht). As the principal method of design, Ricke identified the organization of the house into three distinct spatial zones arranged one behind the other, which Ricke interpreted as being of progressively private character: a semipublic zone, a central zone, and a private zone. Among the wide range of houses of all sizes that were developed on this structural type, two were particularly characteristic: a smaller 40–60 square meters (135–200 square feet) and a larger 90–130 square meters (300–430 square feet) version.

The smaller version met the basic spatial needs of a simple household. The central zone, as the principal living space of the house community, is constituted by a single, nearly square hall (*st ḥms*, "place of sitting"?) that occupies the entire width of the building. A typical element in the room is a low bench or dais constructed against one of the walls: the seat of the head of the household. The hall provides the sole access to the rooms in the back of the house, characteristically comprising two separately entered, nearly square chambers. At Deir el-Medina, one of the rooms leads to the kitchen area in the back of the house. A staircase frequently situated in one

of the back rooms or next to the hall adds the roof as a usable space. More or less temporary structures on the roof may have fulfilled similar functions as the back rooms: storage, sleeping, cooking. The semipublic zone of the house, either a yard or a broad hall protecting the privacy of the house, served as a further setting for various household activities, such as grinding grain or feeding animals. At Deir el-Medina a household shrine was regularly located in that space.

The larger version of the New Kingdom house is the so-called Amarna-villa. That house is generally situated as an elevated, nearly square, solitary building within a large estate that was defined by an enclosure wall. Various additional buildings (granaries, stables, servants' quarters, a well) were set within the enclosed area. Characteristic also was the existence of a garden, with a lake and a private shrine. Among the defined spaces inside the larger house, the following are usually found:

1. A square antechamber built against one end of the façade and entered from a ramp or a flight of stairs that led from the ground level to the elevated level. The area in front of the entrance door was frequently protected by a roof resting on a screen wall.
2. A broad front hall with two or four columns in a row. Windows, possibly decorated with a central papyrus-shaped column, may have opened onto the approach to the house, forming part of the façade.
3. A nearly square central hall with one, two, or four columns. The door that led from the front hall into the central hall established the main axis through the house, further emphasized by the symmetrical arrangement of all the other doorways that opened onto both the front hall and the central hall. The axis terminated at the back wall of the central hall, making the hall a place of rest. The hall was lighted by means of windows located above the level of the surrounding smaller chambers. Among the permanently installed furniture were a dais for chairs of the master and his wife, a support for water jars, and a bowl for embers.
4. A smaller square hall with one column. Furnished similar to the central hall, the room served for private gatherings.
5. A sleeping room with a niche at one end for the bed.
6. A bath with a flat stone basin and a separate toilet, with a toilet seat.

HOUSES. *Plans of various houses.* (a) Old Kingdom priest's house at the funerary complex of Khentkawes at Giza; (b) Middle Kingdom priest's house at the pyramid of Amenemhet III at Dahshur; (c) New Kingdom villa (Q 46/1) at Amarna; (d) Greco-Roman three-storied house (C 50/51) at Karanis. (Courtesy Felix Arnold)

A

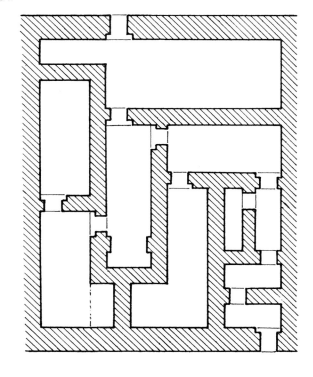

B

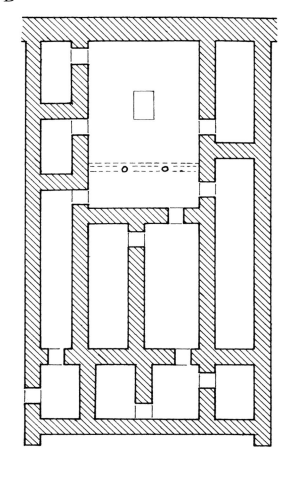

C

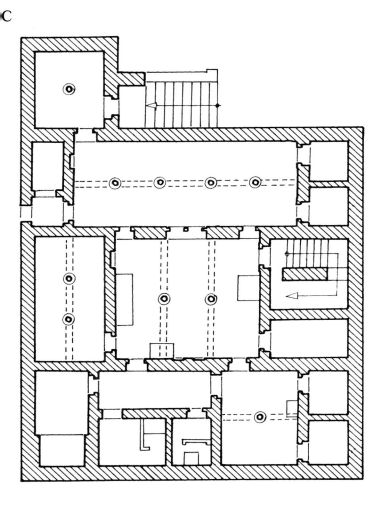

D

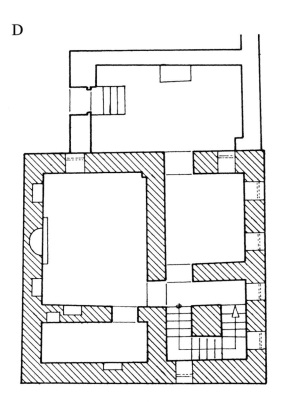

7. A staircase accessible from the central hall led to the roof, where additional private rooms constructed of lighter materials may have existed.

8. Various multifunctional side rooms were also found, which served as extra bedrooms and storage chambers.

As Elke Roik has shown, the Amarna-villa may also have been the type of house depicted in several tombs of the New Kingdom; controversial remains her thesis, however, that all New Kingdom houses were single-storied buildings. Archaeological evidence for a second story has since been recorded both at Tell el-Amarna and at el-Lisht. Several texts (a letter to Ahmose and the minutes on the division of estates) contain additional information on New Kingdom domestic architecture.

Late Period. Domestic architecture of the Third Intermediate Period and the Late period has met little interest among Egyptologists. The few examples studied (at Medinet Habu, Karnak, and Elephantine) suggest that the tradition of the New Kingdom house persisted more or less unchanged for much of the Late period. In examples dating after the First Persian Occupation (from Elephantine), a tendency to develop the design of the house from the position of the staircase, rather than from the character of a central hall, may be noticed. Only additional evidence can verify the postulation of a gradual transition from the house types of the New Kingdom to the types of the Greco-Roman period.

Greco-Roman Period. Several well-preserved settlements of Greco-Roman times, particularly in the Faiyum area (at Karanis and at Dime) but also elsewhere (at Medinet Habu), provide a complete impression of the domestic architecture between the third century BCE and the eighth century CE. The characteristic type of house found at most sites might be called the "tower house," usually higher than it was wide. As multistoried buildings, the houses were designed around a staircase; at each level, one or more rooms are accessible from the staircase. The space between the houses was occupied by various yards, including kitchen areas.

Construction. Housing elements discussed below include the walls, roofing, stairways, temperature control, sanitation concerns, and decoration.

Walls. Traditionally built of sun-dried bricks, a wall thickness of one or one and a half bricks was common; typical brick sizes were 28 × 14 × 9 centimeters, 30 × 15 × 10 centimeters, and 33 × 17 × 8 centimeters (11 × 5.5 × 3.5 inches, 11.75 × 6 × 4 inches, and 13 × 6.75 × 3.25 inches). While thinner walls may be found as minor partition elements, thicker walls sometimes served as status symbols. Historically, a general development, from thicker walls in the Old and Middle Kingdoms (up to six bricks at

Illahun!) to thinner walls in the New Kingdom, has been observed. Openings in walls were used primarily for passage and the ventilation of otherwise closed spaces, lighting being of minor concern. The location of windows high above eye level allowed not only stronger light to enter rooms but also prevented a glaring effect from small openings. Openings were either roofed by small brick vaults or by horizontally placed beams of wood or stone. More rarely, entire frames were constructed of wood or stone. Windows, usually higher than wide, were frequently closed by a wooden (or stone) grille; a wooden shutter has been found at Amarna. Doors, unless left open, were furnished with a wooden door leaf that turned in a stone poleshoe (socket).

Roofs. Two basic methods for the roofing of chambers were practiced. Employing the same building material for the roof as for the walls—mud bricks—rooms were covered by barrel vaults. Widely used both in the Old and Middle Kingdoms (examples were discovered at Abusir, el-Lisht, and Illahun), vaults have rarely been found in New Kingdom domestic architecture. A second method of roofing was the timbered ceiling; onto the wooden beams, reed mats were laid, then covered by mud. Although the use of vaults was generally restricted to a width of 2.5 meters (about 7.5 feet) and the use of timbered roofs to a width of 3.5 meters (about 10.5 feet), supports made the creation of larger spaces possible. While wooden (mostly octagonal) pillar supports placed on stone bases were most widely used in domestic architecture, many examples of plant-shaped stone columns are known. Generally, rooms in houses were supplied with a mud floor, renewed partially or completely every few years. A more luxurious version is the brick pavement found in upper-class houses. Burnt bricks, possibly used as paving, have been found at el-Lisht.

Stairs. The vertical connection between the ground level and the roof area or between different levels in multistoried buildings was achieved by staircases. The steps were generally made of bricks, laid either on brick vaults or on wooden beams. The incline angle was often intended to be similar to our modern staircases (each step about 16–17 centimeters [6.25–6.75 inches] high and 27–30 centimeters [10.5–11.75 inches] deep). Only monumental examples have a much smaller incline angle.

Control of temperature. The principal method of regulating the climate inside the house was its insulation. Relatively thick walls of (unburned!) bricks are a good insulator in themselves. Rooms of central importance were additionally protected by the surrounding side rooms. Openings were minimized, especially on the southern side of the house, which faces the sun for most of the daylight hours. The entrance was preferably located on the northern side, frequently at the back of a portico. Active methods of regulating the temperature included, aside from ventilation, the evaporation of water for cooling and the burning of wood in pottery bowls for heating.

Sanitation. Few sanitary installations have been found in Egyptian houses; a central sewage system did not exist. Only in the houses of the upper class at Tell el-Amarna were small baths and toilets found; all others used temporary installations (such as chamber pots).

Decoration. Judging by the large number of houses studied so far, decoration was not a general practice in Egypt. Some house owners did, however, use decoration as a means of improving their quality of life and for exhibiting their wealth and status. Nearly all the construction elements of a house could be decorated in one way or another. The painting of walls with a black dado, colorful dado lines, and a yellow upper zone was a common practice, particularly during the Middle Kingdom; the whitewashing of walls, and even floors, was found in all periods. Figurative wall decoration was rare and usually religious in character (such as the funerary scenes at Illahun or the fertility scenes at Deir el-Medina). A significant element for decoration were the entrance doors into the central living room; a wooden lighting grille above the two door leaves was frequently decorated with various symbols. Large windows were sometimes supplied with a plant-shaped central support, such as a papyrus-bundle column. The beams of the ceiling were sometimes painted. Columns of nearly all shapes of Egyptian architecture have been found in houses.

[*See also* Gardens; *and* Palaces.]

BIBLIOGRAPHY

Bietak, Manfred, ed. *House and Palace in Ancient Egypt: International Symposium in Cairo, April 8 to 11, 1992.* Vienna, 1996. Gives an overview of the current state of research.

Borchardt, Ludwig, and Herbert Ricke. *Die Wohnhäser in Tell el-Amarna.* Berlin, 1980.

Bruyère, Bernard. *Rapport sur les fouilles de Deir el Médineh 1934–35.* Cairo, 1939.

Dunham, Dows. *Second Cataract Forts.* 2 vols. Boston, 1960–1967.

Endruweit, Albrecht. *Städtischer Wohnbau in Ägypten.* Berlin, 1994. A detailed discussion of the influence of the climate on Egyptian domestic architecture.

Husselman, Elinor. *Karanis Excavations of the University of Michigan in Egypt, 1928–35: Topography and Architecture.* Ann Arbor, 1979.

Kemp, Barry. *Amarna Reports.* 5 vols. London, 1984–1989. Includes detailed studies on various topics relating to domestic architecture.

Lacovara, Peter, ed. *Deir el-Ballas: A Preliminary Report on the Deir el-Ballas Expedition 1980–1986.* Winona Lake, Ind., 1990.

Ricke, Herbert. *Der Grundriß des Amarna-Wohnhauses.* Leipzig, 1932.

Roik, Elke. *Das altägyptische Wohnhaus und seinë Darstellung im Flachbild.* Frankfurt, 1988.

Tietze, Christian. "Amarna I–II." *Zeitschrit für Ägyptische Sprache und Alterumskunde* 113 (1985), 48–84; 114 (1986), 55–78. A study on the socioeconomic aspects of the houses at Amarna.

von Pilgrim, Cornelius. *Untersuchungen in der Stadt des Mittleren Reiches und der Zweiten Zwischenzeit.* Elephantine, 18. Archäologische Neröffenlichungen, Deutsches Archäologisches Institut, Abteilung Cairo, 91. Mainz, 1996. A well-founded treatment on the development of a typical Egyptian settlement and its house types.

FELIX ARNOLD

HUMOR AND SATIRE. Ancient Egyptian civilization lasted more than three thousand years, but confrontations with increasingly hostile and powerful foreign powers began taking their toll as the Ramessid period came to an end. Eventually these outside forces eclipsed Egypt in the ancient world, and what was once a great power became a region incorporated into other great civilizations. Despite its demise, ancient Egypt left a rich legacy for the following generations of humankind, and its arts and letters have provided access to and insight into one of the earliest advanced societies in history. From this valuable source, modern humankind has learned many details about the ancient Egyptians, including the inner workings of their society, government, religion, history, art and architecture, and literature. Not immediately apparent in this material, and therefore more difficult to discern, are the feelings and the emotions that the people expressed. What instilled fear in their hearts? What made them feel safe? What induced them to anger and rage? Why did they laugh, and why did they cry?

Statuary, reliefs, and texts can provide some insight into these questions, but, since much of the material at our disposal derives from official or religious sources, it tends to reflect the eternal and infinite rather than the immediate and the finite. Still, one can identify certain gestures among mourners in a funerary scene that clearly depict sadness and despair, even though such representations may be formulaic. Some of the attendees, such as those depicted in the tomb of Ramose, even have tears falling from their eyes. In religious texts, false etymologies use plays on words, and in one the word for humankind (*rmṯ*) is derived from the tears (*rmwt*) of the god. The young widow of Tutankhamun, Ankhesenamun, in a letter to the Hittites requests the foreign king to send a prince for her to marry. By so doing, she implicitly expresses fear and anxiety for her own welfare as well as concern for her country. Interplay among the characters in literary works also provides insight into human emotions. The *Contendings of Horus and Seth* relates that the god Amun-Re retired to his tent feeling exceedingly sad over the continuing battles between Horus and Seth, who were vying for the throne of Osiris. Although the setting of the story is the realm of the divine, the traits of the gods and goddesses are clearly human, since the Egyptians anthropomorphized their deities to a great extent.

One of the divine characteristics that also reflected human personality was humor, and the same text contains several illustrative interactions. Many of the confrontations between Horus and Seth seem to border on burlesque. In one, the two contenders agree to a naval battle, and Seth is tricked into constructing his ship out of stone, which of course sinks, causing him to lose that round. In the *Destruction of Mankind*, the goddess Hathor takes on a very undignified role when she becomes drunk and then can be easily fooled by Re. The Demotic tale of Setna Khaemwase also contains passages with comedic touches. In one, characters playing a game quickly lapse into a slapstick incident, and one keeps hitting the other over the head with the game box, pounding him into the ground. Such episodes must have amused readers. It is likely that some of these texts, whether popular or religious, had humor as one of the intended layers of interpretation. The number of copies available for many of them, as well as their longevity, suggest their wide and lasting appeal. A strong oral tradition ensured that the stories reached a large segment of the population.

It is possible to search for references to humor in written work, and to track down specific instances of the word "laugh" and its derivatives, (*sbi, sb ssbjt*). They occur in a wide range of genres, including religious, literary, monumental and nonliterary texts. The Pyramid Texts inform us that laughter and shouting accompany the king's ascension to heaven (Spell 1149) and that when sorrow ends, laughter begins (Spell 1989). The divine snake in the *Shipwrecked Sailor* laughs at the puny mortal who promises to do and provide things this demigod already controls. Likewise, in the later *Contendings of Horus and Seth*, Horus laughs at the gathering of gods who think they know more than he does. Laughter occurs in other stories, a temple inscription, and a eulogy, but another passage in the *Contendings* is extremely informative and supplies the reason for the laughter. Here the author records that the god Amun-Re was amused when his daughter Hathor came before him behaving in a lewd manner.

This instance is further evidence that low buffoonery may have been one of the staples of Egyptian humor, and other examples can be found among graffiti, papyri, and statuettes. However, one must always be cautious in regard to interpreting material from another culture. Cross-cultural studies of contemporaneous societies are difficult enough, but they become much more complex when dealing with an early culture such as Egypt, where the language ceased to be used and the civilization died out almost two millennia ago. Today we may think that we see obvious attempts at humor, but perhaps our observation is influenced by personal or cultural bias, and we see something the ancient artisan never intended. For example, a sculptural group from a larger assemblage of servant statuettes from the sixth dynasty, now in the Oriental Institute Museum, depicts two individuals. At first glance, the figures appear to be frolicking, but perhaps they are engaging in activity of a sexual nature, fighting, or exhibiting dominant-over-submissive behavior. A small New Kingdom sculpture from Amarna that portrays monkeys grooming each other may be a simple genre scene or a thinly disguised parody of the royal family. A papyrus of the twenty-first dynasty now in the Turin Museum that depicts men and women engaged in exaggerated sexual activity may be another example of lowbrow humor; the accompanying text would support such an interpretation. Some scholars, however, have pointed out that the focus of the activity is procreation and fertility, and that the number of related illustrations appears to be similar to the number of vignettes in certain mythological papyri and so-called religious books. Thus, this papyrus may be susceptible to more than one explanation.

In fact, the ancient Egyptians in all likelihood created these works with multiple layers of interpretation. Researchers of art and architecture have attempted to demonstrate that much of the creative output of the ancient Egyptians clearly exhibits multivalence, and recent investigations of literature show several simultaneous "registers." So, while the last example under discussion may illustrate ancient Egyptian humor, that interpretation may be only one of many and may not represent the major focus. A sexually graphic graffito inked on the wall of a cave near Queen Hatshepsut's mortuary temple at Deir el-Bahri clearly depicts a woman in a submissive pose being approached from behind by an ithyphallic male. Again, burlesque may have been intended by the artist. However, the female figure wears royal headgear, the graffito is near the queen's temple, and the paleography of adjacent inscriptions suggests a date in the eighteenth dynasty. Such information is strong evidence for relating the female to Hatshepsut. If this attribution is correct, then perhaps the scene is a satirical statement of the artist against the queen who opposed tradition and proclaimed herself king. That private individuals expressed such feelings in regard to the reigning monarch is perhaps also indicated in the statuette of the monkeys mentioned above, as well as in a later New Kingdom letter. In the latter, the writer refers apparently to the reigning pharaoh Ramesses II as "the old general."

Satire or irony seems to have been an effective tool of the Egyptians, and it is particularly evident in portrayals of foreigners. The tomb of Tutankhamun contains several items that incorporate traditional enemies in a compromising fashion. They appear on the king's footstool and on the bottom of his sandals and his walking stick, where they will be trod on by him or pushed into the ground. Four of their heads project out from beneath the base of an unguent jar, trapped for eternity. A similarly unpleasant fate awaits those enemies depicted on the bottom of the footboard of coffins of the later periods; there, they are eternally trampled by the deceased. The heads of enemies are sculpted below the windows in the high gate of the outer wall surrounding the mortuary complex of Ramesses III. These foreigners then would be subject symbolically to the dominance of the Egyptian ruler and members of the royal family and entourage, who would be standing at the window above the sculptures. That this tradition had longevity in Egypt is evident from the bound prisoners from the Archaic period at Hierakonpolis. Carved on the side of the door socket, they were under the feet of those who passed as well as being constantly covered by the doors as they were opened and closed. The eighteenth dynasty temple of Hatshepsut may also present a satirical portrayal and comment on the wife of the ruler of Yam. While he stands lean and dignified, she appears grossly overweight. A small donkey waits patiently nearby, with the label designating it as the transportation of the queen.

Foreigners and enemies, however, are not the only ones subjected to satire or irony. A popular text that focused on the positive aspects of the scribal profession portrayed all the other jobs available to Egyptians below the elite class as extremely undesirable; today it is often referred to as "The Satire on the Trades." In the *Story of the Eloquent Peasant*, the title character frequently resorts to satirical comments and retorts in his communications with his upper-class opponent. One may also see satire, parody, and irony in several sketches on ostraca, as well as illustrations on papyri. Most such scenes depict animals in roles not characteristic for them. In one of these reversals, a hippopotamus stands in a tree, while a bird climbs a ladder set between the branches. Sometimes the reversals are compounded with anthropomorphized activities. Scholars have seen in some of these drawings elements in later fables, such as those of Aesop. In one vignette on the Turin Papyrus, cats and mice battle one another in a scene reminiscent of those found on the walls of temples and tombs. Here, however, the participants are animals, and the apparent victors are the traditionally weaker species, the mice. An apparent satire on class distinction may well have been the motive for another scene on papyrus in which an elite mouse mistress sits, while her lower-class feline beautician adjusts her coiffure. An unrelated reversal that occurs in a Middle Kingdom letter may also contain some satirical wit, for here the writer replaces the traditional epistolary ending that wishes the addressee well with one that conveys evil.

As noted above, the Egyptians did not always explain in their texts what caused them to laugh. They did, however, occasionally tell a joke. In recorded correspondence from the Ramessid period, one can find an example. In it, a man named Thutmose writes to another whom he feels had slandered him because of a joke Thutmose had told to a high tax official. Fortunately for us, Thutmose repeats his apparently offensive joke, which can be paraphrased thus. "You are like the wife blind in one eye who had been married for twenty years, and then her husband decided to leave her for another woman. However, when he confronted her, he told her the reason for his defection was that she was blind in one eye. She responded to him: 'Is this what you've learned in our twenty years together?' "

Detecting such situations in art is much more difficult for the modern viewer, since the bulk of the material available to us is more formal and/or official, and any intention of humor would undoubtedly be of much less importance than the major focus and might violate decorum. Despite this problem, it is sometimes possible to discern humor in what may first appear to be a typical scene of everyday life on the wall of a tomb. We are especially fortunate when a text accompanies a scene. The specifying nature of the inscription can sometimes help determine the more generic nature of the illustration. On a wall of the eighteenth dynasty tomb of the official Paheri, the artisans illustrated a banquet scene, not uncommon in the repertoire of funerary vignettes. In addition to the figures at the affair, the painter also provided texts near some of the participants that represented their speech. The resulting banter among the people reveals that the women at the apparently dignified gathering are in fact drinking rather heavily, and that one humorously notes that she is parched and her throat is like straw. Apparently Paheri not only wanted his tomb to have the traditional illustrations that were necessary for the afterlife; he also intended that he would be entertained by lively and humorous interactions. An Old Kingdom tomb supplies another example of a fairly typical scene. Here, two men sculpt statues, ostensibly for the tomb owner. What distinguishes this portrayal is the text that records the dialogue between the figures. One of the craftsmen complains about how long his work has been taking, while the other retorts, perhaps rather derisively, that his coworker is carving stone (a hard and therefore time-consuming material), not wood (a softer medium). Both these scenes may represent ancient Egyptian jokes embedded into traditional forms of art whose primary purpose was within the realm of the funerary religion. They reaffirm the notion that even though the ancient Egyptians may not have focused on humor in their artistic and literary creations, it was an important aspect of their culture.

BIBLIOGRAPHY

Brunner-Traut, Emma. "Satire." In *Lexikon der Ägyptologie*, 5: 489–491. Wiesbaden, 1982. A useful summary with references to discussions in other studies.

Guglielmi, Waltraud. "Spott." In *Lexikon der Ägyptologie*, 5: 1169–1173. Wiesbaden, 1982. A good summary and extensive notes.

Guglielmi, Waltraud. "Der gebrauch rhetorischer Stilmittel in der Ägyptischen Literatur." In *Ancient Egyptian Literature: History and Forms*, pp. 465–497. Leiden, 1996. Discusses some aspects of satire, parody, and comedy.

Loprieno, Antonio. *Ancient Egyptian Literature: History and Forms*. Leiden, 1996. Several essays refer briefly to the subject (that of Guglielmi referred to above is more specific). Jorn Tait, "Demotic Literature: Forms and Genres"; Antonio Loprieno, "Defining Egyptian Literature, Ancient Texts and Modern Theories"; Stephen Quirke, "Narrative Literature"; Richard Parkinson, "Types of Literature in the Middle Kingdom."

Silverman, David P. "Humor." *Egypt's Golden Age: The Art of Living in the New Kingdom 1558–1085 B.C.* Boston, 1982. Pages 277–211 contain a concise treatment of the subject with examples from the accompanying exhibition.

van de Walle, Baudouin. *L'humor dans la littérature et dans l'art de l'ancienne Égypte*. Leiden, 1969. An extensive investigation of the subject of humor.

van de Walle, Baudouin. "Humor." In *Lexikon der Ägyptologie*, 3: 73–77. Wiesbaden, 1979. A condensation of the author's earlier monograph on the subject, with additional notes.

DAVID P. SILVERMAN

HUNTING desert game and the animals of the Nile Valley and its adjacent marshes was the original (Paleolithic) form of food gathering in ancient Egypt. The domestication of some animals and the slaughter of domesticated animals replaced hunting during and after the Neolithic period. Rudiments of the original hunt were, however, preserved in the slaughter ritual, and animals selected for slaughter were caught, bound, killed, and then dissected according to the ancient hunting traditions. The hunting of animals in the wild continued, however, as a special event, although the main focus was no longer the gathering of food but the dominance of the hunter over the game. The task of the hunt came to be seen as a testament to the physical superiority of the hunter over the spiritual powers of the animal world. A successful hunt qualified the hunter as a leader and it especially legitimized the power of the ruler or king (as, for example, the royal hunts portrayed on the chest of Tutankhamun or the hunting scenes of Ramesses III in Medinet Habu). The importance of the hunt in qualifying the powers of Egypt's ruler resulted in an eventual reservation of the hunt as a privilege for the king. For example, during the height of the Old Kingdom, only the king was allowed to go hunting equipped with bow and arrow, and he had the reserved right to hunt specific game animals—above all the wild bull and the lion. Other instances of royal hunting privileges included the harpooning of the hippopotamus in the Nile Delta's marshes, bird-hunting with throw sticks in the papyrus thicket, and the spear-hunting of fish with two-pronged spears.

In the hunting scenes of private tombs from the Old Kingdom, the tomb owner was not shown as the hunter.

He participated in the hunt only as a spectator, while the members of his household joined as helpers (for example, in leading the hounds, handling the bent sticks, or lassoing game). Only during the fifth dynasty do nonroyal tomb owners join actively in the hunt (the first documented examples being Niankhkhnum and Khnumhotep in Saqqara), where the first depictions of fishing and of bird-hunting in the papyrus thicket were also found. The nonroyal tomb owner in his role as hunter was then given the same qualifying symbols as the ruler. The adaptation of royal hunting privileges for nonroyal tomb owners became evident toward the end of the Old Kingdom, when they were shown hunting with bow and arrow (the first known depiction is the rock tomb of Ankehtifi in Moʻalla).

The ritualistic interpretation of the hunt in ancient Egypt means that hunting was not considered a sport or recreation. An evaluation of hunting as a sport is possible only after the rituals have lost meaning; thus, during the Middle Kingdom, the king and his noble officials went hunting for the first time as a recreation. The concept of open and closed seasons for hunting was unknown to the Egyptians. In depictions of hunting scenes from the Old and the Middle Kingdom, the hunt was portrayed mostly in spring—in the mating season and when the young are born.

Hunters and Hunting Costumes. Typical hunting costumes were first documented during the late prehistoric period on the Lion Hunt Palette, on which the expedition hunted lion and desert game. The hunters are dressed in furs belted with animal tails. Some wear a headdress of ostrich feathers. Their hunting equipment consists of bows and arrows, spears, bent sticks, and lassos. Only the leader of the expedition shoots at the lion. Circumstances were somewhat different by Old Kingdom times. The noble tomb owner (Niankhkhnum, Khnumhotep) of that period wore the three-sectioned kilt for desert hunting; it was also worn during the hunt in the papyrus thicket and is almost identical to the royal *shendyet*-kilt (šnḏwt). The accompanying hunters and beaters were dressed in the so-called ribboned kilt. Specialized hunters, used mostly for leading the hounds (*nu* [*nw*], "hunters"), wore a special costume that clearly identified them. It consisted of a knee-length dress that covered the upper body. The seam on the top is cut below the arm on the one side; on the other side, it is tied in a knot above the shoulder. The dress is usually in multicolored stripes; but sometimes the stripes are uniformly white. Since the costume is knotted above one shoulder, like a panther skin, it may well have been a dress made of fur or animal skin or a fabric imitating such materials.

During the Middle Kingdom, the hunter wore a long kilt with a wide gap in the front, behind which a bunched-up leather leaf is visible. In some cases, a ribbon crosses

HUNTING. *Fowling depicted on a relief from the tomb of Mereruka at Saqqara, sixth dynasty.* (Courtesy David P. Silverman)

the upper body. This hunting costume can be identified as the Nubian mercenary dress, worn from the beginning of the Middle Kingdom. During the New Kingdom, tomb owners were shown wearing the Egyptian courtier's costume and riding a chariot to the hunt.

Game. Aside from birds and fish, the most frequently sought animals were the hippopotamus, hunted with harpoons in the papyrus marshes, and the desert animals in areas around the Nile valley. The most popular region for hunting game in Egypt was the flat desert area, where the conditions for ambush, the foremost hunting method, were favorable. There are accounts of hunts in the Wadi Hammamat, a desert valley in the Eastern Desert, in the Faiyum Oasis, and in the Giza area, near Memphis. As the game became depleted, the hunt sometimes extended into foreign lands, where they were often part of war campaigns. Royal inscriptions from the New Kingdom tell of hunts in neighboring countries for lion, elephant, and rhinoceros.

Game is shown in detail in the hunt depictions from the Old Kingdom onward. During the Old Kingdom, many wild animals were hunted: antelope cows, Isabella gazelle, Dorkas gazelle, bow-legged antelope, Mendes antelope, stag, ibex, mane sheep, hyenas, wild dogs, foxes, and hares but also lions, leopards, and ostriches. To identify the landscape as a desert, the hunt illustrations include zorils (a skunklike animal), porcupines, hedgehogs, and desert rats; with the possible exception of the hedgehog, those were likely not regarded as game. In the hunt illustrations of the Middle Kingdom, wild donkey, giraffe,

HUNTING. *A hippopotamus hunt on a relief from the tomb of Mereruka at Saqqara, sixth dynasty.* (Courtesy David P. Silverman)

and various monkeys were shown, as well as some unusual hunt animals (such as the mythical beasts whose habitat was believed to be in the desert).

Hunting Tools and Methods. The hunting methods of the historic period were, in the main, the same as those of the prehistoric. The hunting weapons had also changed little since Neolithic times (arrows, spears, and harpoons, as well as flat curved clubs). Traps and nets were used for hunting birds; collapsing nets were used for catching waterfowl. In the marsh thickets, birds were hunted with throw sticks. Fish were caught with nets, wicker traps, fishing rods, and spears, and the hippopotamus with harpoons. Desert game was pursued by trapping, by ambush, or by chase.

There is very little documentation for trapping in the historic period, in which animals were caught either dead or alive in traps, nets, pits, tight enclosures, and other manmade structures. In an Old Kingdom tomb, two lions were shown being transported in cages on sleighs, and they were probably caught by trapping. In the historic period, most hunts took place as a single-file ambush, in which hunters with varying types of equipment participated. Hounds (and probably hunting leopards) were also used. Many depictions document that the ambush took place in the flat, open landscape of the desert. Fences and

nets were erected to close off the area on two sides, with lateral barricades set up parallel. From the opposite open sides, the hunters and beaters would approach with their hounds, herding the game with cries and by beating sticks. While the royal hunter shot the choicest game (wild bull and lion) with bow and arrow, the other participants fell upon the game with bent clubs, axes, or lassos; some caught it with bare hands.

The ambush hunt was replaced by the chase hunt only during the New Kingdom, when the horse-drawn chariot was first used. The hunter rode in the chariot and gave chase to the game that tried to escape at top speed from both a hail of arrows and the accompanying hounds. The lion hunt became part of the royal hunt from the middle of the eighteenth dynasty onward. A special variation of the lion hunt was the hunt for a single lion from a chariot, in which the king killed the lion with a lance while riding in the chariot. The iconography of this image was probably adapted from Mesopotamia.

Hunters' Language and Hunting Gods. No special hunters' language has been found. The exaggerated accounts of royal prowess in the hunt cannot be taken as "huntsman's slang," because such accounts were written in order to praise the king. The victorious hunt of the king metaphorically made "game" of Egypt's enemies, and they fled in horror from the attacking king. They also ran like "herds of game" from the attacking ruler, it was said.

Some gods, too, went hunting (Horus, Onuris, Sched), although Egypt had no specific god of the hunt. The goddess Neith was, however, linked to the hunt as a hunt deity. Possibly, the hunt was the domain of the lion goddess Sekhmet. Desert game was sacrificed to her, and to the goddess Bastet in the temple, yet during the feast of Bastet, lion hunting was forbidden.

[*See also* Sports.]

BIBLIOGRAPHY

Altenmüller, Hartwig. *Die Jagd im Alten Ägypten.* Hamburg, 1967.
Altenmüller, Hartwig. "Jäger," "Jagd," "Jagddarstellungen," "Jagdmethoden," "Jagdritual," "Jagdtracht," and "Jagdzauber." In *Lexikon der Ägyptologie,* 3: 219–236. Wiesbaden, 1975.
Decker, Wolfgang, and Michael Herbst. *Bildatlas zum Sport im alten Ägypten,* Handbuch der Orientalistik, Erste Abteilung, 14. Leiden, New York, and Cologne, 1994.

HARTWIG ALTENMÜLLER
Translated from German by Elizabeth Schwaiger

HYGIENE. In ancient Egypt, as in modern times, hygienic practices, whether good or bad, had a profound effect on the health status of the population. Many aspects of the environment affected the physical and mental well-being of individuals, and the range of evidence available allows an examination of hygiene from both the public and personal aspects.

In the public sphere, climate had a far-reaching effect. During the fifth century BCE, the Greek writer Herodotus, in book II of his *Histories,* was of the opinion that the health of the Egyptians was due to the lack of variability in their weather. Certainly, the constant sunshine provided the body with vitamin D, yet the intensity of the heat encouraged the rapid breeding of flies and other insects, which spread infections among the population. The Nile River played a central role in the life of the ancient Egyptians, being at once the source of drinking and washing water, a means of travel and transport, and most importantly the provider of the essential irrigation waters, without which agricultural activities could be severely curtailed. The Nile waters were even then unhygienic, harboring the endoparasitic worms that caused much disease. The schistosome worm in the Nile is one of the most prominent health hazards even in present-day Egypt, affecting human physical and mental development, and research has shown that the disease it causes, schistosomiasis, was present in Egypt from at least Predynastic times. Infestation by these worms, which enter the body through the feet of unsuspecting waders in infected waters, often leads to general ill health, increased susceptibilities, and, in extreme cases, death. Infestation by hookworms often leads to anemia—from blood loss—resulting in weakness and debilitation. The guinea worm enters the body in an immature form in drinking water and then matures in the stomach, later burrowing through the abdominal wall to mate.

As with developing societies generally, the ancient Egyptian transition from nomadic food collection into a sedentary agricultural life had its consequences. Nomadic groups periodically move, leaving behind parasite-ridden waste; sedentism, however, results in the accumulation of animal and human fecal and other waste matter, with its consequent effects. Defecation in fields and the use of animal feces as fertilizer meant that parasites, such as hookworms, tapeworms, and roundworms, could complete their life cycles and infect new human hosts through food crops; any fecal waste deposited along the banks of the Nile provided good breeding grounds for flies, which carried the filarial worms responsible for onchocerciasis ("river blindness"). Evidence from tomb paintings seems to suggest that some musicians were blind, possibly as a result of this type of eye disease.

For the ordinary ancient Egyptian, housing may have been overcrowded, with inadequate ventilation and poor sanitation. In many households, animals shared human living quarters. Such conditions favored infectious diseases, such as tuberculosis, and promoted other chest infections. As outlined above, defecation generally took place outdoors—in the fields, in the deserts or near the home—but there is evidence that some of the elite had planned sanitation. Housing representing several levels of society has been excavated at Tell el-Amarna (ancient Akhetaten), an eighteenth dynasty site in Middle Egypt. In some of the better houses there, a stone or wooden seat with a keyhole-shaped opening served as a latrine, with a removable bowl for waste underneath.

Household waste was disposed of, unhygienically, in the vicinity of the home; thus, food remains and other rubbish attracted scavengers, many of them carrying transferable diseases. Permanent housing in villages, towns, and cities enabled fleas and bed bugs to encounter new human hosts. While in most cases these creatures were little more than irritants, they could cause skin diseases. Concern with ridding the household of parasites is evident from "recipes" in the Ebers Papyrus, which suggest smearing infested rooms with a mixture of charcoal and fleabane or utilizing a solution of natron. More seriously, the *Xenopsylla cheopis* flea that carried *Pasturella pestis,* the agent of bubonic plague, could gain access to humans when its host, the black rat, invaded grain storerooms.

Sources suggest that the ancient Egyptians were particularly concerned with cleanliness and grooming. The Greek historian Herodotus wrote that the Egyptians "set cleanliness over seemliness," and he noted that the Egyptians washed their linen garments frequently. In reality, however, personal cleanliness was not only a means of attaining good health but an indicator of status and rank. Cleanliness meant being Egyptian, for foreigners were believed to be dirty and unkempt. The ancient Egyptians were aware of the need to wash frequently and did so at least once a day: some texts mention washing before and after meals. The priests were required to wash at least twice a day. Some of the wealthier people had private washing facilities. One house at the Amarna site had a bathing area, with stone slabs forming the base and a splashback for a shower; water was poured over the bather from a jug, as the waste water drained away through an outlet in the wall. The majority of the population, however, bathed in the Nile waters, which exposed people to further disease conditions, since the Nile was also used as a sewage-and-waste disposal system. Soap, as we know it, was not used, but the ancient Egyptians employed natron—a naturally occurring salt—as a cleansing agent. Natron came from several areas of Egypt, the most notable being the Wadi Natrum in the Faiyum district.

Following their ablutions, the Egyptians often rubbed unguents into the skin. These unguents, oils fragranced with frankincense or myrrh, prevented the skin from drying out in the hot, sunny climate. The Egyptians believed that oils prevented wrinkles. The wealthy had access to imported oils, while the ordinary people used castor or linseed oil. Curative recipes in the Ebers Papyrus express the ancient Egyptian concern with body odor, and it is thought that they used douches and genital fumigation for personal freshness. From the earliest times, cosmetic items, palettes, and eye paints were included as important components of funerary equipment, reflecting their importance in daily life. Both males and females paid a great deal of attention to their appearance, and this included the use of eye paint. The most frequently used eye paint was called *msdmt* and was made from the minerals galena or stibnite; the other type, called *w3dw*, was made from the mineral malachite. Apart from being decorative, the eye paint protected the eyes from the glare of the sun and had some medicinal properties. In some of the medical papyri, *msdmt* is recommended for eye problems; it may have acted as a disinfectant. In a letter from the nineteenth dynasty, the draftsman Pay begs his son not to neglect him for he "is in darkness" (i.e., blind), and he asks his son to bring him treatment for his eyes in the form of an unguent made from honey, ocher, and galena. Evidence from human remains reveals that henna was used for various cosmetic purposes; an examination of the mummy of Ramesses II revealed that the elderly pharaoh's red hair was achieved through the application of henna. In the British Museum, London, a mummified

arm has beautifully manicured nails, colored a rusty red with henna.

Care of the hair was extremely important to the ancient Egyptians. A depiction of the eleventh dynasty queen Kawit on her sarcophagus shows her servant at work dressing her hair. It is suggested that any depictions of individuals with unkempt hair must indicate either a state of mourning or low status—therefore the uncleanliness of the individual concerned. A variety of oils and unguents were used to dress the hair; the examination of the bodies of a group of soldiers or archers from the eleventh dynasty indicated that their thick curls were adorned with grease. From the examination of human remains, the deduction was that some individuals retained their natural hair while others chose to wear wigs. Excavations have revealed a variety of hair colors and qualities, including carefully dressed natural tresses measuring up to 27 centimeters (11 inches) in length, as observed on a body from the Gabati cemetery site in central Sudan, which also yielded wooden combs. Evidence from tomb paintings show a variety of dressed hair styles, many employing pins or flowers as decoration. There is little evidence to suggest how regularly the ancient Egyptians washed their hair. From an examination of statues, it is clear that some of the wealthier preferred to shave their heads and wear wigs. This may have been undertaken for comfort in the hot Egyptian climate, but it may also have been an attempt to be relieved of head lice. There are several reports of lice eggs discovered during the examination of ancient hair—on the hair of the weaver Nakht, during the autopsy of his mummy in Toronto in 1974 for example, and on Nubian bodies dating to the sixth century BCE. The earliest example of lice so far found on ancient Egyptian hair is of Early Dynastic date. Contrary to popular conceptions, nits and their adult form, lice, are not evidence for poor hygiene, but rather the opposite, for head lice cannot travel on dirty hair shafts. Infestation with lice, either on the hair or body, may cause dermatitis from scratching. Lice may also result in the transmission of the more serious typhus and relapsing fevers. It is difficult to determine the prevalence of such diseases in ancient Egypt as no evidence is retained on the skeleton. Whatever the reason for wearing wigs, there is no doubt they constituted an important commercial industry. Research has indicated that most Egyptian wigs were made from human hair, many being of elaborate construction. An exemplary wig at the British Museum, consisting of a mass of light-colored curls atop numerous dark-colored plaits, is constructed from over 120,000 human hairs. Despite the preoccupation with hair care, baldness was evidently a fact of life in ancient Egypt, to judge from the recipes contained in the Ebers Papyrus, one of which recommends a cure, using a mixture of fats from a lion and a hippo.

Herodotus wrote that Egyptian priests shaved their

bodies every other day; again, the prevention of lice infestation is postulated, however, the act may have held religious significance as a symbol of purification. Depilatory equipment, metal tweezers, razors, knives, and small whetstones, helped the Egyptians fastidiously pluck and shave unwanted hair. In the Middle Kingdom *Story of Sinuhe*, Egyptian standards of cleanliness are compared with the lesser hygienic habits of the foreigners that Sinuhe encountered on his travels, when he says: "Years were removed from my body. I was shaved and my hair was combed." From the nineteenth dynasty onward, priests shaved their heads completely. The history of facial hair can be charted from Predynastic times, when figures of wood or clay suggest that Egyptian men then favored beards. Those Predynastic beards, as evidenced on the Narmer Palette, may have been purely symbolic, however. Certainly, as with the unkempt hairstyles noted above, facial hair eventually became indicative of a low rank in life but, during the Old Kingdom, neat moustaches were very much in vogue among the upper classes, as can be seen on the statue of Prince Rahotep. As with unkempt hair, facial hair may also have indicated a state of mourning. For example, eighteenth dynasty depictions of King Akhenaten in an "unclean" state, with facial stubble, has been interpreted as the king's outward display of grief following the death of one of his daughters. In Egyptian religious concepts, facial hair came to be a divine attribute of the gods, with deities depicted wearing plaited beards and the dead and mummified pharaoh adorned with a false beard, secured by cords. While barbering was probably undertaken within the home, it is possible that there were itinerant barbers.

The examination of Egyptian mummies undertaken so far seems to indicate that most Egyptian males were circumcised. The practice may certainly relate to a state of ritual purity, but there can be little doubt that hygiene was an important motivating factor. The surgical procedure of circumcision is not mentioned in the extant medical texts and is depicted on only two occasions. The better known scene is that from the sixth dynasty tomb of Ankhmahor at Saqqara, which seems to show two young men being circumcised; it has been suggested, however, that this is an initiation scene, showing the shaving, preparation, and circumcision of a *ḥm-k3* priest. The second circumcision scene, now very badly damaged, is in the temple of Mut-en-Asheru at Karnak. During the Old and Middle Kingdom, Egyptian boys were probably circumcised between the ages of six and twelve years, although Weha, an eleventh dynasty man from Naga ed-Deir, reports being circumcised with 120 other "men." Perhaps only royal personages, the nobility, and priests were routinely circumcised during these periods, but in later periods the procedure may have become routine for all Egyptian males. It is not clear whether the procedure involved the actual removal of the foreskin or merely a ritualistic "cut." From at least the Late period, priests had to be circumcised in order to attain the state of purity deemed necessary for the execution of their duties in the temple. Again, foreigners who were not circumcised were looked down upon by the Egyptians and were regarded as unclean. Despite the fact that full female circumcision (as practiced in modern Sudan) is known as "pharaonic circumcision," there is no direct evidence for it in ancient Egypt. Nevertheless, the Classical author Strabo believed that the Egyptians circumcised their daughters, for he wrote; "the Egyptians circumcise the males and excise the females." It is difficult to assess mummified female bodies, distorted by the mummification process, for evidence of the excision procedure.

As in many other ancient societies, Egypt had a high infant mortality rate. Poor standards of hygiene led to dysentery, diarrhea, and gastric disorders resulting in infant deaths. Puerperal fever and other complications of giving birth, exacerbated by a lack of hygiene, contributed to maternal mortalities. Excavations at the Gabati cemetery in Central Sudan have revealed the burials of several adult females with a fetus or newborn baby, a testament to the hazards of childbirth in ancient times. Women were regarded as "unclean" after giving birth, and the event was followed by a period of cleansing or purification. Evidence from the Westcar Papyrus suggests that the new mother underwent a period of seclusion from her family for up to fourteen days to attain a state of purification. Women were also regarded as "unclean" during their times of menstruation; it is not clear, however, whether it was the woman herself or the menstrual flow that was regarded with disfavor. Generally, there is little information about menstruation from ancient Egyptian sources, as texts were written by men. Notably, the Middle Kingdom *Satire of the Trades* regarded as unfortunate the washerman who must clean women's bloodstained clothing.

Dental health was very much influenced by hygiene practices or the lack of them. Inadequate oral hygiene is implicated in the two main forms of dental disease: periodontal disease and dental caries (cavities). Both conditions are related to the formation of plaque, a sticky film in which bacteria proliferate on the teeth. Plaque irritates the gums, causing gingivitis, the first stage of periodontal disease. Left unchecked, this inflammation travels into the gum, destroying the fibers holding the tooth in its socket; eventually the tooth may fall out. The molars are most commonly affected, since they are less readily cleansed by the action of the tongue and saliva. Tooth decay, if left untreated, can also lead to the loss of an affected tooth, through the formation of a dental abscess. Amenhotpe III and Ramesses II feature dental abscesses as part of their dental health profile. Sometimes unremoved plaque calcifies to form calculus (or tartar), which creates gum pockets wherein decay can intensify. Diet is another important causative factor in the development of periodontal disease and dental decay, since certain foodstuffs promote the rapid growth of plaque. Roman historians suggested that the ancient Egyptians used a type of "toothpaste" made from the roots of plants. It is possible that, as now used in parts of Africa, twigs and sticks served as rudimentary but effective toothbrushes. Rags may also have been used to clean the teeth. Then, as now, people were concerned with halitosis, or bad breath, and several medical papyri recommend chewing pellets of aromatic spices and honey to improve the situation. It is possible that cinnamon, having mildy astringent properties, was used as an antiseptic mouthwash. Ritual evidence suggests that the king's oral hygiene also included natron, to purify his mouth, as part of his morning toilette.

[*See also* Birth; Dental Care; Disease; Hairstyles; Medicine; *and* Toiletries and Cosmetics.]

BIBLIOGRAPHY

Filer, J. *Disease*. London, 1995. Surveys the health status of the ancient Egyptians and Nubians.

Filer, J. M. "The SARS excavations at Gabati, Central Sudan, 1994–5: C: The Skeletal remains." *The Sudan Archaeological Research Society Newsletter* 8 (1995), 23–27.

Filer, Joyce. "Revealing Hermione's Secrets." *Egyptian Archaeology* 11 (1997), 32–34. Presents the findings from a new examination of this well-known mummy.

Filer, Joyce. "The Gabati Cemetery. An Ancient Nubian Population Revealed." *Minerva* 10.2 (1999), 31–34.

Fletcher, J. A. "A Tale of Hair, Wigs and Lice." *Egyptian Archaeology* 5 (1994), 31–33. Explores hair and hygiene in ancient Egypt.

Nunn, J. *Ancient Egyptian Medicine*. London, 1996. Offers an excellent overview of medical practices and practitioners in ancient Egypt.

JOYCE M. FILER

HYKSOS. The term *Hyksos* (Ὑκσωζ), the Greek rendering of Egyptian *ḥḳꜣw-ḫꜣswt*, means "rulers of the foreign countries" and should not be confused with "Shepherd Kings" (a popular etymology according to the first-century CE Roman-Jewish historian Flavius Josephus). "Hyksos" was originally a common designation for foreign rulers, but it became—according to the Turin Canon and to inscriptions on scarabs and the royal protocol on a doorjamb—the official designation of at least the first three of the six kings of the fifteenth dynasty (although the Turin Canon lists all six with this designation). After King Khayan, this strange title was possibly dropped, which could be seen as a sign of a political trend toward a more thorough Egyptianization.

Egypt's fifteenth dynasty was of Near Eastern origin. According to the Turin Canon, it ruled Egypt for 108 years (c.1664–1555 BCE). Strictly speaking, the term *Hyksos* should be used only for these kings and not as an ethnic designation, as introduced by the third-century BCE Greco-Egyptian historian Manetho.

Memory about the Hyksos. Other than the Hyksos kings of the fifteenth dynasty, some Theban kings of the sixteenth and seventeenth dynasties were designated "Shepherd Kings." They also ruled at the same time as, and were more or less dependent on, the fifteenth dynasty for their lineage. The seventeenth dynasty was again of Egyptian descent. The kings of the sixteenth dynasty were considered to be a minor Hyksos dynasty and were probably vassals of the fifteenth dynasty.

The Hyksos takeover of Egypt is presented here (see Wadell 1956) according to Manetho, and following Josephus, as an invasion during the reign of the ephemeral king Tutimaeus,

> In his reign . . . invaders of obscure race marched in confidence of victory against our land. By main force they easily seized it without striking a blow; and having overpowered the rulers of the land, they then burned our cities ruthlessly, razed to the ground the temples of the gods, and treated all the natives with a cruel hostility, massacring some and leading into slavery the wives and children of others. Finally they appointed as king one of their number whose name was Salitis. He had his seat at Memphis, levying tribute from Upper and Lower Egypt, and always leaving garrisons behind in the most advantageous positions. Above all he fortified the district to the east, foreseeing that the Assyrians . . . would one day covet and attack his kingdom.
>
> In the Saïte (Sethroïte) nome he found a city very favourably situated on the east of the Bubastite branch of the Nile, and called Avaris. . . . This place he rebuilt and fortified with massive walls, planting there a garrison. . . . Their race as a whole was called Hyksos, that is king-shepherds.

After a prolonged war with the Egyptians, the Hyksos were driven from Egypt and confined to the Delta city of Avaris. In an attempt

> by siege to force them to surrender, blockading . . . giving up the siege in despair, [the king] concluded a treaty by which they should all depart from Egypt. . . . On these terms the Shepherds, with all their possessions and households complete . . . left Egypt and journeyed over the desert into Syria.

Avaris was a big fortified place in the Delta, east of the Bubastic branch of the Nile, in keeping with the archaeological remains of Tell ed-Dabʿa. Manetho's account of the destruction of temples and other atrocities has been doubted by scholars and was most probably an exaggeration. The many royal Middle Kingdom statues found in Tanis, but most probably transported originally to Avaris, can be seen as a sign of the destruction of Egyptian monuments in the Hyksos period. It is also thought that the

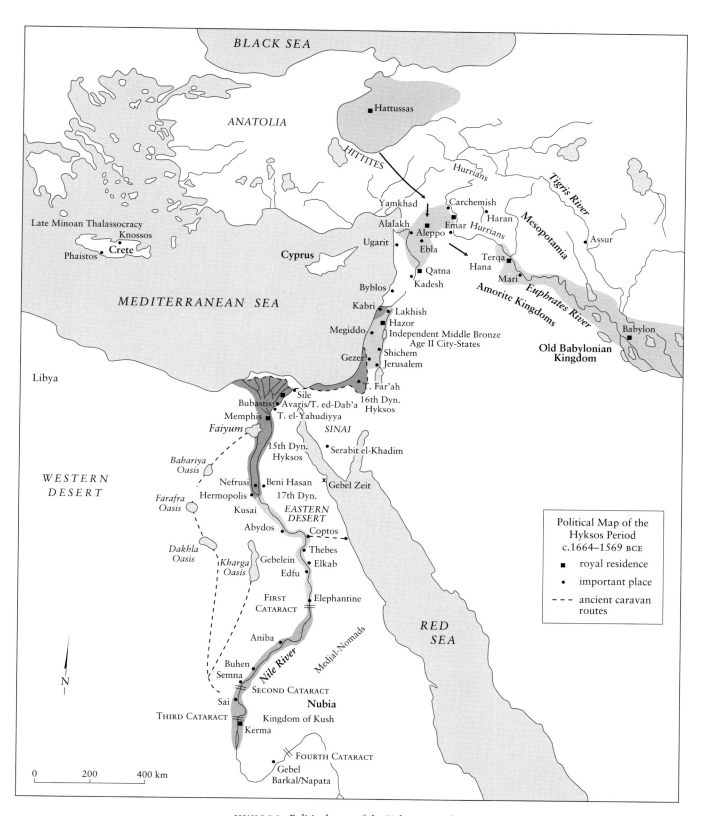

BLACK SEA

ANATOLIA

■ Hattussas

HITTITES

Hurrians

Tigris River

Mesopotamia

Yamkhad

■ Carchemish

Haran

Late Minoan Thalassocracy

Knossos

Crete

Phaistos

Alalakh

■ Emar *Hurrians*

Aleppo

■ Assur

Ugarit

Ebla

Cyprus

Terqa ■

Hana

Mari

Amorite Kingdoms

Euphrates River

■ Babylon

MEDITERRANEAN SEA

Qatna

Kadesh

Old Babylonian Kingdom

Byblos

Kabri

Lakhish

Hazor

Megiddo

Independent Middle Bronze Age II City-States

Shichem

Gezer

Jerusalem

T. Far'ah

Libya

Sile

16th Dyn. Hyksos

Bubastis

Avaris/T. ed-Dab'a

Memphis

T. el-Yahudiyya

Faiyum

SINAI

Bahariya Oasis

15th Dyn. Hyksos

• Serabit el-Khadim

Farafra Oasis

Nefrusi

• Beni Hasan

X Gebel Zeit

Hermopolis

17th Dyn.

EASTERN DESERT

WESTERN DESERT

Kusai

Dakhla Oasis

Abydos

Coptos

Kharga Oasis

• Thebes

Gebelein

• Elkab

Edfu

FIRST CATARACT

• Elephantine

RED SEA

| Political Map of the Hyksos Period c.1664–1569 BCE |
| ■ royal residence |
| • important place |
| - - - ancient caravan routes |

Aniba

Medja-Nomads

Nile River

Buhen

Semna

SECOND CATARACT

Sai

Nubia

THIRD CATARACT

Kerma

Kingdom of Kush

FOURTH CATARACT

• Gebel Barkal/Napata

0   200   400 km

N

HYKSOS. *Political map of the Hyksos period.*

many private and royal Middle Kingdom statues abroad may have been traded by the Hyksos dynasty.

Hyksos Rule in Egypt. The rise of Hyksos rule can be traced to the major influx from the Levant into Egypt's temple economy and the royal and private households of the twelfth and the thirteenth dynasties, especially those near the royal residence (at Itjtawy, el-Lisht) or at Illahun. Their large settlement in the northeastern Nile Delta (Tell ed-Dab'a, later Avaris) was inhabited by soldiers, shipbuilders, craftsmen, and trading agents from Syria-Palestine. It became a specialized settlement at the northeastern entrance of Egypt for organizing and controlling Egyptian mining expeditions and trade with the Levant, Cyprus, and to some extent the Aegean. The Egyptian officials responsible for this activity ("Overseers of Foreign Countries" or "Overseers of Retenu") were peoples of West Semitic language. Their tombs were adjacent to their palatial residences, and some had monumental limestone statues portraying them in their native dress and coiffure. The later destruction of such statues indicates political turmoil in that region. Their nearly exclusive control over foreign commodities, soldiers, ships, and connected installations in the eastern Delta gave them powerful positioning for making policy.

The thirteenth dynasty was not stable; it consisted, more or less, of a continuum of usurpers with very short reigns that averaged three years. The power brokers of that period were administrators and generals, some of them of foreign origin. Toward the end of the eighteenth century BCE, parts of the Delta broke with thirteenth dynasty rule. By a few monuments, the kingdom of Nehesy "the Nubian" is known. His monuments are only in the northeastern Delta, between Bubastis and Tell el-Hebwa. He seems to have resided in Avaris, where he created an Egyptian interpretation of a local cult of the Syrian storm god Hadad (Baal-Zaphon), syncretizing him with the Egyptian storm god Seth, who became from that time the dynastic god "Seth, lord of Avaris" or "Seth, lord of *R₃-₃ḥt*" ("door of the fertile land"). The name Nehesy is known from several monuments as "oldest king's son" before he came to reign. He was possibly part Egyptian, based on his mother's purely Egyptian civil name. His power rested, however, on the large population of Near Easterners, who had continuously settled in the northeastern Delta before his reign. Many kings' names of the fourteenth dynasty may not be Egyptian, and several are West Semitic. The large number of non-Egyptian names suggests that several small kingdoms existed in the northeastern Delta during that time, but only one, with Avaris as capital, has been documented. It probably became the core of the later kingdom of the Hyksos. This would explain why the kings of the fourteenth dynasty were originally called *ḥḳ₃w-ḫ₃swt* ("rulers of the foreign countries"). This title led to the mistake that this dynasty originated from the town of Xois (according to the Manethonian tradition). [*See* Manetho.] There is, however, no indication that Xois was an important city during the Second Intermediate Period.

The transition from the late Middle Kingdom to the fifteenth dynasty (and the Second Intermediate Period) remains unclear. It may have begun with the union of several petty kingdoms in the northeastern Delta or with the takeover by Salitis of Memphis, the traditional capital, as well as the Middle Kingdom royal residence, Itj-tawy—so that he would be crowned as pharaoh. Whatever the cause, the late thirteenth dynasty rulers either withdrew to Upper Egypt or abdicated to a new local dynasty, a phenomenon that was parallel to the dissolution of the fourteenth dynasty in the Delta. At that time, Lower Nubia was left to the Sudanese kingdom of Kush. A stela of the local Theban king Neferhotpe III shows that hordes of Near Easterners destabilized the Theban area. It may have been only a matter of time until Upper Egypt came under the control of the North.

The Fifteenth Dynasty. The six Hyksos in Manetho's epitomes have their equivalent in the six Hyksos on a fragment of the Turin Canon. Only the name of the last king, Ḥamudi, was preserved. To equate the six Hyksos names from Manetho's excerpts with those from monuments is very difficult because of corrupted versions in the epitomes. For the beginning of the fifteenth dynasty, Manetho attributes nineteen regnal years to Salitis. From a genealogy of priests, the name Shalek *(Š₃rk)* has been proposed as the first Hyksos king, who lived one generation before Apophis. The names *M₃'-ib-R'* and *šši* on numerous scarabs with a wide distribution have never been found on monuments. Inclusion into the main Hyksos dynasty may therefore be doubtful; the same applies to the name *Mr-wsr-R' I'ḳb-ḥr* (Ya'akob-har), whose scarabs were found from Kerma in the Sudan to Shiqmona in northern Palestine.

Seuserenre Khayan (Apachnan from Manetho's list) must have been an important ruler, since monumental architecture is known from his reign, such as an inscribed block from Gebelein. Stone vessels have been found in Knossos and in Boghazköy that were probably diplomatic gifts from Khayan, sent abroad. He also usurped statues of the Middle Kingdom. On a stela from Tell ed-Dab'a, containing the royal names of Khayan, there is evidence of the king's oldest son Yanassy (Yansas-aden); probably he can be identified with Iannas from Manetho's list (who according to Josephus, reigned after Apophis; according to the third century CE historian Africanus, Khayan ruled under the name Staan, two reigns before Iannis).

The most important Hyksos was Apophis (Apopy), who had a long reign (c.1605–1565 BCE). He probably held suc-

HYKSOS. *Gold diadem of a Hyksos princess.* It is designed with representations of rosettes and heads of oryxes. (The Metropolitan Museum of Art, Lila Acheson Wallace Gift Fund, 1968. [68.136.1])

cessively the pronomina *ʾз-ḳnn-Rʿ*, *Nb-ḥpš-Rʿ*, and *ʾз-wsr-Rʿ*. An architrave from Gebelein also shows his name. The Rhind mathematical papyrus is dated to his thirty-third regnal year. Manetho's epitomes attribute either sixty-one or fourteen years to his rule. As the opponent of the kings Sekenenre and Kamose of Thebes, Apophis should be placed near the end of the Hyksos period. Most likely, he was the immediate predecessor of Ḥamudi (Khamudy), the only Hyksos name preserved in the Turin Canon. The length of his reign can be approximated from the reverse of the Rhind mathematical papyrus, dated to Year 11 of an unmentioned king—who can only be Ḥamudi.

The succession of Khayan, Yansas-aden, Apophis, and Ḥamudi is probably correct. The dynastic placement of Seker-her (Sikru-Haddu, "memory of the god Hadad") is problematic. He must have been (according to a monumental doorway with his full titles) one of the six Hyksos of the fifteenth dynasty.

Nearly all the Hyksos names have been convincingly decoded as West Semitic (Redford, 1970, Ryholt, 1997, and Schneider, 1998), with some differences in interpreting the etymology. The suggestion that some of the names may be Hurrian or even Aryan is not convincing. Besides the above-mentioned names of the fifteenth dynasty, many more scarabs are known with West Semitic names, such as ʿAmu, Yakʿammu, Yakbeʿam, and Yakubaʿal; some of them also carried the title of Hyksos, like ʿAnat-her, User-ʿAnat, and Semqen. Probably the above-mentioned

scarabs with the names Maa-ibre Sheshy and Mer-userre Yaʿa kub-har should be placed within this group, rather than among the kings of the fifteenth dynasty. Some Egyptologists place most of the obscure kings under the sixteenth dynasty. Their frequency in Palestine (Iʿaqeb-her and Yakbeʿam occurred even in northern coastal Palestine) leads to the suspicion that there were a number of rulers in southern Palestine around Sharuhen or even as far north as Tel Kabri, who were vassals to the fifteenth dynasty kings, or even partly independent. It is unclear whether the sixteenth dynasty designation "Shepherd Kings," according to the Africanus version, is correct, or if the sixteenth dynasty kings reigned in Thebes (Eusebius) as Ryholt (1997) maintains. Without doubt, there were, under the umbrella of the fifteenth dynasty rulers, a series of vassals in southern and coastal Palestine, in Middle Egypt, and in Thebes. (In Thebes, they also can be identified within the seventeenth dynasty.) Such was the political system of the Hyksos, and typical of the Amorite kingdoms in Syria and the city-states in Palestine. We know little about the conditions in the central and western Delta at that time; probably vassals were installed there, too.

The Hyksos soon took pharaonic status and titles and probably used Egyptian scribes and officials for administration. It seems, however, that they adapted the administration to their own tradition. No vizier is known, but the office of the chancellor (*ʾimy-r-ḥtm.t*), with the West Semitic name *Ḥ3r*, seems to have had prime importance; scarabs with his name have a wide distribution, from southern Palestine to Kerma in Sudan. The sciences and literature were continued, and several important papyri were kept in Avaris: the mathematical Rhind Papyrus, the literary Westcar Papyrus, and some medical papyri.

The chancellor's scarabs and a similar wide distribution of certain types of pottery (of Tell el-Yahudiyya ware) show the extent of Hyksos commercial and political influence. The presence of such seals and pottery in Lower Nubia and Sudan and the paucity of such objects in Upper Egypt indicate that the Hyksos kingdom in northern Egypt and the southern kingdom of Kush established direct relations, without Upper Egypt participating in this trade. Such commerce would make strongholds necessary, controlled by the Hyksos. Such a station was set up on the commanding rocks of Gebelein, 28 kilometers (17 miles) south of Luxor, where two blocks of monumental architecture with the names of Khayan and Apophis were found (it is unlikely that those blocks were transported from Lower Egypt just to be incorporated as fill there). Another such stronghold was Nefrusi in Middle Egypt.

In southern Palestine, the widespread Hyksos scarabs and Tell el-Yahudiyya ware indicate a Hyksos realm of influence. Central inland Palestine shows a distinctly different pottery scatter, a sign of cultural and political distinction, independent of the Hyksos. Nonetheless, the enormous fortifications in the south of Canaan that are dated to the late Middle Bronze Age could be taken as some evidence of protection against the Hyksos.

According to the Speos Artemidos inscription of Hatshepsut, the Hyksos ruled without Re and, according to the Sallier Papyrus, King Apophis did not serve any god but Seth. This may be an exaggeration since the Hyksos kings used the prenomens constructed with Re and the *z3-Rʿ*-title ("son of Re"), at least from Khayan onward. They seem to have followed some Canaanite cults that incorporated Egyptian traits and showed acculturation (according to archaeological evidence from a temple precinct in Avaris). The Hyksos also tolerated the continuation of local traditional cults in Egypt but probably failed to maintain them.

The End of Hyksos Rule. Under Khayan and the early reign of Apophis, the rule of the Hyksos reached its peak. Resistance against those kings started from their remotest vassal, Thebes, which then controlled the region between Elephantine and Cusae, to the south of Hermopolis. The beginning of the seventeenth dynasty there seems to coincide with the beginning of Hyksos rule—and this suggests that the seventeenth dynasty may have been installed by the Hyksos. Yet the names of its kings, such as Intef and Montuhotep, suggest Theban nationalism. In the Ramessid-era Papyrus Sallier I, in the tale of Apophis and

Sekenenre, a problem arose between the Hyksos ruler and his Upper Egyptian vassal; the end of the story is not preserved, but the mummy of King Sekenenre Taʿo shows several deadly wounds caused by a Syrian-Palestinian battle axe. An encounter on the battlefield between this king and the forces of his overlord Apophis was possible. At Deir el-Ballas in Upper Egypt, near Naqada, a castle was constructed by Sekenenre Taʿo that served, according to the excavator Peter Lacovara, for this king and his successors Kamose and Ahmose, as a campaign residence against the Hyksos. Inscriptions on Tablet Carnarvon I and the two stelae of Kamose, found at Karnak, tell that at the beginning of Kamose's reign, conditions were peaceful; in his third year, he began a rebellion against the Hyksos ruler Apophis. The devoted vassal of the Hyksos Teti, son of Pepy, was defeated at Nefrusi. A surprise attack to the north then opened a route to Avaris. Apophis attempted to resume a former strategic relationship with the king of Kush (Kerma), inviting him to attack in the south of Egypt while Kamose was still busy in the north; but the messenger, who had avoided the Nile Valley, was intercepted along the oasis route.

Avaris was not taken by Kamose, but his stela reported that plentiful booty was taken from hundreds of ships filled with gold, lapis lapis lazuli, silver, turquoise, innumerable bronze battle axes, *b3k*-oil, incense, fat, honey, precious woods, and other products from "Retenu" (Lebanon/Palestine). Kamose claimed to have taken everything from Avaris, although this seems highly exaggerated. It is also unlikely that the ships were not turned back before the Thebans could advance to Avaris. The listing of the products of Retenu is valuable for its information about goods from Canaan. Kamose seems to have died that year, since no records survive for him beyond Year 3 of his reign. Ahmose, probably his brother, succeeded to the throne as a child under the tutelage of his mother Ahhotep, so it took some time before warfare with the Hyksos was resumed. That could not have happened before the eleventh year of the reign of King Ḥamudi, who must have succeeded Apophis, after the Year 3 of Kamose, although the exact date is undetermined. Most likely, he started his reign later than Ahmose. According to paleographic evidence, the final assault on Avaris happened only from Ahmose's eighteenth regnal year onward, but not much later.

The entry on the reverse of Rhind Papyrus states that Memphis (Heliopolis) was the first city to be taken in Ahmose's offense against the Hyksos. Two days later, the Thebans took the frontier fortress Sile (probably Tell el-Hebwa). For this operation they must have bypassed Avaris along the river and severed connections between Avaris and Palestine. The length of the siege of Avaris is unknown, owing to limited information. The naval officer

Ahmose, son of Abn, mentions in his autobiographical inscription in his tomb in Elkab, some battles in which he was personally involved, and "then one took Avaris." (More information can be expected from the study of numerous relief fragments, with representations of the warfare around Avaris, found recently by Stephen Harvey at the Ahmose pyramid-temple at Abydos.)

Manetho's work, as related to us by Flavius Josephus, reported the ancient Egyptians in despair because of the long siege, so they agreed to a free retreat by the Hyksos to Palestine. The archaeological record at Tell ed-Dab'a revealed that the majority of the town escaped destruction by fire and seems to have been abandoned; within the citadel, however, we have evidence of destruction and violence.

After the conquest of Avaris, Ahmose constructed within the Hyksos citadel his own headquarters, containing two palaces on high platforms—a big one and a small one. Those installations probably replaced his former campaign residence in Deir el-Ballas and served as a new residence for the campaigns he continued against the Hyksos in southern Palestine. Surprisingly, parts of his new palace compound in Avaris imitated Aegean ashlar façades with wooden elements. A side entrance had painted decorations and a portico. Rooms of the small palace had Minoan-style wall paintings: bull-leaping, bull-grappling, hunting, acrobatics, and emblematic griffins. The use of scenes typical to Minoan palaces suggests a throne room, similar to that known from the palace at Knossos. The similarity of emblems shared with Knossos includes a half-rosette frieze. The Minoan paintings probably reflected a new political agreement between Egypt—which could provide the luxury goods of Africa, especially gold—and the most formidable sea power of that time, the Minoan Thalassocracy, which could provide Egypt some security at sea. Lacking a seagoing fleet at that time, Egypt probably needed the help of a sea power.

After the reconquest of Avaris and the eastern Delta region, the Egyptians of the early New Kingdom were still vulnerable. The Hyksos had not been thoroughly defeated, especially since several sites show that they must have had an intact domain to the northeast of the Delta in southern Palestine. There, a subdynasty of the main Hyksos existed (probably the sixteenth dynasty). Southern Palestine was the main olive oil and wine source for the Hyksos, as known from the many amphoras in Avarais from that region. Great were the resources and economic strength of this remaining Hyksos kingdom, to which the Avaris Hyksos withdrew; thus the potential of a reconquest of Egypt from this nearby base still existed in the early New Kingdom. The attack by Ahmose on Sharuhen in southern Palestine was then a logical move for the stabilization of his reign. According to the biography of his namesake Ahmose, son of Abu, it took three years to take Sharuhen. The assaults on the other towns in southern Palestine were, perhaps, not less difficult. The Middle Bronze Age city-states in inland Palestine were not attacked until the time of Thutmose III. After the destruction of the Hyksos kingdom in southern Palestine, the successors of Ahmose focused their attention immediately to the north, to Syria, where another new and formidable power, the kingdom of Mitanni, had begun to infiltrate the important city-states there. Egypt, after a long period of isolation, was fully entangled in the mainstream of Near Eastern politics during the eighteenth dynasty.

Archaeological Sources. In archaeological terms, the presence of the Hyksos rule in Egypt can be assessed through the data from sites that were a specific variant of the Syrian-Palestinian Middle Bronze Age culture. These sites were found east of the Pelusiac branch of the Nile River, along the eastern edge of the Delta. They represent something similar to a cultural province that outlined the core, or the homeland, of the Hyksos rule in Egypt. The most important, and northernmost site was Tell ed-Dab'a (Avaris) which had the longest history of continuous settlement. The Syrian-Palestinian Middle Bronze Age culture there dates to the late twelfth dynasty (c.1800 BCE), when a massive influx came to the region. Before that, only a few sherds of Levantine origin were found in the stratigraphy of an otherwise purely Egyptian culture. Perhaps the size and singularity of the early settlement at Tell ed-Dab'a can be explained best as an open trading zone for the Levant—comparable to Naucratis for the Greeks in the Late period. Besides Tell ed-Dab'a, the Middle Bronze Age IIA (Middle Bronze Age I) is only represented by some few camp sites without architectural features in the Wadi Tumilat, perhaps originating from migrating nomads. Some tombs that date to the end of this period are known at Farasha.

All other known sites are dated to the time of the Hyksos rule, especially to the second half of this period. One of the most important strategic sites was Tell el-Yahudiyya, with a rampart fortification covered by a stucco slope. North of that site were the cemeteries of Inshâs and another settlement at Ghita. In the Wadi Tumilat were cemeteries at Kua, a bigger settlement with tombs at Pithom, and more tombs at Tell es-Sahaba. (Remains of Middle Bronze Age culture from Bubastis are unverified.)

The position of the Hyksos sites shows that during their rule the route along the Pelusiac branch of the Nile was important for sea connections to the Levant. The land route along the Wadi Tumilat—a traditional track to the central and southern Sinai—was also important. Interestingly, no evidence exists for the use of the *via maris* or the turquoise mines at Serabit el-Khadim during this period. A connection to the Red Sea has been suggested but not verified. Some contacts to the galena mines at Gebel Zeit can be postulated according to hawk-shaped Tell el-Yahudiyya ware that has been found in the eastern Delta. Since Middle Bronze Age sites are not known from other parts of Egypt, this suggests that the land was otherwise controlled by vassals and by occupied strongholds.

The sites, in particular Tell ed-Dab'a, show that long before the Hyksos, Near Easterners lived in the Nile Delta. The camp sites at Wadi Tumilat show that they were nomads pasturing their flocks. The stable settlement at Tell ed-Dab'a, with its Syrian middle-room houses (dated to the Middle Bronze Age IIA period), as well as house burials and temple constructions, demonstrate that an urban population of a different background was in residence there. Some of the ceramic and architectural features point toward northern Syria as their origin. This source is also indicated by a locally made cylinder seal, with a representation of the northern Syrian storm god. Another part of the population may have originated from southern Palestine, from where the majority of trade originated. A high percentage of graves having weapons and copper molds suggests that many settlers were soldiers and metalworkers. The martial features in the burial customs continued until the Hyksos period. Pairs of donkey burials were found in front of tombs, indicating the use of caravans.

An Egyptian administrative palace of the early thirteenth dynasty shows that the officials who resided there were Near Eastern. The cemetery attached to the palace has syncretic features of Syrian-Palestinian Middle Bronze Age and Egyptian burial traditions. Even high officials who controlled the administration of trade and other enterprises with the Levant were of Near Eastern origin. A few held the title of "Overseer of Foreign Countries" and had colossal limestone statues set up in the chapels of their tombs, depicting them as Near Eastern dignitaries, with red mushroom-shaped coiffures, yellow skin, and the traditional throw stick. A blending of ideology was also present in Canaanite temples and cult installations within Egyptian mortuary chapels, showing that syncretism between the two cultures developed both before and during the Hyksos period. The position of tombs within houses and the location of graveyards in the midst of settlements is, however, an ancient Near Eastern feature.

The location of Avaris in a northerly position at a navigable Nile branch and the listing of numerous ships at Avaris in the Second Kamose Stela makes it clear that maritime activity was an important part of this community living in Egypt. With the beginning of the Hyksos period, the settlement area of Avaris doubled or tripled in size, and in the eastern Delta most of the sites date only to this period. There were also changes in some classes of pottery, especially in the Tell el-Yahudiyya ware. All the evidence suggests that a massive influx of people came to Avaris.

Archaeological evidence in Egypt reveals that intense trade occurred with southern Palestine throughout the Second Intermediate Period—with the main imports olive oil and wine. New animals were introduced, including the horse and, shortly before the Hyksos period, woolbearing sheep. Contacts with the northern Levant were, however, poor during the Hyksos period, owing to the destabilized condition of the coastal Syrian towns. Yet trade with Cyprus flourished, and the ceramic records of mutual imports from Egypt in Cyprus were, perhaps, only a side effect of an increased demand for copper by the Hyksos. Trade with Cyprus reached a peak toward the end of the Hyksos period, especially at Tell ed-Dab'a and, to a lesser extent, farther inland. Fragments of huge storage jars show that commodities, such as fruits, nuts, or other organic matter, were imported in large quantities. The archaeological record also shows that trade between the Hyksos-dominated North and Upper Egypt was very poor and that during the later phase of the Hyksos period imports from the Memphite area came to an end. This lack of trade prompted an increased isolation of the eastern Delta from the rest of Egypt, and resulted in economic disadvantages for the North, which explains its eventual downfall.

The impact of the Hyksos on ancient Egypt should not be underestimated. They were perceived as a foreign dynasty, so their political relations and acts of power must have caused great internal irritation. Their rule therefore stimulated a political nationalism by the time of the rulers of the late seventeenth dynasty. Egypt benefited from the Hyksos trading network that included the southern Levant and Cyprus, as well as some technical innovations in the ceramic and metal industries. The long contact with a Near Eastern culture also had its impact on Egypt in the fields of literature, music, and perhaps indirectly in language innovations. From those influences, Egypt became, in the New Kingdom, more involved with the eastern Mediterranean than ever before.

[See also Ahmose; Dab'a, Tell ed-; Fifteenth Dynasty; Foreign Incursions; Kamose; Pithom; Second Intermediate Period; and Yahudiyya, Tell el-.]

BIBLIOGRAPHY

Alt, A. *Die Herkunft der Hyksos in neuer Sicht.* Sitzungsberichte d. Sächsischen Akademie der Wissenschaften, 101.6. Leipzig, 1954.

Bietak, M. "Hyksos." In *Lexikon der Ägyptologie*, 3:62 ff. Wiesbaden, 1978.

Bietak, M. *Avaris and Piramesse, Archaeological Exploration in the Eastern Nile Delta.* Ninth Mortimer Wheeler Archaeological Lecture, The British Academy. Oxford, 1981. Included in *Proceedings of the British Academy,* London, 65, pp. 225–290. 2d enl. ed. Oxford, 1986.

Bietak, M. "Egypt and Canaan during the Middle Bronze Age." *Bulletin of the American Schools of Oriental Research* 282 (1991), 28–72.

Bietak, M. *Avaris, The Capital of the Hyksos—Recent Excavations at Tell el-Dab'a.* The first Raymond and Beverly Sackler Foundation Distinguished Lecture in Egyptology, British Museum Publications. London, 1996.

Gardiner, A. H., "The Defeat of the Hyksos by Kamose: The Carnarvon Tablet No. 1." *Journal of Egyptian Archaeology* 3 (1916), 95–110.

Giveon, R. "The Hyksos in the South." In *Fontes atque pontes: Eine Festgabe für Hellmut Brunner,* edited by M. Görg. Wiesbaden, 1986.

Habachi, L. *The Second Stela of Kamose and His Struggle against the Hyksos Ruler and His Capital.* Glückstadt, 1972.

Oren, E. D. ed. *The Hyksos: New Historical and Archaeological Perspectives.* University Museum Symposium Series. Philadelphia, 1997.

Van Seters, J. *The Hyksos: A New Investigation.* New Haven, 1966.

Redford, Donald B. "The Hyksos Invasion in History and Tradition." *Orientalia* n. s. 39 (1970), 1–51.

Redford, Donald B. *Egypt, Canaan, and Israel.* Princeton, N.J., 1992.

Ryholt, K. S. B. *The Political Situation in Egypt during the Second Intermediate Period c.1800–1550 B.C.* CNI Publications, 20. Copenhagen, 1997.

Säve-Söderbergh, T. "The Hyksos Rule in Egypt." *Journal of Egyptian Archaeology* 37 (1951), 53–71.

Schneider, T. *Ausländer in Ägypten. während des Mittleren Reiches und der Hyksozeit.* Ägypten und Altes Testament, 42. Wiesbaden, 1998. Follows O. Rössler's transcription system.

Wadell, W. G. *Manetho.* Loeb Classical Library. London, 1956.

Weinstein, J. "Hyksos." In *The Oxford Encyclopedia of Archaeology in the Near East,* edited by E. M. Myers et al., vol. 3, pp. 133–136. New York, 1997.

MANFRED BIETAK

HYMNS. [*This entry surveys the major types of ancient Egyptian hymns, with reference to their origins, themes, metrics, verse points, and sources of documentation. It comprises three articles:*

Nile Hymns
Osiris Hymns
Solar Hymns

For related discussions, see Lyric.]

Nile Hymns

Besides the sun, the inundation of the Nile is the next most important natural phenomenon in Egypt. Yet while many hymns to the sun are known, only six different Nile hymns are known from the pharaonic period.

The first is the great Nile hymn, which is generally but inaccurately attributed to the poet Kheti. The large number of surviving copies (four papyri, two writing tablets, and seventy ostraca) shows that this text was popular with the people and highly appreciated by writers. According to the main manuscripts, this hymn has 136 verses, divided by rubrics into fourteen strophes. Most probably, this hymn of high literary value and beauty was sung during the celebrations at the coming of the flood, which began to rise around the heliacal rising of the star Sirius, near 19 July. The hymn is intended to encourage the god Hapy to come to Egypt and to give it his blessing. Careful examination of the available manuscripts shows that the great Nile hymn is not an "exceptionally obscure and corrupt . . . composition," as Gardiner characterized the text in 1935 (*Hieratic Papyri in the British Museum,* third series, I, p. 46); on the contrary, its contents, formal structure, and metrics are carefully composed.

The first of this hymn's three main parts is formed by strophes I–X (22+54+22 verses). Here the progress of the flood is followed from its emergence near the island of Elephantine in the South (I, 2) via the Faiyum in Middle Egypt (VII, 3) and Heliopolis in Lower Egypt (VIII, 2; IX, 1), to the place where the waters mix with those of the Mediterranean (X, 3). Then the Nile hides his image (I, 3, *sšmw*) in order to return the next year. Hapy is praised as a universal god. The blessings of the inundation are the basis of life, prosperity, and health in Egypt. But Hapy satisfies the waterless hill country outside Egypt too, with the rains (I, 7–8). The catastrophes resulting from too low (II, 5–III, 2) and too abundant inundation (IX, 1–12) are sketched. These passages must reflect real experience: there is food for neither man nor animal, nor raw materials for industry. Everyone is poor and loses his dignity. Offerings to the gods in the temples are reduced. The social and ethical order is turned upside down. "A million perish among men" (II, 8). Hapy is here perceived as a demonic sovereign god "who makes one rich, and the other poor; but there is no possibility to argue with him. Who gives satisfaction, who cannot be intimidated and restricted by boundaries" (VII, 7–10). In the middle of this first main part, it is said that Hapy is welcomed in the person of the king, escorted by children (VI, 3–4).

The second main part consists of strophes XI–XII (sixteen verses). The theme here is the festivities on the occasion of the ceremonial welcome of the king in his role of the god Hapy. People sing and make music in procession; the whole country revels. Again children are mentioned. Together with the sixteen verses of this part, the children may be an allusion and foreshadowing to the sixteen children—symbolizing the sixteen cubits of the ideal level of the Nile inundation—who have been known since Roman times as *putti.*

The third part is formed by the prayer that concludes the hymn (strophes XIII–XIV, twenty-two verses). Hapy is urged to rise. The offerings that are presented to Hapy and to the other gods are the products and gifts of the inundation itself (XIII, 1–12). The last strophe incites people to extol the Ennead, which presides over the cavern of the inundation in Kher-aha (Heliopolis), and to perform the ritual for the king, who is named "son of Hapy." The hymn ends with a rhythmic refrain: "Be green [the color of the water of the first stage of the inundation, before changing to reddish brown] and come! Be green and come! Hapy, be green and come!"

Most authors date the great Nile hymn to the Middle Kingdom; however, the role awarded to the king in the hymn fits the New Kingdom much better. The ritual identification of the king with Hapy is found for the first time in texts of the eighteenth dynasty. The whole atmosphere of the hymn is closely related to texts from the Amarna period, and Akhenaten is often addressed by the name of Hapy.

Another Nile hymn is found on ostracon Deir el-Medina 1675; no other manuscripts of this text are known. Rubrics divide its ninety-three verses into nine strophes. In some respects this hymn is closely related to the great Nile hymn, and Fischer-Elfert (1986) is convinced that its author has used that text as a model. The same themes appear, often in the same wording. In other respects, the lesser Nile hymn exudes much more the atmosphere of the Amarna hymns. The detailed portrayal of nature in strophes II, III, VI, VII, and VIII stands out, as does the description of human behavior and social relations in strophes IV and VIII. Like the great Nile hymn, this text ends with an invocation to Hapy: "Come to Egypt with your products (*mi r km.t m inw=k*). Hapy, do not be sluggish (*wsf*). Keep yourself from being too heavy (*dns*), so that the living beings are diminished (*'nd*)" (VIII, 85–86 to IX, 88–89). Compare the great Nile hymn: "Come to Egypt (*mi r km.t*) to make live men and animals with your products (*m inw.k*) of the fields" (XIV, 7–8), "If he is sluggish (*wsf*), noses stop up, everybody is poor" (II, 5–6), "Who is too heavy (*dns*) so that people are diminished (*'nd*)" (IX, 3). In this text too, the king is mentioned: "Young men praise their Lord" (IV, 42); however, nothing seems to point out a ritual role of the king as (son of) Hapy. The structure of the lesser Nile hymn has not yet been studied in detail. Fischer-Elfert suggests that perhaps the hymn follows the succession of the three seasons *ȝḫ.t*, *pr.t*, and *šmw*. This Nile hymn undoubtedly dates from the New Kingdom.

A shorter Nile hymn (30 + 11 verses) is part of a rock inscription near Gebel es-Silsila, about 68 kilometers (40 miles) north of Aswan. Four kings from the New Kingdom (Sety I, Ramesses II, Merenptah, and Ramesses III) dedicated this text to the god of the inundation. After the royal titulary, the main text honors first the king, called "Good god," but with the epithet "beloved of Hapy," and the focus shifts swiftly onto the latter. Hapy is praised in phrases closely related to the great Nile hymn. His mysterious character is emphasized. The hymn is followed by a decree for offerings and a "list of this oblation which is presented to all gods and Nun on that day of throwing the Book of Hapy [into the river]." Although the word "praise" (*dwȝw*) is not used explicitly in this text, it is obvious from the liturgical context that it is a Nile hymn.

The hieratic ostracon Gardiner 28 has a short Nile hymn (about twenty-eight verses) in praise of the inundation of the year of Ramesses II's first *sed*-festival. Hapy is praised mainly as provider of food, and the hymn concludes with praise of the king.

Only eight lines of a Nile hymn are known from ostracon Deir el-Medina 1105. It mentions the mysterious character of Hapy, who is also Ptah-Tatenen. Finally, some words of the beginning of an unknown Nile hymn are preserved on an unpublished ostracon from Deir el-Medina, inventory number 11677.

All these hymns praise the Nile not as river, but for its annual fertilizing, regenerating flood. The inundation was venerated as a god named Hapy (*ḥ'py*). Strictly speaking, Nile hymns can be defined therefore as religious chants to Hapy. He was believed to be both the god who initiated the inundation of the Nile, and the physical water of the flood itself. All manuscripts of Nile hymns date from the New Kingdom, as do the hymns themselves. Though the blessings of Hapy are described in the Old Kingdom Pyramid Texts (Spell 581; R. O. Faulkner, *The Ancient Egyptian Pyramid Texts*, Oxford, 1969, p. 235) and in the Middle Kingdom Coffin Texts (Spell 317–321; Faulkner, *The Ancient Egyptian Coffin Texts*, vol. 1, Warminster, 1973, pp. 240–250), hymns to the inundation from these periods have not been preserved. However, this does not mean that they did not exist then. Life, health, and prosperity in Egypt have always been totally dependent on the annual inundation of the Nile. The Nile hymns express the religious feeling that people owe all daily blessings to the inundation. Good and bad floods are life and death to the Egyptians: that is one of the most crucial themes in Nile hymns. Especially in the practical religion of the common people, the cult of the inundation, with its famous Nile festivals, played an important role. Another characteristic of Nile hymns is the close relation to the king and to royal hymns. In the New Kingdom especially, the king ritually represents the god of the annual inundation; in the liturgy of the Nile festivals, he played Hapy's role. This is the context in which we have to place the Nile hymns. These hymns, aiming at encouraging the inundation to rise, formed (together with offering lists) the main contents of the "Books of Hapy," which were thrown into the river. The reason that all preserved Nile hymns from pharaonic Egypt date from the New Kingdom must be related to the revival of the cult of the inundation in the nineteenth and twentieth dynasties. This may have resulted from the expected second coincidence of the civil new year's day and the heliacal rising of the star Sirius in 1313 BCE.

BIBLIOGRAPHY

Assmann, Jan. "Nilhymnus." In *Lexikon der Ägyptologie*, 4: 489–496. Wiesbaden, 1982. An elaborate article on the great Nile hymn, showing a different opinion on genre and dating of the text.

Barucq, André, and Francois Daumas. *Hymnes et prières de l'Égypte ancienne*, pp. 504–506. Littératures anciennes du Proche-Orient, 10. Paris, 1980. French publication of Ostracon Gardiner 28.

Bonneau, Danielle. *La Crue du Nil, divinité égyptienne à travers mille ans d'histoire (332 av.–641 ap. J.–C.).* Études et commentaires, 52. Paris, 1964. A good survey of all matters relating to the cult of the inundation, with frequent references to the pharaonic period. The Nile festivals are treated in chapter 5, pp. 361–420.

Černý, J. *Hieratic Ostraca*, pl. IXa. Oxford, 1957. Publication of Ostracon Gardiner 28.

Fischer-Elfert, Hans-Werner. *Literarische Ostraka der Ramessidenzeit in Übersetzung.* Wiesbaden, 1986. Study of the small Nile hymn of ostracon Deir el-Medina 1675, pp. 31–62, and ostracon 1105, pp. 29–30.

Foster, J. L. "Thought Couplets in Khety's 'Hymn to the Inundation'." *Journal of Near Eastern Studies* 34 (1975), 1–29. The most recent English translation and study of the formal structure of the great Nile hymn.

Gasse, Annie. *Catalogue des ostraca hiératiques littéraires de Deir el-Medina*, vol. 4, fasc. 1, nos. 1676–1774. Cairo, 1990. Volume 1 gives translation, philological commentary and interpretation. For the structure of the hymn, see pp. 169–171, together with the integral translation in annex table II. The question of dating the great Nile hymn is treated in chapter 6, pp. 186–190. Ostracon 1754 is part of ostracon Deir el-Medina 1176, and ostracon 1767 is the same as ostracon Deir el-Medina 1192; ostracon 1745 can be added to the list of manuscripts.

Kitchen, Kenneth A. *Ramesside Inscriptions.* Vol. 1, pp. 85–89. Oxford, 1975. Republication of the rock inscriptions near Gebel es-Silsila.

Kitchen, Kenneth A. *Ramesside Inscriptions Translated and Annotated: Translations.* Oxford, 1993. For translation of the Gebel es-Silsila texts, see pp. 72–76.

Kitchen, Kenneth A. *Ramesside Inscriptions: Notes and Comments*, pp. 69–77. Oxford, 1993.

Maspero, G. *Hymne au Nil.* Bibliothèque d'étude, 5. Paris, 1912. The first publication of the great Nile hymn. Since then, at least twenty-one new translations of the text have been published with readings and interpretations of the text that diverge, often considerably.

Mathieu, B. "Études de métrique égyptienne I: Le distique heptamétrique dans les chants d'amour." *Revue de l'égyptologie* 39 (1988), 63–82. The most recent study of metrics in ancient Egypt, with a reasoned list of metrical units, pp. 71–77.

Mathieu, B. "Contraintes métriques et production textuelle dans l'Hymne à la Crue du Nil." *Revue de l'égyptologie* 41 (1990), 127–141. Discussion of the metrics of the great Nile hymn, which is set up by heptametric distichs consisting respectively of four and three accentual units. Red dots mark the end of each verse.

Plas, Dirk van der. *L'hymne à la crue du Nil.* Vol. 2. Egyptologische Uitgaven, 4. Leiden, 1986. An new edition of the manuscripts of the great Nile Hymn.

DIRK VAN DER PLAS

Osiris Hymns

The figure of Osiris makes its first appearance in the written record during the Old Kingdom: on the tomb stelae as a god to be invoked for offerings, and in the Pyramid Texts as the divinity with whom the dead king is identified to symbolize his entry into the divine world of the gods. In the Old Kingdom stelae, however, it is not Osiris but Anubis who is the prime object of the petitions. Similarly, it is interesting to see that Osiris is not at this time a major figure, except in the one specific instance of his coalescence with the deceased king. Actual hymns to Osiris are not found until the Middle Kingdom, and they flourish in the New Kingdom.

In the Osirian hymns the subject matter falls into two distinct divisions—events leading to the triumph of Horus (the awarding of the land of Egypt to Horus as King), and Osiris' rulership of the Duat, the realm of the dead. The first portion of this material is best seen in the longest and most connected narration of Osiris' life to survive from ancient Egypt, the stela of Amenmose (Louvre C286). It comprises a fairly long poem opening with a section that describes the many centers for the worship of Osiris, from ancestral Busiris and Heliopolis, to Herakleopolis, and finally to Abydos. He is called a god of primeval times and foremost of the Nine Great Gods; and the culmination of his praises is, "He gave earth food." Then the joyful reaction of the entire universe is described: earth flourishes because of his guidance; he "goes forth in peace" to receive the adoration of the gods and the nations, bearing the scepter of Geb, noblest of the Ennead, and conquering his enemies. Next described is the transfer of function in governing the creatures of the world, and especially Egypt: Geb presents all the creatures of earth to Osiris, who rises in splendor upon the throne of Egypt, bringing light and abundance, and providing a "pattern" for governing.

Then there is an interesting leap in the flow of the narration: the murder of Osiris by his brother Seth is entirely omitted. The poem immediately moves to the heroic resurrection brought about by Osiris' sister-wife Isis, who through her mystical power ("magic") joins the scattered pieces of Osiris' body, resurrects the god, and receives his seed to become the mother of Horus. Then Isis takes the child Horus to the Ennead sitting in the court of Geb. Called "the Lords of Truth," they determine that Horus is the rightful ruler of Egypt (and the earth)—he is the king. Like Osiris before him, Horus goes forth bearing the scepter and mace of Geb to rule earth and heaven in order to continue the abundance originally brought on by Osiris. The climax of the poem is a paean to Horus as ruler and a damnation of the unnamed Seth as a destroyer and criminal overcome by Horus. The chorus of praise ushers in a golden age of justice and right—"the land is at peace under its master . . . the back is turned on iniquity." In the final section, the proceedings of the Ennead are noted and officially recorded, and the happy verdict is passed on to Osiris, since he, though confined to the underworld, now rules his earthly kingdom vicariously through his son.

The contents of the stela of Amenmose have been presented at length because this is the most detailed rendering of the myth of Osiris to survive from Egypt's great period (as opposed to the much more extensive material from Greco-Roman times). But it nevertheless presents events only up to the time when Osiris becomes king of the dead.

The fundamental theme of the Osiris myth, of course, is death and resurrection. Osiris defeated death, and he lives forever in the next life. He thus gave the hope of a similar resurrection to all ancient Egyptians, who came to identify each deceased person as "an osiris," one who merged with the figure of the god Osiris and like him staked claim to eternal life. Just as the sun-god Re gave a pattern or regularity to life by the cycles of light, dark, and renewed light, so Osiris gave a similar pattern to the rhythms of life and death through renewed life.

The hymns presenting the second portion of the Osirian material—the rule in the kingdom of the dead—do not have a similar single source to encapsulate the myth. There are, nevertheless, many hymns representing this phase of the story of Osiris (primarily from the New Kingdom *Book of Going Forth by Day* (*Book of the Dead*). From them collectively one can gain a composite picture of Osiris as king of the dead. Most hymns from the Egyptian tradition are constructed as a pastiche of phrases and epithets referring to the god they praise. Since many of the laudatory terms appear to be interchangeable among several gods, it is often difficult to separate the characteristics of a specific god and to provide him with a distinctive personality. This trait of ancient Egyptian poetic composition is what tends to make Egyptian hymns repetitious and lacking in interest to the modern ear. Often, much of the hymn is taken up with a list of cult centers (with appropriate laudatory language) and an identification of the god in his many forms and in his fusion with other gods.

Nevertheless, amid the repetitiousness (and unlike the connected narrative from the stela of Amenmose) one can extract from these hymns some of the most important traits connected with the god as he rules the underworld. Osiris is praised as the powerful ruler of the Sacred Land, sitting on his great throne in the underworld, about which the dead crowd in order to praise him and participate in the offerings and gifts given him. He presides over the tribunal of judges in the Hall of the Two Truths where the newly arrived dead are given judgment. He is, above all, just. He is usually mentioned as being present when the sun god Re passes through the underworld, undergoing the rejuvenation that restores his youth and vigor for the new dawn. The dead stand to receive a glimpse of him, the god of light, in the otherwise dark realm of Osiris. Osiris is also identified with other deities like Khentyamentiu, Andjeti, and Sobek, as well as by epithets like Wennefer ("the Eternally Perfect") or Weredj-ib ("the Weary-hearted," i.e., "dead"). He is often fused with well-known gods like Horakhty or Atum. Most of the traditional Osirian characteristics gleaned from pictorial art are also present in the hymns—the two forms repeating or complementing each other.

[*See also* Myths, *article on the* Osiris Cycle; *and* Osiris.]

BIBLIOGRAPHY

Texts
Moret, A. *BIFAO* 30 (1931): 725–730 and pls. 1–3. The "Stela of Amenmose," Louvre C286.
Naville, Edouard. *Das Ägyptische Totenbuch der XVIII, bis XX, Dynastie.* 3 vols. 1886; reprinted, Graz. 1971.

Translations
Assmann, Jan. *Ägyptische Hymnen und Gebete.* Zurich, 1975. See especially pp. 443–460.
Barucq, André, and François Daumas. *Hymnes et prières de L'Égypte ancienne.* Paris, 1980. See especially pp. 73–114.
Faulkner, R. O., ed. and trans. *The Egyptian Book of the Dead (The Papyrus of Ani).* 1994.
Foster, John L. *Echoes of Egyptian Voices.* Norman, Okla., 1992. See pp. 40–46.
Lichtheim, Miriam. *Ancient Egyptian Literature.* Vol. 2. Berkeley, 1976. See pp. 81–86.

Commentary
Griffiths, John G. In *Lexikon der Ägyptologie*, pp. 623–633. Wiesbaden, 1982. With extensive bibliography.

JOHN L. FOSTER

Solar Hymns

Ancient Egyptian texts of adoration addressed to the sun god are called "solar hymns" by modern scholars. They are distinguishable from ancient Egyptian hymns addressed to other deities not only by their subject but also by their structure, language, and purpose.

The sun god is often addressed in solar hymns simply as Re ("Sun"), but he also appears in more specific identities associated with one or more of the phases of the daily solar cycle: in the morning as Khepri ("Evolving One"), or Harakhty ("Horus of the Akhet," the space between the netherworld and the visible horizon); during the day as Re, Horus ("Far One"), or Harakhty; and at sunset as Atum ("He Who Finishes"). The choice of name also reflects the various roles of the sun god as creator (Atum), source of light and life (Re), and ruler of the universe

(Horus). Since the same functions are associated with the creator and supreme deity, Amun, this god also appears as the object of solar hymns, usually in the form of Amun-Re or more elaborate combinations such as Amun-Re-Harakhty. Solar hymns of the Amarna period are addressed to the sun disk (the Aten); their title, however, indicates that the deity worshipped in these hymns is not the disk itself but the divine force of light manifest in it.

Like other hymns, those addressed to the sun god typically have a bipartite structure, consisting of a title followed by the hymn itself. The title is normally in the infinitival form *dw3 X in Y*, "worshiping X by Y," or *rdjt j3w n X jn Y*, "giving praise to X by Y," where X and Y are the names of the sun god and the worshiper, respectively. The body of the hymn, addressed to the god, is often introduced by the words *.nd̲ h̲r.k* "hail to you." In most cases the hymn itself contains no mention of the worshiper; a third section is sometimes added for this purpose, usually with a prayer for assistance.

Solar hymns typically are associated with a particular part of the sun's daily cycle, specified in the hymn's title with a phrase such as *m wbn.f* "in his rising" or *m h̲tp.f* "in his setting" added after the god's name. The hymn itself, however, often makes reference to the three parts of the solar day: sunrise, daytime, and sunset. Each phase, in turn, is associated with the process of life itself: the sunrise with creation and birth; daytime with triumph over the forces inimical to life; and sunset with death and the promise of new life. The most important of these is sunrise, the beginning of the Egyptian day. The use of solar hymns in that setting is reflected in the lexical root shared by the verb *dw3* "worship" and the noun *dw3w* "morning," and in the posture of Egyptian worship—hands raised with the palms facing outward—which may derive from the gesture, often depicted in Egyptian art, of baboons facing the rising sun.

Solar hymns employ the metric structure typical of Egyptian verse, with lines of two to four feet (units of stress, in Egyptian) arranged into couplets or triplets expounding a central theme. Their language makes extensive use of clauses and sentences with verbal predicates, which describe the evolution and motion of the sun god, as in the following from the *Book of Going Forth by Day* (*Book of the Dead*):

> Hail to you, Re in your rising,
> Atum in your ultimate setting!
> You rise and shine on the back of your mother [Nut],
> having appeared as the king of the gods. (BD 15 Ani)

Such predicates are found less often in other kinds of Egyptian hymns, which typically employ more static epithets of the god, as in the following from the Berlin Papyrus:

> Hail to you, Ptah, father of the gods,
> Tatenen, eldest of the original gods,
> holy god, elevated of form,
> great of terror, who is on the great throne. (Berl. 3048)

The distinctive language of the solar hymns reflects the nature of the sun god himself. Unlike the other Egyptian gods, who embody the unchanging forces and elements of nature, the sun god was viewed as a divine force continually in process, evolving each day from birth to death and each night from death to rebirth. The function of the solar hymns was not only to celebrate this daily cycle but also to participate in it, thereby helping to ensure its continuation. In this respect, too, hymns to the solar deity differ from those addressed to other gods, whose more stable nature was worthy of celebration but did not need the constant reaffirmation demanded by the more transitory character of the sun god. Hymns directed to the sun god as Amun-Re often combine the two kinds of language, with epithets reflecting the god's unchanging nature as eternal creator (Amun) and verbal predicates emphasizing the continual evolution of his manifestation as the sun (Re).

Solar hymns are first attested in their typical form in the New Kingdom, but the genre is prefigured by a short "morning litany" that appears in the Pyramid Texts of the Old Kingdom:

> You awake in peace, Purified One, in peace.
> You awake in peace, Horus of the East, in peace.
> You awake in peace, Eastern Ba, in peace.
> You awake in peace, Harakhty, in peace.
> Though you go to rest in the night bark
> you awake in the day bark,
> for you are the one who looks down on the gods:
> there is no god who looks down on you. (Pyr. 1478–79b)

The earliest attested solar hymns belong to a cycle intended for recitation at each hour of the day. This hourly ritual first appears in the temple of Hatshepsut at Deir el-Bahri, although its language is suggestive of a Middle Kingdom original.

During the course of the New Kingdom the genre developed in two different thematic directions. The traditional, and oldest, type of solar hymn is liturgical in character, based on the hourly ritual that helped to ensure the continuation of the solar cycle. Texts of this kind typically describe the daily evolution of the god in cosmic terms, as the triumph of light over darkness, motion over inertia, life over death, and order over chaos. They remained in use into the Ptolemaic period, but became progressively associated with the kind of "restricted" knowledge embodied in the netherworld texts of royal tombs. Solar hymns of a more personal kind developed alongside the traditional texts in the eighteenth and nineteenth dynasties. These relate the solar cycle directly to the sphere of human activity and experience, concentrating on the themes of light and motion as the source of human life and development. As such, they are less liturgical than celebratory in nature, recognizing the relationship between a beneficent god and his creation as worthy of worship and praise.

In keeping with its cosmic focus, the traditional solar hymn describes the sun god in relation to the forces of nature, themselves divine, and is therefore inherently polytheistic in character. The more personal hymns celebrate the relationship between the solar deity as creator and the world as his creation, and thus tend toward a monotheistic view of divinity. This trend is visible, outside the genre, as early as the poem in praise of the beneficent (and unnamed) creator at the end of the *Instructions for Merikare*, perhaps of late Middle Kingdom composition; it culminates in the monotheistic "Hymn to the Aten" of the Amarna period, which is also the ultimate expression of the personal type of solar hymn. This theme disappears from solar hymns after the nineteenth dynasty.

Solar hymns are the best-represented of all Egyptian hymns. They appear on the walls of temples (Deir el-Bahri, Edfu), on stelae and stelophorous statues, in liturgical papyri and those of literary character such as the Cairo "Hymn to Amun-Re," and on ostraca. Solar hymns are also frequent in funerary contexts—on pyramidia from private tombs, in the doorways of tombs (for example, the Hymn to the Aten), among netherworld texts such as the *Book of Day and Night*, and in the *Book of Going Forth by Day* (Spell 15)—where they allow the deceased to participate in the daily solar cycle.

Most Egyptian religious texts, particularly those of the funerary genre, were normally reproduced without much change once they had been created. In contrast, each solar hymn is a unique, individual creation rather than a canonical composition. This is true even for Spell 15 of the *Book of Going Forth by Day*, unlike the other spells in that funerary corpus. Despite their individuality, however, solar hymns, both liturgical and personal, are often built around a standard core of themes and phrases.

[*See also* Amun and Amun-Re; Aten; Myths, *article on the* Solar Cycle; *and* Re and ReHorakhty.]

BIBLIOGRAPHY

Assmann, Jan. *Liturgische Lieder an den Sonnengott*. Münchner Ägyptologische Studien, 19. Munich and Berlin, 1969. Study and translation of liturgical solar hymns.

Assmann, Jan. *Ägyptische Hymnen und Gebete*. Zurich and Munich, 1975. Translations of more than 100 ancient Egyptian solar hymns, with an extensive introduction.

Assmann, Jan. *Sonnenhymnen in thebanischen Gräbern*. Theben, 1. Mainz am Rhein, 1983. Study and translation of solar hymns found in tombs.

Scharff, A. *Ägyptische Sonnenlieder*. Berlin, 1922. An early study of solar hymns.

Stewart, H. M. "Traditional Egyptian Sun Hymns of the New Kingdom." *Bulletin of the Institute of Archaeology, University of London* 6 (1967), 29–74. Study of the core themes and phrases common to many solar hymns.

Zandee, J. "Prayers to the Sun-God from Theban Tombs." *Jaarbericht van het Voorziatisch-Egyptische Genootschap "Ex Oriente Lux"* 16 (1959–1962), 48–71. Study and translation of solar hymns in the doorways of several major tombs.

Zandee, J. "Hymnical Sayings Addressed to the Sun-God by the High-Priest Nebwenenef, from his Tomb in Thebes." *Jaarbericht van het Voorziatisch-Egyptische Genootschap "Ex Oriente Lux"* 18 (1964), 253–265. Translation of an important solar hymn, with commentary.

JAMES P. ALLEN

I

ICHNEUMON, the Egyptian mongoose (*Herpestes ichneumon*), is a predator of the civet family (Viverridae) which looks rather like a marten. The length of its body is about 65 centimeters (25 inches) and the length of its tail about 45 centimeters (15 inches); its short legs allow it to move swiftly and sinuously. The ichneumon's coat is dun colored. In tomb decorations of the Old Kingdom it often appears in papyrus thickets; it is rather precisely distinguished in these early works from genets, wild cats, and other similar animals, in contrast to the less rigid New Kingdom depictions, in which it is no longer so carefully differentiated. In the Late period temple at Kom Ombo, a lion is depicted clambering up a papyrus stalk—the normal, if somewhat unrealistic, convention for portraying the ichneumon. The ichneumon was highly valued in ancient Egypt as a killer of mice and, even more, of snakes. It haunted riverine terrain and preyed on bird's eggs; it was reputed also to eat the eggs of crocodiles.

The ichneumon was venerated as a sacred animal. In accordance with its various aspects, it was associated with several different deities and connected with their myths. As the *ḥȝtri*-ichneumon (a Semitic loan word meaning "weasel"; Coptic *shathoi*), its large, wide-open eyes make it the complementary "light" figure for the blind *'m'm*-shrew deity of Letopolis and, in mythology, it represents the seeing side of Horus-Mekhenti-en-irty. As the *'ḏ*-ichneumon ("tracker")—corresponding to the Greek *ichneumon*—it is the snake-killing companion of Atum of Heliopolis (Hesychios), known from the Pyramid Texts and Coffin Texts until the *Physiologus* (chapter 26, parallel to the otter in chapter 25) and eventually to the medieval Arab writers Hayat al-Hayawab and Ibn Manzur al-Ifriqi. The Horus or Atum ichneumon—known from Letopolis and Heliopolis, respectively—was worshiped all over the country, particularly in the Nile Delta: in Buto, Herakleopolis Magna, Athribis, Sais, and Hibis. In later times, the ichneumon was assigned to the goddess Wadjet (documented only in isolated examples before Aelian), but probably as a substitute for the otter, which had originally belonged to Wadjet (or Leto) as the *uraeus* god (of royal snakes), but which had become rare. Finally, the king was said to be "beloved" of the *ḥȝtri*-ichneumon or was deputized for by the ichneumon as Sol Invictus (Lat., the Unconquerable Sun).

The following texts testify to a cult of the ichneumon: the *Book of Going Forth by Day*, the *Book of That Which Is in the Underworld*, the *Book of Caverns*, and certain magical texts; furthermore, there are ichneumon mummies (particularly from Bubastis) and votive offerings, mainly from the Late period. In addition, there are small bronze statuettes and bronze sarcophagi in the shape of an ichneumon. For the sake of clarity, these may be distinguished from the more common shrew-sarcophagi as follows: the ichneumons have a long head, close-set ears, a tail that hangs down to the ground, and fur that is long and coarse. By contrast, the shrew is long-snouted, with upright ears that have two folds, a tail stretched out horizontally, and mythological decorations placed on its back. The otter has a blunt snout, wedge-shaped tail, and webbed feet, and it stands in the "praying" (scenting) position. In publications and museums, ichneumons, otters, and shrews are usually labeled as these or other animals by guesswork alone.

BIBLIOGRAPHY

Brunner-Traut, Emma. "Spitzmaus und Ichneumon al Tiere des Sonnegottes." *Nachrichten von der Akademie der Wissenschaften zu Göttingen* (1965), 123–163.

Brunner-Traut, Emma. In *Festschrift für Siegfried Schott zu seinem 70. Geburtstag*. Wiesbaden, 1968.

EMMA BRUNNER-TRAUT
Translated from German by Julia Harvey

IHNASYA EL-MEDINA. *See* Herakleopolis.

IKHERNOFRET a high palace official, at the end of the twelfth dynasty during the reigns of Senwosret III and Amenemhet III. The autobiographical section of Ikhernofret's commemorative stela erected at Abydos (now in the Berlin Museum) tells us that he grew up and studied at the royal palace and eventually acquired important administrative responsibilities that culminated in his being promoted to "Overseer of the Seal," or chief treasurer.

The text of of his stela recounts Ikhernofret's activities at Abydos, where he was sent by King Senwosret III to refurbish the cult statue of the god Osiris, the shrine that housed the statue, and the bark that carried them. While at Abydos, Ikhernofret took the opportunity to participate in the festival of Osiris, personally "leading the great procession" and "following the god in his footsteps." From this text, one gets the impression that an actual mock battle was staged, with some festival participants acting as followers of Osiris and others playing enemies of the god. Although brief, Ikhernofret's account is one of the few narratives of such a festival from pharaonic Egypt.

Ikhernofret is also important because of the number of commemorative stelae left in his chapel at the pilgrimage site of Abydos. The main monument in the chapel was the previously mentioned stela, which contained a representation of the king and the god Osiris, as well as the autobiographical account. Also included in the chapel were stelae belonging to some of his working acquaintances and subordinates, from fellow administrators to members of the priesthoods of Abydos. These stelae mention Ikhernofret either generally, as part of the formulaic prayers usually encountered on such monuments, or specifically, as protector or patron. In Ikhernofret as patron, we see a true act of piety in which one man, whose stela at Abydos assured him spiritual participation in the sacred rites there, wished to have close friends share in one of the most important religious acts of their time.

BIBLIOGRAPHY

Leprohon, Ronald J. "The Personnel of the Middle Kingdom Funerary Stelae." *Journal of the American Research Center in Egypt* 15 (1978), 33–38. A prosopography of the individuals found on Middle Kingdom commemorative stelae.

Lichtheim, Miriam. *Ancient Egyptian Literature; A Book of Readings.* Vol. I: *The Old and Middle Kingdoms.* Berkeley, 1973. pp. 123–125. Contains a description and translation of Ikhernofret's stela.

Simpson, William Kelly. *The Terrace of the Great God at Abydos: The Offering Chapels of Dynasties 12 and 13.* New Haven, 1974. A seminal study of the groups of commemorative stelae found in chapels at Abydos.

RONALD J. LEPROHON

ILLAHUN (also called Lahun, Kahun, or El-Lahun), a site on the desert edge, beyond the cultivation, to the northeast of the Bahr Yusuf, where it curves to enter the Faiyum Depression (29°14′N, 30°59′E). Although the site has remains from the Predynastic period to the Muslim era, it is dominated by the Middle Kingdom, twelfth dynasty pyramid of Senwosret II (r. 1897–1877 BCE) and its associated town.

Comprehensive exploration and excavation of Illahun was conducted by W. M. Flinders Petrie from 1887 to 1889 and in 1914. His published descriptions and plans lack detail; although finds were plentiful, little attempt was made to record context. Since 1989, N. B. Millet of the Royal Ontario Museum and architect J. E. Knudstad, with their small team, have been reexamining specific areas of the town, as well as the pyramid, to recover some precise architectural details.

The royal pyramid originally measured 106 meters square (about 300 feet square) and had a height of 48 meters (about 150 feet). Its innovative construction incorporated a natural knoll of rock to support a framework of crossed limestone cribbing walls, infilled solidly with mud bricks, the whole finally encased in dressed masonry. Clearance on the eastern face revealed this bedrock core to have been substantially enhanced with coursed limestone masonry beneath the now-missing casing. A wealth of construction detail not recorded by Flinders Petrie remains to be recovered in future clearance. The entrance shaft is on the southern side, which is unusual, and close by are four shaft tombs for near relatives, with that of Princess Sit-Hathor-Yunet yielding superb jewelry. The Illahun pyramid complex includes eight solid rock-cut *mastaba*s, a subsidiary pyramid on the northern side, and a temple against its eastern face.

There is no trace of a causeway leading to the valley temple ruins, 1.2 kilometers (some three-quarters of a mile) distant on the eastern axis of the pyramid. In 1888 and 1889, immediately to the north and east of this temple, Flinders Petrie excavated the town he called Kahun, ancient Hetep-Senusret ("Senusret is content"), an outstanding example of early town planning. It was built to house the administrators of the royal cult and the appended estates; this included the priests and bureaucrats, their families and dependent personnel, and the craftsmen and laborers with their families. Some important papyri were found there, ranging in subject from temple archives to medicinal (including the gynecological and the veterinary), as well as mathematics, literary texts, private business affairs, letters, and horoscopes.

Only an estimated half of the town was left to be excavated by Flinders Petrie. It measured 384 meters (about 1,200 feet) on the northern side and at least 335 meters (950 feet) on the western side. It was enclosed by a 3-meter- (10-foot-) thick mud-brick wall, which had only one gate preserved, that on the eastern side. The function of the wall was probably enclosure rather than defense. The town was built in two phases: an initial compound, with a smaller addition built on the western side. The town was subdivided by straight streets, 4 meters (13 feet) wide, with central, stone-lined drains—into its blocks, mainly residential buildings were grouped by size. Ten large houses or mansions, each 42 × 60 meters (130 feet × 190 feet), with up to seventy rooms, had the favored position on the higher northern side. Re-examination of Flinders Petrie's so-called acropolis has revealed a fairly standard mansion plan, and clearly his postulated "king's residence" must be sought outside the town. The rest of the town's space was densely occupied by a variety of smaller housing, as in the western enclosure, where about 150 houses of three to seven rooms were arranged along

ILLAHUN. *Pyramid of Senwosret II, twelfth dynasty.* (Courtesy Donald B. Redford)

eleven parallel streets. All buildings were probably single storyed, having stairs to either flat roofs of timber that were covered with mats and mud or to roofs with mud-brick vaulting. All rooms and open courts were paved with mud bricks, and the walls were plastered and white-washed; some had decorative painting. Population estimates, based on the average house occupancy and the grain-storage capacities, vary from three thousand to five thousand.

BIBLIOGRAPHY

David, A. Rosalie. *The Pyramid Builders of Ancient Egypt: A Modern Investigation of Pharaoh's Workforce.* London and New York, 1986. Along with a general introduction to the Middle Kingdom, the book describes Flinders Petrie's excavation campaigns and uses the finds to reconstruct life in the town.

Kemp, Barry J. *Ancient Egypt: Anatomy of a Civilization.* London, 1989. Chapter 4, "Model Communities," outlines the development of town planning and the relationship of the socioeconomic hierarchy to urban structure.

Petrie, W. M. Flinders. *Illahun, Kahun and Gurob.* London, 1891.

Petrie, W. M. Flinders, Guy Brunton, and M. A. Murray. *Lahun II.* London, 1923.

Uphill, Eric P. *Egyptian Towns and Cities.* Aylesbury, 1988. Part of the Shire Egyptology Series, this is a concise, well-illustrated introduction to urban development in Egypt, with good bibliography.

ROSA A. FREY

IMHOTEP (Gr., Imouthes), the master builder of the third dynasty, was the chief architect of King Djoser (ruled c.2687–2668 BCE) during whose reign the first pyramid (the Step Pyramid) was built at Saqqara, the necropolis of Memphis, which was then the capital of Egypt. Whether or not this monumental tomb construction was the architect's concept or his king's, this remarkable innovation was surely planned and erected under the direction of Imhotep. The third-century BCE Egyptian historian Manetho attributes this stone building to him. He was also the high priest of Heliopolis. Throughout his life, which reportedly lasted until the end of the dynasty (c.2649 BCE), he was greatly honored. This was demonstrated by the discovery of his name inscribed on the base of a statue of Djoser (Cairo, the Egyptian Museum JE 49889), a singular indication of his extraordinary standing at that time. Over a millennium later, during the New Kingdom, he was venerated and described in contemporaneous literature as the patron of scribes, and in the Turin Papyri as the son of Ptah, chief god of Memphis. Hornung (1982) cites a chronological list dating to that era that names Imhotep as the earliest Wisdom teacher. In the Late period, veneration evolved into deification; Imhotep had his own temples and priesthoods. During this final stage of native rule, he was glorified for his skills as a physician and healer. The Greeks,

IMHOTEP. *Statue of Imhotep in the Brooklyn Museum of Art.* (Courtesy Stephen Phillips)

after conquering Egypt, associated him with their god of medicine, Asclepius, and continued to build temples dedicated to him. Imhotep's reputation survived into the era of the Arab invasion of North Africa during the seventh century CE.

Although presumably buried in North Saqqara, near the pyramid of Djoser, Imhotep's tomb remains unlocated and the evidence of his life's accomplishments can only be deduced from records based more on legend than fact. Despite this paucity of information, there is little doubt that Imhotep was one of the most important personalities of ancient Egypt, an early version of a Renaissance man. Although a considerable number of his statues survive from the New Kingdom, Imhotep is best known today from a large quantity of Late period bronze statuettes depicting him as a shaven-headed, seated priest holding a roll of papyrus on his knees. These artifacts were undoubtedly made as votive representations intended to endow their owners with erudition.

BIBLIOGRAPHY

Grimal, N. *A History of Ancient Egypt.* Translated by I. Shaw. Oxford, 1992.

Hornung, E. *Conceptions of God in Ancient Egypt.* Translated by J. Baines. Ithaca, N.Y., 1982.

Wildung, D. *Imhotep und Amenhotep-Gottwerdung im alten Ägypten,* MÄS 36, Munich and Berlin, 1977.

Wildung, D. "Imhotep." In *Lexikon der Ägyptologie,* 3: 145–148. Wiesbaden, 1980.

JACK A. JOSEPHSON

IMMORTALITY. *See* Afterlife.

IMPERIALISM. At the most basic level, imperialism is about power—the domination of one society over others, whether cultural, economic, political, or a mixture of these. A common characterization of imperialism is of a territorially expansive state exercising control over other polities, ranging from other states to nonstratified societies. While there is a considerable and growing literature on ancient imperialism, some have objected to the use of the concept, arguing that it applies only to the modern domination of the third world by the West. We need not, however, be limited to concepts and terms that existed in antiquity. Few today would doubt that religion played a central role in ancient Egypt, yet the Egyptians had no word for religion. The use of the term does not imply a one-to-one correspondence between ancient and modern imperialism. Yet there is broad consensus in the utility of the concept in various regions and at various times.

Ancient and Modern Imperialism. Wallerstein's *The Modern World System* (New York, 1974) stressed the need for the European center to dominate a subordinate periphery. It was often in the interest of ancient empires, however, to promote peripheral complexity in order to mobilize distant resources, especially where transportation was difficult. Thus, the presence of colonists might indicate a trading colony, and peripheral elite emulation of the core often reflects the manipulation of outside symbolism in internal prestige systems more than core dominance. In order to conclude that an empire existed, we must have direct evidence for control. Such evidence does exist for ancient empires, including Egypt; it varies from extremely intrusive incorporation of peripheries into territorial empires, to hegemonic empires adopting a strategy of minimal intervention.

Definitions of imperialism often focus on the degree of central control vs. peripheral autonomy, reflecting different levels of political and/or economic domination. Three key variables in determining imperial outcomes are: logistical considerations, or distance and transport obstacles between center and incorporated area; the nature of the local polity and society, notably its complexity and willingness to cooperate; and imperial goals—geopolitical considerations, trade routes, and resource extraction. These factors emphasize the political and economic costs and benefits of imperial expansion. Some scholars, however, question the economic returns of modern and ancient empires, arguing that ideological considerations like prestige and religion drove the pace and nature of conquest. In this way, Egyptian imperialism has been characterized as driven by an ideological imperative to expand Egypt's physical borders and cultural boundaries.

Empire and Ideology. Barry Kemp (1997) has argued that the expansion of the Egyptian state through imperial conquest fits a scribal, bureaucratic value system, articulated in a royal ideology glorifying expansion and acculturation, in both Nubia and Syria-Palestine (see the response by Smith 1997, pp. 301–307). A genre of texts does speak explicitly of an ideological goal to extend the borders of Egypt. Their formulaic expressions, however, belong to an idealized realm that often extended the sphere of Egyptian control to abstract, mythical boundaries. Thus, not only do "heaven and all the foreign lands which god has created serve" the New Kingdom pharaoh Hatshepsut, but "commands are sent to an unknown land, and they do everything that she commanded." These declarations refer to the limits of royal authority in general, an assertion of the political and cosmological power of the king rather than an actual policy of expansion.

The ideological topos applied to external interactions was aimed at legitimizing royal authority to an internal audience, and it was often divorced from the practical functioning of empire and international relations. In particular, the royal theology of *maat* (*mȝʿt;* "order, goodness") linked the king's defeat of foreign enemies with the sun god's defeat of the cosmological forces of *isfet* (*isft;* "chaos, evil") in the netherworld. In the state ideology, foreigners represented the earthly forces of *isfet* which threatened to destroy Egypt's inner peace and prosperity, and so they are depicted in a negative light as destructive and uncivilized. Thus Hekanefer, Prince of Miam, appears in the topos of "pacified Nubian" in the Theban tomb of Huy, viceroy of Kush under Tutankhamun. During the ceremonial presentation of tribute (*inw*), Hekanefer and the other Egyptianized Lower Nubian princes don "barbaric" Nubian accouterments (leather sash, jewelry, wig, feathers) over an Egyptian kilt. In the same ceremony, the gifts, emissaries, and even princesses of Babylon are presented as just another example of a "pacified" enemy bowing down to the pharaoh, much to the Babylonian king's consternation! Yet at the same time, Hekanefer's tomb and the monuments of other Nubian princes all portray the owners as completely Egyptian, and diplomatic correspondence with Babylon is couched in terms of equality. In the same way, literary texts such as the *Story of Sinuhe* present foreigners like the ruler of Byblos as civilized, positive actors. The value of the imperial ideology lay not in territorial incorporation and acculturation, but rather in the king's prestige at home as pacifier of Egypt's foreign enemies.

Empire and the Political Economy. Kemp (1978; 1997) particularly argues against economic return as a prime motive in imperialism. During the New Kingdom, for example, much of the revenue from imperial taxes and tribute in Nubia was consumed locally through a temple and estate redistribution system similar to that of Egypt itself, and thus was of no obvious economic benefit outside Nubia. We can understand the profitability of Egypt's empire by looking at staple and wealth finance in the ancient state economy. This model makes a distinction between bulky, low-valued foodstuffs, which were costly to transport (staple production), and high-value to bulk luxury goods, which can be moved long distances efficiently (wealth production). Staple production was captured in Syria-Palestine by co-opting an already complex series of polities with existing redistributive state economies, and in Nubia by remodeling the economy and taxation along Egyptian lines. For the latter, the local reinvestment of taxes in staples would have underwritten most or all of the costs of the settlements, entrepôts, forts, and staff required for the exploitation of trade routes and natural resources.

The exchange of wealth goods is often regarded as small-scale gift exchange reinforcing social relations, and thus as of little importance to the overall economy of ancient states. The exchange of wealth goods, whether between states or in internal redistributive systems, did have an important social dimension. Tribute lists from the reign of Thutmose III (c.1450 BCE), however, show that the amounts of gold extracted from Nubia, when converted into labor values, represented a substantial resource to the state economy. Just the Nubian gold dedicated to the temple of Amun at Thebes, the most important state temple of the time, represents a year's labor for 12,500 unskilled workers, or salary for 6,250 skilled craftsmen or 2,273 overseers, artists, or scribes. And this figure does not include the value of gold flowing directly into the royal treasury, nor other Nubian prestige goods like ivory and ebony from the savannas and forests of central Sudan. The prestige economy was especially powerful when combined with a materialization of ideology, the conversion of wealth into objects embued with social symbolism. Sumptuary goods obtained through Egypt's imperial and long-distance exchange networks legitimized the position of the king through display in ceremonies like the presentation of tribute, and reinforced patronage relationships through the distribution of largess in awards of the "gold of valor." Nubian gold was especially important to cementing Egypt's foreign relations with major Near Eastern powers, and in the international trade for wealth goods, like the coveted stone lapis lazuli from Afghanistan.

Historical Overview. Egypt's long relationship with its neighbors shows a complex pattern of interactions, which can sometimes be characterized as equal exchange, especially with Syria-Palestine, but often—particularly with Nubia—as an empire shifting from territorial to hegemonic strategies in various regions and contact situa-

tions. Both exchange networks and imperial expansion secured control over key trade routes and sources of luxury goods desired by the Egyptian state. These included ebony, ivory, incense, and gold from Nubia, and wood (especially cedar), wine, olive oil, resins, incense, silver, and lapis lazuli from the Near East.

Late Predynastic and Early Dynastic periods. The earliest evidence for Egyptian territorial expansion dates to the late Predynastic and the Early Dynastic periods. The Calcolithic through Early Bronze Age I (EB I, c.3300–3000 BCE) in Palestine shows a steady increase in exchange with Egypt. Excavations in southern Palestine at sites like Tell Erani and Nahal Tillah revealed Egyptian settlements dating to the late EB I, with characteristic architecture, burial practices, and material culture, including locally produced Egyptian-style pottery and seal impressions. Eighteen potsherds found in southern Palestine were incised with *serekh*s, the niched palace façade associated with the emergence of Egyptian kingship. Three of these sherds name the first dynasty king Narmer. These sites dominated an important trade route linking Egypt to Syria-Palestine. The discovery of large numbers of Levantine imports in the late Predynastic royal cemetery at Abydos, notably in tomb Uj, attests to the importance and volume of trade between the two regions.

The Lower Nubian A-Group civilization also shows evidence of growing exchange during the same period. A-Group rulers based at Qustul borrowed, or perhaps shared, motifs of Egyptian kingship like the Horus falcon and *serekh* façade. This peaceful interaction ended with Egyptian conquest sometime before the end of the first dynasty. A relief with captive peoples and towns dominated by a falcon above a *serekh*, found at Gebel Sheikh Suleiman, has been attributed to king Djer, although the reading is debatable. Regardless, the A-Group civilization disappears archeologically at this time, implying the forced depopulation of Lower Nubia. References to slave-taking in later texts might provide a motive for this draconian policy. A small community of presumably enslaved Nubian laborers is attested at the Second Cataract in the Old Kingdom Egyptian settlement at Buhen. Raids farther south into Upper Nubia are mentioned as early as the reign of Khasekhemwy.

Old Kingdom. The Egyptians maintained direct control over Lower Nubia from the second dynasty to the fifth. Raids continued into Upper Nubia during the Old Kingdom; for example, Snefru mentions taking seven thousand slaves and one hundred thousand herd animals during one such incident. There was, however, no attempt at conquest past the Second Cataract. During the fourth dynasty, several imperial settlements were established. The only well-documented example is at Buhen. The large numbers of seal impressions found there indicate tight administrative control from Egypt. Similar occupations suggested at Ikkur and Aniba are disputed, but Quban apparently had an Old Kingdom component. These settlements were abandoned by the end of the fifth dynasty, and the C-Group, who seem to have come from Upper Nubia, resettled Lower Nubia. The biographies of expedition leaders from Aswan reflect a shift in Egypt's Nubian policy from empire to diplomacy and exchange. Traveling both by land and along the Nile, individuals like Harkhuf negotiated for safe passage and escorts in order to secure and transport valuable trade goods from Upper Nubia to Egypt.

In contrast to the continuing Egyptian presence in Nubia, the Egyptian colonies in southern Palestine were abandoned long before the start of the Old Kingdom. Although a few military campaigns are attested, the Egyptians mostly engaged in peaceful exchange with Syria-Palestine. Both texts and archeological evidence emphasize sea-borne trade with the coastal Levantine cities, especially at Byblos and Ugarit. Elite emulation is often cited as evidence for an Egyptian empire, or at least individual colonies; there is no evidence, however, for direct Egyptian control. Instead, local leaders adapted Egyptian architectural and stylistic motifs to bolster their prestige and authority at home.

Middle Kingdom. Some Egyptologists, and especially Syria-Palestinian archeologists, suggest a large-scale Egyptian imperial presence in Syria-Palestine during the Middle Kingdom. This so-called empire is reconstructed mostly by the presence of twelfth dynasty Egyptian statuary of high officials like Thuthotpe (c.1870 BCE) from Megiddo, an important center strategically located in central Palestine, or the statuary and sphinxes of kings and princesses found at various Syrian sites. All of this statuary came, however, from later or disturbed contexts. Most of the pieces have funerary inscriptions that suggest a likely origin in the cemeteries or temples of Egypt. Since similar statuary was exported to the Kerman capital in Nubia by the Hyksos during the Second Intermediate period, it is likely that most, if not all, of the statuary found in Syria-Palestine was also exported later. Thus, a northern empire proves to be ephemeral.

Lebanese and Syrian centers such as Byblos and Ugarit were treated as important trading partners, and their elites adopted many Egyptian motifs and practices. The royal tombs at Byblos show a variety of luxury goods naming kings of the late twelfth dynasty. Hieroglyphic inscriptions show that the Byblian rulers adopted Egyptian titulary, while finds and the architecture of the temple complexes show substantial Egyptian influence. This need not indicate formal Egyptian domination, though. The control and manipulation of Egyptian symbolism would reinforce royal and elite patronage relationships

and legitimize their authority over the populace. These local rulers were in effect co-opted by the Egyptians through mutual benefit and the exchange of gifts. Military campaigns were presumably mounted only when Egyptian interests were threatened. Later Middle Bronze Age Palestinian civilization was heavily dependent on trade. A complex settlement hierarchy developed in this period, anchored by major trade gateways at Hazor in Galilee and Tell ed-Dab'a, ancient Avaris, in the Nile Delta. This Delta site apparently began as a Palestinian mercenary and/or trading colony, to become the capital of the Hyksos during the Second Intermediate period.

In Lower Nubia, Egypt engaged in territorial conquest backed up by a chain of fortresses on a scale that dwarfed the modest working settlements of the Old Kingdom. The Second Cataract of the Nile provided a hardened frontier, with the great fortified towns of Buhen and Mirgissa at either end of the rapids, and six forts at strategic points running a short distance south to Semna. The well-preserved walls at Buhen provide an insight into the "state of the art" in fortifications, including complex systems of revetments, bastions, and towers. The Semna inscription of Senwosret III declares that no Nubians could travel north from the Second Cataract without permission from the Egyptian garrison commander at Semna, and even then only if they were on a trading or diplomatic mission. A series of dispatches from the forts found at Thebes indicates that even small groups of Nubians were tracked through the desert and turned away when they tried to cross the border.

The forts played a multifaceted role in the Nubian policies of the Middle Kingdom: on the one hand, they supported punitive campaigns to the south; and on the other, they were a static defense to prevent violation of the boundary by the growing power of Kush, a Nubian kingdom centered at Kerma, just south of the Third Cataract. On the economic side, the fortresses and their garrisons regulated and facilitated riverine and overland trade, monitored the local population, and exploited the natural resources of the area. In contrast to the Old Kingdom, the Egyptians allowed the native C-Group to stay, if closely watched and somewhat restricted in their activities and interactions. The C-Group preserved their distinctly Nubian culture, probably as a kind of passive resistance to the Egyptian invaders.

By the end of the twelfth dynasty, Egyptians—some in positions of considerable authority in the imperial administration—began to be buried in large numbers in Nubia. Women and children also appear in the fort cemeteries. This pattern indicates staffing by permanent settlers who now regarded Nubia, not Egypt, as their home, resulting in greater autonomy for the forts and a savings to the central administration. The fortress of Askut documents this change through the modification of uniform barracks blocks into normal houses, and evidence of an ancestor cult similar to that attested later at Deir el-Medina. Even though the forts were now manned by settlers, seal impressions show that they were run down to the mid- to late thirteenth dynasty under tight administrative control from the Department of the Head of the South at Thebes, and even the royal residence at Itjtawy at the entrance to the Faiyum. These sealings show the highly compartmentalized administrative system present at all of the forts, with separate seals for granaries, treasuries, the "upper fort," storehouses, provisions, and the "labor prison."

New Kingdom. Lower Nubia came under Kerman control around 1680 BCE during the Second Intermediate Period, but it was reconquered early in the reign of the seventeenth dynasty king Kamose, around 1570 BCE. Early in the eighteenth dynasty, Lower Nubia was made over in the image of Egypt under a new acculturation policy. Within a short time, Nubian settlements and cemeteries disappear, with a few exceptions toward the end of the eighteenth dynasty; they are replaced by a completely Egyptian cultural complex. The continuing presence of Egyptians in Nubia, demonstrated at Buhen textually and at Askut archeologically, may help to explain the rapid acculturation of the Nubian elite, who gradually brought the rest of Nubian society into the Egyptian cultural sphere. We know from cemeteries like Fadrus and the inscriptions of Nubian elites like the princes of Miam (Aniba) and Tekhet that Nubians quickly adopted Egyptian names and were fully incorporated into the local bureaucracy. They are always depicted as Egyptians on their own monuments, contrasting with their appearance as topical foreigners in scenes showing the presentation of tribute, discussed above.

The viceroy (Fr., "king's son") of Kush had two "deputies," one for Wawat and one for Kush—Lower and Upper Nubia, respectively. In Lower Nubia, large private and temple estates managed by the elite replaced the more egalitarian socio-economic structure of the C-Group. The once dispersed population was concentrated in towns, often located at the old Middle Kingdom forts. Egyptian gods—usually Horus, Lord of such a place, or Hathor, Lady of that place—probably replaced native deities in each community. Pliant chieftains became good Egyptian officials in the colonial bureaucracy. These native princes may have been drawn from the seminomadic Medjay, who were often used as mercenaries by the Egyptians. Nubians could rise as high as the rank of deputy in the colonial administration, or find a favored place at court, like the fan-bearer Maiherpri, who was given the rare privilege of burial in the Valley of the Kings. Although these individuals and their families did well from the co-

lonial system, C-Group cemeteries such as the important site of Fadrus show that the bulk of the population became impoverished peasants, like their counterparts in Egypt.

The fate of Upper Nubia is less clear. Recent excavations show that Kerma itself was sacked and burnt, probably under Thutmose I. His armies pushed upriver as far as Kurgus, near the Fifth Cataract, where he placed a boundary inscription similar to that of Senwosret III at Semna. The ruler of Kush's sons survived, however, and their rebellions forced Thutmose II and Hatshepsut to mount campaigns to crush them. The native line was finally replaced by an Egyptian administrator during the reign of Thutmose III. The local leaders who remained loyal to Egypt are depicted in hybrid dress similar to that of the Lower Nubian princes like Hekanefer, which may indicate that they were also acculturated but donned Nubian accouterments for ideological reasons. A series of fortified temple-towns, similar to those in Egypt, was established from Sai to Sesebi, but recent surveys reveal a dearth of Egyptian sites in the area from the Third to the Fourth Cataract in the fertile Dongola Reach. Local rulers in this area, like the princes of Syria-Palestine (see below), may have been allowed a degree of autonomy as long as the trade and tribute flowed steadily northward.

The Nubian colonial system implemented under the early kings of the eighteenth dynasty functioned smoothly for about five hundred years, until the waning days of the twentieth dynasty. Officials continued to be appointed to both local and regional offices throughout Lower Nubia. The temple and other estates continued to produce the surpluses that fueled the colonial infrastructure. Major new building projects were undertaken into the nineteenth dynasty, like the massive carved temples of Ramesses II and his wife Nefertari at Abu Simbel. The system came crashing down when Penhasi, the viceroy of Kush under Ramesses XI, marched north with his elite Nubian colonial troops and sacked the town of Hardai in Middle Egypt. He was chased back into Nubia by the general Herihor, who despite several attempts was never able to reassert Egyptian control over Nubia.

Egypt's New Kingdom imperial policy in Syria-Palestine was also one of territorial conquest, but not of acculturation as in Lower Nubia. This change in policy may be due in part to the period of Hyksos domination, along with the geopolitical threat from the Mitanni Empire, based in northern Syria. Military control began as Ahmose and his successors expanded into southern Palestine. Egyptians maintained the upper hand against Mitanni, controlling coastal Lebanon and Syria as far north as Ugarit and inland to the Syrian city-states of Qatna and Qadesh. A chain of fortresses was built along the northern coast of Sinai to Gaza, a key Egyptian center. Many conquered cities remained unfortified after the destruction of their Middle Bronze Age walls, presumably as a deliberate policy to keep Palestinian cities vulnerable to Egyptian military force. The Egyptian presence in Syria-Palestine north of Gaza was limited to small garrisons; local affairs continued in the hands of independent vassal states and Egyptian military, diplomatic, and commercial officials acted as liaisons. The Amarna Letters provide a good idea of regional politics in Syria-Palestine in the late eighteenth dynasty. They reflect the use of Near Eastern diplomatic conventions in establishing their imperial infrastructure. Conquered cities were seen as vassals and could not treat with outside powers. They were required to supply periodic tribute and food for military campaigns. Southern Syria, Lebanon, and northern Palestine served as an interaction zone for trade and competition between Egypt and Mitanni, Mitanni and the Hittite Empire (based in central Turkey), and finally the Hittites and Egypt after the collapse of the Mitanni. Egyptian vassals did some tentative realigning after the fall of Mitanni, promoting intercity conflict and seeking clandestine meetings with the Hittites which in some cases led to defections, including the key coastal city of Ugarit. The presence of Egyptian envoys after the Hittite conquest suggests a continuing flexibility characteristic of points of contact between peripheries dominated by competing centers.

Letters from Syrian-Palestinian vassals accusing the pharaoh of neglecting allies have traditionally been interpreted as indicating weakness on the part of Akhenaten (c.1353–1335 BCE), who was too absorbed by domestic matters and his great religious reform to maintain the empire. Recent studies strongly suggest that this policy of nonintervention was actually a clever manipulation and part and parcel of the vassal system, in which intercity competition was allowed as long as the overall system functioned; rival cities could squabble as long as it did not disrupt the imperial system. Local rulers also focused their aggression on other locals, not the Egyptian administration, in a classic example of divide and conquer. This policy provided a highly efficient means of exploitation. The hegemonic imperial system adopted by the Egyptians was largely self-supporting, requiring a minimal expenditure of resources to maintain the small number of garrisons and a system of gift exchange to bind local rulers. Outright conquest would come at a high cost to Egypt, while the city-states were easily co-opted with the Egyptians providing only the top layer of administrative and military control.

Egyptian activity in Syria-Palestine seems to have increased during the Ramessid period. Sons of local rulers were taken as hostages to Egypt and trained at court in a classic method of co-opting elites, reminiscent of modern British imperialism. Otherwise, there was no particular interest in acculturation. Egyptian architecture, symbolism, and practices were adapted to suit local needs, and were used to create and maintain prestige at home more than to please their Egyptian overlords. An administrative center was established at Gaza in southern Palestine, with military commanders at Jaffa and Beth Shean. Excavations at Beth Shean provide a rare example of an Egyptian colonial site in the Levant. In Syria and Lebanon, garrisons were established along the Mediterranean coast at Kumidi, Sumur, and Ulasa. A chain of fortresses was also established by Ramesses II along the northern coast of Africa. It has been suggested that at the end of the Ramessid era, the Egyptians settled military captives from the Sea Peoples in coastal Palestine to protect Egyptian interests there, establishing the group later known as the Philistines.

Third Intermediate Period and the Late and Ptolemaic periods. During the Third Intermediate period, Egypt mounted military campaigns, diplomacy, and trade to both north and south, but this activity never led to direct control. In the Late period, Egypt was itself incorporated into large-scale empires. Rulers of the Napatan kingdom of Kush adopted pharaonic royal titulary and many religious and cultural features from Egypt, eventually incorporating Egypt into a large-scale empire reaching from the Butana in central Sudan into Syria-Palestine. The Kushite pharaohs of the twenty-fifth dynasty were defeated by the Assyrians, who briefly incorporated Egypt into their own extensive empire. Later Egypt came under Persian domination, but it became independent under Greek Ptolemaic rule. Egypt again became an imperial power during this period. Only a small part of Lower Nubia came under Ptolemaic control, but Palestine and the northern coast of Africa west to Cyrene in Libya, as well as Cyprus, some Aegean islands, and parts of coastal Anatolia, were annexed. By the mid-second century BCE, most of the empire was lost, and Egypt was finally absorbed into the Roman Empire in 30 BCE.

[*See also* Mesopotamia; Nubia; Persia; Syria-Palestine; *and* Trade and Markets.]

BIBLIOGRAPHY

Adams, William Y. *Nubia: Corridor to Africa.* London, 1977. A detailed survey of Nubian history from the earliest times through the Islamic period, with considerations of interactions with Egypt. More thorough than O'Connor (1993), but less accessible for the general reader.

Bass, G. F. "Oldest Known Shipwreck Reveals Bronze Age Splendors," *National Geographic* 174 (1987), 692–733. Presents preliminary results of the 1300 BCE shipwreck found off the coast of Turkey at

Ulu-Borune, which is critical for understanding the nature and volume of trade in the eastern Mediterranean.

Bleiberg, Edward. *The Official Gift in Ancient Egypt.* Norman, Okla., 1996. A consideration of the Egyptian economy from a substantivist point of view, followed by an in-depth study of the economic and social dimensions of *inw*, often translated as "tribute" in an international context.

Conrad, Geoffrey W., and Arthur Demarest. *Religion and Empire.* Cambridge, 1984. The authors argue for religious ideology as the prime mover for Aztec and Inca expansionist imperialism.

Curtin, Philip D. *Cross-cultural Trade in World History.* Cambridge, 1984. Discusses the phenomena of trade and trading colonies, or diaspora, in Africa, the ancient eastern Mediterranean, pre-Columbian Americas, and exchange between Europe and Asia.

Doyle, Michael W. *Empires.* Ithaca, 1986. A cross-cultural analysis of the causes and patterns of imperialism, notable for a model stressing the combination of factors from both conqueror and conquered in determining imperial outcomes.

Kemp, Barry J. "Imperialism in New Kingdom Egypt (c. 1575–1087 B.C.)." In *Imperialism in the Ancient World,* edited by P. D. A. Garnsey and C. R. Whittaker, pp. 7–57, 283–297. Cambridge, 1978. A consideration of Egypt's Nubian and Syro-Palestinian empires, combining textual and archeological data.

Kemp, Barry J. "Why Empires Rise." *Cambridge Archaeological Journal* 7 (1997), 125–133.

Levy, Thomas. *The Archaeology of Society in the Holy Land.* New York, 1995. Chapters by specialists, with detailed analytical discussion of the major archeological and historical periods of ancient Palestine, including interactions with Egypt.

Liverani, Mario. *Prestige and Interest: International Relations in the Near East ca. 1600–1100 B.C.* Padua, 1990. An insightful, wide-ranging comparison of textual evidence from Egypt and the great powers of the Near East, contrasting ideological pronouncements emphasizing the internal prestige of the ruler with diplomatic correspondence reflecting political and economic interest.

Loprieno, A. *Topos und Mimesis.* Wiesbaden, 1988. An innovative study contrasting Egyptian references to foreigners in both the more mundane everyday mimesis, where they appear in a more positive light, and ideologically charged topos, which depicts them in highly negative terms.

O'Connor, David. *Ancient Nubia: Egypt's Rival in Africa.* Philadelphia, 1993. Provides a general introduction to the civilizations of ancient Nubia, including Egypt's empire. Less detailed than Adams (1977), but with many illustrations and photographs.

Redford, Donald B. *Egypt, Canaan, and Israel in Ancient Times.* Princeton, 1992. A comprehensive critical survey of Egypt's interactions with, and empire in, Syria-Palestine.

Säve-Söderbergh, Torgny, and Lana Troy. *New Kingdom Pharaonic Sites.* 2 vols. *Swedish Journal of Egyptology* 5. 2 and 3 (1991). A valuable consideration of Egyptian imperialism and the principality system of the New Kingdom. Includes a thorough analysis of several key Nubian sites that illustrate the acculturation of Nubians, especially the important cemetery at Fadrus and the tomb of Djehutyhotep, prince of Tekhet.

Schreiber, Katharina. *Wari Imperialism in Middle Horizon Peru.* Ann Arbor, Mich., 1992. Includes a useful cross-cultural discussion imperial dynamics.

Sinopoli, Carla. "Archaeology of Empires." *Annual Review of Anthropology* 23 (1994), 159–180. A broad survey of archaeological approaches to imperialism, with an excellent bibliography.

Cusick, James, ed. *Studies in Culture Contact: Interaction, Culture Change, and Archaeology.* Carbondale, Ill., 1998. Essays discussing contact dynamics, ranging from the ancient Mediterranean to the modern colonization of the New World. Useful for its focus on the conquered, and includes a paper on Egypt and Nubia by Stuart T. Smith.

Smith, Stuart T. *Askut in Nubia: The Economics and Ideology of Egyptian Imperialism in the Second Millennium* BC. London, 1995.

Smith, Stuart T. "State and Empire in the Middle and New Kingdoms." In *Anthropological Analysis of Ancient Egypt,* edited by Judy Lustig, pp. 66–89. Sheffield, 1997.

Smith, Stuart T. "Ancient Egyptian Imperialism: Ideological Vision or Economic Exploitation?" *Cambridge Archaeological Journal* 7 (1997), 301–307.

STUART TYSON SMITH

INHERITANCE. The Demotic law book from Hermopolis West (beginning third century BCE) contains inter alia a chapter (fragmentary toward its end) on inheritance; many cases are presented, each provided with an appropriate decision. It begins with an intestate (no will) succession for fields, gardens, slaves, temple prebends, properties, then it devolves generally upon the son qualified, *šr ꜥ3* ("oldest son"). Whenever other descendants required a part thereof, different situations might arise. Yet, usually the *šr ꜥ3* (in the absence of sons, a daughter) played the major role in the succession. He or she received more benefits and his or her share normally exceeded that of any other heir.

In translating *šr ꜥ3* always by "eldest son," the point may be missed in a given succession. Indeed, passages in the law book, as well as a pertinent proviso in marriage contracts, indicate that the first born is not necessarily the favorite, yet the *šr ꜥ3* did come from among the descendants. The law book also presents the situation of an estate definitively left to a son other than the *šr ꜥ3*, and other situations as well. In fact, this theoretical treatise provides various circumstances whereby the succession might also be established by the last will, which could be in written form.

The documentation further affords vivid glimpses of ancient Egyptian inheritance practices. One Demotic papyrus (Papyrus Moscow, from Akhmim, 70 BCE) amply records a *donatio mortis causa:* A father undertakes the division, effective upon his death, of his estate (97 *arouras* of fields, several amounts of money, other revenues, movables, etc.) among his six sons, taking into consideration his wife and his daughter. In so doing, he impressed his last will ultimately upon his *šr ꜥ3*, thus appointing him (perhaps tacitly) as the executor-to-be.

If an estate passed unsplit to the heirs, they could jointly run its management so that everyone received a part from its yield. One Demotic papyrus (Papyrus Leiden, from Memphis, 257/256 BCE) illustrated that state of affairs. In a community of heirs (two sons and one daughter) the *šr ʿȝ* drew up a title for his sister, acknowledging her one-fourth in houses, revenues, and other property inherited from their parents and other ancestors; yet, the other brother as well as their mother gave their accord. Since no individual parts were given, there was no actual division.

Texts from earlier periods do not yield such informative details. They disclose, however, that a community of heirs existed in one form or another, perhaps to save the estate from fragmentation. Usually the estate was under the control of an administrator/trustee (*rwḏ*) who could be one of the heirs. In the fourteenth-century BCE succession narrated by the scribe Mose in his tomb inscription at Saqqara, a woman, Urnero, was appointed by an official from the supreme council to assume that responsibility on behalf of her five brothers and sisters. Apparently the task was not easy. Indeed, various examples bespeak litigations conspicuously initiated by the heirs opposing the administrator in question. In the dispute recounted by the scribe Mose, an official from the supreme council was called upon to carry out the partition of the estate among the six coheirs.

A series of Demotic papyri exists on which a lawsuit was based, with a record of the proceedings at the trial. That record (Papyrus British Museum 10591 *recto*) is the most elaborate of judicial proceedings from the ancient world. In 181/180 BCE, some family arrangements were made by one Petetum for the offspring of his two successive marriages. Upon his death, there was at first no division of his real estate among his two sons; the elder, Tuot, seems to have kept control of it. In 174/173, however, the younger brother, Tefhape, wanted his share. Quarrels arose, and the elder brother's wife, Chratiankh, countered by starting legal proceedings against him. Her claim was mainly founded on her marriage settlement, made by her husband and confirmed by his father, who, as she alleged, pledged the land to her as security. At court, she claimed the land for her son (by Tuot), who was then under age but upon whom the land should devolve in the future.

Many occurrences from Hellenistic and Roman times relate the specific Egyptian legal device called *katoché*, which gave the advantage to the children, with regard to the devolution of their father's estate: Since during his lifetime, they enjoyed a claim to his property; he was then not able to dispose of it as he pleased without their accord; after his death, their claim became a property title. Chratiankh was obviously implying that *katoché* in favor of her son. As for the defendant, he justified his claim—especially since his elder brother had made a deed of apportionment to him, which had been confirmed by her. Thereupon the judges decreed that the younger brother should be put forthwith in possession of his share. This trial came to be at Siut in 170 BCE.

Children inherit, normally, from their father and mother individually; likewise, the father and mother inherit, each from his and her own family. This shows that the thought of inheritance in direct line was deeply rooted in the people's mind. In principle, then, husband and wife do not inherit from each other. Yet, as an Egyptian woman could legally represent her husband in many dealings, she appears sometimes to be addressed by him in connection with the devolution of his property. One papyrus (Papyrus Kahun I, 1; from the nineteenth to the eighteenth century BCE) reports on two last wills publicly made by two brothers. One had granted his property (including slaves) to his brother; years later, that brother passed it to his own wife, on condition that she in turn confer it on the child she prefers. Since the Ramessid period, however, the wife could be allocated, if not all her husband's property acquired during marriage, then at least a third. More favorable arrangements could also be envisaged by the man if he wished.

In textual material, some offices yielding income (revenues in kind) are recorded as being conveyed from one family member to another, thus hinting at inheritance. Papyrus Kahun VII, 1 (from the nineteenth century BCE) reports of two such house-documents (*imit-pr*, "what is in the house," not a testament *ipso iure*). The first had been made by the chief of a priest guild for his wife, but in the second, he replaced his deed by establishing a new one, conferring his position on his son from her. As to his house property, he granted it to other children.

Particularly interesting is a conveyance (the Stèle Juridique de Karnak from the seventeenth century BCE) regarding the office of governor in Elkab. This office was held within a family and the grandfather was succeeded by one of his sons, who later died without descendants. The office then devolved on one of his brothers, and afterward on this brother's son, a certain Kebsi. Kebsi ceded it in a house-document to his brother Sobeknakhte "from son to son, from one family-successor (*iwʿ*) to another" for 60 gold-*deben*. The deed thus took on the form of a sale, and as such it would be on firm ground, more than just a *donatio mortis causa*. A plethora of Demotic and Coptic deeds, from later times, convey, bequests that use the same device. In the last case, Kebsi asserted, "neither son/daughter, brother/sister, nor any relative shall claim the office" given to his brother. That is a clause (*bebaiosis* declaration) inserted into the deed, stressing the nonexistence of claims on the part of presumptive heirs. The usage of that clause in a wide variety of conveyances points out that presumptive heirs had claims on one's property, in general, but also when no inheritance was in view. In transactions from later periods bearing on loans, the debtor promised to fulfill all engagements toward his creditor; in so doing, he frequently involved his children's responsibility. In case of his untimely death, his heirs were then under obligation to clear his debts.

Against this background, some texts from the workmen's community at Deir el-Medina (thirteenth to twelfth century BCE) can be displayed now. One papyrus from a family archive adds to the documentation on testaments. It records the oral deposition of one Naunakhte, a workman's wife, before the local council (*qnbt*), whose clerk penned the document. Naunakhte bequeathed only to those of her children (four sons plus four daughters in all) who had supported her in her old age and disinherited the others (yet not of their father's property). Especially remarkable is that Naunakhte decided on her own succession among her children. Accordingly, she split up her property in various bequests, so that neither the favorites nor the disinherited received equal parts. One son, for example, was rewarded a bronze bowl more than other heirs, whereas a disinherited son got a compensation (tools and utensils worth 40 *deben*). Barely one year later, her husband and children appeared before the local council and gave consent; evidently it was requisite that her "writings be [carried out] exactly."

Three cases deserve special attention because of their common feature: a father disjoins his property for his siblings. In Ostracon Gardiner 90, the father grants his "benevolent" son the rights to the work of ten slaves obtained (inherited?) from his own mother. In Ostracon Deir el-Medina 108, a father drawing up a house-document in favor of his children declared: "Concerning all [my] things, they are shares of all [my] children." Thereupon his implements, household goods and other property as well as his rights (to recurring provisions of cereals, etc.) are apportioned to four sons and two daughters; this took place "in the presence of witnesses." Papyrus Cairo 58092 (*verso*) recounts that one day a father made a statement "regarding his places [immovables] of his father [presumably inherited] in order to give them to his children." The text lists some buildings, a ground, a pyramid, and more, precisely measured; it also names five sons and one daughter, each being allotted a specific portion. They had still to pronounce, "If we turn up to contest, we should get 100 blows [a thrashing] and lose our share." Obviously, after everyone was put in his or her allotment, each assured never to dispute with one another about the inheritance. Such an assurance used to be given mutually by heirs upon partition, as was revealed also by the Demotic and Coptic documents. In all these cases, it was the father who in his lifetime undertook the division of his estate among his siblings. Yet, that he definitively gave it away and remained empty-handed is doubtful. Rather, he plausibly would have complete control of his affairs for as long as he lived (as in a living trust); only after his death would his legacy, it seems, become effective.

One record (Ostracon Gardiner 103) reveals a father who left for his children (probably *mortis causa*) a house, whereas after hesitation he assigned a son another dwelling. Then that legatee argued that the dwelling had been donated by one ancestor for the cult of a local god. He sought, therefore, redress asking for a new and just partition.

In one papyrus (Papyrus Cairo 58092 *recto*), regulation reads: "Let the effects be given to him who [cared for] the interment, says the Pharaoh's rule"; it appears to have applied among the inhabitants, and an authoritative precedent came about eventually: a son, who provided coffins and saw to his mother's funeral, inherited her estate to the exclusion of others. That precedent, too, was set as a rule, and it was cited repeatedly when inheritance disputes occurred. Accordingly, the speaker in the Cairo Papyrus, who alone had arranged his mother's interment, laid claim on her property. As his brothers and sisters object, he wrote to the local authorities explaining his position. In Ostracon Petrie 16, a man was alleged to have furnished a deceased woman with a coffin; hence he got her part in a building. Then, his son pretends to this part, but her daughter is challenging him. As no relationship point is indicated between the two parties, the father and son might have been outsiders (or distant relatives) who put forward their claim and supported it by quoting the aforementioned precedent.

There were three more conflicts about houses (presumably inherited). All were decided by the local council through divine ordeal. Notwithstanding the fragmentary state of the texts, each time someone was pleading his own claim, yet in the end was turned down. Moreover he was to swear not to dispute any longer the rightful heir's position. In the presence of an heir, then, any other claimant to the property had to withdraw and acknowledge the heir's prerogative.

BIBLIOGRAPHY

Allam, S. *Hieratische Ostraka und Papyri aus der Ramessidenzeit. Urkunden zum Rechtsleben im alten Ägypten*, 1. Tübingen, 1973.

Allam, S. "Familie und Besitzverhältnisse in der altägyptischen Arbeitersiedlung von Deir-el-Medineh." *Revue Internationale des Droits de l'Antiquité* 30 (1983), 17 ff.

Allam, S. "La Personne adoptive en Égypte pharaonique." In *Le Droit de la famille en Europe: son évolution depuis l'antiquité jusqu'à nos jours: Actes des Journées Internationales d'histoire du Droit*, edited by R. Ganghofer, pp. 783 ff. Strasbourg, 1992.

Allam, S. "Vom Erbrecht in Altägypten." *Kemet* 6. 4 (October 1997), 22 ff.

Clarysse, W. "Prolemaic Wills." In *Legal Documents of the Hellenistic World*, edited by M. Geller and H. Maehler, pp. 88 ff. London, 1995.

Mattha, G., and G. Hughes. *The Demotic Legal Code of Hermopolis-West*. Cairo, 1975.

Mrsich, T. "Erbe." In *Lexikon der Ägyptologie*, 1: 1235–1260. Wiesbaden, 1975.

Pestman, P. "The Law of Succession in Ancient Egypt." In *Essays on*

Oriental Laws of Succession, edited by J. Brugman, et al., pp. 58 ff. Leiden, 1969.

Pestman, P. "'Inheriting' in the Archive of the Theban Choachytes (2nd cent. BC)." In *Aspects of Demotic Lexicography: Acts of the Second International Conference for Demotic Studies, Leiden 19–21 September 1984*, edited by S. Vleeming, pp. 57 ff. Leuven, 1987.

Seidl, E. "Vom Erbrecht der alten Ägypter." *Zeitschrift der Deutschen Morgenländischen Gesellschaft* 107.2 (1957), 270 ff.

Till, W. *Erbrechtliche Untersuchungen auf Grund der koptischen Urkunden*. Sitzungsberichte der Österreichischen Akademie der Wissenschaften, 229.2. Vienna, 1954.

S. ALLAM

INSECTS. As the most numerically abundant class of animals, insects were represented in Egypt by bees, flies, various biting insects, locusts, and beetles. The Egyptian bee (*Apis mellifica fasciata;* in Egyptian, *bit*) was an integral part of the king's titulary from the earliest periods of Egyptian history. The term *nsw-bity* is conventionally translated "King of Upper and Lower Egypt" but literally means "he who belongs to the sedge and the bee," the papyrus, a sedge plant, being associated with Upper Egypt and the bee with the Nile Delta; a wide variety of other evidence suggests a close connection between the bee and Lower Egypt. The Lower Egyptian city of Sais had a "Mansion of the Bee" where Osiris was worshiped, and the name of the Delta city Chemmis (*3ḫ-bit* in Egyptian) meant "thicket of the bee." The Lower Egyptian goddess Neith was associated with the bee.

There are other religious associations of the bee. According to the ancient Egyptians, bees came into being from the tears of the sun god Re. The bee may also have had some sort of connection with the goddess Hathor, because eating honey was forbidden in Dendera, where she was worshiped. The creator god Khnum was said to work busily like a bee. Many priests of Min had titles connected with honey collection. The goddess Nut appears as a bee at least once.

The earliest evidence for the domestication of bees in Egypt is a scene in the sun temple of Newoserre Any of the fifth dynasty which contains the earliest representations of beekeeping. In ancient times, and even today, the Egyptians built beehives from cylindrical tubes of dried mud or dung stacked one on top of another. Beekeepers seem not to have worn protective gear when tending the hives, but rather smoked the bees into a stupor before extracting the honeycomb. In present-day Egypt and in Greco-Roman times (and possibly earlier as well), beehives were moved from place to place by boat or donkey to increase honey production. A honeycomb found in a tomb at Deir el-Medina was analyzed, and the pollens that the bees which produced it had consumed were identified as primarily those of Egyptian plum and persea, with traces of other plants. A special "white honey" obtained in the Delta during the New Kingdom was probably destined only for the use of the king and temples. In a tax-collection scene in the tomb of the vizier Rekhmire at Thebes (tomb 100), honey is brought only from cities in Upper Egypt north of Thebes. Wild honey was collected during hunting expeditions in the desert, even in Nubia. Honey also was part of the tribute offered to the Egyptian king by vassals in the Near East.

Because sugar was unknown to the ancient Egyptians, honey was the sweetener of choice. During the Old Kingdom, however, its use is suggested to have been restricted to the pharaoh's table and as a temple offering, because it is not mentioned in private tombs or texts. By the New Kingdom, the use of honey was certainly more widespread, figuring among the daily rations of men participating in military and commercial expeditions.

Honey was the most common ingredient in Egyptian medicine, appearing approximately five hundred times in the roughly nine hundred known prescriptions. The Egyptians used it to treat a wide variety of problems. Honey occurred frequently in eye-salves, in ointments for treating wounds and burns, and in medicines to be taken internally which otherwise would have been too bitter to swallow. Modern scientific tests have demonstrated that honey is indeed an effective killer of bacteria and fungi, and the Egyptians seem to have regarded it as having magical properties as well, for honey was said to be sweet for man but bitter for the evil dead and demons, who were repelled with potions containing honey.

Like honey, beeswax was used in medicine, principally to anoint open wounds. Wax was also used to make magical figurines and *shawabti*s, as a cosmetic ingredient, as an adhesive, for coating painted surfaces, and in the embalming of mummies.

The common housefly (*ꜥff* in ancient Egyptian; the word survives in Egyptian Arabic as a verb referring to the swarming of insects on food) would have been a ubiquitous nuisance in ancient Egypt. It is difficult to impossible to identify the species of fly depicted in Egyptian art, but it has been suggested that the Egyptians may have been familiar with the families Muscidae and Calliphoridae. A scene in the tomb of Niankhchnum and Khnumhotep depicts what may be a horde of flies swarming about a fisherman as he guts his catch. Both men and women are depicted holding fly whisks in tomb paintings, and two horsehair fly whisks were found among the treasures in Tutankhamun's tomb. In a section devoted to ridding the house of pests, the Ebers Papyrus recommends a salve composed of some sort of bird fat to ward off the "bites" of flies.

Flies were not regarded in an entirely negative light by the Egyptians. Fly excrement and blood appear in a num-

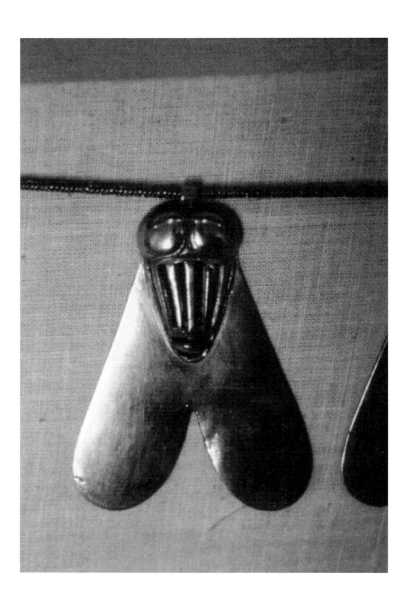

INSECTS. *Golden fly in the Cairo Museum.* (Courtesy
David P. Silverman)

ber of medical prescriptions, but never flies themselves.
Gold fly pendants were awarded to soldiers and military
officers who distinguished themselves in battle (it has
been suggested this was due to the fact that their persistence in battle was reminiscent of a fly's behavior). During
the eighteenth dynasty, such men recounted their military
valor and listed the number of gold flies the king awarded
them, beginning in the reign of Thutmose I, but later this
came to be a reward bestowed on any civil servant. The
housefly was also depicted on common amulets throughout Egyptian history, but their significance is unknown.

Mosquitoes, fleas, and gnats are insects (*ḥmy, ḥnws,*
and *ḥnms* are Egyptian names for stinging insects) that
could have disturbed the Egyptians in their sleep by biting, the identity of the third plague that afflicted Egypt in
the *Book of Exodus,* from Hebrew scriptures. According

to the ancient Greek historian Herodotus, the Egyptians
of marshy areas used the nets with which they caught fish
as netting to protect themselves from mosquitoes or gnats
during the night; a bed belonging to the fifth dynasty
Queen Hetepheres, found in her tomb, seems to have had
netting. The inhabitants of Upper Egypt, Herodotus reports, were protected from noxious insects by sleeping in
towers, for the winds kept them from flying up high. It
has been suggested that Herodotus is simply referring to
the custom of sleeping on rooftops, but another possibility is that the people slept in mud-brick towers that may
have doubled as granaries, as is common today in Upper
Egypt (similar towers are depicted in ancient Egyptian
art). The Ebers Papyrus gives a prescription of oil rubbed
on the body to keep away some sort of biting insect (*ḥnws*).

The best-known association of locusts (Egyptian *snḥm,*

Schistocerca gregaria or *Acrydium peregrinum*) with Egypt is their appearance as the eighth plague mentioned in the *Book of Exodus*. Ancient Egyptian texts noted the locust's destructive behavior as a threat to crops. In tomb scenes, locusts are depicted in the Nile marshes, the fields and gardens, and in one case in the mouth of a hedgehog, and several grasshopper-shaped cosmetic boxes have been found. In a single representation, a boy is depicted catching a grasshopper with a net. The term "locusts" is used metaphorically to stand for the numerous soldiers of the Egyptian king, and another time "locust" stands for the leader of foreign enemies. "Locust" also appears as a male personal name.

A number of beetles were known to ancient Egyptians (belonging to the superfamilies Scarabaeoidea and Diversicornia), although the sacred scarab (*Scarabaeus sacer*) is the best known. These beetles inhabit soil, dung, or decaying plant and animal substances. The scarab often feeds on dung, and has the peculiar characteristic of rolling dung destined to be food into a round ball that can reach the size of a small apple, and then rolling it to a safe storage place underground. The female scarab buries her eggs in pear-shaped balls constructed entirely underground. The ancients erroneously believed that the scarab laid its eggs in the former type of ball. Their Egyptian name (*ḫprr*) is related to a verb (*ḫpr*) which means "to become." The scarab was worshiped as a god, Khepri, and had a close association with Re, representing the sun god when he rose from the underworld at the eastern horizon in the morning and descended below the western horizon in the evening, analogous to the behavior of the beetle rolling its food-ball.

Scarab-shaped amulets were the most common amulet worn in ancient Egypt. Besides their protective function, these amulets are often inscribed with the reigning monarch's name on the ventral side; they were used as seals pressed into mud clumps used to seal containers and doors. Most of these scarab amulets have been found in the excavation of palaces and settlement sites, even in the Near East; they therefore play an important role in the dating of sites and remains.

[*See also* Bees and Honey; *and* Scarabs.]

BIBLIOGRAPHY

Bacher, Ilona. "Die Fliege in Kultur und Religion der alten Ägypter." M.A. thesis, University of Munich, 1993. Nearly impossible to obtain, this is the only extensive work dealing exclusively with the fly in Egyptian culture and religion.

Chouliara-Raïos, Hélène. *L'abeille et le miel en Égypte d'après les papyrus grecs.* Greece, 1989. Contains information derived primarily from Greek sources on the bee and honey in Greco-Roman times.

Hornung, Erik, and Elisabeth Staehelin. *Skarabäen und andere Siegelamulette aus Basler Sammlungen.* Ägyptische Denkmäler in der Schweiz 1. Mainz, 1976. Offers extensive bibliographic references on scarabs.

Houlihan, Patrick F. *The Animal World of the Pharaohs.* Cairo, 1996. Pages 187–194 are devoted to insects.

Keimer, Ludwig. "Pendeloques en forme d'insectes faisant partie de colliers égyptiens." *Annales du Service des Antiquités de l'Égypte* 32 (1932), 129–150; 33 (1933), 97–130, 193–200; 37 (1937), 143–172.

Kritsky, Gene. "Beetle Gods, King Bees and Other Insects of Ancient Egypt." *KMT* 4.1 (1993), 32–39. Popular article covers beetles, praying mantis, locusts, dragonflies, butterflies, bees, and flies.

Leclant, Jean. "L'abeille et le miel dans l'Égypte pharaonique." In *Histoire, Ethnographie et Folklore*, edited by R. Chauvin, pp. 51–60. Traité de biologie de l'abeille, 5. Paris, 1968. A discussion of bees and honey in pharaonic Egypt.

Rand Nielsen, Elin. "Honey in Medicine." In *Sesto Congresso Internazionale di Egittologia: Atti*, vol. 2, pp. 415–419. Turin, 1993.

Raven, Maarten J. "Wax in Egyptian Magic and Symbolism." *Oudheidkundig Mededelingen uit het Rijksmuseum van Oudheden te Leiden* 64 (1983): 7–47.

Tufnell, Olga. *Scarab Seals and Their Contribution to History in the Early Second Millennium B.C.* Studies on Scarab Seals, 2. Warminster, 1984.

Ward, William A. *Pre-12th Dynasty Scarab Amulets.* Studies on Scarab Seals, 1. Warminster, 1978. Contains an appendix on scarab beetle biology and behavior by Sadek Ibrahim Bishara.

Ward, William A., and William G. Dever. *Scarab Typology and Archaeological Context: An Essay on Middle Bronze Age Chronology.* Studies on Scarab Seals, 3. San Antonio, 1994.

NICOLE B. HANSEN

INSIGNIAS were emblems of status, derived from professional tools whose practical functions had become secondary to symbolic ones. They include thrones, scepters, staves, and standards. Class, office, and gender dictated which insignias a person possessed. In mortuary contexts, however, private and royal persons possessed divine insignias, since all aspired to divinity in the afterlife. Coffin Text Spell 75 invested the deceased with divine insignias. Middle Kingdom coffins depicted insignias in groups, called object friezes, which encircled the mummy, with crowns painted by the head, sandals by the feet, scepters by the hands, and staves along the body's length. Model insignias also accompanied mummies in their coffins.

Thrones. Commoners had few possessions, and out of necessity they sat on the ground. Restricted to the upper classes, chairs were thus a status symbol. Thrones, which were ritual chairs, were restricted to gods, goddesses, and royalty. A deity (*nṯr*) sat on the block throne (Figure 1), a seat in the form of a cube with sides often decorated with the "enclosure" hieroglyph (*ḥwt*), and thus representing the term "temple" (*ḥwt-nṯr*), which meant "enclosure of a god." A throne decorated with the palace façade invested its occupant with a palace. A throne covered with plumage associated its occupant with the lofty falcon of Re-Horakhty, who was "variegated of plumage."

Kings sat on block thrones decorated with motifs of universality. The knotted-plants motif (Figure 2), a hieroglyphic monogram for "unity of the Two Lands" (*zmꜣ-*

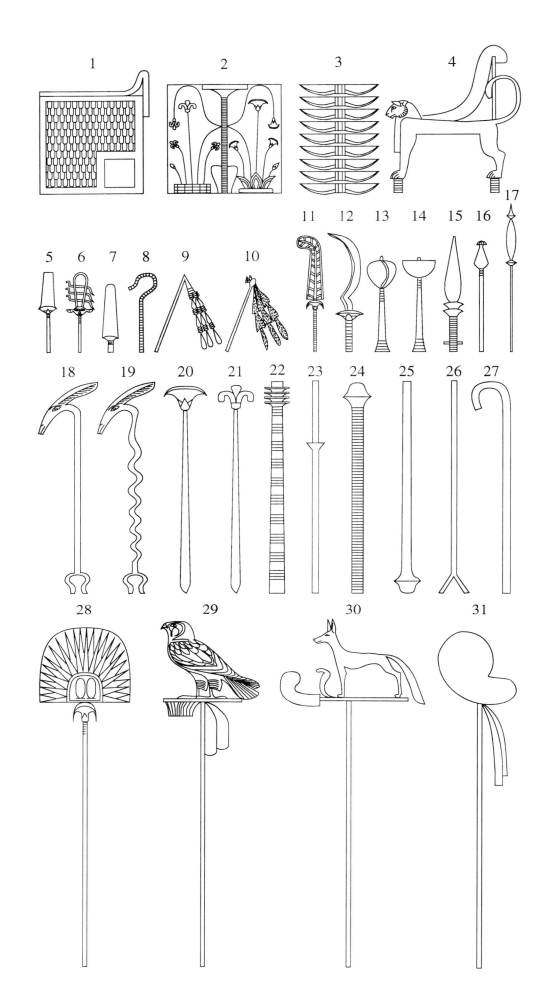

t3wy), signified dominion over Upper and Lower Egypt. It depicted the sedge plant of Upper Egypt tied with the papyrus of Lower Egypt to a windpipe representing "unity" (*zm3*). Some thrones portrayed Seth, Thoth, Horus, or Nile gods tying these plants. Other royal thrones emphasize victory by displaying Nubian, Asiatic, Libyan, and Aegean prisoners bound by unification plants. Elsewhere these enemies were transformed into nine bows (Figure 3), which represented the sum of Egypt's enemies, since bows meant "enemies," and nine, the tripling of three, represented "plurality of pluralities." Nine bows figured on the king's footrest and sandals, so that he might trample his enemies. Lapwings, symbolizing subject people, were also figured under the king's feet. Sometimes kings sat on the lion throne (Figure 4), comprised of two lions supporting a seat. This iconography evoked the horizon, since Shu and Tefnut guarded the horizon in leonine form. The vignette to Spell 17 of the *Book of Going Forth by Day* depicted them as lions whose backs form a horizon where the sun rises and sets. By rising from or sitting on a lion throne, the king appeared to rise and set like the sun god, emphasizing his role as heir to the throne of Atum, the deity who created Shu and Tefnut as his resting place in the abyss.

Scepters. Symbolic scepters derived from professional tools. Men used them more than did women, and kings more than officials and deities. The most typical male insignia was the *aba*-scepter (Figure 5), a flat paddle on a papyrus-umble handle, resembling a fly-swatter. Used like a wand, it served in the consecration of offerings and the supervision of ship-building. As a hieroglyph, it represented "govern" (*ḥrp*), and "control" (*sḥm*); therefore, it is also called the *kherep*- or *sekhem*-scepter. The *sekhem*-scepter was sacred to Anubis in the temple of Hu (known as the "Enclosure of the *Sekhem*" (*ḥwt-sḥm*), and to Osiris at Abydos. As a hieroglyph, it expressed "power" and any deity's stellar manifestation. When consecrating offerings, the king used two *sekhem*-scepters: one for Seth, and another for Horus. Elsewhere, Horus and Seth appear as "the Two *Sekhem*s" (*sḥmwy*).

◀ ━━━━━━━━━━━━━━━━━━━━━━━

INSIGNIAS. *Insignias discussed in the text of this article:* (1) block throne; (2) knotted-plants motif; (3) nine bows; (4) lion throne; (5) *aba*-scepter; (6) *sekhem*-scepter (depicted as a sistrum); (7) *ḥts*-(or *3mts*-) scepter; (8) crook; (9) flail; (10) fly-whisk; (11) ostrich-plume fan; (12) scimitar; (13) piriform mace; (14) lentoid mace; (15) *mks*-scepter; (16) lotus scepter; (17) Ramessid baton; (18) *w3s*-staff; (19) *d'm*-staff; (20) papyrus staff; (21) sedge staff; (22) *djed*-pillar staff; (23) *mks*-staff; (24) *3ms*-staff; (25) herald's staff; (26) *aby*-staff; (27) *a'wt*-staff; (28) sunshade; (29) Horus standard; (30) Ophois standard; (31) *šdšd*-standard.

Sometimes the *sekhem*-scepter hieroglyph represented the sistrum (Figure 6), a musical rattle that was sacred to Hathor and was carried by her priestesses. It had a metal loop with jingles mounted on a cow-goddess-faced handle. Women also carried the *ḥts*- or *3mts*-scepter (Figure 7), whose hieroglyph means "finish" (*ḥts*). Its form was derived from the lettuce plant and may have related to the cult of Min, to whom that plant was sacred. It was used, like the *aba*-scepter, for consecrating offerings. Additional hieroglyphic values were "graciousness" (*j3mt*), "ornament" (*ḥkr*), and "harem lady" (*ḥkrt*), which may derive from the scepter's similarity both to the tree hieroglyph (*j3m*) and to the spear-point hieroglyph (*ḥkr*), which object decorated archaic palace gates.

As a pair, the crook and flail (Figures 8, 9) were insignias of kingship and might be carried only by kings, Osiris, and gods identified with them. Other deities could proffer them but did not keep them. Both insignias derived from the iconography of Andjety, who later became Osiris of Busiris. Sacred models of them were kept in Heliopolis. The crook was a cane with hooked handle, sometimes gold-plated and reinforced with blue copper bands. It probably derived from the shepherd's crosier. Its hieroglyphic value was "rule." The flail was a rod with three attached beaded, strands. It possibly derived from a shepherd's whip, although it may have served for collecting incense gum. For unknown reasons, a flail is figured floating above the upraised hand of Min and other ithyphallic deities. Certain sacred animals carried the flail on their backs.

In silhouette, the flail resembles the fly-whisk (Figure 10), a stick with three pendant animal pelts. Despite their similar appearance, they are not interchangeable. Hieroglyphically, the fly-whisk designated "protect" (*ḥwj*). Ladies carried them, often reimagined, in the New Kingdom, as bent lilies or papyrus umbels. The ostrich-plume fan (Figure 11), with its papyrus-umbel handle, had the same phonetic value as the fly-whisk and could stand hieroglyphically for "protect," and royal guards may have carried it for this reason. It could also represent the "breath of life" when held by Isis, Nephthys, or Horus, who waved it over the corpse of Osiris in order to revive him.

The forms of some scepters derived from weapons. Montu and Amun sometimes proffered the scimitar (Figure 12) to the king when he was depicted on temple pylons smiting enemies. The word "scimitar" (*ḥpš*) was etymologically connected to the "strong arm" (*ḥpš*) of Horus or Seth. Seth's strong arm was the foreleg of a bull, represented in the sky by the Big Dipper. Kings also carried maces associated with Ophois, the "Opener of Ways," and the Eye of Horus. The piriform mace (Figure 13) served as a hieroglyph for "bright" and for "lightning." The lentoid mace (Figure 14) had fallen out of all but ritual use by dynastic times. A wooden club called the *mks*-scepter (Figure 15), not to be confused with the *mks*-staff (see below under "Staves"), was employed in combat even after the old stone maces were obsolete. Other mace-like scepters included the lotus scepter (Figure 16), representing the fruit of a lotus, and its derivative form, the Ramessid baton (Figure 17), held by the king when directing festival processions.

Staves. Like scepters, staves are sticks, but they stand as tall as a person's chest from the ground. They derived from walking sticks, fighting canes, and tent poles. Gods carry the *wȝs*-staff (Figure 18), often erroneously called a "scepter;" its forked base may have been intended for controlling serpents, and its animal-headed apex may personify a desert creature like the Seth-animal or a gazelle. Seth possessed a sacred *wȝs*-staff emblem in his temple at Ombos, and Montu retained another one which acted as the emblem of Thebes. The *wȝs*-staff, in fact, is a hieroglyph for "Thebes" (*wȝst*) as well as for the word "dominion." In Egyptian reliefs, *wȝs*-staffs served as vertical borders to scenes, supporting elongated "sky" hieroglyphs and standing on elongated "earth" hieroglyphs, which served as the horizontal parts of the frame. They seem therefore to represent the pillars of the sky, hence dominion over the entire universe. The *dʿm*-staff (Figure 19) is identical to the *wȝs*-staff except that its shaft undulates. Its hieroglyphic value is "electrum," a precious natural alloy of gold and silver, and it is associated with Geb, god of the earth. Coffin Text Spell 469 also associated it with Orion, who used it to defeat the demons. Only goddesses personifying the eye of the sun god hold the *wȝs*-staff. These goddesses may also carry the papyrus staff (Figure 20), representing goddesses of Lower Egypt like Wadjet, Tefnut, Bastet, Sakhmis, and Neith, who protected the infant Horus in the marshes. Because it grows in water, the papyrus plant, symbolized the sun's first ascension from the abyss. The sedge staff (Figure 21) parallels the Papyrus staff, representing Upper Egyptian manifestations of the solar eye goddess, such as Nekhbet, Rat-tawy, Tjanenet, and Mut. The *djed*-pillar staff (Figure 22), a column with four cavetto-cornice capitals, hieroglyphically represented "stability." Originally a focus of the cult of Ptah, who was called "August *djed*-Pillar," it was soon transferred to Sokar and Osiris. On the last day of Khoiak, during the Sokar festival, the king ceremonially erected a *djed*-pillar and proclaimed the resurrection of Sokar-Osiris, whose shrine at Giza had four *djed*-pillars, one at each corner.

Staves carried by ordinary mortals included the *mks*-staff (Figure 23), having the form of a pole with a hand guard for cane battling. Old Kingdom officials are portrayed holding the *mks*-staff in the left hand and the *ʿbȝ*-

scepter in the right. Its name meant "protect it." Another object with a similar name, often conflated with the *mks*-staff, is the *ȝms*-staff (Figure 24), which resembles a tent pole wrapped with a strap and topped by a cap. Some Middle Kingdom coffins depict them in groups of four, one for each direction of the compass. Its name meant "grasp it." The herald's staff (Figure 25) is a pole with a wider base than apex. Its hieroglyphic values were "word" and "speak," as is appropriate, since heralds pounded such staffs when they made official speeches. Its butt end therefore had a cap on it, so that it might make a louder noise when pounded. Thoth, as the herald of the gods, had two of them, and four are sometimes represented on Middle Kingdom coffins, perhaps so that the deceased's arrival in the afterlife as a god might be announced in the four corners of the universe. The *aby*-staff (Figure 26) had a forked butt end designed for snake control and boat propulsion. These staves were carried in the desert and on boats but were also associated with the status of an eldest son, since the hieroglyph for that person shows a man walking with an *aby*-staff. The *aʿwt*-staff (Figure 27), a pole with a curved apex, also related to desert travel and animal husbandry. Its hieroglyphic value was "hoofed desert animals." Several magical funerary statues of Tutankhamun, from his intact tomb, show him walking with this staff, perhaps indicating his journey across the Western Desert to the next life.

Standards. Standards (*jȝwt*) are staves with heraldic emblems mounted on their apices. Their earliest representations appear atop images of Naqada II boats. Rather than being carried by the person whose status they represented, they were carried in that person's vicinity by others of lower status. The origin of the heraldic standard was perhaps a sunshade (Figure 28). Most sunshades were plumed fans mounted on poles to protect one's eyes from solar glare; or they may have symbolically protected onlookers from the brilliance of the king or official around whom they were carried. Because of their height, they were highly visible, and this helped people to recognize one's rank from a distance.

A divine standard consisted of a vertical support staff with a horizontally oriented *nṯr* (god) sign atop it. The presence of such insignias behind royalty served to indicate their divine status. The Horus standard (Figure 29) normally represented Horus or the king in the function of Horus, but it could serve as a hieroglyphic sign referring to the king. The Ophois standard (Figure 30) had the jackal of Ophois, "Opener of Ways," riding a sledge on its apex. Ophois standards appeared in pairs, one for Ophois of Upper Egypt and another for Ophois of Lower Egypt. The *šdšd*-standard (Figure 31) was topped by an enigmatic shape, which may have represented the king's placenta, the moon god, Khons, or a throne cushion, according to different Egyptologists. Two Ophois standards, a Horus standard, and the *šdšd*-standard preceded the king during his thirty-year *heb-sed* jubilee festival. Many divine standards were also carried in royal funerary processions, called the "Following of Horus." Often carried behind the king in temple reliefs was his *ka*-standard, which bore the upraised arms of the "*ka*" hieroglyph, inside of which appeared the king's Horus name. Other divine standards served as nome standards, representing the various administrative districts of Egypt, and military standards, representing divisions of troops.

[*See also* Ceremonial Mace Heads; *and* Crowns.]

BIBLIOGRAPHY

Andrews, C. *Amulets of Ancient Egypt.* Austin, 1994. A comprehensive illustrated guide to Egyptian amulets, many of which were miniature representations of insignias.

D'Auria, S., P. Lacovara, and C. Roehrig. *Mummies and Magic: The Funerary Arts of Ancient Egypt.* Boston, 1988. Catalog of funerary objects with informative discussions of Egyptian iconography.

Fischer, H. "Fächer und Wedel." In *Lexikon der Ägyptologie,* 2: 81–85. Wiesbaden, 1977. Briefly covers the subject of ancient Egyptian fans and fly whisks.

Hayes, W. *The Scepter of Egypt.* 2 vols. New York, 1953, 1959. These volumes illustrate and discuss some of the many objects belonging to the Metropolitan Museum, including the Middle Kingdom staves and scepters of Senebtisi from Lisht, and various insignias from other periods.

Kaplony, P. "Zepter." In *Lexikon der Ägyptologie,* 6: 1373–1389. Wiesbaden, 1986. A brief but informative discussion of several Egyptian scepters and staves.

Kuhlman, K. "Thron." In *Lexikon der Ägyptologie,* 6: 523–529. Wiesbaden, 1986. A brief article describing the form and iconography of Egyptian thrones.

Lurker, M. *The Gods and Symbols of Ancient Egypt.* London, 1974. A layman's glossary of ancient Egyptian iconography, with interesting entries on various insignias.

Newberry, P. "The Shepherd's Crook and the So-called 'Flail' or 'Scourge' of Osiris." *Journal of Egyptian Archaeology* 15 (1929), 84–94. This article challenges currently held views on the significance of the crook and flail. It has much useful information but is not entirely successful in proving its thesis, which is that the flail was a tool for collecting ladanum from the cistus plant.

Reeves, N. *The Complete Tutankhamun: The King, the Tomb, the Treasure.* London, 1990. This lavishly illustrated compilation contains numerous illustrations and commentaries on insignias found in the context of an intact royal burial.

Smith, W. *The Art and Architecture of Ancient Egypt.* Edited by W. Simpson. New Haven, 1998. A textbook that gives general background on Egyptian art and iconography.

Wilkinson, R. *Reading Egyptian Art: A Hieroglyphic Guide to Ancient Egyptian Painting and Sculpture.* London, 1992. A manual for interpreting Egyptian art as a hieroglyphic mode of expression; several entries represent insignias.

GEOFFREY GRAHAM

INSINGER PAPYRUS, the primary manuscript for an important Late period Demotic Wisdom text. Purchased in 1895 by J. H. Insinger for the Rijksmuseum in Leiden, the Netherlands, the papyrus lacked its first eight or nine columns when it entered that collection; these have since been identified in the University of Pennsylvania Museum. The Insinger Papyrus's provenance was probably Akhmim, in Middle Egypt. Additional published or known fragmentary versions are today in Berlin, Cairo, Copenhagen, Florence, Lille, and Paris. Each displays minor, but not insignificant, differences. Greek jottings on a papyrus strip used to reinforce Insinger suggest, but by no means prove, an early Roman date; the original composition (and the papyrus itself) may be Ptolemaic.

As probably the latest lengthy Egyptian didactic text, the Insinger Papyrus is firmly in the native tradition, although it possesses unique features. Most of the twenty-five published chapters (called "Instructions") are identified by a heading. In common with the scribes who composed other Late period Wisdom texts, the author of the Insinger Papyrus was much concerned with the nature of god, the qualities of the good or evil man, and the role of the individual in society. On the basis of Karl Zauzich's description in Miriam Lichtheim's *Late Egyptian Wisdom Literature* (1983), pp. 107–109, the still unpublished first chapters of Insinger dealt, for example, with god ("In the hand of god are sustenance, work, and life"); the avoidance of envy; and the effects of wealth ("Property causes praise to come into existence for a fool who is loaded down with stench"). The published chapter headings illustrate the wide range of subjects, which include the following:

    7. self-restraint
    8. avoidance of gluttony
    9. rejection of foolishness
   10. instruction of a son
   11. acquiring protection in life
   12. carefulness in relationships with others
   13. crime and sin (lacks heading)
   14. the inferior and stupid man
   15. warning against greed
   16. caution against miserliness (lacks heading)
   17. strictures on worry
   18. the nature and importance of patience
   19. calmness
   20. warning not "to slight a small thing"
   21. "the teaching not to slight lest you be slighted"
   22. the advantages of staying in one's home town
   23. god and punishment (lacking a heading)
   24. greatness of god
   25. retaliation

The composition also touched on other topics not apparent from the headings; among them, Insinger's view of women—column 7, line 11: "[Even] a wise man is harmed because of a woman he loves." Such negative statements were balanced by the admission that a woman might indeed be good, if difficult to fathom—column 8, line 9: "There is she who is mistress of praise as mistress of the house through her character." In column 12, line 22: "One does not ever discover the heart of a woman any more than [one knows] the sky."

Fate, an important concept in Late period Egypt and in the Greco-Roman world in general, also played an important role in the composition. The chapters often conclude with the line: "The fate and the fortune that come it is the god who sends [or determines] them," as in column 21, line 6.

The Insinger Papyrus shares with the other products of Late period Egyptian wisdom a tendency to organize subject matter and themes loosely; the Insinger Papyrus, however, seems to be more tightly structured than most. The climax of the work appears to be the striking hymn to god in the Twenty-fourth Instruction (cols. 31–32, lines 9–21). While the sayings are generally monostichs, that is, "single sentences that are grammatically and logically complete and self-contained," they can be paired, forming a sort of couplet (Lichtheim, 1983, pp. 1, 110). For example, "A fool before whom there is no stick has no concern in his heart" and "A fool who has no concern gives concern to him who sends him [on an errand]." An unusual feature of the Insinger Papyrus is that the total number of individual sayings is given at the end of each chapter or section.

The tone of Insinger is rather more elevated than that of other Late period didactic texts. It is often contrasted with the Wisdom text of Onkhsheshonqy, which is characterized by more practical, earthy, and self-interested sayings. For example, Onkhsheshonqy column 16, line 5: "Do not drink water in the house of a merchant; he will charge you for it." The author of the Insinger Papyrus assumed, at times, a mildly humorous or ironic attitude, declaring, for example, "A son does not die from being punished by his father." There was also a marked fondness for paradoxes (which are not often found in older Wisdom texts). For example, "There is the one who lives on little so as to save, yet he becomes poor" and "There is one who does not know, yet the fate gives [to him] wealth."

The relationship between the Insinger Papyrus and earlier works, such as Amenemope and Ptahhotep, is not completely clear. While a few direct borrowings have been identified, the debt of the Insinger Papyrus to its predecessors is probably one of similarities in attitude and subject matter, rather than in close verbal parallels or quotations. Significant questions remain, as well, concerning the possible contact between Late Egyptian Wisdom, represented by such texts as the Insinger Papyrus, and other traditions—as, for example, those preserved in Hellenistic, Hermetic, and Jewish didactic literature.

BIBLIOGRAPHY

Text Editions and Facsimiles

De Cenival, F. "Fragment de Sagesse apparentée au Papyrus Insinger (P. Université de Lille III Inv. P. dem. Lille 34)." *Cahiers de recherches de l'Institut de papyrologie et égyptologie de Lille* 12 (1990), 93–96.

Houser, Jennifer R. "Missing Fragments of P. Insinger in the Collection of the University of Pennsylvania Museum (E16333A and E16334B)." In *Seventh International Congress of Egyptologists, Cambridge, 3–9 September 1995*, edited by Christopher Eyre, p. 88.

Lexa, František. *Papyrus Insinger.* 2 vols. Paris, 1926. Includes hand copy and glossary.

Smith, M. "Weisheit, demotische." In *Lexikon der Ägyptologie*, 6: 1197–1198. Wiesbaden, 1986. A useful list of the manuscript witnesses to Insinger.

Suten-Xeft, Le Livre Royal. 2 vols. Leiden, 1899–1905. Photographic reproduction of the Insinger Papyrus.

Volten, Askel. *Kopenhagener Texte zum Demotischen Weisheitsbuch.* Copenhagen, 1940.

Volten, Askel. *Das Demotische Weisheitsbuch, Studien und Bearbeitung.* Copenhagen, 1941. The recently identified columns are not yet published, but a detailed description by Karl-Theodor Zauzich is in Lichtheim (1983), pp. 167–109.

Translations

Lichtheim, Miriam. *Late Egyptian Wisdom Literature in the International Context: A Study of Demotic Instructions.* Orbis biblicus et orientalis, 52. Freiburg, 1983. An invaluable translation and discussion of Insinger.

Thissen, H. J. *Demotische Weisheitstexte*, vol. 3.2. *Texte aus der Umwelt des Alten Testaments*, edited by Otto Kaiser, et al., pp. 280–319. Gütersloh, 1991.

Monographs and Articles

Quack, J. "Korrekturvorschläge zu einigen demotischen literarischen Texten." *Enchoria* 21 (1994), 63–72.

Ritner, Robert. "A Misinterpreted Passage in Insinger." *Enchoria* 11 (1982), 113–114.

Schneider, T. "Hiob 38 und die demotische Weisheit." *Theologische Zeitschrift* 46 (1991), 108–124.

Williams, Ronald. J. "The Morphology and Syntax of Papyrus Insinger." Ph.D. diss., University of Chicago, 1948.

Zauzich, K.-Th. "Pap. Dem. Insinger." In *Lexikon der Ägyptologie*, 4: 898–899. Wiesbaden, 1982. With bibliography listing earlier text editions, translations, and studies.

Zauzich, K.-Th. "Paläographische Herausforderungen II." *Enchoria* 21 (1994), 90–100.

Dating

Jasnow, Richard. *A Late Period Hieratic Wisdom Text*, pp. 36–42. Studies in Ancient Oriental Civilization, 52. Chicago, 1992. On the connection between earlier and later Egyptian wisdom.

Mahé, J. P. *Hermés en Haute Égypte.* Vol. 2. Quebec, 1982. Heavily utilizes Insinger and other Egyptian didactic texts in his analysis of the classical Hermetic corpus.

Pezin, M. "Premiers raccords effectués sur les documents démotiques de Lille." *Cahiers de recherches de l'Institut de papyrologie et égyptologie de Lille*, 8 (1986), 89–98.

Quack, J. *Die Lehren des Ani: Ein neuägyptischer Weitheitstext in seinem kulturellen Umfeld*, pp. 204–205. Orbis biblicus et orientalis, 141. Freiburg, 1994. Notes possible quotations from or allusions to the Wisdom of Any in Insinger.

Sanders, Jack T. *Ben Sira and Demotic Wisdom.* Society of Biblical Literature Monograph Series, 28. Chicago, 1983. Presents the case for the dependence of Ben Sira on Insinger, but see also the review by H.-J. Thissen, *Enchoria* 14 (1980), 199–201.

Worp, K. "The Greek Text on the P. Dem. Insinger; A Note on the Date." *Oudheidkundige Mededelingen uit het Rijksmuseum van Oudheden te Leuven* 63 (1982), 39–40.

RICHARD JASNOW

INSTRUCTION OF PTAHHOTEP. The *Instruction of Ptahhotep* is arguably the most famous of the early examples of Wisdom Literature. It was probably composed in the Old Kingdom during the sixth dynasty, but the ten extant copies of the text date no earlier than the Middle Kingdom, with the majority of the texts dating from the New Kingdom. The longest and most complete text, the Prisse Papyrus of the Bibliothèque Nationale in Paris, is the version most often quoted and dates from the Middle Kingdom. Excerpts from this well-known text may also be found in didactic texts from the New Kingdom and Late period.

Traditionally, the author of these maxims is believed to be a vizier named Ptahhotep who lived during the reign of Izezi, a pharaoh of the fifth dynasty. There is no proof of this, and the text may be pseudepigraphical, as is the case with other examples of Wisdom Literature.

The text consists of thirty-seven maxims, a prologue, and an epilogue. In general, these maxims provide the reader with rules on how to conduct oneself in life: limit pride, exhibit self-control, know one's place in society, and be generous and thoughtful toward others. In short, one must adhere to the principles of *maat* in order to succeed. Possessing good speech is paramount in the practice of these rules; through well-selected words and restrained action, one can achieve a life filled with respect. The *Instruction of Ptahhotep* not only offers examples of right behavior but also provides day-to-day situations in which the righteous man will triumph over the unrighteous man.

Furthermore, this *Instruction* spends a great deal of effort in specifying the class situation in Egyptian society. The text advises the reader to know his place in society, and not to wish for that which others have. Some of the maxims provide us with clues as to the treatment of women in society, as Ptahhotep commands the reader to keep the wife happy in the home, but restrict her from power. This flat view of women will change over the development of Wisdom Literature: New Kingdom texts, such as the *Instruction of Amenemope* treat women with more respect and devote significantly more space to consideration of them.

We also learn through this text that wealth comes from the gods, and that a man's character is controlled by fate. Here, the attitude of the divine, as in other examples of Wisdom Literature, falls into the abstract. Rather than name a specific god or gods, the author of the text, as in the case of the *Instructions of Kagemni*, chose simply "god" in many instances.

The epilogue of this *Instruction* outlines the advantages of adhering to these rules. As is the case with Wisdom Literature, adhering to the rules outlined will propel its subject to success, respect, and happiness. The principles of *maat* are the key ingredient of these guidelines for the living, which will result in leading the good life.

BIBLIOGRAPHY

Assman, Jan. *Weisheit, Schrift und Literatur im alten Ägypten.* Munich, 1991.

Foster, John. *Thought Couplets and Clause Sequences in a Literary Text: The Maxims of Ptahhotep.* Society for the Study of Egyptian Antiquities Publications, 5. Toronto, 1977.

Lichtheim, Miriam. *Ancient Egyptian Literature.* Vol. I. Berkeley, 1973. The definitive translation of the Prisse Papyrus.

Shupak, Nili. *Where Can Wisdom Be Found? The Sage's Language in the Bible and in Ancient Egyptian Literature.* Orbis Biblicus et Orientalis, 130. Leiden, 1993. Though technical in parts, provides a good background to the Ptahhotep text and links it with other examples of Wisdom Literature.

WENDY RAVER

INSTRUCTIONS FOR MERIKARE. Continuing the Old Kingdom genre of the instruction into the Middle Kingdom, the *Instructions for Merikare* gives a twist to the old formula: this is a royal instruction, from a king to his son. Rather than simply providing guidelines on how to live a life according to the precepts of justice, temperance, and proper action, one finds here the addition of how to rule while practicing these virtues. Thus, this text is the first of a genre that continued throughout Egypt's history and even into the Islamic period.

Since it is known that the pharaoh Khety III preceded Merikare as ruler of Egypt during the Herakleopolitan period, it is assumed that the author of the text was Khety III. As is the case with other examples of didactic literature, the text may be pseudepigraphical, but it was most probably composed in the court of Khety III during the tenth dynasty. It survives in three copies dating to the eighteenth dynasty.

The *Instructions for Merikare* resembles other didactic texts in outlining the rules by which one should live. In its expression of the rules by which one should govern, the text centers on how to be a worthy leader while adapting the advice found in other texts. As in the Old Kingdom's *Instruction of Ptahhotep*, one learns to employ good speech and conservative action in order to receive respect and practice true justice. The reference to the "hothead" (*hnn ib*) as someone to avoid, found in the *Instructions for Merikare*, will recur in later examples of Wisdom Literature.

Expanding on the theme of serving one's public, a personal narrative interwoven in the text appears in which the king tells of events in his lifetime. This is a device that will appear later in the *Instructions of Amenemhet*. In Merikare's *Instructions,* we see reference to the expulsion of foreigners and a description of civil war, a portrait of an Egypt now divided into nomes that before was ruled centrally. Its author mentions the destruction of the nome of This and reports that destroying architecture is a great evil. Since the North and South are at peace during the writing of this text, Merikare receives the advice to continue peace with the South and to strengthen the border of the North against seminomadic Near Easterners. The author goes into great detail in describing this "lowly Asiatic" (a Near Easterner), referring to both his poverty and his wandering.

There is also an abstract reference to "the god," perhaps signifying all divinities rather than a specific god in this text, as well as in the *Instruction of Ptahhotep* and the *Instructions of Kagemni*. However, this "god" plays a more central role in determining the course of a person's life and is a personal deity who guards over humankind and shines, through nature, for all. The text ends with Khety's advice to heed his words in order to live peacefully and happily, both personally and politically.

BIBLIOGRAPHY

Assman, Jan. *Weisheit, Schrift und Literatur im alten Ägypten.* Munich, 1991.

Lichtheim, Miriam. *Ancient Egyptian Literature.* Vol. 1. Berkeley, 1973.

Shupak, Nili. *Where Can Wisdom Be Found? The Sage's Language in the Bible and in Ancient Egyptian Literature.* Orbis Biblicus et Orientalis, 130. Leiden, 1993.

WENDY RAVER

INSTRUCTIONS OF A MAN FOR HIS SON,

an anonymous teaching text, known from about 140 fragments on papyrus, ostraca, a leather manuscript, and a wooden tablet, all of New Kingdom date. A running version is still lacking, and the state of preservation in many parts of the text remains deplorable. An early twelfth dynasty date of composition is fairly certain.

The *Instructions* can be divided into two distinctive parts of uneven length. The first eight chapters are concerned with the importance of perfect speech (chapter 1); a long treatise on the central figure of the king and the necessity of following and praising him ensues (chapters 2–8). Pharaoh represents the life-dominating power; deities of destiny like Renenet and Mesekhnet are relegated to the very beginning and end of one's life. The king is the guarantor of wealth, a sedentary way of life, social re-spect, a tomb, and a happy afterlife. This applies to those subordinates loyal to him; opponents run the risk of being annihilated physically and of being deprived of remembrance by future generations. The king's power transcends the borders of Egypt.

The second part of the text (chapters 9–24), which is still marred by many lacunae, deals with the role of proper speech (*mdt*) in different social situations and constellations. One of its primary fields of application is the fair treatment of petitioners and litigants in court (esp. chapters 9, 12, and 19). Every single pronouncement has to be in accordance with the principle of *maat* (*m3't;* "order," "justice," chapters 9 and 13). Speech has to be delivered sparingly and must conform to the ideal of the silent man (*grw;* chapter 12). Practiced in an overindulgent way, it may turn into "fire" (*ht*), especially in a dispute with an ignoramus (*hm;* chapter 19). Proper speech is the first behavioral requisite of any member of the elite who wants to keep his household and office running well. Conforming to this ideal guarantees friendship, social acceptance, and a clientele (chapters 20 and 21).

Thus, the overall theme of the second part of the teaching is a treatise on the principle of "speaking *maat*" (*dd-m3 't*) and displaying vertical solidarity with one's subordinates. As is known from countless autobiographies, "speaking *maat*" is to be complemented by "doing Maat" (*iri-m3't*), treated extensively in the second part of the contemporary *Loyalist Instruction.*

The readership and audience for the *Instructions* must have lain within the highest echelons of society. The title, the *Instructions of a Man for His Son,* contains a hint of the *couche sociale* as addressee by using, in reversed order, the elements of the well-attested sociological term "son of a (gentle)man" (*s3[n] s*); a female audience can safely be excluded.

Many of the topics treated in the second part of the text occur elsewhere, but the emphasis on speaking *maat,* as well as the scope of this main subject, is unique to this text. Contrary to such teachings as those of Ptahhotep, Anii, and Amenemope, the *Instructions of a Man* is made up of only two main topics (loyalism and speech) in different facets.

There is strong evidence that this instruction was composed as the central text of a triptychon that once consisted of the *Instructions of Khety,* the *Instructions of a Man for his Son,* and the *Loyalist Teaching.*

BIBLIOGRAPHY

Fischer-Elfert, H.-W. *Die Lehre eines Mannes für seinen Sohn: Eine Etappe auf dem "Gottesweg" des loyalen und solidarischen Beamten des Mittleren Reiches.* Ägyptologische Abhandlungen, 60. Wiesbaden, 1999. Enlarged text with translation and commentary.

Helck, W. *Die Lehre des Djedefhor und die Lehre eines Vaters an seinen*

Sohn. Kleine ägyptische Texte. Wiesbaden, 1984. Text and translation.

HANS-W. FISCHER-ELFERT

INSTRUCTIONS OF AMENEMHET,

INSTRUCTIONS OF AMENEMHET, an early Middle Kingdom work, written probably not too long after the reign of Amenemhet I, founder of the twelfth dynasty. Its author is unknown. It survives in several New Kingdom papyri and writing tablets, and in a great many New Kingdom ostraca from Deir el-Medina, written as exercises by the boys in the local school. (The basic text occurs on Papyrus Millingen, now lost but copied by J. Lopez.) The ostraca, having been copied by schoolboys, are full of errors and misreadings (or mishearings), but they sometimes help with individual words or phrases. The ending of Papyrus Millingen is missing but can be supplied from alternative sources to complete the text with some reliability.

This piece is termed a *sbȝyt* by its author; hence its traditional title of "instructions," that is, a didactic piece purporting to pass on some sort of wisdom or teaching from the author to his audience. The didactic genre of Egyptian literature comprises a fairly wide range of writings. In fact, this work is really a kind of testament or apologia by a dead father (Amenemhet) to his son (the heir apparent, Senwosret)—thus presenting a variant on the basic situation of the *sbȝyt:* the wisdom of a father (usually gained from high office and public service) passed on to a son.

In this piece, the speaker is the late King Amenemhet I, who has apparently been assassinated in a palace coup. He speaks to his son, Senwosret, from beyond the grave, much like the ghost of Hamlet's father. The burden of his words and the reason for his appearance are his desire to communicate to his son the circumstances of his death. He presents an extended justification for his reign and his good deeds, as well as a veiled but fairly circumstantial description of the coup that resulted in his death while the son was away from the palace. His tone is bitter and disenchanted: Do not trust anyone, he says, implying that the conspiracy began in the harem. The apparition concludes his visit with words of encouragement to Senwosret, who will reign with the dead king's spirit at his side, helping him to rule.

Because of this situation, the piece has sometimes been described as propaganda supporting the throne and in favor of Senwosret I as successor to the dead king. This may well be; but it is also important to remember that the "testament" is a piece of literature, written in verse, and shaped to make a point, whether for the purpose of persuasion or not. Its presentation of the historical situation is molded by literary concerns and should not be relied on, without confirmation, as historically true. The "facts" of this piece, indeed, do not agree with the purported situation at the beginning of the *Story of Sinuhe.* As literature, the account is particularly rich in imagery, in colorful and concrete phrasing, and in the drama of the situation.

All in all, the *Instructions of Amenemhet* is a fine piece of Middle Kingdom literature, "complete," and giving momentary insight into events in the palace toward the beginning of the twelfth dynasty.

BIBLIOGRAPHY

Texts

Foster, John L. "The Conclusion to *The Testament of Amenemhat, King of Egypt.*" *Journal of Egyptian Archaeology* 67 (1981), 36–47; pl. 4–11.

Helck, Wolfgang. *Der Text der "Lehre Amenemhets I, für seinen Sohn."* Kleine Ägyptische Texte. Wiesbaden, 1969. Parallel text edition.

Posener, Georges. *Catalogue des ostraca hiératiques littéraire de Deir el Médineh.* Vol. 3. (nos. 1267–1675). Documents de Fouilles, Institut français d'archéologie orientale du Caire, 20. Cairo, 1977–1980. Supplement to the Helck edition.

Translations

Foster, John L. *Echoes of Egyptian Voices.* Norman, Okla., 1992. See pp. 36–39.

Lichtheim, Miriam. *Ancient Egyptian Literature.* Vol. 1. Los Angeles, 1973. See pp. 135–139.

Parkinson, R. B. *The Tale of Sinuhe and Other Ancient Egyptian Poems 1940–1640 B.C.* London, 1997. See pp. 203–211.

Simpson, William Kelly. *The Literature of Ancient Egypt.* 2d ed. New Haven, 1973. See pp. 193–197.

JOHN L. FOSTER

INSTRUCTIONS OF AMENEMOPE,

INSTRUCTIONS OF AMENEMOPE, Wisdom text that dates from about the twentieth dynasty, known from one ostracon (the oldest manuscript), four wooden tablets, and two papyri, the basic manuscript being Papyrus British Museum 10474 of the Persian period. Its author, Amenemope, introduces himself as the overseer of fields and grains. The addressee is his youngest son, the overseer of cattle Hor-em-maakheru. The text is divided into thirty numbered chapters; each line of its text is written separately (stichically) and contains a metrical verse.

The whole text is permeated by conceptions of the Ramessid period's dominant religious conception, which Egyptologists usually term "personal piety." Amenemope discusses the personal relationship between the individual and his or her god. There are two basic ways of approaching one's god. One is by refraining absolutely from zeal and pietism. Instead, one has to rely on a god's free will and action without interfering in his plans. The person practicing this behavior is called the "truly silent one." The other approach is taken by the "hot one," who pushes too eagerly on his way to reach the god. He manifests his nature by speaking with a "hot mouth" and shows a strong inclination toward aggression and strife. Direct contact with him is to be avoided because "god knows how to answer him" (5, 17). The "hot one" seems to maintain a special relationship with the moon god Thoth. Thus, one serious implication of his behavior is social isolation and even bad luck for his family and progeny. (This characterization of the "hot one" reflects the current Egyptological view, but alternative interpretations are certainly to be sought.)

Another main topic of the *Instructions* centers on material possessions and wealth, which are addressed in so-called "better-sayings": "Better is bread with a happy heart than wealth with vexation" (9, 7–8). The principles are that property acquired by illicit actions will not endure overnight; and that modesty in every sphere of daily life will result in personal happiness and social acceptance.

Amenemope is not interested in the status of women in family or society, thus displaying a marked contrast to the *Instructions of Anii.* He offers a maxim (chapter 25) about proper behavior toward physically handicapped or mentally deranged people, those who "are in the hands of god," a circumlocution for "being possessed by a manifestation of a god." Here belong the blind, the dwarf, and the lame. His warnings seem to criticize widespread attitudes that are perceivable in the roughly contemporaneous *Satirical Letter* of Papyrus Anastasi I.

As an official of the agricultural administration, Amenemope also warns against falsifying the grain measure and moving the markers on the borders of plots by swearing false oaths and thus insulting the moon god. Decent behavior and abstaining from gluttony when invited by one's superior is another topic.

Amenemope's teaching is the most influential Egyptian Wisdom text that has found its way into Hebrew scriptures (*Prov.* 22.17–23, 11). *Proverbs* 22.20b even refers to "thirty chapters," also mentioned at the end of *Amenemope* (27, 7). This number does not correspond to *Amenemope* 22, 17–23, 11 but has to be taken as a reference to the text extending to 24, 22 (Römheld 1988).

BIBLIOGRAPHY

Budge, E. A. W. *Facsimiles of Egyptian Hieratic Papyri in the British Museum.* 2d series. London, 1923. Plates 1–14 reproduce Papyrus British Museum 10474.

Lichtheim, M. *Ancient Egyptian Literature,* vol. 2: *The New Kingdom.* Berkeley and Los Angeles, 1976. See pp. 146–163.

Römheld, D. *Wege der Weisheit: Die Lehren Amenemopes und Proverbien 22, 17–24, 22.* BZAW 184. Berlin and New York, 1988.

Shirun-Grumach, I. "Die Lehre des Amenemope." In *TUAT III.2.II, Weisheitstexte II,* edited by O. Kaiser, pp. 222–250. Gütersloh, 1991.

HANS-W. FISCHER-ELFERT

INSTRUCTIONS OF ANII. This Wisdom text, presumably from Ramessid times (nineteenth dynasty) according to its language (literary Late Egyptian) is currently known from five papyri, nine ostraca, and one wooden tablet (containing only a title). Its author, a scribe by the name of Anii, purports to be attached to the mortuary temple of Nefertari (First Lady of Ramesses II?) in Western Thebes. His maxims are addressed to his son (and future scribe) Khnonshotep, which is only known from a dramatic dialogue between father and son at the end of the composition. Apart from this text, Anii may have turned to a wider audience in order to be located in the middle echelons of the literary elite.

The text is divided into chapters of uneven length, which are connected by means of identical or similar key words. The beginning is still missing. The subjects Anii presents to his pupil are as follows:

1. Acquire a perfect character and behavior. This may be done by keeping calm in situations of trouble and discussions.
2. Strive for perfect speech in public affairs. This is one of the central goals in any official's education and ensuing career. Discretion and correctness in transmitting messages also belong here.
3. Be versed in writings.
4. Refrain from opposing your superior and always keep to your own standing within the social and bureaucratic hierarchy.
5. Try to avoid having strife with other people.
6. Be on friendly terms with the policeman of your quarter. This may also imply bribery.
7. Shun married women and also ladies from outside your settlement whom nobody knows. These maixims refer to adultery and perhaps sexual adventures with prostitutes.
8. Respect your mother who nurtured you for three years and put you in school. Make offerings to your parents when they have passed away and found their final abode in the West. Worship your ancestor ghost duly so that he does not interfere in your household and any of your business affairs.
9. Marry as soon as you have acquired your own property and have a son. Do not rely on other people's belongings or on those of your own parents. Keep your property together, and do not waste it on people in need.
10. Do not reproach your wife as long as she acts according to what you expect her to do.
11. Refrain from drunkeness.
12. Prepare for your own burial and existence in the beyond as death may snatch you at any time.

13. Mind your cultic obligations toward "your (personal) god" by performing his feast (of thanksgiving?) in due course. Adore him quietly and abstain from false piety. Offer to him daily, do not question his oracles. He is the sun in the sky, with his statues upon earth.

The instruction ends with a dialogue between Anii and his son which is unique in ancient Egyptian wisdom literature. Here, Khnonshotep declares his inability to conform to his father's advice by stating that he is still much too young to put them into action. Anii contradicts him vehemently by referring to different kinds of beasts that have been domesticated by man. Even a crooked stick in the field may be made straight and turned into a noble's mace, thus, even an ill-disposed character may be taught successfully.

The text fits neatly into the Egyptian tradition of didactic literature. One of its major characteristics is its author's stress on a phenomenon called "personal piety" by Egyptologists. This is a reverent approach to one's own god, selected from the pantheon, and is typical of the pre-Amarna period and Ramessid times. Recently, international influences have been proposed for some features of the text (Quack 1994).

BIBLIOGRAPHY

Quack, J. F. *Die Lehren des Ani: Ein neuägyptischer Weisheitstext in seinem kulturellen Umfeld. Orbis Biblicus et Orientalis*, 141. Freiburg and Göttingen, 1994.

HANS-W. FISCHER-ELFERT

INSTRUCTIONS OF HORDJEDEF.

Wisdom Literature, often referred to as "didactic literature" or simply "instructions," spans the history of ancient Egypt from the Old Kingdom to the Late period. This genre consists of a series of instructions, generally given from father to son. The purpose of the texts also remains the same throughout the history of Egypt: to guide the recipient of the texts to live the "correct life," in order to prosper both in this life and in the afterlife. Although the Wisdom Literature generally offers the names of both author and recipient, it is agreed that the texts are probably pseudepigraphical.

Representing the earliest known example of Wisdom Literature in Egypt, the brief *Instructions of Hordjedef* provides its recipient with basic advice to be used in everyday life. Only the beginning survives, and even this was pieced together from various ostraca dating from the New Kingdom, as well as from one wooden tablet dating from the Late period. The numerous though fragmentary examples of this text evidence its popularity throughout the ages and support the theory that it may have been used as a common scribal text. Miriam Lichtheim has dated the text's composition to the fifth dynasty, based on its archaic language and stylistic qualities.

From what can be gleaned from the text, it was important to establish oneself in order to establish the household. The text advises the reader to choose a suitable wife to raise a family, one who is a "mistress of her heart." One takes a suitable wife in order to raise a son for inheritance and to continue the traditions of the family.

One must also prepare for burial, because eternal life holds a higher importance than temporal existence. The text devotes more attention to death and the preparation for death than any other topic, adding that the funerary priest was important to the maintenance of the tomb. These themes appear again in the *Instructions for Merikare*, as well as in other examples of Egyptian literature.

Supposedly, the text was written by Hordjedef, the son of Khufu of the fourth dynasty, for his son, Au-ib-re. Hordjedef, whose unfinished *mastaba* is situated in the Giza necropolis, had the reputation of a man of letters during his lifetime. His character took on somewhat mythical stature through Egyptian history; he is involved in many literary episodes relating to the period of Khufu. He is perhaps best described in Papyrus Chester Beatty IV, dating from the New Kingdom, where he is remembered as a great writer.

Although Egypt was rich in its Wisdom Literature, it must be noted that this genre is not confined only to Egypt. Similar sentiments surface as well in the Wisdom Literatures of Mesopotamia and in the Bible's *Book of Proverbs*.

BIBLIOGRAPHY

Assman, Jan. *Weisheit, Schrift und Literatur im alten Ägypten.* Munich, 1991. A good overview of Wisdom Literature in ancient Egypt.

Lichtheim, Miriam. *Ancient Egyptian Literature.* Vol. 1. Berkeley, 1973. Currently the definitive translation of the Hordjedef text.

WENDY RAVER

INSTRUCTIONS OF KAGEMNI.

The fragmentary Wisdom text represents the conclusion of a more lengthy instruction, now lost. The identity of its author is also lost, but the text refers to a man named Kagemni, whose name matches that of a vizier during the reign of Sneferu who was buried near the pyramid of Teti at Saqqara. Like other examples of the Wisdom Literature, such as the *Instructions of Hordjedef* and *Instruction of Ptahhotep*, this text is probably pseudepigraphical.

Only the concluding portion of the text survives; it is preserved in the Prisse Papyrus, now in the Bibliothèque

Nationale in Paris, and this papyrus also includes a version of the *Instruction of Ptahhotep*. Although The *Instructions of Kagemni* dates to the Middle Kingdom, the actual composition of the instruction may date to the latter part of the sixth dynasty.

The surviving portion of the text shows Kagemni receiving instruction on the benefits of restraint and the disadvantages of impropriety. According to the instruction, one should refrain both from idle chatter and from gluttonous behavior at the table, for modesty is the key to prosperity. The text also advises the reader to eat with economy when company is present in order to give the appearance of self-sufficiency. Likewise, the instruction guides proper behavior when eating with a glutton and drinking with a drunkard and advises one to act gently in order to win favor with those considered to be harsh. This behavior would not only lead one to be well liked among his peers but also win respect from them.

Curiously, the author adds that no one knows what action god chooses when he punishes. Although Egypt was a society in which its people believed in many gods, we see "god" rather than "gods" here. Perhaps this refers not to a singular god but rather to a divine principle. This abstraction surfaces in other examples of Wisdom Literature, such as in the *Instructions for Merikare* and the *Instruction of Ptahhotep*.

The play on opposites found in this text (modesty and moderation versus gluttony and pride) sets the groundwork for future examples of Wisdom Literature in which opposite forms of behavior are prominent in describing the "happy man," the man who chooses to avoid the pitfalls of life and live virtuously. Furthermore, there is in this text the appearance of the "silent man" as having virtue. This "silent man" also appears in the *Instruction of Ptahhotep* but becomes much more established in the Wisdom Literature, particularly in the *Instruction of Amenemope*, dating to the New Kingdom.

The final portion of the text narrates what happened after the instruction was received. The vizier, who may be either the author or Kagemni, summoned his children and told them to follow the teachings given to them. The last line reveals that Kagemni was made mayor of the city and vizier after Sneferu became king.

BIBLIOGRAPHY

Federn, W. "Notes on the Instruction of Kagemni." *Journal of Egyptian Archaeology* 36 (1950), 48–50.

Gardiner, A. H. "Kagemni Once Again." *Journal of Egyptian Archaeology* 37 (1951), 109–110.

Lichtheim, Miriam. *Ancient Egyptian Literature.* Vol. I. Berkeley, 1973. The standard translation of this work.

WENDY RAVER

INSTRUCTIONS OF KHETY, a text also known as *Dua-Khety*, is generally referred to as the *Satire on the Trades*. Khety was praised as a famous author. The text represents an early version of a theme later popular in the literature of the Ramessid era: the elevated status of the scribe in respect to other professions. The text is specified as an instruction, and its popularity reflects its use as a teaching tool with an obvious slant at the humorous, satirical depiction of the sorry lot of those who are not scribes. It is perhaps the most copied text, represented in four New Kingdom papyri, two writing boards, and several hundred ostraca (a scholar in 1981 counted 247 ostraca!), but the presumed original is dated in the Middle Kingdom.

The prologue, after identifying the work as an instruction, describes the narrative frame. The author takes his son Pepy from the northeastern town of Tjel to the royal residence, to place him in the school for magistrates among the select children of the officials, and advises him to study hard: "I shall make you love books more than your mother." There follows a description of the other walks of life, each deprecated in respect to that of a scribe (that is, an accountant): the mason, goldsmith, coppersmith, carpenter, jeweler, barber, reed-cutter for arrows, potter, bricklayer, builder, vintner, field hand, weaver, arrowmaker, messenger, furnace-tender, sandalmaker, washerman, fowler, fisherman, and tenant farmer. Then there is general advice about the boy's future classmates, respect for his mother, honoring father and mother, and wishes for success.

The satirical or humorous aspect of the description of the other professions cannot be denied. The coppersmith at his furnace has fingers like a crocodile's claws and stinks more than fish excrement. The carpenter has to work by lamplight into the night. The barber shaves until night but must be up early to find clients. The bricklayer works outdoors in the wind, ill-dressed for such work. The vintner is weary under his shoulder-yoke. The weaver is shut up inside and is beaten if he stops; he has to bribe the doorkeeper to let him out for a break.

There follow general instructions for proper deportment, for being circumspect, securing understanding, honoring parents, and associating with appropriate persons of one's own station. Frequently an ostracon will have the verses relating to a single profession inscribed. The popularity of the text led to extreme cases of text corruption, and so it has not been always easy to translate.

BIBLIOGRAPHY

Brunner, Hellmut. *Die Lehre des Cheti, Sohnes des Duauf.* Ägyptologische Forschungen 13. Glückstadt and Hamburg, 1944.

Brunner, Hellmut. *Altägyptische Weisheit: Lehren für das Leben.* Zürich and Munich, 1988. With introduction and translation.

Gugliemi, Waltraud. "Berufssatiren in der Tradition des Cheti." In

Zwischen die Beiden Ewigkeiten: Festschrift Gertrud Tausing, edited by Manfred Bietak et al., pp. 44–72. Vienna, 1994. Discussion in detail of four passages in the Miscellany literature and Papyrus Chester Beatty IV, V, and the later development of the themes of the satire on the professions. With remarks on the concept of satire in general and references to satire from Ben Sira through the Middle Ages.

Helck, Wolfgang. *Die Lehre des Dwȝ-Htjj. Textzusammenstellung.* 2 vols. Kleine Ägyptische Texte. Wiesbaden, 1970. The main current edition of the preserved texts, with commentary and translation.

Hoch, James. "The Teaching of Dua-Khety: A New Look at the Satire of the Trades." *Society for the Study of Egyptian Antiquities Journal* 21–22 (1991–1992, issued 1995), 88–100. A major interpretation of the text.

Lichtheim, Miriam. *Ancient Egyptian Literature: A Book of Readings*, vol. 1: *The Old and Middle Kingdoms*. Berkeley, 1973. Extensive bibliography.

Posener, Georges, "L'auteur de la Satire des Métiers." In *Livre du Centenaire de l'IFAO (1880–1980)*, pp. 55–59. Cairo, 1980.

Seibert, Peter. *Die Charakteristik.* Ägyptologische Abhandlungen, 17. Wiesbaden, 1967.

Simpson, William K., ed. *The Literature of Ancient Egypt: An Anthology of Stories, Instructions, and Poetry.* new ed. New Haven, 1973.

Williams, Ronald J. "Scribal Training in Ancient Egypt." *Journal of the American Oriental Society* 92 (1972), 214–221.

WILLIAM KELLY SIMPSON

INTERPRETATION OF EVIDENCE. Material remains demonstrate *that* there once existed an ancient high culture in Egypt. Knowing *what* those remains are, and *how* and *why* they were created, is a different matter. The first level of knowledge concerns the collecting of empirical data, the evidence; the other levels concern the interpretation of the evidence. This is performed not only by acknowledged professional scholars, Egyptologists, but also by a heterogeneous group of nonprofessionals, as well as critics of both groups, ranging from scholars in other disciplines to esotericists. Since the same objective data may result in debates among Egyptologists, as well as among Egyptologists and non-Egyptologists, there is clearly a fundamental epistemological problem. This encyclopedia of Ancient Egypt is the first to explicitly explore the problematic interpretation of evidence in this field of human sciences. The seven-volume *Lexikon der Ägyptologie* (Wiesbaden 1975–1992) ignores the subject. Focusing on some essential aspects of this extremely complex issue from a general theoretical and methodological perspective thus seems warranted.

Evidence of human existence concerns two fundamentally different but mutually influencing kinds of data. First, there is the ecological, or natural, data—the geographical, geophysical, climatological, and environmental circumstances that precondition human existence in a particular area (it may be called human-independent data). Second, there is human-dependent data—artifacts and the results of actions. Knowledge of past, or fossilized, human activity can, beyond merely mortal remains, only be obtained through artifacts—those objects that reveal human intentional behavior. The "intentional behavior" reflects "culture," and as such displays a specific cognitive confrontation and wide-ranged interaction of humankind with the cosmos, as expressed in its material culture. An artifact as such is a given, observable to anyone; however, as a cognitive-processual outcome of a hominid, it needs *interpretation*, which may be defined thus by: "Theoretical or narrative account of facts, texts, persons, or events that renders the subject-matter intelligible" (*The Oxford Companion to Philosophy*, Oxford/New York, 1995, p. 414).

Any culture is a complex, dynamic system of several parallel, interacting, and intersecting subsystems—including the economic, social, religious, linguistic, material culture, and, centrally, the psychological subsystems. Any cultural evidence, then, comprises not only the several multilinear levels or dimensions of significance, ranging from the very concrete to the highly abstract, but also becomes a node in the linking of a number of subsystems. For example, a wooden container of a certain shape belongs to the material culture subsystem because of its materials and technological aspects. Yet a mummified body inside makes it a coffin, and part of its iconography (pictures of deities) and texts relate it to the religious subsystem; another part relates it to the social and economic subsystems, showing the owner in certain roles. In conjunction with other (funerary) artifacts, a collective psychological attitude toward death might show, and quality distinctions in materials and/or manufacture might indicate further economic and/or social stratification. Variations over time in all the aspects of the example above reveal that it concerns a dynamic system, in which the interactions of a society with a certain phenomenon—death—vary, or co-vary, on several levels in different subsystems. So, a coffin or any other funerary object does not inform on *the* funerary ideas of *the* Egyptians at any time, but only on *some* funerary ideas of *certain* Egyptians during a *certain* time. It implies that *the* interpretation of evidence does not exist but depends on the interpreter's questions. In short, artifacts are encoded sign systems of very diverse (un)conscious information on human interaction with (un)reality. This is their universal binding factor at any time and any place.

Correct decoding of evidence by a modern interpreter may be hampered by several factors. First, there is the unavoidable incompleteness of cultural materials; only a sample remains of the original, full cultural volume. This sample, too, is only partly known; the rest may yet be discovered. From the known artifactual volume only a part may be published. In actuality, the acquisition of knowledge is one big statistical undertaking, based on select or aselect or a mix of such samples from the past "reality." That means for high(er) levels of interpretation, only inferential statistics can be used, which, at best, may support but not prove an interpretation. Second, the modern scholar takes an outside, or etic, stance toward the ancient Egyptian evidence (in contrast to an ancient Egyptian who had an inside, or emic, position). In other words, the same cognitive framework does not exist in relation to the cosmic environment the ancient Egyptian once had. Consequently, an ancient Egyptian's access to, and thus interpretation or understanding of, Egypt's cultural output had far greater intimacy and subtlety than Egyptologists can hope to attain. Third, our own bias/preference for an "-ism approach" to the data, as formulated in methodological and/or theoretical discussions in archaeology since the 1960s, self-evidently, results in different interpretations of the same evidence: for example, (neo-)Marxism interprets the collapse of the Old Kingdom differently from (post-)processualism, cognitive-processualism, or structuralism. Fourth, although obviously not all evidence should be taken at face value—for instance, because of an unequal interpretative weight of the sources—the impossibility (ensuing from the three points above) of drawing a line with respect to the "correct" interpretation, or decoding, of the data creates further uncertainty and thus disagreement.

This unavoidably leads to a sobering definition of evidence as "that body of belief, often of an observational sort, which supports some less well-established hypothesis" or "theory against a background of shared but unformalizable assumptions about the nature of the world and degrees of evidential support" (*The Oxford Companion to Philosophy*, p. 254).

The overwhelming amount of surviving sculpted, painted, drawn, and written evidence (almost exclusively from temples and tombs) seems to cover in a more or less recognizable way almost all physical, social, and ideological (i.e., religious and political) aspects of ancient Egyptian existence. Numerous representations of a tomb owner observing all kinds of activities by subordinates show such subjects as cattle breeding, musical performances, ship building, hunting in the desert, fishing and bird catching, and more. On temple walls, the king's always triumphant military exploits are shown, his performing of all necessary rites before deities (offering food, flowers, clothing, a statuette of Maat, the goddess of righteousness and good order, etc.); there are even scenes revealing his divine conception. At closer scrutiny, and first of all, by far the greatest majority of those representations appear to be exclusively related to the *elite*. Further, the unrealistically tall sizes of the main actors and, consequently, the lack of perspective in the two-dimensional representations are striking. The protagonists, especially

women, are usually represented with (hyper)slim, idealized, bodies in the prime of life, without traces of aging or physical flaws. Finally, the number of subjects and/or the various stages of activities appear to be limited in such a way that only a conscious selection from life was represented. Therefore, the unavoidable major conclusion is that, although part of the scenes can be taken literally (i.e., what was visually observable—fauna, flora, foreign peoples, herds, waterways, wars fought, etc.), the remaining "typical Egyptian" features fall under what was conscious ideological distortion, in varying degrees and for various reasons, reflecting a metaphorical ordering of the cosmos in Egyptian terms and forms.

In the mass of representational sources, a certain repetitiousness in themes and an idealization in the circumstances and the styles, at the expense of specificity and/or individual realism, looks so vast that the latter seem to have been ignored. This can be best explained by the ideology of the fundamental, multifaceted concept of *maat*—the ideal, well-balanced, hierarchized, mainly cyclical conditions of the divine sphere—operating on a parallel level on earth: in ruling the cosmos and humankind, the creator god with accompanying deities protected all against the disintegrating forces of chaos; this was mirrored by Egypt's king and his elite governing his land and its inhabitants. Several aspects of this ideology, evidently conceptualized by and for Egypt's elite, were visualized and symbolized in architecture and its decorations. This concept also explains the unrealistic and hierarchically scaled sizes of protagonists, their youthful appearance, the repetitive character of certain iconographic programs that show the king as only mediator between gods and humankind, and the king's—Egypt's—superiority over enemies, as expressed by battlefield scenes, New Kingdom scenes of Mediterraneans and Near Easterners bringing tribute, and the subjugation of exaggeratedly negroid Nubians. All this is expressed in homogeneous, traditional, apparently unchangeable artistic conventions, in an artistic canon. Supplemented by textual evidence, the representational sources therefore reflect fundamental Egyptian ideas concerning kingship, the elite, religion, and the social and political order in general.

Yet, in many cases, closer scrutiny appears to contradict Egypt's universal tendency toward idealization. Examples from the fourth dynasty show the far from ideal, obese, statue of Hemiunu, and the realistic portrait bust of Ankhhaf. Although these deviations were possible, which relativizes the absolute character of ideology, simultaneously, they underscore its fundamental role concerning kingship: Old Kingdom royal sculpture of the fourth dynasty and later shows an unfaltering idealization of the rulers, demonstrating an ideology-based opposition between royal and nonroyal (private). It appears to exist between the elite and nonelite, too. In Old Kingdom tomb scenes there are presented several physical deformities (varying from baldness to abdominal hernias), as well as transient and dangerous moments (fighting boatmen falling overboard into the water with lurking crocodiles). Yet in the scenes the seemingly immobile, watching tomb owner is never in danger. Even an opposition in degrees of danger between domestic and wild animals is observable: delivering cows are assisted by men, and half-born goats, threatened by a waiting dog or feline, are in reach of a man swinging a protective stick; but delivering hippopotami have to protect their young against crocodiles. Irrespective of this ideological opposition aspect, the subjects—without further demonstrable symbolism—represent exemplary, not historically unique, reality. There also exists opposition in beauty between male and female: only men can be represented idealized *and* obese in the same tomb. Women (the "queen" of Punt and the pregnant queens Ahmose and Mutemwia—all eighteenth dynasty—excepted) are normally represented slim, although in varying degrees over time, which reveals the instability of a prevalent ideal of beauty. Typical for the Egyptian culture is that these opposites are relative: the elite dwarf Seneb is ruthlessly shown with his too short legs; Seneb's nonconformity to physical *maat* demonstrates that the concept was either less fundamental to artistic conventions or that it was open to interpretation (i.e., it comprises a graduated pluralism in meaning and application).

In Middle Kingdom portraits of Sesostris III and Amenemhet III, the royal–private opposition seems to be flatly contradicted by their careworn faces; however, the situation is more subtle, since the royal body shows still unbroken youthful vigor. Evidently the rugged faces were valued as reflecting a positive quality of the king, experience, concomitant to a new aspect of royal dogma, with the hardships of kingship described in royal *Instruction* texts (for example, those for Merikare and Sesostris I by Amenemhet I). It was still in line with an apparently adapted *maat*-concept in royal ideology, most plausibly explained by the—at least for royalty and the elite—traumatic experience of the First Intermediate Period. The shift in royal ideology during the New Kingdom was the king's explicit sportive character: shooting, rowing, driving (Amenhotpe II), and hunting (Thutmose III, Amenhotpe III). It was necessitated by the new military-aggressive aspect of kingship, which resulted from the, again traumatic, occupation by the Hyksos during the Second Intermediate Period, who were cast out of Egypt by military force. Then the king regained his youthful physiognomy.

The idealized visual representation of the king is not only supported by but also relativized by literary texts, revealing human weaknesses: the cruel Khufu (Cheops, in

the Papyrus Westcar), the homosexual Pepy II (Papyrus Vandier), and the debauching Amasis (Demotic Chronicle). Inconsistencies between nonwritten and written, or literary (in contrast to documentary or administrative), sources are a warning against taking any such texts at face value. The inventory of sins in the *Book of Going Forth by Day* (*Book of the Dead*), Spell 125, does not reveal the goodness of the elite but all the once-current vices; although this text cannot be completely true, the situation is more complicated in the case of the First Intermediate Period's "autobiographies," which repeatedly mention, for example, the excellent measures taken by nomarchs against ravaging famines. The so-called Lamentation Texts seemed to complete a picture of total political and socioeconomic crisis. Recent reevaluation of the archaeological material from the Qau region in Middle Egypt has demonstrated that those texts reflect a literary *topos* only current in the very limited, elite stratum of the highest administrators who were stressing their capability to deal efficiently in case of calamities. If those texts were true, the archaeological record should show a far-reaching historical reality, revealed by an increase of poor and badly made tombs for the victims. Quite the reverse is the case.

This example of archaeology correcting textual evidence has been balanced by cases in which archaeological data itself was wrongly interpreted. For example, W. M. Flinders Petrie initially dated his Predynastic finds at Naqada to the Middle Kingdom; Gertrude Caton-Thompson misread the chronological sequence of the prehistoric Faiyum-A and -B cultures. Pierre Montet, finally, was misled by the overwhelming Ramessid and twenty-first dynasty evidence in Tanis and identified it as the Ramessid capital Pi-Ramesse, and consequently with the Hyksos capital Avaris—which according to texts preceded it, notwithstanding the fact that no strata earlier than the twenty-first dynasty were present. These cases have since been redressed by the reconsideration of the available evidence and/or by new fieldwork.

In contrast to these unintentional cases of misunderstanding the evidence, some attention should be given to examples of deliberate misconstruing and the distorting of data; merely to prove a predisposed idea, some have simply ignored the weight of counterarguments. Examples vary from ideas cherished by fundamentalist Christians—that Khufu (Cheops), the builder of the Great Pyramid at Giza, is really the Old Testament figure Job or that Ptolemaic funerary papyrus fragments are really the *Book of Abraham*—to those like Immanuel Velikovsky, with his revised biblical–Egyptian chronology. Afrocentrism is one of the most influential but disputable offshoots on the burgeoning tree of pseudo-Egyptology, and the most recent and manipulative in this respect is Martin Bernal's Black Athena-thesis, which claims that Greece was twice "colonized" from Egypt and that, consequently, the Greek civilization originates from "black" Egyptians. Such assertions are based on interpreting out-of-context materials and attaching unbalanced weight to select passages of, for example, Herodotus. There, the Egyptians were called "black" and "woolly haired," so the interpretation of Egyptian civilization might be "obviously" and "fundamentally African," and from there armies of Sesostris might allegedly march to the Black Sea; archaeology then "proves" that the Hyksos fled to Greece and were buried in Mycenaean shaft tombs; linguistic data further bolsters those "facts," with the etymology of the name *Athena* deriving from Egyptian Hut-Net (*Ḥwt-Nt;* "House of [the goddess] Neith") as one of the cornerstones. Disregarded was the Greeks' own subtle terminology for skins darker than their own, that in the Old Kingdom not a single representation of a black (sub-Saharan) person is found in either royal or private tombs, and that in the New Kingdom a sharp difference between the Egyptians' and the Nubians' physiognomy was made.

Various factors in the interpretation of Egyptian art led Egyptologists to the point of denying the existence of "real" art, since symbolism and craftsmanship were stressed. The focus in classical sources, such as Herodotus or Plato, was on an allegedly extreme traditionalism and uniformity, the fact that the Egyptian word *hmt* only means "craftsmanship" and that "artists" did not sign their work. The limitation in subject matter should neither underestimate the individualistic aspects of patrons (the iconographic program of not a single royal tomb or temple is identical) nor of artists (the execution in size, style, and details of not a single scene is interchangeable). One should instead think of the endlessly repeated, yet always different, scenes used in Christian art: "Madonna with Child," "Crucifixion," "Last Supper," "Last Judgment." Because of, for example, coexisting representations of the sky as a (starry) blue baldachin, as a naked or dressed woman (the goddess Nut), as a cow, or a waterway, the Egyptians' cognitive and intellectual capabilities have been interpreted as reflecting a "multiplicity of approaches" or "many-valued logic" (X is A *and* not-A), allegedly qualitatively different from our two-valued logic (X is A *or* not-A). Cases of the former also occur in Western (religious) thought—Jesus Christ conceived as a throned King, a Shepherd, and a Lamb—so there is no fundamental, but rather a gradual, difference.

From the point of view of the mechanics of cultural evolution, the ultimate interpretative level of evidence concerns a general and, over time, an increasing complexity of cultural expression, exemplified by the "dissolvement" from synthetic (i.e., compact) to analytical (i.e., loose or differentiated) stages or organizations of

language, script, governmental institutions and corresponding functions, number of deities, temple building and iconography, funerary customs, literary genres, and artistical style—from idealized to "realistic." This phenomenon, in a descriptive analogy from thermodynamics, may be summarized by the term *entropy*, defined as a measure for the decreasing amount of free "cultural energy" in the "closed" system of Egyptian culture, necessary for its continuation as a system. The multilinear, pulsating intensity of this entropy (for example, the alternation of initially "negentropic" Kingdoms developing toward "entropic" Intermediate Periods) can be described in terms of "dissipative and self-organizing structures" in nonlinear dynamic systems, as developed in modern chaos theories. Chaos here only concerns the susceptibility of the system's initial stage(s), to the incipiently, hardly observable "disturbances of equilibrium," and, in their long term, their unpredictable behavior and effects. In this light, the birth, life, and death—or rather the (almost irrecognizably slow) transformation or replacement of any local and/or temporal variety of human culture into/by another—appears to be the fundamental and universal mechanism/model of human evolution.

[*See also* Afrocentrism; *and* Kingship.]

BIBLIOGRAPHY

General Theoretical and Methodological Issues

Adams, William Y., and Ernest W. Adams. *Archaeological Typology and Practical Reality: A Dialectical Approach to Artifact Classification and Sorting.* Cambridge, 1991. All theoretical and methodological issues concerning the ordering and processing of data and its interpretation; extensive bibliography and glossary.

Hodder, Ian. *The Archaeological Process: An Introduction.* Oxford, 1999. Basic issues, including the interpretation of material culture and the propagation of nondichotomous thinking in archaeology.

Renfrew, Colin, and Paul Bahn. *Archaeology: Theories, Methods and Practice.* London, 1991. Survey of all aspects and problems of modern archaeology as a discipline (especially chapter 12, on explanation, a review of "-isms" in archaeology); extensive bibliographies per chapter.

Renfrew, Colin, and Ezra B. W. Zubrow, eds. *The Ancient Mind: Elements of Cognitive Archaeology.* Cambridge, 1994. Collection of interdisciplinary articles on general theoretical and methodological issues with respect to the archaeological approach of (ancient) systems of cognition (chapters 1, 2, 3, 6, and 8 are of special interest for Egyptology).

Shanks, Michael, and Christopher Tilley. *Re-constructing Archaeology: Theory and Practice.* 2d ed. London, 1992. Concerns interpretation as a construct about, rather than a reconstruction of, the past.

Specific Issues

Baines, John. "On the Status and Purpose of Ancient Egyptian Art." *Cambridge Archaeological Journal* 4.1 (1994), 67–94. Discussion demonstrates that "art" is a useful term in ancient Egyptian context.

Bianchi, Robert Steven. "An Elite Image." *Chief of Seers: Egyptian Studies in Memory of Cyril Aldred,* edited by Elizabeth Goring, et al., pp. 34–48. London, 1997. Discusses problems in art-historical approaches with respect to the elite character of the data.

Bietak, Manfred. *Avaris. The Capital of the Hyksos: Recent Excavations at Tell el-Daba'*. London, 1996.

Binsbergen, Wim M. J. van. "Black Athena: Ten Years After." *Talanta: Proceedings of the Dutch Archaeological and Historical Society* 28–29 (1997). See below, Lefkowitz (1996).

Englund, Gertie, ed. *The Religion of the Ancient Egyptians: Cognitive Structures and Popular Expressions*. Uppsala, 1987. Collection of various articles on the "pragmatics" of Egyptian religious cognition and practice.

Frandsen, Paul J. "On Categorization and Metaphorical Structuring: Some Remarks on Egyptian Art and Language." *Cambridge Archaeological Journal* 7.1 (1997), 71–104. Discussion of inalienable and interactional properties of mental images in Egyptian art in relation to the metaphorical structure of reality.

Harpur, Yvonne. *Decoration in Egyptian Tombs of the Old Kingdom: Studies in Orientation and Scene Content*. London and New York, 1987. Analytical study of the iconographic organization of elite tombs.

Hornung, Erik. *Conceptions of God in Ancient Egypt. The One and the Many*. Translated by John Baines, London 1983. (Original title, *Der Eine und die Vielen*. Darmstadt, 1971). Pages 237–243 deal with "logic"; a contrary view is presented in Van Walsem (1997, pp. 320–322).

Kemp, Barry J. *Ancient Egypt: Anatomy of a Civilization*. London and New York, 1989. In-depth analysis of the mechanics, and the ideological and interpretational aspects of state and culture formation.

Lefkowitz, Mary R., and Guy MacLean, eds. *Black Athena Revisited*. Chapel Hill, 1996. Collection of critical studies on Afrocentrism. See above, van Binsbergen (1997).

Loprieno, Antonio, ed. *Ancient Egyptian Literature. History and Forms*. Problem eder Ägyptologie, 10. Leiden, 1996. Comprehensive and detailed study on literary sources and their interpretation.

O'Connor, David B., and David P. Silverman, eds. *Ancient Egyptian Kingship*. Problem eder Ägyptologie, 9. 1995. Collection of penetrating studies on various aspects of the evolution of kingship, with reassessments of older interpretations.

Quirke, Stephen. "Translating *Ma'at*." *Journal of Egyptian Archaeology* 80 (1994), 219–231. A review discussion of Jan Assmann's *Ma'at: Gerechtigkeit und Unsterblichkeit im alten Ägypten* (Munich, 1990). A masterly summary in English of the book's contents and an examination of the difficulties in interpreting the many facets of this concept.

Robins, Gay. *Proportion and Style in Ancient Egyptian Art*. Austin, 1994. Fundamental study on the function of the grid and proportions, demonstrating the variations allowed by this seemingly rigid framework.

Van Walsem, René. "The Interpretation of Iconographic Programmes in Old Kingdom Elite Tombs of the Memphite Area. Methodological and Theoretical (Re)considerations." *Seventh International Congress of Egyptologists, Cambridge, 3–9 September 1995*, edited by Christopher Eyre, pp. 1205–1213. Oxford, 1998.

Van Walsem, René. "The Struggle against Chaos as a "Strange Attractor" in Ancient Egyptian Culture. A Descriptive Model for the "Chaotic" Development of Cultural Systems." *Essays on Ancient Egypt Honour of Herman te Velde*, edited by J. van Dijk, pp. 317–342. Groningen, 1997. Discussion of the use of terms from the natural sciences by Egyptologists and their implications for Egyptian cognition/logic; discusses some central ideas in chaos theory and their applicability to cultural systems.

RENÉ VAN WALSEM

INTOXICATION. The state of intoxication through the drinking of alcoholic beverages was viewed by the ancient Egyptians with either approval or disapproval, depending on the context. Beer and, to a lesser extent, wine were staples of the diet, and the Egyptians were very familiar with the aftereffects of alcohol. Intoxication to the extent of losing control was discouraged in many ancient Egyptian sources, but this disapproval was aimed at the loss of control from excessive drinking rather than at the state of intoxication itself. Intoxication was considered good, even desirable, in many contexts in ancient Egypt, not only as an enhancer of pleasure and companionship but also as a means of communion with the dead and the gods. The Egyptian word for "intoxication, drunkenness" (*tḫt*) derives from the verb "to be drunk" (*tḫi*), from which also come the words for "habitual drinker, drunkard" (*tḫw*) and, by extension, the verb "to be confused" (*tḫtḫ*). Other common terms related to intoxication include the verb "to be, become drunk" (*nwḥ*) and the terms for "drinking party" (*'t ḥnḳt*, literally "beer-house"), "drinking-place" (*mswr*, originally "drinking bowl") and "place of intoxication" (*st n tḫy*).

As in many aspects of Egyptian life, moderation was considered important in drinking. Intoxication was acceptable in a variety of settings, if not taken to extremes. Much of the evidence for Egyptian attitudes toward intoxication comes from the New Kingdom, although both earlier and later evidence suggest a certain consistency across time. Intoxication as a form of anesthesia in medical procedures is known from Egyptian medical texts, but far more sources attest to drinking for pleasure. Wisdom texts, songs, love poems, and stories describe the joys of intoxication, either for the sheer pleasure of drunkenness or for the conviviality it inspired. Beginning at the top of the Egyptian social order, monumental and literary texts sometimes record kings' (often solitary) enjoyment of intoxication, which is also commemorated in Old Kingdom workers' names (e.g., Khufu-is-drunk, Menkaure-is-drunk, Sahure-is-drunk). Among the nonroyal population, drunkenness often accompanies seduction and sexual activity; however, intoxication is more commonly associated with parties and social life. Drinking parties were considered an ideal leisure activity by the Egyptians, though one more open in practice to elites than to members of the lower orders. Such gatherings are illustrated, in somewhat idealized and symbolic form, in eighteenth dynasty tomb scenes of banquets, where intoxication was enjoyed by both men and women, and was accompanied by feasting, dancing, and music. Drinking parties could be held within families but could also involve friends and neighbors; even the most informal social gatherings in Egypt resulted in some degree of drunkenness. Voluntary ab-

INTOXICATION. *A servant presents wine to the official Nebamun, his wife Ipuky, and their daughter at a banquet, eighteenth dynasty, reign of Amenhotpe III-IV.* This is a copy (by Nina de Garis Davies) of a painting in the tomb of Nebamun and Ipuky at Thebes. (The Metropolitan Museum of Art, 30.4.106)

INTOXICATION. *Image from a Theban tomb showing one of the less pleasurable consequences of overindulgence, New Kingdom.*

stention from alcohol was exceptional enough to make a serious statement: thus, in the Third Intermediate Period stela of Piya, for example, Tefnakhte abstains from drinking as a gesture of contrition. Some texts lament the time when a person will be unable to become drunk, either through old age or death; this is especially common in elegiac songs urging the hearer to enjoy life while alive.

Beyond drinking for the sake of pleasure, intoxication in ancient Egypt often had religious implications. The gods themselves became intoxicated on occasion; the best example of this comes from the *Book of the Heavenly Cow,* in which Hathor (as the eye of Re), to avert her destruction of humanity, is tricked into drunkenness through the use of beer dyed red to look like blood. Through this myth, as well as her associations with music, dancing, and pleasure, Hathor was known as the "Mistress of Intoxication" and was particularly associated with drinking. Other goddesses, including Mut, Sakhmet, Tefnut, Bastet, and the beer goddess Menqet, were also associated with drunkenness. Specific religious festivals are linked with intoxication: the great Valley festival and Opet festival at Thebes, as well as the aptly named Festival of Intoxication and the Festival of the Offering of Intoxication. Drinking was also associated with funeral rites; some scholars interpret the drinking represented in tomb banqueting scenes as being designed to permit communion with the spirit of the deceased. Far from being a sign of disrespect, intoxication put the drinker into an altered state that facilitated contact with the gods and the dead.

An excessive level of intoxication, leading to a loss of control, was looked on with varying degrees of mild disapproval—the drunken person was viewed mostly with amused contempt or slight alarm, while efforts were made to warn the young against getting drunk too much or too often. Again, much of the information on this subject comes from the New Kingdom. Images of guests vomiting at parties are sometimes found in banqueting scenes in elite tombs of the eighteenth dynasty (e.g., the Theban tombs of Djeserkaraseneb [tomb 38] and Neferhotep [tomb 49]), showing the aftereffects of excessive drinking. Textual sources reflect concerns over the undisciplined behavior that could arise from intoxication. The maxims of Any cite hurting oneself, childish behavior, and the disapproval of companions as the dangers of excessive drinking, while the *Miscellanies* warn against injuring others and having sex with prostitutes while drunk. Documentary texts of the New Kingdom also associate violence and prostitution with intoxication. These pitfalls of intoxication were seen as the result of the loss of self-control—the *Miscellanies* liken a drunken man to a boat with a crooked steering-oar, a house without bread, even a shrine without its god—and reflect larger Egyptian preoccupations with the maintenance of order. Sources from later periods show similar concerns: Demotic wisdom texts warn of the aftereffects of drinking, both physical and mental, while the Demotic tale of Amasis shows that even kings were not exempt from the results of too much drinking. Greek writers such as Herodotus and Athenaeus often described what they saw as the prevalence of excessive drinking in Egypt, reflecting the cultural differences between Egyptians and Greeks with regard to contexts and amounts of alcohol consumption. Attitudes toward intoxication in Egypt became predominantly negative with the coming of Christianity.

[*See also* Banquets; *and* Erotica.]

BIBLIOGRAPHY

Brunner, Helmut. "Trunkenheit." In *Lexikon der Ägyptologie,* 6: 773–777. Wiesbaden, 1986. Essential reference.

Darby, William J., Paul Ghalioungui, and Louis Grivetti. *Food: The Gift of Osiris.* 2 vols. London, 1977. The chapters on wine and beer contain some useful information, but should be used with caution, particularly with regard to ancient Egyptian sources.

Darnell, J. C. "Hathor Returns to Medamûd." *Studien zur Altägyptischen Kultur* 22 (1995), 47–94. Useful reference for religious festivals involving intoxication.

Geller, Jeremy. "From Prehistory to History: Beer in Egypt." In *The Followers of Horus: Studies Dedicated to Michael Allen Hoffman, 1944–1990,* edited by Renée Friedman and Barbara Adams, pp. 19–26. Egyptian Studies Association Publication, 2. Oxford, 1992. Brief discussion of beer and drunkenness.

Gugliemi, Waltraud. "Die Biergottin Menket." In *Aspekte spätägyptischer Kultur: Festschrift für Erich Winter zum 65. Geburtstag,* edited by Martina Minas and Jürgen Zeidler, pp. 113–132. Aegyptiaca Treverensia, 7. Mainz, 1994.

Helck, Wolfgang. *Das Bier im alten Ägypten.* Berlin, 1971. Classic study on beer in its lexicographical, social, ritual, medical and mythic contexts; essential references for intoxication.

Spalinger, Anthony. "A Chronological Analysis of the Feast of *thy.*" *Studien zur Altägyptischen Kultur* 20 (1993), 289–303. References for the Festival of Intoxication.

Wilson, Hilary. *Food and Drink in Ancient Egypt.* Aylesbury, 1988. Useful summary in English of evidence for alcoholic beverages.

TERRY G. WILFONG

INUNDATION. *See* Nile.

IPUWER. The *Dialogue of Ipuwer and the Lord to the Limit* is known from a fragmentary nineteenth dynasty manuscript from Saqqara, containing seventeen columns of about fourteen lines each (Papyrus Leiden I.344 *recto*). It is uncertain how many lines are lost at the end (possibly no more than eight), and the manuscript may not have been a complete copy of the composition. At least one column is missing from the start. The extant composition comprises around 650 metrical lines. A sage, Ipuwer, is mentioned as a protagonist in the surviving manuscript, but without title, although a nineteenth dynasty tomb relief (the "Daressy Fragment") mentions an "Overseer of Singers Ipuwer." He is presumably a fictional character rather than a historical figure.

The poor preservation and publication of the manuscript have hindered interpretation, and the unity of the text and the identity of the speakers have been controversial issues. The date of composition has been disputed, largely because the text has often been considered a reflection of historical events of either the First or Second Intermediate Period. Internal evidence suggests a date in the thirteenth dynasty, although, according to some scholars, the text may have been subjected to redactional criticism.

The text is a lament about the state of the land, a well-attested literary genre in the Middle Kingdom. Ipuwer is addressing the "Lord to the Limit," who replies with at least two speeches. The dialogue apparently takes place before an audience—perhaps the Lord's entourage—who are also addressed by the sage. The "Lord" is apparently the king, although an identity as the creator god has been proposed; the text's concerns are theodic, but the Lord is probably a representative of the creator god rather than the god himself.

The extant text opens with two long laments in short stanzas, describing the reversals in society:

> Look, he who was loafless is a lord of a storeroom;
> his storehouse is furnished with the property of someone else.

Injunctions to destroy the enemies of the country and to remember happier times follow, and then Ipuwer speaks

a discursive complaint about the creator's justice in allowing such disorder to flourish:

> Look, why did He seek to shape [mankind],
> when the meek are not set apart from the savage
> so that He might have brought coolness upon the heat?

After another nostalgic section describing social calm, with the refrain "It is so good when . . . ," the Lord replies, but Ipuwer seems to dismiss his attempted justification with a parable. The manuscript ends as the Lord replies once more. To judge by better preserved examples of the genre, the debate probably continued until a positive resolution was reached.

The *Dialogue*'s description of mankind's vicissitudes throws incidental light on social attitudes of the period, as well as on wider cultural concerns. The *Dialogue* has usually been discussed for its presumed historical aspects, but it is arguably an ahistorical composition dealing with the well-attested Middle Kingdom literary theme of theodicy; there has been little discussion of its literary quality, which is considerable.

BIBLIOGRAPHY

Barta, Winfried. "Das Gespräch des Ipuwer mit dem Schöpfergott." *Studien zur Alatägyptischen Kultur* 1 (1974), 19–33.

Fecht, Gerhard. *Der Vorwurf an Gott in den "Mahnworten des Ipu-wer."* Abhandlungen der Heidelberger Akademie der Wissenschaften, Phil.-hist. Kl., 1. Heidelberg, 1972. Detailed study of parts of the composition, with new readings.

Gardiner, Alan H. *The Admonitions of an Ancient Egyptian Sage, from a Hieratic Papyrus in Leiden.* Leipzig, 1909. Standard edition of the text.

Helck, Wolfgang. *Die "Admonitions" Pap. Leiden I 344 recto.* Kleine Ägyptische Texte. Wiesbaden, 1995. Recent edition of the text, but incorporating speculative emendations and restorations; generally unreliable.

Otto, Eberhard. *Der Vorwurf an Gott: Zur Entstehung der ägyptischen Auseinandersetzungsliteratur.* Vorträge der Orientalistischen Tagung in Marburg: Ägyptologie. Hildesheim, 1951.

Parkinson, R. B. *The Tale of Sinuhe and Other Ancient Egyptian Poems 1940–1640 BC.* Oxford, 1997. Recent translation, see pp. 167–199.

R. B. PARKINSON

IRON. In ancient Egypt, iron ores were plentiful and were used for pigments, particularly in the form of ochers and hematite; they were also used as amulets, beads, and weights, chiefly the hematite or occasionally the magnetite forms. For much of dynastic times, however, the high temperatures required to smelt iron from ores and the difficulties in working it kept it from being used as a metal. Finds of iron in Egypt before the mid-first millennium BCE are rare. Most are artifacts made of meteoric iron, as is the famous iron dagger from the tomb of Tutankhamun; the ancient Egyptians knew of the nonterrestrial origin of this metal and called it *biȝ m pt* ("copper from heaven"). Iron obtained from meteorites is readily distinguishable from other iron because of its high nickel content.

The technology for iron manufacture may have originally been developed in the Near East as an outgrowth of bronze working. Iron could be produced incidentally in furnaces, since for bronze, copper ores were smelted with iron-containing fluxes. Iron usage was only slowly adopted throughout the Near East during the second millennium BCE, even though iron deposits were plentiful in the region. In Egypt, significant deposits were known in the Eastern Desert and in the Sinai, but they do not appear to have been mined until after pharaonic times. Instead, the metal was imported from Greece, Cyprus, Anataolia, and possibly Nubia.

Ancient smiths needed to overcome a number of difficulties to begin large-scale iron manufacturing. The metal requires very high temperatures (1200°C) to separate it from the rest of the ore, necessitating a change from open-bowl furnaces to shaft furnaces. Ancient furnaces then produced the metal by mixing the ore with charcoal and firing it to produce a "bloom"—a lump of iron, slag, and charcoal. The cooled iron would be broken up and hammered into shape or remelted. Tools, weapons, and other iron objects were made by alternate heating and hammering, producing what is known as wrought iron. By quenching, a process in which hot iron is plunged into cold water, the iron could be made hard. Two ax heads are known from Egypt that had the characteristic restructuring of the metal edge that indicates quenching, a technique unusual in pre-Roman times.

Wrought iron was not significantly stronger than hardened bronze (a copper alloy), but it was far less brittle—a quality that made it ideal for sword blades—which seems to have been the impetus for its widespread adoption. The earliest iron blades, set in bronze hafts, have been discovered in Luristan, to the northeast of Syria-Palestine. The Hittite Empire, in iron-rich Anatolia, seems to be the earliest home of large-scale iron working. Iron objects are known from Egypt with increasing frequency throughout the later New Kingdom; however, iron does not appear to have been produced in Egypt on a large scale until the end of the Third Intermediate Period. This lack of iron has been suggested for the weakening of the New Kingdom and Egypt's economic downturn during the Intermediate Period.

Iron objects are associated with Egypt's twenty-fifth dynasty and its reoccupation of Lower Nubia—and it may be that the impetus for iron working in Egypt spread there from Nubia. Nonetheless, since an iron-producing center that was dated to the first millennium BCE was discovered in Gerar in Palestine, that may yet point to a Near Eastern origin for Egypt's iron working. The technology might even have been introduced into both Egypt and Nubia by Greek mercenaries. In the Nile Delta, iron smelting sites have been discovered at Naucratis and Defenneh. The great quantities of imported wood required for the furnaces, as well as access to foreign trade, would have made the Delta an ideal center for iron working. Foreign craftsmen, particularly Greeks resident there, probably facilitated the growth and development of the iron industry.

Iron was, in fact, produced in large quantities in Nubia. Vast iron slag heaps are found at Meroë, and an iron foundry was excavated by P. L. Shinne and F. J. Kense (1982) in the ancient town. Iron artifacts have been found in Nubian tombs and foundation deposits of the Napatan period, and other iron-producing centers are thought to have existed at Napata, Kawa, and Tabo. Iron working at Meroë appears to have been localized in one or more industrial quarters, where a series of small, shaft furnaces were enclosed in a large baked-brick structure. Iron has been claimed as the source of the wealth and power of the Meroitic kingdom; access to iron ores, rich vegetation, and positioning at major trade routes did offer Meroë strategic advantages.

BIBLIOGRAPHY

Shinnie, P. L., and F. J. Kense. "Meroitic Iron Working." *Meroitica* 6 (1982), 17–28.

Tylecote, R. F. *A History of Metallurgy*. London, 1992.

PETER LACOVARA AND
YVONNE J. MARKOWITZ

IRRIGATION. Conversion of the Nile floodplain and delta to "perennial" irrigation began in 1833, with the benefit of modern technology. An increasing number of river barriers impounded water in Egypt, raising the low-water level 3 meters (10 feet) or more to carry it over long distances in great canals; this permitted two or even three plantings per year. This effort culminated with the Aswan High Dam (completed in 1971), which holds back all the Nile waters for distribution over the country at any season. For at least four thousand years before that, Egyptian irrigation was of "traditional basin" type, whereby the annual pulses of floodwater were manipulated by massive labor and incremental improvements in technology, but without fundamentally changing the natural processes of annual inundation and subsequent flood recession. Earlier, in prehistoric times, inundation and recession were also available for agriculture, even without controls or modifications of any kind. These three kinds of irrigation have been called "neotechnic," "paleotechnic," and "eotechnic," respectively.

The emergence and slow elaboration of paleotechnic irrigation is of substantial interest for Egyptology. It has direct implications for the increasing agricultural production that presumably facilitated population growth during the Old, Middle, and New Kingdoms and in Greco-Roman times. Similarly, it is pertinent for interwoven issues of land tenure and irrigation management, including the discredited but tenacious Wittfogel hypothesis, which claims that centralized control of irrigation will evolve concomitantly with a hierarchical social order and despotic government.

Natural Irrigation. A convex floodplain, such as that of the Egyptian Nile, is inundated naturally, in response to the predictable rhythm of annual runoff. The floods fill the channel first and then spill out at breaks or low points in levees to fill the lower-lying basins with 0.5 to 2.5 meters (1.5 to 8 feet) of water. After the flood crest has moved on downstream, the water level in the basins begins to fall, slowly at first and then more rapidly, moving back to the channel through openings in the levees. Six to eight weeks after the water first enters the flood basins, they are dry again except for marshy low spots (backswamps), mainly near the desert edge. Where the floodplain is narrow, in Upper Egypt south of Dishna, flood basins are comparatively small—probably 10 to 20 square kilometers prior to human modification. In Middle Egypt the floodplain is broad, so that diverging channels such as the Bahr Jusef broke off from the main Nile to channel flood waters toward the opposite desert margin. These secondary channels subsequently helped to drain waters during recession. Flood basins here were much larger—some of them more than 100 square kilometers.

According to the eotechnic model of natural irrigation, early farmers would have been able to broadcast seed on the wet mud of flood basins immediately after recession. Given the abundance of stored moisture in the absorbent clay-silt soil, the crop would grow and mature to harvest without any further addition of water. In Nubia, prior to completion of the Aswan High Dam, farmers sowed the channel banks of the river the moment that the flood began to recede, and sorghum plants were thriving there within a matter of weeks, to ripen without additional water. Various writers have described the utilization of free-draining flood basins in other parts of the African monsoon rain belt, specifically the Senegal, middle Niger, Chari-Logone, and Omo rivers. In each of these cases from the ethnographic present, the wet basin lands are sown as soon as the summer floods recede, with essentially no effort expended to control the influx or egress of water.

The fact that such "recessional agriculture" continued well into the mid-twentieth century and in such diverse areas makes it clear that its productivity was quite satis-factory. For the Senegal River, it normally provides a yield of 300 to 1,000 kilograms per hectare of sorghum, which implies returns per calorie of labor input of between 23.1 and 76.1. In the case of late prehistoric Egypt, a conservative estimate of 600 to 3,000 kilograms per hectare for wheat would provide similar returns with respect to labor. Such high yields reflect the annual renewal of fertility during the flood cycle on good to optimal soil. This certainly does not merit the label "primitive" agriculture, especially when compared with the much lower yields of Mediterranean dry-farming.

Development of Pharaonic Irrigation. What, then, was the incentive to modify and improve on natural irrigation? One likely explanation is that cultivators could compensate for lower-than-average floods by cutting sluices into the levees, or attempt to limit the incursion of unusually high floods by reinforcing levees or plugging up breaks in them. Since excessive wetting of the soil eliminates aerobic bacteria and favors anoxic subsoils that inhibit root development, it would be advantageous to cut sluices in order to drain off superabundant flood waters more rapidly. These quite basic modifications would eventually be converted into wood or masonry gates. Those could be followed by more labor-intensive projects that required considerably more organization and social cooperation: the subdivision of existing flood basins by transverse earthen dikes. Once perfected, multiple artificial basins within one natural flood basin would represent a quantum jump in water control, since each basin could be manipulated on a different schedule. Thus, a mediocre flood might initially be held in one such basin to soak it thoroughly; the water would then be allowed to move on to the next basin, and so on. Canals could also be cut to carry a controlled quantity of water to basins farther down the line. These examples illustrate how manipulated irrigation can reduce the negative effects of year-to-year flood variability.

A second possible explanation is linked to social stratification, which becomes increasingly evident in late Predynastic times. Subsistence risk with respect to the vagaries of the annual flood is reduced when an extended family, a large landowner, or a corporate institution (such as a temple) holds an assortment of unconnected land parcels at different elevations or distances from the river, on soils of different qualities and types, or in different basins. Among groups practicing recession agriculture in tropical Africa, some form of communal land tenure is typical. Most commonly, an extended family holds a portfolio of land parcels scattered across different microtopographies which are reassigned each year as the flood recedes, taking into account which plots have been soaked and which have been under water too long. In this way, risk is reduced for the individual cultivators who comprise the extended family. Such was the case in nineteenth-century Egypt, even though land was owned by rich landlords, but commonly worked by leaseholders with usufruct rights and tithe obligations. The specific parcels were reassigned within a village or kin group after each flood. The Hekanakhte letters (2002 BCE) show how the holdings of a large landowner were scattered across several parts of Egypt, with about half the land in fallow or unimproved pasture. Revenue records of the New Kingdom verify that temple lands were widely dispersed, with taxes assessed on the basis of land quality, including drainage.

As competition for land increased, presumably in the wake of population growth, community groups are likely to have had access to smaller portfolios, with increasing subsistence risk, unless water control was augmented. Institutions such as mortuary estates and temple domains were set up or expanded by royal decree on uncultivated lands, probably used earlier for livestock pasturage. Such holdings would inevitably compete with rural communities for new arable land, and they appear at times to have been connected with new settlements, sometimes involving foreign colonists. In one form or other, the expansion of cultivation must have involved some degree of irrigation development. Large estates, whether private or institutional, typically were graced by ornamental gardens or had commercial plantings, such as vineyards, that required year-round watering. Pictorial evidence shows that such orchards were served by canals, with water stored in tanks or pools; this must have given strong incentive to adopt innovations in water-lifting technology.

These were some of the processes that favored a shift to artificial irrigation. Yet the documentation for increasing manipulation of irrigation in historical Egypt is fragmentary and indirect, presumably because water rules and irrigation management were commonplace information that required little or no written records. Occasional representations on tomb reliefs and other art are thus required to complement the unsatisfactory written record and minimal direct archaeological evidence.

The earliest evidence for artificial irrigation is the mace head of King "Scorpion" (Dynasty "0," c.3100 BCE), which shows the ceremonial cutting of an irrigation ditch or the opening of a levee. The representation is reminiscent of ceremonies inaugurating the irrigation season that were symbolically reenacted well into modern times. The detail is significant: the king holds a hoe, while two attendants stand ready with the traditional fiber basket and a "broom," used until recently to gather and carry dirt. He stands on the bank of a bifurcating waterway that, judging by two adjacent men who carry hoes, represents canals. Between them is a rectangular grid with four rows of parallel lines, surmounted by a palm tree. In analogy with eighteenth-

dynasty garden scenes, these signify rows of irrigated fields, apparently arranged as long lots. The mace head leaves little doubt that canal irrigation, with dispersal of water into geometrically patterned fields via small ditches, was quite familiar. The transition from natural to artificial irrigation had been completed by the end of the Predynastic era.

Scattered information indicates that irrigation canals were well known. For the sixth dynasty, among a number of inscriptions that suggest canal-digging, there is an allusion to Pepi I (c.2354–2310 BCE) using a canal to place a tract of land under water. Such references to canals are textually linked with ponds, wells, and "water conduits" (distribution ditches?), and they appear to refer to the watering of orchards or gardens on institutional estates. However, canals must also have been used to allow barges heavily laden with shaped stone to move from quarries on the eastern side of the Nile to the pyramids and their valley temples on the edge of the Western Desert. This argument is supported by the existence of cut stone revetments, large piers, and extensive artificial basins on the floodplain margin between Giza and Abusir. Such harbor installations, some connecting to rock-cut ramps, would have been linked to one or more transverse canals, since the flood crest was too brief and the inundation too shallow to allow transport barges simply to navigate across the flooded fields.

During the ninth and tenth dynasties, Khety I, ruler of the thirteenth Egyptian nome, rebuilt or enlarged a canal 10 cubits wide, near modern Asyut, replacing the ruined sluice gates with brick structures. The twelfth dynasty nomarch Khnumhotep II appears to have engaged in some sort of public irrigation work in the area of Beni Hasan. Scarabs of King Amenhotpe III (r. 1410–1372 BCE) commemorate the establishment of a new flood basin at Akhmim, suggesting that this was not a routine event.

For a long time, there was a dearth of technology to lift water mechanically, and both Old and Middle Kingdom reliefs show manual lifting or the transport of two buckets of water suspended from a shoulder yoke. A technical aid for this laborious work first appears on art of the Amarna period (c.1350 BCE) in the form of the *shaduf*, or sweep. This is a levering device with a bucket tied to the end of a long pole that can be rotated from a fixed position, to lift water no more than 1.5 meters (5 feet). Although a series of *shaduf*s can actually raise water out of the Nile, it is a slow and inefficient method, capable only of watering a garden plot or filling a small tank. It would take three men a day to water a quarter-hectare, and with the water table 3 to 5 meters (10 to 16 feet) below the surface during the dry season, the *shaduf* could not raise water out of a deep well. First documented in Mesopotamia on an Akkadian cylinder seal (c.2370–2200 BCE), the *shaduf* was introduced from there to Egypt, possibly in the wake of the Near Eastern campaigns of Thutmose III (1504–1452 BCE). It remained the only mechanical lifting device in pharaonic Egypt.

The *saqiya*, or animal-driven waterwheel, is first verified archaeologically in Ptolemaic times, as another introduction from Mesopotamia. The *saqiya* pulled a belt of ropes carrying a series of water-filled jugs 3.5 to 7.5 meters (11.5 to 22.5 feet) up from a well or river. If operated around the clock, one *saqiya* could water between eight and ten hectares. This was the first mechanism capable of irrigating summer crops on a significant scale, and it became a standard feature of Islamic irrigation. It helps to explain the addition of summer sorghum as a new crop under the Ptolemies, as well as the emergence of larger-scale commercial farming in Egypt, which eventually become the breadbasket of Rome.

The Greek-speaking veterans of the Persian Wars who were settled in Egypt to bear arms for the Ptolemies presumably facilitated the introduction of nontraditional agricultural methods. Central here was the development of the Faiyum by Ptolemy II (r. 282–246 BCE), who introduced Mesopotamian-style irrigation. From reconstructed locks at the Faiyum, he had long, high-lying canal systems built around the northern, eastern, and southern perimeters of the basin. New towns with military colonists were built along this new radial irrigation system, which until its decline in later Roman times was well populated and apparently quite productive. Both winter and summer crops were grown in a landscape that also included fallow and saline land parcels. Summer cropping, however, was possible only with *saqiya*s, and salinization could become a problem if sufficient discharge did not continue down the line, so as to drain excess soluble minerals into the shrinking Faiyum Lake. Another limitation of the new lands of the Faiyum was fertility, since they were not directly inundated by the Nile. That could be compensated for only by regular fallow, crop rotation with legumes (such as bersim), or systematic application of bird guano, manure, or human waste. The possibilities for double cropping were circumscribed and, in general, cultivation of these new lands was precarious.

Limitations of Pharaonic Irrigation. The available evidence documents the importance of canals from late Predynastic to Old Kingdom times. Substantial navigation canals must be inferred around Giza, but elsewhere canals appear to have been linked primarily to institutional and private estates, to help irrigate ornamental and commercial plantings that would be harmed by protracted flooding and would therefore be located on slightly higher ground. All pharaonic canals were designed to disperse flood waters rather than for pre-flood irrigation. Summer irrigation would require weirs on the Nile itself,

in order to raise the low-water level, and these were technologically impossible until the nineteenth century CE.

The plantings of Khnumhotep near Beni Hasan, with their date palms, sycomore figs, and vine bowers, appear to have been situated on a Nile levee, judging by boats depicted on the adjacent panel of his tomb reliefs. The essential vegetable gardens of estates or villages would also have been planted on less clayey soils, on levee berms or near the desert edge. For both orchards and garden vegetables the problem was much the same—the Nile or a canal could bring water into immediate proximity, but it still had to be raised to be of use. An alternative possibility (verified archaeologically and textually) was to protect estate gardens from the flood by an enclosing wall, and to dig a basin down to the water table, providing a constant supply of water as well as an ornamental pond. Indeed, ponds or large pools were even more central to the estate enclosure than were sacred lakes on a temple domain.

In sum, orchards and gardens posed a genuine problem of site and water, whereas grain broadcast in the flood basins did not. Their high value fruits, wine, and vegetables may therefore have been the main incentive for the innovative adaptations of Early Dynastic and Old Kingdom irrigation, given that many hundreds of estates were established during the Old Kingdom alone, perhaps two-thirds of these in the Delta. Even so, growers remained dependent on manual lifting until the Amarna period, which probably limited the expansion of orchards and vineyards. The *shaduf* was preeminently suited to the scale of such "plantations" and must have facilitated the commercialization of agriculture.

Beginning with Khety I and ending with the early twelfth dynasty, there are allusions to some sort of public role of local potentates in either maintaining or increasing the supply of water via canals, and a ten-cubit (5.7-meters/18.5-feet) wide canal is quite large. Subsequent twelfth dynasty pharaohs devoted their attention to the Faiyum and perhaps to its agricultural development. They engaged in building activities and founded at least one new town, but their role in water control may have been limited to constructing impoundments at the entrance of the Faiyum to restrict the influx of the excessive floods common at the time. Their interest in the Faiyum was apparently grounded in the royal estates of the area. The role of Amenhotpe III in creating a new basin, implicitly by building one or more transverse dikes, stands out as an unusual intervention; probably it was a favor to his wife's family, whose estates were in Akhmim. The pace of subdivision of the natural flood basins by dikes remains unknown, in part because Middle Kingdom designations that might indicate dikes or dams are ambiguous. Nineteenth dynasty documents referring to temple domains in Middle Egypt suggest that some of the long transverse dikes of this sector may already have been in place, but the Wilbour Papyrus suggests that extensive areas were mainly used for pastoralism, implying that irrigation control was incomplete.

Despite its limitations, the documentation of water control in pharaonic Egypt shows that then—as during the 1800s CE—basin irrigation was the norm and therefore elicited few directives and no explanatory comment. Estate irrigation and commercial crops, representing only a tiny fraction of the arable land, attracted most of the explicit attention. Even here, interventions seem to have been motivated by personal considerations: to reward retainers, to favor family members, to endow institutions, or to generate public support (as in the case of the monarchs of the First Intermediate Period and twelfth dynasty).

Such actions were not part of a rational and sustained public policy, even though increased rural productivity was favored at various levels of government, if only for its economic advantages. The problem lay with the limited efficiency of an archaic state that still lacked a properly defined, vertical bureaucracy to channel national administrative functions down to the level of the nomes and towns. Despite the pharaoh's symbolic power and control over the military and the official cult, implementation of his directives beyond the confines of the capital depended on the cooperation of wealthy families in the provinces, especially in Upper Egypt. There is no evidence for a category of high or mid-level officials charged with directing or overseeing the maintenance or expansion of irrigation. In effect, there was no top-down policy for irrigation development.

The early Ptolemies centralized government administration, and they evidently promoted a complex strategy of economic development that included water control and commercialized agriculture. Fortunately, an immense quantity of extant papyrus documents illuminates how irrigation worked during the Greek and Roman periods—in excessive and repetitive detail. Even so, there is little evidence for official directives, and government representatives appear to have been little more than liaison with local communities. For example, the villagers themselves selected the workers liable for corvée (forced labor) to clean the canals, and they worked under the supervision of a foreman elected from their own ranks. The corpus of Greco-Roman information is congruent with that of the nineteenth century CE, when irrigation was similarly organized and maintained locally. In neither period was competition for water an issue in free-flooding alluvial basins, since the flood crest simply moved downstream from one to another, regardless of what provisions there were for water distribution or withdrawal.

In conclusion, the transition from eotechnic, recessional agriculture to paleotechnic irrigated farming was incremental and took place primarily at the grass-roots level. Providing water for flood-sensitive commercial plantings and market gardens posed a special problem that attracted repeated interest at the government level, and was inadequately resolved until water-lifting technology became available, perhaps two millennia after the first efforts at flood basin modification. Even so, problems of scale limited the growth of commercial agriculture. The Ptolemies promoted summer cropping with the assistance of the animal-drawn waterwheel, but their enterprise eventually declined, in part as a consequence of salinization or depleted soil fertility. Throughout this long transition, it is implicit that natural flood basins were being subdivided by dikes. Yet that process remained incomplete in Middle Egypt as of the twelfth century BCE, and even during Ptolemaic times tracts of unimproved land typically existed within the flood basins.

The underlying process of agricultural intensification was interwoven with parallel trends toward demographic growth and greater sociopolitical complexity. Yet irrigation was never maintained or regulated by an administrative bureaucracy; instead, it functioned at the local level, beyond the purview of the pharaoh. His power was not grounded in the control of water resources, and he derived only indirect benefits from expanding agricultural production or commercialization.

[See also Nile; and Technology and Engineering.]

BIBLIOGRAPHY

Abd al-Rahim, A. "Land Tenure in Egypt and Its Social Effects on Egyptian Society, 1798–1813." In Land Tenure and Social Transformation in the Middle East, edited by T. Khalidi, pp. 237–248. Beirut, 1984. A perspective on the Egyptian countryside at the time of the Napoleonic Survey.

Bonneau, Danielle. Le regime administratif de l'eau du Nil dans l'Egypte grecque, romaine et byzantine. Leiden, 1993. Assembles the fragmentary evidence for water management in Greco-Roman Egypt, which was much the same as in earlier times.

Butzer, Karl W. Early Hydraulic Civilization in Egypt. Chicago, 1976. A brief but comprehensive study of irrigation, development, and demographic growth; rejects the Wittfogel hypothesis.

Butzer, Karl W. Recent History of an Ethiopian Delta. Chicago, 1971. Provides photographic documentation of the Omo River's floodplain and delta, which approximates a prototype for the "primeval" Nile and its initial agricultural settlement.

Eyre, C. J. "The Water Regime for Orchards and Plantation in Pharaonic Egypt." Journal of Egyptian Archaeology 80 (1994), 57–80. A well-documented essay that examines increasing water control and provides a measured critique of the ambiguous terminologies for categories of land used in old Egyptian texts.

Harlan, Jack R., and J. Pasquereau. "Décrue agriculture in Mali." Economic Botany 23 (1969), 70–74. A small classic on eotechnic recessional agriculture, relevant to predynastic Egypt.

Hugonot, J. C. Le jardin dans l'Egypte ancienne. Frankfurt, 1989. Outstanding coverage of orchards, gardens, and water.

Kadary, Sally L. D. Land Tenure in the Ramesside Period. London, 1989. A detailed study of a neglected subject.

Park, Thomas K. "Early Trends toward Class Stratification: Chaos, Common Property, and Flood Recession Agriculture." *American Anthropologist* 94 (1992), 90–117. Although cluttered by too many objectives, this article is nonetheless quite useful in comparing eotechnic irrigation agriculture along the Senegal River with Egyptian circumstances.

Schenkel, Wolfgang. "Les systèmes d'irrigation dans l'Égypte ancienne et leur genèse." *Archéo-Nil* 4 (May–June 1994), 27–35. An overview by a leading specialist on ancient Egyptian irrigation, with sometimes diverging views.

Willcocks, William, and J. I. Craig. *Egyptian Irrigation.* 3d ed. London, 1913. The standard work on traditional basin irrigation and its transformation into perennial irrigation.

KARL W. BUTZER

ISIS. The goddess Isis (or *Aset; ꜣst*) is well attested in the early sources and eventually became the best known of all Egyptian goddesses. It was the theology of kingship that assigned to Isis a special significance. In the Pyramid Texts (1655 a–b), she was viewed as a member of the Ennead of Heliopolis, and other allusions in the Pyramid Texts show that she was constantly linked to the pharaoh in both life and death. Her name, meaning "seat" or "throne," firmly points to her association with sovereignty. An interpretation implying "seat" or "dwelling" with reference to a bond between Isis and the sun god Re is less likely than one that alludes to a link with Osiris, although a precise exegesis is still debated. The throne is certainly a basic symbol of the goddess, being present both in her hieroglyphic name and in her iconography.

Role in the Myth and Ritual of Osiris. Presented as the wife and sister of Osiris, Isis is prominent in his myth and also in the rites associated with his death. In the Pyramid Texts, Osiris is said to have been smitten by his brother Seth in a place called Nedyet or Gehestey; the episode should perhaps be connected with the tradition that Osiris was then drowned by Seth. In a later era, there are allusions to a belief that death by drowning was a blessed fate because it recalled the death of Osiris. In a related legend, Seth is presented as the enemy of Horus; the two figure as hostile brothers, rather like Cain and Abel, and in their feud Seth is said to have torn out the eye of Horus, whereas Seth's testicles were removed by Horus. The pair are also involved in a homosexual episode in which Horus is violated by his brother, but a text recently restored by Leclant shows that Horus too is said to violate Seth. What is clear is that the Horus-Seth myth was conflated with that of Osiris and Seth, with a revision of the family links; Seth as the brother of Osiris became the uncle of Horus. Isis appears in these texts as the mother of Horus, and she is said to give birth to him at Khemmis, a place apparently in the Nile Delta. Her role as the mother of Horus becomes increasingly evident with time, although Hathor

ISIS. *Late period bronze statuette of Isis nursing Horus.* (University of Pennsylvania Museum, Philadelphia. Neg. #S4–143071)

figures occasionally in early allusions to this function. At the same time, Isis protects Osiris against the threats of Seth, and both these functions emphasize her basic significance vis-à-vis the pharaonic divine kingship. The living pharaoh was equated with Horus; he was also regarded as the son of Re. When the king died, he was identified with Osiris, and this illumines the supreme im-

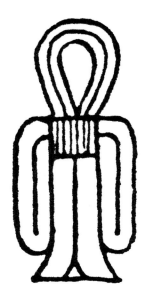

ISIS. *Amulet of the Girdle of Isis, based on the form of the* ankh-*sign and associated with the blood and magical power of the goddess.* (After H. Bonnet, *Reallexikon der ägyptischen Religionsgeschichte.* Berlin, 1952, p. 352.)

portance of Isis in the funerary ceremonies. With her sister Nephthys, she fulfills the part of the mourning falcons and also aids the rites of purification and mummification. To these rites and that of the Opening of the Mouth ceremony was assigned the power of renewing life, and eventually the role of Isis in the myth was specifically to ensure the revival of life in the dead Osiris, including his sexual and procreative potency. This power is alluded to in the New Kingdom *Hymn of Amenmose* and is sculpturally figured in tombs of the same era (see Otto 1968, plates 16 ff.).

It is the close nexus with kingship that distinguishes Isis from the paramours of the Near Eastern deities who are associated with renewed life after death, such as Ishtar, Cybele, and Aphrodite, with the beloved ones of Tammuz (Dumuzi), Attis, and Adonis. This is not to claim that the role of Isis was consistently prominent in Egyptian royal rites. A funerary framework usually attaches to both Isis and Osiris. In the coronation rites, attention is naturally focused on the new king, who is equated with Horus, but since Isis is the mother of Horus (in his forms as Horus the Child and Horus the Elder), she figures in the retrospective aspect of such rites, as indeed does Osiris as his father. Within the mythic pattern, Isis holds a conspicuous lead role in the story of her quest for the lost and slain Osiris. Texts often refer to the anxiety of the search, followed by the relief of the finding. Nephthys joins Isis in the task, while Horus and Geb are also mentioned. The seeking and finding mirror the fear that the body of the

king may be lost in the Nile or in the desert and may thus be deprived of the solace and assurance of due burial rites. The society in which the concept had its origin was probably one of nomads and hunters who feared the dismemberment and dispersion of the body.

Relationship to Other Deities. Isis and her sister Nephthys are closely grouped in funerary rites, not only as the chief mourners but also as sacred performers in roles to which priestesses were assigned. Ambivalence marks the role of Nephthys. She is named as the consort of Seth, in a pair parallel to Isis and Osiris as offspring of Geb and Nut, yet her close relation to Isis brings her to a shared sexual link to Osiris. This is especially clear in two groups of songs assigned to Isis and Nephthys in the Ptolemaic era: the Festival Songs and the Lamentations. In one of these texts Osiris is called the "Bull of the Two Sisters." Plutarch in *De Iside et Osiride* takes this further in an allusion to the adultery of Osiris with Nephthys, albeit through mistaken identity; and he names Anubis as the fruit of their illicit union. Some Egyptian texts also refer to Anubis as the son of Osiris, yet Isis is portrayed as a consistently loyal spouse to Osiris.

Hathor, in contrast, has a basic significance of her own, and a close affinity to Isis. Her name means "House of Horus"; perhaps "house" here refers to the celestial domain of the falcon god (Meeks and Favard-Meeks 1997, p. 236). But her early claim to be the mother of Horus may more probably be implied. A kind of rivalry with Isis emerges here, and also a medium of influence, since the cow-form of Hathor is sometimes transferred in part to Isis. Hathor, like Isis, is a goddess of love, but in a less inhibited form; she is a goddess too of the dance, music, and drunken abandon. An antithesis results, since Isis is a goddess of love in its socially acceptable form, with motherhood as its dominant theme. There are episodes, however, in which Horus and his mother Isis appear in dire conflict: after a violent assault by Horus on his mother, she is said to have cut off his two hands (Spell 113, *Book of Going Forth by Day,* and other texts). A piece of etiology emerges here: the writing of Nekhen (Hierakonpolis) showed two signs interpreted as the hands of Horus, who had an early cult center there. Another story (the *Contendings of Horus and Seth,* 8, 9 ff.) tells how Horus, because his mother favored Seth, cut off her head, whereupon Thoth (according to Papyrus Sallier 4) restored the head of Isis as a cow head—another piece of etiology explaining the bovine headdress of Isis, derived from Hathor.

Nut, the goddess of heaven, was bound to come into contact with Isis, if only through her ubiquity in the funerary domain. Nut gives birth to the sun and stars and swallows them at sunset; this led to her being called "the Sow" with allusion to the sow as a devourer of her offspring. In the Hellenistic era, the connection of Isis and Nut is conveyed in art by depictions of Isis riding on a sow (see Bergman 1974). In the astral world, Isis was at times identified with the bright star Sirius, or Sothis (Sepedet), in the constellation Orion, the latter being equated with Osiris; and their sexual union is said to produce Horus Sopd (Pyramid Texts 632 a ff.).

Attributes. While the throne-sign is a constant feature in the depiction of Isis, her association with Hathor often endows her head with cow horns and sun disk. In a Middle Kingdom text, Isis identifies herself with the *nat*-serpent, the *uraeus* of the royal diadem (Münster 1968, p. 106); and in the *Book of Gates*, the twelfth gate, both Isis and Nephthys appear as *uraei* (Hornung 1992, pp. 306–307). Isis is at times figured as a serpent in the Roman era, together with a serpentine Sarapis. A combined form, Isis-Bat, connects her with the goddess Bat, but Hathor supplies the link, since Bat is a Hathor look-alike, with curling horns and sun disc (see Fischer 1961, p. 7 ff.). From Hathor, too, Isis derives the sistrum, the shaker or rattle used to accompany music in sacred rites; it was probably of African origin. In the Greco-Roman era, Isis was often figured carrying both sistrum and situla (on the latter vessel, see Griffiths 1975 pp. 208–210); it was often shaped like a nippled breast, and some examples relate to the New Kingdom. The same objects were often carried by priestly servants of the goddess (Witt 1997, plates 31–32).

A popular amulet used in a funerary context was explained as "the blood of Isis." It represents the *ankh*-sign, that of life, in a form that suggests a girdle. Spell 156 of the *Book of Going Forth by Day* shows the amulet with the words, "Thou hast thy blood, O Isis, thou hast thy magical power." Perhaps the object is a bandage for use in menstruation. Magical power was often ascribed to the goddess, particularly in the sphere of healing. In the *Story of Re and Isis*, she heals even the god Re by eliciting from him the truth about his name; in the Metternich Stela, she saves Horus.

Several cult centers were assigned to Isis, including Behbet el-Hagar in the Nile Delta, Akhmim, Coptos, and Philae. Where the cult began is uncertain. Her celebrated temple in Philae had its origins only in the last pharaonic dynasties (see Žabkar 1988). Some of these hymns dwell on her warlike power, doubtless in relation to the hazards of the region.

The Universal Goddess. During post-pharaonic eras, the cult of Isis witnessed a remarkable expansion in two ways: spatially, it spread to most parts of the known world; and its spiritual content was much widened in that Isis became a universal goddess who subsumed the functions of many other deities. The spatial expansion was achieved in the Ptolemaic era, not through political pressure by the rulers but by merchants, priests, and private devotees. By that time, the god Sarapis had to some extent replaced Osiris as the consort of Isis. Yet other deities of the Isiac-Osirian circle were still prominent, especially Anubis and Harpocrates, who are among those mentioned in the *Aretalogies* or *Praises of Isis*, in works by Plutarch and Apuleius, and in a massive corpus of inscriptions. In the Isis-Book of Apuleius, Isis claims to be "mother of the universe" and "mistress of all the elements."

A part of this process of expansion was an influx of Greek religious ideas. In particular, Demeter was equated with Isis, a tangible result being the depiction of Isis with sheaves of grain as part of her headdress. The "Isis-knot," however, was a feature of Isiac dress derived from an Egyptian fashion. Whereas the Isiac mysteries were partly based on the Greek model of Eleusis, their elements of initiation and secrecy had Egyptian antecedents. The Hellenistic Isis offers a deeper human approach in the paradigm of the loyal wife and mother; she retains an element of chastisement and validates, on the pattern of Osiris, a faith in immortality.

BIBLIOGRAPHY

Apuleius. *The Isis Book: Apuleius of Madauros.* Edited with introduction, translation and commentary by John Gwyn Griffiths. Études préliminaires aux religions orientales dans l'empire romain, 39. Leiden, 1975. Although highly stylized, the account of Apuleius is probably based on first-hand experience of the cult.

Assmann, Jan. "Death and Initiation in the Funerary Religion of Ancient Egypt." In *Religion and Philosophy in Ancient Egypt*, edited by James P. Allen et al., pp. 135–159. Yale Egyptological Studies, 3. New Haven, 1989. Includes an impressive study of the "Isis-mysteries."

Bergman, Jan. *Ich bin Isis: Studien zum memphitischen Hintergrund der griechischen Isisaretalogien.* Uppsala, 1968.

Bergman, Jan. "Isis auf der Sau." *Boreas* 6 (1974), 81–109.

Bergman, Jan. "Isis." In *Lexikon der Ägyptologie*, 3: 186–203. Wiesbaden, 1980. The first of Bergman's works concentrates on the Memphite background of the Greek Isis *Aretalogies*; the third is an ordered survey of the whole development of the Egyptian cult.

Bianchi, Robert S. "Not the Isis Knot." *Bulletin of the Egyptological Seminar* 2 (1980), 9–31. A fine study which demonstrates that the "Isis knot," though not specifically Isiac in origin, was a popular Egyptian fashion.

Bleeker, C. J. "Isis as Saviour Goddess." In *The Saviour God; Comparative Studies in the Concept of Salvation Presented to Edwin Oliver James*, edited by S. G. F. Brandon, pp. 1–16. Manchester, 1963. Concerned mainly with the Greco-Roman cult.

Bonnet, Hans. *Reallexikon der ägyptischen Religionsgeschichte.* 2d ed. Berlin and New York, 1971. See especially "Isis" and "Isisblut." Of enduring worth.

Borghouts, J. F. *Ancient Egyptian Magical Texts.* Nisaba, 9. Leiden, 1978. A valuable collection of texts with brief notes. Often concerned with Isis and her circle.

Dunand, Françoise. *Le culte d'Isis dans le bassin oriental de la Méditerranée.* 3 vols. Études préliminaires aux religions orientales dans l'empire romain, 26. Leiden, 1973. A thorough and careful conspectus.

Faulkner, R. O. *The Ancient Egyptian Coffin Texts.* 3 vols. Warminster, 1973–1980.

Faulkner, R. O. *The Ancient Egyptian Pyramid Texts.* 2 vols. Oxford, 1969.

Faulkner, R. O. *The Ancient Egyptian Book of the Dead.* rev. ed., edited by Carol Andrews. London, 1985. Indispensable basic works.

Fischer, H. G. "The Cult and Nome of the Goddess Bat." *Journal of the American Research Center in Egypt* 1 (1962), 7 ff.

Frankfort, Henri. *Ancient Egyptian Religion, an Interpretation.* New York, 1948; reprint, 1962.

Frankfort, Henri. *Kingship and the Gods: A Study of Ancient Near Eastern Religion as the Integration of Society and Nature.* Chicago, 1948. Occasionally dogmatic, but sound on Egypt's divine kingship.

Griffiths, J. Gwyn. *Apuleius, Isis-book.* Leiden, 1975.

Griffiths, J. Gwyn. "Isis as Maat, Dikaiosune, and Iustitia." In *Hommages à Jean Leclant*, edited by Catherine Berger, Gisèle Clerc and Nicholas Grimal, pp. 255–264. Institut français d'archéologie orientale du Caire, 3. Cairo, 1994.

Griffiths, J. Gwyn. *The Origins of Osiris and His Cult.* Studies in the History of Religions, 40. Leiden, 1980. For Isis as a key figure in the primal myth, "Nut, Isis and Nephthys," pp. 47 ff.

Griffiths, J. Gwyn. *Plutarch's De Iside et Osiride.* Cardiff, 1970. Unlike the work of Apuleius, Plutarch's essay ranges very widely, often dealing with aspects of Egyptian religion beyond the scope of his chosen theme; but Isis is his central figure.

Hornung, Erik. "Versuch über Nephthys." In *Studies in Pharaonic Religion and Society: In honor of J. Gwyn Griffiths*, edited by Alan B. Lloyd, pp. 186–188. London, 1992. Often in the shadow of Isis, Nephthys is yet far from being a mere doublet or pallid abstraction; she personifies selfless help to others. A learned, lucid, and charming study.

Leclant, Jean, and Clerc, Gisèle. *Inventaire bibliographique des Isiaca. Répertoire analytique des travaux relatifs à la diffusion des cultes Isiaques 1940–1960.* 4 vols. Études préliminaires aux religions orientales dans l'empire romain, 18. Leiden, 1972–1991. An analytical bibliography of great value. Although its coverage is restricted to the years 1940–1969, it deals with the diffusion of the Isiac cults and with many other facets of Egyptian religion.

Meeks, D., and C. Favard-Meeks. *Daily Life of the Egyptian Gods.* London, 1997.

Müller, Dieter. *Ägypten und die griechischen Isis-Aretalogien.* Abhandlungen der Sächsischen Akademie der Wissenschaften zu Leipzig, 53.1 Berlin, 1961. See works by Bergman and Žabkar.

Münster, Maria. *Untersuchungen zur Göttin Isis vom Alten Reich bis zum Ende des Neuen Reiches.* Münchner Ägyptologische Studien, 11. Berlin, 1968. The best and most detailed presentation of the early sources.

Otto, E. *Egyptian Art and the Cults of Osiris and Amon.* London, 1968.

Quirke, Stephen. *Ancient Egyptian Religion.* London, 1992.

Silverman, David P. "Divinity and Deities in Ancient Egypt." In *Religion in Ancient Egypt*, edited by Byron E. Shafer, pp. 7–87. London, 1991. A perceptive analysis of the formative stages of ancient Egypt's religion. On Osiris and his circle, see pp. 44 ff.

Witt, Reginald Eldred. *Isis in the Graeco-Roman World.* London, 1971; reprint, Baltimore, 1997. An attractive study by a classical scholar who was eager to see Isis as "the Great Forerunner" of the "Blessed Virgin Mary."

Žabkar, Louis V. *Hymns to Isis in Her Temple at Philae.* Hanover and London, 1988. An impeccable record of Egyptian texts with transliterations and translations, followed by a rich and discerning commentary. An epilogue on the Isiac Aretalogies is the best discussion hitherto.

J. GWYN GRIFFITHS

ISLAM AND ANCIENT EGYPT. Any continuity from ancient to Islamic Egypt was irretrievably and doubly cut off, first by the adoption of Christianity in Egypt in the fourth century and then, three centuries later, by the Islamic conquest. Memories of the world of the pharaohs had long since been forgotten by Egyptians who had been incorporated into the Greek, the Roman, the Byzantine, and, by the seventh century CE, the expanding Islamic world. Medieval Muslims were aware of this finality, and Islam as a belief and as a legal system enhanced Egypt's rupture with the past. The world of Ancient Egypt was presented in unadulterated Islamic terms, featuring the few righteous Egyptian believers who took the admonitions of the prophets Joseph and Moses to heart, to profess monotheism. Pharaoh, from the time of Moses, was presented as the epitome of unbridled worldly power, of haughtiness, and of *zulm* ("tyranny").

Since the original function of the ancient Egyptian monuments, their cultural and ritual context, and the meaning of the ubiquitous other pharaonic symbols had been forgotten, they all became open to new attributions and interpretations. Thus the pyramids of Giza were turned into Joseph's granary, and the most striking buildings in the Faiyum and in Saqqara were rediscovered as the mansion of Potiphar's wife and Joseph's prison. The incomprehensible hieroglyphs, called "bird's script," "temple script," or even "hieratic" script (*al-qalam al-kāhinī*, "script of the priests"), were imbued with enigmatic meanings. In early Muslim texts on ancient Egypt, an age-old Upper Egyptian or preferably an Ethiopian monk were mentioned, who still understood the mysterious hieroglyphic script. In medieval Islamic sources, exoticism and weirdness were the dominant attributes associated with Egyptian antiquity. Ancient Egypt was turned into a repository of miracles, magic, and treasures, yet also into a land of technical ingenuity and scientific wisdom—a double image that is familiar to us from Hellenistic hermeticism, the Renaissance, as well as Enlightenment Europe. In stark contrast to the new Muslim morality, ancient Egypt—the "Babel of the sorcerers"—epitomized idolatry and paganism; its gigantic monuments; its many gods (some even in animal shape), its mummified bodies of humans, animals, and birds, its uninhibited pictorial splendor, and many more characteristics that went against Islamic tenets provided the Muslims of Egypt and of other countries the strong negative foil that served to make them aware of their own proper religious and legal prescriptions. Egypt's historical discontinuity did not preclude its Muslim historians from trying to integrate the pagan prehistory of their country into the overall salvation patterns of Islam and to discover tokens of divine guidance in an otherwise profoundly heathen world. Conversely, pharaonic symbols and relics might also be significant for latter-day events. Even though the pagan structures of pharaonic Egypt would defy Islam during all the rest of human history, they would finally have to succumb, too: in a seventeenth-century source, we are presented with very modern demolition techniques when King Nebuchadrezzar would blow up the pyramids with black powder at the end of history, thus opening the Egyptian lands to demise in the floods of the Nile.

Water was important for the Muslim view of pharaonic history; only the Flood divided the period of paganism into two distinct halves. Abū Jaʿfar al-Idrīsī (died 1251), the most important medieval Muslim author to inform us about the pharaonic past and its vestiges, devoted a quarter of his extensive treatise on the pyramids to the question of whether the pyramids were built before or after the Flood. The vast majority of the authorities consulted by him on this question favored a pre-Flood date. According to them, the pyramids survived the Flood—although not unscathed—because, according to a fourteenth-century source, the Deluge precipitated the Sphinx, formerly a red idol of the sun, from the top of the pyramid of Khufu (Cheops) and broke it into pieces. The question of who commissioned the erection of the pyramids was hotly debated and, in the long list of potential builders, Aristotle was listed; he was said to have erected the pyramids of Khufu and Khefre as mausoleums for himself and his disciple, Alexander the Great.

The topography of ancient Egypt was eerie, wondrous, and outlandish for the medieval Muslim observer. Awesome spirits—some male and aggressive, some female and seductive—guarded the treasures and secrets of the old magi. The sciences of both alchemy (Ar., kīmiyāʾ) and treasure-hunting (Ar., maṭālib) were closely associated, in early Islamic times, with the pharaonic heritage, notably the Sphinx, a proverbial warden of treasures. Among the thirty miracles of the world that were listed in pertinent medieval Islamic texts, as many as twenty belonged to the land of Egypt, with the pyramids being the first and foremost. Attempts were made to integrate travel to those monuments into the general precepts of Islam. Visiting the miracles of Egypt was declared not only permissible, but was even recommended.

Besides the pyramids of Giza, a few other relics and sites of Old Egypt were consistently granted attention in medieval Islamic writing. These include the ruined site of Heliopolis, with its famous two obelisks; also Memphis, with the so-called arch of lapis lazuli and the monolithic green chapel that was hauled away to downtown Cairo in 1350; Saqqara, with the Step Pyramid and the mummies of the ibises; and, foremost, the Sphinx of Giza. South of Giza, the majestic temple of Akhmim was the key attraction for medieval Muslim geographers, travelers, and encyclopedists; the reason may have been the location of the town and the temple of Akhmim, directly on the caravan route from Cairo on the Nile to the Red Sea ports, from which one could reach Mecca, as well as the emporiums of the Indian trade. There were also the Faiyum, the two mastabas in the Dakhla Oasis, Philae (with Pharaoh's bath), the unfinished obelisk in the quarry south of Aswan, Dendera and Antinoë, and some monuments in the Luxor region, such as the huge temple of Karnak. The image of Luxor was characterized by double sanctity—the ubiquity of the pharaonic monuments and the continuing presence of the local Muslim saint, Sīdī Abū ʾl-Ḥajjāj al-Uqṣurī (died 1244), whose tomb was built into the ruins of the Luxor temple.

It is difficult and sometimes challenging to try to determine the exact dividing line between the miraculous and the scientific geography presented in medieval Islamic texts. Yet geography did exist, as did precise measurement, sophisticated trigonometrical technique, and records of the physical qualities of the building dimensions and materials. Attention was paid to the many inscriptions (in various writing systems) on the pyramids of Giza. Numerous questions were addressed by Muslim authors of the Middle Ages: What is the meaning and the origin of the hieroglyphs? Is there any connection with the Greek alphabet? Then, too, the mysterious interior of the old Egyptian temples, mastabas, and pyramids captivated their curiosity. The pyramid of Khufu became accessible by force as early as the ninth century CE. The story of that event, the expedition of the caliph al-Maʾmūn into the great pyramid, found its way even into the collection called the *Arabian Nights*.

Certain recurrent iconographic features of pharaonic architecture were recorded and interpreted by medieval Muslim authors. The Egyptian sun disk was used in a clever attempt to establish an absolute chronology for the pharaonic remains—seen as a symbolic representation of both the zodiac sign cancer and the eagle; when the star of Altair entered the zodiac of cancer (so one Upper Egyptian scholar of the twelfth century reckoned), those monuments were erected. Using a complicated astronomical argument, he arrived at an age of twenty thousand years for the ancient Egyptian ruins (early by some sixteen thousand years).

The expertise with which the ancient Egyptians worked with difficult materials, such as granite, and their craftsmanship in erecting huge structures, such as pyramids, temples, and obelisks, evoked profound awe among medieval Muslim authors. Did pharaonic architects use ramps to move the stones gradually to their final high position, one asked, with a shrewd sense of reality. Also, that rows of slabs were found, with hieroglyphic inscriptions not only on the visible front but also on the nonvisible inside, was proof to a keen medieval Arab observer that some development occurred in pharaonic history, because the stones must have been used in different epochs yet both times in the hieroglyphic age.

The difficulty for a medieval Muslim author to differentiate precisely and convincingly between reality and fantasy in the description of the pharaonic monuments and of their surroundings, is similar to modern scholarly work. The need is to identify elements of history in the enormous, heterogeneous body of work left to us in Arabic (as well as in Persian, Ottoman Turkish, and other languages) on the history of Egypt before Islam, with a heritage shaped by omnipresent magic, sorcery, pagan lore, and a traditionally based collective imagination. Nevertheless, faint vestiges of Egypt's historical truth exist in medieval Arabic writing. The polymath al-Maqrīzī (died 1442) quoted the now-famous Egyptian king list recorded by the Greco-Egyptian priest Manetho. Apart from that, there are two other intrinsically Islamic renderings of Old Egyptian history in Muslim sources—the traditionist version and the hermetic version. The traditionist version can be traced back to early Muslim scholars and begins with the Flood and the founding of the Egyptian kingdom by Noah's great-grandson Miṣr, the eponym of the country. The hermetic, genuinely Islamic redaction of the history of pagan Egypt is associated with the author al-Wāṣifī/Ibn Waṣīf Shāh of the tenth to eleventh century; it contains a wondrous description of pharaonic events from before the Flood and onward.

Ancient Egypt is volatile, vague, and only faintly recognizable in the pertinent medieval Muslim literature; tangible relics of pharaonic days are rare in the Arabic texts. Tokens of continuity from ancient to Islamic Egypt were limited mainly to the spheres of popular beliefs and practices. The Sphinx is mentioned, unmistakable by virtue of its features and its conspicuous location, an apotropaic idol against the sands of the Western Desert. The continuing awareness that "The West," the western bank of the Nile River, was originally the abode of the dead is clearly traceable in medieval Arabic sources. For average Muslims, from the Middle Ages onward, pharaonic sites otherwise served four main functions that cannot always be easily separated: (1) they were the target of pious iconoclasts who abominated the pictorial pagan heritage (pictures being tabu in Islam); (2) they attracted treasure hunters; (3) they provided cheap, yet excellent building materials; and (4) they have always been favorite areas of tourism. In the Fatimid times of the tenth to twelfth centuries CE, to give one example, bonfires were lit atop the pyramid of Khufu for the "nights of fire," holidays that enjoyed particular support under Egypt's ruling Ismaili-Shiite regime.

In medieval Islamic writings, attempts were made to harmonize the rejection of ancient Egyptian paganism (as embodied in the relics of the Pharaohs) and the urge to preserve the majesty of the architectural patrimony. Those monuments were, it was said, petrified tokens of God's admonition not to forget the futility of human glory and might; in a very sagacious argument, a scholar of the thirteenth century even employed the Companions of the Prophet, epitomes of righteous Islamic behavior, as crown-witnesses against the wanton destruction of any pharaonic monuments. Those men enjoyed resting and praying in the shadow of the pyramids, and they did not mind being interred in their vicinity. Only in the modern age (which can be dated by the decipherment of the hieroglyphs by Champollion) did the tensions inherent in traditional Muslim attitudes vis-à-vis Egypt's pagan heritage become crucial again. The discoveries of the new field of Egyptology and the spectacular excavations of the nineteenth and twentieth centuries provoked new models of thought. Then, knowledge of, and pride in, the pharaonic past had to be harmonized with an Islamic view of history. At first, around the middle of the nineteenth century, the Egyptological (i.e., alien and European) image of ancient Egypt was tenuously juxtaposed with the Islamic. Gradually, efforts at a more effective synthesis were undertaken. Yet before an indigenous and harmonious Egyptian *Geschichtsbild*, founded both on the new scientific knowledge and on the tenets of Islam, could tentatively take root, a wave of secularization conquered the Egyptian institutions of higher learning. The Egyptological model, in the interpretation of Egypt's history before the Roman emperor Diocletian (r. 284–305 CE)—supported by an overriding pharaonicist ideology that derived national pride from the glory and treasures of earliest Egyptian history as well as a large literary corpus and a rich pharaonicizing architecture—seemed invincible for decades. Only since the 1980s, did the incompatibility of certain Egyptological and certain rival Islamic "truths" about pharaonic Egypt reemerge as an increasingly serious problem in Islamic fundamentalist quarters. The golden splendor of the ancient Egyptian kings and the abject reprehensibility of the pharaoh who defied Moses and his prophetic message may not always be easily separable for the pious believer—even in the closing days of the twentieth century.

[*See also* Biblical Tradition.]

BIBLIOGRAPHY

Cook, Michael. "Pharaonic History in Medieval Egypt." *Studia Islamica* 57 (1983), 67–103.

Fodor, Alexander. "The Origins of the Arabic Legends of the Pyramids." *Acta Orientalia Hungarica* 23 (1970), 335–363.

Graefe, Erich. *Das Pyramidenkapitel in al-Makrīzī's "Ḫiṭaṭ."* Leipziger Semitistische Studien, 5. Leipzig, 1911; reprint, 1968.

Haarmann, Maria. "Das moderne Ägypten und seine pharaonische Vergangenheit." Ph.D. diss., University of Freiburg, Germany, 1991.

Haarmann, Ulrich. *Das Pyramidenbuch des Abū Ǧaʿfar al-Idrîsî (st. 649/1251)*. Beiruter Texte und Studien, 38. Beirut, 1991. With comprehensive bibliography on Western language studies on Islam and ancient Egypt, pp. 273–283.

Haarmann, Ulrich. "Medieval Muslim Perceptions of Pharaonic Egypt." In *Ancient Egyptian Literature: History and Forms*, edited by Antonio Loprieno, pp. 605–627. Probleme der Ägyptologie, 10. Leiden, 1996.

Wiet, Gaston. *L'Égypte de Murtadi fils du Gaphiphe: Introduction, traduction, et notes*. Bibliothèque de l'école nationale des langues orientales vivantes, 14. Paris, 1953.

ULRICH W. HAARMANN

ISRAEL. According to the biblical tradition, the word *Israel* derived from Jacob-Israel, the grandson of Abraham the Patriarch (*Gn.* 32.2). During the Second Intermediate Period (1750–1600 BCE), the Hebrews came to the northeast of the Nile Delta. After some centuries there, and a period of servitude in Egypt, they fled under the leadership of Moses. Subsequently, Joshua led them into the land of Canaan in the Levant, along the eastern Mediterranean shore, returning to the land where their Patriarchs had lived.

Reference to Israel is not found in Egyptian records until Merenptah's fifth regnal year (c.1229 BCE); recorded on the Merenptah (or Israel) Stela is reference to the monarch's invasion of Canaan, in which Israelites were encountered. The grandiose claim "Israel is wasted, his seed is not" must be understood as a hyperbolic statement, since the Israelite tribes were not eradicated at the end of the thirteenth century BCE. Merenptah's Stela is now thought to have a pictorial counterpart at Karnak temple, which includes Israelites who are portrayed as Canaanites.

The period of Israel's United Monarchy (c.1040–970 BCE) coincided with the beginning of Egypt's Third Intermediate Period (c.1100–650 BCE), when Egypt was retrenching and not as concerned with international affairs as was the case during the previous New Kingdom. Relations between Egypt and Israel are not well documented in Egyptian sources, although Egypt is frequently mentioned in the biblical books of *Kings* and *Chronicles*, as well as in some Hebrew prophetic literature. Consequently, sources for Egypt's contacts with the kingdoms of Israel and Judah from about 1040 to 586 BCE largely come from the Bible and from some Assyrian records.

The Egyptian *Story of Wen-Amen*, which reflects the geopolitics of the Levant during the reigns of Herihor from Thebes and Smendes from Tanis (1075–1050 BCE), does not mention Israel, although some of the Sea Peoples, who settled along the Levantine coast, were cited. The biblical books of *Joshua* and *Judges* suggest that Israelite tribes had not yet occupied the coastal area, and this was the area visited in Wen-Amen's maritime travels. Thus Wen-Amen's silence on the Israelites may only mean that his travels did not include areas occupied by them.

While there is no direct evidence from either Egyptian or Hebrew sources, it is thought that there were cordial relations between King David, second ruler of the United Monarchy, and the kings of Tanis. Not until the reign of David's son Solomon (c.970–930 BCE), however, is there evidence for direct contact between the two nations. In *1 Kings* 3.1, there is a marriage alliance between Solomon and the daughter of Pharaoh; this is probably the twenty-first dynasty Tanite king Siamun (984–965 BCE). It is uncertain whether the treaty resulted from Egypt's failed attempt to conquer Philistia and Israel, or whether Pharaoh seized Gezer (*1 Kings* 9.16) from the Philistines to support Solomon, Israel's new king; the latter seems likely. Good relations between the two nations meant the free flow of ideas. As Solomon was familiar with the Egyptian Wisdom Literature (*1 Kings* 4.29–30), that may account for the verbal correspondence between *Proverbs* 22 and the *Wisdom of Amenemope*. Trade also then flourished, as judged from the reference to Solomon facilitating horse-and-chariot exchange between Egypt and the Neo-Hittites of northern Syria (*1 Kings* 10.28–29).

Toward the end of Solomon's reign, the twenty-second (Libyan) dynasty was established by Sheshonq (the biblical Shishak). The alliance with Israel was over, as reflected in Solomon's political enemy Jeroboam finding sanctuary at the court of Sheshonq (*1 Kings* 11.40). With Solomon's death (c.931 BCE), Israel split into two kingdoms; David's successors controlled Judah from Jerusalem, and Jeroboam returned from Egypt to become king of the northern state, Israel. In 925 BCE, Sheshonq invaded the Levant. Biblical sources offer only a Judean perspective on that invasion, that King Rehoboam was humbled and his treasury stripped to bribe Sheshonq, thereby preventing an attack on Jerusalem (*1 Kings* 14.25–26; *2 Chron.* 12.1–12). Nevertheless, the city name list—the itinerary of Sheshonq's campaign—at Karnak records a large number of Israelite toponyms (e.g., Megiddo, Tanaach, Rehob, Beth Shean), indicating that Jeroboam suffered a serious blow from his erstwhile protector. A fragment of Sheshonq's victory stela was discovered at Megiddo, and a number of Israelite sites show evidence of having been sacked by Egyptian forces, including Stratum VA/IVB at Megiddo and Stratum VII at Tel Mevorakh. Surprisingly, the Karnak topographical list records the names of nearly seventy toponyms in the Negev. Amihai Mazar (1990) suggests that "Shishak's goal may have been to disrupt the Israelite and Phoenician trade with southern Arabia and restore Egyptian hegemony over this trade as it had been during the New Kingdom."

The next incursion into Judah and Israel was made by Zerah the "Ethiopian (Cushite)" during Asa's reign (910–869 BCE; *2 Chron.* 14.9). At that time, the son of Sheshonq, Osorkon I, ruled in Tanis. (In the past, some scholars thought that Zerah was the Hebrew form of writing Osorkon; this, however, is linguistically impossible.) The text of *2 Chronicles* 14.9, it must be noted, never refers to Zerah as "king," and his army consists of Cushites and Libyans (*2 Chron.* 16.8). More plausibly, Zerah was a mercenary, leading Egypt's army in 897 BCE, when the invasion took place. Kenneth Kitchen has observed (1986) that Osorkon would have been quite old and probably incapable of leading the attack.

In the waning years of the Northern Kingdom of Israel (725–4 BCE), King Hoshea revolted against his Assyrian overlords: "But the king of Assyria found treachery in Hoshea; for he had sent messengers to So, king of Egypt, and offered no tribute to the king of Assyria" (*2 Kings* 17.4). The identity of "So" is problematic, and different interpretations of the text have been proffered; one emended reading is that Hoshea "sent [to] So, to the King of Egypt," So being Sais (Sao) in the western Delta. Alternatively, Donald Redford (1981) has proposed that "So" has been equated with the Greco-Egyptian historian Manetho's epithet *pso*, which is attached to Necho, the name of the twenty-sixth dynasty king. *Pso* would correspond to Egyptian *pa-sau* (*p3 s3w*), meaning the Saite.

While this suggestion has merit, it is not without problems, the principal one being geography. Sais is located around 100 kilometers (64 miles) west of Tanis, the closest seat of power to Israel. At that time, there were concurrent kingships at Sais and Tanis, the twenty-third and twenty-fourth dynasties, respectively. The Tanite ruler was Osorkon IV; the Saite king was Tefnakht. It seems likely that Hoshea would have sought help from the closer source, Tanis. Kitchen (1986) suggested that "So" might be an abbreviation for O(so)rkon IV. Regardless of how "So" is understood, the help either did not come or did no good, for Samaria was destroyed in 722 BCE by the troops of Sargon II, king of Assyria. The Hebrew prophet Isaiah took notice of Hoshea's lack of faith in God, and he denounced the trusting of Egypt for military aid rather than trusting God (*Isa.* 31.1; 19.11–15).

Once Assyria became a real threat to Egypt, the Cushite rulers of the twenty-fifth dynasty had to rethink their relationships with Jerusalem. Taharka came to the aid of Hezekiah of Jerusalem in 701 BCE (*2 Kings* 19.9; *Isa.* 37.19), apparently acting on behalf of his elder brother, Shebitku the king. Yet nothing in the biblical text suggests that Hezekiah sought his help. More likely, the twenty-fifth dynasty kings realized that once the kingdom of Judah fell nothing stood in Assyria's way and that Egypt was next to be conquered. So the Cushites apparently acted out of self-interest. No extant sources from Egypt record Taharka's campaign to Judah, although it may be alluded to on the Kawa stela of Taharka; there, Shebitku orders his brother and a military force to leave Napata and join him in Memphis. Sennacherib's *Annals* do report on Taharka's effort to support Judah, and he claims to have trounced the chariots and infantry of the "king of Ethiopia" at Eltekeh.

The collapse of the Assyrian Empire between 612 and 609 BCE motivated Necho II of the twenty-sixth dynasty (r. 610–595 BCE) to enter the Levant, to influence the geopolitics of the Near East. For a brief period between 609 and 605 BCE, Necho wielded considerable influence on Judah. First, he set off to Charchemish on the Euphrates to aid the remnant of Assyria that was holding up in Haran and to stop the advances of Nebuchadrezzar and his Chaldean armies. The Judean monarch Josiah thought otherwise and tried to stop Necho at Megiddo (near Jerusalem). In a battle that ensued, Josiah was killed. Subsequently, Necho dethroned Josiah's successor, Jehoahaz II, took him to Egypt and replaced him with his brother Eliakim (i.e., Jehoiakim. *2 Kings* 23.33–34). In 605 BCE, Nebuchadrezzar drove out Necho's forces stationed at Charchemish, ending a short period of Egyptian dominance in the Levant; again, Egyptian records of Necho's activities there have not survived, but, along with biblical references, the Babylonian Chronicle documents that presence of Egypt in Syria.

The last period of contact between Egypt and Israel occurred when Zedekiah, facing Nebuchadrezzar's invasion, called on Egypt for military help in 591–589 BCE (*2 Kings* 25.20b; *Ezek.* 17.15). The prophet Jeremiah then reported on the coming of Pharaoh Hophra (Apries), indicating that they could not help Judah's plight because its doom was sealed (*Jer.* 37.5–10; 44.30; *Ezek.* 30.21–22). The ancient historians Herodotus and Diodorus Seculus reported on Apries' failed ventures in the Levant; Egypt's help was futile, Jerusalem fell in 586 BCE and many Jews fled to Egypt for safety—among them were Jeremiah and Baruch, his scribe (*Jer.* 43.5–44.30). Jeremiah then warned Egypt of Nebuchadrezzar's coming invasion, which occurred in 568 BCE.

Whether friend or foe to Israel, Egypt exerted considerable influence over its Levantine neighbor. Egyptian papyrus was the most important commodity received by the Israelites. Even before the Israelites settled in Canaan during the second half of the second millennium BCE, Egypt had economic interests in that region. Egyptian scarabs found in abundance in Bronze and Iron Age sites throughout the Levant attest to Egypt's commercial interests. Interestingly, Egyptian royal scarabs found in both

Israel and Judah are replete with Egyptian motifs—winged discs, Egyptian crowns, and Egyptian hair style. Similarly, the ivories found at Megiddo and Samaria are dominated by Egyptian images.

[*See also* Biblical Tradition; Exodus; Megiddo; *and* Syria-Palestine.]

BIBLIOGRAPHY

Hoffmeier, James K. "Egypt as an Arm of Flesh: A Prophetic Response." *Israel's Apostasy and Restoration: Essays in Honor of Roland K. Harrison*, edited by Avraham Gileadi, pp. 79–97. Grand Rapids, 1988.

Hoffmeier, James K. *Israel in Egypt: Evidence for the Authenticity of the Exodus Tradition.* New York, 1997.

Kitchen, Kenneth. *The Third Intermediate Period in Egypt*, Warminster, 1986.

Mazar, Amihai. *Archaeology of the Land of the Bible.* New York, 1990.

Redford, Donald B. "A Note on II Kings 17:4." *Journal of the Society for the Study of Egyptian Antiquities* 11 (1981), 75–76.

Redford, Donald B. *Egypt, Canaan, and Israel in Ancient Times.* Princeton, 1993.

Yurco, F. "Merenptah's Canaanite Campaign." *Journal of the American Research Center in Egypt* 23 (1986), 189–215.

JAMES K. HOFFMEIER

IVORY is a dense and fine-grained material, ideal for carving in relief or in the round, or for use in thin sheets as inlay or veneer. Ivory can be obtained from the teeth (tusks) of both the elephant and the hippopotamus. The principal substitute for ivory in ancient Egypt was bone, which was widely available and used in many of the same ways. Other types of tusk, such as those of boar or walrus, are not attested from ancient Egypt.

Ivory was used from the earliest periods of Egyptian history; Predynastic (c.4000–3050 BCE) and Early Dynastic (c.3100–c.2686 BCE) sites, such as Hierakonpolis, have yielded some notable finds. Much of this early ivory (although not all) which has been specifically identified is from hippopotamus. These animals must have provided a ready and regular source of tusks when their herds were culled to prevent crop damage. Although some elephant ivory was brought from western Asia, most came from Nubia. Populations of both elephants and hippopotami survived in western Asia into the Late Bronze Age, although both seem to have become extinct by the end of that phase (c.1100 BCE). As ecological factors affected the northerly range of the elephant, ivory increasingly came from the more southerly regions, most probably the African savanna lands between the Nile and the Atbara Rivers. Evidence suggests that elephant ivory use reached its peak in the later eighteenth dynasty, around the reign of Amenhotpe III and documentation is particularly rich at this period (in the Amarna Letters). Ivory was undoubtedly one of the most significant exports of Upper Nubia

IVORY. *Statuette of a gazelle from Thebes, New Kingdom.* As part of an elaborate eighteenth dynasty burial, this statuette served as a symbol for the powers of renewal. (The Metropolitan Museum of Art, Gift of Edward S. Harkness, 1926. [26.7.1292])

in the New Kingdom; however, no documents quantify the trade.

The techniques employed in working ivory were essentially those used in woodworking. Small objects, such as gaming pieces, elements in "cosmetic spoons," furniture (such as the bull legs typical of Early Dynastic graves), and parts of statuettes were all carved in the round from solid pieces of both elephant and hippopotamus ivory. Some large objects of solid elephant ivory have survived, such as the headrest from the tomb of Tutankhamun in the form of the god Shu. Generally, however, tusks seem to have been split into thin panels that were then used as veneer or inlay. Some surviving examples of panels have decoration carved in low relief, with colored staining (principally blue and red). Hippopotamus lower canines were used, in their natural shape, split and stripped of their enamel, as musical clappers or as wands. Hippopotamus incisors, which are straighter, were suited for use as kohl tubes and mirror handles.

IVORY. *Chest decorated with ivory, eighteenth dynasty.* This chest was found in Tutankhamun's tomb and is now in the Egyptian Museum, Cairo. (Scala / Art Resource, NY)

Although examples do survive, there is considerably less ivory from the Third Intermediate, Late, Ptolemaic, and Roman periods. This *may* indicate a decline in ivory working, but it might equally reflect changes in burial practices or the chance of the material's survival. A number of sources of Ptolemaic date indicate that ivory was lavishly used during that period. The Ptolemies acquired their ivory (and live elephants) both from the Kushite kingdom of Meroë and from India.

BIBLIOGRAPHY

Barnett, R. D. *Ancient Ivories in the Middle East.* Qedem, 14. Jerusalem, 1982.

Krzyszkowska, O. H. *Ivory and Related Material: An Illustrated Guide.* Bulletin of the Institute of Classical Studies, Supplement, 59. London, 1990.

Krzyszkowska, O. H., and R. G. Morkot. "Ivory and Related Materials." In *Ancient Egyptian Materials and Technologies,* edited by P. Nicholson and I. Shaw. Cambridge, 1999.

Morkot, R. G. "There are No Elephants in Dongola." *Actes de la VIIIe conference internationale des études Nubiennes, Lille, 11–17. Septembre 1994.* Cahiers de recherches de l'Institut de papyrologie et d'égyptologie de Lille, 17. Lille, 1997.

ROBERT MORKOT

J

JASPER. *See* Gems.

JERUSALEM, most important site of ancient Israel, located close to the western edge of the Judean Desert in the central hill country of Palestine, about 40 kilometers (25 miles) east of the Mediterranean. The town was the center of a Canaanite city-state during the Late Bronze Age, the capital of Israel during the United Monarchy, the capital of the kingdom of Judah during the Divided Monarchy, and the capital of all Israel later on and in the present day. It is situated on a major north–south route through the Judean highlands near the Jordan River. The earliest evidence for its occupation dates to the Late Chalcolithic period, in the mid-fourth millennium BCE.

In Egyptian documents of pharaonic times, Jerusalem is explicitly mentioned only in the Execration Texts of the twelfth and thirteenth dynasties. Jerusalem was first named in the twelfth dynasty Berlin pottery bowl texts (inscriptions e27–28 and f18) from the Middle Kingdom time of Senwosret III and Amenemhet III (1878–1797 BCE). It subsequently was named in the Brussels clay figurine texts (inscription E45) of the early thirteenth dynasty. The toponym used in those documents is *Rushalimum;* two princes are associated with Jerusalem in the earlier group of texts, only one in the later group.

During the New Kingdom, the Egyptian colonial administration in the Levant had little interest in the Judean highlands. Yet Jerusalem was soon one of the few hill-country polities (the other major one being Shechem) to attract serious Egyptian attention. Although Jerusalem is not named in New Kingdom topographical lists, tombs found in the vicinity of the Late Bronze Age town have yielded some Egyptian imports, though in much smaller quantities than were found at sites on the coastal plain and along the main roads. Jerusalem (read as *Urusalim*) is the origin of at least six, and probably seven, cuneiform tablets associated with the New Kingdom diplomatic archive at Amarna (Amarna Letters EA 285–290, probably also EA 291). The letters, whose language and writing indicate that they were written by a scribe of northern (i.e., Syrian) origin, were sent to the king of Egypt by the local ruler, Abdi-Heba. They evidently overlap the end of the eighteenth dynasty reign of Amenhotpe III and the early part of the reign of Amenhotpe IV (Akhenaten). In those documents, the governor of Jerusalem recites a litany of complaints about his current situation, from problems with raiding bands of 'Apiru (for which he seeks help from the Egyptian garrison), to complaints about the activities of Canaanite princes, to a protest that Egypt's Nubian troops (stationed at the Egyptian garrison in Jerusalem) had burglarized the residence of Abdi-Heba. These documents show both the significance of Jerusalem within Egypt's Canaanite domain and the corruption and instability in the region during the mid-fourteenth century BCE.

There is limited evidence for Egyptian activity in the Jerusalem area during the Ramessid era. Biblical references in *Joshua* 15.9 and 18.15 to "the spring of the waters of Nephtoah," located at Lifta near Jerusalem, are sometimes interpreted as originating in the term "the spring of Merenptah" and ultimately in "the wells of Merenptah"—in the hill country—from which, according to Papyrus Anastasi III (*verso* 6.4–5), a military officer arrived in Egypt.

Excavations to the north of the Damascus Gate in East Jerusalem, during the late nineteenth century, uncovered several Egyptian objects, including a fragment of a funerary stela, two calcite (Egyptian alabaster) vessels, and one or two other items possibly of Egyptianized character. An uninscribed serpentine statuette was discovered in the same area in 1975. Gabriel Barkay (1996) has suggested a nineteenth dynasty Egyptian temple outside the Late Bronze Age town as the origin of this material, but the heterogeneous and poorly dated nature of the finds have made it difficult to accept this theory.

From the Bible it is clear that substantial relations existed between Egypt and Israel/Judah during the First Temple period; there can be little doubt that Egypt influenced the development of some aspects of Israelite/Judean culture—including administrative practices and literature—though the extent of such influence has long been a subject of debate. Curiously, Jerusalem is specifically mentioned in connection with Egypt only in the Hebrew scriptures. An unnamed pharaoh is reported in *1 Kings* 9.16 to have destroyed Gezer and given the town as a dowry to his daughter, who was married to Solomon; then Solomon built a special residence for this princess within his Jerusalem palace complex (*1 Kings* 7.8). In the fifth year of King Rehoboam (c.926/925 BCE), "Shishak,

JERUSALEM. *View south from the Wall of Haram.* The Bronze Age city is in the foreground. (Courtesy Donald B. Redford)

king of Egypt, came up against Jerusalem; he took away the treasures of the house of the Lord and the treasures of the king's house" (*1 Kings* 14.25–26; *2 Chron.* 12.2–12). The town is not mentioned in Sheshonq's topographical list at Karnak, evidently because the Egyptian army did not actually enter the town and/or destroy it. The suggestion that the large gold and silver Karnak temple donations made by Sheshonq's son, Osorkon I, came from the Jerusalem Temple is unlikely, considering how few items made of those precious materials are known from Iron Age deposits anywhere in Palestine.

In the art and architecture of first-millennium BCE Jerusalem, there was some indirect Egyptian influence (through Phoenicia). An excellent example is the "Tomb of Pharaoh's Daughter," located in the village of Silwan, on the eastern slope of the Kidron Valley; this tomb probably dates to the second half of the ninth century BCE. The structure, carved out of the natural rock, has an Egyptian-style cornice surmounting its three projecting walls; although the roof is now flat, it originally had a small pyramid. Parallels exist between this tomb and those in the royal cemetery at Salamis in Cyprus. The origin of this architectural style can be traced to Phoenicia but ultimately to Egypt (e.g., the New Kingdom tombs at Deir el-Medina).

Jerusalem came under Ptolemaic Egypt in 301 BCE (according to the Roman-era Jewish historian Josephus, in his *Antiquities of the Jews*, vol. 12, 1–2). Subsequently, the town was captured in 200 BCE by the Seleucids; freed by the Hasmoneans in 164 BCE; conquered by the Roman general Pompey in 63 BCE; then destroyed by a Roman army under Titus in 70 CE. A number of large decorated tombs, constructed during Late Hasmonean and Roman (pre-70 CE) times, have Egyptian-style architectural elements, including pyramids and concave cornices.

[*See also* Israel.]

BIBLIOGRAPHY

Barkay, Gabriel. "A Late Bronze Age Egyptian Temple in Jerusalem?" *Israel Exploration Journal* 46 (1996), 23–43. Presents archaeological evidence for a nineteenth dynasty Egyptian temple in Jerusalem.

Kitchen, Kenneth A. *The Third Intermediate Period in Egypt (1100–650 B.C.).* 2d ed. Warminster, 1986. Offers a detailed analysis of the Sheshonq topographical list.

Mazar, Benjamin, Yigal Shiloh, Hillel Geva, Nahman Avigad, Michael Avi-Yonah, Meir Ben-Dor, Dan Bahat, and Myriam Rosen-Avalon. "Jerusalem." In *The New Encyclopedia of Archaeological Excavations in the Holy Land*, edited by Ephraim Stern, vol. 2, pp. 698–804. New York, 1993. A review of the archaeology of Jerusalem.

Moran, William L. "The Syrian Scribe of the Jerusalem Amarna Letters." In *Unity and Diversity: Essays in the History, Literature, and Religion of the Ancient Near East*, edited by Hans Goedicke and J. J. M. Roberts, pp. 146–166. Baltimore, 1975.

Moran, William L. *The Amarna Letters.* Baltimore, 1992. Letters 285–291 (pp. 325–334) are from Jerusalem.

Rendsburg, Gary. "Merneptah in Canaan." *Journal of the Society for the Study of Egyptian Antiquities* 11 (1981), 171–172. Links the biblical reference to "the waters of Nephtoah" with "the wells of Merneptah," as mentioned in Papyrus Anastasi III.

Ussishkin, David. *The Village of Silwan: The Necropolis from the Period of the Judean Kingdom.* Jerusalem, 1993. Pages 43–62 describe the "Tomb of Pharaoh's Daughter."

Wimmer, Stefan. "Egyptian Temples in Canaan and Sinai." In *Studies in Egyptology Presented to Miriam Lichtheim*, edited by Sarah Israelit-Groll, vol. 2, pp. 1065–1106. Jerusalem, 1990. Disputes (p. 1073) the evidence for a Late Bronze Age Egyptian temple in Jerusalem.

JAMES M. WEINSTEIN

JEWELRY. Items of personal adornment from the Nile Valley are an important part of the history of jewelry. More than mere body ornament, jewelry in ancient Egypt was used to display rank, proclaim wealth, and designate social status. It was also fashioned into powerful amulets, objects of barter and trade, accouterments of daily attire, diplomatic gifts, military honors, and propagandistic tools. The Egyptologist Walter B. Emery once commented that the Egyptians "were greatly addicted to the wearing of jewelry." No doubt his observation was based on archaeological evidence demonstrating that jewelry was worn by the living as well as the dead, by mortals as well as by representations of the gods, and by men as well as by women and children. Since precious metals are eminently recyclable, the body of material from ancient Egypt that has survived probably represents only a fraction of the jewelry produced. This situation is compounded by a long history of tomb robbery. In addition, jewels obtained surreptitiously were often disassembled, the precious stones unmounted, and the metal melted down by a profitable underground network of thieves, craftsmen, and officials.

Our understanding of Egyptian jewelry comes from a variety sources. Most valuable are ornaments recovered during controlled excavations. For example, a Predynastic (Naqada II) diadem from Abydos, now in the British Museum, was discovered in a burial attached to the head of a woman. Composed of gold, garnet, turquoise, and malachite beads, the circlet represents one of the few beaded ornaments where the original pattern of the beadwork was recorded. As a result, the form, method of construction, and use of what would otherwise be a handful of beads are known. Additionally, the archaeological record provides information concerning the sex and social circumstances of the owner. Such knowledge, crucial if we are to determine the role and meaning of jewelry in society, is sadly lacking for most ornaments. Another important resource for the jewelry historian exists in the detailed recording of jewelry and jewelry-making in sculpture, paintings, and reliefs. In fact, some ornaments, such as the heart-shaped *dmḏ*-pendant worn by Old Kingdom officials and Middle Kingdom kings, are known exclusively from representations. The more common situation, however, is an inability to match a known jewel with an ancient image. This is even the case for entire classes of ornament—for example, Tutankhamun was buried with numerous finger rings and ear ornaments, yet the young king is never depicted wearing either form of jewelry.

Texts also supply essential insights into the materials, forms, manufacture, and purposes of jewelry. An interesting jewelry-related vignette occurs in the Westcar Papyrus, which tells the story of a boat trip designed for the amusement of King Sneferu. The rowers, twenty young ladies from the harem, wear fish amulets of turquoise in their hair. With the exertion of rowing, one fish is lost in the lake and all action stops while the waters are magically parted and the amulet retrieved. Although Sneferu ruled during the Old Kingdom, the text dates to the Middle Kingdom. Fish amulets, believed to protect the wearer from drowning, were found in burials contemporaneous with the text. The text, in this case, is in agreement with the archaeological and art historical findings.

Materials and Techniques. A wide range of materials was available to the ancient jeweler, and those selected were chosen for aesthetic, practical, and symbolic reasons. Symbolism was particularly significant, since the bulk of jewelry worn in ancient Egypt served amuletic ends. Gold, considered "the flesh of the gods," was valued for its inherent properties of sunlike brilliance, malleability, and resistance to corrosion. Egypt had both alluvial and quartz-vein deposits of this precious metal, which was eagerly sought by all strata of society. Silver had to be imported from the Near East and the Aegean. A manifestation of "the bones of the gods," silver symbolized the moon and lotus blossom, a flower that defeats darkness and death as it opens under the warming rays of the morning sun.

While casting was a known metalworking technique in ancient Egypt, ornaments of precious metal were more likely to be fabricated from hammered sheet metal, which was cut, shaped, and joined through crimping or soldering. Wirework was primarily accomplished through strip-twisting, as the draw-plate was not available until the Roman period. Handwrought wires were used for securing beads and amulets, chain-making (for example, the loop-in-loop chain), as well as decorating metal surfaces. For jewelry designed exclusively for burial, the metal was often quite thin, as the jewels of the deceased were not subjected to the wear of daily life. Gilding, an inexpensive means of achieving the look of solid gold, was also used to enhance less costly materials such as wood, steatite, and faience.

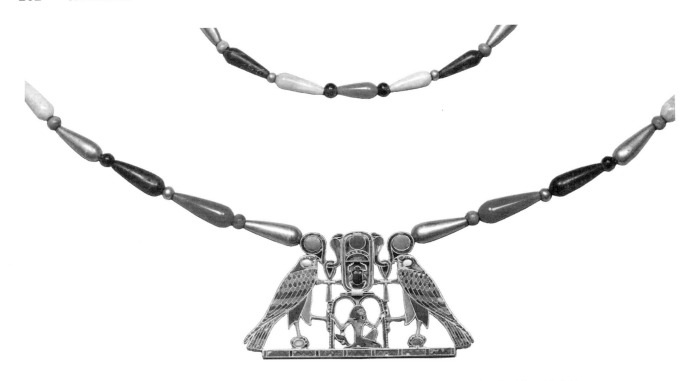

JEWELRY. *Pectoral of the twelfth dynasty princess Sithathoriunet.* It is made of gold and inlaid with amethyst, turquoise, feldspar, carnelian, lapis lazuli, and garnet. In the center of the design is the name of the princess's father, Senwosret II. The whole composition is a rebus that can be read as "The Sun God gives hundreds of thousands of years of life to Senwosret II." (The Metropolitan Museum of Art, Purchase, Rogers Fund and Henry Walters Gift, 1916. [16.1.3])

The stones most prized for jewelry were those nowadays classified as "semiprecious." They included carnelian, green feldspar or amazonite, turquoise, and lapis lazuli. Carnelian and amazonite were obtained locally while turquoise and lapis lazuli were imported from the Sinai and Afghanistan. Other stones—malachite, calcite, banded agate, porphyry, olivine, fluospar, rock crystal, obsidian, hematite, jasper (red and green), and serpentine—were used less frequently. Changing tastes and availability may have influenced the use of some stones—for example, amethyst was thought to be "fashionable" during the Middle Kingdom, while peridot and emerald, obtained from the Red Sea area, were not incorporated into jewelry until the Ptolemaic period. Most stones, however, were selected for their hardness, rarity, and color. In antiquity, color was synonymous with essence—the red-orange of carnelian symbolized power and dynamism; the green of amazonite and turquoise represented regenerative growth; and the brilliant blue of lapis lazuli was associated with the heavens and the life-giving Nile. By the Old Kingdom, a tricolor scheme of red, blue/green, and deep blue had been established for royal and courtly jewels—a color arrangement that eventually became the standard for all mixed-material constructions. In Nubia, Egypt's neighbor to the south, the color palette varied—demonstrating the cultural specificity of certain substances.

The semiprecious, hard stones were used to make a variety of ornaments, including beads, amulets, and pendants. These forms constitute the most popular items of adornment throughout the ancient world. The same stones were also extensively employed as inlay material. Those who could not afford the hard, colored stones for jewelry used steatite (soapstone), a readily available soft stone that was easy to carve and that could be made harder through heating. Hardness was more than a practical matter, as the Egyptians equated this property with endurance and longevity. In addition, firing in a kiln provided the opportunity to alter the neutral color of steatite through the application of glazes in the blue-green and black color range. Although glazed steatite was widely used for beads and amulets, it was rarely employed for inlaying.

Organic substances were utilized for objects of adornment from the earliest of times. Flowers, seeds, shells, resin, and plant fibers were easily manipulated and accessible to all members of society. Patterned shells from the Mediterranean and Red Sea were bartered and can be found in burials far from their source. Cowrie shells, believed to possess amuletic powers, were popular throughout Egyptian history. Pierced and strung as girdles, they were worn by young women to protect and enhance their reproductive capabilities. Facsimiles were even made in precious metal, a practice illustrating the Egyptian penchant for mimicking one material with another. Ivory, obtained from the tusks of the elephant and hippopotamus, was valued for its rarity, symbolism, and visual appeal. A relatively soft material, this animal product was carved into hairpins, finger rings, bangles, cuffs, ear ornaments, amulets, and beads. It was also used as an inlay material and could be dyed a variety of colors. Pearls were not known in Egypt until the Ptolemaic period, although the nacre lining (mother-of-pearl) of the Red Sea oyster was exploited for bangles, rings, ear ornaments, and beads. Rectangular nacre plaques, pierced at the long ends and woven flat in vertical rows, were worn on both arms in sets of three by men of the Nubian Pan-Grave culture; these men were reputed to be skilled archers and resided in Egypt where they were enlisted as mercenaries. This form of ornament and its pattern of use is diagnostic of the culture, demonstrating the role of jewelry in identifying groups of people.

Probably the most commonly used material for jewelry was faience—a non-clay, quartz-based, glazed ceramic that could be modeled by hand or shaped in a mold. When first made, the faience surface gleamed, an attribute reflected in its ancient Egyptian name *ṯḥnt*, meaning "that which dazzles." One of the advantages of faience derives from the range of colors available to the craftsman, whose technical skill increased dramatically during the New Kingdom. For a long time, faience was regarded as an inexpensive, substitute material. New scholarship suggests that the Egyptians believed faience possessed magical properties, based on the dramatic transformation—from dull, white paste to a glimmering substance—that takes place during heating.

Soon after glassmaking was established in Egypt during the New Kingdom, it found application in jewelry production. Like faience, it could be set in molds to produce objects in the round or cut for use as an inlay material. Probably the most famous glass inlays are the brilliant, blue strips of glass incorporated into the *nms* headdress of Tutankhamun's mask. Some glass and stone inlays were employed simultaneously, as in the belt buckle of Queen Nofretari, which demonstrates the primacy of color in material selection. Although the basic constituents of faience and glass are similar (silica-lime-alkali), glass has fewer impurities and requires higher firing temperatures. To fabricate beads—the most ubiquitous of glass ornaments—colored glass rods (about 0.5 centimeter in diameter) were heated over an open furnace and wrapped around a metal rod. One particular bead, the stratified "eye" bead, was developed in Egypt during the reign of Thutmose III. It proved so popular with Egypt's neighbors that both the form and technique were extensively copied. The talismanic blue "eye" bead produced in the Middle East today has its origins in ancient Egypt.

Enameling, the fusion of powdered glass through heating onto a metal surface, derives from the Egyptian predilection for colored surfaces and experience with glassmaking. In many respects, enameling imitates stone-inlaying in that the objective—broad zones of uniform color—can be achieved through either method. Though technically more sophisticated, enameling would have eliminated the need for costly stone imports such as lapis lazuli. In addition, enamels can be set in small and curved areas difficult to fit with cut stones. The final product is also far more refined and delicate.

The earliest known example of enameling in the Nile Valley dates to the twenty-first dynasty. It exists in the form of a circular medallion with stylized palmettes set in the center of a gold bowl. The bowl was recovered from the tomb of General Wendjebauendjed in the 1920s but has only recently been highlighted as one of the earliest examples of the enameler's art. The fact that no jewelry with enamels was found among the royal treasures from Tanis does not establish the medallion as an isolated example—rather, it only emphasizes the incompleteness of the plundered finds and our lack of knowledge of the period. There is, however, ample evidence of an extensive enameling industry during the Ptolemaic period. Enameling appears to be the preferred method of applying color to metal surfaces during that time.

The Craftsmen. To judge by the titles and material resources afforded the various specialties, there was a clear division between the "fine" and "applied" arts in ancient Egypt. The most esteemed artists were sculptors and architects. Of lesser influence were skilled painters, followed by outline draftsmen. At the opposite end in rank and status were craftsmen who created objects of daily life, and, although many items in this category demonstrate extraordinary craftsmanship and aesthetic sensibility, their makers failed to achieve the recognition reserved for large-scale work. The jewelers of dynastic Egypt are known to us from relief, paintings, and stelae. Private tomb decorations are especially valuable in that they illustrate groups of artisans busy at work in spaces that feature workbenches, simple furniture, and tools. A typical vignette occurs in the Saqqara tomb of the sixth dynasty vizier Mereruka. Depicted are jewelry specialists, including weighers, melters, goldworkers, and bead stringers. Finished ornaments, such as a *wsḥ*-collar with falcon ter-

JEWELRY. *Detail of a courtwoman's gold headdress, originally inlaid with carnelian and glass.* It is made of almost nine hundred gold rosettes. It is from Thebes, and dates from the eighteenth dynasty, during the reign of Thutmose III. (The Metropolitan Museum of Art. Purchased with Funds given by Henry Walters and Edward S. Harkness, 1926. [26.8.117])

minals, a diadem with streamers, and a beaded choker are incorporated into the scene. Interestingly, several dwarfs form part of the work crew. Dwarfs are almost always represented in Old Kingdom scenes of jewelry-making, possibly because of their association with Ptah (patron of artisans).

From the New Kingdom, there are several surviving scenes of jewelry production in the tombs of high officials, whose duties included the supervision of temple craftsmen. Probably the most famous occurs in the Theban tomb of Rekhmire (tomb 100), an early eighteenth dynasty vizier of Thutmose III. Rekhmire routinely conducted inspections of Amun temple workshops where the arts of metalcraft and jewelry fabrication proceeded at a rapid pace. Men trained in smithing and bead-drilling, and stringers worked in assembly-line fashion, although

the most skilled of the fabricators undoubtedly practiced their trade in a more relaxed environment. The names and titles of individuals involved in jewelry-making are known from funerary stelae such as the limestone stela of Ahmose, an eighteenth dynasty metalsmith designated "Chief of Metalworkers." The trades in Egypt were hereditary and it is possible that Ahmose's son Meny, who is shown standing to the right of his seated parents, was similarly employed.

The Forms. Although ancient Egyptian jewelry is admired for its aesthetic appeal and craftsmanship, it is the striking and exceptional nature of its iconography that sets it apart from the ornaments of other cultures. Egypt was one of the few societies in world history that did not establish sumptuary laws limiting the use of certain materials to elites. There was an early attempt to restrict powerful motifs, such as the bee and falcon, to the ruling class, but with the passage of time and the democratization of the afterlife as experienced during the First and Second Intermediate Periods, these restrictions were lifted. While jewelry fulfills what has been described as a basic human urge to decorate the body, it also promotes other ends. It is not surprising that in a culture generally characterized as a theocracy, the religious, amuletic role of ornament frequently dominated. During prehistoric times, when beads, amulets, hairpins, and bangles constituted the greater corpus of jewelry, the materials and forms were chosen with the object of protecting the wearer. It is no coincidence that most Egyptian jewelry was designed to encircle, and therefore magically protect, various parts of the body. The head, neck, arms, wrists, fingers, waist, and ankles were all designated as areas in need of safeguarding.

By the end of the Old Kingdom, the basic forms and styles of Egyptian jewelry were well established, although "fads," many in response to foreign influences and new technologies, can be detected in all periods. Probably the most enduring item of jewelry was the beaded broad-collar, a neck ornament worn by both sexes and by a range of anthropomorphic deities. These beaded collars offset the standard Egyptian dress, which consisted of a near-white kilt for men and a plain, colorless linen sheath for women. In a study of Old Kingdom beaded collars that examined both excavated examples and representations of collars in sculpture and relief, Ed Brovarski determined there were two basic types: the *wsḫ*-collar ("the broad one"), which consists of multiple rows of densely spaced tubular beads strung in an upright position, and the *šnw*-collar ("that which encircles"), composed of trapezoidal segments of tubular beads alternately arranged in vertical and horizontal rows. The *wsḫ*-collar was further distinguished by a bottom row of drop pendants, whose shape derives from a long-bodied beetle, an insect believed to possess the power of everlasting life. The two forms of the beaded collar have several characteristics in common that can be applied to Egyptian ornament in general. First, they illustrate a preference for symmetry in that the right half of each collar is a mirror image of the left. This symmetry was expanded to include matched pairs of wristlets, armlets, and anklets. Like the collars, they were usually fabricated from beads woven with linen (flax) threads. Another shared feature is that of graduation, wherein the largest beads were situated in the center with the remainder tapering toward the ends. Both have terminals (end-pieces) that serve to gather the multiple strands of thread into one twist or braid for tying around the neck. Both also have counter-poises, which hang down the back of the neck and were designed to relieve some of the collar's weight.

During the Old Kingdom, another hallmark of Egyptian jewelry was developed—namely, the incorporation of text into the design and fabric of a jewel. The writing of names was particularly important in that the act of setting one's name in a lasting, magical material insured the wearer against decay and destruction. Although nonroyal names and titles, as illustrated in the inscribed terminals of the sixth dynasty architect Impy, are known to exist, most ornaments with text feature divine or royal names. For the ordinary person, a jewel with the name of a deity or king guaranteed the wearer's protection by potent forces. The thousands of finger-ring bezels inscribed with the names of Akhenaten, Nefertiti, and Tutankhamun found in the ruins at Amarna testify to the popularity of such items. Inscriptions could also draw on a rich system of symbols and emblems imbued with special properties. In this category fall such magical signs as the *'nḫ* ("life"), *ḫprr* beetle ("to exist"), *šn* ("protect"), *wḏȝt* ("sacred eye"), and *ḏd* pillars ("stability").

Although the beaded collar remained a staple of Egyptian jewelry, the form evolved so that by the New Kingdom, it included openwork designs composed of signs, amulets, and floral elements made of brightly colored faience. Collars were sometimes worn with a pectoral, a trapezoidal pendant suspended from a necklace of beads. Although representations of the ornament date to the Old Kingdom, the earliest surviving examples were found in the Middle Kingdom burials of the princesses Sithathoriunet (at Illahun) and Sithathor and Mereret (at Dahshur). These jewels, as well as other treasures recovered from the princesses' tombs, represent some of finest ornaments ever crafted in Egypt. Each is fabricated from gold sheet with carnelian, turquoise, and lapis lazuli inlays set in cloisons. The metalwork is "open," with sections of metal worked separately and later assembled and soldered so that negative spaces fill the void between the hieroglyphs and symbols. The back of each jewel has delicately chased linework reiterating the patterns colorfully detailed on the front. The burial of Tutankhamun contained twenty-six pectorals found on the mummy and in several elaborate containers; these are bolder in design and, from signs of wear and ancient repairs, several were worn in life.

Ear ornaments do not appear with any regularity in Egypt until the end of the Second Intermediate Period, although they were worn in Mesopotamia and Nubia much earlier. By the New Kingdom, several forms of the earring were in vogue, including the hoop, the pennanular ring, the stud, and the plug. They were worn by both sexes, although women are more frequently shown wearing them. For some reason, kings were not depicted wearing this form of adornment, although sizable ear lobe perforations have been identified on several royal mummies. There is also an absence of representations of the finger

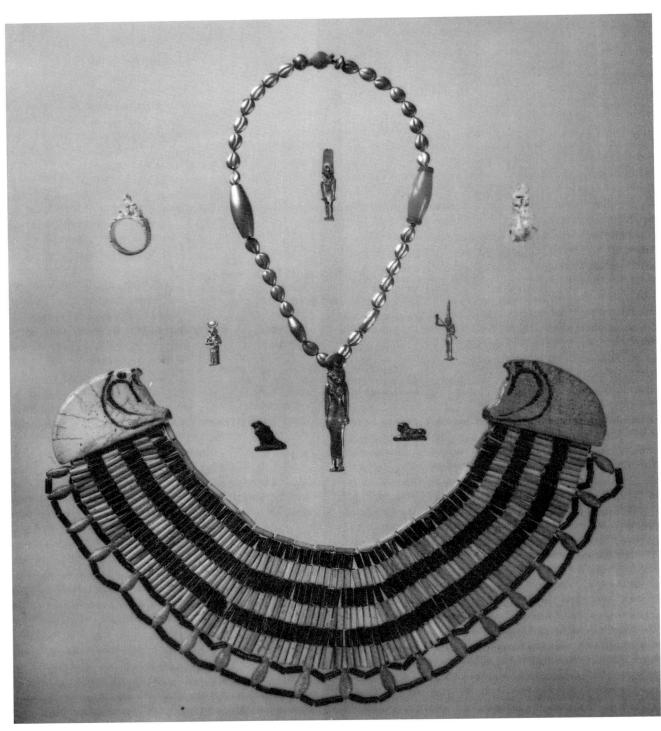

JEWELRY. *Assorted Egyptian jewelry.* At top are gold and chalcedony beads with a gold amulet of the feline goddess Sekhmet, from the twenty-fourth dynasty. At the bottom is a twelfth dynasty faience collar. (University of Pennsylvania Museum, Philadelphia. Neg. # S8–41465)

ring, a jewelry item that came into fashion during the Middle Kingdom. The earliest rings appear to be plain wires, worn on several fingers of each hand. The scarab was eventually threaded onto the wire, forming a central bezel that could be enhanced by a decorative metal surround or collet. By the New Kingdom, rings for elites were elaborate constructions with bezels occasionally incorporating miniature sculptures of horses, divinities, and sacred animals. Less ornamental and more affordable was the stirrup signet ring. Typically cast in multipart molds, the signet evolved from the rigid (nonswivel) scarab ring, whose base was inscribed with signs and/or symbols. Signets were made in faience, as well as in gold, silver, and bronze. Like scarabs, many were commemorative and may have been distributed during festivals or in celebration of the king's accession. New faience formulas developed during the late eighteenth dynasty, which resulted in a more durable faience body, made the wearing of these rings possible. Faience continued to be used for rings throughout the Third Intermediate Period, when the ring style changed to a wide, openwork band.

Egyptians frequently wore jewelry on their wrists, arms, and ankles. Less formal arrangements consisted of strings of beads and amulets, while more traditional decorations were part of coordinated parures, composed of a beaded collar (with counterpoise), wristlets, armlets, and anklets. Wrist ornaments show the greatest variety of forms, with bangles, cuffs and tight-fitting, multistrand, beaded jewels popular during most periods. A distinguishing element that could be added to the latter was the ornamental clasp. Clasps were often made of sheet metal and inlaid with semiprecious stones. Like pectorals, the designs for clasps encompassed hieroglyphic signs, symbols, and emblems. They could also incorporate three-dimensional elements, as in the bracelet clasp (now in The Metropolitan Museum of Art, MMA 26.8.121) belonging to one of Thutmose III's wives; the mini-sculptures in this example are reclining cats of gold and carnelian.

Like most jewelry in ancient Egypt, armlets were worn by both sexes but with less frequency than wrist ornaments. The reason for this may partly reside with practical problems posed by body movement and gravity. To compensate for their weight, armlets need to fit firmly on the upper arm to prevent slipping. A solution to the problem is evident on the highly embellished armlet of Queen Aahhotep of the early eighteenth dynasty (in the Cairo Museum, CG 52642). While the front of this jewel is massive—a hollow box in the shape of a cartouche flanked by two three-dimensional sphinxes—the back of the encircling gold band contains a metal tab, several inches long, designed to secure the armlet in place. With regard to anklets, there appears to be less variety, although one

form—the anklet with claws—protected female wearers against scorpion bites.

The jewelry that has survived from Egypt derives from burials and is therefore funerary in nature. From representations and texts, however, we know that many items that adorned the deceased and were stored in containers in the tomb were also worn in life. Many jewels show signs of wear and repair. Other ornaments, however, were designed exclusively for burial; in this category are decorations so flimsy in construction as to rule out wear, as well as ornaments whose primary function was to protect the wearer during the perilous journey into the next world. Included in this group are barrel-shaped *swrt*-beads that were strung and worn around the neck of the mummy, falcon-headed terminals on broadcollars, and collars—frequently of chased gold sheet—with images of the vulture and cobra goddesses. Some jewels, such as the Gold of Honor necklace and gold 'w'w-bracelet, were prized awards and signs of office—ornaments proudly worn in life and death.

[*See also* Faience; Gold; *and* Silver.]

BIBLIOGRAPHY

Aldred, Cyril. *Jewels of the Pharaohs*. London, 1971.
Andrews, Carol. *Catalogue of Egyptian Antiquities in the British Museum*, vol 6: *Jewellery I*. London, 1981.
Andrews, Carol. *Ancient Egyptian Jewellery*. London, 1990.
Andrews, Carol. *Amulets of Ancient Egypt*. Austin, 1994.
Lucas, A., and J. Harris. *Ancient Egyptian Materials and Industries*. London, 1989.
Ogden, Jack. *Jewellery of the Ancient World*. London, 1982.
Romano, James F. "Jewelry and Personal Arts in Ancient Egypt." In *Civilizations of the Ancient Near East*, edited by Jack Sasson. New York, 1995.
Scheel, Bernd. *Egyptian Metalworking and Tools*. Aylesbury, Bucks, 1989.
Stierlin, Henri. *L'or des pharaons*. Paris, 1993.
Vilimkova, Milada. *Egyptian Jewellery*. London, 1969.
Wilkinson, Alix. *Ancient Egyptian Jewellery*. London, 1971.

YVONNE J. MARKOWITZ

JOPPA (Eg., *Ypw*, Akk., *Yapu*), biblical-era site identified with the city of Jaffa, today an Israeli seaport and joint city with Tel Aviv. On a hill overlooking the Mediterranean Sea, Joppa became an important ancient city because it utilized one of the few natural harbors along the eastern Mediterranean. From 1955 to 1974, Jacob Kaplan conducted a series of excavations there, on behalf of the Museum of Antiquities of Tel Aviv–Jaffa. The earliest evidence for settlement that he found was a rampart in Area C that was dated to the early second millennium BCE (either the Middle Bronze IIA or IIB period). Although Joppa probably had direct maritime contacts with Egypt during the Middle Bronze Age, too small an area of the site from that period was excavated to yield such evidence.

Joppa is not named in any Egyptian texts of the early second millennium BCE. Joppa first appears in Egyptian written sources in the fifteenth century BCE, as entry number 62 in Thutmose III's topographical list in the temple of Amun-Re at Karnak; the list chronicles the places the king claims to have captured during his first Near Eastern campaign. That Joppa's listing probably reflected a real historical event is indicated by Joppa's attestation in a popular story that was included in the nineteenth dynasty Papyrus Harris 500 (now in the British Museum). The hero of that New Kingdom story, Djehuty, captured Joppa for Thutmose III through a ruse, involving the hiding of two hundred soldiers in baskets carried into the city. A gold bowl in the Musée du Louvre in Paris—inscribed with the name Djehuty and the titles, among others, of "Overseer of Foreign Countries" and "Overseer of the Army"—probably belonged to that same individual (though at least one scholar has questioned the authenticity of the bowl).

By the fourteenth century BCE, Joppa had become a major Egyptian military and administrative center in Canaan. It was mentioned in two cuneiform tablets from the diplomatic archives found at Amarna (Amarna Letters EA 294 and 296); these texts indicate that Joppa had an Egyptian stronghold as well as granaries, and EA 296 refers to a local official, Yaḫtiru, who guarded the city gates of Gaza and Joppa. The one Egyptian object of the period found at Joppa is a fragmentary scarab of Tiye, the principal queen of Amenhotpe III; it came from a later context, however, a building (possibly a temple) in Area A that has been attributed to the late thirteenth or early twelfth century BCE.

Joppa's importance to the Egyptian administration of Canaan continued during the thirteenth century BCE. Papyrus Anastasi I, from the second half of the nineteenth dynasty, contains a satirical letter that recounts the adventures of an Egyptian official in Joppa, which is described as having an armory and workshops. Kaplan's excavation of a Late Bronze IIB gate in Area A, Level IV-B, yielded four sandstone doorjamb fragments inscribed with the titles and part of the name of Ramesses II; no wall was found in association with the gate, leading some scholars to conclude that the gate's principal function was ceremonial rather than military. A cuneiform tablet found at Aphek, a large Bronze Age tell near the source of the Yarkon River, contains a letter (dating late in the reign of Ramesses II) from the governor of the Syrian coastal town of Ugarit, Takuḫlinu, to an important Egyptian official, Ḥaya; its principal topic was a transaction involving the purchase of wheat at Joppa for Ugarit.

Joppa remained an important port town throughout the Iron Age and later. Through Joppa came the Lebanese timber for the construction of the First Temple in Jerusalem, as well as for the rebuilding after the Jews returned from the Exile in Babylonia (*2 Chron.* 2.15–16; *Ezra* 3.7). At the end of the eighth century BCE, the Assyrian king Sennacherib conquered Joppa. In the Persian period, Joppa was occupied first by the Persians and then by the Sidonians. For this long period, no textual or archaeological evidence for the nature of Egyptian relations is known. Reference to Joppa in Egyptian texts then occurs in the Zenon Papyri, a large hoard of documents of the mid-third century BCE that were discovered in 1915 at the site of ancient Philadelphia, at the northeastern edge of the Faiyum. Zenon, a Greek from Asia Minor who served as estate manager for Apollonios, the finance minister of Ptolemy II, visited Joppa in 259–258 BCE; among the contents of the papyri is his information on various Levantine places, including Joppa.

[*See also* Canaan; Israel; *and* Taking of Joppa.]

BIBLIOGRAPHY

Dessel, J. P. "Jaffa." In *The Oxford Encyclopedia of Archaeology in the Near East*, edited by Eric Meyers, vol. 3, pp. 206–207. New York, 199. Good recent survey.

Kaplan, Jacob. "The Archaeology and History of Tel Aviv–Jaffa." *Biblical Archaeologist* 35.3 (1972), 66–95. Useful, though somewhat dated, survey.

Kaplan, Jacob. "Jaffa." In *The New Encyclopedia of Archaeological Excavations in the Holy Land*, edited by Ephraim Stern, vol. 2, pp. 655–659. New York, 1993. Summary account of the archaeology of Jaffa (largely a repeat of Kaplan and Kaplan [1992]).

Kaplan, Jacob, and Haya Ritter Kaplan. "Joppa." In *The Anchor Bible Dictionary*, edited by David Noel Freedman, vol. 3, pp. 946–949. New York, 1992. Recent summary of the archaeology of Jaffa, focusing on the authors' own excavations.

Lilyquist, Christine. "The Gold Bowl Naming General Djehuty: A Study of Objects and Early Egyptology." *Metropolitan Museum Journal* 2 (1988), 5–68. Detailed study of the gold bowl of Djehuty in the Louvre; concludes that the item is probably a forgery.

Owen, David I. "An Akkadian Letter from Ugarit at Tel Aphek." *Tel Aviv* 8 (1981), 1–17. Publication of the cuneiform tablet found at Aphek that mentions Joppa.

Singer, Itamar. "Takuḫlinu and Ḥaya; Two Governors in the Ugarit Letter from Tel Aphek." *Tel Aviv* 10 (1983), 3–25. Studies the careers of the two high officials named on the Aphek tablet.

JAMES M. WEINSTEIN

JOSEPH is the personal name of the biblical patriarch and it is also the designation for an ethnic enclave in the central hill country of Palestine ("the House of Joseph"). The etymology of the name is uncertain, although it may have been formulated during the Bronze Age. The Patriarch Joseph is known solely by the novella comprising chapters thirty-seven through fifty of the *Book of Genesis* (and in later intertestamental literature). In this story, Joseph, a younger son of Jacob who was sold into slavery in

Egypt, rose to high office owing to his prediction of a famine and his suggestions for ameliorating its effects. Much of the story's narrative centered upon Joseph's relations with his older brothers, who were first jealous of their father's favorite son, and who were later repentent before one whom they had mistaken for a hard ruler. The Joseph story, as positioned in the Pentateuch (the first five books of Hebrew scripture), acts as a bridge between the Patriarchal traditions (the stories of Abraham, Isaac, and Jacob) and the theme of the Egyptian bondage of the Israelites; but it enjoys the literary integrity of an independent narrative.

Scholarly research has focused on the extent to which the narrative can be treated as historical and the ancient Egyptian portrayal of incidental details. Judgments on the historicity of the Joseph story have ranged from conservative viewpoints to the denial that the story is anything beyond a folktale. (A "Joseph" was, in fact, never mentioned as a vizier or any other high-ranking dignitary in any Egyptian source of any period.) The conservative approach to interpretation has produced reconstructions of the Joseph story that more or less follow biblical chronology. The conventional account placed Joseph and the descents of Jacob to Egypt between about 1900 and 1600 BCE. Scholars who championed this expansive date claimed corroboration through the fact that the Hyksos, who held power in Egypt from about 1665 to 1555 BCE, would presumably have looked with favor on a fellow countryman, thus explaining Joseph's easy rise to authority. (This analysis ignored the clear statement in the narrative that Joseph, a Hebrew, found himself in a court of Egyptians, and that he won status because of his God-given wisdom.) Scholars who attempted to place Joseph in the New Kingdom linked him to the eighteenth dynasty, thus forfeiting a literal acceptance of biblical chronology. These arguments are largely inferential, if not eisegetical.

Any historical assessment of the Joseph story must begin with an empirical examination of the story as seen against its background detail. The unknown author of the *Genesis* account of Joseph has shown himself to be familiar with aspects of the later Judean monarchy. When he described the Egypt in which his story was set, he used Egyptian personal names that were popular from the first millennium BCE to the Ptolemaic period; referred to camels and Ishmaelites, known from the same period, but not common before; employed terms for government officers current in the fifth century BCE; introduced such anachronisms as money, "the Land of the Hebrews," "Goshen" (both of late formulation), the zodiac, and priests' salaries from Pharaoh; and cast Joseph's reforms (ch. 47) in an etiology of the contemporary Egyptian state and economy. The plot pattern around which the whole story was built, namely, the "rags-to-riches" theme, was very popular in folklore—both in Egypt and abroad during the last half of the first millennium BCE.

While there is no evidence for or against a historical Joseph, the unknown author of the Joseph story set his account against the backdrop of the period with which he was most familiar, the fifth to sixth centuries BCE, and is in possession of no earlier source material.

[*See also* Biblical Tradition.]

BIBLIOGRAPHY

Coats, G. W. *From Canaan to Egypt: Structural and Theological Context for the Joseph Story.* Washington, 1976.

Redford, Donald B. *A Study of the Biblical Story of Joseph (Genesis 37–50).* Leiden, 1970.

Schweizer, H. *Die Josefsgeschichte.* Tübingen, 1991.

Vergote, J. *Joseph en Égypte: Génèse Chap. 37–50 à la lumière des études égyptologique récentes.* Louvain, 1959.

Westermann, C. *Genesis, 37–50,* vol. 3. Neukirchen-Vluyn, 1982.

DONALD B. REDFORD

JOURNALS. Egyptological journals—periodical publications containing scholarly articles, notes, and reviews—have been an essential component in the development of Egyptology as a discipline; they have allowed scholars to present their research to colleagues in a timely fashion before monographic publication. Although Egyptologists often publish their work in more general scholarly journals relating to the ancient Near East, specialized Egyptological journals have been (and continue to be) their venue of choice. Although often closely identified with their place of origin, Egyptological journals are generally international, attracting contributors from throughout the scholarly community. Increasingly, specialist journals have come to play an important role in the professional development and advancement of Egyptologists, while nonspecialist journals in Egyptology heighten the profile of the discipline.

In the earliest years of Egyptology, scholars disseminated their findings primarily through monographic publication (often in the form of published "letters" to eminent scholars of the day) or through articles in journals addressed to a more general academic audience. It was not until the mid-nineteenth century that specialist journals began to appear; the earliest major Egyptological journal was *Zeitschrift für Aegyptische Sprache und Altertumskunde,* founded by Heinrich Brugsch in 1863 and edited for much of its earliest phase by Richard Lepsius. Other Egyptological journals followed in subsequent decades, most notably the French *Revue égyptologique,* founded by Eugène Revillout, and *Recueil de travaux relatifs à la philologie et à l'archéologie égyptiennes et assyriennes,* founded by Gaston Maspero. Much English-language work in Egyptology, beginning in the second half of the nineteenth century, was published in the *Proceedings of the Society of Biblical Archaeology*. The turn of the twentieth century saw the beginning of a number of important Egyptological journals, many of which are still published. In Egypt, the Service des Antiquités and the Institut Français d'Archéologie Orientale initiated publication of, respectively, the *Annales* and the *Bulletin*, both of which have remained important venues for Egyptological publication. The Italian journal *Aegyptus* also first appeared in the early part of the century; although emphasizing papyrology, *Aegyptus* also published articles relevant to earlier periods of study. In 1914, two major journals were founded in England: the *Journal of Egyptian Archaeology* and *Ancient Egypt*. The former is the official organ of the Egypt Exploration Society and one of the most important Egyptological journals; the latter did not survive its founder, W. M. Flinders Petrie. These two journals illustrate opposing trends in Egyptological journals in general—the journal as official publication of a learned society versus the journal as platform for its founder and primary contributor. American Egyptology saw the publication of the relatively short-lived *Mizraim*, a journal devoted to Egyptology, papyrology, and ancient law, with Nathaniel Reich as editor and primary contributor. The Belgian Fondation Égyptologique Reine Élisabeth began publishing *Chronique d'Égypte* before World War II as a forum for scholarship in pharaonic, Greco-Roman, and Christian Egypt, a function it still fills. The French journal *Revue de l'Égypte ancienne* lasted for only one year (1932), but it gave rise to the more durable *Revue d'égyptologie*, which remains one of the most important Egyptological journals today.

World War II had an enormous impact on Egyptological journals, both in terms of restrictions on output and in terms of the divided loyalties of an international community of scholars. Most journals experienced limitations in size and frequency, and some suspended publication altogether during the war. The postwar period has seen an enormous increase in journals devoted, entirely or in part, to ancient Egypt, as well as the resurgence of existing journals. Thus, the postwar *Studien zur altägyptischen Kultur* is a major venue for scholarly publication, while the Cairo-based *Mitteilungen des Deutschen Archäologischen Instituts* became especially important for Egyptian archaeology. In North America, where Egyptological articles had previously tended to appear in more general ancient Near East–related journals, such as the *Journal of Near Eastern Studies* and the *Journal of the American Oriental Society*, a postwar boom began in organization-based journals such as the *Journal for the Society for the Study of Egyptian Antiquities, Bulletin of the Egyptological Seminar,* and *Journal of the American Research Center in Egypt*. Egyptological journals of the 1980s and 1990s have placed more emphasis on Greco-Roman and Christian

Egypt. *Enchoria: Zeitschrift für Demotistik und Koptologie* has filled a pressing need for a journal specific to the later stages of the Egyptian language, while a few papyrological journals (like the *Bulletin of the American Society of Papyrologists*) are interacting more and more with Egyptology. Increasing numbers of specialist journals within Egyptology are dealing with language (*Lingua Aegyptia*) or ceramics (*Bulletin de liaison du Groupe International d'Étude de la Céramique Égyptienne; Cahiers de la Céramique Égyptienne*). The proliferation of Egyptological journals in the second half of the twentieth century is not an unmixed blessing to the scholar; although an unprecedented amount of information is available to Egyptologists, it becomes increasingly impossible for any one person to master the literature of the field.

A postwar trend in journals printed from camera-ready copy for quick distribution and regular publication is exemplified in *Göttinger Miszellen: Beiträge zur ägyptologischen Diskussion. Göttinger Miszellen*'s founders, Jürgen Horn and Friedrich Junge, set it up in 1972 as an experiment in encouraging discussion among Egyptologists, and it remains an essential and prolific journal that has done much to facilitate new work among scholars. Other journals have followed this model (e.g., *Discussions in Egyptology*), but tend, on the whole, to attract more work by outsiders than by Egyptologists. Journals begun by students have had a lively if erratic history since the 1980s; *Sarapis*, originating at the University of Chicago, and *Wepwawet*, from University College in London, both combined articles by graduate students with contributions by more established scholars. By their nature, journals intended for discussion rather than definitive publication are often not refereed; while this can facilitate debate among scholars, the increasing emphasis on publication in refereed journals for the purposes of tenure and promotion in the academic world may make scholars less likely to contribute to such publications.

At present, Egyptological journals face an unpredictable future. The ever-increasing interest by nonspecialists has created a demand for journals that are accessible, but with a scholarly foundation. Two very different journals— *KMT: A Modern Journal of Ancient Egypt* and *Egyptian Archaeology*—illustrate the ways that Egyptologists are seeking to meet the demand for more popular periodicals with accessible articles, reports from the field, and current news. In contrast to the demand for popular Egyptological publications, specialist Egyptological journals have suffered from rising publication costs, declining library subscriptions, loss of government subsidies, and an overall decrease in academic sponsorship. Many academic disciplines confronted with similar challenges have turned to the Internet as a cheap and easy means of distributing articles. (*Bryn Mawr Classical Reviews*, which sometimes features book reviews of Egyptological publications, is a good case in point). Some journals, such as *Studien zur altägyptischen Kultur* and *Bulletin of the American Society of Papyrologists*, have turned to the Internet for dissemination of related materials, such as their index, but Egyptological journals in general have not yet taken full advantage of the possibilities of electronic publication and distribution. Online discussion groups devoted to Egyptology, such as Ancient Near East (ANE) and the Egyptologist's Electronic Forum (EEF), have come closest to realizing the potential of modern technology, but they do not fulfill many of the aims of Egyptological journals.

[*See also* Reference Works.]

BIBLIOGRAPHY

Beinlich-Seeber, Christine. "Reihen und Zeitschriften." In *Bibliographie Altägypten 1822–1946.* (*Ägyptologische Abhandlungen* 61.1–3.) 3 vols. Wiesbaden, 1998. Volume 1, pages 3–145, is a monumental survey of journals in which Egyptological articles were published between 1822 and 1946.

Bierbrier, M. L., ed. *Who Was Who in Egyptology.* 3d ed. London, 1995. A patient reader can extract much information about the history of Egyptological journals from this standard reference to the lives and careers of Egyptologists.

Horn, J., and F. Junge. "Eine neue Zeitschrift–Warum?" *Göttinger Miszellen* 1 (1972), 3–5. A description of the rationale behind *Göttinger Miszellen,* by its founders, which addresses the need for journals promoting discussion of Egyptological topics.

TERRY G. WILFONG

JUBILEE. *See* Festivals.

JUDGMENT OF THE DEAD.

Two kinds of judgment of the dead are attested in Egyptian documents: tribunals operating in the underworld in the same continuous manner as tribunals on earth; and in a later version, a single moment for each person after death when a divine tribunal determines whether that individual is worthy of eternal life.

The first version is attested first in late Old Kingdom hieroglyphic tomb-chapel inscriptions with threats to would-be vandals of tombs, and in Hieratic "Letters to the Dead"; references continue in the early Middle Kingdom funerary literature (Coffin Texts). Here the afterlife is a continuation of life on earth; plaintiffs can bring cases to the authorities, who execute justice. The texts do not name the "great god" of the tribunal; he may be the deceased king or the god Osiris, though this is a matter of expression rather than of substance.

In the later version, death marks discontinuity, as a moment determining the immortality of the individual. Here people are either pure or evil; the evil die a second death to become *mut* "dead" (*mt;* "damned"), whereas the good achieve the status of *akh* (*ȝḫ;* "transfigured spirit"). Unerring divine judgment is expressed figuratively by the scales used to weigh precious metals with mathematical objectivity in treasury accounts. This judgment conflates two episodes in the myth of the god Osiris: his resuscitation by his sister-wife Isis after his murder by Seth, and the declaration by the gods that his son Horus was telling the truth in his physical and legal battles with Seth over the inheritance of Osiris. At death, each individual becomes Osiris if declared "true of voice" like Horus; "Osiris (name) true of voice" comes to be the commonest formula for referring to the deceased. In some periods, a word such as "to" before the word "Osiris" can be repeated before the title and name of the deceased, as if to separate the divine and human aspects of the identity surviving death. The very retention of the personal name and official titles marks a limit to the assimilation of the individual to the deity. In early Roman times, identification as Osiris for both men and women was superseded by a system assigning Osiris for men and Hathor for women.

The new judgment appears first in the Middle Kingdom. The term "calculation of differences" later denotes assessment of the individual after death; it occurs already in the phrase "his voice is true in the calculation of differences" on the Abydos stela of an eleventh dynasty general, Intef (Copenhagen Ny Carlsberg Glyptothek AE.I.N.963, lower, line 6). The First Intermediate Period stela of Merer may include a reference to the scales of reckoning but is of uncertain interpretation. Unambiguous references to scales occur in the Coffin Texts (CT) on early to mid-twelfth dynasty coffins (CT 335, "whose eyebrows are the arms of the balance"; CT 452, "that balance of Ra on which Maat is raised"); four coffins of that date bear a text in which the dead are polarized as good and evil (CT 338, "the tribunal which is in Abydos on that night of distinguishing the damned and reckoning the blessed dead"). However, none of these sources attests certainly to "death as judgment time" rather than an afterlife court of appeal. In the *Instructions for Merikare,* a Middle Egyptian literary discourse dated perhaps to the twelfth dynasty, one section (P53–7) warns against wrongdoing with reference to the afterlife: "Do not trust in length of years—they see a lifetime as an hour; when a man is left over after mourning, his deeds are piled up beside him." This might indicate simply a better hearing for the good than for the evil, on the legal principle that those of good character are trustworthy. However, there follows: "As for the man who reaches them without doing evil, he will abide there like a god, roaming (free) like the lords of time." Here the good person undergoes transformation.

The classic exposition of judgment at death comes in the *Book of Going Forth by Day* (the *Book of the Dead*) texts numbered BD 30 and BD 125 by the nineteenth-century

JUDGMENT OF THE DEAD. *Detail of a papyrus of the* Book of Going Forth by Day (Book of the Dead). This is a section of what was originally a continuous roll about 23 meters (72 feet) long. Here, the heart of the deceased is being weighed before Osiris, who is enthroned on the left. The papyrus is from the late dynastic to early Ptolemaic period. (The Metropolitan Museum of Art, gift of Edward S. Harkness, 1935. [35.9.20 (7)])

Egyptologist Karl Richard Lepsius, and the associated illustration in which the heart of the deceased is weighed against the goddess Maat ("what is right"). The two chapters and the weighing illustration are among the most frequently attested elements of the Egyptian funerary corpus, though not every manuscript or burial includes an example. Of the three elements, BD 30 is first attested, on four late Middle Kingdom human-faced heart scarabs (Neferuptah, Nebankh, Dedtu, and one erased), on a late Middle Kingdom or Second Intermediate Period gold plaque, and in both later versions (BD30A and B) among the *Book of Going Forth by Day* coffins of the seventeenth dynasty queen Montuhotpe. In this, the deceased appeals to the heart not to weigh down the balance or testify in a hostile manner before the keeper of the balance. The longer chapter, BD 125, is first attested in the mid-eighteenth dynasty, from the joint reign of Hatshepsut with Thutmose III, in connection with a new burial custom of placing a funerary papyrus with the dead (*Books of the Dead*). In editing earlier *Books of the Dead*, Naville used as the main manuscript the papyrus of Nebseny, dated stylistically to the reign of Thutmose IV (British Museum EA 9900). In the first part, the deceased is led into the "broad court of the Two Maats," to declare innocence of wrongs before the great god (List A), and before the full tribunal of forty-two divine assessors, including Osiris and Ra (List B). The texts conclude with announcements by the deceased of purity and initiation into the afterlife. The declarations of innocence (often called "negative confession" in Egyptology) form the most explicit statement in Egyptian texts of *maat (mꜣʿt;* "what is right"), by delineating its opposite, wrongdoing. However, there is

a culturally specific setting for both series: some denials reflect the precepts of the literary tradition of *Instructions* or *Teachings,* a genre in which a father or master instructs a son or apprentice in the correct way to behave in life; others are related to the priestly oaths of purity taken at the moment of entering priestly service, a genre attested only in later copies but probably in existence earlier. The sequence of declarations varies between manuscripts. In List A, in the *Book of the Dead* of Nebseny, thirty-six declarations of innocence are given, opening with "I have not done evil to anyone" and "I have not slain the sacred herd" (interpreted in some manuscripts as humankind). Other declarations of List A include the religious norms "I have not blasphemed," "I have not harmed the offering-loaves of the gods," "I have not removed the offerings of the blessed dead," and, related, the affirmation of sexual rules "I have not copulated" (in some versions "with a male") and "I have not ejaculated" (in some versions "in the sanctuary of my city god"). Other rules concern probity in administrative measurement: "I have not reduced the aroura land-measure"; "I have not tampered with the counterpoise of the scales."

In List B, the forty-two declarations are tabulated graphically, divided into on the model "O broad of strides, he who comes forth from Iunu, I have not committed evil." The deities before whom List B was to be recited are thus identified not by their primary names but by epithets, sometimes not attested elsewhere, with the addition of a cult center or other place of origin (e.g., cavern, twilight, darkness). All named towns are in Lower or Middle Egypt, a feature that might identify the period and place of redaction as being the Herakleopolitan kingdom of the

First Intermediate Period but, perhaps, more simply reflecting compilation at an unknown date in a northern scribal school, such as Iunu/Heliopolis. The date of composition of BD 125 remains uncertain; there is no precise parallel from the Middle Kingdom, though a positive series of declarations of good character is graphically tabulated on one early twelfth dynasty stela in a manner reminiscent of the List B tabulation. This is the period in which the royal cult complex gained "Osirian" features. The pyramid of Senwosret II at Illahun had a rectangular tree border, with underground chambers on a pattern later echoed by the cenotaph of Sety I at Abydos, while Senwosret III had a major royal cult complex constructed at Abydos South. However, the few sources for funerary literature of the royal family attest to BD 30 but not to BD 125 (heart scarabs, coffin of queen Montuhotpe). It remains possible, then, that the textual edition dates, with the vignette, to the eighteenth dynasty.

The texts and vignettes of BD 30 and 125 may seem to encapsulate an explicit code of ethics, but they are intended to establish a purity analogous to the purity of the priest entering a period of temple service. Therefore, this afterlife codification does not include every precept of didactic literature; some, such as respect for seniors and parents, were evidently not deemed relevant to the aim of entering the underworld. Modern agnostic reading might suggest that, by including declarations of innocence in their burials, the elite may have hoped to secure automatic entry to a good afterlife; when such a question becomes widespread, the questioners already stand outside the particular system of belief. There is no evidence that inclusion of texts exempted anyone from judgment; the texts affirm the desired outcome but insist on judgment. The ethics of providing religious texts for those who could afford them, whatever their biography, seems to receive no explicit treatment in Egyptian sources until the comparison of the damned rich man and the blessed poor man in the Demotic tale of *Setna and his Son,* in which Hellenistic influence may be involved.

The principal vignette to BD 30 and 125 illustrates "truth of voice" in declaring innocence as a weighing of the heart on scales against Maat, before Osiris. Throughout the history of its use, the scene often includes the four sons of Horus as protectors of the internal organs of the deceased after mummification. Weighing vignettes vary in number and role of figures, and in scale within a compositional field, occupying on a papyrus the full height of the roll or only a part. Eighteenth dynasty depictions on papyrus occupy only part of the full height of a roll, and they present the scales as managed by Thoth in baboon form, beside the god Osiris on his throne. In the *Book of the Dead* of Nebseny, this scene is provided as illustration to BD 30; the text of BD 125 occurs farther on in the sequence of the roll, where the "Hall of the Two Maats" becomes a full-height vignette enclosing the tabulated declarations of innocence. Other small-scale weighing scenes of this period and later place Horus in charge of weighing, while Thoth is shown as a scribe declaring or recording the result of the weighing to Osiris. Later eighteenth dynasty versions sometimes make Anubis, god of embalming, the deity in charge of weighing, and they may add nearby a monster called variously Amemet ("Swallower") or Am-mut ("Swallower of the Damned"). The earliest manuscript with Anubis and Amemet is the *Book of the Dead* of Nebqed (Louvre N 3068, reign of Thutmose IV or Amenhotpe III). Here the monster is already the hybrid specified in a caption on the Papyrus of Hunefer (British Museum EA 9901, early nineteenth dynasty): "Its fore as a lion, its rear as a hippopotamus, its middle as a lion." After the Amarna era, the weighing scene tends to occupy the full height of manuscripts, offering opportunities for increasing detail. Ramessid depictions begin to shift the emphasis from the weighing to the declaration of innocence; in the version for Hunefer just cited, Anubis leads the deceased to the scales, which he then oversees alongside Amemet, following which Horus leads the justified deceased to the throned Osiris. This focus on justification recurs in Third Intermediate Period papyri, while in the standard version of the Late to Roman periods (first attested in the tomb of Sheshonq III at Tanis), weighing and justification are given equal importance as an interwoven scene in front of Osiris.

Supplementary figures in more complex vignettes include the goddesses Isis and Nephthys supporting Osiris, and, particularly in the standard Late period version, one or two figures of the goddess Maat. After the Amarna era, features of individuality are added: Shai (allotted life), Meskhenet (birth-brick), and Renenet (nurturing of the deceased). Later vignettes generally include a secondary human figure beside the scales: from the Ramessid era, the *ba*-soul of the deceased; from the Third Intermediate Period, a crouching figure; and from the Late period, evoking Horus and/or Re, a divine child on a scepter. Besides these full-height vignettes, other versions include narrower compositions of stacked horizontal registers, or single excerpts such as the weighing. On coffins of the twenty-fifth and twenty-sixth dynasties, a single band extends over the coffin breast, with the weighing scene over the heart, and, toward the center, the deceased before a line of deities.

The judgment motif continues to be used into Roman times. For example, the weighing and the arrival before Osiris are depicted in a single scene on the papyrus of Kerasher (British Museum EA 9995), and as separate scenes on the coffin of Teuris (weighing along mummy's left side, introduction before Osiris on right side). Texts in

Roman period manuscripts come mainly not from the *Book of the Dead* but from the *Books of Breathing*, including sections of BD 125. In versions of this period (or perhaps slightly earlier), the vignette is often reduced to select elements, and the dead souls are sometimes shown as black shadows or skeletal creatures.

Sometimes the weighing scene (e.g., *Book of of the Dead* of Nebqed) or a part of the text of BD 125 (e.g., *Book of the Dead* of Nebseny, concluding text of BD 125) attracts a vignette of the Lake of Fire. This underworld lake actually judged the dead by scorching the evil but sustaining the good. The vignette shows a rectangle of water with red flaming-torch hieroglyphs and a baboon at each corner. It is more often attached to the separate text BD 126, the appeal to the four baboons (Thoth as justice, at each of the four cardinal points).

Illustrations of a hall for divine judgment also occur in other contexts. The royal Underworld Books of the New Kingdom describe in varying details the fate of the evil and of the blessed dead in the underworld, but they are less often explicit on the place or moment of judgment. In the *Book of Gates*, a version of the night journey of the sun god first attested on the walls of the tomb of Horemheb as king, the central scene of the composition presents Osiris enthroned at the top of a stepped platform with a scales, in part as a mummiform deity; on each of the nine steps is a human figure beneath the collective caption "Ennead of the retinue of Osiris." Beneath Osiris appears a text damning the "enemies," and above him are four inverted gazelle heads labeled *hmhmyw* ("the roarers"). The inscriptions of this scene are distinguished by unusual extension in selection and meaning of signs (cryptography). Above the Ennead, beside the scales, a boat bears a monkey wielding a curved stick to drive off a pig, and the monkey and stick are repeated outside the boat without the pig; this employs the force of ridicule to overpower enemies. This vignette recurs on later sources, sometimes combined with the *Book of the Dead* version (as on the Third Intermediate Period cartonnage Harvard 2230).

Sarcophagi of the thirtieth dynasty attest to another version of the hall of Osiris, in which the enthroned god is offered life by his son Horus.

[*See also* Afterlife; Anubis; Ethics and Morality; Hell; Maat; Osiris; *and* Paradise.]

BIBLIOGRAPHY

Allen, Thomas G. *The Book of the Dead or Going Forth by Day.* Studies in Ancient Oriental Civilizations, 37. Chicago, 1974. The most source-critical translation of *Book of Going Forth by Day* texts into English.

Assmann, Jan. *Ma'at: Gerechtigkeit und Unsterblichkeit im Alten Ägypten.* Munich, 1990. Includes the most important discussion of the judgment of the dead (chap. 4, pp. 92–121, for the tribunals in the afterlife; chap. 5, pp. 122–159, for the judgment of the dead as a single test of purity at entry into a blessed afterlife). See also an extended review by Stephen Quirke in *Journal of Egyptian Archaeology* 80 (1994), 219–231.

Cenival, Jean-Louis de. *Le Livre pour Sortir le Jour: Le Livre des Morts des anciens Égyptiens.* Bordeaux, 1992. A thematic general introduction to the *Book of Going Forth by Day*, with extensive illustrations from the collections of the Louvre.

Faulkner, Raymond O. *The Ancient Egyptian Coffin Texts.* 3 vols. Warminster, 1973–1978. The standard translation into English of the corpus of Middle Kingdom funerary texts, including the passages referring to judgment of the dead.

Faulkner, Raymond O. *The Ancient Egyptian Book of the Dead.* London, 1984. Edition by Carol Andrews, with extensive illustrations from the collections of the British Museum.

Quirke, Stephen. *Hieroglyphs and the Afterlife.* London, 1996. A history of funerary literature, with discussion of the emergence of *Book of Going Forth by Day* texts, including the heart scarabs with "chapter 30" (pp. 102–104, 111–114), and of early examples of the judgment in the *Book*, notably that of Nebqed (pp. 119–123).

Seeber, Christine. *Untersuchungen zur Darstellung des Totengerichts im Alten Ägypten.* Münchner Ägyptologische Studien, 35. Berlin and Munich, 1976. The principal scholarly discussion of judgment vignettes.

Wente, E. *Letters from Ancient Egypt.* Atlanta, 1990. Translations of letters for the context and style of Letters to the Dead, with reference to tribunals in the afterlife.

STEPHEN G. J. QUIRKE

JUSTICE. *See* Crime and Punishment; *and* Law.

K

KA. The complex of ideas concerning the *ka* is one of the most important in Egyptian religion. Since these ideas have no exact analogues in European cultures, it is impossible to translate adequately the word *k₃* and to identify the *ka* with more familiar concepts. Interpretations of the *ka* are numerous, ambiguous, and usually unsatisfactory, and they range from its identification with the Latin *genius* to analogy with "mana."

The word *ka* was expressed by the hieroglyph of two upraised arms, usually considered a symbol of the embrace (or protection) of a man by his *ka*, although other interpretations are possible. A distinction should be made between the internal and external *ka*, as well as between the royal and the human *ka*, since these concepts were qualitatively different.

The idea that there was something securing the physical and mental activities of man arose in Egypt and elsewhere in prehistory. The *ka* (internal *ka*) was one of those entities. Its nature is reflected in numerous words going back to the same root: *k₃j* ("think about," "intend"), *k₃.t* ("thought"), *nk₃j* ("think about"), *k₃j* ("speak"), *k₃.t* ("vagina"), *bk₃.tj* ("testicles"), *nkj* ("copulate"), *nkjkj* ("fertilize"), *bk₃* ("be pregnant," "impregnate"), *nk₃k₃* ("good condition of flesh"). Such words as *ḥk₃*, *ḥk₃.w* ("magic," "magic spells"), *ḥk₃* ("enchant," "be enchanted"), *ḥk₃j* ("sorcerer"), and *ḥk₃(w)* ("god Heqa, personification of magic") reflect the supernatural essence of the *ka*. The reproductive role of the *ka* is obvious, but its connection to thought processes is less clear. The mind was usually related to the *ba* (as in the *Dispute of a Man with his Ba*, where confusion of thought is described as a dialogue with that entity), but the word *ḥmt* ("think" or "to act three together") leads one to suppose that there was also an idea of thinking as a trilateral process, with the *ka* playing some obscure role, along with the *ba*. Owing to the role of the *ka* in thinking, *k₃* could designate human individuality as a whole, and in different contexts it could be translated as "character," "nature," "temperament," or "disposition." Since character to a great extent preordains the life of an individual, *k₃* also means "destiny," or "providence." This use of the word engendered a tradition of interpreting the *ka* as a kind of universal vital force, but this idea is too abstract, and even the examples cited above show that the meaning of *k₃* was far more concrete in each context.

The ancient mind adopted personifications readily. It transformed this "inner motor" into a certain being. It seems that this being (the external *ka*) was primarily associated with the placenta, (the twin of a man), and was born with him. Supernatural associations of the placenta and the umbilical cord are reported by ethnographers in central Africa, but in Egypt such notions were forced out early by more elaborate ideas, and only allusions to them can be traced in dynastic times.

The scenes of the king's birth depict Khnum forming the baby king and his *ka* on a potter's wheel. In Old Kingdom pyramid temples, New Kingdom royal tombs, and the temples of the gods, there are many representations of the *ka* accompanying the king, either as a personified *k₃* sign or as a human form with the *k₃* sign on its head. The *k₃* hieroglyph holds the *serekh* with the Horus name of the king, while the *ka* itself bears an ostrich feather (the symbol of the world harmony, or *maat*) in one hand, and a long staff with a finial shaped like the king's head (*mdw-špsj*) in the other hand. Thus, the royal *ka* is related to the Horus name describing the presence of the sky-god in the king. This portrays the dualism of the king's nature, which combines divine and mortal components: divinity is realized through the *ka*. In a number of cases (especially in the Old Kingdom), the finial is arranged at the level of the head of the falcon on the *serekh*, thus forming a composition structurally and semantically similar to the statues depicting the king with his head embraced by the falcon's wings, and demonstrating his double nature. The relation between the royal *ka* and Horus is apparent in its identification with Harsiese in the New Kingdom (although it could hardly be originally associated with Osirian ideas).

Another, qualitatively different aspect of the *ka* can be seen mainly on the monuments of private persons. The Egyptians were amazed by the fact that depiction can evoke in consciousness an image of the represented. These images were objectified, turned from a part of the psyche into a part of the medium, and identified with the external *ka*. As a result, these representations (at first statues, but also murals) became the main cult objects in tombs and temples. This is further supported by the words *n k₃ n NN* ("for the ka of NN"), which were almost obligatory in the adjacent offering formulas. The most common translation of the word *k₃* as "double" is applicable mainly to this external human *ka*.

KA. *Middle Kingdom statue of King Hor, with the symbol for his* ka *appearing above his head.* (Courtesy David P. Silverman)

Unlike the royal *ka*, the human *ka* was never represented as a separate figure, because any representation itself is the *ka*. This explains the indifference of Egyptian artists to rendering individual features. They did not reproduce the portrait of an individual, but that of his *ka*, who was eternally youthful and in perfect shape.

In an Old Kingdom private tomb, the pictures created an entire world for the *ka*. It is an exact although incomplete copy of the earthly world: only people and objects essential for the owner are depicted. Being a reproduction of everyday life, this "doubleworld" is surprisingly realistic; nothing supernatural, the gods included, is represented. Every tomb formed its own Doubleworld, and their total did not merge into an aggregate next world.

The notion of the *ka* was a dominating concept of the next life in the Old Kingdom. In a less pure form, it lived into the Middle Kingdom, and lost much of its impor-

tance in the New Kingdom, although the *ka* always remained the recipient of offerings.

[*See also* Akh; Ba; Ka-Chapel; *and* Names.]

BIBLIOGRAPHY

Abitz, Friedrich. *König und Gott Die Götterszenen in den agyptischen Königsgräbern con Thutmosis IV bis Ramses III.* Ägyptologsiche Abhandlungen, 40. Wiesbaden, 1984.

Bell, Lanny D. "Luxor Temple and the Cult of the Royal Ka." *Journal of Near Eastern Studies* 44 (1985), 251–294. The most influential modern interpretation of the royal *ka*.

Bell, Lanny D. "The New Kingdom 'Divine' Temple: The Example of Luxor." In *Temples of Ancient Egypt*, edited by Byron D. Schafer, pp. 127–184. Ithaca, 1997.

Bolshakov, Andrey O. *Man and His Double in Egyptian Ideology of the Old Kingdom.* Ägypten und Altes Testament, 37. Wiesbaden, 1997. The most comprehensive study of the human *ka*, with extensive historiographic study.

Bolshakov, Audrey O. "Royal Portraiture and 'Horus Name.'" In *L'art de l'Ancien Empire Égyptien*, edited by Ch. Ziegler, pp. 311–333. Paris, 1999.

Brunner, Helmut. *Die südlichen Räume des Temples von Luxor.* Mainz, 1977.

Greven, Liselotte. *Der Ka in Theologie und Königskult der Ägypter des Alten Reichs.* Ägyptologische Forschungen, 17. Glückstadt, 1954. This and Schweitzer are somewhat out of date but still important.

Lacau, Pierre, and Henri Chevrier. *Une chapelle de Sésostris Iᵉʳ à Karnak.* Cairo, 1959.

Schweitzer, Ursula. *Das Wesen des Ka im Diesseits und Jenseits der alten Ägypter.* Ägyptologische Forschungen, 19. Glückstadt, 1956.

ANDREY O. BOLSHAKOV

KA-CHAPEL. As far as one can judge from incomplete archaeological data, humans never produced burials without monuments marking their location or without cult places. This may not be considered axiomatic only because open cult monuments decay and so disappear much more easily than hidden burials. In Egypt, the functional dualism of the tomb and its division into burial and cult parts (usually substructure and superstructure, although other variants are also possible) is most obvious, owing to the hypertrophy of the latter.

The term "*ka*-chapel" is used mainly in American writing on ancient Egypt and has two meanings. In the narrowest sense, it was the chamber for the bringing of offerings, which contained the false door and the offering stone; in the widest sense, it was the whole complex of chambers in the superstructure open to priests, relatives of the deceased, and passers-by (multiple-roomed chapels). The term is misleading and conceals to some degree the true meaning of the phenomenon, for the notion of the *ka* as related to figurative tomb decoration was later than the earliest chapels and existed in its pure form only in the Old Kingdom. In the Middle Kingdom, the *ka* concept was somewhat profaned and, in the New Kingdom, it was mixed with qualitatively different concepts (see below). Thus, *tomb-chapel* or *cult chamber* (*Kultkammer, Opferkammer*) may be more appropriate terms for this type of architectural structure. The Egyptians designated "*ka*-chapel" by the word *iz*, which they also used for the "whole tomb" and for rooms of varying functions (e.g., offices and workshops), and they never developed more specific terms.

The time when the first *ka*-chapels were built is hard to establish. The earliest *mastabas* seem to have no chapels; their false doors were arranged openly on the façade. Some light (e.g., reed) structures, however, might have been erected in front of the false doors to vanish without any trace. *Ka*-chapels appeared in order to fulfill both ideological and purely practical requirements. The cult place was sacred, owing to its very function, and had to be separated from the surroundings; moreover, offering rituals had to be concealed from strangers. With that, a closed chapel was the best possible means to protect the false door and ritual equipment from vandalism and weathering (this became imperative when vulnerable murals were added).

Ka-chapels of the first dynasties were shaped either as a small court (sometimes roofed) in front of the false door, as a narrow roofed corridor along the eastern façade of the *mastaba* (exterior corridor chapel), or as a similar corridor penetrating into the body of the *mastaba* (interior corridor chapel). The only *ka*-chapel of the third type belonged to Hesyre (third dynasty) and was the first to house numerous mural decorations. From this time, murals were the main factor determining the architecture and appearance of the *ka*-chapels. Narrow corridor chapels with no adequate field of vision vanished, while those resulting from the deepening of the niche where the false door was placed predominated. The only exceptions to this new type were the tombs of the "style of Khufu" at fourth dynasty Giza, with exterior brick *ka*-chapels attached to stone *mastaba*s (they were combined frequently with interior chapels).

The structure of the *ka*-chapel was influenced by both its genesis and ideology. Special attention was always paid to the east–west axis because of the association of the west with the next world. The false door was arranged in the western wall, while the entrance to the *ka*-chapel was placed in the opposite, eastern wall or in the eastern part of the northern or southern wall. In multiple-roomed tombs, the *ka*-chapel was the westernmost chamber of the whole complex. The arrangement of murals conformed to strict rules, which depended on the opposition of the west and the east (e.g., ritual topics were treated on the western wall, while everyday scenes were usually located on the eastern wall). In the second half of the fifth dynasty, multiple-roomed *mastaba*s became numerous; their decoration followed the same rules, although less extensively.

The tightly closed statue chamber, the *serdab*, is usually regarded as an independent component of the tomb, but the cult of statues is identical to that in front of the false door and murals of the *ka*-chapels. There are several Old Kingdom *serdab*s shaped as chapels with statue chambers behind their walls (*mastaba*s of Baefba, Seshemnefer II and III at Giza). The similarity in function of these *serdab*s to those of the *ka*-chapels is proven by the fact that the term *ḥw.t-k₃* applied to them both, as well as to other chambers in the superstructure.

The spatial organization of rock tombs was somewhat different. Because of the technical difficulties of hewing stone, their cult chambers could not be numerous, and rarely exceeded one or two rooms. Such rooms combined the functions of the *ka*-chapels, *serdab*s, and other tomb chambers. Orientation of rock-cut *ka*-chapels was determined by the orientation of the cliff in which they were hewn, and often it differed dramatically from the traditional rules. The false door need not be arranged in the western wall, the entrance need not be opposed to it; moreover, both might be located in the same wall. The rules of the arrangement of murals were similarly modified. In the chapels of Old Kingdom rock tombs, the tradition of carving statues in the wall was developed; later, those engaged statues were adopted in the *mastaba* chapels.

The *ka*-chapel had two main functions. First, it was the offering place where everyday and festive priestly services were celebrated, where offerings where left on the offering stone, and where they were accepted by the tomb owner going forth from the false door. Second, when the first representations appeared, the *ka*-chapel acquired another function—its decorations started to create the world where the *ka*, the "double" of the owner, existed—in the Doubleworld. Decoration of the *ka*-chapel with realistic murals created the Doubleworld, reproducing earthly life and assuring it forever. That idea so elated the Egyptians that during the initial development of murals, they constructed several immured *ka*-chapels, which were isolated and independent from the cult (*mastaba*s of Nefermaat and Rahotep at Meidum). That experiment had no aftermath, and the next life was always regarded as secured both by cult and representations.

Although representations in the *ka*-chapel created the Doubleworld, it would be wrong to suppose that it was regarded as located within that chamber—it existed in another dimension and only touched the earthly world wherever images were placed. Contact of the two worlds in the chapel was reflected in the ritual of Cleaning the Footprints; leaving the tomb, priests wiped up their footsteps to eliminate traces of the earthly in the realm of the Double. (For another interpretation, see H. Altenmüller, "Eine Neue Deutung der Zeremonie des INIT RD." *Journal of Egyptian Archaeology* 57 (1971), 146–153.)

From the first half of the Old Kingdom, exceptional Memphite *ka*-chapels are known for the highest nobility and king's relatives (at Saqqara, Giza, Abusir, Dahshur, Meidum, and Abu Rowash); in the second half of the Old Kingdom, monuments of the lower strata of officialdom and those of nomarchs were also built in the homes (provinces). There were several standard sizes of cult chambers corresponding to the places of their owners in the official hierarchy; however, since decoration of the *ka*-chapels was practically identical, their Doubleworlds were also almost indistinguishable, thus leveling inequality within the ruling class in the next life. Previously, it was supposed that even high-ranking craftsmen could not erect monuments of any significance during the Old Kingdom, but

the 1990s discovery of a cemetery of necropolis artisans at Giza alters this perception.

After a century-long decay of the First Intermediate Period, *mastaba*s of the old types were revived in the Faiyum and near Memphits. Regrettably, they are badly deteriorated, but several well-preserved chapels may be easily mistaken for Old Kingdom monuments (e.g., those of Ihy and Hetep at Saqqara). The main trend of development of the *ka*-chapels, however—beginning from the First Intermediate Period and Middle Kingdom—is represented by rock-cut tombs. Scattered throughout Upper Egypt, rock-cut tombs of those periods are a provincial phenomenon and, thus, several local tendencies coexist in the development of architecture and the decoration of their chapels. Such important necropolises as Hawawish (Akhmim), Meir, Bersheh, and Beni Hasan generally followed traditions of the Old Kingdom, although they deviated from a standard style, owing to provincialism and long independent development. In Thebes (at Tarif, Asasif, Gurna), Armant, and Dendera, the new type of *saff*-tomb appeared, with their chapels cut deeply into the rock and joined to the pillared façade by a narrow corridor. At Qubbet el-Hawa (Aswan) the corridor is longer and the chapel placed in the heart of the cliff seems to be separated further from the world of the living. In addition to rock-cut chapels, the tomb complexes of Qau el-Kebir (Antaeopolis) had free-standing chapels in the valley, which were analogous to the lower temples of royal burial edifices.

From the New Kingdom, the greatest number of rock-cut tombs are known, with the Theban region having the most examples. Among other types of tombs, there was the extensive complex constructed at Thebes for Amenhotep, son of Hapu; like royal monuments, it contained a widely separated cult structure (temple) and hidden burial component (rock-cut chamber). A number of temple-shaped tombs of high officials from later decades was discovered at Saqqara. The most important among them is the complex of General Horemheb, built and decorated prior to his enthronement as last king of the eighteenth dynasty. The increased well-being of the lower classes was reflected in numerous tombs of necropolis craftsmen at Deir el-Medina; the decoration of their chapels was sometimes innovative and less restricted by tradition than decoration in the tombs of high officials.

In spite of the increased number, size, and splendor of New Kingdom tombs, their development marked the end of the *ka*-chapel. The number of religious motifs increased in the decoration of cult chambers during the eighteenth dynasty. Such scenes as funeral processions, which had been of limited importance in the previous epochs, were turned into detailed pictorial narrations. In

Ramessid times, everyday scenes disappeared and representations and texts going back to the *Book of Going Forth by Day* (*Book of the Dead*) prevailed. Thus, the Doubleworld of Old Kingdom tradition declined in use and, accordingly, the term "*ka*-chapel" should not be applied to cult chambers of most tombs after that time.

Egypt's Late period was characterized by a general decline in tomb construction. The widespread use of family vaults and the usurpation of old tombs by new generations made traditional cult chambers useless and nonsensical. Degradation of chapels was mostly a result of the economic difficulty in sustaining a cult. The most remarkable exceptions to that rule were the Theban tombs of the twenty-fifth through twenty-sixth dynasties, which contained superstructures and cult quarters more extensive than any in the history of ancient Egypt. The greatest among them is that of Petamenophis at Asasif.

Of particular interest in the late history of tombchapels was the archaizing tendency of the twenty-fifth through twenty-sixth dynasties, which revived traditions of the Old Kingdom. Carved reliefs in those chapels mimicked decoration of ancient tombs almost exactly, but their owners did not understand the ancient ideology; realistic everyday topics were reinterpreted symbolically, and the resurrection of the Doubleworld in the archaized chapels was suggested only with serious reservations. The last attempt to revitalize old chapel decorations was made in the late fourth century BCE, in the tomb of Petosiris at Tuna el-Gebel (Hermopolis), with its eclectic mix of everyday scenes in the Greco-Egyptian style and religious texts from early Egyptian times.

BIBLIOGRAPHY

Badawy, Alexander. *A History of Egyptian Architecture*, vol. 1: *From the Earliest Times to the End of the Old Kingdom*. Giza, 1954. General review of Early Dynastic and Old Kingdom architecture, with chapters on royal and private tombs.

Bolshakov, Andrey O. *Man and His Double in Egyptian Ideology of the Old Kingdom*. Ägypten und Altes Testament, 37. Wiesbaden, 1997. A study of the *ka* concept as reflected in Old Kingdom tombs, with a brief review of its development. Analysis of the arrangement of representations is less detailed than in Harpur (1987), yet more oriented toward ideology.

Brunner, Hellmut. *Die Anlagen der Ägyptischen Felsgräber bis zum Mittlern Reich*. Ägyptologische Forschungen, 3. Glückstadt, 1936. Out of date but important because of the unique outline of the development of provincial rock-cut tombs in the Old and Middle Kingdoms.

Duell, Prentice. *The Mastaba of Mereruka*. University of Chicago, Oriental Institute. Sakkara Expedition. 2 vols. Chicago, 1938. Publication on one of the largest Old Kingdom multiple-roomed tombs.

Epron, Lucienne, et al. *Le tombeau de Ti*. 2 vols. Cairo 1939–1966. Memoires publiés par les membres de l'Institut français d'archéologie orientale du caire. Publication on the best preserved Old Kingdom multiple-roomed tomb with excellent decoration.

Harpur, Yvonne. *Decoration in Egyptian Tombs of the Old Kingdom: Studies in Orientation and Scene Content*. London and New York, 1987. Excellent work on Old Kingdom tomb decoration; less extensive, but more detailed than Montet (1925).

Kanawati, Naguib. *The Egyptian Administration of the Old Kingdom*. Warminster, 1977. Witty study of the correlation of *ka*-chapel sizes with the social position of their owners.

Kanawati, Naguib. *The Tomb and Its Significance in Ancient Egypt*. Guizeh, 1988. Popular but reliable history of Egyptian tombs.

Lefebvre, Gustave. *Le tombeau de Pétosiris*. 3 vols. Cairo, 1923–1924. Publication of the archaized Ptolemaic tomb of Petosiris.

Martin, Geoffrey Thorndike. *The Memphite Tomb of Horemheb, Commander-in-Chief of Tutankhamun*. London, 1989. Publication of one of the most important funerary complexes of the New Kingdom.

Montet, Pierre. *Les scénes de la vie privée dans les tombeaux égyptiens de l'Ancien Empire*. Strasbourg, 1925. Excellent reference book that traces the development of tomb decoration in the Old and Middle Kingdoms. Its reading should be combined with Harpur (1987).

Petrie, William Matthew Flinders. *Antaeopolis: The Tombs of Qau*. London, 1930. For the tombs with valley chapels at Qau el-Kebir.

Reisner, George Andrew. *The Development of the Egyptian Tomb down to the Accession of Cheops*. Cambridge, Mass., 1936. Detailed typology of early tombs, including chapters on *ka*-chapels.

Reisner, George Andrew. *A History of the Giza Necropolis*. 2 vols. Cambridge, Mass, 1942. Detailed typology of Old Kingdom tombs at Giza, with extensive chapters on *ka*-chapels.

Robichon, Clément, and Alexandre Varille. *Le temple du scribe royal Amenhotpe fils de Hapou*. Fouilles de l'Institut français d'archéologie orientale du Caire. Cairo, 1936. Publication of the eighteenth dynasty cult structure of Amenhotep, son of Hapu.

ANDREY O. BOLSHAKOV

KADESH, written *Kdš(w)* in ancient Egyptian, means "sanctuary" (*qadosh*) in Semitic; it is associated with a number of sites in Palestine, such as Kadesh-barnea (at the eastern end of the Sinai) and another Kadesh located northeast of Lake Hulah in Galilee. The Kadesh that is called both "Kidshu" and "Kinza" in the Amarna Letters of the late eighteenth dynasty, however, is certainly Tell Neby Mend in Syria. Excavations there have unearthed letters on cuneiform tablets referring to a king of "Kinza," a member of the ruling family, attested in the Amarna Letters and other diplomatic records of the Late Bronze Age. These and its location also identify Tell Neby Mend as the "Kadesh-on-the-Orontes," where Ramesses II (r. 1304–1237 BCE) met the Hittites in battle (c.1274 BCE). The name *Qedes* was still connected with localities in the area early in the modern period. While some scholars question the identity of Tell Neby Mend as the Kadesh that opposed Egypt in the mid-eighteenth dynasty, there is no compelling reason to think the Egyptians ever associated "that wretched enemy of Kadesh" with any other place.

The strategic importance of Kadesh-on-the-Orontes lay in its position at the northern end of a broad inland plain (called Coele ["hollow"]-Syria in classical antiquity, and later the *biqá'a*, or "valley," in Arabic); through it, armies had to pass on their way north to inland Syria. The city makes its first appearance in ancient Egyptian records as the ringleader of about 330 Canaanite and Syrian city states allied against Thutmose III (r.1504–1452 BCE). After that coalition's defeat at Megiddo (c.1457 BCE), Kadesh continued to resist. It was still fending off Egyptian control during Thutmose III's last attested campaign (c.1438 BCE), but by the reign of his successor it had been forced to yield: when Amenhotpe II (r. 1454–1419 BCE) approached the city on his "first campaign of victory" (c.1422 BCE), the ruler of Kadesh swore fealty, using a formula that implies a purging of past guilt (see Scott Morschauser's "The End of the *sdf₃-tryt* 'Oath'" *Journal of the American Research Center in Egypt* 25 [1988], pp. 93–103). A generation later, when Egypt under Thutmose IV (r. 1419–1410 BCE) made peace with the Kingdom of Mitanni, vassals on both sides were locked into their allegiances, and Kadesh remained under Egyptian overlordship.

The situation changed drastically during the reign of Akhenaten (Amenhotpe IV, r. 1372–1355 BCE), when the Hittite king Suppiluliumas I precipitated the collapse of Mitanni and replaced it with Hatti as the northern superpower in the Near East. The Hittites had planned (Suppiluliumas wrote) to eliminate their opposition without fighting against Kadesh: but the city's king, Shutatarra, joined the Hittites' enemies and was caught up in their defeat. He was deported to Hatti along with his son (and coregent?) Aitakama, though the latter was eventually allowed to return to Kadesh. In the only letter of Aitakama preserved in the cuneiform archive of Amarna Letters (EA 189), he portrays himself as one of the pharaoh's aggrieved and misunderstood vassals; but in the report of others he emerges less sympathetically—joining another of the pharaoh's vassals in attacking a third, and even encouraging his neighbors to exchange their Egyptian overlord for the Hittite king. Belatedly recognizing Kadesh's defection, the Egyptians twice sent an army to recover it; and twice they were not only defeated but punished with a Hittite raid on neighboring Egyptian vassal territory. Hatti's reluctance to relinquish its serendipitous prize emerged in subsequent negotiations with Egypt, when Suppiluliumas disingenuously claimed that he had taken the city, not from the pharaoh but from the Mitannian king. The all-out war that finally erupted between the two powers ruled out any settlement of differences, leaving Kadesh and other erstwhile Egyptian vassals in Hatti's orbit for the rest of the eighteenth dynasty.

Like others among Hatti's new vassals, Kadesh tried at times to better its situation by defecting to Egypt. One such attempt by King Aitakama was stopped when he was murdered by his own son, Niqmadu, whose rule in Kadesh was subsequently recognized by the Hittite king Mursilis (Murshili) II. A more significant reversal would occur, however, early in the nineteenth dynasty, under Sety I (r. 1314–1304 BCE): the pharaoh's attack on Kadesh is vividly represented at Karnak, where it was written of "the ascent that Pharaoh . . . made to destroy the land of Kadesh and the land of Amurru." This claim is backed up by a stela of Sety I from Tell Neby Mend, indicating by its very presence that Kadesh was restored, willingly or not, to Egyptian control. Though a Hittite *revanche* later in Sety's reign came to nothing, Kadesh was back in the Hittite fold by the early reign of his son, Ramesses II (r. 1304–1237 BCE). Such a reversal—whether brought about by Hittite arms or the city's own political realignment—precipitated a widely publicized campaign to recover Kadesh. Egyptian records show that the critical encounter occurred late in May during Ramesses II's fifth regnal year. Ambiguities in these sources give rise to many obscurities (including details about topography, the battle's chronology, and the disposition of the forces). It seems, though, that Egyptian intelligence was deceived regarding the Hittites' movements, as a result, the pharaoh made camp to the west of Kadesh, without realizing that Hittite forces were concealed nearby. The four divisions of the Egyptian army were spread too far apart to be used effectively when the Hittites unexpectedly attacked. Fortunately, the pharaoh rallied his troops well enough to resist the Hittite onslaught, until relief forces providentially arrived on the scene. At the end of the second day, when it was clear that Egypt's fighting ability had not been broken by surprise, the Hittite king Muwatalli allowed the pharaoh to retire from the field with his army. This gesture (though portrayed as Hittite cravenness in Ramesses II's battle records) was neither cowardly nor humanitarian—merely prudent—since the Hittite king thus spared himself further casualties in an inconclusive engagement. Moreover, Hittite records show that Muwatalli's forces took advantage of Ramesses' retreat by recovering Amurru (the province west of Kadesh) and by occupying previously unconquered Egyptian territory in Upi (in southern Syria, near Damascus).

After that battle, Kadesh remained part of Hatti's empire, and only a few generalized references to that former vassal are to be found in Egyptian records. The city at Tell Neby Mend was destroyed in the twelfth century BCE, probably by the Sea Peoples, who are known from Egyptian sources to have occupied the adjoining territory of Amurru.

BIBLIOGRAPHY

Breasted, James Henry. *The Battle of Kadesh: A Study in the Earliest Known Military Strategy.* Chicago, 1903. This pioneering study, although outdated on a number of points, still has much to offer.
Faulkner, Raymond O. "Egypt: From the Inception of the Nineteenth Dynasty to the Death of Ramesses III." *Cambridge Ancient History,* edited by I. E. S. Edwards, 3d ed., vol. 2, pt. 2: *History of the Middle*

East and the Aegean Region c.1380–1000 B.C., pp. 226–229. Cambridge, 1975. Generally sound, though concise, narrative of events, with a useful survey of bibliography to date.

Gardiner, Alan H. *Ancient Egyptian Onomastica.* Oxford, 1947. Summarizes evidence on the location of Kadesh (prior to modern excavations) and Egyptian activities in the area.

Gardiner, Alan H. *The Kadesh Inscriptions of Ramesses II.* Oxford, 1960. A solid translation, with commentary, of the Egyptian texts that deal with the battle.

Goedicke, Hans, ed. *Perspectives on the Battle of Kadesh.* Baltimore, 1985. Substantial, if occasionally controversial, studies of the battle.

Kitchen, K. A. *Pharaoh Triumphant: The Life and Times of Ramesses II.* Warminster, 1982. A good, if somewhat generalized, account of the battle and its aftermath.

Klengel, Horst. *Geschichte Syriens im 2. Jahrtausend V.U.Z.* Berlin, 1966. The most thoroughly documented study of the history of Kadesh during the Late Bronze Age (although now somewhat dated).

Klengel, Horst. *Syria, 3000 to 300 B.C.: A Handbook of Political History.* Berlin, 1992. More up-to-date but also more concise than the 1966 work.

Murnane, William J. *The Road to Kadesh.* 2d rev. ed. Studies in Ancient Oriental Civilization, 42. Chicago, 1990. Discusses the background of interstate relations in the Near East leading up to the Battle of Kadesh.

Schulman, Alan R. "The 'N'rn' at the Battle of Kadesh." *Journal of the American Research Center in Egypt* 1 (1962), 47–52.

Schulman, Alan R. "The 'N'rn' at Kadesh Once Again." *Journal of the Society for the Study of Egyptian Antiquities* 11.1 (1981), 7–19. This and the 1962 article focus on the identity of the Egyptian relief force that arrived on the territory of Kadesh while the battle still raged.

Vandersleyen, Cl. *L'Égypte* vol. 2: *De la fin de l'Ancien Empire à la fin du Nouvel Empire*, pp. 299–300; 325–327. Paris, 1995. This author opposes the identity of Tell Neby Mend as Kadesh in the mid-eighteenth dynasty.

WILLIAM J. MURNANE

KAMOSE (r. 1571–1569 BCE), last king of the seventeenth dynasty, Second Intermediate Period. Kamose reigned between Sekenenre Ta'o and Ahmose, founder of the eighteenth dynasty, and he probably belonged to their line, although their precise relationship is unknown; he might also be a young brother of Sekenenre rather than his son. In his three-year reign, he recovered a large part of the Egyptian territory that had been lost (through the Hyksos) during the preceding century. Kamose related his campaigns in a long text, of which two thirds is known; the beginning was found on the fragments of a huge stela, dated Year 3 of his reign (and in an almost contemporary Hieratic copy of the beginning of that stela). The second part of the account, was found on a smaller stela, one in perfect condition.

When Kamose became king, Egypt was ruled by the Hyksos leader Aa-woserre Apophis and his Egyptian allies, from the Nile Delta in the north to Cusae, about 30 kilometers (20 miles) south of Hermopolis (el-Ashmunein). In a first campaign, Kamose drove them back beyond Neferusy (near Beni Hasan). In a second campaign, he went against the southern kingdom of Kush, which controlled Nubia as far as the First Cataract of the Nile; he reclaimed the territory up to the south of Buhen. Then he returned to fighting in the North. Kamose related his victory as if he were in front of Avaris, the Hyksos capital in the eastern Delta, terrorizing its inhabitants, while pillaging and destroying the Hyksos fleet. In actuality, after having foiled an alliance between the Hyksos and the Kushite rulers, he apparently recovered only the Nile Valley south to the Faiyum; the story about Avaris might have been only threats or wishes—in which case Kamose probably never did reach Avaris. It is not known whether he reigned beyond his third regnal year. He was buried in Dra 'Abul Naga, in a poor, nonroyal coffin. The mummy within disintegrated when it was uncovered in 1857.

BIBLIOGRAPHY

Habachi, Labib. *The Second Stela of Kamose and His Struggle against the Hyksos Ruler and His Capital.* Abhandlungen des Deutschen Archäologischen Instituts Kairo, 8. Glückstadt, 1972.

Vandersleyen, Claude. *L'Égypte et la Vallée du Nil*, vol. 2: *De la fin de l'Ancien Empire à la fin du Nouvel Empire.* Nouvelle Clio, L'histoire et ses problèmes. Paris, 1995.

CLAUDE A. P. VANDERSLEYEN

KAMUTEF, literally, "bull of his mother," is not exactly the name of a deity, but rather is a functional epithet associated with the name of a deity—usually Amun-Re, or less frequently the combination Min-Amun-Re, or even Min alone. It makes Amun his own father Amun-Re-Kamutef. Kamutef is represented under the appearance of Min, a figure bound up (like a mummy), having an erect penis. Amun-Re-Kamutef is attested at Karnak during the time of Senwosret I, and its ithyphallic depiction dates to the eleventh dynasty. At Coptos during the Middle Kingdom, Min-Kamutef was considered as the son of Isis. The Osirian terminology was thereby introduced into the Coptite theology, and Min-the-son was able to assume the functional name of Horus, and even of Horus-Isis. Kamutef appears in the Hermetic texts under the Greek name "Kamephis."

To impregnate one's own mother was considered incest, a practice attested in the Pyramid Texts. Such an act allowed Geb, who raped his mother Tefnut, to appropriate the royalty of Shu, who was Tefnut's brother and husband and Kamutef's father. Yet to be "Kamutef" is also a way of denying linear time and inverting the succession of generations by uniting the past and the present in one personnage. This personnage, being both father and son of itself, possesses a legitimacy that is not questionable. Helmuth Jacobssohn (1939, 1955) sees in Kamutef a concept employed by the Egyptians to express the continuity of the regeneration of the gods and of the royal dynasties.

Probably, the historical circumstances of the appearance of Amun-Re-Kamutef clarify the significance of this theological construction. Around 2000 BCE, Montuhotep I reestablished the pharaonic power over the entire country. Parallel to his military and political actions, he established his power by means of a new theology whose central figure was Amun, the Theban god who appeared during the reign of his father Antef II. The unifier Montuhotep I is depicted on certain reliefs as adding the feathers of Amun to his crown of Upper Egypt. Amun is not a vague and weak local god; in his first attestations he is a divine and solar king, and an immanent entity, hidden in all things. He presents himself under two forms, a normal and an ithyphallic one, the latter being an appearance borrowed from his companion Min. During the reign of Senwosret I, even the nonithyphallic form of Amun could be described as "Kamutef." The two forms were equally important. Later, they alternated systematically on the walls of the Theban temples.

In the new theocracy, Amun-Re-Kamutef was an expression of the idea of legitimate descent without ancestry, and it kept the royal function safe from dynastic contestation. Although a divinity without ancestors, Amun-Re-Kamutef was not really one of the primordial deities, those solitary and unique gods present at the beginning of the world. Amun-Re-Kamutef is practically absent from the great funerary texts and cosmogonic stories.

The processional image of Min-Amun-Re-Kamutef, a ceremonial object used in the festival of Min, was conserved at Karnak. Following Herbert Ricke (1954), it is customary to attribute to Amun-Re-Kamutef the building constructed by Thutmose III in front of Temple of Mut at Karnak, but this interpretation can be questioned. We know of several priestly titles relating to the cult of the Kamutef-forms of Amun or of Min, but there was no clergy specifically dedicated to this divine aspect.

[*See also* Amun and Amun-Re; *and* Min.]

BIBLIOGRAPHY

Assmann, Jan. "Muttergattin." In *Lexikon der Ägyptologie*, 4: 264–266. Wiesbaden, 1980. With a summary of Jacobssohn's theses.

Bonnet, Hans. *Reallexikon der Ägyptischen Religionsgeschichte.* Berlin, 1952.

Jacobssohn, Helmuth. *Die dogmatische Stellung des Königs in der Theologie der alten Ägypter.* Ägyptologische Forschungen, 8. Glückstadt, Hamburg, and New York, 1939, 1955. See in particular pages 18 ff. The same author summarized his theses in 1978 in *Lexikon der Ägyptologie*, 3: 308–309.

Lacau, Pierre, and Henri Chevrier. *Une chapelle de Sésostris Ier à Karnak.* Cairo, 1956.

Quirke, Stephen. *Ancient Egyptian Religion.* London, 1992.

Ricke, Herbert. *Das Kamutef-heiligtum in Karnak.* Beiträge zur ägyp-

tischen Bayforschung und Altertumskunde, 3. Cairo, 1954. Publication of the excavations of the temple of the Mut precinct, with an attempt at an interpretation and presentation of the information about Mut.

CLAUDE TRAUNECKER
Translated from French by Susan Romanosky

KARANIS. *See* Faiyum.

KARNAK, an ancient site whose name derives from that of a nearby village, refers to a large complex of temples on the eastern bank of the Nile River at Luxor (ancient Thebes) in Upper Egypt (25°43′N, 32°40′E). Early in the twelfth dynasty, Egyptian rulers who had originated in the Theban area inaugurated what was perhaps the first shrine on the site of Karnak. By the New Kingdom, the eighteenth dynasty pharaohs made Thebes the center of the Egyptian empire and Karnak the center of the cult of Amun (the principal divine sponsor and protector of the empire, with his consort Mut, their son Khonsu, and the Theban war god Montu). Karnak retained this central position throughout the New Kingdom, even after the governmental center had been moved to the Nile Delta. Karnak's status as a major sacred center then continued for at least another millennium. In the fourth century BCE, Nektanebo I ordered the construction of a gigantic mud-brick enclosure wall around the main complex centered on the temple of Amun; that wall today encloses some 60 acres (more than 100 hectares) of ruins in varying states of preservation. To the north of the main precinct is a temple to Montu, while to the south lies the temple of the goddess Mut. Excavations outside the eastern enclosure wall disclose the remains of a series of four interrelated temples, constructed at the behest of Amenhotpe IV (later Akhenaten) at the outset of his reign, in what was probably a poor residential area.

Any attempt to present a systematic description of what lies within the Nektanebo walls is complicated by the continuous additions, disassemblings, rebuildings, and alterations that more or less continued until well into Roman times, that is for well over two millennia. The Roman emperor Tiberius, for example, added his name, written in hieroglyphs, to one of the component structures. Thus, any description that proceeds from the present entrance along the central axis of the great temple of Amun runs back through and athwart the chronology of construction, for the growth of the temple was not according to any systematic master plan, nor did it proceed in one direction only.

The temple of Amun—called "most select of sites" (Eg.,

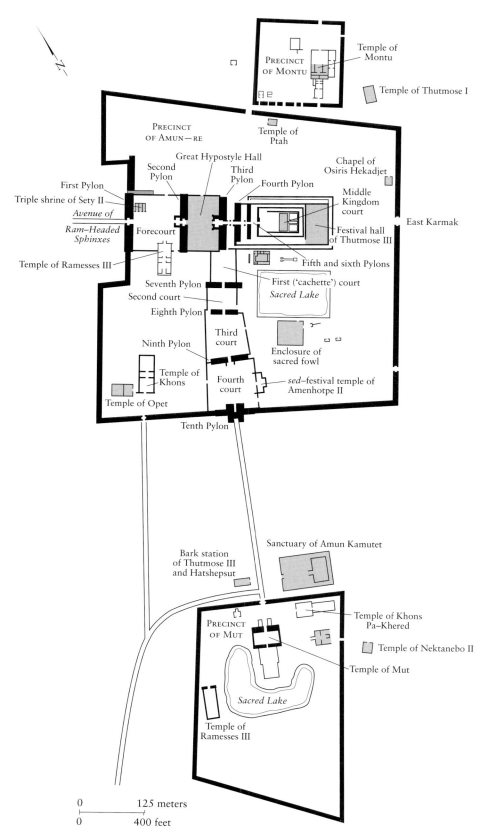

N

Precinct of Montu

Temple of Montu

Temple of Thutmose I

Precinct of Amun—re

Temple of Ptah

Great Hypostyle Hall

Second Pylon

Third Pylon

Fourth Pylon

Chapel of Osiris Hekadjet

First Pylon

Triple shrine of Sety II

Avenue of

Ram–Headed Sphinxes

Forecourt

Middle Kingdom court

Festival hall of Thutmose III

East Karmak

Temple of Ramesses III

Fifth and sixth Pylons

Seventh Pylon

First ('cachette') court

Sacred Lake

Second court

Eighth Pylon

Third court

Ninth Pylon

Enclosure of sacred fowl

Temple of Khons

Fourth court

sed–festival temple of Amenhotpe II

Temple of Opet

Tenth Pylon

Bark station of Thutmose III and Hatshepsut

Sanctuary of Amun Kamutet

Temple of Khons Pa–Khered

Precinct of Mut

Temple of Nektanebo II

Temple of Mut

Sacred Lake

Temple of Ramesses III

0   125 meters

0   400 feet

KARNAK. *Plan of Karnak.*

Ipt-swt)—was the center of the cult of Amun ("the Hidden One"); during the New Kingdom, it was transformed from the worship of a local fertility divinity to the center of the "estate of Amun," a national religious and economic institution that, fed by the fruits of pharaonic conquests and self-promotion, became the single most powerful and influential priestly body in Egypt. Ruler after ruler trumpeted both piety and military success by adding to or rebuilding part of the complex while covering its walls with scenes and inscriptions of military victories, religious ceremonials, and benefactions to and from Amun and other members of the divine community. The temple was the scene of annual, monthly, and other ritual cycles and processions in honor of the Theban triad. Other deities were assigned areas of the complex as "guests"; thus, for example, the northeastern quadrant appears to have been the principal locus of worship for the mortuary god Osiris, said to be "resident in *Ipt-swt*." Amun himself appears in several forms, including the ithyphallic Amun-Kamutef and the solar Amun-Re-Herakhty.

The great temple of Amun consists of a main axis that runs from west to east through a series of six great pylons, or gateways, leading to the main sanctuary. A secondary axis runs to the south from just beyond the Third Pylon, adding pylons Seven through Ten; this axis connects the main Amun complex to the temple of the goddess Mut. From there it originally ran along a sphinx-lined corridor all the way to the Luxor temple of Amun. To the east of this series of pylons, and south of the Amun temple, lies the large "sacred lake." Nearby is a rather intriguing edifice constructed by Taharqa of the twenty-fifth dynasty, which takes some of its influence from earlier structures elsewhere in the complex.

The ancient processional access to the temple was a canal from the Nile, which ended in later times at a quay just west of the avenue of ram-headed sphinxes that lead to the First Pylon. Beyond lies the First Court, which contains, on the north side, a tripartite way-station built by Sety II for the sacred barks of the Triad. Serving a similar function is the much larger tripartite templelike structure of Ramesses III, which protrudes into the open area beyond the southwestern forecourt wall. Access to the open area to the north of the Ramesses III building is gained through the twenty-second dynasty "Bubastite Portal," a gateway bearing numerous ritual inscriptions and scenes. Just outside, to the east, Sheshonq I inscribed a record of his campaigns in Palestine. In the center of the First Court are the scant remains of a structure contributed by the Nubian pharaoh Taharqa (of the early seventh century BCE). Beyond the badly preserved Second Pylon (of the late eighteenth dynasty) lies the Great Hypostyle Hall, a veritable forest of 134 columns. The central aisle is defined by 12 columns some 22 meters (72 feet) high; the other 122 columns are about 15 meters (50 feet) high; the former are topped by open-bud capitals, the remainder by closed papyrus capitals. Light entered the stone-roofed hall through a series of grated clerestories high above ground level. The decoration of the walls of this room belongs to the reigns of Sety I and Ramesses II; it consists of ritual and processional scenes executed in raised reliefs under the earlier king and incised relief by his successor. In contrast to these scenes inside the hall, battle and victory scenes of Sety I decorate the outside surface of the northern wall.

The Third Pylon, built by Amenhotpe III, is of interest not only because the remains suggest its original imposing monumentality and the quality of the decoration but also because of its core, formed of blocks taken from earlier monuments of the twelfth dynasty king Senwosret I and from those of Amenhotpe I, Hatshepsut, and Thutmose IV of the eighteenth dynasty. These earlier structures have been largely reconstructed and now stand in the open area north of the Hypostyle Hall. In similar fashion, Horemheb subsequently dismantled the Aten-temples of Akhenaten on the east of Karnak and used the blocks (*talatat*) in constructing the Ninth and Tenth Pylons on the north–south axis.

The Fourth and Fifth Pylons, built by Thutmose I, originally had pairs of obelisks standing before them; only one of Hatshepsut's and one of her father's remain standing. Beyond the Sixth Pylon of Thutmose III lies the central court that served as the principal sanctuary of the complex. An original shrine of the latter ruler was replaced in the late fourth century by a red granite bark shrine, set up on behalf of Philip Arrhidaeus, the half-brother and successor of Alexander the Great. The last important structure along the main axis of the Amun temple is the Festival Hall of Thutmose III, a building designed to celebrate the king's *sed*-festival. In the northeastern quarter of the Karnak enclosure are a number of chapels to Osiris, dating mostly to the twenty-third and twenty-fifth dynasties; notable among these is the chapel of Osiris-Ruler-of-Eternity, begun in the twenty-third dynasty and augmented in the twenty-fifth. Along the northern enclosure wall is a small temple of the god Ptah.

The four pylons that run to the south of the main temple were built by Thutmose III (VII and VIII) and by Horemheb (IX and X). Some of the side walls were built by later Ramessid rulers, and some traces of twelfth and early eighteenth dynasty structures have been discovered there. Built into the side wall between the Ninth and Tenth Pylons is the *sed*-festival chapel of Amenhotpe I. In the southwestern corner of the enclosure are the remains of a temple dedicated to the moon god Khonsu and a

KARNAK. *Papyrus and lotus columns of the court of the sixth pylon.* The papyrus and lotus are emblems of Upper Egypt and Lower Egypt, respectively. The columns are made of red granite. (Courtesy Dieter Arnold)

smaller building for the goddess Ipet. A large number of statues was found in a cachette between the Seventh and Eighth Pylons.

To the north of the Nektanebo enclosure is the precinct of the Theban war god Montu, which, in addition to the temple dedicated to that god, contains a smaller structure for the cult of the goddess Maat. Built by Amenhotpe III, and later augmented by Ptolemaic rulers, the Montu enclosure is somewhat unusual in that the access is from the north. The remains of a small temple of Thutmose I have been unearthed just outside the southeastern corner of the enclosure. To the south of the south line of pylons lies the enclosure of the temple of Mut, with its atypical horseshoe-shaped sacred lake. Excavations have yielded a large number of statues of the goddess Sekhmet. To the west of the sacred lake are the remains of a temple of Ramesses III.

Karnak is a treasure trove of reliefs and statuary, much of it executed with great skill and aesthetic sensitivity. The subject matter of the reliefs ranges from imperial combat to the relationships between the king and the gods, from religious processions to processions of royal sons, from lists of conquered territories to zoological and botanical themes. The statuary of gods, goddesses, kings, and their wives form a rich repertory; indeed, the long history of the temple makes it an archive of subjects and styles that reveals the richness of Egyptian religious art and allows the critical eye to see the outlines of development and change over the millennia.

[*See also* Temples.]

BIBLIOGRAPHY

The principal work on the Karnak temples, carried out by the Centre franco-égyptien de Karnak, has been published in a series of monographs:

Azim, M. *Karnak et sa topographie.* Cairo, 1998.

Badawy, A. *A History of Egyptian Architecture.* Vol. 3. Berkeley, 1968.

Baines, J., and J. Málek. *Atlas of Ancient Egypt.* Oxford, 1980.

Barguet, P. *Le temple de d'Amon-Re à Karnak.* Cairo, 1962.

Lauffray, J. *Karnak d'Egypte. Domain du divin.* Paris, 1979.

Oriental Institute of the University of Chicago. *The Temple of Khonsu.* Chicago, 1979–1981.

Shafer, B. E., ed. *Temples of Ancient Egypt.* Ithaca, 1997.

Trauneker, C., and J.-Cl. Golvin. *Karnak: résurection d'un site.* Freibourg, 1984.

GERALD E. KADISH

KAWA, a site on the eastern bank of the Nile River, some 100 kilometers (62 miles) upstream from the Third Cataract, occupying a prominent mound that formed over 36 hectares. Excavations were undertaken at Kawa by the Oxford Excavations in Nubia expedition led by Francis Llewellyn Griffith from 1929 to 1931 and, after his death, by M. F. Laming Macadam and Laurence Kirwan in the winter of 1935–1936. Although excavated on a large scale, much of the site remains to be investigated, and at no point were the earliest deposits reached. The oldest artifacts were of the Kerma period, but no structural evidence of that date was revealed. Epigraphic evidence indicates that in Old Egyptian, the town was called *Gem Aten* ("the Aten is perceived"); this strongly suggests that a settlement was founded (or refounded) there during the New Kingdom, either in the latter part of the reign of Amenhotpe III or in that of his son, Amenhotpe IV, better known as Akhenaten.

Griffith's team excavated the well-preserved remains of a stone temple (Temple A) built by, or possibly completed by, Tutankhamun. Temple A remained in use for centuries, and there are inscriptions within it of a number of nineteenth and twentieth dynasty pharaohs, including Ramesses II. The latest attested pharaoh is Ramesses VI (r. 1156–1149 BCE).

On the collapse of Egyptian control of the region, which ended by the early eleventh century BCE, the fate of the town is unknown. It was next mentioned in the extant sources from the time of the Kushite ruler Alara (early eighth century BCE), when there was probably a functioning temple of Amun there. In 690 BCE, the Kushite ruler Taharka, passed through Kawa on his way to Egypt and was appalled at the state of a temple in the town. He ordered the reconstruction of that building and, in 684 BCE, began the construction of a large temple of Amun (Temple T), which was completed in four years by a team of architects and masons brought from Memphis especially for the task. Kawa was a nome capital, and it held a prominent place in the ritualized demonstration of royal power by the Kushite kings. A number of inscriptions, including that of Irike-Amanote (r. 431–405 BCE), carved on the walls of Temple T, record that the town was one of several sites visited by the new Kushite monarchs. At each visit, the king's divine mandate to rule was confirmed by the local god; at Kawa, it was Amun of Gem Aten, depicted as a ram-headed god, with the horizontally twisted horns of the sheep species *Ovis longipes palaeoaegyptiaca.*

The town was inhabited into the early first millennium CE, and from that time additional temples, dwellings, a temple garden, and a wine press are known from excavations. Surface finds from the rest of the site indicate that substantial mud-brick buildings lie buried there. By the fourth century CE, the site was abandoned, having perhaps finally succumbed to the ever encroaching windblown sands, which had constantly threatened to overwhelm it. It has never been reoccupied.

[*See also* Nubia.]

BIBLIOGRAPHY

Macadam, M. F. Laming. *The Temples of Kawa,* vol. 1: *The Inscriptions.* London, 1949.

Macadam, M. F. Laming. *The Temples of Kawa,* vol. 2: *History and Archaeology of the Site.* London, 1955. This work, with *Kawa I,* publish in detail the excavations of the 1920s and 1930s; the prime sources for any discussion of the site.

Welsby, Derek A. *The Kingdom of Kush: The Napatan and Meroitic Empires.* London, 1996. Discussed here and placed in their wider context are Kawa, as a major center of the Kushite state, and the Kushite Temple T.

DEREK A. WELSBY

KEMIT, a schoolboy text compiled at the very end of the eleventh dynasty or the beginning of the twelfth, to assist in the education of young scribes for service in the civil bureaucracy, which had been depleted of talent during the tumultuous First Intermediate Period. Although the extant sources of *Kemit* are confined to the New Kingdom (on a writing board and more than one hundred ostraca), the text is distinguished from other New Kingdom literary documents by being inscribed in archaic fashion in vertical columns in a script that closely resembles early Middle Kingdom Hieratic. None of the documents preserves *Kemit* in its entirety, but through a careful assemblage of the numerous fragmentary ostraca, the complete text has been successfully reconstituted.

The term *kemit*, meaning something like "summation" or "completion," is not found in the text itself, but it is known from the twelfth dynasty "Satire on the Trades" section of the *Instructions of Khety*, where a passage "at the end of *Kemit*" is quoted. The *Kemit* book consists of three independent sections: greetings used in letter-writing, a narrative concluding with a letter, and a selection of phrases drawn from the genre of ideal biography. The text begins with the writer addressing his "lord" in a letter that contains wishes for his well-being, favor with the gods who daily should do everything good for him, a ripe old age, and eventual passing on to the honored state of a deceased person. Although portions of the epistolary formulae are attested as early as the sixth dynasty, the naming of Montu, god of the Theban nome, in the greetings suggests an early Middle Kingdom date.

Because of the considerable difference in time between the date of composition and the date of the preserved copies, there is much that is obscure in this schoolboy compendium, especially in the middle section. Here there is reference to a certain Au, who as a young married cadet, salved with perfumes and garbed in a kilt of blue linen, visits a dancing-girl. The girl, however, realizes the impropriety of the situation and knows that Au's wife must be constantly weeping for her husband, so she urges Au to see to his wife. In response to the dancing-girl's concern, there follows a letter addressed by Au to his wife, imploring her to come north to the place where he speaks of being found by his comrades "like an orphan at the edge of a strange city." The letter concludes with a statement by Au about meeting his father on a feast day (birthday?) while his mother had gone off to the Sycomore Shrine.

The phrases of the ideal biography section emphasize the virtue of respecting one's parents, being quiet, and controlling one's temper. The writer describes himself as a scribe "who is valuable to his lord and most expert in his calling." In the conclusion, the student is urged to become educated in texts, because wisdom serves to advance one's status, and the perquisites of being a scribe at the royal residence ensure that one "can never become miserable in it."

BIBLIOGRAPHY

Barta, Winfred. "Das Schulbuch Kemit." *Zeitschrift für ägyptische Sprache und Altertumskunde* 105 (1978), 6–14. Offers translation and discussion of the structure of *Kemit*.

Posener, Georges. *Catalogue des ostraca hiératiques littéraires de Deir el Médineh.* Documents de Fouilles de l'Institut Français d'Archéologie Orientale du Caire, 18. Cairo, 1951. Publication of the reconstituted text of *Kemit* in hieroglyphic transcription from the hieratic documents.

Posener, Georges. *Littérature et politique dans l'Égypte de la XIIᵉ Dynastie.* Paris, 1956. Discusses *Kemit* as the earliest of a series of literary compositions designed to educate scribes to become loyal civil servants in the bureaucracy.

Wente, Edward F. *Letters from Ancient Egypt.* Society of Biblical Literature, Writings from the Ancient World, 1, edited by Edmund S. Meltzer. Atlanta, 1990. Provides a translation of the *Kemit* book on pages 15–16.

EDWARD F. WENTE

KERMA, a major archaeological site, located below the Third Cataract of the Nile River, in Sudan (19°36′N, 30°25′E). Kerma was the seat of one of the first African kingdoms (2300–1500 BCE), identified in Egyptian texts as Kush from the Middle Kingdom onward. Possibly the land of Iam (mentioned in the sixth dynasty by Hirkhouf) may have been centered around Kerma. The kingdom was blessed by an environment conducive to agriculture and husbandry, and it owed its scope to a privileged geographic situation that assured it a dominant role in the trading networks of Egypt, sub-Saharan Africa, and the Red Sea. Its political importance is evident in the chain of fortresses erected in Lower Nubia by the pharaohs of the twelfth dynasty.

A study of Kerma's ceramics and funerary customs has led to the identification of several chronological phases: Old Kerma (end of Old Kingdom/First Intermediate Period), Middle Kerma (Middle Kingdom), and Classic Kerma (Second Intermediate Period). The territorial boundaries have not yet been established. To the south, Kerma remains have been located up to the Fourth Cataract of the Nile, while to the north, Batn el-Hagar most certainly marked a border. During Classic Kerma, the kingdom of Kush expanded its sphere of power into Lower Nubia and occupied the fortresses of the Second Cataract. Armed conflict, documented in Egyptian sources, seems not to have stood in the way of trade exchange, as witnessed by the archaeological discovery of Egyptian ceramics and seal imprints that belonged to Egyptian administrative services. This development was reflected in the structures brought to light first by G. A. Reisner (1923) and by the expedition of the University of Geneva from 1977 onward. The city of Classic Kerma, surrounded by an imposing system of defences, covered an area larger than 30 hectares. The topography is characterized by causeways and some specific sectors: the religious quarter dominated by the *deffufa*, a temple whose mud-brick walls still rise to 18 meters (55 feet); the palace and its stores; and the harbor quarter, not counting the chapels of the secondary settlement. All these institutions indicate a complex organizational structure, undoubtedly inspired by Egypt, yet whose precise modalities we cannot establish owing to a lack of written sources. The existence of an administrative organization was confirmed by the discovery of local seals and seal impressions. The seals were made of baked clay, and clay reserves were prepared especially for them.

Kerma's funerary customs are distinct from those practiced in Egypt. The dead rest in a bent position on a leather blanket or a wooden bed. The surface of the tomb is marked by a circular tumulus, ceramics, and bucrania (ox skull) deposits. From Middle Kerma onward, chapels are associated with certain tombs. The layout of the necropolis in Classic Kerma indicates the existence of an elite class in the service of the sovereigns who exercised near-absolute power. The last sovereigns are interred in monumental tombs that measure up to 100 meters (320 feet) in diameter, which contain hundreds of human sacrifices and abundant funerary offerings. These include Egyptian pieces, such as the famous statues of Hapydjefa and Sennuwy, most likely acquired during raids into Lower Nubia. Two temples seem important because of their faience decor and painted murals, which blend purely sub-Saharan African elements with others borrowed from Egyptian themes. The city of Kerma was probably destroyed under Thutmose II of the eighteenth dynasty, when all of Nubia fell to Egypt.

[*See also* Nubia.]

BIBLIOGRAPHY

Bonnet, Charles. "Les fouilles archéologiques de Kerma (Soudan). Rapports préliminaires." Geneva, vols. 26–45, 1978–1997. Detailed presentation of the excavations undertaken by the Swiss Mission of the University of Geneva since 1978.

Bonnet, Charles. *Kerma: Territoire et métropole.* Bibliotheque General, 9. Cairo, 1986. Conference at the Collège de France, offering a sound approach to the study of urban development, religious architecture, and funerary customs, principally based on the excavations carried out at Kerma.

Bonnet, Charles, et al. *Kerma: Royaume de Nubie.* Geneva, 1990. Exhibition catalog of the Musée d'art et d'histoire de Genève, dedicated to the excavation work led by the University of Geneva at Kerma. Abundant graphic and photographic documentation on the material, architecture, and urban culture, and on funerary customs; detailed bibliography.

Dunham, Dows. *Excavations at Kerma.* Boston, 1982.

Gratien, Brigitte. *Les cultures Kerma: Essai de classification.* Lille, 1978. Synthesis of what is known of the history of the Kerma culture and its relations with Egypt and other Nubian cultures.

Gratien, Brigitte. *Saï I. La nécropole Kerma.* Paris, 1986. Second important Kerma site, excavated from 1971 to 1978. Based on the research of this necropolis, Gratien defined the main chronological phases of Kerman culture.

Reisner, George A. *Excavations at Kerma.* 2 vols. Harvard African Studies, 5–6. Cambridge, Mass., 1923. Results and interpretation of the excavations undertaken by the author between 1913 and 1916.

Wenig, Steffen. *Africa in Antiquity: The Arts of Ancient Nubia and the Sudan,* vol. 2: *The Catalogue.* Brooklyn, 1978. Exhibition catalog, giving an overview of all successive culture in Nubia, from prehistory to the Christian era; rich iconographic documentation and detailed bibliography.

Wildung, Dietrich, et al. *Sudan: Ancient Kingdoms of the Nile.* Paris and New York, 1996. Exhibition catalog, including the most recent archaeological research with regard to prehistoric periods up to the Meroitic period; rich iconographic documentation. (English version in progress.)

CHARLES BONNET
Translated from French by Elizabeth Schwaiger
and Martha Imber-Goldstein

KHAEMWASET. "The One Who Rises in Thebes" was the son of Ramesses II (r. 1304–1237) by his second great wife Isetnofret. He was born during the reign of his grandfather, Sety I, when his father was prince regent. When he was still a boy of about five, he took part in a Nubian campaign, as shown in a scene in the temple of Beit el-Wali in Nubia; he also accompanied his father to later wars: one in Syria near a fortress called Dapur is recorded on the eastern wall of the Hypostyle Hall of the Ramesseum west of Thebes.

The army, however was not to be the career of Khaemwaset. As a youth he entered into the sacred service of Ptah and Apis at Memphis. He held the titles "Sem of Ptah" (high priest of Ptah) and "Overseer of the Artisans" (high priest of Memphis). He was responsible not only for the administration of the temple and estates of Ptah but also for the construction of royal monuments, including a new temple to Ptah and other building projects of his father throughout Egypt. As high priest of Ptah, Khaemwaset was charged with the proclamation and celebration of his father's *heb-sed*, or thirty-year jubilee. Five of the thirteen other jubilees of Ramesses II were under the charge of Khaemwaset. He supervised the announcement of these as far as Aswan in the south and left records commemorating them in Year 30, 34, 37, 40, and 43 of his father's reign. Three of these records are in the Speos of Horemheb, the last king of the eighteenth dynasty at Gebel el-Silsila, two others in the area of Aswan, and one in the temple of Elkab. During his tours, Khaemwaset had the chance to place his own statues in many temples, as for example in the area of Miniya in Middle Egypt, in Abydos, and in Karnak.

The other responsibility of Khaemwaset was the cult and burial of the Apis bull, the sacred animal of Ptah; under his supervision the deceased bull was embalmed for burial. After the mummified body was decorated, the animal was placed in a huge wooden coffin in a special rock-cut tomb with an underground burial chamber and a funerary chapel above, in the necropolis of Saqqara. Two of these bulls, from the Years 16 and 30 of Ramesses II, were interred in one tomb. The south wall of the burial chamber was decorated with scenes that show Prince Khaemwaset and his father, Ramesses II, adoring Apis. The bull of Year 30 was the last one interred in an isolated tomb. After that, Khaemwaset changed the burial of the Apis bulls: instead of a simple rock-cut tomb, he established a special underground gallery under the desert plateau of Saqqara, which was still in use a thousand years later for burial of the bulls. It is known as the Serapeum, and was discovered and excavated by Auguste Mariette in 1852. Instead of funerary chapels for each bull's isolated tombs, Khaemwaset also built a temple to celebrate the last rites of the deceased bulls. Blocks and fragments from statues with the names of Khaemwaset and his mother Isetnofret have been found by the Serapeum.

Khaemwaset also had a personal interest in the past, especially that of his ancestors and their buildings. From his residence at Memphis, he was able to visit and investigate the royal monuments of the Old Kingdom in this area. Surely because he was impressed by the glorious building of the past, he started to clear the sand from them and to renew the cults of the ancient kings. The pyramids of Giza and other royal monuments at Abusir, Abu Gurab, and Saqqara bear witness to the labors of Khaemwaset. On one face of each pyramid or sun temple, he engraved a standard inscription with the names and titles of their owners, the name of his father Ramesses II, and his own name. The inscriptions inform us of the following: Khaemwaset has done this work through his own desire to restore the monuments of his ancestors, because the names of their owners are not found on the faces of their buildings, and because their temples have fallen into ruin. One inscription is still to be seen on the pyramid of Unas at the necropolis of Saqqara. Khaemwaset may also have done some excavation of the ancient sites. This follows from an inscription engraved by him on three sides of a statue base of Prince Kawab, a son of the King Khufu (r. 2609–2584 BCE), which Khaemwaset discovered in the ruins of a tomb of the fourth dynasty at Giza and placed in a chapel at the necropolis.

Khaemwaset also became famous in popular tradition as a magician and was a subject of folk stories about his wisdom and power. For a thousand years after his death, stories were woven around him, some of which are preserved in Demotic papyri from the Ptolemaic and Roman periods. In the Demotic *Story of Setna*, Khaemwaset searches for a magical book of Thoth that will allow him to understand the language of birds and animals and to charm the earth.

Little is known about the private life of Khaemwaset. He was married, but the name of his wife is unknown. A son of Khaemwaset with the name Ramesses and the title "King's Son" is mentioned on a statue of the prince (now in Vienna); a daughter of Khaemwaset, called Isetnofret after her grandmother, has the title "His Beloved Daughter from His Body."

Khaemwaset was still alive in the Year 52 of his father's reign, but he was dead before Year 60. On one statue from Abydos, now in the British Museum, Khaemwaset is given the title "Senior King's Son, His Beloved," which is well known as the title of the crown prince during the New Kingdom. His younger brother, Merenptah, lived long enough to succeed his father on the throne.

The site of Khaemwaset's tomb is not exactly identified; he was probably buried in the Saqqara necropolis, and not in the catacombs of the sacred bulls, as some Egyptologists assert. His tomb, probably not far from the Serapeum, must have been destroyed when the catacombs were enlarged during the thirtieth dynasty or later in the Ptolemaic period. At that time, the burial of the prince may have been moved into the older section of the Serapeums, which he had built. About 1.5 kilometers (1 mile) northwest of the Serapeum, workers from Waseda University, Tokyo, in 1991 excavated a building in which many blocks and fragments bear the name and titles of Khaemwaset; its purpose is still unknown, but it may be a chapel of the god Sokar.

BIBLIOGRAPHY

Aly, Ibrahim M. "À propos du prince Khâemouaset et de sa mère Isetneferet: Nouveaux documents provenant du Sérapéum." *Mitteilungen des Deutschen Archäologischen Instituts, Abteilung Kairo* 49 (1993), 97–105, pl. 20–23.

Dodson, A. "Of Bulls and Princes: The Early Years of the Serapeum at Sakkara." *K.M.T.: A Modern Journal of Ancient Egypt* 6 (1995), 19–32.

Gomaà, Farouk. "Chaemwese." *Lexikon der Ägyptologie* 1: 897–898.

Gomaà, Farouk. "Chaemwese, Sohn Ramses II. und Hoherpriester von Memphis." *Ägyptologische Abhandlung* 27 (1973).

Kitchen, K. A. *Ramesside Inscriptions: Historical and Biographical.* London, 1979. See pp. 871–899.

Kitchen, K. A. *Pharoah Triumphant: The Life and Times of Rameses II, King of Egypt.* 1982. See especially pp. 89, 103–109.

Kitchen, K. A. *Ramesside Inscriptions: Translated and Annotated, Translations.* London, 1996. See pp. 565–585.

"A Monument of Khaemwaset at Saqqara." *Egyptian Archaeology, the Bulletin of the Egyptian Exploration Society* 5 (1994), 19–23.

Schmitz, B. *Untersuchungen zum Titel s3-Njswt "Königssohn."* Habelts Dissertationsdrucke, Reihe Ägyptologie, 2. 1976. See especially pp. 264, 266, 319–320, 325, 331.

Teeter, E. "Kaemwaset." *K.M.T.: A Modern Journal of Ancient Egypt* 1.4 (1990/1991), 41–64.

FAROUK GOMAÀ

KHAFRE (r. 2576–2551 BCE), fourth king of the fourth dynasty, Old Kingdom. The son of Khufu, Khafre (or Khephren to the ancient Greeks), is best known as the owner of the second pyramid at Giza. As with the other

KHAFRE. *Pyramid of Khafre at Giza.* (Courtesy Dieter Arnold)

kings of that dynasty, written records that date to his reign are scarce; even information on family relationships and the lengths of individual reigns at that time may often be conjectural. Two of his wives are known: Meresankh II, the daughter of his brother Kawab, and his chief wife, Khamerernebty. His eldest son, Menkaure, builder of the third pyramid at Giza, succeeded him. Two other sons are recognized: Nikaure and Sekhemkare. His daughter Khamerernebty II became Menkaure's chief queen. Khafre succeeded his brother, Djedefre, who had ruled for eight years. Ideologically, Khafre continued Djedefre's promotion of the cult of the sun god Re by using the title "Son of the Sun" for himself and by incorporating the name of the god in his own.

Khafre built his pyramid at Giza next to that of his father. His pyramid complex has survived better than many others, in part because of the innovative construction method of using massive core blocks of limestone encased in fine lining slabs. The whole complex served as a temple for the resurrected god-king after his funeral, with statues incorporated into the design of both the mortuary and valley temples. There exist emplacements for more than fifty-four large statues of the king. None of the statues from the mortuary temple has survived, and it has been suggested that they were recycled in the New Kingdom.

All the lining slabs were also removed in antiquity, and with them any inscriptions and reliefs; only the megalithic core blocks remain. Khafre's valley temple, however, is one of the best-preserved from ancient Egypt. Fragments of several statues of the king were discovered there, including the famous diorite statue of the king seated on a lion throne with the falcon of Horus behind his head, reflecting the belief that the king was a living incarnation of that god. Each of the two entrances to this temple were once flanked by a pair of sphinxes 8 meters (26 feet) long. The only remaining inscriptions in the building are around the entrance doorways; they list the king's names and titles, those of the goddess Bastet (north doorway), and those of Hathor (south doorway). Recent work in front of the valley temple has revealed the location of a ritual purification tent and two ramps with underground tunnels that extend toward the valley.

Next to the valley temple, the Great Sphinx lies inside its own enclosure. Its position next to Khafre's causeway and certain architectural details indicate that it was an integral part of the pyramid area; that colossal lion statue with the head of the king, carved out of a sandstone outcrop, represents Khafre as the god Horus presenting offerings to the sun god. From the eighteenth dynasty forward, the Sphinx was a symbol of kingship and a place of pilgrimage, and a small chapel was erected between its paws.

Political events of Khafre's reign can be deduced only from scant archaeological remains and rare inscriptions, which show that his workmen were exploiting the diorite quarries at Toshka in Nubia and that expeditions were sent to Sinai. His name was found on a list of other fourth dynasty kings at Byblos, implying diplomatic and commercial links.

Like his father Khufu, Khafre was depicted in folk tradition as a harsh, despotic ruler. His pyramid complex was used as a quarry in the late New Kingdom, and the lining slabs and statues were removed to adorn other temples and royal establishments. By the Late period, however, the cults of the fourth dynasty kings had been revived, and Giza had become a focus for pilgrimage.

BIBLIOGRAPHY

Hawass, Z. "The Excavation in Front of the Valley Temple of Khafre: The *ibw* and the *R-s'*." *Mitteilungen des Deutsches Archäologisches Institut, Abteilung Kairo.*

ZAHI HAWASS

KHASEKHEMWY (r. 2714–2687 BCE), the last king of second dynasty, Early Dynastic period. According to the Turin Canon, he ruled for twenty-seven years. During the first part of his reign as Hor Khasekhem ("Appearance of the Power") he controlled Upper Egypt only—like his predecessor Peribsen—and he resided at Hierakonpolis. A large funerary enclosure (the "fort") indicates that he intended to be buried there, but no tomb has been located. In the temple area, a fragment of a stela showing a victory over Nubia, three stone vessels with year names ("victory over the papyrus people, unification of Egypt"), as well as two statues (now in Cairo and Oxford) were discovered (Quibell et al. 1900–1902). The scenes on the base of the statues also refer to the victory over Lower Egypt mentioning 47,209 slain northeners (probably a census number). Following this victory, Upper and Lower Egypt became reunited, the king altered his name to Hor–Seth Khasekhemwy ("Appearance of the Two Powers"), and changed his residence to Memphis.

Rainer Stadelmann suggests (*Die Ägyptischen Pyramiden*, 3d ed., 1997, p. 37) that Khasekhemwy's tomb is actually to be identified with the western massives of the Djoser complex at Saqqara. It is more likely, however, that he was buried at Abydos where he built another large funerary enclosure, Shunet el-Zebib, near the cultivated area, and a tomb with fifty-eight chambers at Umm el-Qaab (Petrie 1901). During the first excavation of this tomb in 1896/97 Émile Amélineau found two skeletons in the vicinity of the central limestone chamber. As there are no subsidiary burials, one of these might be the remains of the king.

Investigations by the German Institute show Khasekhemwy's tomb to have undergone several building stages. The first was a copy of the tomb of Peribsen, which was later enlarged by storeroom galleries similar to the second dynasty tombs at Saqqara. A stela from the tomb was discovered at the modern village.

Khasekhemwy's wife was Ni-maat-Hapi. Her name "the *maat* belongs to [the Memphite] Apis [bull]," points to her origin from Lower Egyptian. She outlived him and contributed to his funerary equipment at Abydos together with their son Djoser (Hor Netrj-khet), who succeeded as first king of the third dynasty (Dreyer 1998).

[*See also* Early Dynastic Period.]

BIBLIOGRAPHY

Dreyer, Günter. "Der 1. König der 3. Dynastie." In *Fs. Rainer Stadelmann*. Mainz, 1998.
Petrie, W. M. Flinders. *The Royal Tombs of the Earliest Dynasties*, vol. 2. London, 1901; reprint, Oxford, 1975.
Quibell, James E., et al. *Hierakonpolis*. 2 vols. London, 1900–1902; reprint, London, 1989.

GÜNTER DREYER

KHEFREN. *See* Khafre.

KHEOPS. *See* Khufu.

KHNUM. The god Khnum is well attested, from the earliest period of Egyptian religion to the latest. He played a major role in the Egyptian pantheon. His numerous cult sites are located in the South, for the most part, near the cataract region, with Esna as his cult center. His name seems to be related to a Semitic root meaning "sheep."

Khnum appears some half-dozen times in the Pyramid Texts of the later Old Kingdom (c.2400–2200 BCE), where he is portrayed primarily as a builder—five times of ferryboats and once of a ladder that ascends to heaven. One other passage, quite obscure, depicts him as a deity who "refashions," perhaps the first allusion to his role of creator god, familiar from texts of later periods.

In the Middle Kingdom Coffin Texts (1991–1786 BCE), Khnum is depicted as a creator of men and animals but not yet as a universal creator, a status that he later achieves. In the New Kingdom reigns of Hatshepsut and Thutmose III, he is first portrayed as a fashioner of gods, men, and animals, enacting creation on a potter's wheel, a motif that becomes prevalent in texts and reliefs from the New Kingdom through Roman times and is associated with the divine birth of the pharaoh.

The iconography of Khnum is, for the most part, consistent throughout Egyptian history. He is invariably shown as a ram or a ram-headed anthropomorphic deity. The Egyptians drew this iconography from the now extinct sheep *Ovis longipes,* subspecies *palaeoaegypticus;* it differed from subspecies *palaeoatlanticus,* which did not make its appearance in Egypt until the Middle Kingdom. At that time, the new subspecies came to be used in the iconography of the god Amun. In ovine representations of these two gods, Egyptian artists seem to have kept their iconographic programs separate, with neither exerting influence on the other.

BIBLIOGRAPHY

Badawi, A. M. *Der Gott Chnum* Glückstadt, 1937. The only full discussion of Khnum and all that pertains to him: his name, iconography, cult sites, and religious significance.

Bickel, S. "L'iconographie du dieu Khnoum." *Bulletin de l'Institut français d'archéologie orientale* 91 (1991), 55–67. Gives a detailed discussion of the evolution of the iconography of the god Khnum, from the Old Kingdom through the Ptolemaic period.

Otto, E. "Chnum." In *Lexikon der Ägyptologie,* 1:950–954.

PAUL F. O'ROURKE

KHNUMHOTEP II OF BENI HASAN,

"Overseer of the Eastern Desert," Middle Kingdom. Known to us primarily through his magnificent tomb, which commands a superb view of the Nile Valley from its vantage point in the eastern cliffs of Middle Egypt, the details of Khnumhotep II's life and lineage were presented in an extensive autobiography that runs around the lowest part of the walls of his tomb-chapel. The brightly colored paintings that cover the remainder of those walls bring his world to life. The decoration of his chapel was laid out to echo the Egyptian cosmos on three levels: the local landscape; the Egyptian landscape; and the landscape of the cosmos as a whole.

Khnumhotep II came to power in the twelfth dynasty, in the Oryx nome, in the nineteenth year of the reign of Amenemhet II (c.1910 BCE); he continued into the reign of Senwosret II. He was the only ruler of the Eastern Desert during his lifetime, with the title "Overseer"; he was not a nomarch. His autobiography tells of building funerary chapels and setting up statues in his principal city of Menat Khufu. It describes the building of his tomb, and it emphasizes the close relationship of his family to the royal house. The most famous event of his reign was recorded in a scene on the northern wall of his chapel; that scene shows a gorgeously attired group of Near Easterners from Shu (men, women, and children), who brought eye-paint to Khnumhotep. That depiction of early international trade took place under the auspices of Senwosret II, represented there by a royal scribe.

Khnumhotep had a large family, and he may even have married several times. His principal wife—the mother of his heir and a number of other children—was a princess named Khety. He also seems to have married, or at least to have had children with, an exceptional woman named Tchat, who—whenever she is depicted in his tomb—usually bears the male title of "Sealer."

BIBLIOGRAPHY

Kamrin, Janice. *The Cosmos of Khnumhotep II.* London, 1997. The tomb is studied and analyzed in depth, and the concept of tomb as cosmograph is developed.

Lichtheim, Miriam. *Ancient Egyptian Autobiographies Chiefly of the Middle Kingdom: A Study and an Anthology.* Freiburg, 1988. Includes the most up-to-date translation of Khnumhotep II's autobiography.

Newberry, P. E., et al. *Beni Hasan,* pt I. London, 1893. The primary publication on Khnumhotep II's tomb; includes black-and-white copies of all of the decoration.

JANICE KAMRIN

KHOKHAH, an ill-defined area in the Theban necropolis (25°44'N, 32°36'E). The site is named after a modern village and is located between the Asasif in the north and east and the so-called lower enclosure of Sheikh Abd el-Qurna in the west. The exact meaning of the name Khokhah is unclear, although it has been translated as "peach" or "vault." In Egyptian Arabic, the term is used to describe an "opening in a wall," a "gate," or a "wicket gate," possibly referring to the entrances of the local rock-cut tombs.

The Khokhah area has never played an important role in the history of the archaeological exploration of the Theban necropolis. Nevertheless, the private tombs of the Old Kingdom and the First Intermediate Period and several tombs of the eighteenth and the nineteenth dynasties were systematically investigated and published by Egyptian, British, German, and Hungarian expeditions.

With the exception of el-Tarif, the Khokhah area is the earliest known cemetery in the Theban necropolis. During the end of the Old Kingdom and during the First Intermediate Period, when Thebes was no more than a comparatively unimportant provincial capital, three Theban nomarchs had tombs excavated for themselves—small, single-chamber tombs—in the hills of Khokhah (tombs 186, 405, and 413). After that, Khokhah was not used as a major burial site for more than five hundred years, until the second half of the eighteenth dynasty (c.1450 BCE). Several high and medium rank officials then built their tombs in Khokhah during the time of Thutmose III and Hatshepsut. The area became quite popular during the reign of Amenhotpe III (c.1410–1372 BCE), when some of the most exceptional private tombs in the Theban necropolis were constructed. The unique tomb of the chief steward Amenemhat, also called Surer (tomb 48), was one of the largest and most important private tombs of the New Kingdom. The inner, rock-cut part of the tomb extends for almost 60 meters (190 feet) into the rock; its four main rooms contain seventy columns and pillars to support the ceiling. The dimensions and architectural layout of the tomb closely resemble the architecture of contemporaneous royal temples; however, the majority of private tombs in the Khokhah area can be ascribed to officials of rather modest social rank. For example, the Tomb of Two Sculptors (tomb 181) is well known for the exquisite style and quality of its painted decoration.

Several other private tombs were excavated in Khokhah, which date from the reign of Ramesses II (c.1304–1237 BCE) and later. Some of the Ramessid tombs have unusually elaborate subterranean sections that represent the new religious conceptions of the post-Amarna era, exceeding by far the dimensions of the accessible upper part of the tombs (e.g., tomb 32 of Thutmose and tomb 373 of Amenmessu).

BIBLIOGRAPHY

Kampp, Friederike. *Die thebanische Nekropole.* Theben, 13. Mainz, 1996. Standard publication of the private tombs of Thebes, with up-to-date bibliography.

Porter, Bertha, and Rosalind L. B. Moss. *Topographical Bibliography of Ancient Egyptian Hieroglyphic Texts, Reliefs and Paintings.* Oxford, 1960–1972.

Saleh, Mohamed. *Three Old-Kingdom Tombs at Thebes.* Archäologische Veröffentlichungen, Deutsches Archäologisches Institut Abteilung Kairo, 14. Mainz, 1977.

Säve-Söderbergh, Torgny. *Four Eighteenth Dynasty Tombs.* Private Tombs at Thebes, 1. Oxford, 1957. Contains, among others, the preliminary publication of the Theban tomb of Surer (TT 48).

DANIEL C. POLZ

KHONSU. The primary function of Khonsu in Egyptian religion was as a lunar deity, and so he was portrayed with the symbols of the moon's disk and crescent on his head. Khonsu's name means "the traveler" (*H̱nsw*) and most likely refers to his nightly journey across the sky in a boat. In his role as a moon god, Khonsu assisted the god Thoth, also a lunar deity, in marking the passage of time. Khonsu was also influential in effecting the creation of new life in both animals and humans.

Khonsu was the son of Amun and Mut. Together with them, he formed the family triad worshiped in the area of Thebes in southern Egypt. He was depicted as a mummified youth wearing the sidelock, characteristic of childhood; he is also shown holding the royal symbols of the crook and flail and, like the god Ptah, he frequently wears a *menat*-necklace.

As a divine child of Amun and Mut, Khonsu had close connections with two other divine children: the god of air, Shu; and the falcon-headed sun god, Horus. Because of this association with Horus, Khonsu is sometimes shown with a falcon's head, wearing a headdress with a sun disk and a moon crescent. He was also linked to Horus in his role as a protector and healer.

Khonsu is described in early Egyptian religious texts as a rather bloodthirsty deity. He was mentioned only once in the Pyramid Texts, in the spell known as the "Cannibal Hymn," where he was described as "Khonsu who slew the lords, who strangles them for the King, and extracts for him what is in their bodies." He was mentioned a number of times in the Coffin Texts, where his violent nature was again noted: in Spell 258, he is "Khonsu who lives on hearts"; in Spell 994, he lives on heads; and in Spell 310, he is capable of sending out "the rage which burns hearts."

Although he was mentioned in these earlier texts, Khonsu did not rise to prominence in the Egyptian pantheon until the New Kingdom. During its later days, one of his divine epithets was "the Greatest God of the Great Gods," and he was worshiped at Thebes as "Khonsu-in-Thebes-Neferhotpe." During late Ramessid times, most of the construction at Karnak temple focused on the temple of Khonsu, begun under Ramesses III, which is situated near the *temenos* wall of the temple of the god Amun. One of the ancient Egyptian creation myths is known as the "Khonsu Cosmogony." It is preserved in a Ptolemaic text recorded on the walls at the Khonsu temple at Karnak and explains the connection of the Theban Khonsu to the creation myths of Memphis and Hermopolis.

In his role as a healing deity, however, Khonsu became well known beyond the boundaries of Egypt. A stela, possibly dating to the twenty-first dynasty, records the sending of a statue of Khonsu to Bekhten to cure an ill princess; upon its arrival, the princess was immediately cured. The ruler of the country tried to hold the image hostage, but after experiencing a nightmare in which the god appeared as a golden hawk, he allowed Khonsu to return to his temple in Thebes, where his arrival was met with great rejoicing.

Khonsu's fame as a healer continued into the Ptolemaic period. King Ptolemy IV was healed of an unknown illness though the intervention of Khonsu, and he was so impressed that he called himself "Beloved of Khonsu Who Protects His Majesty and Drives Away Evil Spirits."

Khonsu also had cults at the sites of Memphis, Edfu, and Hibis. At Kom Ombo he was worshiped as part of a different triad, in which he was the child of the crocodile deity Sobek and the divine cow Hathor.

BIBLIOGRAPHY

Brunner, Hellmut. "Chons." In *Lexikon der Ägyptologie*, 1: 960–963. Wiesbaden, 1974.

Quirke, Stephen. *Ancient Egyptian Religion.* London, 1992.

Shafer, Byron, ed. *Religion in Ancient Egypt.* Ithaca, N.Y., 1991.

JENNIFER HOUSER-WEGNER

KHUFU (r. 2609–2584 BCE), second king of the fourth dynasty, Old Kingdom. Very little is known about Khufu (called Cheops in Greek), although he built the most famous tomb in pharaonic Egypt—the Great Pyramid at Giza, one of the seven wonders of the ancient world. His full name was Khnum-Khufwy, which means "[the god] Khnum protects me," Khufu being the short form or nickname. The Turin Canon ascribes to him a reign of twenty-three years, but it may have been much longer. He succeeded his father, Sneferu; his mother was Queen Hetepheres I; and he had three wives. Only one statue of Khufu—a small figurine found at Abydos—has survived, but his name is preserved in inscriptions from various sites in Egypt, Sinai, and Byblos. Khufu may have intended that his son Kawab follow him, but the successor was in fact Djedefre.

Khufu's most important achievement was the building of the Great Pyramid ("The Horizon of Khufu") at a new site, the Giza plateau. Members of the royal family were buried in small pyramids and tombs to the east of the Great Pyramid and officials of the reign to the west. A cult pyramid was discovered to the southeast of Khufu's tomb. The design program of the entire pyramid complex continued to be used until the end of the Old Kingdom.

The construction of the Great Pyramid provides some important insights into the reign of Khufu, notably his ability to command the material and human resources necessary to build his tomb. He organized households and estates from various parts of Egypt to supply the labor, as well as the food, clothing, and housing for the workers. In essence, the building of the Great Pyramid was a national project that must have had a significant socializing effect on the conscripted labor brought to Giza from the hamlets and villages of Egypt. The discovery of the workers' town revealed support facilities, residential areas, and cemeteries for those who constructed and maintained the pyramid complex. In the popular imagination, the Khufu pyramid was built by slaves, but that was not the case; the full-time and the conscripted workers built their own tombs near the pyramid of Khufu and prepared them for eternity, like those of the nobles and officials nearby. From an architectural point of view, the pyramid reveals not only the brilliance and skills of the "Overseer of All the King's Works" and his architects but also the ancient Egyptian achievements in engineering, astronomy, mathematics, and art.

Khufu was remembered by the Egyptians throughout subsequent pharaonic history, and many tales were told about him. The ancient Greek historian Herodotus reported Khufu's character as cruel and impious; the former attribute is perhaps based on traditions about the exactions necessary for the building of the pyramid, and the latter hints that Khufu presented himself as the sun god Re during his own lifetime. The Westcar Papyrus (of Middle Kingdom date) describes Khufu listening to stories about his ancestors and miracles that happened in the past. Khufu sends for the magician Djedi, hoping that he might know about a mysterious document of the god Thoth that could aid in constructing a pyramid. In the twenty-sixth dynasty of the Late period, however, Khufu was worshiped as a god; his name appears on scarabs, and the names are known of two priests of that era who were in charge of maintaining his cult.

[*See also* Old Kingdom, *article on the* Fourth Dynasty.]

BIBLIOGRAPHY

Grimal, Nicolas. *A History of Ancient Egypt.* Oxford, 1992.
Hawass, Zahi. "The Khufu Statuette: Is It an Old Kingdom Sculpture?" *Bulletin de l'Institut français d'archéologie orientale* Extraite des Mélanges Gamal Eddin Mokhtar, T. XCU 1/2. Cairo, 1985.
Hawass, Zahi. *The Pyramids of Ancient Egypt.* Washington, D.C., 1990.
Lehner, Mark. *The Pyramid Tomb of Queen Hetep-heres and the Satellite Pyramid of Khufu.* Mainz, 1985.
Lehner, Mark. *The Complete Pyramids.* London and New York, 1997.
Reisner, G., and W. S. Smith. *A History of the Giza Necropolis.* vol. 2: *The tomb of Hetep-heres, the Mother of Cheops.* Cambridge, 1955.
Trigger, B. G., et al. *Ancient Egypt: A Social History.* Cambridge, 1983.

ZAHI HAWASS

KING LISTS. In distant antiquity, before longstanding, independent eras came into use (such as the Seleucid, Christian, Himyarite, or Muslim eras), people dated by the individual year, naming each year after a significant event occurring in it. A longer timespan was that of the reign of a ruler, and beyond that of rulers in succession. For a local (or wider) "state" administration to be able to refer back in time for fiscal, ritual, propaganda, or historical purposes, it soon became necessary to keep lists of the succession of named years and of the successive monarchs through whose reigns the series extended. Such practices underlie the lists of year-names of kings in early Mesopotamia (Sumerian to Old Babylonian times); and such a document as the Palermo Stone in Egypt (for the first five dynasties); the latter, when intact, displayed several registers of rectangles—one for the events of each year—grouped under headings naming each successive king whose years they were. This was the oldest form of the full king list.

In later Old Kingdom Egypt, and most other places, the practice changed to one of numbering the years of each individual ruler. Then full king lists simply list the names of successive kings with the number of years that each had ruled. In the ancient Near East, this produced the Sumerian King List and the various king lists for Babylonia and Assyria. In Egypt, the major parts of only two such lists survive: the Turin Canon of Kings (from the later nineteenth dynasty), and the Epitome, or summary

KING LISTS. *Relief of a king list, from Abydos.* (Courtesy David P. Silverman)

list, of kings and dynasties with reign lengths and totals, excerpted from the *History of Egypt* written by Manetho in the third century BCE, a millennium later. Rarely, these briefly include other details about a given ruler (as in Mesopotamia). Neither king list gives only names and year numbers, but each has its own internal subdivisions. Broken into numerous fragments (not all of which can be convincingly rejoined), the Turin Canon of Kings is inscribed on the back of a papyrus, the front of which was originally used to record tax receipts from several districts in Egypt. Officers of wells and a fort named after Ramesses II are listed (their names are now lost); no later royal name occurs. From right to left, in accord with the direction of the Hieratic script, these tax returns originally occupied six pages (the present-day "columns" 1–8; I, II, III, IV+V, VI+VII, and VIII). On the back of the papyrus, turning it around through 180 degrees, there were originally eleven columns listing the reigns of gods, of other divine beings, and of kings, down to the end of the Second Intermediate Period. In columns IX and XI only the upper parts are probably correctly placed; the supposed lower parts and column X cannot yet be reconstructed with conviction. It is just possible that the eighteenth dynasty and the founders of the nineteenth originally occupied the lower part of column XI (assuming fragment 163 belongs elsewhere).

Column I may have had an introduction, followed by the reigns of the gods (the first three, Ptah, Re and Shu, are now lost but are attested in Manetho), and then by other divine beings, and (in col. II) by the Glorious (or, Blessed) Spirits, and the Followers of Horus. All these primeval, legendary epochs (with reigns sometimes running into thousands of years) were in practice ancient Egypt's equivalent concept for our modern notion of prehistory, or the Predynastic epoch. Then come what we today term the "historical dynasties," which we conventionally number as did Manetho a thousand years after the Turin Canon was written. The divisions observed in the Turin list are fewer and broader. The heading (II:10) "[?House of] King Mene(s) . . ." opens a continuous list of rulers corresponding to the First to Fifth Dynasties of Manetho, and a now lost total of kings and years reigned. Then follow what we (after Manetho) call the Sixth to Eighth Dynasties, followed by their own total (IV:14–15), and apparently by a grand total (IV:15–17) for the entire span of the First to Eighth Dynasties (our Early Dynastic or Archaic period and the Old Kingdom). Then eighteen rulers (so totaled) correspond to Manetho's Ninth plus Tenth Dynasties (First Intermediate Period). The Middle Kingdom of today's histories is represented (V:11–VI:3) by two separately totaled groups of kings that correspond to Manetho's Eleventh and Twelfth Dynasties. A new heading

(VI:4) introduces a very long series of rulers that certainly includes the Thirteenth and Fourteenth Dynasties of Manetho, to the end of column VIII, bringing us well into the Second Intermediate Period. The chaotic collection of fragments that makes up columns IX–X includes very broken and obscure names (some perhaps semilegendary), plus a fragment from the Fifteenth, or Hyksos, Dynasty of Manetho, and kings with foreign names (fragment 123) of a similarly Levantine origin. Finally, the upper part of column XI would seem to correspond to a line of Theban kings contemporary with the Hyksos, breaking off before the final, famous Seventeenth Dynasty kings (Sekenenre, Kamose) whence sprang the victorious Eighteenth Dynasty and Egypt's New Kingdom and empire. Throughout, after each royal name, there is given the king's length of reign (often now lost), in years, months, and days; in the first two dynasties (ending in the third), lifespans of rulers are also given. For occasional fuller formulae, such as "he reigned/acted for (such a period)," no single overall explanation has as yet been convincingly offered. When compared with first-hand monuments and documents of some of the kings concerned, various figures in the papyrus appear to be correct; others, however, appear to be contradicted by original evidence—the Canon is not infallible. Many figures cannot yet be checked, and many more are lost. As for rulers, it is clear that the Turin list is sometimes incomplete: it has only six kings for the Seventh/ Eighth Dynasties, where the Abydos list has fifteen rulers, while in the Second Dynasty there may be too many (by erroneous duplication). Even so, combined with original documents plus Manetho, the Turin Canon is a valuable aid for chronology before the New Kingdom. Drafted on the back of a discarded tax return, it can hardly be called an official document; but its contents clearly derive from older and "official" sources.

A thousand years later, an Epitome was compiled from Manetho's *History of Egypt*. This divides up the long line of kings into thirty royal houses or "dynasties," after the "prehistoric" epoch of gods, demigods, and other entities. The Second Persian Occupation of Egypt was added as a "Thirty-first Dynasty," possibly to link with Alexander the Great and the Ptolemies. The Epitome's normal usage is to give the following information: (1) the number of the dynasty; (2) the number of its kings; (3) their reputed place of origin (not necessarily the same as their capital city); (4) their names and reigns, but not in all cases (omitted in the Seventh–Eleventh, Thirteenth, Fourteenth, Sixteenth, Seventeenth, and Twentieth and partly in the Twenty-second); and (5) the total years for the dynasty. Manetho's dynasties represent a much greater degree of subdivision than does the Turin Canon. In some cases, this may be carried too far—the Seventh–Eighth and Ninth–Tenth were almost certainly single units. Larger cumulative year totals are included after each dy-

nasty from the Second to the Eighth and after the Eleventh, the end of Manetho's book I, comparable with the fewer such periodic totals in the Turin Canon. But in his book II, only a final total appears for its Twelfth to Nineteenth Dynasties, and in book III there is a similar final total for the Twentieth to Thirty-first Dynasties. For Manetho's Epitome, we are dependent on the recensions of Africanus (c.220 CE) Eusebius (c.320 CE), and George the Syncellus (c.800 CE), usually, but not always, in descending order of accuracy. Much earlier, Josephus (first century CE) cites a few extracts from Manetho's history and series of New Kingdom rulers. Such is the impact of almost five centuries of repeated recopying between Manetho's day and that of Africanus at the earliest, that the regnal and dynastic figures now present in our extant sources for Manetho vary widely in their quality, from great accuracy (corresponding very closely to the first-hand monumental data) to totally corrupt nonsense. In between these extremes lie figures whose units are correct, but in which the tens have been "inflated" by one or more tens of years (more rarely, "deflated" in the same way). When used and tested critically against original and older sources, however, a fair proportion of the data in Manetho can often be utilized in determining or confirming reign lengths of kings. And from the Eighteenth Dynasty onward, we possess no other such compilation.

A second group of documents may be termed "ritual summary king lists." These can give a considerable sequence of kings with certain omissions, such as the obscurer rulers in the intermediate periods, or proscribed rulers such as Queen Hatshepsut and the Amarna kings. They do not include regnal years or other details. Nevertheless, such long sequences are true lists, derived from full lists but serving cultic purposes, as the reigning king's official royal ancestors. The first document here is the "Table of Kings" engraved under the image of Thutmose III in the Karnak temple of Amun at Thebes (now in the Louvre). Thutmose III offers to sixty-two kings (thirty-one each to left and to right), seated in four registers on three walls. There is no overall chronological sequence, but specific groups of rulers are in order (as with the Sixth, Eleventh, and Twelfth Dynasties). Many rulers from the Thirteenth to Seventeenth Dynasties occur, possibly because of their being Theban kings who wrought benefactions for the god Amun.

The second group of documents is also monumentally carved in stone. In his great memorial temple at Abydos, Sety I shows himself offering to the names of seventy-six kings in two rows (still all intact, ending with his own name), in straight chronological order, omitting the Ninth, Tenth, and Thirteenth to Seventeenth Dynasties, Queen Hatshepsut, and the Amarna kings. Ramesses II includes a similar (but damaged) list in his own temple nearby, simply adding his own name to the whole. In each case, the tableaux are part of the rites of the royal ancestors, a roll of all kings who preceded the reigning pharaoh. In imitation of his royal masters, the learned lector-priest Tjunuroy included a similar two-row tabulation of rulers in his own tomb-chapel at Saqqara (now in the Cairo Museum). Except for numbers 13 to 22 (erroneously given in straight sequence), the fifty-eight rulers (four names are lost) are engraved in retrograde order, from Ramesses II back to the late First Dynasty (no room for more).

This is no accident but rather reflects the usage current in the actual rite of invoking past kings in the daily temple rituals and rituals for festivals, which is preserved for us in our third group of documents, surviving ritual papyri. In the relatively well-preserved IX Chester Beatty Papyrus, for example, King Ramesses II invokes his ancestors, beginning with himself and his father and grandfather, then proceeding backward through the Eighteenth Dynasty to its predecessor Kamose, two kings of the Middle Kingdom, and in summary "all the kings of Upper and Lower Egypt." Such lists could, of course, be drawn from full lists of the Turin Canon type in the "House of Life" or ritual research wing of temple libraries.

Retrograde cultic king lists were not unique to Egypt. In thirteenth-century BCE Ugarit in North Syria, we have a retrograde list of more than thirty kings of Ugarit, running back from the thirteenth to the nineteenth century BCE; one segment of the famous Assyrian king list (first millennium BCE) also had a retrograde section, based on the ancestry of Shamshi-Adad I. In the early days of Egyptology in particular, the Abydos and Saqqara lists served as a useful outline sequence of principal rulers to help interpret the sequences of the Turin fragments, to link up with the dynasties of Manetho, and to form a basic framework for kings met with on the newly discovered monuments.

Finally, we have a crowd of lesser documents that are not true king lists, but mere "king groups." Minor collocations of only three or four kings' names (with or without other royalties) are omitted here.

At the Ramesseum and Medinet Habu, their memorial temples in Western Thebes, Ramesses II and Ramesses III both include scenes of the festival of Min, showing portable statuettes of themselves and their predecessors being carried in the great procession. Ramesses II has a full retrograde sequence from himself back through to the beginning of the Eighteenth Dynasty (excluding Hatshepsut and the Amarna kings) and thus of the New Kingdom, plus Nebhepetre Montuhotep as founder of Theban greatness and thus of the Middle Kingdom, and Menes, as founder of the dual monarchy and in principle (for us today) of the Early Dynastic and Old Kingdom. Ramesses III updates his set of predecessors but abbreviates it to himself, his father Setnakhte, and the last "legiti-

mate" Nineteenth Dynasty predecessor Sety II, adding only Merenptah and Ramesses II before him. Much later, under Ramesses IX, the temple archivist Imiseba includes the cartouches of twelve kings in a scene of the bark-shrine of Amun, in two rows and a column. The bottom row, retrograde, had Nebhepetre Montuhotep II as Theban founder, plus Sekenenre and Wadjkheperre Kamose and the Eighteenth Dynasty founder Ahmose I. Above these, the series in the upper row continues with Thutmose II and III, and Amenhotpe II, then Setnakhe, founder of the Twentieth Dynasty. He is followed (in the end column) by his successors Ramesses III, IV, VI, and probably VII or IX. Remarkably, the later Eighteenth and entire Nineteenth Dynasties were not selected for inclusion.

Kings honored in private tomb chapels appear in Theban tomb 19 of Panehsy, whose two rows of royalties include the Eighteenth and Nineteenth Dynasties down to Sety I (with the usual exclusions); Tomb 2 of Khabekhnet, with Nebhepetre, and late Seventeenth and early Eighteenth Dynasties; Tomb 359 of Anherkhau, with Montuhotep II, early Eighteenth Dynasty, and his own king, Ramesses IV. One offering table of Paneb lists ten kings from Nebhepetre, Senwosret I, and all the accepted New Kingdom kings to Sety II; one of Kenhirkhopshef has an untidy listing of Nebhepetre and the Eighteenth and Nineteenth Dynasties down to Ramesses II.

Other minor documents include a fifth dynasty palette with six Old Kingdom royal names; a Middle Kingdom graffito in the Wadi Hammamat, naming three kings and two princes (as if kings) of the fourth dynasty; and the West Theban ostracon Cairo Cat. 25,646, naming the usual New Kingdom list from Ahmose I to Ramesses II, among other minor pieces. None of the foregoing three groups (or any of the minor bits omitted here) contributes much to establishing the chronology of Egypt; their main value is as witnesses to the importance of the kingship in Egyptian religious life.

[*See also* Chronology and Periodization.]

BIBLIOGRAPHY

Fairman, H. W. "The Kingship Rituals of Egypt." In *Myth, Ritual and Kingship*, edited by S. H. Hooke, pp. 74–104 (esp. 100–104). Oxford, 1958. Important study for Egyptian kingship as related to temple rituals, not least those that include "king list" elements.

Gardiner, Alan H., ed. *Hieratic Papyri in the British Museum*. 3d Ser. London, 1935. Official publication of the Chester Beatty Hieratic papyri II-XIX, with translations, including the "king list" element in festival temple-rituals (cf. pp. 90–97).

Kitchen, K. A. *Ramesside Inscriptions Translated and Annotated: Translations*. Vols. 1–2. Oxford, 1993–1996. These include translations of the Sety I king list at Abydos (Vol. I), and of the Turin Canon and Ramesses II king list at Abydos (Vol. II).

Kitchen, K. A. *Ramesside Inscriptions Translated and Annotated: Notes and Comments*. Vols. 1–2. Oxford, 1993–1998. These two volumes provide bibliographies and commentary for the translations cited above.

Kitchen, K. A. "The King List of Ugarit." *Ugarit-Forschungen* 9 (1977/ 78), 131–142. English publication of the retrograde king list from Ugarit, including comparisons with the Egyptian and Mesopotamian king lists.

Redford, Donald B. *Pharaonic King-Lists, Annals and Day-Books*. Mississauga, 1986. The major work on the whole subject of the nature, history and function of Egyptian king lists, and other related compositions (annals, etc.)

Waddell, W. G., ed. *Manetho*. Loeb Classical Library. Cambridge, Mass. and London, 1940. The standard edition of the works of Manetho in Greek text with English translation.

KENNETH A. KITCHEN

KINGSHIP. No pharaonic agreement formalized the royal institution on the banks of the Nile. Rather, this institution of kingship was defined through a series of practical and doctrinal contributions inherited from the unpredictable events of history and the talents of thinkers on kingship, who constructed, in a wholly empirical progression, the elements of a doctrine of power and of the state. In this manner, storytellers and theologians, enlisted by members of the court, took on the role of occasional jurists.

It is difficult to discern a unified trend in this development during three thousand years of history. There is great variety in the formulation of doctrines through myths, titularies and royal phraseology, theogamic exposés, lists of kings, Wisdom and oracle texts, the use at court of royal dreams, edicts of restoration, and other genres; some texts are a blend of genres—the *Instructions of Amenemhet*, for example, includes Wisdom Literature, biographical, and funerary texts—and the ideas may be set down in definitions, axioms, enumerations, verdicts, or repetitions of previously used or partially renewed themes and metaphors. Nonetheless, this complex diachronic corpus reveals a work of public law, and its disparate elements, though fragmentary, form the body of a unified doctrine. Specific points of law are examined: the theocracy of power, the dual nature of the king, the collection and bestowal of the five royal names, the definition of the royal office and of the kingdom, or the modes of establishing successors. They are not addressed with the coherence and clarity characteristic of a treatise, nor is there an attempt to formulate and explore domains that up to that point had remained outside the field of reflection, such as coregency or the status of the crown prince. Similarly, we find no trace of opposing doctrinal interpretations that would have to be reconciled, but rather an abrupt juxtaposition of formulas or antithetical facts. For example, the royal lists on the one hand aim to exclude pretenders to the throne, but on the other to reconcile contradictory facts by integrating foreign kings with the indigenous kings through endorsing "acts of force" or through inventing fictitious dynasties that will assuage the Egyptian concern with filiation; such lists deliver a

structure of ideology in exchange for the acceptance of a certain fiction. However, nothing is expressed in a discursive fashion. The classification of names (that is, the structure of the lists), or the exclusion or inclusion of a name, assume the value of historical verdicts or stand in for a philosophy that we struggle to unravel. For example, in regard to the duality of the king "in the flesh" and in his function, we find no evidence that the Egyptians pondered whether the royal succession is in the hands of the king, or beyond his grasp; or, in other words, has the titleholder of power become so as a result of the intent of his father or predecessor, or by divine will?

This abstruse framework in the end created a constitutional custom, albeit uncodified, and out of it emerges a definition of kingdom and the status of the king (including, as a counterpoint, that of his adversaries), as well as the two main modes of devolution of power. We will look at several controversies provoked by the adverse conditions that forced the monarchy to face the issues of coregency, the divinity of the king, and the fate of members of the royal lineage excluded from power; we will continue with a study of the impact of kingship on Egyptian culture and history.

The Pharaonic Institution. The kingdom is seen in Egyptian documents as a nourishing and living unit. Its organic metaphor is often tripartite, like its geographic reality. The *Story of Truth and Falsehood* uses the exaggerated image of an ox as a symbol of the country: the giant beast faces upstream, its nose is in the south, and the tip of its tail lies in the Nile Delta. Later on, at Kom Ombo and Edfu, Egypt is described as the Eye of Horus or of Osiris, whose different parts (at Kom Ombo) are signs used to write fractions which, when added, constitute the image of the complete eye. In Ptolemaic temples, where theological elaborations of earlier eras are generally recapitulated, processions of nomes bring the scattered members of Osiris to the temple to reassemble them. Reconstituting the body of the dismembered god was the equivalent of re-creating the unity of Egypt. The lexical clue stems from the assimilation of the names of nomes and those of the divine members: the vocabulary of geography and that of anatomy were largely similar. Later on, the metaphor of the sedge and the bee, indicating the dual monarchy of the Two Lands, expresses the perfection of a totality and not the contingency of two separate units. Initially associated with two chronological strata of sovereignty, the sedge and the bee were subsequently given territorial meaning with relation to Upper and Lower Egypt; however, the dissociation is purely rhetorical. Similarly, when Queen Hatshepsut is called the "forward rope of Upper Egypt" and the "hind rope of Lower Egypt," the nautical metaphor, again binary, expresses the impossibility of dividing the kingdom. Egypt, made up of elements joined together, like the universe or a ship, presents a cohesion that denies any possibility of dismemberment. Finally, distinct but nonseparate elements are designated by names and expressions translating a collective entity. The kingdom comprises "men, cattle of mankind" (*Instructions for Merikare*), the subjects whose master or king the sovereign is, and even the artisans. Thus, an ensemble of words or images serves to indicate the unity of the land and the ensemble of all the members of a community—the kingdom. The homogenous and consistent effort at metaphorical description in Egypt elevates the unity of the kingdom, although the variety in metaphors is an indicator of indecision with regard to the concept of the kingdom.

Several times the jurists of the kingdom emphasize the link between the subjects and their king. They justify the order of power by affirming that the sovereign Amenemhet III is the "creator of humans," that Ahmose "infuses the noses of women with the breath of life." In addition to this image of royal paternity, which binds the subjects of the king in fraternal unity, an august metaphor whose affective composite is undeniable—the king as "bridegroom of Egypt" (Ramesses II)—strengthens the link between king and kingdom. The image of paternity combined with the matrimonial metaphor illuminates the collective nature of the kingdom while at the same time basing the royal function on the notion of the king as the source of human life. The union of the kingdom and the king, stemming from the physical body of the latter, creates a lasting harmony and maintains diversity within the unity, while at the same time basing it in loyalty and love. Devotion and proselytism are the components of loyalty to the throne (*Loyalist Teachings*), the foundation of success: "His adversary shall be deprived."

Even so, competitors and enemies threaten the unity of the kingdom and the survival of those under the kingdom's jurisdiction, dispensed only by the king and his functionaries, after the manner of Atum, the creator god. The horror and abnormality of disorganized behavior in the kingdom, whether on the part of internal enemies or of foreigners, appear in the long indictment of Merikare against bad subjects, and further in the stela of King Kamose confronting the king of the Hyksos and his accomplices.

A relatively long work, the *Instructions for Merikare* begins with a typology of the king's opponents, a litany of dissidence and dark machinations, followed by a catalogue of appropriate reactions to the malignity of the agitators. Among numerous expressions referring to the unruly, which are difficult to translate, the author distinguishes the seditious without support, against whom he invokes the death penalty, from the powerful and known rivals, who are better handled by "absorbing them into the domestic circle" in order to rid oneself of them more easily at some later time. The tribunal eloquence of the

KINGSHIP. *King Merenptah in a characteristic pose representing one of the chief duties of kingship—the smiting of Egypt's enemies.* In this particular example, the enemies are a group of Western Asiatic foreigners. The king's lioness bounds forward to assist him. This relief is on a nineteenth dynasty doorjamb from Memphis. (University of Pennsylvania Museum, Philadelphia. Neg. # S4–143060)

contestants, who "bend" and "persuade" the crowd, is juxtaposed with the masterful speech of the king in his council; its worth stems from his knowledge of ancient writings, so that the power of the king proceeds from the erudite word—"The sword of the king is his tongue."

The portrait of the usurpers is cast in this manner. In the two stelae that recount his reclaiming conquest of Egypt, King Kamose presents the Near Eastern (Hyksos) leader installed in the Delta at Avaris and the Nubian in the South as having unduly seized power. The Hyksos, moreover, is a traitor for having sought a secret entente with the Nubian in order to surround Kamose, who uncovers the conspiracy. Parallel to these intrusions into the kingdom, the king encounters difficulties in persuading the "chieftains" of the kingdom to put an end to the partitioning of Egypt: paying tribute to the Hyksos for pastures and herds, the chieftains are partisans of the status quo. The political and warlike obstinacy of Kamose alone offers resistence to the servile and disloyal logic of the councilors, who are content with a fallacious prosperity founded on pastoral ententes. Kamose postulates the opposing view of the indivisibility of the territory and the autochthony of the legitimate holder of power. Their use of force does not legitimize the insurgents as rulers. The Hyksos kings are called Apophis, the name of the serpent-enemy of Re—always attacking and always defeated—sometimes endowed with the determinative of foreign countries that accompany their proper names in cartouches during the Persian, Macedonian, or Roman periods. The foreign kings installed on the throne are removed from the list of kings. Marked by disgrace and shame, the tyrants are not of the kingdom. There is thus a dual and mechanical awareness of conquest as a crime and of the permanent axis of order provided by the king, an appreciation that is nourished by specific events and not by a cool reflection on power.

By virtue of this, one feels, the execution of power is limited. The principle of *maat* would shield kingship from absolutist tendencies (e.g., the cruelty of Khufu), the only exception being the granting of a pardon (e.g., Senwosret I to Sinuhe). Grace does not override law. Another limitation is that the territorial seat of kingship is indivisible: "I [Hatshepsut] have seized that which god has placed before me: all the countries closed in my fist, the Nine Bows, without anything missing." It is, moreover, nontransferable: "I [Kamose] would like to know the purpose of my power if there is a prince in Avaris and another in Kush, if I am enthroned at the same time as an Asian and a Nubian, each holding a piece of Egypt and if they share that land with me." These phrases are used by the jurists of kingship to confirm that the king cannot diminish the power of his successor by allowing the kingdom to be attacked. The king does not dispose the kingdom of which he is simply in charge. Thus, the basic rules of kingship, which contain the whim of the king and the disposal of the territory, lead to its reinforcement.

The mechanisms of royal succession are another instrument of diminishing the king's control in order to protect the kingdom. The devolution of the kingdom reveals a coexistence of patrimonial customs and divine decision-making. On the one hand, succession is established by blood line, determined successively by primogeniture, masculinity, and collateral lineage. The firstborn may die, and the eldest surviving sibling take the crown, in the manner of Merenptah, thirteenth son of Ramesses II. A royal daughter may become the depository of monarchic function until her marriage legalizes the royal status of the pretender to the throne. Yet, while women are chains in the link of transferring power, matrilineal elements remain subordinate to a principle of patrilineal devolution. It is further true that women are not in principle excluded from power, since in Manetho's *Epitome* (fr. 8, 9, 10) we read that during the reign of Binothris (second dynasty) "it was decided that women could hold royal power." However, the practice contradicts the principle. While the Old and the Middle Kingdoms come to an end under the reign of queens—Nitokerty (sixth dynasty) and Sobekneferu (twelfth dynasty)—these reigns inaugurate periods marked by a collapse of power. Other reigns by women, such as those of Hatshepsut and of Twosret in the New Kingdom, mark crises in dynastic succession and are eliminated from the memory of the kingdom in the royal lists: selective amnesia, and perhaps a certain decorum, play a role in the composition of these lists. To this we should add some thoughts on the theology of power. The creator god, whose representative on earth is the king, has a human body in his role as creator of human beings, which is incompatible with the feminization of certain titles of the titularies and the language of royal phraseology. And yet, hereditary succession with a preference for masculine primogeniture arises from the necessity to preserve the territorial integrity of the kingdom, that is, the possessions of the national house. Thus, in the *Contendings of Horus and Seth*, the young Horus's management and upkeep of his father's herd is superior to that of his uncle and rival Seth reflecting the term defining the royal office, *iat*, a homophone of the word for "cattle," *iaut*. The point of the story is to give greater value to a succession from father to son than from brother to brother, by transposing into mythic literature the pastoral mores that have remained active. The kingdom, like the cattle, cannot be seized by someone who has not "increased" or maintained it. This coherence has a corollary in the indivisibility of property to the exclusive advantage of the son. The transmission of regal function reflects successor models practiced in a family system where patrilineage dominates over chattels and goods.

Still, a system of inheritance in which masculine primogeniture prevails over the eldest in a collateral line, failing a descendant in direct line, acts like a mechanism of extension in the succession—first to the son, then to

KINGSHIP. *Head of a king in profile.* This is a sculptor's model, in plaster, from the Ptolemaic period. (The Metropolitan Museum of Art, Rogers Fund, 1907. [07.228.7])

the brothers and nephews, in order to avoid leaving the seat of power vacant. From this perspective, the king owes his power to a custom more powerful than his own will. Although Antef II could affirm; "I have transmitted this heritage to my own son," or Sety I could declare on the subject of his son Ramesses; "Crown him as king . . . Place the *uraeus* on his head," the transfer of royalty is beyond the individual influence of the reigning king. Behind the apparent transfer from monarch to monarch lies the automatic accession of the successor upon the death of the king to continue the office: "The falcon has flown toward the sky and a new one has risen in his place," a clear equivalent of the European funereal cry, "The king is dead!" that is followed immediately by the triumphant call, "Long live the king!" The Egyptians were the first to distinguish the royal office, in its permanence, from its transitory holder of office.

If the devolution of the kingdom is enmeshed in customs, it is no less embedded in royal predestination: "I am born of Re, although raised by Menmare [Sety I, his father]," Ramesses II states antithetically. In more circumstantial fashion, the doctrine of predestination is affirmed for all phases of life: "I have conquered when I was a newborn, noble in the egg, ruler although still a suckling baby. Then he [the god] raised me to the rank of lord of the Two Parts when I was still an uncircumcised child and proclaimed me lord of the *rekhyt,* image before the people. He made me resident of the palace when I was still an adolescent . . . Now that I have become like Horus, responsible for myself [lit., "he who counts upon himself," i.e. an adult] . . . I shall undertake works in the temple of my father Atum." The generations of kings, in the course of their lives, perpetuate in the flesh the divine imprint that they constitute and, from a king to the son who carries in him the personality of the father, the natural identity reflects the fact that they come from the same divine principle. Having become similar but radically different from the common masses, they find within themselves the capacity to reign, a kind of natural right to succession.

Parallel to the myth of divine filiation is the liturgy of theogamy (Hathepsut at Deir el-Bahri and Amenhotpe III at Luxor), where the king is shown to be of royal blood from his mother and to have earthly incarnation through the unification of the god and the queen, confirming the right of birth as well as the illicit seizure of power. Queen Hatshepsut knew how to exploit the liturgical resources of royalty to fulfill her own pretension to the throne at the expense of young Thutmose III. The divine decision underlies the pharaonic institution, although this is irregularly expressed throughout history.

The jurists of Egyptian kingship made an effort to disassociate the sovereign from sovereignty to protect the kingship from potential weaknesses of the king, from his premature death, or an absence of an heir to the throne. "O Horus who is in Osiris the king!" This axiom, in which a new principle progressively replaces the older principle, distills the idea of dynastic continuity and the permanence of the pharaonic institution. Under these conditions, the statutory succession does not exclude recourse to other means in order to counter a threatened break in the royal line. The old King Akhtoy (tenth dynasty) confesses, "The monarchy is a wonderful institution, [but] it has no son, it has no brother who might maintain the monuments"; he thus acknowledges that the royal function is not necessarily hereditary, as Diodorus Siculus maintained (I, 43, 6). From scattered fragments one can thus establish a profile of the pharaonic royal institution.

Approaches to Kingship. Beyond an essentially chronological technical study of texts to collate information on the co-regencies and their refutations, the greatest debate among scholars seems to pertain to the question of the degree of power granted during a king's lifetime to his successor. Therefore, the status of the crown prince or presumptive successor and the question of his replacement in the case of royal incapacity will be analyzed here.

The right of the successor, which defines the place of the latter in the kingdom, rests on the natural identity between the king and his "eldest son" and on the place of the "mastery" of the son next to that of the father—in other words, on the coexistence of powers in the administration of the kingdom. As regards the natural identity, the royal ideology has above all borrowed from the Heliopolitan religion. Legend attributes the paternity of all kings to Re, the masculine god of Heliopolis, whose light chases the night away. Regardless of the substitutions in persons that follow, in the real father there is the presence of a divine power that is transferred, at the time of begetting, to his descendants, who will illuminate the country by their own brightness. This natural identity, by which like breeds like, implies that the attributes of kingship are projected onto the eldest son at the moment of creation. The arrangement of coexisting powers in the kingdom is by degrees. Note the informal exercise of power by Senwosret I at the end of the reign of his father Amenemhet I, going through the enthronement of Prince Sety as "eldest son" and "hereditary prince," who does not exercise all the royal prerogatives but discharges mainly military and territorial responsibilities, along with less defined roles such as the cult of Maat and the obligation of nurturer, until the time of the anticipated investiture, when the living king commands the crowning of his presumptive suc-

cessor to ensure the hereditary transfer of the monarchy at the beginning of the dynasty. This projection into the future finds its opposite in the manifestations of the cult of ancestral kings, whose official witnessing begins in the Middle Kingdom, affirming the principle of solidarity among kings across time.

However, the hereditary prince who has become king, and the designated successor in case of royal incapacity, are not always one and the same. All is handled as if a given king's inability to reign were to open the way for another to insinuate himself into the administration of the kingdom. Owing to the youth of King Thutmose III, Queen Hatshepsut multiplies the events legitimating her takeover: pretended investiture by her father Thutmose I, descent through Amon in keeping with the scenario of theogamy, and recourse to the oracle of the god at Thebes. Without erasing either the image or the name of Thutmose III from contexts associated with rituals and eponymy (titulary and date in reference to his name), Hatshepsut fully exercised power and relegated the young king to the role of a figurehead. This governing by two identical yet distinct rulers did not create a contradiction for the queen's jurist, since each was given his or her own mode: "He departed toward the sky and united with the gods. It was his son [Thutmose III] who rose in his place as king of the Two Lands. He governed on the throne of his progenitor, while his sister, the wife of the god, Hatshepsut, took care of the Two Lands as she saw fit. Egypt worked with bowed head for her, the radiant seed of the god who had procreated her."

Another topic of study is the role and fate of the pharaoh's younger children and other members of the royal lineage excluded from the succession. At times, the rivalries between groups of descendent erupt into violence, ending in regicide. The successors to Amenemhet I and Ramesses III are born in the harem, and the origin of the mother plays a role in the intrigues in the royal entourage. However, short of such a coup d'état, there are two paths open to these junior royals. During periods of territorial expansion, political appointments are created to respond to the new needs of the kingdom's administration, and the new titles tend to become hereditary, sowing the seeds of the fragmentation of authority. Still, unity is preserved for several reasons. An indivisible sovereignty continues to be a prize worth pursuing, and the granting of command makes it possible both to satisfy and to differentiate political ambitions. The religious power of the king is in itself a unifying element, since the local chieftains depend on him for regular ritual needs. Time, too, is a factor in the dispersion of the members of a line; in these groups an erosion of power takes place. Finally, simple loyalty to the king is often a stabilizing factor. In a period when there is no territorial expansion, however, the divisions of power lead to a proliferation of kingdoms without a future, as during the First Intermediate Period or at the end of the Libyan dynasty.

Finally, there is the controversy on the divinity of the king and its perception by the Egyptians, which has been studied by Georges Posener with a rare intellectual balance. In his book *De la divinité du pharaon* (1960), Posener departs from the commonly held view by showing that the current image of the god-king is excessive, constructed as it is mainly from official and religious sources. Posener shows that this image is not the only one we can derive from these sources. Some writers—Moret, Jacobson, and Frankfort—tend to present the king in the image of an organizer of the universe. Others, by contrast, observe that the official sources themselves portray an image of human kings whose posterity has preserved the memory of the names of men received at birth rather than of the regal names given at the time of anointment—kings endowed with diminutives, suffering the intrigues of the harem and tripping over their chariots. One should be careful, however. The vocabulary of the protocols (onomastics, titles, and epithets) is undoubtedly useful to affirm the divinity of the king; however, it cannot alone serve to determine the degree of divinity that the Egyptians accorded their king. When the king confronts the gods, the energy of the gods is exchanged for manufactured products offered by the king. It has also been shown that the king of fable is neither a miracle-worker nor omniscient; he may be a cruel despot (Khufu) or may indulge in nocturnal escapades (Pepy II). The negative influence of the royal entourage, the deceitful actions through breaking an oath, the rage of the king against his servants, and the tale of his indulgences round out the all-too-human and at times unpleasant image of the royal character (e.g., King Sisebek of Vandier Papyrus). What should we conclude? On the one hand, there is no natural incompatibility between the king and the gods: the gods too have failings and weaknesses. On the other hand, the resemblance depends on the identity of the situation: it is not the man who is honored in the king but the incarnate power. Hence the double nature of the royal personage.

The discrepancy between expectation and that which is possible is enormous. The king, perceived as the only intermediary between gods and men as keeper of the universe, cannot be simultaneously present everywhere, and so he delegates his religious powers to specialists. The existence of the clergy in Egypt is based fundamentally on this practical notion of delegating royal powers. At the same time, the victorious king *urbi et orbi* is a fiction. While there are some athletic and enterprising kings, many others—women, child-kings, elderly or sickly kings—avoided the field of battle. Royal invincibility in battle is another fiction; only foreign sources (the Bible, the An-

nals of Assurbanipal) or archeological evidence (mummy of Sekenenre) document defeat, unthinkable to the Egyptians. Animal assimilations of kings, warrior scenes on bas-reliefs in the temples showing the oversized king overpowering a crowd of dying or fleeing enemies, are magic tricks, continuously conjuring against inauspicious forces, while sometimes poorly reflecting stark military realities.

The King in History and Culture. The deciphering of the pharaoh's name, enclosed in a cartouche, delivered the key to the civilization of ancient Egypt. Moreover, by being on a par with the kingdom, the names of Egyptian kings provided a chronological framework to the course of Egyptian history.

In Egyptian documents events are dated according to the years of the reigns; these are placed in order of succession and are classified into groups. The names of the kings determine the outline of their history; in the Ramesseum, the names of Menes, Montuhotep, and Ahmose provide a periodization in relation to the cult of ancestral kings. Yet the outline created by Egyptologists has almost obscured that of the Egyptians by designating the periods introduced by these names as Old, Middle, and New Kingdom. The dynasties of Manetho, without doubt based on an even older outline in units called "houses" in the Turin Canon of Kings, continue to underline Egyptian history, in spite of the reoccurrence of royal names, a repetition of an older cycle into a newer one.

The magic keys to understanding pharaonic civilization, the names of the kings and the pharaonic regime, are also its linchpin. For more than three thousand years the pharaonic institution knew no alternative, regardless of pharaonic vagaries and different types of access to power and the origin of the holders of power. Criticisms were formulated only in reaction to certain reigns. Since Khufu and Pepy II, the royal image had been subjected to negative portrayal in stories. King Akhtoy exposes himself to self-criticism, qualifying his own reign as a "time of suffering." Later still, the question of royal responsibility is thought of in terms of social injustice and of the opulence of temples in Papyrus Vandier. The same approach is found in the Demotic Chronicle. Indeed, the impossibility of dethroning a king is inscribed in the ritual of the Confirmation of Royal Power. Negative sentences with regard to contesting the throne serve, by denying the impossible, to confirm the evidence of monarchic continuity. The history of Egypt is pharaonic.

The foreign policy of territorial expansion is directed to the maintenance, pursuit, and achievement of cosmic order. Representative of the creator god on earth, liturgical agent of the memory of the original facts, the king's role is to perpetuate on earth, by cultic and warlike acts, the creation, the "first time." Confined to the walls of the temples, historical memory conveying the dominant position of the king and of Egypt vis-à-vis the rest of the world becomes a cult memory, producing archetypes and blunting the uniqueness of the event.

Many aspects of the pharaonic culture are informed by the person of the king. In two-dimensional art, among the conventions of design that reflect the orientation role of the king, scenes are often organized according to a structure where the king faces the god, to whom a concrete offering is made to ensure longevity, happiness, and health for the king. In war and the hunt, the king faces his enemies and prey in a similar manner. The king is the equal of the gods, and his heroic size expresses the difference between his status and that of his subjects, his foreign enemies, and the animals he hunts in the marshes or desert. The proportional relations between the king and other figures are influenced by the antagonism that is active in the universe and that has to be reduced, in the literal sense, to render the universe habitable. Finally, the other symbolism of confrontation between royal order and the contortions of the vanquished, both men and animals, underlines the tensions between adverse worlds in which the king must vanquish chaos to perpetuate order. Political codes and cosmogonic reflections are transposed visually in the rituals of kingship. On a larger scale, art and literature depend on the state. An entire literature was developed in the royal dispensaries, extolling loyalty to the king and his divine ascendancy and exalting his physical strength; art was never so buoyant as during periods of power when the planned economy of the state guided inspiration.

The liturgical value of the numeral four confers rituals, spells, and perhaps even town plans their efficacy within the universe. In the rituals of the *sed*-festival an arrow is shot in the four directions of the horizon; the king makes a ritual walk around the field, which "he consecrates four times." The former expresses the cosmic triumph of the king and the latter his power over the Egyptian ground derived from his identity with the creator god. The circular ideogram of the town cut into four quarters along two orthogonal axes was possibly a definition of the universe, linked to the town organized into four sections. In reference to solar orientation, this urban quadripartition of cults reflected the idea of a totality of the area submitted to their influence. Finally, the quadrangular character of the statue bases and their inscription in a cubic or paralleliptic setting facilitated the installation and orientation of these movable pieces according to the cardinal points within buildings that were themselves oriented in this manner.

The architectural expression of the monarchy is crushing and sumptuous. The monumental cult practiced by a king to ensure the security of the universe addresses the creator god in his local forms. This is reflected in the sinking into the ground of certain buildings, perhaps in relation to a quest for the depths of Nun, as found in the temples of Nubia; integrated in the cosmos, they offer a minimal surface exposed to the forces of destruction. From this follows their placement on a mound and the construction of surrounding walls of undulating brick beds imitating the cosmogonic wave. Water supply for the territory springs from royal initiative, though its administration is delegated to local officials. Finally, if the management of borders through erecting fortresses serves exclusively to reinforce power, the importance of the urban phenomenon leads to the question about its genesis: were royal cities spontaneous, or planned, as implied by an epithet of Cambyses "He Who Establishes the Towns"? Kings certainly participated in the founding of various cities of Egypt: Menes built the fort of the White Wall all the way to Alexandria; the workers' villages in the necropolises of the Memphite region, at Illahun, and Deir el-Medina may have been planned by the royal establishment. The architecture and urbanism bear witness to an ongoing process in which technical investigation and administrative and liturgical imperatives come together to effect a monumental transposition in stone of the circumstances of the world and the reinforcement of the monarchy.

[*See also* Coregency; Cults, *article on* Royal Cults; Encomia; Harem; Legitimation; Palaces; Queens; Royal Family; Royal Roles; Sculpture, *article on* Royal Sculpture; State; *and* Titulary.]

BIBLIOGRAPHY

Bonhême, Marie-Ange, and Annie Forgeau. *Pharaon: Les secrets du pouvoir.* Paris, 1988.

Derchain, Philippe. "Mittes (suite)." *Revue d'Égyptologie* 46 (1995), 89–92. At Kom Ombo, the image of the offering can be interpreted as a summary map of Egypt, as the eye of Horus.

Diodorus Siculus. *The Library of History of Diodorus of Sicily, I.* Translated by C. H. Oldfather. Loeb Classical Library. London and Cambridge, Mass., 1989.

Frankfort, Henri. *Kingship and the Gods: A Study of Ancient Near Eastern Religion as the Integration of Society and Nature.* Chicago, 1948. Comparative study of Egyptian and Mesopotamian kingship. The king is understood as the "king-pin" of the universe.

Herodotus. *The Persian Wars*, vols. 1–2. Loeb Classical Library. London and Cambridge, Mass., 1921.

Hornung, Erik. *Geschichte als Fest: Zwei Vorträge zum Geschichtbild der frühen Menschheit.* Darmstadt, 1966. On the ritualist king: history as realization of the myth among the Aztec of Latin America and the ancient Egyptians. A feast for the mind.

Hornung, Erik. "Pharao ludens." *Eranos* 51 (1982), 479–516.

Hornung, Erik. "Pharaon." In *L'homme Égyptien*, edited by Sergio Donadoni, pp. 337–373. Paris, 1992.

Leclant, Jean. "Les 'empires' et l'impérialisme de l'Égypte pharaonique." In *Le concept d'Empire*, edited by Maurice Duverger, pp. 49–68. Paris, 1980.

Lorton, David. "Towards a Constitutional Approach to Ancient Egyptian Kingship." *Journal of the American Oriental Society* 88 (1979), 460–465.

Manetho. *The Aegyptiaca of Manetho: Manetho's History of Egypt.*

Translated by W. G. Waddell. Loeb Classical Library. London and Cambridge, Mass., 1940. A history of Egypt written in Greek by Manetho, an Egyptian priest of hellenized Sebennytos, at the request of Ptolemy II. A work known only from excerpts.

Moret, Alexandre. "Du caractère religieux de la royauté pharaonique." In *Annales du Musée Guimet*, Bibliothèque d'Études, 15. Paris, 1902. The king is thought of as a still imperfect god.

Murname, William J. *Ancient Egyptian Coregencies*. Studies in Ancient Oriental Civilization, 40. Chicago, 1977.

Obsomer, Claude. "La date de Nesou-Montou (Louvre Cl)." *Revue d'Égyptologie* 44 (1993), 103–140. Refutes the generally accepted idea of a ten-year co-regency between Senwosret I and his father Amenemhet I.

O'Connor, David, and David P. Silverman, ed. *Ancient Egyptian Kingship*. Problème der Ägyptologie, 9. Leiden, 1995. Several contributions regarding the general character of Egyptian royalty and its historical inscription.

Posener, Georges. *De la divinité du pharaon*. Cahiers de la Société Asiatique, 15. Paris, 1960. A close look at the sacred character of the pharaonic monarchy, underlining its human aspects.

Posener, Georges. *Littérature et politique dans l'Égypte de la XIIe dynastie*. Paris, 1969.

Robin, Gay. "A Critical Examination of the Theory That the Right to the Throne of Ancient Egypt Passed through the Female Line in the 18th Dynasty." *Göttinger Miszellen* 62 (1983), 67–77.

Vallogia, Michel. "Amenemhat IV et sa corégence avec Amenemhat III." *Revue d'Égyptologie* 21 (1969), 107–133.

Vernus, Pascal. "Le concept de monarchie dans l'Égypte ancienne." In *Les monarchies*, edited by E. Le Roy Ladurie, pp. 29–42. Paris, 1986.

MARIE-ANGE BONHÊME

Translated from French by Elizabeth Schwaiger

KINSHIP. A system of kinship is a universal feature in human societies, but because the European kinship system is for us self-evident, it may be difficult for us to understand that people living in other times and cultures may have a different understanding of kinship and a different attitude toward their relatives. The ancient Egyptians, for example, had no word for "parents," but this does not mean that they had no concept of parents. The designation and categorization of relatives are culturally coined. Moreover, in most cultures there are differences between the "terms of address" used in speaking to relatives, and the "terms of reference" used in speaking about them. There are various systems of kinship (though these are always bilateral, from an individual's point of view), and various rules of descent, which affiliate an individual at birth with a certain group of relatives while others are excluded. Terms of kinship are always connected with certain distinct patterns of social relations and behavior, but to detect these patterns in Egypt's societies through its long history is very difficult, simply because we cannot ask the people. We can, however, describe the distinctive ways in which the ancient Egyptians designated their relatives. Their terms of kinship are modeled in a symmetrically ordered bilateral system. Neither the gender nor the age of an individual played a role in the way he or she designated degrees of kinship.

Basic Kinship Terms. The core of Egyptian kinship terminology is a group of four elementary roots: *Jtj*, *mwt*, *z3/z3.t* (in the New Kingdom often replaced by *šrj/šrj.t* "little one"), and *sn/sn.t* denoting the relationships of "father," "mother," "son/daughter," and "brother/sister," respectively. Note that the terms for male and female (lineal) descendants and (lateral) siblings are built from the same two roots, differentiated only grammatically by the feminine gender ending -*t* (translated literally, the Egyptian word for "daughter" is "female son," and for "sister," "female brother"). In addition to these six basic terms, there were four more terms for relations by marriage (affinals): *šm* and *šm.t*, "parents-in-law" (and, reciprocally, son/daughter-in-law?); *ḥm.t*, "wife, woman"; and *h3jj*, "husband, man." These terms were used to describe the basic relationships, built around the individual's "family of orientation" in which he or she was born, and the "family of procreation," which is established when an individual marries.

Use of the Kinship Terms and System. There were two ways to describe further degrees of relationship. The first involved adding the basic terms to compound and descriptive kinship terms. By this means, even the most remote degrees of relationship could be described precisely from the point of view of an individual (usually labeled "Ego" in kinship charts drawn by anthropologists). For example, *z3 sn.t=f* means "son of his (Ego's) sister," equal to the Western system's "nephew"; *z3 nj sn.t nj.t mwt nj.t mwt=f* means "son of the sister of the mother of Ego's mother," or "son of his mother's aunt"; and *z3.t nj.t sn.t nj.t ḥm.t=f* means "daughter of Ego's wife's sister." This is an excellent way to speak referentially about kin relations, but it seems rather impractical for addressing a relative.

The second way to describe degrees of kinship was to use the six basic terms with extended meanings. Scholars have detected the range of these extended meanings by checking ancient Egyptian genealogies on more than two thousand Middle Kingdom stelae. If, for example, a woman is labeled "daughter" by a man (Ego) while her mother's name is different from the name of Ego's wife but is exactly the name of another daughter (whose mother is Ego's wife!), this may be taken as proof that *z3.t* "daughter" could also be used for the relationship of "daughter's daughter," that is, "granddaughter."

Accordingly, the extended meanings of basic kinship terms can be established as follows:

mwt = mother, grandmother (etc.), mother-in-law
jt = father, grandfather (etc.), father-in-law
z3 = son, grandson, great-grandson (etc.), son-in-law
z3.t = daughter, granddaughter (etc.), daughter-in-law

sn = brother, uncle (father's/mother's brother), cousin (father's/mother's brother's/sister's son), nephew (brother's/sister's son), brother-in-law

sn.t = sister, aunt (father's/mother's sister), cousin (father's/mother's brother's/sister's daughter), niece (brother's/sister's daughter), sister-in-law

The patterns are quite simple and clear: lineal ascendants can be called "father" and "mother" like parents, and lineal descendents could be designated like children. Collateral relatives in descending or ascending generations (children of siblings, siblings of parents, children of parents' siblings, siblings of the wife, and consorts of the siblings) are designated like siblings. The term *sn/sn.t* is a classificatory term and polysemic by extension (like "uncle" and "aunt" in English), designating siblings (and their children), uncles/aunts, and cousins. But unlike "Hawaiian" (classificatory) systems of kinship, which generally tend to merge relations on the same generational level (father=uncle, brother=cousin), the Egyptian system clearly separates lineal and collateral relatives in ascending and descending generations. Accordingly, the Egyptian terminology belongs to the same group of descriptive kinship systems as European systems. All degrees of relation are named bilaterally without differentiating the father's or mother's side; moreover there existed kin groups on one's father's and one's mother's side in regard to whom one had certain rules of behavior, rights, and obligations. The individual was a member of an extended family and a specific kindred via patrilineal and matrilineal lines. In ethnographic terms, the ancient Egyptians had a bilateral cognatic kinship system.

The elementary kinship terms were used alone and in compounds from the end of the Old Kingdom, and the origins of the system are lost in the mists of history. There is no sign of a change in terminology from the Old to the Middle Kingdom, and the system continued into the New Kingdom. The main new feature, from the mid-eighteenth dynasty, was the extension of the designation *sn/sn.t* "brother/sister" to married couples, perhaps echoing the rather frequent dynastic brother–sister marriages in the family of King Ahmose at the beginning of the New Kingdom. The marriage relationship thus turned into a fictive blood relationship, incorporating the consort into the group of *sn(.t)*-relatives.

In historical times there existed no lineages with unilineal descent, or clans in the narrow sense of the term (and of course no tribes), but only cognatic descent groups and extended families. There are no traces of matriarchy—not even signs of matrilineal descent—but there is ample evidence for patriarchy and patrilineal rules of inheritance from Old Kingdom times. A person could also inherit property from his mother's side, and he could have certain obligations to his mother's family.

Terms for Kin Groups and Social Groups Not Based on Kinship. From the Old Kingdom there were extended family households with the family of the master of the house as the core, and including such relatives as aunts or children's families, as well as servants. But there were many more social groups recognized beyond the core and extended family. The individual was part of manifold interwoven hierarchical networks consisting of relatives, friends, superiors, and—at least for some—inferiors. Accordingly, there existed a number of designations for social groups, which are recorded since the First Intermediate Period (the Old Kingdom is not very informative on kinship matters).

Exclusively used for kin groupings is *mhwt*, meaning "sib, clan" in a broader sense—the "family" beyond the core family. These are groups of families and of relatives who are more or less closely tied through common male or female relatives or ancestors (e.g., the "Ahmose and Ahmose-Nofretari clan" at the end of the seventeenth dynasty and early in the eighteenth). *Mhwt* is first mentioned in Papyrus Brooklyn 351446 from the time of Amenemhat III and is common until Coptic times.

The famous letters written by Hekanakhte early in the twelfth dynasty mention the *ḫrjw*-people, "relatives (like aunts or uncles) living in an extended family household," a term commonly used for a social kin-tied group below the level of *mhwt*. It is possible that in large elite households the dependents were part of the *ḫrjw*. They were fed by the head of the family but were also liable for punishable offences he committed.

Ḥ3w are "relatives" in general, or kindred, and this term is rather frequent through all periods. The earliest records are in the tomb of Shemai and Idi at Kom el-Koffar near Coptos (eighth dynasty) and on a ninth dynasty stela (now in Kraków) of a man working at Edfu who speaks about his benefits for his *ḥ3w*-relatives in the time of famine. *Ḥ3w*-relatives could inherit a man's property and took part in his funeral ceremonies.

Not exclusively designating kin groups were the following five terms.

3bwt, "domestic group, extended family," consists of relatives on the father's and the mother's side, parents, siblings, and children, perhaps excluding the wife and her relatives, but including servants; the term is recorded only in juridical documents of the late sixth dynasty and apparently went out of usage after that.

Whjjt, "village community," or a group of families living at a certain place, is recorded from the beginning of the twelfth dynasty.

Hnw, "tenants, co-residents, adherents," comprises all members of an extended household, regardless of kin ties. Autobiographical inscriptions state that a child and a widow have no *ḥnw*-people for their sustenance and protection, because they do not have a household of their own.

Wḥdwt "herd, horde, troop, gang" is a social group bound together by a common place of work (e.g., the employees of the temple of Osiris at Abydos) or a common idea (e.g., the followers of the gods Horus or Seth).

Ḫt, "group, corporation," is a term with very similar meaning but much older. It is first used for the heavenly corporation (i.e., the stars) of gods, deceased humans—of which the King became a member (or head) after death, according to names of royal funeral endowments from the first and second dynasties, such as "Horus is the first of the corporation" (King Den) or "Horus is the star of the corporation" (King Enedjib). Later, the meaning of the term shifts to "generation," that is, "group of the same age, sharing the same social rights and obligations."

It should be emphasized that some of this last set of terms seem not to be very distinctive in meaning and merge into one another. This is due to the fact that we have no ancient definition of even one of the terms, and they seem to have been used rather loosely and not very systematically throughout Egyptian history.

Attitudes Concerning Relatives, Kinship, and Society. A man's wife and her relatives were his affinals and a kind of foreign element in his household. The head of the family did not belong to the kin group of his wife and could not dispose of their property. Only the children linked father and mother by blood with each other's relatives, and the individual belonged to the group of relatives (the "house") of his father and to that of his mother as well. There was a strong emphasis on patrilineal descent. Some professions tended to be transmitted from father to son—for example, priestly offices or handicrafts.

No rules for marriage preference can be found in the written record, nor is there evidence for special roles of cross-cousins or the mother's brother, as in many other societies. Yet autobiographical inscriptions throughout Egyptian history show the special care of a man for his parents and siblings, and stress the relationship between father and son.

Wedding ceremonies seem not to have been considered worth recording. We know that there was serial monogamy, and because of a high rate of female mortality in childbirth, some men seem to have had several spouses. Therefore, many men—from the twelfth dynasty to the early eighteenth, at least—preferred maternal filiation for the sake of differentiating among half-siblings and legitimizing their claims to inheritance from their mothers as well as fathers. The pharaohs—and, following their example, some members of the elite—were polyga-

mists throughout Egyptian history. Men were seriously warned in literary teachings against adultery with married women. The crime was punished juridically with the death penalty for both the man and the woman, according to Papyrus Westcar and the *Instructions of Anii;* and it was prescribed ethically by society because it affected the rights and interests of the deceived husband. The woman's own rights were not considered, and rape seems not to have been a culpable crime. Women were revered as wives and mothers, but a young unmarried woman was metaphorically equated with a wild lioness who is dangerous to men and has to be tamed—psychological judgments typical of an androcentric society.

Ancient Egyptian society was not preferentially stratified by kinship from the Old Kingdom onward. Social hierarchy and order were determined by rank and status, not by kinship. Kinship played its role underneath a visible overlay of court etiquette and ideology, governmental acts, and administration. Only when royalty and the court center were in trouble, and in times of conflict such as the First and Second Intermediate and the Late period, did kinship and kin-groups move into the realm of such written records as autobiographies. The core family of a couple and their (unmarried) children seems to have played a main and independent role, thrusting kin-groups and relatives more and more into the background. In the autobiographies, kinfolk are always the object of a man's concern, not a group that could help him. But, of course, they played a role, and nepotism found its way into the record during all periods. The remembrance and funeral cult for ancestors typically seems not to have survived more than three or four generations, but for the New Kingdom we have some evidence that the family (of the elite at least) gathered at the family tomb on certain festival days to celebrate together with their ancestors.

[*See also* Family; *and* Social Stratification.]

BIBLIOGRAPHY

Bell, Lanny. "Family Priorities and Social Status: Preliminary Remarks on the Ancient Egyptian Kinship System." In *Sixth International Congress of Egyptology. Abstracts of Papers*, pp. 96–97. Turin, 1991. Only an abstract.

Bierbrier, Morris L. "Terms of Relationship at Deir el-Medina." *Journal of Egyptian Archaeology* 66 (1980), 100–107.

Feucht, Erika. *Das Kind im alten Ägypten. Die Stellung des Kindes in Familie und Gesellschaft nach altägyptischen Texten und Darstellungen.* Frankfurt and New York, 1995.

Fitzenreiter, Martin. "Zum Ahnenkult in Ägypten". In *Göttinger Miszellen* 143 (1994), 51–72. On ancient egyptian attitudes towards ancestors and the role of ancestor worship.

Fitzenreiter, Martin. "Totenverehrung und soziale Repräsentation im thebanischen Beamtengrab der 18. Dynastie." In *Studien zur Altägyptischen Kultur* 22 (1995), 95–130. On ancestor worship and the development of theban tombs.

Franke, Detlef. *Altägyptische Verwandtschaftsbezeichnungen im Mittleren Reich.* Hamburger Ägyptologische Studien, 3. Hamberg, 1983. The basic reference work on the ancient Egyptian terminology of kinship and kingroups was a Ph.D. thesis in German (see review by Gay Robins in *Bibliotheca Orientalis* 41 (1984), 602–606).

Franke, Detlef. "Verwandtschaftsbezeichnungen." In *Lexikon der Ägyptologie*, 6:1032–1036. More recent recapitulation, with new literature.

Robins, Gay. "The Relationships Specified by Egyptian Kinship Terms of the Middle and New Kingdoms." *Chronique d'Égypte* 54.108 (1979), 197–217. Study of kinship terms, not reliable in every aspect concerning the extended meanings.

Whale, Sheila. *The Family in the Eighteenth Dynasty of Egypt: A Study of Representation of the Family in Private Tombs.* Australian Centre for Egyptology Studies, 1. Sydney, 1989.

Willems, Harco. "A Description of Egyptian Kinship Terminology of the Middle Kingdom c. 2000–1650 B.C." *Bijdragen tot de Taal-. Land- en Volkenkunde* 139 (1983), 152–168. Good and reliable overview, in English.

DETLEF FRANKE

KIYA, highly favored secondary wife of Akhenaten, tenth king of the eighteenth dynasty. Believed by some scholars to be of foreign origin, she is occasionally identified with the Mitannian princess Tadu-Khepa (less likely, Gilu-Khepa).

In formal inscriptions, Kiya may be recognized from her unique epithet, which occurs in both a full form— "Greatly beloved wife of the king of Upper and Lower Egypt, who lives on Truth, Neferkheprure-waenre, the goodly child of the living Aten who lives for ever and eternity, Kiya"—and in variously abbreviated versions. Her name can be recognized as "The Noble Lady" mentioned in wine-jar dockets from Tell el-Amarna; a memory of her under this title evidently occurs in the Late Egyptian *Story of the Two Brothers* (Papyrus d'Orbiney, British Museum).

Kiya's name first occurred in conjunction with the earlier form of the Aten cartouches, indicating that she was in favor before the ninth or the tenth year of Akhenaten's reign. Her influence seems to have extended until Year 11 (and perhaps as late as Year 16), when her name finally disappeared from known records. She evidently bore at least one daughter for the king and, it has been suggested, a son—the future Tutankhamun. This achievement may well have hastened her downfall—of which there are indications in the appropriation of her monuments and in the damage occasionally found to images of her eyes. It is significant that this suspected decline in popularity coincided with an increase in the status of Nefertiti, her rival in the king's affections, who adopted a different title at about this time.

Kiya's image is characterized in relief sculpture by her large domed earrings and by a curious, open-backed, Nubian-style wig. As a result, her features have been identified in three youthful sculptor's studies in gypsum (two are now in the Berlin Museum and are attributed to the workshop of Thutmose at Tell el-Amarna; the third is in the Pushkin Museum, Moscow) and in an unfinished (and partially altered) head of quartzite (in the Berlin Museum, also from the Thutmose workshop).

In reliefs from both Tell el-Amarna and Hermopolis, Kiya's name and titulary have been partially erased and replaced by texts that relate to Meritaten, Akhenaten's eldest daughter by the Great Royal Wife Nefertiti (Hanke 1978). Inscriptional evidence would similarly identify Kiya as the original and intended owner of both the coffin and canopic jars from tomb 55 in the Valley of the Kings (Perepelin 1968 and 1978) that had been altered for subsequent reuse, evidently by Akhenaten himself.

BIBLIOGRAPHY

Gabolde, Marc. "Baketaton fille de Kiya?" *Bulletin de la Société d'Égyptologie, Genève* 16 (1992), 27–40.

Hanke, H. R. *Amarna-Reliefs aus Hermopolis.* Neue Veröffentlichungen und Studien. Hildesheim, 1978.

Harris, John R. "Kiya." *Chronique d'Égypte* 49 (1974), 25–30.

Jørgensen, Mogens. "Kija," Papyrus. *Ægyptologisk tidsskrift* 17/2 (December, 1977), 27–31.

Krauss, Rolf. "Kija-urprüngliche Besitzerin der Kanopen aus KV 55." *Mitteilungen des Deutschen Archäologischen Instituts, Abteilung Kairo* 42 (1986), 67–80.

Manniche, Lise. "The Wife of Bata." *Göttinger Miszellen* 18 (1975), 33–38.

Perepelin, Yuri Y. *Taina zolotogo groba.* Moscow, 1968.

Perepelin, Yuri Y. *The Secret of the Gold Coffin.* Mosow, 1978.

Reeves, C. Nicholas. "New Light on Kiya from Texts in the British Museum." *Journal of Egyptian Archaeology* 74 (1988), 91–101.

van Dijk, Jacobus. "Kiya revisited." In C. Eyre. ed., *Seventh International Congress of Egyptologists, Cambridge, 3–9 September 1995. Abstracts of Papers* (London, 1995), 50.

NICHOLAS REEVES

KOM OMBO (Eg., *Nbt;* Gr., *Ombos*), a site on the eastern bank of the Nile River, in the Kom Ombo basin, a large fertile area to the south of Gebel el-Silsila (24°27′N, 32°56′E). Kom Ombo was sited at the terminus of two caravan routes—one running westward through Kurkur Oasis to Tomas in Nubia; the other, from Daraw through the Eastern Desert, regaining the Nile at Berber. Those routes were regularly used in early modern times, although how old they are is uncertain. The Kom Ombo basin has significance in the Nile Valley archaeology of the Late (Upper) Paleolithic (c. 15,000–12,000 BCE). In the 1920s, Edmund Vignard identified and excavated prehistoric sites having a stoneworking industry he named Sebilian. Vignard's work has been revised by that of P. E. L. Smith and Fekri Hassan, who have also identified two other industries in the region, Silsillian and Sebekian, which coexisted with the Sebilian.

Little is yet known of the town during the dynastic period, and there has been little excavation of the ancient site beyond the clearance of the temple. New Kingdom

KOM OMBO. *Antique photograph (c.1876) of the ruins of the Augsutan double gate in front of the pronaos of Ptolemy XII.* The photograph was taken by the Bonfils family. (University of Pennsylvania Museum, Philadelphia. Neg. # T2–949c)

blocks have been noted, and an eighteenth dynasty gateway (now destroyed) was reported by Champollion in the early 1800s. In the Ptolemaic period, Kom Ombo was a training center for the elephants used in the Ptolemaic armies, which were brought along the Red Sea from Ethiopia. The construction of the surviving temple was begun in the reign of Ptolemy V Epiphanes (204–180 BCE), the decoration continuing to be added by the later Ptolemies and the Roman emperors. An inscription in Greek records that members of the local military claimed a significant part in the construction of the temple of Harwer (equated with Apollo), in the reign of Ptolemy VI Philometor (180–145 BCE). The foremost part of the precinct collapsed from the eastward movement of the river, which was stopped in 1893 by the building of a stone embankment.

The temple, built of sandstone from Gebel Silsila, is an elegant and interesting architectural construction, actually comprising two independent but conjoined temples.

The western is dedicated to Harwer (Horus the Elder) with his consort Tasenetnofret (the good sister, a manifestation of Hathor) and their child Panebtawy (the Lord of the Two Lands), and the eastern to the crocodile-headed god Sobek, Hathor, and their child Khons. Two completely independent temples may have originally occupied the site, with some indications that Sobek may have been the preeminent deity in the eighteenth dynasty. The temple has two axes, with two suites of rooms and sanctuaries. The relief sculpture is typical of the Ptolemaic and Roman periods, with very deeply carved sunken relief on the exterior walls and columns, and fine quality *bas*-relief on the interior walls. Much of the relief is covered with a very thin layer of plaster, and the original color survives in many places. Inlay was used for the eyes of some of the most important figures. The columns of the hypostyle hall have a variety of richly carved floral capitals. The decoration of the inner rooms depicts Ptolemy VI and Cleopatra

KOM OMBO. *Contemporary view of the temple at Kom Ombo.* (Courtesy Dieter Arnold)

II, and Ptolemy VII with Cleopatra II and Cleopatra III. The columns of the outer court bear images of the Roman emperor Tiberius. Some of the most interesting late decoration is to be found in the northern part of the outer passage, running around the temple proper. One relief depicts the Roman emperor Trajan offering a set of implements (which are traditionally said to be surgical instruments, although this identification is disputable). The reliefs along the remainder of this wall depict some of the Antonine emperors, the last being a roughly incised scene of the short-lived emperor Macrinus and his son Diadumenianus (217 CE). At the center of the back wall of the temple proper, between colossal images of the presiding triads, is a shrine for the ordinary people (as the colossal aegis of Hathor occupies the same position at Dendera): a *naos*-shaped niche, containing a seated figure, is flanked by a pair of eyes, a pair of ears, and images of the four winds. These take the form of an eight-headed and eight-winged cat, an eight-winged falcon, a cow and (now damaged) a many-headed snake.

A *mammisi* stands to the west in the usual relation to the main temple; it was decorated in the reign of Ptolemy VII (r. 145–116 BCE). A small chapel dedicated to

the goddess Hathor stands on the southern side of the main temple; it is now used for storing mummified crocodiles, sacred to the god Sobek, which were found in the necropolis. Surrounding the temple are large mounds of the city, unexcavated.

BIBLIOGRAPHY
de Morgan, Jacques, et al. *Kom Ombos.* 2 vols. Vienna, 1909.
Gotbub, Adolphe. *Textes fondamentaux de la théologie de Kom Ombo.* Institut français d'archéologie orientale du Caire, BdE 47/1. Cairo.

ROBERT MORKOT

KUSH, the name of a district and a political entity, since the twelfth dynasty; it was south of the Second Nile Cataract and would eventually give its name to all of Upper Nubia, present-day northern Sudan. During the Old Kingdom, however, the biography of Harkhuf at Aswan implied that during the sixth dynasty, Upper Nubia had only one important kingdom, called Yam, from which the Egyptians obtained a variety of exotic Central African products. Following the First Intermediate Period, Yam was replaced in the texts by the vague polity of Kush (*k3s*,

$k_3\check{s}$), first named on the stela of Senwosret I at Buhen, which commemorated his conquest of Lower Nubia. On the stela, Kush headed a list of ten Upper Nubian toponyms, personified as bound captives; they presumably represented the districts south of Buhen. In other official contemporary references, however, Kush was singled out as the only power in Upper Nubia, and it was usually modified by the adjective *khesy* ($\hbar s[y]$; "vile," "wretched"). Its prominence has suggested that its first position in the Buhen list does not indicate that it was the most northerly of the named principalities, as was once suspected, but rather that it was the leader of an Upper Nubian coalition of small states.

During the Middle Kingdom, one or more undated Egyptian campaigns against "wretched Kush" were recorded during the twelfth dynasty reign of Senwosret I (1971–1928 BCE). No others were listed until the reign of Senwosret III (1878–1843 BCE), when they clustered in the eighth, ninth, twelfth, sixteenth, and nineteenth years of his reign, probably as a result of his fort-building activities at the Second Cataract of the Nile. Two successive "rulers of Kush," Awawa and his son Utetrerses (?), were named in the Execration Texts, revealing that Kush had a hereditary monarchy; these texts were magical inscriptions written on ceramic pots or on small figurines that were intended to neutralize Egypt's enemies. The long intervals of time during which Kush was not mentioned in texts, however, have suggested that Kush's relations with Egypt were primarily peaceful and that its rulers, like their predecessors at Yam, were the chief middlemen in the Nile trade that connected Egypt with central Africa. As Egypt's power declined during the Second Intermediate Period, Kush extended its influence northward, as was revealed by stelae of Egyptian officials at Buhen who acknowledged their service to its kings—one of whom, Nedjeh, was named. By the seventeenth dynasty, however, Kamose, king of Thebes, went to war with the Kushites in Lower Nubia, as he did with the Hyksos kings in the Nile Delta, in an effort to expel both from traditional Egyptian territory.

Archaeological evidence virtually confirms that the capital of Kush was located at present-day Kerma, Sudan, about 650 kilometers (420 miles) upstream from Aswan and about 20 kilometers (12.5 miles) upstream from the Third Cataract, on the eastern bank of the Nile. There, vestiges were found of a large ancient settlement (name still unknown) first excavated by George A. Reisner from 1913 to 1915, who published *Excavations at Kerma. Harvard African Studies 5–6* (Cambridge, Mass., 1923); annually, since 1977, the site has been worked by C. Bonnet, (who has published annual reports since 1978 in the journal *Genava*). The site includes an inner city, surrounded by a defensive wall and *fosse*, and an outer city that is still poorly known. The inner contains successive palaces, a religious sanctuary with a massive mud-brick platform (the Western Deffufa), and a residential area with rectangular and circular dwellings. To the east, a huge cemetery of tumulus graves includes several royal tombs, 90 meters (about 300 feet) in diameter and two large mud-brick funerary temples (the best preserved called the Eastern Deffufa). The city flourished from c.2500 to 1460 BCE; then it was destroyed by fire. Brigitte Gratien's study of Kerma's distinctive material culture, published in *Les cultures Kerma* (Lille, 1978), revealed that its geographic distribution—ultimately spreading from the Fourth Cataract to Aswan—coincided with that of the known expansion of the historical kingdom of Kush. Egyptian imported objects found at Kerma have indicated that it was heavily involved in trade with the Theban and the Hyksos kingdoms. Its destruction coincided with the recorded conquest of Kush by the pharaohs of the early eighteenth dynasty.

With the overthrow of Kush, Upper and Lower Nubia became a single Egyptian province that was governed by a viceroy called the "King's Son of Kush and Chief of the Southern Foreign Lands." At that time, the Egyptians understood the name Kush to designate, loosely, all of Nubia. Viceroy Huy, for example, reported that his authority extended from Nekhen (Upper Egypt) to the Fourth Cataract. Lower Nubia, however, was known as Wawat (w_3w_3t). Both Kush (Upper Nubia) and Wawat supplied differentiated annual taxes of gold, slaves, cattle, and agricultural produce, although Kush continued to supply precious raw materials from the far south: ivory, animal products and skins, exotic woods, aromatic resins and gums, precious stones, and the like. Each region had its own Egyptian "deputy," who was responsible to the viceroy; the viceroy also controlled a provincial army, whose field officer was called "Commander of the Archers of Kush." Nubian princes were raised at court in Egypt, Egyptianized, and returned to Nubia as district governors. The number of such districts has been suggested by the three "chiefs of Wawat" and the six "chiefs of Kush" who were represented in Huy's tomb. Traditionally, Nubia also supplied mercenary troops to the Egyptian army; the diplomatic archive from Tell el-Amarna has revealed that during the late eighteenth dynasty, the pharaohs stationed Kushite troops in the Near East to defend their northern empire.

The Egyptians faced military disturbances in Kush throughout the New Kingdom. By the beginning of the twentieth dynasty, Egypt had withdrawn from Upper Nubia; by the end of that dynasty, royal authority had ceased in Lower Nubia, and Viceroy Panehesy had become independent. His title was then temporarily assumed by the Theban high priests, but it had little meaning beyond northern Wawat. Although for the next two centuries the events in Kush are little known, through lack of historical sources, Egypt continued to use Kushite troops in Palestine, and biblical texts indicate that Sheshonq I (of the twenty-second dynasty) employed *kushim* (in Hebrew) in his sack of Jerusalem (c.925 BCE); the army in Judah of his successor Osorkon I was led by a Kushite general named Zerah (c.897 BCE).

In the eighth century BCE, Kush was reunited under a native Nubian monarchy centered at Napata, which in 712 BCE conquered Egypt and became its twenty-fifth dynasty. Egypt and Kush were then reinterpreted as the original "Two Lands": Egypt was "the Northland" (ta-mehy; *t₃-mḥy*) and Kush was "the Southland" (ta-resy; *t₃-rsy*). The first of the Napatan kings to be honored in Egypt was Kashta (ruled c.755–735 BCE). His son Piya (Pi[ankh]ya, ruled c.735–712 BCE), conqueror of Upper Egypt, spoke of "widening Kush." His brother Shabaqa (r. 712–698 BCE) consolidated his victories, established the court at Memphis, and was credited with founding the Kushite regime in Egypt. Because the Kushites believed that they were the sons of the primeval Amun of Napata, and (erroneously) that they were the heirs of the great pharaohs of the eighteenth dynasty, they consciously attempted to revive or re-create the culture of the ancient past in Egypt; their age, therefore, marked the beginning of Egypt's last great cultural renaissance. Their texts reveal a passionate religiosity and a devotion to the Egyptian gods. During the reign of Taharqa (690–664 BCE), the Assyrians began attacking Egypt in almost annual campaigns, beginning in 671 BCE; in Assyrian texts, he is constantly referred to as "king of Kush" (*ka-si/ši, ka-su/šu, ku-si/šu*). By 663 BCE, the Assyrians had driven him, his successor Tanutamun (Tanwetamani; ruled 664–656 BCE) and their dynasty from Egypt forever.

With that expulsion, the Kushite court returned to Napata, eventually settling at Meroë, about 250 kilometers (180 miles) to its southeast; there, the Kushite state endured for another millennium, perhaps at times extending its territories well up the Blue and White Niles. The names of more than seventy rulers of Kush after Tanutamun are known today from pyramids at Nuri, el-Kurru, and Gebel Barkal (all within the Napata district), and from Begrawiya (ancient Meroë) in Sudan. For four centuries, the culture of Kush closely followed the Egyptian model, employing the Egyptian language and writing for inscriptions; that phase is known as the Napatan period. After the third century BCE, however, the culture—now called Meroitic—became infused with new Central African artistic ideals. The Meroitic language and writing soon replaced Old Egyptian; unfortunately for scholarship, Meroitic has not yet been deciphered. Throughout its long existence, the people of Kush continued to call their kingdom Kush—*kš* or *Ikš* in Egyptian and *qes* in Meroitic.

Although the Greeks always called Kush by their own term (*aithiopia*, "land of burnt faces"), the original name continued to be used by non-Greeks. The hieroglyphic text of the Roman prefect Cornelius Gallus (when at Philae in 29 CE), spoke of "pacifying the chiefs of Kush (*kš*)." In the late first century CE, Josephus, the Hebrew historian of Roman-era Palestine, transcribed the Hebrew name of Kush (*koš*), son of Ham (*Gen.* 10.6–7), into Greek as "Khousaios," explaining that "the Aithiopians, his subjects, are to this day called by themselves and by all in Asia Khousaians." In the fourth century CE, the Christian king Ezana of Axum recorded in Ge'ez his victory over "the towns of the Kasu." Jewish and Arab chroniclers, well into the Middle Ages, continued to speak of "a land of Kush" or "Kushaye," far up the Nile, and of a city southwest of Dongola, named "Kusa" or "Kusha."

[*See also* Kerma; Meroë; Napata; *and* Nubia.]

BIBLIOGRAPHY

Adams, William Y. *Nubia: Corridor to Africa*. Princeton, 1977. Still the outstanding work on Nubian archaeology and history, although outdated in parts, especially chapter 8, on Kerma.

The Brooklyn Museum. *Africa in Antiquity: The Arts of Ancient Nubia and the Sudan*. 2 vols. Brooklyn, 1978. The best resource for ancient Nubian art, culture, and bibliography.

Eide, Tormond, Tomas Hägg, Richard H. Pierce, and Lazlo Török, eds. *Fontes Historiae Nubiorum: Textual Sources for the History of the Middle Nile Region between the Eighth Century B.C. and the Sixth Century A.D.* 3 vols. Bergen, 1994–. New translations of texts relating to Nubian history after the fifth century BCE, with full commentaries and bibliography of the most recent research.

Kemp, Barry. "Chapter 10: Old Kingdom, Middle Kingdom, and Second Intermediate Period in Egypt." In *The Cambridge History of Africa*, vol. 1: *From the Earliest Times to c. 500 B.C.* Edited by J. D. Clark, pp. 658–769. Cambridge, 1982. Outstanding presentation of the data on Egypt's relations with Nubia before the New Kingdom.

Kendall, Timothy. *Kerma and the Kingdom of Kush, 2500–1500 B.C.: The Archaeological Discovery of an Ancient Nubian Empire*. Washington, D.C., 1997. Overview of the history of the Kerma excavations and scholarship (to 1995), with full bibliography.

Kitchen, K. A. *The Third Intermediate Period in Egypt (1100–650 B.C.)*. Warminster, 1973. The outstanding resource on this period.

Moran, William L. *The Amarna Letters*. Baltimore, 1992.

O'Connor, David. "Chapter 12: Egypt, 1552–664 B.C." and "Appendix: The Toponyms of Nubia and of Contiguous Regions in the New Kingdom." In *The Cambridge History of Africa*, vol. 1: *From the Earliest Times to c. 500 B.C.*, Edited by J. D. Clark, pp. 830–940. Cambridge, 1982. Outstanding presentation of the evidence for Egypt's relations with Nubia during and after the New Kingdom, with discussion of the interpretation of Nubian toponyms in Egyptian texts.

State Archives of Assyria. 12 vols. Helsinki, 1987–1995.

Vantini, Giovanni. *Oriental Sources Concerning Nubia: Collected and Translated by Giovanni Vantini*. Heidelberg and Warsaw, 1975.

TIMOTHY KENDALL

KUSHITE PERIOD. *See* Twenty-fifth Dynasty.

ABOVE
The three most famous pyramids at Giza. They were built by the fourth dynasty kings Menkaure, Khafre, and Kheops. (Erich Lessing / Art Resource, NY)

RIGHT
The Great Sphinx of Giza. A mythical animal with the body of a lion and the head of a man, this fourth dynasty monument is partly sculpted out of a natural knoll and partly built. Between its paws is a granite stela, placed there by Thutmose IV. (Erich Lessing / Art Resource, NY)

Predynastic vase. Decorated with a ship and animals, this painted pottery vessel is now in the Aegyptisches Museum, Berlin. (Erich Lessing / Art Resource, NY)

ABOVE

Geese. From the *mastaba* tomb of Atet at Meidum, this fourth dynasty fresco is executed in tempera on plaster. It is now in the Cairo Museum. (Scala / Art Resource, NY)

RIGHT

Statue of Thutmose III (1504–1452 BCE), in the Luxor Museum, Egypt. (Giraudon / Art Resource, NY)

Old Kingdom statue of a scribe writing on papyrus. This figure is of painted limestone, with inlaid eyes, and it dates from the fourth or fifth dynasty. It was found at Saqqara and is now in the Louvre Museum in Paris. (Erich Lessing / Art Resource, NY)

Painted wood sculpture of a woman grinding grain to prepare bread. From the fifth dynasty, this sculpture is now in the Museo Archeologico in Florence, Italy. (Nimatallah / Art Resource, NY)

Eighteenth dynasty wall painting, showing the scribe Nakht with his family hunting in the Nile marshes. A detail of a wall painting in the tomb of Nakht at Qurna. (Erich Lessing / Art Resource, NY)

ABOVE

Queen Ankhesenpaaten and King Tutankhamun (r. 1355–1346 BCE). A detail from the back of the Golden Throne of Tutankhamun. The Queen is holding a salve-cup and spreads perfumed oil on her husband's collar. The throne is now in the Cairo Museum. (Scala / Art Resource, NY)

RIGHT

Various funerary figurines, from the New Kingdom to the Greco-Roman period. They are made of painted limestone, faience, calcite, basalt, and painted wood. They are now in the Aegyptisches Museum, Berlin. (Erich Lessing / Art Resource, NY)

The goddess Hathor places a magic collar on Sety I. From Thebes, this painted bas-relief is now in the Louvre Museum in Paris. (Giraudon / Art Resource, NY)

A pharaoh portrayed as the god Osiris. The fourteenth-century relief is from Abydos. (Erich Lessing / Art Resource, NY)

Acrobatic female dancer. From Deir el-Medina, this eighteenth dynasty painting on limestone is now in the Museo Egizio in Turin. (Alinari / Art Resource, NY)

The temple of Ramesses II at Abu Simbel. (Erich Lessing / Art Resource, NY)

Peasant couple harvesting. In the cemetery of Deir el-Medina, this wall painting is in the vaulted tomb chamber of Sennutem, a necropolis officer of the early Ramessid period. (Erich Lessing / Art Resource, NY)

Nineteenth dynasty relief of the goddess Maat, now in the Museo Archeologico, Florence. (Scala / Art Resource, NY)

Sarcophagus from the twentieth dynasty, now in the Museo Gregoriano Egizio, Vatican City. (Scala / Art Resource, NY)

The sun god Re traveling in his solar bark and engaged in the daily killing of the serpent Apophis, representing the sun's victory over darkness. A detail from the coffin of Nespawershepi, a chief scribe of the twenty-first dynasty. It is now in the Fitzwilliam Museum, Cambridge, UK. (Werner Forman / Art Resource, NY)

Second-century BCE lotus- and papyrus-columns from the temple at Kom Ombo. This was one of the "healing" temples to which pilgrims came to regain their health. (Erich Lessing / Art Resource, NY)

Kiosk of Nektanebo I, a king of the thirtieth dynasty. Formerly on the island of Philae in the Nile, this structure and the rest of Philae's surviving architecture were moved to the nearby island of Agilkia during the 1960s. Philae was then about to become permanently flooded by the 1970s construction of the Aswan High Dam. (Erich Lessing / Art Resource, NY)

The goddess Nut spreading her wings in protection over the deceased. A detail from a painted wood coffin, of the twenty-first or twenty-second dynasty, now in the British Museum, London. (Werner Forman / Art Resource, NY)

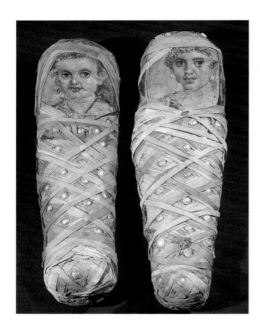

ABOVE

Two child mummies from the Greco-Roman period. Their portraits are on painted canvas and date from about 50 CE. The mummies are from Hawara, in the Faiyum, and are now in the Aegyptisches Museum in Berlin. (Erich Lessing / Art Resource, NY)

RIGHT

Funerary portrait from Hawara, in the Faiyum. Painted on canvas, it dates from about 50 CE. It is now in the Aegyptisches Museum in Berlin. (Erich Lessing / Art Resource, NY)

L

LAKES. A lake is a large, natural, permanent body of water that has a source sufficient to maintain its water level above the discharge rate. In Egypt, during historical times, the climate was arid and there were only two such lakes of any significance: Lake Karun and Lake Mariotis. Earlier, in the Pleistocene epoch, when there were several humid episodes in northern Africa, there were lakes throughout the eastern Sahara, particularly where the western oases are today. The former lake areas had been important resources for hunter-gatherers during the Pleistocene.

Lake Karun (Lake Moeris of classical writers; Eg., *Mr-wr*; Ar., *Birket Qarun*). Today the lake fills the northern side of the Faiyum Oasis, toward the western end (centered on 29°28′N, 30°36′E). It currently stands at 44 meters (135 feet) below mean sea level. The water source is the Bahr Yussuf, a channel that leaves the Nile River just north of Dairut, flowing northward, parallel to the Nile, until passing westward through a gap in the limestone hills at Illahun. It is the central geographical feature of the Arsinoite or twentieth nome.

The Faiyum. The Faiyum basin had been in existence and inhabited during the Pleistocene. The evidence from Paleolithic sites on the northern side of the lake indicates Stone Age life along the edge of a much larger body of water than exists today. These hunter-gatherers would have utilized the lake for fishing and as a water attraction for hunted animals; the lake and its marshy borders have been a center of fishing and fowling ever since. There were two periods of great activity in the Faiyum; the twelfth dynasty and the Ptolemaic period. When Amenemhet I moved his court from Thebes to el-Lisht, he and his successors instituted a land reclamation scheme in the Faiyum that resulted in the draining of large marshy areas. This was principally accomplished by the regulation of the inflow at Illahun, making available large tracts of rich, arable soil. Many of the royal funerary monuments of that dynasty are in the vicinity of the Faiyum. At the close of the dynasty, the area ceased to be of national importance, remaining so until the third century BCE. At that time, Ptolemy II realized the rich potential of the Faiyum region by reducing the lake level to about its present size. Considerable land was thus reclaimed, and extensive irrigation works were constructed under his reign. A number of large important towns were then established, primarily around the southern side of the depression, which functioned mainly as centers for the new agricultural produce. A major inhabitant of the region's waters was the crocodile and, as the god Sobek, was worshiped as chief deity of the Faiyum.

Lake Mariotis (Ar., *Behiret Maryut*) A part of the changing Delta formation of the Nile River is a series of lakes connected to the Mediterranean Sea: el-Manzala, el-Buruillus, Edku, and Maryut are the largest. They are shallow and swampy and, while fish are taken, there is little settlement nearby or other economic use of them. The westernmost, Lake Mariotis, has considerable historical importance. At its greatest extent, the lake was some 45 kilometers (28 miles) long, lying to the south and west of Alexandria, parallel to the Mediterranean coast and less than a kilometer (a half mile) south of it. Centered at 31°08′N, 29°55′E, the lake was connected to the Nile system under the Ptolemies by a number of small canals, to become a major access to Alexandria, bringing products of the surrounding area and the produce of the Nile Valley. These were then exported to the Mediterranean world from Portus Mareotis, on the southern side of Alexandria. The land around this lake was rich, and the resultant agricultural production was important to the Alexandrian economy. The area adjacent to the lake produced wines and olives of high quality; the white wines were particularly notable and are mentioned by the Roman poets Horace and Virgil, and others. Several amphora-production centers that were located around the lake also attest to the great wine production, since amphoras were the wine containers for shipping. Several Greco-Roman towns and sites were located along the lake's borders on the high ground. It was recorded that there were eight islands in the lake with luxurious villas. Present-day Alexandria is a major summer resort area for Egyptians, and it would seem that the area of Lake Mariotis served a similar function in ancient times; wealthy Alexandrians probably owned properties in the region and went there for holidays.

The Western Desert. Egypt's Western Desert (the eastern end of the Sahara) has the remains of many lakes; the only ones that exist today are from uncontrolled well production, a result of human error. Many of the ancient lakes existed for considerable periods—during the long moist episodes of the Pleistocene and early Holocene. Evidence for human occupation near the lakes, or playas, indicates their use as resource areas. The present-day desert oases are the remnants of such lakes.

Wadi Natrun. Situated to the west of the Nile Delta, 75 kilometers (about 47 miles) northwest of Cairo, Wadi Natrun was one of the most important of the remnant lakes. It fills a narrow depression, some 60 kilometers (about 40 miles) long, with a varying number of small lakes that are 23 meters (70 feet) below sea level. The lakes are fed from the water table of the Nile. The area has been of considerable importance throughout Egyptian history as a major source of natron (a naturally occurring combination of sodium carbonate and sodium bicarbonate), used in mummification, and soda (sodium oxide), used for glass manufacture. The natron occurs in solution in the lakes, forms a crust around the edges of the lakes, and is deposited on the bottoms. Natron was important in ancient Egyptian medicine, ritual, and crafts.

[*See also* Faiyum.]

BIBLIOGRAPHY

Cosson, A. de. *Mareotis*. London, 1935. An account of the history and importance of Lake Mariotis.
Kleindienst, M. R., C. S. Churcher, M. M. A. McDonald, and H. P. Schwarcz. "Geomorphological Setting and Quaternary Geology of the Dakhleh Oasis Region: Interim Report." In *Reports from the Survey of Dakhleh Oasis, Western Desert of Egypt 1977–1987*, edited by C. S. Churcher and A. J. Mills. Oxford, 1999.
Said, Rushdi. *The Geology of Egypt*. Rotterdam and Brookfield, 1990.
Wendorf, F., and R. Schildt. *Prehistory of the Nile Valley*. New York, 1976. Chapter 11 is by Bahay Issawi, concerning Faiyum geology; chapter 12 is on the prehistory of the Faiyum Depression.

ANTHONY J. MILLS

LAND AND SOIL. Ancient Egypt comprised four dominant physiographic provinces: the Nile Delta, the Nile Valley, the Western Desert, and the Eastern Desert. These incorporate many landform features, including mountain ranges (Red Sea hills), desert oases (Kharga, Dakhla, Bahariya, Farafra), basins (Qattara Depression, Faiyum), wadis (Natrun, Hammamat), coastal lagoons (Burullus, Manzalah), coastal beach deposits (Mediterranean and Red Sea coasts), inland plateaus (Diffa, Gilf Kebir), inland and coastal dune fields, river terraces, geziras, and desert hills. Sedimentary histories of these features range from Precambrian to Quaternary and, specifically for the exposed sedimentary units, from the Mesozoic Tethys Sea erosion/deposition to the Recent pre-Aswan Dam sedimentation.

These landforms and their associated sediments played diverse roles in the culture of ancient Egypt. Of great significance was the symbolic dualism, composed of complementary opposites, embodied in the stark contrast between Nile alluvium and desert. The rich agricultural land, *kmt* ("black land"), exemplified fecundity and life; the arid, barren desert, *dšrt* ("red land"), denoted sterility and death. Also symbolic and basic to Egyptian civilization was the dualistic division between the Nile Delta as Lower Egypt and the Nile Valley as Upper Egypt. Less symbolically, the various sediments also contributed to Egyptian civilization in a number of practical ways. From a basic soil classification context, Egyptian sedimentary units may be divided into coarse-grained and fine-grained sediments.

Fine-Grained Sediments (Silts and Clays). Silts and clays served numerous cultural functions. Before the construction of the Aswan Dam, the Nile River had the most consistent yearly flooding cycle of all the great rivers of the world. Annual flooding maintained Egyptian soil productivity by depositing sediments that added new nutrients (organics, phosphates, nitrates, and carbonates) to the system, and by providing a downward flux in the vadose zone (the zone between surface and water table) that removed undesirable evaporitic salts. The dominant agricultural sediments, located on alluvial flats, consisted of oxidized overbank Nile silts that were distributed throughout the floodplain. Natural levees were used for agriculture and settlement. The regular yearly inundation was arguably the single most important factor in the development of ancient Egypt's unique civilization.

Two clay source types dominated Egyptian ceramic production: (1) the terrigenous-alluvial-lacustrine muds/clays, most importantly Nile silts, also wadi and desert clays; and (2) the calcareous sediments, especially marl muds, clay limestones, and some lag deposits.

The first source type included ubiquitous unconsolidated Pleistocene/Holocene brown silty muds (clay + silt) of the Nile alluvial floodplain consist of oxidized facies that are terrigenous-alluvial and lacustrine. Reduced sediment facies are composed of gray-black reducing muds from lagoonal, fluvio-lacustrine canal, and buried paleofluvio-lacustrine deposits; these generally contain a higher clay content than the oxidized sediments. Silty to sandy muds form in wadis, in response to local processes of soil formation (pedogenesis) during valley aggradation and are generally associated with older river terraces. Desert clays also occur as gray kaolin clays from Lower Cretaceous Nubian Sandstone deposits and closed-basin lacustrine deposits (Pliocene estuarine "plastic" clays from el-Kharga).

The second source type consisted of calcareous sediments derived from Cretaceous to Recent consolidated and unconsolidated facies: Upper Cretaceous to Paleocene variegated shales, phosphate formations (Dakhla), chalks, mudstones, and calcareous shales; Eocene marls; Oligocene and Miocene calcareous shales and clayey limestones; yellowish lag clays from the alteration of limestones (*tafl*); and Pleistocene paludal facies (marsh sediments) of calcareous silty or clayey fine sandy muds. They originate from fresh-water, brackish-water, marine, or K-horizon (caliche, calcrete) desert soils. When present in any quantity in ceramic pastes, they impart a distinctive calcium carbonate and mudstone texture to the fabric.

Mud brick was the most common building material in ancient Egypt. Mud-brick source sediments were dominated by the ubiquitous alluvial and fluvio-lacustrine, fine-grained, oxidized brown Nile silts; reduced black-gray canal and harbor-lacustrine muds; and yellowish aeolian, quartz-impregnated, fine-grained wadi alluvium. These source sediments were utilized alone or mixed with other organic and inorganic materials, such as sand, straw, and dung, to produce mud bricks. Mud plasters, mud mortars, and *terre pisée*, also important for construction, were produced from the same materials.

Coarse-Grained Sediments (Sands and Gravels). Coarse-grained sediments were also exploited for various purposes, including construction, use as abrasives, glass production, and use as ceramic temper. Architectural foundations generally consisted of aeolian sands or alluvial gezira sands and gravels used for leveling and load-bearing prior to construction. In sedimentary environments such as the Nile Valley and Delta, the dominant sediment consisted of silts containing montmorillonite clay. Montmorillonite holds up to about twenty-eight times its weight in water. This capacity generally wreaks havoc with stone construction because seasonal wetting and drying cause alternate swelling and shrinking of the ground. Foundation sands and gravels aid with wall stabilization under these conditions. Foundation sands also served as a religious symbol, representing the primeval mound of first creation. In addition, sands and gravels were used in construction ramps and for tomb-shaft fill; sand was used in various mechanisms for moving monolithic stones.

Alluvial, marine, and dune sands were used as abrasives for a variety of purposes, including stone-quarrying and stone-working. These sediments are naturally well sorted and composed mostly of quartz (Mohs Scale of Hardness, 7).

Various sand sources (alluvial, marine, aeolian) were used in glass production. These natural sands were mixed with additional calcite (limestone or mollusk shells), plant ash, coloring materials, and natron to make glass.

A variety of materials were used as ceramic temper, most notably sands, gravels, and rock fragments from the following sources: (1) aeolian sands derived from inland dunes consisting of fine sand to granule-sized, very well-rounded, frosted and iron-stained clear quartz sands; (2) coastal dune sands composed of well-sorted quartz

sands where the iron oxide from the surface of the older dune sands has been eroded; (3) beach sands and silts composed of moderately well-sorted, coarse silt to sand-sized quartz with secondary feldspar, heavy minerals, and large-grained muscovite mica; (4) colluvium found on and at the base of sedimentary and igneous rocks cliffs, consisting of poorly sorted admixtures of angular sedimentary, metamorphic, and igneous rock fragments, as well as rounded and frosted aeolian quartz sands and rounded and frosted quartz sands from cross-bedded dune sandstones (colluvial sands may also contain calcrete fragments and fossiliferous biocarbonates); (5) alluvial sands and gravels from the Pleistocene geziras and Holocene Nile main and distributary channel sediments; and (6) coarse-grained brackish or fresh-water shells associated with lagoonal, marsh, and fluvial environments.

[*See also* Natural Resources; *and* Nile.]

BIBLIOGRAPHY

Al-'Izz, Abu. *Landforms of Egypt.* Cairo, 1971. Basic geology of Egypt; sediment distribution and landform evolution is presented.

Butzer, Karl W. *Early Hydraulic Civilization in Egypt.* Chicago, 1976. A groundbreaking study in the cultural ecology and the hydrogeo-archeology of the Nile Basin.

Butzer, Karl W. "Modern Egyptian Pottery Clays and Predynastic Buff Ware." *Journal of Near Eastern Studies* 33 (1974), 377–382. Geologic clay-paste sources for pottery are discussed in relation to predynastic ceramics.

Butzer, Karl W., and Carl L. Hannen. *Desert and River in Nubia.* Madison, 1968. Summarizes the geomorphic evolution of the Nile Basin and describes major sedimentary formations.

Lucas, A., and J. R. Harris. *Ancient Egyptian Materials and Industries.* 4th rev. ed. London, 1989. The primary reference book on the subject.

Nordstrom, H. A., and J. Bourriau. "Ceramic Technology: Clays and Fabrics." In *An Introduction to Ancient Egyptian Pottery*, edited by D. Arnold and J. Bourriau, pp. 143–190. Mainz, 1993. Ancient Egyptian ceramics are discussed in relation to paste and temper sources.

Said, R., ed. *The Geology of Egypt.* Rotterdam, 1990. A series of articles on the detailed geology and stratigraphy of Egypt, including the distribution of sediments and basement tectonics.

MAURY MORGENSTEIN
AND CAROL A. REDMOUNT

LANDHOLDING. Taking possession of the soil is the first defining act of a culture. In a society based on agricultural production, like that of Egypt, the countryside is the first and most important means of production. Thus, not only the physical geography of the country but also the legal form of appropriation of land are decisive in all social and cultural features.

Terminology. In addition to texts focusing on landed property, such as land lists, tax documents, wills, contracts of hire and sale, and donations, there is evidence for the system of landholding within the language itself. Egyptian has many expressions for different classes of land as a result of the people's long practical experience in exploitation of the river-dominated landscape.

Physical qualities. The most important term for a unit of arable land is *3ḥ.t*, usually rendered *ahet*. Like other terms for fertile arable land, its etymology does not reflect a special agricultural purpose, but rather the overwhelming importance of water: *3ḥ.t* is derived from *ḥ3j* ("to flow"). *3ḫ.t*, another word for "arable land," comes from *w3ḥj* ("being inundated"); *b'ḥ* ("inundated land") is from the verb *b'ḥ* ("to inundate"). Other expressions focus on the fertility of the soil as dependent on the changing levels of inundation: thus, *q3j.t*, still surviving in Coptic ⲣⲓⲉ, is the term for ordinary land of normal agricultural quality, but it literally means "highland," as opposed to *ḫrw* ("low level land"). In similar way, in later texts *m3w.t* ("new land," "island") is presumably related to low level ground no longer submerged by the river beyond the period of inundation; *3ḫ-qj* and *3ḫ-m3w* are the Demotic equivalents of γῆ ἤπειρος and νῆσος in Greek papyri.

Besides *q3j.t* ("normal agricultural land"), some other terms are attested in the New Kingdom for other classes of land. *nḥb*, presumably "fresh land," is attested in the land list of the Wilbour Papyrus as the most fertile class of land, providing double the quantity of taxable corn coming from *q3j.t* land. Between these two classes is *tnj* land, furnishing one and one-half the quantity of *q3j.t* land. These three terms are presumably restricted to the naturally irrigated lands used for growing cereals. But besides these, Egyptian agriculture recognized land appropriate for the cultivation of vegetables (*ḥzp.t?*), fruit-bearing trees like date palms and sycomore *figs* (*'.t n.t-ḥt, ḥntš*), and vines and olive trees (*k3m*). These may have been artificially irrigated throughout the year and smaller in extent than the cereal-growing lands.

The growing of flax for textiles is attested early. Cultivation of flax and barley may have taken place on the same fields: Hekanakhte's first letter to his steward Merisu tells us that land previously planted with flax could later have been used for growing cereals.

Administrative terms. The word *jḥwt/'ḥwt*, attested since the Old Kingdom, is the most important term for taxable lands on behalf of a "land-owning" institution, without any distinction of physical or ecological status. Accordingly, a word derived from *jḥwt—jḥwtj*—means "farmer," not in view of his concrete work but of his tax-producing services.

Larger units of such *jḥwt*-lands existed. The most important of them was the *rmnjt*-domain, which combined several *jḥwt*-plots in the possession of the same land-owning institution. These plots might be contiguous, but by no means needed to be.

All lands in Egypt in agricultural use were registered in special records kept in the offices of the treasury and the granary, as is attested in the New Kingdom inscription of Mes in Saqqara. In the New Kingdom, great land-owning institutions, like the temple of Amun, had their own inventories of their landed property. Thus, the land was divided among many authorities; however, there was a governmental interest in uniting all these lands in one register. The vizier was concerned with all matters of landed property.

Historical Evolution

Early Dynastic period and Old Kingdom. As in many economies based on tribal organization, agriculture in predynastic Egypt may have taken place within the narrow bounds of small villages and may have been restricted to subsistence production. Before the large stone monuments from the third dynasty onward could be erected, a profound change must have taken place within a short time, so that traditional agricultural production developed into a centrally managed enterprise with large surpluses. Seals of the first dynasty prove the delivery of revenues from Lower and Upper Egypt. Since the time of King Adj-ib the existence of royal vineyards under the authority of the Lower Egyptian treasury (*pr-dšr*) is attested. Large estates run by officials came into being, at the latest, by the end of the third dynasty. Meten, an official flourishing at the beginning of the fourth dynasty, was responsible for many such estates in various regions of the Delta. From the biography of Weni, about two hundred years later, we learn that the personnel of these estates had to join military campaigns. Large estates—the basis of wealth in the Old Kingdom—are represented by figures of humans bearing goods in nobles' tombs as part of their funerary endowment.

Although in later times temples administered the domains that supported them, this might not have been true in the Old Kingdom. The funerary temple of King Neferirkare Kakai in Abusir had its own domains. Whereas it depended on deliveries of supplies from the palace, and it may be that the palace took part of the income collected from these domains.

During the second half of the Old Kingdom, beginning with Userkaf, the Palermo Stone reports donations of land made by the king for the benefit of certain gods or their temples. There are donations of 2, 23, 24, 44, or 54 *arourae*, but in one case, probably a gift to the sun god Re, the enormous quantity of more than 1,704 *arourae* is reported.

First Intermediate period and Middle Kingdom. The *ḫbsw*-fields ("plowlands"), mentioned in the tomb of the nomarch Kheti in Asyut as the object of an irrigation project, played an important role in Middle Kingdom agriculture. Being attached to the *w'rt*, the royal administrative departments of the Middle Kingdom, they may have been actual "crown property, administered by officers of the pharaonic government" (Hayes). These fields may have been tilled with the help of compulsory labor. A granary was attached to these fields, and the two formed an economic unit.

In addition, there were the *šdw*-fields, which are mentioned several times as belonging to smallholders (*nḏsw*). It is not known if these *nḏsw* were private owners of their plots, but considering the development of pharaonic landholding, this seems unlikely. In the eighteenth dynasty these fields are mentioned as the area for apportionment of smallholdings (*s3ḥ*); the usufruct of plots of five, ten, or in one case thirty-two *arourae* is given by the king to priests and other officials. Plots of such size are attested in the late New Kingdom as parts of institutional holdings. Nevertheless, in the Middle Kingdom there were smallholders who managed their fields to a certain degree independently, like the *ka*-priest (*ḥm-k3*) Hekanakhte.

New Kingdom and later. With the New Kingdom we see the temples appearing not only as owners of land but administering lands independently of the crown. Like the king, the large temples—for instance, that of Amun-Re at Kamak—had their own granaries and treasuries. At first sight this appears to be a bipartition of the land between king and temples, still evident in the terms βασιλικὴ γῆ and ἱερὰ γῆ of Hellenistic Egypt. Earlier, scholars believed that the large possessions belonging to the temple of Amun brought about the fall of the New Kingdom, acting as a cancer in the body of the Egyptian state, but no one knows exactly how much of the land the temples actually possessed. The great Harris Papyrus of Ramesses III mentions 1,071,780 *arourae* (295,007.44 hectares) as the total amount of land in the possession of all the temples of Egypt. This would be equivalent to one-eighth of the arable land of modern Egypt. But it is not clear whether the king included in this figure only that land he himself gave to the temples, or whether he wanted to reconfirm all the temples' landed property.

On the other hand, on examining the entries of text A of the Wilbour Papyrus, one does not get the impression that in the mind of the Egyptians all land should belong to the king. Like the Harris Papyrus, this important land list of the New Kingdom begins its enumeration of the great land-owners of Egypt with the temple of Amun, going on with the temples of Heliopolis and Memphis and the smaller temples. Only after this does it turn to some fields belonging to the reigning king, the most important of them being the "*ḥ3-t3*-fields of Pharaoh." And it is specifically these fields that frequently lie within the grounds of the temples, administered by priests. So the king of the New Kingdom does not seem to have been the sole possessor of all land, but he was—alongside the gods—*one* of the possessors, being godlike himself; and it was he and his officials, especially the vizier, who controlled the land

in the name of his divine parents, allotting to them the fertile soil.

Private Property. What about all the people who were not kings or gods—did some of them hold landed property as private possessors? In the Old Kingdom, the domains represented in the nobles' tombs are part of their funerary endowments, and this resembles more the possession of a god than the private property of a living person. Living persons of the Old Kingdom might have had at their disposal lands and gardens of remarkable size; they even were able to buy and inherit them, as Meten did. But they held these lands in their capacity as officials of the king, and even buying land is no proof of the existence of private property in a society where it was possible to buy high governmental offices together with their income. So, too, great officials in the New Kingdom held large domains only in trust for a land-owning institution like a temple. Therefore, since no living person could be a private owner of land—the king being an owner only in the capacity of godlike person—one could say that the soil of Egypt was the property of the community, as manifested in the form of divine beings.

The terms for "plot of landed property" in the New Kingdom, *p(s)št* and *dnjt*, elucidate what the Egyptians thought about property. It is possible to translate the expression for the disputed plot in the litigation of Mes, *t3 psš.t n Nšj*, as "the property of Neshy," but *sensu stricto* the meaning is "the share of Neshy." In the mind of an Egyptian, property had the connotation of "share," being a personal right of usufruct resulting, for example, from assignment by a king. Such assignments could be made to soldiers, to priests, and to other officials, frequently in an amount of three or five *arourae* (0.827 or 1.378 hectares) or some multiple of these. The Wilbour Papyrus notes such smallholders, who all held their plots not as private property but under the prerogative of a land-owning institution.

With the end of the New Kingdom, sales of such smallholdings, called *3ḥwt nmḥww* ("fields of the commons"), became frequent. The gods of Kamak—Amun, Mut, and Khonsu—helped by means of mighty oracular utterances to confirm the acquisitions of smallholdings exercised by the great Theban families of priests. From some of these documents one has the impression that the price of land declined within a short time: in year 16 of Siamun, an *aroura* (no land quality stated) cost 1.1 *deben* (1 *deben* being 91 grams) of silver, but by the time of Takelot I the price was 0.1 *deben* of silver for an *aroura* of *q3jt*-land, and 0.05 *deben* of silver for an *aroura* of *št3-tnj* quality. This may have resulted from a large offering of land owing to the high cost of grain production, which made independent farming more and more difficult for these smallholders. Such holdings may have been under the prerogative of a temple that was not affected by the sale. In Demotic and Abnormal Hieratic contracts concerning sales of land, this land belongs to a temple both before and presumably after the sale, the recompense being given for the right to use the land under the authority of the temple.

The same is true of contracts of land leases. The contracts of the twenty-sixth dynasty normally have a duration of one year, and they result in a division of the yield between lessor and lessee in three (sometimes four) parts, the lessor getting one part. The lessor brought in the land only, and the lessee the means of production, such as oxen and seed. The lessor had to pay the dues to the temple, because, just as in the case of sale contracts, the leased land could belong to a temple. Although no contracts of land leases of the New Kingdom are preserved, leases may have been in use then. The word used in the Demotic contracts for "lease," *sḥn*, has the meaning "to order, to charge," and in this authoritative sense the term is attested in the New Kingdom in reference to commanding tenant farmers to cultivate the fields. "You are charged (*sḥn*) by too many fields," it is stated in Papyrus Turin A, in regard to the fatal blows afflicting the unfortunate tenant farmer. That the Egyptian tenant farmers regarded "their" fields as a burden and tried to run away from them is attested in a tradition beginning with Middle Kingdom and lasting until Greco-Roman times.

BIBLIOGRAPHY

Baer, Klaus. "The Low Price of Land in Ancient Egypt." *Journal of the American Research Center in Egypt* 1 (1962), 25–45. Deals with pharaonic documents that give the price of land and discusses the changing price level in relation to prices of slaves, grain, and cattle, and in relation to the rent of land remaining after taxes.

Endesfelder, Erika. "Königliches Boden-Eigentum in der Frühzeit." In *Grund und Boden in Altägypten: Untersuchungen zum Rechtsleben im Alten Ägypten*, edited by Schafik Allam, pp. 261–274. Tübingen, 1994. Discusses seals and annalistic tablets from the Early Dynastic period presumably containing names of land-administering institutions.

Eyre, Christopher J. "Feudal Tenure and Absentee Landlords." In *Grund und Boden in Altägypten: Untersuchungen zum Rechtsleben im Alten Ägypten*, edited by Schafik Allam, pp. 107–133. Tübingen, 1994.

Gardiner, Alan H. "The Inscription of Mes: A Contribution to the Study of Egyptian Judicial Procedure." In *Untersuchungen zur Geschichte und Altertumskunde Ägyptens*, edited by Kurt Sethe, vol. 4, pp. 1–54, 1905. Publication of a text in a New Kingdom tomb in Saqqara concerning a litigation on landed property, cited in this article.

Gardiner, Alan H. *The Wilbour Papyrus*. Vol. 1, *Plates;* vol. 2, *Commentary;* vol. 3, *Translation;* vol. 4, *Indexes.* Compiled by Raymond O. Faulkner. Oxford, 1948. Edition of the most important land list of the New Kingdom, with commentaries on the system of Egyptian landholding in the late New Kingdom as elucidated by the Wilbour Papyrus and related documents.

Hayes, William C. *A Papyrus of the Late Middle Kingdom in the Brooklyn Museum.* Brooklyn, 1955. Publication of a document dealing with fugitive people; pp. 27–29, commentary on the term *ḥbsw*.

Helck, Wolfgang. *Zur Verwaltung des Mittleren und Neuen Reiches.* Probleme der Ägyptologie, 3, 1958. Pages 89–170, essay on the administration of land and of agricultural production from the beginning of the Middle Kingdom to the end of the New Kingdom.

Hughes, George R. *Saite Demotic Land Leases.* Studies in Ancient Oriental Civilization, 28, 1952. Publication of seven Saite papyri concerned with land leases. The author discusses the form of leasing contracts in Saite times.

Hugonot, Jean-Claude. *Le jardin dans l'Egypte ancienne.* Frankfurt am Main, 1989.

James, Thomas Garnet Henry. *The Hekanachte Papers and Other Early Middle Kingdom Documents.* Publications of the Metropolitan Museum of Arts, New York, Egyptian Expedition, 19. New York, 1962. Publication of some documents concerning a Middle Kingdom household, providing various information about landholding and agricultural matters.

Janssen, Jacob J. "Prolegomena to the Study of Egypt's Economic History during the New Kingdom." In *Studien zur Altägyptischen Kultur*, 3, 1975. Pages 139–153, discussion of the most important New Kingdom documents relating to agriculture.

Katary, Sally. *Land Tenure in the Ramesside Period.* London and New York, 1989. Discussion of the figures of the Wilbour Papyrus based on statistical evaluation.

Menu, Bernadette. "La notion de propriété privée des biens fonciers dans l'Ancien Empire égyptien." In *Recherches sur l'histoire juridique, économique et sociale de l'ancienne Égypte*, edited by B. Menu, pp. 43–73. Paris, 1982.

Menu, Bernadette. "Le régime juridique des terres en Égypte pharaonique." In *Recherches sur l'histoire juridique, économique et sociale de l'ancienne Égypte*, edited by B. Menu, pp. 1–42. Paris, 1982.

Posener-Kriéger, Paule. "Les Papyrus d'Abousir." In *State and Temple Economy.* Orientalia Lovanensia Analecta, 5, pp. 133–151. Leuven, 1979. Contains conclusions on the economic relations between palace and temples, based on the archive of the funerary temple of king Neferirkare Kakai in Abusir.

Römer, Malte. "Gottes- und Priesterherrschaft in Ägypten am Ende des Neuen Reiches." In *Ägypten und Altes Testament*, edited by Manfred Görg, vol. 21, 1994. Deals with landed property in the New Kingdom, the *nmḥww* and their fields, and the price of land.

MALTE RÖMER

LANGUAGE. Primarily, Egyptian is a language of the fusional type, using "fused" morphemes with the potential for more than one function or internal modification—compare Eng. "deep, depth"—as opposed to agglutinating languages such as Turkish or Sumerian, or isolating ones such as Chinese. As a secondary feature, Egyptian shows a tendency to agglutinate affixes, such as its suffix pronouns (*-s* "she, her"), which also form a "suffix conjugation" (*rdi-s* "may she give") as opposed to the fusional old perfective (*rdi.ti* "she was given"). Lexical meaning usually adheres to bi- or triconsonantal root morphemes (*r-d̲-i̯* "give"). The language has a preference for a strict word order (like English): the clause and sentence constituents subject (S), verb (V), and object (O) follow a basic word order of VSO, with a strong tendency toward the alternative SVO order which, in the course of linguistic history, supersedes the VSO order. Alongside the sentences with a verbal predicate, there are non-verbal sentences, either with a nominal predicate or, rather frequently, with an adverbial phrase as predicate (*sš m niwt* "the scribe was in town", *sš* "scribe" as subject, *m* preposition "in," *niwt* "town"). Attributes, adjectives, and relative phrases follow their reference noun. [*For a more detailed description, see the article* Grammar.]

Linguistic Relations and Contacts
Temporal extension, geographic range, and language family. Egyptian was the majority language of the inhabitants of the lower Nile Valley at least during the last four millennia BCE and the first half of the first millennium CE. After the Arab conquest of the Egyptian Nile Valley in the early seventh century, it remained the language of the Christian minority (Copts) until well into the Middle Ages, surviving as the liturgical language of the Coptic Church into the present. It became extinct as a vernacular in the seventeenth century. Egyptian first appeared in writing in the form of captions and label texts on stone and pottery objects from the late Predynastic and Early Dynastic periods (thirty-second to twenty-seventh centuries BCE); it went out of written record in the first half of the fourteenth century CE.

Egyptian is considered a branch of the group of African and Near Eastern languages called Afro-Asiatic (or Hamito-Semitic). Despite many scholarly differences as to detail or categorization, there is a consensus about the other main branches: (1) Semitic as the largest group, with the subgroups Akkadian and Eblaitic (the oldest), Northwestern Semitic (with Aramaic, Ugaritic, Early Canaanite/Hebrew), and Southwestern Semitic (Arabic, and Semitic languages of Ethiopia); (2) Berber, spoken in North Africa from Mauritania to Libya; (3) Cushitic, in Sudan, Somalia, parts of Kenya and Ethiopia; (4) Chadic, in Central Africa around Lake Chad, including Hausa; (5) Beja, in the area between the Nile Valley and the Red Sea; and (6) perhaps Omotic, in Ethiopia north of Lake Rudolph. Within this group, only Egyptian and Semitic have a major literary tradition; the others show little or no documented historical depth. The group as a whole is much more disparate than the Indo-European language group; interestingly, Egyptian shows some grammatical (isomorphism) and not a few lexical relations (isoglosses) with Indo-European. To explain this, the hypothesis has been offered (Kammerzell 1994) that Egyptian evolved in the Late Neolithic Nile Valley out of contact between a Near Eastern language group (Paleo-Levantine), which influenced Indo-European, and an African language group (Paleo-Saharanic). When first becoming historical (i.e.,

appearing in written documents), Egyptian still displays features of affinity with the other Afro-Asiatic languages: (for example sentences with nominal predicate: the "suffix conjugation" old perfective/stative; *nisba*-adjectives, the forms of participles or personal pronouns; the feminine marker -*t*). However, it differs already from them in structure (e.g., no cases, no "prefix conjugation") enough to make us assume an autonomous evolution of at least a thousand years.

Linguistic contact. The intensity of the contact between speakers of the different languages of the ancient Near East and Africa depended very much on time and social evolution. The invention of writing in Late Predynastic Egypt had probably been stimulated by the evolution of early cuneiform writing in Mesopotamia (Sumer), knowledge of which diffused along trade routes. However, documentation for Early Dynastic and Old Kingdom linguistic contacts is scarce and restricted to names of persons and places in the Levant and Nubia. This is due to Egypt's "splendid isolation" at the time, resulting from its unique position in the area as a territorial state and a power with little need to negotiate. During the last part of the Old Kingdom, foreign interpreters served in the Egyptian provincial administration. Libyan dogs' names are preserved for posterity in the First Intermediate Period. In the Middle Kingdom, migrant tribes from Moab are depicted and their chieftain's name given, and the Semna Dispatches report the movements of Nubians passing through the region of the Second Cataract forts.

The picture changes radically during the Hyksos rule and especially in the New Kingdom (sixteenth to eleventh centuries BCE). Egypt fights for hegemony in the Near East and against the rising empires in Mesopotamia (Egyptian *Nhrn*, Canaanite *Naharina* "Two Rivers") and Anatolia (Hittites). Its imperialist move into Palestine and Syria and up the Nile into the territory of modern Sudan, and finally the balance of power among the Late Bronze Age states, brought about close contact and demographic displacement, extensive long-range trading activities, and more or less stable international relations. Contingents of Nubians (since the Middle Kingdom), Levantines, and Sea People served in the Egyptian army. Prisoners of war served as laborers; they themselves or their descendants were allowed to settle and worked their way up in court or civil service. Interstate correspondence made use of Akkadian (Amarna archives); Ramesses II's treaty with the Hittites is bilingual. Linguistic borrowing now appears on a large scale: "loan words" were frequently employed in the diplomatically active, militarily expansive, and culturally open society of the New Kingdom—words such as *ʾbry* "stallions," *ym* "sea," *mrkbt* "chariot," *slq* "snow," *ḏd* "olives." Mostly Old Canaanite or Akkadian (Middle Assyrian or Middle Babylonian) but also Nubian, Libyan, Hittite, Hurrian, or Aegean in origin, these words reflect particular modes of expression (of administrative officials, soldiers, merchants, or gardeners); they accompanied imported goods and technologies, particularly luxury items, military equipment, and administrative procedures (chariots, weapons, horses, fortifications, corvée labor, and tributes); they named newly introduced agricultural and manufactured products (plants and animals, vessels). These loan words were not marked as foreign but were treated as if native to the language.

In the first millennium BCE, when the Egyptian Upper Nile colonies had become independent (kingdoms of Napata and Meroë) and Egypt itself a middling power among the states of the Near East and the Mediterranean rim, both object and subject of geopolitical currents, the period of translations and multilingual texts begins: the stelae of Carian and Phoenician mercenaries, of Darius I ("Canal-stelae" in Egyptian, Old Persian, Akkadian, Elamitic), the Egyptian-Greek decrees of the Ptolemies (Rosetta Stone, Canopus Decree). Later we find the Egyptian-Greek-Latin text of Cornelius Gallus, the Roman prefect in Egypt. In postdynastic times, under the reign of the Ptolemies and as a province of the Roman Empire, Egypt became an intensely multicultural and multilingual country. Greek loan words and personal names appeared in Egyptian texts; documents and records were composed in both Greek and Egyptian (Demotic). The full impact of bilingualism on Egyptian is displayed by its latest stage, Coptic: the proportion of Greek words in its vocabulary is considerable, especially content words, but even a number of function words such as ⲁⲗⲗⲁ "but" or ⲕⲁⲧⲁ "according to"; in specific texts, such as New Testament translations, the proportion of Greek is extremely high. In the Middle Ages, the twilight of Coptic as a living language, there are again bilingual texts, now Coptic-Arabic.

A certain number of Egyptian words have found their way into European languages. They include nouns such as adobe, elephant, ebony, and lily, and names like Susan or Onofrio (cf. Černý 1971).

Writing and Scripts

Hieroglyphs. At first—and in monumental and other representative inscriptions up to the very end of Egyptian civilization—the language is written with signs of pictorial appearance which the Greeks called *ta hieroglyphika grammata* ("the sacred carved letters"). The hieroglyphic writing system emerged in Late Predynastic and Early Dynastic times, together with the principles of large-scale representational art; hieroglyphs are stylized pictures of living beings, of objects and parts thereof. When used as writing signs, the principles of pictography apply only in sign plays and for calligraphic considerations. Instead, the signs are members of conventionalized sets, and the number of signs in actual use is limited (200–300 in normal texts). In Ptolemaic times the sign-producing processes were revived, multiplying the number of signs to reach several thousand.

Hieroglyphic pictograms primarily represent sequences of phonemes (the smallest phonetic element that distinguishes meaning). They are conventionalized in historical times, but originally they were derived from the name of the object depicted by disregarding its meaning (the rebus principle, as in writing the word "belief" with the pictures of a bee and a leaf; cf. Davies 1987, p. 31); sometimes, mostly in Greco-Roman times, they were also derived by the *acrophonic principle,* by which one represents the object by means of the first consonantal phonogram of its name. Unlike Sumerian (and later Akkadian) syllable signs, which stand for whole syllables of one or two consonants with one or two vowels, hieroglyphic graphemes (the smallest written element that distinguishes phonemes, morphemes, and other elements of the language or writing) basically represent only consonantal phonemes, usually one to three, irrespective of syllable boundaries (hence, "phonograms"). Most frequent are graphemes that are biconsonantal, or represent two consonantal phonemes.

The elementary graphemes, those phonograms that represent one phoneme, cover the language's whole set of twenty-four phonemes; they are not used like an alphabet, however, but as "complementary" signs to facilitate reading the biconsonantal (around eighty) and triconsonantal graphemes. Over time, the bond between graphemes and the phonemes they referred to was bound to be weakened by the effects of historical sound change; as a consequence, a new set of elementary graphemes came into use during the New Kingdom. Since these signs were developed out of some of the biconsonantal graphemes accompanied by their complementary monoconsonantal signs, they are known as "group writing" signs (sometimes called "syllabic").

Beside the graphemes which represent phonemes, there are hieroglyphic pictograms that can be used iconically, either to classify words according to their semantic field or to represent the actual entity depicted. The former are called "semograms" or "determinatives"—graphemes that assign phoneme groups representing meaningful morphemes, that is, words, to classes of meaning, and the latter are "logograms" or "ideograms." During most of dynastic times, the set of signs is conventionalized; in postdynastic times, the sign-producing processes were revived in grand style as "Ptolemaic writing." Nevertheless, these graphemes can cover the whole range from narrow specificity—the pictogram of a locust, for example, classifying as semogram/determinative the word for "locust"—to extreme generality, as in the pictogram of an arm with a stick classifying all kinds of action. When categorizing units of perception denoted by words into abstract classes such as "human beings," "animals," "minerals," "fluids," and so on, the Egyptian system of classification shows considerable affinity to modern ones. One should take note that among the writing systems of the world, Egyptian hieroglyphs thus exhibit the most explicit system of culturally structuring the perceived world.

The Egyptian writing system as such differs from alphabetic systems only in a shift in information redundancy. The Egyptian units may be incompletely encoded phonemically, but they provide direct semantic information.

Being miniature pictures, the hieroglyphic graphemes are closely linked to representational art and play an integral part in representation (cf. Baines 1984). As pictures, they follow the representational rules and conventions of Egyptian two-dimensional art; as signs, they are arranged—usually within the constraints of readability—according to calligraphic considerations. Arranged either in lines or in columns, of large size or small, they can be read from right to left (the normal orientation) or from left to right, depending on the esthetic or organizational needs of their representational context. Only during the last phase of Egyptian civilization do the signs lose their ability to express speech and thought as graphemes. At the same time, their pictorial features gain importance in the Late and postdynastic periods, when they are used on a large scale in plays of signs which combine word meaning, iconic meaning, and sign arrangement, including acrostics. Known as cryptography, this method of artfully blending iconic and linguistic meaning gave rise to the concept of an Egyptian symbol writing which from late antiquity until the beginning of Egyptology dominated heuristic approaches to Egyptian writing.

Cursive forms. Through simplification, the pictorial signs of the hieroglyphic script were adapted to writing with ink and brush. Moderately simplified "cursive hieroglyphs" were in use since the Middle Kingdom for a certain kind of funerary texts (Coffin Texts), and from the eighteenth dynasty on for the manuscripts of the *Book of Going Forth by Day* (*Book of the Dead*) and the painted *Book of That Which Is in the Underworld* (*Amduat*) decoration on the walls of royal tombs.

For everyday purposes, the hieroglyphic signs were abbreviated still further. Hieratic, as this type of script was named by the Greeks, was the Egyptian script proper for one and a half millennia, employed to record administrative and business documents, letters, and literary, scientific, and religious texts, usually written on sheets or rolls of papyrus, potsherds, and small fragments of stone (ostraca). The Hieratic signs have lost their pictorial appearance to a large extent, but as graphemes they follow the same functional principles as hieroglyphs do. They can be written in columns (a grouping that falls into disuse during the Middle Kingdom) or in lines, but unlike hieroglyphs, they invariably read from right to left. In this they differ from cursive hieroglyphs, which do the opposite and used to be read backward compared to the apparent orientation of the signs. In the orthography of words and phrases, hieroglyphic and Hieratic texts can differ considerably. For scholarly purposes, Hieratic signs are customarily transcribed into hieroglyphs to improve their readability.

At the beginning of the Late period, another type of cursive writing took the place of Hieratic for everyday purposes, for texts of legal and administrative character, and also for belles-lettres. This script was called Demotic by the Greeks: *ta demotika grammata*, "the popular letters," vs. *ta hieratika grammata*, "the priestly letters"—since Hieratic had become confined to religious texts in the Late and postdynastic periods. In principle a derivative of Hieratic, Demotic is a highly cursive script, and morphemes or words are frequently written as phonogram complexes largely drawn from group writing signs in combination with semogram complexes, both contracted to a kind of shorthand. This method of writing hardly permits a sign-by-sign analysis of the graphemes. Although it remains possible for scholars to transcribe Demotic into hieroglyphs, the outcome is no longer an adequate reproduction, and too unwieldy to be of use.

Coptic. In conjunction with the decline of pagan Egyptian civilization during Roman rule and the gradual loss of the intertextual connecting line to the indigenous tradition, a new writing system was devised. It made use of the twenty-four letters of the Greek alphabet, supplemented by six signs taken from Demotic: this is the Coptic script. Coptic breaks with the pictorial character of the graphemes and becomes an alphabetic writing which denotes vowels as well as consonants. It is documented in a number of dialects, which, however, may represent not local varieties of the language but variant conventionalized grapheme sets deriving from local traditions, as Loprieno (1981) has argued.

Influences. The Egyptian writing system seems to have stimulated the development of the Western Semitic alphabetic scripts. In their earliest form (Proto-Canaanite, or Proto-Sinaitic, since its first known documents were found in the Egyptian turquoise mines of Sinai), they contain a large percentage of signs borrowed from Egyptian (cf. Gardiner 1916). As in Egyptian, only the consonantal phonemes are recorded, while vowels remain undenoted (at variance with cuneiform principles, which denote both), and the set of Egyptian monoconsonantal elementary graphemes may have provided a model for the restricted set of signs typical of alphabetic scripts. Via the relationship with the later Canaanite or Phoenician alphabet that formed the basis for the Greek and Latin alphabetic writing system, Proto-Canaanite—and thus Egyptian—"lives on" in Western writing systems.

Even after the end of Egyptian political supremacy along the upper Nile, Egyptian continued to contribute heavily to the communication means and writing systems of an important ancient African civilization. Centered in modern Upper Nubia and the Sudan, it was known to the Egyptians as "Kush," and to the classical authors as "Ethiopia." During the Cushitic and Napatan periods of this strongly egyptianized civilization (from the early eighth through the late third century BCE, including the phase of Cushitic reign in Egypt itself, the twenty-fifth dynasty, with Napata in the Fourth Cataract area as its capital), Egyptian language and writing was the official language of its decorum texts. From the late third century BCE until well into Late Antiquity (Meroitic period, with Meroë in the Sixth Cataract area as its capital), the native tongue itself, "Meroitic," was written in a cursive and a hieroglyphic script: the sign classes of both were derived from Egyptian graphemes, the cursive coming from Early Demotic. The Meroitic writing system, however, is quite different from Egyptian: vowels as well as consonants are denoted, and it is basically a syllabic system of the "Devanagari" type, in which a grapheme represents a consonantal morpheme plus the vowel *a*, unless followed by the vowel graphemes *i*, *o*, or shwa—usually transliterated as *e* or "zero." Although the signs are quite readable and documentation is plentiful, the language itself is not yet fully understood: apart from some morphological features and the meaning of some words and standard phrases, the majority of the texts remain untranslatable.

Egyptian Linguistic Knowledge

The linguistics of speech. Usually there is no need to render explicit the rules and phenomena of one's own language unless one has to teach it, help others learn it, learn another language: explicit rendering of a language is necessitated by linguistic contact. Thus, it comes as no surprise that grammatical exercises of some kind cannot be found before the Ramessid era and appear again in the Ptolemaic period. Implicitly, however, every conscious speaker of a language has a large amount of knowledge, and this holds true for Egyptian speakers too.

Egyptian has terms for "speech" and "writing," but not for "language" as an abstract, rule-governed system. The Egyptian linguistics of speech may be subdivided into rhetoric and etymology. Rhetoric—"perfect speech" (*md.t nfr.t*)—is taught by giving normative rules of how to form well-balanced paragraphs (*tz.w*, "knots"; in writing, marked by verse-points), which are closely akin to the prose rhythm of classical antiquity, and by giving advice on rhetorical strategy (cf. the "disputant" in the *Instruction of Ptahhotep*) and examples of well-formed speech.

Egyptian etymology has a strong similarity to the etymological approaches of the Pre-Socratics, Plato, and the Stoic philosophers: although things and living beings are not identical with their "names" (*rn*), the latter are indelibly connected to their essence. This means, first, that phonetic resemblance points to essential relationship, and second, that analysis of sound leads to the essence of things: the god Re is the great "cat" (*mjw*) since he is the one "who is identical (*mjw*) with his creation" (Coffin Texts IV 286/287ff.). This is usually but inadequately termed "word plays." Thus, language itself offers a natural system of ordering things and beings, reproduced in the so-called onomastica, which comprise "all things which exist," as the *Onomasticon of Amenemope* claims. Consequently, language allows one to manipulate and create things by manipulating and creating names and words—the cognitive foundation of magic.

Linguistics of writing. Any adequately elaborated writing system calls for a minimum of conscious action on the part of those who establish or improve it. Speech is produced as a continuous flow of sounds; it is no trivial act to break the chain of sounds into units that can be shaped into a meaningful written form—the more so, if one is dealing with monoconsonantal alphabetic signs (e.g., *jqr* "excellent"). The ways in which semograms/determinatives are used display a conscious division of lexically meaningful units—lexemes—and relationally meaningful units, or morphemes: the closed sets of conjugation carriers and conjugation endings, of simple prepositions, demonstratives, and personal pronouns are not categorized into classes of meaning. Early writing (late Predynastic and Early Dynastic) shows a mixing of logograms with phonetic complements and phonemic writing with semograms. Conventionalization furthers the following development: a specific grapheme group ending with a semogram is assigned to each word ("schematogram"); all grammatical derivates of a word keep the same graphic nucleus; and functional morpheme signs are postponed. Sign grouping has become a "visual morpheme."

In pursuit of the possibilities inherent in their writing system, Egyptian intellectuals did not stop at throwing the net of linguistic categorization by means of iconic classifiers (semograms; see above) over the world and its objects. Hieroglyphs are signs used to write down meaningful units of the language referring to things, but to an equal degree, they are signs that depict units of visual perception. Writing something can simultaneously mean depicting something, but the nature of the writing system means that this is usually depicting something else. Writing can thus be made to refer to meaning on two different levels; this is the basic principle on which cryptography (enigmatic writing) or the play of signs work. As a further consequence, if depictions are writing signs conveying units of meaning different from their pictorial appearance, the units of perception depicted can by themselves be considered signs of yet another script—the world and its order of things can become the script of god. The Egyptian priestly elite is thus the founder of a unique branch of language philosophy that has been called "philosophy of writing" (Sauneron 1972). But there is another consequence of these impressive accomplishments, which turned out to be of major negative impact (cf. Sternberg-el-Hotabi 1994). On the one hand, the progressive complexity of hieroglyphic writings left progressively fewer people able to write and read it, so that the priestly elite itself contributed to the eventual fall of the Egyptian civilization it had tried to preserve. On the other hand, their attempts to make the world speak in its own language lie at the root of the image of Egyptian as a picture writing to be interpreted only metaphorically and symbolically, an image which for centuries was the major obstacle to regaining access to the language.

Language and Society. Egypt was the first territorial state in history, a monarchy legitimized by cosmology, founded on a society of growing complexity based in its turn on a wide-reaching division of labor. This basic structure forced Egypt to develop a complex and effective administration. From Early Dynastic until postdynastic times, its ruling class was centered on a royal court, and civil service was its principal path to advancement and financial gains. Language constituted the adhesive force and the communicative flux of this society.

Its organization was founded on and doubly bound to theological reasoning, and much effort was spent on formulating, writing, and rewriting decorum texts, official and self-fashioning verbal representations. Speaking well and well-regulated eloquence were called for in councils (*qnb.t*), a prerequisite to court office and an integral part of etiquette. Independently of the individual's standing in society, it conveyed prestige and granted social acceptance. The ability to read and write was the entrance ticket to a career and to professional advancement; there were schools (*'.t-sb3*) in the royal residence and connected to the temples, but formal education was short and followed by sometimes very long on-the-job training. Professional specialization was common; the administrative officials were trained mainly in Hieratic, while priests and temple officials, designers, and specific groups of artisans and workmen commanded both Hieratic and hieroglyphic scripts with varying degrees of proficiency.

In the Middle Kingdom, the growing density of educational facilities led to the emergence of literary texts designed to further social self-fashioning (teachings and complaints) and to provide entertainment (fictional narratives); a selection of these texts was to become school reading in the New Kingdom. During periods of instability of the central administration (Intermediate periods), and toward the end of Egyptian civilization, literacy decreased, as did the general level of knowledge. Literacy has been calculated as 1 percent of the population of 1 to 1.5 million, on the basis of adult male office-holders in the Memphite necropolis of the Old Kingdom (cf. Baines 1984). These figures allow for possibly higher rates in the New Kingdom, but they presumably underestimate the size of the gray area of nonprofessionals on the periphery of a society that rated literacy as highly as Egyptian society did.

Language History and Language Stages. Attested by texts from around 3000 BCE to the Middle Ages, Egyptian is the language with the longest documentation in human history. Egyptian grammar had a very long time indeed to change and evolve. For research purposes, this long continuum was divided by early modern linguists into stages roughly linked to the periods of Egyptian history. These stages were then treated as synchronic cuts and found more or less systematic description in the form of philological grammars. Traditionally, Old Egyptian, Middle Egyptian, Late Egyptian, Demotic, and Coptic were considered such stages, and there is an apparent linguistic demarcation line that separates Old and Middle Egyptian as the older group from the younger group of Late Egyptian, Demotic, and Coptic. Since these stages were given strong typological outlines in the respective grammars, the language's history has usually been explained along the lines of major differences between spoken and written language (the cataclysm theory): while the written language remained unchanged, spoken forms did change, and it was only after centuries that these changes surfaced in writing. This theory, however, needs to be judged in the light of the following considerations.

First, colloquial language differs from its written counterpart not only in grammar, but also in the content of the messages conveyed; when writing one obeys different linguistic norms. In learning to write, the users of the language also learn unconsciously to observe the unwritten rules governing expression in any particular kind of text—that is, they adopt another register. Although these registers are determined by tradition, they are also subject to change through the very use that the community makes of language.

Second, writing does not evolve at the same pace as the spoken language: changes in the structure and pronunciation of words and forms are not necessarily mirrored in written usage. In the same way, changes in written forms need not reflect changes in other linguistic forms. The members of a community using a given language usually do not recognize changes in their language as linguistic innovations, and innovations emerge so slowly that even outside observers can recognize them only by comparing forms in texts that are separated from each other by long intervals of time.

Thus, the differences especially between Standard (Classical) Middle Egyptian and Late Egyptian—taken as representative of the later group—are not so fundamental as is widely assumed: all Late Egyptian forms and expressions were basically present in Middle Egyptian. The main difference from Middle Egyptian is that Late Egyptian is dominated by forms that were rarely used before even if they were present, and that usages characterizing Middle Egyptian were finally abandoned. In short, linguistic change in Egyptian can be characterized as change in the frequency with which given forms were used, accompanied by shifts in their roles within the network of linguistic relations. Although the abandonment of earlier writing conventions is a specific characteristic of New Kingdom texts, earlier forms do in fact persist in the texts for a long time. The relationship of the conventional writing symbols (graphemes) to the phonetic segments that differentiate lexically distinct linguistic items (phonemes) is not as clearly defined as in Middle Egyptian, making it possible for linguistic changes to remain unrecognized. Adjustments in written forms then make gradual evolutionary changes appear to have been abrupt.

Developments in forms and morphology can be observed already in earlier periods, in those texts lacking stylistic pretensions or representing textual genres less burdened with tradition, such as letters and administrative records. Late Egyptianisms in such texts, or in literary and theological texts of a later date, do not betray an author's unconscious "slipping" into colloquial language; rather, they are symptoms of language evolution.

Scope of linguistic stages. Temporal linguistic demarcation is thus less real than has been generally assumed. In all periods there is a considerable amount of overlap in the use of various register grammars. On the one hand, a number of grammatical features from previous stages may be preserved; on the other, features of the dominant grammar of the period to follow may appear. For diagnostic purposes and with a certain degree of simplification, one can classify text grammars by the proportion of linguistic expressions of previous stages they contain (sometimes veiled by their written form). The most culturally significant texts have the highest proportion of such traditional forms; from the texts of daily life through literary to ideological and theological works, the proportion of these forms increases constantly, because the latter reside in the linguistically more protected higher registers of the hierarchy of textual expression. The "Middle Egyptian" of Ramessid theological texts disguised by Late Egyptian writing habits is thus nothing but a manifestation of a perfectly normal use of language. It is only at the end of the twentieth dynasty that we perceive the emergence of a seemingly "purified" Middle Egyptian, which shows all the signs of a language expressly taught in schools; this learned scholastic Middle Egyptian will continue for the rest of ancient Egyptian history in roughly the same role Latin played in Europe.

The following classification is used here to distinguish the groups and stages of Egyptian language history, and the linguistic registers during same periods; besides periods and levels of texts (registers), main classifying parameters are sentence structure and orthography.

1. *Earlier Egyptian*

a. Old Egyptian (twenty-seventh to twenty-first century BCE), in use during the Old Kingdom; subdivided into Archaic Old Egyptian (twenty-seventh to twenty-second centuries), the medium of the Pyramid Texts, and Standard Old Egyptian (twenty-fifth to twenty-first centuries), the language of the monumental inscriptions of royal and private individuals.

b. Middle Egyptian (twenty-third century BCE to fourth century CE). It is subdivided into:

- Standard or Classical Middle Egyptian (twenty-third to fourteenth century BCE), used starting in the sixth dynasty for letters, in some autobiographies and funerary texts (Coffin Texts) of the Late First Intermediate Period, in most texts of the Middle Kingdom, and up to the early eighteenth dynasty in decorum texts;
- Late Middle Egyptian (twentieth to thirteenth century BCE), first attested in the Hekanakhte papers, then, e.g., in the Great Hymn to the Aten in the Amarna period, or the literary hymn to Amun (Papyrus Leiden I, 350rt); it is characterized by Middle Egyptian sentence structure and orthography and a more or less sparing use of Late Egyptian forms, words, and writings;
- "Neo"-Middle Egyptian (eleventh century BCE to fourth century CE); the language of religious and decorum texts from the late New Kingdom to the end of pagan Egyptian civilization, which is based on Standard Middle Egyptian structure and orthography but is only learned as a second language and has a linguistic and writing development of its own.

2. *Later Egyptian*

a. Late Egyptian (fifteenth to seventh century BCE), subdivided into:

- "Medio"-Late Egyptian (fifteenth to twelfth century BCE), used, e.g., for the letters of the early eighteenth dynasty, in the Amarna boundary stelae, and the story of the *Doomed Prince;* it is a language that shows a basically Late Egyptian sentence structure with a variety of Middle Egyptian syntactical elements and forms, and still uses Middle Egyptian orthography as a rule;

- Late Egyptian proper (fourteenth to seventh century BCE), the language in use during the late New Kingdom (nineteenth and twentieth dynasties) and the Third Intermediate Period for business, everyday affairs, literature, and some decorum texts; it shows a pure Late Egyptian sentence structure with Late Egyptian forms and writings; occasional Middle Egyptianisms in grammatical forms and orthography disappear progressively.

b. Demotic (seventh century BCE to fifth century CE), the language of business transactions, everyday affairs, and literature from the Late period to the end of pagan Egyptian civilization. Unlike all previously mentioned terms for those language stages and language variants documented in both monumental (hieroglyphic) and cursive (Hieratic) texts, "Demotic" is applied simultaneously to both a stage and a script. Demotic grammar is clearly a derivative of Late Egyptian. Demotic is subdivided into:

- Early Demotic (seventh to fourth century BCE), in use during the twenty-sixth dynasty and the Persian rule;
- Middle Demotic (fourth to first century BCE), in use during the reign of the Ptolemies, in the fields of administration and everyday affairs competing with Greek, and supplying literature for those still Egyptian-minded;
- Late Demotic (first century BCE to fifth century CE), in use under Roman rule but progressively giving way to Greek; it already follows Coptic grammatical principles, even if still written in Demotic script.

c. Coptic (first to seventeenth century CE) is the language of Christian Egypt, written in Greek alphabetic signs and a few adapted Demotic signs for Egyptian phonemes absent from Greek. From a variety of Coptic dialects (such as Akhmimic, Fayyumic, Lycopolitan), Sa'idic and Bohairic emerge as the two main literary dialects; Sa'idic, mainly used in Upper Egypt and documented since the fourth century, is the language of early autochthonous Coptic literary writing; Bohairic, attested first in the fourth century, is of Lower Egyptian (Delta) origin. Competing with Arabic since the seventh century CE, Coptic was gradually superseded by it, but in its Bohairic variant it survives to the present as the liturgical language of the Coptic Church.

Recovery of the Language

Decipherment. While a working knowledge of Egyptian survived for quite a while in Coptic (a Coptic-Arabic grammar appeared as late as the thirteenth century CE), knowledge of the ancient writing system declined progressively during the first centuries CE and fell into final oblivion in late antiquity. The latest dated hieroglyphic text is a stela of a holy bull from 340 CE; the latest Demotic text is from 452 CE; both are in the temple at Philae. Dynastic Egyptian literature, the written documents of a whole civilization, historical and religious, monumental and cursive, fell silent. All that remained was a faint remembrance and a widespread and deeply rooted notion of the symbolic nature of Egyptian writing; the latter had been fostered by hieroglyphic decorum inscriptions, especially cryptography, of Ptolemaic and imperial Roman times. The notion was put into words by the Egyptian priest and grammarian Chairemon in the first century CE, and perpetuated and transmitted to posterity by Neoplatonic philosophers, the pagan apologetes, and the Church Fathers. It was only when the Neoplatonists of Renaissance Florence rediscovered and translated Horapollon's *Hieroglyphika* and the *Corpus Hermeticum* that things Egyptian returned to the minds of European intellectuals. Their interest in symbolic writing and universal principles led to first attempts at decipherment and kept curiosity alive well into the Enlightenment, but it also encouraged a line of study that would prove to be an obstacle to success. Erroneous as these early attempts were, they nevertheless paved the way: it was Athanasius Kircher in the seventeenth century who launched the idea that Coptic was the language of the hieroglyphic inscriptions, and in the mid-eighteenth century, J. J. Barthélemy came to think of the "cartouche" rings as enclosing royal names—an idea that became the starting point for the eventual decipherment.

The conditions for the final breakthrough were created by the discovery of an Egyptian commemorative stela written in hieroglyphic, Demotic, and Greek, erected in honor of King Ptolemy V Epiphanes and dated to his ninth year of reign, corresponding to 27 March 196 BCE. The stela, now in the British Museum, became famous under the name of the Rosetta Stone; it was unearthed in 1799 by soldiers of Napoleon Bonaparte's Egyptian campaign. Incidental as the finding itself may have been, it was not incidental that Napoleon's army was accompanied by Vivant Denon and his scholars, the "travel academy" that would later publish the *Description de l'Égypte*, a veritable gold mine for future studies. It was not incidental either that the stela found the attention it deserved; the time had come, the age of the symbolically minded and the Platonists was waning, and the era of empiricism had begun to flourish. With the Rosetta Stone as its key, the final phase of the recovery of the Egyptian writing system in the early nineteenth century centered on three persons: the Swedish diplomat and orientalist Johan Åkerblad, a pupil of the celebrated Sylvestre de Sacy; the British scientist Thomas Young, a proponent of the undulatory theory of light; and the French professor, schoolteacher, and librarian Jean-François Champollion.

Following de Sacy's method, Åkerblad concentrated on the Demotic section and succeeded in identifying all the proper names occurring in the Greek text, a morpheme (the pronominal suffix for "him, his") and a few alphabetically written words in their Coptic spelling. He was thus the first to overcome the age-old prepossession with the symbolic character of the Egyptian signs—an accomplishment not to be underestimated—and to put the hypothesis of phonemic writing on a sound basis. He carried his alphabetic approach too far, though, and failed to make further progress.

Young, too, started with the Demotic script, but he then proceeded to the hieroglyphic. He realized that the two were related, which meant that neither represented a symbolic type of writing, and that they contained different types of characters, phonemic and others. With the help of passages from the *Book of Going Forth by Day*, he established the equivalence of hieroglyphic and Hieratic signs. He identified allophony, the determinative for feminine names in late texts, and, back again on the Rosetta Stone, the name of King Ptolemy in the hieroglyphic section and the phonematic value of the name signs.

While Åkerblad and Young represented the traditional type of the polymath, in Champollion the modern type of scholar, whose strength is singlemindedness, entered the stage. Having devoted all his life to the study of Oriental languages, writing systems, Coptic, and things Egyptian, he eventually won the race to decipher the hieroglyphs. Where his forerunners had made ventures into the unknown, he turned to systematic analysis. His method was based on the assumption that the hieroglyphic system worked on phonemic principles, on independent checks of name pairs (first Ptolemy and Cleopatra, then other names and titles of Ptolemaic and imperial Roman Egypt), and finally on the proof that even the names of earlier times (Ramesses and Thutmose) were written by using the same principles. After his initial breakthrough, his knowledge and experience brought further progress in a rush; within only two years, between his *Lettre à M. Dacier relative à l'alphabet des hiéroglyphes phonétique* of 1822 and the amazingly well-informed *Précis du système hiéroglyphique* of 1824, he discovered the basic principles of the entire Egyptian writing system, amassed a huge amount of data, and identified not a few grammatical structures.

Grammar and philology. As happens very often in new areas of knowledge, Champollion had learned so much, had broadened the horizons to such a degree and gained such deep insights, that nobody else was equipped to take things further or even to discuss them on the same level. The situation improved only in 1837, when Richard Lepsius's penetrating reexamination of Champollion's decipherment proved it to be sound; from 1838 on, Samuel Birch translated and edited Egyptian texts, publishing a *Dictionary of Hieroglyphics* in 1867; in 1855, Heinrich Brugsch wrote the first grammar of Demotic.

The scientific basis for modern knowledge of the Egyptian and Coptic language was finally established by Adolf Erman, who in 1880 published his *Neuägyptische Grammatik*, and by his colleagues (including Ludwig Stern) and pupils, who later were to be known as the "Berlin School." Most of the eminent philologists and grammarians of the time either belonged to the Berlin School directly or were in close connection with it: J. H. Breasted, K. Sethe, G. Steindorff, W. Spiegelberg, F. Ll. Griffith, B. Gunn, and later H. Grapow. In 1897, Erman launched the *Wörterbuch der ägyptischen Sprache*, a lexicographic task that would last more than half a century and in which scholars from almost every country participated. Among these was Alan Henderson Gardiner, an offshoot of the Berlin School—he was a student of Erman and Sethe—and at the same time its crowning glory. He was the last of the giants of the founding generation of Egyptian philology. There is almost no area of the field he did not improve by important contributions; his *Egyptian Grammar* (first published 1927, third edition 1957), both a manual and a gold mine of details and linguistic insights, is still an indispensable tool for learning Egyptian and translating and analyzing Egyptian texts.

The following phase, which lasts to the present, has been one of increasing sophistication in a variety of aspects. A growing multitude of scholars edited texts, published text-specific grammars, and developed theories of Egyptian syntax. Egyptian phonology has become an object of research, and channels to general linguistics have been opened. A leading figure in these undertakings has been Hans Jakob Polotsky, who formulated the paradigm that allowed the various stages of Dynastic Egyptian and Coptic to be described on the same grounds and by the same notions. Although well prepared now to merge into general linguistic knowledge, the Egyptian language still has not a few dark corners awaiting illumination.

[*See also* Decipherment; Egyptology; Literacy; *the composite articles on* Grammar *and* Scripts; *and the biographical entry on* Champollion.]

BIBLIOGRAPHY

Baines, John. "Schreiben." In *Lexikon der Ägyptologie*, vol. 5, cols. 693–698. Wiesbaden, 1984. English summary of the author's concepts of decorum principles, institutions, prestige, and stability of Egyptian writing.

Baines, John. "Communication and Display: The Interpretation of Early Egyptian Art and Writing." *Antiquity* 63 (1989), 471–482.

Černý, Jaroslav. *Language and Writing*. In *The Legacy of Egypt*, edited by J. R. Harris, vol. 2, pp. 197–219. Oxford, 1971. Rich in examples of borrowings of Egyptian vocabulary into Western languages.

Davies, W. Vivian. *Reading the Past: Egyptian Hieroglyphs*. London, 1987. Highly informative and well illustrated, an excellent introduction to language, scripts, writing principles, and decipherment.

Fischer, Henry G. "Hieroglyphen." In *Lexikon der Ägyptologie*, vol. 2, cols. 1189–1199. Wiesbaden, 1977. Concise English rendering of the functions and uses of Hieroglyphs.

Gardiner, A. H. "The Egyptian Origin of the Semitic Alphabet." *Journal of Egyptian Archaeology*, 3 (1916), 1–16.

Goldwasser, Orly. *From Icon to Metaphor: Studies in the Semiotics of Hieroglyphs.* Orbis Biblicus et Orientalis, 142. Fribourg and Göttingen, 1995. Study of the determinative system and its value for examining Egyptian conceptual categories.

Hintze, Fritz. "The Meroitic Period." In *Africa in Antiquity: The Arts of Ancient Nubia and the Sudan, I, The Essays,* pp. 89–105. Brooklyn, N.Y., 1978.

Hoch, James E. *Semitic Words in Egyptian Texts of the New Kingdom and Third Intermediate Period.* Princeton, 1994. The basic recent publication on lexical borrowings into Egyptian.

Iversen, Erik. *The Myth of Egypt and Its Hieroglyphs.* Copenhagen, 1961.

Junge, Friedrich. "Sprache." In *Lexikon der Ägyptologie,* vol. 5, cols. 1177–1187. Wiesbaden, 1984.

Junge, Friedrich. "Zur 'Sprachwissenschaft' der Ägypter." In *Studien zu Sprache und Religion Ägyptens,* vol. 1, *Sprache,* pp. 257–272. Göttingen, 1984.

Kammerzell, Frank. *Panther, Löwe und Sprachentwicklung im Neolithikum.* Göttingen, 1994. Most recent essay on origin and prehistory of the Egyptian language along the lines of Collin Renfrew, *Archaeology and Language: The Puzzle of Indo-European Origins* (London, 1989).

Loprieno, Antonio. *Ancient Egyptian: A Linguistic Introduction.* Cambridge, 1995. A comprehensive treatment of Egyptian through all stages with many glances at the genetic frame.

Polotsky, Hans Jakob. "Egyptian." In *At the Dawn of Civilisation,* edited by E. A. Speiser, pp. 121–134, 359–363. London, 1964. Case studies; although reflecting an older stage of knowledge, this essay still gives a proper impression of the language.

Pope, Maurice. *The Story of Decipherment: From Egyptian Hieroglyphs to Linear B.* London, 1975.

Sass, Benjamin. *The Genesis of the Alphabet and Its Development in the Second Millenium B.C.* Wiesbaden, 1988.

Sauneron, Serge, ed. *Textes et langages de l'Égypte pharaonic: Cent cinquante années de recherches 1822–1972.* Bibliothèque d'étude, 64. Cairo, 1972. Account of the state of linguistic knowledge at the time; many aspects of the language are treated in essays of varying quality.

Schenkel, Wolfgang. "The Structure of Hieroglyphic Script." *Royal Anthropological Institute News* 15 (1976), 4–7. Concise treatment of the principles and mechanisms of hieroglyphic writing.

Schenkel, Wolfgang. "Schrift." In *Lexikon der Ägyptologie,* 5:713–735. Wiesbaden, 1984. Comprehensive study of all aspects of the Egyptian writing system, in German.

Schenkel, Wolfgang. *Einführung in die altägyptische Sprachwissenschaft.* Orientalistische Einführungen. Darmstadt, 1990. A comprehensive introduction into a variety of aspects of the language; history of the language and language research. Extensive bibliographical notes in the remarks.

Sternberg-el-Hotabi, H. "Der Untergang des Hieroglyphenschrift. *Chronique d'Égypte* 69 (1994), 237–241.

Stricker, Bruno H. "De indeeling der Egyptische taal-geschiedenis." *Oudheidkundige Mededelingen uit het Rijksmuseum van Oudheiden te Leiden* 25 (1944), 12–51. The basic essay concerning the differentiation of language stages.

FRIEDRICH JUNGE
with Heike Behlmer

LAPIS LAZULI. *See* Gems.

LATE PERIOD. [*This entry surveys the Late period of ancient Egyptian history, with reference to that period's major kings, main historical events, and significant cultural and social developments. It comprises four articles:*

An Overview
Twenty-sixth Dynasty
Thirtieth Dynasty
Thirty-first Dynasty

For related discussions, see Achaemenids; *and* Persia.]

An Overview

The Late period is one of the best-documented periods of Egyptian history, but it raises problems that are unknown to students of the earlier periods. A great advantage is the existence of a connected commentary written by an intelligent outsider: the historian Herodotus of Halicarnassus in Asia Minor visited the country in the 450s BCE and left his account in Book II of his *Histories.* Another asset is the wealth of sources on stone, potsherds, and papyrus, not merely in Hieratic and Demotic but also in the other languages of what had become a polyglot country: Aramaic and Phoenician, Cypriote and Lycian, Greek and Carian, and even some other languages that have yet to be identified. On the other hand, much of the archaeology of this period is lost (for example, hardly any of the great cities of the Delta have been excavated scientifically) or ignored (this is true of some of the art of the period). Traditionally the Late period has been neglected by Egyptologists, but in recent years aspects of it have become fashionable. Good comprehensive treatments, however, are still rare.

Historical periods do not begin overnight, but it is convenient to recognize the accession of Psamtik I in 664 BCE as the sign of a new dispensation over Egypt. At the beginning of his career Psamtik was merely the governor of Sais in the west central Delta. He made a virtue out of necessity in posing as the loyal vassal of the Assyrians, who had made an attempt at conquering the entire country in 667. Behind this smokescreen he was able to unite most of the principalities of the Delta, and to extend his power to Memphis and Middle Egypt. In his ninth year, he was able to pull off his greatest coup. His daughter, Nitocris, was adopted by the Theban authorities as the adoratress, or god's wife, of Amun; in effect, she became the head of the Theban clergy, a post which carried with it considerable economic and political power within Upper Egypt. This can be seen as a form of dynastic marriage, with the daughter of an ambitious ruler marrying another who was even more powerful. In this case, the other ruler happened to be a god, but the political effect was the same as if he had been human. This settlement could not have been reached without the support of the powerful Theban

Montuemhat, and it is no surprise to find that this character, together with his family, profited greatly from the rise of the new regime. After 656 BCE, the twenty-sixth dynasty was in effective control of Egypt.

Psamtik needed an army, and in some ways his career resembles that of the adventurer Mohammed Ali at the beginning of the nineteenth century CE. He turned to the forefront of military technology, which was in the hands of the Greeks and their cousins, the Carians of Asia Minor. Mercenaries from both communities were easily induced into his service, since pharaoh had a reputation as one of the most generous employers on earth. This made good sense militarily, but it had the consequence of reminding the traditional Egyptian warrior class, who are known by Herodotus's term *machimoi* or "warriors," that they were no longer in the forefront of things. The alienation of the native military caused by this decision produced a fault-line running through society, and led to recurrent problems for the dynasty. The history of this period oscillates between expansive foreign ambitions and the need to pander to the interests of the traditional intelligentsia, whether aristocrats, priesthoods, or the *machimoi*.

Expansionism is the keynote of the reign of Psamtik's son Necho (r. 610–595), whose exploits involving Phoenicians circumnavigating Africa are recounted by Herodotus. The threat from Asia was no longer the Assyrians but a resurgent Babylonia, and Necho sent an army to the aid of his former overlord to fight the new menace. This army was defeated by Nebuchadnezzar of Babylon at Carchemish in 604. Expansionism is also seen in the Nubian campaign of Psamtik II in 595, where the army was composed of Ionians, Carians, and possibly Phoenicians, as well as Egyptians. However, military activity in Nubia was comparatively safe. Action of a more dangerous sort can be seen at the end of the reign of Apries (589–570), when an expedition to conquer Greek Cyrene on the Libyan coast led to a mutiny by the army and the deposition of the pharaoh himself. Events of this sort may have happened in earlier Egypt, but the sources are silent. However, the deposition of Apries is unlikely to have been unique in pharaonic history.

Apries's successor, Amasis, is the survivor of the dynasty; he succeeded in occupying the throne for forty-four years (570/69–526), almost until the eve of the Persian conquest in 525. Amasis survived because he was able to balance forces which were in danger of tearing the state apart, and it is instructive to see how this was done. Amasis was the choice of the army, and it was vital for him to appeal to the *machimoi* who had supported him. At the same time, he needed to keep his throne in an international world where alliances could be made and broken very quickly. For the first decades of his reign, the main threat to Egypt's independence came from Babylonia, but after 538 the problem lay with Persia, whose expansion appeared unstoppable. A series of alliances were made with middling powers in the Aegean world, notably Lydia and the Greek island of Samos. These succeeded in diverting enemy attention away from Egypt, since the powers in question were easier targets, and they also provided outlets for the activities of pharaoh's foreign mercenaries. A more serious venture was the occupation of Cyprus, probably because of the island's importance as a naval base. In the meanwhile, Amasis could busy himself rebuilding the Egyptian economy. This was done to improve its defensive position, as well as to reconcile the population to the regime.

But the example of Apries made it clear that the affections of the native Egyptians had to be carefully cultivated. In Herodotus Amasis appears almost as a comical figure, a fool, but one with a heart full of common sense. He gets drunk at night, but makes the point to a visiting Greek that this releases tension, like an archer who relaxes his bowstring to make it more efficient. He is not exactly reverent toward the niceties of religion, but he is careful not to give the impression of atheism or hostility. This is not a purely Greek tradition, however, as is well shown by a Demotic tale which features Amasis drinking on a heroic scale in defiance of his courtiers' advice. (This is in fact a parody of the well-known New Kingdom genre known as the *Königsnovelle*.) The resulting hangover threatens to paralyze the mechanism of government, and the king proceeds to embark on an affair with the wife of a boat-captain. However, this is not just a titillating story. What Amasis is doing is to harness the Egyptians' traditional penchant for satire to his own propaganda aims. The times did not require an aloof god-king, which the unfortunate Apries had given the impression of being, so much as a human whom the traditional *machimoi* could identify with. A lovable rogue is not the obvious target for assassination attempts; instead, the instinct is to rally to his defense, especially when the threat comes from abroad.

The growing prosperity of Egypt in the twenty-sixth dynasty is shown by the increasing numbers of contracts drawn up on papyrus. At the beginning of the dynasty most contracts must have drawn up in the script known as Abnormal Hieratic, which was descended from the Hieratic of the later New Kingdom. However, the period shows the steady spread of Demotic, a new and (to the Egyptians' way of thinking) simplified script which probably originated in Memphis or the Delta. By the middle of Amasis' reign, the triumph of Demotic is complete. This centralizing of record-keeping, and with it economic life, must have benefited Egypt's prosperity considerably. A good index of this prosperity is temple-building, which reached a peak under Apries and Amasis, and which principally affected the Memphite region and the Delta, although there was also a major rebuilding program at Abydos. The impressive extent of this program can be grasped from the incomplete list of monuments given by Kienitz (1953). Another feature of this reign is a social change, under which marriage documents, which had previously been drawn up between the groom and the father of the bride, are now drawn up simply between husband and wife. This may have been a deliberate reform, but it is more likely to have been the culmination of a trend that was already under way. Meanwhile, the growing wealth of Egypt helped to provoke another process, that of foreign immigration. This in itself was not a new phenomenon: New Kingdom Egypt, for example, saw immigration on a considerable scale, and it is possible that the country acted as a magnet to foreign settlers at most periods of its history. However, it is in the Late period that the process can be documented most closely. The best-known community of immigrants is the various types of Greeks, notably from the Ionian coast of Asia Minor and the more adventurous states of the mainland. Because of the later power of Greek culture, we might be tempted to assume that they were the most influential community in Egypt, but an Egyptian contemporary might not have seen things this way. Like other foreign communities, however, the Greeks were entrepreneurial and successful, and this earned the enmity of the more conservative element among the Egyptians. Amasis dealt with this problem imaginatively, by giving the Greeks the city of Naucratis, not far from Sais, as a trading monopoly. This satisfied both sides. Herodotus states that Naucratis was founded at this point, but the city probably existed as early as Psamtik I.

Closely allied with the Greeks were the Carians, who came from the Asian mainland opposite the island of Rhodes. Both communities originated as mercenaries, though they later extended themselves into associated trades. It is quite possible that several generals of the period, who appear in our sources with excessively loyalist or pious names, are foreigners from one or other of these communities. Until recently the Carians were almost unknown, but a flood of light was released by the discovery by the Egypt Exploration Society of a series of stelae in the Egyptian style, taken from a cemetery which was used by the Carians of Memphis. These turned out to be bilingual, and the subsequent decipherment of the Carian language has yielded a wealth of information about the assimilation of the Carians to the manners and culture of their hosts. A third community with military associations is probably the Cypriote, which has left several inscriptions in its unique linear script, a survival from the world of the Myceneans. Some of these (for example, those at Abydos) may be Saite in date, while others, such as those at Karnak, are known to be fourth century.

Not all immigrants were warlike. From the opening up of the country under the first Saite kings, much of the commercial life of Egypt had been in the hands of traders from the Near East, in particular from the coast of Phoenicia. The Phoenicians kept their traditional language, which is recorded from some sites in Egypt, particularly Abydos. The characteristic amphorae of Tyre and Sidon are found in archaeological contexts, for example at North Saqqara. Obviously, the quiet activities of trade have left less of a mark in the historical record than other, more martial arts, but this should not lead us to underestimate the importance of such a community, many of whom may have become extremely wealthy. They might then have been in a position to penetrate the native ruling class through marriage and commercial influence. Even Amasis had a queen who bore the name Takheta, which means "the female Hittite." There were no Hittites worth speaking of in the sixth century BCE, but she may well have been from a wealthy immigrant family from Syria or Anatolia. This person even became the mother of the last king of the dynasty, Psamtik III, who ruled for six months in 526/5 BCE.

Together with the Phoenicians, we may consider the large numbers of Near Eastern immigrants who were attracted to Egypt. Many of these seem to have been active in economic life, and this state of affairs was helped by the increasing use of Aramaic as a lingua franca. This must have been widely used in Egypt, and it is well attested in inscriptions; indeed, it can almost be considered as the second language of the country, at least by the time of the Persian Occupation in 525. The later stages of the Egyptian language show many loan words from Aramaic, whereas, interestingly, there are very few words of Greek origin. The latter permeated the written language only with the adoption of Christianity and the Scriptures.

The Jews form something of a special case among the immigrants from the Near East. Linguistically they were just another part of the Aramaic diaspora, although Hebrew may well have been used for liturgical purposes. The troubled history of Palestine at this period is well documented in the Bible, and there would have been a steady influx of Jewish political or economic refugees into the land of Egypt. Some of these communities prospered there, and it is against this background that we should view the well-known story of Joseph. Though the Bible sets this story at an earlier period, Donald Redford (1970) had no difficulty in showing that, in the form in which we have it, this story is a product of the Late period. The tale of an immigrant who was able to beat the Egyptians at their own games—running the economy and interpreting dreams—would have been irresistible to a community trying to make its way in the new world beside the Nile.

The best-documented Jewish settlement in Egypt is that on the island of Elephantine, opposite the city of Aswan at the First Cataract. The origins of this community may have been military (Aswan being a frontier region), but it was probably augmented by other settlers. The township had its own temple to the Jewish god, and it is possible to reconstruct much of its domestic history, thanks to a series of Aramaic documents on leather and papyrus. These cover much of the fifth century BCE, and they record marriages and divorces, house purchases, wills and transfers, litigation, and petitions to the authorities. A few texts, such as the biography of the Persian king Darius (522–486 BCE), and an Egyptian tale about a sorcerer which had been translated into Aramaic, give fascinating glimpses of the community's taste in literature. Details of these unique documents can be found in the publication by Bezalel Porten (1996). In general, the Jewish community at Elephantine shows a refusal to accommodate itself to Egyptian thinking, and a reluctance to intermarry; but this is to an extent an ideal image of the community as it would like to imagine itself. In practice, a Jewish woman from Elephantine was able to swear in court by the name of an Egyptian goddess, and the same woman turns out to have a weakness for Egyptian husbands taken from the more muscular professions. There may have been more activity of this sort than we are led to believe: the exclusivity of the Jews in Egypt must have been relative, not absolute.

There were other ingredients in this melting-pot of nations: immigrants from Libya and Anatolia, Arabians, and, as so often in ancient Egypt, settlers from Nubia. The latter go almost unnoticed in our sources, since Nubians were always part of the Egyptian scene. Nevertheless, it is likely that the majority of Nubians did jobs of low social status until, after a few generations, they were able to merge into the general population.

The presence of such a complex society raises problems of interpretation for the modern scholar. Equally important, it must have raised acute practical difficulties for the Egyptian authorities. How could such a society be made to function, and what were the most effective ways to keep it together? In practice, many of these communities must have brought with them their own traditions, covering such matters as civil and family structure and religious rituals. It is likely that many of these traditions were tolerated by the authorities, as long as they did not clash head-on with Egyptian practice. (The final days of the Jewish community at Elephantine have left us a series of reports and petitions designed to settle precisely such an incompatibility of religious observance, which had led to severe local differences.) In the end, however, Egyptian criminal law must have been given preference over local idiosyncrasies. Murder of a sacred animal, for example, could be a serious crime under Egyptian law, and it is unlikely that a Carian could evade such a law simply by pleading that baboons and ibises were unknown back in his homeland. It is no accident that one of the first acts of

the emperor Darius, when he assumed control of Egypt in 522 BCE, was to draw up a complete codification of the law as it stood in the final year of Amasis. Systemization of this sort was probably essential, under the Achaemenid kings if not already under the Saites.

Law may command obedience, but it does not necessarily go to the heart. Armed force is one way of unifying a country, but a more effective solution can be to resort to a shared culture. The Egyptians who found themselves in a new situation, where strange languages were heard in the streets and immigrants grew to wealth and power, could be forgiven for falling back on their own culture, which they knew was millennia old. (In their enthusiasm and defensiveness they were not above adding extra millennia to their history, as is clear from Herodotus and from the exaggerated accounts preserved by other Greek writers.) This native culture was not only old, it was distinctive. In matters such as the belief in immortality, the elaborate care of the dead, the worship paid to animals, magical practices, and the theology of the transcendent nature of kingship as embodied in the pharaoh, it was unique in the ancient world. It is no coincidence that it is precisely these aspects—especially the first four—that are stressed during this period. It is almost as if the ruling elite had made a decision to use Egyptian culture as a form of adhesive, to bind together peoples who had come from differing traditions and backgrounds, and to reinforce the Egyptians' sense of identity against a world which no longer put their country at the center of things. This concentration on culture and religion (which to the Egyptians was quite inseparable from culture) may have been conscious, or it may have been instinctive. Either way, it was deeply felt, and it was effective.

This finds an echo in a famous passage quoted by Herodotus (II, 18). There the answer to the question "Who is an Egyptian?" is given by the oracle of Amun at Siwa: an Egyptian was anyone who lived downstream of Elephantine and drank the water of the Nile. The interesting point about this answer is that the idea of an Egyptian is not defined in racial terms. To the Egyptians, race and culture were closely identified, and it did not matter who one's parents might have been. The answer is geographical, giving the traditional limits of Egypt proper, but there is a subtext, to the effect that the definition is also one of culture. An Egyptian was someone who spoke Egyptian, worshipped the immemorial gods and goddesses in their temples, thought like an Egyptian, knew his or her history, and, when the bright day was done, went into the presence of Osiris surrounded by the protective powers of the hieroglyphs. The visual, cultural, and magical attraction of Egyptian culture was strong, and the ruling classes were determined to keep it that way. Most immigrants aspire to greater things, for their children if not themselves, and the way ahead was clear to them: it was to become a Greek Egyptian, or a Carian one, perhaps even a Jewish one. The monuments of the fifth-century Greek and Carian settlers show the absorption of Egyptian gods, burial practices, and iconography, while the Aramaic stelae from the same period show whole phrases adopted from Egyptian rituals and translated into the host language. Double-naming is common, at least at the beginning. Thereafter, it comes as no surprise to find that the Egyptian names start to predominate. The ancient culture of the pharaohs was adept at turning people into Egyptians.

The Persian conquest in 525 BCE marked the end of Amasis' dreams of glory, but in the long term it made surprisingly little difference. Egypt was integrated into a world empire for the first time—a state reflected in the grand opening of the Achaemenid equivalent of the Suez Canal in 497/6. There was an Iranian governing class grafted on top of the administration, and a Persian satrap in overall command. But this governor frequently needed to be recalled, in case he was tempted to declare his independence. The administration of the country continued in Egyptian, and in the time-honored mode of inspired chaos, as is shown by the informative Demotic text known as the *Petition of Petiese*, which dates from 509 BCE. As the period of Persian rule proceeds, one sees the gradual process of assimilation extended even to Iranian officials, who are shown worshiping Egyptian gods such as the Apis bull and dedicating stelae in hieroglyphs. One is sometimes tempted to wonder who has conquered whom. In 404 BCE, the Persian garrisons realized the inevitable and left the country.

The Late period has its architectural masterpieces, such as the tomb of Montuemhat at Thebes and the lesser-known Saqqara complex of Khetbeneit-erboni II, daughter of one king (either Psamtik II or Apries) and wife of another (Apries or Amasis). Above all, it was an age of personal piety. The individual, faced with a world of disquieting change, turned to his relationship with the gods. The serene portraiture of its sculpture, the austere impressiveness of the funerary complexes of Saqqara, Abusir, and Thebes, the selective re-creation of Old, Middle, and New Kingdom motifs and their integration into a distinctive idiom, can all be seen as aspects of this introversion. The same is true for some of the Wisdom Literature written in Demotic, which is powerful and deserves to better known. There is a tendency to absorb Near Eastern practices, especially in the fields of omen-interpretation and astrology, but there too the foreign elements are quickly naturalized. These achievements are essentially aspects of the redefining of pharaonic culture within a changing world; this culture survived through the period of independence under the twenty-ninth (399–380) and

thirtieth (380–343) dynasties, and the brief return to Persian rule after 343 BCE. It was still powerful and creative when Alexander the Great put an end to the Late period in 332 BCE and ushered in the Hellenistic world. The Egypt that had emerged from the regime of Psamtik I was still vigorous and recognizable six hundred years later, when Cleopatra sailed along the Nile.

[*See also* Herodotus.]

BIBLIOGRAPHY

Bothmer, Bernard V. *Egyptian Sculpture of the Late Period, 700 BC to AD 100.* Brooklyn, 1960. Ground-breaking survey of Late Egyptian art.

Braun, T. F. R. G. "The Greeks in Egypt." In *Cambridge Ancient History*, 2d ed., vol. 3, part 3, pp. 32–56. Cambridge, 1986. Study of several immigrant communities in Egypt.

Depuydt, Leo. "Regnal Years in Achaemenid Egypt." *Journal of Egyptian Archaeology* 81 (1995), 151–174. Improved chronology of documents from the period of Persian occupation.

Der Manuelian, Peter. *Living in the Past: Studies in Archaism of the Egyptian Twenty-sixth Dynasty.* Chicago, 1994. Analyzes the Late period artistic and linguistic revival and its conventions.

Elgood, P. G. *The Later Dynasties of Egypt.* Oxford, 1951. Standard historical narrative.

Gardiner, Alan. *Egypt of the Pharaohs.* Oxford, 1960. Chapter 13 is useful for literary sources.

Grimal, Nicolas. *A History of Ancient Egypt.* Oxford, 1992. Pages 334–382 present a readable account of the period.

Gyles, Mary F. *Pharaonic Policies and Administration, 663 to 323 B.C.* Chapel Hill, 1959. Concentrates on political history.

James, T. G. H. "Egypt: The Twenty-fifth and Twenty-sixth Dynasties." In *Cambridge Ancient History*, 2d ed., vol. 3, part 2, pp. 677–747. Cambridge, 1991. Sets the period into the context of the preceding Nubian domination.

Johnson, Janet H., et al. *Life in a Multi-cultural Society: Egypt from Cambyses to Constantine and Beyond.* Chicago, 1992. Series of detailed studies on ethnicity and cross-cultural influence.

Kienitz, Friedrich. *Die politische Geschichte Ägyptens vom 7. bis zum 4. Jahrhundert vor der Zeitwende.* Berlin, 1953. Full lists of inscribed monuments and other sources.

Leahy, Anthony. "The Earliest Dated Monument of Amasis, and the End of the Reign of Apries." *Journal of Egyptian Archaeology* 74 (1988), 183–199. Improves chronology of Amasis' coup d'état.

Lloyd, Alan B. *Herodotus Book II: A Commentary.* 3 vols. Leiden, 1975–1988. Covers almost all aspects of Late period culture and society.

Lloyd, Alan B. "The Inscription of Udjahorresnet, a Collaborator's Testament." *Journal of Egyptian Archaeology* 68 (1982), 166–180. Biographical text exemplifying native reaction to the Persian conquest.

Lloyd, Alan B. "The Late Period, 664 to 323 BC." In *Ancient Egypt: A Social History*, edited by Bruce G. Trigger et al. Cambridge, 1983. Chapter 4 is an authoritative treatment, especially of classical sources.

Masson, Olivier. *Carian Inscriptions from North Saqqâra and Buhen.* London, 1978. Primary edition of bilingual texts from Memphis.

Mathieson, I., et al. "A Stela of the Persian Period from Saqqâra." *Journal of Egyptian Archaeology* 81 (1995), 23–42. New evidence for Iranian presence in Egypt.

Porten, Bezalel, et al. *The Elephantine Papyri in English.* Leiden, 1996. Complete new edition with commentary.

Ray, John D. "The Achaemenid Period in Egypt." In *Cambridge An-*

cient History 2d ed., vol. 4, part 1, pp. 254–286. Cambridge, 1987. Emphasis on social history, with bibliography.

Ray, John D. "Soldiers to Pharaoh: The Carians of Southwest Anatolia." In *Civilizations of the Ancient Near East*, edited by J. M. Sasson et al., vol. 2, pp. 1185–1194. New York, 1995. Account of a mercenary community which emigrated to Egypt.

Ray, John D. "Amasis: The Pharaoh with No Illusions." *History Today* 46/3 (March 1996), 27–31. Emphasizes the use of propaganda.

Redford, Donald B. *A Study of the Biblical Story of Joseph.* Leiden, 1970. Sets the narrative firmly into its Egyptian context.

JOHN D. RAY

Twenty-sixth Dynasty

The last significant and relatively long-lasting period of native Egyptian unity, the twenty-sixth dynasty, ruled between 664 and 525 BCE. In particular, the twenty-sixth dynasty—also known as the Saite period—has about it the air of a siege mentality. Its founding pharaoh, Psamtik I (r. 664–610 BCE), had won control of Egypt through a judicious alliance with Assyria. Within a short time, by effectively cementing his relationship with Assurbanipal of Assyria, Psamtik was able, slowly but inexorably, to move from his domain in the western Nile Delta to all of Lower Egypt. Then, after crushing some troublesome Libyans to the west, he secured the services of hardy Greek and Carian mercenaries and placed them in key military garrisons at the borders of Egypt. After nine years, Psamtik peacefully took over Thebes, the religious and political center of Upper Egypt, which from the early eighth century BCE had been in the hands of the Kushite pharaohs of the twenty-fifth dynasty.

The foreign policy of Psamtik I and his son Necho II (r. 610–595 BCE) was based on the proximity of their home city, Sais, in the Delta, and its necessary commercial and political relations with eastern Mediterranean states. For the first time in centuries, Egypt conquered territory in Palestine (under both rulers) and secured effective naval control over the coast to the northeast of the Delta. Indeed, for the first time Egyptian texts reveal a relatively sizable number of Egyptian "admirals," thereby indicating just how crucial the sea was for the nascent dynasty. Alliances with Polycrates of Samos and with the state of Lydia helped cement the Saite dynasty's outward-looking, aggressive policy. Moreover, the large number of Hellenic mercenaries who came to Egypt intensified the interaction of Greek culture with that of the Nile Valley, a cultural interaction that can be inferred as well from the increasing number of Jews who left their homeland, Judah, to settle at Elephantine and in Egypt's north (probably at Memphis). Unlike the previous dynasty, that of Psamtik and his successors was, by economic and military circumstances, forced to deal in a complex of foreign relations with the other nations and peoples of the day.

The power of Assyria went into a slow decline after Psamtik I's elevation to the throne of Egypt. From the 620s BCE, Egypt was still aligned to the Assyrian empire and was faced by the growing threat of new contenders for superpower status. In one way, and remarkably, both Psamtik and Necho II managed to stave off the continuous advances of the Babylonians, now led by Nabopolassar and his son Nebuchadrezzar. We must keep continually in mind that Egypt had no sources of iron, the then-newly advantageous metal for the technology of war. In addition, Egypt's gradual reliance on foreign soldiers—mercenaries—to strengthen the state meant that a portion of the state's revenues were paid to hired soldiers who were ultimately loyal only to themselves or to their division leader, rather than to the king of Egypt. Certainly by 610 BCE and onward, the Saite kingdom's control over the southern Levant was contested. It was one thing for Egypt to conquer the small state of Judah led by Josiah in the Battle of Megiddo in 609 BCE, another for Egypt's forces to meet those of Nebuchadrezzar. In 605 BCE, the Egyptian forces were crushed by the Babylonians, and from that time onward Egypt failed to regain control over any portion of the Near East. The conquest of Jerusalem by Babylonia in 597 BCE also meant that Necho II could not seek any important ally in southern Palestine; noteworthy are the later erasures of his name, quite possibly instigated by his successor Psamtik II (r. 595–589 BCE), a result of his failures abroad. Although Necho II had begun a canal from the Red Sea to the Mediterranean—note once more the maritime policy of this dynasty—he had been unable to complete it.

The old enemy of Sais was that of the kingdom of Kush to the south (in Sudan). Although robbed of their territory north of Aswan and Elephantine, Kushite monarchs continued to pose a problem for the Egyptian state. Not surprisingly, then, difficulties occurred at the southern boundary during the Saite dynasty; in fact, in the reign of Psamtik II, a massive Egyptian expedition was sent into Kush to break, once and for all, its military power. Psamtik II's expedition followed in principle that practice of an earlier Egyptian monarch, Kamose (ruled c.1571–1569 BCE), who had also been faced with a threat from the south—from the Nubians. Kamose was then also facing the Hyksos to his north. In both cases, the Egyptian state was caught between two foes, on two fronts. Under Psamtik II, the Saite policy was different in one way from that of Kamose: instead of moving first to the north, Psamtik rid Egypt of the Kushite threat in the south. Soon after, a massive expurgation policy against the twenty-fifth (Kushite) dynasty pharaohs occurred, in which as many monuments of those kings as possible were attacked and their names erased.

When Psamtik II died, his successor Apries (r. 589–570

LATE PERIOD: TWENTY-SIXTH DYNASTY. *Relief fragment from the twenty-sixth dynasty.* The relief, which depicts a nautical scene, is from the rock-cut tomb of Nespakashuty, who was the vizier of Upper Egypt during the reign of Psamtik I, the first pharaoh of the twenty-sixth dynasty. The tomb is at Deir el-Bahri. (The Metropolitan Museum of Art, Rogers Fund, 1923. [23.3.468])

BCE) attempted to consolidate his sphere of influence over the eastern Mediterranean islands, rather than face the might of Babylonia to his north and east. Certainly, with the eventual fall of Judah, after the sacking of Jerusalem in 587 or 586 BCE, Egypt had no potential land ally. At this time, the philo-Hellenic attitudes of the twenty-sixth dynasty became preeminent, those that Apries' successor (and opponent), Amasis (r. 569–526 BCE), also continued. The instability of Egypt then was evident in the short civil war that took place as Nebuchadrezzar finally penetrated Egypt in 568 BCE. Amasis took care to strengthen contacts with the Greeks and with Lydia as well, while he stayed apart from the rivalry of Babylonia, the Medes, and the Persians. Internally, he came increasingly to rely on the foreign contingents in his army. Yet, just prior to his death, Persia—under Cyrus and Cambyses—became the deciding factor.

The popular traditions surrounding Amasis would be worthwhile to bring into this discussion. The ancient Greek historians Diodorus Siculus and Herodotus reported on this king's fondness for drinking; indeed, the "human" aspect of the pharaoh was stressed in those accounts. That this attitude was not one of a later reconstruction can be seen from a fragmentary Demotic tale, *Amasis and the Skipper,* a literary narrative that contrasted to no small extent with another native Egyptian tale (Berlin Papyrus 13598), in dealing with the death of Psamtik I, among other things. In the latter account, the formality of the pharaoh's role was what counted, whereas in the former, the alcoholic depiction of Amasis was quite unexpected, if not shocking.

Such local literary productions seem to have been devised during the Saite period; as such, one may see an indigenous revival of the art of storytelling, with the protagonist being the king. One major concomitant of this was the rapid spread of the new system of writing in

Egypt: Demotic. As can be seen from both accounts above, as well as from other more mundane papyri of this era, the older forms of writing—in particular, Hieratic—were abandoned and a more rapid and flexible system of cursive writing was used. As an example, one can mention an Egyptian account in Demotic of a Nubian conflict dated to regnal Year 41 of Amasis. Such a description would previously have been immortalized on a freestanding stone stela, carved with hieroglyphs. The expansion of the Demotic script appears to have been a product of the successful reunification of Egypt under Psamtik I, as this script was apparently developed in Lower Egypt, if not at Sais itself, in the context of the revival of a civil service. In Upper Egypt, the more archaic, abnormal hieratic script was abandoned later than in Lower Egypt, undoubtedly caused by its later annexation by the successful diplomatic activity of Psamtik I.

Under this modification of Egypt's writing system—aimed toward a more effective rendition of the vernacular—the art of writing was continued on the great revival of statuary that prevaled during the twenty-fifth dynasty. Since the Saite pharaohs had been of a Delta origin, not surprisingly, they depended on Old Kingdom norms for their inscriptions as well as for their depictions. Whether in reliefs or in freestanding sculpture, the statuary of the Saite dynasty overtly reflected their dependence on age-old northern norms, especially those at the great cemetery of Saqqara. Those tombs of the fifth dynasty and the sixth formed, in essence, free and available templates for the artisans to copy; they were of great importance, since the private officials of the twenty-sixth dynasty were also buried at Saqqara. Although such "archaizing," if it can be called that, had been part of the twenty-fifth (Kushite) dynasty as well, the emphasis on Old Kingdom models by Psamtik I and his lineage went considerably further. The archaizing tendencies extended beyond the plastic arts and script. Old cultic texts were recopied, and orthography aped old-fashioned, if not obsolete, renderings of words. Archaic terms and phrases, titles long-since defunct, and long-abandoned methods of dating were self-consciously resuscitated and prominently displayed in new creations.

In the twenty-sixth dynasty, a great use was made of Old Kingdom models and moreover, an increasing flexibility occurred in the hieroglyphic writing system; also at that time, the first evidence of a simplified, alphabetic-style script is known in Egypt. A further example of such changes having occurred within the Saite period, rather than in the preceding dynasty, can been seen in the revival of the squatting type of figure, a mark of the great Memphite school of sculpture from the fourth dynasty to the sixth. Finally, mention may be made of the realistic portraiture of this time; often attributed as "brutal," the sculpted heads of the twenty-sixth dynasty stand alone as witness to the highly developed art that was begun under Psamtik I.

In contrast, at Thebes, the tombs of the elite of the Saites reflected New Kingdom antecedents. That is to be expected if only because there the nobles of the eighteenth dynasty to the twentieth were buried. Yet it cannot be ignored that private tombs at Thebes also borrowed extensively from the models of the Old Kingdom as well as the New Kingdom. Perhaps a better interpretation is a fusion, as represented by the Southern Egyptian approach to art and writing, in contrast to the Northern. Even such lowly texts as the offering lists reveal this eclecticism. At Saqqara, in the North, offering lists were virtually duplicates of feast lists, which could be found in many an Old Kingdom lintel or architrave; at Thebes, there were copies of eighteenth dynasty lists, as well as those of the earlier age. Significantly, at the capital, Sais, a different and local tradition obtained, thereby indicating that the twenty-sixth dynasty was not solely reliant on old models for their outlook on religious life.

The twenty-sixth dynasty ended under the extremely short reign of Psamtik III (r. 526–525 BCE), son and successor of Amasis. As the opportune time for the Persians to attack the Nile Valley, they, unlike the Babylonians, routed the Egyptians and their foreign soldiers. With the help of some native Egyptians who were disgruntled by Amasis' seizure of the throne, Cambyses of Babylon took Egypt and successively imposed his governorship.

[*See also* Amasis; Apries; Archaism; Grammar, *article on Demotic grammar;* Necho II; Psamtik I; *and* Scripts, *article on Demotic script.*]

BIBLIOGRAPHY

Bothmer, Bernard V., Herman De Meulenaere, and H. W. Müller. *Egyptian Sculpture of the Late Period. 700 B. C. to A. D. 100.* Edited by Elizabeth Riefstahl. Brooklyn, 1960. A remarkable volume concerned with the art of Egypt during the specified period; although dated, it remains paradigmatic.

Der Manuelian, Peter. *Living in the Past: Studies in Archaism of the Egyptian Twenty-Sixth Dynasty.* London and New York, 1994. A complex but valuable work covering questions of art and language during the Saite period.

Freedy, K. S., and Donald B. Redford. "The Date of Ezekiel in Relation to Biblical, Babylonian and Egyptian Sources." *Journal of the American Oriental Society* 90 (1970), 462–85. This useful study links the foreign relations of the Saite dynasty with its Assyrian and Babylonian competitors.

Kitchen, Kenneth A. *The Third Intermediate Period in Egypt (1100–650 BC).* Warminster, 1973. An extremely significant work that covers the period in some detail.

Spalinger, Anthony J. "The Concept of Monarchy during the Saite Epoch—An Essay of Synthesis." *Orientalia NS* 47 (1978), 12–36. A study of the twenty-sixth dynasty with a sociohistorical view.

ANTHONY J. SPALINGER

Thirtieth Dynasty

The First Persian Occupation over Egypt lasted from 525 until 404 BCE, when the country regained its independence. Egypt's independence, however, continued to be overshadowed by the former colonial power, and no native ruler was in any position to forget this. In reality, the country was far from unified, and a series of princes emerged, mainly in the Nile Delta, who might well be described as warlords or even freedom fighters. Such people have a habit of not wanting to share their freedom very widely, and the brief rule of Amyrtaeos (twenty-eighth dynasty) was followed by a coup d'état staged from the city of Mendes in the central Delta. This is conventionally known as the twenty-ninth dynasty (c.399–380 BCE), although the situation has several features in common with the political structure that prevailed in the Third Intermediate Period. In addition, the threat from Persia remained real. The major figure of this dynasty is Hakoris (r. 392–380 BCE), who made an alliance with Evagoras of Salamis in Cyprus and was able to impose his rule over most of Egypt. It is possible that even his reign was interrupted by one or more usurpers. Ancient Egypt is sometimes seen as an unbroken sequence of dynasties, but the reality was more complex: dynasties took many forms.

The last king of the dynasty, Nepherites II, was deposed after a reign of a few months. The usurper was Nekhtenebef, a governor the city of Sebennytos in the north-central Delta, who is conventionally known as Nektanebo I (r. 380–363 BCE)—essentially a military commander—and he was a shrewd one. A Late period Wisdom text includes the maxim, "Great is a great man, if his great men are great," and the strength of the new regime lay precisely in this detail. Some of Nektanebo's appointees may have been foreign mercenaries, but others were undoubtedly related to him, and therefore to the old military aristocracy. These included the vizier Harsiese, and another, Petineit, whose tomb excavation at Saqqara has been published by Bresciani (1980). Petineit seems to have been a descendant of a vizier of Psamtik I, whose original tomb he adapted for his own burial. There were generals of the caliber of Wahibre (known from a sphinx now in Vienna) and Tjaharpto. In practice, this regime can be described as a military junta. The junta's twin aims were to avoid anarchy at home and to defend the country abroad against the revenge of Persia.

From the first year of the reign comes the Naucratis Stela, a magnificent work of art now in the Cairo Museum. Naucratis was a major trading center, and in the stela's text the new king assigns one-tenth of the revenues on riverine traffic, plus the same on local manufactures, to the temple of Neith at Sais. This was not mere window dressing: the point of the exercise was to stimulate the wealth of temples in order to revitalize the economy. Temple industries and landholdings were important sources of taxation, and this taxation paid for the defense of Egypt. In addition, temples were able to deliver loyalty to a usurper pharaoh by nevertheless representing him as the choice of the gods. A program of temple building was initiated, which was to put the two Nektanebos alongside Ramesses II at the top of the list of royal temple founders. There was hardly a cult center that was not the object of their activities, and an entirely new sanctuary was added at Iseum (Beḥbeit) near Sebennytos. The art of the period—precise relief on dark background, sculpture in the round, and architecture—is characterized by reticence and careful draftsmanship, and it has several of the more introverted features of the art of the Middle Kingdom. It is worthy of serious study.

In 375 BCE, the Persians struck. The preceding dynasty had been inclined to turn to the power of Sparta for defense, but the Persians entered into a pact with Athens, which had recovered from its defeat in the Peloponnesian War. The Persian forces, led by Pharnabazus and the Athenian Iphicrates, found the mouths of the Nile barricaded, but they were able to force a landing near the Mendes branch. Iphicrates was for pressing on to Memphis, but the Persian commander overruled him. During the resulting delay, the Nile flooded, and the invaders, disoriented, were forced to evacuate the country. Nektanebo had reason to believe that his piety had brought this flood, and piety became one of the keynotes of the intellectual life of the period. Quiet conformity with "the way of the god," as a contemporary biography puts it, was the key to survival and prosperity.

Nektanebo's son, Teos or Tachos (r. 362–361 BCE), may have felt that quiet piety was unexciting, and immediately on his accession he launched an aggressive campaign into Phoenicia. He had the advantage of surprise, but of nothing else. His advisors were Agesilaus, the aged king of Sparta, and the Athenian admiral Chabrias, but these two disagreed openly. The atmosphere of chaos and distrust is confirmed by the autobiography of a priest, Onnofri, son of Painmou, who was denounced during the expedition by forged letters accusing him of treason. Chabrias advised the king to finance his campaign by confiscating wealth from the temples. Some of this wealth was turned into gold and silver coins to pay Greek troops—the first coinage ever struck by an Egyptian pharaoh. Theoretically, pharaoh could do this, but he was carrying Nektanebo's policy of cooperation with the temples to an unworkable extreme. The army mutinied and installed as pharaoh Tachos's young nephew, Nekhtharnehbo, conventionally known as Nektanebo II. The expedition returned to Egypt, and Agesilaus went home with a fortune.

Nektanebo II had learned that the temples could be a

good friend, but a terrible enemy. He continued the temple-building program with vigor and with the same quality of design. In addition, the propaganda value of the priesthood was exploited increasingly. In many temples, statues of the dynasty were installed, which themselves received divine worship, together with their own priesthood. (In this scheme the disgraced Tachos was replaced by Nektanebo's father, Tamos.) The inclusion of the regime into the religious pantheon was deliberate, emphasizing both Nektanebo's piety and the reverence due to him. Another innovation was the cult of Nektanebo the falcon (which is well exemplified by a cult statue now in New York); this embodies a visual pun on the king's name, Nḫt-Ḥr-ḥb, in that the falcon is Horus (Ḥr), and the king holds a scimitar (nḫt) together with the sign for festival (ḥb).

Nektanebo II is famed in later tradition as a magician, and it is clear that this image was not a personal idiosyncrasy but an item of deliberate policy. The king wished to show himself as the agent of piety, who could converse with the gods and obtain their goodwill. Unlike his irreligious uncle, he epitomizes the age. This romanticized image is the subject of a story, The Dream of Nektanebo, which survives on a papyrus in Leiden. Though written in Greek, this tale is clearly Egyptian, and fragments of a Demotic version are now known. There, the king is shown as defending Egypt with model boats in magical bowls. Unfortunately, there is still one gap in the temple-building scheme, that of Onouris, the god of the capital city, Sebennytos, and it is implied that it was this omission that caused the gods to give eventual victory to the Persians. It is also made clear that this was not the king's fault, but the result of human failing at the temple itself. In the end, Nektanebo's magic may have let him down, but his reputation lived on among his people.

The Dream of Nektanebo is dated to the night of 5 July 343 BCE, which must be close to the date of the Persian invasion and the Second Persian Occupation. This time there was to be no respite, and the country once again became a Persian province, a state of affairs which lasted until the arrival of Alexander the Great in 332 BCE. Nektanebo fled, and his unused sarcophagus later found its way to Alexandria, where it was used as a public bath; it is now in the British Museum. Yet Nektanebo was not forgotten. In the Greek Romance of Alexander, written in early Ptolemaic Alexandria, he takes the place of Aristotle as Alexander's tutor. Alexander kills him out of boredom, but as he dies he confesses that he is really Alexander's father. He had flown over the sea to visit Alexander's mother: perhaps an echo of the cult of Nektanebo the falcon. In this folkloric way, Egypt was able to deny the reality of foreign conquest, and Nektanebo gained the romantic immortality that his magic deserved. He was the last

native Egyptian to rule Egypt until the Officers' Revolution of 1952 CE.

[See also Achaemenids; Nektanebo; and Persia.]

BIBLIOGRAPHY

Bresciani, Edda, et al. Saqqara I: Tomba di Boccori. La Galleria di Padineit. Pisa, 1980. Publishes tomb of an important vizier under Nektanebo I.

de Meulenaere, H. "Les monuments du culte des rois Nectanébo." Chronique d'Égypte 35 (1960), 92–107. Examines mechanism of loyalist propaganda.

Lichtheim, Miriam. Ancient Egyptian Literature. Vol. 3. Berkeley, 1980. Pages 86–89, translation of Naucratis Stela, with comments.

Olmstead, A. T. History of the Persian Empire. Chicago, 1966. Chapters 28 and 29 integrate period into general history of the Near East.

Ray, John D. "Egypt: Dependence and Independence, 425–343 BC." In Proceedings of the Groningen 1983 Achaemenid Workshop, pp. 79–95. Leiden, 1987. Concentrates on diplomatic relations with the Achaemenid Empire.

Ray, John D. "Nectanebo, the Last Egyptian Pharaoh." History Today 42.2 (Feb. 1992), 38–44. Deals with the personality of the last native pharaoh, and his role in later literature.

Ritner, Robert K. The Mechanics of Ancient Egyptian Magical Practice. Chicago, 1995. Thorough survey of Egyptian magic, with emphasis on the Late period.

Stoneman, Richard. The Greek Alexander Romance. London, 1991. On the role of Nektanebo II in later fiction.

Traunecker, Claude. La chapelle d'Achôris à Karnak. 2 vols. Paris, 1981. Contribution to the architectural history of the period.

von Kaenel, F. "Les mésaventures du conjurateur de Serket Onnophris et de son tombeau." Bulletin de la Société Française d'Égyptologie 87–88 (1980), 31–45. Edits a fragmentary but informative text about the political situation during the campaign of Tachos.

JOHN D. RAY

Thirty-first Dynasty

The thirty-first dynasty, more properly known as the Second Persian Occupation (343–332 BCE), includes the years between the reconquest of Egypt by Persia under King Artaxerxes III Ochos and the succeeding conquest by Alexander the Great (after his defeat of Darius III).

The last pharaoh of the thirtieth dynasty, Nektanebo II (361/60–343 BCE), had managed to repel two attacks by the Persian invaders—one in 358 BCE by an army led by Artaxerxes (then a prince), and the second in 351 BCE, led by the then-crowned Artaxerxes. Nektanebo finally suffered defeat when the Persian king retook Cyprus and Sidon and then reached Pelusium, with the help of the betrayal by Mentor of Rhodes. The Persian commander Bagoas first took Pelusium and eventually the other cities of the Nile Delta and Memphis. Nektanebo fled into Nubia with his treasure. (The episode of the ephemeral sovereign Khabbash, perhaps an Ethiopian or a Libyan, mentioned on the the satrap-stela of Ptolemy, should probably be placed between 344 and 343 BCE.)

As in the case of Cambyses, who conquered Egypt in 525 BCE, classical authors accuse this new conqueror of acts of violence and brutality. Artaxerxes is reported to have killed the Apis bull, offering in its stead an ass for the adoration of the Egyptians; he is also said to have killed the bull of Heliopolis and the ram of Mendes, as well as sacking temples and cities. In fact, recent excavations at Mendes have shown that the city underwent violent destruction and desecration at about this time (c.343–342 BCE). Artaxerxes died in 338 BCE, killed by the eunuch Bagoas, who in 336 BCE also killed Arses, who had succeeded his father.

There is little that we can say for certain about Egypt during the decade of the Second Persian Occupation. We know that under Darius III, Egypt was ruled by the satrap Sabakes, who fought and died at Issos, and by the satrap Mazace. At the battle of Issos, in the army that the Persians fielded against Alexander of Macedon, there were some Egyptians. One was the noble Samtowatefnakht of Herakleopolis, whose autobiographical stela (the "Stela of Naples") recounts how he survived the battle unscathed, and how Arsafe, his city's god, protected him, allowing him to return to his homeland. In 332 BCE, the satrap Mazace ceded the satrapy to Alexander without a fight.

The rule of the Achaemenids thus came to an end, and Egypt became a province of the empire of Alexander the Great, though still administered as a satrapy. The second-century CE Greek historian Arrian (Flavius Arrianus) informs us that Alexander made the Egyptian Petesi satrap in Egypt, together with Doloaspis; in the text of a Demotic ostrakon found in Saqqara by a British archaeological expedition, a certain "Petesi the satrap" is appointed (*P3-di-1st p3 ihstrpny*), who may be identified with the "Pateesis" of Arrian's text.

[*See also* Achaemenids; Alexander; Nektanebo; *and* Persia.]

BIBLIOGRAPHY

Bresciani, Edda. "Persian Occupation of Egypt." In *The Cambridge History of Iran*, vol. 2, pp. 502–528. Cambridge, 1985.

Bresciani, Edda. "L'Égypte des satrapes d'après la documentation araméenne et égyptienne." *Comptes rendus de l'Académie, Inscriptions et Belles-Lettres*, 96–108. Paris, 1996.

Bresciani, Edda. *"Letteratura e Poesia dell'antico Egitto. Cultura e società attraverso i testi."* Turin, 1999.

Briant, P. *Histoire de l'Empire Perse.* Paris, 1996.

Burstein, Stanley. "Foreigners in the Documents from the Sacred Animal Necropolis, Saqqara." In *Life in a Multi-Cultural Society*, edited by H. S. Smith, p. 296. Chicago, 1993.

Elgoed, P. G. *Later Dynasties of Egypt.* Oxford, 1951.

EDDA BRESCIANI
Translated from Italian by Robert E. Shillenn

LAW. Whoever deals with Egyptian law must avoid two dangers. The first is applying contemporary categories without regard for the differences between the world to-day and that of the Egyptians. It would be meaningless to distinguish among civil, public, and criminal pharaonic law. Of course, the people who built the pyramids were acquainted with such regulations, or more exactly, with regulations mixing some of these aspects. But in this regard as in others, the Egyptians had criteria of their own. So it is more profitable to discover theirs than to cling to current classifications.

The second error lies in extending data which are relevant only for a limited place or time to the whole country or to all periods. I would like to stress the differences existing between the Mesopotamians, who wrote on clay tablets, and the Egyptians who used engraved hieroglyphs only for a selective publishing of documents, and for other purposes, preferred papyri or ostraca, materials which have survived only when buried in the cemeteries on the desert borders, out of the reach of the inundation (e.g. at Saqqara, Abusir, or Deir el-Medina). In Mesopotamia, we have an overabundance of information concerning all aspects of human life, but in Egypt, we must tackle sparse and incomplete data, often difficult to connect. The hazards of the transmission of texts dictate whether we are well informed about any aspect of Egyptian law (e.g. anything pertaining to the organization and protection of the funeral estates), and less, or not at all, according to the period, about some other aspect.

Hp, "Law"? The first difficulty comes with the term commonly rendered "law." We often forget that *hp* admits the same range of translations ("rule," "regulation," "habit," "rite," "ceremony," and even "cycle" of a planet) as *nt-ꜥ* does (translated, also arbitrarily as "custom"). The underlying idea common to both terms is that of recurrence, exemplified by the movements of celestial bodies, as well as by the behavior of earthly beings. To put it in another way, *nt-ꜥ* and *hpw* belonged basically to *maat*: literally "the one who steers," the embodiment of the order given to the organized world by the demiurge at the origin of the cosmos (therefore, "[cosmic] order" rather than "justice"). This is the reason that both were supposed to have existed from the very beginning of time. Owing to these everlasting laws, each pharaoh had, in principle, no more power than his most prominent officers: according to many laudatory epithets, he shares with his dignitaries, he could only "apply, enforce" (*iri hpw*), "fix" (into writing) (*smn hpw*) or "regenerate, revive" them (*smnḫ, swꜣḫ hpw*), even if, in reality, it is certain that he did issue rules of his own.

Most of the "decrees" (*wḏ[t](-nsw)*, "[king's] order")—preserved through copies on stelae, archives on papyrus, and, in one case, in the original found among the accounting papyri of the pyramid of Raneferef at Abusir—contain only specific provisions. Though "broadcast" to many officers, from the vizier to the relevant local authorities, the only aim of many of them was to protect some divine or funerary estate, together with its belongings and staff, against theft or requisitioning by other authorities or institutions (Coptite decrees of Neferirkare, Pepy I and II, Horus Demedjibtauy or Nebkheperre Antef; for the New Kingdom, decrees of Nauri, Kanais, Hermopolis, Armant, and Elephantine). In the case of the original *wḏ-nsw* of Abusir, the "decree" was issued for the purpose of allotting select portions of meat from the divine offerings to different persons, probably as a life annuity. Moreover, we also possess a few *wḏ-nsw* addressed to only one person, which reduces them to mere letters of instructions (for example, Turin Papyrus 1896, a command of Ramesses XI to send beads and flowers to make garlands, addressed to the viceroy of Kush). But, apart from these "decrees" with restricted provisions, if any, there are at least two others which fit better into what we mean by "law," since they concern the population of Egypt as a whole, or at least in part.

In his "decree" still standing before the tenth pylon at Karnak, Horemheb lists a few abuses an "individual" (*nmḥy*) could suffer at the hands of palace or army officers, in the countryside or when delivering wood as fuel to the kitchen of the palace. In each section of the text, after giving a detailed example of the abuse committed against the *nmḥy*, he states that such behavior on the part of the authorities represents an offense, forbids them accordingly to do so "from today onwards," under such penalties as flogging and cutting off their noses, and, in some cases, requiring the redress of the damage inflicted on the *nmḥy*. Seven paragraphs, built on the same pattern (setting out, nonretrospective prohibitions, penalties, and indemnities), but dealing with unrelated topics, are still recognizable on the stela: unlawful requisitioning of boats (1–2) and "(maid) servants" belonging to the *nmḥy* by palace officers (3); the seizing of hides by soldiers (4); the "squeezing" of people living alongside the river to supply food for the king and his retinue during their trip to Thebes on the occasion of the yearly Opet festival (5); the harvesting of fodder in private fields by palace servants (6); and the use of false measures to exact more taxes in the markets (7).

The second example is a *wḏ-nsw* found near the seventh pylon at Karnak, in which Sety II forbids the "prophets" of the whole country to require a "trifle" (a euphemistic term for bribery) from the bearers of divine statues, a provision probably aimed at cleaning up oracular practices.

The conclusion that all these "decrees," with either specific or more general provisions, fell into the extensive and rather vague concept of *hp*, although they represented newly issued measures, and, thence, that the statement according to which the pharaoh only revived everlasting rules was a mere fiction, may be drawn from the fact that each Ramessid *wḏ-nsw* comprising a punishment introduces it by the phrase "the *hp* shall be enforced against him by." An early variant of this formula actually bears "this *hp*"—clear evidence that in the late Middle Kingdom in an Abydene "decree," as in the more developed Ramessid formula—*hp* could only refer to the very provision, if not to the punishment alone, contained in the "decree."

Conversely, in the Cairo Papyrus 58092, the litigant, who probably felt less concern about the theoretical connection between *hpw* and *maat*, explicitly states to the living king (Ramesses III) the *hp* he put forward to claim the property of the deceased. In this case, it was a general rule over inheritance, and not a measure restricted to a few protected persons: " 'It is to the one who has buried that the goods shall be given' says the '*hp*' of the pharaoh." But the Demotic expression "the *hp* of the written document" shows that a *hp* could also find its origin in the will of both parties to a private agreement, as well as in that of the pharaoh.

Summarizing, I propose to define *hp*—usually translated as "law," which is certainly too narrow—as every kind of rule, either natural or juridical, general or specific, public or private, written or unwritten. That is, in an administrative or legal context, every source of rights, such as "law," "decree," "custom," and even "contract."

Application of *hpw*. The important thing is that Egyptian legal documents always refer to a "rule" (*hp*), whether they concern proceedings or the way judgments were passed: for example, the time allowed to the vizier to settle complaints about fields (if they happen to be near his office, three days; elsewhere, two months); the registration of transfers of property to the "office of the district reporter," both done *m* or *mi ntt r hp*, "according to the rule," textually "like what corresponds to the *hp*"; or the obligation under which the vizier was laid to judge the claimant "in close accordance with this *hp* which is in his hand." Moreover, it is this basic principle that the pharaoh stated first when solemnly addressing a newly promoted vizier: "You shall see to it to do everything according to the *hp*, and to do everything according to its own righteousness." As I interpret it, he had to treat each case (a formulation large enough to comprise judgments as well as administrative decisions) according to the established rule, but without sticking to the letter of the law and being unfair.

For instance, when dealing with a runaway peasant girl registered for statute labor, the Brooklyn Papyrus 35.1446 (a list of detained persons from the end of the Middle Kingdom) refers to "the law (*hp*) pertaining to one who runs away without performing his service," to allow the release of her relatives put in prison as security for her return. In other cases, involving women as well as men, this document cites "the law pertaining to one who deliberately deserts for six months," "the law pertaining to those who flee the prison," and "the law pertaining to deserters."

This is why it once was argued that the forty leather *sšmw* depicted lying before the vizier Rekhmire in his tomb could represent rolls containing law codes. But since then, it has been pointed out that the same rare word occurs in the *Satire of the Trades* with the meaning of "rods" (to flog culprits). Therefore, the existence in Egypt of true law codes cannot be demonstrated, at least as some extensive organized system issued by the king. This rules out "the *hpw* of the prison" alluded to by the *Admonitions of Ipuwer* or, much later, the so-called *Code of Hermopolis* (a Demotic collection of *hpw* about farming and leasing), which were probably rules compiled for the needs of the administrative practice without royal approval.

The rules applied to everyone in Egypt, without discrimination by class or sex. The *hpw* quoted by Brooklyn Papyrus 35.1446 were applied in the same way to both men and women, and the penalties fixed by the decree of Nauri to protect Sety I's temple against embezzlement could, in principle, affect everybody involved in such a crime, from the viceroy of Kush to "anybody [else] sent to Nubia on the king's behalf." Clearly in the opinion of the Egyptians, one person was equal to another, as is illustrated by the comparison of dignitaries who had to pass sentences with a "pair of scales" that weighs "without tilting" (regardless of the social standing of people). This is a common phrase found in many laudatory biographies from the Old Kingdom to the Late period.

As a result, it is possible that Egypt never experienced slavery in the Roman sense before the Ptolemaic period. The difference among such categories as *hmw* ("slaves"), *b3kw* ("servants"), *sdmw-ꜥš* ("those who listen to their master's call") or *mrt* ("underlings") is still unclear. Although these dependents (often foreigners claimed as war booty) were obliged to work their entire lives for other people or institutions, they enjoyed the same legal status as other people did, at least in some respects. For instance, during the Ramessid period, two "slave girls" (nevertheless both termed "citizen"), were able to sell their own property. In both cases, it was their master who bought the land. But the document adds that they could have sold it to an "outsider," which means that the master would not have been allowed to take advantage of his position to influence them, a clear indication that his permission was not needed (Cairo Stela 27-6-24-3). Thus, in practice, it was probably more the labor of dependents and their potential offspring that belonged to their master than their actual persons, even though the earlier status of some slaves may have been less favorable because the

first meaning of *hm* was "body." This is the reason why "days of servant" or "slave" per month during a year, and not the dependent himself, could be sold (Papyrus Gurob II, 1 and 2, Berlin Papyrus 9784 and 9785, all dating from the reign of Akhenaten), allotted to the people of Deir el-Medina for brewing (e.g. Campbell Ostracon 6), bequeathed (Gardiner Ostracon 90), misappropriated (Horemheb's Decree §3), divided between several institutions (the funeral estate of Sheshonq I's father received the "fourth part of a confectioner"), or given back to the "servant" to set him free (Adoptions Papyrus, dating from the reign of Ramesses XI).

Like "slaves," women, either married or widowed, had, during the New Kingdom, (and probably before) complete legal authority to manage their own assets. As far as we can see from the Deir el-Medina sources (ostraca, Naunakhte's documents), they were allowed to sell, buy, or bequeath anything they owned without their husband's approval (if married), or without the assent of anyone (if single). They could also appear beside, or even before, men among the witnesses to an agreement or a will. Likewise, if there was no will at their father's or mother's death, the shares of the estate inherited by the daughters were equal to those of the sons. Nevertheless, it was the husband who had the right to manage the property acquired by a couple during their married life. Should he die or "repudiate" (*h3ꜥ*, "drop") her, the wife received a third of all property belonging to the couple, the two other parts being retained by her husband or given to his heirs, according to a rule often alluded to by texts (Turin Papyrus 2021, Adoptions Papyrus, for instance).

Courts of Justice. What is known about pharaonic courts (during the Old Kingdom, *d3d3t*, and since the Middle Kingdom, *knbt*, "corner" of a building, with reference to the spot where officials often held audiences for lack of a permanent room) varies considerably with period or location.

Sources. Much information about the *knbt* of the workmen of the Theban necropolis or about "the great *knbt* of the Southern Town" (Thebes) is available from the ostraca of Deir el-Medina and the papyri found in the precinct of the temple of Medinet Habu, the administrative seat of the west bank since the end of the twentieth dynasty (e.g., in the Tomb Robbery documents). For courts existing elsewhere in the country, data are more scanty, but they generally correspond to what is known about those of the Theban area. The information about the connection between the local *knbt* of Memphis and "the great *knbt*" in Heliopolis is drawn from the Inscription of Mes, engraved in his tomb at Saqqara (excerpts of five lawsuits over fields, which lasted from Horemheb to Ramesses II). This matches the evidence about the links existing between the local *knbt* of Deir el-Medina and "the great *ḳnbt*" of Thebes, the southern counterpart of the Heliopolitan high court. The first mention of the "great court of Heliopolis" is found in the Inscription of Mes. As for that of Thebes, its members are still attested during the twenty-fifth dynasty. Even if the great courts did not disappear simultaneously, both were certainly created at the same time, probably when the office of the vizier was split in two. They were already extant when Horemheb chose trustworthy people to sit in "the two great towns of Upper and Lower Egypt" to listen to the inhabitants' complaints. For the "commission of enquiry" (*st-śmtr*) formed after the "harem conspiracy," which was supposed to have put an end to Ramesses III's reign, the source is the Turin Papyrus, supplemented by papyri Lee, Rollin, and Rifaud.

The following sections will present, I hope, a coherent reconstruction of the dispensation of justice in Egypt (that is, the composition, powers, and functioning of the courts), at least from the New Kingdom onward. It remains to be seen whether this information, which is acceptable for the period extending from Amenhotpe III to the end of the twentieth dynasty, conforms with the scanty data available from earlier and later periods.

Composition. Until specialized courts and "judges" (*n3 wptyw*, the Ptolemaic *laocrites*?) sitting in permanent rooms ("judgment houses") developed under the twenty-sixth dynasty, there had been no professional magistrates in Egypt. "Courts," or "court of auditors," were formed with "officers" (*śrw*), who held administrative as well as judicial duties, and sat "as a court constituted to judge" (Horemheb's Decree right side 6) depending on the circumstances. This means that any [royal] "appointee" could be a member of a *ḳnbt*, according to the interpretation Ramesses II gave to this term before his soldiers at Kadesh. What distinguished the *śr* (connected with the root *wśr*, "powerful") from the "feeble" (*nmḥy*) was that the former received "food" (*k3w*) from the king, and was thus supposed to partake in his divine "*k3*-substance."

The workmen of "the (king's) tomb," who were given monthly grain rations, were also considered *śrw*, and held this position in the *ḳnbt* of their community, even though most of them were barely able to write their own names. On ostraca, they appear, either individually or as "the entire gang," after their authorities: usually, the "two great ones of [the] gang," the "chief of medjays" (Nubian policemen), and the "two scribes of the tomb." The latter acted both as clerks and as representatives of the vizier, and collected complaints and kept an eye on compliance with *hpw*. Sentences or orders were executed by the "two doorkeepers of the tomb," who served as bailiffs of the local court with the scribes' authority, seizing the property of debtors in default of payment, and bringing to court whoever had to appear before it, sometimes with the help of medjays.

According to Horemheb's (Decree right side 7) or to Papyrus Gurob II (*ḳnbt* of *Pr-Wsir* in the Faiyum during Amenhotpe III and IV's reigns) and Berlin Papyrus 3047 (Theban *ḳnbt* under Ramesses II), other local "courts" throughout the country were similarly constituted, with the *śrw* of the place ("mayor," "prophets," ordinary "priests") attended by "scribes" acting as clerks; in particular, the "scribe of the mat" was responsible for the keeping of the land register.

"The great *ḳnbt*" of Thebes and that of Heliopolis both consisted of the most prominent civil or military officers of Upper or Lower Egypt under their vizier's command. In Thebes, in addition to the "first prophet of Amun" and the "mayor," who were already members of the local *ḳnbt*, there were "prophets," "overseers," high-ranking military officers, "scribes" attached to the vizier, and some "royal cup-bearers," foreign domestics of the pharaoh sent from distant Piramesse, to watch over his interests.

The commission (perhaps fictitiously) appointed by Ramesses III to deal with the harem conspiracy was exclusively formed of men whom the pharaoh could trust, mainly "cup-bearers" and military officers. But they had to investigate a family case inside a secret place. In a similar occurrence, more than a thousand years earlier, Pepy I had appointed Weni alone, attended by one *s3b* (an administrative title translated, without evidence, as "judge"), to "hear" the testimony of a queen in his harem and to put her deposition into writing.

Powers. Important lawsuits, such as those involving land or influential people—for instance, the wife of a Ramesses II dignitary accused of opening the pharaoh's storehouses to steal costly supplies (Ashmolean Museum Ostracon 1945–37)—were brought directly to the "great *ḳnbt*," after a written complaint had been laid before the vizier. Lesser cases were left to local courts.

The powers of the courts were notarial, and concerned litigation and punishment.

Notarial powers. Because most Egyptians were illiterate, they put every deed of any importance before their local "court," and the scribes of the *ḳnbt* wrote it down before witnesses. Whenever the deed (sale, will, or donation) entailed some change of ownership over land, a bill of transfer, termed *imyt-pr* (inventory of "what is in the house"), was drawn up and sent to the vizier, who "sealed" and stored it after approval. Thus, all data about every plot situated in his district were gathered at the vizier's "office," which secured the fulfilment of agreements by both sides and the compliance of third parties.

Among the covenants submitted to "courts," sales required elaborate proceedings, because the Egyptians were not acquainted with money before their last kings started minting coins to pay their foreign mercenaries. A "compensation," expressed by a metallic standard (from the

New Kingdom on, copper *dbn* of 92 grams), was fixed, and this "price" (*swnt*) was paid by the direct or postponed delivery of various commodities valued at an equivalent total amount.

Like chattels or real estate, "office" (*i3t*) together with tilled fields which were indissolubly and indivisibly ("from son to son (or) heir to heir") assigned to their holder's sustenance, could be the subject of such sales, donations, or wills executed by the *imyt-pr* ("inventory"): for example, that of the "mayor" of Elkab (Cairo Stela 52453, seventeenth dynasty); those of ordinary "priest" or "controller of phyle" (Kahun papyri, late Middle Kingdom); that of "soul-servant" of a deceased (contracts of the twelfth dynasty nomarch Hapidjefa's tomb in Asyut). Moreover, not only "days of servant," but also of boat, and probably donkey, were subject to transfer by sale, will, or donation. What is now known as a rental was understood as a sale by the Egyptians, who applied the concept of "days of working" to joint ownership to determine the share, or in case of embezzlement, to fix the compensation according to the length of time during which one had been deprived of the use of his property (Decree of Nauri, 47–50 [boats]; Horemheb's Decree §§1–3 [boats, servants]).

Powers of litigation and punishment. But the court had mainly to judge (*wpi*) whether the person who appeared before it, either as a litigant or as a person kept in detention pending trial, was "righteous" (*m3'ty*), or "guilty" (*'d3*). Most of the lawsuits arose from disputes over inheritance (Cairo Papyrus 58092, Turin Papyrus 2021), or from failure to fulfill written or oral agreements through insolvency or unwillingness. The defaulter usually took an oath before the *knbt* to pay his debts before an appointed day or be beaten (usually 100 blows) in addition to a fine doubling what was owed in the agreement or deed put forward by the claimant (Chicago Ostraca 12074, IFAO 388, Gardiner 106, etc.). So the borderline between litigation and punishment was certainly not as clear as it is now.

With regard to punishments for criminal offenses, the powers of courts were limited. Except in a few minor cases, they had only to pronounce on the guilt of those who appeared before them, and imprison the culprits until the vizier or, in the most serious cases ("great crimes worthy of death," such as pillaging tombs), the pharaoh disposed of them because any punishment, from the amputation of limbs to the death penalty, had to be passed by the king himself (Turin Indictment Papyrus *recto* 2, 3).

Functioning. The functioning of courts is well covered in the Tomb Robbery documents and the Inscription of Mes. Because there were no examining magistrates in Egypt, the preliminary investigations of cases had to be carried out by the whole court, either by the local *knbt* or by the "great court" under the vizier's control, depending on the case's importance. Thus, it was the *śrw*, acting as a body (or some of them sent as a commission), who had to verify such things as the condition of the tombs said by informers to have been looted (Abbott Papyrus), or to question witnesses and suspects (often by harshly beating them) to see whether their statements tallied (Brooklyn Museum Papyrus 10052, 10053), or to hear the depositions of litigants, or to examine the "(written) evidence" (*mtrt*) produced by both sides in a dispute over an inheritance (Cairo Papyrus 58092). Whenever it investigated or settled matters, the "great *knbt*" could send out a commissioner to arrange details, such as hearing witnesses or partitioning land, in conjunction with the nearest local court. So, as far as we can see from Mes's account, the "great *knbt*" was not a court of appeal to which litigants thwarted by the local *knbt* could refer. Both courts had to act in a complementary way, as departments of the same government service situated at different levels usually do.

To sum up concerning the composition of powers and functioning of the Egyptian courts until the end of the New Kingdom, it can be said that *knbt* had not yet grown into independent organs specialized in the dispensation of justice. Probably as a result of their main duties concerning land tenure (a sensitive matter in Egypt), the courts were still an ordinary part of government.

Evidence of Corruption. "Do not compromise yourselves with people! Do not accept rewards from others!" Such were Horemheb's instructions to his newly appointed officers (Decree right side 5). But was this system efficient enough to allow people to live peacefully?—maybe, until the middle of the nineteenth dynasty. Nevertheless, evidence about the low morals of *śrw* grew more abundant from Ramesses II's reign onward. The Inscription of Mes relates that a register could be forged. Papyrus Salt 124 contains a complaint lodged against a "great one of [the] gang," who having bribed the vizier to get his job, had been stealing furniture from tombs, beating his subordinates and making love with their wives, near the end of the nineteenth dynasty. Four of the people appointed to investigate the harem conspiracy were convicted of having sexual intercourse with the wives of some of the defendants and were accordingly deprived of their titles and punished with mutilation. The Turin Indictment Papyrus has a long list of embezzlements committed by the priests of Elephantine. The Tomb Robbery Papyri also describe the looting of graves and temples during the reigns of Ramesses IX and XI, sometimes with the complicity of officials who took bribes to keep silent and released those who were under arrest.

In such conditions, the system of *knbt* deteriorated from the middle of the twentieth dynasty onward. This led to the development of oracles as a means to settle disputes between litigants as well as a means to determine guilt.

Eventually, the king's officers were replaced by professional judges, drawn from the clergy, to pronounce sentence at the "portal-where-justice-is-given" (*rwt-di-Mȝ't*) in Ptolemaic temples. Indeed, who could be more able and willing to administer justice than the god himself, "the vizier of the feeble," who "does not take bribes from the guilty, and [never] says 'bring written evidence!'" (*Praise of Amun*, dating from Merenptah, nineteenth dynasty).

[*See also* Administration, *articles on* State Administration *and* Provincial Administration; Crime and Punishment; Family; Inheritance; Marriage and Divorce; Officials; Prices and Payment; Slaves; Tomb Robbery Papyri; Women; *and* Work Force.]

BIBLIOGRAPHY

Allam, Shafik. "Egyptian Law Courts in Pharaonic and Hellenistic Times." *Journal of Egyptian Archaeology* 77 (1991), 109–127. Further data about the dispensing of justice from the Saite period onward.

Bakir, Abd el-Mohsen. *Slavery in Pharaonic Egypt.* Cairo, 1952. A comprehensive collection and translation of the relevant sources until the Greco-Roman times.

Černý, Jaroslav. "The Will of Naunakhte and the Related Documents." *Journal of Egyptian Archaeology* 31 (1945), 29–53.

Černý, Jaroslav. *A Community of Workmen at Thebes in the Ramesside Period.* Cairo, 1973. Still the basic work about Deir el-Medina and the people who dug the tombs of the kings.

Černý, Jaroslav, and T. Eric Peet. "A Marriage Settlement of the Twentieth Dynasty: An Unpublished Document from Turin." *Journal of Egyptian Archaeology* 13 (1927), 30–39. Translation and comment of Papyrus Turin 2021.

Gardiner, Alan H. *The Inscription of Mes.* Untersuchungen zur Geschichte und Altertumskunde Ägyptens, 4, pt. 3. Leipzig, 1905. The only full translation of this important document available in English.

Gardiner, Alan H. "Four Papyri of the 18th Dynasty from Kahun." *Zeitschrift für Ägyptische Sprache und Altertumskunde* 43 (1906), 27–47. Documents about the selling of "days of servant."

Janssen, Jac. J. *Commodity Prices from the Ramessid Period.* Leiden, 1975. A detailed study of the economic life in Deir el-Medina which will remain unequalled for a long time. Of special interest are pp. 101–111 ("The Money"), 494–509 ("The Transactions"), and 531–532 ("Joint Property").

Janssen, Jac. J., and P. W. Pestman. "Burial and Inheritance in the Community of Necropolis Workmen at Thebes (Pap. Boulaq X and O. Petrie 16)." *Journal of the Economic and Social History of the Orient* 11 (1968), 137–170.

McDowell, A. G. *Jurisdiction in the Workmen's Community of Deir el-Medina.* Leiden, 1990. The best and most up-to-date study of the dispensing of justice—through "court" (pp. 143–179) or oracle—in the settlement of the necropolis workmen. The author has succeeded in disregarding modern categories and prejudices to produce a cautious and nuanced survey of the working of the *ḳnbt* of Deir el-Medina and of the "great *ḳnbt*" of Thebes.

Nims, C. F. "The Term Hp, 'Law, Right', in Demotic." *Journal of Near Eastern Studies* 7 (1948), 243–260.

Peet, T. Eric. *The Great Tomb-Robberies of the Twentieth Egyptian Dynasty.* Oxford, 1930. Publishes and translates the main documents about the pillaging of the Theban necropolis. To be supplemented by J. Capart et al., "New Light on the Ramesside Tomb-robberies," *Journal of Egyptian Archaeology* 22 (1936), 169–193.

Pestman, P. W. "The Law of Succession in Ancient Egypt." In *Essays on Oriental Law* (*Studia et Documenta ad Jura Orientis Antiqui Pertinentia,* vol. 9), pp. 58–77.

Pestman, P. W. "Marriage and Matrimonial Property in Ancient Egypt." Papyrologica Lugduno-Batava, 9. Leiden, 1961.

Pestman, P. W. "Remarks on the Legal Manual of Hermopolis: A Review Article." *Enchoria* 12 (1984), 33–42.

Théodoridès, Juliette, et al., eds. *Vivre de Maât: Travaux sur le droit égyptien ancien.* Louvain-la-Neuve, 1995. Essays of Aristide Théodoridès; contains many French excellent translations of texts alluded to here.

JEAN-MARIE KRUCHTEN

LEATHER. The first evidence in ancient Egypt for "leather" (*dḥr*) occurs in Neolithic graves of the Badarian (c.5500–4000 BCE) period. These Predynastic dead were provided with leather aprons and cloaks, occasionally decorated with painted geometric designs in black, blue, white, and yellow, as well as sandals, cosmetic bags, and cushions (their leather covers stuffed with vegetable matter). Leather, throughout Egypt's history, was manufactured mainly from the skins of calfs, gazelles, goats, and sheep. Predynastic leatherworkers tanned skins by drying, smoking, salt curing, and coating in ocherous earths. Sometimes skins were softened by the use of dung, fat, and urine; they were tanned by the use of oils and they were tawed with alum (any of a group of astringent mineral salts). Although a rather stiff leather, alumed goatskin sandals were found at Mostagedda and at Thebes in Upper Egypt. The seat of a stool from Tutankhamen's New Kingdom tomb was also of goatskin, but his sandals were of calfskin.

From a Predynastic tannery at Gebelein in Upper Egypt, pieces of leather were found to be treated by a liquor made from the pods of the acacia tree (*Acacia arabica*), also found there, that contained about 30 percent tannin. A scene in the New Kingdom tomb of the vizier Rekhmire at Thebes probably shows a leatherworker removing a skin from a similar tanning liquor. Before tanning, skins were stripped of hair and flesh by flint scrapers (later by metal scrapers) after a long soaking in brine; they were then steeped in clean water to remove the salt, dirt, and blood. The tanning process included one or more soakings in the tanning liquor. After tanning, hides were dyed red, yellow, or green. They were then stretched and dried over wooden trestles and smoothed with stones. Alum was basic to the finish, acting as a mordant for fixing dyes to leathers. The dyes used included kermes, a purple-red color made from dried female insect bodies

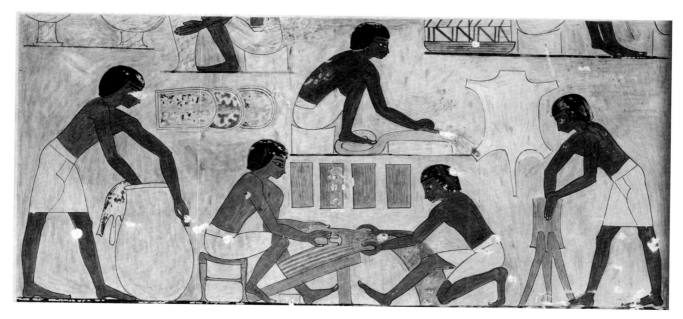

LEATHER. *Depiction of leatherworkers.* This is a copy of a painting in the eighteenth dynasty tomb of the vizier Rekhmire at Thebes. The workers soak and scrape the skins and make them pliable over a wooden horse. (The Metropolitan Museum of Art. [35.101.2])

(genus *Kermes* or *Coccus ilicis*), and madder, a red created from the roots of the madder plants *Rubia peregrina* and *Rubia tinctorium*. Yellow may have been obtained from the rind of the pomegranate (*Punica granatum*); green from a combination of the woad plant (*Isatis*) with yellow.

The production of footwear has accounted for many of the known leather artifacts. An example of a shoe developed from a sandal design was unearthed at Illahun, a twelfth dynasty workers' town in the Faiyum, although a cobbler's shop has not yet been discovered there. In the tomb of Rekhmire, wall scenes show workers cutting hides into sandal soles and straps with a semicircular bronze knife. This knife cut around a hide's circumference to make lengthy thongs, which were used for stitching leather; they were also twisted into ropes, particularly for ships' cordage. Leather or rawhide thongs were used to lash handles to adze and ax blades, and for making furniture joints. Other leather working tools included copper and bronze awls for piercing holes, horns for the enlargement of holes, and bone (later copper) needles and bodkins for sewing and assembling leather pieces. (Replica and reconstructed ancient tools perform well on both thick and thin leathers.) These tools and techniques produced leather goods for many purposes. Military personnel were supplied with leather footwear, loincloths, shields, body armor, quivers, and wrist guards. Chariots had floors of interlaced leather strips, as did stool and chair seats. Chariot wheel coverings, axle bearings, harnesses, and decorative bodywork were also of leather. Leather was also fashioned into funerary goods, bracelets, dagger sheaths, wall hangings, writing materials, box coverings, mirror cases, and clothing.

Leatherworking is depicted in private tombs that date from the fifth to the twenty-sixth dynasty at Giza, Saqqara, Deshasheh, Beni Hasan, and Thebes. Workshops were likely established near these cemeteries, since commissioned work by the wealthy conferred prestige and favor on highly skilled leatherworkers. An illustration in the fifth dynasty tomb of Ti at Saqqara depicts sandals being offered for sale. A sandalmaker's workshop is shown in the twelfth dynasty tomb of Amenemhet at Beni Hasan in Middle Egypt. One of this nomarch's titles, "Overseer of Horns, Hooves, Feathers, and Minerals," probably indicates a responsibility to collect leather taxes for the government. This, in turn, implies that all leather goods possessed recognized values. For example, the price of a pair of shoes during the New Kingdom equaled 1 to 2 *deben*, a standard weight in copper. The system of payment for work by the state, by high officials, and by the temples included leather goods, often leaving workers with surpluses that could be traded for necessities or other goods. A regular international trade in leatherwork is not certain, but in the eighteenth dynasty Theban tomb of Huy, viceroy of Nubia, and in the nineteenth dynasty temple of

Ramesses II at Beit el-Wali in Nubia, leather furniture and shields are shown being brought into Egypt as tribute.

BIBLIOGRAPHY

Brunton, Guy, and Gertrude Caton-Thompson. *The Badarian Civilisation and Predynastic Remains near Badari.* London, 1928. Authoritative account of the excavation of leather goods from Badarian graves.

Carter, Howard. *The Tomb of Tut.Ankh.Amen.* London, 1923. Describes the leather artifacts and the circumstances surrounding their discovery and excavation.

Davies, Norman de Garis. *The Tomb of Rekh-mi-Rē' at Thebes.* New York, 1962. Illustrates and interprets New Kingdom leatherworking scenes.

Harris, J. R. *Lexicographical Studies in Ancient Egyptian Minerals.* Berlin, 1961.

Lucas, Alfred. *Ancient Egyptian Materials and Industries.* 4th rev. ed. by J. R. Harris. London, 1962. Offers a comprehensive discussion of techniques and materials employed by ancient Egyptian leatherworkers; extensive references. (A revised edition is in preparation.)

Petrie, W. M. Flinders. *Deshasheh.* London, 1898. Illustrates and interprets Middle Kingdom leatherworking scenes.

DENYS A. STOCKS

LEATHERWORKING. *See* Leather.

LEBANON, the northern Levantine region along the eastern Mediterranean coast that was an important source of coniferous woods (especially cedar), resins, wine, oil, and various finished goods for Egypt. The major coastal towns of ancient Lebanon (Akk., *labnanu,* Heb., *lĕbānôn*) developed around natural harbors and became wealthy through trade with the Mediterranean world and the Near East. Four narrow and roughly parallel north–south ecological zones (the coast and coastal plain; the Lebanon Mountains; the Biqa' Valley, and the Anti-Lebanon Mountains) encouraged the development of independent political entities, rather than a unified country. Lebanon's ports and towns were never a military threat to Egypt, whose interests in the region were largely economic and political. On occasion, however, Lebanese ports served as launching points for Egyptian military campaigns against enemies to the north and east.

Pharaonic Egypt's relations with Lebanon are historically fragmentary and based largely on textual sources. Because the principal Bronze Age and Iron Age coastal towns (Tyre, Sidon, Sarepta, Beirut, and Byblos) mostly lie under present-day cities, the excavation of Lebanon's ancient settlements is rarely possible. Byblos (today's Jebail) and Kumidu (Tell Kamid el-Loz, situated in the southern part of the Biqa' Valley) are the only two Bronze Age towns to have had significant excavation; Sarepta (today's Sarafand) is the one Iron Age coastal town.

Analyses of wood from the late Predynastic settlement at Maadi near Cairo indicated that Lebanese cedar had been imported into Egypt by the late fourth millennium BCE. The oldest inscribed Egyptian object found in Lebanon is a broken stone vessel from Byblos that contains the name of Khasekhemwy, the last king of the second dynasty (r. 2714–2687 BCE). This item was probably a gift to a Byblos ruler or temple; in the Bronze Age and Iron Age, Egyptian kings regularly sent gifts to the temples and political authorities of important Lebanese towns, as part of their effort to maintain favorable commercial and political ties.

Egypt's relations with Lebanon intensified during the Old Kingdom, when timbers of Lebanese cedar were imported into Egypt in considerable quantities, and a wealthy Egyptian state and its nobility wanted to acquire sometimes exotic goods. A fifth dynasty relief in the mortuary temple of Sahure at Abusir, for example, shows a Near Eastern bear and flask. Stone vessels, statuary, reliefs, and other large objects inscribed for fourth, fifth, and sixth dynasty kings and officials have been found at Byblos—whose principal goddess, Baalat Gebal, the Egyptians linked with their own goddess Hathor. In addition, an axhead inscribed with the name of Khufu was found at the mouth of the nearby Adonis River. The collapse of Egypt's Old Kingdom and the destruction of Byblos in the late third millennium BCE temporarily ended Egyptian activities on the Lebanese coast.

Egypt's contacts with Lebanon were restored in the eleventh dynasty and flourished once again in the twelfth. The *Story of Sinuhe* names Byblos as that Egyptian official's first stop, after he fled Egypt following the death of Amenemhet I. At Byblos, during the twelfth and thirteenth dynasties, local officials employed both Egyptian writing and political titles. Egyptian and Egyptianized objects were numerous in that period at Byblos; outstanding objects include an obsidian jar inscribed with the name of Amenemhet III and an obsidian box with the name of Amenemhet IV. A small diorite sphinx inscribed with the cartouche of Amenemhet IV was found during some modern construction work in Beirut, and several Lebanese coastal cities (including Byblos and Tyre) were mentioned in the Egyptian Execration Texts.

Egyptian–Lebanese connections remained close well into the late eighteenth century BCE. A relief fragment depicting the Byblos mayor Yantin, along with a cartouche of Neferhotpe I (r. 1747–1736 BCE), comes from that site, while a fragmentary statue of Khaneferre Sobekhotpe IV (r. 1734–1725 BCE) was discovered at Tell Hizzin in the northern Biqa' Valley. Archaeological evidence for relations during the latter half of Egypt's Second Intermediate Period is meager, but the prominent mention in the Kamose Stela at Karnak of three hundred ships of cedar

LEBANON. *Mountain face, Lebanon Range.* (Courtesy Donald B. Redford)

filled with gold, silver, semiprecious stones, oil, and other valuables indicates that the Hyksos rulers of the fifteenth dynasty traded extensively with Lebanon and Syria.

The New Kingdom pharaohs of the early eighteenth dynasty (especially Thutmose III) incorporated Lebanon into Egypt's Near Eastern empire. The coast and coastal plain became part of the district of Canaan, whose administrative headquarters was at Gaza on the southern Palestine coast; the southern Biqaʿ Valley was allocated to a second district, whose operational center was at Kumidu; the northern Biqaʿ Valley was assigned to a third district, headquartered at Sumur on the Syrian coast. New Kingdom texts sometimes refer to the region of Lebanon as *rmnn* (*rbrn*, in the *Story of Wenamun*). Throughout the New Kingdom, Byblos seems to have been the principal center of Egyptian activity on the Lebanese coast.

The Amarna Letters from the reigns of Amenhotpe III and IV (Akhenaten) include a substantial number of messages sent to the Egyptian court by the mayors of the major Lebanese coastal towns: at least sixty-seven cuneiform tablets from Rib-Hadda of Byblos (Amarna Letters EA 68–95, 101–138, 362); ten from Abi-Milku of Tyre (EA 146–155); two from Zimreddi of Sidon (EA 144–145); and three from Ammunira of Beirut (EA 141–143). The letters document disputes and conflicts between the leaders of the various towns, threats to the stability of the region caused by Abdi-Ashirta and Aziru (successive rulers of the Syrian kingdom of Amurru) and a resurgent Hittite empire, and Egypt's general neglect of those events. Finds at the Egyptian administrative center at Kumidu included several cuneiform letters (two evidently sent by Amenhotpe III) as well as a variety of Egyptian imports and Egyptianized objects from the "treasury" building (apparently part of a local royal cemetery).

Later Egyptian texts indicate that in the early nineteenth dynasty, Sety I and Ramesses II reasserted Egyptian military control in Lebanon. Sety I's name appears on a fragmentary stela from Tyre, while Ramesses II's name has been found on a fragmentary stela, doorway blocks, and several calcite (Egyptian alabaster) vessels from Byblos; on a calcite jar from a rock tomb in downtown Beirut; on a stela fragment from Tyre; a rock stela from Adlun; and on three rock stelae carved in the Nahr el-Kalb, just north of Beirut. Later on in the dynasty, Lebanese place names (including Beirut, Sidon, Sarepta, and Tyre) are mentioned in Papyrus Anastasi I, while a dispatch for the ruler of Tyre is noted in the *Journal of a Frontier Official*.

The incursion of the Sea Peoples into the eastern Mediterranean in the early twelfth century BCE ended Egyptian authority everywhere in the northern Levant. No royal statuary or stelae of the twentieth or twenty-first dynasty, for example, are attested in Lebanon. The *Report of Wenamun,* from the end of the New Kingdom, records the inhospitable reception given that Egyptian priest by the prince of Byblos, Zekerbaal, who had no reason to fear Egyptian retribution. That a brisk trade between Egypt and the towns of Phoenicia (as the later Greeks called the Lebanese coastal area) continued for at least a while, despite the change in relationship between the two parties, is evident from the mention in the *Wenamun* text of seventy ships in the harbors of Byblos and Sidon that were trading with Smendes (r. 1076–1050 BCE), the first king of the twenty-first dynasty.

Evidence for a major revival in Egyptian political activity in Phoenicia in the early twenty-second dynasty occurs in the form of several pieces of royal sculpture from Byblos. Two of these items are a fragmentary statue of Sheshonq I (r. 931–910 BCE), reinscribed in Phoenician with a dedication by the local ruler, Abibaal; and a broken statue of Osorkon I (r. 910–896 BCE), which was reinscribed by Abibaal's successor, Elibaal.

Renewed ties with Phoenicia and the extraordinary expansion of Phoenician maritime trade around the Mediterranean world in the Iron Age and later led to the dispersal of Egyptian objects and cultural influence as far away as Greece, Carthage on the North African coast, and the Iberian Peninsula. Egyptian influence on Phoenician culture in its homeland and abroad was substantial, especially in the minor arts (such as ivories, scarabs, amulets, jewelry, and bronze figurines), as well as architecture and religion. In the Persian period, for example, Phoenician dignitaries were buried in huge anthropoid stone sarcophagi of Egyptian form. In addition, the Saite dynasty's Necho II (r. 610–595 BCE) employed Phoenician sailors to circumnavigate Africa, while Psamtik II (r. 595–589 BCE) hired Phoenician mercenaries to serve in his military. The cities of Naukratis and, later, Alexandria became the major emporia for Egyptian trade with Phoenicia.

[*See also* Syria-Palestine; *and* Wenamun.]

BIBLIOGRAPHY

Chéhab, Maurice. "Relations entre l'Egypte et la Phénicie des origines à Oun-Amon. In *The Role of the Phoenicians in the Interaction of Mediterranean Civilizations,* edited by William A. Ward, pp. 1–8. Beirut, 1968. Useful though somewhat outdated history of Egyptian–Lebanese relations until the early eleventh century BCE.

Chéhab, Maurice. "Noms de personnalités égyptiennes découverts au Liban." *Bulletin du Musée de Beyrouth* 22 (1969), 1–47. Convenient catalog of objects found in Lebanon (especially at Byblos) that contain Egyptian royal and private names.

Hachmann, Rolf. "Kamid el-Loz 1963–1981. German Excavations in Lebanon, Part I." *Berytus* 37 (1989), 5–187. Detailed summary in English of the excavations at Kumidu.

Leclant, Jean. "Les relations entre l'Egypte et la Phénicie du voyage d'Ounamon à l'expédition d'Alexandre." In *The Role of the Phoenicians in the Interaction of Mediterranean Civilizations,* edited by William A. Ward, pp. 9–31. Beirut, 1968. Survey of Egyptian–Phoenician relations from the early eleventh century BCE to 332 BCE.

Lipiński, Édouard, et al. *Dictionnaire de la civilisation phénicienne et punique.* Turnhout, 1992. Valuable compendium of basic information on Phoenician culture, accompanied by bibliographies for each entry; numerous entries relate to Egypt.

Moran, William L. *The Amarna Letters.* Baltimore, 1992. Includes translations of the Amarna Letters from Lebanon.

Ward, William A. "Egyptian Objects from the Beirut Tombs." *Berytus* 41 (1993–1994), 211–222. Finds include a jar containing the cartouches of Ramesses II.

Ward, William A. "Archaeology in Lebanon in the Twentieth Century." *Biblical Archaeologist* 57 (1994), 66–85. Convenient recent survey of archaeological activity in Lebanon, with some references to Egyptian connections.

Weinstein, James M. "Egyptian Relations with the Eastern Mediterranean World at the End of the Second Millennium BCE." In *Mediterranean Peoples in Transition: Thirteenth to Early Tenth Centuries BCE: In Honor of Trude Dothan,* edited by Seymour Gitin, Amihai Mazar, and Ephraim Stern, pp. 188–196. Jerusalem, 1998. Includes a discussion of Egyptian relations with coastal Lebanon from the end of the New Kingdom through the early Third Intermediate Period.

JAMES M. WEINSTEIN

LEBENSMÜDE. *See* Man Who Was Weary of Life.

LEGITIMATION. The legitimacy of effective political systems usually rests on an ideology or worldview shared by those who hold power within the whole system. The ancient Egyptian worldview was constructed around the cosmic role of the king, who mediated between humans and deities, maintained order in the face of chaos, and embodied the supreme religious, political, military and legal authority—even if in practice he delegated much of his authority to others. The legitimation of this system worked on two levels: the legitimation of the office of kingship and the legitimation of individual holders of the office, the two often to some extent overlapping. The institution of kingship remained fundamental to Egyptian ways of thought for three thousand years, but that concept did not remain unchanged. Different aspects of the office were emphasized during different historical periods, which provided new interpretations, with increasing complexity.

The legitimation of kingship had to be an ongoing process, to prevent the role of monarchy becoming devalued with time and its authority diminished. The legitimacy of the office had to be maintained, no matter the shortcomings of any office holder. The concept of kingship had to provide stability, regardless of any incompetent rulers, disputes over the succession, or, ultimately, foreign conquest. Kingship was maintained by repetition of ritual performance, by royal display embodied in the creation of monuments (and probably in ephemeral forms now lost), and through the authority of myth.

From Predynastic times, the king was an embodiment of the god Horus, a relationship that was visually displayed in the king's Horus name, the oldest part of the royal titulary. Later, with the increasing prominence of the cult of Osiris, the king was identified with Horus, son of Osiris, who inherited the kingship from his murdered father. The king was also the heir of the gods who had originally ruled Egypt before they withdrew from earth. He was the son of Re and that god's earthly representative. The myth of the king's divine birth—first referred to in surviving evidence in a literary text of the twelfth dynasty—made him the physical son of Re (or by the eighteenth dynasty of Amun-Re), who had impregnated the king's human mother with his divine seed. Epithets were devised that filiated the king to other deities, and images were made that depicted him being suckled by goddesses who transferred their divine essence to him through their milk. The divine aspect of kingship that was inherent in the office itself was carried from one king to the next by the royal *ka* (life-force).

From the nineteenth century, Egyptologists' understanding of the legitimation of individual kings was clouded by the mistaken belief that the right to the throne passed through the female line. That notion went back to the work of late nineteenth-century anthropologists, such as Sir James Frazer, who hypothesized, for example, in *The Golden Bough* (1900), that in their earliest stages of development human societies were matriarchal; only later, after the discovery of the male role in procreation, could patriarchal systems come into being. Therefore, looking for surviving traces of Egypt's original matriarchal system seemed valid. Due to a misunderstanding of Egyptian kinship terms, Frazer thought that the whole of Egyptian society had a system of matrilineal descent; in his view, although descent appeared to pass from father to son, men married their sisters, so descent actually passed from a man to his sister's son, who also happened to be his daughter's husband. Frazer viewed this proposed matrilineal system as a survival from an original matriarchy, although in historic times Egypt was in fact patriarchal. Frazer's ideas on the evolution of Egyptian society did not become widely accepted, not only because such a system would have been unworkable but also because it could be shown that brother-sister marriage had not been widespread; in fact, it could only be plainly demonstrated in the royal family, where kings often married their (half-)sisters. There, Frazer's notions lingered into the late twentieth century, to help ameliorate the perceived problem of incest. Although nowhere specifically formulated, the

hypothesis developed that the right to the throne passed through the female line from one royal "heiress" to the next, so that the king—even if he was the son of his predecessor and his principal wife—had to legitimize his claim to the throne by marrying the heiress. To maintain matrilineal descent, the heiress had to be the daughter of the previous king as well as the heiress that king had married. Thus the heiress would normally be the (half-)sister of the king whom she married. The heiress did not become king (ruler) herself—since apart from a very few exceptions, Egypt's rulers were male—but the heiress did bring the office of king to the man she married and, in this way, she made his rule legitimate.

The theory of legitimation through marriage with the royal heiress became received knowledge, especially in English and German Egyptological literature, but for most of the twentieth century it was not subjected to rigorous examination in any publication. For that hypothesis to be true, there would have to have been an unbroken line of heiresses in direct descent from one another; in fact, such a line did not exist. For example, although the first four kings of the eighteenth dynasty married (half-)sisters, many of the remaining kings married women of nonroyal origins. A study of the titles and insignia of kings' consorts has shown no difference between those given to queens of royal and nonroyal birth, except that the former have the titles "king's daughter" and "king's sister" that the latter do not. Thus, none of the titles and insignia that have been variously suggested as marking the royal heiress were in fact unique to the women of royal birth. On monuments, there was no difference in the status of kings who married their (half-)sisters and those who did not; nothing suggests that the first group were regarded as more legitimate than the second. Finally, none of the myths that legitimized kingship incorporated the role of the royal heiress. The king claimed his office through his relationship to various deities. Although the goddess Isis played an important part in the myth of Osiris as his sister-consort and the mother of Horus, her role cannot be equated with the hypothetical heiress. Nor was there an heiress to bring the throne to Horus, whose inheritance of the kingship was unambiguously stated to be as the son of Osiris. Taken together, the evidence shows that the heiress theory will not stand up to scrutiny—and that it should be discarded—as have been the late nineteenth-century suppositions on the development of early human societies.

With the rejection of the heiress theory, the ways in which individual kings achieved legitimacy must be found elsewhere. In the Egyptian view of things, inheritance of office ideally passed from father to son in both the royal and nonroyal spheres. There were, however, many examples of kings who were not the physical sons of their predecessors; such kings could be officially appointed as heir, as Horemheb claimed to have been, but in most cases the record is silent concerning the transfer of office. Nevertheless, kings referred to their predecessors as *it*, "father/ancestor," even without physical descent. Their mythical line of descent would have been embodied in the notion of the royal *ka* (*k3*), which carried the divine aspect of kingship from one holder to the next.

Four New Kingdom monarchs—Queen Hatshepsut, Thutmose III, Horemheb, and Ramesses II—have left accounts of their elevation to the throne. Although Hatshepsut's claim to have been appointed the heir of her father, Thutmose I, cannot be strictly true (since he was succeeded by his son, Thutmose II, to whom Hatshepsut was married), the terms in which she expressed her legitimacy would at the time have had to seem valid in order for her claim to be effective.

A general theme in texts relating to the king was that he was chosen by the gods to rule Egypt. That idea was incorporated into the more specific accounts: Hatshepsut and Thutmose III, for example, gave dramatic versions of their selection by an oracle of Amun. Horemheb, who was not the son of his predecessor, told of his recognition and promotion by Horus of Hnes, Horemheb's local deity, who presented him to Amun during the annual Opet festival at Thebes. In more conventional terms, Ramesses claimed to have been chosen by Re, "while I was yet in the egg." In addition, both Hatshepsut and Ramesses recounted the ways they were presented by their father to his court, as his heir. To become king, the chosen individual underwent ritual in which the insignia of Re, the crowns and *uraeus*, and the full, fivefold titulary of a king were given, including the forms of the names that embodied the king's relationship to the gods. Thutmose III's account probably referred, as well, to the instruction of the king in special and highly restricted knowledge about the gods. Hatshepsut and Horemheb stressed the king's role in providing for the cults of the gods, while Ramesses' account was embedded in his dedication text of the temple of Sety I at Abydos, the whole purpose of which was to record his establishment of the cult of the newly dead, deified Sety I. Thutmose III referred to the subjugation of foreign lands and the extending of Egypt's borders.

Serving the gods and vanquishing enemies were fundamental acts that the king had to perform repeatedly to maintain legitimacy. Kings built, renovated, and added to temples; commissioned statues of the gods and ritual furniture for their cults; established offerings; and endowed temples with land, livestock, and personnel. In theory, kings performed the rituals for the deities in their temples; in practice, they provided priests to act in their place. The ideal relationship between kings and deities was shown in temple reliefs, where a king performed the cult for the deities and the deities acknowledged the king in speech and actions, embracing him and handing him the symbol of life and the insignia of kingship. The gods' words to the king often referred to the subjugation of Egypt's enemies, and they relate to the king's role as the maintainer of *maat*, "the correct order of the universe," against the constant encroachment of chaos; the forces of chaos haunted the desert and foreign lands that surrounded the ordered world of Egypt, so that the hunting of desert animals and Egypt's aggression against foreigners were actually ritual acts that kept chaos at bay. The ritual aggression of the king was expressed both visually and textually, in temple and palace decoration, as a proclamation of legitimacy both to the gods and to those humans who had access to these buildings.

Specific rituals of kingship that confirmed the king's legitimacy were the *sed*-festival and the Opet festival. The *sed*-festival is known from the first dynasty onward, usually occurring around the king's thirtieth regnal year and every three years thereafter. The king performed rituals relating to the dual kingship of Upper and Lower Egypt that led to his regeneration, as was dramatically shown in the youthful images of Amenhotpe III that were produced after his first *sed*-festival. Although most kings never celebrated a *sed*-festival, temple reliefs and texts often promised the king *sed*-festivals as part of the symbolic system that expressed the legitimacy of his rule.

From the reign of Hatshepsut comes the first evidence of the Opet festival. This celebration took place annually at Thebes, in the temple of Luxor, to which the sacred boats of Amun, Mut, and Khonsu were brought from Karnak. The king underwent rituals that renewed his divine aspect—the royal *ka*—and thus confirmed the legitimacy of his rule. Later generations sometimes denied the legitimacy of earlier kings, by excluding their names from the ancestral king lists and by destroying their names and images.

BIBLIOGRAPHY

Baines, John. "Kingship, Definition of Culture, and Legitimation." In *Ancient Egyptian Kingship*, edited by David O'Connor and David P. Silverman, pp. 3–47. Leiden, 1995. A fundamental introduction to the concepts of kingship and legitimation in ancient Egypt.

Bell, Lanny. "Luxor Temple and the Cult of the Royal *Ka*." *Journal of Near Eastern Studies* 44 (1985), 251–294. A seminal article about the cult of the divine king at Luxor temple and the renewal of divine kingship through the annual opet festival.

Gardiner, Alan H. "The Coronation of King Haremhab." *Journal of Egyptian Archaeology* 39 (1953), 13–31. A translation and discussion of Horemheb's account of his accession to the throne.

Gundlack, Rolf, and Hermann Weber, eds. *Legitimation and Funktion des Herrschers vom ägyptischen Pharao zum neuzeitlichen Diktator.* Stuttgart, 1992.

Murnane, William J. *Texts from the Amarna Period in Egypt*, pp. 230–233. Atlanta, 1995. A translation of Horemheb's account of his accession to the throne.

Otto, Eberhard. "Legitimation des Herrschens im Pharaonischen Ägypten." *Saeculum* 20 (1969), 385–411. A classic article on the legitimation of kingship.

Robins, Gay. "A Critical Examination of the Theory That the Right to the Throne of Ancient Egypt Passed through the Female Line in the 18th Dynasty." *Göttinger Miszellen* 52 (1983), 67–77. Challenges the established view that the kingship of ancient Egypt passed through the female line of the royal family and that kings could only legitimize themselves by marrying the royal "heiress."

Silverman, David P. "The Nature of Egyptian Kingship." *Ancient Egyptian Kingship*, edited by David O'Connor and David Silverman, pp. 49–87. Leiden, 1995. A synthesis of kingship and the divinity of the king.

GAY ROBINS

LEPSIUS, KARL RICHARD (1810–1884), pioneering Egyptologist and leader of the Prussian expedition to Egypt of 1842–1846. Born in Naumburg in Saxony, the son of a regional government official, Lepsius was educated in Greek and Roman archaeology at the universities of Leipzig (1829–1830), Göttingen (1830–1832), and Berlin (1832–1833). His interest and facility in ancient languages were proved early in his life. In 1833, while in Paris, he attended lectures on the history of Egypt by Jean Letronne, the French classicist and archaeologist who had taken an early interest in the work of Jean-François Champollion on the decipherment of ancient Egyptian language.

Lepsius was attracted to the study of Egyptology, then in its infancy, but he resisted concentrating on Egyptian language until the posthumous appearance of Champollion's *Grammar* (1836–1841), when it became possible for him to undertake a systematized approach to it. Lepsius made a comparison of the various systems of translation then in use, in an attempt to discover to his satisfaction the one that was most likely to be correct. In 1836, he visited Italy, where he was able to meet Ippolito Rosellini, who had led the Tuscan contingent attached to Champollion's expedition to Egypt. The result of their discussions concerning the work of Champollion resulted in Lepsius's publication *Professeur I. Rosellini sur l'alphabet hiéroglyphique Lettre á M. le Professeur I. Rossellini etc.*, in which he expanded on Champollion's explanation of the use of alphabetical signs in hieroglyphic writing. If he was not the sole individual who recognized the principal on which the ancient language was organized, he certainly contributed one of the most helpful additions to the original theory.

In 1842, with the proposal of Johann Eichhorn, then Prussia's minister of instruction, and the recommendations of the scientists Alexander von Humboldt and Robert Wilhelm Bunsen, King Frederic William IV of Prussia commissioned a scientific mission to investigate the remains of ancient Egypt in the Nile Valley. The staff of the expedition consisted of surveyors, artists, draftsmen, and a plaster molder—the best equipped and qualified of any scholarly group to follow the French Egyptologists in the entourage of the Napoleonic army's campaign in Egypt forty years earlier. The Prussian expedition assembled in the Egyptian seaport of Alexandria in September of 1842 and had reached Giza by early November. Altogether they spent more than six months at Giza, Abusir, Saqqara, and Dahshur. Lepsius later explained the length of time devoted to the investigation of this area by noting that, with the exception of the pyramid studies of Richard H. Vyse and John S. Perring (1835–1837) and the cursory examination of the area by the French-Tuscan expedition under Champollion and Ippolito Rosellini (1828–1829), they were the first to study and record what was essentially material from the Old Kingdom, a foundation for the study of Egyptian history. As an example of the thoroughness of their work, in the area from Abu Rowash to the Faiyum region, they discovered the remains of 67 pyramids and more than 130 tombs of nobles.

In May 1843, they encamped in the Faiyum, at the ruins of the Labyrinth, where they carried out excavations and remained for several months. In the process, they made the first detailed plans of that monument. They traveled through Middle Egypt with stops at a number of sites, including Beni Hasan and Bersheh, as they made their way up the Nile River, hardly pausing at Thebes on the way to Nubia. The custom at the time, dictated by the realities of travel on the Nile, was to move with dispatch to the south, then to examine the monuments in more detail on the return journey down river.

The work of the party in what was called Ethiopia (Upper Nubia) must stand as the earliest thorough investigation and modern record of that area. Lepsius, with a small company, separated from the main party at Khartoum and ascended the Blue Nile past Sennar. His intention was to explore the country but also to make a study of the regional languages. When they descended the Nile, they were at Thebes by 2 November 1844. They camped for four months at Qurna, on the western bank, to investigate the tombs and temples and then spent another three months on the eastern bank, at the temples of Karnak. The length of time that they devoted to important centers of Egyptian antiquity indicates the serious attempt they made to observe and record as much as possible.

Lepsius made a side trip, by way of the Coptos road to Sinai, then went back to Thebes before the group set out northward, making lengthy stops at the principal sites on the way. The Nile Delta was explored as far east as Tanis during their journey from Cairo to the Mediterranean seaport of Alexandria. They returned to Europe along the eastern shore of the Mediterranean, by way of Beirut, Damascus, Baalbek, and Constantinople (Istanbul), arriving at Trieste in January of 1846.

In a summary of the accomplishments of the Prussian expedition, Lepsius characterized the earlier French–Tuscan excursion as one of "discovery," whereas he maintained that the importance of his own work was in the opportunity he was given to expand and develop a history and chronology of ancient Egypt. He also pointed out that Champollion had only ascended the Nile to the Second Cataract, whereas his exploration more completely included the Nubian monuments. He emphasized the contributions that his expedition made to the understanding of geography, the ancient Egyptian language, and Egyptian mythology. In simple fact, Lepsius, with a carefully chosen team of specialists, was able to take more time and care in investigation and recording than anyone had before him. He was instrumental in adding depth and detail to any further understanding of Egyptian antiquities.

Although the main concerns of the expedition were the recording of monuments and texts in copies, squeezes, and casts, they had also carried out some limited excavations to facilitate their investigations. In the course of the expedition, Lepsius also collected more than fifteen thousand antiquities and plaster casts to take back to Europe.

The chief result of the study was the monumental twelve-volume *Denkmäler aus Ägypten und Äthiopien*, with its nearly nine hundred plates. Although the text did not appear until after Lepsius's death, compiled from his notes by Edouard Naville and others, this work has continued to be a standard reference on the monuments of Egypt and Nubia and is an indispensable research tool for modern scholars. The plans, maps, and drawings of tomb and temple walls are of a high degree of accuracy and reliability. Often they are the only record of monuments since destroyed or later reburied.

Lepsius was made a professor at the Berlin University in 1846 and codirector of the Egyptian Museum in Berlin in 1855. He edited the *Zeitschrift für Äegyptische Sprache und Ältertumskunde*, one of the most important early periodical journals on Egyptian antiquity for many years. Following the early progress of Champollion, he ranks as one of the fathers of the modern study of Egyptology and one of the early giants in the development of the discipline, essentially laying the groundwork for the chronological study of Egyptian history. He is considered the founder of the "German school" of methodical research on the language, antiquities, and archaeology of ancient Egypt.

[*See also* Champollion, Jean-François].

BIBLIOGRAPHY

Bierbrier, M. L. *Who Was Who in Egyptology*. 3d rev. ed. London, 1995.
Ebers, George. *Richard Lepsius: ein Lebensbild*. Leipzig, 1885.
Lepsius, Dr. (Karl) Richard. *Letters from Egypt, Ethiopia and the Peninsula of Sinai*, translated by Leonora and Joanna B. Horner. London, 1853.

WILLIAM H. PECK

LETTERS. *See* Correspondence.

LETTERS TO THE DEAD. *See* Correspondence.

LIBYA. To Egypt, the land west of the Nile Valley was the least interesting of its neighbors. Already part of the Sahara by the early historic period, it did not have the mineral deposits that made Nubia, the Eastern Desert, and even the Sinai worth the effort of exploring and revisiting. The borders of Egypt are effectively defined by the sea to the north and east, and by a succession of cataracts on the Nile to the south, but the expanse of desert to the west, beyond the Western Desert, must have seemed endless. Especially in the earlier period of ancient Egyptian history, the term "Libyans" was often used to refer to people ("Tjemehu," "Tjehenu") who lived within the boundaries of what is now Egypt. It is, however, likely that the chain of oases that runs from north to south, more or less parallel to the Nile Valley, provided an informal natural frontier beyond which few Egyptians ever ventured. [*See* Western Desert.]

These oases, from Bahariya via Farafra and Dakhla to Kharga, are the most important feature of the Western Desert. They served as an alternative to the Nile as a trade route and as a means of communication from north to south, and they offered the possibility of uncontrolled access to the valley at various latitudes. Several episodes testify explicitly to such uses, but the danger of attack from the west was apparently not regarded by the Egyptians as sufficiently serious to warrant the installation and maintenance of permanent garrisons. Indeed, there is little archaeological trace of occupation of the oases between prehistoric times and the period after the New Kingdom. An interesting exception is the Dakhla Oasis, which was extensively settled in the Old Kingdom, perhaps with a view to exploiting its agricultural potential as well as controlling trade. The largest site seems to have been Balat, at the eastern end of the oasis, where a governor's palace and fortress of the sixth dynasty have been identified. Harkhuf, an official on mission to Nubia in precisely that period, used the oasis route to avoid hostile Nubians in the region between the First and Second Cataracts, traveling south from Kharga via the desert road known as the Darb el-Arbain, which brought him back to the Nile by way of the Selima Oasis. During this expedition he showed his concern for stability in the region by trying to restore peace between the Nubian ruler of Yam and the leader of the Tjemehu Libyans. Apart from strategic considerations, one of the most valued features of the oases seems to have been the wine they produced, which in the New Kingdom was probably second only to the vineyards of the Nile Delta in its importance to the Egyptian court.

There is no evidence that any of the different ethnic groups who made up the Libyan population in the pharaonic period were literate. Before the fifth century BCE, when the Greek author Herodotus included an account of the country and its peoples in his *Histories*, our knowledge depends on Egyptian sources. These are mostly official records which have no interest in presenting the Libyans as anything more than rebels to be crushed or as bearers of tribute. To date, virtually no archaeological evidence that might help to balance the picture has emerged from Libya itself before the foundation of Cyrene by Greek colonists in about 630 BCE. Disappointing as this is, it does suggest that the population of Libya before that turning point was largely nomadic, since nonsedentary societies rarely leave much of an imprint on the archaeological record.

Until the eighteenth dynasty, and to some extent also later, the words *Tjehenu* and *Tjemehu* were used to designate both particular regions west of Egypt and their occupants. Tjehenu referred to the area west of the Nile Delta as far south as the Faiyum, and these people, although always portrayed as foreign, may originally have been related to the Egyptians of the Delta. Tjemehu denoted an area that stretched south into Nubia, certainly as far as Wadi el-Sebua and perhaps as far as the Third Cataract. This clear distinction, formulated during early contacts, soon gave way to less precise usage, to the point where the two words became interchangeable. Control of these people and access to their animals seem to have been the Egyptians' main concern, and most of the evidence for this period consists of records of Egyptian aggression.

The earliest of these records are two ceremonial palettes of the Protodynastic period, votive objects used to notify the gods of signal royal achievements. The Libyan Palette, one of the earliest inscribed examples, takes its name from a single hieroglyph representing the word "Tjehenu." On one side there are symbolic depictions of royal conquests of settlements, and on the other appear registers of animals and fruit- or oil-bearing trees, presumably some of the booty acquired. The Battlefield Palette shows the bodies of the slain below a bound and yoked figure being led away. Although the object is uninscribed, the captive has been identified as Libyan because he wears the penis sheath often associated with these people in Egyptian iconography. From the Old Kingdom, a notable scene showing a conquered Libyan chieftain has survived in the mortuary temple of the fifth dynasty king Sahure. It also includes his family and registers of animal booty or tribute which expand on the theme encountered on the Libyan Palette. The reuse of the same scene—without acknowledgment—by Pepy I about 150 years later, and again by Taharqa 1,600 years after that, is a salutary reminder that such records owe more to general conceptions of kingship and its portrayal than to historical reality. For the Middle Kingdom, the introductory setting to the fictional *Story of Sinuhe* makes reference to the return from Libya of an expedition with captives and cattle.

There was also undoubtedly a steady trade in cattle and other goods, although the extent of this is difficult to ascertain because of the limitations of the evidence. Distinctive oasis wares, which might have been used in the manufacture of vessels to transport wine or other liquid or dry commodities, are only just beginning to be identified by ceramic studies. Libyans also appear as bringers of "tribute" in Theban tombs of the mid-eighteenth dynasty, and an inscription from the reign of Hatshepsut, according to which the Libyans supplied ivory and leopard skins, suggests that they also acted as middlemen, using the oasis route to bring these exotic products from much farther south. The continuing potential of this route for communications hostile to Egypt is evident at the end of the Second Intermediate Period. A stela set up at Karnak by King Kamose describes an alliance between the Hyksos in the Delta and the kingdom of the Kush in Nubia. Since Kamose himself controlled Upper Egypt, this alliance could only have come into being through correspondence conducted by another route, and the stela does indeed record the capture of a messenger in one of the oases.

Until the eighteenth dynasty, the extant evidence offers no hint of a serious threat to Egypt from the west. That changed with the arrival of new ethnic groups, of which the most important were the Libu—whose name has given us, through Greek, the modern word "Libya"—and the Meshwesh. The latter people are generally regarded as ancestors of those inhabitants of Libya whom Herodotus calls "Maxyes." Egyptian depictions of these new Libyans are perhaps best observed in a scene from the *Book of Gates* preserved in the tomb of Sety I, where they appear with a Nubian, a Near Easterner, and an Egyptian as one of the four races of mankind. Their characteristic features are pale skin, plaited hairstyle, long pointed beard, and extensive body painting or tattooing. They wore long, open, brightly colored cloaks with geometric patterns.

They also have in common with earlier depictions of Libyans the penis sheath, and feathers were worn in the hair to indicate chieftain status.

Like their predecessors, the Libu and the Meshwesh seem to have been nomadic and pastoral peoples, depending largely on cattle, sheep and goats for their subsistence. There is evidence from Mersa Matruh to suggest that they possessed a primitive ceramic technology, but the bronze weapons they used in battle against the Egyptians were almost certainly acquired through trade rather than locally produced. These groups seem to have moved east through Tjehenu country from Cyrenaica (in present-day Libya), where they could have been resident for a considerable period, beyond the cognizance of the Egyptians, until disturbed by the arrival in North Africa of the Sea Peoples. The exact ethnic and cultural relationship between the latter and the Libu and Meshwesh is uncertain. On at least one occasion, in the reign of Merenptah, they joined forces to attack Egypt. The relevant distinction ultimately is that the Sea Peoples were mostly deflected away from Egypt, whereas many Libyans settled there.

Until the mid-1980s, serious hostilities between Egypt and the newcomers to Libya were regarded as having begun in the nineteenth dynasty. The extant record is patchy, however, and the publication of a fragment of painted papyrus from Tell el-Amarna, which shows a Libyan warrior killing an Egyptian, may indicate that there was conflict in the time of Akhenaten. Some Libyans, perhaps prisoners of war, had already been enrolled in the Egyptian army by this time, since they appear in tomb reliefs at Amarna as part of the king's bodyguard. Following a preemptive strike into Libya by Sety I, recognition of real danger from the west is implied by the construction, under Ramesses II, of a network of forts along the western Delta and the Mediterranean littoral as far as Mersa Matruh, 300 kilometers (185 miles) west of Alexandria, to protect the vulnerable coastal route into Egypt. No major clashes are known during his sixty-seven-year reign, but inscriptions at Karnak and elsewhere record that his successor, Merenptah, was confronted in his fifth year of reign by a coalition made up of approximately two-thirds Libyans and one-third Sea Peoples. The presence of women, children, and cattle shows that this was a whole population on the move, not merely an attempt at military conquest. An interesting detail to emerge is that the Libyans, unlike the Egyptians, did not practice circumcision. Some Libyans had already occupied the Farafra Oasis, and the importance of the oasis route for communications is again apparent, since their attack on the Delta was launched in concert with a prearranged Nubian rebellion in the South of Egypt. Both were crushed.

The Libyans are known to have tried again to enter Egypt in Years 5 and 11 of Ramesses III. The Egyptian victories in these battles are recorded in the king's mortuary temple at Medinet Habu and summarized in the posthumous account of his reign given in the Harris Papyrus. From the official Egyptian point of view, as it has come down to us, the story ends there, with the crushing defeat of the invaders and the settlement of captives in camps, followed by the beginning of a process of acculturation, which involved teaching them the Egyptian language. Yet the Harris Papyrus also records that Ramesses III built new enclosure walls to protect temples in Middle Egypt, and documents from the workmen's village at Deir el-Medina show that even Thebes suffered disruptive raids down to the end of the twentieth dynasty, despite its religious importance and southerly location. At least some of these raids involved Libyans, and it is clear from what followed after the New Kingdom that significant numbers had succeeded in settling in Egypt, especially in the Delta, and that their descendants gradually took control of parts of the country and eventually of the whole of Egypt.

The lack of archaeological evidence makes it impossible to suggest what effect Egyptian culture may have had on that of the Libyans prior to the late New Kingdom. Libyan captives brought to Egypt might serve in the army or on building projects, as in the case of the temple of Ramesses II at Wadi el-Sebua. Rising through the ranks of the army was one way in which individuals could better themselves, and the example of the army commander Herihor shows that some people of Libyan background had risen to positions of great power by the end of the twentieth dynasty. Herihor added the offices of "Viceroy of Kush" and high priest of Amun to that of army commander and went on to claim royal status. It is this development, rather than the accession of Sheshonq I at the start of the twenty-second dynasty, that marks the real beginning of the period of Libyan rule in Egypt. This lasted for some four hundred years, until the reunification of Egypt by Psamtik I, himself of Libyan descent, in 664 BCE. The New Kingdom had ended with the effective division of Egypt into two parts—the North ruled by the twenty-first dynasty successors of the Ramessid kings, and the South by the high priests of Amun—but recognition of the Libyan dimension is arguably more important to our understanding of developments.

One of the striking features is the retention of Libyan names, such as Sheshonq, Osorkon, and Takeloth, within the new military elite. Another is the survival throughout the period of Libyan tribal titles, as well as their feather symbols of authority, among the chiefs of the Meshwesh and the Libu in Egypt itself. A patchwork of small principalities developed in the Delta, each governed by a local ruler. Under strong kings they might be kept in check, but the tendency toward fragmentation is shown at its most extreme in a stela set up by the Nubian king Piya of the twenty-fifth dynasty, which lists five kings and a plethora of Libyan chiefs, each in control of his own small part of Egypt. It is hard not to see an echo of the tribal structure of Libyan society in this. A decline in the prestige of the kings, who were often no more than paramount chiefs, was inevitable.

The Libyans seem to have had no artistic or architectural tradition of their own, and the elite culture of the period remained wholly Egyptian. Nonetheless, some features of the period—such as lengthy genealogies and the increased importance of women within the priesthood and in the governing class generally—may owe something to a Libyan heritage. The same may be true of changes in burial customs, involving less advance preparation for the afterlife.

Little is known of contact between Egypt and Libya in this period, but the advent of the twenty-sixth dynasty and the suppression of the Libyan chiefdoms marked the end of an era in Egyptian history. Interest in the oases seems to have been renewed, with the construction of temples at Hibis in the Khargeh Oasis and more remotely at Siwa, where an Egyptian presence is visible for the first time. The Greek foundations of Cyrene in Libya and Naucratis in Egypt introduced a new element into the relationship between Egypt and its western neighbor.

[*See also* Osorkon; Sheshonq I; Third Intermediate Period; *and* Western Desert.]

BIBLIOGRAPHY

Baines, J. "Contextualizing Egyptian Representations of Society and Ethnicity." In *The Study of the Ancient Near East in the 21st Century*, edited by J. S. Cooper and G. M. Schwarz, pp. 339–384. Winona Lake, 1996. Emphasizes the importance of ethnicity in understanding the Libyan period in Egypt.

Bates, O. *The Eastern Libyans*. London, 1914. Dated but still classic anthropological study.

Giddy, Lisa. *Egyptian Oases: Bahariya, Dakhla, Farafra and Kharga during Pharaonic Times*. Warminster, 1987.

Hölscher, W. *Libyer und Ägypter*. Glückstadt, 1955. Detailed survey of textual and iconographic evidence.

Jansen-Winkeln, K. "Der Beginn des libyschen Herrschaft in Ägypten." *Biblische Notizen* 71 (1994), 78–97. Important discussion of the Libyan features of the twenty-first dynasty.

Kitchen, K. A. *The Third Intermediate Period in Egypt (1100–650 BC)*. 3rd edn. Warminster, 1996. Comprehensive chronological and political account of this period of Egyptian history.

Leahy, A. "The Libyan Period in Egypt: An Essay in Interpretation." *Libyan Studies* 16 (1985), 51–65. Argues that the Libyans in Egypt retained elements of their cultural background that had a significant impact on Egypt in the first millennium BCE.

O'Connor, D. "The Nature of Tjemhu (Libyan) Society in the Later New Kingdom." In *Libya and Egypt c.1300–750 BC*, edited by A. Leahy, pp. 29–113. London, 1990. Detailed analysis of the New Kingdom evidence.

Osing, J. 1980. "Libyen, Libyer." In *Lexikon der Ägyptologie*, 3: 1015–1033. Wiesbaden, 1979. Very dense and informative review of the topic.

Ritner, Robert K. "The End of the Libyan Anarchy in Egypt: P. Rylands Cols. 11–12." *Enchoria* 17 (1990), 101–108. Discusses the disappearance of Libyan titles.

Selincourt, A. de. *Herodotus, The Histories:* Book IV. Harmondsworth, 1954.

Spalinger, A. J. "Some Notes on the Libyans of the Old Kingdom and Later Historical Reflexes." *Society for the Study of Egyptian Antiquities Journal* 9 (1979), 125–162.

ANTHONY LEAHY

LIMESTONE, the most important stone used in ancient Egypt. Limestone is a sedimentary rock composed of calcium carbonate ($CaCO_3$) in its pure form (3 on the Mohs Scale of Hardness); however, it almost never occurs in that form but is usually of varied composition, most often combined with magnesium carbonate ($MgCO_3$, magnesite) to form dolomite ($CaMg[CO_3]_2$; 3.5–4 on the Mohs Scale of Hardness), as well as other minerals. These substances cause a variation in the texture and hardness, so depending on the composition, the hardness varies between 3 and 5 on the Mohs Scale. As a sedimentary rock, limestone is produced either by organic or inorganic processes, and it is often a highly fossiliferous rock (composed of the calcium carbonate shells of mollusks and other marine animals).

From the earliest dynasties, limestone was widely utilized, owing to its widespread occurrence in and around the Nile Valley and the surrounding deserts. Ease of quarrying and carving, the ability of harder forms to accept a polish, and its structural strength allowed it to be used for the construction of large buildings—pyramids and temples. The world's first large-scale structures, the Old Kingdom pyramid complex of Djoser, was constructed entirely of limestone. Limestone continued to be the preferred stone into the early New Kingdom, when it was gradually replaced by sandstone (Clark and Engelbach 1930, pp. 12f). Present-day experiments have demonstrated that Egyptian workers could easily quarry and sculpt limestone with copper tools, whereas hard stones, such as granite, basalt, or quartzite required working with stone tools. [*See* Stoneworking.]

Numerous quarries were operated within the Mokattum Formation (a Middle Eocene limestone deposit), with important sites at Giza, Saqqara, and Illahun (on the Nile's western bank); Gebel Mokattam near the Citadel in Cairo; Gebel Tura near Tura village; and Gebel Hof near el-Masara village. Other major sources are within the Samalut Formation (Middle Eocene), the Minia Formation (late Lower Eocene to early Middle Eocene), and the Drunka Formation (Lower Eocene). Some limestones are coarse grained and are used mainly as core materials in structures; others, notably the dense variety of the Mokattum Formation, known as "Tura" Limestone, was the preferred finishing stone and facing for the Old Kingdom pyramids. Limestone was so easily obtained that it be-

LIMESTONE. *Statuette of the God Tutu, from the thirtieth dynasty.* (The Metropolitan Museum of Art, The Theodore M. Davis Collection, Bequest of Theodore M. Davis, 1915. [30.8.71])

came almost the only stone for buildings other than temples—used in constructing elite homes and palaces.

Limestone statues of all sizes were commonly sculpted, since fine-grained, dense varieties are easily carved, to allow fine detailing. Examples include the famous Old Kingdom seated statue of Djoser, as well as Rahotep and his wife Nofret, Nakhtmin's wife, and the New Kingdom bust of an unnamed queen of Ramesses II. For statuary, a pure, nearly white, dense limestone was generally selected; sometimes it was finished with a medium-to-high polish, whereas at other times it was smoothed and painted. The most famous painted limestone sculpture must certainly be the New Kingdom painted head of Queen Nefertiti, found at Akhetaten (Tell el-Amarna).

Innumerable votive stelae were carved in limestone, the only stone easily obtained that would allow precise carving of hieroglyphs and highly detailed funerary scenes. Probably for the same reasons, limestone was chosen in New Kingdom wall facings—for example, the great processional scenes in the Luxor Temple and the sculpted relief scenes in the Saqqara tombs of Maya and Horemheb.

Limestone is known from Egyptian written sources under a number of names: *ꜥyn, inr-n-ꜥin, inr-ḥḏ, inr-ḥḏ-nfr,* and *inr-ḥḏ-nfr-n-ꜥin.*

[*See also* Calcite.]

BIBLIOGRAPHY

Clarke, Somers, and R. Engelbach. *Ancient Egyptian Construction and Architecture.* London, 1930, repr. New York, 1990.

Erman, Adolf, and Hermann Grapow. *Wörterbuch der Aegyptischen Sprache.* 6 vols. Berlin, 1982.

Harrell, James A. "An Inventory of Ancient Egyptian Quarries." *Newsletter of the American Research Center in Egypt* 146 (1989), 1–7 (plus cover photo).

Lesko, Leonard H., and Barbara Switalski, eds. *A Dictionary of Late Egyptian.* 4 vols. Berkeley, 1982.

Russman, Edna R. *Egyptian Sculpture—Cairo and Luxor.* Austin, 1989.

Schulz, Regine, and Matthias Seidel. *Egypt—The World of the Pharaohs.* Cologne, 1998.

CLAIR R. OSSIAN

LION. *See* Feline Deities; *and* Felines.

LISHT, EL-, two pyramid cemeteries of the twelfth dynasty on the western bank of the Nile, some 50 kilometers (31 miles) south of Cairo (29°23′N, 31°9′E). They received the name el-Lisht from a nearby modern village. There are indications that Itjtawy, the royal residence city of the twelfth dynasty, was located to the east of the cemeteries under the village. A broad wadi separates the northern cemetery, dominated by the pyramid of Amenemhet I, and

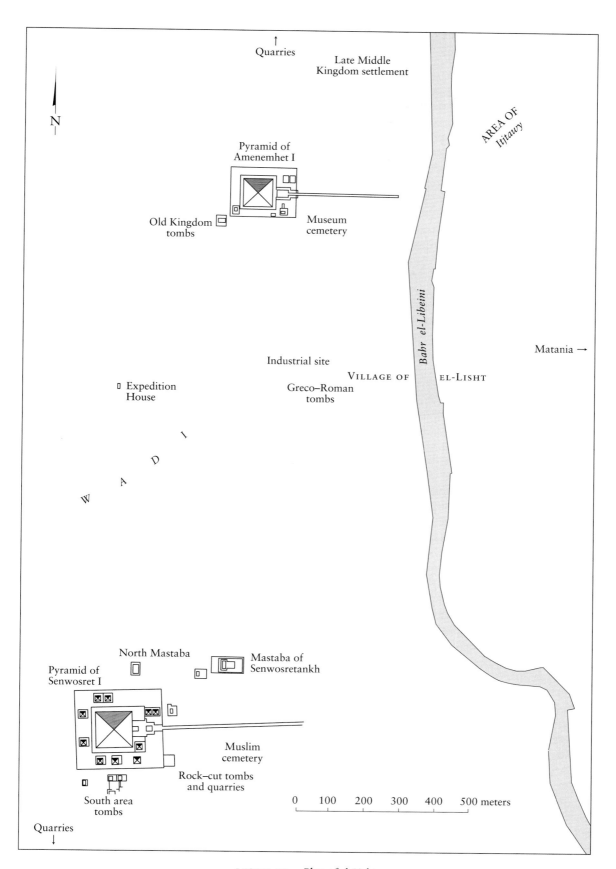

Quarries
↑

Late Middle
Kingdom settlement

N

AREA OF
Itjtawy

Pyramid of
Amenemhet I

Old Kingdom
tombs

Museum
cemetery

Bahr el-Libeini

Matania →

Industrial site

Expedition
House

VILLAGE OF   EL-LISHT

Greco–Roman
tombs

W
A
D
I

North Mastaba

Mastaba of
Senwosretankh

Pyramid of
Senwosret I

Muslim
cemetery

Rock–cut tombs
and quarries

South area
tombs

0   100   200   300   400   500 meters

Quarries
↓

LISHT, EL-. *Plan of el-Lisht.*

the southern cemetery, with the pyramid of Senwosret I. Excavations were carried out by the French Institute (J.-E. Gautier, 1894–1895), The Metropolitan Museum of Art, New York (A. M. Lythgoe, 1906–1914, A. Lansing and A. Mace, 1914–1934, and D. Arnold, 1984–1991), and the Egyptian Antiquities Organization (Ahmed Abdel-Hamid, 1991–1994).

The pyramid of Amenemhet I was the successor to an earlier royal tomb project begun by this king at Gurneh and abandoned when the court was moved to the Itjtawy. The poorly preserved pyramid complex shows symptoms of the loss of Old Kingdom tradition. The pyramid was 84 by 84 meters (276 by 276 feet) wide and 59(?) meters (about 195 feet) high with a slope of about 54 degrees. The core of rough fieldstone blocks contains numerous reused, decorated blocks from Old Kingdom temples (Khufus, Khafre, Userkaf, Unas, and Pepy II). The sloping entrance corridor from the north is cased with granite blocks, some of them being reused architraves with the name of Khafren. The small burial chamber was found robbed. A vertical shaft in its floor disappears into the groundwater but seems to lead to the canopic chamber. The foundation trenches of a modest pyramid temple in front of the eastern side of the pyramid contained reused blocks depicting Amenemhet I and Senwosret I as co-regents. Except for a granite altar and two false doors of Amenemhet I, nothing remains of the temple. No secondary or queens' pyramids were built. The foundations of a small valley chapel were found above the edge of the cultivation. The area east of the pyramid is now covered by a huge modern cemetery.

Under Senwosret I, the builders succeeded in re-creating the Old Kingdom tradition. This king's pyramid complex is an excellent successor to the prototypes of the fifth and sixth dynasties, with the name "United are the seats of Kheperkare." The pyramid was 105 by 105 meters (345 by 345 feet) wide and 61.25 meters (201 feet) high, with a slope of 49°24'. The core is built of small fieldstone blocks retained by a grid of skeleton walls. Some areas still show the casing blocks. The name of the pyramid was "Senwosret overviews the Two Lands." The sloping entrance passage from the north is cased with granite and disappears below 48 meters (156 feet) into the groundwater. The burial was robbed by thieves when discovered in 1882. Decorated blocks of the entrance chapel were found above the pyramid entrance. Important remains of the architecture and decoration of the pyramid temple and its granite altar were preserved to the east of the pyramid, suggesting that the temple closely followed the prototypes, except for the absence of front storerooms. Gautier discovered ten complete seated limestone figures of Senwosret I, buried in pharaonic times. An inner stone enclosure wall was decorated with one hundred relief panels showing offering-bearing fertility figures, surmounted by the palace façade, with the royal names and the Horus falcon. An outer brick enclosure surrounded the small pyramids of Queen Neferu, Princess Itakayet, and seven more pyramids and the subsidiary pyramid of the king. The causeway had side walls and a roof of stone; it contained statues of the king in Osirid shape, standing in side niches. The valley temple has not yet been found.

The pyramids are surrounded by a few tombs of contemporary and slightly later officials, as well as thousands of shaft tombs and surface burials of the twelfth and thirteenth dynasties and the much later Roman period. The southern cemetery contains three major tombs. Northeast of the cemetery of Senwosret I lies the monumental tomb enclosure of Senwosretankh; there, a *mastaba* is decorated with the early paneling motif and a burial chamber is inscribed with Pyramid Texts. North of the causeway are the remains of the tomb enclosure of Imhotep, with a sarcophagus pit inscribed with Coffin Texts. A wooden shrine and two wooden royal statuettes were preserved in a cache in the enclosure wall of the tomb. Southeast of the pyramid of Senwosret I, the tomb enclosure of the vizier Montuhotep was discovered, containing remains of statuary, relief decoration, and a beautifully decorated and inscribed sarcophagus. The cliffs southeast of the pyramid of Senwosret I contain numerous rock-cut tombs of the twelfth dynasty, some of them with beautiful, but heavily damaged, wall decoration.

The tombs of the northern cemetery were less monumental. The tomb of the vizier Antefoker was found southeast of the pyramid of Amenemhet I. The undisturbed burial of Lady Senebtisi (southwest of the pyramid) produced important information about a middle-class burial of the Middle Kingdom. From the Middle Kingdom onward, a settlement of tomb caretakers, funerary craftsmen, fishermen, and farmers spread over the partially abandoned and robbed northern cemetery, and this site is providing important information on domestic architecture and the life of the lower classes.

BIBLIOGRAPHY

Arnold, Dieter. *The South Cemeteries of Lisht, I: The Pyramid of Senwosret I.* New York, 1988.

Arnold, Dieter. *The South Cemeteries of Lisht, III: The Pyramid Complex of Senwosret I.* New York, 1991.

Arnold, Felix. *The South Cemeteries of Lisht, II: The Control Notes and Team Marks.* New York, 1990.

Gautier, J.-E., and G. Jéquier. *Fouilles de Licht.* Cairo, 1902. On the excavation of the pyramid of Amenemhet I.

Hayes, W. C. *The Texts in the Mastabeh of Sen-Wosret-ankh at Lisht.* New York, 1937.

Lansing, A., and W. C. Hayes. Report. *Bulletin of the Metropolitan Museum of Art* 28 (November 1933), 9–38.

Mace, Arthur C., and Herbert E. Winlock. *The Tomb of Senebtisi at Lisht.* New York, 1916.

Note: Excavation reports for el-Lisht appeared in the *Bulletin of the Metropolitan Museum of Art* 2 (April 1907), 61–63; 2 (July 1907), 113–117; 3 (May 1908), 83–84; 3 (October 1908), 184–188; 9 (October 1914), 107–111; 16 (November 1921), 5–19; 17 (December 1922), 4–18.

DIETER ARNOLD

LITERACY. Because of all the monumental inscriptions that survive from ancient Egypt, it is clear that the Egyptians were exposed to, if not surrounded by, writing to a greater degree than other communities of the ancient Near East. Although Egypt was primarily agricultural, which would generally indicate a low literacy rate, such exposure to, and high regard for, writing presumably would have made more ancient Egyptians motivated to comprehend it. Recent estimates of literacy, based on officials with scribal titles who were buried in certain Old Kingdom cemeteries, are very low—less than 1 percent. This perception is based on the limited survival rates of ancient monuments, however, and also on a lack of careful and thorough excavation and publication. The number of bureaucrats in any ancient period and place may indeed have had little correlation with literacy rates in general.

The way literacy is defined affects our estimates of literacy rates in different parts of Egypt and in different historical periods. *Literacy* refers to the ability to read and write, but clearly there are many grades of literacy; far more people are able to read than write. If signing one's name is enough to prove literacy, then it is impressive that so many witnesses could do so in ancient Egypt. If the ability to write was so rare, then it is equally impressive that both men and women would undertake to write letters to deceased relatives, both male and female, to communicate their discontent. Surely, they could have screamed to the heavens rather than take the time to scribble their plaintive messages discreetly on bowls of offerings. The fact that many people who could write did not do so might be used to lower a literacy rate unfairly, just as the large number of mistakes and inconsistencies found in surviving texts would unreasonably lower our estimation of their writing skills.

The site in Egypt that has been most productive with respect to inscribed ostraca and papyri, as well as having the best preserved tombs and dwellings, is Deir el-Medina, the village of the workmen of the New Kingdom royal necropolises in Western Thebes. Evidence from this one site indicates that not only those with scribal titles but also the foremen, many of the draughtsmen, common workmen (quarrymen and carpenters), and wives were also literate.

In the history of ancient Egyptian philology, considerable advances were made in understanding Demotic texts before recognizing the phonetic values of hieroglyphs. Demotic is a difficult, abbreviated handwriting system that bears little similarity to the hieroglyphs from which its groups evolved. Similarly, the intermediate stage of writing between cursive hieroglyphs and Demotic, which we call Hieratic, was an entity in its own right that developed out of, but separately from, hieroglyphic writing. By the late New Kingdom, Hieratic represented what was studied and learned first by students who may not have learned the old, formal, monumental, hieroglyphic system. Hieratic, for the ancient Egyptian, was much quicker to use, presumably easier to learn, and allowed more freedom of expression. Writing with reed brushes on broken pieces of pottery or on limestone sherds, using ink made from soot, meant that there was little expense necessary; writing merely required the free time and an inclination or necessity to communicate or record, after having received a reasonable amount of training.

The literacy rate among ancient Egyptian women was undoubtedly much lower than that among men. Despite this trend, there was a goddess of writing, Seshat, and a feminine form of the word for scribe, which shows that this activity was acceptable for women. It is clear, however, that there were comparatively few positions in which women would have been able to use this skill. Some princesses, queens, priestesses, and businesswomen were literate, but women were notably absent from the records concerning education or formal schooling. In several instances, women were depicted in tombs with scribal equipment beneath their chairs. There are letters from different periods sent by women that could have been written for them by professional scribes; there are several examples of letters from one woman to another. A few ostraca from Deir el-Medina have survived that were addressed to wives who should have been able to read them without assistance, for example, Neferhotep's note to his wife that told her to send him some beans for his bread which, without beans, was not agreeable enough to deserve recognition. Women were occasionally shown selling goods at market, and even the ancient Greek historian Herodotus noted as a novelty, women doing the shopping. Because women were involved in at least simple commercial transactions that would require some use of arithmetic, it is likely that these women would have learned to read and write as well.

Queens in the sixth dynasty, noble women in the Middle Kingdom, and priests' wives in the New Kingdom had their own copies of the funerary literature connected with each period. Possession of these documents demonstrates that these women understood their importance, expected to be able to read in the afterlife, and would have had no impediments to achieving literacy. In a Late period story written in Demotic about Prince Khaemwaset, one of the sons of Ramesses II, Ahwere, the wife of an earlier prince, is said to be able to read aloud the spells from an ancient book recovered by her husband, and to be able to write, though not as well as her husband. The wives of some priests of the twenty-first dynasty may have been involved in the selection of spells for their *Book of Going Forth by Day* (*Book of the Dead*), and, based on internal evidence, may even have authored new spells that appeared for the first time in their manuscripts. Other than these examples, none of the authors known from ancient Egypt were women.

Thoth was the god who invented writing, or the "words of God" for the ancient Egyptians, and he is often shown with a papyrus roll in one hand and a reed brush in the other, writing what had to be recorded or composing one of the sacred books attributed to his authorship. The goddess Seshat was also a patroness of writing and is frequently shown recording royal names on the leaves of the sacred persea tree.

It is noteworthy that many statues of men have been found in a seated position writing on a papyrus roll on their knees, or, more dramatically, with their garments covered with legible hieroglyphs. Even great generals are shown in this writing posture, but lacking arms or armor. The fact that the vast majority of statues were inscribed is significant in itself; the identifying texts were apparently considered to be at least as important as the artists' portrayal of the owner, and perhaps more so. This lack of a distinct portrait may help to explain why so many statues were reused by later generations, who merely substituted their own names for those of the original owners. This practice was prevalent among those preparing the statues of succeeding kings that were to be erected in cult and mortuary temples.

The importance of writing in an agricultural society should not be minimized since clearly the land documents and wills of those in ancient rural areas were as important to their owners as they would be to farmers today. Only those who owned nothing and lacked all hope of possessions would have been passed over in this system. It is inconceivable to some scholars that this underclass would have been more than 99 percent of Egypt's population, and it is not unreasonable to estimate that at least 5 percent of the population of ancient Egypt would have been literate.

Among the most common graffiti encountered along pathways, quarry sites, or remote desert areas, are addresses to passersby to wish for a thousand loaves of bread, as well as beer, oxen, and fowl for the named writer. Possibly, this exercise was magical, but it is more likely that the writers would have expected that some proportion of travelers would have been able to read the request. Scratching one's name on a favorite seat was far less magical but would have intimidated trespassers and legitimized a person's claim to the property if disputes arose. The presence of the name points to the expectation that others would be able to attest to the written claim by being able to read.

Deir el-Medina was an exceptional village. The written material on papyri and ostraca recovered from this single site is enough to provide hundreds of fragments of literary works in both Middle Egyptian and Late Egyptian, as well as a variety of historical, magical, and religious texts. A huge quantity of nonliterary material in varied handwriting attests to a high rate of literacy in this village. A large number of inscribed stelae belonged to both the men and the women of the village, and graffiti can be found wherever the most prolific writers among the workmen went. Because the site was long occupied, an abundance of writing material remains. The workmen used sherds for writing practice and had access to writing supplies provided for their work in the royal tombs. Their jottings from memory or for expedience littered the village area and its cistern, which seems to have been used as a dump. The abandonment of the village was sudden and complete. Neither the artisans nor the marauders that caused their displacement could have been concerned about the written material left behind.

A book collector and scribe from Deir el-Medina, Kenherkhepeshef, not only collected a large number of papyrus scrolls but also read and annotated them and even replaced an original scribe's name with his own. He also copied historical texts from temple walls, presumably for his own enjoyment, and composed a few original texts as well. Of course, his best "books" had been written and copied by others, not from this small village, but from the major religious center across the river, which has unfortunately yielded no papyri of its own, though far more important works were produced there. Every fragment we have serves to show how much has been lost. The fact that some of Kenherkhepeshef's books were later cut up and used as scratch paper by an unappreciative yet literate heir shows how vulnerable such rolls were.

There have been numerous, though generally isolated, finds of papyri in tombs and at temple sites in many different locations in Egypt, and there are many papyri whose provenience is unknown. Tombs and mortuary temples provide more paleographic material than cult temples, palaces, or administrative centers because they had less traffic and tended to be left alone. The detailed record keeping in the fifth dynasty Abu Sir Papyri, which refers to only one mortuary temple, indicates how much additional work of this type, at comparable sites, must have been done that has not survived. Until the 1980s and 1990s, the Giza necropolis was viewed as an elitist enclave, but now that the tombs and dwellings of working class people are being uncovered nearby, scholars' perception of the literacy rate will change based on the quantity of written material. The Kahun Papyri from a Middle Kingdom building site in the Faiyum are fragmentary and diverse and show how much more has not survived. The reference in the *Admonitions of Ipuwer* to the *hpw* ("laws" or "precedents") being trampled in the streets during unsettled times is another indication of the vulnerability of papyri.

The destruction of papyri has occurred in many ways: papyri were wrapped around bodies which were later burned for fuel, Demotic papyri were erased or otherwise reused by the Greeks, pieces of papyrus were used by ancient embalmers to stuff crocodiles, and huge amounts of papyri were lost by modern excavators since the 1800s. Many more papyri could have been destroyed before the modern era by those with other uses for them; scholars are fortunate that any of this fragile material remains.

From what little survives of wills and titles to property, it is clear that an extensive bureaucracy and archive would have existed throughout ancient Egypt. The cuneiform letters found at Tell el-Amarna (called the Amarna Letters) demonstrate the need to have had palace archives from all periods and also the clear evidence that these have generally perished. The survival of the baked clay cuneiform tablets emphasizes the fragility of papyri and leather rolls that were occasionally used by the Egyptians. Far fewer ostraca would have survived in the more humid North, because of the action of occasional rainstorms on the ink and the flaking of potsherds from moisture, salts, and heat.

Many commodities prepared for tomb, palace, and home use were labeled by their producers (such as the winemakers) to be read later by butlers, priests, or other servants in other parts of the country. The prevalence of writing on everyday commodities is another indication of the importance of literacy in ancient Egypt. That it was not always easy to convince students to keep working at their reading and writing can be gleaned from some of the exercises that they had to copy, such as the "Satire on the Trades," which compares the exalted position of a scribe to all the various alternative occupations—and which were described by scribes in the worst possible light.

BIBLIOGRAPHY

Baines, John. "Literacy and Ancient Egyptian Society." *Man,* n.s. 18 (1983), 572–599.

Baines, John, and Christopher J. Eyre. "Four Notes on Literacy." *Göttinger Miszellen* 61 (1983), 65–96.

Bryan, Betsy M. "Evidence for Female Literacy from Theban Tombs of the New Kingdom." *Bulletin of the Egyptological Seminar* 6 (1984), 17–32.

Janssen, Jac. J. "Literacy and Letters at Deir el-Medina." In *Village Voices: Proceedings of the Symposium "Texts from Deir el-Medîna and Their Interpretation": Leiden, May 31–June 1, 1991,* edited by R. J. Demarée and Arno Egberts, pp. 81–94. Leiden, 1992.

Lesko, Leonard H. "Some Comments on Ancient Egyptian Literacy and Literati." In *Studies in Egyptology: Presented to Miriam Lichtheim,* edited by Sarah Israelit-Groll, vol. 2, pp. 656–667. Jerusalem, 1990.

Lesko, Leonard H. "Literature, Literacy, and Literati. In *Pharaoh's Workers: The Villagers of Deir el Medina,* edited by Leonard H. Lesko, pp. 131–144. Ithaca, 1994.

Velde, Herman te. "Scribes and Literacy in Ancient Egypt." *Scripta Signa Vocis: Studies about Scripts, Scriptures, Scribes and Languages in the Near East Presented to J. H. Hospers by His Pupils, Colleagues and Friends,* edited by H.L.J. Vanstiphout, pp. 253–264. Groningen, 1986.

Wente, Edward F. "The Scribes of Ancient Egypt." In *Civilizations of the Ancient Near East,* edited by Jack M. Sasson, vol. 4, pp. 2211–2222. New York, 1995.

LEONARD H. LESKO

LITERATURE. Ancient Egyptian literature—written through all the various phases of the Egyptian language (Old, Middle, and Late Egyptian, Demotic, and Coptic)—can be documented for a period of almost three thousand years, from the Pyramid Texts of the fifth and sixth dynasties (c.2300 BCE) to the pieces written in Coptic during the early Christian era. This article will consider Egyptian literature only through the end of the New Kingdom.

It is necessary to distinguish between two definitions of literature: (1) anything written down, and (2) belles-lettres, or writings that include an imaginative and creative dimension, even though their primary purpose may be more utilitarian (a prayer, a letter, a moral instruction). This article will confine itself to the second definition, with the understanding that what was "literary" to the ancient Egyptian reader and what is literary to the modern reader do not necessarily coincide; and the boundaries between Egyptian literature falling under the first definition and that falling under the second are not yet clear. That is, one asks where the tomb biography should be placed, for it certainly is a major kind; and a similar question applies to the letter, since examples exist that are certainly literary. Thus, while certain kinds of ancient Egyptian literature seem to correspond with modern genres—lyric, narrative, and hortatory or didactic (the wisdom texts)—others may need to be included. Similarly, some texts are currently misplaced by modern scholars, for example the "magical texts," which are after all lyric pieces with the specific purpose of protecting a person against maleficent forces or beings.

Egyptian literature is a literature in ruins. Much survives—enough to appreciate, evaluate, and comment on it—but surely what now exists must be only a fraction of what was written, and there is no way to tell how much has been lost. There are probably multiple representatives of all the major kinds of literature undertaken by the ancient writers; but in no case do we really have a fullness of examples appearing steadily from the Old Kingdom until the end of the New (and on into the Late, Classical, and Coptic periods). The lyric is well represented, particularly by hymns and prayers; there are moral instructions ("teachings") from all three kingdoms; yet the narrative, once it appears in the Middle Kingdom, is represented by few examples, many of them fragmentary. Nevertheless, among this literature occur masterpieces that can be set without shame beside those of other ancient literatures: *Sinuhe,* the *Shipwrecked Sailor,* Akhenaten's Hymn to Aten, and the *Instructions of Amenemope.* And others might be cited.

Finally, Egyptian literature is largely an anonymous literature. No authors' names are attached to most of the pieces, nor does any named author for certain have multiple titles attributed to him (except possibly Khety of the Middle Kingdom). The lyrics and narratives, in particular, are not attributed to any authors (except for Akhenaten's hymn, which need not have been composed by the king). It is the instructional (or "wisdom") pieces that bear names; there are at least two lists of authors' names, both from the New Kingdom, one from a papyrus and the other from a stone block. The first of these includes the names of Imhotep, Hordjedef, Neferti, Khety ("the best of them"), Ptahemdjehuty, Khakheperresonb, Ptahhotep, and Kaires; these, in fact, form a list of the sages of ancient Egypt. Some of them can be connected with surviving works, while others cannot. The stone block depicts two registers of such famous men, including some of those just named and adding Ipuwer to the list; but most do not have writings attributed to them. Thus, there is only a partial match between the famous men named in ancient Egyptian sources and the list of surviving pieces of literature. An author as famous as Imhotep has no surviving text attributed to him, and most texts are now anonymous.

The problem of attribution is compounded by the fact that the surviving pieces attributed to specific authors may well be pseudonymous, since connecting compositions with famous names made for wider circulation; and disentangling genuine from pseudonymous works becomes a very difficult undertaking. Names often appear at the ends of compositions; but they are those of the copyist, and most texts clearly say so.

Genre. Did the ancient Egyptian writers think and compose in terms of *genre?* The answer to this question is yes. Although it is not yet clear whether some of the familiar forms used by the ancient Egyptians (again, the tomb biography) were thought of as "literature" (in the sense used here), there are well represented types of literature that modern readers can distinguish as familiar genres.

These are the lyric, the narrative, and the instruction (i.e., the wisdom literature). Modern disagreements tend to center on whether or not a piece is literary and not on which genre it belongs to. This confusion has been increased until recently by the tendency of some scholars to omit most of the pieces in the lyric genre from consideration as literature.

Confusion also arises through modern terms applied to some of the ancient texts. Perhaps the best example is the Pyramid Texts (PT). They are a mélange of various kinds of writing; but the locale is constant (royal pyramids), and their purpose throughout is to aid the "dead" king in his journey to the otherworld to live forever with his siblings, the gods. But among the individual spells—all with the same overarching purpose—are lyric poems (like PT 261 or PT 216). Both pieces are small units that are complete in themselves, imaginative, metaphoric, and lyric: the first likens the king to a bolt of lightning flashing across the sky, and the second places the king in the protecting arms of Atum in the otherworld as the dawn light causes the stars—the king, Orion, and Sothis—to disappear. The overall *purpose* of the Pyramid Texts should not be confused with the *form* of their discrete parts (a dictum that applies also to "magical texts," some of which are lyrics in form while embodying the purpose of asking protection).

A similar problem of genre occurs with the tomb biographies, which sometimes contain narrative (cf. those of Weni and Harkhuf in the Old Kingdom) but seem (to modern eyes) not to be literary in the way that the narrative of *Sinuhe* is. Most tomb biographies, of course, tend to be lists of titles and accomplishments; but the "Catalogue of Virtues" seems to be literary, however stereotypic.

Examination of the three major ancient genres reveals a practice of the ancient Egyptian writers which, for want of a better term, can be called "embeddedness." This well-known practice has important implications. It is the practice of including ("embedding") material which by itself would belong to one genre in the context of another. The practice does not occur so much among lyric pieces; but in some instructions and in several of the narratives it is quite apparent, and it sometimes makes the primary genre of a piece of literature questionable. Perhaps the best example of embeddedness is the *Tale of Sinuhe.* Its primary genre is, of course, narrative. But within this discourse (it is, after all, a "telling"—*dd.f*) occur letters from and to the king, an encomium (also of the king), a song of victory at the defeat of the hero of Retenu, and a prayer of supplication by the princesses. These pieces from the lyric and epistolary genres take up a good portion of the total work; they are embedded in the narrative.

Another example occurs with the piece usually called the *Eloquent Peasant.* Here it is more difficult to decide whether the work should be called a narrative or an instruction. The enveloping story is of the peasant taking his goods to market and encountering obstruction, with the subsequent happy outcome. But the bulk of the work consists of the peasant's nine pleas for justice, which certainly belong to the instructional or didactic literature. In this case, the embedded material seems to be the reason for the framing narrative. We also see the remnants of such embedding in the *Shipwrecked Sailor*.

There is also the issue of subtypes of literature, or subgenres. These are usually quite clear. For instance, the great bulk of the lyric genre consists of hymns and prayers—they form the majority of pieces of surviving ancient Egyptian literature. But there are clearly other kinds of lyrics: love songs, harper's songs, praises of the king (encomiums) and other persons, fragments of work songs, and perhaps others.

There is a similar variety in the instructions. The basic kind is the teaching, which consists of a series of moral observations, or maxims—the wisdom of a father gathered and passed on to a son (Ptahhotep, Amenemope). But the genre is by no means limited to this. We have the so-called instruction of King Amenemhat, which in fact is not a series of maxims but rather a kind of apologia for his life, a testament for his son. There is the *Man Who Was Weary of Life*, which is a philosophical probing of the value of life here and beyond. Or there is the *Prophecy of Neferti*, which is a wise man's vision of the disasters to overcome Egypt preceding the Middle Kingdom. Or, the "instruction" by Khety for his son Pepy, which in fact urges the son to study hard at school and consists of a series of portraits of the misery of those in humble occupations (the "Satire on the Trades"), and provides only a few of the traditional maxims toward the end.

Finally, there is variety in the narratives as well. These include stories of the gods (myths), and a division of the tales that seems to group them into stories of the mundane or everyday, characterized by verisimilitude (*Sinuhe*, *Wenamun*); and there are stories of the marvelous and faraway (the Westcar Tales, the *Contendings of Horus and Seth*, the *Shipwrecked Sailor*). In almost every case the narratives are stories of adventure.

There are other genres or subgenres: the tomb biography; the letter, some examples of which are certainly literary (those in *Sinuhe*, the *Lament of Menna*, and the "literary letter" of Papyrus Anastasi I); and the "schoolboy writings," a mixture of prayers, encomiums, descriptions, and observations on the life of the student.

Finally, indications of genre do exist, but they are not used carefully enough by the ancient authors to be entirely useful to modern scholars. That is, not all works of a given kind bear the same identifying tag, and sometimes the tag occurs where it is misleading. The instructional

literature usually bears the tag *sbȝyt* ("teaching"), but not always; and some other pieces are called by this name. Narratives often are identified by *ḏd.f*, but not all of them; and many kinds of "nonliterary" pieces do have this tag. Lyrics can have the word *dwȝw* ("praising"), to identify hymns and prayers, or *sḥm-ib* ("heart's delight"), which appears for certain love-songs along with *ḥst* ("song"). Unfortunately, none of these terms is fitting in every case.

Historical Development. Egyptian literature, in the sense used here and based on surviving examples, develops only during the late Old Kingdom (sixth dynasty), with the lyrics embedded in the Pyramid Texts and certain of the narrative tomb biographies (if these turn out to be "literary"). It continues with more and more examples of the main genres on through the Middle and New Kingdoms (and on into the later periods of Egyptian history).

The main genres are not, however, all steadily enriching streams. Certainly the lyric genre is there from the beginning of known Egyptian literature; and one sees this genre developing from the desire to "speak" the king into the otherworld. It is religious activity of this sort that seems to bring forth the earliest Egyptian lyrics—attempted manipulation of the gods and their world. From that time on lyrics, especially in the form of hymns and prayers, are abundant.

The instructional literature may or may not go back to the late Old Kingdom, depending on whether the early instructions are composed by the authors whose names are attached to them (like Hordjefef, Kagemni, or Ptahhotep), or whether these instructions are in fact pseudonymous. It is extremely difficult to determine; and as with several pieces of major Egyptian literature, there is still disagreement on dating of texts. At any rate, the instructions seem to have their source in the desire to make permanent the ways of the fathers. The genre is well documented from both the Middle and New Kingdoms. The instructional literature is, in fact, the written repository of the wisdom of the culture, hence the honor of having one's name attached to such a work.

Literary narratives are not met with until the Middle Kingdom, when some of the finest are written (*Sinuhe*, the *Shipwrecked Sailor*. This genre also continues into the New Kingdom, although many of the later examples are fragmentary and seem to be lesser efforts than those of the Middle Kingdom. As the form of *Sinuhe* suggests, the literary narrative could have stemmed as readily from the tomb biography as from a love of adventure and storytelling for its own sake.

It should be reiterated that Egyptian literature is rife with problems of date and authorship. Dating a piece of literature can depend on internal evidence, like the use of language or the mention of specific happenings (but note the backdating of the Westcar Tales and *Neferti*), or on the dating of the papyrus, ostracon, or wall on which the piece was found. And authorship is often plagued (as mentioned before) by the problems of pseudonymous attribution.

Verse Form. Egyptian literature is apparently a verse literature, although the assertion is still in dispute. This conclusion stems from the use of the "verse points" (the red dots marking the text at intervals in many of the papyri and ostraca). If one attempts to reconstruct a viable eclectic text from many surviving copies—as occurs, for instance, with the Hymn to the Nile, one of the most copied texts surviving from antiquity—one places all copies of like passages together in a parallel-text version of the work, lining up the verse points. This process is well known, of course; and the positioning of like passages in parellel aids in deciding which of alternate readings is the better or more nearly corresponds with the ur-text. If one then places the lines one under the other, each line ending in a verse point—that is, sets the text as verse—one discovers that each verse-pointed line is a grammatical clause, and that two such clauses complete a sentence. These are the "thought couplets," whose structuring is the basis of ancient Egyptian verse; and the couplet thus is seen to be the ancient Egyptian verse sentence.

There are variations in the couplet structuring, in the narrative genre in particular and less often in the lyric and instructional genres. The couplet can be varied by occasional use of triplets, quatrains, single lines, and two-element lines; but in no case do these variations overwhelm the basic couplet structure so as to destroy the underlying couplet rhythm. This structural patterning pervades the works of literature from beginning to end.

Here the concept of embeddedness becomes especially relevant. It has been difficult for scholars to determine which pieces are constructed in verse and which in prose, and there is still a good deal of disagreement about the boundaries of the two kinds of literature. First of all, there has been a tendency to limit ancient Egyptian "poetry" (i.e., verse) to the lyric genre—songlike works—with the other two major genres being relegated to prose construction. If one takes an ancient Egyptian lyric (like the Hymn to the Nile, which can be shown to be written in couplets, or verse), and then moves to establish the patterning of, say, *Sinuhe*, one finds that exactly the same general patterning of the couplet pervades this narrative. The idea of embeddedness becomes useful because of the several lyric passages embedded in Sinuhe's narrative. The structuring of the tale continues unchanged from the enveloping narrative through the lyric passages (and even the letters) and back to the narrative. All genres are found to be composed in this couplet form.

It is possible that the *mdwt nfrwt* ("fine speech" or "elegant expression") often met with in conjunction with the Egyptian literary texts may refer to just this structuring in terms of the thought couplet, joined with all the traditional usages of literary embellishment.

Style. The style of ancient Egyptian literature is as varied as the purposes of its authors. Nevertheless, there are some characteristics that can be mentioned as playing a fundamental role in the formation of ancient Egyptian literary works. First of all, there is the ancient division into recognizable genres, even though the boundaries of those genres are not perfectly clear to the modern eye. Then there is the structuring device of the thought couplet. The couplet is not merely a verse sentence that is two clauses long; it also can organize meaning—basically within the couplet, but also continuing into larger structures consisting of couplets—in terms of similarity and contrast, of likeness and difference, between the two halves of the couplet. An earlier (and not quite accurate) term for this is "parallelism of members." In the couplet form the author could express likeness and difference in terms of sound values, word choice, grammatical constructions, and rhetoric. Several of the characteristics of Egyptian verse stem from this basic *twoness* of the couplet. Such elegant playing with language can be clearly seen in the nine complaints of the Eloquent Peasant as he tries to formulate his conception of justice. The nine set pieces seem repetitious and overblown to the modern reader, who wants to get on with the story, until he realizes that the peasant is working all the variations on the implications of the couplet form as he tries to utilize the *mdwt nfrwt* to persuade Rensi of the justice of his cause.

Egyptian verse utilizes all the literary armament of most world literatures: careful word choice, word play (punning), simile and metaphor, alliteration (and thus, presumably, assonance), and the other devices of belles-lettres. Word play is an especially common device, often used to work the variations on a single word or closely related group of words, as in the peasant's eighth complaint, where he explores the single word *maat* (*mȝʿt*): "Do justice for the Lord of Justice, who is the justice of his justice!" A like emphasis is given the word *sḏm* in the *Instruction of Ptahhotep*, where the author plays on the various meanings of the word in its meanings of "to hear" and "to obey."

Comparisons (especially simile and metaphor) are also freely used. The *Man Who Was Weary of Life* is full of this imaginative language. In fact, the man's third song, toward the end of the piece, is entirely a series of comparisons attempting to define his longing for death: it is "like the fragrance of myrrh" or "like a clearing sky."

The style of Egyptian pieces, as one would expect, is more a function of the individual author's intention than a set of predetermined rules. At one end of the spectrum of style there are highly patterned passages like those just mentioned, but at the other end there is a spare and unadorned style, though still structured by the couplet. A good example of the spare style would be the section early in *Sinuhe*, describing his flight from home to the relative safety of Amunenshi's court in Retenu; the passage is characterized stylistically by a series of *sḏm.n.f*s, but little more.

There are one or two other devices that are characteristic of ancient Egyptian style. The first is intermixture—apparently haphazard—of discourse in the second and third persons. This seems to occur only in the lyric genre and may be limited to hymns. A god will be addressed directly (as, for instance, in the opening "you"-form of Leiden Hymn 90), and then the presentation will turn to the third person (the "he"-form). Direct address is followed by third-person description within the single poem, an interchange that occurs rather regularly.

A second aspect of this phenomenon has been called the "participial style" and is contrasted with the "verbal style." That is, new stanzas (as indicated by rubrics in the ancient texts) often open with a participle (the "who"-form) rather than a verbal form such as either the *sḏm.f* or the *sḏm.n.f*. The verse lines of the participial style are augmented by non-verbal clauses. Whichever form is chosen by the author, it is continued for the balance of the stanza.

Although special tags indicating the genre or type of a given piece (*sbȝyt*, *dwȝw*, etc.) are erratically used, there is one characteristic form of some consequence. This is the *sḏm.n.f*, which has long been called the "narrative verb form"; it seems indeed to be employed for the purposes of narration, but limited in literature to the narrative genre. Its use is rare or absent in the lyric and instructional genres.

The tone (the attitude of the author toward his work) of Egyptian literature is as various as the authors composing it—that is, the tone is specific to the purpose of the individual work. This is a truism, but the range of tone is quite extensive in surviving Egyptian literature. There is the debilitating despair of the *Man Who Was Weary of Life;* there is the pedagogical stance of most of the maxim texts; the excitement of adventure and far places in many of the stories; the humility of the prayers; and the awe and joy expressed in the hymns, reaching to near-ecstasy in Akhenaten's Hymn to the Sun. Given what is at most a pitiful remnant of what ancient Egyptian literature must have been, there is still a rich range of attitude and emotion in the pieces we have.

Finally, there seem to have been no radical changes in style in Egyptian literature as it unfolded from the Old Kingdom through the New. There were some changes in the language itself from Old Egyptian to Middle Egyptian; and there was a marked change from Middle Egyptian to Late Egyptian. Yet the Egyptian style was more a function of the individual author's purpose—within the limits of the thought couplet, with its patterning of likeness and difference—than of changes in the language.

Sources. How much of ancient Egyptian literature survives? That is impossible to tell. So often the Egyptian texts are fragmentary: papyri are tattered, hardly legible, and ridden with lacunae; ostraca (which were often used for "scrap paper" by both workmen and schoolboys) are faded, abraded, and broken; and the walls on which the hieroglyphic signs were once carved are razed, broken, or fallen. Even so, every now and then pieces of ancient texts appear—usually only fragments—the readings of which will fill lacunae in known texts or offer confirmations or variants of known readings. Rarely, an entire new text will appear. New material, some of it literary, is regularly recovered from the sands and tombs of Egypt and offers the prospect of further study.

Modern scholars are limited by what has been recovered, by the vagaries of preservation, and by the physical condition of the items. While there is no way to assess the amount of missing literary work, one can determine the find-spots and the places in which literature was preserved by the ancient Egyptians. The surviving literature seems to derive from court, temple, schoolroom, and tomb. In addition, there must surely have been a rich oral tradition in Egypt, but by its very nature it no longer exists, except for tantalizing hints in the written literature.

The more affluent Egyptians were buried with a copy of the *Book of Going Forth by Day* (the *Book of the Dead*), a New Kingdom compilation of prayers, hymns, and spells (much like the royal Pyramid Texts of the Old Kingdom) which were meant to facilitate the deceased's passage to the otherworld and to ease his journeying within it. There are innumerable copies of this work, and they exhibit many variants in both wording and choice of spells. Another source, from Deir el-Medina in Western Thebes, consists of a large cache of New Kingdom ostraca from the scribal school, numbering in the thousands, which was the trash heap for writings no longer wanted and thus disposed of in a large pit. The recovered pieces include many passages, usually fragmentary, of the literary texts the schoolboys were set to copying as they became literate and familiar with the Hieratic script. Among these were some entirely new texts (e.g., Menna's *Lament*, a letter to his wayward son) and many fragments of what must have been the classics of the Egyptian tradition—at least according to the teachers at Deir el-Medina. There have also been small collections of papyri, from tombs and temples especially, with more or less complete copies of other literary texts. In many cases the find spot is unknown or undocumented, since the papyri were purchased rather than excavated under controlled conditions.

Study. Egyptology, as a field of scientific study, is not much more than a century and a half old. The hieroglyphs were deciphered in 1822 by Jean-François Champollion, and the tomb of King Tutankhamun was discovered in 1922. The study of the Egyptian language during this time has been somewhat overshadowed by the stunning finds of the archeologist and the visual splendors of the ancient civilization. Nevertheless, students of the language have been working with the rules of grammar, the range of meanings of words (which often have had to have their very denotations established), and the sequences of sentences in the language. This is an ongoing effort. But because of this effort to rescue the language, and because of the similar effort to establish the facts of the history of ancient Egypt—from its own point of view—ancient Egyptian literature has tended to be the handmaid of Egyptian linguistics and history. If one looks at the early translations of Egyptian literary works, one finds them halting and often inaccurate. Improvement has come with the establishment of a tradition of translating these works so that previous attempts can provide comparative readings for later scholars to work with. Only in the past twenty-five or thirty years has there been a burst of activity centering on Egyptian literature itself, and this has resulted in a wide-ranging investigation of the specifically literary texts and the literary language in which they are expressed.

[*See also* Biographies; Funerary Literature; *the articles on* Hymns; Narratives; Oral Tradition; Wisdom Tradition; *and articles on particular literary works.*]

BIBLIOGRAPHY

Texts
Note: Bibliographical details, sources, and critical commentary for ancient Egyptian literature can be found in *Lexikon der Ägyptologie,* edited by Wolfgang Helck, Wolfhart Westendorf, and Eberhard Otto. 7 vols. Wiesbaden, 1975–1992. For parallel texts, see volumes in the series Kleine Ägyptische Texte, edited by Wolfgang Helck.
Blackman, A. M. *The Story of King Kheops and the Magicians.* Edited by W. V. Davies. Reading, 1988.
Koch, Roland. *Die Erzählung des Sinuhe.* Bibliotheca Aegyptica, 17. Brussels, 1990.
Parkinson, R. B. *The Tale of the Eloquent Peasant.* Oxford, 1991.

Translations
Foster, John L. *Love Songs of the New Kingdom.* New York, 1974; reprinted, Austin, Tex., 1992.
Foster, John L. *Echoes of Egyptian Voices.* Norman, Okla., 1992.
Foster, John L. *Hymns, Prayers, and Songs: An Anthology of Ancient Egyptian Lyric Verse.* Atlanta, 1995.
Lichtheim, Miriam. *Ancient Egyptian Literature.* 2 vols. Los Angeles, 1973–1978.
Parkinson, R. B. *The Tale of Sinuhe and Other Ancient Egyptian Poems 1940–1640 BC.* Oxford, 1997.
Parkinson, R. B. *Voices from Ancient Egypt.* Norman, Okla., 1991.
Simpson, William Kelly ed. *The Literature of Ancient Egypt.* New ed. New Haven, 1973.

Studies
Burkard, Günter. *Überlegungen zur Form der Ägyptischen Literatur.* Wiesbaden, 1993.
Loprieno, Antonio, ed. *Ancient Egyptian Literature.* Leiden, 1996. Includes an excellent, extensive, and up-to-date general bibliography.
Mathieu, Bernard. *La poésie amoureuse de L'Égypte ancienne.* Cairo, 1996.

JOHN L. FOSTER

LOAN WORDS. *See* Vocabulary.

LOOMS. *See* Weaving, Looms, and Textiles.

LOTUS. Blue and white water lilies, *Nymphaea cerulea* and *Nymphaea albicans,* were native to the Nile River in antiquity. Egyptologists have universally called them "lotus," despite the fact that botanists reserve that apellation to the pink genus *Nelumbo,* which probably entered Egypt with the Persian conquest c.522 BCE. Since this misnomer

LOTUS. *Faience chalice in the form of a lotus, from Aniba, eighteenth dynasty.* (University of Pennsylvania Museum, Philadelphia. Neg. # S4–143065)

is so entrenched in the literature of Egyptology, we will follow that convention for ease of comprehension.

The blue lotus is day blooming, opening shortly after dawn and again closing tightly in mid-morning. Each blooms for three days. The petals are blue with coloration most intense at the periphery. The calyx is a brilliant yellow and the blossom has a pleasing aroma to supplement its attractive appearance. Its distribution along the Nile favored Upper Egypt, while papyrus grew in the marshes of the Delta. They became the symbols of Upper and Lower Egypt respectively, owing to this geographic distinction. The blue lotus's day blooming mimics the sun appearing in the blue sky—a botanical reflection of the cosmic daily rebirth of the sun and of rebirth in the afterlife. It was a perfect multilevel symbol of the complex intertwining political and religious belief system and thus its appearance in ancient Egyptian literature and imagery was ubiquitous.

The lotus is mentioned in the Ebers Papyrus, where it is designated as a poison. The hieroglyphic name *sšn* is reinforced by depiction of the blossom. Modern toxicological analysis has identified four potent narcotic alkaloids in *Nymphaea*—nymphaeine, nuciferine, nupharidine, and alpha-nupharidine. They are found only in the blossoms and rhizomes (roots) and are soluble in alcohol but not in water. Hieroglyphic texts do not designate color unless a blue pigment was used. The narcotic properties (and potential for poison), are confirmed in modern texts on herbal medicine and toxopharmacology. Nevertheless, the fiction that the lotus is innocuous persists in the literature of both Egyptology and standard botany, perpetuating an error from the Napoleonic era.

The association of wine and lotus blossoms becomes increasingly common from the New Kingdom throughout the later dynasties, in depictions of banquets and in funerary-offering depictions. Modern wines have an alcohol content in the 10 to 17 percent range. It is reasonable to believe that ancient wines did, too, and thus could dissolve the narcotic alkaloids. The Egyptians may well have appreciated the effect of lotus-enhanced wine.

Women are depicted in ancient Egyptian scenes harvesting lotus blossoms and extracting the essence with a twisted cloth press. The ultimate use was not indicated, but it could have been for perfume, medicine, or to enhance wines. The latter is supported by numerous New Kingdom banquet scenes showing young female servants pouring an unidentified liquid from tiny vials into much larger wine bowls. The inclusion of so many open blue lotuses in such scenes further indicates they were held during the very early morning, in the brief period in which they bloomed; this biological clock functions the same for the cut blossom as for the intact plant.

The white lotus is night blooming and its image is en-

countered primarily on drinking vessels. These containers probably were for daily use, whereas the blue lotus vessels were reserved for ritual purposes.

[*See also* Flora; *and* Flowers.]

BIBLIOGRAPHY

Harer, W. Benson, Jr. "Pharmacological and Biological Properties of the Egyptian Lotus." *Journal of the America Research Center in Egypt* 22 (1985), 49–54.

W. BENSON HARER, JR., M.D.

LOWER EGYPT, or *T3-mḥw* ("the land of the papyrus plant," "the northern land"), comprised essentially the Nile Delta. It constituted half of the cultural and political duality that formed the totality of ancient Egypt. According to the dualism that permeated ancient Egyptian thought, the Egyptian state was a unity composed of two separate but equal and balanced opposites: Upper Egypt—the narrow, geologically defined Nile Valley; and Lower Egypt—the flat, broad Nile Delta, whose fan shape reminded Herodotus of the Greek letter *delta* (Δ). According to the mythic paradigms of divine kingship and political unity accepted in ancient Egypt, these two archetypal geopolitical divisions were unified into a single entity through the person and office of the pharaoh: under the sovereignty of the king as ruler of Upper and Lower Egypt, "The Two Lands" became one. Official tradition held that Lower and Upper Egypt were united by Menes, a semilegendary figure revered as the first king of unified Egypt. This same Menes is also credited with founding Egypt's first capital, Memphis, at the juncture of Lower and Upper Egypt.

Lower Egypt's tutelary deity was Wadjet, the cobra goddess, one of the Two Ladies protecting the pharaoh. Wadjet's cult was associated with the site of Buto, present-day Tell el-Fara'in, which is identified with "Pe and Dep," the semimythical Predynastic twin capitals of Lower Egypt and the location of Lower Egypt's traditional shrine (an archetypal, pavilion-type shrine, known as the *pr-nw* or *pr-nsr* and shaped like a box with a domed roof with high posts on either side). The "souls of Pe" were mythical falcon-headed figures connected with Buto. The heraldic plant of Lower Egypt was the papyrus, and the Red Crown, or *dšrt*, symbolized Lower Egypt as a political entity. Iconographically, all these symbols could represent Lower Egypt.

Like Upper Egypt, Lower Egypt had its own system of nomes or provinces by Old Kingdom times. The first Lower Egyptian nome was located around Memphis, also the nome capital, and it occupied a transitional zone between the Delta and the Nile Valley. Both the number and boundaries of Lower Egyptian nomes were more fluid than those of Upper Egypt, and not until Greco-Roman times was the definitive number of twenty Lower Egyptian nomes established. Political, communication, and transport lines in Lower Egypt followed Delta watercourses, which shifted, sometimes significantly, over time. Movement north and south was comparatively easy; east to west was problematic. Sites in Lower Egypt were positioned along watercourses, often creating a dynamic and symbiotic interplay between site formation and channel development. This active shifting of watercourses and settlements has contributed to the development of Lower Egypt's complex and inadequately understood settlement pattern.

Physical Development and Characteristics. Recent research, including radiocarbon-dated material from deep estuarine cores and borings, places the origin of the present Delta at about 6500–5500 BCE, in an era of decelerated sea-level rise. The data show an abrupt transition at that time throughout the Delta from sand-dominant to mud-rich deposits. The transition reflects a major depositional change that transformed the region from a partially vegetated sandy plain to a rich, silt-covered floodplain. The slower rate of sea-level rise, combined with regional fluctuations in Holocene climate and associated flood levels, resulted in growing accumulations of Nile silt and the creation of a broadening, seasonally flooded, fertile alluvial plain in the Delta. Sea-level rise reduced the river-course gradient, leading to the formation of a system of meandering Nile distributaries and increased overbank silt deposition. Over the past approximately eight thousand years, evolution of the Delta plain has continued, resulting in average silt depositions now measuring 10–15 meters (32–50 feet), with local thicknesses (below Lake Manzalah) up to 50 meters (162 feet). The rate of sedimentation varied over time, with accumulation increasing during times of rising sea levels or lower river discharge, and decreasing during times of sea retreat or higher river discharge. Today the Delta comprises some 22,000 square kilometers (14,500 square miles) of fertile floodplain, twice that of Upper Egypt, with a Mediterranean coastline some 225 kilometers (140 miles) long. Its radius from coast to apex area at Cairo is approximately 160 kilometers (100 miles); elevation decreases from 18 meters (55 feet) above sea level at Cairo to 1 meter (3.2 feet) or less along the coast. Butzer (1974) estimated Delta territory in antiquity at about 17,000 square kilometers (10,540 square miles), accounting for 58 percent of ancient Egyptian territory. The current Nile apex, where the river splits into two modern branches, lies about 25 kilometers (16 miles) northwest of Cairo and 38 kilometers (24 miles) north of Memphis. Tousson (1925) placed the ancient apex farther south at Boulaq; Butzer (1974) put it some 60 kilometers (38 miles) upstream of Memphis.

The ancient Delta constituted a distinctive ecozone with highly individual geomorphic and biotic attributes. Its natural flood regime differed from that of the Nile Valley, as floodwaters spread over multiple distributaries with resulting lower flood crests and correspondingly lower natural levees. Large portions of the Delta were inundated and uninhabitable for several months each year. Many basins tended to form seasonal or perennial swamps and remained marshy long after floodwaters drained off; papyrus swamps developed where permanent fresh waters remained. Scattered Pleistocene sand mounds, known as "geziras" or "turtlebacks," and sand flats representing stabilized ancient dune fields formed topographic highs above most flood levels. These provided favored sites for ancient settlement. To the north, the Delta grew increasingly marshy before merging with coastal lagoons, wetlands, salt flats, lakes, and sand dunes. Brackish lagoons evolved into lakes when cut off from the sea by silt and sand bars that were formed by the eastward longshore sea currents. Coastal lagoons generally never extended south of the modern 2-meter (6.5-foot) contour line. The northern reaches of the Delta seem to have been settled only marginally, at best, for most of antiquity, and major Delta harbors apparently lay mostly inland along main Nile channels rather than on the coast.

Natural Delta development and environment changed in response to the interplay of Nile branches, eustatic sea level, and coastal processes. The southeastern Mediterranean, including the Delta shoreline, was characterized by a very low tidal range, north to northwest offshore winds active during much of the year, and a large-scale counterclockwise circulation pattern that drove water masses eastward. With time, active coastal processes interacted with Nile sediment discharged at the coast, to produce the arcuate coastline shape, with its coastal barriers and dune fields. Wetlands of marsh and shallow lagoons then formed landward of the sand barriers and dune fields. Northern Delta cores suggest that these wetlands shifted continuously; according to Said (1993), Lake Manzaleh probably originated during the seventh century CE.

The Delta lies in a highly arid region subject to unpredictable annual fluctuations in Nile flow. Egypt's dynastic era began after its climate had become hyperarid and stream discharge was significantly reduced; aridification reached its present level by about 4500 years before present. Water management was a basic and constant challenge for even the earliest settlers. Development and modification of the natural Delta flood regime continued and increased throughout historical times, along with agricultural intensification, land reclamation, and a growing population. All peaked in Ptolemaic times. Intensive development required technological advances in irrigation and drainage and was possibly hindered by endemic diseases, such as malaria.

For much of the Holocene, a number of diverging Nile channels, whose location, size, and existence varied over time, have crossed the Delta. As many as seven principal and five secondary Nile mouths are attested in variously dated texts and maps, located between the Pelusiac branch on the east and the Canopic on the west. Deep coring suggests that western and central Nile Delta distributaries dominated during late prehistoric times, building out subdeltas beyond the modern coastline. The eastern branches were unimportant initially, carrying little sediment, and the northeastern coastal zone filled in only during or after the New Kingdom when the shoreline pushed out 30–40 kilometers. Butzer (1974) proposed three initial major Nile branches, debouching at approximately the classic Rosetta, Sebennytic, and Damietta mouths. Bietak (1975) reconstructed five major branches during the Ramessid period: "the western river" (Canopic), "the water of Ptah" (Bolbitine/Rosetta), "the large river" (Sebennytic), "the water of Amon" (Phtametic/Bucolic/Damietta), and "the water of Pre" (Pelusiac?). The ancient Greek historian Herodotus mentioned five principal branches: the Canopic, Sebennytic, Mendesian, Saitic (Tanitic), and Pelusiac. Strabo and his contemporaries in antiquity enumerated seven: the Canopic, Bolbitine (Rosetta), Sebennytic, Phtametic (Damietta), Mendesian, Tanitic, and Pelusiac. Today, only two principal Nile channels, the Damietta and Rosetta, remain active. According to Said (1993), the Pelusiac branch began silting up during a period of low Niles in the second millennium BCE, when it became separated from the sea by a series of accretional coastal sand ridges. The Canopic branch silted up as a result of the reexcavation of the Bolbitine (Rosetta) branch about 300 BCE. The other Nile branches disappeared during the eleventh, thirteenth, and seventeenth centuries CE, during times of exceptionally low Nile discharge.

Lower Egypt in Egyptological Research. Until recently, Lower Egypt was underinvestigated and largely ignored by traditional Egyptological scholarship. Only within the last two to three decades have our knowledge and understanding of the Delta advanced significantly, partly from renewed interest in the region, partly due to the adoption of a broader, more contextual view of Egyptian archaeology, and partly because of the development and application of more sophisticated analytical techniques and technologies.

Following an initial flurry of archaeological investigation approximately a hundred years ago, largely driven by biblical concerns, the study of Lower Egypt became a research backwater as a bias developed in Egyptology toward Nile valley material. Borghouts commented as recently as 1986 that: "In many respects our idea of the history of Egypt is . . . the history of the region starting with Heliopolis and stretching further south deep into the Sudan. Our view of the history of the Delta is indeed meagre when compared to that."

Two main factors account for the marginalization of Delta research. First, geological and geomorphological studies of the area were limited in number and scope until recently. The physical development and characteristics of the Delta were consequently misunderstood and misinterpreted for many years. Earlier scholars assumed that Lower Egypt remained an uninhabitable, inhospitable swamp until relatively late in Egyptian history. They also believed that archaeological remains were deeply buried by centuries of flood deposits. Such preconceptions and misconceptions were reinforced by an object-oriented view of Egyptian culture and archaeology, which focused on cemeteries, temples, and the recovery of museum-quality objects, inscriptions, and monumental architecture—material present primarily in Upper Egypt. By comparison, the alluvial Delta, with its lack of natural resources, predominantly urban remains of decayed mud bricks, and complicated stratigraphic sequences was of little interest.

Recent research and fieldwork has begun to rectify the situation, although Delta history and archaeology remain poorly understood in general. While much cultural material lies deeply buried, often far below today's high water table, even this may be recovered through use of appropriate techniques, such as pumping, coring, and remote sensing. Other finds are easily accessible and surface surveys have produced significant results. A survey by van den Brink (1993) in the eastern Delta recorded ninety-two sites in two seasons and documented a shift to a more clustered, possibly more hierarchically structured Old Kingdom settlement pattern from an earlier linear, egalitarian pattern.

Many sites are known almost solely through texts, and Delta archaeology in general is complex and problematic. Careful research programs correlating textual and archaeological data wherever possible are required for interpretation, since earlier cultural levels are often underrepresented archaeologically, and stone structures and statues erected at one location often served as quarries for others. Our information on the Delta remains enormously fragmentary and our knowledge of its occupational character, patterns, intensity, and development is limited. A large proportion of Delta sites have been destroyed or severely damaged since 1800, limiting opportunities to gather further data. Egypt's burgeoning population and its industrial and agricultural development pressures threaten remaining Lower Egyptian sites. Despite best efforts and intentions, few will likely survive much longer. It is imperative that additional research and preservation take place as soon as possible.

History and Settlement. Lower Egypt was influenced, to varying degrees at different times, by its geographical position: north was the Mediterranean Sea with its maritime routes; east was the Sinai Peninsula and Syria-Palestine; west was the Libyan frontier. Although the coast was generally inhospitable, the Delta became increasingly receptive to Mediterranean influences, and internal Delta harbors became important for foreign ventures, especially during and after the New Kingdom. Protection of the permeable and vulnerable eastern and western borders was a constant concern. Substantial contacts with Canaan are attested as early as Predynastic and Early Dynastic times; during the Second Intermediate Period, Canaanite Hyksos ruled Egypt from their eastern Delta kingdom. Old Kingdom assaults by Libyan peoples from the Western Desert are recorded, apparently resulting from deteriorating desert ecological conditions. By Ramessid times, Libyans attempted to settle in the Delta, and Ramesses II built a series of forts to guard the western border. In the Third Intermediate Period, dynasties of Libyan origin ruled Egypt. Traditionally, and especially in times of weak central government, the Delta was both refuge and magnet for populations to its east and west, and migrant Libyans and Near Easterners settled permanently or briefly.

In antiquity, Lower Egypt was especially famed for its wine, cattle, and marsh hunting grounds teeming with fish and wild birds. When fully developed, the Delta was a lush land of agriculture, horticulture, viticulture, and stock raising. Cattle herding was economically important from earliest through Roman times; a quarter of Lower Egyptian nome symbols included cattle.

Important Lower Egyptian centers such as Buto and Maadi existed already in the Predynastic period. Earlier scholars believed in the literal reality of Egypt's symbolic geography and reconstructed a prehistoric northern kingdom; recent research, however, has invalidated this hypothesis. Increasing numbers of established towns and cult centers are known to have existed in Early Dynastic times, and archaeological data from the eastern Delta suggest locally dense settlement patterns. Nome capitals, known from Old Kingdom times, served as religious centers and seats of provincial bureaucracy and political power. Some, such as Bubastis and Mendes, remained stable for millennia; others shifted location or came into being as the sociopolitical and economic structure of the Delta changed with fluctuating political fortunes, shifting population patterns, and moving water channels. Occasionally remnants of ancient centers lie within modern cities, proof of remarkable occupational continuity and importance. Old Kingdom records attest numerous estates and royal land grants in the Delta, some linked to the founding of new villages, suggesting that territory was freely available. By the New Kingdom, especially in Ramessid times, Lower Egypt increasingly dominated Egyptian

political and economic life, partly due to its proximity to the Mediterranean world. In the first millennium BCE, the Delta became the economic heartland of the politically splintered country. Rival families from different Delta cities competed for power, and small city-based principalities throughout the Delta began a period of growth and prosperity that continued into the early centuries CE. Population increased substantially during Ptolemaic times, especially in the Alexandria-Naukratis sector. Various Nile channels were maintained by excavation, and intensified irrigation and wetland-drainage projects substantially modified the Delta surface. Delta land was still available for new colonists.

The Memphite area was always one of the most populous and renowned of Egypt. Memphis was the royal residence and capital of Egypt during Early Dynastic and Old Kingdom times and continued to be a major administrative center throughout Egyptian history. Many later kings maintained palaces there, and Memphite temples were among the most important in Egypt. Its harbor and workshops played major roles in foreign trade. Only Thebes compared to Memphis in political, economic, and religious importance. Although the city remains largely unknown, buried beneath modern fields and villages, the magnificent Memphite cemeteries extend more than 30 kilometers (19 miles) along the desert's edge, hinting at both city size and shifting urban foci through time. Just northeast of Memphis was Letopolis (Ausim), capital of the second Lower Egyptian nome. Ancient Heliopolis (Tell Hisn), center of the influential sun cult and capital of the thirteenth Lower Egyptian nome, lay northwest of modern Heliopolis.

Major settlements west of the Rosetta Nile branch included the important Predynastic site of Merimda Beni-Salama; Terenuthis (Kom Abu Billu), controlling approaches to the Wadi Natrun; and Imu (Kom el-Hisn), capital of the third Lower Egyptian nome, at least from New Kingdom times. In the twenty-sixth dynasty, Naukratis was founded as a Greek trading post; Amasis granted the city a monopoly over Greek trade with Egypt. Also Greek was Alexandria, founded in 332 BCE by Alexander the Great. Never a true Egyptian city, Alexandria served as chief city and seaport of the Hellenistic world. On the mouth of the Canopic Nile branch was Canopus (Aboukir), one of the few sites located on the Mediterranean coast.

The area east of the former Tanitic Nile arm encompasses some of the best known and most completely explored territory to date. Major ancient settlements included Bubastis (Tell Basta), founded by at least Old Kingdom times, capital of the eighteenth Lower Egyptian nome during the Late period, seat of the twenty-second Daphnae (Tell Defenneh) dynasty, and cult city sacred to the cat goddess Bastet. Northeast was a substantial urban sector, densely populated from at least Middle Kingdom times, incorporating the Hyksos capital of Avaris (Tell ed-Dabʾa) and the great Delta residency of the Ramessid kings, Piramesse (Qantir). Farther north lay Tanis (San el-Hagar), residence and burial place of the kings of the twenty-first and twenty-second dynasties, and Late period capital of the nineteenth Lower Egyptian nome; Imet (Tell Nabasha/Farʾun/Bedawi), nome capital of a district divided during the New Kingdom; and a series of late Predynastic–Early Dynastic sites, including Minshat Abu Omar. Other significant settlements in the northeastern Delta included Leontopolis (Tell el-Yahudiyya), Per-Sopdu (Saft el-Hinna), Tell Retabah, and Pithom (Tell el-Maskhuta) in the Wadi Tumilat, Tell Hebwa, Tell el-Herr, and, on the former Pelusiac branch and Mediterranean shore, Pelusium (Tell Farama).

In the northwest-central portion of the Delta was Sais (Sa el-Hagar), the residence city of the twenty-sixth dynasty and the ancient cult center of Neith, ideologically important Buto, occupied from Predynastic times, and Xois (Sakha), the poorly known capital of the sixth Lower Egyptian nome and putative seat of the fourteenth dynasty. Farther south and east are Athribis (Tell Atrib), capital of the tenth Lower Egyptian nome; Leontopolis (Tell el-Muqdam), capital of the eleventh Lower Egyptian nome during the Ptolemaic period; and Diospolis (Bela-mun), capital of the seventeenth Lower Egyptian nome. To the north lay Sebennytos (Samannud), capital of the twelfth Lower Egyptian nome and seat of the thirtieth dynasty; Iseum (Behbeit el-Hagar), site of a major Isis temple; Hermopolis Parva (el-Baqliya), capital of the fifteenth Lower Egyptian nome; Mendes (Tell el-Rubʾa), capital of the sixteenth Lower Egyptian nome and the possible seat of the twenty-ninth dynasty, and its twin city Thmuis (Tell el-Timai), which rose to prominence in Greco-Roman times at the expense of Mendes.

[*See also articles on various Lower Egyptian sites.*]

BIBLIOGRAPHY

Aufrere, S., and J.-Cl. Golvin. *L'Égypte Restituée, Tome 3: Sites, Temples et Pyramides de Moyenne et Basse Égypte*. Paris, 1997. Useful archaeological overview summarizing our knowledge of different sites by region.

Baines, I., and J. Málek. *Atlas of Ancient Egypt*. New York, 1984. Invaluable summary of a variety of information, including regional and site synopses.

Bietak, M. *Tell ed-Dabʿa II*. Vienna, 1975. A masterful historical geographical study of the eastern Delta, from an archaeological perspective, that includes reconstructions of former Nile channels based on modern contour maps.

Borghouts, J. F. "Surveying the Delta: Some Retrospects and Prospects." In *The Archaeology of the Nile Delta: Problems and Priorities*, edited by E. C. M. Van den Brink, pp. 3–8. Amsterdam, 1988.

Butzer, K. "Delta." In *Lexikon der Ägyptologie*, 1: 1043–1052. Wiesbaden, 1974. Concise, detailed summary of physical development and characteristics of the Delta, incorporating selected cultural and economic data.

James, T. G. H. *Ancient Egypt: The Land and Its Legacy*. Austin, 1990. A general overview of various geographical regions of ancient Egypt, reviewing major sites and excavations, and including a chapter on the Delta.

Said, R. *The River Nile: Geology, Hydrology and Utilization*. New York, 1993. A major synthesis dealing with the origin, evolution, and hydrology of the Nile River, including sections on the Delta.

Sestini, G. "Nile Delta: A Review of Depositional Environments and Geological History." In *Deltas: Sites and Traps for Fossil Fuels*, edited by M. K. G. Whateley and K. T. Pickering. Boston, 1989. Reviews geological history and summarizes modern environments and processes, as well as subsurface stratigraphy and structure.

Stanley, D. J., and A. G. Warne. "Sea Level and Initiation of Predynastic Culture in the Nile Delta." *Nature* 363 (1993), 435–438. Correlates recent research into development of modern Nile Delta and the first Predynastic settlements in the region.

Stanley, D. J., and A. G. Warne. "Nile Delta in its Destruction Phase." *Journal of Coastal Research* 14 (1998), 794–825. Comprehensive review of geomorphology, hydrology, and development of the Nile Delta from geologic to modern times.

Tousson, O. *Mémoire sur l'Histoire du Nil*. Cairo, 1925. Extensive work dealing with numerous aspects of the Nile River, especially important for Arabic sources.

Van den Brink, E. C. M., ed. *The Archaeology of the Nile Delta: Problems and Priorities*. Amsterdam, 1988. Important collection of articles dealing with the archaeology of the Nile Delta, comprising the proceedings of a seminar held in Cairo in 1986.

Van den Brink, E. C. M., ed. *The Nile Delta in Transition: 4th.–3rd. Millennium B.C.* Tel Aviv, 1992. Invaluable collection of articles dealing with the archaeology and geology of the Nile Delta in the fourth to third millennia BCE, comprising the proceedings of a seminar on the topic held in Cairo in 1990.

Van den Brink, E. C. M. "Settlement Patterns in the Northeastern Nile Delta during the Fourth–Second Millennia B.C." In *Environmental Change and Human Culture in the Nile basin and Northern Africa until the Second Millennium B.C.*, edited by Krzyzaniak, M. Kobusiewicz, and J. Alexander. Poznan, 1993. Presents results of an archaeological and palaeogeographical survey of 90 square kilometers in Sharqiya governorate in the northeastern Delta, concentrating on the late Predynastic–Early Dynastic and Old Kingdom finds.

Wilson, J. A. "Buto and Hierakonpolis in the Geography of Egypt," *Journal of Near Eastern Studies* 14 (1955), 209–236. Interesting study and comparison of modern provinces and ancient Egyptian nomes in the Nile Valley and Delta.

CAROL A. REDMOUNT

LUXOR, the name attached today both to the present-day metropolis of the region that was ancient Thebes and to the temple, situated beside the Nile's eastern bank, which adjoins the town (25°41′N, 32°24′E). It derives from the Arabic *al-uksur*, "the fortifications," which in turn was adapted from the Latin *castrum*, which referred to the Roman fort built around the temple in the later third century CE. The temple's earlier name, in Egyptian, was *ipt rsyt*, the "southern sanctuary," referring to the restricted "holy of holies" at the temple's southern end, wherein its principal god dwelt. This being was a fertility god, and his statue was modeled on that of the similarly endowed Min of Coptos. He was called "Amun, preeminent in his sanctuary" which was later shortened to "Amenemope."

Despite the presence of elements from Middle Kingdom buildings reused in its construction, the Luxor temple can be traced back no earlier than the eighteenth dynasty. Perhaps the earliest reference to it in ancient records comes from the twenty-second year of the reign of Ahmose (c.1548 BCE), on a pair of stelae left at Maâsara quarry, in the hills east of Memphis; this text records the extraction of limestone for a number of temples, including "the mansion of Amun in the Sou[thern] Sanctuary." When that building was constructed, and what it looked like, are both unknown, for structural evidence appears at Luxor only during the joint reign of Hatshepsut (c.1502–1482) and Thutmose III: these elements are built into the triple shrine erected by Ramesses II (c.1304–1237) inside his first court, which reuses elements from an original chapel dedicated by these mid-eighteenth dynasty rulers. This small building had apparently been the last of six "rest stops" built along the road that brought Amun and his circle of gods from Karnak to Luxor every year during the Opet festival. Although the axis of Ramesses II's courtyard is skewed vis-à-vis the rest of the temple, so that it aligns with the road to Karnak outside, the shrine is situated in a way that maintains an axial relationship with the sanctuary inside the temple—a peculiarity that might suggest that the Ramessid triple shrine was deliberately rebuilt on the same spot as its eighteenth dynasty predecessor. No other remains of a Thutmosid temple at Luxor can be identified, nor is it clear whether it was this building or an earlier one that witnessed the god Amun's alleged "prediction" of Hatshepsut's kingship in the second year of an unspecified ruler; although many fragments dating to Thutmose III have been found recycled in later buildings on the site, it cannot yet be proved that they originally came from there. Thus, any remnants of a mid-eighteenth dynasty temple at Luxor are still to be sought beneath the present temple.

Most of the temple of Luxor in its present state was built by Amenhotpe III (c.1410–1372) in three phases. First was the temple proper, at the south end of the site. Behind a columned portico lies the entrance to what was originally another columned hall, flanked by a number of chapels that accommodated the processional shrines of Amun (west) as well as Khonsu and Mut (east) when they visited Luxor during the Opet festival. The columns inside the hall were removed in later antiquity when this room was transformed into the sanctuary of the Roman fort: an apse, painted with figures of Diocletian (284–305 CE) and his three coregents, was inserted into the back wall at this time (blocking the earlier doorway), with the emperors'

entourage painted onto the plaster that covered the pharaonic reliefs throughout the rest of this room (see John Baines and Jaromír Malek, *Atlas of Ancient Egypt* [Oxford, 1980], p. 87, for nineteenth-century paintings of these Roman decorations, which are now nearly all destroyed). The small chapels at the sides of the original hall have been identified as belonging to the divine king's processional shrine (east) and his *ka*-statue (west), when they were lodged inside the temple during the Opet festival. Beyond the modern doorway that now cuts through the bottom of the Roman apse is the temple's offering hall: its walls are carved with offering scenes that feature Amenhotpe III, sometimes accompanied by a priestess called the "god's wife"; and a doorway at the room's southeast corner led originally to a passage through which provisions and river water were introduced. The room that opens to the south of the offering hall was the "bark sanctuary" that accommodated the boat-shaped processional shrine of Amun of Luxor, along with that belonging to Amun of Karnak on its annual visit. The door that now connects this room with the "holy of holies" to the south is a modern descendant of a doorway inserted during Greco-Roman times: in Amenhotpe III's original plan, these areas did not connect except symbolically, through a gigantic false door (of which virtually nothing remains) on the bark sanctuary's south wall. The room itself is now filled by an open-ended shrine that was inserted at the instance of Alexander the Great, probably in recognition of the Luxor temple's role in Amun's begetting the pharaoh (Alexander equated Amun with Zeus and regarded him as his own heavenly father).

This "divine birth" was ritually reenacted in a pair of rooms east of the bark sanctuary and the offering hall. In the so-called birth room the scenes that show Amenhotpe III being engendered by Amun and then recognized as king by other divine beings are prototypes for those found inside the *mammisi* or birth-houses that were regularly attached to temples in Greco-Roman times. Themes of recognition and coronation also dominate in the room to the south, beside the bark sanctuary; and along the east walls of both these rooms are niches to hold statues of some of the divinities associated with the cult at Luxor. Such a transition to the temple's role as a divine residence is not haphazard, for it is in the southeast corner of the birth suite that we find the only access to the "southern sanctuary" proper. In this restricted area dwelt Amun of Luxor, his statue kept inside a commodious chapel, with statues of other divinities lodged in niches off the outer rooms of this suite. The architecture of the suite's central hall, with its twelve columns (perhaps corresponding to the hours of the day and the night), along with the reliefs carved in this room and Amun's inner sanctum, are suggestive of the cyclical regeneration of nature, which includes the god himself when he is symbolically brought

LUXOR. *The colonnade of Tutankhamun at the temple of Luxor.*

back to life through the Opening of the Mouth ceremony performed by his son, the king. These themes in the late eighteenth dynasty decoration of the Luxor temple may well anticipate the more complex "rebirths" that would be enacted later, when the god of Luxor regularly took part in the Feast of the Decade.

The second phase of Amenhotpe III's work at Luxor involved the construction of a "sun court" in front of his temple. His third and final phase, the processional colonnade, was unfinished at his death, but its decoration was completed after the Amarna period by Tutankhamun, Ay, and Horemheb (with the latter usurping his two predecessors' work here, as well as most of their restorations inside the temple): its lowest register is inscribed with a notably detailed depiction of the Opet festival procession from Karnak to Luxor, and back again. Although the colonnade was conceived as a glorified entranceway, Ramesses II went on to build a courtyard in front of it, with statues placed between the columns of its porticoes, and obelisks (along with other colossal statues set in front of its pylon. With these additions, the plan of the Luxor temple was formally complete. Subsequent alterations at various points inside and around the temple did not substantially alter its appearance during pharaonic times. More significantly, the road to Karnak was refurbished and lined with new sphinxes by Nektanebo I (380–363

BCE); and a number of new buildings adorned the courtyard in front of the temple in late antiquity, of which a chapel dedicated to Serapis by Trajan (98–117 CE) is the best preserved.

With Diocletian's building of the Roman fort around the temple, much of the complex must have been placed off limits to the native clergy, although evidence from within the temple proper shows alterations that permitted access to the offering hall and sanctuary areas. The christianizing of Luxor is marked by the occasional introduction of religious symbols into the pagan reliefs and by the construction of churches—most of them in the areas around the temple, but in one case on the east side of its first court. Following the Islamic conquest of Egypt, this structure was superseded by the mosque of Abu'l-Haggag, the Muslim patron saint of Luxor, who continues to be venerated at this site today.

[*See also* Karnak.]

BIBLIOGRAPHY

Abd el-Razik, Mahmud. *Die Darstellungen und Texte des Sanktuars Alexanders des Grossen im Tempel von Luxor.* Deutsches Archäologisches Institut, Archäologische Veröffentlichungen, 16. Mainz, 1984. Publication of the reliefs on Alexander the Great's bark sanctuary.

Abd el-Razik, Mahmud. *Das Sanktuar Amenophis' III. in Luxor-Tempel.* Waseda University Studies in Egyptian Culture, 3. Tokyo,

1986. Publication of the reliefs inside the bark sanctuary of Amenhotpe III.

Barguet, Paul. "Luxor." In *Lexikon der Ägyptologie*, 3:1103–1107. Wiesbaden, 1980. A survey article, in French, that includes references to much older literature.

Bell, Lanny. "Luxor Temple and the Cult of the Royal Ka." *Journal of Near Eastern Studies* 44 (1985), 251–294. Convincingly explains the role of Luxor Temple in the ritual engendering of the pharaoh that took place each year during the Opet festival.

Bell, Lanny. "The New Kingdom 'Divine Temple': The Temple of Luxor." In *Temples of Ancient Egypt*, edited by Byron E. Shafer, pp. 127–184, 281–302. London and New York, 1998. This study considers how the different parts of the temple functioned in connection with its basic ritual purposes.

Brunner, Hellmut. *Die südlichen Räume des Tempels von Luxor.* Deutsches Archäologisches Institut, Archäologische Veröffentlichungen, 18. Mainz, 1977. Publication of the reliefs inside the "southern sanctuary" inside Luxor Temple.

Epigraphic Survey. *Reliefs and Inscriptions at Luxor Temple.* 2 vols. Oriental Institute Publications 112, 116. Chicago, 1994, 1998. Definitive publication, with translations and commentary, of the reliefs of Luxor Temple's great processional colonnade, including fragments that can be reintegrated into the standing walls.

Gayet, Albert J. *Le temple de Louxor.* Mémoires publiés par les membres de la Mission Archéologique Française au Caire. Paris, 1894. Very poor, but still indispensable, collection of drawings of reliefs from the temple proper.

Habachi, Labib. "The Triple Shrine of the Theban Triad in Luxor Temple." *Mitteilungen des Deutschen Archäologischen Instituts, Kairo* 20 (1965), 93–97. Account of the materials, dating originally to Hatshepsut and Thutmose III, that were recycled into Ramesses II's shrine in the first court at Luxor.

Kuentz, Charles. *La face sud du massif est du pylône de Ramsès II à Louxor.* Cairo, 1971. Publication of Ramesses II's reliefs on the back wall of his pylon.

Lacau, Pierre, and Henri Chevrier. *Une chapelle d'Hatshepsout à Karnak.* 2 vols. Cairo, 1977–1979. Publication, with translations and commentary, of the reliefs and inscriptions that document the Opet procession from Karnak to Luxor during Hatshepsut's reign.

Monneret de Villard, Ugo. "The Temple of the Imperial Cult at Luxor." *Archaeologia, or Miscellaneous Tracts Relating to Antiquity* 45 (1953), 85–105. This thorough account of the Roman's transformation of this room also decisively rebuts earlier opinions that identified it as a Christian church.

Murnane, William J. "False Doors and Cult Practices inside Luxor Temple." In *Mélanges Gamal Eddin Mokhtar*, vol. 2, edited by Paule Posener-Kriéger, pp. 137–148. Institut Français d'Archéologie Orientale, Bibliothèque d'Étude, 97.2. Cairo, 1985. This study traces how the bark sanctuary was connected to the "holy of holies" and other parts of the temple, from Greco-Roman times back to the eighteenth dynasty.

el-Saghir, Mohammed, Jean-Claude Golvin, Michel Reddé, el-Sayed Hegazy, and Guy Wagner. *Le camp romain de Louqsor.* Mémoires de l'Institut Français d'Archéologie Orientale, 83. Cairo, 1996. Fundamental publication of the remains of the Roman fort built around Luxor Temple in the latter third century CE.

WILLIAM J. MURNANE

LYRIC. The literature of ancient Egypt is rich in its wide variety of lyric poetry. The lyric is a poem or verse utterance, which tends to be imaginative, subjective (expressing the feelings, emotions, and views of the speaker), and melodic or rhythmic in structure. As applied to ancient Egypt, lyric expression is embodied in several kinds of poem. The large majority of surviving examples are hymns and prayers—praises, reminiscences, and requests of the various deities or of the pharaoh, who was the god-king of Egypt. These poems can express delight in the creation, a longing for transcendence, a simple joy in the light of day, or thankfulness for divine protection; they can express a need for guidance, a petition for favor, or a request for protection; they can simply ask for purity of heart and the power to serve god or king well. As with the literatures of other civilizations, Egyptian hymns and prayers express the gamut of religious emotion.

There are also other kinds of Egyptian lyric poetry. One group, which overlaps the lyrics abovementioned, includes the royal hymns and prayers, encomiums, and even battle songs that were addressed to the ruler as leader and god-king. Another group includes the small corpus of love songs from the New Kingdom. There are also the lyrics known as harper's songs—generally found in tombs and seemingly advocating a *carpe diem* ("sieze-the-day") attitude. Then there are the lyrics found scattered among the Pyramid Texts, which were composed to aid in the king's resurrection and assumption into the afterlife but which occasionally presented pieces describing the imagined beauty and awe of the king's figure, streaking across the sky as a bolt of lightning or fading as a star in the dawn light. There are lyrics connected with the rituals of the priests as they conducted various services. There are at least fragments, in the tombs, of work songs, marsh songs, and banquet songs. Further, there is a whole group of "Hymns to the Crown" and still another of what are usually classed with the "magical spells" but which often are in the form of lyrics. Finally, there is a body of lyric poems that stem from the scribal schools; these can be variously embodied as hymns, prayers, descriptions, meditations, and praises of various sorts, but they emerged from the school training of the educated and literate Egyptian. Such pieces were either copied by students or written by teachers for the students as they learned.

Subdivisions of the lyric genre are sometimes, but not invariably, marked by special titles or phrases indicating their kind. For instance, hymns or prayers are often called *dw3w* ("a praising," followed by the deity's name) and are almost always introduced by the phrase *ind ḥr.k* (literally translated, "Hail to thy countenance!"). Similarly, some of the love song collections seem to have introductory titles or phrases, such as *rw nw t3 sḥmḥ-ib 3* ("Utterances of great heart's joy") or *tsy nḏm* ("sweet sayings"), although they seem more to be specific metaphorical titles rather than genre markers. One harper's song (for Neferhotep on

Papyrus Harris 500) even is introduced by *ḏd.n p₃ ḥsy n bnt* ("spoken by the singer with the harp"), an introductory tag usually found in Egyptian literature among the narratives. One obvious word in ancient Egyptian, *ḥzy* ("song"), seems not to be used as an indication of genre or kind. What all this amounts to is the fact that, except for the use of *dw₃w* for hymns, no reliable indicators exist to point out the various kinds of lyric.

The structure of the poems in the lyric genre, like the narratives and wisdom writings, seems to be based on the use of two-line units, or couplets. This can be deduced from those lyric texts which have red "verse points" written into the text. The verse sentence in such poems seems to take up the length of two verse points each. That is, the typical Egyptian verse sentence is two verse-lines long. There are variations—triplets and quatrains—but the basis for the forward movement of the meaning is the couplet. Where verse points are included in the text, this procedure by the Egyptian poet is demonstrable. In the many lyric texts lacking verse points placed there in antiquity, however, the couplet structure is inferred but not proved. There may be other means of structuring the poetry; but the only one seen so far is that just described. It can be added that the "litanies" which have survived (like the "Victory Song of Weni" in his sixth dynasty tomb biography) are structured in three-line units; but these are divisible into the couplet plus the repeated refrain that together make up the litany structure. In addition, hymns are composed in what is called "nominal style"; that is, the clauses constituting the verse lines are almost completely composed of participles and nonverbal clauses; only rarely do verbal clauses occur. The remaining literary devices, of which there are many—imagery, figurative language, word play, alliteration, etc.—are displayed in conjunction with the couplet structure.

Another trait of the Egyptian lyric is embeddedness—its employment as part of the other two types of literature, the narratives and the wisdom texts. This fact points out a striking characteristic of Egyptian literature: structurally, the genres and subtypes can be intermixed. To take an obvious example, in the *Story of Sinuhe* there are three clear instances of lyrics, one in the royal encomium to Senwosret I spoken by Sinuhe as he stands before Amunenshi, another in the song of victory after Sinuhe defeats the hero of Retenu, and the third the song of the princesses as they ask the king to pardon Sinuhe. Since this kind of intermingling of literary kinds occurs throughout Egyptian literature, it indicates that all three of the major genres employ the same couplet structuring to convey their meaning.

Hymns. By far the largest of the lyric categories are the hymns (including prayers) to the various deities. Typically, the individual hymn has a short prose introduction

naming the person offering the hymn, his position, and his relationship to the deity. This is followed by the verses of the hymn proper in which the deity—in a series of lines which are near to the stereotype for each separate god—is called upon, his (or her) status among the deities is named; his origin, power, and usual activities are mentioned; any special epithets associated with the god are referred to; centers of the god's cult are listed; and references to major alternative manifestations often appear (for instance, Thoth as ibis or baboon). Usually, major events in the myth of the god are referred to or described as the hymn proceeds with its main job of praising the god. Not all these items appear in every hymn; but the list is characteristic.

The deities with the most hymns composed for them are Osiris, Re, and Amun-Re. Because of their number it will be best to present only selections.

The "Great Hymn to Osiris" from the stela of Amenmose in the eighteenth dynasty is the most extensive of the many praises of Osiris. The Osiris hymns in general concentrate on the death and resurrection of Osiris, after which he is made ruler of the afterworld, king of the dead. His fundamental significance, of course, is that he provides an example for the ancient Egyptian of defeating death, of living eternally after the death in this world. In fact, the deceased became "an osiris" in the next world and was called that in the copies of the *Book of Going Forth by Day* (*Book of the Dead*), a New Kingdom collection of spells, hymns, and other religious matter having to do with resurrection. The "Great Hymn," as it is usually termed, concentrates not so much on Osiris in the afterlife as upon that god as an exemplary king in this life, the finest of the Ennead of gods, who takes the throne of Egypt at the behest of Geb, his father, and who brings food to humankind; but he is murdered by his jealous brother, Seth. His wife/sister Isis searches for his mutilated body, restores it, and breathes life back into the dead god. At this point in the hymn, attention is turned to Horus, the posthumous son of Osiris and Isis, who is brought up in seclusion by his mother; and when of age he is brought before the grand tribunal of the Ennead to claim his birthright—the land of Egypt. Horus is proclaimed king of Egypt, bringing in another golden age, one of justice and joy under his governance. The poem thus concentrates primarily, not upon Osiris as resurrected king and ruler of the afterlife, but upon the rule of Egypt, with the god-sanctioned succession of the divine son following his divine father upon the throne of Egypt. The son rules in this life while the father rules in the next.

Where the usual hymns to Osiris are often a series of epithets and myth-bearing phrases heightening the god, Amenmose's hymn is largely a narrative in lyric form—that is, it tells a story, the fundamental myth of Osiris. But at the beginning there is a prologue in which the earlier mentioned characteristics of the deity addressed occur. The poem begins by mentioning the many names and incarnations of the god, and his mysteries celebrated in the temples; and these are followed by the enumeration of his several cult centers, his presiding over the last judgment of the individual in the afterworld in the Hall of Two Truths, and his original gift to men—"food." Then the narrative portion commences.

Of the many hymns to Re, most (like those in the Memphite tomb of Horemheb or in the Theban tomb of Kheruef) celebrate the sun god's passage across the sky and his subsequent journey through the underworld to bring his light to those in the afterlife, as he is rejuvenated in order to rise the next dawn. Some of these sun hymns emphasize praise for the god, while others are more personal, asking Re for succor and prosperity in the afterlife (tomb of Horemheb). The sun hymns found in the *Book of Going Forth by Day* (especially chapter 15; Ani Papyrus and others) emphasize the daytime journey of the sun across the sky—rising as Horakhty ("Horus of the Two Horizons"), crossing the sky as the mature Re, and finally going to rest in the western horizon as Atum ("the Old One"). A similar journey through the underworld shows Re bringing his light to those "in their coffins." Some of these hymns emphasize the sky-trip in the day-bark or the night-bark, where Re is attacked by the serpent of chaos and disorder, Apepi (or Apophis) in the mythic battle between light and darkness, or between order and disorder. Re and his crew have been victorious to date in this diurnal battle; but the forces of light could conceivably be defeated, and the result would be collapse of the cosmic order. This fact lends a touch of uncertainty to the smooth running of the cosmos, and invests the many hymns to the rising sun with a very real joy at the sight of the dawning sun each day. Re is often hymned as the divinity who is self-created, the first being, creator of the cosmos, and creator of all other gods. Particularly in those sun hymns in the *Book of Going Forth by Day*, the personal connection with the one offering praise is often included:

> May you transfigure my spirit,
>   make sacred the osiris, my soul!
> Be praised in triumph, O Lord of the gods,
>   be exalted in the midst of your wonders!
> Pour your rays over my breast like the daylight!
>   (Ani Papyrus, chapter 15)

The culmination of the sun hymns which offer worship to the traditional gods (that is, excluding the sun hymns of the Amarna period) are the hymns to Amun-Re, the great god whose worship flourished in the imperial Egypt of the New Kingdom. Once again there are many examples of hymns to this god; and in them the theology of the ancient Egyptians seems to have reached its most intricate and developed form. One major series of such hymns occurs in the *Cairo Hymns to Amun-Re* (in Papyrus Boulaq XVII) where the god is praised in all his various incarnations as the other major gods of Egypt and where the major events of his myth are presented. Another of the longer and more complex hymns occurs on the Cairo Papyrus 58032, the *Hymn to Amun-Re* (often called "Credo of a High Priest of Thebes"). This hymn, like the "Cairo Hymns," praises the deity through his activities in the world and his splendid ordering of the cosmos. But perhaps the most interesting of the hymns to Amun-Re are those collected as the *Leiden Hymns* in Papyrus Leiden I, 350 *recto*. The papyrus is incomplete, but enough survives to show that the work is a major contribution to ancient Egyptian sacred poetry. Here the poems are set off by numbers indicating that there were at least thirty in the complete manuscript, of which some eighteen survive entire, or in part. They present the nature and power of the god in his many aspects; and together the individual poems give a rounded picture of the deity. The creatures are seen offering their gifts. Thebes is presented as the locus of the god's worship, and in another of the hymns is described as the prime city of Egypt. There is a lovely hymn at sunrise where the Nine Great Gods appear out of chaos to offer their praise to the new day. Another morning hymn praises the god in the form of Horakhty. Others celebrate his self-creation, power, lordship over creation, as well as his mercy and compassion, his birth, and his forms. The overall sequence offers as full a presentation of Amun-Re as survives from Egypt.

There are hymns to virtually every god of ancient Egypt—Ptah, Thoth, Isis, Hathor, Khnum, and so on. There is even one to Hapy, the god of the Nile inundation, attributed to Khety, the Middle Kingdom author who also is reputed to have written the *Instruction* that bears his name. After one reads a good number of the hymns, there is a feeling of sameness and repetitiousness (one scholar remarked that they are all scissors-and-paste productions). To a degree this is true, but not entirely. The Egyptian gods all were made by the Creator God (whatever his name) from the same divine material when he formed the universe. In this sense they have the same attributes and natures, which in turn elucidate the same series of images and metaphors in their hymns; and this is the source of their repetitiveness. On the other hand, each god is known for certain special characteristics and certain unique events in his career; and it is these one looks to for the individual personalities of the various gods. What is generic to their common divinity will be repeated from hymn to hymn; what belongs to their personal myth will be expressed in differing phrases, images, metaphors, and symbols.

One group of sun hymns, in addition, deserves special mention. These are the Amarna hymns, and their importance is due to the theology they embody. They stem from the religious revolution inspired by King Akhenaten, who came to the throne in the mid-fourteenth century BCE toward the end of the eighteenth dynasty. His "heresy" emphasized the concept of the one god of the universe, with resulting corollaries that the other gods of the traditional Egyptian pantheon simply did not exist, and that neither belief in Osiris nor elaborate funeral ceremonies were necessary. Several of the courtiers buried at Akhetaten, the new capital city of Akhenaten, include in their tombs variations of what seems to have been the core of Akhenaten's "teaching," painted or carved on their walls. The tomb of Ay, who later became pharaoh for a short time, offers the most extensive version of this belief in the form of a hymn known as the "Great Hymn to Aten." Aten is the name for Akhenaten's understanding of the sun god; and this hymn, with the king himself as the putative speaker or singer, is one of the gems of ancient Egyptian literature. It celebrates "light" with an almost ecstatic fervency, and takes joy in the multiplicity of creatures and the fecundity of the earth. Aten is portrayed as one, alone, the creator, universal, loving, paternal, divine, and beautiful. He is presented as the divine light, the opposite of darkness and disorder; and in fact the basic imagery of the poem is a fairly regular contrast between light and darkness, not only as daily phenomena, but also as principles lying at the heart of the cosmos. Aten floods the earth with light at his rising each day; when he sets, the earth lies in a darkness like death; he provides for all creatures; he supervises generation, even of the chick in the egg; he governs all lands, not only Egypt; he provides the proper place for each creature; he sends Hapy to water the land—as a river in Egypt, as rain in Asia; he is alone, shining in the heavens but also in Akhenaten's heart. And in the final stanza, the king asks Aten to "lift up the creatures" for his sake. Both the tone of joy and the delight in a sole god are fundamentally quite unlike the traditional sun hymns.

Hymns to the King. Another major group of lyrics attaches to the person and function of the pharaoh. The oldest of these occur among the Pyramid Texts of the late fifth and the sixth dynasties of the Old Kingdom. These ancient texts are concerned with the deceased king's resurrection and entry into heaven so that he may take up his eternal life among his fellows, the gods. Most of the pieces ("spells" or "utterances") involve magical means and supernatural conjurations—some by imitative, or sympathetic, magic—to assist the king in accomplishing the transition; but here and there are sections with true lyric imagination. It, of course, is not clear if the "lyric" pieces were thought to be such by the ancient priests themselves; but they nevertheless clearly fit the Egyptian lyric category. An examples of this is in Spell 261 of the Pyramid Texts where the king is likened to a flash of lightning which streaks across the night sky and presages the storm. The intent of the piece is to visualize the king's awesome power and his presence in the sky—just where the thrust of the Pyramid Texts wants to place him, as a heavenly being. But this purpose is fused here with spectacular imagery and metaphor in order to produce a vivid portrait of the risen king. A similar lyric use occurs in Spell 216 of the Pyramid Texts, where the king is visualized as a star fading in the quiet of the dawn. As the various stars disappear, so does the star representing the king. Yet—using the analogy of sympathetic magic prevalent in these spells—as Orion and Sothis go to the underworld, so does the king. The final stanza indicates that they all end up comforted in the arms of their father Atum.

The two preceding lyrics are short single scenes; but most of the Pyramid Texts are longer, more complex, and often full of beings, places, and activities which are difficult to interpret. Yet one hymn, while its prime purpose is aiding the king's resurrection, still works as a lyric. This is the piece grossly miscalled the "Cannibal Hymn" but which can more accurately be titled the "Resurrection of King Unas" (Spells 273–274 of the Pyramid Texts). The poem opens with cataclysm in the heavens and on earth as King Unas is seen ascending into the sky. He has turned his back on earth; and his helpers are gathering lesser deities to be eaten as his sacrificial meal—their power entering Unas' body to enhance his own power among the other gods. Much of the hymn is given to the sacred meal, during which the inert body of the king rises up to partake of his "communion." The poem ends with a celebration of the king's power—his resurrection accomplished—and his attainment of eternal life beyond the vagaries of life on earth.

There are other lyrics connected with the figure of pharaoh as well. These are the praises, encomiums, adulations, and prayers which come from the scribal tradition and survive from the "schoolboy miscellanies" of the New Kingdom. They seem to be straightforward in their praise of the king—even conventional and repetitive. Ramesses II and Merenptah are both lauded as warrior kings (Papyrus Anastasi II), with foreign enemies falling before them. And one might note that it is not their armies which are praised, but the kings themselves; the power is concentrated in the person of the divine king himself. The king lives on *maat;* he is the very image of Re; he (in this case, Merenptah) is the foremost ship of the line, a scimitar, a ready javelin. And his palace is magnificent. These are the collections in the papyri. One or two ostraca also offer this sort of royal encomium as well, as in the celebration of an unknown king's jubilee (Ostracon Wilson 100) celebrated upon his entry into Thebes.

Finally, there are, more specifically, battle songs. The earliest of these is the piece known as the "Song of the Victorious Army" from the tomb of Weni in the sixth dynasty of the Old Kingdom, identifiable from its poetic form as a litany wherein the refrain is repeated every other verse line. This is of some importance since the poem shows (along with the less certain "Catalogue of Virtues") that lyric poetry was composed during the Old Kingdom. The refrain in Weni's litany is "The army returned in triumph," and is followed in each instance by a line narrating the destruction the army caused among its enemies. While this poem centers on the army itself, another group of lyrics from the Middle Kingdom does, once more, concentrate upon pharaoh, in this case Senwosret III (Papyrus Kahun LV.1). There are four lyrics, all but the first in litany form; and in them the king is seen as a conquering hero, a purveyor of joy to gods and men, the embodiment of greatness, and protector of his people. The lyrics at times rise to vivid poetry: the king is "a sunshade to help keep cool in summer" or "a warm dry nook in winter."

A small group of lyrics related to the pharaoh are the "Hymns to the Crown" (Papyrus Moscow B1). These celebrate the powers inherent in the various royal crowns—the Red Crown, the White Crown, the Double Crown—as well as the powers inherent in the *uraeus* snakes that adorn them.

A final group of compositions, which often are actually in lyric form, are sometimes found among the texts termed "magical spells" (like the lyric poems found among the Pyramid Texts). These are pieces (as in Papyrus Harris I) with the specific intent to ward off danger—spells to protect from snakes, crocodiles, lost love, toothache, and so on.

Love Songs. A quite different category of lyrics are the love songs from the Ramessid period of the New Kingdom. They are the only example of clearly secular lyrics to survive from Egypt. Whereas the hymns and prayers, the praises, encomiums, and battle songs discussed so far all celebrate either divinities or the divine king (and thus have a primarily religious orientation), the love songs celebrate love between men and women (sometimes, boys and girls)—human love rather than divine love. The individual songs are short, usually only twenty to thirty verse lines. And in them we have expressed the entire range of the feelings of romantic love. They are idyllic, tender, humorous, even satirical, sometimes naive, almost always graceful; and the speakers range from self-sacrificing in the service of love, pure of heart, hesitant, or intensely passionate, openly physical in their desire, even at times given to lust, sexual innuendo, and bawdy. The situations are perennial, too; the young woman walking down the road and seized by confusion when suddenly meeting her lover, Mehy, as he rides by; the couple sitting together in the garden to catch the evening breeze; a lover cataloging the charms of his girlfriend head to toe; a girl coaxing her lover to go swimming with her by promising to wear her new swimsuit which goes sheer in the water; a woman thinking passionately of her absent lover as she lies in bed.

One of the reasons for the charm of the love songs, in addition to the attractive lovers and situations, is the multitude of sense impressions they contain. They are full of images of flowers, gardens and orchards, leisurely living, and the activities of young sophisticates. One sequence begins its individual poems with reference to various orchard trees—the pomegranate, the fig, the sycomore—and the love theme develops out of these citations. Another follows a young woman—a birdcatcher's daughter—as she lures her lover out into the marshes and fields where she spends her time trapping birds. The teeming life portrayed in the love songs is the verbal equivalent of the lush, nature-filled, and banquet-filled scenes of daily life that were painted or carved in the tombs of the nobles at Thebes; and the two together offer a full and detailed portrait of the New Kingdom lives of the well-to-do on their farms and estates. And this nearness to the rhythms and locales of everyday life makes the love songs among the most accessible of all extant ancient Egyptian literature—no dogma or politics or social formalities come between the reader and their world. The love songs are perhaps the world's earliest example of the literary kind, the pastoral.

The speakers of the songs are both male and female, divided about equally. This may be one of the earliest instances in world literature where the two sexes converse on an equal footing. This is not to say that women composed some of the songs. The songs are anonymous; and one cannot prove the sex of the authors. The probability is that the authors were male, simply because of the social conditions at that time. Women rarely wrote, although there surely were literate women at the palace and in the priesthoods. At any rate, the poets imagined their speakers to be of both sexes, and often had couples speaking back and forth to each other—bantering, flirting, exchanging words of love and longing, or just passing the time of day. Other sequences of the love poems seem to present discreet situations from poem to poem. Still others, like that of the birdcatcher's daughter from the second song cycle of Harris Papyrus 500, present a carefully worked out series of glimpses of a young woman's mind as she endures a love affair that ends badly; but the sequence is actually narrative from poem to poem.

There are only about fifty love songs; and they survive in four small collections: Papyrus Chester Beatty I, Papyrus Harris 500, Papyrus Turin 1966, and Ostracon Cairo 25218, augmented by Ostracon Deir el-Medina 1266.

Harper's Songs. Still another very small group of lyrics are termed "harper's songs." There are only half a dozen examples, and they survive primarily in a funerary context. Only the poem from the tomb of king Intef, introduced, "In front of the singer with the harp" does not fit this situation because it occurs on Papyrus Harris 500 among the collections of love songs. There is, of course, an affinity between the two types of songs, as will become clear. The harper's songs affirm life and intense living in the midst of a literature that is filled with the themes of death, resurrection, and eternal life. Like the love songs, these works embrace living fully in the present physical world, upon "drinking life to the dregs." Their theme is *carpe diem*, "seize the day!"

The song from Intef's tomb can be taken as an example. It is in two parts, a first stanza lamenting the desolation of life and the certainty of death:

> There is no return for them
> to explain their present being,
> To say how it is with them,
> to gentle our hearts
>   until we hasten to the place where they have gone.

And a second stanza exhorts the listener (in this case, Intef) to forget the reality and imminence of death and to "follow your heart's desire while you live!" Enjoy myrrh, fine linen, perfumes today; for Osiris does not hear the wailing of those who are about to die, and weeping does not save the heart from the grave.

The harper's songs are particularly interesting because they seem to negate a fundamental belief of ancient Egyptian civilization—the life after death. In them, the end of life is the grave, not the afterworld. Thus there is a discrepancy, it seems, between the *carpe diem* attitude of the songs and their situation in tombs, where the remainder of the material on the walls and ceilings is one grand hymn to eternal life. In the tomb of Inherkhawy (tomb 359 in Western Thebes), the tomb owner seems to claim, in a short preface to his harper's song, that he was "a man redeemed through abundance of good offered by God himself." And the singer for the deceased priest Neferhotep (tomb 50 in Western Thebes), in the first of his three harper's songs, finds it necessary to castigate those who have erroneously exalted life on earth and belittled the City of the Dead, which "loathes disorder" and is "without a rebel."

Just where the harper's songs fit in the intellectual universe of the ancient Egyptian is not yet clear, since the clash of skepticism and faith seems unresolvable.

Other Songs. There are hints of a few other kinds of lyric, gleaned mainly from wall paintings in the tombs. Work songs, songs for hunting in the marsh, banquet songs—these are all possible songs or, better, snatches of songs; for they are seen as bits, not complete compositions, hinting at the fullness just barely hinted at on the walls. They would be a fine addition to the many varieties of lyric described above. At any rate, the genre of ancient Egyptian lyric poetry that survives is extensive, with poems of real power.

[*See also* Encomia; *and the composite article on* Hymns.]

BIBLIOGRAPHY

Assmann, Jan. *Ägyptische Hymnen und Gebete.* Zurich, 1975.

Barucq, André, and François Daumas. *Hymnes et Prieres de l'Égypte Ancienne.* Paris, 1980.

Foster, John L. *Echoes of Egyptian Voices: An Anthology of Ancient Egyptian Poetry.* Norman, 1992.

Foster, John L. *Hymns, Prayers, and Songs: An Anthology of Ancient Egyptian Lyric Verse.* Atlanta, 1995. The apparatus includes sources of texts and translations for all selections.

Lichtheim, Miriam. *Ancient Egyptian Literature.* 2 vols. Los Angeles, 1973, 1978.

Loprieno, Antonio. *Ancient Egyptian Literature.* Leiden, 1996.

JOHN L. FOSTER

M

MAAT. The ethical conceptions of "truth," "order," and "cosmic balance" are encompassed in the Egyptian term *maat*, and the personification of those principles is the goddess Maat (*M3't*). The goddess represented the divine harmony and balance of the universe, including the unending cycles of the rising and setting of the sun, the inundation of the Nile River, the resulting fertility of the land, and the enduring office of kingship; she was considered to be the force that kept chaos (*isft*), the antithesis of order, from overwhelming the world. Hence *maat* was a complex, intertwined, and interdependent sense of ethics that tied personal behavior—such as speaking truthfully, dealing fairly in the market place, and especially sustaining obedience to parents, the king, and his agents—to the maintenance of universal order. To transgress one aspect of *maat* threatened to encourage chaos and overwhelm order. To live according to *maat* was also fundamental to personal existence. The *Instruction of Ptahhotep* (sixth dynasty) vowed: "There is punishment for him who passes over its [*maat's*] laws." The *Instructions for Merikare* (ninth dynasty) said: "Do *maat* so that you may endure upon Earth."

Maat and the King. One of the primary duties of the king was to maintain the order of the cosmos, effected by upholding the principle of *maat* through correct and just rule and through service to the gods. In turn, the people of Egypt had an obligation to uphold *maat*, through obedience to the king, who served as the intermediary between the divine and profane spheres. The *Instructions of Kagemni* record "do *maat* for the king, for *maat* is what the king loves"; the negative confession that was recited by the deceased, as his or her soul was judged against *maat*, included the profession "I have not disputed the king." The sense of fealty to the king and its association with personal responsibility for the balance of the universe may help explain why there are so few periods of social unrest in Egypt—for to act against the king was to risk the stability of the cosmos. The association of government and *maat* reached even the lower levels of government. Viziers who dispensed justice in the name of the king wore a pendant in the form of the goddess Maat, which both alluded to their association with the goddess and their inspiration to act justly.

One of the clearest indications of the association of the king and the goddess Maat was the ritual of her presentation to the other gods. This ritual, which symbolized the dedication of the king to uphold the principles inherent in *maat* is first attested in the New Kingdom reign of Thutmose III (r. 1504–1452 BCE), although textual references suggest that it may be traced to Hatshepsut. The greatest number of examples from the eighteenth dynasty come from the early reign of Amenhotpe IV (r. 1372–1355 BCE), who assumed the poorly understood epithet *'nh m m3't* "Living as truth." The presentation of Maat was commonly depicted on the walls of Ramessid-era temples, especially in areas that were accessible to the public, which suggests that the ritual served as a symbol of royal legitimacy. This sense of the ritual being a royal prerogative has been verified in that only kings, one queen (Nefertiti), and a few others of quasi-royal status (Prince Osorkon and the "Gods' Wives of Amun" of the twenty-fifth dynasty and the twenty-sixth) have been depicted presenting Maat to a god in nonfunerary contexts (a few tomb scenes, however, show nonroyal individuals presenting the image of the goddess).

Kings were considered to be imbued with *maat*. From the Old Kingdom reign of Sneferu (fourth dynasty) onward, the concept of *maat* was a common part of the royal titulary; many kings claimed the epithets *nb m3't*, "Possessor of *maat*," and *h m M3't*, "who arises in *maat*." Most of the Ramessid kings compounded their prenomen or nomen with *maat*. From the time of Sety I onward, many kings were depicted presenting a rebus of their prenomen to the gods thereby directly equating themselves with *maat*.

The deity Maat pervaded the world of the gods. She was considered to be the daughter of the sun god Re and she was the Eye of Re, so parts of her body were equated with Re's body. She was also the "food of the gods," and the gods claimed to have "gulped down Maat." Maat served as the archtypical food offering for the gods, as suggested by offering scenes in the tombs of Merenptah, Sety II, Twosret, Sethnakhte, and Ramesses III, as well as at the Small Temple at Medinet Habu where *nw* vessels (normally associated with wine or other liquid offerings) are shown presented to the god—yet the offering scene is labeled as presenting Maat. Thoth had an especially close association with Maat, and the two deities are often shown paired.

The Goddess Maat. Representations of the goddess Maat are attested as early as the middle of the Old King-

MAAT. *The goddess Maat wearing the Feather of Truth in her headdress.* She is weighing the heart of Userhet, an official during the reign of Sety I. This is a detail of a copy (by Norman de Garis Davies) of a painting in Userhat's tomb at Thebes (tomb 51), dating from the nineteenth dynasty. (The Metropolitan Museum of Art, 15.5.18)

dom, initially in theophoric names. She is shown in the form of an idealized female, wearing a sheath dress and her characteristic emblem—an ostrich plume (phonogram m_3ʿ)—on her head. The symbolism of the emblem is uncertain, although the same emblem is shared by the god Shu, who in some cosmologies is her brother.

Temples and Cult of Maat. Despite the great importance placed on Maat, there is no evidence for a temple dedicated to her that predates the New Kingdom construction of the temple to Maat at Karnak North by Amenhotpe III. Textual references suggest that other temples of Maat were located at Memphis and at Deir el-Medina. The Karnak structure was used for the coronation of Queen Hatshepsut and, perhaps, for the investiture of some kings. The Tomb Robbery Papyri indicate that the court that met to investigate the robberies of the royal tombs during the reign of Ramesses IX convened at the Maat temple. Although texts refer to priests of Maat in the ranks wʿb, ẖry-ḥbt, and ḥm-nṯr, nothing is known about a cult specific to the goddess. The title i, "overseer of the

domain of Maat," suggests that lands and resources were held by the Maat temple, but nothing more is known of their extent or administration. In temple cult-offering scenes, Maat usually stands behind the king or behind the recipient. She rarely acts as the recipient of offerings.

Maat and Funerary Beliefs. Both the goddess Maat and the conception of ethics inherent in *maat* are most closely associated in the funerary realm—for correct behavior during life was a requisite for eternal life after death. Spell 816 of the Coffin Texts relates that Maat was associated with the Opening of the Mouth ceremony. By the New Kingdom, Maat was credited with being able to grant a good burial, and she is invoked in *ḥtp di nsw* offering formulas. Her association with rebirth is most clearly illustrated by Chapter 125 of the *Book of Going Forth by Day* (*Book of the Dead*), first attested in the reign of Amenhotpe II, which shows the weighing of the heart against a small figure of Maat (or the feather emblem) to evaluate the worthiness of the deceased. In the New Kingdom and onward, Maat was increasingly associated with sun hymns and solar imagery, in reference to the deceased's union with the cycle of the sun and, hence, eternal rebirth. Maat, or a dual form (Maaty), was pictured in the solar bark with her father Re. Sun hymns on the portals of private Theban tombs, such as that of Neferhotep (tomb 49), refer to the deceased presenting Maat to the sun god. By the twentieth dynasty, Maat acquired distinctively funerary associations, particularly in Thebes, through her fusion with Imntt, the goddess of the west. The Theban necropolis was referred to as *st M3ʿt*, "the place of Truth," and "the place for those who have done Maat." The peak over the Theban necropolis was referred to as "the great peak of the West in this its name of Maat." Ramessid epithets of Maat included "Mistress of the necropolis"; "Mistress of the West"; and "Mistress of the West who resides in the necropolis." By the Ramessid period, the association of the deceased with Maat was so strong that the transfigured *akhs* (souls) were, like the god themselves, considered to consume and live upon *maat*.

BIBLIOGRAPHY

Assmann, Jan. *Maat: Gerechtigkeit und Unsterblichkeit im alten Ägypten.* Munich, 1990. A broad-ranging study of *maat* and its implications for ancient Egyptian society.

Assmann, Jan. *Egyptian Solar Religion in the New Kingdom: Re, Amun and the Crisis of Polytheism.* Translated from the German by Anthony Alcock. London and New York, 1995. A further expostulation of Assmann's controversial theory that from the mid-eighteenth dynasty, *maat* as an ethical concept leading to salvation was eroded, as people sought automatic atonement directly from the gods.

Hornung, Erik. *Conceptions of God in Ancient Egypt: The One and the Many.* Translated from the German by John Baines. Ithaca, 1982. The standard work on the theory of Egyptian religion.

Lichtheim, Miriam. *Maat in Egypian Autobiographies and Related Studies.* Orbis biblicus et orientalis, 120. Freiburg, 1992. Handy source for the way *maat* is reflected in professions of personal worth.

Teeter, Emily. *The Presentation of Maat: Ritual and Legitimacy in Ancient Egypt.* Studies in Ancient Orient Civilization, 57. Chicago, 1997. A study of the role of *maat* in the offering cult and her relationship to the king.

EMILY TEETER

MAGIC. [*This entry comprises four articles:* An Overview; Magic in Medicine; Magic in Daily Life; *and* Magic in the Afterlife.]

An Overview

The concept of "magic" has proved to be a most difficult category for modern Egyptology, with little agreement regarding the definition or scope of supposedly magical practices. The designation of "magic" has been applied subjectively to any actions or recitations deemed "non-religious" by individual authors. Following the early anthropological theories of James G. Frazer (*The Golden Bough*, 1910) and Bronislaw Malinowski (*Magic, Science and Religion and Other Essays*, 1948), "magic" is most frequently distinguished from "religion" on the basis of the former's "blasphemous," threatening attitude (as opposed to "proper" humility) and its immediate, limited, and personal goals (contrasted with rites and prayers for general well-being). Unfortunately, such distinctions are inadequate for ancient Egypt, where a threatening attitude may be adopted in orthodox public rituals for general benefit, and identical texts and rites may serve either personal or general ends. Seeking to avoid this problem, many scholars have adopted the term "magico-religious," while others have urged the abandonment of any category of magic. A working definition of *magic* as "any activity which seeks to obtain its goal by methods outside the simple laws of cause and effect" has been proposed by Ritner (1993, p. 69) and adopted in subsequent reference works (M. Depauw, *A Companion to Demotic Studies*, Brussels, 1997, p. 109).

Justification for the retention of the concept derives not from modern Egyptology but from indigenous terminology. In the Christian period, the Coptic term *hik* was equated explicitly with Greek *mageia* and Latin *magia* as a designation for impious and illegal sorcery. Coptic *hik* is the descendant of pharaonic (*ḥq3*), whose pre-Christian associations were, however, neither impious nor illegal. Attested from the Old Kingdom through the Roman era, *heka* represented a primary cosmic force and, personified as Heka, the eldest son of the universal creator. In this capacity of child deity, Heka was venerated as the junior member of local triads at Heliopolis in the Old Kingdom, the Memphite necropolis in the New Kingdom, the western Delta in the Third Intermediate Period, and Esna in Hellenistic times. His pivotal theological significance, substantially formulated before the Middle Kingdom, was recognized well beyond these local cult sites.

As detailed in the recitation "To Become the God Heka" (Coffin Text Spell 261), Heka was believed to have been formed "before duality had yet come into being" as the force that at once animated, compelled, and protected the gods and subsequent creation. Antecedent to the Creative Word (Hu), Heka infuses the creator's projected images, or *ka*-spirits, with his "magical" vitality, in keeping with the likely meaning of his name as "He who consecrates the *ka*-spirit." Representing the principle of consecrated imagery, Heka is styled "Lord of *ka*-spirits" in Coffin Text Spell 261, and the association recurs in Spell 648, where the "millions of *ka*-spirits within his mouth" serve as "powers" which instill fear in the gods, create the mountains, and knit the firmament together. The description of Heka's empowered imagery "within his mouth" reflects the close link between Egyptian magic and the word, whether spoken or written. His fundamental association with cosmic dynamics is indicated by the emblematic spelling of his name, from the twentieth dynasty onward, with the hieroglyph for "power." At the Roman temple of Esna, his primacy was stressed by a folk etymology explaining his name as "the First Work." In Greco-Egyptian magical papyri of late Roman date, *heka* is translated by both *hiera mageia*, signifying "holy magic," and *hiera* or *theia energeia*, meaning "holy" or "divine power." Ironically, these last mentions are contemporary with the Coptic Christian denigration of *hik/heka* as irreligious, demonic sorcery. In marked contrast to Western and orthodox Coptic notions of magic, Egyptian *heka* was considered neither supernatural nor unholy, representing instead the divinely sanctioned force that initiated, permeated, and sustained nature itself.

Heka's creative role is repeated daily, for he accompanies the sun god Re on his cyclical voyage, protects the enthroned Osiris in the netherworld, and by prayer invokes the continued separation of heaven and earth. His protective duties entail a corresponding destructive role, and Heka's power to frighten even the gods is an invariable feature of his theological descriptions. Heka's threatening character has been noted above in connection with the Coffin Texts and was already evident in the earlier Pyramid Texts, where the appearance of the deity causes the sky to tremble and the earth to quake (Spell 472). In the first example of a recitation technique that would be continued into Coptic times, a formal curse against recalcitrant spirits is said to be uttered not by the human speaker, but by a higher authority: "It is not I who says this against you, O gods; it is Heka who says this against you, O gods" (Pyramid Text Spell 539).

With similar orthodoxy, the hostile power of *heka* might be tapped for cosmic, state or even personal cursing rites. The legitimacy of such practice is specified in the literary *Instructions for Merikare*, which lists magic among the fundamental benefactions allotted by the creator to humanity, in company with the creation of heaven, earth, air, food, and proper government: "It was in order to be weapons to ward off the blow of events that he made *heka* for them (humanity)." The "Execration Texts," attested from the Old Kingdom through the Late period, illustrate the unity of state and private cursing practice. Anticipating the use of the so-called voodoo doll, these texts comprise lists of names of foreign rulers, Egyptian enemies, and hostile forces inscribed on red pottery or on figures of bound prisoners, rendered harmless by ritual torture and burial. While the updated lists of foreign rulers certainly derived from the state chancellery, the names of condemned Egyptians may have been influenced by private sponsorship, as was surely the case with isolated figures designed to curse individuals and families. Ad-

dressing the practitioner, a late cursing ritual pairs state and divine enemies with "all foes male and female whom your heart fears" (Papyrus British Museum 10188, col. 28/17–18). In response to such techniques, "Oracular Amuletic Decrees" offered divine protection against any potential male or female magician (*hekay*). Closely related to such execration rituals are "love" spells, which are first attested in Ramessid times and become particularly common in Demotic and derivative Greek papyri. Borrowing the imagery and mechanics of cursing magic, "love" spells are equally spells of domination, ensuring that the victim can neither eat nor sleep, but only follow the magician's client "like an ox after grass" (Ostracon Deir el-Medina 1057).

The force of *heka* is thus morally neutral, and even foreign enemies and demons might be said to possess or utilize *heka*. Unlike the classical and later Christian use of *mageia* or *magia*, the Egyptian term does not serve primarily as a term of disparagement to mark cultural boundaries, distinguishing inferior, foreign "witchcraft" from positive, local "religion." Individual cases of *heka* might be described as "bad" or "evil" from the perspective of the intended victim, but no general categories of "white" or "black" magic are documented in Egyptian sources. Attempts to isolate such distinctions have proved unsuccessful (see Ritner 1993, pp. 20–21, 30–35). In the reign of Ramesses III (c.1198–1166 BCE), a harem conspiracy made use of standard execration techniques with manipulated wax figurines in a failed attempt to replace the monarch with a prince Pentaweret, but the surviving interrogation records constitute a trial for treason, not sorcery. The manuals of magic used by the conspirators were orthodox compositions taken from the royal archives, and the practitioner was a priest, the customary magician in Egyptian society.

As made evident by the previous references to the Pyramid Texts, Coffin Texts, Execration Texts and Oracular Amuletic Decrees, the practice of magic in Egypt was closely associated with written manuals detailing recitations, obligatory ingredients, and ritual performance—corresponding to a tripartite categorization of magic as speech, inherent property, and rite. Spell collections, whether designed for state or royal ritual, medical healing, exorcism, cursing, or even agricultural security, were accorded sacred status as "emanations (*b3w*) of Re" and were products of the "House of Life" (*pr-'nḫ*), or temple scriptorium. Composed, compiled, and stored in the scriptorium, such magical texts were exclusive temple property, jealously guarded to prevent misuse by outsiders, whether foreign or native. Restrictions applied even to simple fording spells, as indicated by the Harris Magical Papyrus (Papyrus British Museum 10042, col. 6/10): "First spell of enchanting all that is in the water, concern-

MAGIC: AN OVERVIEW. *A twelfth dynasty magic "wand" made of ivory.* Such amulets, inscribed with magical symbols, served to ward off snakes, poisonous insects, and other hidden dangers. (The Metropolitan Museum of Art, Theodore M. Davis Collection. Bequest of Theodore M. Davis, 1915. [30.8.218])

ing which the Chief Lector Priests say: 'Do not reveal it to others.' A veritable secret of the House of Life."

The strong emphasis in Egyptian magic on written texts necessarily restricted the range of professional practitioners to members of the literate, temple-affiliated elite, who are currently estimated as comprising no more than 1 percent of the population. Old Kingdom tomb scenes may indicate that simple charms were memorized and recited by illiterate farmers and herdsmen, though representations and the Harris Magical Papyrus suggest the presence of a specialist, with the herdsmen performing only protective gestures. Rare mentions of a prophetic "wise woman" (*rht*) are found in private records from the cloistered and highly literate New Kingdom artists' colony at Deir el-Medina, which substituted community participation for professional priests in typically restricted ritual roles. Otherwise, magicians are explicitly designated as members of the priestly hierarchy, including the "Prophet of Heka" (*ḥm-nṯr Ḥq3*), the "Chief of Secrets" (*hri-sst3*), and especially the "Chief Lector Priest" (*ḫri-ḥb ḫri-tp*), who was entrusted with the sacred scrolls and who recited hymns and incantations during formal temple ceremonies as well as during private apotropaic and funerary rites. In abbreviated form (*ḫri-tp*), the title becomes the standard term for "magician" from the New Kingdom onward and appears in transcription in both Akkadian (as *khartibi*) and Hebrew records (cf. *Genesis* 41.8: *hartumim*) to designate Egyptian magicians.

As the imagistic principle represented by *heka* underlies all ritual, whether conducted in a temple or private

setting, so the same ritual specialist could serve either public or private interests. This dual role would have created no professional difficulty. With the exception of the very highest ranks, Egyptian priests were not on duty throughout the year, but served in groups or "phyles" in rotation. With four and, after year 9 of Ptolemy III (238 BCE), five such phyles serving in rotation, priests will have had at least three-quarters of the year off duty, with opportunity and incentive to create a lucrative "private" practice. The classical and medieval conception of magicians as itinerant and unaffiliated practitioners on the social fringe has no validity in pharaonic Egypt, where groups of off-duty priests had the training, temple access, authority, and established clientele requisite for the role of community magician. As authors, editors, and custodians of ritual texts, their monopoly on the profession was unassailable.

The best evidence for the accouterments of the professional magician derives from the find of an intact "magician's box" in a twelfth dynasty tomb shaft beneath the northern storerooms of the Ramesseum. Measuring eighteen by twelve by twelve inches, the chest was labeled on its cover as belonging to a "Chief of Secrets" and contained twenty-three fragmentary papyri, a bundle of reed pens, four broken ivory apotropaic wands, and an assortment of beads, amulets, and figurines. The papyri and writing instruments are again indicative of the importance of literacy in Egyptian magic, and the subjects of the Ramesseum Papyri (P. Ram.) reveal the range of the specialist's concerns: medico-magical treatments for eye disease, stomach complaints, and constricted urination (P. Ram. III); recipes for procreation, pregnancy, and newborns (P. Ram. IV); remedies for muscular pains and stiffness (P. Ram. V); formal hymns to the crocodile deity Sobek (P. Ram. VI); incantations for protective amulets (P. Ram. VII); exorcisms of afflicting ghosts (P. Ram. C); a dramatic ritual text concerning the cult of Osiris (P. Ram B); an archaic funerary liturgy (P. Ram. E); as well as spells against headache (P. Ram VIII), serpents (P. Ram IX-X) and for general protection (P. Ram XVI-XVII). The further inclusion of literary texts (P. Ram. I, II, A, and D) suggested to Gardiner that "the tomb-owner combined with the sterner purposes of his profession the function of a local story-teller and entertainer" (*The Ramesseum Papyri* [Oxford, 1955], p. 1).

The prominence of medical spells within the Ramesseum corpus reveals the close association between magician and physician (*snw*), whose training was also tied to the temple scriptorium and whose methodology combined both "rational" and "magical" treatment strategies, with charged substances (magic by property), incantations (magic by speech), and ritual actions (magic by rite). From the introductory sections of Papyrus Ebers (c.1550 BCE), it is evident that even prescriptions with no specified magical component were routinely accompanied by standardized spells for applying remedies, loosening bandages, and drinking potions (cols. 1/1–2/6). A century later, Papyrus Hearst provides similar generic spells for measuring ingredients (cols. 13/17–14/4) or applying oil (col. 14/4–7). Medical compendia might also include spells seemingly more appropriate for the community magician. Papyrus Ebers contains an incantation "to prevent a kite from robbing" (col. 98/2–6), though this may have been collected to protect the pharmacist's herb garden. Physicians with distinctly theological backgrounds included the "priest of Sakhmet" (*w'b Shmt*), the goddess of plague and disease, and the "controller of Selqet" (*hrp-Srqt*), goddess of scorpions and snakes. The class of healer known as the "amulet-man" (*s3w*) was perhaps illiterate, though in company with the priests of Sakhmet and regular physicians they were trained to take the pulse and are attested at court. It was a priest of the destructive deity Sakhmet who gained access to state execration rituals and attempted the overthrow of Ramesses III.

The Ramesseum spells for childbirth and neonates are paralleled in the "Magical Spells for Mother and Child" (Papyrus Berlin 3027) of early New Kingdom date; they were recited not by anxious mothers but by lector-priests (*hri-hb*) or "magicians of the nursery" (*hq3y n k3p*). Closely related to such spells are the apotrapaic wands recovered from the magician's box, which are formed from hippopotamus tusks and engraved with a series of animal spirits. While determined by the material, the shape of these pieces is probably intended to represent a knife, comparable to those typically held by the engraved figures. Similar magical knives are well attested from the Middle Kingdom, and inscribed examples state that the figures offer protection from all evil forces. Signs of wear suggest that they may have been used to delineate defensive circles around a child's bed. As the protectress of children, mothers, and the bedroom, the leonine goddess Beset served similar ends, and her image is found both on these knives and as an individual bronze figure within the Ramesseum cache. The remaining items from the box illustrate the varied functions of magic in daily life. Female figurines probably served to enhance fertility; beads and a bronze uraeus (wrapped in hair) formed protective amulets; an ivory herdsman recalls the early scenes of fording rites noted previously and is further evidence for the participation of trained magicians in agricultural contexts.

As noted by John Barns in his edition of Papyrus Ramesseum IV (*Five Ramesseum Papyri* [Oxford, 1956], p. 25), the high incidence of magical treatments in this early corpus refutes the still common notion that magic increased over time, "corrupting" Egyptian religion and medicine. In the form of amulets and manipulated figurines, the use of magic continued with no *qualitative* change from Predynastic through Coptic times. Innovative forms and the demands of an expanding wealthy class did produce a *quantitative* increase in magical texts and objects, but the orthodox position of magic within religion and medicine remained constant. The invention of magical knives in the Middle Kingdom represents a new application of customary magical mechanics, not a new significance for the concept of magic itself. Late predilection for love spells does not signal "a spirit that is strikingly different" from earlier times, but rather a continuation of traditional execration practice, following Ramessid and earlier precedent (*contra* Borghouts, 1974, p. 17). Examples of the techniques of coercive spell, charged substance, and rite are found in all extant medical texts, and similar features pervade the funerary literature of all periods. As "practical theology" designed to compel individual salvation, the Pyramid Texts, Coffin Texts, and *Book of Going Forth by Day* (*Book of the Dead*) are inherently magical, as are the attendant grave figures, *shawabti*s, protective bricks, amuletic images, and other tomb accessories.

In addition to apotropaic knives and love spells, magical innovations include the oracular procedure termed *ph-ntr*, meaning literally "to reach" or "to petition" a god. Although this term is often applied to private and even hostile conjurations, it serves to designate any oracular consultation of a divine image, even the temple-sponsored statue processions that functioned as formal tribunals, fully equivalent to a court of law. Temple oracles were a typical feature of New Kingdom religious practice, and they assumed additional prestige with the subsequent decline of royal authority. The manifestation of the god was addressed directly, and by appropriate signs or documents a response was granted. Ascribed to the patronage of Heka, the "Lord of oracles, Lord of revelations," such procedures were not simply legal, but the source of local legality. Private adaptations are first attested in the Ramessid period. In the harem conspiracy against Ramesses III, the plotters "began to petition god (*ph̠-nt̠r*) for the derangement of the people." In a less hostile context from the reign of Ramesses IX, the necropolis worker Qenna from Deir el-Medina was granted an excused absence "in order to petition god" with the assistance of a lamp allotted from the village storehouse. Qenna's use of a lamp to evoke divine visions is paralleled by numerous revelatory spells in the magical papyri of Hellenistic Egypt, whether surviving in Demotic or in Greek adaptations. Like their native antecedents, the Demotic rituals are termed *ph̠-nt̠r* and are evidence of direct continuity with earlier practice. Hostile use of the *ph̠-nt̠r* was countered in post-Ramessid times by the extensive Oracular Amuletic Decrees, descendants of "royal decrees" of protection issued by individual gods against detailed lists of ills (cf. Papyrus Turin 1993, 7/6–10). From the Amuletic Decrees derive the similarly detailed "Self-Dedication Texts" of the Ptolemaic era.

Also extending from the New Kingdom through Hellenistic times are the healing stelae known as "*cippi* of Horus," which combine traditional ritual techniques with newly standardized imagery and spells to prevent or allay the effect of snakebite and scorpion sting. Produced for general distribution, or in larger scale as public benefactions, the healing stelae were not read, but placed in contact with water that was drunk by the sufferer. The notion that magical power can be consumed is found as early as the Pyramid Texts (Spells 273–274), while Coffin Text Spell 341 records the transfer of the power of inscribed imagery to ingested fluids: "This spell is to be spoken over seven sketched eyes of Horus, washed off in beer and natron and drunk by the man." In similar fashion, incantations are drawn on the hand and licked off by the practitioner (Coffin Text Spell 81), so that standard descriptions of magicians include any "who shall lick off his spell" (Coffin Text Spell 277; *Book of Going Forth by Day* Spell 149e). On the basis of such magical mechanics, the term for "swallow" acquires the nuance "to know" by the New Kingdom. The licking or drinking of charged fluids remains a basic technique for subsequent Late Egyptian, Demotic, Greco-Egyptian, and Coptic magical rites.

The techniques of Egyptian magic have been noted frequently above, with reference both to ritual mechanics such as licking, swallowing, or image manipulation and to recitation devices like threats and blame-shifting ("It is not I who says . . ."). Perhaps the most common ritual technique is circumambulation (*phr*), used to enclose and defend sacred space or to ensnare hostile forces. Circular processions accompany funerary rites and a wide variety of temple rituals and are performed by private homeowners armed with sticks to avert the "plague of the year" at the dangerous calendrical cusp. Similarly protective are the circles scratched into the earth with apotropaic knives. In contrast, an execration ritual to protect the temple scriptorium (Papyrus Salt 825) confines wax figures of enemies within a jar encircled by the practitioner. So basic is the association of "encircling" with magic that the term *phr* comes to mean "enchant" in Demotic and Coptic. Other common ritual techniques include knots, numerological and color symbolism, necromantic intercessions, and the bivalent action of spitting or the purely hostile acts of breaking, trampling, burning, reversal, and burial.

Of recitation techniques, none is so basic as the explicit identification of the practitioner with one or more deities ("I am deity NN"). By recasting the speaker, and often the client, as a god, such equations confer divine authority on the incantation and link the fate of the client with that of a divine prototype. In medical texts, the patient is almost invariably identified with the youthful Horus, whose recovery from assaults by Seth and his confederates serves as the pattern for all healing. From the Pyramid Texts onward, identifications often take the form of lists, associating each of the client's body parts with that of a deity so that "no limb of his is lacking a god" (Socle Behague h14). Direct identification with a deity is integral to Egyptian magical recitations into Coptic times, and it permeates Greco-Egyptian spells by means of the untranslated native phrase *anok* ("I am"). Similar in purpose is the abbreviated mythological episode, or "historiola," which provides a divine precedent for the desired result: as the deity triumphs in the tale, so the client will triumph likewise. The link between client and god may be either implicit or expressed by direct identification. As the spell's beneficiary is qualified by divine associations, so the opponent is equated with demonic forces. To ensure efficacy, all parties are identified as specifically as possible. For humans, the pattern is typically "NN whom the woman NN bore." Nonhuman entities may also be given filiation: "cold, son of a cold" (Papyrus Ebers, col. 90/16). Hostile spirits are listed as inclusively as possible, with strings of male and female pairs often concluded by the term *et cetera* (*ḥmt-r₃*). The language of the spell constitutes "performative speech," often using the past tense to declare that the desired result has been accomplished.

As early as the Pyramid Texts (Spell 281), incantations may include unintelligible vocables, to be understood as either "magical words" or as transcriptions of foreign recitations (cf. Harris Magical Papyrus, cols. 7/12 and 12/1–5). Syncretistic by nature, Egyptian conjurations readily assimilated Semitic, Cretan, Nubian, and ultimately Greek elements, which were incorporated within canonical manuals at all periods. Later collections may display a higher percentage of such borrowings, but even in these compendia the underlying methodology of recitation and praxis remains primarily Egyptian. As demonstrated above, the Demotic and Greek language spells of Roman date are the direct inheritors of traditional Egyptian magic. Old Coptic spells continue the tradition, and the development of the Coptic script in part derived from the magicians' desire to specify vowels within exotic incantations. Despite a shift of deity, native techniques continue within Coptic and medieval Islamic magical practices, though the practitioner is now suspect, and his practice at variance with official theology.

BIBLIOGRAPHY

Studies

Borghouts, J.-F. "Magical Texts." In *Textes et langages de l'Égypte pharaonique*, vol. 3, pp. 7–19. Bibliothèque d'Étude, 64 3. Cairo, 1974.

Borghouts, J.-F. "Magie." In *Lexikon der Ägyptologie* 3:1137–1151.

Kákosy, László. *Zauberei im alten Ägypten*. Budapest, 1989.

Koenig, Yvan. *Magie et magiciens dans l'Égypte ancienne*. Paris. 1994.

Kropp, Angelicus. *Ausgewählte koptische Zaubertexte*. 3 vols. Brussels, 1930–1931.

Lexa, François. *La Magie dans l'Égypte antique*. 3 vols. Paris, 1925.

Ritner, Robert K. *The Mechanics of Ancient Egyptian Magical Practice*. Studies in Ancient Oriental Civilizations, 54. Chicago, 1993.

Ritner, Robert K. "The Religious, Social, and Legal Parameters of Traditional Egyptian Magic." In *Ancient Magic and Ritual Power*, edited by M. Meyer and P. Mirecki, pp. 43–60. Leiden, 1995.

Ritner, Robert K. "Egyptian Magical Practice under the Roman Empire: The Demotic Spells and Their Religious Context." In *Aufsteig und Niedergang der römischen Welt*, edited by W. Haase, vol. 2.18.5, pp. 3333–3379. Berlin, 1995.

Sørensen, Jørgen. "The Argument in Ancient Egyptian Magical Formulae." *Acta Orientalia* 45 (1984), 5–19.

Translations

Betz, H. D., ed. *The Greek Magical Papyri in Translation Including the Demotic Spells*. 2d ed. Chicago, 1992.

Borghouts, J.-F. *Ancient Egyptian Magical Texts*. Nisaba, 9. Leiden, 1978.

Meyer, M., and R. Smith, eds. *Ancient Christian Magic: Coptic Texts of Ritual Power*. New York, 1994.

ROBERT K. RITNER

Magic in Medicine

Standard discussions of medical practice in ancient Egypt typically distinguish between rational therapy ("medicine") and the use of incantations and rites ("magic"). On the basis of this modern categorical bias, rational treatments have been the focus of detailed study, while magical aspects are often marginalized and their significance to the ancient audience is undervalued. The prevailing attitude is exemplified by the primary edition of Papyrus Edwin Smith, which isolates Case 9, in which the physician recommends a comforting spell for a terminal skull fracture, as a "characteristic product of the recipe-hawking physician (as contrasted with the surgeon) . . . our surgeon's sole relapse into the superstition of his age (Breasted 1930, p. 217)." Despite this harsh judgment, the features of the case are not aberrant in composition and include a preliminary physical examination and (rational) treatment with a compress and bandaging. In this as in other instances, "magical" and "rational" treatments are paired, and the two methodologies are complementary, not in conflict.

The physician's use of ritual and spell is in keeping with ancient medical education, which was affiliated with the temple scriptorium (*pr-ʿnḫ*), a repository for medical and other sacred texts. Medicine, like all sciences, fell under the patronage of the god Thoth, although other deities might be seen as healers, including Amun, Isis, and Horus, as well as the deified sages Imhotep and Amenhotep son of Hapu. Priesthoods of these benign gods might be expected to include religious healers, but the most notable physician-priests are associated with potentially threatening goddesses: Sakhmet, goddess of disease, and Selqet, goddess of scorpions and snakes. The priest of Sakhmet is mentioned explicitly in both the Edwin Smith (col. 1/6) and Ebers (col. 99/2–3) papyri as a medical practitioner likely to take a measurement of the pulse, in common with the standard physician (*swnw*) and even the amulet-seller (*zꜣw*). This "amulet-man" noted in Papyrus Ebers might find state service as well, and amulet-men of the king of Upper and Lower Egypt are attested at court. The "controller of Selqet" treated scorpion sting and snakebite, and groups of these professionals were enlisted by the state to accompany mining expeditions, where noxious animals posed a constant danger. The handbook of such a specialist is now preserved in the Brooklyn Museum (47.218.48 and 47.218.85). Dating to the thirtieth dynasty or early Ptolemaic period, the manual provides not only a "rational" analysis of snakes by name, description, and relative toxicity, but also a "magical" analysis of the reptiles' divine associations. As expected, treatment incorporates both strategies, with incisions, emetics, topical applications, and recited spells. Magical spells against snakebite are the oldest medical remedies known from Egypt, preserved in large number within the Pyramid Texts (spells 226–244, 276–299, 314, 375–399, 499–500, 501, 538, etc.) and subsequent literature adapted from daily life for funerary purposes. These incantations include the first examples of unintelligible glossolalia, or "abracadabra" words, presumably representing foreign or divine speech (Pyramid Text Spell 281).

Within the more narrowly defined medical literature, spells are a regular and undifferentiated feature. The earliest preserved medical treatise, the Kahun Papyrus of the twelfth dynasty (c.1850 BCE), deals with both gynecology and veterinary medicine. A series of six prescriptions (nos. XXVI–XXXI) to determine whether a woman will conceive includes physical examinations, anointing, fumigation and, in prescription XXX, a fragmentary spell. Nothing formally distinguishes this manner of treatment, which is labeled simply "another instance" like those that precede and follow it. The Ramesseum Papyri III–V (c.1786–1665 BCE) are poorly preserved, but the combination of "rational" and "magical" therapy is again evident, with ingested recipes charged by spells recited over stems of onions (III, 5), flax knots placed at a child's throat (III, 33–34, and cf. IV, iii/5), fumigations and recitations over an image of a child (IV, 23–24), recitations over ointment at childbirth (IV, 30), and incantations over beer (IV, iii/4 and iv/1). Papyrus Ramesseum V preserves no spells, but its reliance on oil of hippopotamus, crocodile, lion, mouse, donkey, and lizard seems motivated by magical associations, rather than by purely physical properties. Medical spells appear also in contemporary Middle Kingdom magical manuals, with Papyrus Turin 54003 offering spells against snakebite, eye problems, and swallowed fishbones.

The use of magic in Case 9 of the Edwin Smith Papyrus (copied c.1550 BCE) has been discussed above. Further incantations against the "plague of the year" were added by the original scribe on the verso of the papyrus. As noted in a perceptive study by Wilson (1952), the relative paucity of magic in this "Surgical Papyrus" is likely due to the nature of the injuries under consideration. Most are simple fractures of obvious origin and straightforward treatment. Had the text dealt with the more mysterious problem of internal disease, magic would have been more prominent, as is the case in the corresponding Ebers Papyrus, copied by the identical scribe. In both papyri, infection is attributed to "something entering from the outside," depicted as a demonic figure with antennae.

The Ebers Papyrus (also c.1550 BCE) is a compilation of remedies and theoretical discussions, and it freely joins "rational" and "magical" methodology. The magical component of the papyrus is evident from the very beginning, as the first three sections detail the "First spell for applying remedies on any limb of a man" (col. 1/1–11), "Another spell for loosening any bandage" (col. 1/12–2/1), and a "Spell for drinking a remedy" (col. 2/1–6). Each spell contains a brief mythological episode, known as a "historiola," which assimilates the patient and his fate to the successful healing of a deity and offers protection against "the stroke of a god, the stroke of a goddess, from a dead man, a dead woman, from a male adversary, a female adversary," etc. All spells are recommended as "truly effective—(proved) millions of times." The introductory position of these generic spells indicates that their use is to be understood in all subsequent remedies without any further specification. By implication, even recipes lacking explicit magical features would still have been accompanied by standard healing incantations. Thus, the absence of spells from individual sections of the Edwin Smith, Ebers or other medical papyri should not be used as evidence of an exclusively rational approach, and the supposed contrast between the "recipe-hawking" and rational physician is fallacious.

The Ebers Papyrus contains seventeen incantations and two birth prognostications generally treated as magical. In addition to the three introductory spells, the papyrus prescribes incantations coupled with potions for treatment of diarrhea (§ 48, col. 15/16–16/6) and roundworm (§ 61, col. 18/21–19/10). An exorcism of *whdw* conjures the principle of corruption believed responsible for natural aging and decay (§ 131, col. 30/6–17). The *whdw* or unexpelled residue of bodily waste, is commanded to leave the body as spittle or vomit and thus "perish just as you came into being." Further exorcisms expel bewitchment (§ 733, col. 88/13–16), bald patches (§ 776, col. 92/13–16), illness in the female breast (§ 811, col. 95/7–14), and prevent a kite from robbing (§ 848, col. 98/2–6). Paralleling the use of magic as a last resort in Case 9 of the Smith Papyrus, the "instructions for the swelling of the vessels" caution the physician against physical treatment, but provide a recitation for enchanting the fatal illness (§ 873, col. 108/9–17).

Several incantations are recommended for ophthalmological treatments. For blindness, the principle of substitution underlies a topical treatment with fluid extracted from pig's eyes accompanied by a statement "as magic" that the practitioner has "brought these which are put in the place of those" (§ 356, col. 57/17–21). The selection of pig's eyes evokes (and counteracts) the myth of the blinding by Horus by a black pig (Coffin Text Spell 157 and *Book of Going Forth by Day* [Book of the Dead] 112). A spell against "white spots" in the eyes recounts a historiola of the floundering of the solar bark recited over the gall bladder of a tortoise, an enemy of Re and his ship (§ 360, col. 58/6–15; cf. *Book of Going Forth by Day* Spell 161). Word association (paranomasia) forms the crux of a spell to "expel the collecting of water in the eyes (cataracts)," which invokes the presence of vigor (*w3d*) by the application of malachite (*w3d*, § 385, col. 60/16–61/1; cf. *Book of Going Forth by Day* 160). In most spells, cures are effected by means of direct identification between patient and deity, either completely ("I am Horus"; "It is not I who recites but the goddess Isis") or in part ("My head is the head of Anubis, . . . my nose is the nose of Thoth . . ., there is no limb of mine lacking a god").

Representative examples of the pairing of rational and magical procedures are afforded by the three treatments offered for the common cold (cols. 90/14–91/1). The first remedy is simply date wine to be drunk by the patient, and the second involves ground plant material inserted into the nostrils. The third (§ 763), "Another exorcism of a cold," consists of a spell against the personified "cold, son of a cold, who breaks bones, throws down the skull, who hacks in the bone-marrow, who places illness in the seven holes in the head." Using performative speech, the cold is urged to flow out of the patient by means of a recitation over a mixture of the milk of a woman who has borne a male child and fragrant gum, placed in the nose. While a rational basis is easily found for the insertion of soothing gum into sore nostrils, the spell itself and the use of mother's milk derive from magico-religious concepts. The "milk of a woman who has borne a male child" is symbolic of the curative milk of the goddess Isis, who healed her infant son Horus by this divine liquid. Healing spells generally associate the sufferer with Horus, the prototypical patient, and episodes of his mythical healing are often recited as historiolae within the body of an incantation. The need for this mother's milk probably inspired the creation in the New Kingdom of specialized vases in the shape of females suckling an infant son. By the magical principle of images, milk poured from these vessels derived from the body of "a woman who has borne a male child."

The same fluid is used in two exorcisms for burns (§§ 499–500, col. 69/3–7), which comprise variants of a common historiola relating the burning of Horus on the desert. Additional variants of the spell appear in Papyrus British Museum 10059 (§§ 47–48, cols. 14/14–15/4) of the eighteenth dynasty, and in Papyrus Leiden I 348 (§§ 37–38 vo. 3/1–3/5) from the nineteenth dynasty. The use of such mother's milk is found throughout the medical papyri in treatments for burns, the eyes, nose, muscles, swellings, *wḥdw*, and pediatrics, surviving even in the Coptic Chassinat Papyrus (ninth century) in a cure for the ear. The substance passed into the Greek Hippocratic corpus, the works of Dioscorides and Pliny the Elder, and European medical manuals from the twelfth to fifteenth centuries, with its last attestation in an English herbal of 1671.

The blend of medical and magical treatments characteristic of Papyrus Ebers is equally evident in the related Hearst Papyrus (c.1450 BCE), which duplicates almost one hundred sections of the older text and adds further generic spells to be used when measuring medicines (§§ 212–213, cols. 13/17–14/4) or applying oil (§ 214, col. 14/4–7). Later papyri maintain a similar admixture, with spells prominent in Papyrus British Museum 10059 (c.1350 BCE), Berlin Papyrus 3038 and the Chester Beatty Papyri V–VIII and XV (all c.1300 BCE), and Papyrus Carlsberg VIII (c.1200 BCE). Spells treat the full range of human ills, including headache, eye disease, scorpion sting, internal disease, and rectal problems. As in the Middle Kingdom, medical treatments also appear in the purely magical papyri of Ramessid date. Papyrus Leiden I 348 includes incantations for head and stomach aches, accelerating childbirth, dispelling bad dreams, and healing burns. The cosmopolitan nature of New Kingdom and Ramessid society favored the incorporation of foreign elements within Egyptian magical treatments, and spells in Northwest Semitic dialects and even Cretan speech (Linear A) are recorded in Papyrus British Museum 10059 (§§ 27–33, cols. 10/6–11/7).

Magical and medical techniques continue to be joined in the latest medical papyri. Like its ancient predecessor from Kahun, the Roman-era Papyrus Berlin 13602 treats gynecological matters with physical therapy and spells. Reflecting the broader international influence during the Greco-Roman eras, the many medicinal spells of the London and Leiden Magical Papyrus (third century CE) combine Greek terminology for ingredients with native and even Nubian (*verso* col. XX) incantations. As is evident from this survey, medical texts of all periods utilize magical elements, and there is no justification for suggestions of an increase of magic in later times.

Textual material is accompanied at all periods by healing amulets, and, as noted previously, the amulet seller might also perform a limited physical examination. Since most patients will have been illiterate, written texts were commonly adapted as unread phylacteries, tied as a small packet suspended from the client's neck. Other amuletic forms were generated by evolving medico-magical needs. In the Middle Kingdom, ivory wands carved from hippopotamus tusks served as "magical knives," decorated with apotropaic figures and used to delineate a protective circle about mothers and newborn infants. Secondarily, the knives appear in funerary contexts, where they ensure the rebirth of their deceased owner. The New Kingdom mother and child vases have been discussed above, and a further anthropomorphic vessel type was created for unguents associated with pregnancy. Combining the physical attributes of a human female and a hippopotamus, the vases represent the body of the goddess Taweret, whose fluids could be used to ensure elasticity of the skin. A funerary adaptation of this sort is found among the alabaster vessels of Tutankhamun, where an unguent jug provided with the head and breasts of Hathor guaranteed that the reborn king would be nourished by the goddess herself. So-called "Bes-jugs" of the Late period represent a similar adaptation for divinely charged contents.

A further innovation of the New Kingdom is the round-topped healing stela, or "*cippus* of Horus." Designed to avert or heal the wounds of snakes, scorpions, or other dangerous animals, the stelae may be traced from the eighteenth dynasty to the Roman era. Typical examples depict a central image of the youthful Horus trampling multiple crocodiles beneath his feet while grasping in both hands wild animals of the desert: snakes, scorpions, lions, and gazelles. A protective head of Bes appears above Horus, and rows of additional divine figures fill subsidiary vignettes. Depending on the size of the stela, two or more standardized texts cover all remaining surfaces. Such stelae were erected for both public and private benefit, and smaller, portable examples were carried on caravans, with examples attested from Nippur, Byblos, Hama, Meroe, Auxum, and Rome. *Cippus* spells appear on a large-scale statue of Ramesses III, placed by royal beneficence at a caravansary at Almazah in the Delta east of modern Cairo. Like the spells of the phylacteries, the texts of the *cippi* were unread; their power was acquired instead by pouring water over the words and images and ingesting the charged fluid. Larger stelae were erected above basins intended to collect the curative water. The most famous large-scale *cippus* is the Metternich Stela, now in the Metropolitan Museum of Art in New York (MMA 50.85), commissioned in the reign of Nectanebo II (c.360–343 BCE) by the priest Nes-Atum to replace texts taken from the temple of the Mnevis bull in Heliopolis. This collection of fourteen incantations gleaned from temple scriptoria provides several new historiolae but follows standard spell techniques. One celebrated spell (§ 3, 11. 9–35) uses the traditional identification of deities with the patient's bodily members to heal an injured cat ("You cat here, your head is the head of Re . . . there is no limb of yours lacking a god"). In the thirtieth dynasty and the Ptolemaic period, the *cippus* was incorporated within public healing statues, which represent a priestly donor covered by carved incantations presenting a stela of Horus. The bases of such statues also feature basins for the reception of water offerings, which in turn became a healing drink for the supplicant.

In later Hellenistic times, *cippus* imagery also appears on carved gems, popular healing or protective amulets that were distributed throughout the Greco-Roman world. Such gems mingle native imagery with contemporary foreign elements to produce an "international style" of occult iconography once attributed to syncretistic Gnostics. Even in these late products, ancient Egyptian magical and medical concepts may be preserved, and the uterine amulets in particular reflect older gynecological practices.

The long association of the temple with the science of medicine produced new forms of sacred healing. By the later New Kingdom, rear walls of major temples had become popular shrines for divine petitions, and penitential hymns proclaimed the deity's role in inflicting and curing maladies. In the Hellenistic eras, temples and sanctuaries of sacred animals became pilgrimage sites where clients practiced incubation to receive curative visions. A sanatorium was constructed at the temple of Dendera; Deir

el-Bahri became an incubation center for Imhotep and Amenhotep son of Hapu; and the ibis catacombs of Tuna el-Gebel received donations in return for miraculous cures. The technique of incubation, or ritual sleep, need not represent Hellenistic influence, since texts from the First Intermediate period onward already signal the existence of oracular dreams. The association of temple and healing shrine is perhaps clearest at Kom Ombo, focus of the popular cult of "Horus the good doctor." On the Antonine enclosure behind the rear wall of the sanctuary, a relief combines contemporary medical instruments with the ancient Eye of Horus (*wḏȝt*), at once the amuletic symbol for curing, the hieroglyphic representation for medical measurements, and the purported origin of the pharmaceutical symbol ℞. The healing powers of the ancient temples are still invoked in modern folk rituals for fertility, entailing baths in the sacred lakes and ingested powder scraped in large gouges from temple walls.

[*See also* Medicine.]

BIBLIOGRAPHY

Breasted, James H. *The Edwin Smith Surgical Papyrus.* Chicago, 1930.

Daressy, Georges. *Textes et dessins magiques.* Catalogue Général des Antiquités Égyptiennes du Musée du Caire. Cairo, 1903.

Dawson, Warren R. "A Strange Drug." *Aegyptus* 12 (1932), 12–15.

Edwards, I. E. S. "Kenhikhopshef's Prophylactic Charm." *Journal of Egyptian Archaeology* 54 (1968), 155–160.

Erman, Adolf, *Zaubersprüche für Mutter und Kind.* Berlin, 1901.

Grapow, Hermann. *Von den medizinischen Texten.* Grundriss der Medizin der alten Ägypter, 2. Berlin, 1955. See pp. 11–26.

Lacau, Pierre. "Les statues 'guérisseuses' dans l'ancienne Égypte." *Monuments Piot* 25 (1921–1922), 189–209.

Ritner, Robert K. "A Uterine Amulet in the Oriental Institute Collection." *Journal of Near Eastern Studies* 43 (1984), 209–221.

Ritner, Robert K. "Horus on the Crocodiles: A Juncture of Religion and Magic in Late Dynastic Egypt." In *Religion and Philosophy in Ancient Egypt,* edited by W. K. Simpson, pp. 103–16. New Haven, 1989.

Ritner, Robert K. *The Mechanics of Ancient Egyptian Magical Practice,* Studies in Ancient Oriental Civilizations, 54. Chicago, 1993.

Sauneron, Serge. "Le rhume d'Anynakhté (Pap. Deir el-Médinéh 36)." *Kemi* 20 (1970), 7–18.

Steiner, Richard C. "Northwest Semitic Incantations in an Egyptian Medical Papyrus of the Fourteenth Century B.C.E." *Journal of Near Eastern Studies* 51 (1992), 191–200.

Wilson, John A. "A Note on the Edwin Smith Surgical Papyrus." *Journal of Near Eastern Studies* 11 (1952), 76–80.

ROBERT K. RITNER

Magic in Daily Life

Beyond the enclosed precincts of formal temple ritual, private individuals often had recourse to an array of religious practices now deemed "magical." Especially at times of personal crisis, "magic" served to cure disease, ease childbirth, and defend against attack by enemies, beasts, or demons. More generally, such methods might be employed at any time for a variety of purposes: to ensure the fertility of husbands, wives, fields, or livestock; to safeguard the continued health of family members and animals; to curse opponents; to compel love and respect from sexual partners or supervisors; to empower the corpse in funerary ceremonies; or to send and receive messages from deceased ancestors. The use of magic in these circumstances was legal, normative, and by no means in opposition to state religion.

Utilizing the coercive yet orthodox religious principle of *ḥqꜣ*, these private rites parallel official temple cult in both mythology and manipulation of "consecrated imagery," and for good reason. The community magician was typically a member of the literate priesthood, whose temple obligations claimed no more than a quarter of the year. Serving in groups or "phyles" in rotation, the priest when off duty might supplement his income by offering his ritual skills to private clients. With literacy restricted to an estimated one percent of the population, it was the same close-knit community of temple-affiliated scribes who composed, edited, and guarded the rituals and recitations of temple magic, and who in the formal role of "lector-priest" (*ḥry-ḥb*) might perform such rites for state, temple, or private purposes.

Known exceptions to this rule are few and confined to the otherwise atypical workmen's village of Deir el-Medina, which lacked any resident priesthood. Living apart from the Nile community at government expense, the literate artisans served as their own priests. Dockets on the *verso* of Papyrus Geneva MAH 15274 record their communal use of magical manuals for daily concerns: "Today (came) the scribe Panetcher giving the spell for extracting the poison to the scribe of the royal tomb Paneferemdjedet" (*verso* II/1–6). A further docket (*verso* V) may record the specific antivenom spell employed by the scribes. Even these manuals probably derived from a temple source and were simply copied, not composed, by the scribes at Deir el-Medina. Evidence of a temple origin is clear in Papyrus Chester Beatty VIII, which became the property of the scribe of the royal tomb Kenherkhepeshef, and which states that "this writing was found in the library, (in) a room of the temple" (col. 4/3), and that the spell "is to be recited by the chief lector-priest" (*verso* 7/7). As skilled craftsmen, the artisans of this village were quite capable of fashioning amuletic images for magical purposes, and one letter preserves the request to "make for me a *wrt*-demon, since the one that you made for me has been stolen and thus works a manifestation of Seth against me" (Ostracon Deir el-Medina 251).

A few ostraca from the same site reveal the existence of local "wise women" (*rḫt*), who are unattested elsewhere in Egypt. Functioning as a medium or diviner, the "wise woman" is consulted on matters of curses and possession:

"I have gone to the wise woman and she told me: 'The wrath of Ptah is with you . . . because of an oath by his wife'" (Ostracon Gardiner 149). The scribe Kenherkhepeshef writes to a woman of the village: "Why did you fail to go to the wise woman on account of the two infants who died while in your care? Inquire of the wise woman about the death of the two infants, whether it was their fate or their destiny" (Ostracon Letellier).

The records of such consultations contain no reference to the practitioner's apparatus or literacy. In contrast, most evidence of magic in daily life indicates a reliance on recited spells, precise ritual, and charged, amuletic substances. The discovery of a Middle Kingdom "magician's box" from a tomb beneath the Ramesseum has provided an example of the range of materials and textual sources used by a typical practitioner. In addition to twenty-three papyri comprising hymns, detailed exorcisms, funerary rites, and spells to promote fertility and cure a variety of illnesses, the box contained writing materials, dolls, divine and serpent figures, human hair, amulets, and beads.

The interdependence of public and private magic is well illustrated by rites to protect agricultural and residential property. In Roman-era Esna, a statue of the deity Heka was carried from the temple and made to circumambulate the local fields to ensure their productivity. In Theban tomb paintings of the New Kingdom, depictions of harvest rites show comparable bark processions among the fields under the patronage of Amun, Mut, Khonsu, and the harvest goddess Renenutet, whose image is erected beside both state and private granaries. These agricultural ceremonies for public and private benefit are descendants of the ancient royal jubilee rite of "encircling a field" (*pḥrr šꜣ.t*), enacted to confirm the protection and possession of the land by the royal celebrant.

Similar rites of protective encircling are performed by homeowners at the critical juncture of the new year. On the verso of Papyrus Edwin Smith, the second incantation against the annual threat of disease stipulates that the spell is to be recited "by a man with a stick of *ds*-wood in his hand while he goes outside, going around his house. He cannot die by the plague of the year" (col. 18/15–16). This private ritual, appended to a formal treatise on medicine, is paralleled not only by the agricultural and jubilee processions, but also by a wide variety of official circumambulation rites intended to maintain the sacred space of cities, temples, and burial grounds. In the Greco-Egyptian magical papyri of Roman date, such magical circles are made even about individual plants that the magician harvests for his spells, and the basic term for "encirclement" (*pḥr*) acquires the nuance "to enchant" in both Demotic and Coptic. From the Archaic era to the Roman era, the methodology and purpose of the "magical circle" remain constant, whether enacted for royal, temple, or private property.

Other instances of agricultural magic include a "spell to prevent a kite from robbing" added to the collection of medical recipes in Papyrus Ebers (§ 848, col. 98/2–6) and exorcisms of noxious animals from the fields in the Harris Magical Papyrus (British Museum 10042 § X, col. 10/1–11/1). The former rite diverts the attention of plundering birds by a spell invoking the falcon deity Horus that is recited over a cake atop a branch of acacia wood. Horus reappears in the latter "spell of the herdsman" to protect his cattle from "lions, hyenas and all manner of wild animals with long tails, who eat flesh and drink blood." The protection of valuable cattle was a matter of great concern, as indicated by numerous fording spells which guard against the crocodiles that infested marshes and canals. Old Kingdom tombs often depict such a fording scene: a reluctant herd is enticed into crossing the water by a herdsman who carries a calf on his back, while a spell is recited on boats or ashore by others who make protective gestures. Though it has often been assumed that the herdsmen themselves recite the spell, the find of an ivory figurine of a herdsman carrying a calf among the objects of the Ramesseum "magician's box" suggests that even in such mundane circumstances the recitation was done by professionals. Closer examination of the Old Kingdom scenes reveals a distinctly dressed figure who acts as speaker and supervisor.

Temple authority over anti-crocodile spells is explicit in the Ramessid Harris Magical Papyrus (British Museum 10042), the first text of Egyptian practical magic published after the decipherment of hieroglyphs (1860). Entitled "Good Spells to Chant Which Drive Away the Swimming One," the collection includes twenty-three incantations of varying character, including formal hymns attested on temple walls, brief invocations, and seeming rigmaroles in glossolalia or foreign language. Such spells represent restricted knowledge, "concerning which the Chief Lector Priests say: 'Do not reveal it to others.' A veritable secret of the House of Life" (§ K, col. 6/10). In the cited passage, a secret recitation imbues an egg of clay with the cosmic force of the egg of the primordial Ogdoad. Placed "in the hand of a man in the prow of a ship," the charged egg is thrown if a crocodile should surface. As in the Old Kingdom fording scenes, there is a distinction between professional reciter and gesticulating actor. If recitation might be limited, however, apotropaic gestures certainly were made by all individuals, being perhaps the most common feature of popular magical practice. Even the depictions of Egypt's enemies show such gestures, with the *mano cornuta* raised in vain against the crushing blow of Ramesses III at Medinet Habu.

Images of defeated enemies are a staple of Egyptian magic. In royal and sacerdotal contexts, prisoner figures are incorporated into door sockets, paving stones, footstools, throne bases, sandal bottoms, coffin bottoms, canes, jar handles, linch pins, and even oar stops, so that the most mundane acts of walking, sitting, or riding are ritualized, rendering the image seized, crushed, or throttled. State and private interests intersect in the more formal execration ceremonies performed with prisoner images, which extend from elaborate assemblages inscribed with the codified "Execration Texts" to smaller groups and individual figurines. Made of stone, wood, clay, wax, or dough, prisoner figurines are typically inscribed with the personal name of the intended victim and are then misused by binding, piercing, spitting, burning, and, most importantly, by premature burial. In the systematic state assemblages, enemies are represented by red pots or figures on which are inscribed the five sections of the "rebellion formula" that enumerates the potentially hostile rulers of Nubia, Asia, and Libya, as well as outcast Egyptians and generally destructive forces (evil speech, plots, dreams, etc.). The presence of personal names on jars enclosing deposits of these rituals suggests that private donors may have played a role, perhaps influencing the selection of outcast Egyptians. Just such a mixture of state and private vendetta is recorded in the late ritual against Apophis (Papyrus British Museum 10188), in which the practitioner is instructed to abuse figures of the enemies of Re, pharaoh and "all foes male and female whom your heart fears" (col. 28/17–18). Personal enemies are surely represented by often crudely produced individual figures and by smaller groups portraying cursed families. From Ramessid to Hellenistic times, execration methodology was adapted for so-called love spells, which simply constitute compulsion spells for a different goal. In such spells, the victim is made helpless, unable to eat, drink, or rest, while compelled to follow the magician "like an ox after grass" (Ostracon Deir el-Medina 1057).

Prisoner imagery may also be adapted for nonroyal clients on objects directed against demons and disease. During the Middle and New Kingdoms, protective circles were sketched around a child's bed with so-called apotropaic wands or knives, whose efficacy is enhanced by representations of defensive spirits said to offer "protection by day and protection by night." Typical examples, like those from the Ramesseum box, display files of knife-wielding animals in company with Taweret and Beset, but examples now in the Metropolitan Museum of Art, New York and Paris (MMA 15.3.197; Louvre 3614 + MMA 26.7.1288) add scenes of prisoners devoured by a lion, Taweret, and a cat. In funerary contexts, hostile forces are averted from the deceased by the image of a divine prisoner named *Nkiw-mn.t*, "The Vanquished One at the Stake," used as a vignette in New Kingdom papyri; in Hellenistic times, subjugated prisoners are painted on the cartonnage beneath the feet of individual mummies.

Whether in sleep or in death, the resting body was considered particularly vulnerable, and extant spells to protect the bedchamber are varied and elaborate. From the early New Kingdom, a Berlin papyrus (Papyrus Berlin 3027) published as "Magical Spells for Mother and Child" preserves rituals of the "magician of the nursery" against childhood diseases inflicted by possessing spirits. The most famous of these spells (Text C) banishes any vampiric male or female demon "who comes in the darkness and enters in furtively" with face reversed, intent on kissing, quieting, and stealing the child. Protection is made with onions and honey, "which is sweet to mankind but bitter to the dead."

From Ramessid Deir el-Medina, Ostracon Gardiner 363 contains a ritual against ghosts "recited over four *uraei* made of pure [. . .] clay, with flames in their mouths. One is placed in [each] corner [of any bedroom] in which there is a man or woman sleeping with a man [or woman]." Similar fire-spitting *uraei* are depicted as protectors of the cardinal directions in temple reliefs and papyri, "shooting fire . . . in the darkness" (Papyrus Salt 825, col. XIX). Probably associated with such spells are two artifacts in the British Museum, one a rearing clay serpent from a house at Amarna (EA 55594) and the other a pair of gilt *uraei* entwined about the leg of a bed (EA 21574).

A Brooklyn Papyrus (47.218.156) of early Ptolemaic date contains two rituals to save the sleeper "from anything bad and evil, any fear, any terror, any dead man or any dead woman" who, as an incubus, would inject poison-laden semen into the ears. Originally designed for a pharaoh, the texts are adapted for commoners. A similar spell intended for a King Psamtek survives only in a Ptolemaic copy (Brooklyn Papyrus 47.217.49), but it signals the existence of a Saite original. Such defensive rituals were further elaborated in Ptolemaic times to safeguard the rest of the sacred falcon at Edfu, who was the beneficiary of both a "Protection of the Bedroom" (*s3 ḥnk.t*) and an annual "Protection of the House" (*s3 pr*), performed just before the New Year like the private ritual of P. Edwin Smith, noted above.

Much as disgruntled ghosts were thought to represent a threat to the living, so the blessed dead might bestow protection and fertility. Contacted directly by "Letters to the Dead," inscribed figurines, or by "necromantic" divinatory rituals with lamps and cups (cf. *Book of Going Forth by Day* Spells 134, 148, and 190), the dead are implored to fight on behalf of the living, with the results revealed in dreams. Belief in the continued sexual potency of the deceased is explicit in Coffin Texts Spells 576 and 619 and underlies the fear of incubus assault. When pla-

cated, departed ancestors can ensure the fertility and health of their descendants: "Let a healthy son be born to me, for you are an able spirit" (Chicago Jar Stand).

Health maintenance certainly entailed the most common applications of magic in daily life. From the simple wearing of amulets to complex rituals, medicine employed a wide variety of magical treatments. Drugs were chosen for their mythological correspondences as well as for perceived biological properties. Occasionally administered in specialized containers representing curative deities (Isis, Taweret, Bes), they were invariably accompanied by standardized spells when measured or applied to bandages. Many treatments combined "rational" and "magical" strategies, with plant and mineral substances "charged" by spell and rite. In most such cases, the patient is equated with the youthful Horus, whose cure is sanctioned by the gods.

Magical techniques predominate in remedies for expelling the venom of snakes and scorpions, the affliction most frequently noted in healing texts. Antivenom spells are attested from the Pyramid Texts through modern times, and the ancient specialist was a trained priest, the "controller of (the scorpion goddess) Selqet." A popular innovation of the later New Kingdom was the antivenom stela or "*cippus* of Horus," used well into Roman times. Engraved with divine figures and spells, the stelae were brought in contact with water subsequently drunk by the patient.

Emphasis on deity as the ultimate source of salvation from illness led to a new development in the Third Intermediate Period. Ramessid protective spells might be headed "A Royal Decree of Osiris, Foremost of the Westerners" (Papyrus Turin 1993, vo. 7/6–10), but during the theocratic Libyan era (twenty-first to twenty-third dynasties) divine sponsorship was formalized. By petitioning the cult statue during official processions, clients received "oracular amuletic decrees" issued by the local god(s) that promised security from a detailed list of illnesses, gods, *weret* and *wrt* and other demons, as well as magicians, snakes, and ill-intentioned oracles. Written on long, thin strips of papyrus, the decrees were rolled and inserted into tubular amulet cases suspended from a cord worn about the petitioner's neck. Probable descendants of this practice are the Ptolemaic documents from Memphis and the Faiyum known as "Self-Dedication Texts," in which the suppliant vows perpetual servitude to the deity in exchange for protection from itemized ills.

The temple setting for these late practices underscores the continued role of magic within sanctioned daily religion. Thus it is perhaps fitting that the final documents of traditional religion, preserved in Demotic and Greek translations, comprise manuals of practical magic, with rituals for oracles, healing, love and cursing.

BIBLIOGRAPHY

Edwards, I. E. S. *Oracular Amuletic Decrees of the Late New Kingdom.* 2 vols. Hieratic Papyri in the British Museum, 4. London, 1960.

Erman, Adolf. *Zaubersprüche für Mutter und Kind.* Berlin, 1901.

Jankuhn, Dieter. *Das Buch "Schutz des Hauses" (s3-pr).* Bonn, 1972.

Pinch, Geraldine. *Magic in Ancient Egypt.* London, 1994.

Ritner, Robert K. "O. Gardiner 363: A Spell Against Night Terrors," *Journal of the American Research Center in Egypt* 27 (1990), 25–41.

Ritner, Robert K. *The Mechanics of Ancient Egyptian Magical Practice.* Studies in Ancient Oriental Civilizations, 54. Chicago, 1993.

Ritner, Robert K. Review of *Magic in Ancient Egypt* by G. Pinch. *Journal of Near Eastern Studies* 57 (1998), 298–299.

Sauneron, Serge. *Le papyrus magique illustré de Brooklyn.* Brooklyn, N.Y., 1970.

Wainwright, G. A. "The Earliest Use of the Mano Cornuta." *Folklore* 72 (1961), 492–495.

ROBERT K. RITNER

Magic in the Afterlife

From earliest prehistoric times until the very end of indigenous Egyptian religion, burial customs provide unmistakable evidence of conscious efforts by survivors to influence the fortunes of the deceased, whether by deposited artifacts, associated texts, or ritual performance. The most pervasive feature of such magic for the afterlife is the inclusion of grave offerings within the tomb. Designed to sustain the corpse physically, spiritually, and socially, funerary offerings exhibit a wide variety of forms, extending from simple deposits of food to elaborate tomb assemblages such as that of Tutankhamun, which comprises objects of daily life and of ritual. By transferring tangible artifacts of the earthly world to the spiritual realm of the dead, all such offerings represent magical practice. Early Dynastic (Archaic) burial customs underscored this functional transition by ritually breaking or "killing" deposited objects in order to assimilate them to their deceased owner (Ritner 1993, p. 148).

In what is perhaps the single unifying "scriptural" text from Egypt, the standard funerary prayer focuses primarily on the offering process. Attested from the Old Kingdom through Hellenistic times, the prayer provides a theoretical basis for funerary offerings, in which "an offering which the king gives" to (or in the company of) attendant deities is in turn transmitted to the cult and *ka*-spirit of the deceased. While actual objects may be physically presented via this system of "reversion of offerings," the funerary prayer represents a magical supplement. By the act of reciting a common list of invocation offerings (literally, "the going forth of the voice"), the ritual performer ensures that the deceased beneficiary is provided with the underworld equivalent or intangible essence of the object named: "a thousand loaves of bread, a thousand jugs of beer, a thousand oxen, a thousand fowl, a thousand vessels of alabaster, a thousand bolts of cloth, and every-

thing good and pure on which a god lives." Uttered both by official *ka*-priests, formally contracted to provide the service, and by pious visitors to the tomb chapel ("O you who pass by this tomb"), the invocation is characterized as a simple "breath of the mouth" without hardship for the speaker, but with enduring benefit for the dead (tomb of Pahery). Such an understanding is in accord with the basic, imagistic principle of Egyptian magic (*ḥḳȝ*), which postulates a manipulable link between any given object and its representation in word or image.

The spoken offering prayer is typically supplemented by yet other images, including engraved texts of the prayer itself and menus of desired products, as well as depictions of such goods produced and borne by attendants or piled on stands or tables. The offering slab alone may contain a series of supplemental images, being at once provided with physical offerings, carved in the shape of the word for "offering" (*ḥtp*), inscribed with the funerary prayer, and decorated with relief images of flowing jugs, bread loaves, haunches of beef, fowl, or flowers. In any individual tomb, the series of deposited offerings, relief depictions, and textual recitation constitutes an intricate system of magical reinforcements serving the religious goal of a beatified afterlife. One must reject the common assumption that "decorative" scenes of daily life in tombs of the Old through New Kingdoms are in some sense less religious or magical than later tomb depictions of deities and underworld scenes. Egyptian tomb art is primarily functional, not decorative, and scenes of estates and crop production are intended not merely as testimonials to earthly wealth, but as objects—and status—to be transferred to the next life. Like the common banquet scenes that depict the deceased partaking of his offerings in the hereafter, the so-called scenes of daily life have their true functional locus in the afterworld. The later preference for underworld scenes is discussed below.

As food offerings are complemented by an array of consecrated imagery to maintain the nourishment of the deceased, so deposited staves, scepters, jewelry, and other insignia of status are complemented not only by tomb depictions of estates, personal triumphs, and servants, but also by an evolving set of three-dimensional servant figures. In the first and second dynasties, tombs of royalty and high officials are surrounded by numerous subsidiary (*sati*) burials of retainers, who were slain to accompany their masters. In conformity with the less destructive principle of imagistic substitution, actual sacrifices are replaced in the Old Kingdom by individual stone sculptures which represent servant figures performing a variety of activities: grinding grain, baking, brewing, butchering, playing harps, or dancing. By the First Intermediate Period, the collapse of royal sculptural workshops led to the substitution of often crude wooden figures, typically arranged in complex group settings depicting granaries, breweries, slaughterhouses, households, or boats. Such figures were simplified in the New Kingdom into all-purpose servant images, known initially as *shawabtis* (*šwbty*), or "persea-wood figures." By simple phonetic metathesis, the term was later transformed to *ushabtis* (*wšbty*), or "answerers" associated with Spell 472 of the Coffin Texts and Spells 6 and 151h of the *Book of Going Forth by Day* (*Book of the Dead*). Should the deceased be called upon to perform any work in the necropolis, whether cultivation, irrigation, or corvée, the figure is to answer on behalf of its owner: "I shall act; here I am." Made of wood, stone, faience, or even mud, such figures multiply in number, often with one *ushabti* for each day of the year and an additional set of figures representing foremen. In keeping with the general democratization of Egyptian funerary customs, the wider availability of servant *ushabti*s allowed not merely maintenance but improvement of social status for the deceased. A reminiscence of these servant figures by the Greek satirist Lucian in his tale "The Lover of Lies" (*Philopseudes*) served as the inspiration for "The Sorcerer's Apprentice," recounted in a poem by Goethe and a symphonic piece by Paul Dukas, which was featured in a section of Walt Disney's animated film *Fantasia* (1940).

The distinguishing feature of Egyptian mortuary practice was the physical preservation of the corpse itself. With the elaboration of funerary structures and equipment, natural desiccation in the arid sands was necessarily replaced by artificial techniques of mummification. The complex process of mummification is at once a form of "medical" intervention to arrest the decay believed to be engendered by the corruptive agent *wḥdw*, and a "magical" process to ensure a primary repository for the *ka*-spirit, otherwise resident in supplementary *ka*-statues, in relief or painted depictions of the tomb owner, or even in simple spellings of his name. Mummification techniques are correspondingly a mixture of rational treatment (the draining of bodily fluids and application of drying natron salts) and magical incantations, amulets, and rites.

The spells and rituals associated with mummification are preserved in a series of mortuary texts successively inscribed on tomb walls, coffins, deposited papyri, or directly on the mummy bandages themselves: the Old Kingdom Pyramid Texts, the First Intermediate Period and Middle Kingdom Coffin Texts, the New Kingdom *Book of Going Forth by Day*, and the Late period *Books of Glorifications* (*s3ḫ.w*) and *Books of Breathings* (or *Breathing Permits*). Although this funerary literature contains general theological expositions and insights into the broader religious concerns of society, the explicit purpose of these texts is one of practical theology, with coercive ritual and incantations for the benefit of the individual tomb owner.

Early scholarly classifications notwithstanding, Egyptian funerary texts are hardly separable from other ritual texts commonly designated as magical, and both groups make use of identical methodology in spell and praxis. Particularly common in the recitations of both are the "historiola," or brief mythological precedent for the desired result, and the use of lists equating the spell's beneficiary or his body parts with a series of deities. Starting in the New Kingdom, underworld literature returns to the tomb walls, with elaborate, illustrated guides to the underworld (*Book of That Which Is in the Underworld* [*Amduat*], *Book of Caverns, Book of Gates*, for example) in royal tombs and in vignettes derived from funerary papyri in private tombs. Such depictions have often been linked to the rise of a new sense of popular piety, but as in earlier wall scenes, the purpose of these tomb illustrations is to reinforce the status of the deceased in the underworld. While the format may be new, the sentiment is traditional, and the textual sources for the representations may well extend back to the Middle Kingdom or First Intermediate Period. Insofar as the wall scenes are charged images supplemental to funerary texts and offering ritual, they are as magical as their predecessors.

The numerous spells against snakes and scorpions in mortuary literature represent an obvious link to magical practices in daily life. On occasion, the transmission of older funerary spells into later collections is accompanied by greater detail, so that the terse Spell 260 of Pyramid Texts is recast as a resurrection spell as Spell 1 of the Coffin Texts, and, as Spell 169 of the *Book of Going Forth by Day*, it is further designated as the recitation that accompanies the installation of the funerary bier. The pivotal role of magical efficacy underlying all funerary recitations is emphasized by common incantations to secure *heka* for the deceased (Coffin Texts, Spells 342, 350, 392, 402, 426, 491–492, 495, 499–500, 572–573, 705, and 1017, and *Book of Going Forth by Day*, Spell 24) and to prevent him from garbling a spell (Coffin Texts, Spell 657, and *Book of Going Forth by Day*, Spells 90, 110a3S1 and a4S).

Amulets and other charged substances are often prescribed by the ritual associated with individual mortuary spells, and tangible examples of such items are typically interred with the corpse as magical protection. The use of *ushabti*s in conjunction with *Book of Going Forth by Day*, Spells 6 and 151h has been noted above. The most important funerary amulet was certainly that of the heart, associated with *Book of Going Forth by Day*, Spells 29B and 30. Fashioned as a heart or scarab (symbol of becoming and transformation) and bearing the text of the relevant spell, such amulets served as substitute hearts. Considered the central organ of the physical body and the seat of thought, memory, and emotion, the heart was not removed during mummification. Supplementary amulets, spells, and vignettes both preserved the heart's vitality and coerced it to remain silent regarding past misdeeds when it was weighed against *maat* ("truth") in the judgment hall of Osiris (*Book of Going Forth by Day*, Spell 125).

By virtue of its form, the burial mask assimilates the corpse to Osiris, and the companion "Spell for a Secret Head" (*Book of Going Forth by Day*, Spell 151a–c) equates individual body parts with a list of gods. Other amulets associate the deceased with the protection of a particular deity, such as the *djed*-column of Osiris (*Book of Going Forth by Day*, Spell 155), the red jasper knot (*Book of Going Forth by Day*, Spell 156) and gold vulture (*Book of Going Forth by Day*, Spell 156) of Isis, and the Heliopolitan broad collar with falcon-headed terminals (*Book of Going Forth by Day*, Spell 158). Green (*w3d*) feldspar amulets of papyrus columns (*Book of Going Forth by Day*, Spells 159–160) confer the quality of raw vigor (*w3d*), while the single most common funerary amulet, the Eye of Horus (*wd3.t*), guarantees general health and soundness (*wd3*). More specific assistance is offered by the headrest amulet that aids the deceased in his ascent to the sky (*Book of Going Forth by Day*, Spell 166), the snakehead amulet that offers coolness against the inflammation of snakebite (*Book of Going Forth by Day*, Spells 33–35), the *ba*-amulet that ensures the safe return of the spirit to the corpse (*Book of Going Forth by Day*, Spell 89), and the later hypocephalus that restores bodily warmth (*Book of Going Forth by Day*, Spell 162).

If the amuletic sections of the *Book of Going Forth by Day* contain protections placed directly within the wrappings of the corpse, Spell 151d–g records spells and instructions for creating a larger defensive perimeter of the tomb interior, with four "magical bricks" surmounted by protective images placed in niches at the four cardinal directions. An extra exemplar of Spell 151f found in the doorway of the "treasury" of Tutankhamun's tomb is designed to repel the enemy of the deceased king, and is probably the source of the fictional "Curse of King Tut," supposedly promising "death on swift wings" for any desecrator of the tomb. Although Tutankhamun's curse is a fabrication of the press, genuine tomb curses are attested from other sites and eras. Such curses are typically from private tombs and are largely confined to the Old Kingdom.

Thus, in the tomb of Nikaankh at Tihna, the owner threatens violators with a complaint before the underworld tribunal: "As for any man who will make disturbance, I shall be judged with him." The door support of the steward Meni adds an immediate, earthly punishment: "A crocodile be against him in the water; a snake be against him on land, he who would do anything against this [tomb]. Never did I do a thing against him. It is the god who will judge." In the tomb curse of Ankhmahor from Saqqara, notions of retribution and ghostly manifes-

tation are combined in the closest approximation to the vengeful mummy of Hollywood films.

> As for anything that you might do against this tomb of mine of the West, the like shall be done against your property. I am an excellent lector-priest, exceedingly knowledgeable in secret spells and all magic. As for any person who will enter into this tomb of mine in their impurity, having eaten the abominations that excellent *akh*-spirits abominate, or who do not purify themselves as they should purify themselves for an excellent *akh*-spirit who does what his lord praises, I shall seize him like a goose, placing fear in him at seeing ghosts (*akhs*) upon earth, that they might be fearful of an excellent *akh*-spirit. I shall be judged with him in that noble court of the great god. But as for anyone who will enter into this tomb of mine being pure and peaceful regarding it, I shall be his protective backer in the West in the court of the great god.

The most extensive tomb curse is found in a proclamation of the twenty-first dynasty for the funerary estate of the deified eighteenth dynasty architect, Amenhotep, son of Hapu. Desecrators are warned that they will lose all earthly positions and honors, be incinerated in execration rituals as enemies of the gods, capsize, drown, and decay at sea without heirs, tomb, or offerings. Lacking a proper funerary cult, they will die a second death and lose all hope of immortality: "They will starve without sustenance and their bodies will perish."

As implied by the curse of Amenhotep, the rituals of embalming and burial are critical for the beatification of the deceased. Divine associations are conferred both by the spells recited by funerary priests and by the utensils and apparatus employed. A calcite vase from the tomb of Tutankhamun is sculpted with the head and breasts of the nurturing cow goddess Hathor, so that its unguents constitute the restorative fluids of the goddess herself. Similarly representative vessels depicting Isis, Taweret, and Bes are used in curative magic. Imagery of the sky goddess Hathor reappears on one of Tutankhamun's three funerary biers. As the mummy was placed atop this couch designed as the celestial cow, it was ritually elevated into the heavens with the sun god Re in a reenactment of *The Myth of the Heavenly Cow*. The double lion bed served a similar purpose. Representing the paired horizon deity Aker or Ruty or the twins Shu and Tefnut, the bed positions the corpse as the central sun disk in the hieroglyphic symbol for "horizon," thereby linking the deceased with the solar circuit. The remaining bed, shaped like the hippopotamus goddess, Taweret, assured the rebirth of the corpse as it was passed in ceremony through the body of this goddess of pregnancy.

The burial reenacts a mythic prototype as well, with masked "Anubis men" carrying the corpse, now transformed into Osiris by invocations, ritual masking and offerings symbolic of the defeated Seth. The Opening of the

Mouth ceremony restores the senses to the body and is effected with both an adze and a ram-headed wand named, appropriately, "Great of Magic."

Even after burial, interaction with the deceased employed a variety of "magical mechanics." In addition to the continuing offering cult, necromantic consultations were possible, and instructions for such rituals are contained in the *Book of Going Forth by Day*, Spells 148 and 190, designed to ensure that the deceased is received by the gods "so that it can make known to you what fate befalls it." Visualization of the dead could be accomplished by the technique of scrying, using a bowl painted with figures viewed through a volume of oil. Direct assistance for the deceased is promised in the rubrics of many spells in the *Book of Going Forth by Day* that might be performed by the living on behalf of dead relatives. Conversely, the custom of "letters to the dead" comprises petitions from the living for assistance from the underworld. Inscribed on ostraca, linen, papyri, and on bowls once containing propitiatory offerings, the "letters to the dead" echo the phraseology of personal correspondence among the living, with a mixture of casual pleasantries, complaints, and requests. The numinous position of the beatified dead gave them authority and influence in matters of divine petitions and tribunals, demonic possessions, healing, and fertility. Thus, writers request that the dead litigate against personal enemies, intervene on behalf of suffering descendants, and ensure the pregnancy of surviving daughters. Other notes contain reproaches: "Will you remain calm about this?" "What have I done against you?" As indicated by a text from the First Intermediate Period, the response to such letters could be expected in a dream: "Please become a spirit for me [before] my eyes so that I may see you in a dream fighting on my behalf."

In exceptional cases, necromantic consultations were institutionalized, as in the cults of the saintly healers Imhotep and Amenhotep son of Hapu. At Deir el-Medina, the deceased ruler Amenhotpe I was worshipped as patron of the village and consulted in regular processional oracles. By the reign of Ramesses II, an oracle of Ahmose, founder of the eighteenth dynasty, was functioning in Abydos, and subsequent to his own death Ramesses II became the presiding spirit of oracular procedures in both Egypt and Nubia. In literature, deceased rulers are often loquacious, as in the *Instructions of Amenemhet*, and in the autobiographical Harris Papyrus and the Turin Indictment Papyrus, related by the deceased Ramesses III. Necromantic consultations were extended in later times to nonroyal spirits as well, including those drowned in the Nile, and thus especially linked to the fate and numinosity of Osiris, and the mummified remains of sacred animals, for whom "letters to deities" now replaced the older "letters to the dead."

Even the depredations of tomb robbers may attest to the pervasive character of traditional magical practices, for the willful destruction of the name, image, or mummy of the tomb owner conforms to old execration ritual. Perhaps motivated by fear of "an excellent *akh*-spirit," such injuries crippled the deceased spirit by removing his magical system of empowered supplemental imagery.

[*See also* Amulets; Book of Going Forth by Day; Book of That Which Is In the Underworld; Coffin Texts; Funerary Figurines; Mummification; Pyramid Texts; *and the composite article on* Offerings.]

BIBLIOGRAPHY

Allen, Thomas George. *The Book of the Dead or Going Forth by Day.* Studies in Ancient Oriental Civilization, 37. Chicago, 1974.

Andrews, Carol. *Amulets of Ancient Egypt.* London, 1994.

D'Auria, Sue, et al. *Mummies and Magic: The Funerary Arts of Ancient Egypt.* Boston, 1988.

Faulkner, R. O. *The Ancient Egyptian Pyramid Texts.* Oxford, 1969.

Faulkner, R. O. *The Ancient Egyptian Coffin Texts.* 3 vols. Warminster, 1973–1978.

Gardiner, Alan H., and Kurt Sethe. *Egyptian Letters to the Dead Chiefly from the Old and Middle Kingdoms.* London, 1928.

Grinsell, L. V. "The Breaking of Objects as a Funerary Rite." *Folklore* 72 (1961), 475–491.

Ritner, Robert K. *The Mechanics of Ancient Egyptian Magical Practice.* Studies in Ancient Oriental Civilization, 54. Chicago, 1993.

Ritner, Robert K. "Necromancy in Ancient Egypt." In *Magic and Divination in the Ancient World,* edited by Leda J. Ciraolo. Gröningen, forthcoming.

Silverman, David P. "Magical Bricks of Hunuro." In *Studies in Honor of William Kelly Simpson,* edited by Peter Der Manuelian, vol. 2, pp. 725–41. Boston, 1996.

Wente, Edward F. "A Misplaced Letter to the Dead." *Orientalia Lovaniensia Periodica* 6/7 (*Miscellanea Vergote,* 1975–1976), 595–600.

ROBERT K. RITNER

MALACHITE. *See* Gems.

MANETHO (*fl.* 290–260 BCE; his name in Egyptian is *Mry.n ntr c₃* ["beloved of the great god"]), Egyptian priest of Sebennytos in the Nile Delta and general savant. Manetho was reputed to have written widely on such subjects as the history, religion, cult, medicine, and natural history of the Nile Valley. Some works credited to him, such as the "Sothis-book," may be pseudepigraphical, yet there can be little doubt that he was the author of a three-volume history of Egypt, the *Aegyptiaca,* in Greek, for the edification and instruction of non-Egyptians. Although contemporary attestations are lacking, Manetho was historical, and he lived during the early period of the new Ptolemaic regime in Egypt; this makes it tempting to construe his work as a response to Ptolemy II's initiative to create a databank, a research library at Alexandria, which ideally would store the history, literature, religious lore, and science of the known world.

Although no longer extant, the *Aegyptiaca* may be reconstructed as the latest stage in the evolution of the Egyptian king-list tradition. As such, it became the successor to the New Kingdom king list (now represented by the Turin Canon) and the culmination of the tendencies that were part of that fluid tradition. Little under the rubric "Manetho" was actually original with him; he just translated into Greek and transmitted his contemporary Egyptian tradition. Curiously, it was not the extant monuments and stelae (which Manetho above anyone would have been able to read) but the contents of temple archives in Demotic that he used as sources. Thus his material came from legends, romances, mythological tales, and Midrashic interpretations—not, apart from the king list itself, from sober historical texts. Beginning with the deity Ptah (Hephaestos) as world-creator, Manetho divided the king list into groupings of gods, demigods, heroes, and thirty human dynasties. The last continued an earlier Egyptian concept of (royal) "houses," which constituted one of the organizing principles of the Turin Canon. Manetho used the king list as a skeletal framework into which he inserted material (often folkloristic) at the appropriate points, for example, after the mention of a king. The entry for each king was accompanied by the length of his reign in years. In some cases, narrative material that spanned the reigns of several kings was added at the end of the dynasty to which it belonged.

The king-list tradition, as reflected in Manetho's work, showed an extension of some trends already begun in the Turin Canon:

1. The division into dynasties was derived partly from the association of groups of kings with a particular site (Diospolis, Herakleopolis, or Memphis) and partly from accurate memory of family units;
2. A sectioning of the list into groupings of nine kings owes much to the mythological concept of the Ennead as the ideal ancestor dynasty;
3. Since the throne of Egypt, hypothetically, could be occupied by only one king at a time, dynasties that had been collateral had to be represented as consecutive.

While the original *Aegyptiaca* did not long survive—it may still have been available in the early years of the Christian era, although that remains moot—an abridgement, the *Epitome*, was made early in the second century BCE, by culling kings' names, lengths of reigns, and salient historical information. The latter comprised misinterpreted annalistic material, folklore, and biblical and classical cross-references, entered after the fashion of glosses. During the Judeo-pagan polemic that had originated in Alexandria,

the *Epitome* was much used as a reference work to bolster the cases of either side; such use continued into the period that included both the Jewish revolt against the Romans and the rise of the fathers of the Christian church. The Jewish historian Josephus (of the late first century CE), who knew both the *Epitome* and the original *Aegyptiaca*, used extensive quotations from the sections that treated the Hyksos and the eighteenth dynasty. During that acrimonious polemic in Alexandria and because of a prior chronological agenda, the lengths of pharaonic reigns and other numerical summations suffered considerable distortion. That the *Epitome* survived at all was due to its use by the Christian philosopher Julius Africanus (of the early third century CE), who employed it for the Egyptian section of his synchronistic chronicle of world history to 221 CE; this was then quoted by Eusebius (260–340 CE), who incorporated his own version (which also survives in a distorted Armenian version).

Manetho's other works (on religion, on culture, and his citicisms of Herodotus) have not survived. There is no reason to think that Manetho's name was used on any pseudepigraphical literature that was masqueraded as the genuine *Aegyptiaca*.

[*See also* King Lists.]

BIBLIOGRAPHY

Helck, W. *Untersuchungen zu Manetho und den Aegyptischen Koenigslisten.* Berlin, 1956.

Krauss, R. *Das Ende der Amamazeit.* Hildesheim, 1978.

O'Mara, P. "Manetho and the Turin Canon: A Comparison of Regnal Years." *Göttinger Miszellen* 158 (1997), 49–62.

Redford, Donald B. *Pharaonic King-lists, Annals and Daybooks.* Mississauga, 1986.

Redford, Donald B. "The Name Manetho." In *Egyptological Studies in Honor of Richard A. Parker,* edited by L. Lesko. Hanover and London, 1986.

Thissen, H.-J. "Manetho." In *Lexikon der Agyptologie,* 3: 1180–1181. Wiesbaden, 1980.

Waddell, W. G. *Manetho.* Loeb Classical Library, 1940.

DONALD B. REDFORD

MANICHAEAN TEXTS. The adherents of Manichaeism taught that evil was eternal and co-equal with good and that the visible world had been created not by the supreme God, but by a lesser deity, or even by Satan. They supported their cosmogony with an elaborate mythology drawn from pre-Christian and non-Judaic sources. The discovery in 1929–1930 in Egypt of a handful (probably seven; the number is not yet certain, owing to the dispersion of the manuscripts and the vicissitudes of war) of Coptic manuscripts with Manichaean texts, probably in the ruins of ancient Narmuthis, near Medinet Madi in the Faiyum, caused great and justified sensation. They contain many important texts not known in other languages, and they reveal an aspect of Coptic literature not previously known.

This is not the place to deal with the vicissitudes of the codices after discovery, although they justify the fact that some of the texts are still unpublished; that we cannot even draw a detailed list of the codices and of the works they contained. Before discovery they had already suffered very much during more than thirteen centuries of storage in a cellar, where they had become almost carbonized. As a result, we will never recover the texts in their entirety. What was saved, or may in future be recovered, is of great value for our knowledge of Manichaeism and of the Manichaean communities in Egypt. Only a small part of the text was published between the date of the discovery and World War II; after a long pause, work has been resumed on the edition of what did not perish during the war (notably, a facsimile edition of the part in Dublin), but the material is very fragmentary. The codices are difficult to date; Polotsky proposed the fifth century CE. They are very precisely executed, with "inscriptiones," "subscriptiones," current titles, and decorations, as was customary in the Manichaean community.

Other invaluable information on Egyptian Manichaean communities comes from the documents and artifacts found in the extraordinarily rich excavations of the village of Kellis, where one such community lived. In this case, however, the archeological work is still in progress, so I will make only brief remarks on this material after my discussion of the Faiyum documents.

The Coptic Manichaean codices of the Narmuthis find contained, from what is actually known, the following works. The Codex of the Psalms, now in Dublin, has been published only in part in the edition by C. R. C. Alberry under the title *A Manichaean Psalm-Book* (Stuttgart, 1938; *Manichäische Handschriften der Sammlung A. Chester Beatty*, vol. 2). This is a huge volume (more than 500 pages) of psalms—that is, liturgical hymns—which are combined in a number of groups, with a complete index of incipits (first lines) at the end of the volume. The groups were as follows (cf. Krause, 1991): group 1, twenty-five psalms, title lost; group 2, psalms 26–33, entitled "of Herakleides"; group 3, psalms 34–82 (not certain), entitled "Synaxis"; group 4, psalms 83–105, "of the Soul"; group 5, psalms 106–118, title lost; group 6, psalms 119–130, "for Sunday"; group 7, psalms 131–135, "of father Herakles"; group 8, psalms 136–149, title lost; group 9, psalms 150–154, "of the Passover"; group 10, psalms 155–162, "Various"; group 11, psalms 163–164, title lost; group 12, psalms 165–170, title lost; group 13, psalms 171, "of lord Syrus"; group 14, psalms 172–199, "various"; group 15, psalms 200–205, "of the night"; group 16, psalms 206–217, "of Herakl[es or -ides]"; group 17, psalms 218–241, "of the Bema"; group 18, psalms 242–276, title lost (called "of Jesus" after their content); group 19, psalms 277–286, "of Herakleides"; group 20, psalms 287–289, "various"; group 21, psalms 290–297, title lost; group 22, psalms 298–333, "Sarakoton"; group 23, psalms 334–340, "of Herakleides"; group 24, psalms 341–360, "of Thomas"; and last (ungrouped) psalms. The accurate systematic organization of these poetic compositions shows an important aspect of the activity of the Manichaean elite in liturgy and in literature, and also (as is well known) in the accurate making of the codices; the same may be said for the Kephalaia.

Two huge volumes contain the famous Kephalaia, or part of them. These are texts that relate the discourses of Manichaeus (this appears to be the form of the name used in Egypt) to his disciples, but they were not written by him. One of the volumes is now in Berlin (one folio is in Vienna) and has been published for the most part by Hans J. Polotsky and Alexander Böhlig as *Manichäische Handschriften der Staatlichen Museen Berlin*, vol. 1. Kephalaia (Stuttgart, 1935), and vol. 2, *Lieferungen 11/12* (Stuttgart, 1966). The other manuscript volume is now in Dublin and is still unpublished; therefore, information on its content is not certain.

The Kephalaia are a group of anecdotes that report discourses by Manichaeus to his disciples during their meetings. Their character and contents vary. Some are historical narratives: Keph. 1, on the advent of the apostles from the beginning to Jesus and Manichaeus; Keph. 17, on the three ages of the world (the first man, his advent, and the destruction of the idols); Keph. 18, on the five wars of good against evil; Keph. 76, on the mission of Manichaeus; and Keph. 77, on the four kingdoms. There are numerous descriptions of the heavenly personages of Manichaen mythology: Keph. 7, on the the five fathers; Keph. 10, the fourteen aeons; Keph. 11, the Fathers of light; Keph. 16, the five greatnesses; Keph. 20, the name of the Father; Keph. 21, the Father of greatness; Keph. 26, the first man and the envoy; Keph. 28, the twelve riders of the Father; Keph. 38, the light-nous; Keph. 46 and 66, the envoy; Keph. 50, the words God, rich, and angel; Keph. 51 and 53, the first man; Keph. 55, 57, and 64. Adam; Keph. 56, Saklas; Keph. 60, the four Fathers; and Keph. 67, the Illuminator. Comments on religious behavior include Keph. 79 and 81, on fast; Keph. 81, judgment; Keph. 87 and 93, charity; and Keph. 88 and 91, catechumens.

There are detailed explanations of Manichaean imagery: Keph. 2, on the similitude of the tree; Keph. 4, the four great days and great nights; Keph. 5, the five hunters of the light and the four of the darkness; Keph. 6, the five treasures; Keph. 8, the fourteen vehicles; Keph. 29, the eighteen thrones of the Father; Keph. 30, the three vestments; Keph. 36 and 49, the wheel of the king of honor; Keph. 42 and 43, the three vehicles; Keph. 45, the vehicles; Keph. 61, the vestment of water; Keph. 62, the three stones; Keph. 72, the vestments; Keph. 85, the cross of light; Keph. 90, the fifteen ways; and Keph. 95, the cloud. Explanations of concepts are found in Keph. 3, on happiness, wisdom, and force; Keph. 9, the kiss of peace; Keph. 14, silence, fast, peace, day, and stillness; Keph. 19, the five departures; Keph. 31, the call; Keph. 34, the ten works; Keph. 35, the four works; Keph. 39, the three days and two deaths; Keph. 41, the three battles; Keph. 47, the four great things; Keph. 63, love; Keph. 78, the four works; Keph. 80, righteousness; and Keph. 84, wisdom. Explanations of natural elements include Keph. 37, on the three zones; Keph. 44, tides; Keph. 59, the elements which wept; Keph. 65, the sun; Keph. 68, fire; Keph. 69, the zodiac and the stars; Keph. 71, the elements; Keph. 73, the envy of matter; Keph. 74, the living fire; and Keph. 94, the purification of the four elements.

A third codex was divided between Dublin (about fifty sheets, published by Hans J. Polotsky as *Manichäische Homilien* [Stuttgart, 1934; *Manichäische Handschriften der Sammlung A. Chester Beatty*, vol. 1]) and Berlin (an unconserved block, now probably lost). It contained an interesting collection of four texts, dealing with the vicissitudes of Manichaeus and his disciples, both in the historical past and in the apocalyptic future. Despite Polotsky's title *Manichäische Homilien*, they are not homilies in the current sense of the word. The first of the four is the *logos* of the prayer—that is, a lamentation in the form of a prayer for the death of Manichaeus, probably written by his disciple Salmaios. The second is the *logos* of the great war, an apocalyptic narrative of the persecutions of the Manichaeans, their triumph with the reestablishment of the Manichaean church, and finally the coming of Jesus and the final judgment, the return of Jesus to the realm of the light, and the destruction of the material world; this text was possibly written by the disciple Kustaios. The third is a narrative of the persecution of Manichaeus by Bahram I and Bahram II, and his crucifixion. Finally, there is an apotheosis of Manichaeus, of which only a few pages remain, very damaged.

All the other texts of this cache are unpublished. Much was lost around 1945, so we have only some preliminary accounts made before the war. They comprised a *Synaxeis manichaeorum*, partly in Dublin and partly in Berlin; an *Opus historicum manichaeorum*, codex in Berlin and mostly lost; and the *Epistulae Manichaei*, codex in Berlin and mostly lost.

The Kellis documents (from the name of a village in the Dakhla Oasis, now called Ismant el-Kharab) are still being found in excavations in progress from 1987. They include codices on wooden boards, papyrus and parchment codices, private letters, and inscribed wooden boards. The languages are Greek, Coptic, and Syriac; the texts are mostly nonliterary, but there are many "classical" texts, liturgical and religious (Manichaean) texts, and translation tools providing equivalence of vocables, and

other linguistic evidence. The date is probably mid-fourth century CE, and the owners probably belonged to a missionary cell of the first stage of Egyptian Manichaeism.

A last important document is the impressively small Greek codex now at Cologne University (Inv. 4780), a wonderful work in miniature that contains the life of Manichaeus from childhood to youth. It illustrates the origins of Manichaean ideas in an environment surprising for scholars. Its religious-historical implications have been widely investigated.

The Medinet Madi codices, together with the new documents, are important sources for the history of Manichaeism in Egypt. According to one Middle Iranic document, around 250 CE, Manichaeus sent his disciple Adda to Egypt with some scriptures, to preach the new religion. Other important persons mentioned in our sources (notably the *Acta Archelai*) are Pappos, Thomas (possibly the author of some psalms), and especially Skythianos. The last, a rich Saracen merchant, settled in Egypt to found Manichaean communities, coming from the Red Sea caravan route to the city of Hypsele, not far from Siout (Assiut). It is notable that the Medinet Madi texts are written in what appears an Assiutic dialect.

Manichaeism spread very fast in Egypt, as in other countries of both the east and the west. When Diocletian issued his famous edict of 31 March 297, he happened to be in Alexandria; a papyrus fragment dated to the late third century (P.Ryl. III 469) warns people against Manichaean propaganda. In about the same epoch, Alexander of Lykopolis wrote his tractate *Against the Manichaeans*, and later the bishop Serapion of Thmuis, a friend of Athanasius, wrote another.

Interesting features of the Manichaean organization in Egypt (as elsewhere) are the very active role of women, and the possibility (though recently rejected) that the *electi* resided in monasteries of a sort, possibly providing an example to Pachomius for the creation of monastic communities. Recent studies have pointed to the proximity of the Gnostic Nag Hammadi texts to parts of Manichaean doctrine, which surely was born in a Gnosticizing (partly Christian) environment. Several late documents, the last from the seventh century CE, testify to the existence of so-called Manichaeans in Egypt until the Arab invasion of the mid-60s. It is uncertain whether real Manichaean communities were meant, or whether this was simply a scornful name applied to any isolated heretic groups or persons.

BIBLIOGRAPHY

General works

McBride, D. "Egyptian Manichaeism." *Journal of the Society for the Study of Egyptian Antiquity* 18 (1988), 80–98.
Polotsky, Hans J. "Manichäismus." In his *Collected Studies*, pp. 699–714. Jerusalem, 1971.

Ries, Julien. *Les études manichéennes: Des controverses de la Reforme aux decouvertes du XXᵉ siècle.* Louvain-la-Neuve, 1988.

Tardieu, Michel. *Le Manichéisme.* Paris, 1981.

Vergote, Jozef. "L'expansion du manichéisme en Égypte." In *After Chalcedon,* edited by Van Roey, pp. 471–478. Leuven, 1985.

On the Medinet Madi Codices

"Codex Manichaicus Coloniensis." In *Atti del Simposio Internazionale, Studi e Ricerche, Cosenza.* Cosenza, 1986.

"Codex Manichaicus Coloniensis." In *Atti del Secondo Simposio Internazionale (Cosenza, 27–28 Maggio 1988).* Cosenza, 1990.

Giversen, Søren. *The Manichaean Coptic Papyri in the Chester Beatty Library,* vol. 1: *Kephalaia: Facsimile Edition.* Geneva, 1986; vol. 2: *Homilies and Varia: Facsimile Edition.* Geneva, 1986; vol. 3: *Psalm Book, Part I: Facsimile Edition.* Geneva, 1988; vol. 4: *Psalm Book, Part II: Facsimile Edition.* Geneva, 1988.

Krause, Martin. "Zum Aufbau des koptisch-manichäischen Psalmenbuches." In *Manichaica Selecta,* edited by A. Van Tongerloo and S. Giversen, pp. 177–190. Leuven and Lund, 1991.

Robinson, James M. "The Fate of the Manichaean Codices of Medinet Madi, 1929–1989." In *Studia Manichaica, II. Internationale Kongresse zum Manichäismus,* edited by G. Wiessner and H.-J. Klimkeit, pp. 19–62. Wiesbaden, 1992.

Schmidt, Carl, and Hans J. Polotsky. "Ein Mani-Fund in Ägypten: Originalschriften des Mani und seiner Schüler." *Sitzungsberichte der Berliner Akademie* (1933), 4–90.

On the Kellis Documents

Gardner, Iain. "A Manichaean Liturgical Codex Found at Kellis." *Orientalia Lovaniensa Periodica* 62 (1993), 30–59.

Koenen, Ludwig. "Manichäische Mission und Kloster in Ägypten." In *Das romisch-byzantinische Ägypten, Akten Symposium Trier 1978,* pp. 93–108. Mainz, 1983.

Koenen, Ludwig, and Cornelia Romer. *Der Kölner Mani-Kodex: Abbildungen und diplomatischer Text.* Papyrologische Texte und Abhandlungen, 35. Bonn, 1985.

Koenen, Ludwig, and Cornelia Romer. *Der Kölner Mani-Kodex: Über das Werden seines Leibes, Kritische Edition.* Opladen, 1988.

TITO ORLANDI

MAN WHO WAS WEARY OF LIFE. This tale outlines a conversation between a man eager to die and his *ba* ("personality/spirit"). The *ba* was just one component of the Egyptian soul: it was the aspect of soul that represented the deceased. The *ba* was usually depicted as a bird with the head of the deceased person. Here, the man and his *ba* discuss the good and bad aspects of death.

This papyrus was found with the *Story of Sinuhe* and the *Eloquent Peasant* in a twelfth dynasty Theban tomb. Whereas numerous examples of *Sinuhe* and the *Eloquent Peasant* survive, only this one example of this difficult text remains.

The text is divided into two parts. In the first, which exists in a fragmentary state, the man seems to be experiencing a suffering so great that he wishes to die. He wants his *ba* to lead him to death before his time; this may imply suicide, but also suggests that the man simply waits impatiently for his inevitable end. The *ba*, however, wishes to leave him because of his request. This, for an Egyptian,

was a fate worse than death, for the *ba* continues the soul in the afterlife. The man attempts to cajole the *ba* into staying by offering it conditions that would make another *ba* envious. In response, the *ba* states that the man should rejoice in the festivals and in life, and not worry about burial, for pain exists in death, too. Although preparation for the afterlife was a cornerstone of Egyptian faith and practice, the *ba* tells its owner that time will eradicate the tomb.

The man's answer to the *ba* consists of four poems, each different in style. In the first, each verse begins with, "Lo, my name reeks," and continues describing the low state of his character. In the second, he refrains from describing his plight and chooses instead to describe the plight of his community; he lives in a society where robbery and plunder are commonplace, and his fellow citizens are cold and cruel. The third poem begins, "Death is before me today," adding positive similes for the coming of death. In contrast to the vile comparisons to the man's name, there are beautiful allusions, such as the smell of a lotus flower and the fragrance of myrrh. Finally, a poem of only three stanzas concludes this section, beginning, "Truly, he who is yonder will be a living god," and then highlighting the anticipated afterlife where justice prevails.

After imploring the man once more to stop anticipating death, the *ba* decides to stay with the man until death finally comes. After death, he promises, the two will be united. Although some may say that the man inevitably chose suicide, the text in no way implies this. He seems to have elected a natural death, thus being able to participate in the benefits of an afterlife after all.

BIBLIOGRAPHY

Brunner-Traut, E. "Die Lebensmüdc und sein Ba." *Zeitschrift für Ägyptische Sprache und Altertumskunde* 94 (1967), 6–15.

Faulkner, R. O. "The Man Who Was Tired of Life." *Journal of Egyptian Archaeology* 42 (1956), 21–40.

Goedicke, Hans. *The Report about the Dispute of a Man with his BA (Papyrus Berlin 3024).* Baltimore, 1970.

Lichtheim, Miriam. *Ancient Egyptian Literature.* Vol 1. Berkeley, 1973.

WENDY RAVER

MARKETS. *See* Trade and Markets.

MARRIAGE AND DIVORCE. In ancient Egypt, both marriage and divorce were relatively informal and private matters between individuals. In general, the state took no interest in either marriage or divorce, so there was no official documentation of unions or their dissolution. There also seem to have been no specific marriage ceremonies in ancient Egypt, although there probably were informal family celebrations of the union, and more formal festivities for royal marriages. Marriage in ancient Egypt might best be described as cohabitation with intent to reproduce, since maintenance of the household unit and the production of children and heirs were strongly emphasized. Marriage within the royal family also had political and religious implications; such marriages differed from those among nonroyals in terms of partner choice, rates of polygamous marriage, and other factors. Divorce was the dissolution of the marital union by the departure (either voluntary or forced) of either husband or wife, and the disposition of property from within that unit. There was no inherent stigma in divorce, and in certain periods it seems to have been very common.

In practice, the mechanics of marriage and divorce in ancient Egypt reflected the role of social influences—the family and the community—and the traditional roles of men and women in Egyptian society. Although a marriage could be initiated by a man or woman, and both would theoretically be equal partners within the relationship, men tended to figure more prominently in the processes of marriage because of their more visible roles in society. In many cases, the woman's family probably played an important role in arranging the union, and the husband sometimes gave gifts to the bride's family as part of the process. Once married, husband and wife would tend to follow the standard social roles for men and women: the husband would work outside the home and earn income, while the wife would administer the household, care for the children, and do other kinds of domestic work. The basic assumption of Egyptian marriage was that women would look after the home and children, and men would support wives and offspring—an ideal that was perhaps not so practical for non-elite households. In later periods, the husband's responsibility for spousal support was clearly articulated in annuity contracts on the woman's behalf, but this seems to reflect earlier, if unwritten, custom. Women had considerable property rights in marriage: they retained control of the property they brought into the marriage; they were the regular inheritors of substantial portions (at least one-third) of their husband's property; and they could enter into financial transactions and legal agreements on their own. Where women acted through male representatives, this was not due to formal restriction on their own actions. Archaeological evidence from joint burial assemblages often highlights social and economic inequities between husband and wife. It is hard to get a balanced idea of the emotional dynamics of Egyptian marriages from textual evidence; the nature of these sources is such that records were made primarily when things went wrong, and this characterizes the majority of texts relating to marriage. Although it is not common, letters and other texts sometimes attest to great love and af-

MARRIAGE AND DIVORCE. *Serpentine statuette of a family couple.* A nineteenth dynasty official and his wife embrace each other in a gesture expressing mutual love and affection. (The Metropolitan Museum of Art, Rogers Fund, 1907. [07.228.94])

fection existing between husband and wife; even these texts, though, tend to be the result of misfortune (such as the deeply felt letters written to dead spouses).

The termination of marriage came about for a variety of reasons, the most basic being incompatibility. The emphasis on reproduction within marriage made infertility a concern that could weaken the marriage, but divorce was not the only solution to a childless marriage: adoption was quite common. Adultery seems to have been considered the greatest threat to marriage, more from concern for property and inheritance rights than from notions of sexual fidelity. No distinction was made between "legitimate" and "illegitimate" children in ancient Egypt, and children born through adulterous relations would be legal heirs to both parents, threatening the inheritance of the members of the married household. Although family and community members often aggressively pursued instances of suspected adultery, it was not, as far as can be determined, something that was usually punished. No specific "legal" grounds for divorce were necessary, although the excuses of adultery, infertility, physical defects, and incompatibility were sometimes cited. Divorce was most commonly initiated by the husband, although in the later period cases of women initiating divorce are found; the divorced spouse might be abandoned or thrown out of the house, depending on the situation. Surviving documentation relating to divorce tends to concern especially complex cases; divorces by mutual consent were probably not documented. Remarriage after divorce was very common, and it was not unusual for both men and women to divorce and remarry more than once.

Remarriage after divorce or bereavement was common in part because being married was seen as the ideal state for an adult in ancient Egypt. Most unmarried adults encountered in Egyptian documentation were single because of the death of a spouse or divorce; individuals who never married seem to have been rare. Certain religious offices (such as that of the God's Wife of Amun as it developed in the Third Intermediate Period) were occupied by intentionally unmarried individuals, but this is clearly atypical. Still more unusual was a situation such as that of Hatshepsut after she assumed the titles and roles of king. Having taken on the attributes of a male king, the widowed Hatshepsut clearly could not marry, but she needed someone to take on the duties traditionally carried out by the king's principal wife. Ultimately, Hatshepsut's daughter Neferure took on some of these duties for her mother, in effect acting as king's principal "wife," but this situation was likewise exceptional.

Egyptian terminology for marriage and divorce reflects the informal and home-centered nature of the relationship. Phrases translated as "to marry" include "to establish a household" (*grg pr*), "to enter a household" (*ʿq r pr n*) and, in later periods, "to live together" (*ḥms jrm*) with someone. Marriage is also described as the act of a man "taking" a wife (*jṯ*, later *ṯ3y*) or "making" someone a wife (*jr (m) ḥm.t*), and in later periods women are sometimes described as "taking" a husband as well. Parents are sometimes described as giving a woman (*rḏj m* [later *r*] *ḥm.t*) as wife to someone. Less legalistic is the use of the term *mnj* ("to moor") as a metaphorical expression for marriage. The terminology for the partners in a marriage contrasts the roles of men and women. The word for husband (*h3y/hy*) is used in contexts in which a woman is the textual focus and it is necessary to identify her partner. In the majority of cases, though, the man is the center of interest, and thus the terms for "wife" are much more fre-

quently encountered and more complex in usage. The most common words for "wife" are *ḥm.t* (also *st-ḥmt*) and *ḥbsw.t;* in the New Kingdom, the word "sister" (*sn.t*) is also used for wives in monumental inscriptions (though never in legal contexts). The term "married woman" (*ḥm.t ṯ3y*) is also used. In addition, the titles "citizeness" (*ʿnḫ.t n njw.t*) and "mistress of the house" (*nb.t pr*) generally indicate a woman who is married. Sometimes a woman is simply described as being "with" a man; this occurs in contexts in which the same woman also described as being the *ḥm.t* of a man, and thus seems to indicate "wife" as well. There was no special terminology for divorce: a husband would "leave," "abandon" or even "cast out" (all covered by *ḫ3ʿ*) his wife, while a wife could "go away" from or "abandon" (*šm*) her husband. A divorced woman was called a *wḏʿt*, "an adjudged one (?)."

The documentation associated with marriage and divorce in ancient Egypt was concerned primarily with property—safeguarding the property held before marriage, clarifying the division of property obtained within the marriage, and ensuring the support and inheritance of spouses and children. There was no record of the marriage or divorce itself, and what documents survive tend to show situations in which something has gone wrong and are thus atypical of the majority of marriages and divorces. In earlier periods, documents pertaining to marriage or divorce are texts relating to property disposition, division of property, and inheritance (especially the *jmy.t pr*). In later periods, the types of documents associated with marriage become more standardized; the Demotic *sẖ n sʿnḫ* and *sẖ.w n ḥm.t* (respectively, an annuity contract made for a wife by her husband, and guarantees to the woman's parents of her marriage property) are the most common.

Given the definitions of marriage in ancient Egyptian society, there was nothing inherent in the relationship to prevent polygamy—a man could, in theory, cohabit with more than one woman in pursuit of offspring. Polyandry, in which one woman has multiple husbands at the same time, is unattested. In practice, however, polygamy was uncommon outside of the royal family; cases of polygamy among nonroyals are uncommon and often ambiguous. The Egyptians tended toward multiple marriage in the form of serial monogamy rather than polygamy, since the ease and acceptance of divorce—as well as the mortality rate—made marriage and remarriage the most common pattern for individuals with multiple spouses. The infrequency of polygamy may also be a function of the expense of keeping additional wives and their children; the domestic dynamics of having multiple wives and the physical limitations of the home could also be limiting factors. Definite cases of polygamy are rare, in part because of the imprecision of terminology used: reference to a "second" or "third" wife could easily be taking into account a dead or divorced "first" wife. The existence of different legal terms for wives—*ḥm.t* and *ḥbsw.t* are suggested to be for first and subsequent (but not necessarily simultaneous) wives, respectively—suggests that some distinction was made, but the first wife in such cases could easily be divorced or deceased. The primary reasons for polygamy in nonroyal contexts seem to be to produce children, but divorce in cases of infertility seems to have been more common. Another possibility in case of infertility was the introduction of a female slave into a household to bear children to her owner; although any resulting children could then take on the status of heirs, it is doubtful that their slave-mother would have been regarded as their father's "wife." Older scholarship frequently refers to the existence of concubinage in ancient Egypt, but this term, with its loaded associations, is probably best avoided.

Conversely, polygamy was the norm, and perhaps even the rule, for the king. Multiple, simultaneous marriages by the king are attested from the Old Kingdom onward (possibly even earlier). The obvious reason for this trend is the emphasis on the production of heirs—the more wives, the greater chance of producing a viable heir who would survive the reigning king to succeed him. In the case of long-lived kings, this was a major consideration—Ramesses II survived twelve of his sons (by multiple wives) to be succeeded by Merneptah, the thirteenth. Polygamy by the king also followed mythological precedent and served to set the king apart from the rest of the population. In spite of the multiplicity of royal wives, one wife was designated as the king's principal wife (king's great wife), who fulfilled many important ceremonial and ritual functions. The king's principal wife was not necessarily a lifetime title, and the transfer of this title from one wife to another could be used to disfavor or "demote" an existing principal wife. For a combination of theological, political, and logistical reasons, divorce from the king was not practical, and demotion was an acceptable alternative. The majority of the king's wives were secondary in rank and importance. These secondary wives lived with servants and children in dwellings designated as *ḥnr/ḥnr.t*. Often suggestively translated as "harem," these are now understood simply to be the separate households (literally, "enclosures") in which secondary wives, offspring, and servants would live and which the king might visit. Surviving records suggest that the secondary wives were not left idle in these residences, but were involved in weaving and other activities, in addition to raising their children. A large group of secondary wives with children who could be heirs was not without danger for the king, as is seen in the so-called harem conspiracy involving the wives of Ramesses III.

King's wives often came from within the royal family, or from among the high elite; such marriages could cement alliances and secure the king's power base. Another source of king's wives could secure alliances on a larger scale: diplomatic marriages. Such marriages first became common in the eighteenth dynasty, not surprising given the increasing emphasis on maintaining international relations, and continued to be significant factors in international politics through the Third Intermediate period. The majority of Egyptian diplomatic marriages involved daughters of foreign rulers coming to Egypt to marry the ruling king; such marriages were often initiated by a request (or demand) from Egypt. Egyptian kings often prominently commemorated these marriages to foreign princesses; for example Amenhotep III issued scarabs to announce his marriage to the Mittanian princess Gilukhepa. The reluctance of Egyptian kings to send out their own daughters was noted by foreign rulers, who appear to have been willing to make do with nonroyal Egyptian women, perhaps passing them off as princesses. The single known instance of a diplomatic marriage initiated by an Egyptian royal woman was Ankhesnamun's request to marry the son of Hittite king Šuppiluliumas, but this attempt was unsuccessful and ended in the death of the Hittite prince.

In addition to looking outside Egypt for wives, Egyptian kings are also notable for the practice of marrying within their closest family—to sisters and, less frequently, daughters. Brother–sister marriage had extensive mythological precedent for the Egyptians. The mythology of kingship was especially rich in this tradition: Osiris and his sister Isis, Seth and his sister Nephthys. The "heiress theory"—that kings married their sisters because kingship descended through the female line—has been convincingly disposed of by Gay Robins (1993) as an artifact of scholarship, an attempt by earlier Egyptologists to deal with their discomfort at the frequency of incest in the Egyptian royal family. While it seems likely that brother–sister marriage would have had the political advantage of keeping power within a close family circle, the mythological precedents for the practice and its value in setting the king off from the general population seem to have been important factors as well. Brother–sister (and also father–daughter) marriage is perhaps best attested in the royal family of the New Kingdom, specifically the eighteenth dynasty, but it can be found in other periods of Egyptian history as well. Sibling marriage was frequently practiced by the Ptolemies, among whom brother–sister marriage seems to have had the advantage of restricting the scope of family power and fortune, while firmly identifying the Ptolemies with earlier Egyptian traditions and divine precedents.

Outside the royal family, brother–sister marriage was extremely uncommon through most of Egyptian history.

The marriage of half-siblings was less uncommon, and marriages within the extended family were relatively frequent. The issue is slightly confused by the New Kingdom use of the terms of sibling relations for married couples, as well as the more poetic use of the terms for "brother" and "sister" (*sn* and *sn.t*) as endearments between lovers. Such usage is clearly metaphorical, and terms of sibling relationship for marriage partners are not used in this manner in legal contexts. Jaroslav Černý's investigation of possible cases of consanguineous marriages demonstrated that there were only a very few instances in which full-sibling marriage among nonroyals of the pharaonic period was a possibility, if not a certainty. The only attested spread of the practice of brother–sister marriage to the population of Egypt at large occurred in the Roman period. Census returns from the second century CE show an astonishing proportion of over 25 percent of the inhabitants of the Faiyum town of Arsinoe involved in full-sibling marriages, with slightly lower rates in other parts of the Faiyum and significantly lower rates elsewhere. Even though these figures are not necessarily representative of Roman Egypt as a whole, this population appears to have been one of the few in human history in which incestuous marriage was a social norm. The reasons for this apparent surge in sibling marriage in Roman Egypt are still unclear, but it is possible that this has something to do with the perception of brother–sister marriage as a specifically Egyptian practice and a marker of some sort of Egyptian identity.

Although not formally restricted, marriage partners tended to come from similar social backgrounds; women would often marry men in the same occupation as their fathers, for example, and people would often marry within their town and even within their extended family. Such choices reflect the patterns in social relations involved in marriage, where family and neighbors would have been involved in the decision in some capacity. Parents seem to have played an active role in arranging some marriages, but often the decision was left to the individuals. Outside of the high elite circles where alliance with the royal family was a possibility, marriage does not seem to have been acknowledged as a means of upward social mobility. Marriages between slaves, not surprisingly, seem usually to have been arranged by their owners. Marriages between slaves and free persons did occur, but the ultimate status of the partners (and their resulting children) was ambiguous at best. In cases where a slave woman is brought into a household to bear children for a free man, it is uncertain whether this relationship would have been categorized as a marriage, especially if the man already had a wife. Egyptians could and did marry foreigners, especially in the New Kingdom and later. Except for royal, diplomatic unions, marriages with foreigners most often took place between Egyptian men living abroad and foreign women, or (probably more frequently) between Egyptian women and non-Egyptian men who were resident in Egypt. Representational evidence for the latter sharply contrasts the differences between the Egyptian wives and their foreign husbands.

[*See also* Children; Family; Gender Roles; Harem; Inheritance and Disenfranchisement; Kinship; *and* Women.]

BIBLIOGRAPHY

Allam, Shafik. "Quelques aspects du mariage dans l'Égypte ancienne." *Journal of Egyptian Archaeology* 67 (1981), 116–135. Major study of aspects of marriage and divorce in Pharaonic and Greco-Roman Egypt, with useful references.

Černý, Jaroslav. "Consanguineous Marriages in Pharaonic Egypt." *Journal of Egyptian Archaeology* 40 (1954), 23–29. Classic study of brother–sister marriage in the Pharaonic period.

Clère, J.-J. "Un mot pour 'mariage' en égyptien de l'époque ramesside." *Revue de l'égyptologie* 20 (1968), 171–175. Discussion of terminology for marriage.

Eyre, C. J. "Crime and Adultery in Ancient Egypt." *Journal of Egyptian Archaeology* 70 (1984), 92–105. Study of the dynamics of adultery within Egyptian society.

Helck, Wolfgang. "Die Tochterheirat ägyptischer Könige." *Chronique d'Égypte: Bulletin périodique de la Foundation égyptologique Reine Elisabeth* 44 (1969), 22–26. Survey of evidence for father–daughter marriage among kings.

Janssen, Jac. J. "Marriage Problems and Public Reactions (P. BM 10416)." In *Pyramid Studies and Other Essays Presented to I. E. S. Edwards*, edited by John Baines, T. G. H. James, Anthony Leahy and A. F. Shore, pp. 134–137. Occasional Publications, 7. London, 1988. Examination of a document relating to a problematic marriage at Deir el-Medina.

Johnson, Janet H. "The Legal Status of Women in Ancient Egypt." In *Mistress of the House, Mistress of Heaven: Women in Ancient Egypt*, edited by Anne K. Capel and Glenn E. Markoc, pp. 175–186, esp. 179ff. New York 1997. Crucial survey of documentary material, with a generous selection of texts in translation.

Johnson, Janet H. "Annuity Contracts' and Marriage." In *For His Ka: Essays Offered in Memory of Klaus Baer*, edited by David P. Silverman, pp. 113–132. Chicago 1994. Study of documentation associated with marriage in the fourth century BCE.

Lüdeckens, Erich. *Ägyptische Eheverträge*. Ägyptologische Abhandlungen, 1. Wiesbaden, 1960. Collection of Demotic documents concerning marriage-related property.

Meskell, Lynn. "Intimate Archaeologies: The Case of Kha and Merit." *World Archaeology* 29 (1998), 363–379. Groundbreaking study of archaeological evidence relating to status within marriage in ancient Egypt.

Montserrat, Dominic. *Sex and Society in Graeco-Roman Egypt*. London, 1996. Chapter 4 includes a survey of the evidence for marriage and divorce in Greco-Roman Egypt.

Pestman, P. W. *Marriage and Matrimonial Property in Ancient Egypt: A Contribution to Establishing the Legal Position of the Woman*. Papyrologica Lugduno-Batava, 9. Leiden, 1961. Important study of the economic aspects of marriage, with special reference to Demotic and Greek documents from the later periods.

Robins, Gay. *Women in Ancient Egypt*. London, 1993. Essential study for marriage and divorce in the pharaonic period.

Rowlandson, Jane, et al., eds. *Women and Society in Graeco-Roman Egypt: A Sourcebook*. Cambridge and New York, 1998. Chapter 4 includes translations of Greco-Roman period documents relating to marriage and divorce.

Scheidel, Walter. "Incest Revisited: Three Notes on the Demography of Sibling Marriage in Roman Egypt." *Bulletin of the American Society of Papyrologists* 32 (1995), 143–155.

Schulman, Alan R. "Diplomatic Marriage in the Egyptian New Kingdom." *Journal of Near Eastern Studies* 38 (1979), 177–193. Survey of evidence for the practice of diplomatic marriage from the Hyksos king Apophis to Ramesses II.

TERRY G. WILFONG

MASKHUTA, TELL EL-. *See* Pithom.

MASKS. The ancient Egyptian worldview was characterized by an abiding sense of liminality. A philosophical and physical engagement with permeable boundaries—with respect to finite and infinite time or space, life and death, or the human and divine spheres—is discernible in their religious texts and rituals. Living persons in ancient Egypt might have employed transformational (so-called mortuary) spells to assume nonhuman forms on earth. Masked priests, priestesses, or magicians, in the physical (dis)guise of divine beings, such as Anubis or Beset, assumed such identities to exert the powers associated with those deities and thereby to ensure the success of dramatic cultic (re-)enactments. The construction and use of masks and other facial coverings for mummies emphasized the ancient Egyptian belief in the fragile state of transition that the dead would successfully transcend in their physical and spiritual transfer from this world to their divine transformation in the next. In their use by both the living and the dead, therefore, masks would have played a similar role in ancient Egypt, by effecting the magical transformation of an individual from the mortal to the divine state.

Although there are numerous examples in art, dating from the Predynastic palettes (such as the Two-Dog Palette in the collection of the Ashmolean Museum, Oxford) and onward, of depictions of anthropomorphic beings with the heads of animals, birds, or fantastic creatures, which might represent humans dressed as deities, such figures were more probably understood as images of the gods themselves. This interpretation is especially true for any three-dimensional figure or statue (such as the Middle Kingdom female figure from Western Thebes, now in the collection of the Manchester Museum, sometimes referred to in earlier literature as a leonine-masked human but which must certainly have been regarded as an image of the demoness Beset). Two-dimensional represen-

MASKS. *New Kingdom canopic mask from Thebes.* Made of cartonnage, this mask is possibly from the cache of Tutankhamun's embalmer. (The Metropolitan Museum of Art, Theodore M. Davis Collection, Bequest of Theodore M. Davis, 1915. [30.8.231])

tations are more difficult to interpret with such certainty, however, because they may have been designed as intentionally ambiguous. For example, one of the most commonly rendered mortuary scenes depicts the mummification of a body by a jackal-headed being. The scene may document the actual mummification rites performed upon the individual for whom the funerary scene was commissioned, or it could be interpreted as commemorating that episode of the embalmment by the jackal god Anubis in the mythic account of the death and resurrection of the god of the dead, Osiris, whom the deceased wished to emulate. That such two-dimensional scenes were encoded with dual meaning (because they could refer to specific or mythic events) also accounts for ambivalence in the interpretation of the depictions of ceremonies that were presumably carried out by priests on behalf of the king as part of royal or temple rituals. An example of one such ritual is the procession of composite animal/human figures, identified in the accompanying texts as the souls of Nekhen and Pe, who carry the sacred bark in a procession detailed on the southwestern interior wall of the Hypostyle Hall at Karnak Temple. Such scenes can be interpreted either as literal records of the historic celebrations performed by masked or costumed priests or as a visual actualization of faith in the royal dogma, which claimed categorically that the mythic ancestors of the god-king legitimized and supported his reign.

Examples of ritual masks from the archaeological record are rare, perhaps owing to the fragile and perishable materials of which they may have been constructed. Although a fragmentary Aha or Bes-like face of cartonnage was recovered by W. M. Flinders Petrie at the Middle Kingdom town site of Kahun, incontrovertible evidence for use by the Egyptians of masks in rituals conducted by the living has been preserved only from the Late period. A unique, ceramic mask of the head of the jackal-headed god, Anubis, dated to after 600 BCE (now in the collection of the Roemer Pelizaeus-Museum, Hildesheim), was evidently manufactured to serve as a head covering. There are indentations at each of the sides of the object, which would have allowed for it to be supported atop the shoulders, lifting the snout and upraised ears of the jackal head above the actual head of the wearer. Whereas two holes cut out at the jackal's neckline would have allowed the wearer to view straight ahead, peripheral vision would have been limited, necessitating assistance, as explicitly depicted in a temple relief at Dendera. This scene from the Ptolemaic temple of Hathor presents an "X-ray" view of the head of a processing priest, who wears just such a jackal mask, that covers his head and projects above his shoulders and who is accompanied and assisted by a companion priest. A description of a festival procession of Isis, which was led by the god Anubis (presumably a similarly masked priest), that took place not in Egypt but rather in Kenchreai, is provided by the second-century CE author Apuleius in *The Golden Ass* although no textual evidence is preserved from any period in Egypt that explicitly corroborates this custom.

Among the elaborate precautions taken by the ancient Egyptians for the preservation of the body after death, the protection of the head was of primary concern. The equipment of the deceased with a face-covering fabricated of sturdy material not only provided a permanent substitute for the head in case of physical damage but preserved that countenance in an idealized form, which presented the deceased in the likeness of an immortal being. Gilt flesh tones and blue wigs associated the dead with the glittering flesh and the (semiprecious gemstone) lapis lazuli hair of the sun god; specific features of a mask—eyes, eyebrows, forehead, and the like—were directly identified with individual divinities as is explained in the *Book of Going Forth by Day* (*Book of the Dead*), Spell 151B, so that the deceased would arrive safely in the beyond and gain acceptance among the other divine immortals in the council of the great god of the dead, Osiris. Initially, the prerogative of royalty, masks used to cover the dead were manufactured henceforth throughout Egyptian history for the elite class without respect to sex.

As early as the fourth dynasty, attempts were made to stiffen and mold the outer layer of linen bandages that covered the faces of mummies and to emphasize prominent facial features in paint. The earliest masks, which were manufactured experimentally as independent sculptural works, have been dated to the Herakleopolitan period (late First Intermediate Period). Those early, hollow masks were of wood, fashioned in two pieces held together with pegs, or of cartonnage (layers of linen or papyrus stiffened with plaster) that had been molded over a wooden model or core. The faces of both men and women, with their overexaggerated eyes and enigmatic half-smiles, were framed by long, narrow, tripartite wigs, kept secure by a decorated headband. The masks' "bibs" extended to cover the chest, as well, and both male and female examples were supplied in paint with elaborate, beaded and floral-motif necklaces or broad collars that served not only an aesthetic function but also satisfied an apotropaic requirement as elucidated in funerary spells. The elongated masks evolved into anthropoid inner coffins, first appearing in the twelfth dynasty. Hollow or solid masks (sometimes diminutive in size) were also created by pouring clay or plaster into a generic, often unisex, mold to which ears and gender-specific details were added. Masks became increasingly more sophisticated during the New Kingdom and Third Intermediate Period, when royalty were equipped with masks of beaten precious metal (like the solid gold mask of Tutankhamun or the series of gold and silver masks excavated at the necropolis of Tanis). Masks of all types were embellished with paint (generally, red flesh tones for males and yellow, pale tones for females) or gilt, as well as by the addition of composite, inlaid eyes or eyebrows, details that elevated the cost of the finished product. Indicators of social status—hairstyles, jewelry and costume (depicted on body-length head covers)—are often helpful in dating masks but the idealized image of transfigured divinity, which was the objective of the mask-covering, precluded the individualization of masks to the point of portraiture, which resulted in a formal sameness or hieroglyphic quality in the anonymous facial features of mummy masks from all periods of Egyptian history.

The use of permanent face coverings for the dead continued as long as mummification rites were practiced in Egypt. With regional preferences, cartonnage and plaster masks were equally popular in the Ptolemaic period; the cartonnage masks became only one element of a complete suit of separate cartonnage pieces that covered the wrapped body, a set that included a separate cartonnage breastplate and separate cartonnage footcase. Roman-period plaster masks exhibit Greco-Roman influence only in their coiffures, patterned on styles current at the imperial court. Both beards and mustaches on the males and elaborate coiffures on the women were highly modeled in relief.

An alternative to the cartonnage or plaster mask, introduced in the Roman era, was the so-called Faiyum portrait. Such portraits were initially chiefly recovered from cemeteries in the Faiyum and first archaeologically excavated in 1888 and 1910–1911 by Flinders Petrie at Hawara but have since been found at sites throughout Egypt, from Marina el-Alemain in the North to Aswan in the South. These paintings in encaustic (colored beeswax) or tempera (watercolor) on wooden panels or linen shrouds were executed in a painterly technique adopted from the Hellenistic artistic milieu, with results stylistically comparable to contemporary frescoes at Pompeii and Herculaneum in Italy. Nevertheless, such two-dimensional paintings occupied the same position on a decorated mummy and served the same ideological function as traditional three-dimensional masks.

The immediate appeal of the portraits to late nineteenth- and early twentieth-century collectors, however, encouraged a tendency to isolate the paintings from their funerary contexts. The paintings were initially studied by classicists and art historians who, basing their conclusions on details in the paintings alone (hairstyles, jewelry, and costume), identified the portraits as being those of Greek or Roman settlers who had adopted Egyptian burial customs. Although the portraits appear, at first, to capture the unique features of specific individuals, perhaps only the earliest examples of the genre (dating from the first half of the first century CE) were painted from live models, whereas the same generic quality that permeates the visages of the cartonnage and plaster masks persists, upon closer study, within the corpus of Faiyum portraits that have been preserved. Successful attempts have been made, however, based on the analysis of brush strokes and tool marks and the distinctive rendering of anatomical features, to group the portraits according to schools and to identify some individual artistic hands.

A link might nevertheless be traceable between the ultimate funerary function of the Faiyum portraits and a cultic use for the paintings while their owners were yet alive. Evidence from the portraits themselves—that the upper corners of panels were lopped at an angle to secure a better fit before being positioned over the mummy, that there

MASKS. *Mummy mask of Khnumhotep, a twelfth dynasty steward from Meir.* (The Metropolitan Museum of Art, Rogers Fund, 1912. [12.182.131c])

are signs of wear on paintings in areas that would have been covered by the mummy wrappings, and that at least one portrait (now in the British Museum) was discovered by Flinders Petrie at Hawara still within a wooden Oxford-type frame—indicates that the paintings had a domestic use prior to inclusion within the mummy wrappings, that they were probably hung within the home.

The cultic and funerary functions of the Faiyum portraits and the inclusion of iconographic elements (such as the gilding of lips, in accordance with funerary Spells 21 to 23 of the *Book of Going Forth by Day*, to ensure the power of speech in the afterlife), as well as the iconographic allusions to traditional deities (such as the sidelock of Horus worn by adolescents, the pointed-star diadem of Serapis worn by men, and the horned solar crown of Isis worn by adult females), in addition to the fact that these portraits, like all masks, were but one component of the overall design of the complete mummy decoration, emphasize a continuity of native Egyptian tradition. Although these two-dimensional painted faces were the products of the Hellenized cultural world of Roman Egypt, they fall toward the end of a continuum of a desire to permanently preserve the faces of the dead in an idealized and transfigured form that began in the Old Kingdom and continued to the end of paganism in Egypt.

The very latest examples of funerary masks are actually painted linen shrouds, the tops of which were pressed into a mold to produce the effect of a three-dimensional plaster mask. Examples of that type, which may date as late as the third or fourth centuries CE, were first excavated in 1894–1895 by Edouard Naville, within the sacred precinct of the mortuary chapel of Queen Hatshepsut, and were initially incorrectly identified by him as the mummies of Christians, probably of the Coptic (Christian) monastery for which the modern site, Deir el-Bahri, is named. Eventually, H. E. Winlock correctly identified the iconography—particularly the ubiquitous representation of the bark of the Egyptian funerary god Sokar—on further examples of that type to be consistent with pagan Egyptian funerary traditions, although certain motifs, such as the cup held in one hand, seem to presage the final transition from pagan mask to Coptic icon painting and the portraits of Byzantine saints.

BIBLIOGRAPHY

Bierbrier, Morris, ed. *Portraits and Masks: Burial Customs in Roman Egypt.* London, 1997.

Borg, Barbara. *Mumienporträts: Chronologie und Kultureller Kontext.* Mainz, 1997.

Celenko, Theodore, ed. *Egypt in Africa.* Indianapolis, 1996. See the chapter "Masking," pp. 68–77.

Corcoran, Lorelei H. *Portrait Mummies from Roman Egypt (I–IV Centuries A.D.): With a Catalog of Portrait Mummies in Egyptian Museums.* Studies in Ancient Oriental Civilization, 56. Chicago, 1995.

D'Auria, Sue, Peter Lacovara, and Catharine H. Roehrig, eds. *Mummies and Magic: The Funerary Arts of Ancient Egypt.* Boston, 1988.

Doxiadis, Euphrosyne. *The Mysterious Fayum Portraits: Faces from Ancient Egypt.* New York, 1995.

Ritner, Robert Kriech. *The Mechanics of Ancient Egyptian Magical Practice.* Studies in Ancient Oriental Civilization, 54. Chicago, 1993.

Shaw, Ian, Paul Nicholson, et al. "Mask." In *The Dictionary of Ancient Egypt.* New York, 1995.

Walker, Susan, and Morris Bierbrier, with Paul Robert and John Taylor, eds. *Ancient Faces: Mummy Portraits from Roman Egypt.* London, 1997.

LORELEI H. CORCORAN

MASTABA. *See* Architecture; *and* Tombs.

MATHEMATICS. Knowledge about ancient Egyptian mathematics has been derived from a limited number of written sources, the most complete of which is the Rhind Mathematical Papyrus, written in Hieratic script by the scribe Ahmose during the Hyksos period, at about the middle of the sixteenth century BCE. The scribe was actually copying an earlier work, assembled during the Middle Kingdom, in the second half of the nineteenth century BCE, which itself was certainly drawing on earlier material, some of which probably dated back to the Old Kingdom. The document is best regarded as a teacher's or student's manual; it reveals, among other things, that the Egyptians had a counting system to base ten. Their notation for fractions, unlike ours, did not allow for numerators greater than one, except in the case of the fraction 2/3. Historians of mathematics have long presumed that such a restriction must have impeded the development of Egyptian mathematical thought. In this article, such condemnation will be rejected; instead, an account will be given of what the Egyptians were able to achieve (bearing in mind the scantiness of the surviving material, which undoubtedly fails to cover the full extent of their knowledge).

First to be considered will be the basic operations of arithmetic: addition, subtraction, multiplication, and division. If only whole numbers were involved, addition and subtraction posed no problems. Multiplication at its simplest consisted of repeated doubling. Suppose, for example, it was required to multiply some number by 37. The procedure would be to double that number and to continue doubling the result until a value was obtained for thirty-two doublings. This value, when added to the value obtained for four doublings, together with the original number, would give the answer to the multiplication. In effect, intermediate multipliers were obtained by partitioning 37 into 32 + 4 + 1. An alternative method was to take advantage of the base-ten system by introducing multiples of 10 into the calculation. Intermediate multipliers could then be obtained by partitioning 37 into 1 + 2 + 4 + 10 + 20. Partitioning numbers in this way lies at the very heart of Egyptian arithmetic.

Division was performed as a multiplication sum in reverse. If it was required to divide some number by 37, the instructions were to treat 37 so as to obtain that number. The divisor then became the number to be multiplied, and appropriate multipliers had to be found for 37, so that the products, when added together, gave the required result. Suppose the number to be divided was 47. Since 37 = 36 + 1, it would have been apparent that 37 multiplied by 1 + 1/4 gives 46 + 1/4, with a shortfall from 47 of 3/4, or

1/2 + 1/4. It follows that the remaining multiplications needed to bring the total up to 47 are 1/2 × 1/37 = 1/74 and 1/4 × 1/37 = 1/148. The answer to the division of 47 by 37 would then be written as 1 + 1/4 + 1/74 + 1/148.

The division of 47 by 37 is the same as multiplying the fraction 1/37 by 47. The Egyptians were adept at handling unit fractions, so their methods are discussed here in more detail. The addition of fractions with unit numerators (1) over different denominators was done just as one would today, by finding a common multiple for the denominators. An example is provided by problem no. 7 in the Rhind Mathematical Papyrus, where it is required to multiply 1/4 + 1/28 by 1 + 1/2 + 1/4. The working shows how to obtain the result by multiplying out and then taking 28 as a common multiple, so that the only fractions to be added at the end are halves and quarters, leading to an answer of 1/2. In fact the creator of the problem would have known quite well that 1/4 + 1/28 is equal to 2/7, since doubling of 1/7 features in a table at the beginning of the papyrus in which all odd-numbered fractions are doubled up to 1/101. He would also have known that 1 + 1/2 + 1/4 is equivalent to seven quarters (7/4), so that the answer to his sum has to be 2/7 × 7/4, or 1/2. Like many of the problems in the Rhind Mathematical Papyrus—which was designed to train scribes in the various mathematical procedures needed for their work—this one was constructed not to obtain an answer by the most direct method but to illustrate a technique.

A procedure that is fundamental to Egyptian arithmetic involves finding different series of fractions that together sum to unity (add up to 1). A number of examples occur in the Rhind Mathematical Papyrus, and it is likely that others were listed elsewhere in tables for reference. Fractional series fulfilling this condition could have been found without difficulty by selecting a number with several factors, partitioning it into components that were multiples of those factors, and then dividing by the chosen number. Suppose the chosen number was 30; it can be partitioned into 20 + 6 + 3 + 1, 20 + 5 + 3 + 2, or 15 + 10 + 3 + 2. Dividing through by 30 will give 2/3 + 1/5 + 1/10 + 1/30, 2/3 + 1/6 + 1/10 + 1/15, and 1/2 + 1/3 + 1/10 + 1/15, all of which sum to unity. These series are all used in the Rhind Mathematical Papyrus. The most formidable series of this sort arises as a corollary of problem no. 23. It consists of the eight terms 1/3 + 1/4 + 1/8 + 1/9 + 1/10 + 1/30 + 1/40 + 1/45, but it may have been obtained by putting together two four-term series: 1/3 + 1/9 + 1/30 + 1/45 and 1/4 + 1/8 + 1/10 + 1/40, each of which sums to 1/2 and, with the addition of 1/2, forms a five-term series summing to unity.

Series summing to unity play an essential role in the Rhind Mathematical Papyrus table for doubling odd-numbered unit fractions. Doubling a fraction is the same as dividing the denominator of that fraction by 2; in the case of fractions with denominators not greater than 29, work was provided to show how this was done. In all cases but one, the intermediate multipliers used in the division were taken from the fractional series obtained by repeated halving of 2/3. In the case of 2/13, the intermediate multipliers were from the series obtained by repeated halving of 1/2.

For most higher denominators, the scribe gave only the answer, together with information showing that 2, the numerator of the doubled fraction, has been in effect partitioned into 1 plus a fractional series summing to unity. For example, to double 1/67, multiply 67 successively by 1/40, 1/335, and 1/536 to get respectively 1 + 1/2 + 1/8 + 1/20, 1/5, and 1/8. The series 1/2 + 1/4 (= 2 × 1/8) + 1/5 + 1/20 sums to unity, since 20 partitions into 10 + 5 + 4 + 1, so that the addition of 1 gives the 2 of the doubling process. To take a simpler example, 2/7 = 1/4 + 1/28, because multiplying through by 7 gives 7 × 1/4 = 1 + 3/4 = 1 + 1/2 + 1/4, 7 × 1/28 = 1/4, and 1/2 + 1/4 + 1/4 sums to unity.

The evidence suggests that in the division, care has been taken to choose fractional multipliers not just from the 2/3, 1/3, 1/6 . . . or the 1/2, 1/4, 1/8 . . . series, but in such a way as to give the most elegant result (i.e., with not more than four fractions, with denominators that are if possible even numbered and not too large, so as to facilitate subsequent calculations). Trial and error with different multipliers would have been exceedingly time-consuming, but in the Robins and Shute (1987) commentary on the Rhind Mathematical Papyrus, the authors suggested a possible shortcut procedure, which would involve the partition of 2 into 1 with a series of fractions that sum to unity, as given for each example by the scribe.

Other arithmetical techniques employed by the ancient Egyptians included the summing of arithmetical and geometrical progressions, the solving of linear equations, and the use of reciprocals. The most awkward equation tackled in the Rhind Mathematical Papyrus, in problem no. 31, is $(1 + 2/3 + 1/2 + 1/7)x = 33$, the solution of which is equivalent to evaluating 33 × 42 ÷ 97. To lessen the burden of a long string of fractions, the scribe arranged to deal with the smaller ones separately. He found that the coefficient of x in the equation, when multiplied by 14 1/4, fell just short of 33, so he expressed that shortfall as the sum of six unit fractions.

The Egyptians obtained reciprocals by dividing numbers, integral or fractional, into unity. The reciprocal pairs of numbers that occur in the Rhind Mathematical Papyrus are 1 + 1/2 + 1/4 and 1/2 + 1/14 (problem nos. 9, 63), 4 + 1/2 and 1/6 + 1/18 (problem no. 67), and 2 + 2/3 and 1/4 + 1/8 (problem no. 71). Their modern equivalents are 7/4 and 4/7, 9/2 and 2/9, and 8/3 and 3/8. Tables of reciprocals were probably available for scribal use, but none has survived. Perhaps the main interest of reciprocals lies not in what we know the Egyptians did with them, but in what they might have done, since a single cuneiform tablet (Plimpton n.322) shows that the Babylonians knew that reciprocals could generate so-called Pythagorean triples (i.e., three whole numbers such that the square of the largest is equal to the sum of the squares of the other two). The simplest of all reciprocal pairs, 2 and 1/2, yields the simplest of all Pythagorean triples: 3,4,5. The method can be obtained by expressing the Pythagorean relationship as the difference of two squares, factorizing and dividing by the square of the middle term of the triple. Thus, $4^2 = 5^2 - 3^2$ yields $1 = [(1 + 1/4) + (1 - 1/4)] \times [(1 + 1/4) - (1 - 1/4)] = 2 \times 1/2$.

Since, according to the theorem attributed to Pythagoras, Pythagorean triples form the lengths of the sides of right-angled triangles (hence their name), it is pertinent to consider whether the Egyptians knew about this property. As far as the triple 3,4,5 is concerned, it is virtually certain, despite doubts expressed by some historians of mathematics, that they did. Problem no. 1 in the Berlin Mathematical Papyrus (P. Berlin 6619) concerns the areas of three squares, of which the largest has an area of 100 square cubits, so a side is 10 cubits. Its area is equal to the sum of the areas of two smaller squares, whose sides are in the ratio of 1:1/2 + 1/4. It is required to discover the lengths of their sides. These turn out to be 8 cubits and 6 cubits; it follows that the ratio of the lengths of the sides of the three squares is 6:8:10. In other words, they can be regarded as squares based on the sides of a 3,4,5 right-angled triangle. Later, work in Demotic script in the Cairo Papyri includes sloping-pole and rectangle problems (nos. 24–31) that involve the Pythagorean triples 3,4,5; 5,12,13; and 20,21,29.

Another reason for supposing that the Egyptians knew of the 3,4,5 triangle is based on the proportions of the fourth dynasty pyramid of Khafre (Chephren) at Giza and of many of the later Old Kingdom pyramids. The same proportions occur in some pyramid problems included in the Rhind Mathematical Papyrus (nos. 56–59). They show that the eventual conformation of a pyramid was determined by the slope of its faces and the size of its base. The unit measuring slope was the *seked* (*skd*), giving the displacement horizontally for a vertical drop of seven units, seven being the number of palms in a royal cubit, which was the architectural unit of length. The *seked* for Khafre's pyramid is 5 1/4, and a lateral displacement of 5 1/4 units for a drop of 7 is the same as a lateral displacement of 3 units for a drop of 4. A vertical section through a pyramid with this *seked*, passing through its apex and the midpoints at two opposite sides of its base, would produce two identical 3,4,5 right-angled triangles, whose

sides are half the width of the square base of the pyramid, its height, and the length from the apex to the midpoint of one side of the base. It is hard to see any reason for the change, not readily appreciated with the naked eye, from the more primitive *seked* of 5 1/2 occurring in the Great Pyramid, unless it was to incorporate a 3,4,5 right-angled triangle, thereby facilitating the cutting by stonemasons of casing blocks with the correct angle.

The concept of a *seked* can be regarded as a rudimentary form of trigonometry. Two of the greatest Egyptian achievements in mathematics belong to the sphere of geometry; they are (1) the formula, correct and by no means obvious, for the volume of a truncated pyramid that was given in the Moscow Mathematical Papyrus (no. 14) and (2) the formula (approximate as it had to be, but still the best in the pre-Hellenic world) for the area of a circle that was given in the Rhind Mathematical Papyrus (nos. 41–43, 48, and 50). The methods for arriving at these formulas are not extant; nor is it anywhere attested that the Egyptians knew the formula for the volume of a complete pyramid—but they surely must have, since to compute it they had only to reduce the top surface of a truncated pyramid to zero.

The Egyptian method for estimating the area of a circle was to subtract a ninth part from its diameter and square the result, with an error of only 0.6 percent. Attempts have been made to explain the way this formula was obtained by considering problem no. 48 in the Rhind Mathematical Papyrus. This problem is unusual because there is no description of the procedure but simply a calculation accompanied by a diagram, which has variously been interpreted as either a circle or an octagon inscribed within a square. The square is given a side of 9 units, so that if the inscribed figure is a circle, it will have a diameter of 9 units, and its area, according to the Egyptian formula will be 64 square units, as compared with the 81 square units making up the circumscribed square. If the inscribed figure is an octagon, the intention may have been to treat it like a circle, thereby getting an approximate value for its area. If the octagon was meant to have angles located at trisection points along the sides of a circumscribed square with sides of 9 units, its area would be equal to that of five small squares, each with sides of 3 units, plus four triangular half squares together equal to two whole squares also with sides of 3 units, giving an area of $7 \times 9 = 63$ square units. This is close to the area of a square with sides of 8 units or to that of a circle with a diameter of 9 units, according to the Egyptian formula.

Against the above interpretation, it seems evident that the Egyptian scribe was more concerned to prove his methods by showing that they worked than to indicate how those methods were reached. An alternative hypothesis would suppose that the circle whose area was to be determined was not inscribed within a square but super-imposed upon it, being drawn through quarter points along its sides. Such a circle and square would be seen to have approximately equal areas, so that the circle would have been effectively "squared." The relative proportions of the diameter of the circle and the side of the square would be found to be very close to 9:8, as in the Egyptian formula for the area of a circle.

From the discussion above, the competency of Egyptian mathematicians would seem established. Comparisons with Babylonian achievements seem adverse because so much more Babylonian material has survived on their clay tablets than on fragile Egyptian papyrus. If the Moscow Mathematical Papyrus had not survived, no record would exist of the Egyptians' ability to calculate the volume of a truncated pyramid. Other such procedures that were well known to the Egyptians may have left no traces in the record known so far. Then, too, the supposed impediment caused by the use of unit fractions is largely illusory (since these were a notational device, perhaps adopted in part for aesthetic reasons), and not the result of a conceptual block. The ability to manipulate such fractions deftly may have been a source of pride to the Egyptian scribe.

BIBLIOGRAPHY

Chase, Arnold B. *The Rhind Mathematical Papyrus: Free Translation and Commentary with Selected Photographs, Transcriptions and Literal Translations.* Classics in Mathematics Education, volume 8, 1979. A good overview, convenient for the general reader, produced by an enthusiast.

Gillings, Richard J. *Mathematics in the Time of the Pharaohs.* Toronto, 1972; Dover reprint, 1982. A highly readable, personal approach; the Berlin and Moscow problems referred to were transcribed on pp. 161 and 188.

Parker, Richard A. *Demotic Mathematical Papyri.* Providence, 1972. A brief commentary and seventy-two texts from Cairo, the British Museum, and Carlsberg (not all free from Babylonian and Greek influences); the Demotic problems referred to were included.

Peet, Thomas E. *The Rhind Mathematical Papyrus BM 10057 and 10058: Introduction, Transcription, Translation and Commentary.* Liverpool and London, 1923. The definitive publication, the first in English. Reviewed by B. Gunn, *Journal of Egyptian Archaeology* 12 (1926), 123–137.

Peet, Thomas E. "Mathematics in Ancient Egypt." *Bulletin of the John Rylands Library* 15 (1931), 404–441. A straightforward general account by an Egyptologist trained in mathematics.

Robins, Gay. "Mathematics, Astronomy and Calendars in Pharaonic Egypt." In *Civilizations of the Ancient Near East,* edited by J. M. Sasson, vol. 3, pp. 1799–1813. New York, 1995. An up-to-date survey.

Robins, Gay, and Charles C. D. Shute. "Mathematical Bases of Ancient Egyptian Architecture and Graphic Art." *Historia Mathematica* 12 (1985), 107–122. Includes a study of pyramid proportions and a warning against mathematical coincidences.

Robins, Gay, and Charles C. D. Shute. *The Rhind Mathematical Papyrus.* London, 1987, Dover reprint, n.d. Includes color photographs of the *recto* and *verso* of BM 10058 and the *recto* of BM 10057, constituting all the purely mathematical part of the papyrus; the commentary covers selected problems and gives a detailed analysis of the table of doubled odd-numbered unit fractions.

Robins, Gay, and Charles C. D. Shute. "The 14:11 Proportion in Egyptian Architecture." *Discussions in Egyptology* 16 (1990), 75–79. The authors reject the notion that the 14:11 proportion found in the Great Pyramid was chosen to form part of a geometric series with that common ratio.

Robins, Gay, and Charles C. D. Shute. "Irrational Numbers and Pyramids." *Discussions in Egyptology* 18 (1990), 43–53. Despite claims by modern numerologists, irrational numbers such as *pi* and *phi* occur in the dimensions of the Great Pyramid only as mathematical coincidences.

CHARLES SHUTE

MEAT. *See* Diet.

MEDAMUD, a site located 5 kilometers (3 miles) north of Karnak (25°44′N, 32°42′E). Excavations at Medamud were directed from 1925 to 1930 by archaeologists of the French Institut of Oriental Archeology—Fernand Bisson de la Roque, Alexandre Varille and Clément Robichon—who bared various stages of temple construction.

The oldest was a primitive sanctuary that was dated to before the eleventh dynasty. It revealed a strange structure within a polygonal enclosure, which included a courtyard where pylons preceded two deep sanctuaries that evoked tombs. Each was covered by a mound planted with trees. The remains were lost in the 1970s flooding caused by the High Dam at Aswan, and only the architectural plans remain.

A Middle Kingdom temple constructed by Senwosret III, above the primitive sanctuary, is best known for its numerous stones that were reused in later foundations; several portals were thus reconstructed by the French excavators, of which a *sed*-festival porch of Senwosret III demonstrated the royal character of the site. Other less famous pharaohs (Sobekhotpe, Sobkemsaf) also inscribed their cartouches on lintels and gateways—thereby pursuing, copying, or usurping their predecessors' accomplishments. (For example, statues of Senwosret III, the deified ancestor, were found still standing in the Roman period temple.) Sections of columns made of limestone and sandstone (rarely used in the Middle Kingdom), as well as the brick wall base, enabled excavators to draft a hypothetical plan of the temple. Foundation deposits indicated a north–south axis, with a westward opening onto an unknown edifice. The south side was lined with storage space, giving the entire construction a fortresslike aspect.

A New Kingdom temple was built to spread westward on a foundation platform that contained a deposit from Thutmose III. A gateway, dating from Amenhotpe II, still stands on the site. No plan has been drawn of this construction.

MEDAMUD. *Remains of the temple of Montu, Ra'ttawy, and Harpocrates.* The temple dates from the Ptolemaic period. (Courtesy Dieter Arnold)

The first Ptolemies erected a *tribune* and *dromos,* to be used as a new western entrance; some of the stone blocks were dated to Ptolemy III. The front of the temple with the altar of Ptolemy II was also remodeled. On the southwest side of the courtyard, an edifice was built of which only the plan drawing and the foundation deposits remained; many of the construction blocks were found under the present pylon gateway. A *sed*-festival porch of Ptolemy II and another portal of Ptolemy IV, called the "gateway of the mound Djême," combined local royal traditions with Theban funeral rituals to Osiris and the gods of Djême. Those buildings were destroyed in 206 BCE, during the Theban disturbances.

The youngest temple has a long history. The construction began under Ptolemy V, but the building and decoration extended into the Roman period; the last cartouches were dated to the time of Diocletian (r. 284–305 CE). The plan is quite original, but it is based on the oldest directional orientations, with the principal axis west–east for the main temple; it also includes at the entrance: three kiosks; a hall of justice that opens into a big, columned courtyard, called the court of Antoninus Pius; a portal (still standing); a hypostyle; and a sanctuary surrounded by chapels. The secondary axis, north–south, is that of the rear temple, which has a passage that approaches from the courtyard; it is "the house of the great, venerable bull," the god Montu. Four statues of this god and his wife were discovered there (they are connected with the holy cities of Medamud, Thebes, Tod, and Armant). The sacred bull of Montu was said to deliver oracles. A famous scene on the exterior side of the south wall shows a Roman ruler consulting the bull. The farthest enclosure opens westward, to the dromos; that monumental gateway, decorated by the Roman emperor Tiberius (r. 14–37 CE), was also a "place for rendering justice."

Mentions of Montu, the god of Medamud, were made as early as the eleventh dynasty. During the New Kingdom, Montu lost his preeminent role, which then went to Amun; but he recovered full power under the first Ptolemies. Then, in Theban rituals, both Montu and Amun were worshiped as primeval gods. The Coptic Christian churches reoccupied the site at the end of the fourth century CE; small statues of Osiris were, however, found buried under domestic thresholds, from that time.

BIBLIOGRAPHY

Bisson de la Roque, Fernand, et al. *Rapport préliminaire des fouilles de Médamoud (1925–1932).* Fouilles de l'Institut français d'archéologie orientale du Caire, 3–9. Cairo, 1926–1933.

Bisson de la Roque, Fernand, "Les Fouilles de l'Institut francais à Médamoud de 1925 à 1938." *Revue de l'égyptologie* 5 (1946), 25–44.

Carlotti, Jean–François, and Chantal Sambin. "Une porte de fête–sed de Ptolémée II remployée dans le temple de Montou à Médamoud." *Bulletin de l'Institut français d'archéologie orientale* 95 (1995), 383–438.

Robichon, Clément, and Alexandre Varille. "Les fouilles: Médamoud." *Chronique d'Égypte* 27 (1939), 82–87; 28 (1939), 265–267.

Sambin, Chantal. "Les Portes de Médamoud du musée de Lyon." *Bulletin de l'Institut français d'archéologie orientale* 92 (1992), 147–184.

Valbelle, Dominique. "La porte de Tibére dans le complexe religieux de Médamoud." In *Hommages à la mémoire de Serge Sauneron*, vol. 1, pp. 73–85. Bibliotheque d'étude, 81. Cairo, 1979.

CHANTAL SAMBIN
Translated from French By Daniela Bruneau

MEDICINE. Ancient Egyptian medicine can be traced from the origin of the civilization until Coptic times. Knowledge of ancient medicinal practices derives from a variety of sources, including artistic representations; surviving medical treatises and instruments; references in the historical, social, and literary records; botanical information; and not least through paleopathology, the study of the preserved bodies of the Egyptians. From all these resources, it is possible to obtain a fairly accurate picture of the general health and diet of the Egyptian population, the ailments from which they suffered, and the theories and treatment strategies that they devised. While the wealthier classes in all times had access to a complex diet of grains, vegetables, fruit, fish, fowl, cattle, milk, beer, and wine, the basic source of calories for the broader population was grain, received as rations to be made into bread and beer or bartered for other products. Except in times of famine, the nutritional state of the country was healthy, with the average farm laborer producing sufficient kilocalories per year to sustain about twenty adults. Average life expectancy has been estimated at thirty to thirty-six years, although a number of individuals are recorded as reaching the age of sixty, and several octogenarians are known, including kings Pepy II and Ramesses II. The ideal Egyptian age was considered 110 years, as recorded in popular wishes and literature (Papyrus Westcar) and as adopted in the Joseph tale of *Genesis* 50.23.

Mediating between the ideal and real worlds of health was the Egyptian doctor and his many divine patrons: Thoth, deity of healing and science; Sekhmet, goddess of disease; Selqet, goddess of scorpions; Isis, goddess of magic; Horus, the divine physician; and Imhotep and Amenhotep, son of Hapu, two divinized sages and healing saints. The physician was likely trained within a temple setting, and medical treatises were preserved in temple scriptoria. Judging by recorded titles, the medical community was highly stratified from Early Dynastic times, with simple physicians (*swnw*), overseers of physicians, inspectors of physicians, chief physicians, palace physicians, inspectors of palace physicians, and chief palace physicians. All of these hierarchical titles could be further divided among a series of medical specialties, including ophthalmology, dentistry, internal disease, and proctology. References within medical texts suggest a working relationship, or at least a familiarity, with the craft of the embalmer; and embalmers are included within the medical profession as *swnw* in the Late period. Other related fields comprised the pharmacist, bandager, and masseur, as well as the priests of Sekhmet and Selqet, and even amulet sellers, who were trained to take the pulse. Virtually all known medical practitioners are male. Before the Late period only a single female physician is attested: Peseshet of the Old Kingdom (fifth or sixth dynasty). As Peseshet is styled "Overseer of Female Physicians," others must have existed, at least at that time. Women played a greater role as medical auxiliaries, serving as midwives and wet nurses.

Ancient therapeutic intervention is attested both by mummified remains and by wall reliefs with accompanying texts. Perhaps the most pervasive surgical procedure was male circumcision, evident from burials of the Predynastic period onward. In the celebrated tomb of the sixth dynasty vizier Ankhmahor at Saqqara (c.2374 BCE), carved scenes record two stages in the circumcision of a priest; a comparable depiction appears at the Karnak Mut temple complex from the twenty-fifth dynasty, more than a millennium and a half later. A First Intermediate Period stela from Nag ed-Deir (now in the Oriental Institute of Chicago, OIM 16956) indicates that circumcision was the focus of a group initiation, likely performed in late puberty. Human remains show that circumcision was a common, but not universal practice. By Roman times, if not earlier, the rite was restricted to the priestly caste. Mummies have provided evidence of other procedures, including the use of splints, sutures, and trephination. The adaptability of the later Egyptian surgeon is revealed by a relief on the outer enclosure wall of the temple at Kom Ombo, site of the popular worship of "Horus the Good Doctor." Though formerly much disputed, the relief is now believed to depict contemporary Roman-era surgical instruments together with Egyptian amulets and a censer. Earlier medical instruments survive, including scalpels, needles, tweezers, clysters, and measuring vessels.

The most detailed evidence for Egyptian wound and disease treatment is found in seventeen papyrus compendia, in addition to numerous ostraca that record individual prescriptions from the Amarna through the Roman eras. The earliest surviving medical manuscript is the Kahun Papyrus of the twelfth dynasty (c.1850 BCE), which contains both gynecological and veterinary treatments. From this and later papyri, it is clear that most female complaints were attributed to a disordered, and often dislocated, uterus. The wandering uterus was believed to affect the eyes, neck, legs, teeth, and even a woman's inclination to leave bed. Remedies included fumigations, potions, and pessaries. Further passages include birth prognostications and vaginal suppositories to prevent pregnancy. The unique veterinary text records treatments for the eyes of birds, dogs, and cattle. The papyrus contains the only references to the technique of bleeding in Egyptian medical practice, when injured cattle are cut upon the nose and tail to see whether these will heal. The association of veterinary and human medicine is reflected in the use of the title *swnw*, which also designates priestly inspectors of sacrificial cattle in Old Kingdom reliefs. The fragmentary Ramesseum Papyri III–V date to the thirteenth dynasty (c.1786–1665 BCE) and include sections on ophthalmology, gynecology, pediatrics, and the vascular system. From the eighteenth dynasty derive the treatises of greatest significance: the Edwin Smith "Surgical" Papyrus and Papyrus Ebers, both likely copied by the same scribe, about 1550 BCE.

The Smith Papyrus (now at the New York Academy of Sciences) is an incomplete copy of an older reference manuscript, argued to date from the Old Kingdom on the basis of grammatical features and archaic terminology, supplemented by numerous glosses. The surviving text systematically details the treatment of trauma in descending anatomical distribution from the top of the head to the spinal vertebrae, where the scribe ceased copying in midsentence. The preserved forty-eight cases are arranged in a coherent pattern that specifies the "bedside manner" of the Egyptian physician. Following each title, a description of the examination begins with the phrase. "If you examine a man who has . . . ," and continues with a detailed list of symptoms. The process of examination includes visual and olfactory clues, palpation, and a calibrated taking of the pulse. Thereafter, the physician pronounces an oral diagnosis and an assessment of the patient's chances of survival, by stating either, "An ailment which I will treat," "An ailment with which I will contend," or "An ailment not to be treated." When considered feasible, treatment is described in the final section and includes bandaging, splints, poultices, manipulation, and, in one instance, a heated lancet applied to a suppurating tumor. Particularly common is the recommendation to leave the patient "at his mooring stake," an expression clarified by a gloss as indicating enforced bedrest and normal diet until a decisive moment is reached. Surprisingly modern in approach, this determination suggests an awareness not only of the physician's limitations, but of the body's ability to heal itself in certain circumstances. As in other papyri, wounds are treated with honey and copper salts, which have been shown to be effective antibacterial agents in modern clinical trials. In one extreme case where treatment is not advised, a magical spell is recommended, and additional incantations were copied by the same scribe in a separate section on the *verso* of the papyrus. Final additions to the *verso* include brief sections on gynecology and cosmetics, and a second scribe has appended a prescription for a wrinkle remover ("Recipe for Transforming an Old Man into a Youth") and a suppository.

Whereas the Smith Papyrus concentrates on external trauma, the contemporary Ebers Papyrus treats internal disease and includes critical theoretical sections that detail the vascular system and the source and progression of internal illness. The papyrus displays a rudimentary knowledge of the circulatory system, envisioned as a network of vessels centered on the heart and extending to individual organs and then to all body parts. Within the system moved blood, water, air, and the corruptive residue of bodily waste, termed *whdw*. The notion of *whdw* constituted the first empirical, comprehensive disease theory in history, explaining in rational form the onset of disease, aging, and death, and providing the rationale for diet, medicine, and mummification. In practice, the physician tested the soundness of the system by taking the pulse at various points in the body. An excess of *whdw* in the system brought about illness, and the existence of the corruptive agent was seemingly proved by the manifestation of pus in wounds or blisters. To prevent an accumulation of *whdw*, the physician recommended purges and enemas; otherwise the vessels would slowly fill with the residue over a lifetime, producing the onset of old age with failing organs crippled by constricted or blocked vessels. Ultimately, the natural accumulation resulted in death, and the embalmer's attempts to preserve the body were also directed against *whdw* by draining bodily fluids and by removing those organs thought most likely permeated by food residues. Belief in the system of *whdw* was maintained into Hellenistic times, and it was adopted in part by the Cnidian school of Greek medicine and by subsequent Alexandrian enema specialists. The orthodoxy of the Ebers Papyrus is demonstrated by the somewhat later Hearst Papyrus, 100 of whose 260 paragraphs are paralleled in the earlier text.

Ramessid collections include the London Medical Papyrus (BM 10059, c.1350 BCE), Papyrus Berlin 3038 and Papyrus Chester Beatty VI (both c.1300 BCE), and Papyrus Carlsberg VIII (c.1200 BCE). The cosmopolitan character of Ramessid Egypt is reflected in the London Papyrus, which incorporates seven incantations in foreign languages. Six of those spells are in Northwest Semitic dialects, while one is said to be "in the language of Crete (Keftiu, the Biblical Caphtor)." The first and last foreign spells use a Semitic term ("strangulation") to designate the illness, suggesting that the disease was first encountered abroad, with the Egyptian physician adopting both its local name and form of treatment. Hittite sources do record a plague among Egyptian soldiers based in the Near East at the time of the compilation of this papyrus. Further Hittite records show the local adoption of Egyptian medicine, with a steady importation of Egyptian physicians and remedies to the Anatolian court.

One of the most common dangers in Egypt at all periods was injury by snake or scorpion, treated by a specialist known as the "Controller of Selqet." The manual of such a specialist survives from the thirtieth dynasty or early Ptolemaic period. The Brooklyn papyrus on snakebite (47.218.48 and 47.218.85) features a systematic description of snakes by name, distinctive features, toxicity, divine associations, and treatment alternatives, including incisions, emetics, topical salts, and spells.

It is only with the loss of Egyptian independence that stark changes appear in local medical practice and its related pharmacopeia. Egyptians came to dominate the medical field during the Persian Empire, and individual Egyptian doctors are known to have served as court physicians for several Persian emperors. Increased contact produced influences in both directions. During this period, medical astrology was introduced to Egypt, and the Egyptian physicians resident in Persia surely encountered new plants and drugs that were later incorporated into their practices back home. Unfortunately, no general medical treatise of this period survives, and it is only in the Roman period (second century CE) that our documentation resumes. Though poorly published, the Crocodilopolis Medical Book (Papyrus Vienna 6257), in Demotic, is nevertheless an excellent witness to the adaptive nature of the Egyptian physician.

While the theoretical underpinnings of native Egyptian medicine and the ancient treatise format are undisturbed in this late work, the range of new plant and mineral ingredients is striking. This abundance is due less to Greek or Roman cultural domination than to unprecedented international trade that was made possible by succeeding Persian, Ptolemaic, and Roman empires. Egyptian medicinal use of plants had always been extensive, with some 160 distinctive plant products—of which roughly 20 percent have been identified securely or tentatively. In the Crocodilopolis manual, more than sixty new plants and five new minerals now appear in the native pharmacopeia, while about two hundred ingredients are used in this one manual. How many of these newer items had been adopted in the previous Persian or Hellenistic times cannot be known. Additional exotic ingredients appeared in recipes on the *verso* of the London and Leiden "Magical" Papyrus of the following third century CE.

Coptic medicine is best represented by the Papyrus Chassinat from the ninth century CE, containing 237 recipes collected by a physician for his son. Remedies for a variety of illnesses are listed unsystematically, with most concerning the ubiquitous eye diseases still prevalent in the country. Trachoma, trichiasis, cataracts, nearsightedness, inflammation, and abscesses are noted. Additional Coptic recipes are preserved in collections in Berlin, Cairo, London, Manchester, and elsewhere. The collections treat skin diseases, gout, female complaints, teething, adult toothache, wounds, leprosy, jaundice, loss of sleep, and even domestic hygiene. References to surgery are rare, with circumcision and tooth extraction noted explicitly. Although Coptic medicine displays clear influence of contemporary Greco-Roman practice, native elements survive, as indicated by the reliance upon purgatives and the topical use of traditional "magical" ingredients, such as mother's milk and animal excrement. The medical hierarchy, now associated with monasteries rather than temples, included teaching doctors, general practitioners, and senior physicians. Female doctors administered to patients of their own sex. The increased concern for skin ailments in Coptic medicine is striking, and leprosy has been identified in a mummy of the sixth century CE.

Paleopathology constitutes the most innovative investigation of Egyptian medicine and health, utilizing not only dissection, but the more modern techniques of radiography, computed tomography, electron microscopy, differential diagnosis, and DNA analysis. Such examinations have revealed the presence of a variety of ancient diseases, including bilharziasis (*Schistosomiasis*), roundworm (*Ascaris*), guinea-worm (*Dracunculus*), and tapeworm (*Taenia*) infestation, with rare examples of malaria, tuberculosis, smallpox, and carcinoma (cancer). Ancient dental remains have been studied intensively. These show a low incidence of caries (cavities), probably attributable to an absence of refined sugars in the native diet, but extraordinary abrasion throughout the adult population, leading to tooth loss, abscesses, and, exceptionally, osteomyelitis. The cause of such tooth wear is blamed on the native bread, rendered gritty by friable grindstones and ambient sand. Several examples of dental bridges have been recovered from burials, though these may be postmortem cosmetic appliances.

The impact of Egyptian medicine on developing Greek medical theory has been noted above, and further survivals and influences are certain. The Pre-Alexandrian Hippocratic Corpus contains adaptations of Egyptian birth prognoses and a variety of ingredients labeled "Egyptian" that become standard in Greco-Roman medicine.

The most important of the latter was natron, used as a purifying agent in Egypt and subsequently in Greece. Some Egyptian technical terminology was simply translated into Greek, with the term *gs-tp* ("half-head") rendered as *hemikrania* (modern "migraine"). The city of Alexandria must have served as a transmission point, and it can be no coincidence that the Alexandrian Herophilus was the first Greek to adopt the local technique of pulse-taking. The longstanding affiliation between Egyptian medicine and embalming, particularly reinforced in the Late period, provided an environment favorable to Herophilus' pioneering studies in human dissection, which would have been prohibited elsewhere.

[*See also* Dental Care; Disease; Hygiene; *and* Magic, *article on* Magic in Medicine.]

BIBLIOGRAPHY

Bardinet, Thierry. *Les papyrus médicaux de l'égypte pharaonique.* Lyon, 1995.

Darby, William J., Paul Ghalioungui, and Louis Grivetti. *Food: The Gift of Osiris.* 2 vols. London, 1977.

Edel, Elmar. *Ägyptische Ärzte und ägyptische Medizin am hethitischen Königshof.* Göttingen, 1976.

Estes, J. Worth. *The Medical Skills of Ancient Egypt.* Canton, Mass., 1989.

Filer, Joyce. *Egyptian Bookshelf: Disease.* Austin, 1995.

Ghalioungui, Paul. *The Physicians of Pharaonic Egypt.* Mainz, 1983.

Grapow, Hermann, et al., eds. *Grundriss der Medizin der alten Ägypter.* 9 vols. Berlin, 1954–1973.

Kolta, Kamal Sabri. "Medicine, Coptic." In *The Coptic Encyclopedia,* edited by Aziz S. Atiya, pp. 1578–1582. New York, 1991.

Nunn, John F. *Ancient Egyptian Medicine.* Norman, Okla. 1996.

Ritner, Robert K. "Innovations and Adaptations in Ancient Egyptian Medicine." *Journal of Near Eastern Studies* 57 (2000).

Ritner, Robert K., and P. Piccione. "Ancient Egypt." In *Society for Ancient Medicine Review* (vols. 16–24 and continuing). Ann Arbor, 1988–1999 and continuing.

Sauneron, Serge. *Une traité égyptien d'ophiologie.* Cairo, 1989.

Steuer, Robert O. *Aetiological Principle of Pyaemia in Ancient Egyptian Medicine.* Supplements to the *Bulletin of the History of Medicine,* 10. Baltimore, 1948.

Steuer, Robert O., and J. B. de C. M. Saunders. *Ancient Egyptian and Cnidian Medicine.* Berkeley and Los Angeles, 1959.

Till, Walter. C. *Die Arzneikunde der Kopten.* Berlin, 1951.

ROBERT K. RITNER

MEDINET HABU, the area adjoining the cultivation at the southern end of the Theban Necropolis (25°44′N, 32°35′E). The Arabic name Medinet Habu ("City of Habu") was thought to reflect the site's more ancient connection with Amenhotep, the son of Hapu, a respected sage of the fourteenth century BCE, later deified, whose memorial temple was immediately to the north. No trace of this association has come down from ancient times, however, as the site's formal name in Egyptian was either Djeme, "Males and Mothers"—originally with reference to the eight primeval deities, or Ogdoad, whom the ancients believed to be buried there—although the name continued to be used by the site's later Christian inhabitants.

Medinet Habu's most conspicuous standing monument is the great memorial temple of Ramesses III (r. 1198–1166 BCE). On the grounds of this complex, however, are numerous other structures, most notably the so-called small temple (built in stages, from the mid-eighteenth dynasty until the second century CE) and the memorial chapels of the divine votaresses of Amun (twenty-fifth dynasty and twenty-sixth). Among other ancient buildings at the site, but less well preserved, is the memorial temple of King Horemheb (r. 1343–1315 BCE), usurped from his predecessor Ay (r. 1346–1343 BCE), which abuts Ramesses III's enclosure on its northern side. To its east are a number of tomb chapels made for high officials of the later New Kingdom. Most abundantly on the enclosure wall of Ramesses III's temple are the remnants of later mud-brick houses—from the town that engulfed the site beginning in the eleventh century BCE until the site was abandoned in the ninth century CE. Reuse of Ramesses III's temple was made especially apparent by the decorated doorways that were cut into its northern outer wall during early Christian times, when the Holy Church of Djeme occupied the building's second court.

Detailed knowledge of the area's history and function has come from the work begun in 1924 by the Oriental Institute of the University of Chicago, under the direction of James Henry Breasted and funded by the Rockefeller Foundation. By 1933, the entire site had been systematically excavated and its plan recorded; the copying of the reliefs and inscriptions carved on the walls of Ramesses III's temple, however, including its eastern high gate, continued into the 1960s. Recording by the Epigraphic Survey (Chicago House) of the other inscribed structures at Medinet Habu still continues. As the only attempt to document the entire archaeological, architectural, and decorated substance of a such a large site, this unique series of publications is of ongoing value for the study of ancient Egyptian history, religion, and culture.

The great temple of Ramesses III was called the "Mansion of Millions of Years of King Usermare-Maiamun 'United with Eternity in the Estate of Amun on the West of Thebes.'" The precinct, 210 × 315 meters (about 700 feet × 1000 feet), was entered by two stone gates in the mud-brick enclosure wall, on the eastern and the western sides, respectively. The western gate—presumably the normal entrance for employees who lived outside the precinct—was destroyed when the temple was besieged in a civil war, during the reign of Ramesses XI (c.1096). The eastern entrance, approached by a canal, terminated in a harbor, from which important visitors and statues could

MEDINET HABU. *Main gate of the royal palace.* The palace is from the nineteenth dynasty. (Courtesy Dieter Arnold)

enter the temple; the processional way led first between two porters' lodges that were set into a low, crenelated stone rampart, built in front of the main enclosure wall, and then into the precinct, through the high gate. Despite its military features and the bellicose motifs carved on its outer walls, this structure seems to have been only modeled on a fortification, since the pharaoh is shown at play in reliefs inside its upper chambers; these may have served as royal sitting rooms whenever he visited the "Mansion."

The interior of the complex, following the earlier model of Ramesses II's memorial temple (called the Ramesseum), had been divided into an inner and an outer quarter—with most of the outer at the eastern end consisting of a garden, administrative offices, and courtyards of various types (mostly occupied by later structures, although a small sacred lake is extant at the precinct's northeastern corner). Housing for the temple staff had been tucked up against the northern and southern walls of the outer enclosure. The inner quarter, demarcated by another mud-brick wall, enclosed the temple and its adjoining mud-brick service buildings and storerooms (badly ruined if compared with their counterparts at the Ramesseum), along with two wells and (south of the tem-

ple's first courtyard) a small palace. Although symbolically a residence for the deceased king, the small palace had also been used as a functional rest house for visiting royalty; it was even remodeled to make it more usable by its human occupants.

The temple itself is, for the most part, a slightly smaller copy of the Ramesseum. Two pylons lead into an open courtyard, and the temple's cult rooms were constructed to the west of the portico, at the back of the second courtyard. Commemorated on the building's outer walls (the eastern and northern), as well as inside its two courts, were scenes from the wars of Ramesses III; on the southern outer wall, west of the small palace, was inscribed a calendar of annual feasts and offerings (comparable to those found in Ramesses II's temples at Abydos and Western Thebes). Inside, the first courtyard may have been used for assemblies, with the king presiding from the royal balcony of appearances, which was entered from the palace's southern side. The temple also appears to be divided into sections, based on the ideas of cosmic continuity (north) and resurrection (south)—thus, scenes around the second courtyard depict the festival of the ithyphallic fertility god Min (north), balanced by episodes from that of the underworld deity Sokar (south); deeper inside the temple, cult chambers of the solar god Re (north) stand opposite those dedicated to Osiris (south). Other rooms housed the images of other deities (including Sokar and the divine Ramesses II); there was a "treasury," in which were stored temple furnishings and cult apparatus, and also a "slaughter-house" (apparently nonfunctional, in which meat offerings were symbolically prepared). As in memorial temples of earlier Ramessid times (the nineteenth dynasty), the main cult rooms were devoted to the processional shrines of Amun-Re, of Mut and Khonsu (who left their homes in the temples at Karnak to visit the western bank on festive occasions throughout the year), and of a resident form of Amun-Re who was, in fact, the divine Ramesses III. At the very back of the temple, there were included a series of small rooms, entered through low, concealed doorways; these may have been meant to function as crypts.

Even more important than the temple of Ramesses III (whose cult died out with the end of the New Kingdom) was a building, the "Holy-of-Place," that is today most commonly called the "small temple." The core structure that justifies this name was built for Queen Hatshepsut (1502–1482 BCE); and Thutmose III (1504–1452 BCE), over the foundations of an earlier structure; although this last has been ascribed, on slender grounds, to the Middle Kingdom, a safer date for it would be the earlier eighteenth dynasty. Major additions to this Thutmoside building were made from the twenty-fifth dynasty to the thirtieth, culminating under the Ptolemies in an impressive pylon façade (built against mud-brick towers, c.100 BCE): in front of that, Antoninus Pius (138–161 CE) added a portico and a courtyard, but both were left unfinished. The lengthy duration of the cult in this small temple building reflected not only the importance of the Ogdoad, whose tomb was believed to be within the "mound of Djeme," but also a special form of Amun, "primeval one of the Two Lands (i.e., Egypt)," who had the power to re-engender himself; this god's "decade" feast, held at regular ten-day intervals, at least from the time of Ramesses II, accounted for much of the functioning vitality at Medinet Habu, which continued alongside that at the temples of Karnak and Luxor to just before the emergence of Christianity.

Starting in the eighth century BCE, the space to the south of the avenue between the eastern high gate and Ramesses III's temple had been appropriated for tomb chapels that belonged to the Divine Votaresses of Amun—noble ladies, symbolically "married" to Amun-Re, who also represented the royal dynasty that was recognized by the increasingly independent local regime at Thebes. Burial vaults were below ground level, and the superstructures of only two chapels remain today: that of Amenirdis I, sister of the Nubian king Piya (Piankhy) (r. 735–712 BCE) is notable for its elegantly sculpted deco-

ration; beside it (west) is the chapel built for the last of the twenty-fifth dynasty votaresses, Shepenwepet II, daughter of Taharqa (r. 690–664 BCE), after she had adopted Nitokris, daughter of the founder of the twenty-sixth dynasty, Psamtik I (r. 664–610 BCE). Although less well executed than its neighbor, this western structure is more interesting, since it was adapted to contain both votaresses' tombs, along with that of Nitokris's mother. As a group, these later buildings represent not only the political fragmentation of Egypt during the Third Intermediate Period but also the continuing importance of Medinet Habu during the Late period, when it still functioned as headquarters for the "Estate of Amun on the West of Thebes."

BIBLIOGRAPHY

Edgerton, William Franklin. *Medinet Habu Graffiti Facsimiles*. Oriental Institute Publications, 36. Chicago, 1937.

Hölscher, Uvo. *The Excavation of Medinet Habu*. 5 vols. Oriental Institute Publications, 21, 41, 54, 55, 66. Chicago, 1934–1954. Plans of the excavations at the site, with different periods color-coded, along with descriptions of its buildings.

Lichtheim, Miriam. *Demotic Ostraca from Medinet Habu*. Oriental Institute Publications, 80. Chicago, 1957.

Murnane, William J. *United with Eternity: A Concise Guide to the Monuments of Medinet Habu*. Cairo, 1980. An extended guide that summarizes the contents of the primary publications, including a selection of plans and drawings from them.

Nelson, Harold H. "The Identity of Amun-Re United with Eternity." *Journal of Near Eastern Studies* 1 (1941), 127–155. Demonstrates the identity of this deity with the divine Ramesses III.

University of Chicago Oriental Institute. Epigraphic Survey. *Medinet Habu*. 8 vols. Oriental Institute Publications, 8, 9, 23, 51, 83, 84, 93, 94. Chicago; 1930–1970. Facsimile drawings, along with photographs and paintings of the reliefs and inscriptions of Ramesses III's temple and its eastern high gate.

WILLIAM J. MURNANE

MEDITERRANEAN AREA. The nature and extent of relations among Egypt, Cyprus, Anatolia, Crete, the Aegean islands (Cyclades), and mainland Greece increase from late prehistory to the Bronze Age (c.3500–1070 BCE)—albeit with fluctuations and with modern debate concerning the mechanisms and directionality of transmission, the intensity and scope of contact and influence, and the varying preservation and interpretation of archaeological and textual-pictorial evidence. Difficulties and debate also exist regarding complex synchronisms, differing terminologies, and absolute dating for the material culture assemblages of these widely dispersed regions.

The archaeological evidence for Egypt-Aegean contact before the second millennium BCE is sparse and based on Egyptian items, materials, and influences found in the Aegean (mainly Crete and western Anatolia), suggesting that Syria-Palestine, Cyprus, eastern Anatolia, and possibly Libya acted as intermediaries in transmitting items within this region. By the Middle and Late Bronze Ages, evidence exists for both direct and indirect maritime contact between Egypt and the Aegean. The main shipping routes are navigable from May to September; they follow sea currents and winds that go northward and westward, along the Levantine and Anatolian coasts to the Aegean, and those that go southward and eastward, from Crete to Libya and Egypt. A northwestern route likely connected Nile Delta ports, Marsa Matruh (a Late Bronze Age site 290 kilometers/180 miles west of Alexandria), and the Libyan coast with southern Crete (e.g., Kommos).

Middle and Late Bronze Age texts indicate that the state, the temples, and their officials conducted and controlled international trade, while ships' crews practiced small-scale private trade. Archaeological and textual-pictorial sources (e.g., Mari; Avaris; Amarna; Ugarit; Bogazkoy; Theban tombs) reveal increasingly complex international relations and the commercial exchanges of materials and products limited to or abundant in certain locales. These include reciprocal royal and official gifts (luxury items and materials) between nations of equal and unequal status, political alliances, treaties, and diplomatic marriages. The impact of piracy and state-sanctioned private entrepreneurs cannot be ignored in the redistribution of foreign commodities and influences.

Late Predynastic and Early Dynastic. The late Predynastic (Naqada II–III: c.3500–3050 BCE) and the Early Dynastic (Archaic) period (Dynasties "0," 1, 2, 3: c.3050–2632 BCE) encompass the Chalcolithic to Early Bronze Age I–II in the Levant and Anatolia, Chalcolithic II–III in Cyprus, Neolithic to Early Minoan I in Crete, and Neolithic to Early Helladic/Cycladic I on the Greek mainland and Aegean islands.

Cyprus and Egypt. Evidence for early Egypt-Cypriot contact is tenuous. The aceramic period (c.7000–6000 BCE) at Khirokitia and the early Chalcolithic levels at Kalavasos-Ayious yield forty carnelian beads and a carnelian pendant, respectively, which are often assigned Egyptian or Sinai origins; some suggest that slabs with thirty depressions from Lemba-Lakkous and elsewhere represent adaptations (via Cilicia) of Egyptian Senet-game boards (which have grids of thirty squares). These carnelian items could originate from Syrian sources or represent Cypriot red jasper, while thirty depressions on a slab could easily reflect the lunar cycle and not necessarily Egyptian influence.

Anatolia and Egypt. Although the presence of silver in Egypt (e.g., jewelry) and gold in Anatolia might reflect an exchange (albeit probably indirect) of precious metals between these regions, gold sources do occur in Anatolia, while silver is not restricted to Anatolian sources. Better evidence for contact is represented by a loop-handled vessel from Badari (Egypt), which resembles forms in northern Syria and Tarsus (southeastern Anatolia).

The Aegean and Egypt. Early Egypt-Aegean contacts remain unconfirmed, since all late Predynastic and Early Dynastic Egyptian stone vessels in the Aegean were found in later contexts. Possible Egyptian stone vessels, found during the excavation of Final Neolithic period houses (radiocarbon dated to 4135–3375 BCE) at Knossos (Crete), originated from insecure and contested contexts. No connection is thought to exist between Early Minoan I Red Linear decoration on a buff ground (on Aghios Onouphrios ware) and similarly decorated Predynastic to first dynasty pottery from Egypt.

Old Kingdom. The Old Kingdom (fourth to sixth dynasties: c.2632–2191 BCE) parallels Early Bronze III, Chalcolithic III to Early Cypriot I, Early Minoan I to IIA–B, and Early Helladic I–II. Despite little textual information, archaeological data confirm connections between Egypt and the Mediterranean area.

Cyprus and Egypt. Cypriot products remain undetected in Egypt, but may include lumber and possibly copper, transmitted via Byblos. Cyprus yielded possible "Egyptian"-style Senet-game boards (e.g., Sotira-Kaminoudhia), stone slabs with depressions placed in spirals (identified as a Cypriot adaptation of the Egyptian game of Mehen), and faience beads—none of which are necessarily Egyptian. Egyptian seals bearing the names of fourth and fifth dynasty kings (Khafre, Menkaure, and Unas) occur in variously dated and later contexts.

Anatolia and Egypt. An Early Bronze Age (EB II, elsewhere EB III) Cilician pot came from a fourth dynasty tomb at Giza, while silver in Old Kingdom contexts may originate from Anatolia. Anatolia yielded some probable Egyptian exports: ivory, gold, and turquoise from Troy level II, gold from Poliochni, an *ex situ* (purchased) gold cylinder seal bearing the names of Menkaure and Djedkare (fourth and fifth dynasties), a turquoise macehead from an Early Bronze Age (EB II, elsewhere EB III) tomb at Dorak (northwestern Anatolia), and gold leaf from a chair with the titles and cartouche of Sahure (fifth dynasty) from Dorak (tomb 1; problematic in date). Despite later texts citing Egypt as a major gold source, gold is found in Anatolia, while ivory could originate from Syrian elephants; however, the nearest turquoise source is in the Sinai, where Egyptian Old Kingdom mining occurred at Wadi Mughara and Wadi Kharig.

Crete and Egypt. Although Old Kingdom Egypt lacks items from or references to Crete, eighteenth-century BCE Mesopotamian texts and a Neo-Assyrian text (KAV 92) transmitting an inscription of Sargon of Akkad (c.2334–2279 BCE) reveal the name "Kaptara" (Crete?) for a land in the Upper Sea. Excavations at Knossos on Crete have produced an Egyptian Early Dynastic(?) obsidian bowl fragment and a diorite bowl from secure Early Minoan (EM) IIA and II contexts. Other probable Egyptian imports in EM IIA include hippopotamus ivory, amethyst, carnelian, and gold. A *pyxis*, bearing Khafre's name (fourth dynasty), came from a *tholos* tomb at Aghia Triadha, but it might represent an antique that was introduced up to 850 years after Khafre, since the tomb's contents span Early to Middle Minoan.

Greece and Egypt. Greek products and influence are absent in Old Kingdom Egypt, while Early Cycladic II (Keros-Syros culture) artifacts are limited to the Aegean and western Anatolia (despite some from Syria-Palestine in Greece). Evidence concerning the introduction date for Old Kingdom items in Greece is problematic and inconclusive: some scarabs from Camiros on Rhodes displayed the names of fourth and fifth dynasty kings (Menkaure and Unas), but they originated from insecure contexts and may represent twenty-sixth dynasty reissues; later introductions do include an *ex situ* stone bowl from Kythera (Cerigo Island), with the cartouche of the fifth dynasty king Userkaf, and an Old Kingdom statue head from Athens.

First Intermediate Period. The period (seventh to early eleventh dynasties: c.2191–2040 BCE) spans Early Cypriot I–II, Middle Bronze I, Early Minoan III, and Early Helladic III, during which there was a decline in international relations. Several scholars assign the appearance of Egyptian stone bowls and scarabs in Crete to Early Minoan III, while others argue a Middle Minoan I date (twelfth dynasty). In contrast, Egypt lacks this period's Aegean and Cypriot items.

Middle Kingdom. Egypt's late eleventh to thirteenth dynasties (c.2040–1665 BCE) were parallel to Early Cypriot III to Middle Cypriot III, Middle Bronze IIA–B, Early Minoan III to Middle Minoan IIIA, and Early Helladic III to Middle Helladic; there was a revival and increase in international relations.

Cyprus and Egypt. The names "Alasiya" and "Asy" (Isy) appear in Near Eastern texts from the eighteenth to twelfth centuries BCE; they are generally accepted as designating Cyprus or a town in Cyprus. Cypriot pottery increased in Egypt from Middle Cypriot I to II–III times, while Cyprus yielded Egyptian faience and a Nubian-faced pendant in a nineteenth-century BCE tomb at Lapithos. A Late Cypriot context at Enkomi yielded a scarab of Senwosret I.

Anatolia and Egypt. Egypt has many eleventh and twelfth dynasty silver items (e.g., from Montuhotep I's mortuary temple, from Tod, Illahun, Dahshur, and the tombs of Senebtisi, Neferuptah, and Wah), which may have originated in Anatolian mines. Egyptian contact with northwestern Anatolia is attested at Alaca Huyuk, which yielded a plaque with a *djed*-pillar from an eighteenth-century BCE stratum and a Middle Kingdom plaque with a Bes-figure from the earliest Hittite-occupation level. Other Middle Kingdom items from Anatolia occur in later contexts: statuettes from the Hittite capital Hattusas (Bogazkoy), a granite statuette of Sitsneferu (time of Senwosret II) from Adana, and a granite statuette of Keri from a Byzantine cemetery at Kirikkale near Ankara.

Crete and Egypt. Early second millennium BCE and later texts from Egypt (e.g., *Admonitions of Ipuwer*) and from Syria-Mesopotamia (e.g., Mari tablets) designate Crete or Cretans as "Keftiu" and "Kaptara"/"Kaphtor" (a land of the Upper Sea), respectively; Crete lacks indigenous texts. In Egypt, the site of el-Lisht has produced a Middle Minoan I potsherd, Illahun yielded a Minoan-style serpentine lid, and some Middle Minoan IIA–B vessels. Minoan influence is evident at Buhen (tomb K5), where an Egyptian pottery vessel displays Middle Minoan II-type decoration, and on Middle Kingdom scarabs and the ceiling of Hepzefa's tomb (time of Senwosret I), which adopt spiraliform designs. A Middle Minoan IB–II date and Minoan influence were assigned to 153 silver bowls and cups found in four copper chests (two bear Amenemhet II's name) deposited in the foundations of a temple at Tod. Kemp and Merrillees (1980) questioned the twelfth dynasty date for the deposition and contents of the boxes, and through contextual analysis argued that deposition occurred later, at some point between Thutmose III's reign and the Ptolemaic period. Some researchers contest a Minoan derivation for these vessels but retain Syria, Anatolia, and Greece(?) as possible sources.

Egyptian products in Crete include First Intermediate Period scarabs in Middle Minoan IA contexts, locally copied and adapted scarabs, an Egyptian-style clay sistrum from Arkhanes Phourni, gold and Egyptian-derived plaques with a sphinx design at Mallia, a twelfth dynasty diorite statuette of User in context (albeit contested) with Middle Minoan IIB pottery at Knossos, and Middle Kingdom(?) ivory statuettes at Palaikastro.

Greece and Egypt. Egypt lacks Early and Middle Helladic pottery, but the few Middle Kingdom items found in Greece came from later or insecure contexts. The statue of Sonb from Athens and three scarabs of Senwosret from Sparta may reflect later imports.

Second Intermediate Period. The period (fourteenth to seventeenth dynasties: c.1665–1555 BCE) and the advent of the eighteenth dynasty span Late Cypriot IA–B, Middle Bronze IIC, Middle Minoan IIIB to Late Minoan IA, and Middle Helladic to Late Helladic IA.

Cyprus and Egypt. Egypt has some imported and locally copied Late Cypriot I pottery. More than five hundred Cypriot potsherds from Tell ed-Dab'a include White Painted Pendent Line Style, White Painted Cross Line

TABLE 1 *Broad Synchronisms between Egypt, Cyprus, Levant, Anatolia, and the Aegean.*

EGYPT: Absolute dates BCE are "circa" (approx.)	EGYPT: Dates following the chronology in *The Oxford Encyclopedia of Ancient Egypt*	CYPRUS * = system followed here for Cypriot Ages		LEVANT & ANATOLIA Bronze Ages	CRETE Minoan Ages	CYCLADES Cycladic (islands) Ages	GREECE (Mainland) Helladic Ages
		Chronological terminology, sequences, dates, and synchronisms adopted from Albright, Aström, Dickinson, Ehrich (ed.), Evans, Gjerstad, Hankey, Jacobsson, Merrillees, and Warren.					
3500–3300	Late Predynastic	Chalcolithic		Chalcolithic	Neolithic	Neolithic	Neolithic
3300–3050	(or Naqada II–III)	**Merrillees:**	Gjerstad:	EB I	-(EM I?)	-(EC I?)	-(EH I?)
3050–2850	Dynasty 1	*Chalc.II	EC IA	EB II	EM I	EC I	EH I
2850–2687	Dynasty 2	*Chalc.II	EC IB	EB II	EM I	EC I	EH I
2687–2632	Dynasty 3	*Chalc.III	EC IB	EB II	EM I	EC I	EH I
2632–2510	Dynasty 4	*Chalc.III	EC IC	EB III	EM I–IIA	EC I–II	EH I–II
2510–2374	Dynasty 5	*EC I	EC IC	EB III	EM IIA-B	EC II	EH II
2374–2191	Dynasty 6	*EC I	EC II	EB III	EM IIB	EC II	EH II
2191–2165	Dynasties 7–8	*EC I	EC II	EB IV/MB I	EM III	EC IIIA	EH III
2165–2040	Dynasties 9–10 vs. 11	*EC I–II	EC III	EB IV/MB I	EM III	EC IIIA	EH III
2040–1998	Late Dynasty 11	*EC II–III	EC III	MB IIA	EM III	EC III A	EH III
1998–1991	Civil strife				MM IA	EC III B	MH early
1991–1895	Early Dynasty 12	*EC III	EC III	MB IIA	MM IA	EC IIIB	MH early
1895–1786	Late Dynasty 12	*MC I		MB IIA	MM IB/ MM IIA	EC IIIB MC early	MH middle
1786–1700	Early Dynasty 13	*MC II		MB IIB	MM IB/ MM IIB	MC early	MH middle
1700–1665	Late Dynasty 13	*MC III		MB IIB	MM IIIA	MC late	MH late
1664–1555	Hyksos Dyns."14"-15 Theban Dyns.16–17	LC IA	Aström: *LC IA:1	MB IIC	MM IIIB LM IA	MC late LC I	MH late LH I
1555–1482	Early Dynasty 18 (Ahmose-Hatshepsut)	LC IB	LC IA:1–2 *LC IB	MB IIC LB IA	LM 1A LM IB	LC I LC II	LH I LH IIA
1482–1452	Early Dynasty 18 (Thutmose III yr.22+)	LC IIA	*LC IB	LB IB	LM IB	LC II	LH IIA
1452–1410	Mid-Dynasty 18	LC IIA	*LC IIA:1	LB 1B	LM II	LC II	LH IIB
1410–1382	Mid-Dynasty 18 (Amenhotpe III)	LC IIB	*LC IIA:1 *LC IIA:2	LB 2A	LM IIIA1	LC III early	LH IIIA1
1382–1365	Late Dynasty 18 (Amenhotpe IV)	LC IIB	*LC IIB	LB 2A	LM IIIA2	LC III early	LH IIIA2
1365–1323	Late Dynasty 18	LC IIB	LC IIB-C:1	LB 2A	LM IIIB	LC III middle	LH IIIB1
1323–1237	Early Dynasty 19	LC IIC	*LC IIC:1	LB 2B	LM IIIB	LC III middle	LH IIIB1-2
1237–1201	Late Dynasty 19	LC IIIA	*LC IIC:2	LB 2B	LM IIIB/C	LC III late	LH IIIB2/C1
1200–1149	Early Dynasty 20	LC IIIB	*LC IIIA:1	Iron 1A	LM IIIC	LC III late	LH IIIC1
1149–1076	Late Dynasty 20	LC IIIC	*LC IIIA-2	Iron 1B	LM IIIC	LC III late	LH IIIC2-3
1076–1000 BCE	Early Dynasty 21 (Smendes-Psusennes)	Geometric I	*LC IIIB:1 *LC IIIB:2	Iron 1B	subminoan	LC III final	LH IIIC3? submycenaean

Style, White Painted V, White Painted Alternating Broad Band and Wavy Line Style, White Painted Composite Style, Red on Black, Plain Ware, Cypriot Bichrome Ware, and local imitations of Cypriot pottery. That site and 'Ezbet Helmi have later Cypriot pottery: Base Ring I, White Slip I, White Painted VI, Red Lustrous Wheelmade Ware, and Red Slip Wheelmade Ware. Although Cyprus yielded some Hyksos-style (fifteenth dynasty) scarabs and Tell el-Yahudiyya had juglets of possible Egyptian origin, Jacobsson (1994) asserts that they probably represent later imports.

Anatolia and Egypt. Egypt lacks obvious Anatolian imports, but an obsidian vase fragment with Khyan's car-touche (fifteenth dynasty) occurs in occupation debris at Bogazköy; it is *ex situ* and may reflect later Egypt-Hittite relations.

Crete and Egypt. Minoan contact with Egypt increased in the late fifteenth and the seventeenth dynasties. At el-Lisht, a pot with birds and dolphins reflects Middle Minoan III decoration. Tell ed-Dab'a (Avaris) yielded a Middle Minoan IIIA/B potsherd, an Aegean/Minoan-style gold pendant from a tomb, and a niello dagger with Minoan motifs. Late Hyksos period debris from the palace area at Tell ed-Dab'a yielded Middle Minoan IIIB to Late Minoan IA contact with Egypt through thousands of fragments of paintings that are Minoan in their techniques of production, style, and themes. The nationality of the painters (i.e., Egyptian versus Minoan) and the direction of influence (i.e., which culture influenced the other) has been debated, since comparable Minoan frescoes are either a little later in date (e.g., Late Minoan IA/Late Cypriot I Theran frescoes on Akrotari), or mostly later in date (e.g., Middle Minoan IIIB–Late Minoan IIIA frescoes from Knossos and elsewhere).

Some Egyptologists argue strongly for a Minoan origin for, and Minoan artists producing, the Avaris frescoes. Earlier and contemporary Egyptian paintings (mostly from tombs) differ in technique, style, and themes from the Avaris and Aegean palace frescoes. The Avaris paintings incorporate Minoan techniques of *buon fresco* (background color), *secco* (later colors), and stucco relief on lime plaster, in contrast to the less frequent Egyptian use of gypsum plaster to prepare surfaces for painting. Other Minoan techniques include pressing stretched strings into wet plaster to outline the borders of compositions. The selection of colors—black, white, yellow, red, blue—for background and details follow Minoan rather than Egyptian preferences (which uses green more frequently). The Avaris frescoes are Minoan in their style and composition of details, elements, and themes for large and small-scale images: red backgrounds (with trees, hills, and figures), Cretan flora (e.g., dittany), bull-leapers, winged griffins, bulls, flying gallop motif (MM II origin), maze/labyrinth designs, conical rhyton, acrobats, Minoan-style garments (kilts, belts, boots, flounced skirts), persons with blue-tinted shaven scalps, and black curled locks of hair. As in the Theran and Knossos compositions, the Avaris frescoes contain Egyptian elements: Nile vegetation (palms, blue papyrus, reeds, *w3ḏ*-lily), landscapes with rivers, and wildlife (leopards, lions, antelopes, hunting dogs); some Aegean plants (e.g., crocuses) are noticeable by their absence.

In Crete, Middle Minoan III to Late Minoan I/IA contexts contain Egyptian items: an ivory figurine, a Hyksos scarab, and seven Egyptian vessels of calcite (alabaster, marble), porphyrite, and faience from Mallia, Mavrospelio, Katsamba, Knossos, and Akrotiri. A stone lid from Knossos bears the cartouche of a Hyksos ruler (Khayan), which appears alongside Middle Minoan III pottery. Mallia contains locally adapted images of the Egyptian hippopotamus deity (Taweret) reconfigured as a Minoan fertility spirit.

Greece and Egypt. To date, no Early to Middle Helladic products appear in Egypt, whereas some Egyptian items in Greece may date to the advent of Late Helladic I.

New Kingdom: Eighteenth to Twentieth Dynasties. The Early eighteenth dynasty of Ahmose to Thutmose III (c.1555–1452 BCE) spans Late Cypriot IB–IIA, late Middle Bronze 2C to early Late Bronze IB, Late Minoan IA–B, and Late Helladic I–IIA.

Cyprus and Egypt. The Late Bronze Age Cyprus-Minoan script has similarities to Cretan Linear A, but it remains undeciphered and lacks identifiable references to Egypt; Near Eastern and Egyptian texts mention "Alasiya" (probably Cyprus). Late Cypriot I pottery occurs throughout Egypt (e.g., Saqqara, Sedment, Meidum, el-Balabish, Deshasheh, Abydos, Shellal, Riqqeh, Rifeh, Aniba), and consists of imported and locally copied jars, jugs, juglets, tankards, pilgrim flasks, spindle bottles, and some bowls and arm-shaped items. These vessels display various styles: Base Ring I, White Painted Pendent Line, Cross Line Style, White Painted VI, White Slip I–II, Black Slip II, and Red Lustrous Ware (the last was initially equated with Syria, but has since been shown to be Cypriot). Late Cypriot I contexts yield Ahmose's name on a scarab (Akhera) and a serpentine jar fragment (Koulia-Teratsoudhia). Five scarabs of Thutmose III occur in Late Cypriot IIIA, in IIIB:1, and in broader Late Cypriot contexts at Enkomi, Kourion, and Maroni.

Anatolia and Egypt. Silver items in Egypt may originate from Anatolia or elsewhere, while texts mention Hittite gifts given to Thutmose III during his campaigns in Syria-Palestine. Egyptian items in Anatolia are equally sparse, but may include scarabs from Bogazkoy.

Crete and Egypt. Although inscriptions in Linear A (undeciphered) and Linear B from Crete contain evidence for relations with the Near East, their interpretation remains problematic and they lack definite references to Egypt. The suggestion that a Semitic loan-word (*A-ku-pi-ti-jo*) in a Linear B tablet (Bb1105) from Knossos means "Egyptian" is tenuous. New Kingdom texts record contact with "Keftiu" (Crete), which is described either as an island in the middle of the sea or a place near Asia. Minoan products and influence in Egypt include a Late Minoan IB alabastron (bag-shaped vessel) from Sedment (tomb 137), an imitation Late Minoan 1A–B alabastron from Aniba, copies of Late Minoan I pottery from Abu Ghurob, potsherds from Late Minoan I jars, bowls, and ewers, and an Aegean-derived niello dagger from Queen Ahhotep's tomb (from the time of Ahmose). A second phase of Minoan-style frescoes at Tell ed-Dab'a was dated to the time after Ahmose's destruction of Avaris. During Hatshepsut's reign, Theban tombs begin depicting people from Keftiu.

Egyptian amphoras at the coastal site of Kommos in southern Crete assist arguments for direct maritime contact between Egypt and Crete. Late Minoan I and IB contexts yielded thirty-one Egyptian containers of calcite (alabaster), basalt, porphyrite, faience, and pottery, an amulet, a scarab, and a *Tridacna* shell. Other probable Egyptian exports to Crete included amethyst, carnelian, ebony (African blackwood), hippopotamus and elephant ivory, African fauna (monkeys, oryx/antelopes?, cranes?), and possibly rock crystal and ostrich eggs (from Libya?).

Late Minoan 1A paintings from Cretan and Aegean palaces display Egyptian influence in various motifs and iconography: papyrus, reeds, *w3s/w3ḏ*-lilies, palms, monkeys picking flowers, antelopes, and tall poles outside shrines (similar to the flagstaffs fronting Egyptian temple pylons). Parallels between Egyptian and Aegean art include depictions of women with light-colored skin (cream: i.e., untanned) and men with darker-colored skin (red-brown: i.e., tanned).

Greece and Egypt. Some Late Helladic IIA (Mycenaean) pottery was found in Egypt at Saqqara, Illahun, Abu Ghurob, Sedment, and Dra Abul Naga, while Late Helladic I–II and IIA contexts in Greece provide seven calcite (Egyptian alabaster) and faience containers, scarabs and seals, and a cosmetic spoon. Late sixteenth-century BCE shaft graves IV–V at Mycenae yielded dagger blades with inlaid Nile landscapes and hunting scenes. The Theran frescoes also included a Nile landscape. Thutmose III's name appears on a granite offering stand and on a basalt statue from later contexts at Salonica, as well as on twenty-sixth dynasty reissues of scarabs from Camiros (Rhodes).

Mid-Eighteenth Dynasty. The time of the kings Amenhotpe II and III (c.1452–1382 BCE) spans Late Cypriot IIA–B, Late Bronze 1B–2A, Late Minoan II–IIIA:1, and Late Helladic IIB–IIIA:1.

Cyprus and Egypt. Late Cypriot I–II pottery (e.g., Base Ring I–II and Red Lustrous ware) continues to be found in Egypt. The analysis of Base Ring juglets reveals an oily substance (scents or ointments) and possibly opium. Stratified Late Cypriot IIA:2 contexts reveal various Egyptian items in Cyprus: calcite (alabaster), glass, and faience vessels; jewelry of bronze, gold, and silver; and scarabs. These and later contexts reveal the names of Amenhotpe III and/or Queen Tiy on a ring, a scarab, and a commemorative scarab.

Anatolia and Egypt. Inscriptions in Akkadian, Hittite, and Egyptian record the names of Anatolian countries and peoples: "Arzawa" (southern Anatolia), "Khatte/Khattuša" (central Anatolia), "Kaška" (northeastern Anatolia), and "Arusna" (northwestern Anatolia). Two letters cite the exchange of gifts and messages between Amenhotpe III of Egypt and Tarkhundaradu of Arzawa: a daughter was promised in marriage to Amenhotpe III, while in exchange Amenhotpe discussed the dowry and sent a greeting gift of gold, 317 linen pieces (garments, mantles, other items), 10 containers of sweet oil, 13 ebony chairs with ivory and gold overlay, and 100 ebony pieces. Several Late Helladic IIIA burials at Panaztepe near Troy contained Egyptian gold, an alabastron, a scarab from the eighteenth dynasty, and a scarab of Amenhotpe III.

Crete and Egypt. Amenhotpe III's statue base from Kom el-Hetan lists toponyms for Crete and places in Crete: "Keftiu" (Crete) is described as an obscure northern country near Asia, while the remaining places include "Lyktos" in eastern Crete, "Amnisos" in northern Crete, "Knossos" in central Crete, "Kydonia" in western Crete, and "Phaistos" in southern Crete. Although no Late Minoan II pottery is known from Egypt, the Egyptian textual-pictorial record reveals much Minoan influence and products in Egypt. One ostracon bears a reference to "the Keftiuan." A medical papyrus transcribes a remedy in the Keftiu language for recital to cure an "Asiatic [Near Eastern] disease." Wall scenes depict ships of Keftiu in a royal dockyard. Theban tombs display Keftiu bringing elaborate metal vessels (animal-shaped rhyta, jars, jugs, bowls), ingots, leather, and cloth; these Minoans have long, multiple locks of black hair and wear short kilts (with multicolored patterns, tassels, and a belt), and sometimes boots or sandals with leg bindings. In the vizier Rekhmire's tomb, a painter replaces a Keftiu kilt with a plainer kilt, which some scholars suggest reflects the Mycenaean seizure of Crete and the replacement of Minoan emissaries in Egypt. Minoan patterned textiles (depicted in Aegean frescoes), which figure among Aegean exports to Egypt, probably inspired the identical patterning found on ceilings in Egyptian tombs. Aegean-style decoration also appears on a wooden cosmetic-jar lid from Saqqara.

In Crete, Egyptian influence in Late Minoan II and IIIA:1 is less widespread, but includes thirty Egyptian containers of calcite (alabaster), diorite, pottery, frit, and porphyrite, a scarab (of Amenhotpe III and Queen Tiy), and Egyptian-style lapis lazuli amulets and beads. More broadly dated Late Minoan I–II and II–IIIA:1/A contexts produced twelve calcite (alabaster), gypsum, and diorite containers from Knossos, while Amenhotpe III and Queen Tiy appear on scarabs and a seal from Khania, Knossos (Sellopoulo), and Aya Triadha.

Greece and Egypt. Near Eastern texts use several names for Mycenae and places in Greece and western Anatolia. Hittite texts mention the kingdom of "Ahhiyawa" in western Anatolia (possibly Homer's Achaeans: Mycenaeans), a coastal city named "Millawanda"/"Milawata" (Miletus?), and a treaty with "Tarwisa" (Troy?) and "Aleksandu" (Alexander) of "Wilusa" (Ilion?). Amenhotpe III's statue base lists places and peoples associated with Mycenae. These places are described as obscure northern countries, while other Egyptian texts mention islands (the Cyclades) in the midst of the "Great Green" (Mediterranean).

Although only a few Late Helladic IIB vessels occur in Egypt, more evidence exists for Egyptian contact with Greece. There are similar themes in Egyptian and Aegean art, such as paintings of cattle in a marsh (e.g., Amenhotpe III's Malqata palace and Mycenaean pictorial vessels). Late Helladic II and later contexts at Mycenae and Argive Heraion yielded many Egyptian items: a jug, bowl, and alabastron of stone, calcite (alabaster), and faience, six fragmentary plaques of Amenhotpe III, eighteenth dynasty scarabs, a flying-gallop motif on a niello inlaid dagger, and an Egyptian (?)-transmitted ostrich egg (mounted in a Minoan-style gold and faience casing). Other broadly dated items include the cartouches of Amenhotpe III and/or Queen Tiy on an ape figurine, a faience vase, and scarabs from Mycenae, Ayios Elias, and Ialysos (Rhodes); Camiros (Rhodes) and Sounion yielded twenty-sixth dynasty reissued scarabs with Amenhotpe III's name. Lambrou-Phillipson (1990) reports an unprovenanced eighteenth dynasty–style anchor in the Marine Museum of Piraeus (Attica).

Late Eighteenth Dynasty. The time of Amenhotpe IV to Horemheb (c.1382–1323 BCE) covers Late Cypriot IIB, Late Bronze 2B, Late Minoan IIIA2–B, and Late Helladic IIIA2–B1.

Cyprus and Egypt. Amenhotpe IV's archives at Tell el-Amarna (the city of Akhetaten) contain correspondence, the Amarna Letters, from the king of Alasiya (Cyprus), detailing gifts of copper ingots, oil, wood, horses, and ivory sent to Egypt (EA 33–40); he mentions attacks against Egypt by the Lukka and some Cypriots and requests the return of captured Cypriots. Other texts refer to Cypriot traders residing in Egypt. A text from Ugarit notes the Cypriot manufacture of ships for Egypt. Imported and locally copied Cypriot ceramics in Egypt consist of mainly closed forms (juglets, flasks, bottles, a bull-vase) and some bowls in Base Ring II, White Slip II, and Red Lustrous ware. Letters from Alasiya mention Egyptian emissaries residing in Cyprus: for example, Egyptian envoys were delayed for three years awaiting the production of copper which was halted, owing to the death (by a plague) of copper workers. Other Cypriot letters request (reciprocal) Egyptian gifts: an ebony bed, gold, silver, good oil, and a chariot-and-horse team. The king of Alasiya even councils the Egyptian king (Amenhotpe IV or a successor) against making a treaty with Khatte, which was then an enemy of Alasiya. Egyptian items appear throughout Cyprus: glass, faience, and a late eighteenth dynasty bead with a Nubian-style head. Broadly dated and later contexts yielded a silver ring with Amenhotpe IV's cartouche at Enkomi, a faience scepter head with Horemheb's name at Hala Sultan Tekke, and bronze and ivory "weights" with Nubian heads at Enkomi and Kalavassos-Ayios Dhimitrios.

Anatolia and Egypt. Evidence for Egypt-Anatolian contact increases. Texts from Amarna and Khatte record an exchange of messengers and correspondence. King Shuppiluliumas of Khatte sends a greeting gift of silver stag-and-ram-shaped *rhyta* and two silver disks (ornamented? with trees) to Amenhotpe IV, Smenkhkare, or

Tutankhamun. Another letter reports a Hittite prince sending a greeting gift of sixteen men. Both Hittite and Egyptian texts record the dispatch of Egyptian presents and emissaries to Khatte and include requests for the Egyptian ruler to send gold, a piece of lapis lazuli, gold and silver statues, and a furniture stand. Egyptian objects in Anatolia include a calcite (Egyptian alabaster) vase at Bogazkoy, and an eighteenth dynasty scarab in later Phrygian levels at Fraktin (central Anatolia). A shipwreck (late eighteenth dynasty) at Ulu Burun near southern Anatolia contains Egyptian items bound for northwestern Anatolia, Rhodes, or Greece: three gold and silver rings, a plaque, six scarabs, a gold bezel, a hematite weight, and five bronze tools (adze, axe, chisels).

Egypt-Hittite relations were initially cordial in the late eighteenth dynasty. A Hittite text reports that King Shuppiluliumas sent an emissary to Egypt to determine whether Tutankhamun's recently widowed queen (Ankhesenamun) was serious regarding her unprecedented request to marry a Hittite prince. Egypt's relations with Khatte deteriorated when the Egyptian escort murdered the Hittite prince en route to Egypt, thereby permitting Ay to usurp the throne. Egypt and Khatte then battled for control of Syria. Ay's donation stela from Giza refers to a district called "The Field of the Hittites," which may indicate an area settled by Hittite captives; a Hittite text records the outbreak of plague among Egyptian captives brought back to Khatte, which subsequently infected the Hittite population.

Crete and Egypt. Although Egypt-Minoan contact continued, Late Minoan III pottery in Egypt is virtually indistinguishable from Late Helladic (Mycenaean) IIIA:2 and IIIB pottery at Tell el-Amarna and Sedment. Minoan/Aegean influence appears through the transference of painted decoration, albeit in purely Egyptian motifs, to the floors and dadoes in the Malqata and Amarna palaces of Amenhotpe III and IV. Egyptian products appear in Crete, including an ivory seal and eleven pottery and calcite (alabaster) containers.

Greece and Egypt. Late Helladic (Mycenaean) IIIA:2 and IIIB pottery increased dramatically throughout Egypt during and after Amenhotpe IV's reign, at Tell el-Amarna, Deir el-Medina, and Saqqara. A chapel of the king's statue at Amarna yields a fragmentary painted papyrus, depicting a battle scene in which two soldiers (wearing Mycenaean-style helmets, with boar tusks, and dappled ox-hide[?] tunics) may represent Greek mercenaries employed by Egypt. Egypt and Greece contain similar artistic elements (which continue in the thirteenth century BCE), such as gestures, postures, and details in illustrations of bulls, cows, horses, goats, monkeys, lions, and hunting scenes. Egyptian items appear in stratified Late Helladic IIIA:2 contexts in Greece.

Nineteenth Dynasty. The reigns of Ramesses I to Queen Twosret (c.1323–1201 BCE) parallel Late Cypriot IIC:1–2, Late Bronze 2B, Late Minoan IIIB–B/C, and Late Helladic IIIB1–2/C1.

Cyprus and Egypt. Despite textual attestations for a Hittite seizure of Cyprus early in the dynasty, evidence exists for continued contact (via Ugarit) between Egypt and Cyprus. Late Cypriot IIC pottery appears in Egypt at Kom Rabia (Memphis), while Egyptian products appear in Late Cypriot IIC:1–2 and IIIA:1 contexts: calcite (alabaster), glass, and faience containers, a pendant, a gold diadem (with a Nubian face), faience, and scarabs. In Late Cypriot IIA:2 and IIIA:1, an *ex situ* amphora handle from Hala Sultan Tekke bears Sety I's name, while five scarabs of Ramesses II occur.

Anatolia and Egypt. Egypt-Hittite contact consists mainly of warfare in Syria until the ratification of a peace treaty in the twenty-first year of Ramesses II. Huge Egyptian facilities have been excavated at Pi-Ramesses (northeastern Delta) for chariotry and metalworking (furnaces, tools, and smelting channels—from the time of Sety I and Ramesses II). The foundry contains a stone mold for producing Hittite-style shields, which may reflect the presence of Hittite craftsmen under Egyptian supervision. Sety I's and Ramesses II's battles against the Hittites brought much booty to Egypt, and Hittite captives appear as soldiers, laborers, craftsmen, and other personnel in palace and temple workshops. In contrast, an early nineteenth dynasty granite stela fragment, from a palace in Hattusas (Bogazkoy), probably represents booty from the Egypt-Hittite war (possibly from the Syrian city of Kadesh). Around Year 18 of his reign, Ramesses II granted sanctuary to Urhi-Teshub (formerly "Great King" of Khatte: Murshili III), who had been deposed and exiled by his uncle, Hattushili III. After a period of heightened tension concerning Urhi-Teshub and a realignment of Syrian-Mesopotamian countries backing either Egypt or Khatte, Ramesses II and Hattushili III established peace and exchanged letters, messengers, and gifts. Copies of the treaty survive in both Khatte and Egypt, demarcating the Egypt-Hittite border and stipulating the nature of relations between Egypt, Khatte, and each other's vassal states, including mutual military assistance against external and internal threats.

From about twenty-two thousand cuneiform documents at Bogazkoy, over one hundred letters and copies of letters represent correspondence exchanged between the royal families of Egypt (Ramesses II and Queen Naptera) and Khatte (Hattushili III and Queen Puduhepa), including a reply from Ramesses II to a Hittite vassal ruler (Kupanta-Kurunta of Mira). Ramesses II and royal family members send greeting gifts to Khatte, such as gold necklaces and cups, dyed and undyed linen items (gar-

ments, tunics, cloaks, bedspread), furniture, and boxes inlaid with gold and lapis lazuli. A text from Year 34 of Ramesses II records the stabilization of commerce with Khatte, noting that a man or woman leaving on business to Syria could reach Khatte in confidence, owing to Ramesses II's establishment of peace.

Hittite relations with Egypt include the visit of a Hittite prince to Egypt, and the marriage of Ramesses II (in Year 34 and in 40/45) to two Hittite princesses who are accompanied by personnel, their belongings, and gifts (gold, silver, copper, stone vessels, slaves, horses, cattle, goats, sheep). King Merenptah later sends grain to Khatte to relieve a famine, while Egyptian influence in Anatolia is known from the human-headed sphinx statues at Alaja and Bogazkoy and the royal symbol of a winged disk displayed over Hittite kings.

Crete and Egypt. Although Egypt-Minoan contact declines in this period, Late Minoan IIIB contexts in Crete produce an Egyptian ceramic jar from Kommos and a faience scarab from Poros.

Greece and Egypt. Late Helladic (Mycenaean) IIIB pottery increases throughout Egypt, virtually replacing Cypriot wares—even Cyprus contains high proportions of the pottery. Egyptian products in Late Helladic IIIB Greece include eight alabastra and bowls of calcite (Egyptian alabaster), diorite, porphyrite, and faience; a figurine; three scarabs; faience beads; amulets (Bes figures; crocodiles); and six plaques from Langada (Kos), Mycenae, Perati, Dendera, and Pylos. Perati has yielded scarabs of Ramesses II, while an unprovenanced granite statue of Unnufer is probably a later import.

Early Twentieth Dynasty. The time of Sethnakhte to Ramesses VI (c.1200–1149 BCE) spans Late Cypriot IIIB, Iron Age 1A, Late Minoan IIIC, and Late Helladic IIIC:1.

Cyprus and Egypt. Small quantities of Late Cypriot IIC–IIIA pottery appear in Ramessid contexts at Memphis (Kom Rabia), while some Egyptian pottery of the dynasty is reported from Hala Sultan Tekke in Cyprus. Late Cypriot IIIA:1–2 contexts in Cyprus yielded Egyptian glass, faience, and calcite (Egyptian alabaster) containers; scarabs; a pendant; and a staff terminal. Late Cypriot levels at Enkomi contain a scarab of Ramesses III and an ivory game box with an Egyptian Senet-game board on one side and a twenty-square game on the other.

An overview of Egypt-Cypriot relations reveals Late Cypriot pottery at over fifty New Kingdom Egyptian sites, in contrast to a broader variety of Egyptian products in Late Cypriot contexts at Akanthou, Aradhippou, Apera, Cesnola, Dromolaxia, Enkomi, Ayios Iakovos, Hala Sultan Tekke, Kazaphani-Ayios Andronikos, Klavdhia, Kouklia-Teratsoudhia, Kourion-Bamboula, Kourion, Limassol, and Maroni. The Egyptian items include Nile perch (*Lates niloticus*); vessels of calcite (Egyptian alabaster), faience, or glass; pottery amphorae; a bronze razor; kohl containers of glass and faience; jewelry of gold, silver, electrum, bronze, glass, and faience (amulets, rings, a collar, pendants of Ptah, Taweret, cats, and flies); scaraboid and scarab seals; a bronze statuette of Amun; and possibly ostrich eggs and ivory.

Anatolia and Egypt. Egypt-Hittite contact ends during this period, when invasions by the Sea Peoples (and the displaced peoples) destroy Khatte and other Levantine states. West Anatolians number among the Sea Peoples who attack Egypt's borders. In Anatolia, a late New Kingdom statuette is known from Karamugh near Edessa (which probably was introduced later). Better provenanced Egyptian products come from a merchant ship of contested nationality (Syrian, Cypriot, or Aegean), which sank at Cape Gelidonya, near southern Anatolia, about 1200 BCE. The wreck contains four Egyptian scarabs; a plaque; and some weights (matching Egyptian standards) out of a cargo of storage jars; lead scraps; bronze and stone tools; a cylinder seal; jewelry; unworked crystal; ingots of copper (one ton), of bronze, and of tin.

The Aegean and Egypt. Although no Late Helladic IIIC or sub-Mycenaean pottery is found in Egypt, increasing Aegean contact occurred through Libyan and Sea Peoples' invasions of Egypt's western and eastern borders. Some Egyptian items appear in Late Helladic IIIC:1 contexts in Greece, such as scarabs, cartouches, and an alabastron (tomb 124 at Perati), but could easily reflect heirlooms predating this period. Broadly dated Late Helladic/Late Mycenaean IIB–III contexts yielded eighteen Egyptian containers of stone, pottery, and glass, ten scarabs, and two amulets.

The Sea Peoples. The successive maritime piracy, coastal raids, mass migrations (e.g., Mycenaean diaspora), and settlement of the Sea Peoples and other displaced peoples (c.1232–1191 BCE until c.1100 BCE), destroyed or destabilized empires, kingdoms, regions, and cities throughout the eastern Mediterranean (Mycenae; Khatte; Alasiya; Levantine towns), but these groups and their movements remain complex and incompletely understood. Various groups of Sea Peoples and raiders are encountered in fourteenth-century BCE texts, which mention the "Meshwesh" (Libya), "Shardana" (northern Syria), "land of Danuna/Denyen" (Cilicia in southeastern Anatolia), and "Lukka" (Lycia in southwestern Anatolia). The Shardana, Meshwesh, and Lukka reappear alongside several new peoples—the Shekelesh (southern Italy?), Teresh (Lydia in western Anatolia), and Ekwesh (near western Anatolia)—who represent Libyan allies in an invasion of Egypt's western Delta in Year 5 (c.1232 BCE) in the reign of Merenptah. Later, despite repelling another Libyan invasion (c.1194 BCE), Ramesses III confronts and barely defeats a massive overland and maritime invasion of "Djahi" (Palestine) and Egypt's Delta, by raiders and Sea Peoples in Year 8 (c.1191 BCE). The invaders included already known enemies (Shardana; Teresh; Shekelesh; Danuna/Denyen) and new foes (Peleset [Anatolia?/Aegean?]; Tjeker [Troad]; Weshesh [Troy?]), many of whom were captured and placed in Ramesses III's army. By 1100 BCE, these Sea Peoples and raiders appear settled in Palestine (Peleset [Philistines]; Tjeker), northern Syria-Palestine (Danuna/Denyen), Sicily (Shekelesh), Sardinia (Shardana), and possibly Etruria (Teresh?).

Late Twentieth Dynasty. The time of the late twentieth dynasty to the early twenty-first corresponds to Iron Age 1B, Late Cypriot IIIA:2 to IIIB:1–2, Late Minoan IIIC and the sub-Minoan period, and Late Helladic IIIC:2–3 and the sub-Mycenaean period. Although Egypt lacks contemporary Cypriot or Aegean pottery, Late Helladic/Late Minoan IIIB/C and IIIC contexts in the Aegean yielded Egyptian items: fourteen scarabs, ten figurines and amulets, seven calcite (alabaster) and glass containers, two cartouches, and a stone pendant. Late Cypriot IIIA:2 and IIIB:1–2 contexts on Cyprus produced a seal (with a Nubian head), scarabs, and calcite (alabaster), faience, and glass containers from Kition and Enkomi. One of the few accounts of Egyptian activity abroad is the *Journey of Wenamun*, written about 1076 BCE, which relates the return journey from Byblos (Lebanon) of an Egyptian priest whose chartered ship is driven by a storm to Alasiya (Cyprus); Wenamun locates a townsperson who understands Egyptian, to negotiate with the town's princess in dissuading the townsfolk from killing him and the ship's crew (probably a defensive or retaliatory practice adopted by coastal towns to deal with unknown foreign maritimers who could represent sea raiders).

Egypt and the Mediterranean then entered a "dark age," regarding international relations, although some texts and artifacts indicate continued trade with the Levant. Soon, the Macedonian Greeks, under Alexander the Great, incorporated Egypt into their plans of empire. Under the Ptolemies, and later under the Romans, Egypt became an important province in an expanding circum-Mediterranean trade empire. With the Arab conquest of the mid-seventh century CE Egypt became one of the several Islamic lands around the Mediterranean basin; it then became a special province of the Ottoman Empire.

[*See also* Crete; Cyprus; Hittites; Mycenae; *and* Sea People.]

BIBLIOGRAPHY

Beckman, G. *Hittite Diplomatic Texts.* Society of Biblical Literature, Writings from the Ancient World, 7. Atlanta, 1996. A corpus and translation in English of some fifty Hittite texts, with a bibliography and index.

Betancourt, P. P. *The History of Minoan Pottery.* Princeton, 1985. An excellent historical discussion, corpus, typology, decorative motifs, and analysis of utilitarian and luxury Minoan (Cretan) pottery from c.3000–1200 BCE; an index of items in museums (arranged by sites).

Blieberg, E., and R. Freed, eds. *Fragments of a Shattered Visage; The Proceedings of the International Symposium of Ramesses the Great.* Monographs of the Institute of Egyptian Art and Archeology, 1. Memphis, 1993. A multi-authored study of Ramesses II's reign, including results from excavation at Piramesse (Qantir).

Bourke, S., and J.-P. Descoeudres, eds. *Trade, Contact, and the Movement of Peoples in the Eastern Mediterranean. Studies in Honour of J. Basil Hennessy.* Mediterranean Archaeology Supplement 3. Sydney, 1995. A multi-authored volume with articles on Cyprus and faience in the eastern Mediterranean, the Late Bronze Age Vasilikos Valley in Cyprus, and Egyptian amphorae from Late Cypriot Cyprus.

Cline, E. H. *Sailing the Wine-Dark Sea: International Trade and the Late Bronze Age Aegean.* BAR International Series 591. Oxford, 1994. A study and reference work with chapters on previous scholarship, sections dealing with Late Bronze Age trade throughout different regions of the Mediterranean and surrounding areas, trade mechanisms, routes, products, and shipwrecks; useful catalog organized by area and types of artifacts, a bibliography, and illustrations.

Davies, W. V., and L. Schofield, eds. *Egypt, the Aegean and the Levant: Interconnections in the Second Millennium BC.* London, 1995. This multi-authored volume contains an up-to-date treatment of Egypt-Aegean relations.

Dickinson, O. *The Aegean Bronze Age.* Cambridge World Archaeology. Cambridge, 1994. An introduction to the Aegean with references, maps, site plans, photographs and drawings of artifacts, chronological tables, an index, and bibliography.

Ehrich, R. W., ed. *Chronologies in Old World Archeology.* 3d ed. 2 vols. Chicago, 1992. This two volume work provides a synthesis and synchronisms of the prehistoric to 2000–1500 BCE material cultures of the regions and subregions of the world (e.g., Near and Middle East and Mediterranean area) using sequence dating, relative dating, and absolute dating (calibrated radiocarbon dates); extensive bibliographies, maps, illustrations, data tables, and information on Egypt-Mediterranean relations.

Eriksson, K. O. *Red Lustrous Wheel-Made Ware.* Studies in Mediterranean Archaeology, 103. Jonsered, 1993. An in-depth study of Red Lustrous Wheel-made Ware types, distribution, and chronology.

Gale, N. H., ed. *Bronze Age Trade in the Mediterranean.* Studies in Mediterranean Archaeology, 90. Jonsered, 1991. A multi-authored volume including articles on organic goods in Bronze Age East Mediterranean trade, Bronze Age shipwrecks and trade, Egyptian stone vases from Knossos, and Minoan foreign trade.

Hellbing, L. *Alasia Problems.* Studies in Mediterranean Archaeology, 57. Göteborg, 1979. A study of textual and archeological sources regarding the problems and identity of Alasia (Alasiya) as Cyprus; with an index, bibliography, endnotes, and photographs.

Jacobsson, I. *Aegyptiaca from Late Bronze Cyprus.* Studies in Mediterranean Archaeology, 112. Jonsered, 1994. A corpus of Egyptian items from Late Bronze Cyprus with a catalog arranged by material and artifact type, a section organized by sites with dated contexts, a summary discussion of the catalog and overall conclusions.

Karageorghis, V. *Cyprus from the Stone Age to the Romans.* London, 1982. A summary of Cypriot archaeology and history with 137 maps, drawings of artifacts, site plans, and photographs; with endnotes, a selected bibliography, and an index.

Karageorghis, V., ed. *Acts of the International Archaeological Symposium "Cyprus between the Orient and the Occident," Nicosia, 8–14 September 1985.* Nicosia, 1986. A multi-authored work with articles on the foreign relations of Cyprus in the Neolithic/Chalcolithic periods, the Philia vulture and its foreign relations, the role of Cyprus in the economy of the eastern Mediterranean, Hala Sultan Tekke and its foreign relations, and Ramessid Egypt and Cyprus.

Kemp, B. J., and R. S. Merrillees. *Minoan Pottery in Second Millennium Egypt.* Mainz, 1980. In-depth multi-authored technical studies (mostly in English; one article in German) of Minoan and Minoan-derived pottery from el-Lisht, el-Haraga, Illahun, Buhen, Abydos, Qubbet el-Hawa, and a few other sites in Egypt; with illustrations, references, and an index.

Lambrou-Phillipson, C. *Hellenorientalia: The Near Eastern Presence in the Bronze Age Aegean, ca.3000–1100 B. C. Interconnections Based on the Material Record and the Written Evidence.* Studies in Mediterranean Archaeology Pocket-book 95. Göteborg, 1990. A study of archeological and textual information on interactions between the Eastern Mediterranean and the Near East.

Macqueen, J. G. *The Hittites and their Contemporaries in Asia Minor.* rev. ed. London, 1986. An introduction to the Hittites, with chapters on the historical and geographical background to Anatolia, their origins, and neighbors.

Merrillees, R. S. *The Cypriote Bronze Age Pottery found in Egypt.* Studies in Mediterranean Archaeology, 18. Lund, 1968. An excellent corpus of Cypriot pottery in Egypt with a catalog arranged by sites, analysis of ware types, a discussion of trade, and a historical summary.

Moran, W. L. *The Amarna Letters.* Baltimore, 1992. Translations of 382 letters from Tell el-Amarna (and a few elsewhere), with correspondence between Egypt (temp. Amenhotpe III to Tutankhamun) and Cyprus (Alasiya), Anatolia (Arzawa; Khatte), Mesopotamia (Assyria; Babylonia), Mitanni, and many city-states throughout Syria-Palestine.

Mountjoy, P. A. *Mycenaean Pottery: An Introduction.* Oxford University Committee for Archaeology Monograph No.36. Oxford, 1993. An introduction to Mycenaean pottery with historical background, pottery types, their contextual relationships, and trade.

O'Connor, D., and E. H. Cline, eds. *Amenhotep III: Perspectives on His Reign.* Ann Arbor, 1998. A multi-authored volume with an article on "The World Abroad," sections by J. M. Weinstein on Egypt and the Levant and by E. H. Cline on the Aegean and Anatolia.

Phillips, J. S. "The Impact and Implications of the Egyptian and Egyptianizing Material found in Bronze Age Crete ca. 3000–ca. 1100 B.C." Ph.D. diss., University of Toronto, 1991. A study and corpus of Egyptian(izing) material from Crete (c.3000–1100 BCE) with a discussion of previous scholarship and chronology, a catalog of artifacts arranged by materials, artifact types, and objects organized by sites.

Sandars, N. K. *The Sea Peoples: Warriors of the Ancient Mediterranean 1250–1150 B.C.* rev. ed. London, 1985. A summary of the Sea Peoples, with chapters introducing the historical background and origins of the Sea Peoples, piracy, the Aegean, Egypt, and textual and archaeological sources.

Wachsmann, S. *Aegeans in the Theban Tombs.* Orientalia Lovaniensia Analecta, 20. Leuven, 1987. A discussion of Egyptian artistic conventions, Aegeans and their clothing, wares, and physical types, the Keftiu, islands in the midst of the sea, and Alashia, an index of Theban tombs depicting Aegeans, a discussion of Late Minoan IB and absolute chronology, the Ulu Burun shipwreck.

Weingarten, J. *The Transformation of Egyptian Taweret into the Minoan Genius: A Study in Cultural Transmission in the Middle Bronze Age.* Studies in Mediterranean Archaeology, 88. Partille, 1991. A 200-page study with footnotes, a bibliography, drawings, and photographs.

GREGORY D. MUMFORD

MEGIDDO, present-day Tell el-Mutesellim, an imposing 18-acre site near the southwestern corner of the Plain of Esdraelon (Greek for Jezreel Valley) of northern Israel. The tell guards the northern opening of the Wadi Ara (Nahal Iron) through the Carmel Ridge, thus controlling the principal military and commercial highway connecting Egypt and the Near East in antiquity (called by the Romans, the *Via Maris*). The site is also astride a major north–south road that leads from Akko inland to Jerusalem.

Megiddo (Eg., *Mkt*, Akk., *Magidda*) has been the scene of four excavations: (1) by Gottlieb Schumacher on behalf of the German Society for the Study of Palestine (1903–1905); (2) by Clarence Fisher, then P. L. O. Guy, and finally Gordon Loud for the Oriental Institute of the University of Chicago (1925–1939); (3) by Yigael Yadin, Immanuel Dunayevsky, and Avraham Eitan for the Hebrew University of Jerusalem (in eight seasons between 1960 and 1974); and (4), by Israel Finkelstein and David Ussishkin on behalf of the Institute of Archaeology, Tel Aviv University, starting in 1992.

There are scattered indications from the late fourth millennium BCE at Megiddo of Egyptian contact: for example, a disk-shaped mace head from Stratum XIX of the Early Bronze I period is clearly an import from Egypt. Relations with Egypt are next attested for Egypt's late Middle Kingdom or early Second Intermediate Period. Manfred Görg has suggested that the place-name Megiddo is miswritten as *mky* in the Brussels Execration Texts (entries E37, E62) belonging to the early thirteenth dynasty of the Middle Kingdom. A statuette base of Djehutihotpe, nomarch of the Hare nome, who died during the reign of Senwosret III in the mid-twelfth dynasty, was found with three other Egyptian statuette fragments in the platform of the Stratum VIIB Temple 2048 of the thirteenth century BCE. These objects, long interpreted as indicative of Egyptian rule at Megiddo during the twelfth dynasty, are now generally viewed as "loot," taken from Egypt during the Hyksos period or later. Egyptian small finds are rare in tomb and settlement deposits of the Middle Bronze IIA period (contemporary with most of the twelfth and early thirteenth dynasties), but become numerous in Middle Bronze IIB–C deposits, reflecting the general increase in Egyptian–Palestinian relations during the Second Intermediate Period.

Megiddo was the center of an important Canaanite city-state in the mid-second millennium BCE. Its capture became the strategic objective of Thutmose III's first Near Eastern campaign in the early fifteenth century BCE; a coalition of Canaanite forces headed by the princes of Kadesh and Megiddo then banded together for defense. The campaign, known in considerable detail from the king's *Annals* and his topographical lists at Karnak, as well as from a stela found at Gebel Barkal in northern Sudan, included both the defeat of a Canaanite chariot force outside Megiddo and a seven-month siege. Megiddo ultimately surrendered and, for the next three centuries, become an important Egyptian stronghold. Megiddo is elsewhere mentioned at least twice in connection with Egypt during the fifteenth century BCE. A cuneiform letter found at Taanach contains an order from an individual named Amenhotpe (probably an Egyptian official) to the prince of Taanach to send troops and tribute to the Egyptians at Megiddo. Megiddo is one of at least seven northern Palestinian towns mentioned in Papyrus Leningrad 1116A (lines 68 and 185), and envoys from those towns received grain and beer from Egyptian officials at Thebes in regnal Year 19 or 20 of Amenhotpe II.

Seven cuneiform tablets from the Egyptian diplomatic record office at Tell el-Amarna are from Megiddo (Amarna Letters EA 242–247, 365). These letters are filled mostly with statements of fealty to the Egyptian king from Biridiya, ruler of Megiddo, as well as complaints from Biridiya about Labayu, the ruler of Shechem, whom the Megiddo official describes as a continuing threat to his own town and from whom he wants Egyptian military protection. In EA 244 Biridiya specifically requests a hundred Egyptian archers to defend his town from Labayu, while in EA 365 he seeks the king's attention by bragging about his furnishing of corvée labor for work at Shunama (the biblical Shunem).

Megiddo remained an important Egyptian military and administrative center during the nineteenth and early twentieth dynasties. In addition to its *pro forma* appearance in several Ramessid-era topographical lists, Megiddo is one of a number of Palestinian towns named in Papyrus Anastasi I (line 23.1) from the second half of the nineteenth dynasty. More significant are the numerous Egyptian artifacts—scarabs and amulets; pottery, glass, and stone vessels; ivories and jewelry—from thirteenth and early twelfth century BCE deposits both on the tell and in contemporaneous tombs. Especially notable are three ivory plaques (numbered 379, 380, and 381+382 by the excavators), found in an ivory hoard from the early twelfth century BCE, in the so-called treasury of the Stratum VIIA palace; the inscriptions on the plaques mention a certain Kerker, "singer of Ptah, South-of-his-Wall." An ivory model pen case (item 377 in the same hoard) contains the cartouches of Ramesses III and the title "Royal Messenger to Every Foreign Country"; this object may have belonged to an official named Thutmose. A bronze statue base of Ramesses VI, found out of context in a pit beneath a wall of the thirteenth century BCE, is the last major New Kingdom object with a royal name found in

Palestine; it is generally thought to provide a *terminus post quem* for the demise of the Egyptian empire in Canaan.

Megiddo reappeared in Egyptian records in the tenth century BCE, in connection with Sheshonq's Palestinian campaign in the fifth regnal year of the Judean ruler Rehoboam (c.926/925 BCE), at the beginning of the Divided Monarchy of the Jewish states. Megiddo is in Sheshonq's topographical list (entry 27) at Karnak, and a small fragment of a triumphal stela of the king was recovered by the University of Chicago excavators at Megiddo in a dump left by the Schumacher expedition of the early 1900s. Sheshonq was probably responsible for the destruction of at least a portion of the Stratum VA/IVB town.

Megiddo was part of the northern kingdom of Israel until 732 BCE, when the Assyrians under Tiglath-Pileser III annexed it with much of the rest of that region. Thereafter, the town (represented by Stratum III) became the capital of the Assyrian province of Magiddu, remaining as such until the Assyrians withdrew from northern Israel late in the seventh century BCE. Deposits at Megiddo of the early first millennium BCE contain numerous small Egyptian and Egyptianized objects, especially amulets, figurines, and scarabs.

In 609 BCE, Necho, while leading an Egyptian army up to Carchemish in Syria to support the Assyrians against the Babylonians, encountered Josiah on the plain of Megiddo. In the Hebrew scriptures, Josiah was slain by Egyptian archers (*2 Kings* 23.29–30; *2 Chron.* 35.20–24), though it is unclear whether he died in battle or was executed by Necho. Megiddo reverted to the status of a small town during the Persian period. It was finally abandoned during the fourth century BCE, perhaps as a result of the invasion of the Levant by Alexander the Great.

[*See also* Syria-Palestine.]

BIBLIOGRAPHY

Gonen, Rivka. "Megiddo in the Late Bronze Age—Another Reassessment." *Levant* 19 (1987), 83–100. A useful re-analysis of the stratigraphic history of the Late Bronze Age strata (IX–VIIA), contemporary with Egypt's New Kingdom empire.

Görg, Manfred. *Untersuchungen zur hieroglyphischen Wiedergabe palästinischer Ortsnamen.* Bonner Orientalische Studien, n. s., 29. Bonn, 1974. Pages 137–155 contain a detailed discussion of the place-name Megiddo in Egyptian texts.

Guy, P. L. O. *Megiddo Tombs.* Oriental Institute Publications, 33. Chicago, 1938. Presents numerous Egyptian small finds in Megiddo's Middle and Late Bronze Age tombs.

Kempinski, Aharon. *Megiddo: A City-State and Royal Centre in North Israel.* Munich, 1989. Historical and archaeological study, with a strong bias for advocating an Egyptian presence at the site in various periods.

Lamon, R. S., and G. M. Shipton. *Megiddo I: Seasons of 1925–1934.* Oriental Institute Publication, 42. Chicago, 1939. Publication of the Iron Age II and Persian period strata.

Loud, Gordon. *Megiddo II: Seasons of 1935–1939.* Oriental Institute Publications, 62. Chicago, 1948. Publication of the Bronze Age and Iron Age I strata.

Loud, Gordon. *The Megiddo Ivories.* Oriental Institute Publications, 52. Chicago, 1939. Presents the great ivory hoard found in the Late Bronze Age palace.

Moran, William L. *The Amarna Letters.* Baltimore, 1992. Includes excellent translations of the letters from Megiddo.

Shea, William. "The Conquests of Sharuhen and Megiddo Reconsidered." *Israel Exploration Journal* 29 (1979), 1–5. First major publication to argue that Thutmose III captured, but did not physically destroy, Megiddo.

Tufnell, Olga. "The Middle Bronze Age Scarab Seals from Burials on the Mound at Megiddo." *Levant* 5 (1973), 69–82. Analysis of the scarabs found in the tombs of the early second millennium BCE.

Ussishkin, David. "Notes on Megiddo, Gezer, Ashdod, and Tel Batash in the Tenth to Ninth Centuries B. C. *Bulletin of the American Schools of Oriental Research* 277/278 (1990), 71–91. Pages 71–74 offer a discussion of the discovery and significance of the Sheshonq stela fragment.

Ussishkin, David. "Megiddo." In *The New Encyclopedia of Archaeological Excavations in the Holy Land,* edited by Ephraim Stern, vol. 3, pp. 461–469. New York, 1993. Valuable survey of the stratigraphic history of Megiddo.

JAMES M. WEINSTEIN

MEIDUM, site on the western bank of the Nile River, 65 kilometers (40 miles) south of Cairo (31°10′E, 29°23′N). A step *mastaba* and a royal cemetery were constructed there from the transitional years of the third to fourth dynasty. The step *mastaba* is the last royal tomb that was built in steps (begun with seven steps and enlarged to eight), with a base length of 120.75 meters (365 feet), a height of 85 meters (256 feet), and a slope of 75 degrees. The entrance is located 16 meters (50 feet) high on the north side and slopes to the crypt built on ground level. The small crypt is covered by the oldest known corbeled roof. The builder was probably Sneferu. In the fifteenth to seventeenth years of his reign, the step structure was transformed into the first real pyramid, with a base length of 144.32 meters (440 feet), a height of 92 meters (285 feet), and an inclination of 51 degrees, 51 minutes. At the same time—probably under the influence of solar aspects—a new type of pyramid complex was developed, replacing the older type and culminating in the Djoser complex at Saqqara. The new concept included a valley temple (unexcavated), a causeway, an east–west oriented enclosure surrounding the pyramid, and a small cult place in the center of the eastern side. Its western court contains the offering table, flanked by two uninscribed stelae. To the north and the south of the pyramid were ruins of smaller subsidiary pyramids of unknown function. Important remains of construction ramps have been observed there. A theory about an alleged collapse of the pyramid casing during the con-

MEIDUM. *The pyramid of Meidum.* (Courtesy Dieter Arnold)

struction created much scholarly confusion, but it has been proven wrong.

Mastaba no. 17, northeast of the pyramid, is the majestic tomb for an important member of the royal family. The huge building 52 by 105 meters (165 by 330 feet) is constructed of rough field stones with a wide cult place at the southern end of the eastern side (13.5 meters/32 feet), now destroyed. The spectacular, stone-cased crypt contains a granite sarcophagus that is 5 meters (16 feet) high.

A mastaba field to the north of the pyramid consists of a dozen brick *mastaba*s of the early fourth dynasty. Of great importance for the development of tomb architecture is the *mastaba* of Nefermaat and Atet (no. 16). Two offering niches are built into the brick core and cased with limestone; they were decorated with the first line decorations of subjects from everyday life. The decoration of the door frames was executed with incised figures that were filled in with colored pastes. The tomb façade displays a rich panel pattern. The *mastaba* of Prince Rahotep and Princess Nofret (no. 6) contained a pair of painted, life-size seated figures of the couple, in a unique state of preservation, masterpieces of Old Kingdom sculpture.

Excavations at the site were originally by W. M. Flinders Petrie in 1891 and 1909; Alan Rowe (Eckley B. Coxe Expedition) in 1929–1930; and the Egyptian Antiquities Organization.

BIBLIOGRAPHY

Borchardt, L. *Die Entstehung der Pyramide an der Baugeschichte der Pyramide von Mejdum nachgewiesen.* Brussels, 1928.
El-Khouli, Ali, et al. *Meidum.* Warminster, 1999.
Petrie, W. M. Flinders. *Medum.* London, 1892. *Meydum and Memphis.* London, 1910.

DIETER ARNOLD

MEIR, a present-day village approximately 7 kilometers (4 miles) west of Qusiya, the site of ancient Cusae, capital of the fourteenth Upper Egyptian nome. The village (27°27′N, 30°45′E) gives its name to the important cemetery situated southwest of it. The necropolis of Meir (27°25′N, 30°43′E) extends about 1.6 kilometers (1 mile) north to south, along the high limestone ridge of the Western Desert. There are three main levels; the most renowned is the middle terrace, which encompasses the decorated tomb chapels of influential local officials, notably the nomarchs (provincial governors) of the late Old Kingdom and the Middle Kingdom.

The cemetery of Meir was excavated by members of the Egyptian Antiquities Service during the last quarter of the nineteenth century. The site was already badly disturbed, since it had long been a source of clandestine digging for antiquities and easily quarried stone. From 1910 to 1915, Sayyid Khashaba held the official government concession for excavations in the area that included Meir and extended approximately 80 kilometers (50 miles) from Dairut to Deir el-Gandala on both banks of the Nile. During that time Ahmed Kamal conducted excavations for Khashaba, and he published preliminary reports in the *Annales du Service des Antiquités de l'Égypte* soon after each season. The reports document the discovery at Meir of numerous funerary objects—coffins, canopic chests, statuettes, and models—primarily of Middle Kingdom date. The objects from Khashaba's share of the finds are dispersed in numerous Egyptian and foreign museums, including The Metropolitan Museum of Art, New York.

Most current knowledge of the tombs of Meir derives from the well-documented activity of Aylward M. Blackman, who conducted the only thorough study of the architecture and decorative program of the tombs. This project took place under the aegis of the Archaeological Survey of the Egyptian Exploration Fund (EEF), later Society (EES). In five seasons, between January 1912 and spring 1950, Blackman made copies of the scenes on the walls of the decorated tomb chapels of the middle terrace; he published most of them in a series of six volumes.

In his 1912 survey, Blackman divided the necropolis into five groups of rock-cut tombs, each series separated by a ravine (wadi). The five groups, labeled A to E from north to south, comprise fifteen decorated chapels: A 1–4, B 1–4, C 1, D 1–2, and E 1–4. Nine of these decorated tombs date to the sixth dynasty (A 1–2, D 1–2, E 1–4), and six were cut in the twelfth dynasty (A 3, B 1–4, C 1). Two decorated tombs on the east bank at Qusair al-Amarna also belonged to Old Kingdom officials of Cusae, and these tombs were partially reused in the New Kingdom.

The earliest known Old Kingdom tomb, A 1, belonged to Niankhpepi, whose additional names included Sobekhotep, by which he is often referred, and Hepi-kem ("Hepi the black"). He was an "Overseer of Upper Egypt"—a title used almost exclusively by nomarchs at that time—and an overseer of the priests of Hathor of Cusae. In 1894, several wooden statues were found in a pit in his tomb (A 1)—a standing statue inscribed with his name and titles (CG 60), an unusual figure of a male porter carrying a chest and basket, and some two dozen wooden models

MEIR. *One of the rock-cut tombs at Meir.* (Courtesy Dorothea Arnold)

depicting food-preparation activities (CG 236–254) and boats (CG 4880–4893)—all of which represents the only intact group of Old Kingdom models recorded from Meir.

As for Niankhpepi Sobekhotep's successors, there is some confusion because of the repetition of the name Pepiankh (including one of the tomb owners at Qusair al-Amarna) and the lack of full genealogy. These Old Kingdom officials buried at Meir and Qusair al-Amarna encompassed at least three generations from the reign of Pepy I to Pepy II.

The Middle Kingdom Group B tombs were further cleared in 1918 by Howard Carter. According to unpublished field notes in the Griffith Institute in Oxford, Carter documented eleven tomb-chapels in the middle terrace of Group B, thus augmenting Blackman's four decorated chapels with seven undecorated ones, as well as eleven undecorated rock-cut tombs that consisted of only single chambers with burial pits. The published record for Meir provides an incomplete picture of the site as a whole.

The first nomarch of the twelfth dynasty line at Cusae is Senbi I. His tomb-chapel, B 1, is decorated with finely painted reliefs, including scenes rendered in a naturalistic manner, particularly of the desert hunt. The owners of the other Middle Kingdom chapels were another Senbi (referred to as Senbi II) and four men named Ukhhotep (in most schemes I–III, since the Ukhhotep who owned A 3 is not considered to have been a nomarch). In the tomb-chapel of Ukhhotep II (B 4), there is an illustrated list of his predecessors, representing a total of fifty-nine local rulers with their wives, apparently going back to officials of the Old Kingdom. Because of its poor state of preservation—as well as lack of corroborative information—this list is not helpful in reconstructing the chronology of the nomarchs.

Tomb-chapel B 4 also included the cartouche of Amenemhet II, which is the only occurrence of a king's name in the tombs. The correlation of the genealogy of the rulers of Cusae with the kings of the twelfth dynasty hangs on this date, but the royal associations are not consistently accepted. A general sequence based largely on Blackman's attributions would place Senbi I (tomb B 1) in the reign of Amenemhet I, the first ruler of the twelfth dynasty; Senbi II, the owner of B 3 and grandson of Senbi I, within the reigns of Senwosret I and Amenemhet II; and Ukhhotep III, the owner of C 1 (the last of the series of decorated tombs), in the reigns of Senwosret II and Senwosret III.

Two statue groups of Ukhhotep III that were originally carved for his tomb (Meir C 1) are now in the Egyptian Museum, Cairo (CG 459) and the Museum of Fine Arts, Boston (accession number 1973.87). Both granite statues depict Ukhhotep standing between two of his wives, Nebkau and Khnumhotep, and accompanied by his daughter Nebhethenutsen. These women and many others are depicted in the scenes and inscriptions on his tomb walls, where five wives and seven concubines are mentioned (see Blackman, *Meir*, vol. 6). Ukhhotep III's tomb, C 1, is of interest for many reasons. The painting style has been called mannerist and includes unusual color hues, such as the light green between white and darker green on Ukhhotep's striped (or pleated) cloak. Women play prominent roles in the scenes, and many take part in traditionally male activities, which may reflect their ties to the local cult of the goddess Hathor. The mention of multiple wives raises the strong possibility of polygamy, usually practiced only on the royal level. It has often been noted that Ukhhotep usurped other royal prerogatives in the iconography of his funerary material, such as the unification symbol (*smȝ tȝwy*) and the heraldic plants of the North and the South. Also uncommon is his bold pose, holding the *ankh* sign of life.

Many of the high officials buried at Meir held the title "Overseer of the Priests of Hathor," whose cult was central to the town; however, neither the temple of Hathor nor the actual town of Cusae have been uncovered. Several Greek literary papyri attributed to Meir were purchased by Wallis Budge in 1888–1889 for the British Museum, and among them is Aristotle's *Constitution of Athens*. Numerous Roman mummy masks uncovered at Meir attest to the reuse of some of the older tombs at that time.

BIBLIOGRAPHY

Allam, Schafik. *Beiträge zum Hathorkult (bis zum Ende des Mittleren Reiches).* Münchner Ägyptologische Studien, 4. Berlin, 1963. Detailed discussion of the cult of Hathor of Cusae from the Old Kingdom to Greco-Roman times (see pp. 23–41).

Blackman, Aylward M. *The Rock Cut Tombs of Meir.* 6 vols., the last two with Michael Apted. London, 1914–1953. These volumes of the Archaeological Survey of Egypt (ASE 22–25, 28–29) remain the basic source for the decorated tombs at Meir.

Freed, Rita. "Group Statue of Ukh-hotep II and His Family." In *Mummies and Magic: The Funerary Arts of Ancient Egypt*, edited by Sue D'Auria, Peter Lacovara, and Catharine H. Roehrig, pp. 121–122. Boston, 1988. Useful synopsis of information and earlier bibliography for the statues of Ukhhotep, owner of Meir C 1.

Hayes, William C. *The Scepter of Egypt*, vol. 1. New York, 1953. The large number of Middle Kingdom objects from Khashaba's Meir excavations are included in the relevant sections (see geographic index, under "Mir").

James, T. G. H., ed. *Excavating in Egypt: The Egypt Exploration Society 1882–1982.* Chicago and London, 1982. Includes background to Blackman's work at Meir as well as reference to the British Museum acquisition of papyri from Meir. See discussion of the Greco-Roman Branch.

Kessler, Dietrich. "Meir." In *Lexikon der Ägyptologie*, 4: 14–19. Clearly presented analysis of historical and archaeological background to site, with extensive bibliography, also incorporated within the footnotes.

O'Connor, David. "Sexuality, Statuary and the Afterlife; Scenes in the Tomb-chapel of Pepyankh (Heny the Black): An Interpretive Essay." In *Studies in Honor of William Kelly Simpson*, edited by Peter Der Manuelian, vol. 2, pp. 621–633. Boston, 1996. Detailed analysis of one wall in Meir A 2 with scenes of manufacturing wooden statues and objects.

Porter, Bertha, and Rosalind L. B. Moss. *Topographical Bibliography of Ancient Egyptian Hieroglyphic Texts, Reliefs, and Paintings*, vol. 4: *Lower and Middle Egypt*. Oxford, 1934. The entry on Meir (pp. 247–259) outlines the basic scenes in the decorated tombs relying heavily on Blackman—but without benefit of *Meir V-VI*, published in 1953. Numerous objects in various museum collections are cited.

Simpson, William Kelly. "The Middle Kingdom in Egypt: Some Recent Acquisitions." *Boston Museum Bulletin* 72 (1974), 100–116. Well-illustrated discussion of the two group statues of Ukhhotep in Boston and Cairo.

BARBARA A. PORTER

MEMPHIS, a site with visible remains in the center of the floodplain of the western side of the Nile (29°51′N, 31°15′E). Memphis is some 23 kilometers (14 miles) due south of central Cairo, extending from north to south about 4 kilometers (2.5 miles) and from east to west (maximum) 1.5 kilometers (almost 1 mile) around and between the modern villages and towns of ʿAziziya, ʿEzbet Gabri, Mit Rahina, Bedrashein, and Shinbab. This area represents only 10 percent of the city at its greatest extent, perhaps in the Ptolemaic period. The names given to the city by the pharaonic Egyptians—*ỉnbw-ḥḏ* ("white walls"), *Mennefer* (named after the pyramid and mortuary temple of King Pepy I; hence *Memphis* in Greek; *Moph* or *Noph* in Biblical Hebrew; *Manf* in Arabic), *Ḥwt-kȝ-ptḥ* (hence Greek *Aigyptos*, or *Egypt* in English), and *ʿnḫ-tȝwy*—were used, variously, for the metropolitan area as a whole or for specific quarters and temple enclosures. The city was described in some detail by the ancient historians Herodotus, Strabo, and Diodorus Siculus, and it is mentioned as well by many writers of the first three centuries CE.

Traditionally founded in c.3000 BCE by Menes, the legendary figure credited with the creation of a politically unified Egypt, Memphis served as the effective administrative capital of the country during the Old Kingdom, then during part, at least, of the Middle and New Kingdoms (with Itjettawy and Thebes), during the Late period, and again in the Ptolemaic period (along with the part city of Alexandria), until it was eclipsed by the foundation of the Islamic garrison city of Fustat on the Nile and its later development, al-Qahira (now Cairo). The identity of the site of Memphis was lost in the seventh century CE, when under Islam it ceased to be a bishopric, until the sixteenth century, when it was tentatively identified by François de Pavie and, later, by other European travelers; its location and identity remained a matter of debate, however, until firmly established by the Napoleonic Commission in 1799. The commission carried out the first fieldwork at the site, which was limited to mapping, measuring, and in some cases removing the few monumental statue fragments then visible above ground. Major excavations were subsequently undertaken by Jean-François Champollion and Ippolito Rosellini (1828), Karl Richard Lepsius (1843), Joseph Hekekyan (1852–1854), Auguste Mariette (1857–1862), William M. Flinders Petrie for the British School of Archaeology in Egypt (1907–1914), Clarence Fisher for the Pennsylvania University Museum (1915–1923), Rudolph Anthes, for the same museum (1955–1956), and through the years by many officers of the Egyptian Antiquities Service (later called the Egyptian Antiquities Organization, now the Supreme Council for Antiquities). Since 1980, the site has been at the heart of a regional survey by the Egypt Exploration Society, which has posited a constantly shifting position for both river and settlement and has suggested that the original foundation lies to the north, near the Early Dynastic elite necropolis at North Saqqara.

The unrivaled geographical location of Memphis—both commanding the Delta heads while being at the confluence of the important trade routes across the Eastern and Western Deserts—meant that there was no alternative capital possible for any ruler with serious ambitions to govern both Upper and Lower Egypt. Even before the emergence of the Neolithic culture (Naqada II, the Gerzean) in Upper Egypt and its eventual domination of the Delta communities, several sites in the region were important centers of trade (such as Maadi) or showed a flourishing and distinct farming plus hunting-gathering lifestyle (such as al-Omari). The city of Memphis lies in an unusually narrow stretch of the Nile Valley (rarely more than 7 kilometers/4.5 miles wide) from the Faiyum to the Delta, which is marked by the spread of royal funerary (pyramid) clusters from Meidum to Giza on the western bank of the Nile. The abnormal constriction of the floodplain there was almost certainly a factor in the notional and symbolic boundary between Upper and Lower Egypt, set at Ainu (Helwan), directly opposite Memphis.

The city of Memphis, at least from the second millennium BCE, was one of the most cosmopolitan in Egypt, attracting foreign mercantile and seafaring communities during the eighteenth dynasty and the nineteenth; reflecting this ethnic diversity, Near Eastern cults are attested (those of Baʿal, Astarte, and Resheph). From the seventh century BCE, three hundred years before the arrival of Alexander the Great and his forces, foreign quarters and minorities (Syropersikon; Hellenomemphites, and Karomemphites) are known; according to Herodotus, Greek mercenaries were brought to Memphis as a household regiment during the twenty-sixth dynasty. Even the Hyksos dynasty, reviled in the political propaganda of the Theban revival, seems to have been accepted at Memphis.

The Site. The Memphis ruin field has been divided into ten mounds (*tells* or *koms*), with intervening pools (*bir-*

kas) that before about 1900 were submerged by the Nile's summer floodwaters. The local *kom* names have been retained by archaeologists for convenience, and they are (from north to south) 'Aziz, Tuman, Dafbaby, Fakhry, Nawa, Arba'in, Rabia', Qala', Helul, and Sabakha.

No settlement trace earlier than the First Intermediate Period (a small cemetery on the west, at Kom Fakhry) has so far been recovered from the ruin field. Much past excavation concentrated on the central Ptah temple and its immediate environs (that by Champollion; Lepsius; Hekekyan; Mariette; Petrie; and Anthes), on the ceremonial palace and temple of Merneptah to the southeast on Kom Qala' (that by Flinders Petrie; by Clarence Stanley Fisher), or on the residential palace of Apries and its enclosure to the north on Kom Tuman (that by Flinders Petrie). None of those structures has been firmly dated before the Ramessid period, and the earlier phases of occupation may well be buried beneath the western part of the ruin field and the fields between it and the escarpment of the Libyan desert.

Ptah temple. The outline of the Ptah temple is well established, though only the western gate has been exposed and recorded in detail, so little is known of its internal arrangements except at the southeastern corner. The temple was conceived on a grand scale (the total area enclosed [275,000 square meters], is similar to that of the final layout of the Amun-Re enclosure at Thebes). The mud-brick enclosure wall was defined by the excavation of Flinders Petrie, and he and others recorded more than twelve colossal statues, including two sphinxes, on its perimeter. Those were mostly from the axial gateways, and the most famous (the travertine statue of Ramesses II found in 1821) stood before the southern gate. Two colossal granite statues of that king were also found there in the 1950s; they have been restored for display in the grounds of the museum at Mit Rahina. A travertine sphinx was also found by Flinders Petrie near that spot, but it was on the inside of the southern wall.

The western gate does not show an orthogonal plan but was an attempt to reconcile the alignments of the southern and western walls of the enclosure. The granite-faced pylon with its unusual three-aisled entrance has been excavated, as well as part of the hypostyle hall behind it. Pedestals have been found for at least five statues fronting the pylon, and fragments of three of these are still on site; the most southerly had been placed on a reused granite block that bears an important inscription of Amenemhat II of the twelfth dynasty. Colossal statues of the god Ptah were also found there, as well as numerous dyad and triad statues of Ramesses II with other deities. Little is known of the architectural details of either of the other gates. A line of seated statues was found near the eastern gate; and a colossal granite statue, now standing outside the main Cairo railway station, also came from there. A large granite sphinx, now in the University Museum, Philadelphia, was found by Flinders Petrie near the presumed position of the northern gate.

In the southwestern corner of the enclosure is a building identified as the embalming house of the Apis bulls; it contains a number of limestone and travertine slabs, called "beds," for the embalming ritual that occurred before the mummified remains of the bulls were taken to the Saqqara *serapeum* for burial. The surviving material there dates to the Late period, and it was probably built over earlier structures of similar function. A little to the south, across the present tourist road to the museum at Mit Rahina, stands a small cube-shaped sanctuary (sometimes called an "oratory") that houses statues of the deity Ptah and two female deities (Mennefer and the temple wall, or *tjesmet*, personified) both dandling the infant King Sety I.

Other temples. Several other temples were found in the vicinity of the Ptah enclosure. At the southwestern corner stood a temple of Ptah (the precise form of the deity is uncertain); southeast of that was a temple of Hathor; and outside the southern gate of the enclosure stood another small temple, probably of Ptah and Sakhmet. To the west stood an (unidentified) temple on rising ground, near the village of Mit Rahina. To the east, a small temple inscribed by Merneptah was found in the early 1900s, next to the large palace excavated by Fisher. None of these sites in the central and eastern areas has been dated to earlier than the start of the nineteenth dynasty.

Other Sites. The First Intermediate Period (or early Middle Kingdom) cemetery to the west, on Kom Fakhry, was excavated in advance of road-building in the 1950s; it consists of a series of vaulted tombs in brick and limestone that belong to priestly officials. The tomb orientations and painted scenes are comparable to burials at Saqqara and Giza, as well as at Ihnasya, Dendera, Edfu, and Mendes. From 1984 to 1991, an excavation by the Egypt Exploration Society on Kom Rabia' revealed habitation levels of the thirteenth to the nineteenth dynasty, with a distinct break in occupation at the end of the thirteenth dynasty, which corresponds to an apparent hiatus in the use of the Saqqara necropolis.

To the north at Kom Tuman, the impressive remains of a massive (at least 20,000 square meters) brick platform still loom above the village of 'Ezbet Gabri. It was extensively excavated by Flinders Petrie, who established that it was the foundation for an elevated palace of King Apries of the twenty-sixth dynasty, and it is contained within a large enclosure that he described as a (military) camp. Probably, that was the Persian and Hellenistic citadel and fort known to ancient Greek writers as Leukon Teikhos ("white fortress"), perhaps because of its proximity to the old town of Inbuhedj. East of the fort, there is evidence for a temple of Mithras (a favorite cult of Roman sol-

MEMPHIS. *Fallen granite colossus of Ramesses II found near the temple of Ptah at Mit Rahina, a modern village on the site of ancient Memphis.* (Courtesy Dieter Arnold)

diery); a theater, mentioned in a papyrus letter, may have stood nearby. Along the eastern edge of the ruin field are the remains of the Roman-era river wall, and the Nilometer at Memphis, famous in antiquity, was surely located nearby. (The New Kingdom port of Perunefer, with its foreign communities and institutions, is assumed by many to be at or near Memphis, but it has not been securely identified.) There are many other traces of the Ptolemaic and Roman occupation of Memphis, including faience factories on Kom Helul and Kom Rabia' and a bathhouse on Kom Sabakha.

Several Christian churches are known archaeologically, and even after Memphis was depopulated in the seventh century CE, some of its institutions remained important: for example, the Nilometer readings continued for a while to be taken there. Some pagan cults survived, but it is clear that with the establishment of Christianity as Rome's state religion, much religious emphasis shifted to the desert-edge monasteries, especially to the important monastic town of Apa Jeremias at Saqqara. An outlying part of the conurbation, the island of Tammuh, was still a focus of both Christian and Jewish faiths in medieval times, but the main places of pilgrimage, such as Sign Yusuf ("Joseph's prison") at Saqqara, replaced Memphis' metropolitan center.

There are documentary references to an East Memphis (Eg., *Inebhedj Iabtet;* Gr., *Arabias tou Memphitou*), which must refer to an enclave on the eastern bank of the Nile, from Helwan to the quarrying centers of Tura and Ma'sara. In the Early Dynastic period, there was also a large eastern-bank cemetery near Ezbet al-Walda, directly opposite and complementing the elite necropolis at North Saqqara, although the custom of eastern-bank burial seems to have been discontinued after the third dynasty. Interestingly, this area to the east of Memphis was still administered by the municipality of Giza, not by Cairo, when the Ottoman Empire ruled Egypt, from the sixteenth to the nineteenth century.

BIBLIOGRAPHY

Anthes, Rudolph. *Mit Rahineh 1955.* Philadelphia, 1959.
Anthes, Rudolph. *Mit Rahineh 1956.* Philadelphia, 1965. Excavation reports on two seasons' work by the University Museum, University of Pennsylvania. The 1955 report contains John Dimick's survey map.
Jeffreys, D. G. *The Survey of Memphis,* part 1: *The Archaeological Report.* London, 1985. First of a series of *Survey of Memphis* volumes, describing the results of the preliminary site survey.
Jeffreys, David, and Ana Tavares. "The Historic Landscape of Early Dynastic Memphis." *Mitteilungen des Deutschen Archäologischen Instituts abteilung Kairo* 50 (1994), 143–173. A discussion of recent fieldwork in the region, leading to some new questions.

Jones, M. "The Temple of Apis in Memphis." *Journal of Egyptian Archaeology* 76 (1990), 141–147. A reappraisal, following several seasons of fieldwork, of the Embalming House of the Apis bulls.

Kemp, B. J. "The Palace of Apries at Memphis." *Mitteilungen des Deutschen Archäologischen Instituts abteilung Kairo 33* (1977), 101–108. A discussion of Petrie's work at this site and a summary of the subsequent erosion.

O'Connor D. B. "Mirror of the Cosmos: the Palace of Merenptah." In *Fragments of a Shattered Visage: The Proceedings of the International Seminar on Ramesses the Great*, edited by E. Bleiberg and R. Freed, pp. 167–198. One of several discussions by the author of the functional and ideological role of ancient Egyptian temples.

Petrie, William M. Flinders. *Memphis.* Vol. 1. London, 1909. The first excavation report, based on work from 1907 onward.

Petrie, William M. Flinders. *The Palace of Apries.* Vol. 2. London, 1909.

Petrie, William M. Flinders. *Meydum and Memphis.* Vol. 3. London, 1910.

Porter, B., and R. L. B. Porter. *Topographical Bibliography of Ancient Egyptian Hieroglyphic Texts, Reliefs and Paintings*, vol. 3: *Memphis.* 2d ed., in two parts, revised by J. Malek. The definitive reference collection of inscribed material in and from pre-Islamic Egypt. Part 1 covers Abu Rawash to Abusir; part 2 covers Saqqara to Dahsnur. The ruin field (Mit Rahîna) is discussed in part 2, pp. 830–875.

Thompson, Dorothy J. *Memphis under the Ptolemies.* Princeton, 1988. An excellent introduction to the textual and archaeological evidence for Hellenistic Memphis.

Zivie, Alain-Pierre. *Memphis et ses nécropoles au nouvel empire. Nouvelles données, nouvelles questions.* Paris, 1988. A collection of papers (not all in French) discussing aspects of the settlement and cemeteries of Memphis.

Zivie, C. M. "Memphis." In *Lexikon der Ägyptologie*, 4:24–41. Wiesbaden, 1982.

DAVID G. JEFFREYS

MEMPHITE THEOLOGY. *See* Myths, *article on* Creation Myths.

MENDES

MENDES (modern Tell el-Rub'a), the largest surviving city-mound in the Nile Delta, located about 35 kilometers (21 miles) east of Mansura in the Daqahlieh plain (30°9′N, 31°6′E). Originally joined to Tell Timai, the overall site measures about 3 kilometers (2 miles) north to south and averages 800–900 meters (some 2400–2700 feet) east to west. Initially called *'npt*, "place of verdure," the name *Mendes* derived from *Pr-b3-nb-Ddt*, "House of the Ram, lord of the 'Abiding Place.'" Both the ram god and the fish goddess (Hat-Mehit, "She who is preeminent among the fishes") were honored at the site; the temple of the ram stood in the northern sector of the town, and Hat-mehyet possessed a cult center on the eastern side, overlooking the harbor and the Mendes branch of the Nile River.

The site was visited by Auguste Mariette in 1867 and was first dug by Edouard Naville in 1892; but it was not until the 1960s that formal excavations were undertaken. In several campaigns from 1963 to 1980, an expedition from New York University under the direction of Bernard V. Bothmer and Donald Hansen investigated the northwestern enclosure. In 1990, Robert Wenke and Douglas Brewer from the universities of Washington and Illinois began yearly excavations in the earliest levels; and in 1991, a team from the University of Toronto undertook extensive excavations in the temple and royal necropolis, which continues as of 1998.

As early as the Naqada III period, a settlement existed at that site, founded on a series of levees. The town flourished and, by the sixth dynasty, a necropolis covering about 150,000 square meters/yards surrounded the shrine of the ram god. Most of the tombs there consisted of mudbrick *mastabas*, but a small number had stone-lined burial chambers and access passages. Recovered mortuary stelae revealed that the tomb occupants represented the priesthood of the ram god, members of the civil service, and some hereditary nobility. At least part of the cemetery had been destroyed by fire toward the close of the sixth dynasty. Concomitant to the conflagration, vandals had desecrated burials, smashed stelae, and left corpses sprawled between the tombs. Use of the site ended soon after the Old Kingdom came to a close and, although Mendes was frequently mentioned in the Coffin Texts, no trace of the Middle Kingdom has yet turned up in the excavations.

The city experienced heightened prosperity during the New Kingdom; Thutmose III restored the temple, and Ramesses II added a forecourt and a pylon. Merenptah and Ramesses VI were represented on objects recovered from the site and, presumably, Nessubanebdjed (now known as Smendes), founder of the twenty-first dynasty, was a native. In the ninth century BCE, the city became home to a Libyan chiefdom that held power for generations. The Saite kings honored Mendes, and Amasis added a large sanctum with four *naoi* to the temple. In the fourth century, BCE, Nepherites of Mendes, an erstwhile freedom-fighter against the Persians, founded the twenty-ninth dynasty; he was buried at the site in a pit topped by a limestone *mastaba*. When the Persians recaptured Egypt in 343 BCE, the city was committed to destruction, as was vividly reflected in the excavations. Restored by Ptolemy II in c.275 BCE, Mendes prospered in the third century BCE as a center for wine and perfume manufacture, with trade links throughout the Mediterranean. After 200 BCE, however, the Mendes branch of the Nile weakened, and the inhabitants began to relocate. Although a priesthood survived into the first century CE, and the temple was later used as a Christian church, domestic occupation had largely ceased by mid-Roman times.

BIBLIOGRAPHY

Bothmer, Bernard V. et al., eds. *Mendes.* Vols. 1 and 2. Warminster, 1976–1982.

MENDES. *Granite naos of the Ram-god of Mendes, from the reign of Amasis, twenty-sixth dynasty.* (Courtesy Donald B. Redford)

Meulenaere, Herman de. "Mendes." In *Lexikon der Ägyptologie*, 4: 43–45. Wiesbaden, 1982.

Redford, Donald B. "Three Seasons in Egypt. III. The first Season of Excavation at Mendes." *Journal of the Society for the Study of Egyptian Antiquities* 18 (1991), 49–79.

DONALD B. REDFORD

MENES is the Greek form of the name of the legendary first human king of Egypt, as given by the third-century BCE Egyptian historian Manetho; alternative forms are Min (as given by Herodotus), Minaios (as given by Josephus), and Menas (as given by Diodorus Siculus). Other variants are also attested. The various Greek forms un-doubtedly render the Egyptian name *Mni*, found in the Abydos and Turin king lists, although the etymology of the name is uncertain. Some have proposed a connection with the verb "to endure"; others have wished to connect it with the Egyptian indefinite pronoun *mn*, meaning "so-and-so"—that is, as a substitute for a forgotten name. James Allen (1992) has sought to link the name Meni with the Egyptian name of the city of Memphis (*Mn-nfr*), which Menes is said to have founded.

It is unclear which, if any, of the known first dynasty kings is to be equated with Menes. Both Narmer and Aha have been identified with Menes. Narmer's claim rests on his earlier historical position and on the Narmer Palette, which has been interpreted as showing the king in the act of conquering Lower Egypt. Aha's claim is based on the occurrence of the game-board hieroglyph (phonetic *mn*) on objects bearing Aha's name, the interpretation of which is not entirely certain. The New Kingdom king lists and the Manethonian tradition do preserve at least some genuine material on the first dynasty, but it is uncertain whether there exists an unbroken tradition of knowledge on the part of the Egyptians about the foundational king that could connect the name *Mni* with any historical person. What can be affirmed is that it is probably Narmer, rather than Aha, who is to be regarded as the first king of the first dynasty, since the name Narmer heads the sequence of kings given in the necropolis sealings of the kings Den and Ḳaʿa.

According to Manetho, Menes founded a dynasty of eight kings from This. Manetho gives Menes a reign of about sixty years (sixty-two years in Africanus, sixty in Eusebius); his principal achievement is said to have been the foundation of Memphis, on land reclaimed from the Nile by means of the construction of an immense dike. Manetho reports that Menes campaigned abroad; he is said by Pliny to have invented writing, and by Diodorus Siculus to have been the first law-giver and to have established the divine cults in Egypt. Finally, again according to Manetho, Menes was carried off by a hippopotamus.

[*See also* Narmer.]

BIBLIOGRAPHY

Allen, J. P. "Menes the Memphite." *Göttinger Miszellen* 126 (1992), 19–22.

Wilkinson, T. A. H. *Early Dynastic Egypt.* London, 1999.

STEVE VINSON

MENKAURE (r. 2551–2523), fifth king of the fourth dynasty, Old Kingdom. Menkaure was the throne name of the son of Khafre and the grandson of Khufu, the fourth and second kings of the fourth dynasty, respectively. He also bore the Horus name Kachet, the Nebty name Ka, and the golden falcon name Netjeri. He built the smallest pyramid at the Giza plateau, which is called "Menkaure Is Divine." The pyramid is remarkable because it is the only one of the fourth dynasty that was partially constructed of limestone blocks encased in granite. Menkaure planned to cover the entire surface with granite, but he died suddenly; only sixteen courses were clad with granite. The pyramid was completed by his son and successor Shepseskaf, but the temples had architectural additions that were made during the fifth and sixth dynasties. This suggests that the cult of Menkaure was very important and perhaps differed from the cults of Khufu and Khafre.

At the pyramid's entrance, an inscription records that Menkaure died on the twenty-third day of the fourth month of the summer and that he built the pyramid. It is thought that this inscription dates to the time of Khaemwase, high priest of Memphis and son of Ramesses II, during the nineteenth dynasty. Excavations have revealed a pair of statues of Ramesses II on the south side of Menkaure's pyramid. The statues were made of granite; one represents Ramesses as king, while the other is Re-Atum. The name of Menkaure is written in red ocher on the ceiling of the burial chamber of the middle subsidiary pyramid (QIIIB). Richard H. Vyse (1784–1853) found a basalt sarcophagus in the main pyramid and, inside it, the skeleton of a young woman. The sarcophagus was lost in the Mediterranean between the ports of Catagena and Malta when the ship *Beatrice* sank after setting sail on 13 October 1838. The lid from the wooden anthropoid coffin found inside Menkaure's pyramid still exists.

Menkaure's principal queen was Khamerernebti II, who is portrayed with him in a group statue that was found in the valley temple. It is believed that she was buried in a Giza tomb (GIIIa). Shepseskaf completed the pyramid complex of his father with mud bricks and left an inscription inside the valley temple indicating that he built the temple for the memory of his father. Menkaure ruled for eighteen years. The objects found in some storage rooms of the temples show that the king's cult was maintained and that the valley temple also functioned as a palace. A decree of Antyemsaf of the sixth dynasty indicates that the valley temple was in use during his reign; a decree of Pepy II was found on the valley temple vestibule, awarding privileges to the priests of the pyramid city. In the adjacent open court and in the area just east of the temple lie the remains of the Old Kingdom houses. The personnel responsible for maintaining the cult of the deceased king lived there. The Giza pyramid complex was used until the end of the Old Kingdom. The statuary program found inside the complex displays the superb quality of arts and crafts. The triads found in Menkaure's valley temple suggest that his pyramid complex was dedicated to Re, Hathor, and Horus. In addition, they show the king's relationship with the gods and are essential to his kingship, indicating both a temple and palace function. The name of Menkaure was found written on scarabs dated to the twenty-sixth dynasty, which may imply that he was worshiped in that period.

Little else known about Menkaure's reign. The textual and archaeological evidence of the Old Kingdom indicate that the palace of Menkaure was located near his pyramid and not at Memphis. Menkaure exploited granite from Aswan and sent expeditions to Sinai. The Greek historian Herodotus mentioned that Menkaure died suddenly and

MENKAURE. *Pyramid of Menkaure at Giza, fourth dynasty.* (Courtesy Dieter Arnold)

added that there was an oracle from the Buto statue that foretold that he would live for six years. Menkaure started to drink and enjoy every moment of his remaining years; however, Menkaure lived for twelve years, thus disproving the prophecy. Herodotus also said that Menkaure's daughter committed suicide and that the Egyptians loved Menkaure more than his father and grandfather. The Late period tales were based on Menkaure's reputation during the Old Kingdom. He ruled with justice, gave freedom to his officials to carve statues and make offerings, and moderated the firm rules.

BIBLIOGRAPHY

Edwards, I. E. S., C. J. Gadd, and N. G. L. Hammond, eds. "Early History of the Middle East." In *The Cambridge Ancient History.* 3d ed. Cambridge, 1971.

Gardiner, A. H. *Egypt of the Pharaohs: An Introduction.* Oxford, 1961.

Hallo, W. W., and W. K. Simpson. *The Ancient Near East: A History.* New York, 1971.

Hawass, Z. "The Programs of the Royal Funerary Complexes of the Fourth Dynasty." In *Kingship in Ancient Egypt,* edited by D. O'Connor and D. Silverman. Leiden, 1996.

Hawass, Z. "The Pyramids." In *Ancient Egypt,* edited by David Silverman. London, 1997.

Kanawati, N. *The Egyptian Administration in the Old Kingdom.* Warminster, 1977.

Petrie, W. M. F. "From the Earliest Kings to the XVth Dynasty." In *A History of Egypt,* vol. 1. 11th ed. rev. London, 1924.

Reisner, G. A. *Mycerinus: The Temples of the Third Pyramid of Giza.* Cambridge, 1931.

ZAHI HAWASS

MERENPTAH (r. 1237–1226 BCE), fourth king of the nineteenth dynasty, New Kingdom. Merenptah was the thirteenth son and successor of Ramesses II. Having assumed high military functions during his father's reign, he became heir to the throne after the death of his elder brothers. He was middle aged on his accession and reigned for about ten years.

Merenptah was not renowned for his building program. All religious centers had been restored or rebuilt by his predecessors, and new temples had been erected under the reign of his father, thus Merenptah achieved only compulsory monuments. His rock-cut royal tomb in Western Thebes included splendid wall decorations and had sarcophagi of excellent workmanship, indicating that the royal workshops were very skillful during that time. The ruins of his funerary temple in Thebes, although mostly destroyed, show the plan of an extended precinct.

MERENPTAH. *Statue of Merenptah in the Cairo Museum.* (Courtesy David P. Silverman)

The building material as well as the reinscribed statues of kings and gods, however, were mostly reused from the adjoining temples of Amenhotpe III, in spite of the reopening of sandstone quarries at Gebel es-Silsila. There, a great donation to the Nile god Hapy is celebrated on a large stela. The limestone quarries at el-Babein were reopened with the dedication of a rock-cut chapel to the goddess Hathor. Other building activities are attested in major Ramessid centers: in Memphis, a sanctuary to Ptah and a magnificent palace; at Heliopolis, a temple preceded by a commemorative column (once surmounted by a statue, it anticipated on the triumphal columns of the Roman period); in the Nile Delta, statues and blocks bearing his name were moved from Piramesse and found reused in Tanis and surrounding sites.

Merenptah's reign is marked by the invasion of the Libyans who were bound in a coalition with the Sea Peoples; Merenptah successfully repelled these groups in his fifth regnal year. Reports of the victory have been inscribed on columns and stelae in Egypt and Nubia. The confederacy of western foes, mainly Lebu and Meshwesh, also included newcomers from the Mediterranean—the Sea Peoples, comprising the Akawash, Turash, Luka, Shardana, and Shekelesh. The battle took place at Pi-yer, on the western border of the Nile Delta, and ended with the triumph of the Egyptian army. Six thousand soldiers were slain, and nine thousand prisoners taken. The chief of the Libyans fled, members of his family were captured, and a great booty was seized by the Egyptians.

The fame of the king is due to the unique mention of

Israel in Egyptian sources, which occurs on the Victory Stela once placed in Merenptah's mortuary temple at Thebes (now in the Cairo Museum). In this report, the Libyan defeat is followed by the capture of Palestinian cities and the devastation of Israel. Scenes presumed to illustrate that campaign and attributed to his reign, actually belong to a cycle of scenes depicting episodes from the Near Eastern wars of Ramesses II. Recent scholarship agrees that Merenptah is not the pharaoh of the biblical *Book of Exodus*. His mummy was found in the tomb of Amenhotpe II, which was used as a royal cache during the twenty-first dynasty, in the Third Intermediate Period.

[*See also* Sea Peoples.]

BIBLIOGRAPHY

Redford, D. B. *Egypt, Canaan, and Israel in Ancient Times.* Cairo, 1993.
Sourouzian, H. *Les monuments du roi Merenptah.* Sonderschrift des Deutschen Archäeologischen Instituts, Abteilung Kairo, 22. Wiesbaden, 1989.
Vandersleyen, C. *L'Egypte et la Vallee du Nil.* Paris, 1995.

HOURIG SOUROUZIAN

MERERUKA (short form Mery) held the office of vizier around 2360 BCE, at the end of the reign of Teti and the beginning of that of Pepy I. He was probably a son-in-law of King Teti, since he was married to an "eldest bodily royal daughter," Watet-khet-Hor/Seshseshet by name. Mereruka's own background has not been clearly established. An "Acquaintance of the King" named Nedjet-em-pet/Tit, appears as his mother in the decoration of his tomb. She may be the same lady as an identically named woman whose tomb was found not far from his. Naguib

MERERUKA. *Statue of Mereruka at Saqqara.* (Courtesy David P. Silverman)

Kanawati (1996) identifies this latter Nedjet-em-pet as Mereruka's mother. Another candidate for Mereruka's mother is Nedjet-em-pet, who was the wife of an "Elder of the Hall" named Mer(er)uka from Giza (Harper 1987). The question of Mereruka's lineage remains unsettled.

The tomb of Mereruka lies in the Teti cemetery at Saqqara. It abuts the *mastaba* of the vizier Kagemni, which has led to the conclusion that Mereruka followed Kagemni in that office. It is one of the great tombs of the Old Kingdom, with a total of thirty rooms: twenty were designed for Mereruka himself (Section A), five for his wife, Watet-khet-Hor (Section B), and five for his son Meriteti (Section C). The section erected for Meriteti was, for a short time, usurped by Pepiankh/Memi, another son of Mereruka's, but was reclaimed later by Meriteti. The decoration of Mereruka's *mastaba* is executed in painted raised relief. The representational program includes conventional themes as well as others derived from the royal domain. Of special interest are the scenes showing a man and woman siting on a bed in the so-called birth room and the representation of hunting in the papyrus thickets in the gate room. At the entrance to the tomb, the tomb owner is depicted before an easel at which he draws the representations of the seasons, an indirect association between the tomb's occupant and the sun god.

BIBLIOGRAPHY

Duell, Prentice. *The Mastaba of Mereruka.* 2 vols. Oriental Institute Publications, 31, 39. Chicago, 1938.

Harper, Yvonne. *Decoration in Egyptian Tombs of the Old Kingdom.* London and New York, 1987.

Kanawati, Naguib. *The Teti Cemetery at Saqqara.* Australian Center for Egyptology, 8. Warminster, 1996.

Nims, Charles F. "Some Notes on the Family of Mereruka." *Journal of the American Oriental Society* 58 (1938), 638–647.

Porter, Bertha, and Rosalind L. B. Moss. *Topographical Bibliography of Ancient Egyptian Hieroglyphic Texts, Reliefs and Paintings.* Oxford, 1981.

HARTWIG ALTENMÜLLER
Translated from German by Elizabeth Schwaiger

MERIKARE, one of the last kings of the Herakleopolitan period, the ninth and tenth dynasties (c.2165–2040 BCE). That period is known chiefly for the strife between the Herakleopolitans in the north of Egypt and the Thebans in the south of Egypt. The Turin Canon of kings, a papyrus in the Egyptian Museum (Museo Egizio) in Turin, Italy, lists eighteen Herakleopolitan kings, but most of them were ephemeral rulers for whom little or no further evidence exists. Contemporary evidence for Merikare suggests that he was the most important and longest reigning king of that period. His connection with the struggle against the Thebans is evident from the biographical in-

scription of the nomarch Khety in a tomb at Asyut in Middle Egypt, the nomarchs of which supported the Herakleopolitans. The much destroyed text describes scenes of conflict in which Merikare's name is prominent. The same inscription also tells of the renovation of the temple of Wepwawet, the local god, by order of the king.

Merikare's pyramid was called "The Pyramid which is Flourishing of Places," known from the titles of officials who served its cult and who were buried at Saqqara. Although not yet identified, an unexcavated pyramid at Saqqara close to that of King Teti of the sixth dynasty may prove to be Merikare's. The name of Merikare was immortalized in a literary work, *Instructions for Merikare*, the author of which is purported to be his father, a king whose name is lost. The author advises his son on kingship, but there are also remarkable passages of regret as to actions taken in his own reign. All the preserved papyri on which this work was written has been dated to the New Kingdom, but the literary form suggests that it was composed in the early Middle Kingdom, perhaps not long after the Thebans triumphed.

[*See also* Instructions for Merikare.]

BIBLIOGRAPHY

Lichtheim, Miriam. *Ancient Egyptian Literature: A Book of Readings.* Berkeley, 1973. Contains a description and translation of *Instructions for Merikare.*

Malek, Jaromir. "King Merykare and His Pyramid." In *Hommages à Jean Leclant,* edited by C. Berger, vol. 4, pp. 203–214. Bibliothèque d'études, 106. Cairo, 1994. The known facts about Merikare are included in Malek's article.

DIANA MAGEE

MERNEITH (early third millennium BCE), a queen of the first dynasty, mother of King Den. She was probably the wife of King Wadji and perhaps a daughter of his predecessor King Djer, in whose tomb at Abydos two objects with her name were found. She seems to have reigned for her son Den when he was still a minor, and she was therefore buried like a ruler at Abydos Umm el-Qaab.

In Old Egyptian, she was *Mrt-Nt* ("beloved of Neith"). She is not mentioned in the king lists, but her special position is indicated by seal impressions from tomb 3503 at Saqqara (Emery 1954, pl. 55), which show her name with a royal *serekh*, next to the Horus name of Djer and by impressions of the seal of the royal necropolis of Abydos discovered at Den's tomb, where she is listed among the first dynasty kings after Den; her title "King's Mother" is on the same level as the royal Horus-falcons. On the Palermo Stone, her name is partly preserved in the headline of Den's reign.

According to the excavation report of W. M. Flinders Petrie, *The Royal Tombs of the First Dynasty* (London,

1900), her tomb is one most carefully built. It consists of a central chamber, surrounded by store chambers and forty-one subsidiary burials. Like a king, she had two stelae (one now in Cairo) adorning it, but on them her name was written without the *serekh*. The authenticity of a baboon statue, of unknown provenance, inscribed with her name (Kaplony 1966, p. 91ff.) has been doubted by Seipel (1980, p. 38f.).

BIBLIOGRAPHY

Dreyer, Günter. "Ein Siegel der frühzeitlichen Königsnekropole von Abydos." *Mitteilungen des Deutschen Archäologischen Instituts Kairo* 25 (1969), 1–21.

Emery, Walter B. *Great Tombs of the First Dynasty.* Vol. II. London, 1954.

Kaplony, Peter. *Kleine Beiträge zu den Inschriften der ägyptischen Frühzeit.* Wiesbaden, 1966.

Seipel, Wilfried. "Untersuchungen zu den ägyptischen Königinnen der Frühzeit und des alten Reiches." Ph.D. diss., Hamburg, 1980.

GÜNTER DREYER

MEROË, an ancient polity also known as Kush, developed along the Nile River immediately to the south of Egypt. Meroë flourished during the latest period of ancient Egyptian history, being, in the main, contemporary with the Ptolemies and the Romans. The Egyptians had various names for the area to their south, one of them being Ta Seti: ("the land of the bow") in reference to the skillful use of that weapon by the inhabitants, who seemed to have called their country Kash or Kush—so this term was also used by the Egyptians. Classical writers used the name Meroë taken from the town that became the residence of a line of rulers originally based farther north, at Napata. During the twenty-fifth dynasty, these kings had ruled Egypt, before retreating in the mid-seventh century BCE back to Napata; and from there they ruled until moving south to Meroë.

Archaeological evidence shows Meroë to have been inhabited as early as the eighth century BCE. Although the local rulers were buried there from shortly after 300 BCE, the date is uncertain for when the royal residence was moved to this new capital; most probably, it was about the sixth century BCE. The city that became the royal residence—and both male and female rulers are known—is situated on the east bank of the Nile, some 200 kilometers (125 miles) north of the junction of the Blue Nile and White Nile.

Meroë, which may have had a population of about 10,000, consisted of several well-defined areas. The first has the remains of a large temple, dedicated to the god Amun, and a processional way that leads to the east, flanked by at least four smaller temples. The second is an area of large stone buildings surrounded by a massive wall, considered to be the royal residence. The third is a large area of small, domestic mud-brick buildings and the area that was devoted to iron smelting, for which the town was famous. Excavations by J. Garstang from 1910 to 1914 provided information about the temples and palaces; later excavators, from 1965 to 1976, studied the domestic and iron-working areas, as well as several small temples.

After the withdrawal of the last Kushite king from Egypt, the frontiers between the two states varied with the stationing of their armies. A fort on the island of Dorginarti in the Second Cataract may have been an Egyptian and Persian frontier outpost, but by the end of the fourth century BCE, Meroë laid claim to Aswan.

During Ptolemaic times in Egypt, the situation south of Aswan was somewhat fluid; both Ptolemaic and Meroitic rulers left traces of building activity in the temples of that region. Later, with Roman rule in Egypt, the frontier was drawn at Aswan. As a result of an attack by Meroë in 24 BCE, in which Aswan was captured and statues of Rome's Emperor Augustus were pulled down and perhaps taken away, the Romans invaded and reached Napata. On their way back to Egypt, they left a garrison at Qasr Ibrim. After their defeat, Meroë sent envoys to Augustus to arrange a treaty, and by it the frontier was placed at Hiera Sykaminos (Ar., Maharraqa). No evidence exists that the statues of the emperor were recovered; the finding of a bronze head of Augustus at Meroë in the 1910 excavations suggests that they were taken as trophies of war.

Many sites of the period are to be found along both banks of the Nile. They consist of towns and villages with associated cemeteries and a number of temples and stretch from Garba, near Maharraqa in the north to Sennar on the Blue Nile; a total distance of 2,000 kilometers (some 1,250 miles). The only part where monuments are found away from the river is in the wide stretch of open grassland to the east of Meroë and between the rivers Nile and Atbara. Here, in the "Island of Meroë" of the classical writers are found the most dramatic and impressive buildings at Musawwarat es-Sofra and Naqa, where several temples still stand.

The culture of Meroë was heavily influenced by that of Egypt. The rulers adopted the titulary of Egyptian pharaohs, and the early inscriptions were in Egyptian. The art and architecture were closely similar to that of Egypt, though certain distinctive features make it possible to see the difference between Egyptian and Meroitic art. Kings were buried under pyramids, although this custom had long been abandoned in Egypt. Temples were similar to Egyptian constructions, and many of the gods worshiped were the same—the god Amun being especially venerated and treated as the state god. There were distinct Meroitic gods, of whom the best known is the lion-headed Apedemek, for whom several temples of a distinctive style were built.

The inhabitants of Meroë developed their own writing system. It was a simplified form of Egyptian hieroglyphs, being a selection of twenty-three Egyptian signs, and it was used as a syllabary. A modified form of these signs, often known as Meroitic cursive, was used for most inscriptions. The phonetic values of the Meroitic signs are known but with the exception of a few words, many texts cannot be translated.

The long line of rulers of Meroë—many of whose burial places can be identified—provides a thread of history from the end of the twenty-fifth dynasty in Egypt. (c.650 BCE) to the middle of the fourth century CE. The last royal burial is to be dated to the first half of the fourth century. An inscription of Aezanes, king of Axum, found somewhat later at that town in modern Ethiopia, claims that he ruled over Kasu (the kingdom of Kush). There is evidence for destruction in some of the temples at Meroë, and the finding of an Axumite coin and two fragments of Axumite inscriptions in the excavations have supported the view that Aezanes's army attacked and looted the town, in about 350 CE, bringing its kingdom to an end.

[See also Kush; and Nubia.]

BIBLIOGRAPHY

Adams, William Y. *Nubia: Corridor to Africa.* London, 1977. The most detailed account of Meroë; gives full references.

Shinnie, P. L. *Meroe: A Civilization of the Sudan.* London, 1967. Slightly out of date but still useful. Gives an overall survey of the culture and its history.

Shinnie, P. L., and Rebecca J. Bradley. *The Capital of Kush I: Meroe Excavations, 1965–1972.* Berlin, 1980. Describes the first years of the new excavations. The second volume is now in press.

Welsby, Derek A. *The Kingdom of Kush: The Napatan and Meroitic Empires.* London, 1996. The most up-to-date account of Kushite (Meroitic) culture.

PETER L. SHINNIE

MESOPOTAMIA. For more than four millennia, Mesopotamia and Egypt were the two most highly developed, complex societies in the ancient Near East. Egyptian culture coalesced in the Predynastic period and remained more or less homogeneous throughout pharaonic time, with the notable exceptions of the Intermediate Periods. Mesopotamia, situated at the geographic crossroads of Europe, Africa, and Asia, contained a varied and changing cultural domain. These two civilizations came into contact when their expanding hinterlands met in the Syria-Palestine region. At other times, trade through buffer zones in Syria-Palestine and around the Arabian Peninsula mediated and filtered influences. The intensity of their interchange fluctuated, but several periods—Late Uruk, Late Bronze Age, and Iron Age—were noted for their exceptional activity. In the fourth millennium BCE (Late Uruk), the urban society of southern Mesopotamia exerted a strong influence on the less-developed culture of Egypt. Afterward, however, the trend reversed, and Egypt became the primary donor.

The term *Mesopotamia*, first used by the ancient Greeks, means "the land between the rivers" and designates the geographical area defined by the Tigris and Euphrates rivers (roughly equivalent to present-day Iraq). Mesopotamia has three ecological regions: a marshy southern swampland, where the Tigris and the Euphrates come together before emptying into the Persian Gulf; the great central alluvial plain that stretches to the north of modern Baghdad; and the northern limestone plateau of the Jezirah, through which the Euphrates cuts a narrow valley and the Tigris waters fertile countryside. Mesopotamia's alluvial plain needed irrigation for widespread agricultural production, but in the north, rainfall permitted dry farming; in the south, the people of the marshes supported themselves by fishing and herding. Lacking such natural resources as minerals, stone, and hardwood, the Mesopotamian economy depended almost entirely on agriculture and animal husbandry. From the rivers, mud and clay were abundant and were used extensively for ceramics, building, artistic expression, and as the medium for the cuneiform writing system—the earliest known.

Northern Mesopotamia lies within the region called the Fertile Crescent, which includes the Zagros Mountains and the land between them and the Mediterranean coast. There, the first permanent human settlements were based on the domestication of animals and plants during the ninth through seventh millennia BCE. Southern Mesopotamia does not reveal widespread settlement until the sixth millennium BCE. In the fourth millennium BCE, the settlement of southern Mesopotamia was extensive, resulting in the building of large-scale urban centers with monumental architecture; by the end of that millennium (Late Uruk period, c.3600–3100 BCE), cuneiform writing was developed on clay tablets.

The earliest written sources known, from the third millennium BCE, refer to the southern alluvial plain as "Sumer," a group of competing city-states. Toward the end of the third millennium BCE, the Akkadian state unified the southern and northern alluvial plain; it was distinguished from the preceding Sumerian period by the use of Akkadian, a Semitic language. In the Jezirah, the region later known as Assyria, an independent society developed in close concert with that of the south. In the second millennium BCE, southern Mesopotamia (Sumer and Akkad) coalesced into the entity of Babylonia. By the mid-second millennium BCE, Babylonia and Assyria were locked in a complex and interdependent relationship that

MESOPOTAMIA. *Limestone bas relief of a lion-headed eagle on a human-headed bison.* From Tell al Ubaid.

lasted until the Babylonian defeat of Assyria at the end of the seventh century BCE. The fall of Babylon to Persia in 539 BCE signaled the end of the great, native powers of Mesopotamia; this was followed soon after by Persia's expansion and defeat of Egypt in 525 BCE.

As noncontiguous regions, interactions between Egypt and Mesopotamia could occur through either direct or indirect contacts. Early contact has been determined by the presence of foreign artifacts and elements, later by textual references. More difficult to describe are the types of exchanges and social processes that underlay their relations, which ranged from trade to military confrontation and diplomacy, as well as their long-term cultural impact.

Textual documentation includes royal records of military campaigns, everyday administrative documents, letters, and semihistorical narratives, which were effected for a specific purpose and audience. Portable objects that circulate easily, and thus can enter a region without any direct contact with the culture of origin, can be distinguished from immovable elements such as architecture and burial customs, which suggest more direct connections or the presence of foreign populations. Though elusive, artistic evidence—traced through shared or borrowed forms, compositions, and motifs—may calibrate the extent to which a culture adopted or modified foreign elements. Uncertainties in absolute chronologies and historical synchronisms among different cultures have resulted in multiple competing dating systems, as based on a high, middle, low, or ultra-low point of reference. The conclusions drawn, therefore, are not final but open to reinterpretation.

Fourth Millennium BCE. During Egypt's Predynastic Naqada II b–d and Naqada III periods (contemporary with Late Uruk), imported objects, local imitations, and the incorporation of foreign elements attest to extensive Mesopotamian influence. A significant number of Egyptian objects, including ivory knife handles, slate palettes, and architectural elements, exhibit links to Greater Mesopotamia. Nearly all appear in the Naqada II d through Naqada III contexts, although a Mesopotamian cylinder seal from a Naqada II b burial suggests earlier ties. A few motifs that occur on indigenous Egyptian objects are known from Late Uruk seals and the sealings of Susa in southwestern Iran (ancient Elam), in southern Mesopotamia, and in Syria-Mesopotamia (Habuba Kabira, Jebel Aruda). These motifs include fantastical creatures, such as serpent-necked felines and lion-griffins, two snakes entwined around rosettes, a human figure mastering animals, and boats with high prows; there are also stylistic traits such as highly modeled relief and animals with linear patterning on their bodies, as well as compositional strategies such as animal files that appear for the first time. Possibly, such visual forms entered Egypt either on seals or on seal impressions that secured imported goods, although the only Mesopotamian seals found in Egypt are of a nonfigural, "schematic" type. The Mesopotamian motifs were quickly Egyptianized in the early dynasties, as seen on the first dynasty Narmer Palette, in which the entwined serpent necks of the leashed felines symbolize the unification of Upper and Lower Egypt. The Mesopotamian-style cylinder seal—adopted in Egypt in the first to third dynasties—was carved with hieroglyphs, not Mesopotamian-inspired representational scenes. Mesopotamia may have left its impact on the Egyptian tradition, however, in its (potential) contribution to the development of the hieroglyphic writing system. That a complex system of writing appeared in Egypt only slightly later than its development in Mesopotamia, immediately following the period of intense Late Uruk contacts, suggests that the two developed at related moments when ways of storing information became critical to the maintenance of complex urban society. While the notion of writing may have been derived from Greater Mesopotamia, Egypt's subsequent hieroglyphic form had an entirely indigenous character.

Although debates surround the mechanisms and extent of Mesopotamian influence in Predynastic Egypt, direct contact appears to have occurred. Objects and/or people are thought to have traveled from Mesopotamia to Egypt by way of the Red Sea and along the Wadi Hammamat into southern Egypt. Archaeological evidence from Syria and the Nile Delta indicates that a northern path also existed. The Late Uruk period is characterized by clay cones inserted into mud brick walls and by crudely fashioned bevel-rimmed bowls that were associated with centralized distribution. Examples of both have been found not only in Mesopotamia but also in the east at Susa, as well as in Syria, at Habuba Kabira and Jebel Aruda. At Buto in the Nile Delta, clay cones made from local fabric but typologically similar to Greater Mesopotamian examples, present the possibility of an Uruk "colony"; no examples of bevel-rimmed bowls, however, have yet been excavated at Buto.

Mud-brick architecture with elaborately recessed niches, as exemplified in Egyptian funerary *mastabas*, recalls Mesopotamian temple façades. The earliest examples are from the first dynasty reign of Aha at Saqqara and Naqada, although their ultimate inspiration may have been the Naqada II b–d evidence from Buto, where the clay cones imply mud-brick architecture despite no surviving structures. The niched façade, like the cylinder seal, was Egyptianized, and as such it endured as an essential element in funerary architecture.

The evidence and settlement patterns from archaeological sites in southern Mesopotamia, western Iran, and Syria comprise a complex but loosely integrated supraregional interaction system during the Late Uruk period. The exact nature of the "Uruk expansion" in Syria and Egypt, and its relationship to southern Mesopotamia and Susa, remains incompletely articulated; nevertheless, the finds at Buto provide a common link with contemporaneous developments in Mesopotamia. The long-term impact of such connections appears to be both subtle and complex; for example, there is the formation of an Egyptian information storage system that developed independently into both the artistic canon and the hieroglyphic script, as well as the possibility that certain fundamental aspects of Egyptian visual arts, such as fantastical creatures, appear to be derived from Mesopotamian stimuli.

Third Millennium BCE. Connections between Egypt and Mesopotamia during the third millennium BCE remain elusive. An Egyptian presence is known from Byblos on the coast of Lebanon and inland at Ebla in Syria through stone vessels inscribed with the names of Old Kingdom pharaohs, whereas Mesopotamian Early Dynastic artifacts have been found at Mari on the middle Euphrates and Akkadian period artifacts at Tell Brak, farther north. With the unification of southern Mesopotamia under the Akkadian kings (c.2350–2100 BCE), military expansion to the northwest reached as far as Anatolia and the Mediterranean under Sargon (2334–2279 BCE) and Naram-Sin (2254–2218 BCE), who both claimed to have controlled Ebla. At Ebla, a lid of Pepy I (sixth dynasty,

2354–2310 BCE) provides a chronological link with material of the Akkadian period found at Tell Brak in eastern Syria. As will be the case in the early second millennium BCE, Ebla appears to be the link between these two civilizations but has yet to reveal all the answers. To what extent the Akkadian experiences outside their territory relates to the new artistic expressions of open landscape and naturalistic rendering of anatomy, seen for example on the stele of Naram-Sin, remains undetermined.

The distribution of the semiprecious stone lapis lazuli in both Egypt and Mesopotamia demonstrates their participation in a shared long-distance trade network. Lapis lazuli was imported from mines in the area of Badakhshan (in present-day Afghanastan); first known from northern Mesopotamia during the Late Ubaid period (c.4000 BCE), by the Late Uruk period lapis lazuli occurs exclusively in southern Mesopotamia and seems related to trade relations with Elam to the east. In Egypt, the stone was found in graves of the contemporaneous Naqada II period. Its marked decline in the first part of the Early Dynastic period (c.2900–2600 BCE) in Mesopotamia is paralleled by its absence during the first through third dynasties in Egypt (c.3050–2600 BCE), with a resurgence in the later Early Dynastic period (c.2600–2350 BCE) and in the fourth through sixth dynasties (c.2600–2200 BCE). A similar pattern of availability has been charted for obsidian, a dark volcanic glass, imported into Egypt from the coastal regions of the Arabian Peninsula and East Africa. The absence of both materials just before the Old Kingdom may indicate a major disruption in the trade routes through Iran and around the Arabian Peninsula. Lapis lazuli found in Mesopotamian Early Dynastic III levels (c.2600–2350 BCE) at Mari, one bead of which is inscribed with the name of the Mesopotamian king Mesanne-padda, suggests that trade relations may have resumed using Syria as the primary route. The shared pattern of lapis lazuli importation suggests that the two regions participated as independent parties in the same long-distance trade network and that their interests may have intersected in Syria.

Second Millennium BCE. Throughout the Near East and the eastern Mediterranean, the second millennium BCE was an age of extensive international interactions. The period can be divided into two primary phases, corresponding to the first and second halves of the millennium, with a period of uncertainty around mid-millennium. The first half corresponds to the Isin-Larsa and Old Babylonian periods in southern Mesopotamia and the Old Assyrian period in the north. Under King Hammurabi (c.1792–1750 BCE), Babylon expanded to the northwest, eventually conquering Mari. The city-state of Assur also looked to the northwest, establishing trading colonies in Cappadocia (central Anatolia) and briefly ruling parts of north-

ern Syria. At the same time, Middle Kingdom interest and influence grew along the Levantine coast. Finds at Byblos and Ebla resume the pattern established during the Old Kingdom. For example, a ceremonial mace inscribed with the name of a lesser-known thirteenth dynasty pharaoh Harnedjheryotef (c.1770–1760 BCE) was discovered in the "Tomb of the Lord of the Goats" at Ebla. Economic documents and letters from the archives at Mari attest to the close connections between the Middle Euphrates states and the coastal states, such as Ugarit and Byblos.

Exchanges were primarily those of trade, restricted to direct contact between contiguous regions. Egyptians referred in general to the region of Syria as "Retenu," and their understanding of the people from this land, called "Asiatics," was based primarily on knowledge of the small city-states of Syria-Palestine rather than those of Mesopotamia. "Asiatics" (Near Easterners) were listed as servants in thirteenth dynasty texts and many of them have West Semitic names, indicating their likely Levantine origin. Wall paintings in the twelfth dynasty tomb of Khnumhotep III at Beni Hasan (reign of Senwosret II, 1897–1877 BCE) also depict nomadic "Asiatics" led by a man with the West Semitic name of Abi-Shai. Cylinder seals from this period in Syria exhibit an intermingling of Mesopotamian and Egyptian imagery, reflective of the overall social situation in which those cultures interacted. During this time, the Egyptian winged disk appeared in Syria, and was taken into Hittite and Mitannian art of the mid-second millennium BCE, finally emerging in Assyrian art, in which it often represents the state god Ashur. A sculptural head of a ruler found at Susa but made in Babylonia in the nineteenth or eighteenth centuries BCE (sometimes identified as Hammurabi), exhibits an expressive rendering of care and weariness in the lines of the face unique in Mesopotamian art; but that was also found in sculptures of the Egyptian kings Senwosret III (r. 1878–1843 BCE) and Amenemhet III (r. 1843–1797 BCE).

Disruptions in the mid-second millennium BCE correlate with the collapse of the Middle Kingdom and the subsequent control of Lower Egypt by foreigners known as the Hyksos. Although not fully understood, the middle part of that millennium was clearly a time of population movement and active interaction throughout the eastern Mediterranean region. Comparisons of material culture from Ebla and the Hyksos capital of Avaris at Tell ed-Dab'a in the Egyptian Delta suggest that the Hyksos came from northern Syria. The two-wheeled chariot first appeared in Egypt around this time—an innovation attributed to the Hurrian-speaking people from northwestern Mesopotamia and Anatolia—yet a general lacuna in the documentation from Assyria and Babylonia shrouds their role in the international arena during that time. After the sack of Babylon at the beginning of the sixteenth century

BCE, by the central Anatolian Hittite kingdom, a foreign group of rulers called Kassites emerged in southern Mesopotamia. Assyria fell under the jurisdiction of the expansionist Mitannian federation, a conglomeration of partly Hurrian city-states centered on the (still-unlocated) site of Washshukanni in the Khabur region of northern Syria, until the Hittite state under king Shuppiluliuma I defeated the Mitannian armies in the fourteenth century BCE. The heartland of the Mitannian state area, at the bend in the Euphrates, was known to Egyptians as "Naharin."

In the second half of the millennium (Late Bronze Age, c.1600–1100 BCE)—in the Near East, the Middle Assyrian period in the north and the period of Kassite rule in the south, but in Egypt, the New Kingdom—widespread diplomatic relations solidified into highly formalized behavioral conventions; soon contact and conflict intensified in the contested area of Syria. Warfare, trade, diplomatic relations, and interdynastic marriages, all well-documented in texts and artifacts, sustained an era of unprecedented internationalism among Egypt, Mesopotamia, Syria-Palestine, Cyprus, Anatolia, and the Aegean. Merchants and diplomatic messengers traveled between the royal courts, conducting joint-ventures in trade and political alliances. An archive with the correspondence of foreign rulers and Egyptian rulers, written in the *lingua franca* of Akkadian and found at Akhenaten's (Amenhotep IV, r. 1372–1355 BCE) capital at Amarna in Middle Egypt, provides a window onto intensifying international relations in the mid-fourteenth century BCE. Those letters document, for the first time, direct relations among the rulers of Egypt, Babylonia, and Assyria. Through these exchanges, Egypt received as gifts foreign princesses from Babylonia and Mitanni, despite its refusal to reciprocate in kind. The Amarna archive also included several cuneiform examples of Mesopotamian literature. Monumental celebratory inscriptions, such as the annals of Thutmose III (r. 1504–1452 BCE) inscribed on the walls of the temple at Karnak, record tribute brought by Assyria and other Near Eastern states. Egyptian alabaster (calcite) vases found at the Assyrian capital of Assur further attest to both trade and diplomatic ties.

A group of ivory, gold, and alabaster (calcite) luxury goods, which were produced in an international artistic tradition and which may have been exchanged as gifts between rulers, indicates important cultural exchanges at the royal level. The simultaneous development in Egypt and Assyria of historical (primarily battle) narrative in both written and visual forms—in particular, the image of the king in the chariot overcoming enemies or hunting wild animals—cannot be unrelated. Early eighteenth dynasty reliefs from Abydos that date to the reign of Ahmose (c.1569–1545 BCE) suggest that the stimulus originated in Egypt; however, in light of Minoan-style wall paintings in the Hyksos palace at Tell ed-Dabʿa (Avaris) in the Delta, the role of Minoan Crete complicates the situation.

First Millennium BCE. In contrast to the second millennium BCE, during which contacts between Mesopotamia and Egypt appear multidimensional, in the first millennium BCE, contacts appear primarily confrontational. Assyrian royal annals, Babylonian chronicles, and Egyptian monumental inscriptions provide detailed narratives of both military campaigns and political events; however, the self-serving interests of those texts are usually apparent. For example, the inscriptions of the Nubian rulers of the twenty-fifth dynasty present themselves as sole rulers of a unified Egypt, whereas Assyrian records recount numerous fragmented polities ruled by a multitude of petty dynasts and clearly distinguish between Egypt (Muṣur) and Nubia/Kush (Meluḫḫu/Kūsu).

Egypt and Assyria, after emerging from a "dark age" that followed widespread destructions at the end of the second millennium BCE, embarked on expansionist policies that brought them into continual conflict. Assyria, with increased military strength, concentrated attention on the critical trade cities of Syria and Palestine that were traditionally under Egyptian control. The ninth century BCE Assyrian kings Ashurnasirpal II (r. 883–859 BCE) and Shalmaneser III (r. 858–824 BCE) extended the state in all directions. Sargon II (r. 721–705 BCE) recorded that he was the first Assyrian ruler to reach the Egyptian border in Palestine. Under Sennacherib (r. 705–681 BCE), Assyria began a systematic consolidation of its territories to the west. At the same time, the Nubian rulers Shabaqa (r. 705–690 BCE) and Taharqa (r. 690–664 BCE), whose twenty-fifth dynasty had previously supported Assyria's claims, began stirring discontent among the restless rulers of the small Levantine city-states. In retaliation, Sennacherib's son Esarhaddon (r. 681–669 BCE), after quelling the Levantine rebellions, invaded Egypt in 674 and again in 671 BCE, pushing as far south as Memphis. His death en route to Egypt in 669 BCE allowed Taharqa to reestablish rule in lower Egypt, prompting Esarhaddon's successor Ashurbanipal (r. 669–627 BCE) to return to Egypt in 667/666 BCE. Despite Assyria's strength in Mesopotamia, it remained unable to securely rule Egypt. With the growing threat of Babylonia and Elam, Assyria relinquished hopes of subduing Egypt and instead formed a diplomatic alliance. The Egyptian king Necho II (r. 610–595 BCE) sent troops to aid the Assyrians in 609 BCE, challenging the Neo-Babylonian kings, only to be defeated by both Nabopolassar (c.625–604 BCE) and Nebuchadrezzar II (r. 604–562 BCE). When Persia conquered Babylon in 539 BCE and Egypt in 525 BCE, both regions were incorporated into the larger Persian Empire.

Despite the intense military interactions between

Egypt and Mesopotamia, the two remained staunchly anchored within their own cultural traditions. A clay *bulla* found in the palace of Sennacherib at Nineveh and impressed with both the royal seal of Shabaqa and an Assyrian-style seal documents Egyptian–Assyrian cooperation. Three large statues of Taharqa were found in fragments on the mound of Nebi Yunis at Nineveh, possibly in the palace of Esarhaddon. Their presence indicates a knowledge of Egyptian art forms by the Assyrians, although it appears to have had little effect on Assyrian art. Ashurbanipal looted the temple treasury at Thebes in 664/663 BCE, and booty lists record large quantities of goods, including two large "pillars cast in silver." Two border monuments erected by Esarhaddon—a rock relief at Nahr el-Kelb in Lebanon and a stela at Zincirli (ancient Sama'al) in northern Syria—record his defeat of Taharqa. The Nahr el-Kelb relief is situated directly next to a New Kingdom relief of Ramesses II, a juxtaposition that epitomizes the way Assyria defined itself in opposition to Egypt's imperial tradition. The rounded stela shape of the frame and the static image of Esarhaddon stands in stark contrast to the square portico frame and dynamic smiting figure of Ramesses, the great Egyptian imperialist of six hundred years earlier.

Summary. Egypt and Mesopotamia represented two of the most powerful and influential civilizations in the ancient Near East for more than four millennia. Although not geographically contiguous, relations between them are documented in the archaeological, textual, and artistic record. Chains of interaction followed both a northern route that led through Syria and down the coast of Palestine and a secondary southern route around the Arabian Peninsula. Relations appear generally unbalanced, with Mesopotamia taking the lead during Egypt's formative period of the fourth millennium BCE, and then Egypt predominating in the second millennium BCE. Until the fourteenth century BCE, evidence for direct contact is minimal, with the possible exception of a late fourth millennium BCE Uruk "colony" in the Nile Delta. By the end of the second millennium BCE, however, textual documents explicitly detail relations between rulers, messengers, and merchants. During that period (Late Bronze Age), the types of exchanges included trade, diplomacy, and warfare, which heralded an international age of cultural exchange. In the first millennium BCE, military conflict formed the primary mechanism of interaction, and control of the Syria-Palestine area became a dominant concern of both states. With the increased emphasis on conflictual contact came a decrease in long-term cultural impact. The Persian occupations and subsequent Greek conquest incorporated both Egypt and Mesopotamia into their larger empires, causing Egypt's eventual shift toward the Hellenized world.

BIBLIOGRAPHY

Bietak, Manfred. *Avaris: The Capital of the Hyksos. Recent Excavation at Tell el-Dabʿa. The First Raymond and Beverly Sackler Foundation Distinguished Lecture in Egyptology.* London, 1996. Good introduction to the Delta city from the twelfth to the eighteenth dynasty by the head of the excavations.

Gates, Marie-Henriette. "The Palace of Zimri-Lim at Mari." *Biblical Archaeologist* (June 1984), 70–87. Basic introduction to the Old Babylonian period at Mari.

Hallo, William W. and William Kelly Simpson. *The Ancient Near East: A History.* San Diego, 1971; 2d ed. Fort Worth, 1997. Informative parallel histories of Egypt and Mesopotamia.

Kantor, Helene, J. *The Aegean and the Orient in the Second Millennium B.C.* Fiftieth anniversary reprint. The Archaeological Institute of America, 1. Boston, 1997. One of the most influential studies to address foreign relations through artistic evidence. First published in 1947, it is somewhat out of date.

Kantor, Helene J. "The Relative Chronology of Egypt and Its Foreign Correlations before the First Intermediate Period." In *Chronologies in Old World Archaeology*, 3d ed., edited by R. Ehrich, pp. 3–21. Chicago, 1992. A comprehensive treatment of archaeological evidence for connections between Egypt and the Near East from early prehistory to 2000 BCE.

Kitchen, K. A. *The Third Intermediate Period in Egypt (1100–650 B.C.).* 2d rev. ed. Warminster, England, 1986. Detailed history of a lesser-known period of Egypt, with extensive coverage of the Assyrian impact.

Kuhrt, Amélie. *The Ancient Near East c. 3000–330 BC.* London and New York, 1995. Historical overview of Mesopotamia, Egypt, Anatolia, Syria, and the Levant, including discussion of textual sources. Excellent bibliography.

Matthiae, Paolo. *Ebla: An Empire Rediscovered.* Garden City, N.Y., 1980. General account of the excavations at Ebla by the head of the excavation team.

Moorey, P. R. S. "From Gulf to Delta in the Fourth Millennium BCE: The Syrian Connection." *Eretz-Israel* 21 (1990), 62–69. Basic review of archaeological evidence for a Syrian route in the Late Uruk period.

Moran, William L. *The Amarna Letters.* Baltimore and London, 1992. Accessible translation of the internationally exchanged letters found in Egypt that detail the colorful melodramas of the Late Bronze Age.

Oren, Eliezer D., ed. *The Hyksos: New Historical and Archaeological Perspectives.* Philadelphia, 1997. A collection of essays representing the most recent scholarship.

Pettinato, Giovanni. *Ebla: A New Look at History.* Baltimore and London, 1991. Synthetic overview of the archaeological and textual evidence from Ebla. Originally published as *Ebla: Nuovi orizzonti della storia,* 1986.

Pittman, Holly. "Constructing Context: The Gebel el-Arak Knife, Greater Mesopotamian and Egyptian Interaction in the Late Fourth Millennium B.C.E." In *The Study of the Ancient Near East in the Twenty-First Century: The William Foxwell Albright Centennial Conference*, edited by J. S. Cooper and G. M. Schwartz. 1996. A highly theoretical study of artistic relations concentrating on a Predynastic carved knife handle; comprehensive bibliography for the fourth millennium BCE.

Redford, Donald B. *Egypt, Canaan, and Israel in Ancient Times.* Princeton, 1992. Engaging historical narrative, though sometimes idiosyncratic in its interpretations.

Sasson, Jack M. "Letters at Mari." In *Ebla to Damascus: Art and Archaeology of Ancient Syria*, exhibition catalog, edited by H. Weiss, pp. 198–203. Washington, D.C., 1985. Brief introduction to the Old

Babylonian period letters found at Mari, with translations of several examples.

Smith, William Stevenson. *Interconnections in the Ancient Near East: A Study of the Relationships between the Arts of Egypt, the Aegean, and Western Asia.* New Haven and London, 1965. Now out of print, this monumental study of sweeping breadth covers more than three millennia of artistic exchanges.

Wilhelm, Gernot. *The Hurrians.* Warminster, England, 1989. Detailed survey, including chapters on history, society, religion, and literature, as well as one on art and architecture written by Diana L. Stein. Originally published as *Grundzüge der Geschichte und Kultur der Hurriter.*

MARIAN H. FELDMAN

MIDDLE EGYPT, the modern name for a region of the Nile Valley. It comprises an area from the Eastern Mountains of Gebel Abu Foda, north of Asyut, to the entrance of the Faiyum Depression. Its main features are the Nile River, which flows through the east of the region, and a broad stretch of cultivated land to the west of the Nile. The relief of the prehistoric landscape was carved out by Pleistocene epoch branches of the Nile. Deep trenches and sandy alluvial deposits were created, especially in what became the center of the cultivated land and on the Western Desert's border. Today, these trenches and deposits are covered with earth that has been deposited since that time by the annual Nile floods. From approximately 3000 BCE onward, these floods provided ideal conditions for agricultural settlements. The riverbed of the Bahr Yusuf follows the original path of one of these ancient arms of the Nile on the periphery of the Western Desert. Originally it branched off from the Nile north of Asyut; now it is fed from a man-made canal at Dairut, south of Malawi. In the New Kingdom, the Egyptian name for the Bahr Yusuf was Temet; the later Greek name was Tomis Potamos. The river flowed into the Faiyum Depression and was probably deep enough for boats in ancient times, at least in the lower reaches. After the New Kingdom, there were large swamps west of the Bahr Yusuf, especially in the Faiyum estuary. The overflow from the Nile floods and from the Bahr Yusuf collected in these swamps. The Nile runs parallel to the Eastern Mountains (the Minia formation consists of a brittle fossiliferous limestone) that cross through Middle Egypt. In front of and behind the rocky formations to the west of the Nile, intermittent alluvial deposits create temporary islands. On the eastern bank, between the steep sometimes terraced grades of the Eastern Mountains, there are coves, some of which widen into bays in the Amarna valley, near Shekh Abade or south of Minia. The eastern coves are in a floodwater-free gravel base from the Pleistocene, on the fanned-out alluvial deposits in wadi beds, or in the shelter of a high plateau before the steep escarpment of the Eastern Mountains. West of the Nile Valley, the limestone mountains are completely eroded in many places, so there is a gradual transition to the desert. In these locations, modern farmland now covers the ancient desert, although a strong northwest wind frequently deposits sand on the rocky desert ground as shifting sand dunes.

Since the seventeenth century, travelers have visited such Middle Egypt tourist destinations as el-Minia, Beni Hasan, el-Bersheh, Tell el-Amarna, Hermopolis, and Tuna el-Gebel. The first scientific study of the area was attempted by the scholars of Napoleon Bonaparte's expedition to Egypt in 1798–1799; their survey maps, published in the atlas of the *Description de l'Égypte,* show many hills of ruins that are no longer there. Volume 4 of the *Description* (edited by M. Jomard) contains a discussion of Middle Egypt's landscape. The layers of cultivated soil were superficially studied by the Egyptian Antiquities Department prior to twentieth-century land development, but the desert borders were explored in the late nineteenth century, with support from the British Egypt Exploration Fund. A systematic survey of the desert borders was carried out in the 1950s by Werner Kaiser (1961) and Karl Butzer (1961). Only since that time has the cultivated land from Malawi south of the Faiyum estuary been surveyed for traces of settlements and cemeteries. A great number of present-day villages in the cultivated region are located on mounds or hills that were sites dating to Roman or more ancient times. The many mounds and hills, now eroded, can be verified by fragments of pottery found in the surrounding fields.

Prehistoric data are surprisingly rare for Middle Egypt, from Asyut to just outside of Herakleopolis. On the western side of the Nile, near Tuna el-Gebel, tools from the Middle Paleolithic were found, and Upper Paleolithic and Mesolithic stone tools were discovered on the limestone terrace near Sawada, opposite el-Minia. There is no specific evidence of settlements. Cemeteries from the Neolithic period of Naqada II were found beneath the stone pyramid of Zawiet el-Maietin/Kom el-Ahmar and beneath the Ramessid-era temple of Shech Abade at Antinoöpolis.

Middle Egypt comprises the nomes (provinces) of ancient Egypt that developed from the end of the second dynasty—the thirteenth to twentieth nomes. From the Old Kingdom onward, the nomes of Egypt were recorded, and for each, the capital, the deity, the territory specifications, the hinterland data, the canal connections, and the sacred lake were listed. After the third dynasty, Middle Egyptian nomes were inscribed on the tombs and temple walls. Some nomes developed into major provincial centers.

Many village names are recorded from the period of Ramesses V in the Wilbour Papyrus. Some present-day villages, especially those at the flood-protected center of the cultivated land, have therefore been settled continuously since the New Kingdom, possibly even longer. Among the ancient villages whose locations are verifiable—by comparing Arabic, Coptic, and Greek names—are Ashruba (called Sharope) in the New Kingdom, Aba el-Waqf (ancient Opet), Shulqam (ancient "barn of the qemau plants"), and Shusha (ancient Kasha). The name of present-day el-Fashn on the Nile is probably derived from an ancient word for "fortress." The Wilbour Papyrus also contains notes on the landscape of northern Middle Egypt during the New Kingdom. It describes small forests at the center of the cultivated land, with sycomore figs, tamarisks, and other trees. There were meadows, shrubbery, and also isolated swamps and ponds. Between these natural areas were found different types of arable land: "new" land (land recovered after Nile floods) with high-quality sediments; then farther from the Nile were the "highland fields," which required the heavy physical labor of lifting and carrying water for irrigation. Smaller farmsteads and country houses surrounded the densely built villages and hill (tell) settlements. The settlement patterns in the southern part of Middle Egypt are assumed to be similar to those in the North. Only for some villages, especially those at the center, does the etymology of their names indicate a continuity, at the very least, from the New Kingdom onward. The population numbers in these villages were only fractions of today's. The Wilbour Papyrus probably provides an incomplete list of settlements and farmsteads, so it is difficult to estimate the population density of that period. Efforts at establishing the animal and game populations of Middle Egypt's desert borders, based on Old and Middle Kingdom tomb scenes, were not successful. The majority of the population were most certainly farmers. Among those listed as field owners were soldiers, grooms, a police officer, and, in some cases overseers, a physician, a "carrier of the branding mark," a coppersmith, and an embalmer.

Raised causeways linked the settlements that were usually located at the flood-protected center of the cultivated land and connected settlements to Nile ports. The dikes had to be repaired after each annual flood, a task carried out by conscripted farmers. The east–west causeways that cut across the Nile Valley and the drainage ditches next to them can be traced right into modern times. The Wilbour Papyrus contains a list of dikes for the New Kingdom. If today's settlements in the cultivated land are shown to be of ancient origin, then the system of dikes, causeways, and roads can be assumed to have similar continuity. As early as the New Kingdom, the entire irrigation system in Middle Egypt was probably based on these ancient Egyptian causeways. From Ptolemaic times onward, the swamps near the entrance to the Faiyum were regulated with dams and then brick walls.

The traditional nomes of Egypt, immortalized in religious and cult standards of deities, were gradually superseded by new organizational structures during the Old Kingdom. The districts and their administrations were not always of equal stature; some were mere subdivisions of a greater administrative unit. Changes in these units arose naturally from constant changes in the course of the Nile. Villages on the western bank of the Nile—such as Hardai/Kynopolis and its port near el-Qeis—could be categorized as once belonging to an eastern district. In the fifth dynasty in northern Middle Egypt, south of Herakleopolis, there was an autonomous "goat" district, with a "goat" city as the district center. It is known solely from the tombs of the "goat" district administrators, near Dishashe, southwest of Herakleopolis. During the fourth and fifth dynasties, "Land Overseers" were sent from the palace to control individual districts in Middle Egypt on the pharaoh's behalf. Others, given the title "Head of Commissions," could be dispatched to various districts. A list in a necropolis south of Tehna el-Gebel mentions the Faiyum oasis as one of the administrative regions. An administrator was once mentioned for the "districts in the middle," although the districts do not comprise the whole of Middle Egypt. In the sixth dynasty, administrators were usually titled "Great District Chief." Toward the end of the Old Kingdom, there were a number of administrative reforms. For a time, Cusae seems to have been the seat of the "Overseer of Upper Egypt," who was directly subordinate to the king. Some of the district boundaries were changed after the Old Kingdom. Neferusi, a city on the southern border of the sixteenth district, replaced Hebenu to the north as district center, and Sako and Hardai—originally two separate but nearby centers for different districts—were amalgamated into one large administrative center at an important Nile port at the mouth to Gebel et-Teir. A radical administrative reform was introduced by Sesostris I, creating new territories and subdivisions. From the Middle Kingdom onward, the governor (referred to by Alan H. Gardiner and others as "mayor") of an administrative center with surrounding lands (referred to by Farouk Goma'a and others as "county") fulfilled the role of administrator, even though the title "Great District Chief" continued to be handed down. Thus the entire eastern desert region was the domain of the newly appointed "Head of the Eastern Desert" with a seat near Beni Hasan; the "spine of the Nile" formed the administration boundary. The administrator of the Eastern Desert had to oversee the extraction of all products—mainly minerals, ores, and stone—from the Eastern Desert and their transport to the pharaoh in el-Lisht. This does not mean that the eastern and western sections of the sixteenth district were administered independently. The western was home to the administrator's "older relative"—by definition, an official of higher rank. In addition, there were legally independent military installations in Middle Egypt (called "gubernatorial fortresses" by Goma'a and others) and also the pharaoh's harbors, managed by a civil servant or a general with the title "Governor."

The pyramid districts on the Faiyum estuary presented a unique case of economic independence during the Middle Kingdom. In the late Middle Kingdom, the future Middle Egypt vassal of the Delta-based Hyksos ruler in Avaris gained a dominant position in Neferusi. During this period, too, the region of Hermopolis was probably integrated into the larger domain called the "Region of Neferusi"; its southern border seems to have been far south of Cusae and it stretched to Tihna el-Gebel in the north. After the Delta-dwelling Hyksos and their Middle Egyptian allies were overthrown by Thebes, the "Region of Neferusi" remained intact, although Hermopolis gradually returned to the status of administrative center. To the north of Neferusi lay the Hardai territory, which had previously been described as "district of Input" or "district of Sako." Next came the territory of Herakleopolis. The area farther north—the old twenty-first and twenty-second nomes—were already part of the "district of Memphis." The area near Mer-Tem (present-day Meidum), a governor's seat, was most likely a subdivision or subdistrict. During the Ramessid era, the "district of Aphroditopolis/Atfih" to the northeast was probably still independent of Memphis. Each region had its own fortresses and ports. All were, however, under the direct control of the king.

After the New Kingdom, Hardai's northern section was added to this region as an autonomous administrative territory, forming the "district of Per-medjed/Oxyrhynchos." Its administrator took on the old religious title of the nineteenth Upper Egyptian nome. To the south, the old description "district of Neferusi" had been replaced with "tosh-district of Hermopolis." From this developed the Greek *nomos* names of Hermopolite, Kynopolite, Oxyrhynchite, Herakleopolite, and Aphroditopolite with their subcategories, the toparchies. Thus the Cussite, the region around the old fourteenth district center, became a mere toparchy of Hermopolite. From the Third Intermediate Period onward, Middle Egypt—up to just outside of Herakleopolis—was ruled and administrated by Thebes; the Greeks, too, considered the districts of Middle Egypt to be part of the Upper Egypt of Thebes. The area of Antinoöpolis, founded by the Roman emperor Hadrian, became an autonomous nome, and the former harbor city of Hermopolis took on the significance formerly held by the category called *metropolis*. From Diocletian onward, the toparchical structure changed when a new subcategory based on the Latin *pagus* district was introduced. New Roman administration centers emerged (e.g., Theodosioupolis north of Hermopolis).

Middle Egypt played an important role in ancient history. Its agrarian resources and quarries supplied the royal court with materials, ships, and human labor. Middle Egyptian fortresses and harbors on either side of the dangerous Nile cataracts controlled traffic on the river and later on the Bahr Yusuf. Although Middle Egypt is barely mentioned in the Old Kingdom accounts of the struggle between the Herakleopolitan regime, which had allied itself with Asyut, and Thebes, the governors in Middle Egypt and the Thebans must have reached some kind of agreement that made the attack on the North possible in the first place. Their independence—which is manifest, for example, in the autonomous calendar and in the inscriptions on their ornate rock tombs—reached a peak immediately after the unification under Montuhotep I of the eleventh dynasty. The district governor Neheri of Hermopolis was among those who then joined in the civil strife that erupted at the close of the eleventh dynasty. Neferusi must have been an important fortress even then, second only to Asyut. King Kamose needed to defeat the master of Neferusi before he could move against the Hyksos ruler to the north. The Thoth temple at Hermopolis was the most important Egyptian religious center, at all times, and there each governor would also act as religious leader. Akhenaten's choice of Middle Egypt as the site of his New Kingdom palace, to the south of Hermopolis, was influenced by the good harbor—so important for his capital. New Kingdom officers were buried in the necropolis of Tihna el-Gebel. From the Ramessid era onward, mostly foreign soldiers were buried in this region.

During the Third Intermediate Period, the authorities at Thebes created a series of fortresses on the rocky cliffs along the Nile, to fend off attacks from the north. Along the Bahr Yusuf, other fortresses were enlarged and even the Hermopolis town center was surrounded by a wall. By the end of the twenty-third dynasty, the independent Libyan kings of Hermopolis and of Herakleopolis were embroiled in a bitter feud. Although defeated by King Piya, the king of Hermopolis was able to maintain his position until the Saite reunification and remained territorially autonomous. From the Saite period onward, troops of foreign soldiers were deployed at these fortresses. Aramaic-speaking groups were stationed at Hermopolis, with Arabian Hagraeans nearby. Several village names indicate that there were also Syrian settlements. Evidence exists for Persian descendants of the First and Second Persian Occupations, as well as increasingly, a Greek population in Ptolemaic times.

[*See also* Amarna, Tell el-; Beni Hasan; Bersheh; Herakleopolis; Hermopolis; *and* Oxyrhynchus.]

BIBLIOGRAPHY

Butzer, Karl W. "Archäologische Fundstellen Ober-und Mittelägyptens in ihrer geologischen Landschaft." *Mitteilungen des Deutschen*

Archäologischen Instituts Cairo 17 (1961) 54–68. Survey of desert borders in Middle Egypt.

Butzer, Karl W. *Early Hydraulic Civilization in Egypt.* Chicago, 1976. For information on landscape, settlement reconstruction and flood dike systems in Middle Egypt.

Description de l'Égypte. Several volumes and atlas. Paris, 1809–1828. First major land survey.

Gardiner, Alan H. *Ancient Egyptian Onomastica.* London, 1947. A collection of the traditional lists of sites and deities, which also appear on the temple walls.

Gardiner, Alan H. *The Wilbour Papyrus.* London, 1948. 4 vols. Commentary and information on the Wilbour Papyrus, especially in vol. 2.

Gomaà, Farouk. *Mittelägypten zwischen Samalut und dem Gebel Abū Sir.* Wiesbaden, 1991.

Helck, Wolfgang. *Die altägyptischen Gaue.* Wiesbaden, 1981. For general information of the districts of Ancient Egypt.

Kaiser, Werner. "Bericht über eine archälogische-geologische Felduntersuchung in Ober-und Mittelägypten." *Mitteilungen des Deutschen Archäologischen Instituts Cairo* 17 (1961), 1–53. Survey of desert borders in Middle Egypt.

Kessler, Dieter. *Historische Topographie der Region zwischen Mallawi und Samalut.* Wiesbaden, 1981. Information on cultivated land.

Sauneron, Serge, and Jean Yoyotte. "Traces d'établissements asiatiques en Moyenne Egypte ous Ramsès II." *Revue de Egyptologie* 7 (1950), 70–76. For information on foreigners in Middle Egypt.

DIETER KESSLER

Translated from German by Elizabeth Schwaiger and
Martha Imber-Goldstein

MIDDLE KINGDOM (c.2000–1650 BCE). The heritage of ancient Egyptian civilization is popularly associated with the pyramids of the Old Kingdom and the monumental temples, decorated tombs, and Tutankhamun's golden mask of the New Kingdom. The Middle Kingdom has left comparatively few impressive remains for modern eyes. Some may recall the name of Sinuhe, though unaware that—contrary to the popular romance and motion picture—he was a Middle Kingdom man.

If we could ask an early New Kingdom courtier for the most prominent people of the past five hundred years, he might reply, "Kings Nebhepetre Montuhotep, Sehotepibre Amenemhet (I), Kheperkare Senwosret (I), Khakaure Senwosret (III), Nymaare Amenemhet (III), and then the much traveled Sinuhe, and Khety, the scribe." When asked why, he would probably explain that he knew most of them from their stories in the books and that Montuhotep was worshiped at his temple at Deir el-Bahri; Senwosret was a god in Nubia, and Amenemhet was one in the Faiyum. Indeed, early in the New Kingdom, the mortuary complex of Montuhotep I at Deir el-Bahri and the temple of Amun at Karnak, established by Senwosret I, were the most prominent landmarks on the Theban landscape. Amenemhet I, Sinuhe, and Khety were familiar as literary figures, protagonists of three famous texts: respectively, the *Instructions of Amenemhet* for his son Senwosret, the *Story of Sinuhe,* and the *Satire on the Trades.* Today, Senwosret III and his son Amenemhet III are known to almost every visitor to a major Egyptian collection only by their impressive statuary.

Our picture of the Middle Kingdom is formed by the arts of the ancient scribes and sculptors. Thus, the heritage of the Middle Kingdom is not monumental but nevertheless immortal: literature and faces. The faces of many people—royal and nonroyal—portrayed in stone, express concern and intent, and the texts offer sense and meaning.

Cultural History. Many chronologies of ancient Egypt attempt to equate cultural stages with the spans of dynasties. This custom often leads to questions whether, for instance, the Middle Kingdom began with the eleventh or twelfth dynasty, or whether the thirteenth dynasty belonged to the Middle Kingdom or to the Second Intermediate Period. Clearly, the answer depends on one's point of view. If one is speaking about royalty and royal families, it might be right to define breaks in terms of dynasties. But political, ideological, and technical developments evolve differently, and not simultaneously. The Middle Kingdom, defined as a cultural-historical entity, has no sharp limits.

In the political sense, the Middle Kingdom began about 2040 BCE, when the Theban lord Nebhepetre Montuhotep became sole ruler after about a hundred years of disunity, and the Herakleopolitan tenth dynasty came to an end. The Second Intermediate Period—defined as the time Egypt was under divided rule—commenced in the last fifty years of the thirteenth dynasty with the rise of local non-Egyptian (but Egyptianized) rulers in the eastern Nile Delta (the fourteenth dynasty). The collapse of political authority came only after the dissolution of cultural unity, when Syro-Palestinian rulers, called "Hyksos" by later tradition, usurped (at about 1650 BCE) the throne at Memphis. They held it for about a century, while the ruling political-administrative system of the thirteenth dynasty continued in a Theban-centered state labeled the seventeenth dynasty.

In the ceramic sequence, the different Lower and Upper Egyptian assemblages of the First Intermediate Period were replaced with uniform inventory by the early years of Amenemhet II; the styles started to separate again, with strong Syro-Palestinian influences and imports into the eastern Delta, by at least the first half of the thirteenth dynasty. In art, the Old Kingdom tradition prevailed against local styles late in the eleventh dynasty and were augmented in the twelfth dynasty by new types of statuary, such as squatting and cuboid forms. One change that marks the Middle Kindom apart from the Old Kingdom is the greater use of stone for temple-building in the twelfth dynasty. This corresponds to the growing importance of the temple as a social and economic institution, and of the role of the gods. Brick buildings are to

MIDDLE KINGDOM. *Statue of Nebhepetre Montuhotep I, at the Cairo Museum.* (Courtesy David P. Silverman)

be found in the twelfth dynasty to an unparalleled extent, as indicated by the pyramids or the Nubian fortresses.

Funerary culture changed markedly late in the sixth dynasty, when the Coffin Texts tradition began and anyone could aspire to become Osiris after death. A specialized funerary industry, increasingly and nationwide, produced the coffins, plaster masks, servant statues, and models—and doubtless the ideas associated with them—from their Memphite roots. Several religious conceptions (connected with the goddess Hathor of the human *ba*-soul) are attested on popular stampseal amulets for the first time, well before scarab seals appeared in the eleventh dynasty. Another major shift came around the time of Senwosret III, when significant changes were made in the underground design of the royal tomb, and the long tradition of decorated rock-cut tombs for the higher elite

came to an end—for about 230 years, at least in the provinces. These trends accompanied changes in religious belief: for example, the idea of a difficult and dangerous journey to the netherworld, and of a free-moving *ba*-spirit.

The explicit ideology of ruling a harmonious society was the main achievement of the Middle Kingdom. These concepts were expressed in literary works like the *Loyalist Teaching* and the *Instructions of a Man for His Son*, which later became classics that were repeatedly copied. While in the Old Kingdom the pharaoh acted laconic and in solitude, nevertheless he was gracious to his courtiers. He engaged his nobles in dialogue and gave reasons for his actions. Kings not only displayed but also explained themselves. The major ideological and intellectual change between the Old Kingdom and the Middle was a movement from implicit statement to explicit reasoning, which was related to the spread and diversification of the written word and writings. The pharaonic regime in the reign of Senwosret I promulgated eloquently—by charisma and speeches, temple inscriptions and literature, by arguments and threats—a policy that could be defined by three elements. First, there was the desire for commemoration, using stone as the medium to promote cultural identity and remembrance. Second, there was the determined promulgation of an element of ideal social behavior: "to act reciprocally for the one who has acted before," and to remember. Third, loyalty to the pharaoh guaranteed the well-being of all, while opposition brought annihilation. This was an intolerant program: everyone was concerned and involved, and there was no room for neutrality. Its reflection prevails in the autobiographies of the elite and in literature. Once formulated, it led to irrevocable developments and was impressed on the collective memory of future Egyptian societies. Amenemhet I had coined his Horus-name in a manner appropriate to the new spirit of the age, "Repeater of Birth: Creation" (*Wehem Meswet*); his son, Senwosret I, used the Horus-name "Active One in Creation" (*Ankh Meswet*), and brought forth renaissance and restoration. His vast temple-building program made kingship omnipresent.

The social foundations of the Middle Kingdom lay in the system of ruling of the eleventh dynasty. People were tied to the ruler by personal fidelity, conviction, charisma, and material rewards—at least, this is the impression derived from comparing the inscriptions authorized by King Antef II, his chancellor Tjetji or Rediukhnum of Dendera. The king and his companions shared common ideas and views, and the Theban territory was enlarged by their military force and their persuasive powers. The spiritual and social unity between king and courtiers is made visible in the layout of the necropolis of Montuhotep I at Deir el-Bahri, where the royal mortuary complex is surrounded by the tombs of his followers, who are also depicted in the reliefs of the royal tomb.

These attitudes had parallels in other regions, and on a smaller scale. After the decline of Old Kingdom rule, things did not change very much for the common people outside the royal residental quarters. Local potentates, however, managed to gather groups of followers, promising security and welfare to their partisans, in exchange for their civil and military support. Bonds of fidelity developed which rewarded the loyalist with income and security. These relationships mirror the concern of the pharaoh for his subjects at a local level. Both patrons and followers spoke proudly in their autobiographies about the benefits of their actions and their own prosperity. Late in the eighth dynasty, and in the absence of centralized authority, the elites in Middle and Upper Egypt tried to assert elements of royal ideology, tied to local and re-

gional networks and often in competition with each other. Finally, they became trustworthy adherents of the Herakleopolitan or Theban kings. The relationship between the pharaoh, courtiers, and underlings in the twelfth dynasty was modeled after these socio-political systems. Unfortunately, archaeology allows only a glimpse into the conditions prevailing in the country. From the late eleventh to mid-twelfth dynasty, there are few upper-class decorated tombs in the provinces (Aswan, Thebes, Qaw el-Kebir, Rifeh, Asyut, Bersheh, Beni Hasan, and Meir)—the tombs of the court circles in the Memphite region were largely destroyed for their stone. Hence the overwhelming majority of tombs from the Middle Kingdom have few written words. They offer much in other spheres of culture, but are silent about the professions, names, private histories, and personalities of the individuals buried within.

There are four major sources of texts for the study of Middle Kingdom administration and bureaucracy: the inscriptions about successful government expeditions in the Sinai, at Hatnub, Wadi Hammamat, and Wadi el-Hudi, and the numerous rock inscriptions and graffiti (within and outside the Nile Valley, along the caravan and mining routes, and near the Nubian fortresses). Then there is the corpus of more than two thousand inscribed stelae, donated by kings as well as inferior "nobodies," and mostly erected at the holy site of Abydos. Another group consists of administrative papyri, with lists of workers' names; accounts of provisions, tools, work, and activities at the royal court; building projects; administrative decrees; juridical trials; wills; liveries, and simple letters (Reisner Papyri, papyri from Illahun, and Papyrus Brooklyn 35.144, etc.). The very existence of a large amount of papyri dealing with these matters has led some Egyptologists to a rather sinister vision of a rigid and over-regulated government, and a "prescriptive" society. However, there is no reason to assume that regulation, control, and bureaucratic complexity were features typical only of the late twelfth dynasty. It was only then that minor officials and state servants had the possibility and the wealth to donate stelae and/or other inscribed objects of their own. The interpretation of an all-pervasive administration overestimates the capabilities and intents of the courtly elite and bureaucrats. They eagerly tried to control the royal and governmental sector, but there was room for private property, interests, and enterprise, even within the households of extended families and their servants. The economic concept of redistribution seems to have been dominant only in the royal, government, and temple sectors of economy. There were various interwoven economic levels from family and village to temple and the royal palace, with different economic modes in coexistence, ranging from redistribution to free commerce. The slow process of growing possibilities and emerging prosperity of the lower and middle classes can be demonstrated by the evidence for the so-called soldiers of the town regiment (*'nḫ nj nwt*); early in the twelfth dynasty, they are mentioned only as groups in lists of participants on government expeditions, but later on, they appear as individual owners of stelae or statues.

Funeral Culture, Society, and Sociology. Careful analysis of cemeteries, tombs, and funerary customs and culture can yield evidence for the existence of social inequality and stratification far beyond the simple two-tiered model of a society divided into producers and managers. This was, however, the ancient Egyptian elites' abstract view of society, which consisted of nobles (*pat*) and common people (*rekhyt*). Literary texts like the *Loyalist Teaching* speak only of a nonproductive managerial class (ranging from vizier to petty priests like Hekanakhte) and their servants and dependent workers, "who produce that which exists"—a division of society that is depicted in decorated noble tombs since Old Kingdom times, where there seems to be no place for an intermediary and independent middle group or class.

Research in Riqqeh, Haraga, and Abydos North demonstrated that there were at least three distinct levels of grave type, size, and wealth in certain Middle Kingdom cemeteries. There were three different types of burials: surface graves, with or without a coffin; shaft graves, usually with a coffin deposited in a subsurface chamber accessible by a rectangular shaft; and tombs, with the burial within several coffins and a stone sarcophagus in a stone-mantled subsurface chamber accessible by a corridor. Additional status markers were the surface architecture of the tombs and the equipment of the funerary complex with (inscribed) stone objects like sarcophagi, statues, and stelae. There seem to have been no restrictions of access to cemetery areas. Semiprecious materials like amethyst and carnelian and even gold and silver, have been recovered throughout the cemeteries. A middle class may have been represented by the owners of the shaft tombs, but there are usually no inscriptions in the tombs, so one can never be sure whether the owner was an upper servant or minor official, or a true middle-class, "independent townsman." The reality of a middle class of minor officials, professionals, craftsmen, and prosperous servants is beyond doubt, but evidence is scant for the existence of a middle-class economically and hierarchically, independent from the rulers and outside the state sector. Individuals depicted on their own inscribed objects, who had no official or professional titles, could have belonged to it.

While the proof for an independent middle class is elusive (or simply not mentioned in the texts), clear social distinctions existed between the ruling group of the royal court and provincial elites, as well as working people. Papyrus Boulaq 18 from the thirteenth dynasty offers insights about administrative matters at the Theban royal court and the ranking of officials and servants. There were inner and outer parts of the palace, each with its own officials and servants—those serving the royal family and those in charge of government affairs under the supervision of the vizier. The hierarchy at court was intricate and sanctioned by courtly discipline and custom. Below the king and his vizier, we can distinguish the highest officials (like the chief treasurer and high steward), various ranks of courtiers and the local elite, as well as medium- and low-ranking government officials. Outside the scope of the papyrus are the semiofficial and nonofficial tiers. Administration and policy were handled by three departments (vizierate, treasury, and military affairs), supplemented by officials working on the local level, and those dealing with religious matters and the economics of the temples. Clearly there existed some upward mobility—less in the twelfth dynasty, and more in the thirteenth dynasty. The grandfather of three kings (Neferhotep I, Sihathor, and Sobekhotpe IV) in the thirteenth dynasty was of the same social stratum as the origins of some of their highest officials: he was a rank-and-file "soldier of the town regiment." Knowledge of religious and professional matters was passed on from father to son by the priests and artisans, and one can often find relatives working in related administrative or economic branches. For the higher offices, the king had to confirm inheritance. Social tiers or groups of related rank and status seem to have functioned like peer groups, with prevailing and preferential horizontal connections and relations. There were no restricted classes or a caste system (as suggested by Herodotus II, 164), and because personal success was bound to favor from above in the hierarchy, even common people and Egyptianized foreigners could advance at court, in the administration, or in the army.

Social stratification also extended to the afterlife. Theoretically, by means of ritual and religio-magical knowledge, anyone could—and perhaps did—aspire to become Osiris after death. Practically, the access to this knowledge, the possibility of performing appropriate rites, and the acquisition of coffins and mummification were restricted; even the afterlife was not egalitarian but hierarchical. In real life, one looked for patrons in the higher levels of society. Accordingly, people both high and low looked for intermediaries, like the deified local saint Heka-ib at Elephantine Island, to communicate with the superior gods in the hereafter, and put *shawabti*-figures in their graves to serve the dead.

Art. Anyone looking at Greek or Roman statuary could easily identify social types that correspond to certain personalities: the young, athletic aristocrat (the *kouros*), the politician, the emperor, or the philosopher. For the ancient viewer, the portrayal of a bearded, long-haired man served to represent, according to popular conventions, a

MIDDLE KINGDOM. *Red granite block bearing the figure, name, and titulary of Senwosret-ankh, a high priest of Memphis from the twelfth dynasty.* This block was found in his *mastaba* at el-Lisht. (The Metropolitan Museum of Art, Museum Excavations, 1932–1933; Rogers Fund, 1933. [33.1.13])

philosopher. But ancient Egyptian sculpture does not provide immediate insight into the meaning of its messages. Certainly, it is easy to identify social types like a king, a god, or an official, but little can be said about the character and mood of the subject intended by the sculptor and his customer. It is even not clear if this is portraiture at all. The wigs, crowns, clothing, ears, and the whole body of the statues are clearly stylized. The anonymity of the sculptor and his subject requires close scrutiny.

Fortunately, many inscribed royal sculptures exist, representing beyond doubt Senwosret III and Amenemhet III. The suggestion of a long coregency of Senwosret III with his son Amenemhet III offers new insight into their portrayals. The elite mentality is displayed in these faces, frequently and more or less exactly copied and recited by contemporaries and posteriority. Senwosret III's expression appears "strong," because we have a certain idea of this king's reign and mentality, whereas the same face labeled Amenemhet IV might be called "resigned," "bitter," or "weary" by us. The wide range of modern speculations on the meaning of Middle Kingdom royal and nonroyal statuary probably does not accurately reflect the views of the ancient artisan and his public about the meaning behind the faces.

The numerous royal and nonroyal faces of Middle Kingdom statuary express ethical values and character traits rather than naturalistic portraits—that is, how a member of the elite or even a king ought to be represented. They display rank, self-confidence in harmony with hierarchy, intellectual and economic prosperity, and well-being—in short, the ideal personality. In a society so rigorously held by the ideal of "perfection" (*nfr*), rank, and decorum, it seems inconceivable that statuary could display mental and physical indisposition, bad temper, or any other negative mood. Egyptian art was made to order, so it is understandable that its meaning had to be acceptable to the customer and the public.

Literature. While the stony faces display the character and mood of reigning, literature aims at the mind. For the Egyptians, papyrus was a writing material intended not for eternity but for daily use. Ironically, papyri survived much better than many stone buildings, and thus their words became immortal. The twelfth dynasty seems to have been fertile ground for literature, favorable for scribes to conceive discourses and tales. The scribes formulated teachings, thoughts, and insights, ageless and familiar to anyone living in an autocratic monarchy. Their writings are shaped by the society they belonged to: aristocratic and bureaucratic, courtly, male-centered, and martial.

Some common themes and patterns can be identified throughout the Middle Kingdom: the love of perfect speech; and a penchant for literary protagonists of rather low (or even marginal) social level (the *Eloquent Peasant;* the *Shipwrecked Sailor;* the wizard Djedi in the Westcar Papyrus; Neferti; Khakheperreseneb; Ipuwer; and the anonymous "man"), or, at the highest level (King Merikare, King Amenemhet I). These are literary devices showing a predilection for the uncommon, which clearly enhanced the attraction of the plot. It would be a mistake to say that the audience for literature originated from the same low social levels as some of the literary heroes. The heroes are not simply common people, but those fictionally equipped with extraordinary talents. Some texts mirror the courtly and scribal ambience of their audience, like the story of the adventures of the palace official Sinuhe, or the instructions of Vizier Ptahhotep, of Prince Hordjedef for Kagemni, and the *Satire on the Trades.* In their train of thought, these works formulate cultural values—how to think, and how to behave as a member of the elite.

The literary texts of the Middle Kingdom make room for fantasy—more so than any royal commemorative inscription—but nevertheless they promote the values of the nobility. This is clear in texts like the *Loyalist Teaching*—one of the earliest treatises about responsibility and sense of duty among the managerial elite. "Fight for his [the King's] name . . . he is life to the man who gives praise to him," as well as "Fight for the working men . . . they are a flock, good for their lord!" are the two central devices that dictate action.

Another favorite theme is that of troubles and despair. Both can have many causes and dimensions, and affect the individual in various ways. Chiefly, troubles and despair are connected with events before the rise of the twelfth dynasty (as in the *Prophecies of Neferti* and the *Eloquent Peasant*), but they are also the point of departure for Sinuhe's flight, for the shipwrecked sailor's adventure, or for the laments of the anonymous man to his *ba*-soul, and for the lament of Khakheperreseneb to his heart. The reasons for the ancient Egyptians' love of the desperation theme are not well understood, because some of the laments seem to finish abruptly (or have lost their endings). But clearly, they attracted an audience with their vivid descriptions of turmoil, anxiety, and their resolution—situations familiar in any time. The story incorporating the exhortations of a king in despair (significant for the Egyptians' love of the extreme)—who even reports that he was killed in an attack by his conspiratorial courtiers (displaying the human elements inherent in divine kingship), was highly popular in the New Kingdom and was chosen by teachers as an appropriate text for school.

It seems beyond doubt that most of the texts were produced for the love of skilled readings in courtly circles of the Middle Kingdom and that they were not written at the times of their fictional events. Scholars are not unanimous about the dates of the *Instruction of Ptahhotep,* the *Instructions for Merikare* and the *Admonitions of Ipuwer. Ptahhotep* offers a mixture of early Old Kingdom and Middle Kingdom traits, but it is metrically Old Kingdom. *Merikare* lacks definite criteria for determining if it is a work of the late tenth dynasty or early twelfth dynasty. The dialogue of Ipuwer with the Lord-of-All (presumably the king) reveals distinct themes and the lexicon of the First Intermediate Period, but it includes later features and titles as well. Its historical setting is open to question.

Recent Views. The traditional view of the Middle Kingdom was shaped by the works of J. H. Breasted, A. Gardiner, H. E. Winlock, W. C. Hayes, G. Posener, W. Helck, and J. von Beckerath, to name but a few. The research of archaeologists, philologists, and historians in the past twenty years has developed or changed the understanding of the Middle Kingdom in many ways, and here the names of J. Assmann, the Arnolds, O. D. Berlev, M. Bietak, E. Brovarski, H. G. Fischer, D. Franke, B. Kemp, D. O'Connor, R. Parkinson, S. Quirke, W. Schenkel, W. K. Simpson, S. Seidlmayer, P. Vernus, W. A. Ward, and H. Willems should be mentioned.

The absolute chronology of the twelfth dynasty, once the backbone for the chronologies of the entire ancient Near East, is now open for discussion. The relative and absolute chronology of the Middle Kingdom will remain uncertain with the sources currently available. The unfinished royal tomb in the valley west of the Ramesseum is ascribed now (by Dorothea Arnold) to Amenemhet I's Theban years, challenging a reassessment for the transitional period of late eleventh to early twelfth dynasty.

One recent challenge is Claude Obsomer's argument against coregencies in the twelfth dynasty. Most of the traditional evidence in favor of a coregency of Amenemhet I with his son Senwosret I have lost credibility, but discussion will continue. Another problem is the recent lengthening of the reign of Senwosret III (by eleven or twenty years), just when most scholars assumed that Senwosret III did not reign longer than nineteen years.

The excavations in the Middle Kingdom cemeteries and the cenotaph area at Abydos, and the publication of material, mostly stelae, from this site by D. O'Connor and W. K. Simpson have stimulated a new period of growth for Middle Kingdom research. The publication of the dozens of statues and stelae from the sanctuary of Hekaib on Elephantine Island by L. Habachi has provided a deeper understanding of many facets of Middle Kingdom culture. Excavations by C. von Pilgrim will carry this work forward. Surveys by the Darnells on the desert routes between Western Thebes and Nag Hammadi have brought to light forgotten, much-traveled communication lines, with rock inscriptions of great importance. Specialized research in the Faiyum has revealed enormous works projects to enlarge the area of arable land and increase fertility, with dams and a huge reservoir, probably begun in the reign of Amenemhet III.

Lake Nasser has brought archaeology and the documentation of antiquities in Lower Nubia to an end, but research on the excavated, rescued, and recorded material goes on. Moreover, the complexities of Egyptians in Nubia and foreigners in Egypt continue to fascinate scholars.

One of the most astonishing discoveries is the annals of Amenemhet II at Memphis, which give evidence for far-reaching military enterprises on the orders of this king—even to Cyprus, some philologists believe. Amenemhet II has experienced a veritable renaissance, from a nobody to an energetic ruler.

Research has changed our picture of the thirteenth dynasty, too. It is no longer viewed as a period of decline, but as a period that had to accommodate many problems: more than a single royal family, foreign intrusions, cultural diversity, a large bureaucratic apparatus, and growing martial and military influence. The fifteenth dynasty reign of the Hyksos gave important stimuli to Egyptian culture that shaped society: the custom of usurpation of other people's statuary, the horse and the chariot, and intensified international relationships and trade. The recent discovery of Minoan wall paintings at Avaris (Tell ed-Dabʿa), the capital of the Hyksos, has raised many new questions. The seventeenth dynasty became a focus for speculation on the sequence and grouping of kings, for example, the placement of King Antef.

New work on autobiographic inscriptions, administrative and literary papyri, and ostraca is in progress. Urgent tasks are, for example, the complete rerecording of the inscriptions in the rock-cut tombs at Asyut, as well as an inventory of neglected Middle Kingdom sculpture. Analyses of material culture, excavated long ago, or just recently, have yielded fascinating and promising results. Excavations in the Nile Delta, at Memphis, Dahshur, el-Lisht, Bersheh, Abydos, Thebes, Elkab, and the region of Aswan are making enormous contributions to Egyptology, especially where settlements and cemeteries can be excavated together (as at Tell ed-Dabʿa, Elephantine Island).

[*See also* Amenemhet I; Amenemhet III; Montuhotep I, Nebhepetre; Senwosret I; Senwosret III; Sobekneferu; Thirteenth Dynasty; Twelfth Dynasty; *and articles on the various literary works mentioned in this article.*]

BIBLIOGRAPHY

Overviews

Franke, Detlef. "Erste und Zweite Zwischenzeit—Ein Vergleich." *Zeitschrift für Ägyptische Sprache und Altertumskunde* 117 (1990), 119–129. Comparative study of socio-political and ideological traits of the First and Seond Intermediate Periods.

Franke, Detlef. "The Middle Kingdom in Egypt." In *Civilizations of the Ancient Near East*, edited by J. M. Sasson, vol. 2, part 5, pp. 735–748. New York, 1995. Overview article treating major kings and events, with bibliography.

Vandersleyen, Claude. *L'Égypte et la vallée du Nil.* Paris, 1995. Vol. 2, pp. 37–39, 43–55. General outline, with archaeological and textual sources.

Textual Sources and Literature

Assmann, Jan. *Ma'at: Gerechtigkeit und Unsterblichkeit im Alten Ägypten.* Munich, 1995. Study of the fundamental mental and ethical values underlying Middle Kingdom societies.

Lichtheim, Miriam. *Ancient Egyptian Autobiographies Chiefly Of The Middle Kingdom.* Freiburg and Göttingen, 1988. Translations of many important texts.

Parkinson, Richard B. *Voices from Ancient Egypt. An Anthology of Middle Kingdom Writings.* London, 1991.

Parkinson, Richard B. *The Tale of Sinuhe and other Ancient Egyptian Poems 1940–1640 BC.* Oxford, 1997. Recent and reliable translation of Middle Kingdom tales and Wisdom Literature.

Art

Assmann, Jan. "Das Bildnis in der ägyptischen Kunst: Stile und Funktionen bildlicher Selbstdarstellung." In *Stein und Zeit: Mensch und Gesellschaft im Alten Ägypten*, edited by Jan Assmann, pp. 138–168. Munich, 1991. Development and function of Egyptian sculpture, Old to New Kingdom.

Fay, Biri. *The Louvre Sphinx and Royal Sculpture from the Reign of Amenemhet II.* Mainz, 1996.

Spanel, Donald B. *Through Ancient Eyes: Egyptian Portraiture.* Birmingham, 1988.

People and Administration

Franke, Detlef. *Personendaten aus dem Mittleren Reich.* Ägyptologische Abhandlungen, 41. Wiesbaden, 1984. Prosopographic dossiers for people of the Middle Kingdom who appear on more than one inscribed object.

Franke, Detlef. *Das Heiligtum des Heqaib auf Elephantine: Geschichte eines Provinzheiligtums im Mittleren Reich.* SAGA, 9. Heidelberg, 1994. The history of Heqaib's sanctuary as part of Middle Kingdom cultural history.

Obsomer, Claude. *Sésostris 1ᵉʳ: Étude chronologique et historique du règne.* Brussels, 1995. Basic study on his reign and on coregencies, with translations of all relevant sources.

Quirke, Stephen. *The Administration of Egypt in the Late Middle Kingdom: The Hieratic Documents.* New Malden, 1990. Analyzes the administrative papyri of the Middle Kingdom: Boulaq 18, Brooklyn 35. 1446, Illahun papyri, etc.

Ward, William A. *Index of Egyptian Administrative and Religious Titles of the Middle Kingdom.* Beirut, 1982. Useful in concordance with the reviews of D. Franke and W. K. Simpson, and especially H. G. Fischer's additions and corrections.

Wegner, Josef W. "The Nature and Chronology of the Senwosret III/Amenemhet III Regnal Succession." *Journal of Near Eastern Studies* 55 (1996). Publication and discussion of the year date "39" of Senwosret III from his mortuary complex at Abydos-South.

Nubia and Nubians

Meurer, Georg. *Nubier in Ägypten bis zum Beginn des Neuen Reiches.* Berlin, 1996. Concise summary of the facts and problems.

O'Connor, David. *Ancient Nubia: Egypt's Rival in Africa.* Philadelphia, 1993.

Smith, Stuart T. *Askut In Nubia: The Economics and Ideology of Egyptian Imperialism in the Second Millenium BC.* London and New York, 1995.

Second Intermediate Period

Franke, Detlef. "Zur Chronologie des Mittleren Reiches Teil II: Die sogenannte 'Zweite Zwischenzeit' Altägyptens." *Orientalia* 57 (1988), 245–274. Research on the relative chronology of dynasties 13–17.

Ryholt, Kim. *The Second Intermediate Period in Egypt, c.1800–1550 B.C.* Copenhagen, 1997. A study with challenging results.

Hyksos

Bietak, Manfred. *The Capital of the Hyksos: Recent Excavations at Tell ed-Dab'a.* London, 1996. Report on the Austrian excavations to 1995.

Hein, Irmgard, et al. *Pharaonen und Fremde: Dynastien im Dunkel.* Vienna, 1994. Excellent entries on the Hyksos period for an extraordinary exhibition.

Archaeology and Society

Garbrecht, G., and Horst Jaritz. *Untersuchung antiker Anlagen zur Wasserspeicherung im Fayum, Ägypten.* Braunschweig, 1990.

Orel, Sara E. *Chronology and Social Stratification in a Middle Egyptian Cemetery.* Ph.D. dissertation, Toronto, 1993. Research on the cemetery of Beni Hasan.

Quirke, Stephen (ed.) *Middle Kingdom Studies.* New Malden, 1991. Important contributions by J. Bourriau, D. Franke, R. Parkinson, and S. Quirke.

Richards, Janet E. *Mortuary Variability and Social Differentiation in Middle Kingdom Egypt.* Ph.D. dissertation, University of Pennsylvania, 1992. Statistical analysis of grave types in the cemeteries of Riqqeh and Haraga and of a small-scale survey excavation at Abydos North.

Seidlmayer, Stephan J. *Gräberfelder aus dem Übergang vom Alten zum Mittleren Reich.* SAGA, 1. Heidelberg, 1990. Basic analysis of funeral data from cemeteries to establish an archaeological and chronological frame for the timespan from the sixth to early twelfth dynasty.

Tooley, Angela M. J. *Middle Kingdom Burial Customs: A Study In Wooden Models and Related Materials.* London and Ann Arbor, 1991.

Wiese, André B. *Die Anfänge der ägyptischen Stempelsiegel-Amulette: Eine typologische und religionsgeschichtliche Untersuchung zu den 'Knopfsiegeln' und verwandten Objekten der 6. bis frühen 12. Dynastie.* OBO, Series Archaeologica, 12. Freiburg and Göttingen, 1996. Research on typology and mental worlds associated with the stamp seal amulets, an object typical of the First Intermediate Period and originating in popular magico-religious concepts.

DETLEF FRANKE

MILITARY. [*This entry discusses the Egyptian military, with reference to its chronological development, and its constitution, organization, and methods of operation. It comprises two articles:*

An Overview

Materiel

For related discussions, see Foreign Incursions; Forts and Garrisons; *and* Imperialism.]

An Overview

When compared with other ancient cultures of Africa and the Near East, Egypt held a privileged position owing to exceptional ecological conditions: a constantly warm climate, a river serving as the artery of the country, natural borders—the Mediterranean Sea in the north, the First Cataract of the Nile in the south, and desert mountains in the east and west—and rich resources of raw materials in the adjacent desert regions. But Egypt's geography also laid the ground for internal conflict whenever the monarchical state failed: the division of the Egyptian Nile Valley in south and north, or Upper and Lower Egypt, reflected not only regional differences but also ethnic variety, favoring decentralization and fragmentation in periods of political instability (the so-called Intermediate periods).

Warfare and Its Ideological Premises. The relative isolation of the "enclosed" land or *miṣru(m)*, as Egypt was called by its Semitic neighbors, strongly affected its view of the foreign world, its conception of war, and its cultural identity. Generally, military aggression was presented as the response to foreign interference with Egypt's interests abroad—trade and the exploitation of resources, and later also the preservation of foreign provinces and alliances—or to unauthorized immigration. In official display, these challenges to Egyptian foreign policy represented various forms of "border violation," the inexcusable assault on the state's integrity, which justified the decision to wage war whenever it was considered necessary.

Egypt's relative invulnerability enhanced a political ideology that propelled a dual model of the world, separating Egypt from all those living beyond its borders, who were treated as "vile enemies," as antipodes of the Egyptian idea of culture. This conception is most directly illustrated in the pictorial motif of the king smiting his enemies, a stereotype of the state's superiority that remained central throughout Egyptian history, depicted on artifacts, stelae, and temple walls.

Egypt, nonetheless, was neither free of immigration nor without susceptibility to foreign influences. Contacts with Palestine and Syria, the Libyan desert, and Nubia were basic aspects of Egyptian culture from its beginnings, but reflections of these cultural interrelations in the state's self-display vary considerably from period to period. While cross-cultural links were officially denied during the Old Kingdom, their signs became ubiquitous during the New Kingdom. This suggests that Egypt's international role shaped to a considerable degree its internal view of the state and of the foreign world, on a par with the cultural and political changes the Near East underwent in the course of history.

Already during the Old Kingdom, the monarchy maintained foreign troops, composed mostly of Libyan and Nubian deportees or prisoners of war; to a limited degree, mercenarism too may have already been practiced. Skilled in using the bow and the spear, these foreign soldiers built up the elite combat troops fundamental to the striking power of the Old Kingdom army. In official representations, however, their importance is not brought to the fore. Apart from their presence in the Egyptian army, there is not much more information on the impact of foreign cultures on the military during this period. This sharply contrasts with historical evidence from the New Kingdom, where we find abundant references to adopted foreign military practices, techniques, equipment, and organization. Again it becomes obvious that in the earlier periods, the official acknowledgment of cross-cultural adaptations was interpreted as a sign of weakness inappropriate to a state that claimed superiority over its neighbors; in the mature state, by contrast, they served as means to prove equality of specialization within an international network of major powers and alliances.

Prerequisites of Warfare. Those who happened to provoke Egyptian aggression usually had to reckon with strategies of "total warfare"—scorched earth, extinction, and large-scale deportation. This policy, however, was exercised only when the enemy declined to surrender and to accept Egyptian hegemony with its toll of extensive economic sacrifices. In general, military confrontation was applied only after diplomatic negotiations and a policy of intimidation had failed, and it mainly addressed towns and cities together with their economic hinterlands. Thus, fortification architecture and techniques of siege had become the basic means of warfare by the third millennium BCE.

Siege warfare. In Egypt, fortified constructions go back to the period of the establishment of the state (the southern fort of Elephantine, the island north of the First Cataract of the Nile, may even date as early as the first dynasty, although most recent archaeological evidence rather suggests a later date). The most striking example of the state's expertise and versatility in defense is the chain of fortresses erected at the Second Cataract in Nubia during the twelfth dynasty. Based on calculations of living and storage space, these strongholds could accommodate several hundred soldiers. According to the official correspondence sent to the military headquarters at Thebes from Semna, one of the fortresses at the Second Cataract, these military bases entertained a dense intelligence network monitoring every movement and activity of the local population.

Siege warfare triggered technical innovations such as movable ladders (Old Kingdom) and domes which gave shelter to as many as three soldiers (from the Middle Kingdom); later came towers and ramparts, as well as specific tools to perforate fortification walls, like the battering ram (from the eighth century BCE). Its success, however, relied heavily on the logistics of the warring parties and the strategies undertaken to prevent or facilitate movement to and from the besieged city. Thus, seizing a city meant starving it out, which could take years—the siege

of Sharuhen, a late Hyksos stronghold in southern Palestine, lasted three years—depending on its storage capacities. According to textual evidence from the eighteenth dynasty, the so-called *Annals of Thutmose III,* the construction of a second ring of walls erected around the city under siege prevented its inhabitants from seeking assistance; at the same time, it provided the besiegers with elevated shooting platforms. The tale of *The Capture of Joppa,* a fictional text from the same period, gives insight into stratagems applied in warfare; as the story tells it, the besieged enemy, avid for riches, is duped by the Egyptians, who send baskets filled with soldiers instead of tribute into the city, very much in the manner of Homer's Trojan Horse.

Effects of the pitched battle. Pitched battles anticipated siege warfare, but before the Ramessid period (nineteenth and twentieth dynasties) they do not seem to have had much impact on the outcome of a war. Large-scale combat employing both infantry and chariotry in the open field became usual during the nineteenth dynasty, turning the Egyptian military from an elitist to a professional institution. From casualty figures and data on the size of armies, it can be argued that before the Ramessid period military encounters were mainly a question of scare tactics, and, when it came to fighting, of the use of long-range weapons such as bow, spear, and javelin. With the introduction of the sword, hand-to-hand combat became crucial, which might explain the much higher numbers of fallen enemies reported in battle accounts of the later New Kingdom. In order to record the adversary's losses, it was common practice to cut off the hands—later, also the penis—of the slain enemies. During the reign of Thutmose III the battle of Megiddo claimed only eighty-three fallen soldiers on the enemy's side, but the death toll among the Libyans maintained by Ramesses III after his first big campaign against his western neighbors exceeded 12,500.

Detailed information on fatalities among the Egyptians themselves comes only from the New Kingdom. According to the administrative record, 900 men died during one of the expeditions sent by Ramesses IV to the quarries in the Eastern Desert. Thus, it seems likely that casualties were a daily routine for enterprises involving large armies, although it was common to deny any mishaps, including the loss of lives, in battle and expedition reports, because this would corrupt the claim of absolute success by the king and his delegates.

Otherwise, references to casualties are very scarce. In an expedition report from the Old Kingdom, the official in charge emphasizes that he went to Nubia at his own expense in order to recover the corpse of his father, who had been killed during an official mission. The assumption that Egyptians who died abroad on duty were transported back to Egypt for a regular burial is indirectly confirmed by the fact that priests and embalmers took part in expeditions. Further evidence may come from name tags found in an Old Kingdom cemetery, which seem to identify seamen and the superiors under whose command they lost their lives. One mass burial of slain soldiers was found at Thebes, dating to the early Middle Kingdom.

Seasons of warfare. For expeditions to Nubia, the more temperate winter and spring months were preferred. Campaigning in western Asia, however, usually took place during the summer, after bringing in the harvest. Like anywhere else in the ancient Near East, this was the time of the year when manpower was not needed for cultivation, and an army was easy to supply with fresh resources along its line of march through allied territory: during the New Kingdom, Egypt's Syro-Palestinian vassals were obliged by treaty to supply troops in transit with food, commodities, and fodder for their animals. Sometimes they were also required to provide transport ships.

Specialization of the Military. In a land whose culture depended in many ways on the river running through it, shipping and navigation were essential to the state, guaranteeing fast flow of information, smooth traffic of expedition corps and their materials and goods, and easy transfer of troops. As a result, Egypt had formed a navy by the time of the Old Kingdom.

Navy. Seagoing ships between the Levant and Egypt are known from the Old Kingdom, and later documentation suggests that by the same time, Egyptian shipbuilding and the navy already benefited from West Semitic expertise. Originally rooted in the expedition and building department, the navy never achieved complete independence; in fact, it existed for almost two thousand years until it became a strike force of the military (twenty-sixth dynasty, the so-called Saite period); even then, its top executives directed merchant and cargo-vessels as well as warships. Although it is usually taken for granted that Saitic Egypt already maintained the Greek trireme, a highly specialized war craft developed in seventh-century Corinth, the introduction of the Greek ship in Egypt may have taken place later, during the Ptolemaic period. Thus, it seems likely that the Egyptian navy did not specialize as a purely military unit before Hellenistic times. It did, however, always serve logistic purposes as well as strategic ones, and in this respect, some information can be drawn from historical battle accounts given by several pharaohs: Kamose (seventeenth dynasty) who attacked the Hyksos capital, Avaris, in the Nile Delta by water; Ramesses III (twentieth dynasty), who repelled raiding pirates, the so-called Sea Peoples, from Egyptian shores; and Piye (twenty-fifth dynasty), who, during his campaign against an expanding Libyan kingdom in the western Delta, captured Memphis from its harbor. Warships provided parapets for the protection of the rowers. Their soldiers, however, do not seem to have acquired specialized combat techniques connected with sea and river navigation; historical battle reports and military ranking suggest that troops stationed on warships were considered just another kind of army contingent, deployable both on water and on land.

Infantry. The ambivalence characteristic of Egypt's navy also holds true for the army. Throughout Egyptian history, the army also performed civil tasks, especially in large-scale operations such as corvée labor in the quarries. Soldiers transported raw stone and completed monuments back to Egypt, moved expedition goods, reclaimed cultivable land, and supplied building projects with mud brick, stone, and other raw materials. Thus conscripted labor battalions were not necessarily the same as military levies. Accordingly, the highest echelons of the army have to be viewed as organizers, administrators, and strategists of mass deployment rather than as combat-tested warriors. Unlike the commanders of the chariotry, they usually relied on bureaucratic expertise, which quite often enabled them to take over crucial positions within the state administration at some point in their careers. This prerequisite of military leadership changed as late as the beginning of the first millennium BCE, when a new military elite gained authority. It relied strongly on the ideals of foreign-rooted warrior societies, which started to penetrate Egyptian culture from Ramessid times, when large-scale deportations of prisoners of war from Libya and the Mediterranean coasts became routine. Simultaneously, mercenarism began to bear heavily on the structure of the army.

Mobile troops. Although the coordination of large armies and their maintenance were intrinsic to the organization of the Egyptian state from its beginning, chariotry (New Kingdom) and cavalry (eighth century BCE) were late innovations brought to Egypt via Syria and Palestine by cultures more advanced in terms of armament and military organization: the Hurrians in the second millennium BCE and the Assyrians in the first.

Mounted scouts exploring enemy territory and troop movements and thus safeguarding the army in transit were of paramount importance to the Egyptian foreign intelligence service from the beginning of the New Kingdom. The fact that the potential of mounted troops was not discovered at the same time may have stemmed from technical factors: the Egyptian striking weapons—bow, spear, and javelin—did not favor hand-to-hand combat, a technique that became more important at the turn of the first millennium BCE, when the sword began to affect warfare. Before the Ptolemaic period, little more is known about the cavalry than its existence after the Assyrian occupation at the end of the Third Intermediate Period (twenty-fourth to twenty-fifth dynasties). Through the twenty-sixth dynasty, no specific ranking was developed for the command of this new military branch, a fact that may show indirectly that the cavalry was not yet a fully established force of the army.

Wagons and horses became known in Egypt during the Middle Kingdom by virtue of foreign booty from and intercultural contacts with the Near East, but it was not until the eighteenth dynasty that the breakthrough of the chariot as a weapon took place. This development was part of a general "modernization" and professionalization of the Egyptian army, displayed in new military titles and purely military careers. The so-called Hyksos, West Semitic immigrants from Palestine who at the end of the Middle Kingdom built an autarchic kingdom in the Nile Delta and southern Palestine, are held responsible for the import to Egypt of the chariot, the most innovative military achievement in the Near East during the first half of the second millennium BCE. It is more probable, however, that its introduction was a consequence of Egypt's increased dialogue with the more complex political systems that were emerging in the Near East at that time. The resulting international competition was also at the root of a substantial change in Egypt's foreign relations, which had an impact on the military and its weaponry. This process was undoubtedly accelerated and intensified by the West Semitic infiltration into Lower Egypt from the end of the twelfth dynasty on.

Chariotry did not, however, play any major role in the military conflict that accompanied the reunification of Egypt and the conquest of Hyksos territories at the beginning of the New Kingdom. Owing to the geography of the sites of combat, the Nile Delta and southern Palestine, warfare against the Hyksos was dictated by the conditions of water and land. Although chariots are mentioned in contemporary historical texts such as the Kamose inscription, named after the king who fought the first successful campaign against the Hyksos, Egypt's military strength relied solely on its navy and Nubian bowmen. In this source, chariots do not appear as striking weapons, but rather as precious status objects in a king's booty. Thus, at first the chariot served military commanders primarily as a superior, fast operational platform; it was not yet deployed in formations during military actions. Its strategic advantage, however, was soon recognized. Thutmose III, famous for his multiple campaigns to Nubia and Syria that led to the establishment of an empire, seems to have benefited fully from this new army branch in his wars against the kingdom of Mitanni and its allies. His account of the Battle of Megiddo, a town in the Palestinian hill country where he encountered the unified forces of a Syro-Palestinian coalition, claims that the Egyptian army was able to seize 924 chariots, including the luxury ve-hicles of the princes, as well as more than two thousand horses. Provided that the opposing parties relied on similar troop strength, these numbers also give an idea of the size of the Egyptian chariotry in the early New Kingdom. About two hundred years later, the inscriptions recording the Battle of Qadesh, fought by Ramesses II against the Hittites, an expanding kingdom of Anatolian origin, refer to mobile forces more than double that size.

The ratio of chariotry to infantry as complementary units of the army is generally assumed to be 1:10 for the entire Near East before the emergence of cavalry. The mobile guards accompanying expedition security forces were, however, smaller. As an example, in the time of Ramesses IV, the chariotry that escorted Egyptian corvées sent out for quarry work consisted of fifty chariots supervised by one officer. For the care and maintenance of horses and vehicles, twenty stablemasters were in charge, each being responsible for at least two teams and one spare horse.

Beginning in the middle of the eighteenth dynasty, the chariotry became structurally independent from the rest of the army and developed its own ranking and a fixed curriculum for the higher echelons. Although the strategic importance of the new military branch is still a disputed issue, the military careers of chariotry officers make it very likely that the chariotry was indeed the superior strike force of the Egyptian army during the New Kingdom. Further evidence comes from administrative texts listing the standard equipment of a chariot: one to two bows, two to four quivers attached at both sides of the chariot (providing eighty arrows altogether), a spear and/or a javelin, as well as axe and shield for close combat. Both horses and warriors were protected by leather armor, which could be reinforced by plates of bronze and other strong materials. This suggests that chariot combat required special training that allowed the soldier to operate from a vehicle moving at speed.

Organization and Logistics. Chariot warfare also demanded professionalization. The chariotry needed grooms and stablemasters for the care and training of the horses as well as for the maintenance of the vehicles. A chariot's crew consisted of a charioteer and a bowman until late in the second millennium BCE; from that time on, they were usually joined by a third man, the shield-bearer.

But there were also substantial modifications in the organization of the infantry. A more sophisticated structure was imposed on the army, probably adapted from Egypt's Near Eastern neighbors. Its command staff, traditionally division commanders and generals, was increased by a number of field officers, such as the standard-bearer, the commander of bowmen, and the commanders of forts. From these positions, a shift into the more prestigious higher ranks of the chariotry was quite common.

Army size and composition. The size of an army could vary considerably, depending on time and purpose. Based on official inscriptions, the smallest unit of mobile troops during the New Kingdom consisted of fifty, and the largest of more than two thousand chariots. Numbers related to infantry are even more impressive. In the Old and the Middle Kingdom, an expedition army included from a few hundred up to twenty thousand men, a figure that does not seem unrealistic in view of the immense manpower and organization dedicated to the building of the pyramids and other major public projects undertaken in these periods. Owing to their intended employment, these armies consisted of large work forces and only few militarily specialized units: in one case, 17,000 corvée workers were escorted by only 1,030 trained soldiers.

During the New Kingdom, the regular size of an army contingent was fifty, headed by a noncommissioned officer. Five contingents built up a company under the supervision of a troop commander, assisted by a military scribe for managing provisions and other logistic purposes. A division, or army, of 5,000 soldiers, therefore, was composed of twenty companies, at the head of which were twenty officers and twenty administrative supervisors, directed by one top military commander, as is documented in one of the expedition reports of Ramesses IV. For campaigning, when all four divisions of the infantry were called to arms, 20,000 soldiers got on the move. They were led to war by the four major gods of the monarchy, Amun, Re, Ptah, and Seth, symbolized in military banners each representing one of the four divisions, whose bases were located at Thebes, Heliopolis, Memphis, and Piramesse, the royal residence. In contrast with the numbers given in Old and Middle Kingdom sources, the Ramessid quotas count only military units. This supports the assumption that large-scale combat was a development of the latter third of the second millennium BCE.

Although Egypt had used mercenaries, primarily Nubians but also Libyans, since the formation of the state, the expanding foreign interests of the New Kingdom, which was gradually transformed into an imperial power, led to an increase of foreigners in the Egyptian army. In the Ramessid period, when the settlement of defeated armies became a political routine, the quota of foreigners in an Egyptian division was considerable: 3,100 mercenaries from the Mediterranean coast, Libya, and Nubia—in comparison to only 1,900 Egyptian bowmen.

Conscription and stationing. Mass conscription was practiced at all periods. Under the coordination of towns and nomes, organized state service developed early, forming, alongside tax administration, one of the major sectors of bureaucracy. According to sources from the Middle and the New Kingdom, evasion of compulsory work and desertion were punished severely: not only the perpetra-

tors but also their families were assigned to state labor, serving a much longer term than required under regular conditions. This punishment was tantamount to the existential annihilation of the deserter, because keeping an entire family away from their land meant economic ruin and eventually poverty.

Early in the second millennium BCE, military service was due at the age of twenty; in later periods, recruits were much younger. How long or how often an ordinary soldier had to serve we cannot assess. It seems reasonable, however, to assume a rotation practice similar to the one used in the Old Kingdom for corvée workers, whose gangs alternated in ten-month cycles. In Ramessid times, campaigning armies seem to have relied heavily on reservists, soldiers who pursued their private lives in their towns and villages until they were called to arms, either for exercise or for military operations. According to the Greek historian Herodotus in the first millennium BCE, Egypt's forces rotated on a one-year basis and built up units of 2,000 men each. It is possible that the reservist practice used in the New Kingdom already followed a similar pattern.

In earlier times, royal elite troops were stationed both at the residence of the king, traditionally situated in the north, and at Thebes, the capital of Upper Egypt. From the First Intermediate Period to late in the Middle Kingdom, nomarchs—at first politically independent governors of the southern nomes of Egypt—constantly maintained local troops, although these were theoretically at the king's disposal at all times. An army entirely organized and controlled by the state government was an innovation of the New Kingdom, when centralization became a major issue in all administrative departments.

Remuneration and rewards. Already during the Old and Middle Kingdom, the deployment of large work forces relied on a sophisticated administration which ensured the smooth realization of state enterprises and the steady supply of provisions for their troops. In terms of campaigning, the introduction of chariotry in the New Kingdom required even more logistic efficiency. Based on estimates of the rations of the forces of Alexander the Great, an ancient army consisting of 10,000 men and 2,000 horses would have required daily about fourteen tons of grain, eighteen tons of fodder, and 95,300 liters of water. The daily ration of grain for one soldier would be 1.4 kilograms. From Middle Kingdom sources, it appears that an ordinary workman or soldier received a basic bread wage of ten loaves a day. Depending on rank and function, these rations could be increased: a commander of a work force, for instance, could expect a salary of 100 loaves, the head of an expedition as many as 200 loaves. Provision lists show that allowances could be paid out in different commodities, such as cakes, beer, wine, and so on. This is indirectly confirmed by the mention of brewers, millers, bakers, and butchers as part of expedition armies. On the basis of the minimum bread wage calculated according to a specific weight ratio, a soldier of the Middle Kingdom would have been restricted to the meager portion of 0.6 kilogram of grain per day. Therefore, it seems likely that he had to rely on a complementary diet. A quarry inscription from the early twentieth dynasty supports this hypothesis, recording—apart from the minimal ten bread loaves—a daily ration of three jars of beer, two units of meat, and three cakes.

Apart from food rations, at least from the Middle Kingdom on, remuneration and reward for military service consisted of goods, land endowments, and cattle. Later sources leave no doubt that a share of the eventual booty was a most promising incentive for joining the army. Thus, reward materialized not only in the "gold of honor" granted by the king as a mark of distinction, but also in slaves and foreign goods. Land allocated to soldiers was probably exempted from taxes, in analogy with endowment customs known from the first millennium BCE. According to Greek historians, members of the military class of the Late period, called *machimoi* in Greek, received tax-exempt plots of land of twelve *aruras* each (33,078 square meters) in return for a rotating military service on a one-year basis.

Bravery and skills were the basis for appointment into the higher echelons of the professional army, for Egyptians and foreigners alike. Veteran top officers often entered the high bureaucracy.

Weaponry. Weapons industries were the business of the government. The most common projectiles—arrowheads made of stone—could be produced everywhere in the Nile Valley and whenever they were needed. State workshops were established for weapons requiring more complicated means of production. Early in the New Kingdom these workshops were attached to the temples, but they subsequently became part of the royal treasury and military headquarters. In the New Kingdom, one big arsenal, the fort of Sile, was situated at Egypt's northeastern border and functioned as the point of departure for campaigns in Palestine and Syria.

Throughout Egyptian history, bow and spear, and from the Middle Kingdom also the javelin, were the prominent long-range weapons. Maces, clubs, axes, and daggers—later, also the sword and the scimitar—were used for hand-to-hand combat. The first real cutting weapon, the long sword made of bronze or iron, did not appear in Egypt until the late second millennium BCE. The Old Kingdom simple bow, made of a single pole of lithe wood, was replaced at the beginning of the New Kingdom by the more highly developed Near Eastern composite bow, constructed of several glued layers of wood, horn, sinew,

and bone. The production of projectiles also became more sophisticated: while spearheads and arrowheads were first made of flintstone and bone, bronze soon became the primary material. In the later New Kingdom, the shape of projectile points varied greatly, depending on their intended impact when penetrating their target.

Although in official display the weaponry depicted in use by Egyptian soldiers does not show any significant changes until the New Kingdom, archaeological evidence shows that already during the Middle Kingdom more advanced metallurgy and weapon industries of the Near East had entered Egypt through cultural exchange or as booty. Besides the most striking weapon of Near Eastern origin—the light, two-wheeled chariot drawn by a team of horses—significant Middle Kingdom imports were javelins with socketed heads, chisel-shaped axes, and so-called duck-bill axes. This discrepancy between representational and archaeological evidence makes it advisable to treat iconographic data with the utmost caution. In a culture where tradition and iconicity ruled the artistic media, outdated modes may have dominated official display, even in cases in which they had probably already been abandoned and replaced by more modern imports. In the military sphere, this holds especially true for defensive weapons and body armor. Excavations at Piramesse, for example, brought to light molds used for the production of bronze fittings of Hittite figure-eight and trapezoidal shields, but in royal war scenes, Egyptian soldiers are never represented holding this foreign shield type. The same lack of iconographic evidence characterizes the use of body armor developed in the Near East. Mentioned in an Egyptian booty list of the time of Thutmose III for the first time, heavy body armor was available only to the military elite, probably to the higher ranks of the chariotry; during the New Kingdom, however, it must have been more common than historical sources give us to believe. Armor was made of scales of bronze applied in closely packed rows on knee-length, short-sleeved leather or linen shirts. Gold and silver were used for ceremonial body armor reserved for the king and his family, while scales made of yellow and red glazed pottery probably imitated the more precious versions. Helmets arrayed with scales of boar's tusks imported from the Aegean were also part of the defensive armament. Apart from the Aegean type, there was also a double-horned, hemispherical helmet, known from contemporary war scenes; it was characteristic of the Shardanu, a "Sea People" who continuously raided Egypt's coast during the Ramessid period and formed special task forces in the Egyptian army once taken prisoner. Full body armor as developed in the Aegean probably did not enter the country before the twenty-sixth dynasty, when the first Greek mercenaries were established in Egypt.

[*See also* Battle of Kadesh: Sources; Foreign Incursions; Forts and Garrisons; Hittites; Hyksos; Imperialism; Kush; Lybia; Mitanni; Nubia; Persia; Royal Roles; Sea Peoples; *and* Syria-Palestine.]

BIBLIOGRAPHY

Berlev, Oleg, D. "Les prétendus 'citadins' au Moyen Empire." *Revue d'Égyptologie* 23 (1971), 23–48. Discusses the military organization of the Middle Kingdom.

Bietak, Manfred. *Avaris, the Capital of the Hyksos: Recent Excavations at Tell el-Dab'a.* London, 1996. An introduction to the history and archaeology of the Second Intermediate Period.

Christophe, Louis-A. "L'organisation de l'armée égyptienne à l'époque Ramesside." *Revue du Caire* 39 (1957), 387–405. Organization and structure of the Egyptian army in Ramessid times.

Curto, Silvio. *The Military Art of the Ancient Egyptians.* Turin, 1971.

Darnell, John Coleman. "The *kbn.wt* Vessels of the Late Period." In *Life in a Multi-cultural Society: Egypt from Cambyses to Constantine and Beyond,* edited by Janet H. Johnson, pp. 67–89. Studies in Ancient Oriental Civilization, 51. Chicago, 1992. Egyptian warships during the Late period and the controversy of the introduction of the Greek trireme to Egypt.

Drews, Robert. *The End of the Bronze Age: Changes in Warfare and the Catastrophe ca. 1200 B.C.* Princeton, 1993. A detailed analysis of the impact of the Sea Peoples' migrations within the Mediterranean world at the end of the second millennium BCE. Notwithstanding its broad historical and archaeological basis, this book's argument—that the disappearance of long-established cultures was rooted solely in their technological backwardness—seems problematic.

Eyre, Christopher J. "Work and the Organisation of Work in the Old Kingdom." In *Labor in the Ancient Near East,* edited by M. Powell, pp. 5–47. New Haven, 1987.

Gnirs, Andrea M. "Ancient Egypt." In *War and Society in the Ancient and Medieval Worlds: Asia, the Mediterranean, Europe, and Mesoamerica,* edited by Kurt Raaflaub and Nathan Rosenstein, pp. 73–107. Cambridge, Mass., 1999. A general introduction to the history of Egyptian warfare.

Kendall, Timothy. *Kerma and the Kingdom of Kush, 2500–1500 B.C.: The Archaeological Discovery of an Ancient Nubian Empire.* Washington, D.C., 1997.

Landström, Björn. *Ships of the Pharaohs: 4000 Years of Egyptian Shipbuilding.* Garden City, N.Y., 1970.

Liverani, Mario. *Prestige and Interest: International Relations in the Near East ca. 1600–1100 B.C.* Padua, 1990. With a strong focus on Egypt during the New Kingdom, discusses ideological attitudes as well as various aspects of intercultural relations including warfare and diplomacy among the powers of the Near East during the late second millennium. Besides its illuminating historical analysis, this volume also provides extensive specific bibliography.

Leahy, Anthony. "The Libyan Period in Egypt." *Libyan Studies* 16 (1985): 51–65. A socio-historical essay on the Libyan element in Egyptian society from the end of the New Kingdom.

Littauer, Mary, and J. H. Crouwel. *Wheeled Vehicles and Ridden Animals in the Ancient Near East.* Leiden, 1979.

Müller, Dieter. "Some Remarks on Wage Rates in the Middle Kingdom." *Journal of Near Eastern Studies* 34.4 (1975), 249–263.

Redford, Donald B. *Egypt, Canaan, and Israel in Ancient Times.* Princeton, 1992. A diachronic study of international relations in the ancient Near East, with emphasis on the late second and the first millennium BCE.

Säve-Söderbergh, Torgny. *The Navy of the Eighteenth Egyptian Dynasty.* Uppsala, 1946.

Sandars, Nancy K. *The Sea Peoples: Warriors of the Ancient Mediterranean, 1250–1150 B.C.* Rev. ed. London, 1985.

Schulman, Alan R. "The Battle Scenes of the Middle Kingdom." *Journal of the Society for the Study of Egyptian Antiquities* 12 (1982), 165–183. Presents iconographical and historical evidence on warfare during the Middle Kingdom.

Schulman, Alan R. "Chariots, Chariotry and the Hyksos." *Journal of the Society for the Study of Egyptian Antiquities* 10.2 (1979), 105–163.

Shaw, Ian. "Battle in Ancient Egypt: The Triumph of Horus or the Cutting Edge of the Temple Economy?" In *Battle in Antiquity,* edited by Alan B. Lloyd, pp. 239–269. London, 1996. A historical overview of Ancient Egyptian warfare and its political implications.

Shaw, Ian. *Egyptian Warfare and Weapons.* Buckinghamshire, 1991. A short, general introduction.

Smith, Stuart T. *Askut in Nubia: The Economics and Ideology of Egyptian Imperialism in the Second Millennium B.C.* London and New York, 1995. Discusses Egyptian foreign policy in Nubia until the beginning of the New Kingdom on the basis of the archaeological record of Askut, a Middle Kingdom fort in Nubia.

Spalinger, Anthony. "The Military Background of the Campaign of Piye (Piankhy)." *Studien zur Altägyptischen Kultur* 7 (1979), 273–301. A historical analysis of Egypt's political situation at the end of the Third Intermediate Period and its military encounters with the Nubian kingdom of Kush.

ANDREA M. GNIRS

Materiel

From the Nile Valley's earliest residents, Paleolithic hunter-gatherers, to the armies of the Third Intermediate Period, military weaponry played a central role in the life, economy, and culture of ancient Egypt. People's need to hunt for food, as well as to protect themselves from wild animals and hostile individuals, required continuous development and improvement of weaponry from whatever resources were available.

From the Paleolithic to Early Dynastic times, weapons were made of wood, bone, and stone, and there was no difference between implements used for hunting or warfare. Although copper began to be used in Egypt toward the end of Neolithic times, lithic materials continued to be preferred for weaponry well into the Old Kingdom, and beyond that for certain weapons. There is evidence that siege weaponry was used in earlier periods, but in the New Kingdom, as Egypt expanded its hegemony south into Nubia and north into Asia, siege equipment was more consistently utilized.

Hand-held Offensive Weapons. Those weapons used in hand-to-hand combat and not designed to be thrown or slung in some manner are classified as "hand-held."

Sticks and clubs. Various sticks are depicted in the hands of fighters and hunters on the famous painting from tomb 100 in Naqada, dated c.3300 BCE. Some of the sticks are curved at the top, not unlike a shepherd's crook, and others are forked at the bottom, like the *w3s* and *d'm* staffs of later times. In time, these crude weapons gave way to more sophisticated ones, although the *w3s* and *d'm* continued with more symbolic significance. The word for "club" was probably *3ms*, judging from the determinative used.

Maces. The mace, a stick with a stone mounted on its end, is attested very early in Egypt. The principal word for mace is *ḥd*, which is attested as early as the Old Kingdom; earlier, it was probably restricted to the pear-shaped mace, based upon the determinative used in the writing of this word. Another word, *mnw*, is used for the disk-shaped mace, to judge from the determinative used.

The mace, seen in the hand of Narmer as he is dispatching the enemy chieftain (on the Narmer Palette), continued as a weapon. In the Late period, including Greco-Roman times, kings are shown brandishing maces in the head-smiting motif on temple walls. Disc- and oval-shaped mace heads are found in the Naqada I and II periods. Pear-shaped maces are found from as early as the fifth millennium BCE at Merimde, a Neolithic site in the Nile Delta. This form of mace head occurs on the famous Hunters' Palette from the late Predynastic period (c.3200 BCE). The large carved ceremonial mace heads of Kings Scorpion and Narmer are also pear-shaped. This shape continued to be used through pharaonic history and beyond: the royal head-smiting scenes, from Narmer to those depicting Roman emperors, consistently display it. The mace (and club) probably had a more ceremonial function after the Old Kingdom, despite Thutmose III's boast on the Gebel Barkal stela regarding his victories in the Near East: "It was my mace (*ḥd*) which overthrew the Asiatics [Near Easterners], my club (*3ms*) which smote the Nine Bows."

Axes. The earliest form of ax was the hand-held implement from Paleolithic times, in Egypt going back to c.100,000 B.P. When the stone blade was first affixed to a handle is not known, but at that point of development the ax became a deadly weapon. The earliest portrayal of an ax, on the Hunters' Palette, shows a figure-eight-shaped double blade. During the Old Kingdom copper blades were introduced. The ax blades were long and rounded, as evidenced by those used by soldiers in the battle scene from the sixth dynasty tomb of Inta at Deshesheh. This type of blade was still in use during the Middle Kingdom, as evidenced in the tomb of Senbi at Meir. During the Old Kingdom a semicircular blade was also used, for example by soldiers in a siege scene from the sixth dynasty tomb of Khaemwaset at Saqqara. It is this blade that is pictured in writing the Egyptian word *mibt* ("ax"), which is found as early as the third dynasty. In the Middle Kingdom the word *mibt* is replaced by *minb*, but the same determinative is used, as it is in the New Kingdom. From the twelfth dynasty on, the word *3khw* is found; written with a different sign. The duck-bill blade is the ax shown in the tomb

of Khnumhotep at Beni Hasan, where it is carried by the Asiatics (Near Easterners) entering Egypt. This blade was at home in Bronze Age Syria-Palestine. In the two Old Kingdom battle scenes mentioned above, the ax is use by Egyptian soldiers against their enemies and to hack up the city wall. In the New Kingdom, the blade, like the ceremonial one of King Ahmose, is much more narrowly shaped.

Spears. Hand-held stabbing weapons, based on lithic blades that have survived, can be traced back to Paleolithic times. The earliest artistic representation of a spear is on the Hunters' Palette. Spears were regularly used in military contexts in later times as well: for example, the Egyptian soldiers on Hatshepsut's mission to Punt are shown carrying spears and shields on the Deir el-Bahri reliefs, as are troops following Tutankhamun as he drives his chariot on the "painted box." Some of the Near Eastern men carry spears in the Beni Hasan tomb painting, and the Shasu-Bedouin in the Sety I reliefs at Karnak brandish spears and axes against Egyptian forces. Spears were ideally suited as a defensive weapons in siege warfare; Syrian-Canaanite defenders can be seen jabbing at Egyptian troops trying to scale city walls in siege scenes from the Ramessid era. The principal Egyptian word for "spear" is *ḥnty*.

Lances. In essence, the lance is a type of spear with a much longer shaft, although the blades could also be significantly longer than spear blades. Such a weapon appears in siege scenes from the Middle Kingdom Beni Hasan tombs, in which a portable defensive structure covers a group of soldiers who attack a fortified city with a large lance, in the manner of a battering ram. The lance also served hunters to finish off a wounded animal while standing on a chariot; a dramatic hunting relief from Medinet Habu depicts Ramesses III stabbing a downed wild bull.

Swords and daggers. These two implements were of great military importance throughout pharaonic times. These weapons are similar in construction but different in length and usage. A sword is generally defined as longer than 40.5 centimeters, and a dagger is shorter. [The advent of metallurgy appears to have been closely connected to the development of the sword and dagger.] The primary words for dagger are *mtpnt* and *b(3)gsw*; however, the hieroglyph *tp*, meaning "first," probably derives from an archaic word for "dagger" and occurs as early as the first dynasty. The third dynasty relief of King Sekhemkhet at Wadi Maghara (Sinai) shows a dagger tucked in the monarch's belt. These early daggers were made of copper and had no midrib. The dagger's usefulness as a weapon would have been in hand-to-hand combat, and it enjoyed continued use throughout Egyptian history, typically appearing on the person of the king. The surviving daggers of royalty, like those of Tutankhamun and Ahmose, which have gold blades and highly ornate handles, probably had a more ceremonial than practical function.

As copper gave way to bronze in the third millennium BCE, daggers in Egypt evolved into swords. Surviving examples from the Middle Kingdom look exactly like the daggers of earlier centuries. Swords, however, did not enjoy wide usage in Egypt until the New Kingdom. Longer double-edged swords appear to have come to Egypt from Anatolia, where experimentation with iron swords can be traced back to the early third millennium BCE. Such swords appear in Egypt in the hands of Aegean mercenaries serving in the Egyptian army in the Ramessid period and in the hands of the Sea Peoples during their invasion of Egypt. During the New Kingdom, the words *msw* and *nkn* occur meaning "sword." Such swords were used for both stabbing and thrusting.

Sickle swords. The other type of sword found in the New Kingdom is the sickle sword (*ḫpš*), which is written by depicting the actual sword for the determinative. The curved shape of this blade gives it its name. It is different from the more recent Arab and Turkish scimitar, in which the sharpened edge is on the outside of the curvature, whereas the cutting edge of the *ḫpš*, is on the inside of the C-shaped blade. It was used for hacking, not for stabbing; in fact, its point was not sharp. It is the hacking usage of this weapon that has led some experts on military weaponry to propose that the sickle sword evolved from the ax. The sickle sword, attested as early as 2500 BCE in Mesopotamia, is found in Egypt beginning in the New Kingdom and was particularly popular in the Ramessid era.

Medium-Range Weapons. These weapons are thrown; long-range weapons, by contrast, are propelled. Medium-range weapons allowed an individual to attack another individual or a fortified structure from a distance. No doubt the earliest and most readily available such weapons were unworked stones, thrown at or dropped from a height on an attacker. The latter practice continued throughout Egyptian history; siege scenes from the eleventh and twelfth dynasties show defenders on city walls hurling stones at attackers.

Throw sticks. These wooden implements come in several forms: some are made of a round narrow branch, and others are wider and flatter. The latter type looks much like an Australian boomerang. An interesting statement in the *Story of Sinuhe* suggests that these weapons did return when thrown. Commenting on Sinuhe's flight to western Asia and subsequent return to Egypt, King Senwosret I says, "Look, Sinuhe has returned as an Asiatic." The word for "Asiatic" (ʿꜣm) is written, as it always is, with the throw-stick determinative, the word being a homonym for throw-stick (ʿꜣm/ʿmꜣ), which uses the same sign. The

statement suggests that throw-stick returned to the thrower if it did not hit an object. The stick with the narrower surface was not designed to return.

The throw-stick was typically used for fowling in marshes. The small golden shrine of Tutankhamun portrays the king flinging his throw-stick in a marsh scene, a motif known as early as the Old Kingdom. Among the scores of weapons and implements found in the tomb of Tutankhamun was a collection twenty-one throw-sticks, demonstrating that the fowling scene on the shrine is not just a meaningless artistic motif.

As early as the Hunters' Palette, some of the men hold throw-sticks in their upraised hands, as if ready to throw them. If this weapon could be used in hunting larger land animals, then it surely could be used in military contexts. As evidence for the latter, among the soldiers attacking a walled city in the tomb of Khety from Beni Hasan are several who are hurling throw-sticks. Interestingly, the sticks are shown with the round part out rather pointing toward the thrower, as is the method used with the Australian boomerang. In addition, two of the Asiatics in the troop shown in Khnumhotep scene at Beni Hasan are shown carrying throw-sticks along with a spear and a bow. Soldiers depicted on reliefs from Hatshepsut's funerary temple at Deir el-Bahri bear throw-sticks, and a servant in the eighteenth dynasty tomb of Kenamun in western Thebes is depicted carrying a bow-case in one hand and a boomerang in the other. Thus, there is ample evidence that throw-sticks (or boomerangs) were used as military weapons in most periods of Egyptian history.

Javelins. While the spear is a thrusting weapon, the javelin is a smaller spear that is used for throwing. Its range, however, was limited to the strength of the warrior who threw it. The *Story of Sinuhe* well illustrates the limitations of the javelin. When the champion of Retenu duels with Sinuhe, the attacker has an armful of javelins (*nsyw*) which fall short of hitting the Egyptian hero; meanwhile, Sinuhe is able to cut him down with an arrow from his bow. Large quivers for carrying javelins are painted on walls of twelfth dynasty Beni Hasan tombs. Beginning with the nineteenth dynasty, quivers for javelins were mounted on royal chariots. Sety I, in a battle scene at Karnak, is poised to throw a javelin at a Libyan chieftain.

Long-Range Weapons. This class includes those that rely on some means of propelling a ballista (or missile) a distance that exceeds the effective range of medium-range weapons. Inasmuch as there is no evidence from pharaonic times that catapulting devices were used, the bow and sling served as artillery.

Bows and arrows. Although the bow is the most sophisticated long-range weapon in ancient Egypt, it has a long history. Small projectile points from the Paleolithic (c.40,000–30,000 years ago), the Aterian industry, appear to be too early to have been arrowheads. Alternatively, these may have been points for a primitive type of dart or javelin that was hand-thrown. The origin of the bow and arrow can be securely dated to the Late Paleolithic period, c. 10,000–12,000 BCE (Hoffman 1979, p. 67). The archers depicted on the Hunters' Palette either hold the bow in one hand and clutch three arrows in the other, or they stand with the arrow notched and ready for firing. These earliest depicted bows are double convex in shape and look like the hieroglyphs used for writing the words *pdt* and *iwn*. Another type of bow from predynastic and early dynastic times is the arcus, with only a single curvature. Made of a single piece of wood, these bows are called "simple" or "self" bows. They continued in use well into the New Kingdom, long after the introduction of the more powerful composite bow.

The origins of the composite bow, made from laminated wood, horn, and sinew, remain problematic. Not until sometime in the New Kingdom does the composite bow make its appearance in Egypt. An incised block from Mari, dating to the Early Dynastic period, contains the earliest known illustration of a composite bow. It is thought that the composite bow gradually worked its way around the Fertile Crescent and was introduced to Egypt by the Hyksos. This view is tempting, but evidence is lacking. In fact, after decades of excavations at Tell ed-Dab'a, the Hyksos capital Avaris, no bows have come to light, though the tombs of warriors have revealed other weapons.

Composite bows are distinguishable in artistic representations from self bows by their somewhat triangular shape when not drawn. When fully drawn, the tips of the bow curl out. Another discernible difference between the two is the method of attaching the string to the tips. The string on the self-bow is wrapped around the tip many times, while the composite bow has notches on the tips where looped strings were secured.

The combination of materials is what gave the composite bow its strength. It had an effective range of 160 to 175 meters (500 to 600 feet) and, according to classical sources, an exceptional shot could attain a distance of 500 meters (1500 feet!). The power of this bow enabled arrows with larger, bronze heads to be used. Surely the deadly force of the composite bow affected the nature of warfare in many ways, including the need to develop body armor.

Because of the laminate construction of composite bows, they were sensitive to heat and moisture and thus were usually stored in cases. Two types of cases are attested in New Kingdom Egypt: one was carried, and the other was attached to the body of a war chariot. These could be made of leather or wood, and ornamented, as is the surviving case from the tomb of Tutankhamun. A larger bow-shaped box was also found in this tomb which contained seven composite bows, as well as throw-sticks, clubs, sticks, and arrows. This bow box is called "unique" by the antiquarian archery expert W. E. McLeod (1982, p. 61).

During the New Kingdom, the composite bow gradually replaced the self-bow as the weapon of choice in battle. However, the self-bow continued to be used, especially in hunting contexts. Retaining the older type of weapon in the hunt may be attributed to the sense of sport and tradition that goes with hunting. Arrows consist of three parts: arrowhead, shaft, and fletching. To be effective, arrows had to be made of a light, straight material. In Egypt, a reed of some sort was the usual material, although wooden shafts have also survived. Until the New Kingdom nocks were cut into the shaft, but starting in the eighteenth dynasty, wood, bone, or ivory nocks were inserted into the shaft.

The introduction of metals did not completely replace lithic points. Flint projectiles were easy to produce, cheap, and effective. Included in the cache of weapons in the tomb of Tutankhamun were more than three hundred arrows of seven different types. Most were reed-type with bronze and wedge-shaped or chisel-shaped flint points. There were also nine reed arrows with ivory tips. Some arrows made of wood were sharpened to a point, while others flared to a blunted tip; the latter was apparently used for hunting fowl. There are a number of words for arrow—*šsr, stw, swnt,* and *'h3w*—but whether these terms denote different arrow types is not clear. Arrows from ancient Egypt have been found with and without fletching. By adding feathers to the end of the shaft, the arrow obtained greater stability and accuracy. Two, three, and four vanes of feathers have been found on Egyptian arrows.

The quiver makes its appearance in Egypt during the Middle Kingdom, apparently introduced from Syria-Palestine (Yadin 1963, p. 165). This view is supported by the fact that the Egyptian word for "quiver" (*ispt*) is etymologically related to Semitic terms for "quiver": *ispatu* (Akkad.), *'spt* (Ugar.) and *'asppah* (Heb.)

Slings and stones. As a boy, the king of Israel, David (c.1000 BCE), was not the only warrior in the Near East to realize that the sling-and-stone was an effective, inexpensive weapon. Slings were used from the Tigris-Euphrates region to the Nile Valley. They were made from a variety of materials. Discovered in the tomb of Tutankhamun was a sling made of linen. Palm fibers are used by present-day Egyptian peasants and may have been used in ancient times too. Middle Kingdom scenes from Beni Hasan show slingers standing alongside archers attacking a fortified city, indicating the effective range of the sling.

It has been estimated, based on ethnographic study of slingers in the Middle East, that a speed of 100 to 150 miles per hour could be attained by an accomplished slinger, and a target at a distance of 50 meters (150 feet) could easily be struck.

Personal Defensive Equipment

Parrying stick. Military history is essentially the record of developing new and improved weaponry for which countermeasures followed; each weapon had its defensive counterpart. Perhaps the earliest defensive weapon in hand-to-hand combat was the parrying stick, or *mks,* which was used to blunt the blows of a stick, club, or mace. Tomb 100 from Hierakonpolis shows two warriors fighting, both brandishing sticks; one figure has a shorter (parrying) stick for a defense, while the other has what appears to be an animal-hide shield. Certainly by the first dynasty, the parrying stick had a nodule that served as a guard to protect the defender's hand. In most scenes in which a monarch carries a mace, including head-smiting ones, he usually holds a parrying stick in the left hand.

Shields. Shields were primarily a defensive implement against the spear, sword, and dagger. The black-and-white painted shields in models and painted scenes in pharaonic times indicate that cowhides were probably the most common material. This observation is supported by the fact that the word *ikm,* "shield," is typically determined with a sign identified as a cowhide. Alternatively, there are examples of *ikm* from the New Kingdom with the sign for an ingot of metal, indicating that copper or bronze (depending on the period) was also used to cover shields. The tomb of Tutankhamun contained wooden shields, some of which had leather or animals skins over them. The combining of wood and leather made the shield a more effect defensive tool, and a metal protective surface would be especially useful against arrows fired from composite bows. Shields varied in size from relatively small to long enough for a man to stand behind. There are examples from the Middle Kingdom of soldiers wearing a type of body armor. Under straps that cross on a warrior's midsection, an oval shield is worn. This appears to be designed to protect soldiers against arrows.

Helmets. Helmets make their appearance in the eighteenth dynasty. The word for "helmet" is *dbn,* also written with the sign for an ingot of metal, suggesting that bronze was probably the material used for helmets in the New Kingdom empire period. Surprisingly, battle scenes do not usually show Egyptian soldiers wearing helmets. Sherden mercenaries in Ramessid times are identified by their horned helmets. On the chariot of Thutmose IV, Canaanite charioteers are shown wearing helmets. The tomb of Kenamun contains a scene showing eight helmets along with a pair of chariots (and associated trappings),

shields, bows, and swords. The available evidence suggests that the helmet was closely connected to charioteers, possibly because they could not both drive a chariot and hold a shield for protection. The *ḫprš,* or blue crown, often worn by the pharaohs in military settings could have been a protective helmet.

Body armor. Coats of mail were developed for charioteers for the same reason as helmets were. The advent of the composite bow is another possible factor in the development of body armor. The above-mentioned scene from the tomb of Kenamun includes a detailed painting of a coat of mail; its gold color suggests that bronze was the metal from which the scales were made. Some surviving bronze scales from Amenhotpe III's palace at Malkata in western Thebes confirm this interpretation. Canaanite charioteers wear scaled armor in the Thutmose IV chariot. In one instance, an arrow has penetrated the back of the shoulder of an escaping warrior, showing that mail armor was not completely effective. The booty list of the *Annals* of Thutmose III includes a "a fine, bronze coat (*mss*) for fighting." The use of the "leather" determinative with *mss* indicates that bronze scales were secured to a leather garment; such garments were also made of linen, as a fragment of cloth on the Malkata scales reveals.

Mobility

Navy. Mobility is essential to a successful military, regardless of the period of history. Because the Nile played such an important role in transportation, the navy was vital to moving supplies and personnel north and south, and out to the Mediterranean for campaigns to the Levant. Not until the New Kingdom did the Egyptian navy become more than just a means of transporting troops (Säve-Söderbergh 1946). The biography of Ahmose Si Abena of Elkab traces the career of a navy man who moved up through the ranks. His reports about battles against the Hyksos demonstrate that he was directly involved in actual combat and not just in transport duties. Reliefs of the Sea Peoples invasion of Egypt by sea feature the Egyptian navy in pitched battle against this maritime coalition, with Egyptian archers firing arrows at the enemy's armada.

Chariotry. Much of Egypt's military success, which enabled it to establish its empire in the Near East, must be attributed to its chariotry. The wheel was known in Egypt prior to the New Kingdom, but the chariot does not appear in Egyptian records until the beginning of the eighteenth dynasty. Wheeled vehicles are first attested in Sumer as early as the end of the fourth millennium BCE and are more widely known there in the succeeding millennium and a half; it is generally believed that the horse and chariot were subsequently introduced to Anatolia, Syria, and Palestine prior to arrival in Egypt with the Hyksos. W. M. Flinders Petrie believed that the Hyksos were able to overwhelm Egypt easily because they possessed the chariot, but this understanding, though frequently averred in the secondary literature, lacks archeological support.

After two decades of excavations at Tell ed-Dab'a, no traces of chariots have been found, and only some horse teeth from the latest Hyksos period (seventeenth dynasty) have been discovered. King Kamose of Thebes in his stela brags that he will take away the *ti nt ḥtry* of the Hyksos monarch. While this expression has been translated "chariotry," the hieroglyphic determinative for "chariot" is absent, raising a question as to whether "chariotry" is the correct translation. Furthermore, it has been argued that the context of Kamose's boast does not support this interpretation (Schulman, 1980, pp. 111–113). Consequently, the first unambiguous reference to a chariot in Egyptian literature is found in the tomb biography of Ahmose Si Abena, who refers to following the chariot of King Ahmose on foot while campaigning against Avaris. Thanks to an important discovery of painted fragments from a funerary structure of King Ahmose at Abydos in the early 1990s, evidence now exists showing Egyptian chariotry in action. Another fragment depicts a fallen warrior in Syro-Canaanite attire. These fragments make it clear that horses and chariots were in use in the late seventeenth and early eighteenth dynasties, substantiating Ahmose Si Abena's claim. Presently, the archaeological record does not precisely tell us when the chariot arrived in Egypt, or under what circumstance.

The most common word for "chariot" is *wrr(y)t*, which is found in the Ahmose text and continued in used throughout the New Kingdom and beyond. Unlike the word for "horse," *ssm(t)*, whose etymology is Semitic (*sûs* in Hebrew or *sisu* in Akkadian), *wrr(y)t* does not derive from a Semitic root. Although an Indo-European root cannot be ruled out for *wrr(y)t*, it looks like an Egyptian word. Only a century into the eighteenth dynasty is the common Semitic term for "chariot" (*mrkbt*) found in Egyptian texts, and then rather infrequently; and it never supersedes *wrr(y)t*. The term *ḥtry*, meaning "chariotry," a distinct military unit, does not occur until the time of Amenhotpe III. Prior to this, *ḥtry* applies to a yoke or span of draft animals (which was likely intended in the Kamose text), oxen or horses, and hence "chariot."

First and foremost, the chariot is a vehicle for speedily transporting the rider. Since chariots (and horses) were costly, their use was limited to royalty, aristocracy, and the military elite. The Egyptian chariot was light enough that even a single man could carry a chariot, and it could be placed on boats for transport.

The chariot was closely linked with the military, although it had less strategic value than is commonly thought (Schulman 1980, pp. 114–120). Essentially, a chariot provided a moving platform from which an archer could shoot at the enemy, and it could be used in mopping-up operations and chasing down fleeing infantry. There were distinct terms for "chariot warrior" (*snny*) and "charioteer" (*ḳṯn*). The Egyptian chariot as a military vehicle was always equipped with a bow case (even during the Amarna period), and, in the nineteenth and twentieth dynasties, a case for holding javelins was added. The tombs of Amenmose and Kenamun in the Theban necropolis display equipment a charioteer would typically use, including bow, quiver, sword, whip, and helmet.

The chariot was primarily connected to military activity. Nevertheless, hunting was a favorite sport of Egyptian royalty and nobility, and both can be seen pursuing desert game while riding in their chariots. The horses are shown in the same rearing stance found in military scenes where the king attacks his enemies. The kings of the eighteenth dynasty, especially Amenhotpe II (Sphinx Stela) and Amenhotpe III (Hunt Scarab), boasted about their hunting prowess. The sportsman motif, where the king is shown hunting on a chariot, is popular throughout the New Kingdom: it occurs on several objects from the tomb of Tutankhamun. During the Ramessid era and down to the reliefs of Ramesses III at his funerary temple, Medinet Habu, the chariot-hunter motif remained popular.

The chariot can be divided into three parts: the body; the yoke, saddles and harness; and the bridle. Information about these components can be gleaned from numerous painted scenes and reliefs. In addition, a number of chariots have actually survived, including six from the tomb of Tutankhamun, the body of one belonging to Thutmose IV, the chariot of Yuya—all of which are on display in the Cairo Museum—and one in the museum in Florence, Italy. A number of eighteenth dynasty tombs (e.g., Puyemre, Menkheperresenb, and Hepu) contain workshop scenes in which artisans prepare, shape, and carve wood, as well as tanning and cutting leather for various components of the chariot.

Analysis of the chariot in the Florence museum shows that the body, yoke, wheel hub, and saddle yokes were made of elm, which most likely came from the Lebanon-Syria area (Botti 1951, pp. 192–198). Birch was found in the axle, wheel, and floor. The pole was made of willow, while the wheel spokes were of plum. None of these trees is indigenous to Egypt; the closest source of birch is eastern Anatolia. These different foreign woods demonstrate that a complex international trade system furnished the materials for making chariots in Egypt. Local leather was used for the bridle and harness. The floor of the chariot was made of rawhide thongs that were secured on a frame, arranged like the strings of a snowshoe, so that the floor could sustain the weight of the occupants while being extremely light. Leather straps were also wrapped around the wheel to help hold it together and provide a bit of cushion between the wooden wheel and the hard ground. The bodies of chariots, especially those of royalty, could be decorated with gold foil, making the vehicle splendid indeed.

The earliest chariots in Egypt had four-spoked wheels. The transition to the six-spoked wheel, which became standard during the second half of the eighteenth dynasty, was reached after brief experimentation with the eight-spoked wheel, which is found during the reigns of Thutmose III and Thutmose IV. Except for a few anomalies, such as a chariot scene of Akhenaten where an eight-spoked wheel is seen, the six-spoked wheel prevailed into the Third Intermediate Period (1069–650 BCE; cf. Spalinger 1981, pp. 52–53). It has been suggested that the reason for the move from four to six spokes was the addition of the chariot warrior to the chariot during the time of Thutmose III (Hoffmeier 1976, pp. 43–45); the additional weight on the chariot would have necessitated a stronger wheel.

The chariot may not have originated in Egypt, but during the New Kingdom, Egypt mastered its use and construction. Consequently, even in later periods Egyptian chariots were in demand in the Levant. During the twenty-first dynasty, King Solomon of Israel was a middleman in the trade of Egyptian chariots and horses to Syria and Anatolia (*1 Kings* 10.28–29).

[*See also* Equines; *and* Ships and Shipbuilding.]

BIBLIOGRAPHY

Arnold, D., and J. Settgast. "Erster Vorbericht über die vom Deutschen Archäologischen Insitut Kairo im Asasif unternommenen Arbeiten." *Mitteilungen des Deutschen Archäologischen Instituts, Abteilung Kairo* 20 (1965), 47–61.
Bonnet, Hans. *Die Waffen der Völker des alten Orients.* Leipzig, 1926.
Botti, G. "Il carro del sogno." *Aegyptus* 31 (1951), 192–198.
Gardiner, Alan H. *Egyptian. Grammar.* 3d ed. Oxford, 1969.
Harvey, Stephen. "Monuments of Ahmose at Abydos." *Egyptian Archaeology* 4 (1994), 3–5.
Hayes, W. C. *The Scepter of Egypt.* 2 vols. New York, 1953, 1959.
Hoffmeier, James. "Hunting Desert Game with the Bow: A Brief Examination." *Society for the Study of Egyptian Antiquities Newsletter* 6.2 (1975), 8–13.
Hoffmeier, James. "The Evolving Chariot Wheel in the 18th Dynasty." *Journal of the American Research Center in Egypt* 13 (1976), 43–45.
Hoffmeier, James. "Weapons of War." In *International Standard Bible Encyclopedia*, edited by G. W. Bromiley, vol. 4, pp. 1033–1043. Grand Rapids, Mich., 1988.
Hoffmeier, James. "The Chariot Scenes." In *The Akhenaten Temple Project*, edited by D. B. Redford, vol. 2, pp. 35–45. Toronto, 1988.
Littauer, M. A., and J. H. Crouwel. *Wheeled Vehicles and Ridden Animals in the Ancient Near East.* Leiden, 1979.
Littauer, M. A., and J. H. Crouwel. *Chariots and Related Equipment from the Tomb of Tut'ankhamun.* Oxford, 1985.
McLeod, W. E. *The Self Bows and Other Archery Tackle from the Tomb of Tutankhamun.* Oxford, 1982.
Sandars, N. K. "Later Aegean Swords." *American Journal of Archaeology* 67 (1963), 117–153.
Säve-Söderbergh, Torgny. *The Navy of the Eighteenth Egyptian Dynasty.* Uppsala, 1946.
Schulman, A. R. "Chariots, Chariotry and the Hyksos." *Journal of the Society for the Study of Egyptian Antiquities* 10 (1980), 105–153.
Schulman, A. R. "Egyptian Representations of Horsemen and Riding in the New Kingdom." *Journal of Near Eastern Studies* 16 (1957), 263–271.
Shaw, Ian. *Egyptian Warfare and Weapons.* Buckinghamshire, 1991.
Spalinger, A. J. 1981. "Notes on the Military in Egypt during the XXVth Dynasty." *Journal of the Society for the Study of Egyptian Antiquities* 11 (1981), 37–58.
Yadin, Yigael. *The Art of Warfare in Biblical Lands.* New York, 1963.
Yadin, Yigael. "The Earliest Representation of a Siege Scene and a 'Scythian Bow' from Mari." *Israel Exploration Journal* 22 (1972), 89–94.

JAMES K. HOFFMEIER

MILK. Cow's milk *irtt ḥdt* was highly valued and was by no means considered nourishment only for young children or medical patients. Milk's perishable nature and the low yield of Egyptian cows (1–4 liters/quarts), prevented it from being a staple food, however, although dairy cows were raised in rural areas for a village's self-sufficiency. The act of milking was portrayed on tombs and coffins; the cow's hind legs were bound, and the milk was drained from the udder side ways into wide bowls. Instead of massaging the udder to stimulate milk production, the calf was often tied to its mother's front leg. For transport and storage, the milk was poured into clay pitchers that had narrow openings sealed with foliage. The drinking of goat and donkey milk, mentioned in Egyptian medical texts, was rarely illustrated and seems to have been considered unpleasant.

It is unclear into which other products milk was processed: *smi* was probably curdled milk or curd, but possibly cream, since it was formed by letting the milk stand overnight. Aside from "fresh" *smi*, there was milk with salt added, to enhance taste and to support clotting (curdling). A relatively expensive commodity, *smi* was listed next to oils, fats, and honey as an offering. It was also mentioned in delivery documents for the *sed*-festival and as additional rations in *hin*-measures for workers. Whether real cheese was produced is questionable, despite its easy manufacture from letting curd stand and from pressing and despite its being familiar to the neighboring Near Eastern peoples. Other milk products were *sšr* ("whey"), *i₃tt* ("cream" ?), and *srw* (Demotic *sr*, Coptic *CIP*, "butter"). There are but two mentions of "new" vessels for setting milk. The boiling of milk was a peculiarity of bedouin cuisine. In medicine, milk and *smi* were primarily used as cough medicine. In the Horus and Seth myth, Hathor healed the wounded eye of Horus with gazelle milk. Preserved "marsh bowls," anthropomorphic

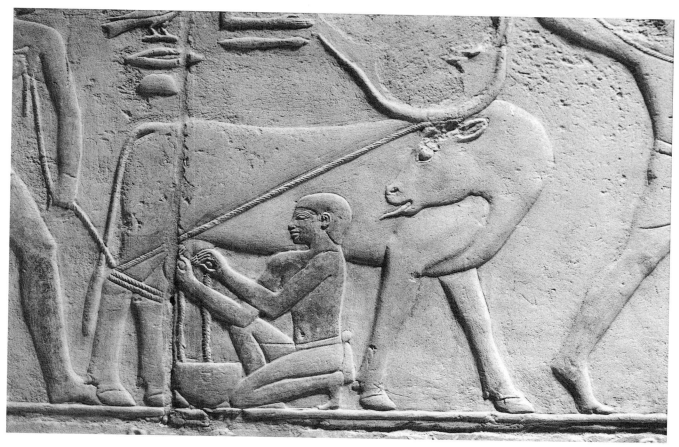

MILK. *Detail of a painted limestone relief featuring a protesting long-horned cow being restrained with a rope and milked.* From the tomb-chapel of the sixth dynasty vizier Kagemni at Saqqara. (© Patrick Francis Houlihan)

vessels with arms and perforated breasts, and others in the form of Taweret have, with some assurance, been identified as milk pitchers.

Milk had a widely religious significance. It symbolized purity and rejuvenation. Nursing by the sacred cows bestowed "divine status and royal status." In the New Kingdom, herds belonging to the temple and others imported from Syria and Nubia provided both cooked and fresh milk for feasts and offerings. For them, the king supplied pails, made of fine metals and copper, and he commissioned milk carriers. Large amounts of milk—more than two full pails—were used for the Sokar feast and the Nile offering. An unrelated ritual consisted of extinguishing torches in milk basins ("milk lakes") in the sanctuary of Deir el-Bahari; in the offering ritual, milk served as food. For the milk offerings of Greco-Roman times, milk was given metaphoric names, such as "sweetness," "life-blessing," "white Eye of Horus," and "perfection." For the Abaton rites, milk was brought daily to Osiris (in 365 bowls) and to the trees of the *mnt3* grove, as a libation, a custom that continued to influence the Meroitic offering tablets of the first and second centuries CE.

For the care of the dead, milk appeared on the offering list and in the name of estates. It was poured onto the ground in front of the coffin sled, for purposes of purification. In transfiguration texts, the dead wish for milk from divine cows, mainly those of Hesat and Sechat-Hor, who also appear as local deities.

BIBLIOGRAPHY

Bossneck, Joachim. *Die Tierwelt des Alten Ägypten.* Munich, 1988.

Darby, William J., Paul Ghalioungui, and Louis Grivetti. *Food: The Gift of Osiris.* New York, 1977.

Guglielmi, Waltraud. "Käse"; "Milch(wirtschaft)"; "Milchopfer"; and "Sauermilch." In *Lexikon der Ägyptologie,* vol. 4. Wiesbaden, 1982.

WALTRAUD GUGLIELMI

Translated from German by Elizabeth Schwaiger

MIN, the Greek form of the name of the god whom the Egyptians called Menu. One of the oldest of the Egyptian

MIN. *Relief sculpture of the god Amun-Min.* The supreme deity Amun is here identified with, and depicted as, the more ancient fertility god Min. This relief is from the eighteenth-dynasty Red Chapel of Hatshepsut and Thutmose III at Karnak, and is now at the Open Air Museum, Karnak. (© Photograph by Erich Lessing / Art Resource, NY)

deities, he was associated with fertility, and specifically, male sexual potency. He was also the god of the desert, especially the wastelands to the east of Coptos and Akhmim, his chief centers of worship. His protection was sought by those who traveled through those inhospitable regions in search of gold, perfumes, and incense in the lands toward Arabia, and he was specially revered by laborers who worked the Eastern Desert mines.

Min is one of the few Egyptian gods whose iconography can be traced into the Predynastic period. At that time, he was represented by an enigmatic emblem—a horizontal line with a disk in the center, flanked by two hemispherical projections. This symbol has been variously identified as a meteorite, a bolt of lightning, an arrow with barbs, the bolt of a door, or two fossilized shells. It appears on palettes, earthenware vessels, and mace heads, as well as on standards. Later, it was incorporated into the hieroglyph for Min's name and the symbol for the fifth nome of Upper Egypt, whose capital was Coptos. Among the earliest anthropomorphic representations of the god are three pillar-like colossal limestone statues excavated at the temple of Min at Coptos by W. M. Flinders Petrie, which date from the late fourth millennium BCE. Now in the British Museum, they are among the few examples of divine sculpture from the beginning of the Early Dynastic period. These damaged statues, executed in a strikingly minimalist manner, depict a male figure whose left hand grasps at a space formerly occupied by a stone phallus. The fifth dynasty Palermo Stone records that in the first dynasty a royal decree commanded a statue of Min to be carved; the sculpture was probably similar to the ones at Coptos. Much later, a Ptolemaic temple of Min and Isis (still extant) was built at Coptos by an official named Sennuu for Ptolemy II, and the Roman emperor Claudius constructed a small temple to Min, Isis, and Horus at el-Qal'a, to the north of Coptos.

The other chief center for the cult of Min was Akhmim, in the ninth nome, on the eastern bank of the Nile. There is a rock chapel dedicated to him at el-Salamuni, to the northeast of Akhmim, which was most likely the creation of the eighteenth dynasty king Thutmose III; it was decorated by Nakhtmin, the "First Prophet of Min." West of Akhmim were two companion temples dedicated to Min and Repyt (Triphis), the goddess who was considered to be his consort. Both temples probably date from the Greco-Roman period, but might possibly be older. There was also a temple of Isis and Min at Buhen in Upper Nubia, built by Thutmose's successor Amenhotpe II (the "North Temple"); it is now removed to Khartoum.

In pharaonic art, Min appears as a human figure, standing upright and wrapped as a mummy, holding his erect penis in his left hand. The earliest known example of this ithyphallic depiction is most likely an ink drawing on a stone bowl found in the tomb of Khasekhemy (died c.2687 BCE). The other iconographic characteristics of Min are the flail that he holds in his upraised right hand, and the distinctive crown that he wears; the crown is tall and double-plumed, with a long ribbon in the back. Later, Min's crown was taken over by Amun. Lettuce (*Lactuca sativa*) was associated with Min, possibly because it was believed to be an aphrodisiac or, perhaps, because of the resemblance that its milky sap bears to human semen. Lettuces are sometimes depicted on an offering table adjacent to the god, which stands between him and his sanctuary. Depictions of Min's sanctuary resemble the tents that desert-dwellers used, and New Kingdom reliefs on temple walls illustrate the ceremony of raising the tentpoles for Min. As lord of the Eastern Desert, Min was sometimes depicted in the company of gods of foreign origin, such as Reshep, Qedeshet, and Anat. Some scholars have identified him with the being described by the Pyramid Texts as "the one who raises his arm in the East." As an embodiment of male sexuality, Min was complemented by the goddess Hathor, who was associated with the libidinous aspects of the feminine.

During the Middle Kingdom, Min was assimilated into the Horus-myth. Sometimes he was identified as the son of Isis; at Abydos he was called "Min-Horus-the-victorious," the powerful conqueror of Seth. Alternately, Isis was pictured as his wife, with Horus as their child. By New Kingdom times, however, Min was equated with Amun, especially with the primordial creative aspect of the latter deity. Min-Amun-Re was given the appelation Kamutef, which literally means "bull of his mother"—that is, one who impregnates his own mother so that she gives birth to himself. This aspect of the supreme deity Amun, depicted exactly like the mummiform, ithyphallic Min, emphasized the eternal and self-subsistent character of divine and pharaonic power. A ceremony honoring Min, featuring a procession of a statue of the god, sometimes took place during the royal coronation as a means of ensuring the king's potency. Similar rituals occurred during *sed*-festivals (royal jubilees); a twelfth dynasty limestone relief now in the Petrie Museum in London shows Senwosret I celebrating his *sed*-festival, holding an oar, and (the inscription reads) "hastening by boat to Min, the god in the midst of the city." At Medinet Habu, the second court of the temple of Ramesses II (nineteenth dynasty) shows a similar festival, during which the pharaoh worships this agricultural divinity by harvesting a sheaf of wheat. Another ritual involved annointing a statue of the god with a life-giving mixture of bitumen and various burnt ingredients. Popular worship of Min was of a riotous nature. The Greeks associated him with Pan, their own rustic god of unbridled male *eros*, and during Ptolemaic times they renamed Akhmim as Panopolis ("Pan's city").

[*See also* Kamutef.]

BIBLIOGRAPHY

Bleeker, Claas J. *Die Geburt eines Gottes*. Leiden, 1956.
Gauthier, Henri. *Les fêtes du dieu Min*. Cairo, 1931.
Gauthier, Henri. *Le personnel du dieu Min*. Cairo, 1931.
Germer, Renate. "Die Bedeutung des Lattichs als Pflanze des Min." *Studien zur Altägyptischen Kultur* 8 (1980), 85–87.
Ogdon, J. R. "Some Notes on the Iconography of Min." *Bulletin of the Egyptological Seminar* 7 (1985–1986), 29–41.
Wilkinson, R. H. "Ancient Near Eastern Raised-arm Figures and the Iconography of the Egyptian God Min." *Bulletin of the Egyptological Seminar* 11 (1991–1992), 109–118.

EUGENE ROMANOSKY

MINERALS. Although the fertile soil of the Nile Valley is regarded as the basic factor for the emergence of the ancient Egyptian civilization, the rich and abundant variety of mineral resources in the deserts surrounding the narrow strip of cultivation also played an important role. If copper was the only mineral resource that was in any sense essential to Egypt's cultural development, few of the most striking characteristics of pharaonic culture—from mummification to cosmetics—could have come into be-

ing without the existence of an abundant and diverse supply of other minerals.

Sources of Metals. The Egyptians were able to obtain copper, gold, and tin (the last from cassiterite) within their own territory; silver, lead, and iron were, however, almost certainly obtained either through trade or pillaging. The principal Egyptian copper-producing regions were in the Eastern Desert (both Egyptian and Nubian), in the Sinai Peninsula, and in the Wadi Arabah region, 30 kilometers (25 miles) north of Eilat. Both native copper and copper ores were available. The copper mines at the Wadi Arabah constitute the earliest metallurgical workshop known, since they have been dated to the fifth or sixth millennium BCE by the associated Neolithic pottery of the Qatifian culture. Although the method of copper extraction was described by the site's archaeologists as unsophisticated, possibly iron ore was already being added, as flux, deliberately. These Chalcolithic (Copper Age) mining and metallurgical operations were probably undertaken by the local inhabitants of the southern Palestine area, rather than by Egyptians, yet Wadi Arabah was likely one of the main sources of copper used by Egyptians in the late Predynastic period.

By the Ramessid period (c.1307–1070 BCE) of the New Kingdom, Egyptians mined copper at the site of Timna in the Wadi Arabah (probably equatable with the Old Egyptian toponym Akita), and a chapel was constructed there for the goddess Hathor, who was particularly associated with mining and quarrying areas. Work seems to have stopped suddenly at Timna, during the reign of Ramesses V of the twentieth dynasty. Mining in the Late period is as yet unsupported by site evidence, despite the abundance of bronze statuettes of that date.

Based on analyses of Egyptian copper-containing ceramic glazes, the copper deposits in the southeastern part of Egypt's Eastern Desert were being exploited as early as the first dynasty. Dated to the Early Dynastic period and Old Kingdom, Wadi Dara is the site of one of the earliest known copper mining sites in Upper Egypt. It includes the remains of a miners' camp, comprising five or six separate workgangs, each with its own equipment for processing copper ore, to obtain the copper.

At Buhen, on the western bank of the Nile, near the Second Cataract, is the site of an Egyptian copper-working settlement, with evidence for its existence well before the nearby Middle Kingdom fortress; some seal impressions (and a number of somewhat ambiguous radiocarbon dates) suggest that copper was being processed at Buhen as early as the Early Dynastic period. Two sixth dynasty graffiti in the Wadi Allaqi indicate that Egyptians were exploiting Nubian gold at least as early as the Old Kingdom.

From the Old Egyptian terminology used to describe

the different types of gold, three basic regions are known: "gold of Koptos," from mines in Egypt's Eastern Desert, in the Wadi Hammamat to Abbad region; "gold of Wawat," from Nubia's Eastern Desert, via the Wadis Allaqi and Gabgaba; and "gold of Kush," from Sudan and Ethiopia. Surveys undertaken from 1989 to 1993 by a combined Egyptian Geological Survey and Munich University team studied about 130 ancient gold-mining sites in the Eastern Desert. There are scant archaeological traces of Predynastic and Early Dynastic exploitations of gold, but the few known sites are found throughout a large area of the Eastern Desert, some as far south as Lower Nubia (where the site of Deraheib in the Wadi Allaqi may even include a Neolithic gold-mining settlement). At least nineteen gold mines are known from the Old and Middle Kingdoms, including the important multiperiod mining site of Bakari, a few kilometers (miles) to the north of the Edfu–Marsa Alam road, where gold may have been mined continuously from the Predynastic period through medieval times. Bakari, which has only been cursorily investigated, may prove to be the gold-mining equivalent of the famous Timna copper mines, in terms of the opportunity to observe changing mining and processing strategies over long periods of time.

Most of the archaeological evidence for ancient Egyptian gold mining suggests that the principal sources during the Old Kingdom were in Egypt's Eastern Desert (i.e., the "gold of Koptos"). Nonetheless, a number of texts (e.g., the stela of Sa-Hathor, a gold-washer sent to Nubia in the reign of Amenemhet II) suggest that the "gold of Wawat" may have been an increasingly important source from the Middle Kingdom to the late New Kingdom. Given that the Koptos gold began once more to be mined in large quantities from at least the Ramessid period onward, it is not clear if the twelfth dynasty switch to the "gold of Wawat" (and perhaps also to the "gold of Kush") resulted from such factors as the temporary depletion of Egyptian gold or the lack of technological ability to exploit the known sources, or whether processes of political change caused Nubia to be, at certain periods, safer for Egyptian miners. The Turin Mining Papyrus, a twentieth dynasty map of gold mines and siltstone quarries (now in the Museo Egizio, Turin, Italy), probably shows the Bir Umm Fawakhir gold mines in the Wadi Hammamat and may, therefore, show Egypt's renewed interest in the "gold of Koptos" during the late New Kingdom.

During the Middle Kingdom, the primary functions of the string of twelfth dynasty Egyptian fortresses in the Second Cataract region of Nubia must have been military and commercial. At least a few served as bases for the procurement and processing of metals—as evidenced by copper slag heaps near Qubban, some gold-processing remains at Askut, the proximity of the Serra fortress to the

gold-mining region of Wadi Hagar Shams, and the presence of riverside gold mines at Saras and Duweishat (the latter probably dating to the twelfth dynasty).

During the New Kingdom, copper was imported from Alashiya (Cyprus), where the principal mines were located in the Troodos mountains. The use of Cypriot copper was indicated in textual references—by the depiction of ox-hide ingots in tomb paintings (showing the arrival of foreign tribute), such as in the eighteenth dynasty tomb of the vizier Rekhmire at Thebes—and also by finds of copper ingots in the Ulu Burun shipwreck (off the coast of Turkey), along with other products connected to both Cyprus and Egypt. Although both lead and silver could in theory have been extracted from galena (lead sulfide), an ore that occurs widely in the Eastern Desert, it seems that both metals were imported from an early date. The Egyptian galena may, then, have been used only as a source of black pigment for eye paint. Good quantities of iron ore, such as hematite and magnetite, also occurred in the Eastern Desert, the Western Desert, and the Sinai Peninsula (Bahariya Oasis, for example, still mined for the iron ores hematite, limonite, and goethite). During the pharaonic period, however, those deposits seem to have been exploited only for pigments or flux (for copper processing), rather than for the extraction of iron itself. Iron was processed and worked in the Late period, judging from W. M. Flinders Petrie's excavation of large amounts of iron slag at the Late period sites of Naukratis and Daphnae (although at least some may have derived from copper smelting).

Sources of Gemstones. From the Chalcolithic period onward, the Egyptians sought to exploit the resources of the Sinai Peninsula. Three types of copper-based minerals were obtained from the Sinai: turquoise, malachite (a banded green stone used for decorative stonework), and native copper. The principal ancient Egyptian sources of such materials were located in the central southern part of the peninsula at Bir Nasib, Mughara, and Serabit el-Khadim. Many of the hieroglyphic inscriptions at the Mughara and Serabit el-Khadim mines refer to the procurement of a substance called *mefk3t*, a term which was formerly translated as malachite but now is taken to mean turquoise. Possibly, the main focus of Egyptian operations at both sites was the mining of copper and malachite, with turquoise perhaps only a convenient by-product.

The deep blue gemstone lapis lazuli (*ḥsbd [m3ʿ]*; composed mainly of the blue alumino-silicate mineral lazurite) was frequently used in jewelry and in decorative treatments at least as early as the Naqada phase of the Predynastic period (c.3500 BCE), yet no sources of the stone are known within Egypt itself. Only one major source was used in ancient times, a group of at least four quarries in the region of Badakhshan in northeastern Afghanistan. Lapis lazuli appears to have been exported from Badakhshan to the early civilizations of the Near East and Egypt from at least the fourth millennium BCE. Possibly the Old Egyptian term *tfrr*, sometimes used instead of *ḥsbd*, might be a reference to the region of Tefreret that was to the south of the Caspian Sea; the stone might have passed through this region on its way to Egypt. Some of the earliest examples of lapis lazuli in Egypt certainly suggest a Near Eastern trade link (e.g., the Mesopotamian cylinder seal incorporated into a necklace of lapis lazuli beads from a late Predynastic grave at Naqada).

The majority of Egypt's gemstones were obtained from the Eastern Desert, including the numerous types of quartz. Rock crystal (known in Old Egyptian as *mnw ḥḏ*) is a colorless, transparent form of quartz crystal, which can still be found in the Western Desert between the Faiyum and Bahariya Oasis, as well as in the Sinai. Traces of smoky quartz—a brownish-grey crystalline variety, occasionally used for funerary vessels in the Early Dynastic period and Old Kingdom—have been found in a Roman-era gold mine, at Romit in the Eastern Desert, but no earlier work sites have yet been identified. Chalcedony is a variant of quartz that comprises thin, parallel-oriented layers; it occurs in a number of colors, ranging from the translucent red or orange hues of carnelian (produced by the presence of tiny amounts of iron oxide) to the more brownish red of sard. Much of the surface of the desert between the Nile Valley and the Red Sea is strewn with water-worn pebbles of carnelian and sard. Varieties of chert in the Eastern Desert include a group of brightly colored (opaque red, green, yellow, or brown) cryptocrystalline quartz gemstones known as jasper. Green and yellow jasper often occur both beside and within deposits of red jasper. Egyptian forms of jasper are somewhat speckled and veined compared with those found elsewhere. Both red and green jasper were used for beads from Neolithic times—from the Badarian period onward. Red jasper was particularly popular for New Kingdom earrings and for hair-rings. Chert and the variety called flint were quartzes used for fine stone tools. In many respects, the peak of flint working was in the late Predynastic period, when such fine artifacts as ripple-flaked knives were produced. Nevertheless, flint was still commonly used in pharaonic times for tools, weapons, and occasionally even jewelry (including skillfully worked bangles). Amethyst, the violet crystalline form of quartz, was used mostly during the Middle Kingdom and the Roman period. The Wadi el-Hudi region, some 35 kilometers (20 miles) southeast of Aswan, was the primary location for amethyst mining in Egypt from the eleventh dynasty until the end of the Middle Kingdom. Late in that period, the principal Egyptian amethyst mines may have been at the

northern end of the Gebel el-Asr gneiss quarries (the so-called Khephre diorite quarries), in the Western Desert about 65 kilometers (40 miles) northwest of Abu Simbel. During the New Kingdom, amethyst was much less commonly used for jewelry, and it is likely that there was a temporary cessation of mining. By the Roman period, however, amethyst had regained its popularity (or availability); apart from Site 12 at Wadi el-Hudi, there are Roman amethyst quarries in the Safaga region near Gebel Abu Diyeiba.

Hematite, an opaque iron oxide, with both reddish-earth and gray to black crystalline varieties, occurs almost everywhere in Egypt, but it was perhaps quarried in the Eastern Desert from the Late period onward. In earlier periods, it may have been obtained from the Sinai Peninsula or from the Aswan region. The type of hematite favored during the pharaonic period was black in color, with a metallic luster, but its source has not yet been found.

No ancient garnet quarries have been found within Egypt—perhaps because its occurrence is not restricted to only one or two areas. Yet lumps of a red mineral substance (identified as *ḥmȝgt*) were shown as items of Nubian tribute in the eighteenth dynasty tomb of Rekhmire at Thebes.

Perhaps the rarest mineral sought by the Egyptians was peridot, the light green transparent gem-quality form of olivine, which is perhaps the material described by as *prḏn*. The only known Egyptian source is the island of Zabargad (Saint John's Island), situated in the Red Sea, some 80 kilometers (50 miles) southeast of the Ptolemaic and Roman port of Berenike. Zabargad was probably also the main source of peridot for the whole ancient Mediterranean region. Although the more opaque yellow-green olivine was used in jewelry from the Predynastic period onward, peridot does not appear to have been used until the Ptolemaic period, when it became a popular material for intaglios and cabochons.

Sources of Eye-paint. Many naturally occurring minerals were used by the Egyptians both as pigments and for cosmetics (especially eye-paint). Some pieces of pyrolusite (a natural black ore of manganese obtained from the Sinai Peninsula) from the Predynastic site of Maadi in Lower Egypt are thought to have been used as a pigment or eye-paint. The two most common ingredients of eye-paint were, however, malachite (copper carbonate) and galena, (lead sulfide). Their ground pigments appear to have been mixed with water to form a paste and were probably applied with the fingers until the introduction of the "kohl pencil" during the Middle Kingdom.

Malachite occurs both in the Eastern Desert and in the Sinai Peninsula; indications of ancient work sites were found alongside the procurement areas of copper and turquoise. From the Badarian period onward, malachite was primarily mined as copper ore or to be ground into powder for use as a green eye-paint. It has been found in Predynastic graves not only as pigment stains on palettes and grinding stones but also occasionally in the form of raw material, placed in small linen or leather bags (as well as with kohl that was stored in shells, reeds, leaves, or jars). Malachite was almost certainly used, from at least the fourth dynasty onward, as one of the essential ingredients in the production of the pigment called "Egyptian blue." It was very occasionally used as a green pigment, although green frit seems usually to have been preferred. The green malachite-based form of eye-paint (*w3dw*) seems to have been used only until the middle of the Old Kingdom, when it was replaced by the black galena-based form of kohl (*msdmt*). Many sources of galena occur in the Eastern Desert, some easily accessible from the Wadi Hammamat (including at least one Predynastic mine). The main archaeological remains, in terms of the procurement of galena, is the work site at Gebel el-Zeit, on the Red Sea coast, dating primarily to the Second Intermediate Period.

Sources of Natron, Alum, and Mica. In addition to gemstones, metals, and pigments, a number of other minerals were used by the Egyptians; prominent among these were natron, alum, and mica. Natron, a naturally occurring compound of sodium carbonate and sodium bicarbonate, is best known for its use in the desiccation stage of mummification, but it was also an important ingredient in medicine and in the production of glass and faience. It is currently obtainable from three main sources: Wadi Natrun (in the Western Desert), the Delta province of Beheira (about 20 kilometers [12 miles] to the west of ancient Naukratis), and the Elkab region of Upper Egypt; it seems likely that all three of those deposits were worked in ancient times. As far as ancient glass production is concerned, it is not clear whether, as has often been suggested, ready-made glass was imported from the Near East during the New Kingdom, in which case the procurement of natron might have been largely for embalming and medicinal use. The Old Egyptian terms *ḥsmn* and *bḏ* were used to refer to "natron," but the divine status of the substance is suggested by the possibility that the word *natron* derives from some form of the Old Egyptian word *ntr* ("god").

The question of the Egyptians' use of alum is somewhat contentious, since few definitely attested archaeological instances exist for ancient Egypt; but it was mentioned in texts in connection with astringent materials, and there are indications that it was being mined in ancient times. Alum occurs in the Kharga and Dakhla oases, and may have been the mineral from which the Egyptians extracted cobalt, the principal colorant used to make blue glass from the New Kingdom onward (although it has also

been suggested that the source of cobalt was Persia or Asia Minor). No cobalt was known to be used in Egyptian glass or faience between the eleventh and seventh centuries BCE, and even when it was used again in later periods, it occurred in association with a different group of minerals, thus perhaps indicating that a non-Egyptian (perhaps Persian) source was being used from the Late period onward. As well as its connections with glassmaking, alum was also used as a mordant in the dyeing of textiles and animal skins. Like natron, it probably also had medicinal uses. Although it was taken for granted that the Egyptians used alum for the tawing of leather, it seems that alum may not have been used for that purpose in Egypt until as late as Roman times. The Mesopotamian records of trade in Egyptian alum date mainly from the first millennium BCE.

From the Predynastic period onward, mica—a type of potassium aluminosilicate, which usually splits into glistening, translucent sheets—was used to a small extent for beads, pendants, and mirrors. The Metropolitan Museum of Art in New York has Middle Kingdom mica pendants and a New Kingdom necklace that incorporates mica, but its use in pharaonic Egypt is fairly infrequent. Most examples of worked mica derive from Upper Nubian sites of the Classic Kerma period (c.1750–1500 BCE), in the form of decorative plaques sewn onto leather caps. Deposits of a type of mica called muscovite have been recorded at Rod Um el-Farag in the Eastern Desert, but there is no indication that they were exploited in ancient times. A deep adit close to the Roman amethyst mines at Wadi el-Hudi, about 35 kilometers (20 miles) southeast of Aswan, had been identified as a mica mine, but no modern confirmation exists.

The Power of Minerals. The control and efficient exploitation of mineral resources was undoubtedly important to the early Egyptian state of the fourth and early third millennia BCE. Even before the unification of the Two Lands, the late Predynastic Upper Egyptian "protostates," such as Naqada and Hierakonpolis, may have prospered to a large degree through their grip over the gold mines in the wadis of the Eastern Desert. Many centuries later, during the New Kingdom, the economic prosperity of the Egyptian empire of the late second millennium BCE was partly based on the quantities of gold obtained from the mines of southern Egypt and Nubia, which were particularly productive in the time of Amenhotpe III (c.1410–1372 BCE). Both the Annals of Thutmose III and the Amarna Letters emphasize the importance of gold in Egypt's relations with its Near Eastern neighbors.

It is worth noting that the Egyptian exploitation of minerals transcended both politics and economics. The procurement of metals and gemstones was regarded as one of the king's obligations for the maintenance of divine harmony (*maat*), but it was also part of an ambitious project for the reenactment of the creation of the world. This "cosmic" theory of minerals is attested by a series of reliefs and inscriptions on the walls of the Greco-Roman temples at Dendera, Edfu, and Philae. In the temple of Hathor at Dendera, rulers were shown presenting precious metals and stones to the goddess; at the bases of the walls of the so-called silver-room (or side-room XI), there are depictions of a row of kneeling personifications of the regions from which specific metals or precious stones were obtained. According to the accompanying hieroglyphic captions, the purpose of those reliefs was not merely to depict the donation of exotic materials to the cult of Hathor but symbolically or metaphorically to reassemble the entire range of special minerals known at the time—gold, silver, copper, galena, lapis lazuli, turquoise, emerald, jasper, calcite, q' mineral (black schist?), carnelian, and microcline (a green feldspar, amazonite)—so that the temple could magically replicate the original divine act of creation. The incorporation of similar scenes into the decoration of the temples at Edfu and Philae suggests that the creation of an actual microcosm, by means of the collection of minerals, was a fundamental aspect of Egyptian religion.

[*See also* Calcite; Copper; Diorite and Related Rocks; Gems; Gold; Iron; Quarries and Mines; Quartzite; Silver; *and* Toiletries and Cosmetics.]

BIBLIOGRAPHY

Aston, Barbara G., James A. Harrell, and Ian Shaw. "Stone." In *Ancient Egyptian Materials and Technology,* edited by P. T. Nicholson and I. Shaw. Cambridge, 1999.

Aufrère, Sidney. *L'univers minéral dans la pensée égyptienne,* 2 vols. Cairo, 1991.

Castel, Georges, Georges Soukiassian, and Georges Pouit. *Gebel el-Zeit I: Les mines de galène (Egypte, IIe millénaire av. J.-C.).* Cairo, 1989.

Chartier-Raymond, Maryvonne, Brigitte Gratien, Claude Traunecker, and Jean-Marc Vinçon. "Les sites miniers pharaoniques du Sud-Sinaï: quelques notes et observations de terrain." *Cahiers de Recherches de l'Institut de Papyrologie et d'Egyptologie de Lille,* 16 (1994), 31–80.

Gardiner, Alan, T. Eric Peet, and Jaroslav Černý. *The Inscriptions of Sinai* II. 2d ed. London, 1955.

Hume, W. F. *Geology of Egypt* II. Cairo, 1937.

Hussein, Abdel Aziz A. "Mineral Deposits." In *The Geology of Egypt,* edited by Rushdi Said, pp. 511–566. Rotterdam, 1990.

Klemm, R., and D. D. Klemm. "Evolution of Methods for Prospection, Mining and Processing of Gold in Egypt." In *Proceedings of the First International Conference on Ancient Egyptian Mining and Metallurgy and Conservation of Metallic Artifacts,* edited by Feisal A. Esmael, pp. 341–354. Cairo, 1998.

Lucas, Alfred. *Ancient Egyptian Materials and Industries.* 4th ed., rev. by J. R. Harris. London, 1962.

Ogden, Jack. "Metals." In *Ancient Egyptian Materials and Technology,* edited by P. T. Nicholson and I. Shaw. Cambridge, 1999.

Rothenberg, Beno. *Were These King Solomon's Mines? Excavations in the Timna Valley.* New York, 1972.

Sadek, Ashraf I. *The Amethyst Mining Inscriptions of Wadi el-Hudi.* 2 vols. Warminster, 1980–1985.

Shaw, Ian, and Rob Jameson. "Amethyst Mining in the Eastern Desert: A Preliminary Survey at Wadi el-Hudi." *Journal of Egyptian Archaeology* 79 (1993), 81–97.

Vercoutter, Jean. "The Gold of Kush." *Kush* 7 (1959), 120–153.

IAN SHAW

MINES. *See* Quarries and Mines.

MIRGISSA. *See* Forts and Garrisons.

MIRRORS. The earliest Egyptian mirrors were highly polished copper disks with a short stem that probably served to provide better anchorage for the handle. They appeared in the region of Memphis during the Early Dynastic period. Some writers have suggested that other materials (stone, mica) or other methods (water in a hand-held container) were used to reflect an image during the prehistoric era, but there is hardly any evidence to substantiate this. A number of Egyptian mines, particularly in Sinai, provided the copper used in the making of these mirrors from prehistory until the end of the Middle Kingdom. Metal was more frequently imported from the Near East and Cyprus during the New Kingdom. Copper working is delicate because it becomes fragile when beaten, and it was superseded around the twelfth dynasty by bronze, which was probably introduced into Egypt through the trading port of Byblos. It is difficult to explain why this metal, an alloy of copper and tin, should have arrived so late in Egypt, whereas in Asia it had been discovered by around 3500–3200 BCE. It is unlikely that the mirror disks or bronze handles are earlier than the Middle Kingdom.

Copper disks of the Early Dynastic period are cordiform (heart-shaped); whereas throughout the Old Kingdom, an elliptical outline soon became the norm. Lotiform disks are rarer; bronze examples were discovered at Abydos. Disks no more than a millimeter thick were simply beaten into shape, but thicker ones were cast, then beaten and polished. The reflecting quality could be enhanced by a patina of gold or silver. From the optical point of view, the disks were concave, convex, or a combination of both. A very few plated bronze disks have been recorded.

Handles. No mirror handles of the Early Dynastic period have been discovered, but this is perhaps an accidental absence. Mirrors from the Old Kingdom might have a wooden handle in the form of papyrus, into which the stem of the metal disk slid, to be fixed to the handle by a rivet. The papyriform column becomes the commonest decoration for mirror handles. The depiction of a complete mirror in the tomb of Kagemni at Saqqara prove the

MIRRORS. *Bronze mirror from the eighteenth dynasty.* The disk of the mirror symbolizes the sun. Its handle is in the form of a woman wearing a cowrie girdle, a symbol of fertility. This type of mirror may have been devoted to the goddess Hathor. Height: 23 centimeters (9 inches). (The Metropolitan Museum of Art, Gift of Miss Helen Miller Gould, 1910. [10.130.1311])

ḥm, serves as the handle of a wooden model and is often found on walls of tombs and temples.

At the end of the Middle Kingdom, materials used for handles become completely diversified: handles in ivory, stone, glazed clay, and earthenware, as well as bronze, silver, gold, and silver-plated bronze. Handles are often inlaid with metal, earthenware, or stone, or plated with gold or silver. Disks and handles in bronze may have varying proportions of tin. The bronze handles are either solid or hollow, cast by the lost wax process, which imparts a unique quality to each piece and leads to the development of more elaborate outlines. In certain cases, bronze handles are made in several pieces joined together, as can be seen in New Kingdom statuettes: the arms are sometimes cast separately, then attached by a mortise-and-tenon joint.

Feminine statuette handles constitute an outstanding innovation of the New Kingdom. About a hundred mirrors of this kind have been recorded. To these should be added many handles of the same type in wood and ivory (sometimes in bone) that have now lost their disks. These maidens carry a simple or enlarged papyrus flower capital, or more rarely a palm or a "fleur-de-lys" emblem. These elements are integrated through arm positions and graceful attitudes, especially when the maiden holds the end of the papyrus umbels with both hands. These statuettes give precious sociological and chronological information, especially concerning the hairstyles worn by young girls. Some of the maidens carry a bird, cat, or child, which should be taken into account as symbolic objects. Even though these statuette mirrors are found in Egypt, Palestine, and Nubia, they were all produced in Egyptian workshops. The quality of their workmanship can vary a great deal; some mirrors are made with care and finely engraved, while others are more roughly finished. Handle statuettes of the god Bes were also produced in the New Kingdom, along with a fretwork-type handle, which shows great mastery of technique, being made up of a group of royal figurines surrounded by snakes and various significant hieroglyphs.

From the twenty-fifth to the twenty-sixth dynasty, a new type of mirror emerged. The handle, either flat or column-shaped, was surmounted by the head of Hathor, sometimes combined with a moon crescent that surrounds the circumference of the disk. The latter is engraved with an offering scene made by a *semsyet mut* to a feminine divinity seated under a canopy. This ritual presentation gives the subject a votive character. The flat papyriform-handled mirror used in this engraved ritual is equipped with a transversal bar at the base; actual objects of this kind have not yet been discovered. Hieroglyphic *ḥm*-type mirrors, sometimes surmounted by the head of Hathor, must have existed during the Ptolemaic period for cult use.

existence of the outline only at the beginning of the sixth dynasty. Other representations at Deir el-Gebrawi and at Thebes date from the late seventh dynasty. Disks mounted on standards, often decorated with *wḏȝt,* also appear in the Old Kingdom in Saqqara and Mendes. The first handles representating human heads—believed to be of Hathor—date from the beginning of the Middle Kingdom; they soon develop the cow's ears typical of Hathor and are combined with a papyriform capital. During this period the papyriform column increases in size and carries a falcon or leopard head, and exceptionally that of an ibex or serpent. A very pure form, that of the hieroglyph

Inscriptional Evidence for the Word for "Mirror."

No word for "mirror" has come to light before the end of the Old Kingdom, and no reference occurs in the Pyramid Texts. In the Middle Kingdom, the first periphrase ('nkh m33 ḥr) is found that refers to this object; this evolves into 'nkh n m33 ḥr, accompanied by a determinative indicating the material and color. On sarcophagus friezes, the papyrus column and, more frequently, the mirrors on standards often occur in pairs or fours. In this context, the inscriptions imy ḏ.t, nṯry, Iwny and m3ʿtj are found, plainly indicating a reference to the sun god Re, clearly present in the disk shape. These religious or symbolic terms were closely related to the funereal function of the object, which was generally placed in tombs near the deceased. In the New Kingdom and during the Ptolemaic period, the term 'nkh, which also stood for "mirror," is accompanied by the determinative ḥm. In the Saite era, the expression wn-ḥr, wnwj-ḥr appears; it is also to be found, with spelling variations, in the Ptolemaic period. Finally, itn followed by the determinative already referred to, or simply by a circle, also designates "mirror" in this era. The expression 'nk pr or 'nkh m pr.f, as well as a large number of portrayals of objects found in the excavations, shows that the Egyptians carefully protected the mirrors with leather or woven fiber covers or even kept them in boxes or carrying cases.

Archaeological Context.

Most of the disks or mirrors were placed in tombs as close as possible to the deceased—man, woman or child. Only a few mirrors have been found in a religious context. Likewise, few mirrors have been discovered in civil buildings, probably because of the lack of urban excavations. Sometimes the owners of these mirrors had their name and title engraved on the disk near the stem; the titles ḥm ntr ht-ḥr and Šmsjt Mwt are women's, while those indicating various positions in the hierarchy of the state (3tjʿ, mr ḥm-ntr) are men's.

Depictions of Mirrors.

Mirror are represented in various situations, not always strictly related to real-life cosmetic activities. In a scene concerning metalcraft in the tomb of Wr-iri.n.i (sixth dynasty), a disk is shown together with vases and tools. In the tomb of Itti/Sdw at Deshasheh (sixth dynasty) is a mirror with a cover that leaves the handle exposed, placed next to a pair of finished sandals in a basketry workshop. The tomb of Kagemni at Saqqara, dated at the beginning of the sixth dynasty, shows the oldest depiction of a mirror with handle—the papyrus column type.

On stelae, as in certain scenes on tomb wall paintings, the mirror is found in funereal contexts. It is placed near the deceased, man or woman, under his seat or nearby with other objects. It is also found among offerings to the deceased.

At Thebes, in the tomb of Intefiqer and his wife, a Hathor priestess is inscribed with a caption referring to an unusual offering scene. A mirror is presented together with a vase to the deceased, who inhales the perfume of a lotus flower. The accompanying text refers to the "tent of purification," confirming the funereal context, since this is a reference to the ritual of rebirth. This emphasizes the symbolic importance of the object. (It should be noted that mirrors were also used in the interpretation of dreams, especially in foretelling the sex of a child.)

In the mastaba of Mererwykai (Mrr-wi-k3i), a mirror with a papyriform handle depicts a dance the meaning of which is not yet understood. The name of the deity Hathor associated with this dance indicates that it was reserved for her. The ritual nature of this dance to Hathor suggests that some mirrors were strictly for this function. The expression ink m ḥrt ḥwr leads us to believe that certain objects were specially designed for these activities. No other text confirms this, unless the owner's inscription ḥem neter Hathor (ḥm ntr Ḥ.t ḥr) emblazoned on certain mirrors, mentioning the use, indicates a ritual character.

On sarcophagi of the Middle Kingdom, disk and papyrus mirrors, with or without cases, as well as disks on standards, are illustrated singly, in pairs, or in fours on friezes. An eye is often engraved on the disk. The material used in the reflecting surface is indicated by the colors white, yellow, red-brown, or pink, and an accompanying text confirms it is made of gold, silver, electrum, or copper.

In the New Kingdom tomb of Kenamun (Kn-Imn), mirrors are presented as offerings to King Amenhotpe II at the New Year celebration. This seems to refer to an annual presentation by the royal workshops, as opposed to the productions of temple or personal workshops. According to a custom documented in Middle Kingdom funereal monuments, on many of the stelae and tomb walls of private individuals a mirror was painted or carved near the deceased or his wife, for whom the monument was intended.

An anonymous stela found at Abydos, dated about 700 BCE, shows a woman offering a mirror to the sun god Re-Horakhty. Two other stelae bear an identical scene: on the first a smsjt Mwt offers a mirror to Re-Horakhty, and on the second, Mut and the goddess of the Nile are the recipients. Finally, the fish goddess Mehit of Thinis receives the offering of a mirror on a bronze plate. These documents are related to votive mirrors dated between 700 and 500 BCE, on the disks of which a ritual offering of the mirror to the goddess Mut is engraved. This gift is made by a woman, bearing the title Šmsjt Mwt, to the deity seated on a highly decorated canopied dais supported by hathoric columns. Apotropaic symbols such as udjat (wḏ3t) are found on certain earlier mirrors, including the face of the god Bes or an ibis. The allusions to heavenly bodies, sun-disk and moon-crescent, and heads of Hathor and Horus which are parts of the handles as well as of the engraving on the disks, are all elements found in Egyptian sun symbolism. This ritual, known to have been founded in the Saite era, develops on temple walls from the reign of Ptolemy II until the reign of the Roman emperor Caracalla. The sacred gestures involving two mirrors are presented by the king himself to Hathor or Isis, as well as to all the goddesses assimilated with Hathor and their hypostases. The two mirrors represent shining heavenly bodies, the sun and moon being the "luminaries" (*ḥȝty.ty*) offered to bring exultation to the goddess; the one that is the eye of Re is intended to calm and contribute to the keeping of the force of light. The goddess returns this light to the king, thus ensuring his supremacy over the universe. The gesture associates the king with the disk. The roots of the ritual are very ancient, as can be observed in the development of scenes where the mirror is represented; it may have originated in Memphis. The god Ptah, the creator, was considered to be the original caster of mirrors.

BIBLIOGRAPHY

Bénédite, G. *Miroirs.* Catalogue Générale des Antiquités Égyptiennes du Musée du Caire, 44001–44102. Cairo, 1907.

Bianchi, R. S. "Reflections of the Sky's Eyes." *Source: Notes in the History of Art* 4.2/3 (1985).

Évrard-Derriks, C. "Le miroir représenté sur les peintures et bas-reliefs égyptiens." *Orientalia Lovaniensia Periodica* 6/7 (1975–1976), 223–227.

Hickmann, H. "La danse aux miroirs: Essai d'interprétation d'une danse pharaonique de l'Ancien Empire." *Bulletin de l'Institute d'Égypte* 37 (1954–1955), 151–190.

Husson, C. *L'offrande du miroir dans les temples égyptiens de l'époque greco-romaine.* Lyon, 1977.

Lilyquist, C. *Ancient Egyptian Mirrors.* Münchener Ägyptologische Studien, 27. Munich and Berlin, 1979.

Munro, P. "Eine Gruppe spätägyptischer Bronzespiegel." *Zeitschrift für ägyptische Sprache und Altertumskunde* 95 (1969), 92–109.

CLAIRE DERRIKS

MITANNI. As one of the four great powers of the ancient Near East and a powerful northern Mesopotamian kingdom, the Mitanni controlled an extensive peripheral empire during most of the Late Bronze Age. The kingdom of Mitanni resulted from the unification of several small states of northern Mesopotamia by a group of Indo-Aryans who had detached themselves from the main Aryan migration south into India. Their cultural impact had been limited to the introduction of a number of personal names of Sanskritic origin, to several words of Sanskritic affiliation, and to a few Vedic deities (in theophoric names and in a treaty). Although the Mitanni state languages remained local Hurrian and Akkadian, the Indo-Aryan political and military roles became dominant.

The term *Mitanni* came from the earlier *Maitani* and the Old Egyptian *Ma-ta-ni*; it was also known as *Ḫurwuḫe/Ḫurruḫe* (in Hurrian), *Ḫurri* (mainly in Hittite), *Ḫuru* (in Egyptian), *Ḫanigalbat* (and variations on that in the Akkadian of Babylonia, Assyria, and Nuzi), and *Naharina* (in West Semitic, "river land,"—the most common designation in Egyptian). Unlike the other major civilizations of the ancient Near East, knowledge of the kingdom of Mitanni comes almost exclusively from its neighbors: from the Amarna Letters; from Egyptian, Hittite, Babylonian, and Assyrian records; and from its vassal kingdoms of Alalakh (in northern Syria), Arrapkha (east of the Tigris River, principally from the town of Nuzi), and Khana (on the middle Euphrates River and the lower Khabur). Six tablets were found at Tell Brak in the heartland of Mitanni, but only two mention the kings Artashshumara and Tushratta.

The earliest mentions of Mitanni as Ḫanigalbat occur in a tablet from the reign of the Babylonian king Ammisaduqa (1582–1562 BCE; then spelled Ḫabingalbat) and under Year 3 of the Akkadian version of the annals of the Hittite king Hattushilish I (c.1575–1540 BCE). By that time, Mitanni was strong enough to launch an invasion of Anatolia that almost extinguished the Hittite kingdom.

Mitanni fought the Hittite kings Hattushilish I and Murshilish I (c.1540–1530 BCE) for control of northern Syria, reversing the Hittite victories over Babylon by defeating Murshilish I upon his return. Then Khana joined Mitanni as a client state. Ḫantilish I (c.1530–1500 BCE) was then ousted from Syria, but a third competitor soon appeared on the scene—Egypt, led by Thutmose I, who invaded northern Syria in c.1525 BCE. He fought Mitanni and reached as far east as the Euphrates River. At this point, most likely, Ilim-ilimma I, an offspring of the old local dynasty, was installed as king of Halab. A few years later, Ilim-ilimma was assassinated, probably by a pro-Mitanni faction. His son Idrimi fled to Ammiya (now Amyūn in Lebanon), at that time under Egyptian rule. He was able (evidently with Egyptian support) to build ships, recruit an army, land on the shore of his ancestral domain, establish himself at Alalakh, and resist the Mitanni king Parattarna for seven years. A shift in Egyptian foreign policy under Hatshepsut, however, deprived Idrimi of Egyptian backing, and he submitted himself to the overlordship of Parattarna. The road to northern and central Syria—and to Palestine as far as the Egyptian border fortress of Sharuhen—was then opened to the Mitanni. Men with Indo-Aryan and Hurrian names were soon appointed rulers of many southern Syrian and Palestinian city-states; they were left in place after the reconquest of these areas by Egypt. Their successors used the same onomastic tradition in the Amarna period. Ḫuru first became an Egyptian designation for Syria and, during the nineteenth dynasty, specifically for Palestine. About the same time, Mitanni acquired a new client state, at the expense of Hatti—Lowland Cilicia (in Hittite, *Adaniya*, in Ugaritic, *Qṭy;* and in Egyptian, *Qadi*). Its contingent—along with troops from Qidshi, Ḥuru, and Naharina—participated in the defense of Megiddo against Thutmose III in 1482 BCE.

Thutmose III's reconquest of Palestine and southern Syria went rather easily, but the campaigns in central Syria were more difficult. In 1472 BCE, however, the Egyptian army invaded northern Syria, northeast to the Euphrates River, and imposed its overlordship on the local states. This did not last very long; Mitanni, probably under the new king Saushshatar, made a crushing comeback in 1463 BCE, to reconquer not only northern Syria but also Tunip and Qidshi. Only Amqa and Upi remained in the hands of Egypt. Saushshatar was successful on other fronts as well; in the northwest, he extended his sovereignty over the large and strategically important kingdom of Kizzuwadna; in the east, he sacked Assur and reduced it to vassalage; and in the far north, he defended the vassal state of Ishuwa from invasion by the Hittite king Tudhaliyash I.

Under one of Saushshatar's successors (Parattarna II or Artatama I), Tudhaliyash I forced Kizzuwdna back into the Hittite fold. This opened for him the passes to northern Syria. Both Hatti and Mitanni sent emissaries to Amenhotpe II to gain Egypt's friendly neutrality (probably in his twenty-third regnal year). Hatti soon concluded a nonaggression pact with Egypt, the Kurushtama treaty. A few years later, in the first regnal year of Thutmose IV, the hard-pressed Artatama I of Mitanni made far-reaching territorial concessions to Egypt: he ceded to it Tunip, with the southern part of its domain (Qatna, Qidshi, and Takhshi), and he agreed to the extension of Egyptian sovereignty upon the hitherto neutral kingdom of Ugarit. The sacrifice paid off: after initial success, Tudhaliyash I was pushed out of Syria by Mitanni's troops, which no longer had to be split on two fronts. The century-long enmity between Egypt and Mitanni was then replaced by an *entente cordiale* which lasted for sixty years. Three generations of Egyptian kings (Thutmose IV, Amenhotpe III, and Amenhotpe IV) married princesses from Mitanni. Under Amenhotpe IV and his ally and father-in-law Tushratta of Mitanni, their joint troops cooperated in reversing the political affiliation of Nuḫašše, Tunip, and Amurru, which had been brought about by the Hittite king Shuppiluliumas I's foray into Syria.

This was to be Tushratta's last success. A few years earlier, the eastern part of his kingdom had been seized by a rival claimant, Artatama II (probably his brother), who established his capital at Taidi. Two years after his Syrian foray, Shuppiluliumas I invaded Mitanni from the north; he sacked its capital, Washshukanni; he crossed into Syria; and he conquered both its Mitanni zone and the areas previously ceded to Egypt by Mitanni. Soon after this, Tushratta was killed by one of his sons, and his kingdom was annexed by Artatama II. Yet another son of Tushratta, Shattiwaza, escaped to Anatolia, presented himself to Shuppiluliumas, and with his military assistance regained his father's domain. Although he had to cede part of it to Hatti by an agreement with Artatama II, Shattiwaza was appointed heir to the remaining part of his kingdom (much of which had been taken over by the newly liberated Assyria). Troops of Naharina still fought on the Hittite side in the Battle of Kadesh (Qidshi), but some twelve to fifteen years later, King Adad-narari I of Assyria made that state his tributary. After two unsuccessful revolts—the second one, against Shalmaneser I, had massive Hittite assistance—by 1250 BCE, Mitanni (Ḥanigalbat) had been completely incorporated into the Assyrian empire.

[*See also* Battle of Kadesh; Foreign Incursions; Mesopotamia; *and* Shuppiluliumas.]

BIBLIOGRAPHY

Astour, Michael C. *Hittite History and Absolute Chronology of the Bronze Age.* Studies in Mediterranean Archaeology and Literature, 73. Partille, 1989. Chapters 10–14, 27, 33, 34, 36, 37, 39, and Charts II and IV deal with the chronology of Mitanni and its synchronisms with Ḥatti, Alalakh, and Egypt, with their military and diplomatic interactions, and with territorial changes in Syria until 1386 BCE.

Diakonoff, I. M. "Die Arier im Vorderen Orient: Ende eines Mythos (Zur Methodik der Erforschung verschollener Sprachen)." *Orientalia* NS 41 (1972), 91–120. First published in Russian, *Vestnik drevnej istorii,* 1970, no. 4, 39–63. A minimalization of the role of the Indo-Aryans in the Near East.

Finkel, Irving L. "Inscriptions from Tell Brak 1984." *Iraq* 47 (1985), 187–201. Two tablets from Mitanni, pp. 191–198.

Finkel, Irving L. "Inscriptions from Tell Brak 1985." *Iraq* 50 (1988), 83–86. A period letter from Mitanni.

Illingworth, N. J. J. "Inscriptions from Tell Brak 1986." *Iraq* 50 (1988), 87–108. Two tablets from Mitanni, pp. 96–108.

Kammenhuber, Annelies. *Die Arier im vorderen Orient.* Heidelberg, 1968. A minimalization of the role of Indo-Aryans in the Near East.

Klengel, Horst. "Mitanni: Probleme seiner Expansion und politischen Struktur." *Revue hittite et asiani-que* 36 (1978), 91–115.

Klengel, Horst. *Syria, 3000 to 300 B.C.: A Handbook of Political History.* Berlin 1992. See Chapter 3: "The Period of Mittanian and Egyptian Domination (c. 1600–1350)."

Liverani, Mario. "Ḥurri e Mitanni." *Oriens Antiquus* 1 (1962): 253–257.

Mayrhofer, Manfred. *Die Indo-Arier im alten Vorderasien. Mit einer analytischen Bibliographie.* Wiesbaden, 1966.

Mayrhofer, Manfred. *Die Arier im vorderen Orient—ein Mythus?: mit einem bibliographischen supplement.* Vienna, 1974. Rejoinder to Kammenhuber and Diakonoff above.

O'Callaghan, Roger T. *Aram Naharaim: A Contribution to the History of Upper Mesopotamia in the Second Millennium B.C.* Analecta Orientalia, 26. Rome, 1948. Ch. IV, pp. 51–92, "The Mitanni Kingdom." Dated, but a useful general survey.

Rouault, Olivier. "Cultures locales et influences extérieures. Le cas de Terqa." *Studi micenei ed egeo-anatolici* 30 (1992), 247–256. Information on the status of Ḫana as a vassal of Mitanni, from unpublished Terqa tablets.

Wilhelm, Gernot. "Parrattarna, Saušatar und die absolute Datierung der Nuzi-Tafeln." *Acta Antiqua Academiae Scientiarum Hungaricae* 26 (1976), 149–161.

Wilhelm, Gernot. *The Hurrians.* Translated from German by Jennifer Barnes. Warminster, 1989. A slightly updated translation of *Grundzüge der Geschichte und Kultur der Hurriter*, Darmstadt, 1982. The chapter "History," pp. 7–41, includes the history of Mitanni.

Wilhelm, Gernot. "A Hurrian Letter from Tell Brak." *Iraq* 53 (1991), 159–168.

MICHAEL C. ASTOUR

MNEVIS. *See* Bull Gods.

MOʿALLA. *See* Ankhtifi of Moʿalla.

MODELS. Ancient Egyptian models, small-scale representations of objects and people from everyday life, may be miniature tools and vessels left in foundation deposits at temples. They may be votive or trial pieces, or scale models representing architectural elements of temples, such as column capitals or monumental gateways. The term *model* is more usually used in Egyptology to refer to figures of household servants performing cooking tasks; farm laborers tending animals and crops; and men involved in manufacturing processes. They can also represent individual items of food or offering vessels substituting for real offerings, as well as tools and weapons. There are models of religious paraphernalia for ensuring the safe passage from death to rebirth, such as the *pzš-kȝf* set (originally a flint knife used in the Opening of the Month ceremony), the seven sacred oils tablet, or sets of miniature libation jars and bowls. Through their outward appearance, imitating objects from life and offerings of food and drink, as well as substituting for depictions of these in tomb decoration, these models were believed to sustain the dead in their afterlife within the tomb magically, providing the food, drink, clothing, shelter, and transport that would be needed for continued existence. The most important categories of models, offering bearers and boats, are discussed separately below.

Predynastic and Early Dynastic (Naqada II to Third Dynasty, 3500–2632 BCE). Models from the Predynastic period are rare. Their function within burials, in the absence of other evidence, is assumed to be the same as that of later models. Made from pottery, they comprise figures carrying offerings, figures within large vats perhaps intended as brewers, boats which may or may not have a crew, houses, and beds. Surviving Early Dynastic period models include large pottery jars modeled to imitate dome granaries, and ivory or bone boats.

Old Kingdom (Fourth to Sixth Dynasties, 2632–2206 BCE). Limestone statuettes of servants appeared in the mastaba tombs of the elite at Giza during the late fourth dynasty, but became more common at Saqqara and Giza in the fifth and sixth dynasties. Models of that date are of single figures, most frequently engaged in the tasks of preparing foodstuffs; the most common is a female miller kneeling to grind grain on a quern stone. Other activities include sifting, forming dough cakes, attending a bread oven, straining beer mash, preparing beer jars, cooking or stewing meat, butchering a cow, and carrying pots or sacks. Manufacturing activities include throwing pots on a slow wheel and heating a forge through a pipe. Domestic life is represented by figures of wet-nurses and harpists. Structural models are of granaries comprising rows of tall conical silos, made either of stone or, more frequently, of pottery. Boat models are of wood. Usually, only two or three servant figures were placed in a single tomb, but the tomb of Djasha at Giza contained sixteen figures, while a group of more than twenty figures is said to have come from the tomb of Nykau-Inpu at Giza.

The diffusion of models into more and more elite burials during the long reign of Pepy II at the end of the sixth dynasty resulted in stone servant figures becoming smaller and degenerate in form, and in the appearance of the use of wood for either single figures or pairs of figures. The best preserved and largest collection of such wooden models came from the tomb of Nyankh-Pepi-kem at Meir. It comprised seventeen scenes of millers, bakers, oven attendants, beer mashers, jar cleaners, duck roasters, offering bearers, cattle carrying sacks, and a man with a hoe; there were also eight boats. Contemporary with models entirely of wood are those that incorporate certain elements, such as jars or quern stones, which were made of stone and set into the wooden models.

First Intermediate Period (Seventh to Tenth Dynasties, c. 2206–2040 BCE). First Intermediate Period models are distinguished from their predecessors by being entirely of wood, and, for the first time, they comprise small groups of figures engaged in allied processes on the same wooden base, such as milling and baking, or brewing and bottling. Also at this time the square granary appears, usually with peaked corners and an internal courtyard in front of a row of flat-roofed silos. The intact tomb of Ini at Gebelein (eighth dynasty) contained a food preparation model, a granary, miniature granary sacks, and two boats.

Middle Kingdom (Eleventh to Twelfth Dynasties, 2134–1786 BCE). Most extant models of wood are from the Middle Kingdom, a time of wealth and prosperity for the provincial elite. The period spanning the end of the

MODELS. *Wooden model of a funerary bark, twelfth dynasty.* This model was made for Chancellor Wekhotpe from Meir. It shows him three times, dressed in his official garment (left), as a statue (right), and as a mummy (center). (The Metropolitan Museum of Art, Gift of J. Pierpont Morgan, 1912. [12.183.4])

eleventh dynasty and the beginning of the twelfth saw an increase in the power of provincial nobles. A reflection of this trend is seen in the number and diversity of models from all the major provincial cemeteries. A typical elite burial of the Middle Kingdom would have included at least two boats, a granary, a pair of offering bearers, a bread and beer preparation scene, and a butchering scene. Often these models were duplicated, probably to ensure a plentiful supply of offerings. Perhaps the largest collection of Middle Kingdom models came from the tomb of Djehutinakht at Bersheh, which contained thirty-three scenes, twelve offering bearers, and fifty-five boats. Paralleling this tomb is that of Karenen at Saqqara, which contained fourteen scenes, a procession of offering bearers, and eight boats. Similarly, the tomb of Tjawy at Beni Hasan contained eleven scenes, an offering bearer, and two boats.

The activities represented by Middle Kingdom models fall into five categories: agriculture and animal husbandry; food preparation; industrial processes; offering bearers; and boats. Models of men hoeing the soil, ploughing with cattle, raising calves, herding and force-feeding cattle have been found most frequently at Asyut, Bersheh, Meir, and Beni Hasan, perhaps reflecting the agricultural wealth of this region in Middle Egypt. Industrial processes comprise spinning and weaving, woodworking and metalworking, and the manufacture of pottery and stone jars. Workshop models of this type come most frequently from Saqqara.

By the reign of Senwosret II, fourth king of the twelfth dynasty, the influence of the provincial elite began to decline because of royal intervention, and there was a concomitant decline in the number and diversity of models. However, the materials from which they were made increased, so that models from the twelfth dynasty Faiyum sites are of wood, faience, and various stones. Alongside the traditional wooden models of kitchen and cooking scenes, granaries, offering bearers, and boats are models of foodstuffs—fruit, vegetables, cuts of meat, cereal grains, and various types of bread—made of blue or green faience or painted cartonnage.

Second Intermediate Period, New Kingdom and Later (1786–931 BCE). With the demise of models came the rise of the *shawabti* figure, perhaps developed from mummiform figures commonly found on twelfth dynasty funerary boats. Inscribed with chapter 6 of the *Book of Going Forth by Day* (*Book of the Dead*), these figures took over many of the functions of models. An eighteenth dynasty variation of the *shawabti* is in the form of a miller. Isolated models continued to be used into the Late period, most notably boat models and figures of mourners.

The Meketre Models. Theban tomb 281 belonged to Meketre, chancellor to Montuhotep I, reunifier of Egypt in the eleventh dynasty. A niche in the entrance corridor of the tomb contained the finest collection of models ever found. These models are unique for their size, quality of craftsmanship, and attention to detail. The Meketre models are probably the product of a northern workshop, perhaps at Lisht, and probably date to the reign of Amenemhet I—hence their notable differences from other late eleventh and twelfth dynasty models from the Theban necropolis. There are nine scenes, each contained within a walled room, as well as two offering bearers and thirteen boats. Unique to this group are the two walled gardens and the inspection of a herd of cattle by Meketre and his officials. The gardens contain model sycamore fig trees surrounding a copper-lined pond, overlooked by a colonnade and windows. The roofs have copper rain spouts. The group also includes a spinning and weaving shed and a carpentry shop. The quality of the figures in these models allows the identification of tasks depicted in other, less accomplished models.

Offering Bearers. Offering bearers are the largest models, in terms of height, of all model types and are among the earliest to be found. Predynastic period offering bearers are simple pottery figures with hollowed heads, or figures carrying hollowed receptacles. Usually these are single figures, but a rare example is known of a row of bearers, possibly from Naqada. Later bearers tend to be more carefully made than other model types, and some are on a par with figures of the tomb-owner. This implies that offering bearers were regarded by the Egyptians as more important than the generic producers of food and drink. During the Old Kingdom, depictions in relief of women carrying baskets on their heads are found on royal mortuary monuments and later in private tombs. These women are given hieroglyphic labels identifying

them as mortuary estates, or land and servants assigned by the dead person as the producers of the funerary offerings. Models of offering bearers, women carrying baskets on their heads and holding flowers or fowl, may have been substitutes for the relief and painted mortuary estates or the servants of those estates.

Offering bearers are usually female, but male porters are found. Indeed, Old Kingdom stone bearers are all male; often they are dwarfs carrying sacks or jars. Male bearers tend to carry religious items such as sensors and libation jars, or scribal equipment, in contrast to the females, who carry food items.

Generally, female offering bearers are single figures, but they can be found in pairs, either two single figures or two figures sharing a single base. This pairing may represent the concept of Upper and Lower Egypt or their titular goddesses, or the two staples of Egyptian diet, bread and beer. Other offering bearers are found in processions, in single or double file, comprising a mixture of both sexes. The finest of this genre is the so-called Bersheh Procession from the Middle Kingdom tomb of Djehutinakht at Bersheh, consisting of three female bearers led by a shaven-headed priest. A similar though smaller procession was among the Meketre models, complementing the two larger offering bearers from that tomb. The largest procession is of (originally) twenty figures, from the tomb of Karenen at Saqqara.

Model Boats. Boat models were believed to provide transport along the river Nile, Egypt's main artery of communication. George A. Reisner in *Models of Ships and Boats* (Cairo, 1913) organized model boats into seven categories:

1. Square-cut craft with two rudders (Old Kingdom)
2. Craft with curling stern and one rudder (Middle Kingdom)
3. Papyrus raft/skiff (Predynastic period onward)
4. Papyriform wooden craft (Old to Middle Kingdom)
5. Papyriform wooden craft with raised finials (Early Dynastic onward)
6. Solar barks (twelfth dynasty)
7. Divine barks (New Kingdom onward)

Five further categories of New Kingdom vessels, from Dilwyn Jones's *Model Boats from the Tomb of Tut'ankhamun* (Oxford, 1990) have a deeply curved hull profile. Each type of boat had a different purpose: types 1–3 were used for transport, fishing, and leisure; types 4, 5, 7, and sometimes 2 were used for funerals or on symbolic pilgrimages to sacred sites, such as Abydos; and types 6 and 7 represented highly specialized religious craft, used to traverse the heavens and underworld in the company of the gods.

Two models were usually placed in the tomb, one

rigged for sailing south with the prevailing wind and placed facing south, the other equipped for rowing north with the current of the river and placed facing north. In some tombs, flotillas of from four to more than fifty models have been found, consisting of pairs of different types of boats.

The earliest boat models are from the Predynastic period, and are made of pottery, ivory, and bone. All are hollow canoe forms, some with raised finials closely resembling the depictions of boats on painted pottery and in tomb 100 at Hierakonpolis; others are similar to Reisner's types 3 and 5. Wooden boats appeared in the fourth and fifth dynasties at sites in Upper and Lower Egypt, becoming common at the end of the sixth dynasty. These models are carved from a single piece of wood, with masts, spars, rudders, oars, and cabins made separately and attached with pegs. Additional details are shown in paint: red and yellow for planking, white for deck details, and black for cordage. Old Kingdom boats have a more or less hollow hull, while First Intermediate period and Middle Kingdom boats tend to have solid hulls with a flat base to facilitate standing upright in the tomb.

Three important sixth dynasty groups of boats consist of eleven models from the tomb of Kaemsenu and sixteen boats from the pyramid of Queen Neith, both at Saqqara. Both these groups comprise types 1, 3, 4, and 5. The third group of eight boats, from the tomb of Nyankh-Pepi-kem at Meir, differs only in the inclusion of model sailors to crew the vessels, a feature common from the end of the sixth dynasty.

Thirteen boats came from the Middle Kingdom tomb of Meketre at Thebes. Two of the seven type 2 boats were kitchen tender boats for the preparation of meals on long journeys. Fishing and hunting in the papyrus swamps was done from a pair of type 3 skiffs, and for deeper water a small type 2 boat was provided. Meketre's type 5 ritual boats differ from most others in the provision of paddles and sails. Painted tomb scenes of the funeral and pilgrimage journeys indicate that ritual craft were usually towed to their destination.

From twelfth dynasty burials at Bersheh and el-Lisht have come the peculiar type 6 boat models. Devoid of crew, they carry instead the standards and emblems of solar deities, and were probably intended to allow the deceased to travel in the company of those gods.

A unique pair of early New Kingdom boats from the burial of Queen Ahhotep, mother of Ahmose, at Dra Abu Naga (Thebes), is of gold and silver and resemble type 7 craft. One of the boats was found resting on a model wheeled carriage. Such carriages, it is known from tomb paintings, were used to transport boats around impassable sections of the Nile.

Fragments and whole boat models have come from the eighteenth dynasty tombs of Amenhotpe II and Thutmose III in the Valley of the Kings, but it was not until the discovery of the tomb of Tutankhamun that a complete collection of New Kingdom boats was found. Comprising thirty-five boats, they form three flotillas of twenty-four traveling craft based around three larger state vessels. There are also types 3, 5, and 7 craft in the collection. The latest wooden boat model from a burial context is the type 7 craft from the twenty-first dynasty tomb of the priests of Amun at Deir el-Bahri (Bab el-Gasus).

Boats can be helpful as a dating tool. Type 1 models are not found after the end of the sixth dynasty, when they are replaced by type 2. Type 4 boats with elongated finials and bipod masts are found during the late sixth dynasty to First Intermediate Period. Type 2 models with a high stern angle are generally of the First Intermediate Period or early Middle Kingdom, while a curled rudder fork on a low-angled stern indicates a twelfth dynasty date.

Geographical and Social Distribution. Models have been found at sites from Aswan in the south to Abusir in the north. It is probably only the damp conditions of the Nile Delta that prevents the placing of models farther north, since models, albeit of pottery, have been found at the Dakhla Oasis site of Qila' el-Daba, indicating how widespread the practice was. Predynastic models have come from such sites as Abadiya, el-Adaima, and Naqada, while Old Kingdom stone servant figures have come from the *mastaba* fields of Giza and Saqqara. Late Old Kingdom models of both stone and wood have been found at Saqqara, Dahshur, Meidum, Sedment, Dara, and Qubbet el-Hawa (Aswan). First Intermediate Period and Middle Kingdom models come from both capital and provincial cemeteries the length of the Nile, such as Saqqara, Sedment, el-Lisht, Riqqeh, Beni Hasan, Bersheh, Meir, Rifeh, Asyut, Hawawish, Sheikh Farag, Gebelein, Qubbet el-Hawa, and the Theban necropolis, to name but a few.

Only the elite in Egyptian society, those in the secular and religious professions, had models in their tombs. This elite group were buried in *mastaba* tombs, in rock-cut tombs with a decorated superstructure, and in shaft tombs with one or more subterranean chambers at the bottom. Characteristic of provincial cemeteries is the arrangement of the high-status rock-cut tombs in a good stratum of rock with the shaft tombs of provincial court members below in the foothills. It is from this latter tomb type that most models have survived. Rarely do models occur in pit tombs, a form of simple shaft, except for pottery miniature agricultural implements and tools.

Excavation of these different tomb types indicates that models were placed in a variety of locations: pits outside the tomb enclosure or shaft mouth; niches cut in the floor of the entrance corridor to the superstructure; *serdabs* (statue chambers) within the *mastaba* superstructure, tomb shaft, or burial chamber; and the burial chamber proper. Some intact tombs, such as that of Nakht at Asyut (Middle Kingdom) had some models placed in the tomb chapel, the area accessible to the living and most vulnerable to the attentions of tomb robbers. It is the discovery of such intact deposits that is most instructive, but sadly most tombs have been robbed and their contents stolen, scattered, or smashed, leaving archaeologists the task of putting the pieces together again.

BIBLIOGRAPHY

Arnold, Dieter. *Der Tempel des Königs Mentuhotep von Deir el-Bahri,* vol. 3: *Die Königlichen Beigaben.* Mainz, 1981. Publication of the models belonging to Nebhepetre Montuhotep I.

Arnold, Dorothea. "Amenemhat I and the Early Twelfth Dynasty at Thebes." *Metropolitan Museum Journal* 26 (1991), 5–48. The most up-to-date and authoritative discussion of the Meketre models.

D'Auria, Sue, et al. *Mummies and Magic: The Funerary Arts of Ancient Egypt.* Boston, 1988. Exhibition catalog, covering Old and Middle Kingdom models, including those of Djehutinakht of Bershah.

Bourriau, Janine. *Pharaohs and Mortals: Egyptian Art in the Middle Kingdom.* Cambridge, 1988. Exhibition catalog, with a section on models.

Breasted, James H. *Egyptian Servant Statues.* Washington, 1948. Out of print, but available in specialist libraries, this is the first work dedicated to models.

Garstang, John. *The Burial Customs of Ancient Egypt as Illustrated by the Tombs of the Middle Kingdom.* London, 1907. Out of print, but available in specialist libraries. This is the publication of the important provincial cemetery at Beni Hasan, where hundreds of models were found.

Jones, Dilwyn. *Boats.* London, 1995. Authoritative and up-to-date work dedicated entirely to pharaonic boats.

Landström, Björn. *Ships of the Pharaohs: 4000 Years of Egyptian Shipbuilding.* London, 1970. Excellent color illustrations of model boats.

Petrie, W. M. Flinders. *Gizeh and Rifeh.* London, 1907. Publication of the intact burial of two brothers at Rifeh.

Petrie, W. M. Flinders, and Guy Brunton. *Sedment.* 2 vols. London, 1924. Publication of the models from the Sedment cemetery.

Robins, Gay, ed. *Beyond the Pyramids: Egyptian Regional Art from the Museo Egizio, Turin.* Atlanta, 1990. Exhibition catalog with entries on models from Asyut.

Spanel, Donald B. "Ancient Egyptian Boat Models of the Herakleopolitan Period and Eleventh Dynasty." *Studien zur Altägyptischen Kultur* 12 (1985), 243–253. Discusses the use of model boats as a tool for dating.

Tooley, Angela M. J. *Egyptian Models and Scenes.* Shire Egyptology, 22. Princes Risborough, 1995. Most recent work concerning models, their chronology, functions and place in funerary culture.

Vinson, Steve. *Egyptian Boats and Ships.* Princes Risborough, 1994.

Winlock, Herbert E. *Models of Daily Life in Ancient Egypt from the Tomb of Meket-Re' at Thebes.* Cambridge, Mass., 1955. Out of print, but available in specialist libraries, this remains the best source of information concerning the highly detailed models of Meketre.

ANGELA M. J. TOOLEY

MONEY. *See* Coinage; *and* Prices and Payment.

MONKEYS AND BABOONS. The prehistoric Egyptians of the fourth millennium BCE were familiar with monkeys, including the imposing and dangerous baboons and the African long-tailed monkey. Both animals were linked with the rejuvenation rituals and festivals of the Upper Egyptian chieftain, at the Predynastic stage, then later to those of the Early Dynastic Egyptian Horus-King. Since that time, they had a permanent place in ancient Egyptian religion as one of the more important animal forms into which the gods might be transformed. The word "baboon" may be derived from ancient Egyptian, probably from a linguistic root that characterized its sexual activity.

During early Old Kingdom times, baboons and monkeys may still have lived in the southern part of Upper Egypt. Nowadays, their range is limited to southern Arabia (hamadryas), Ethiopia (monkeys), and the steppes of the Sudan (baboon). Whether it is possible to conclude from tomb paintings that there were still indigenous monkey populations during the Middle Kingdom is doubtful. During the New Kingdom, monkeys were usually imported from Nubia and the land of Punt (roughly present-day Eritrea). In the Late period, the monkeys for the sacred temple troops were usually brought by ship for the temple of Ptah at Memphis, from Alexandria or from the South. Others were born in Egypt, but in the temple troops the rearing was probably only partially successful. The following types of monkeys were found in the Late period animal necropolises: hamadryas or sacred baboon (*Papio hamadryas*), baboon (*Papio cynocephalus anubis*), green monkey (*Cercopithecus aethiops*), red monkey (*Cercopithecus patas*), and the barbary ape (*Macaca sylvanus*).

Investigations into the animal necropolises of Saqqara and, above all, Tuna el-Gebel have revealed that because of the unfavorable living conditions, the life expectancy of the animals was very limited. Hardly any of some two hundred specimens examined reached their sixth to tenth years. Undernourishment, limited freedom of movement, and lack of light led to rickets, degenerative bone diseases, and probably tuberculosis. Even when trouble was taken to mend the broken bones of baboons or to feed them when they had jaw ailments, knowledge and care concerning the keeping of animals seems to have been limited. In Tuna el-Gebel there is no definite proof of hamadryas baboons. Yet in Western Thebes, eight out of eighteen specimens appear to have been hamadryas. Attempts have been made to extract reproducible DNA sequences from monkey mummies, to get genetic information, as has been done with human mummies. One problem with this technique is the widespread contamination of samples from human interference in ancient times, which had occurred during the mummification process.

A symbiosis of human and monkey has often been inferred from the many Egyptian wall paintings, going as far back as the early Old Kingdom, which show monkeys engaged in various human activities. Care must be taken when drawing conclusions about daily life from such variable and traditional images. In one tomb scene, from the fourth dynasty royal cemetery at Meidum, a boy is shown with a baboon and a green monkey on leashes, which is probably impossible. Scenes in which similar monkey keepers have four or more baboons and monkeys on leads are thematically related, and they often include a dog. The scene showing monkeys (who actually cause destruction and chaos) at markets cannot be accurate; neither is the monkey biting a thief in the leg—even if it is assumed that monkeys fulfilled a kind of policing function at markets. Trained monkeys are shown to perform dances and music there. In scenes of the fig harvest, baboons are shown climbing dom palms and throwing the fruit down, but only for themselves. There were no trained monkeys in Egypt, let alone baboons involved in the date and fig harvests. Monkeys were not present at winepresses or beer making, nor were they "guardians of the clothes bag" or helping with the morning toilet in the women's chambers. Both monkeys and baboons appear unrealistically in the rigging of sea-going boats and boat-building scenes. Egyptian wall paintings are not accurate scenes of everyday life, but artificially arranged images in accordance with the expectations of the tomb owners, for whom the monkeys in the pictures may have originally had a completely different religio-theological function. The scenes of the reversed world on ostraca and papyri, particularly common during the New Kingdom, with monkeys portrayed in playful human poses, must have been derived from mythical scenes, and were not there just to entertain. Little monkeys were readily used as decorative elements on the handles of toilet articles and as toys. They also appear on scarabs and as statuettes. Occasionally they are depicted holding the nut of a dom palm. The common combination "monkey–dom palm" had its own religious foundations; this is shown, for example, by a small stone object from an animal necropolis on which four monkeys holding dom palm nuts are grouped around a column.

Young monkeys were certainly kept as pets in the houses of the upper class, but they were unlikely to have been kept in the immediate living areas, despite the depiction of green monkeys (as well as cats, geese, and ducks) under the chair of the wife of a tomb owner. Green monkeys are dangerous animals, and they must have been kept firmly on leads, as is usually the case in tribute scenes. What is debatable, but quite possible, is that the green monkeys under the chair represent male sexuality, a symbolism that may be inferred from the analogous portrayal of the tomb owner's wife in the role of the sun god's consort.

Green monkeys and hamadryas baboons were imported from the land of Punt, as was shown in the New Kingdom representations and texts of the expedition of Queen Hatshepsut or in the (Middle Kingdom) *Story of the Shipwrecked Sailor*. Baboons also appear unrealistically in the pictures of Nubian tribute, either on the heads of the Nubians or around the necks of giraffes. At first they must have come via central African trade routes; baboons and green monkeys were later exported from Egypt to the Assyrian court and to Syria, or taken as booty by the Assyrian king Assurbanipal after the sacking of Thebes. A few Egyptian monkey keepers even appear in the Assyrian city of Nineveh.

Since ancient times monkeys have been employed as ritual animals in religious proceedings. The "humanness" of the baboons may have contributed to the early identification of the deceased ruler with the baboon. It is possible that mummified baboons were used to represent the deceased royal ancestors of the Predynastic chieftain. On the occasion of the rites to renew the physical world and the person of the chieftain, the individual ancestors were ritually deified in the form of baboons and received cultic offerings; the erection of wooden kiosks containing ancestor baboons at the great *sed*-festival of royal rejuvenation may have developed from this. A figure of a baboon as the image of King Narmer, erected by an official, implicitly suggests the transformation of the king into a baboon, no doubt as part of a rejuvenation festival. The king was identified with a baboon god, known as the "Great White One." Some scholars think that the title "Great White One" derives from the silver-gray mane of a dominant hamadryas. Yet statuettes of baboons and green monkeys, deposited in front of Early Dynastic sanctuaries, have been interpreted as votive offerings to the cult.

Small Early Dynastic plaques show the king or priests (Iwenmutef priests) performing the Opening of the Mouth ceremony and transfiguration before monkeys. The king walks in front of a baboon with a vessel; the baboons receive wine jars. Rites involving monkeys are documented by illustrations, as well as by later religious texts that describe the danger of monkeys "who cut off heads." The image of a baboon with raised tail serves as the hieroglyph for "enraged"; the baboon's wildness made it into a dangerous, apotropaic intercessory, being the primordial creation in a mythical landscape.

As primeval animals, baboons and green monkeys were an (essential) part of the Egyptian cosmogony. The earliest gods are sometimes depicted with baboon's heads. Hapy, one of the Four Sons of Horus, who was connected

MONKEYS AND BABOONS. *The god Thoth is represented by these baboons on the early Ptolemaic tomb of Petosiris, a priest of Thoth, at Tuna el-Gebel.* (Courtesy of David P. Silverman)

with mummification, was a baboon-headed canopic god. Baboonlike creatures guarded the mythical "Lake of Fire" and were then transferred to the newly created cosmic space. The baboon became an aspect of the sun god Re and of the moon god Thoth-Khonsu, as well as a stellar constellation. The green monkey was an aspect of the invisible primeval god Atum, particularly in the form of a monkey shooting with bow and arrow. The observation that baboons greet the rising sun in the morning by barking gave rise to a favorite theme in sculpture, painting, and relief—of the baboon worshiping the sun with raised hands. As companions to the sun god, monkey demons appeared in the royal netherworld texts. Alongside the helping role was the dangerous aspect of the baboon, whose form could be assumed by the enemy of the gods

(Apophis, Seth). Sexual potency and prowess were the characteristics of the baboon god Bebon; he was closely related to the baboon god Baba, who had red ears, blue hindquarters, and the features of Seth. As a god with equal rights in the council of the gods, Baba was ridiculed there.

The squatting baboon, under whose image the scribes of the royal residence did their writing, became an early, visible, protective form of the important Egyptian god Thoth. The baboon of the god Thoth (also called Isdes) became the assisting god in the judgment hall in the hereafter. Thoth's representative cult locations were the towns of Hermopolis in Upper and Lower Egypt. In the temple forecourts of these towns stood images of the protective (city) god Thoth-baboon. The cosmic role of the baboon as the animal of the moon god Thoth eventually resulted in his identification with the moon god Khonsu. Statues of Khonsu in the shape of a baboon stood in front of the Theban Khonsu temple. In the Late period, the god Thoth-Khonsu became an important nocturnal oracle god. This baboon god statue, to whom written petitions for the priests were submitted, was called Metasythmis, Greek for the "hearing ear."

From the New Kingdom onward, temple statues of baboons appear in the cult—usually a maned baboon. The baboons squat on a raised platform, often accessed by a flight of stairs; they are often holding *wḏȝt*-eyes. In the Hermopolis of Middle Egypt, giant quartzite baboons belonging to Amenhotpe III were found, possibly once grouped around a sacred lake. Sacred temple monkeys were kept for the rejuvenation of the baboon gods connected with the annual festival. Late period titles, such as "Priest of the Living Baboon" or "Priest of the Osiris-Baboon," were held by people who served gods in the court of the sanctuaries that had the form of baboon statues. The group responsible for the god also looked after the sacred temple monkeys. A temple of the god Osiris-Baboon, from the time of Alexander IV, son of Alexander the Great, lies at the entrance to the underground ibis and monkey cemeteries at Tuna el-Gebel (called in Egyptian a "resting place for the ibis and the baboon"). The well-preserved sanctuary in front of the monkey necropolis at Saqqara near Memphis was probably dedicated to the same god. Other large statues of monkeys stood in the entrance area to the animal cemeteries. Numerous figurines were recovered depicting baboons and, more rarely, green monkeys. In the temple of Babylon in Old Cairo, a statue of a green monkey once stood in the forecourt as the town god. The two ensign gods "Baboon on the Standard" and "Green Monkey on the Standard" formed part of the processions at the great Egyptian festivals.

There was no personal worship of monkeys in Egypt. The ritual interment of sacred monkeys, which were deified only after they had died and which had been kept exclusively as ritual animals in the temples, may well have begun with the monkeys buried in a tomb from the time of Amenhotpe III in the Valley of the Kings in Thebes. The animals had probably been used during the *sed*-festival of that ruler. Not until the twenty-sixth dynasty were sacred baboons buried in the ibis necropolis near Tuna el-Gebel. In the early Ptolemaic period, monkey mummies are found alongside those of ibises and falcons in almost every animal necropolis. The highest quality burials are those in the well-documented baboon galleries of Memphis at Saqqara, as well as those at Tuna el-Gebel, Abydos, and the Valley of the Monkeys (Wadi Gabbanet el-Girud in southwestern Thebes), all probably from the late Ptolemaic and early Roman periods.

Sacred temple baboons bore individual names; there is no evidence for that with regard to green monkeys. The sacred temple baboons of the Ptolemaic period at Saqqara have their genealogies inscribed on their coffins, and often their dates of birth, installation, and death. At Tuna el-Gebel, the well-known spell to the sky goddess Nut from the Pyramid Texts is regularly found on pre-Ptolemaic coffin lids. The deified baboon first appeared there as "Osiris-Baboon, justified," with no individual name; the first time a personal name appeared was on a piece of linen from the twenty-sixth or twenty-seventh dynasty. A painted Ptolemaic linen shroud is the only proof that in Tuna el-Gebel the name of the animal's mother was recorded. Otherwise, the names of the sacred baboons of the Ptolemaic period there are known from the stone false-door slabs of the coffin niches, from ritual scenes in the cult chambers of the sacred baboons, and from papyri that mention the cultic places of specific sacred baboons in the galleries. According to these texts, the Hermopolitan baboons were often named "Thoth-has-come," "Thoth-is-the-one-who-has-given-him," "Thoth-has-been-found," or "the-strong-featured-one-has-come."

From the twenty-sixth dynasty onward, mummified baboons were buried in wooden coffins. Under the first two Ptolemies, the coffins of baboons buried in special rooms were then placed into costly limestone sarcophagi. Later, the practice of simple wooden coffins returned. Only in Tuna el-Gebel, and during the reigns of Ptolemy I and Ptolemy II, were there individual baboon cult areas in fairly large rock-cut chambers. One special room at the foot of the entrance steps served a statue cult of the gods Thoth-Baboon and Thoth-Ibis. Nocturnal petitions would also have been presented here. The rock-cut chambers were lined with stone blocks and decorated with ritual scenes. They belonged to deified baboons separately identified by names in the form "Osiris-Baboon–*Name*–justified." In front of the (often several) chambers' cult areas, was a four-step staircase, with offering stands and libation slabs. The cult areas had been sold to priestly families who lived off the income from petitioners and the donations from the state on the occasion of religious festivals. The baboons were probably the sacred animals of the town god of Hermopolis, Thoth-Baboon. Deified, they became Osiris, divine company for the town god Thoth-Baboon on the occasion of the Osiris festival. Then, transformed into Osiris-Baboon, they were subsequently reborn. Like the god, the baboons partook of the resurrection of the god Osiris.

The majority of the baboons buried in the wall and floor niches of the animal necropolises were probably members of the monkey colony kept in the temple precincts. In late Ptolemaic times, new cult areas were no longer created, so new monkeys were buried in the old baboon cult chambers. Sacred monkeys continued to be present in Egyptian temples, but lavish monkey burials seem to have ceased in the first century CE.

[*See also* Thoth.]

BIBLIOGRAPHY

Houlihan, Patrick F. "Harvesters or Monkey Business?" *Göttinger Miszellen* 157 (1997), 31–43.

Keimer, Ludwig. "Pavian und Dum-Palme" *Mitteilungen des Deutschen Archäologischen Instituts Kairo* 8 (1938), 42–45.

Kessler, Dieter. *Tuna el-Gebel II. Die Paviankultkammer G-C-C-2.* Hildesheimer Ägyptologische Beiträge. Hildesheim, 1998.

Nerlich, Andreas G., et al. "Osteopathological Findings in Mummified Baboons from Ancient Egypt." *International Journal of Osteoarchaeology* 3 (1993), 189–198. A study on illness in baboons.

Perizonius, Rutger, et al. "Monkey Mummies and North Saqqara." *Egyptian Archaeology* 3 (1993), 31–33.

Smith, Harry S. *A Visit to Ancient Egypt. Life at Memphis and Saqqara (c. 500–30 BC).* A description of a baboon gallery in an informative book on Late period Memphis and its cemetery.

Störk, Lothar. "*Pavian.*" In *Lexikon der Ägyptologie*, 4:915–920. Wiesbaden, 1982.

Vandier d'Abbadie, J. "Les singes familiers dans l'ancienne Egypte." *Revue d'Egyptologie* 16 (1964), 147–177; 17 (1965), 177–188; and 18 (1966), 143–201. Leading study of tomb scenes, ostraca, vessels, and other materials showing monkeys.

DIETER KESSLER
Translated from German by Julia Harvey and Martha Goldstein

MONOTHEISM. Attention has been given to the issue of monotheism in ancient Egyptian religion since the early days of Egyptology. One idea proposed was that Egyptian religion was originally monotheistic and only secondarily developed into a polytheistic system, following the principle of nineteenth-century anthropology that the simple precedes the complex in cultures. According to this view, intellectuals and initiates were thought to have retained a belief in a primitive monotheistic deity while accepting the multiplicity of gods and goddesses as mere personifications of divine attributes; that is, there was one god for the wise and many for the common folk. Theologically, the solitude of the primeval god Nun before the Creation was adduced in support of an underlying primitive monotheism.

This interpretation was challenged by discoveries in the Early Dynastic royal cemeteries at Abydos and by the publication of the Old Kingdom Pyramid Texts, and it was alternatively proposed that monotheism developed from a preexistent polytheism. Some scholars have maintained that even as early as the Old Kingdom there was a nameless divine being behind the multiplicity of gods, whereas others have regarded Egyptian religion as only gradually moving toward monotheism. Since Egyptian religion was a historically developed rather than a revealed religion, polytheism has been seen by some as surviving along with the emergence in the New Kingdom of a transcendent deity who could be manifest in many forms.

The Term "God." The situations in which the Egyptian word for "god" was used in a way suggestive of a monotheistic deity are basically two: personal names and the Wisdom Literature. In the Early Dynastic period and during the Old Kingdom, there existed personal names containing the word "god." Being given to a child at birth, theophoric personal names were spontaneous expressions of joy and devotion to the god of whom the parents had asked the gift of a healthy child. In some of these names the Egyptian term for "god" appears to be used in an abstract way—for example, "god is gracious," "whom god loves," "whom god fashioned," or "god lives." But paralleling such names are others that mention a specific god, such as "Khnum is gracious," "beloved of Re," or "Ptah lives"; this suggests that when the term "god" was used in naming a child, the parents were thinking not of an abstract divinity but rather of a specific local deity to whom they had prayed. There are, in fact, personal names that instead of using the masculine word "god," employ the feminine word "goddess," as in "may the *ka* of the goddess exist," or "great is the goddess." Nowhere does evidence exist to suggest that "goddess" was ever employed as an abstract term in Egypt. So, by analogy, it is probable that when "god" appears in personal names, the speaker was thinking of the deity closest to him—one embodying all divine attributes, but not the sole divinity. In interpreting these early names, it is also possible that "my god" rather than "god" is the proper translation, owing to the fact that in Old Egyptian the first person singular pronoun was regularly omitted in writing.

Monotheism has also been held by some scholars to be present in the Wisdom Literature, where as early as the *Instruction of Ptahhotep*, the term "god" seems to be used in an abstract sense. Some have supposed that the authors of Wisdom texts, being of the elite, were acquainted with the concept of a transcendent monotheistic deity. It should be stressed, however, that in all Wisdom texts the polytheistic element is also present: use is made of the word "gods" in the plural, and specific deities are also named. Since Wisdom Literature was composed for the benefit of the elite scribal class and not intended for broad public dissemination, its polytheistic element was hardly a concession on the part of the sages to appeal to a polytheistic public. Moreover, later Wisdom texts actually mention specific deities even more frequently than earlier Wisdom texts, casting doubt on any supposed trend toward monotheism. It is most unlikely that references to various deities or to gods in the plural were mere turns of phrase. In both the *Instructions for Merikare* and the *Instructions of Ani* there are references to caring for the cultic needs of the gods; these must be concrete deities who possessed temples and priests.

In composing a Wisdom text, the writer desired to make his work comprehensible to bureaucrats throughout the land, not just at the royal residence in Memphis or at Thebes. Along the Nile there were many towns, villages, and districts, each with its primary local deities; and in any given community a person would tend to invest the local deity with the highest attributes possible. One must also reckon with mobility as bureaucrats moved from one part of Egypt to another. Because it would have been inappropriate to name a specific god as dominant throughout the text, recourse was had to the vaguer, less precise word "god" instead. Circumstances would change in place and time, so it was best for the author of a Wisdom text to use the neutral "god" in generalizing for the reader's benefit.

Henotheism. The approach to the divine in the Wisdom Literature is related to the concept of henotheism, whereby a writer, speaker, or devotee selects a god as his or her own single almighty deity, without, however, denying the existence of other gods and goddesses, any of whom might be seen by someone else as the principal deity. Superficially, this might look like monotheism, but it is not; the Egyptians did not impose a universally exclusive god except during the Amarna period, when Akhenaten selected the Aten and curbed the cults of traditional deities. Of the terms that have been utilized to describe Egyptian religion, "henotheism" seems to be the most appropriate. It implies that when an Egyptian honored a god or goddess in hymn or in prayer, he or she treated that deity, at that moment, as though the deity possessed the characteristics of a sole divinity, with all other gods and goddesses —even the mighty ones—paling into insignificance. The deity who is being addressed at the moment stands out as all-important. The fact that more than one god could be called "king," or "lord," of the gods does not reflect a stage between polytheism and monotheism.

A nice illustration of the way a devout Egyptian might single out even a goddess as the object of his devotion occurs in the tomb inscription of the Ramessid scribe Simut. Although initially Simut speaks of the god who guided him early in life as an unnamed male deity, the bulk of the text describes his selection of the goddess Mut to be his patron (to whom he bequeaths all his property), because he found Mut to be at the head of the gods, greater than any other deity, with all that transpires at her command (Wilson, 1970).

It can be argued that the very existence of the god depended on differentiation, such as took place initially at Creation, and that it was therefore impossible to have a deity who was totally one and absolute to the exclusion of others once the existential realm had come to be. Only at the very beginning of Creation was there exclusive unity, which became lost in the differentiating process, when even the Creator became distinguished from the many other deities of the pantheon. A return to the primal monistic state would have meant the very negation of ex-

istence. Thus, the Egyptian view of Creation and of the existential realm presented a serious impediment to the development of monotheism from polytheism.

A god could be a unity, as revealed in theophany or epiphany, or when honored by an individual in prayer or hymn, but he/she was also manifold in nature, capable of appearing in numerous forms. A typically Egyptian thought structure involved thinking in pairs. Within this structure, a deity could be both the one and the many. This concept has been termed "complementary thinking," whereby opposites, instead of contradicting each other logically, complement each other in expressing reality. For monotheism to have developed would have required a radical change in this complementary thought pattern, which permitted the divine, on the one hand, to be a unity in the individual encounter, and, on the other hand, to possess many forms of appearance and attributes.

Summodeism. During the New Kingdom, particularly in the Ramessid period, hymns were composed that describe a divinity who is a kind of universal super-transcendent god, of whom all other deities are merely secondary emanations. This kind of theology, with its notion of an abstract transcendent god who stands above all other deities and whose true nature cannot even be fathomed by either gods or humans, has been regarded as reflecting a crisis in the traditional polytheism; however, it certainly is not monotheism, since the existence of many deities—even though of lesser quality—is still not denied. Here the term "summodeism" best describes the situation in which there is a supreme god heading a polytheistic pantheon, whose multitude of deities exist as hypostases of the high god by virtue of his transforming himself into the many.

Although Ramessid theologians may have been thinking about divinity along such lines, henotheism with its implicit polytheism nevertheless prevailed in the practice of religion. There is a letter written by the high priest of Amun during the reign of Ramesses IX (translation in Wente, 1990, pp. 38–39) that illustrates how even the top ecclesiastical figure adheres to polytheism when he invokes the blessing of Montu as well as of Amun-Re, king of the gods, for recipients of his letter. In correspondences penned by the elite during the late Ramessid age, there is constant mention of numerous deities. The fact that in these letters one finds the writer saying, "I'm all right today; tomorrow is in god's hands," might suggest a belief in the existence of a monotheistic deity because the term "god" is modified by the definite article just as in Coptic biblical literature, where it is used in reference to the monotheistic god of the Bible. However, the Ramessid-era expression about tomorrow's being in god's hands occurs in letters that also regularly contain invocations to numerous named deities. Such a collocation in letters written by officials at the end of the New Kingdom does not suggest monotheism, let alone summodeism—which, unlike henotheism, was largely confined to the realm of theology without seriously altering traditional religious beliefs and practices.

Akhenaten's Monotheism. Although the Aten is attested as a god prior to Akhenaten's reign, Akhenaten's institution of the cult of the Aten as sole deity is unique in the history of Egyptian religion. What he did was to single out this god—who was manifest in the sun disk and its radiating rays of sunlight—from among the others, to be the object of veneration. The Aten was the sun god, and the solar disk was the form in which this divinity appeared. In fact, over the course of Akhenaten's reign one can trace a development that reflects the king's role in implementing a radical new theology. Although other deities were initially still recognized, Akhenaten soon ordered the abrogation of their cults; the persecution of traditional deities, particularly those of Thebes, intensified, as the name and representation of the god Amun were expunged from monuments throughout the land. Even the plural word for "gods" was frequently erased. The king, who had earlier dropped the name Amenhotpe in favor of Akhenaten, had the didactic name of the Aten revised so that it no longer contained elements suggestive of polytheism.

The Amarna theology, as revealed in texts and scenes from tombs and temples, supports the idea that it constituted a form of monotheism. The Aten was about as close to an absolute god as the Egyptians got. He was a jealous god who did not tolerate other deities. Texts speak of the living Aten beside whom there is no other; he was the sole god. The Amarna religion can be described as monotheistic in the sense that it was an established religion whose theology was articulated by Akhenaten, who alone comprehended the true nature of the Aten. In effect, his theology became the religion. By proclaiming the universality and unity of Aten and rejecting the traditional pantheon, Akhenaten was negating the old polytheistic religion.

There are some qualifications to Akhenaten's monotheism. The king, for example, was himself a god and had his own high priest. Whereas Akhenaten in his inscriptions never called himself "god," but only "son of god," there are clear cases in which he is referred to as "god" by his subjects, in such expression as "my god who made me" or "the god who fashions people and makes the Two Lands to live." Akhenaten was not directly identified with the Aten, but since Aten was Re, therefore his son (who was the son of Re and also occasionally identified as Re) was of the same essence as his father, the Aten. The monotheism of Amarna comprised a father–son relationship, in which the son was the incarnation and image of the sun god, daily reborn as the Aten was reborn. In fact, the dual process of the Aten's daily self-creation and his simultaneous regeneration of Akhenaten constituted the focal point of Amarna theology, according to Žabkar (1954).

What is more, Akhenaten's queen Nefertiti also received divine attributes. At Amarna she appears as a deity along with the Aten and Akhenaten in funerary offering formulae, and there are praises and prayers to the king that are paralleled by ones directed to his queen. Hymns to the Aten can be introduced by the words, "Adoration of the Aten, Akhenaten, and Nefertiti." There thus seems to have been a triadic relationship among the Aten and his children, Akhenaten and Nefertiti. It is quite possible that in developing his religion, Akhenaten was familiar with a much older theology surrounding the creator god Atum and his two offspring, the god Shu and the goddess Tefnut, who were consubstantial emanations of the creator god, providing life and order as energizers at Creation. Thus the Aten filled the role of Atum, while Akhenaten was Shu, the god of air, light, and life, and Nefertiti was equivalent to Tefnut, who symbolized the correct order of the world. The Shu-aspect of Akhenaten is iconographically evident in the four-feathered crowns sometimes worn by the king; and Nefertiti's name, which means "the beautiful one has returned," possibly equates her with Shu's twin sister Tefnut, who according to mythology returned to Egypt as a charming woman after going south as a ferocious lioness.

The king and queen worshiped the Aten directly, whereas commoners generally approached the Aten only through the intermediation of the king. Absent from the Amarna scene were those processions of portable barks containing images of the gods that had traditionally been adored by the populace. Instead, the king and queen were the objects of popular veneration as they moved about the city of Akhetaten in procession. Evidence from two letters found at Amarna, however, indicates that a commoner could directly implore the Aten in prayer to bestow benefits, so that it would be wrong to suggest that Akhenaten had a monopoly on piety.

There are a few minor points that have been adduced as qualifications to Akhenaten's monotheism. In his boundary stelae of Year 5 of his reign, the king mentions that he found the site of Akhetaten belonging to no god or goddess—a tacit admission of the existence of other deities besides Aten. The early date of this proclamation may, however, not yet reflect the fully developed Aten theology with its exclusion of polytheism. In Amarna texts, the concepts of "fate," "fortune," and *maat* (*mꜣˁt;* "justice") tend to be personified as goddesses, but such deifications are of a different order than deities of cosmic nature and hardly constitute a serious objection to the characterization of the Aten as a monotheistic divinity. Although some inhabitants of Amarna bore theophoric names that contained the names of traditional deities, this phenomenon has its analogy in the persistence of old theophoric names among Coptic Christians. It has also been pointed out that in private homes and chapels at Amarna, documents have been unearthed that attest to the retention of traditional gods and goddesses as household deities. It is possible, however, that such evidence should be assigned to the reign of one of Akhenaten's successors, Smenkhkare and Tutankhamun.

All in all, Amarna theology can be considered monotheism because it proclaims "the unity of god" and excludes the constellations of older polytheistic deities. Like Judaism, Christianity, and Islam, it was an established religion, founded on the revelation of the Aten to Akhenaten, who alone knew the Aton and anathematized the old polytheistic tradition. The degree to which Amarna theology influenced Israelite monotheism has been much debated. Although there is some similarity between the Great Aten Hymn and Psalm 104 in the negative evaluation of nighttime and in the treatment of nature as nondivine, responding to the life-giving activity of the divinity who constantly nurtures creation, the peculiar theocracy inherent in the triadic relationship of the Aten, Akhenaten, and Nefertiti bears absolutely no resemblance to the god of the Hebrew scriptures.

[*See also* Akhenaten; Aten; Divinity; *and* Religion.]

BIBLIOGRAPHY

Allen, James P. "The Natural Philosophy of Akhenaten." In *Religion and Philosophy in Ancient Egypt*, edited by William Kelly Simpson, pp. 89–101. Yale Egyptological Studies, 3. New Haven, 1989. Regards Atenism as natural philosophy rather than religion, suggesting that Akhenaten, not the Aten, was the god of the new religion.

Assmann, Jan. *Egyptian Solar Religion in the New Kingdom: Re, Amun, and the Crisis of Polytheism.* Translated by Anthony Alcock. London and New York, 1995. Treats the emergence of a high transcendent deity during the New Kingdom, particularly as revealed in Ramessid hymns.

Assmann, Jan. *Moses the Egyptian: The Memory of Egypt in Western Monotheism.* Cambridge and London, 1997. Traces the origins of Moses' monotheism to Akhenaten's religious revolution.

Hornung, Erik. *Conceptions of God in Ancient Egypt: The One and the Many.* Translated by John Baines. Ithaca, 1982. Provides a good summary of the monotheism debate among historians of Egyptian religion, arguing that monotheism was not a possible development from polytheism except through the radical reforms of Akhenaten.

Johnson, W. Raymond. "Amenhotep III and Amarna: Some New Considerations." *Journal of Egyptian Archaeology* 82 (1996), 65–82. Discusses the possible identification of Akhenaten's father Amenhotep III with the Aten, and Akhenaten and Nefertiti as the divine pair Shu and Tefnut.

Morenz, Siegfried. *Egyptian Religion.* Translated by Ann E. Keep. Ithaca, 1973. Deals with the basic characteristics of Egyptian religion, divine immanence and transcendence, and Atenism as a trinitarian theology.

Murnane, William J. *Texts from the Amarna Period in Egypt.* Society of Biblical Literature Writings from the Ancient World, 5. Atlanta, 1995. Convenient up-to-date translations of texts relating to the Amarna period.

Redford, Donald B. *Akhenaten, the Heretic King.* Princeton, 1984. An overview of Akhenaten's reign, important for its discussion of documentation from Thebes pertaining to the early years of Akhenaten's reign before the move to Amarna.

Silverman, David P. "Divinity and Deities in Ancient Egypt." In *Religion in Ancient Egypt: Gods, Myths, and Personal Practice*, edited by Byron E. Shafer, pp. 7–87. Ithaca and London, 1991. Discusses types of deities, divine kingship, and monotheistic tendencies in the reign of Akhenaten.

Wente, Edward F. *Letters from Ancient Egypt.* Society of Biblical Literature Writings from the Ancient World, 1. Atlanta, 1990. Provides translations of letters of the Ramessid era (pp. 111–204) and the two letters from Amarna in which a commoner addresses the Aten directly (pp. 94–96).

Wilson, John A. "Akh-en-Aton and Nefert-iti." *Journal of Near Eastern Studies* 32 (1973), 235–241. Concentrates on divine aspects of the king and the queen at Amarna.

Wilson, John A. "The Theban Tomb (No. 409) of Si-Mut, Called Kiki." *Journal of Near Eastern Studies* 29 (1970), 187–192.

Žabkar, Louis V. "The Theocracy of Amarna and the Doctrine of the Ba." *Journal of Near Eastern Studies* 13 (1954), 87–101. A well-documented discussion of the theology surrounding the father–son relationship between the Aten and Akhenaten.

EDWARD F. WENTE

MONTU (*Mnṯw*), a local Upper Egyptian solar deity who became state god. This came about because of his association with the victorious King Nebhepetre Montuhotep I of the eleventh dynasty (r. 2061–2011 BCE), who had successfully reunified Egypt, bringing an end to the instability of the First Intermediate Period. The king's name means "Montu-is-satisfied." During the twelfth dynasty, the deity Montu became subordinated to another Upper Egyptian deity, Amun, to assume the role of war god. Cult centers were maintained for the worship of Montu at four sites within the Theban region, the fourth Upper Egyptian nome (province): Armant, southwest of modern Luxor on the western bank of the Nile; Medamud, northeast of Luxor, inland from the eastern bank; Tod, southwest of Luxor on the eastern bank; and Karnak, north-northeast of Luxor, adjacent to the northern side of the great temple of Amun. The temples date from the Middle Kingdom at all these sites, except for Karnak, where the earliest structure is New Kingdom and is securely attributed to Amenhotpe III (r. 1410–1372 BCE).

Montu is most commonly represented as a falcon-headed man, whose wig is surmounted by a solar disk, with a double *uraeus* (royal cobra crown) behind which two tall plumes extend vertically. In later periods, Montu also appears with a bull's head and a plumed solar headdress, as a manifestation of the Buchis bull of Armant. A bull sacred to Montu was also revered at Medamud.

In addition to iconography, in temple reliefs, the inherent solar aspect of Montu (as the composite sun deity Montu-Re) is shown by his symmetrical pairing with the sun god Atum of Lower Egypt, frequently escorting the king into the presence of Amun. The name of Montu's chief city, Armant n Iuny (Old Eg., *Iwny*), and Atum's Heliopolis Iunu (Old Eg., *Iwnw*), or On, sounded so similar to the Egyptians that the former was referred to as On-of-Montu or Iunu-Mentu (*Iwnw Mntw*), for clarification.

Montu's veneration as war god began during the Middle Kingdom. In the *Story of Sinuhe*, Montu was praised by the tale's hero after he defeated the "strong man" of Retjenu. During the New Kingdom, the warrior pharaohs of the eighteenth dynasty, in particular, sought to emulate Montu. The Gebel Barkal stela of Thutmose III (r. 1504–1452 BCE) describes the king as "a valiant Montu on the battlefield." Royal warships were adorned with striding Montus, brandishing maces or spears, each figure styled as lord of one of his four cult centers. There is a mythological basis for the use of the god's image in defense of the king, the earthly son of the sun god Re. A hymn on the Armant stela of Usermontu, from that era, described Montu as "the raging one who prevails over the serpent-demon Nik," and the one "who causes Re to sail in his bark and who overthrows his serpent enemy." Later in the New Kingdom, Ramesses II's personal identification with Montu was so strong that a cult statue—using his throne name Usermaare Setepenre, compounded with the epithet "Montu-in-the-Two-Lands"—was venerated in the king's honor during his lifetime.

Montu has been depicted in the company of three consorts: Tjenenet, Iunyt, and Rettawy. He has also been paired in texts with another "raging" god, Seth, perhaps as a contrast between controlled and uncontrolled divine aggressiveness.

BIBLIOGRAPHY

Borghouts, J. F. "Month." In *Lexikon der Ägyptologie*, 4, 200–204. Wiesbaden, 1982. Scholarly essay in English with extensive bibliographical references.

Mond, Robert, and Oliver H. Myers. *Temples of Armant: A Preliminary Survey*. London, 1940. Report of the excavation of Montu's temples by the Egypt Exploration Society.

Watterson, Barbara. *The Gods of Ancient Egypt*. New York, 1984. A survey of Egyptian deities for the general reader, with Montu discussed on pp. 190–191.

Werner, Edward K. "The God Montu: From the Earliest Attestations to the End of the New Kingdom." Ph.D. diss., Yale University, 1985. The principal study of Montu.

Werner, Edward K. "Montu and the 'Falcon Ships' of the Eighteenth Dynasty." *Journal of the American Research Center in Egypt* 23 (1986), 107–123. Analysis of Montu's image as a decorative motif on royal warships, as preserved in relief, painting, and actual models from the tomb of Amenhotpe II.

EDWARD K. WERNER

MONTUEMHET, an exceptional personality who lived in the transitional period during which the Kushite domination of Egypt came to an end (twenty-fifth dynasty) and the Saite dynasty assumed power. His name and titles are found on fifteen statues, more or less well conserved and of very high quality. An admirable head of a statue, attributed to him with great probability, gives us his portrait (Cairo Museum no. 647); the powerful traits are those of an elderly man, with a face full of experience and gentlemanly guile. He took pride in his numerous titles: first and foremost "Prince of the City (Thebes)" and "Governor of Upper Egypt"; designated simply as "Fourth Prophet of Amun," he in fact directed all of the Theban clergy. The interminable lists of his traditional titles hardly furnish precise facts that are "historical" in the modern sense of the term, but it is known that his direct power extended "from Elephantine in the South up to Hermopolis" in Middle Egypt, therefore including the Theban region and that of Abydos, where his name is attested.

Contrary to what is sometimes claimed, he was by no means of Kushite descent. He was the son of a prophet of Amun and Montu, named Nsiptah, and his mother's name was Istenkheb. His family, of which we have knowledge of five generations, had occupied very high positions in Egypt. Montuemhet and his relatives were Thebans who were allied to the Kushites. Politically adroit, Montuemhet came to very good terms with the Divine Adoratrices; these "wives of the god Amun" were princesses of the Kushite royal family. Active under Taharqa (r. 690–664 BCE), after the fall of Thebes he figures among the princes who received the investiture of Assarhadon the conquering Assyrian. He went on to support Psamtik I the Saite, who in 656 BCE imposed his own daughter Nitocris upon Thebes as Divine Adoratrice. He took part in an oracular ceremony in 651 BCE, but he disappears from inscriptions about 648 BCE. Three wives are known: Shepenmont, Neskhonsu—the mother of Nsiptah, who inherited his titles—and finally Oudjarenes, of the Kushite royal family, with whom he had a son named Pasherienmut. Montuemhet's glory is attested by his vast tomb at Thebes (tomb 34), a jewel of the Asasif, on the western bank of Thebes; currently in ruins, it is in the process of restoration, offering vestiges of wonderful reliefs.

BIBLIOGRAPHY

Leclant, Jean. *Montuemhet, quatrième prophète d'Amon, prince de la Ville*. Bibliothèque d'étude, 35. Cairo, 1962.

Parker, Richard A. *A Saïte Oracle Papyrus from Thebes in the Brooklyn Museum (Pap. Brooklyn 47.218.3)*. Providence, 1962.

Russman, Edna R. "Relief Decoration in the Tomb of Montuemhet." *Journal of the American Research Center in Egypt* 31 (1994), 1–19.

Russman, Edna R. "Montuemhet's Kushite Wife." *Journal of the American Research Center in Egypt* 34 (1997), 21–39.

JEAN LECLANT
Translated from French by Susan Romanosky

MONTUHOTEP I, NEBHEPETRE (r. 2061–2010 BCE), a king of the eleventh dynasty and the founder of the Middle Kingdom. He was one of three pharaohs

MONTUHOTEP I, NEBHEPETRE. *Granite head of Montuhotep I, eleventh dynasty.* This head belongs to one of the king's *heb-sed* statues that once flanked the causeway leading to his mortuary temple at Deir el-Bahri. (The Metropolitan Museum of Art, Rogers Fund, 1907. [07.228.34])

whom the ancient Egyptians venerated above all others for having brought unity to their nation and an end to the chaos of civil disorder. He is included in a procession of royal statues depicted on the Ramesseum's Second Pylon (from the nineteenth dynasty) with Menes, the founder of the unified Egyptian state (c.3000 BCE) and Ahmose, the ultimate victor over the Hyksos and founder of the New Kingdom (1550 BCE). Montuhotep was revered for his victory over his Herakleopolitan rivals, which brought an end to the First Intermediate Period. All of Egypt was then brought under Theban control and the Middle Kingdom was established. He was the son and successor of Nakht-neb-tep-nefer Antef III and Queen Yah, possibly the great-great grandson of Tepya Montuhotep, putative founder of the eleventh dynasty at Thebes.

The king's choice of names has caused scholars some confusion. When he came to the throne in 2060 BCE, Montuhotep I ("Montu-is-satisfied") used the Horus name Se'ankhhibtowy ("he-who-causes-the-heart-of-the-Two-Lands-to-live"), which he retained until the fourteenth year of his reign. The war begun by his predecessors against the kings of Herakleopolis was vigorously pur-

sued until the city fell in 2040 BCE. As his victories mounted, Montuhotep assumed more elaborate titles: Horus Netjeryhedjet, Two-Ladies Netjeryhedjet, King of Upper and Lower Egypt Nebhepetre, and Son of Re Montuhotep. Some time before his thirty-ninth year of reign, with reunification realized, he adopted and retained the full five-part titulary of a traditional pharaoh: Horus Sematawy ("uniter-of-the-Two-Lands"), Two-Ladies Sematawy, Horus-of-Gold Qashuty ("high-of-plumes"), King of Upper and Lower Egypt Nebhepetre, and Son of Re Montuhotep. In addition to restoring order within Egypt, inscriptions refer to his campaigns in Nubia and the adjacent desert areas to restore Egyptian control there.

The principal monument of Montuhotep is his mortuary temple, set into the bay of cliffs at Deir el-Bahri in the Theban necropolis. The structure was derived from the traditional tombs with courtyards, as used by his ancestors. The base of the temple is a large, asymmetrical terrace in the form of an inverted T, which rose about 5.5 meters (18 feet) above its courtyard and was fronted by a roofed colonnade. The temple is symmetrical and was based on a core structure once thought to be a small pyramid. Around that structure was a walled-in pillared hall, enclosed by a colonnade. Behind it, a peristyle court led directly to a hypostyle hall that was cut into the cliff, at the back of which a stone sanctuary had been constructed. Two burial chambers had been prepared for Montuhotep: the first was beneath the garden courtyard in front of the terrace; the second was excavated deep into the cliff. His queens, Tem and Neferu, were also interred within the complex. Half a millennium later, Queen Hatshepsut had her own mortuary temple constructed next to that of her royal precedessor, using its design as her prototype.

Upon his death about 2010 BCE, after a reign of fifty-one years, Nebhepetre Montuhotep I was succeeded by his eldest surviving son by Queen Tem, Montuhotep II (r. 2011–2000 BCE).

BIBLIOGRAPHY

Arnold, Dieter. *Der Tempel des Königs Mentuhotep von Deir el-Bahari.* 2 vols. Mainz, 1974. Arnold rejects the central pyramid proposed by E. Naville (1907–1913) and accepted by H. E. Winlock (1947).

Arnold, Dieter. *The Temple of Montuhotep at Deir el-Bahari.* New York, 1979. Publication of the excavation records of H. E. Winlock, as well as recent findings.

Hayes, William C. *The Scepter of Egypt,* pt. 1. New York, 1953. Chapter 10 includes discussion of numerous objects from the king's mortuary temple at Deir el-Bahri.

Hayes, William C. "The Middle Kingdom in Egypt." In *The Cambridge Ancient History,* 3d ed., vol. 1, pt. 2, pp. 464–531. Cambridge, 1971.

Naville, Édouard. *The XIth Dynasty Temple at Deir el-Bahari.* 3 vols. London, 1907–1913.

Winlock, Herbert E. *Excavations at Deir el Bahri 1911–1931.* New York, 1942.

Winlock, Herbert E. *The Rise and Fall of the Middle Kingdom in Thebes.* New York, 1947.

EDWARD K. WERNER

MOON. *See* Astronomy; *and* Myths, *article on* Lunar Cycle.

MORTUARY CULT. *See* Cults, *articles on* Royal Cults *and* Private Cults.

MORTUARY LITERATURE. *See* Funerary Literature.

MORTUARY TEMPLE. *See* Temples.

MOSES (Heb., *mōše(h);* Gr. *mouses*), the Hebrew law-giver who led the *bene Yisra'el* out of Egypt, and a reputed prince of Egypt. The name *Moses* has generally been de-rived from the Egyptian root *msi* ("to bear"), in the form of a hypocoristikon formed on the theophoric pattern "God X is born." (The biblical derivation, from putative *mašā(h),* "to draw out," is a false folk etymology based on the details of the story.) Such shortened forms involving the elision of the divine element occur with relative frequency in the onomasticon of the New Kingdom. An alternative theory would deny any Egyptian derivation at all, equating the name with Canaanite *Mt > Muš,* the serpent god, son of Ba'al.

According to the Pentateuch, which comprises all that survives of the primary tradition about the man, Moses is a Hebrew secreted at birth by his mother to escape a kind of pogrom, and he was discovered by a daughter of the king of Egypt. Brought up at the court, he acts as Yahweh's agent in coercing pharaoh, by the infliction of a series of plagues, to let the *bene Yisra'el,* enslaved Israelites, go free into the desert to worship their God. Thereafter he acts as law-giver to his nation at Mount Sinai and functions as their tribal leader as far as the border of Canaan. As presently constituted, the narrative sections of *Exodus* in which Moses figures are a pastiche of known folkloristic motifs, deftly woven together in a narrative of some literary effect: the community threatened by a tyrant, the hero cast away in infancy, the contest between magicians, the cosmic miracles, the "magicians' tricks" (inanimate-object-to-snake, parted-water, river-to-blood, darkness, "pillar-of-fire," and so forth—all well known in the folklore of the eastern Mediterranean).

As far as is known, no figure comparable to the biblical Moses is to be found in surviving Egyptian sources, and attempts to identify him historically have proven arbitrary and unconvincing. It has been fashionable at times to find him in the Amenmesse of the outgoing nineteenth dynasty (late thirteenth century BCE); in Ahmose, founder of the eighteenth dynasty (sixteenth century BCE); or in one of the protagonists of the Amarna period (fourteenth century BCE). The alleged link between "Mosaic monotheism" and the belief system of Akhenaten has proven impossible to sustain. Similarly, any connection between the biblical figure of Moses and the *Shasu Yahweh* of eighteenth dynasty toponym lists is yet to be demonstrated.

Whatever roots of the tradition extend back in time, the full-blown Mosaic account belongs to the latest stage in the development of the *Exodus* story. In earlier literature outside the Pentateuch, although the *Exodus* is a prominent element in the collective memory of the Levantine communities, Moses scarcely appears. In pursuing the evolution of the tradition, one cannot ignore the folklore later used by discutants in the Judeo-pagan polemic. By the fifth century BCE, a narrative was in existence that linked an "exodus" from Egypt to a pious "clean-up" of Egyptian temples, culminating in an expulsion into the desert of a group of lepers. Once expelled, the lepers organized themselves under the leadership of a renegade priest ("Moses") who thereupon conducted them to Palestine, where they founded Jerusalem. Although this piece of folklore appears to have taken shape as a *midrash* on the dim recollection of the Amarna period, one version firmly links it to the twenty-fourth dynasty and the reign of Bakenrenef (Bocchoris, 717–711 BCE), when a Kushite domination of the Nile Valley loomed. Curiously, in consonance with this travesty of chronology, biblical tradition (*Num.* 12.1) gives Moses a Kushite wife, and post-biblical commentary (Artapanus) brings him into association with the siege of Hermopolis, recalling Piya's siege of the same town around 719 BCE.

[*See also* Biblical Tradition; *and* Exodus.]

BIBLIOGRAPHY

Aurelius, E. *Der Fuerbitter Israels: Eine Studie zum Mosebild im Alten Testament.* Stockholm, 1988.

Černý, J. "Greek Etymology of the Name of Moses." *Annales du Service des Antiquités de l'Égypte* 41 (1941), 349–354.

Denis, A.-M. "Le portrait de Moïse par l'anti-semite Menathon (IIIᵉ s. av. J.-C.) et le refutation juive de l'historien Artapan." *Museon* 100 (1987), 49–65.

Gager, J. G. *Moses in Greco-Roman Paganism.* Nashville, Tenn., 1972.

Griffiths, J. G. "The Egyptian Derivation of the Name Moses." *Journal of Near Eastern Studies* 12 (1953), 225–231.

Marshall, R. C. "Moses, Oedipus, Structuralism and History." *History of Religions* 28 (1989), 245–266.

Siebert-Hommes, J. "Die Geburtsgeschichte des Mose innerhalb des Erzählungszusammenhangs von Exod. I-II." *Vetus Testamentum* 42 (1992), 398–404.

Van Seters, J. *The Life of Moses.* Louisville, Ky., 1994.

Vergote, J. "À propos du nom de Moïse." *Bulletin de la société égyptologique de Genève* 4 (1981), 89–96.

Weinfeld, M. "The Traditions about Moses and Jethro at the Mount of God." *Tarbiz* 56 (1987), 449–460.

DONALD B. REDFORD

MUMMIFICATION. Naturally or artificially preserved bodies, in which desiccation (drying, dehydration) of the tissues has prevented putrefaction, have been discovered in several countries. They are generally called "mummies," although originally this term was applied only to the artificially preserved bodies of the ancient Egyptians. The word *mummy* is derived from the Persian or Arabic word *mumia*, which means "pitch" or "bitumen"; this originally referred to a black, asphalt-like substance that oozed from the "Mummy Mountain" in Persia. This material, credited in the region with medicinal properties, was eagerly sought as a cure for many ailments. The demand eventually led to a quest for an alternative source, and, because the preserved bodies of the ancient Egyptians often have a blackened appearance, these were believed to possess similar properties to *mumia;* consequently, they were used as a medicinal ingredient in medieval and later times (after the mid-seventh-century Arab conquest of Egypt). The term *mumia* or "mummy" was extended to these bodies and has continued in use until now.

Techniques. Human remains (consisting of the skeleton and body tissues) can be preserved indefinitely as a result of environmental and other factors. The dryness of the sand in which the body is buried, the heat or coldness of the climate, or the absence of air in the burial all help to produce unintentional or "natural" mummies. These factors, occurring either singly or in combination, have produced naturally preserved bodies in Egypt, South America, Mexico, the Alps, Central Asia, the Canary Islands, the Aleutian Islands, and Alaska; a different type of preservation also occurs in northwestern Europe, where bodies have been preserved when buried in peat bogs or fens containing lime. There is considerable variation in the extent to which these different environments have been successful in producing "natural mummies." In some areas, this natural process of preservation was intentionally developed by enhancing the existing environmental conditions. Sun, fire, or candle heat were sometimes used to desiccate the bodies thoroughly; other bodies were smoked or cured. Sometimes dry grass and natural materials were used to surround the body and to stuff its cavities, or the burial place provided a sealed environment for the corpse which, by excluding air, prevented decomposition and further deterioration.

The most advanced method of intentional preservation (to which the term "true mummification" is sometimes applied) involved various sophisticated techniques that had been developed throughout a period of experimentation. Ancient Egyptian mummification, which provides the best examples of this method, involved the use of chemical and other agents. In Egypt, a combination of climate and environment, as well as the people's religious beliefs and practices, led first to unintentional preservation of the body and then to true mummification. Because of the scarcity of available cultivatable land, the earliest Egyptians chose to bury their dead in shallow pit-graves on the edges of the desert, where the heat of the sun and the dryness of the sand desiccated the body tissues before decomposition occurred. These natural conditions produced remarkably well-preserved bodies; the skin tissue and hair have often survived, and the corpse retains some likeness of the person's appearance when alive.

History of Mummification in Egypt. Before about 3400 BCE, all Egyptians were buried in pit-graves, regardless of their status or wealth; later, increased prosperity and advances in building techniques led to the introduction of more elaborate tombs for the leaders of the society. These tombs had brick-lined underground burial chambers, which no longer provided the environmental condi-

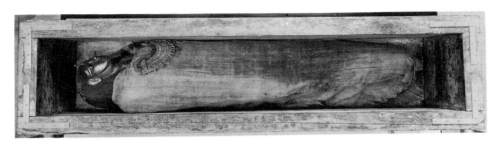

MUMMIFICATION. *Twelfth-dynasty coffin and mummy of Khnumhotep from Meir.* (The Metropolitan Museum of Art, Rogers Fund, 1912. [12.182.131])

tions of the pit-graves that had created the natural mummies. Religious beliefs however, required that the body should be preserved as completely as possible so that the deceased owner's *ka* ("spirit") could return to the tomb and recognize it, reenter it, and thus gain spiritual sustenance from the food offerings placed at the tomb.

Although most of the population continued to be buried in pit-graves, the Egyptians now sought other means to preserve the bodies of the highest classes. There followed a period of experimentation that probably lasted several hundred years. There is some evidence to suggest that these experiments were undertaken as early as the second dynasty (c.2850–c.2687 BCE): the archaeologist J. E. Quibell found a large mass of corroded linen between the bandages and bones of a body interred in a cemetery at Saqqara, perhaps evidence of an attempt to use natron or another agent as a preservative by applying it to the surface of the skin. Another technique involved the production of "stucco mummies," bodies that were covered in fine linen and then coated with plaster, to carefully preserve the owner's body shape and features, particularly the head. In 1891, W. M. Flinders Petrie discovered a body at Meidum dating to the fifth dynasty (c.2513–c.2374 BCE), in which there had been some attempt to preserve the body tissues as well as to re-create the body form. Close-fitting bandages were molded to reproduce the shape of the torso; the limbs were separately wrapped, and the breasts and genitals were modeled in resin-soaked linen. Despite these attempts, however, the actual body had decomposed beneath the bandages, and only the skeleton remained within the elaborately wrapped outer case.

The first convincing evidence of successful intentional mummification occurs in the fourth dynasty (c.2649–c.2513 BCE). In the Giza tomb of Queen Hetepheres, the mother of Khufu, builder of the nearby Great Pyramid, archaeologists discovered a chest containing intentionally preserved viscera which can probably be attributed to the queen, although the previously undisturbed tomb did not contain the owner's body. When these viscera packets were analyzed, it was found that the organs had been treated with natron, the agent successfully used in later times to dehydrate the body tissues. This evidence seems to indicate that the two most important stages of Egyptian mummification—evisceration of the body and the dehydration of the tissues by means of natron—were already in use for royalty. Mummification continued to be practiced in Egypt for some three thousand years, until the end of the Christian era and the arrival of Islam in the country.

The technique gradually became available to the upper and middle classes, and in the Greco-Roman period (c.332 BCE–third century CE) it became increasingly widespread. It was never universally available to the poorer classes, however, and most of the population continued to be interred in simple desert graves, where their bodies were naturally preserved.

According to the Greek historian Herodotus, three main types of mummification were available, and the client chose the method he could afford. The most expensive included elaborate funerary rites as well as a lengthy and complicated procedure to preserve the body. Although this involved many stages, the two steps crucial to arrest the decomposition of the body were evisceration and dehydration of the tissues. The viscera (internal organs) were usually removed from the thoracic and abdominal cavities through an abdominal incision in the left flank; in some cases, the viscera were not extracted at all, and in others they were removed through the anus. The removed viscera were then dehydrated with natron, and either placed in canopic jars or made into four packages and reinserted in the body cavities; some were wrapped in one large packet that was placed on the legs of the mummy. The heart was usually left *in situ*, probably because it was considered to be the location of the individual owner's intelligence and life force. The brain, considered nonessential, was removed and discarded.

After evisceration, the body cavities were washed out with spiced palm wine, then filled with a mixture of dry natron, gum resin, and vegetable matter. The corpse was then left to dehydrate for a period of up to forty days. Natron (hydrated sodium carbonate, $Na_2CO_3 \cdot 10\ H_2O$), the main substance used to pack the body, is found in a dry desert valley called the Wadi Natrun; it is composed of sodium carbonate and sodium bicarbonate and includes some natural impurities. There have been different opinions regarding the use of natron, salt (sodium chloride), or lime (calcium carbonate) as the main dehydrating agent in Egyptian mummification, and there has also been discussion as to whether natron was used in solution (in water) or in a solid state. Assessment of the Greek text that describes the process, along with modern experiments on mummified tissues, has now confirmed that dry natron, which provides the most satisfactory results, would almost certainly have been used to pack the bodies.

After dehydration was complete, the temporary stuffing was removed from the body cavities and replaced with the permanent stuffing and sometimes also the viscera packages. The abdominal incision was then closed, the nostrils were plugged with resin or wax, and the body was anointed with a variety of oils and gum resins, which may have played some part in preventing or delaying insect attack and in masking the odors of decomposition that would have accompanied the mummification process. These stages were, however, essentially cosmetic and had little effect in preventing putrefaction of the tissues. The embalmers then wrapped the mummy in layers of linen bandages, between which they inserted amulets (sacred charms) to ward off evil and danger. A liquid or semiliquid resinous substance was then poured over the mummy and coffin. Finally, the embalmer returned these to the family of the deceased so that the preparations for the funeral and the burial could be made.

The two less expensive methods of mummification that Herodotus mentions did not include complete evisceration. In the second method (which was also used for animal mummification), oil of cedar was injected into the anus, which was plugged to prevent the escape of the liquid, and the body was then treated with natron. Once this was complete, the oil was drained off and the intestines and the stomach, liquefied by the natron, came away with the oil; the flesh had also been liquefied, so only the skin and the skeleton remained. The body was returned to the family in this state. In the third and cheapest method, the body was purged so that the intestines came away, and the body was then treated with natron.

In the long history of mummification in Egypt, there were only two major additions to the basic procedure. From at least as early as the Middle Kingdom (c.2134–1786 BCE), excerebration (brain removal) was practiced on some mummies, and by the New Kingdom (c.1569–c.1076 BCE), this procedure had become widespread. The embalmer inserted a metal hook into the cranial cavity through the nostril and ethmoid bone, and the brain was pulverized to fragments so that it could be removed with a spatula. In some cases, access to the cranial cavity was gained either through the base of the skull or a trepanned orbit (eye socket). Usually, it was impossible to remove the brain completely and so some tissue remained *in situ*. Before mummification was complete, the emptied cranial cavity was packed with strips of linen impregnated with resin, and molten resin was sometimes poured into the skull.

The second innovation was introduced in the twenty-first dynasty (1081–931 BCE), when the embalmers sought to develop a technique that had first been used in the eighteenth dynasty (1382 BCE) in the preparation of the mummy of King Amenhotpe III. Then, the embalmers had attempted to re-create the plumpness of the king's appearance by introducing packing under the skin of his mummy, through incisions made in his legs, neck, and arms. Later, in the twenty-first dynasty, the priests began to use subcutaneous packing not just for the mummies of royalty but for all who could afford this time-consuming procedure. The body cavities were packed through a flank incision with sawdust, butter, linen, and mud, and the four individually wrapped packages of viscera were also inserted into these cavities rather than being placed in canopic jars. Subcutaneous material was also introduced through small incisions in the skin, and the neck and face were packed through the mouth. In this way, the embalmers tried to retain the original bodily contours to some degree, to make the mummy's appearance more lifelike. Artificial eyes were often placed in the orbits; the skin was painted with red ocher (for men) or yellow ocher (for women), and false plaits and curls were woven into the natural hair. These expensive and time-consuming preparations were not retained beyond the twenty-third dynasty (813–711 BCE).

In the Middle Kingdom, the political and economic growth of the middle classes and the consequently increased importance of religious beliefs and practices among all classes of Egyptian society resulted in the spread of mummification to new sections of the population. More mummies have survived from that period than from the Old Kingdom, but it is evident that less care was taken in their preparation.

In the Greco-Roman period (332 BCE–395 CE), when foreign immigrants who settled in Egypt sometimes adopted Egyptian funerary beliefs and customs, mummification again became more widespread. It also became an increasingly commercial venture, and it tended to indicate the deceased owner's social status rather than his religious conviction, with the result that the standards of mummification declined rapidly. Although the bodies

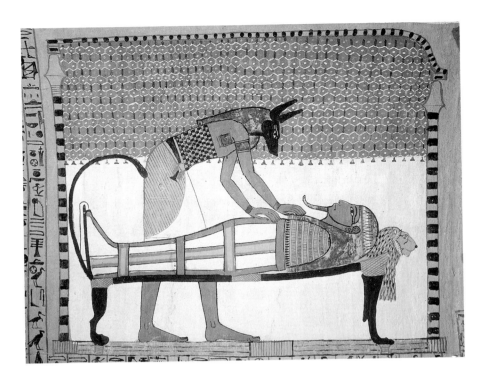

were elaborately bandaged and encased in covers made of cartonnage (a mixture of plaster and papyrus or linen), modern radiographic analysis confirms that they were frequently poorly preserved inside the wrappings.

Sources. Our knowledge of mummification is based on the archaeological evidence provided by the mummies, paleopathological studies of the bodies, painted and carved representations in tomb scenes and elsewhere of some stages of the mummification procedure, and textual references in Egyptian and classical-era accounts. There is no extant Egyptian description of the technical processes involved in mummification. The earliest available accounts occur in the writings of two Greek historians, Herodotus (fifth century BCE) and Diodorus Siculus (first century BCE). Yet, in Egyptian literature, there are scattered references to mummification and the associated religious rituals. One of these, the *Ritual of Embalming*, provides a set of instructions to the officiant who performs the rites that accompany the mummification process, as well as a collection of prayers and incantations to be intoned after each rite. This ritual is preserved in two papyri, probably copied from a common source and both dated to the Roman period (31 BCE–395 CE): Papyrus Boulaq 3 (in the Cairo Museum) and Papyrus 5158 (in the Louvre). References to embalming ceremonies also occur in the Rhind Papyri (discovered by A. H. Rhind in an eighteenth dynasty tomb at Thebes) and in other literary sources, including inscriptions on stelae; however, Herodotus's account remains the most complete literary source.

No paintings or carvings provide an extant, complete record of mummification. Wall scenes in the tombs of Thoy and Amenemope (tombs 23 and 41, respectively, at Thebes) and vignettes painted on some coffins and canopic jars show some stages in the mummification procedure, and in a papyrus that once belonged to Any (nineteenth dynasty, 1315–1201 BCE), a vignette illustrating the *Book of Going Forth by Day* (*Book of the Dead*) shows Anubis, the god of embalming, attending a mummified body inside an embalming booth.

Rituals and Accessories. The mummification procedure was carried out in the embalmer's workshop, known as *wbt* ("place of purification"). Some workshops would have been put up near the individual tombs, but because of the "impure" nature of mummification and its associated dangers, these would have been situated outside the actual tomb enclosure. Other workshops, where larger numbers of bodies were prepared, were located near burial grounds or temple sites.

Although many rites accompanying the mummification process were performed in the embalmer's workshop, one of the most important rituals—the Opening of the Mouth ceremony—was carried out at the tomb. These final rites, which sought to ensure the eternal life of the deceased owner, were an important part of the funeral; with an adze, the priest touched the mouth, hands, and feet of the mummy and of all the representations of the tomb-owner appearing in the tomb, including wall scenes, models, and statues. This action was believed to restore life to the mummy so that the spirit of the deceased could enter and use it; similarly, all the inanimate figures in the tomb would be able to act on behalf of the deceased owner. Modern experiments have shown that optimum results in mummification are achieved after a maximum period of forty days for evisceration and dehydration; however, Herodotus and other sources quote a period of seventy days for mummification, and undoubtedly much of that time would have been occupied with religious and magical rituals. A single ancient Egyptian text, however, records a much longer period, but this undoubtedly included associated rituals and ceremonies.

The embalmers and priests used a range of accessories in the mummification process and associated rites. They placed amulets between the layers of bandages and placed a cartonnage mask, chest, and foot covers over the mummy to give it the necessary physical support. In the actual preparation of the body, the embalmers and their assistants employed a blade of obsidian to make the incision in the flank of the mummy, and they stored the viscera in a set of canopic jars. The body was also treated with plant remains and resins, and the priests used special jars and vessels when they anointed and lustrated the mummy.

Embalmers. Within the distinct group of practitioners who were concerned with the mummification process, Diodorus Siculus stated that there were three main classes who prepared the body for burial. These included the cutter (Gr., *paraschistos*) who made the incision in the flank of the mummy; the scribe who supervised this work; and the embalmer, who belonged to a special guild or organization and was responsible for leading the mummification ceremonies and for wrapping the mummy in bandages.

In fact, the embalmer supervised all the stages of the mummification process. He wore a jackal-headed mask to impersonate Anubis, god of embalming, when he performed the rituals. As highly skilled professionals, the embalmers were a special class of priests who probably had close associations with doctors. Their office was hereditary, and they also employed others, such as the coffinmakers who produced coffins and wooden figurines and other items for the tomb.

In contrast, the cutters, because of the ritual "impurity" (and possible health hazards) associated with making the incision in the corpse and removing the viscera, had the lowest status in society; this group may have included convicted criminals. Other people involved in the mummification procedure and the funeral included the priests of Osiris who performed the rituals, lector-priests who recited the chants and the ritual instructions, and the men who washed and cleansed the mummy and the viscera, prepared the natron and resin, and wrapped the body with layers of linen bandages. The whole process associated with death and burial was a major industry that employed many workers.

Scientific Studies. In recent years, multidisciplinary studies of mummified remains have supplied new information about the process of mummification itself and also about disease, diet, living conditions, and familial relationships in ancient Egypt. It has been shown that natron was used in a dry rather than a liquid state, and that the composition and method of application of the natron could affect the final result. Use of the scanning electron microscope (SEM) to identify insects has provided information about insect attack on the mummies; histology and electron microscopy have supplied evidence about the success or failure of individual mummification techniques; and thin layer and gas liquid chromatography have isolated and characterized the substances that were applied to the mummy bandages.

Several techniques have contributed to the study of disease in mummies. In the 1970s, radiography—a totally nondestructive method—became a major investigative procedure, and later the additional use of computerized tomography (CT) became standard in most radiological investigations of mummies. In addition, dental studies of mummies have provided evidence about age determination, diet, oral health, and disease. Paleohistology, involving the rehydration, fixing, and selective staining of sections of mummified tissue, and paleopathology, the study of disease in ancient people, have developed considerably since the techniques were pioneered in Cairo earlier in the twentieth century by M. A. Ruffer. Endoscopy has now almost entirely replaced the need to autopsy a mummy, since this technique allows the researcher to gain firsthand evidence about embalming methods, and to obtain tissue samples for further study, without destroying the mummy. Histology, transmission electron microscopy (TEM), immunohistochemistry, and immunocytochemistry can then be used to search for evidence of disease in the tissue samples.

Although there have been several studies of bloodgroups in ancient human remains, DNA identification has now largely superseded paleoserology as a technique to examine individual familial relationships; future studies may consider the origins and migrations of ancient populations, and they may be able to identify bacterial, fungal, viral, and parasite DNA as causative agents of disease. Finally, studies have been undertaken to determine the processes of deterioration that occur in mummies so that methods of treatment can be developed to assist curators and conservators in preserving these collections; however, it is essential to ensure that such treatments do not destroy or contaminate any evidence that is yet to be susceptible to future identification and other investigative procedures.

[*See also* Canopic Jars and Chests; *and* Opening of the Mouth.]

BIBLIOGRAPHY

Balout, L., and C. Roubet, eds. *La Momie de Ramsès II.* Paris, 1985. A detailed account of the multidisciplinary study undertaken on the mummy of Ramesses II.

Brothwell, D., and E. Higgs, eds. *Science in Archaeology.* 2d ed. London, 1970.

Cockburn, A., and E. Cockburn, eds. *Mummies, Disease and Ancient Cultures.* Cambridge, 1980; 2d rev. ed. by A. Cockburn, E. Cockburn, and T. A. Reyman, eds., Cambridge, 1998. Major sections on medical and scientific research on Egyptian mummies, within the context of studies on mummies from other areas of the world.

Connolly, R. C., and R. G. Harrison. "Kinship of Smenkhkare and Tutankhamen Affirmed by Serological Micromethod." *Nature* 224 (1969), 325–326.

David, A. R., ed. *The Manchester Museum Mummy Project: Multidisciplinary Research on Ancient Egyptian Mummified Remains.* Manchester, 1979. Description of how a multidisciplinary methodology was established for examining Egyptian mummified remains.

David, A. R., ed. *Science in Egyptology: The Proceedings of the 1979 and 1984 Symposia.* Manchester, 1986. A wide selection of papers presented at the first symposia to focus on studies on Egyptian mummified remains.

David, A. R., and A. E. David. "Preservation of Human Mummified Specimens." In *The Care and Conservation of Palaeontological Material*, edited by C. Collins, pp. 73–88. Oxford, 1995. An account of the various conservation problems relating to Egyptian mummies, with a selection of recommended treatments.

Dawson, W. R., and G. E. Smith. *Egyptian Mummies.* London, 1924; 2d edn., London, 1991. Description of some of the literary, archaeological, and medical sources available for the study of Egyptian mummification.

Diodorus Siculus. *History.* Translated by C. H. Oldfather. Loeb Classical Library. Cambridge, Mass., 1968. See book I, para. 91.

Fleming, S., et al. *The Egyptian Mummy: Secrets and Science.* Philadelphia, 1980.

Garner, R. "Experimental Mummification." In *The Manchester Museum Mummy Project*, edited by A. R. David, pp. 19–24. Manchester, 1979.

Harris, J. E., and K. Weeks. *X-Raying the Pharaohs.* New York, 1973.

Harris, J. E., and E. F. Wente. *X-Ray Atlas of the Egyptian Pharaohs.* Chicago, 1980.

Herodotus. *The Histories.* Translated by A. D. Godley. Loeb Classical Library. Cambridge, Mass., 1946. Book II, para. 86–88, is the most complete ancient literary account of mummification.

Ikram, S., and A. Dodson. *The Mummy in Ancient Egypt.* London, 1998.

Lucas, A. *Ancient Egyptian Materials and Industries* 4th ed., revised and enlarged by J. R. Harris. London, 1962. See chapter 12, "Mummification," pp. 272–326. A revised edition of this major reference work, currently out of print, is planned for 1999.

Pääbo, S. "Molecular Cloning of Ancient Egyptian Mummy DNA." *Nature* 314 (1985), 644–645. Report on pioneering studies undertaken to identify DNA in Egyptian mummies.

Ruffer, M. A. "Histological Studies on Egyptian Mummies." *Mémoires de l'Institut de l'Égypte* 6.3 (1911), 1–33. Account of Ruffer's pioneering work on mummified remains, which established paleopathological studies.

Sandison, A. T. "Human Mummification Technique in Ancient Egypt." In *Science in Egyptology*, edited by A. R. David, pp. 1–8. Manchester, 1986.

Smith, G. E. *The Royal Mummies.* Catalogue général des antiquités du égyptiennes du Musée du Caire, No. 61051–61100. Cairo, 1912. Detailed description of Elliot Smith's pioneering work on the royal mummies, and the information his examinations provided about mummification techniques during the New Kingdom.

Smith, G. E. "Egyptian Mummies." *Journal of Egyptian Archaeology* 1 (1914), 189–206.

ANN ROSALIE DAVID

MUSEUMS. The idea of museums grew out of the imperial cabinets of curiosities that were composed of a disparate range of objects from natural history, to art, to casts of objects from other collections. The eighteenth-century English tradition of the Grand Tour to classical lands hastened the idea of assemblages of similar materials concentrated in galleries, although the prototypes of public galleries were found in private stately homes. Interest in Egyptian art began after Napoleon Bonaparte's military expedition to Egypt in 1798, attended by 167 *savants* led by Dominique-Vivant Denon; it included geographers, botanists, and draftsmen, who mapped and recorded the flora, fauna, and all standing ancient monuments. Their results were published in a series of large folio volumes (1809–1816). These publications and the consequent collection of objects later seized by the British government after winning the Napoleonic Wars (including the Rosetta Stone), brought Egyptian art into the incipient state museums, previously dedicated to gathering classical material, and onto public display. With the appointment of consuls to Egypt, such as Henry Salt (Britain), Bernardino Drovetti (France), and Giovanni Anastasi (Sweden-Norway), competition increased to amass collections of Egyptian art. The French were succeeded in Egypt by Muhammad Ali Pasha, who opened the country to foreign tourism. As a focus for tourists, many ailing and wishing to flee the northern European climate, the Egyptian souvenir trade developed.

The British Isles. The Egyptian collection of the British Museum started with a varied core brought together by Sir Hans Sloane in 1753. The collection grew when the Rosetta Stone and other Egyptian antiquities seized from Napoleon were lodged in the new national museum. The gift of the colossal New Kingdom bust of Ramesses II, jointly presented by the Swiss explorer Jean-Louis Burckhardt and the British consul-general Henry Salt initially awakened the interest of the public in Egyptian art. The first of three large collections, formed through the energy and skill of a former circus strongman and aspiring engineer, Giovanni Battista Belzoni, were sold to the British Museum by Henry Salt for £2,000 in 1823 (the asking price was £8,000). The alabaster sarcophagus of Sety I was sold separately to John Soane whose collection and London home was transformed into a museum. Belzoni, who was undaunted by the difficulties of moving large sculptures from Egypt to Europe, was responsible for claiming the colossal head of the "young Memnon," where the French had failed. Further material for the Egyptian collection in the British Museum was acquired from Henry Salt and from another Salt agent, Giovanni d'Athanasi, after Salt's death. Many important papyri were purchased from Giovanni Anastasi, an Armenian businessman who resided in Alexandria and who also served as consul in Egypt for Norway and Sweden. John Barker, Salt's successor in Egypt in 1833 also provided Egyptian objects for the museum as did the Egyptologist James Burton and numerous private collectors. The Egyptologist E. A. Wallis Budge was employed at the British Museum in 1883, became Keeper in 1894, and aggressively acquired material from Egypt on numerous visits, despite the increasing protest against the removal of antiquities. The Egypt Exploration Fund (later the Egyptian Exploration Society), was created in 1882. Numerous excavations under its auspices resulted in the division of archaeological finds, which were subsequently divided among the subscribing institutions and university museums.

Other Egyptian collections in the British Isles owe their existence to donations by collectors and to the divisions of archaeological finds from Egypt Exploration Society (EES) excavations. University collections were developed at Cambridge, Oxford, University College London, Manchester, Liverpool, and Durham during the nineteenth century. Alumni also showed allegiance to their schools by donating Egyptian artifacts to Eton and Harrow. Private collecting fueled exhibitions early in the twentieth century, such as at the Burlington Fine Arts Club and at Sotheby's public auctions in London.

Cambridge's Fitzwilliam Museum, whose doors opened in 1848, had a substantial classical collection with only a few Egyptian objects, such as twenty-first dynasty coffins. The objects were the gifts of two university college fellows, B. Hanbury and G. Waddington, who traveled to Egypt in 1820 in the wake of Napoleon's army. They were accompanying the army of Muhammad Ali Pasha, commanded by his son, Ismail, in its conquest of Sudan. The monumental granite relief coffin lid of King Ramesses III (1198–1166 BCE) was given to the museum by Giovanni Belzoni, Salt's agent, who hoped in vain for some honorary academic recognition for such a gift. There followed the bequests of the society painters and joint collectors C. S. Ricketts and C. H. Shannon (1937) and of R. G. Gayer-Anderson (1943, 1947, and 1949), who left a small Islamic museum in Cairo in return for permission to remove his substantial collections to the Fitzwilliam Museum.

The Ashmolean Museum at Oxford was enriched by gifts from alumni, especially by the Reverend G. J. Chester (1831–1892), and by material excavated under the auspices of the Egypt Exploration Fund. The Griffith Institute housed within the museum, is a center for provenancing finds and has a premier archaeological library and database. The museum at University College London was largely formed by the archaeologist William Matthew Flinders Petrie, who first bought material (1880–1892) in Egypt, packed it into fifty tea chests, and sold it to the museum; the collection was then augmented annually with material from his excavations. The Manchester and Liverpool university museums were also largely formed by divisions from excavations. A Manchester textile merchant, Jesse Haworth, substantially financed the EEF excavations at the town sites of Illahun and Gurob, accounting for the large amount of daily life material in his home city. Durham owes much of its collection to the fourth Duke of Northumberland, who acquired Egyptian antiquities from auctions, from the third collection of Salt, and from that of James Burton. The Duke's fine Egyptian gold jewelry and scarabs, however, were sold at a Sotheby's auction in 1875. The Eton College collection was created from gifts by former students, and Harrow School owes its collection to the generosity of Sir John Gardner Wilkinson (died, 1875). Edinburgh has a good collection of Egyptian art, some of which was derived from donations by A. H. Rhind (died, 1863).

France. The Louvre's collection began with the temporary collection amassed by Napoleon. Dominique-Vivant Denon then became his director general of museums. The first modern state museum was named the Musée Napoléon from 1803–1814, but the contents were returned to the owners in 1813. The museum was renamed after Charles X, before finally being named Musée du Louvre, with Jean-François Champollion as the original keeper of Egyptian antiquities. The Louvre acquired several distinguished collections: from Salt in 1826 (his second collection, through the agency of Yanni Athanasiou) composed of some four thousand pieces, which sold for £10,000; Bernardino Drovetti's second collection of some five hundred masterpieces in 1827 (Drovetti also sold two other collections to the King of Sardinia [now in Turin] and to the Berlin Museum); from Clot-bey in 1852; from Anastasi in 1857; and from Tyskiewicz in 1862. The government of France acquired the zodiac that was removed from the ceiling of the temple at Dendera, by Sébastien Louis Saulnier, and the Table of Kings from the Great Temple at Karnak, taken by Emile Prisse d'Avennes; this last was transferred from the Bibliothèque National to the Louvre, along with all the other Egyptian holdings in 1922, followed by those of the Musée Guimet in 1946. A long tradition of French excavations in Egypt has continuously increased the holdings in the Louvre. Auguste Mariette's excavations at Saqqara has produced some seven thousand objects for the Louvre. Excavations at Abu Rowash resulted in the images of the ill-fated son of Khufu (r.

MUSEUMS. *The Cairo Museum.* (Courtesy David P. Silverman)

2609–2584 BCE). From Medamud came a large Middle Kingdom find of silver treasures. The Louvre holdings of daily life objects and funerary material are vast, with some one thousand inscribed stelae. As well, numerous smaller collections are kept throughout France.

Germany. The Egyptian collection in Berlin was begun in 1698 with Friedrich III's purchase of material amassed by Giovanni Petro Bellori. It was eventually removed by Napoleon to Paris, only to be returned with pieces added as an interest payment. The purchase, in 1823, by Wilhelm III of General Heinrich von Minutolis's collection was followed in 1828 by the acquisition of some two thousand objects from Giuseppe Passalacqua's collection that had been cataloged by Champollion's brother. Passalacqua became director of the new museum and acquired the collections of Drovetti in 1836 and Saulinier in 1839 bringing the total number of objects to about five thousand. Richard Lepsius made an expedition to Egypt under Wilhelm IV, and he surveyed, excavated, and acquired fifteen hundred objects for the museum (1842–1846). A new museum on Museum Island was opened in 1850, with Lepsius as its director in 1865. Adolf Erman followed Lepsius as director and acquired the Berlin Green Head and the wooden head of Tiye. Excavations by the architect Ludwig Borchardt at the sun temple of Newoserre, at Abu

Ghurob, at Abusir, and at Tell el-Amarna (1911–1914), which produced the bust of Nefertiti and the studio objects of the chief sculptor Thutmose, greatly amplified the collections of the Berlin Museum. The collections were packed into seven underground depots for the duration of World War II, during which two of the depots were destroyed. Much was taken to Russia at the war's end, to be returned in 1958 to the (then) East Berlin museum isle site. In 1967, an Egyptian museum was opened in West Berlin, opposite the Charlottenberg Palace. Plans to unite the two museums at the former East Berlin site are underway.

Other great museums in Germany were created through donations by collectors and by means of membership in the Deutschen Orient-Gesellschaft (DOG), which financed and organized Egyptian excavations. The museum at Munich included material from the Villa Albani (donated in 1815–1816) including the colossal figure of Antinous, material from Ferdinand Michel (1824), and some Roman booty confiscated from Napoleon. Those objects were sold by Cardinal Alessandro Albani to King Ludwig I of Bavaria (r. 1825–1848) to finance the return transport to Rome for the remaining artifacts, since an impoverished France could not pay for the move. Ludwig I also bought antiquities from Drovetti for the Munich museum and in 1837 he purchased half the royal Meroitic gold treasure from the pyramid of Queen Amanishakheto. Soon, F. W. F. von Bissing's purchases from the antiquities trade and his excavations enlarged the museum's collections.

The collection at the Kestner Museum in Hanover was largely acquired from the collector August Kestner (died, 1853), who studied under Jean-François Champollion in Rome and who was further encouraged by Lepsius. The museum at Hildesheim was created through purchases by Wilhelm Pelizaeus who first traveled to Egypt in 1869; he purchased material for himself and at the behest of Hermann Roemer for his home town museum. His support of the Old Kingdom Giza excavations under Steindorff, and later Junker, ultimately led to a large bequest of sculpture to the Museum by Pelizaeus, which bears the two founding names. Frankfurt's Liebieghaus museum owes its rich collection of Roman period mummy masks to C. M. Kaufmann, who acquired them early in the twentieth century in Giza, although they came from tombs in Hermopolis.

Several German university museum collections were created in the nineteenth century largely through finds from excavations. Leipzig's first nonclassical acquisition was the wooden sarcophagus with raised-relief texts from Hed-bast-iru, presented by Lepsius in 1842. Georg Steindorff in 1893 acquired the concession to excavate the officials' cemetery at Giza and thereby greatly enriched the collections with Old Kingdom pieces, including a rare copper alloy, gilt diadem with fretted wood roundels. Middle and New Kingdom material was added to the museum's collection through the Nubian excavations at Aniba. The Heidelberg University Museum owed its creation to the energies of Hermann Ranke and material derived from the excavation at Middle Egyptian sites including el-Hiba, which produced a fragment of the lower part of a limestone statue that depicts a Roman pharaoh with a richly decorated kilt and Herakles club. Objects in the collection also derived from Junker's work in 1927–1928 at Merimda in the Nile Delta, and through Heidelberg's membership in the DOG excavations at Abusir. The museum at Tübingen acquired the Seshemnofer relief from the decorated burial chamber through von Sieglin's 1911 expedition at Giza. The museum also obtained DOG material, especially Old Kingdom reliefs from Abu Ghurob.

Austria. Vienna's Egyptian collection was mainly derived from private benefactions to the imperial collections while the Kunsthistorisches Museum was being built from 1871–1891. With the assassination of Archduke Maximilian (shot in 1867 by Benito Juárez in Mexico), his collection, derived from his father Karl and from his own visit to Egypt in 1855, became the property of the museum. In the twentieth century, the museum received many excavation divisions from Hermann Junker's Old Kingdom excavations at Giza (1912–1929), from Nubia (1961–1965), and from Thebes (since 1960) and the eastern Delta (since 1966).

Italy. The collections of the Museo Gregoriano Egizio in the Vatican were begun by Clemente XIV (1767–1774) and Pius VI (1775–1799), through excavations at the Italian villas Domiziano and Tiburtina. Important sculptural additions were made to the Egyptian collection during the time of Gregory XVI (1838) at Orti Sallustiani, Campo Marzio, and Hadrian's villa. Gregory XVI also transferred to the Vatican many Egyptian sculptures, including the Ptolemaic royal statues found at Sallustiani in 1714. Leon XIII received a large benefaction in 1900 from the Khedive of Egypt. The Museo Egizio of Turin was founded in 1824 with some eight thousand objects collected by Bernardino Drovetti as the first of three collections, which was originally offered for sale to France and finally bought by the King of Sardinia. This collection is composed of some one hundred large sculptures, including those of King Amenhotpe II, a sphinx of Amenhotpe III, a Tutankhamun pair statue (with Amun), Ramesses II, and a posthumous cult statue of Amenhotpe I, as well as some 170 papyri, numerous stelae, sarcophagi, and a wealth of material from tombs and from daily life. Another collection in Rome is the Museo Barrocco, named after the collector. Florence was a main center for the art market from 1824–1838 and, along with Bologna, has a fine collection.

The Netherlands. The National Museum of Antiquities in Leiden owes the foundation of its collection to Wilhelm I who, in 1818, combined two university core collections. Soon, C. J. C. Reuvens was appointed the first professor of archaeology and the first curator; he used the position to make a study of museology. Reuvens acquired 325 objects from Maria Cimba, whose husband was Henry Salt's physician, and whose collection derived from Salt in 1827. Reuvens, in competition with Champollion, succeeded at acquiring the first of three collections composed of 5,675 objects from Giovanni d'Anastasi, the Armenian businessman who also served as Consul in Egypt for Norway and Sweden (1828). He also obtained the collection of J. B. de Lescluze, which had been bought from Jean Barthou, Anastasi's agent, and sold along with various objects from Salt, Drovetti, and Anastasi. Benefactions from the Egyptian government (1893), from the Netherlands consul in Egypt, A. Tj. van der Meulen (1934), excavation divisions, and the acquisition of the greater part of F. W. von Bissing's collection (1939) increased the holdings at Leiden. In Amsterdam, the Allard Pierson Museum's Egyptian collection was largely formed by the banker and excavation financier, C. W. Lunsingh.

Other European Collections. Other major continental Egyptian collections include the Ny Carlsberg Glyptotek in Copenhagen, founded by the brewer Carl Jacobsen (1842–1914) who acquired material by himself and through his curator, Valdemar Schmidt, in the antiquities market and in Egypt. The connoisseur's collection, formed by Calouste Sarkis Gulbenkian in the 1920s and loaned to the British Museum and National Gallery of Art in Washington, D.C., found a permanent home in Lisbon in 1960. Among the highlights are the fine siliceous head of King Amenhotpe III (r. 1410–1372 BCE) and the rare partial bronze figure of King Petubastis (813–c.773 BCE), inlaid with precious metals.

The Musées Royaux d'Art et d'Histoire in Brussels was founded in 1835 and formed its collection similarly to the museum in Leiden. The diplomat and collector Emile de Meester de Ravestein gave many pieces to the museum in 1884; these were followed by the acquisition of mummy coffins, excavated by E. Grèbaut from the necropolis at Deir el-Bahri. With the arrival of the Egyptologist Jean Capart to the museum staff, (1877–1947) efforts were concentrated toward purchasing high-quality works of art from other collections. The museum also subscribed to the EES excavations, receiving divisions in return. In 1935, it received the royal collection of Leopold II, which included a wooden statuette with part of a papyrus, describing the events in the reign of King Ramesses IX (r. 1139–1120 BCE) that completes the so-called Amherst Papyrus preserved in the Pierpont Morgan Library in New York City.

Eastern Europe and the Balkans. In the Athens National Museum, Egyptian material collected by expatriate Greeks, such as Ioannis Dimitriou and Alexander Rostovitz, was reinstalled in the late twentieth century. Among the highlights are the well-preserved twenty-fifth dynasty bronze figure of Takushit, inlaid with precious metals. Other, mostly Roman-Egyptian material is displayed in the Benaki Museum in Athens, named after the collector and founder. There is a small collection in the Czech Republic, in Prague. In Poland, a fine collection assembled by the nobleman Wladyslaus Czartoryski (1828–1894) is in Krakow and another smaller collection is in Warsaw.

Russia. The Pushkin Museum of Fine Arts in Moscow is composed largely of a single collection formed by Vladimir Golenischev. The collection was begun in the 1870s and was originally housed in a private museum in Leningrad before being sold to the state in 1909. It is well known to students of ancient Egyptian language because of the wealth of textual material of its large number of stelae. The Hermitage Museum in Saint Petersburg includes the papyrus with the *Story of the Shipwrecked Sailor*.

Japan. A profound interest in Egyptian art in Japan has resulted in numerous temporary loan exhibitions. Recently, the privately funded Miho Museum opened with works of staggering quality.

Arab Republic of Egypt. The Egyptian Antiquities Service was founded in 1835, but the national collection, stored first in the Ezbakiah Gardens and later in the Cairo Citadel, continued to be used as a source of gifts to visiting foreign dignitaries. In 1855, Khedive Abbas I, ruler of Egypt, presented the remains of the collection to the Austrian Archduke Maximilian. The illicit excavation of the tomb of Queen Ahotpe (1859) in Western Thebes, and its seizure by François Auguste Ferdinand Mariette Pasha (1821–1881), heralded the arrival of the first director of the antiquities service, who was also responsible for moving the national museum to Boulaq (the precise whereabouts are unknown). A high flood in 1878 necessitated a further move to a palace of Ismail Pasha in 1890 (on the site of today's Cairo Zoo) before the move to its present site at Qasr el-Nil in 1902. The architect Ludwig Borchardt installed the collection at the Cairo Museum and conceived the monograph series publication *Catalogue General*. Since its inception, a number of general guidebooks have appeared and computerization of the collections has begun. With the general acknowledgment that the Cairo Museum is overcrowded and poorly accommodated, feasibility studies have been undertaken to examine a one hundred-acre site at junction of Fayoum and Alexandria roads. Other museums in Egypt include the Luxor Museum (designed and built by Dr. Mahmud El Hakim in 1969 and opened in 1975), composed almost invariably of local finds by the Egyptian Department of Antiquities and newly enhanced by the discovery in 1989 of a hoard of twenty-six statues found at the Luxor temple; the Elephantine Museum, enhanced by an annex; and the Nubian Museum at Aswan (1997), which includes many finds from the Nubian salvage campaign during construction of the Aswan High Dam. The Greco-Egyptian Museum at Alexandria has a post-pharaonic Ptolemaic and Roman collection, begun in 1891, although the building was not erected until 1895.

The United States. The main American collections of Egyptian antiquities are in the East: New York's Metropolitan Museum of Art, The Brooklyn Museum of Art, Boston's Museum of Fine Arts, and Baltimore's Walters Art Gallery. The Egyptian department at the Metropolitan Museum of Art was founded in 1906, with Albert Lythgoe as its first director. That same year, an Egyptian excavation procured for the museum Middle Kingdom finds from el-Lisht (1906–1934) and eleventh and eighteenth dynasty finds from the funerary temples of Montuhotep and Hatshepsut at Deir el Bahri (1911–1931). In 1978, the Dendur temple, acquired during the 1960s–1970s building of the Aswan High Dam, was installed in a new wing of the museum. The policy of the department is not to maintain closed storage for scholarly study, but to have the museum's entire holdings on view.

The Brooklyn Museum of Art concentrates its exhibits on high-quality objects. Its collections were largely acquired, beginning with purchases in 1902, from W. M. Flinders Petrie, but substantial excavated material was added to the museum's holdings through support of the Egypt Exploration Fund and its excavations. The museum also supported the Predynastic excavations of Henri de Morgan (1906–1908) in Upper Egypt. The largest donation included the library of the amateur Egyptologist Charles Edwin Wilbour, now the largest library for Egyptology in the Western Hemisphere. The Brooklyn Museum acquired some two thousand objects from the collection of Henry Abbott in 1948.

The Egyptian Department of the Museum of Fine Arts, Boston, was established in 1902 with Albert Lythgoe as its first curator. He enlisted the services of archaeologist George Andrew Reisner in 1905, who excavated at twenty-four sites in both Egypt and Sudan on behalf of the Boston Museum. Thanks to Reisner's work, there is a wealth of fourth dynasty material from the excavations of the Giza cemeteries, including royal Menkaure statues and the painted limestone bust of Prince Ankhhaf. The holdings at the museum are also rich in material from Sudan, including Kerma, Gebel Barkal, Kurru, and Nuri, and from Meroë. The Walters Art Gallery has a large collection of Late period statuary.

Other Egyptian collections in the United States are located in Virginia, Cleveland, and Detroit. University museums with Egyptian collections include the University Museum in Philadelphia, the Oriental Institute Museum of the University of Chicago, the Robert H. Lowie Museum of the University of California, and those at Yale and Princeton universities. In Canada, the Royal Ontario Museum of Toronto has a fine Egyptian collection.

Ethical and Legal Issues in Acquisition. In the late eighteenth and early nineteenth centuries, Napoleon's first systematic attempt to study, collect, and record the antiquities of Egypt initiated a passion for collecting ancient Egyptian objects. Since that time, consular officials competed with one another and with private collectors and tourists for the purchase of works of art. As well, official permits to excavate and remove antiquities from the country could be acquired. An Egyptian law of 1835 prohibited the export of antiquities, but even Abbas Pasha gave antiquities as gifts, emptying the entire contents of the state repository with one generous gift to the Austrian Archduke Maximilian in 1855. A Frenchman, Auguste Mariette—ironically sent to Egypt to acquire early Christian manuscripts, but who excavated the Saqqara Serapeum—was appointed to found a national museum of Egypt in 1859. Voices such as that of the traveler and writer Amelia B. Edwards were raised to stop the wholesale pillage of antiquities. The Egypt Exploration Fund (EEF) was founded as a consequence in 1882 to introduce new ethical standards in scientific excavations. Nevertheless, excavations were often financed by the sale of finds, by subscribing museums, and by individuals, all of whom wished to acquire antiquities. Foreign museums largely ignored antiquities law, to the extent that the British Museum's E. A. Willis Budge purchased twenty-four large crates of antiquities that he illicitly transported from Egypt in 1887, through the military.

In 1952, Egypt's leader, Gamal Abdal Nasser, nationalized native art produced before 1850. Such restrictive laws, combined with the lack of remuneration for chance finds, resulted in illicit trade in Egypt. The government allowed dealers to sell their then-current stock until 1979, and some duplicate material was allowed to leave the Cairo Museum until 1974. The UNESCO accords were drafted in 1970 [and signed by the United States] to stem the illegal import, export, and transfer of cultural property. Nevertheless, these accords cannot be applied to works of art not already recorded in the country of origin or to material from sites unknown. In countries where the accords have not been signed, such as Great Britain, museums follow a voluntary code of resisting the purchase of works of art without provenance. The UNESCO accords have coincided with an increased nationalistic fervor, and with a consequent end to object distributions from excavations, so that historical provenance has become an expensive premium for museums.

In practice, because documentation has always been scarce, most unpublished material is thereby deemed to be illicit. Actions were taken in the 1970s and 1980s to ban even the publication of objects without known historical provenance. In this way, overzealous archaeologists have naively hoped to discourage collecting and to inhibit the increase in value attached to published works of art. This trend, extended in the late twentieth century to discourage conservators from treating unprovenanced works of art on the market, reveals an extreme cynicism for the condition of objects. Another, more moderate, school of thought attaches scholarly value to unprovenanced objects and, rather than suppress the information available, advocates that it should be extracted from the object. The debate is essentially one between the archaeologists and the art historians—who are accustomed to extracting useful information from objects even where archaeological context is absent.

[See also Archaeological and Research Institutions; and Educational Institutions.]

BIBLIOGRAPHY

Dawson, Warren R., and Eric P. Uphill. *Who Was Who in Egyptology.* 2d rev. ed. London, 1972.

Fagan, Brian M. *The Rape of the Nile: Tomb Robbers, Tourists, and Archaeologists in Egypt.* London, 1975.

Moorehead, Alan. *The Blue Nile.* London, 1962, repr. 1980.

Petrie, W. M. Flinders. *Ten Years' Digging in Egypt 1881–1891.* London, 1892.

ELENI VASSILIKA

MUSIC. Texts, representations, and extant instruments shed much light on the circumstances and artifacts of ancient Egyptian music. Clearly, musical culture was a well-developed part of society, yet the nature of the music remains obscure.

Tools of Music. The instruments range from the simple (percussion) to the complex (harps). Their constructions affected the compass of the scales and tunes that could be produced, which evidently differed quantitatively from those known for other ancient cultures. Many of the instruments came to ancient Egypt from the Near East.

Percussion instruments. The most basic percussion sound is produced by clapping hands, an activity often displayed by singers depicted in Old Kingdom tombs, and labeled *m3ḥ*. The earliest instruments in evidence are boomerang-shaped clappers, known in Egypt and southern Palestine in the early fifth millennium BCE. In pharaonic times, clappers were decorated with hands or Hathor faces and labeled ʿwy. Smaller clappers (or castanets) were also used. The rustle of *menat*-necklaces also has percussive aspects.

Drums did not appear until the Middle Kingdom. Barrel-shaped drums, made from hollowed tree trunks, became popular in military bands. Goblet-shaped drums—wheel-thrown pots with skin-covered tops and open bottoms—were introduced about 1750 BCE from the Palestinian region. Circular frame drums (labeled *śr* in tombs) had a skin stretched across a wooden hoop; when they entered Egypt during the New Kingdom period, other percussion instruments lost ground. New drum names (*tbn, ḳmḳm, ḥʿw,* and *śh3t*) were introduced for tambourines and barrel drums in Greco-Roman times but often without consistency.

Percussion instruments are simple in concept but can produce complex rhythmic structures, especially if used in ensembles. One of the largest groups depicted occurs in the Middle Kingdom tomb of the singing instructor Khesuwer. He is shown coaching ten sistrum players and ten hand-clappers; since he has positioned them in neat rows, it was a highly disciplined performance. The sistrum is a metal rattle or noisemaker, consisting of a handle and a frame fitted with loosely held rods; sistrums were jingled, especially in the worship of Isis.

Wind instruments. Owing to their ability to differentiate pitches, wind and stringed instruments can produce more complex music than can percussion instruments.

Both types are known from the beginning of the Old Kingdom. Of winds, we recognize three types: flutes *(m3t)*, parallel double-pipes *(mmt)*, and divergent double-pipes *(wḏni?)*. All were made from reed pipes (or later imitations in bronze), but each type differed in the construction of the mouth-end of the pipe: flutes had a sharp wedge resting just outside the lips; pipes had a loosely attached mouthpiece furnished with double and single vibrating lamellae. Since no mouthpieces have survived, their details are unknown, but extant parallel pipes resemble modern Egyptian folk clarinets with one lamella and, therefore, are called "clarinets." Divergent pipes look like the Greek *aulos*, which had double lamellae like the modern oboe, and are termed "oboi." There were no oboi before the beginning of the New Kingdom, and no clarinets after.

The flutes, clarinets, and oboi had cylindrical bores, and stalks of reed provided adequate material for them, but trumpets flared and required more complex manufacture. The trumpets found in Tutankhamun's tomb were made of silver and bronze, with gold and silver mouthpieces, and were decorated with gold inlay. Although trumpets were primarily military instruments, pictures of Amun, Re-Horakhty, and Ptah gave them sacred associations.

Stringed instruments. Most of the previously mentioned instruments seem to have been adopted in Egypt from the Near East. Egyptian lyres and lutes were also closely patterned on Near Eastern instruments, but their harps *(bnt)* were not. Harps were first used in Mesopotamia about 3000 BCE, but when first seen in Egypt in 2500 BCE, their shapes were uniquely Egyptian. Their construction was more complex than that of wind and percussion instruments, and some used more precious materials. King Ahmose had a harp made of ebony, gold, and silver, and Thutmose III commissioned "a splendid harp wrought with silver, gold, lapis lazuli, malachite, and every splendid costly stone."

There are two main types of harp—arched and angular—and the first type dominated in pharaonic Egypt. Arched harps had a sound box, which was joined smoothly to a curved rod encircled by collars, one for each string. The strings stretched between the collars and a rib in contact with the skin cover of the box. When the collars were rotated, the tension and tuning of the attached strings changed. On angular harps, the rod was stuck through a hole in the oblong box; this arrangement resulted in a sharp angle between the rod and the box.

During the Old and Middle Kingdoms, only arched harps of the shovel-shaped type were used, but sizes and playing positions varied. The New Kingdom brought a plethora of new shapes and sizes, which were more or less equally popular. Some had changed considerably from the

MUSIC. *Representations of Musical Instruments.* (a) Clapper and jingling necklace, Middle Kingdom; (b) circular frame drum, New Kingdom; (c) castanets, New Kingdom; (d) concave frame drum, New Kingdom; (e) goblet drum, New Kingdom; (f) barrel drum, Late period; (g) flute, Old Kingdom; (h) double clarinet, Old Kingdom; (i) double oboe, New Kingdom; (j) trumpet, New Kingdom; (k) thin lyre, New Kingdom; (l) thick lyre, New Kingdom; (m) giant lyre, New Kingdom; (n) lute, New Kingdom. (Courtesy Bo Lawergren)

simple hunting-bow shape of shovel harps, but all had the smooth curve characteristic of arched harps. During the late period, archaized shovel harps were used again, but in the Greco-Roman period the variety of shapes was much reduced.

Angular harps had been invented around 1900 BCE in Mesopotamia and quickly replaced arched harps there, but in Egypt, adoption and complete displacement required more than a millennium. In the end, Egyptian harpists took to it enthusiastically. Athenaeus recounted that an Alexandrian angular-harp player had sent Rome into a state of music madness, with citizens whistling his tunes in the streets. The most significant difference between arched and angular harps was in their complement of strings. Typically, extant Egyptian arched harps have fewer than ten strings, occasionally as few as three. By contrast, extant angular harps typically have twenty-one strings, and sometimes as many as twenty-nine. Because each harp string gives only one pitch, Egypt's slow acceptance of angular harps implies a reluctance to expand the pitch range of their harp music. In the period 2500–1500 BCE, six to ten pitches sufficed, but at the end of the first millennium BCE, twenty-one pitches were required. In Mesopotamia, matters were different: its musicians accepted angular harps quickly, presumably to explore wide-ranging scales. By Near Eastern standards, Egypt was a conservative music culture; this observation confirms Plato's assertion that Egyptians "were forbidden to introduce any innovations in music."

Egypt had three types of lyres: thin, thick, and giant. Thin lyres existed throughout the Fertile Crescent region and the Egyptian lyres were merely the southern extension of this form, devoid of local characteristics. Thin lyres had arisen in northern Syria around 2500 BCE; they were first illustrated in Egypt around 1900 BCE and became common there five hundred years later. The West Semitic name for them was *kinnārum*, and this name is attested in Egypt too, though only once (c. 1200 BCE). An earlier term for the lyre was probably *ḏꜣḏꜣt*, used in the "Admonitions Text" (2152–2134 BCE), where it served as a low-status alternative to the harp *(bnt)*. Since there was only one type of harp (the shovel harp) at that time and thin lyres were widespread along the Fertile Crescent, *ḏꜣḏꜣt* probably meant "lyre." A millennium later, however, in Egypt, that term was instead attached to the angular harp, and *kinnārum* was adopted for the lyre.

Thick lyres had larger dimensions and more strings than thin ones. This type appeared briefly around 1400 BCE in Anatolia, but it lasted from 2000 BCE to the Ptolemaic period in Egypt. Giant lyres flourished during Akhenaten's reign, some large enough to accommodate dual players. Players always wore Canaanite dress, but no giant lyres are yet known from the Palestinian region. The idea of giant lyres with dual players was known in Mesopotamia, since such instruments were engraved on seals from Uruk and Susa around 2500 BCE.

During the New Kingdom, lutes *(gngnti?)* also arrived in Egypt from the Near East, where they had gained popularity in the beginning of the second millennium BCE. They were widely adopted in Egypt, but their popularity was quenched when the country became part of the Hellenistic world. In Greece, lutes had not been used before the third century BCE, and they remained rare long after that date. In Egypt, they returned with Islam in the mid-seventh century CE.

Ensembles and Instrumentalists. During the entire pharaonic period, instruments were often shown in ensembles. A typical Old Kingdom group had singers and hand-clappers, several harps, a flute, and a clarinet. In the beginning, only men played the full range of instruments and women were confined to harps and percussion, but toward the end of the Old Kingdom, other female instrumentalists appeared, and mixed-gender groups become standard during the Middle Kingdom. By the New Kingdom, female groups predominate.

A plethora of musicians' titles throw light on their social organization. Among the best documented are those comprising the *ḥnr*, who sang, danced, and clapped hands in temples, palaces, and funerary settings. They flourished from 2500 to 1500 BCE and in the Ramessid period. Initially, the groups had only female members and overseers, but males joined during the fifth dynasty and became sole overseers during the Middle Kingdom. Royal women often participated. The groups were attached to palaces, temples, and funerary estates, where they provided secular entertainment and sacred singing or performed for the deceased. Female members wore light dresses and hair braided into plaits, with balls dangling from the ends; men wore narrow belts or kilts.

Other titles denote temple songstresses (or chantresses), who served deities like Hathor, Osiris, and Isis. It became fashionable to sing at the Amun-Re temple at Thebes, and many women who dwelt in or near Thebes during the New Kingdom seem to have served there.

Sound of Music. Modern scholars have tried in vain to discover an ancient Egyptian notation system for music, but other, less precise information has come to light.

Notation. Singers in Old Kingdom ensembles usually made arm and hand gestures. Hans Hickmann (1961) claimed that the arm positions communicated pitches to the musicians. Some of his premises, however, seem arbitrary, and others have been invalidated by new research. In particular, gestures that differ in the position of the thumb and index finger were assumed to denote pitches a fifth apart. Moreover, he believed that ancient scales had five pitches per octave, but it is now known that Mesopotamian scales in the second millennium BCE contained seven pitches per octave. Most likely, the gestures were

MUSIC. *Girl musician with harp entertaining guests, from Luxor-Thebes.* (Erich Lessing / Art Resource, NY)

simply spontaneous motor responses common to much music-making, or, perhaps, basic stop or start commands. These chironomic gestures were considered a necessary attribute of singers, as stated in the great Nile hymn (1991–1786 BCE): "They begin singing to the harp for him; female singers are using their hands."

A terra-cotta figurine from the Late period may have musical notation. The figurine shows an angular-harp player facing a scribe, whose writing tablet contains signs. Little has survived besides a few long horizontal lines crossed by numerous vertical strokes. If notation is indeed present, one would expect the length of the verticals to indicate pitches, but the lengths are insufficient to differentiate among the twenty-one strings of the angular harp.

The first definite notation appears on Egyptian papyri from the mid-third century BCE. The notation system and the music are both Greek, since Egypt was then ruled by the Ptolemies.

Musical form. Some tomb texts pertain to musical forms. A song written in an Old Kingdom tomb seems to have been sung antiphonally by two groups, one asking a question and the other answering it. First comes an initial

call and question: "Oh, Western Goddess! Where is the shepherd?" Then the answer: "The shepherd is in the water beneath the fish. He talks to the catfish and greets the *mormyr*-fish." Finally, comes the concluding call: "Oh, shepherd of the Western Goddess." The accompanying scene shows sheep trampling seeds into the field. The calls and the question are written next to the foreman, indicating him as the lead singer. The answer was sung by drivers who urged the sheep across the field. Dating from about 2200 BCE, this antiphonal song is among the oldest known in literature and music. A larger musical form, the rondo, has been suggested for a harper's song (see below).

Circumstances of Music. The abundance of titles meaning "Temple Singer" implies diverse roles for music in the sacred sphere. In its most mundane manifestation, songstresses participated in priestly rituals. But there were also musical extravaganzas like the one staged at the *sed*-festival of Amenophis III. Tomb drawings show long rows of singers, percussionists, and dancers; their music "opened the doors of heaven so that the god may go forth pure."

Several deities were associated with music. Hathor was "mistress of music" and, since Meret incarnated songstresses and brought sacred texts to life, she was the goddess of the vocal apparatus. Bes often played instruments—even abroad, as on a Lycian temple frieze from around 390 BCE in which Bes-clones play the lyre, harp, tambourine, and oboe, and dance. Another deity, the Blind Horus (*Ḥnty-n-irty*), has been identified as the "harp god," but others consider that deity a mere "patron of harp players" and claim that the idea belonged to the realm of popular religion. The choice, however, accords with the fact that many harpists are shown blind or blindfolded.

Music also had an extensive secular role. Representations in Old Kingdom tombs show female family members playing, singing, and dancing for the tomb owner, and in New Kingdom tombs, performers do much the same. Quite a few Old Kingdom tombs offer glimpses of music among farm workers; in some, the workers cut sheaves of barley while a flautist wanders about. Other tombs contain the antiphonal song discussed earlier.

Somewhere between the sacred and profane lie the so-called harper's songs, written in New Kingdom tombs. A harpist (rarely a lutenist) is shown next to the extensive text, which usually begins by describing the inevitability of death and futility of life. The reader is then urged to live for the moment: "Make holiday . . . put incense and fine oil together beside you . . . put music before you . . . give drunkenness to your heart every day." Were these *carpe diem* songs performed in the tomb or intended for life beyond the tomb? Scholars have advocated both views, but most likely a banquet was held in the tomb while the song buoyed the spirits of the participants. The music is unknowable, but a song in Paser's tomb contains a phrase that recurs intermittently seven times. Hickmann suggested that this refrain corresponded to a melodic figure that also, recurred. If so, the form of the music could have been akin to a modern rondo.

Such songs exist in the Old Kingdom tombs too, but those are much shorter and have an entirely different character than the New Kingdom songs. Moreover, the harpist shares the stage with an ensemble. Having analyzed the texts and their visual settings, Altenmüller (1978, p. 20) concluded that the music belonged to a tomb ritual intended to bring back the deceased from the hereafter. During his brief return, the tomb owner was known as "the deified one" and was enabled to join the musicians by the sheer power of their music and Hathor songs.

[*See also* Dance; *and* Sistrum.]

BIBLIOGRAPHY

Altenmüller, Hartwig. "Zur Bedeutung der Harfnerlieder des Alten Reiches." *Studien zur altägyptischen Kultur* 6 (1978), 1–24.

Anderson, Robert D. "Music and Dance in Pharaonic Egypt." In *Civilizations of the Ancient Near East*, edited by Jack M. Sasson, vol. 4, pp. 2555–2568. New York, 1995. Overview by an expert on the Egyptian collection at the British Museum.

Ermann, Adolf. *Life in Ancient Egypt.* New York, 1971. (German original, 1886; translated into English by H. M. Tirard, 1894.) Early discussion illustrates concepts discussed here: *ḥnr* musician-dancers (p. 247), harper's songs (p. 255), and sheep trampling seed into fields (p. 429). The most glaring error is naming the lute *nefer* (p. 253), an error corrected by W. M. Flinders Petrie (*The Wisdom of the Egyptians*, London, 1940, p. 59ff.).

Finscher, Ludwig, ed. *Die Musik in Geschichte und Gegenwart.* 2d ed. Kassel and Stuttgart, 1994–1997. Articles "Harfen (Antike)," "Leiern (Altertum)," and "Mesopotamien (Musikinstrumente)" present recent research on music archaeology.

Hickmann, Hans. *Ägypten.* Musikgeschichte in Bildern 2,1. Leipzig, 1961. The pictorial material is superb, and the author reviews his many, still current, ideas.

Lawergren, Bo. "Distinctions among Canaanite, Philistine, and Israelite Lyres, and Their Global Lyrical Contexts." *Bulletin of the American Schools of Oriental Research* 309 (1998). Shows the intercultural context of Egyptian instruments.

Manniche, Lise. *Music and Musicians in Ancient Egypt.* London, 1991. The only book-length treatment in English. Full discussion of music, its societal role, and instruments (especially the first two), but few references to relevant scholarly literature.

New Grove Dictionary of Music and Musicians, edited by Stanley Sadie. London, 1980. See "Egypt."

Pritchard, James B., ed. *Ancient Near Eastern Texts Relating to the Old Testament.* 3d ed., with supplements. Princeton, 1969. Gives texts of the Hymn to the Nile (p. 373) and a harper's song (p. 467).

Teeter, Emily. "Female Musicians in Pharaonic Egypt." In *Rediscovering the Muses*, edited by Kimberly Marshall, pp. 68–91. Boston, 1993. Discusses groups of women musicians, their titles, place in ensembles, and societal positions; detailed bibliography.

BO LAWERGREN

MUT. The goddess Mut is known primarily as the spouse of Amun-Re, king of the gods; she forms with him and Khonsu the child the Theban triad, from about 1500 BCE until the end of Egyptian religious history. She is, however, not just a vague mother goddess, though she is often represented with the child Khonsu on her lap. She is a stately royal lady, wearing the Double Crown, the two royal crowns of Upper and Lower Egypt, as do some masculine gods. She is the divine queen mother and even queen regnant, a divine female pharaoh who represents kingship with her Double Crown. Beginning in the time of the female pharaoh Hatshepsut, the pharaoh may be called "son of Amun and Mut."

The name of Mut was written with the vulture hieroglyph, but she was not a vulture goddess like Nekhbet, as is often suggested in older literature. She was also represented as an anthropomorphic being with a human head or a lion head. Only very seldom, and evidently secondarily, was she given a vulture head next to a human or lion head. The vulture headdress that she often wears together with the Double Crown is common to many other goddesses and royal women. This vulture headdress, as well as the vulture hieroglyph with which her name was written, is a symbol and ideogram of motherhood, as Horapollo knew: the Egyptian word for "mother" is written with the vulture hieroglyph and is to be read *mwt*. The name of the goddess Mut thus means "mother." (For particulars and problems, see the article by Wolfgang Brunsch in *Enchoria* 8 [1978], pp. 123–128.)

In comparison with other divinities, Mut makes a late appearance in the history of Egyptian religion, or at least in the material that is preserved. So far, no definite proof exists that she played a part in the religion of Predynastic and Early Dynastic times, or even of the Old Kingdom, First Intermediate Period, and Middle Kingdom. The oldest certain attestations date from the Second Intermediate Period and come from Middle Egypt, for example, from Megeb in the tenth Upper Egyptian nome and from Karnak. Whether, when, or how Mut was introduced in this cult center of Amun is not known, but she replaced Amaunet, the "grammatical" female companion of Amun, in the Middle Kingdom in some aspects. Mut is known from the seventeenth dynasty on as "the Great One, Mistress of Isheru."

The precise meaning of the word *išrw* is unknown. Isheru is not only the place and temple where Mut was worshiped in South Karnak, but it is also a term for a lake that surrounds a temple of lion goddesses on three of its four sides. Mythologically, Isheru is the place where these feline deities were appeased, so that their burning wrath was cooled. Leonine goddesses were considered to be representations of the Eye of Re, or the daughter of Re, or the original first feminine being; they had a dual or ambivalent nature in which pacific and creative elements coexisted with fiery, anarchic, destructive, dangerous characteristics. These goddesses had to be pacified with specific prayers or litanies and rituals (see Yoyotte 1980). The festival of the navigation of Mut, together with some other leonine goddesses, on the *išrw*-lake was famous in Thebes and all Egypt.

In Amun's train, Mut was worshiped in many places in the Nile Valley, the Delta, Nubia, and the Western Desert oases. By herself or together with other gods, such as Ptah or Re, she was worshiped near Antinoöpolis as mistress of Megeb; in Memphis, as Mut in the house of Ptah; in Giza, as Mut-Khenty-Abu-Neteru; and in Heliopolis, as Mut-Her-Senutes, the cruel goddess to whom human victims were offered, as Jean Yoyotte (1980–1981) has shown.

In a late Wisdom text (Papyrus Insinger 8, 18–19) one can read: "The work of Mut and Hathor is that what takes place among women, for there are good and bad women among those upon earth." Although Mut is not without malevolent and dissipated traits and remains a leonine goddess who is not always a peaceful cat, she is not, like Hathor, a symbol of sexual excitation. Mut is the matron, the divine mistress of the house. She is the female compassion man meets in his mother, sister, daughter, and—to a certain extent—in his wife; she is not so much the sexual attraction man finds in strange and dangerous women outside the family. Mut was venerated by women and men, and she had both priests and priestesses. The important priestesses called "God's Wives of Amun" had names mostly composed with the name of Mut and were regarded as earthly incarnations of Mut. The femininity of Mut with her royal crowns was authoritative and sometimes also aggressive and terrifying: unlike any other Egyptian goddess, she could be depicted as an aggressive woman with a penis, who frightens off her opponents.

BIBLIOGRAPHY

Capel, Anne K., and Glenn E. Markoe, eds. *Mistress of the House, Mistress of Heaven: Women in Ancient Egypt.* New York, 1996. Good information and references on Mut are in the chapter "Goddesses" (pp. 121–144) in this exhibition catalog, and in entries 61, 64, 65, and 67, written by Richard A. Fazzini.

Naguib, Saphinaz-Amal. *Le clergé féminin d'Amon Thébain à la 21e dynastie.* Leuven, 1990. Chapter on Mut, pp. 75–84.

Troy, Lana. "Mut Enthroned." In *Essays on Ancient Egypt in Honour of Herman te Velde*, edited by Jacobus van Dijk, pp. 301–305. Groningen, 1997.

Velde, Herman te. "Towards a Minimal Definition of the Goddess Mut." *Jaarbericht van het Voor-Aziatisch-Egyptisch Genootschap Ex Oriente Lux* 26 (1979–1980), 3–9.

Velde, Herman te. "Mut." In *Lexikon der Ägyptologie*, 4:246–248. Wiesbaden, 1982.

Velde, Herman te. "The Cat as Sacred Animal of the Goddess Mut." In *Studies in Egyptian Religion Dedicated to Jan Zandee*, pp. 127–137. Leiden, 1982.

Velde, Herman te. "Mut the Eye of Re." In *Akten des Vierten Internationalen Ägyptologisches Kongresses*, pp. 395–403. Hamburg, 1989.

Velde, Herman te. "Mut and Other Ancient Egyptian Goddesses." In *Ancient Egypt, the Aegean, and the Near East: Studies in Honour of Martha Bell*, edited by Jacqueline Phillips. San Antonio, Tex., 1998.

Yoyotte, Jean. "Une monumentale litanie de granit: Les Sekhmet d'Amenophis III et la conjuration permanente de la déesse dangereuse." *Bulletin de la Société Française d'Égyptologie* 87–88 (1980), 46–71.

Yoyotte, Jean. "Héra d'Heliopolis et le sacrifice humain." *Annales d'École Pratique des Hautes Études*, sec. 5, 89 (1980–1981), 29–102.

HERMAN TE VELDE

MUT PRECINCT. The Mut Precinct at Thebes is part of the complex of temples at Karnak (23°43'N, 32°40'E) on the eastern bank of the Nile River, where it lies south of the precinct of Mut's consort Amun. The Mut Temple proper is oriented toward the Amun Precinct and is partially surrounded by a sacred lake of a type called *išrw*, which also became a name for the site. References associating Mut and Isheru are attested as early as the seventeenth dynasty, but the oldest securely dated remains of the site's temples are no earlier than the early eighteenth dynasty reigns of Thutmose III and Hatshepsut.

The Napoleonic expedition, the Royal Prussian Expedition, and some other nineteenth-century explorers mapped parts of the Mut Precinct. Two Englishwomen, Margaret Benson and Janet Gourlay, conducted the first major excavations (1895–1897), concentrating on the interior of the Mut Temple. In the 1920s, the Egyptian Department of Antiquities undertook partial excavations of Temple A in the site's northeastern corner, and of Temple C (built by the twentieth dynasty king Ramesses III), west of the Isheru. Temple C's preserved decoration was later published by the University of Chicago Epigraphic Survey. In 1975, the Institut français d'archéologie orientale du Caire cleared and recorded the site's main entrance. Since 1976, the Brooklyn Museum of Art, under the auspices of the American Research Center in Egypt and since 1978 with the assistance of the Detroit Institute of Arts, has been systematically investigating the site.

Under Hatshepsut and Thutmose III, the precinct probably contained only the Mut Temple and the Isheru. Sections of the western and northern precinct walls of this time, including a stone gateway with the name of Thutmose III, have been uncovered. A later eighteenth dynasty ruler, probably Amenhotpe III, enlarged the Mut Temple, completely enclosing the earlier structure. Amenhotpe III may also have enlarged Temple A, then outside the Mut Precinct and perhaps built earlier in the dynasty, but none of its standing walls predates the nineteenth dynasty.

The Mut Temple's two mud-brick pylons and the first pylon's stone gateway were built no later than the nineteenth dynasty and may have replaced earlier precinct walls. That dynasty's Ramesses II rebuilt Temple A, still outside the Mut Precinct, erecting before its first pylon two usurped colossal statues and two colossal stelae. The text on one of the latter commemorates the renewal of a

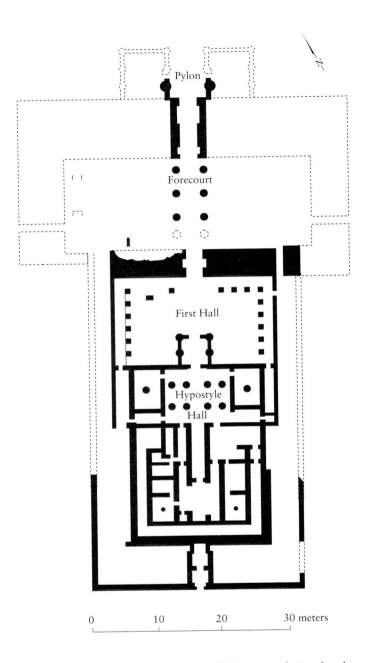

MUT PRECINCT. *Plan of the Mut Precinct.*

temple and seems to identify Temple A as a "Temple of Millions of Years," linked to Amun.

During the twenty-fifth dynasty, extensive work was undertaken at the site. A significant part of the Mut Temple was rebuilt, and a large stone porch was probably erected before its façade. The period may have seen the renewal of Structure B, the site's elevated "pure magazine" (where offerings were prepared and consecrated) to the east of the Mut Temple. Extensive renovations were certainly undertaken for Temple A, which appears to have come to function in part as a *mammisi* for the cult of the birth of Amun and Mut's divine offspring, the god Khons.

This new function of Temple A helps to explain why the twenty-fifth dynasty expanded the Mut Precinct to encompass it, as evidenced by the discovery of mud-brick walls with a stone gateway inscribed for King Taharqa. This dynasty also saw the beginning of a proliferation of small chapels at the site, the earliest of which were dedicated by a major official of the twenty-fifth and early twenty-sixth dynasties, Montuemhat, who was probably in charge of most of the twenty-fifth dynasty work at the site. The thirtieth dynasty also renovated some structures at the site and, possibly, began construction of the final enclosure walls for a fully expanded Mut Precinct.

The Ptolemies renovated the Late period "Contra-Temple," abutting the rear of the Mut Temple, as well as parts of the latter and Temple A. They also built the site's Chapel D, dedicated to Mut and Sekhmet and perhaps also to the Ptolemaic ancestor cult, and the precinct's main entrance. The site's Ptolemaic religious inscriptions are major sources for our knowledge of the goddess and her cult.

The early Roman period appears to have been the time of the construction and renovation of large walls for the Mut Temple and the Mut Precinct. By then, however, houses had come to be built in "fringe" areas of the precinct, and both the temple and habitation remains of the fourth century CE indicate that the site no longer served its original cultic purposes.

BIBLIOGRAPHY

Fazzini, R., "Report on the 1983 Season of Excavation at the Precinct of the Goddess Mut." *Annales du Service des Antiquités de l'Égypte* 70 (1984–1985), 287–307.

Fazzini, R., and W. Peck. "The Precinct of Mut during Dynasty XXV and Early Dynasty XXVI: A Growing Picture," *Journal of the Society for the Study of Egyptian Antiquities* 11 (1981), 115–116.

Fazzini, R., and W. Peck. "The 1982 Season at Mut." *Newsletter of the American Research Center in Egypt* 120 (Winter 1982), 37–58.

Fazzini, R., and W. Peck. "Excavating the Temple of Mut." *Archaeology* 36 (1983), 16–23.

Fazzini, R., et al., *The Brooklyn Museum of Art Archaeological Expedi-tion to the Precinct of the Goddess Mut at South Karnak*, vol. 2: *The Gateway in the First Pylon of the Mut Temple, its Architecture, Religious Texts and Representations.* New York, forthcoming.

Porter, B., R. Moss, and E. Burney. *Topographical Bibliography of Ancient Egyptian Hieroglyphic Texts, Reliefs, and Paintings*, vol. 2: *Theban Temples.* 2d ed., revised and augmented. Oxford, 1972, pp. 255–275.

RICHARD A. FAZZINI

MYCENAE, an ancient city in Argolis, the northeast coast of the Peloponnesian Peninsula of mainland Greece. Classical Greek legend credited the founding of Mycenae to Perseus, the descendant of Aegyptus and his brother Danaus; they had emigrated from Egypt to the Aegean several generations earlier. Thus Mycenae was from its very beginnings linked mythologically to Egypt. Archaeological evidence for contacts between Egypt and Mycenae indicates that they were in contact, indirectly at first, then directly, from the beginning of the second millennium BCE to about 1150 BCE. Recently revived, but unacceptable to most scholars, are the nineteenth-century hypotheses that the wealth in the Shaft Graves at Mycenae (c.1550 BCE) was the result of Mycenaeans helping the Egyptians rid their land of the hated Hyksos; or that the bodies in the graves of Grave Circle A at Mycenae are actually refugee Hyksos; and that the Hyksos conquered the Aegean. In

MYCENAE. *The Lion Gate at Mycenae.* (Courtesy Donald B. Redford)

MYCENAE. *The so-called Treasury of Atreus at Mycenae.* (Courtesy Donald B. Redford)

fact, most of the Egyptian or Egyptianized objects in the Shaft Graves at Mycenae most likely arrived via Minoan Crete, which seems to have been the major Aegean trading partner with Egypt at that time.

Mycenaean pottery from Peloponnesian Greece (the peninsula forming the southern part of the Greek mainland) began to appear with regularity in Egypt by the time of Hatshepsut of the eighteenth dynasty, and Thutmose III states in his *Annals* that the "Prince of Tanaja" (the Mycenaean Greek mainland) sent tribute to Egypt in the form of "a silver *shawabti*-vessel in Keftiuan [Minoan] workmanship together with four bowls of iron [or copper?] with handles of silver." Mycenae is mentioned specifically by Amenhotpe III, on a statue-base list at Kom el-Hetan, along with Tanaja, Keftiu (Crete), Nauplion, Boeotian

Thebes, Messenia, Kythera, Knossos, Phaistos, Kydonia, and perhaps Troy. Fragmentary faience foundation-deposit plaques with the cartouche of Amenhotpe III have been found at Mycenae in fourteenth- and thirteenth-century BCE religious contexts, along with scarabs of his wife. The plaque fragments were found scattered, mostly in secondary contexts; the religious nature of most of those contexts (e.g., in the Cult Center at Mycenae) indicates that the Mycenaeans were still aware of the potentially sacred significance of these particular Egyptian imports. Whether the fragments are the remnants of a royal gift brought by an official Egyptian embassy to the king of Mycenae, in the same manner as the gifts sent by Amenhotpe III to the kings of Babylon, Mitanni, and Cyprus and recorded in the Amarna Letters, is plausible but uncertain.

Strangely enough, the Aegean is not mentioned in any of the Amarna Letters of Amenhotpe III and Akhenaten. There is also little Mycenaean pottery in Egyptian contexts dated to the time of Amenhotpe III, although there is much in contexts dated to the time of Akhenaten; especially at his capital city, Akhetaten (Tell el-Amarna). In addition, few pictorial representations are known in Egypt of the Mycenaeans (as opposed to Minoans); those possibly depicted in the tomb of the vizier Rekhmire are the exception. Despite these observations, other archaeological evidence indicates that Mycenae and the Greek mainland replaced Minoan Crete as the major trading partner of Egypt and the Near East by the thirteenth century BCE; this situation continued until Mycenae was destroyed and New Kingdom Egypt lay in ruins—by the end of the Late Bronze Age, c.1100 BCE.

BIBLIOGRAPHY

Cline, Eric H. "Amenhotep III and the Aegean: A Reassessment of Egypto-Aegean Relations in the 14th Century BC." *Orientalia* 56.1 (1987), 1–36. Discussion of Amenhotpe III and Queen Tiye objects found at Mycenae and elsewhere in the Bronze Age Aegean, with Amenhotpe III's "Aegean List" at Kom el-Hetan in Egypt.

Cline, Eric H. "An Unpublished Amenhotep III Faience Plaque from Mycenae." *JAOS* 110.2 (1990), 200–212. A detailed discussion of the fragments of faience foundation-deposit plaques with the cartouche of Amenhotpe III found at Mycenae.

Cline, Eric H. *Sailing the Wine-Dark Sea: International Trade and the Late Bronze Age Aegean.* Oxford, 1994. An overview of the international trade in the Mediterranean during the second millennium BCE; catalog of Egyptian objects at Mycenae and chapter on Egypt are particularly relevant.

Cline, Eric H. "Egyptian and Near Eastern Imports at Late Bronze Age Mycenae." In *Egypt, the Aegean and the Levant: Interconnections in the Second Millennium BC,* edited by W. Vivian Davies and Louise Schofield, pp. 91–115. London, 1995. Catalog and discussion of Egyptian and Near Eastern imports found at Mycenae.

Pendlebury, John D. S. *Aegyptiaca: A Catalogue of Egyptian Objects in the Aegean Area.* Cambridge, 1930. Original catalog of Egyptian objects found at Mycenae and elsewhere in the Bronze Age Aegean; updated by Cline (1994).

ERIC H. CLINE

MYTHOLOGICAL TEXTS. Any definition of Egyptian mythological texts requires an understanding of the nature of myth. One might define myth as traditional narratives about the gods, the past, and the supernatural domain that lies beyond the scope of the normal human senses and intellect. However, the process of mythologization not infrequently encompasses also what the modern mind would consider historical reality. Historical events and individuals were often mythologized by the Egyptians to underscore the fact that they had a significance beyond the process of history, which placed them within the realm of the heroic, the supernatural, or the superhuman. Often there is no clear division between myth and history,

and it is sometimes a matter of interpretation whether a specific text should be classified as mythological or historical. In general, Egyptian mythological texts articulate the incomprehensible and the marvelous, while attempting to express such phenomena in a rational manner. Certain historical texts reveal a mythological element, making it clear that for the Egyptians there was no sharp distinction between the worlds of myth and of reality. Figures such as Thutmose III, Akhenaten, and Ramesses II were fully historical, but the accounts of their deeds have to an extent transformed them into figures of myth. A large number and variety of mythological texts, and their different forms will be discussed and considered below.

The term *myth* implies a spoken word or statement, and the majority of myths originated in oral tradition. Mythic statements could be a single spoken word (for example, the pronunciation of a divine name), or an extended narrative. The oral element in myth was significant because it permitted a specific myth to develop in accordance with the concepts and experiences that it was intended to express. As myths became more complex and required a certain standard of orthodoxy, recording them became necessary to preserve their correct forms. The earliest written corpus of Egyptian myth was the Pyramid Texts, composed during the fifth and sixth dynasties (c.2500–2200 BCE). These texts experienced a complex development, transmitted at first orally and later in written form. Written and graphic records can be found from the earliest period of Egypt's history. The famous Narmer Palette and the ceremonial mace head of Serk, although intended to illustrate historical events, may be considered mythological texts because they preserved the tradition of past heroic events. In artifacts such as these, as in some of the events of the Early Dynastic period, it is possible to see how history and myth became intertwined to create a semihistorical, semimythological tradition, not unlike that preserved in the *Iliad* of Homer.

The major elements of Old Kingdom myth have been preserved in the Pyramid Texts, whose mythic components span a number of centuries. There is little doubt that the myth of the conflict of Horus and Seth goes back to the Early Dynastic and even the Predynastic period, and that its origins lie in the internal conflicts that eventually led to the unification of the Two Lands. So, too, the killing of Osiris appears to have been rooted in antiquity and gradually developed into the complex form that was finally accepted and connected to the Horus/Seth tradition. The Pyramid Texts further provide certain references to the transformation of Osiris from a demon into a deity, who was beneficent to the deceased. In the earlier periods, such contradictions would have existed side by side without difficulty, but eventually an accepted version emerged, which fixed the myth in written form. This, however, did not prevent the preservation of more primitive elements; one of the positive characteristics of myth is its ability to accept contradictory traditions without having to harmonize them.

The Pyramid Texts were mortuary texts recited during and after the burial of the deceased king. Their mythic traditions had been adapted for specific purposes, such as the resurrection and immortality of the monarch, and an orderly dynastic succession; that is, Horus's burial of his dead father, now transformed into Osiris, ensured that the rightful heir would succeed to the throne. A myth that had originated in political events was thus converted into a ritual which spanned the worlds of the living and the dead. The Heliopolitan priesthood, which was responsible for the compilation of the Pyramid Texts, further conjoined the Osiris myth with the earlier tradition of the conflict between Horus and Seth. Isis and Nephthys, symbolic of the throne and royal authority, were added, possibly at a later date. The texts speak of the mourning of the goddesses over the dead Osiris, which reflected ritual mourning during the royal burial. The association of Osiris with Geb and Nut (primeval deities of earth and sky) as symbols of rebirth grounded this myth even more firmly in the most ancient traditions. The Heliopolitan Ennead, which came out of the conjunction of these deities and myths, was the major accomplishment of the Pyramid Texts for it combined in one system the myth of natural order and the myth that justified the monarchical system.

The scope of the Pyramid Texts, however, goes beyond the Ennead and includes other mythic materials, thus forming a compendium of Old Kingdom myth. One finds, for example, the tradition of the ascent to the sky, where the monarch joins and becomes identified with the sun god Re. Complementing this solar tradition is a more ancient system of symbolism centered on the stars: these astral texts fix the night sky firmly within the corpus of Old Kingdom myth. Finally, mention must be made of those ritual texts that are concerned with the making of offerings to the deceased monarch and protecting him from the various dangers that he might encounter in the next world.

The Pyramid Texts were succeeded in the Middle Kingdom by the Coffin Texts. The collected corpus of Coffin Texts consists of almost 1,200 spells or recitations which were written on coffins. These texts were transmitted through copies on papyrus, which would have served as a source for the scribes engaged in decorating the coffins. Such copies are, however, rare. The texts vary in length from one or two sentences to complex mythological and ritual accounts, most of which were intended to aid in the resurrection of the deceased in the next world. Much of the material in the Coffin Texts was derived from the Pyramid Texts, but their scope is wider, and they were intended not for the use of the dead monarch but for non-royal people, to whom the afterlife was now open. The mortuary nature of these texts did not restrict their contents, and the Coffin Texts are a rich source for the wider mythic traditions of Egypt. Those texts that are clearly connected with the afterlife provide detailed insight into the nature of that life and the process of resurrection. Like the Pyramid Texts, many of the Coffin Texts were rituals used during and after burial, and so they attempted to provide for every need of the deceased during his journey to and sojourn in the next world. Virtually all the gods are mentioned in these texts, but Osiris is one of the most prominent. At the same time, the traditions of the sun god Re are prominent as one of the ritual methods of resurrection. The texts are not orderly expositions of Egyptian myth, but from them it is possible to reconstruct many details of the mythic tradition.

Some of the Coffin Texts were not originally mortuary texts. For example, Spell 148, "Creating One's Form as a Falcon" deals with the pregnancy of Isis and the birth and triumph of Horus. The triumphal aspect of such a spell makes it suitable as a symbol of resurrection, but it is possible that its original use was as a ritual of Horus, or as a text for a woman in childbirth. So also, Spell 80, although concerned with the rebirth of the deceased, stresses important elements of earlier Heliopolitan myth. This breadth of subject matter in the Coffin Texts can be understood when one considers the close connection between myth and the life and experience of the Egyptians. In the Coffin Texts, myths that had given significance to life were now used to give equal significance to death.

During the New Kingdom and until the end of Egyptian civilization, the Coffin Texts were replaced by the *Book of Going Forth by Day* (*Book of the Dead*); the almost two hundred chapters of this work are based partly on earlier texts. There was apparently a collection of texts from which certain recitations could be chosen for any single copy of the *Book of Going Forth by Day,* and some of the versions, written on papyrus, were richly illustrated in accordance with the price an individual could pay. The *Book of Going Forth by Day* is best described as a collection of spells designed to aid the individual in surviving the dangers of the journey to the next world, to ensure his successful judgment before Osiris, and to allow him to move about freely in the afterlife.

Like earlier mortuary texts, the *Book of Going Forth by Day* contains a wide variety of mythological material drawn from other traditions. It places more emphasis than do the earlier texts on the fantastic dangers which were encountered during the journey to the next world, and its presence in the tomb was even more necessary than the earlier texts had been for the protection of the deceased. From a more positive point of view, this work emphasizes the necessity for the deceased to have lived a righteous life if he or she expects to be welcomed into eternity, with the judgment before the tribunal of Osiris a central consideration. Significant in this regard is chapter 75 of the text, the famous "Negative Confession," in which the deceased proclaims his innocence of any sins that would make him unfit to enter eternity. Here one sees proof of the potent concept of morality held by the Egyptians. The mythological nature of the *Book of Going Forth by Day* is evident in the nondogmatic style of its statements. The afterlife is not defined or restricted, but is expressed under a variety of symbols. The deceased is said to live with Osiris, and with Re, among the stars (an ancient concept pre-dating Osiris and the sun god), and/or in the tomb. Since this work was not a statement of orthodox belief but rather a collection of mythological expressions, these contradictory symbols caused no problem, and like all mythic texts, it included various symbolic expressions.

In connection with the *Book of Going Forth by Day*, mention should be made of a collection of royal mortuary texts generally known as the *Book of That Which Is in the Underworld* (*Amduat*). The earliest extant occurrence of this text is on the walls of the tomb of Thutmose I (c.1525–1516 BCE), although it may date from the Middle or even the Old Kingdom. The text describes the nature of the underworld, focuses on the night journey of the sun beneath the earth, and provides the dead monarch with the ritual formulas that he will need to reach his destination. From the twenty-first dynasty onward, this text was also used in private tombs.

The New Kingdom has left behind a number of other mythological texts, one of which is the account of how Re attempted to destroy human beings because they had plotted against him. The destruction is started by the Eye of Re in the form of Hathor, but Re repents and saves humanity by causing Hathor to become drunk on blood-colored beer. This story, written in Middle Egyptian, may have originated in the Middle Kingdom, but the surviving copies come from five royal tombs between the eighteenth and twentieth dynasties; that in the tomb of Tutankhamun is the earliest. It may be debated whether this text is myth or fiction, but its setting in the divine realm places it within a mythological context.

More complex is the Late Egyptian account of the conflict between Horus and Seth. This lengthy narrative, found on Papyrus Chester Beatty I in Hieratic script, had its provenance in Thebes during the reign of Ramesses V (1160–1156 BCE). The story is set in the primeval age of the gods, and the actors in the narrative are the gods themselves. The story, however, is told in a style that is more fictional than mythological. Many of its

events have a serious tone, but it is impossible to escape the conclusion that the story was written for its entertainment value. The gods, far from being the majestic beings that one expects, are frequently mocked by the narrator. The great god, Re-Horakhty ("Re of the Horizon"), is shown sulking childishly, until Hathor playfully exposes herself for his amusement. Seth is portrayed as a churlish individual who is tricked on several occasions, and the homosexual scene between Seth and Horus can hardly be considered a serious mythic narrative. Even Osiris is belittled by the message sent to him by Re-Horakhty, who claims that even without him (Osiris) the grain would still grow. Although the text is a rich source of information about the Horus/Seth conflict, it is unlikely that it was intended for serious purposes.

As mentioned above, historical events and personages were frequently mythologized by the Egyptians. The account of the battle of Megiddo waged by Thutmose III, carved on the wall of the temple of Amun-Re at Karnak, was intended as a historical document, but the narrative is far from objective, owing to the element of heroic myth within it. Definitely mythological is the *Poetical Stela of Thutmose III*, also coming from the Karnak temple. Although the text refers to the historical conquests of Thutmose and to his expansion of Egypt's empire, the narrative is mythological in presenting Thutmose and his deeds as the revelation of the will of Amun-Re. Of a similar nature is the *Stela of Amenhotep III* (r. 1410–1372 BCE) from Western Thebes. Indeed, because of the mythical divinity of the monarch, most Egyptian royal inscriptions have an unmistakable mythic quality.

Liturgical hymns must also be included within the genre of mythological texts. The New Kingdom produced a plethora of mythologically based hymns, one of the most outstanding being the hymn to Osiris on the stela of Amenmose (Louvre C 286). This text is significant not only for its literary merit but also because it contains the most extensive account of the Osiris myth found in Egyptian texts. The hymn preserves traditional formulas by which Osiris was addressed in his rituals and bears testimony to the importance of the god for the wider populace. Although this text is the only copy of the hymn known, it seems likely that it was in common use.

From about 1500 BCE onward, a new phenomenon in mortuary texts began to appear in the solar hymns from the Theban necropolis. These texts were the result of the prominence of Amun-Re, the universal creator god, who had, according to Egyptian tradition, manifested himself in many forms and had taken to himself the functions of many other gods. At times it appears that the other deities are but manifestations of the power of Amun-Re. The Theban solar hymns are unlike the earlier hymnic texts in that their content tends toward an abstract theology and away from pure myth. Nevertheless, such texts belong within the corpus of Egyptian myth because their imagery draws heavily on traditional mythic materials. At the same time, they demonstrate how myth and theology were intertwined by the priesthood to express abstract concepts. Outstanding among these solar hymns are the two hymns from the tomb of the brothers Suti and Hor, dating from the reign of Amenhotpe III. In these texts, Amun-Re is presented as a deity who is both revealed and hidden, the universal creator, god of order, and source of all life. In such texts, Egyptian theology, though expressed mythologically, comes close to a monotheistic understanding of the divine world.

During the rule of Akhenaten—the so-called Amarna period (1372–1355 BCE)—Egyptian theology evolved to its most nonmythological manifestation. Amarna expression was demythologized to articulate a theology that some have considered henotheism, though others have seen it as authentic monotheism. With the exception of a few traditional symbols—excluding Amun-Re—which served to articulate the sun god, the Amarna texts appear free from earlier mythic expressions. Nevertheless, Akhenaten's "myth-free" system was still reliant on myth. The light and rays of the sun, the emphasis on the rising and setting of the Aten, the imagery of the self-begotten deity, and the parental imagery which described the Aten as "mother and father of all created things," all contributed to a new mythological system that aimed to create an abstract theology. No theological system, however, can be completely devoid of myth, and the few mythic elements in Akhenaten's movement testify to the enduring power of myth to influence the composition of religious texts. Most significant in the Amarna system was the myth concerning the monarch and the royal family, which revived a myth of kingship that was as strong as it was in the Old Kingdom. The Amarna concept declared that the king was totally divine, an incarnation of the heavenly deity. The monarch alone knew and revealed the Aten because he had been born from the very body of the god. The Amarna movement thus looked forward to a less mythical way of thinking, but at the same time it looked backward to a way of political thinking whose basis was fully mythological.

The twenty-fifth dynasty produced the Memphite Theology, a work purported to have been copied during the reign of the Nubian king Shabaqa (712–698 BCE), from a worm-eaten document, presumably a papyrus. The text is in the archaic language of the Pyramid Texts and was long believed to be a copy of an Old Kingdom document. It is, however, now generally accepted that the Memphite Theology dates from the twenty-fifth dynasty, and that it was an attempt to strengthen the Nubian kingship on the basis of ancient tradition. The text reiterates the Heliopolitan myth of Geb, the Ennead, Osiris, the conflict between Horus and Seth, and the triumph of Horus. In addition, the Memphite Theology includes a theological exposition of the nature of Ptah, proclaiming him as the supreme deity, the other gods being manifestations of his various aspects. The creative principle in this text is the divine intellect, Ptah, creating all things through the thoughts of his heart and the word of his mouth, a concept of creation that goes beyond the mythical and enters the realm of abstract theology. The Memphite Theology also stresses the royal role of Memphis and affirms the divine legitimacy of the monarchy. Although of late origin, it attempts to reestablish the ancient mythic traditions in which the world of politics was inseparably connected with the cosmic order.

The Theban solar hymns have been mentioned above, but hymns and ritual texts were produced throughout the entire history of Egypt; many of them were inscribed on the walls of temples, reflecting the rituals performed within. Daily rituals were occasions for the recitation of hymnic material that repeated the mythological tradition. Such hymns are found in all major temples, but worthy of note are the New Kingdom texts from the temple at Abydos, a structure which owes its form to Sety I and Ramesses II of the nineteenth dynasty. On the basis of such texts, as well as of similar texts on papyrus, it is possible to reconstruct the daily temple rituals. These were centered on the cult statue of the god of each temple and were a mythologization of the passage of time. Such ritual myth was a means of realizing the divine presence within the world and thus stabilizing it for humans.

The enduring nature of Egyptian myth is shown by the fact that even in the Ptolemaic and Roman periods hymns were produced in the classical format and language. From the Ptolemaic period, for example, there is a Hieratic papyrus of the *Book of Going Forth by Day* which belonged to a woman named Teret (or Tentruty), and which contains a copy of a lamentation of Isis and Nephthys over the dead Osiris (Papyrus Berlin 3008). The details of the text show that the Osiris rituals had not waned in significance since the time of their institution. Ptolemaic temples were richly adorned with hymnic texts, notable among them the hymns to Khnum from the Esna temple, stressing the creative role of the god. The temple at Dendera provides texts from the rituals of Hathor, and the Edfu temple gives evidence for the Horus rituals, particularly the so-called *Play of Horus*, a text which is both political and religious. Finally, mention must be made of the temples of Philae, where the temple of Isis provides hymns rich in both myth and theology. Written under Ptolemy II, these texts continue a tradition dating back to the days of Egyptian independence.

Egyptian mythological texts are important as a stage in

the development of world mythology, but they also yield a wealth of information on Egyptian culture. The entire religious tradition was incorporated into the mythic system, to the extent that the two were inseparable. Egyptian myth reveals a religious mentality which was highly adept at expressing the mysteries of the divine world through a system of complex symbolism. One can discern a religion that was nondogmatic, flexible, and able to satisfy Egyptian spiritual needs for three millennia. Egyptian mythological texts frequently went beyond the expression of the religious and the ritualistic and moved into abstract theology. Concepts of universalism and ideas approaching monotheism become apparent in certain texts, even though such texts retain a tendency to use mythic symbolism.

An integral part of the content of Egyptian texts are those myths that articulate the creation and the structure of the universe. Egyptian creation myths stress the order and the pattern in both the structure of the universe and its origin. The birth symbolism that Egyptian creation myths used underscores the fact that the Egyptians conceived their world as a living organism, in which all components were arranged in an orderly fashion that was a reflection of *maat* ("order"), as opposed to *isft* ("chaos"). In this universe, even political and historical order had been divinely ordained. Hence, the mythologization of historical events and figures was a natural process for the Egyptians, and mythological texts can at times be used to shed light on the historical events of Egypt's past.

Finally, Egyptian mythological texts, especially when combined with the *sb3yt* ("instruction") texts, provide insight into the Egyptian mentality. One can discern a positive outlook on life, the world, politics, nature, and the existence that the Egyptians expected after death. This attitude was also expressed in a highly developed moral code which was an essential part of the Egyptian way of life. This code demanded not only abstention from immoral actions, but also an attempt to lead one's life in a constructive and positive manner. In general, it may be said that the mythological texts—and other texts—provide a picture of a people who grasped the positive values of life and attempted to live that life in a productive and joyful manner.

[*See also* Book of Going Forth by Day; Book of That Which Is in the Underworld; Coffin Texts; Contendings of Horus and Seth; Hymns; Myths; *and* Pyramid Texts.]

BIBLIOGRAPHY

Allen, James P. *Genesis in Egypt: The Philosophy of Ancient Egyptian Creation Accounts.* New Haven, 1988. An excellent study of Egyptian thought on creation, centering on the interpretation of specific texts and stressing the positive theological value of Egyptian creation mythology.

Anthes, Rudolph. "Egyptian Theology in the Third Millennium B.C." *Journal of Near Eastern Studies* 18 (1959), 169–212. This intense study of the Heliopolitan creation tradition and its political implications will provide a good understanding of Old Kingdom myth and a good basis for reading the Pyramid Texts.

Breasted, J. H. *Development of Religion and Thought in Ancient Egypt.* New York, 1959. Published originally in 1912, this is still a classic study of Egyptian religion and myth and merits careful reading; includes numerous quotations from Egyptian mythological texts and orderly exposition of their significance.

Clark, R. T. R. *Myth and Symbol in Ancient Egypt.* London, 1959. A very good introduction to the symbolic nature of myth in ancient Egypt, covering most of the basic types of myth; provides useful background for a reading of the actual texts.

Faulkner, R. O. *The Ancient Egyptian Pyramid Texts.* London, 1969. A translation of most of the available Pyramid Texts; some by their nature will make little sense to the average reader, but still a good primary source for Old Kingdom myth.

Faulkner, R. O. *The Ancient Egyptian Coffin Texts.* 3 vols. Warminster, 1973–1978. A good translation of the Middle Kingdom Coffin Texts, which are rich in mythological material.

Faulkner, R. O., trans. *The Egyptian Book of the Dead.* San Francisco, 1994. Reproduces in facsimile the Papyrus of Ani and provides an excellent translation of the text, with very good commentary.

Forman, W., and S. Quirke. *Hieroglyphs and the Afterlife in Ancient Egypt.* Norman, Okla., 1996. This well-illustrated book contains much information on mythological texts concerned with the afterlife, and is useful for both specialists and general readers.

Grimal, N. *A History of Ancient Egypt.* Translated by Ian Shaw. Oxford and Cambridge, Mass., 1992. An understanding of Egyptian myth is enriched by a knowledge of history, and Grimal provides a thorough account, easily read.

Lichtheim, M. *Ancient Egyptian Literature.* 3 vols. Berkeley, 1973–1980. Contains many mythological texts in readable translation.

Luft, V. *Beiträge zur Historisierung der Götterwelt und der Mythenschreibung.* Budapest, 1978.

Moret, A. *Le rituel du culte divin journalier en Égypte.* Geneva, 1988. Although written around 1900, this is useful for the ritual texts and line drawings it provides, especially texts from the temple of Sety I at Abydos.

Otto, E. *Das Verhältnis von Rite und Mythos im Ägyptischen.* Heidelberg, 1958.

Quirke, Stephen. *Ancient Egyptian Religion.* London, 1992. A well-organized overview of Egyptian religion; useful for what the texts actually say about the world of the divine.

Schott, S. *Mythe und Mythenbildung.* Göttingen, 1956.

Tobin, V. A. "Mytho-Theology in Ancient Egypt." *Journal of the American Research Center in Egypt* 25 (1988), 169–183. A concise, readable account of the nature of the Egyptian mythic corpus, introducing the general content of Egyptian mythological texts.

Tobin, V. A. "Myth and Politics in the Old Kingdom of Egypt." *Bibliotheca Orientalis* 49 (1991), 605–636. Deals with the emergence of Old Kingdom myth from a combination of the natural and political backgrounds.

Tobin, V. A. "Divine Conflict in the Pyramid Texts." *Journal of the American Research Center in Egypt* 30 (1993), 93–110. Interprets the theme of theomachy (conflict of the gods) in the Pyramid Texts and makes reference to the same theme in other ancient cultures.

Wilkinson, R. H. *Reading Egyptian Art: A Hieroglyphic Guide to Ancient Egyptian Painting and Sculpture.* London, 1992. Useful for the study of the actual significance of the written hieroglyphs, many of which are rich in mythological connotations.

Zabkar, L. V. *Hymns to Isis in Her Temple at Philae.* Hanover and London, 1988. A good translation of the hymns to Isis from her temple at Philae, with detailed interpretation of the texts; invaluable reading on Ptolemaic mythological texts.

VINCENT ARIEH TOBIN

MYTHS. [*This article surveys ancient Egyptian myths, discussing their origins and development, what myths reveal about Egyptian beliefs, and the texts and art in which myths are presented. It comprises five articles:*

An Overview
Creation Myths
Osiris Cycle
Solar Cycle
Lunar Cycle

For related discussions, see Mythological Texts *and* Religion.]

An Overview

Although the term "myth" is often used to signify any type of traditional story or legend, for scholars it is highly specific: a myth is a spoken word, statement, or narrative that is used, frequently within a cultic setting, to articulate realities that cannot be defined in a totally rational manner. Myth is a means of sacred revelation, a method of communication that functions through symbolic expression and has its own inner logic—a logic belonging to the realm of the mystical and metaphysical rather than to that of reason and rationality. Although this definition implies that myth has a spiritual purpose, it can encompass a wide variety of topics. There are myths of creation, myths of the gods, historical or semi-historical myths, heroic myths, political myths, myths of national identity, and psychological myths, among others. In all myth the oral aspect is essential, because to the ancient mind the spoken word was a creative force that evoked the reality of the entity or event named. The term "myth" is thus an appropriate one for denoting the statements that the Egyptians made concerning their gods and their environment, since it reflects their consciousness of the reality and the mystery of the divine. Because of its revelatory function, authentic myth does not adapt well to written form. Myths can be recorded in writing, but they then run the risk of becoming dogmatic and unable properly to articulate the continuing revelation of the living world of the divine.

The Western mind often thinks of myth in terms of the Greco-Roman mythic tradition. The latter, however, lost much of its mysterious character under the influence of Homeric and Classical Greek rationalism. Hence, Greco-Roman myths tended to evolve into narrative accounts that provided virtually a universal history but did little to reveal the inner mysteries of existence. Egyptian myth, however, was less concerned with extended narration and was not bound to recount events in an orderly manner; thus, it retained the ability to function as a flexible, symbolic mode of revelation. The Egyptian gods, unlike the anthropomorphic gods of the Greeks, were not understood to be limited to the forms in which iconography portrayed them. Horus was shown with a falcon's head, and Anubis with that of a jackal, but these theriomorphic representations were symbolic means of articulating the sacredness and otherness of the gods. Such iconography was an essential expression of myth, especially within a cultic context. As for the problem of the relationship between myth and cult, some writers suggest that the myth evolved from the cult, while others maintain that the cult grew out of the myth. It is, however, most likely that myths and their cults evolved simultaneously, myth being primary in some cases and cult in others. Once established, myth and cult remained integral to one another and functioned in a complementary manner: the cult dramatized the myth, and the myth verbalized the cultic ritual.

Even before its conjunction with cult, myth had two main sources. One was the natural world, which humans perceived and interpreted by personalizing the natural forces so as to relate to them. The other was historical individuals and incidents, which were idealized and incorporated into myth as heroes or gods and their deeds. It is relatively easy to detect the natural sources of myth, but identifying specific historical elements is often a matter of interpretation. The ultimate sources of myth are highly complex, but in the final analysis, all myths reflect the reaction of the intellect to its background and environment.

Out of the Egyptian corpus of myth one can isolate a number of mythic cycles of primary importance. The earliest of these were the cosmogonic cycles associated with Heliopolis and Hermopolis, both of which evolved out of the observation of nature. The antiquity of these cycles is evident in that they both take their beginning from a fundamental entity, Nun (the primeval waters), the chaos from which creation emerged. The symbol of Nun was derived at an early (probably prehistoric) date from the flooding of the Nile; the primeval mound reflects the emergence of the isolated hillocks that appeared as the waters subsided.

In the Heliopolitan tradition, the god Atum (later Re-Atum) emerged out of Nun, sat on the primeval mound, and performed his creative activity through a combination of masturbation and spitting. From this action there came into being Shu and Tefnut, twin deities of the air, and from their union sprang Geb and Nut, personifications of earth and sky. In these gods, the natural structure of the universe was complete. Geb and Nut then begat the twin couples—Isis and Osiris, and Seth and Nephthys. Through Osiris the Egyptian monarchy became an integral part of the Heliopolitan cycle, and with the defeat of Seth, the god of disorder, by Horus the son of Osiris, the Horus kingship was sacralized by mythological tradition. Both natural and historical sources contributed to this tradition: the cosmogonic elements derived from the natural world, and the political elements from the wars during the Predynastic and Early Dynastic periods. In the murder of Osiris by Seth and the defeat of Seth by Horus one can see reflections of early struggles for the throne, while figures such as Isis, Nephthys, and Hathor have frequently been interpreted as aspects of royal power. This Heliopolitan cycle, with its Ennead of nine gods, developed over an extended period, reaching completion during the fourth or fifth dynasty.

The Hermopolitan cosmogony was less complex than that of Heliopolis, but more pristine in that it was less political. The Hermopolitan cosmogony also began with Nun, but within Nun lived the Ogdoad, eight primal creator deities who later died and went to the underworld. Even after this, however, they retained their power, for it was they who caused the sun to rise and the Nile to flow. This Hermopolitan cosmogony developed in four variations. Two of them stressed the emergence of the world from the cosmic egg, which had been laid either by the celestial goose or by the ibis, the sacred bird identified with Thoth. The two other variations based the creation of the world on the symbol of the lotus from which emerged the sun god Re, either as a child or as a scarab beetle. The major development in the Hermopolitan system was the later grafting on of the god Thoth, who by tradition was self-created, like certain others of the greater gods. In the tradition of Thoth at Hermopolis, the gods of the Ogdoad were his souls. In yet other statements from Hermopolis, the sun god Re was the creator of all things. These different versions within the Hermopolitan cycle illustrate the flexibility of Egyptian myth, which was able to permit contradicting symbols within one tradition.

Among cosmogonic myths, mention must be made of the Memphite tradition preserved in a text known as the Memphite Theology, on the Shabaka stone from the twenty-fifth (Nubian) dynasty. For decades this text was regarded as an Old Kingdom composition, but general opinion now dates it to the twenty-fifth dynasty. The theory of creation that it sets forth is the most abstract and intellectual of all Egyptian cosmogonies, in that it ascribes creation to the divine mind and the utterance of the divine word. In this Memphite tradition, it was Ptah Tatenen ("Ptah of the primeval mound"), the ancient earth god of Memphis, who was the supreme deity and creator, and the gods of the Heliopolitan Ennead were manifestations of him. Ptah was also the founder of ethical order (maat; *m3't*) and of the Horus kingship. This tradition is significant in that it illustrates the ability of the Egyptians to think in quasi-philosophical terms. The basic ideas of the Memphite tradition may have been based on earlier concepts, but its formulation during the Nubian dynasty suggests that the new rulers of Egypt were intent on using it to secure the reestablished unity of the Two Lands.

There were other creation myths and creator deities known to the Egyptians. Very prominent was Amun-Re of Thebes, and during the rule of the heretic pharaoh Amenhotpe IV (Akhenaten), the Aten was recognized as sole creator. At a very early stage, Neith of Sais, often known as "the mother of the gods," may have been a creator mother goddess; at Elephantine at the First Cataract of the Nile, the potter god Khnum was said to have fashioned humanity on the potter's wheel out of Nile mud. The wide variations in cosmogonic myths among the Egyptians do not reflect mythological confusion but are rather a sign of the genius of the Egyptian mythopoeic mind. In the final analysis, all these traditions attempted to articulate the basic truth that the created universe was in some manner dependent on the divine power.

The most enduring of the mythic cycles was that of Osiris, the god of immortality. The origins of Osiris are obscure, and the meaning of his name uncertain, but he was probably known at an early period, although the first mention of his name occurs only in the fifth dynasty. His origin was probably at the city of Djedu (Busiris) in the Nile Delta, but because of his association with the dead king, his chief shrine came to be at Abydos, the earliest dynastic necropolis. Osiris was attached to the Heliopolitan Ennead no later than the fifth dynasty and possibly before, a move which may have been to a great extent political. Certain references in the Pyramid Texts indicate that Osiris may originally have had a demonic nature, but at an early date he became the personification of the dead monarch and a symbol of his rebirth in the next world. According to the myth, Osiris and his sister-wife Isis ruled Egypt, having inherited the kingship from Geb, but Osiris was murdered by Seth, who then seized the throne. The dead Osiris miraculously impregnated Isis, who then gave birth to Horus. Horus, on attaining manhood, fought with Seth to regain the throne; the mythic accounts of the struggle probably reflect the wars of the Predynastic and Early Dynastic periods. Eventually the Heliopolitan Ennead confirmed Horus in his claim to the throne. Horus, in conjunction with Isis, Nephthys, Thoth, and several of the other gods, restored Osiris to life in the underworld, where he reigned as judge and king of the dead. Owing to his connection with the earth, Osiris also took on fertility functions and was responsible for the annual rebirth of the grain. Even the Nile was sometimes considered to be his gift to Egypt, being called "the great efflux of Osiris." Alternatively, the Nile was said to result from the tears of Isis mourning the dead Osiris.

Although the afterlife promised by Osiris was originally reserved for the king and his nobility, evidence from the end of the Old Kingdom suggests that the afterlife was becoming accessible to certain members of the elite, and by the Middle Kingdom to any individual able to provide for himself the proper burial rites. The one who had received proper burial was guided by Anubis to the underworld, where his or her heart was weighed against the Feather of Maat to determine innocence or guilt, and he or she was, it was hoped, adjudged righteous by Osiris and admitted to everlasting life. Because of the ability of Osiris to grant immortality, he attained extreme popularity, and his shrine at Abydos, the site of the celebration of his mysteries, became one of the greatest places of pilgrimage in Egypt. Eventually his worship spread beyond Egypt and became known throughout the Roman Empire.

The role of Osiris made him popular as a god who fulfilled a certain need of the individual, but the function of a state deity was more readily fulfilled by the more universal sun god. The sun god was one of the most ancient of the Egyptian deities, and his influence was felt from the very beginnings of Egyptian religion and myth. His earliest form was Re, the sun god of Heliopolis, and in this name he continued to be central in myth throughout the entire history of ancient Egypt. He was often syncretized with other gods, producing such deities as Re-Horakhty, Re-Atum, Amun-Re, and Khnum-Re. Even during the reign of Akhenaten, the so-called Amarna period, Re did not disappear in favor of the Aten; the designation of the sun god as Re-Horakhty was used during the first half of Akhenaten's reign, and even after that the name Re endured in the Amarna system. When universalism arose in Egyptian thought during the New Kingdom, it was with the sun god that this universalism was associated. The importance of the sun god was a natural development in Egypt because of his prominent visibility and his obvious ability to create and sustain life.

There were various myths associated with the sun god, but these were less important than his daily cycle. The emergence of this cycle was given expression in the myth of his departure from the earth where he had originally lived, specifically at Heliopolis. During his stay on earth, a period that was a type of golden age when humans and gods lived together, Re had been required to put down several rebellions against his authority. Eventually, weary of such problems, he decided to move to the heavens, where each day he crossed the sky in his solar bark; he journeyed through the underworld at night and was reborn on the eastern horizon each morning. His journey was not without danger, for the solar bark was constantly threatened by the monstrous Apep serpent which attempted to disrupt Re's journey. In one tradition, the god Seth had the duty of standing in the prow of the bark and defending Re from his chief enemy. Despite temporary victories by the Apep serpent, apparent in such phenomena as storms and eclipses, the solar bark was always victorious, and cosmic order was constantly maintained.

As with all myth, the importance of such symbols lay not in their details but in their significance. The significance of the Re myth is well expressed in the fact that his chief symbol was the scarab beetle, from which he derived the title Khepri ("the One Who Becomes"). For the Egyptian, the universe was not a static entity, but a living force in a constant state of movement. As Khepri, the sun god was the ideal symbol of this vitality: he was Khepri, the one who comes into being, in the morning at the time of his birth; he was Re, the developed sun god, at noon; and he was Atum, the completed one, in the evening as he descended to rest on the western horizon. The simplicity and beauty of such a mythic expression underlines the Egyptian concept of the unending pattern of light and darkness, the eternal motion, through which the universe and all life moved. The sun hymns in the Theban necropolis and the worship of Re as expressed even in the funerary *Book of Going Forth by Day* (the *Book of the Dead*) give ample indication of the central importance of the solar cycle in all aspects of Egyptian life.

The pharaoh was also an essential element in the Egyptian mythic system. His mythologization was to some extent a political move, and his position was closely woven into the wider fabric of Egyptian myth in order to give the earthly political order a more cosmic and stable position. From earliest times the king was the earthly incarnation of the heavenly Horus, and it is possible that the earthly monarch may have been the actual source of the celestial Horus. In the developed form of the royal myth, the pharaoh was the physical offspring of the sun god, begotten by that deity from his actual body. Pharaoh and sun god ruled Egypt in a partnership, the sun god being the *ntr '3* ("great god"), and the pharaoh the *ntr nfr* ("good god"). The term *nfr* can also be translated as "youthful," and hence the pharaoh could be seen as a "junior" sun god, the lesser member of a political-cosmic partnership. Because of his relationship to the sun god, the pharaoh was the chief priest of all the gods and the chief cultic officer of their rituals, but the priestly power was relegated to the temple clergy. Through this myth of kingship, state and religion were inseparably intertwined, each supporting and validating the other. This theory made the monarch into a sacral figure whose existence was a guarantee of the continuance of cosmic, social, and moral order, and imparted to the Egyptian political order a divine right and character. The Egyptian hegemony was thus truly a "kingdom of God" in a terrestrial setting.

In certain mythological systems, particularly those of late antiquity, eschatological thinking eventually became fairly central. It is sometimes thought that Egyptian myth was free from eschatology, and that to the Egyptian mind all things would endure eternally. For the most part, the Egyptians were not concerned with eschatology, but nevertheless it seems to have been understood that the created universe was not totally eternal, and a few texts speak of the ultimate disappearance of everything, even of the gods. Such texts are few in number, but a Coffin Text (Spell 1130) seems to predict a time when only Osiris and Atum will remain, while chapter 175 of the *Book of Going Forth by Day* states that eventually all things will return to the primeval waters, whence they came. Texts of this nature indicate that there was some awareness of the possibility of the eventual dissolution of the universe, but such negative thinking leads back to a more positive aspect of Egyptian myth: the concept of *maat*. Personified as the goddess Maat, it ensured that this dissolution would not take place or would be postponed, and that the world would continue to exist for "millions of years." In brief, eschatology was not a major element in Egyptian myth, although there were a few traces of it.

In the history of Egyptian myth, the Amarna period is frequently regarded as myth-free. It did, however, have its mythic system—a reaction against traditional myth—and even the visibility of the deity in the Aten, the sun disk, was a form of mythic expression. Unlike traditional myth, Amarna myth did not personify nature but was centered on the Aten; and Akhenaten attempted a demythologization of religion. The Amarna belief system derived from an observance of nature, and its myth was centered on the ontology of the Aten and of the king, not on the natural world. The Aten was almost myth-free but retained a modicum of mythic expression. For example, he was said to beget himself, to be born in the morning, and to rest on the western horizon at evening. The Amarna doctrine of creation was expressed in the mythic symbol of the spoken word, a more sophisticated symbol than that of procreation known in other mythic systems. The Aten was also designated as "father and mother" of everything created, a formula that in virtue of its symbolic nature was a mythical one. The most significant Amarna use of myth, however, is in statements concerning the nature of the

monarch. Akhenaten was presented as the physical son of the deity, the one who had "proceeded" from and was eternally "begotten" by the Aten. The ultimate result of Amarna royal myth was a virtual identification between Akhenaten and the Aten, the king being only slightly below the Aten in stature. Some scholars have seen various expressions of trinitarian myth in the Amarna system, but there is no agreement on any one official Amarna trinity. Mention should also be made of the city of Akhetaten, a mythic expression of the divine presence on earth. This concept of a sacred city constituted what could almost be regarded as a type of realized eschatology. Amarna teachings were not myth-free dogmatic assertions, but rather statements that used a modified form of myth to create an intellectual and abstract religious system.

In the wide variety of Egyptian myth, it is possible to see a logical system wherein the themes reflect a high degree of optimism. Egyptian myth shows a strong affinity for systematization, a search for order that is evident in the traditions of creation: out of chaos comes a comprehensible and organized unity. To articulate this unity, the Egyptian myth-makers did not follow abstract philosophical reasoning but instead relied on observation of the natural world. The continuance of life through procreation provided a natural symbol for the order of the universe, and the symbol of the creative word reveals the Egyptian realization that beyond the natural world there is a divine mind. In this divine mind the Egyptians saw the ultimate reason for the ongoing cycle of the natural world. They could depend on the sun to rise each morning because it was the birth of the sun god and because behind it there lay a supreme intellect. The annual Nile flood occurred because of the cyclical nature of the creation process. The recurring theme of a trinitarian arrangement (in threes) for many of the gods further emphasizes the Egyptian awareness of the natural process of procreation.

This optimism, however, did not blind the Egyptians to the negative forces in the universe. Myths that reflect struggle and tension reveal the awareness of the danger that chaos might erupt. Order was constantly in conflict with disorder, but *maat* was a mythic expression of the confidence that order would prevail. The struggle of Horus and Seth provided an example of this victory of order in both the natural and the political spheres. It was at this point that the divine, natural, and political orders met in the pharaoh. As the offspring of the sun god and himself a god incarnate, the pharaoh was a visible guarantee of stability. When one adds to this the symbol of the sun god, one can appreciate the Egyptian awareness of the existence of a supreme deity and the universalism this deity implies.

Finally, one must take note of the stress that Egyptian

myth placed on the theme of eternal life. It was, of course, Osiris who was responsible for granting this boon, but Egyptian mythological and theological thought gradually developed and the sun god increased in prominence—particularly in his manifestation as Amun-Re—to the point that even the *Book of Going Forth by Day* could open with an adoration of the sun god, an acknowledgment of his power even in the realm of the dead.

The Egyptians, as is testified by their myths, held a very positive outlook on their personal existence and on the stability of their environment. Dogmatic orthodoxy was of relatively little importance, and the variations in mythic expression indicate that they were not bound by the demands of a strict doctrinal system. What was important was the recognition of the reality of the divine world, the assurance that the power of *maat* would sustain the cosmic and political orders, and that the life of the individual would continue even after death. The understanding of existence presented by Egyptian myth must therefore have been a highly satisfying spiritual experience.

Egypt has left behind a wide variety of mythic material. Iconography in tombs and temples contains extensive portraiture of the gods, their cults, and many events of myth. Decorated coffins and elaborate copies of the *Book of Going Forth by Day* can also be useful for gaining an impression of the elaborate Egyptian concept of the divine world. Iconography is of little value without the written text to give it meaning, but the available textual material is sufficient to provide an extensive account of Egyptian myth. The Old Kingdom Pyramid Texts, the Middle Kingdom Coffin Texts, and the New Kingdom *Book of Going Forth by Day* contain an abundance of material on all aspects of Egyptian myth; and although such materials are not systematically arranged, they provide the modern reader with mythic texts as they would have been known to the Egyptians. The tale of the *Contendings of Horus and Seth* contains a New Kingdom fictionalized and even humorous account of this important tradition. Also from the New Kingdom comes the text of the *Destruction of Mankind*, preserved on the walls of several royal tombs. The ancient Greek writer Plutarch provided a complete account of the myth of Isis and Osiris, although one wonders how much of Plutarch's narrative is truly Egyptian and how much has been recast in the form of a Greek myth. A more authentically Egyptian account of the Osiris myth can be found in the *Great Hymn to Osiris*, although the latter text is less a systematic narrative and more a part of liturgy. Finally, the wide variety of hymns and liturgical texts from temples and tombs can add a great deal to an understanding of Egyptian myth as it was used in actual cultic practice.

[*See also* Deities; Mythological Texts; Religion; *and entries on the texts mentioned in this article.*]

BIBLIOGRAPHY

Breasted, J. H. *Development of Religion and Thought in Ancient Egypt.* New York, 1959. Although published originally in 1912, this work is still a classic study of Egyptian religion and myth and is well worth a careful reading.

Clark, R. T. R. *Myth and Symbol in Ancient Egypt.* London, 1959. A very good introduction to the symbolic nature of myth in ancient Egypt, covering most of the basic types of myth.

Faulkner, R. O. *The Ancient Egyptian Pyramid Texts.* London, 1969. A translation of most of the available Pyramid Texts; some will make little sense to the average reader, but this is still a very good primary source for Old Kingdom myth.

Faulkner, R. O. *The Ancient Egyptian Coffin Texts.* 3 vols. Warminster, 1973–1978. This work provides a translation of Middle Kingdom Coffin Texts, which are rich in mythological material.

Faulkner, R. O., trans. *The Egyptian Book of the Dead.* San Francisco, 1994. Very attractive facsimile volume of the Papyrus of Ani; provides an excellent translation of the text, along with very good commentary.

Frankfort, H. *Ancient Egyptian Religion.* New York, 1948. A general and very readable interpretation of the nature of Egyptian myth and religion.

Frankfort, H. *Kingship and the Gods.* Chicago, 1948. A comprehensive treatment of kingship in the wider context of the world of the divine in ancient Near Eastern cultures; a classic study that deserves careful reading.

Frankfort, H., et al. *Before Philosophy.* New York, 1949. A very good exposition of the significance of Near Eastern myth, including material on Egypt.

Griffiths, J. G. *The Origins of Osiris and His Cult.* Leiden, 1980. An exhaustive examination of the tradition and history of Osiris.

Hart, G. *Egyptian Myths.* London, 1990.

Hornung, E. *Conception of God in Ancient Egypt: The One and the Many.* Translated by J. Baines. London, 1983. Many fine insights into the Egyptian theological and mythological mind.

Ions, Veronica. *Egyptian Mythology.* Middlesex, 1968. A very good general overview of the contents of Egyptian myth.

Lichtheim, M. *Ancient Egyptian Literature.* 3 vols. Berkeley, 1973–1980. Contains many mythological and religious texts in a very readable translation.

Quirke, Stephen. *Ancient Egyptian Religion.* London, 1992. An overview of Egyptian religion and myth; easily comprehensible and useful both to the neophyte and to those with some previous knowledge of Egyptian myth.

Shafer, B. E., ed. *Religion in Ancient Egypt.* Ithaca and London, 1991. A very informative work which clearly brings out the importance of Egyptian religion.

Tobin, V. A. "Mythic Symbolism in Egypt and Greece." *Journal of the Society for the Study of Egyptian Antiquities* 17.3 (1987), 106–127. A comparison and contrast of Greek and Egyptian myth; will help the reader to understand the symbolic nature of myth in both cultures.

Tobin, V. A. *Theological Principles of Egyptian Religion.* New York, 1989. A systematic theology of ancient Egyptian religion, stressing the place of creation mythology.

Tobin, V. A. "Myth and Politics in the Old Kingdom of Egypt." *Bibliotheca Orientalis* 49 (1991), 605–636. Deals with the emergence of Old Kingdom myth from a combination of the natural and political backgrounds.

Tobin, V. A. "Divine Conflict in the Pyramid Texts." *Journal of the American Research Center in Egypt* 30 (1993), 93–110. Deals with and interprets the theme of theomachy (conflict of the gods) in the Pyramid Texts, with reference to the same theme in other ancient cultures.

Watterson, B. *The Gods of Ancient Egypt*. New York, 1984. A good introduction to the Egyptian gods and their myths.

VINCENT ARIEH TOBIN

Creation Myths

Creation myths in any culture are not intended as scientific explications of the way in which the universe came into being; rather, they are symbolic articulations of the meaning and significance of the realm of created being. Such myths are to an extent explanatory, but their "explanations" lie in the realm of metaphysics rather than in the realms of science or history. Creation mythology arises primarily out of human curiosity and the experience of the world, and even the most rudimentary culture will have its tradition of creation, whether that creation be spontaneous or the purposeful act of a divine will.

One of the most distinctively Egyptian articulations of creation mythology was the tradition now known as the Heliopolitan cosmogony, which was developed by the priesthood of Heliopolis (Egyptian On), the sacred city of the sun god, situated not far from the ancient capital, Memphis. This mythic system was the product of the Old Kingdom at a time when Egypt had only recently been unified. The Egyptians were aware of the fact that there had been a time when nothing was in existence, for, according to the Heliopolitan tradition, there had been a time when "the sky had not yet come into being; the earth had not yet come into being; humanity had not yet come into being; the gods had not yet been born; death had not yet come into being" (Pyramid Texts, 1466). In this realm of nothingness, a source of creation was necessary. One of the characteristic features of Egyptian creationism is the fact that creation was essentially an act of generation, and for that act a specific generative principle was needed. This generative principle was evident to the Egyptian mind in the yearly flooding of the Nile River, and the procreative powers of the waters suggested the ultimate source of all created being, the "primeval waters." These primeval waters of Egyptian thought were both a negative and a positive entity: negative in that they were boundless, shapeless, infinite and chaotic—all ominous concepts to the Egyptian mentality; but positive in that they contained within themselves a certain potential for being. The creative potential of the primeval waters is evident in their personification as the self-generated god Nun, as expressed in chapter 17 of the *Book of Going Forth by Day* (the *Book of the Dead*): "I am the great god who came into existence by himself, Nun who created his own name as a god in the primeval time of the gods." Thus, for the mythopoeic mentality of Heliopolis, in the beginning there was chaos, but that chaos already contained within itself the potential for order.

That potential was realized when out of the primeval waters there emerged, like the rising sun, the god Atum, the source of all created and generated being. The name Atum bears the double meaning of "totality" and "not to be." Atum was thus at once absolute being and absolute nonbeing, combining within himself these contrasting opposites. This newly emerged deity, sitting on the primeval mound in his form as Re-Atum, the Creator sun god, was frequently depicted as wearing the royal Double Crown of Egypt, symbolic of the fact that with him there came into being the kingship of the Two Lands. The Heliopolitan creation tradition, possibly for strong political reasons, thus combined within itself the created universe and the political order as two inseparable entities. From the political point of view, the Heliopolitan system attempted to create the concept of a sacral kingship, a means of justifying mythologically the newly established monarchy.

The creative power of Re-Atum is brought into action at this point with the generation of the twin couple Shu and Tefnut through Atum's act of masturbation, as is stated in the Pyramid Texts, 1248: "He is Atum, the one who came into being and who masturbated in On. He placed his penis in his fist so that he might have sexual pleasure thereby, so that the twins, Shu and Tefnut, might be born." (According to Spell 76 of the Coffin Texts, Shu and Tefnut were produced by Atum's act of spitting, and probably the two symbols, masturbation and spitting, should be combined in any full account of the myth.) With the birth of the male Shu and the female Tefnut, the Heliopolitan creation tradition moves to the point of differentiating between male and female as the two complementary sources of generation, thus making possible the continuing process of generative creation.

From the union of Shu and Tefnut were born the male Geb and the female Nut, the deities who personified the earth and the sky respectively. Thus, it is at this point in the myth that the universe comes into being, but earth and sky are not simply created things; they are generated divine beings, the source of all else to come. The frequent iconography that portrays Nut as arched over Geb points to the role of these deities as mythic symbols of the continuing generative power of life and creation. The next generation in this creative cycle proceeds to articulate the created universe even further and to admit the reality of the two opposing forces of order and disorder. From Geb and Nut there sprang Osiris and Seth, Osiris embodying within himself the principle of order and Seth representing disorder. With these two were associated their sisters, Isis who became the wife of Osiris, and Nephthys who became the wife of Seth. These nine deities formed the original mythic group of the gods known as the Heliopolitan Ennead. The admission into this group of Seth, the god of confusion and chaos, is highly significant, because it articulates the Egyptian realization of the continual struggle between good and evil, order and disorder, within both the created and the political realms.

The place of humanity within this created order was not the exalted one given to it by Hebrew creationism. According to tradition, Shu and Tefnut once became separated from Atum and lost in the primeval waters. Atum sent out his Eye to look for them, and on their return he wept tears of joy, from which sprang humanity. The Heliopolitan creation myth thus assigns to humanity a certain divine origin, but at the same time the creation of humanity does not appear as a purposeful act. Human beings were little more than the accidental product of a specific emotion of the creator deity, and hence their place within the created order was certainly not intended to be the "crown of creation" one sees in, for example, the Old Testament account of creation.

It is highly significant that the Heliopolitan creation tradition is inseparably connected to the sun god, for each day was in effect a renewal and a repetition of the creation. In the rising of the sun, the Egyptian had the assurance that the created order and the life and sustenance of humanity were eternal and ongoing: the rising of the sun was in essence a sacramental symbol that gave assurance of the stability of the created universe and of the royal political system that governed it.

Hermopolis *(Khmnw)* in Upper Egypt had a cosmogony that was claimed to be the oldest of all the Egyptian creation traditions. The nearby Middle Kingdom necropolis has yielded a number of interesting coffin texts illustrating various aspects of the Hermopolitan creation myth. Like certain other cult centers, Hermopolis was said to be the site of the original primeval mound which emerged from the waters. Like the Heliopolitan myth, the Hermopolitan tradition started with the primeval waters, but within those waters were the eight Heh gods, the Ogdoad, as opposed to the Heliopolitan Ennead. These deities formed four divine couples—Nun and Naunet, Amun and Amaunet, Huh and Hauhet, Kuk and Kauket, names that reflected the basic negative characteristics of the primeval waters: boundlessness, mystery, chaos, darkness, infinity. The Hermopolitan deities were almost always nonanthropomorphic (see, however, the human forms of Amun and Amaunet in the Karnak temple), the males being depicted as having the heads of frogs, and the females, those of serpents. In later traditions concerning the Ogdoad, the specific deities were said to be the offspring of Amun, Shu, or Thoth. Though devoid of specific mythic connotations, the Hermopolitan Ogdoad was expressive of the numinous and mysterious force of the divine creative power. These eight deities created the world together, but eventually they died and took up their abode in the underworld. Even from here, however, they continued to exercise their power, causing the sun to rise each day and the Nile to flow. The Heliopolitan Ennead was the divine group that sustained the world and its political system, but the Hermopolitan Ogdoad appears as a more basic and rudimentary system wherein the gods were the sustainers of the natural order, powers concerned less with politics and more with the essential structure of the created world.

The Hermopolitan myth had several variations—not an infrequent characteristic of myth, which is able to admit the existence of different and even seemingly contradictory symbols within itself. One significant symbol that stands out in two of these variations is the Cosmic Egg, the source from which the world emerged. According to one tradition, this Cosmic Egg was laid by the "Great Cackler," the celestial goose, while another tradition claims that it was laid by an ibis, the bird identified with Thoth. The connection of Thoth with the Ogdoad of Hermopolis developed when the Hermopolitan priesthood adopted that deity and wove him into the fabric of Hermopolitan myth. Thoth thus became yet another symbol of the supreme creator, being himself self-begotten and the source of the Heh gods.

Two other versions of the Hermopolitan myth laid a greater stress on the primeval waters. In one version, a lotus emerged from the waters and opened to reveal the sun god Re in the form of a child. Another variant states that from the lotus there emerged a scarab beetle, symbolic of the sun, and that the scarab beetle then became a male child from whose tears sprang humanity. In this lotus symbolism, it is interesting to note the attempt to graft the creator sun god onto the older symbol of the primeval waters, an example of the syncretizing skill of the Egyptian myth-makers.

From the city of Memphis in the Nile Delta came another of the chief Egyptian cosmogonies, a creation tradition that centered on the god Ptah. Ptah was a very early deity associated with the earth and was frequently portrayed wrapped in the bandaging of a mummy. The chief source for the content of the Memphite cosmogony is the Shabaka stone, erected under the pharaoh Shabaka during the twenty-fifth (Nubian) dynasty. This text, known as the Memphite Theology, claims to be a copy of an archaic scroll, and for a long time it was assumed to reflect the most ancient traditions of Memphis. However, general opinion now tends to date its composition to the time of the twenty-fifth dynasty, and it thus appears to have been one of the latest Egyptian attempts to articulate the creation of the universe. It is certainly one of the most sophisticated and abstract of the Egyptian cosmogonies, expressing creation as an act of the divine will, intellect, and word.

The Memphite tradition does not attempt to set forth

a mythological narrative of creation, but rather presents a theological statement of the nature of Ptah, his relationship to the other gods, and his role as supreme deity and creator. Ptah Tatenen ("Ptah of the primeval mound") was both the source and ruler of all the gods. He was Nun, the father of Atum; he was Naunet, the female counterpart of Nun and mother of Atum; he was the heart (intelligence) and the tongue (creative power) of the Heliopolitan Ennead. The creative process was brought about through the agency of the heart and the tongue, not through physical action and reproduction as in the older Heliopolitan system: "Every word of the god came into being through what the heart mediated and the tongue commanded," as the Memphite Theology puts it. The heart and tongue of Ptah, according to the Memphite tradition, were Atum, and thus Atum was seen as a manifestation of these specific aspects of Ptah. Atum was, in effect, the instrument of the divine will of Ptah. Ptah, therefore, was said to be "the one who had made all things and who had created the gods. He is Tatenen, the one who begat the gods and from whom all things proceeded . . . he is the most powerful of the gods."

All things, according to the Memphite tradition, were the direct creation of Ptah, and the text stresses the fact that he established the cities of Egypt, set up the nomes, appointed the gods to their shrines, and established their offerings. Ptah was thus the creator not only of the universe and its natural order, but also of the social, religious, and political order. In the absence of any real narrative myth in the text, the Memphite tradition takes on a serious theological and philosophical aspect, combined with a political aspect. Horus, in the Memphite Theology, is also an aspect of Ptah, and is moreover personified in the ruling pharaoh. Thus, the Memphite Theology, like the Heliopolitan tradition; combines the world of nature and the world of politics into a single unity—one which, moreover, also has a distinct ethical and moral quality.

The Memphite tradition must be regarded as one of the more important products of the Egyptian mind, because it brings Egyptian thinking about creation beyond the mythological and into the theological realm. The highly abstract nature of the text gives distinct evidence that the Egyptian intellect was capable of dealing with material that would later form the subject of philosophical and theological speculation in the Jewish and Christian worlds. Moreover, one may see an important political aim in this particular cosmogony. Assuming that the text was originally composed during the twenty-fifth dynasty, one might suggest that it was intended as an integral element (i.e., propaganda) in the attempt of the Nubian rulers to revitalize the Egyptian empire and nation.

The traditions outlined above do not exhaust the scope of Egyptian creation mythology. Other centers had their creator deities and myths, some of them at least as ancient as the traditions of Heliopolis and Hermopolis. At Coptos, for example, it was the archaic deity Min who was regarded as creator, and at Elephantine the potter god Khnum was given this position. With the rise of Thebes to prominence during the early Middle Kingdom, Amun (later Amun-Re) of Thebes also took on the position of creator in the Theban mythological tradition. It should also be mentioned that during the reign of Akhenaten, the "heretic" pharaoh of the eighteenth dynasty, the sole deity, the Aten, became the creator and source of all things that exist, although the articulation of the Aten's creative power was expressed in terms that were more theological than mythological.

Egyptian creation mythology is important for its variety of symbolism and for the distinct manner in which the Egyptians were able to integrate and combine different and even seemingly contradictory symbols in their articulation of the emergence and structure of the universe. This peculiar use of mythic traditions gives ample evidence of the fact that the Egyptians themselves must have seen their myths for exactly what myths are intended to be: symbolic statements about phenomena that cannot be fully comprehended by the human intellect. Thus, while the myths expressed and articulated certain concepts about the created order, they did not exhaust that order, and they were able to preserve the sense of awe and mystery that the Egyptians must have felt when contemplating the surrounding world. The Egyptian cosmogonies did not attempt to be dogmatic about the created universe; rather, they encouraged the human personality to experience and marvel at that universe with both the intellect and the spirit.

When the Egyptians contemplated the created universe through their myths and rituals, they would have been aware that the world around them was not simply a collection of material things. The universe was for them an awesome system of living divine beings. The earth, the sky, and the Nile were all entities that had a distinct life-force and personality and drew their life from the original creative power, no matter what name that power may have borne. These living beings were arranged and ordered in a definite system, purposely conceived as in the Memphite tradition, and naturally produced through the process of regeneration as was stressed by the Heliopolitan system. Egyptian creation myth emphasized the fact that there was order and continuity in all things and thus gave the optimistic assurance that the natural, social, and political order would remain stable and secure. The Egyptians were perceptive enough to realize that at times disorder and chaos could become evident in human life and in their environment, but their cosmogonies gave the assurance that such disorder would eventually be overcome by the power of *maat* (*mȝʿt*), that peculiarly Egyptian concept that deified and personified the principle of order (as the goddess Maat) and made it an integral part of the cosmological system.

The concept of creation, for the Egyptians, was not an abstract theory but a reality that gave meaning and significance to their experience of life and of the universe. Behind all created entities, the Egyptians clearly sensed the presence of a divine creative force that not only had acted in the beginning of all things but also continued to act and renew the creation that had originally been brought into being by the divine action and will. Finally, it must also be noted that for the Egyptian mind the divine creative force was primarily neither masculine nor feminine; it was rather a complex and integrated combination of both, for the creative force could be active only when both masculine and feminine were able to act in concert to realize the potential of regeneration. In the final analysis, one might say that the Egyptian creation myths bore witness to the unity, harmony, and singleness of everything that exists.

[*See also* Atum; Geb; Nut; Ptah; Religion; Shu; *and* Tefnut.]

BIBLIOGRAPHY

Allen, James P. *Genesis in Egypt: The Philosophy of Ancient Egyptian Creation Accounts.* Yale Egyptological Studies, 2. New Haven, 1988. An excellent study of Egyptian thought on creation centering on the interpretation of specific texts and stressing the positive theological value of Egyptian creation mythology.

Anthes, Rudolph. "Egyptian Theology in the Third Millennium B.C." *Journal of Near Eastern Studies* 18 (1959), 169–212. A very intense study of the Heliopolitan creation tradition and its political implications. This study will provide the reader with a good understanding of Old Kingdom myth.

Clark, R. T. R. *Myth and Symbol in Ancient Egypt.* London, 1959. A very good introduction to the symbolic nature of myth in ancient Egypt, covering most of the important types of myth.

Frankfort, Henri. *Ancient Egyptian Religion: An Interpretation.* New York, 1948. A general interpretation of the nature of Egyptian religion. Highly useful for an understanding of the Egyptian religious mind.

Frankfort, Henri. *Kingship and the Gods: A Study of Ancient Near Eastern Religion as the Integration of Society and Nature.* Chicago, 1948. A comprehensive and complete treatment of kingship in the context of the world of the divine in ancient Near Eastern cultures. This work will help the reader to see Egyptian myth in the wider context of its time.

Frankfort, Henri, et al. *Before Philosophy: An Essay on Speculative Thought in the Ancient Near East.* Baltimore, 1949. A very good exposition of the inner significance of Near Eastern myth, including material on Egypt and other ancient cultures.

Hart, G. *Egyptian Myths.* London, 1990.

Hornung, Erik. *Conceptions of God in Ancient Egypt: The One and the Many.* Translated from German by John Baines. London, 1983. Contains many fine insights into the Egyptian theological mind and serves as a very good basis for understanding Egyptian religious thinking.

Lesko, Leonard. "Ancient Egyptian Cosmogonies and Cosmology." In *Religion in Ancient Egypt,* edited by Byron E. Shafer, pp. 88–122. Ithaca, 1991.

Quirke, Stephen. *Ancient Egyptian Religion.* London, 1992. A very well organized overview of Egyptian religion; useful for setting creation mythology in its wider setting and for seeing Egyptian myth as a living force.

Tobin, V. A., "Mytho-Theology in Ancient Egypt." *Journal of the American Research Center in Egypt* 25 (1988), 169–183. This article will provide a concise and easily readable account of the nature of the Egyptian mythic corpus.

Tobin, V. A., *Theological Principles of Egyptian Religion.* New York, 1989. A systematic theology of ancient Egyptian religion, stressing the place of creation mythology.

VINCENT ARIEH TOBIN

Osiris Cycle

The invention of writing, in Sumeria and then independently in Egypt, enabled myths first to be recorded, probably toward the end of the fourth millennium BCE (von Soden 1994, p. 31.ff.). By the middle of the third millennium, the names of hundreds of gods and goddesses had been recorded by the Sumerians; soon afterward, the Pyramid Texts were being inscribed by the Egyptians. In both Sumeria and Egypt, a long period of oral transmission must have preceded these writings. In Egypt, the earliest funerary preparations point to a belief in an afterlife, but details of doctrine or a mythical framework are inevitably lacking in such evidence.

The phase preceding the emergence of writing stretches by mere definition into the prehistoric era, but its duration is a matter of surmise. In a well-known essay, Frankfort et al. (1946, pp. 19ff.) designate this phase as that of "mythopoeic thought," a phase with its own logic rather than a "prelogical mentality"; they aver that "it is essential that true myth be distinguished from legend, saga, fable, and fairy tale," although "all these may retain elements of the myth" (p. 15). "Legend" and "saga" share a historical substratum; otherwise, the dictum is acceptable, provided that the possibility of mixed forms is granted. It is more difficult to accept that myth "is nothing less than a carefully chosen cloak for abstract thought" (p. 15). Imagery, though, is rightly stressed; and the symbols are often part of a narrative that is, however piecemeal in its presentation, concerned with "how the world came into being."

Osiris and Heliopolis. The early sources place Osiris in the Great Ennead of Heliopolis and a doctrinal cosmogony can be inferred from the many allusions to this important group. At its head is Atum, the creator god, who appears variously as a scarab beetle, primitive mound, and serpent, but is more commonly figured as anthropomorphic. He has close affinities to the sun god Re and at times appears in the double, syncretized name, Re-

Atum. In the Ennead, he is the father of Shu (air) and Tefnut (moisture), who in turn procreate Geb (earth) and Nut (sky). The separation of earth and sky was ascribed to their father Shu. Geb and Nut are the parents of two marital pairs: Osiris and Isis, and Seth and Nephthys; this arrangement gives the Ennead a total of four marital pairs, leaving Atum at the head in a status of marked isolation. He is the father of the twins Shu and Tefnut but has no wife or consort. He is said to produce his progeny by an act of masturbation or expectoration. This leads to the idea that he is a bisexual being: in the Coffin Texts, he is mentioned with the double pronoun "he-she." Moreover, the masturbating hand was worshiped as the goddess Iusaas, to whom a shrine was devoted in Heliopolis (see Rundle Clark 1959, pp. 41 ff., who believes that the myths about masturbation and spitting are "complementary, not alternative"). Perhaps the idea is that Atum swallows his own sperm and eventually spits it out in the form of developed offspring. There is clear emphasis on Atum's ontological independence; he is apparently self-begotten and needs no female aid in the process of procreation (see Griffiths 1980, p. 186). Should he therefore be regarded as an androgynous deity in the strict sense? Zandee's admirable study (1988) posits this view forcefully, and he adduces many Gnostic parallels. God as mother-father or father-mother is often present in varied periods of Egypt's literature (see Assmann 1983, pp. 119–121, and for iconography, Baines 1985, p. 120). It was especially evident in Amarna and pre-Amarna hymns (see Lichtheim 1976, vol. 2, pp. 86 ff., esp. 91). In Elaine Pagels's *The Gnostic Gospels* (1982, pp. 71–88), there is an eloquent chapter on "God the Father/God the Mother," but with no mention of the strong Egyptian background. In considering the idea in connection with the creator god Atum, one has to face the fact that no semblance of physical bisexuality is present; there is no parallel to Greek hermaphroditism or the Orphic Phanes, where male and female features are combined in one body. Rather, in a process akin to metaphor or allegory, the physical processes described are paradoxical fantasies; they suggest an urge to imagine a bisexual divine being who initiates the whole movement of creation, but who yet remains a totally male figure.

A firmly patriarchal society is reflected, and the same emphasis is seen in the early attitude to fertility in nature, insofar as Osiris embodies this. In contrast to Sumer, where the fertile earth is represented by the mother goddess Ninhursag, Egypt insists on a male deity of earth, Geb; and Osiris, as a figure endowed with chthonic power, also points to male precedence. It is true that after the passage of almost three millennia his sister-wife Isis takes over several of these affinities, thus bringing Egypt more into line with the earth goddesses Demeter, Gaia, Ishtar, and Astarte. In the cultures of those goddesses the sky dei-

ties are male, but for Osiris and Egypt the sovereign of the sky is his mother Nut, and her funerary role is quite dominating, although in a wider context the sun god is the lord of heaven. Immortality as a star implied that the deceased, in his identity with Osiris, was welcomed and protected by his mother Nut; and this meant that the figure of Nut often depicted on the underside of the lid of the sarcophagus was particularly fitting. Her cosmic role in the separation of sky and earth is also depicted frequently in the New Kingdom and later; here she is shown bending over her husband Geb, while Shu separates the two deities cosmically, but thus also prevents their sexual union (see Silverman 1991, p. 24, fig. 13; te Velde 1977, pp. 427–429; and te Velde 1979). This phase of cosmic separation is presented, as in several other mythologies, as a prerequisite of effective life on earth. In a mortuary context, it must mean, as te Velde shows, that rebirth in an afterlife is the analogue suggested. In the early phases of Egypt's development, Geb is viewed as the sovereign whose legacy is bound up with the historical kingship that implicates the rivalry of Horus and Seth. As a representative of the earth, he naturally figures in the ceremony of hacking the earth in Heliopolis (cf. Griffiths 1960, p. 61ff.). In chapter 18 of the *Book of Going Forth by Day*, this rite is connected with the tribunal in which Osiris triumphs over his Sethian enemies, who appear as goats and are slaughtered; their blood is mixed with the earth—a rite the translator, T. G. Allen, renders as "earth-fertilizing." Horus, in one allusion, is vindicated as the successor of Osiris.

Nut, by contrast, is more constantly associated with the afterworld. An interesting suggestion has been made about the "map of heaven" given in a group of early texts: place names ascribed to various parts of the sky (the Winding Waterway, Nurse Canal, Field of Reeds, and Doors Thrown Open) refer to Nut, it is suggested, and "may even have related to her female anatomy" (Lesko 1991, p. 119). Since Nut often personified the coffin, Lesko notes, it is cogent to describe it as "the womb containing the one to be reborn."

The Osirian Group. In the Heliopolitan Ennead, Isis and Nephthys are very close to Osiris. Isis is given some cosmological affinities, especially with heaven and earth; whether she is also a goddess of rain is more doubtful (Münster 1968, p. 198ff.).

At first it seems surprising that Horus, the son of Osiris, is not named as a member of the Ennead. The basic reason was probably the fact of his identification with the living king, who was also the leader of the funerary rites for his father, now equated with Osiris. From this point of view, the deities of the Ennead might be regarded as the ancestors of Horus (cf. Barta 1973, p. 25). With time, many changes and extensions were made and, dur-

MYTHS: OSIRIS CYCLE. *Triad of (left to right) Isis, Osiris, and Horus.* A bronze statuette group from the Ptolemaic period. (The Metropolitan Museum of Art, Rogers Fund, 1942. [42.2.3])

ing the New Kingdom and later, Seth was often displaced by Horus (Hornung 1983, p. 222). In early dynastic history, however, these two rival gods appear together as partners in the divine tutelage of a united monarchy. The queen's title in the first dynasty, according to sealings found by W. M. Flinders Petrie, was "She who sees Horus and Seth." At the end of the second dynasty, King Peribsen opted for a Seth-name, while both deities are associated with the name of Khasekhemwy. A dual god, Horus-Seth, occurs occasionally, doubtless a projection of the dual divinity envisaged in the king (see Griffiths 1960, p. 121ff.; cf. Redford 1992, pp. 36–37). Seth's part in this concept is not maintained except in certain periods, such as under the Hyksos, Ramessids, and Libyans. Thus, a granite group in the Cairo Museum shows Horus and Seth crowning Ramesses III. Seth suffers a process of degradation, although he maintains a radiantly virtuous role as defender of the sun god Re against the attacks of his enemy Apophis. Only in the Greco-Roman period does he

achieve in Seth-Typhon a kind of Satanic persona in the Greek papyri; and even then it is not Satanism in the full Iranian sense of a creator of evil beings. In spite of his book's one-sided title, *Seth: God of Confusion,* te Velde (1967/1976) pays a good deal of attention to this god's multivalent nature, including its favorable facets. He was not able to take account of Leclant's discovery in that the Pyramid Text version of the homosexual episode between the two gods shows them as equally active sexually; indeed, he finds the essential antithesis of the two gods to be one relating to sexuality (Seth) and light (Horus), a rare opposition for which he finds a parallel in Tibet.

Osiris figures in a celebrated creation text, the Memphite Theology, but he is brought into it for the greater glory of Ptah, the god of Memphis, who is lauded in the text as a creator who achieves his task by the force of his divine word. According to this text, in the Nile River, near Memphis, Osiris was drowned (the most likely rendering); he was seen and taken from the river by Isis, Nephthys, and Horus, and received a stately burial in Memphis, a city that housed the royal Residence from the third dynasty onward. Since Osiris makes his first appearance toward the end of the fifth dynasty, a date at the end of the fifth dynasty would suit the origin of the Memphite Theology, but its only source is an inscription dated to 710 BCE, which claims to be a copy of a much earlier original text (see Redford 1992, pp. 399–400, with a searching analysis of the possible results on questions with impact on other cultures). An early origin, however, does not preclude the possibility of later interpolations. Creation by the divine word is a doctrine well known from the Hebrew *Genesis*, as is creation out of nothing; much later, it was found in Gnostic writings and in the *logos* of Stoicism and the New Testament. The Egyptian sources provide at least one antecedent—a fairly neutral word that leaves open the question of precise influence.

The cosmogony of Hermopolis involves four pairs of creator gods, referred to as the Eight, or Ogdoad. Each pair comprises a male and a female deity, and together they are associated with a particular concept—for example Kuk and Kuket with darkness. An urge toward abstract thinking can be discerned here, recalling the early Greek desire to define the basic elements. Nun and Naunet, the primal watery abyss, correspond to a more general Egyptian concept of the origin of things, and the creative egg has several parallels elsewhere, for example, in Orphic thought. The affinities of the Osirian religion, by contrast, are more concerned with the human predicament in its encounter with decay and death. In view of the prominence of Osiris in the concept of the afterlife, any discussion of the cosmology of the Pyramid Texts is bound to offer a cosmology of the afterlife, and this is effectively outlined by James P. Allen (1988, 1989), who states that "although gods may belong to the earth, sky is their domain *par excellence*" (1989, p. 3). Among the gods who enjoy celestial bliss are not only Osiris, the god of chthonic fertility, but also Geb, the actual deity of earth. Osiris is especially associated with the Duat (or Dat), a watery celestial region where he consorts with Orion and Sothis (Sirius), heralds of inundation and fertility. Osiris is lord of the Duat; he is also "Lord of Eternity," and in the Late period the second words of these titles probably sounded alike. In a Theban cosmogony of Ptolemaic date, the Memphite god Ptah is said to travel to Thebes in his form of Khonsu the Great and to create there the divine Ogdoad (whose origin was in Hermopolis). Khonsu, a moon god, had an early cult in Karnak, and in a section of this text devoted to Osiris he is called Khonsu-Osiris. Thoth is also named in this context; he is a god whom the early myth portrays as friendly to both Horus and Osiris, and in the judgment before Osiris he is shown recording

the evidence. (For the Khonsu cosmogony, see Lesko and Parker 1988; also Lesko 1991, pp. 105–107.)

Expanding Functions. A feature of the religion of Osiris was its steadily increasing popularity, with a concomitant tendency to add to the functions ascribed to myth, cult, and symbolism. In addition to the name Khonsu-Osiris, there are many similar combined or syncretized forms; a basic prototype is seen in Osiris-Unas, with the god's name prefixed to the king's, implying identity in the full sense of religious sanction. This formula was eventually applied to every deceased person. Other couplings, such as Osiris-Andjety, point to more specific impacts, possibly including the borrowing of political symbols. Osiris-Apis was a particularly potent fusion in that the early Memphite bull cult conferred on Osiris, albeit in a posthumous context, the stamp of strong physical fertility. Only the dead Apis bull was thus named (the order Apis-Osiris was also used), and Isis was given the title "Mother of the Apis." It was the form Osiris-Apis in Memphis that gave rise to the name Sarapis, a god who became popular under the Ptolemies; it is ironic that this god displaced Osiris to some extent, especially in Egypt itself.

The union of Osiris and Re, exemplified in one notable figure and text (noted above), had a strong doctrinal significance; it alluded to the sun god's nocturnal visit to the Osirian realm of the dead and to the hope of new life symbolized by the arrival of dawn. This concept of enduring force persisted even in the Isiac rite described in the second century CE by Apuleius (*Meta.* 11.23), with its vision of the midnight sun.

Triadic formulations with Osiris were also found, and of these, one of the most influential as attested from the Middle Kingdom onward, was Ptah-Sokar-Osiris. The first two names designate gods of Memphis, and the inclusion of Osiris fortified their funerary appeal. Osirian triads were also commonly formed that do not conjoin the names but mention them in texts or figure the gods sculpturally. The most popular group involves Osiris, Isis (or Nephthys), and Horus, with several forms of Horus being deployed. In the early Christian centuries such family groups sanctioned by religion must have been very familiar, particularly to the theologians of Alexandria (cf. Griffiths 1996, p. 302ff.).

A feature of the great Osirian festival in the month of Khoiak was a rite called the "Raising of the *Djed*-Pillar," which was interpreted as a mark of the new life warranted by the god. The pillar varied somewhat in form, but basically it was a stylized sprouting tree, a part of the lush display of vegetative renewal in the festival itself and also in burial ceremonies. It seems, however, that in origin the pillar had nothing to do with Osiris; its early connections were with Ptah in Memphis, and sometimes it was associated with Re and Khonsu. The priestly leaders of the Osirian faith were clearly very ready to take over attractive elements from other cults.

[See also Hymns, *article on* Osiris Hymns; Osiris; *and articles on other deities mentioned in this article.*]

BIBLIOGRAPHY

Allen, James P. *Genesis in Egypt: The Philosophy of Ancient Egyptian Creation Accounts.* Yale Egyptological Studies, 2. New Haven, 1988. Emphasizes the transference to the celestial regions of many ideas, especially in the Pyramid Texts.

Allen James P. "The Cosmology of the Pyramid Texts." In *Religion and Philosophy in Ancient Egypt,* edited by W. K. Simpson, pp. 1–28. Yale Egyptological Studies, 3. New Haven, 1989.

Anthes, Rudolph. "Mythology in Ancient Egypt." In *Mythologies of the Ancient World,* edited by S. N. Kramer, pp. 15–92. New York, 1961. A valid view of the roles of Geb, Osiris, Horus and Seth.

Assmann, Jan. *Re und Amun.* Freiburg, 1983.

Barta, Winfried. *Untersuchungen zum Götterkreis der Neunheit.* Münchner Ägyptologische Studien, 28. Munich, 1973.

Frankfort, Henri, H. A. Frankfort, John A. Wilson, and Thorkild Jacobsen. *Before Philosophy: The Intellectual Adventure of Ancient Man.* Harmondsworth, 1949; reprint, Chicago, 1977.

Griffiths, John Gwyn. *The Conflict of Horus and Seth.* Liverpool, 1960.

Griffiths, John Gwyn, ed. *The Isis-Book (Metamorphoses, Book XI): Apuleius of Madauros.* Études preliminaires aux religions orientales dans l'Empire romain, 39. Leiden, 1975.

Griffiths, John Gwyn. *The Origins of Osiris and His Cult.* Studies in the History of Religions, 40. Leiden, 1980.

Griffiths, John Gwyn. *Triads and Trinity.* Cardiff, 1996.

Hornung, Erik. *Conceptions of God in Ancient Egypt.* Translated from German by John Baines. Ithaca, 1982.

Jacobsen, Thorkild. *The Treasures of Darkness: A History of Mesopotamian Religion.* New Haven, 1976.

Junge, Friedrich. "Zur Fehldatierung des sogenannten Denkmals memphitischer Theologie." *Mitteilungen des Deutschen Archäologischen Instituts, Abteilung Kairo* 29 (1973), 195–204.

Kákosy, László. "Osiris-Aion." *Oriens Antiquus* 3 (1964), 15–25.

Kákosy, László. *Selected Papers (1956–1973),* pp. 69–79. Studia Aegyptiaca, 7. Budapest, 1981.

Lesko, Leonard H. *The Ancient Egyptian Book of Two Ways.* Berkeley, 1972.

Lesko, Leonard H., and R. A. Parker. "The Khonsu Cosmogony." In *Pyramid Studies and other essays presented to I. E. S. Edwards,* edited by John Baines, pp. 168–175, pls. 33–37. London, 1988.

Lesko, Leonard H. "Ancient Egyptian Cosmogonies and Cosmology." In *Religion in Ancient Egypt,* edited by Byron E. Shafer, pp. 88–122. Cornell, 1991.

Lichtheim, Miriam. *Ancient Egyptian Literature: A Book of Readings.* 3 vols. Berkeley, 1973–1980.

Münster, Maria. *Untersuchungen zur Göttin Isis vom Alten Reich bis zum Ende des Neuen Reiches.* Münchner Ägyptologische Studien, 11. Berlin, 1968.

Redford, Donald B. *Egypt, Canaan, and Israel in Ancient Times.* Princeton, 1992. See especially the discussion of creation myths on pp. 396ff.

Rundle Clark, R. T. *Myth and Symbol.* London, 1959.

Schlögl, Hermann Alexander. *Der Gott Tatenen.* Orbis biblicus et orientalis, 29. Freiburg, 1980.

Soden, Wolfram von. *The Ancient Orient.* Translated from the German by D. G. Schley. Grand Rapids, Michigan, 1994.

Silverman, David P. "Divinity and Deities in Ancient Egypt." In *Religion in Ancient Egypt,* edited by Byron E. Shafer, pp. 7–87. Cornell, 1991. On creator deities, see pp. 33ff.

Tobin, Vincent. "Divine Conflict in the Pyramid Texts." *Journal of the American Research Center in Egypt* 39 (1993), 93–110.

Velde, Herman te. "Geb." *Lexikon der Ägyptologie,* edited by Wolfgang Helck and Wolfhart Westendorf, vol. 2, cols. 427–429. Wiesbaden, 1977.

Velde, Herman te. Seth, *God of Confusion.* 2d ed. Leiden, 1977.

Velde, Herman te. "The Theme of the Separation of Heaven and Earth in Egyptian Mythology." *Studia Aegyptiaca* 3 (1979), 161–167.

Zandee, Jan. "Der androgyne Gott in Ägypten: Ein Erscheinungsbild des Weltschöpfers." *Ägypten und Altes Testament* 14 (1988), 240–278.

J. GWYN GRIFFITHS

Solar Cycle

That the Sun and other heavenly objects should have universally affected human thought is a natural result of life on Earth; and the frequent evidence of their impact on religious thought is also beyond question. A clear example occurs in the *Deuteronomy* warning (perhaps of the seventh century BCE) against the worship of the Sun, Moon, and stars (4.19). Since a prohibition presupposes a practice, we may assume that some Israelites knew of or even indulged in such worship, as did several neighboring peoples.

Physical Effects. If we consider the biological importance for Egypt of various natural phenomena, it is clearly evident that it was not the Sun or any other celestial phenomenon that counted most in physical terms. Rather, it was the Nile River, the great provider of fertility and growth. When the Greek historian Herodotus referred to Egypt as "a gift of the river," he had in mind only the part of Lower Egypt to Lake Moeris, which he regarded as formed by sedimentation through the action of the Nile. Popular misinterpretation has often applied this remark to the whole of Egypt, in a wider sense, and this view is not intrinsically wide of the mark. Yet in the background of religious thought, the import of celestial phenomena is often more dominant. It was the annual inundation of the Nile that ensured fertility, and the worship of Hapy (god of the inundation) specifically honored his blessings. The cult of Osiris also achieved a strong link with water and vegetation, though not in its early phases. A clean cut between the terrestrial and celestial worlds is not a feature of this manner of thinking; what is apparent, rather, is a constant urge to integrate the two aspects and to suggest their interdependence. Thus, the inundation of the Nile was often connected by the Egyptians with the heliacal rising of the star Sothis (the Dog Star, Sirius), seen in the constellation of Orion. A first dynasty ivory tablet from Abydos refers to Sothis as "Bringer of the New Year and of the Inundation." In Pyramid Text 965, Sothis is said to be the daughter of Osiris. In the Pyramid Texts, the nature of the afterworld is often glimpsed, that which the deceased king (identified with Osiris) is said to have experienced. It is situated in the heavens, and yet it contains fields, in particular the Field of Offerings and the Field of Reeds. Water, however, is the chief feature of the sky, and navigation on this water is the method of movement, suggesting that conditions in the terrestrial Egypt are being transferred to the heavens, with a celestial Nile affording the means of transport (see Allen 1989, p. 7).

The Basic Creator-God. The sun god Re is, however, the basic creator god of all, and among his creations are the Nile and even the primal water of Nun from which the earth itself emerged. The Hymns to Re in Spell 15 of the *Book of Going Forth by Day (Book of the Dead)* enlarge on the sun god's sovereignty over heaven and earth. In those hymns, Re is often lauded in his form at sunrise and also at sunset, Atum being the name given to him at the latter stage. Elsewhere three stages are assigned to him—sunrise, noon, and sunset—the names being often designated as Khepri, Re, and Atum. Khepri is a name well suited to denote the arrival of dawn because it implies the process of coming into being. Depicted sometimes as a scarab beetle, the god was regarded as a self-procreated being. A text of the Ramessid era (Pleyte-Rossi, Turin Papyrus 133, 10) refers to the triple positions of these gods during the course of the day: "I am Khepri in the morning, Re in the afternoon, Atum in the evening." Three forms or modes of the sun god are implied—an example, thus, of a modalistic trinity, comparable to the later Christian concept (Griffiths 1996). A liturgical meaning is probably embedded in the Egyptian forms, with allusions to services at morning, noon, and evening; one may also discern references to the divisions of age (child, man, and old man) and to the phases of life (birth, maturity, and death).

The *Book of That Which Is in the Underworld (Amduat),* the *Book of Gates,* and related writings which are profusely illustrated present the nocturnal voyage of the sun god in graphic detail. *Amduat* is concerned with the underworld which Re now enters; it adorns the New Kingdom tombs of kings in twelve sections related to the hours of the night. The sun god is provided with two boats, assigned respectively to the morning and evening. The night journey is by no means plain sailing, for Re is now threatened by demonic forces of darkness led by the serpent Apophis. In this perilous strait, Re's principal defender is none other than the god Seth, whose role in the defeat of Apophis is a far cry from that of a "god of confusion," which te Velde regards as his characteristic activity. The rebuttal of the powers of darkness culminates in the coming of dawn, and the sun god's victory is at the same time interpreted as a celebration of life over death. A natural concomitant of this concept is that a dominant desire of

the deceased is to join the boat of Re and thus to share in his defeat of darkness and death. In the Roman era, Apuleius portrays the Isiac initiate as witnessing the Sun at midnight; the line of symbolism points to a clear connection. (On *Amduat,* see Hornung 1963–1967 and 1984).

Problems of Cult and Myth. Palpable evidence for the cult of Re is most clearly present in Old Kingdom remains of the sun-sanctuaries of several kings of the fifth dynasty. The best known is that of Newoserre at Abu Gurob near Abusir, which features a high obelisk and an altar in the open air, while slaughtering places were provided for the offering of animals; the *sed*-festival of the king is also represented. More intriguing is the evidence for the solar boats, which begins with the first dynasty boat found at Helwan. An impressive example is the solar boat discovered in 1954 near the pyramid of Khufu (Cheops), which his son Djedefra (Ra-djedef) provided in an adjacent rocky cleft. What is intriguing about this boat and similar ones is the definition of its precise purpose in relation to ritual or myth.

To some extent, a similar problem arises with regard to the several other instances of funerary boat-pits; some have proved to be empty; in others, the boats are extant, but they vary considerably in size. Some are full-size realistic objects while others are small enough to be regarded as mere models. The comparative poverty of the owner might explain the choice of the miniature mode, and a magical empowering in favor of a divinely ordained use after death could well be indicated. Even within that purpose, several options suggest themselves. One is the idea that the nocturnal voyage of Re may be imitated, to be followed by his emergence at dawn after the journey through the Osirian underworld where the union of Osiris and Re is achieved. Other ritual journeys might be envisaged, since an early tradition sanctioned visits to the hallowed precincts of Buto, Sais, Heliopolis, and especially Abydos. A kind of second burial at Abydos was the most elaborate option, but the provision of a model boat might suggest an attenuated magical substitute. A sanction for sacral use is indicated by the ancient papyriform design. The empty twin-pit raises the question of the double purpose: eastern and western voyaging was suggested, with northern and southern journeys reserved for the boats in the twin-pits on the eastern face of the pyramid. A total of five boats is attested—a supply sufficient to enable transport in both the funeral and the afterworld. Khufu's extant boat is capacious—43.4 meters (130 feet) long. This seems to favor the least transcendental of the possible explanations: that it was one of the actual boats used in the burial rites (see Jenkins 1980, pp. 160ff.; and Jones 1995, pp. 12–25, 76–78).

Other Divine Roles. Among the celestial phenomena that support the deceased's welfare, special prominence is given to the circumpolar stars. In Egyptian they are called "the never-setting stars," and the term itself points to the enduring nature of their existence; association with them clearly suggests a warrant of immortality. According to Joseph Bradshaw (1990, 1997), there are as many as fifty mentions of these stars in the Pyramid Texts. He shows that Osiris is closely associated with them, taking his throne as king of the dead in the region of the North Pole. He goes on to argue, however, that even Re was not basically a sun god, but a being dominated by circumpolar ideas, a claim rejected by several reviewers of his book.

The sky goddess Nut displays some attributes that are to be expected, but others verging on the bizarre. Her close connection with Nun, god of the primeval waters from which the earth's primal mound is said to have emerged, is in accord with the fact that she is concerned with the basic entities of earth, sky, sun, moon, and stars. The astral beings are often depicted on her body, which figures regularly on the lid of the sarcophagus and on the walls of the sarcophagus chamber. In Pyramid Text 1688, Re is said to come forth from Nut, who bears him daily; and in the New Kingdom papyrus of the priestess Anhai, the god Nun is shown lifting up the boat of Re in his sunrise, in which the sun god is depicted as a scarab beetle. Nut is also credited with a remarkable feat of astral productivity; at sunset she swallows the stars through her mouth, but with the dawn she gives birth to them anew from her vagina. Her swallowing of her star-children leads to her being compared with a sow. A text from the cenotaph of Sety I at Abydos refers to her as "the mother of swine who eats her little pigs." Moreover, the Sun itself, as well as the stars, was a part of Nut's cosmic fertility: according to *Amduat*, at the Twelfth Hour, the Sun appears in the morning "between the thighs of Nut."

The Celestial Cow. A celebrated text found in a number of New Kingdom tombs describes how Re threatened to destroy mankind because of their rebellion against him but eventually decided to deliver them from this fate. The celestial cow is depicted with the various texts, and those texts include instructions for the painting. (The example in Shrine I of Tutankhamun appears in A. Piankoff and N. Rambova, *The Shrines of Tut-Ankh-Amon* [Princeton, 1977], p. 142, fig. 46; a translation of the text accompanies it.)

If we ask who exactly was this cow of heaven, the answer must be Mehet-weret, the divine cow, whose name means "the great flood." The name is written before the cow in the text of Tutankhamun (Hornung, p. 31) and seems to be equated with the heavens in the Pyramid Texts (289c). Yet in Pyramid Text 1344, as Hornung points out, it is Nut that appears as a heavenly cow; and a third cow goddess linked to the heavens is Hathor. Both Nut and Hathor figure several times in the text.

Of much greater import is the interpretation of the myth. Here Re has the leading role, but Hathor is also a key figure, being crucially implicated in the reversal of the story. As the ruling sun god of Heliopolis, Re was regarded as king of the gods; and as the father of Maat, the all-pervading concept of truth, justice, and order (both domestic and cosmic), he was assigned a dominant judicial role—for example, as president of the tribunal of the dead, although Osiris eventually tends to take over this role. In the myth of the Celestial Cow, Re is first presented as old and decrepit, worrying that men are plotting against him; he decides to destroy them, using his fiery Eye in the form of Hathor his daughter. She duly returns to him after slaying men in the desert. For this she is praised by Re, but Hathor's relish for blood induces Re to hit on an astonishing stratagem. He produces beer on a large scale—seven thousand jars—mixed with red ocher to make the beer look like blood. Hathor partakes so avidly of this that in a drunken state she forgets her desire to kill more men. At the same time, Re has evidently changed his mind: instead of destroying mankind, he now wants to save them. In a later section, however, he declares that he is too tired to deal further with them; he withdraws from the earth as the heaven is lifted up. Now the celestial cow is identified with Nut, and Re rides on her back. After this, men on earth resort to strife and warfare, an activity condemned by Re even though they are fighting against his enemies. We are then told "and thus originated slaughter among men"—an example of the etiological urge that marks this myth. The whole affair of the seven thousand jugs of beer is another instance, since it is clearly concerned with a festival of Hathor, a goddess who was known, *inter alia*, as "Mistress of Drunkenness."

The idea of a divine decision to destroy mankind is found in several other ancient cultures. From Babylon, Israel, and Greece come myths that describe the gods as using a catastrophic flood as the medium of destruction. The difference in Egypt is due to the fact that there the annual inundation of the Nile was seen as a boon rather than a bane; the destroying medium is now the fiery eye of the sun god, suggesting the burning heat of the desert. The saving of a remnant is found in all the myths, but unlike the Egyptian example, the others accord this privilege to favored human beings—Utnapishtim in Babylon, Noah in Israel, and the pair Deucalion and Pyrrha in Greece. If we look at the moral issues, we find that Utnapishtim and Noah are excepted from doom because of their piety. But as for the human transgressions that have aroused the anger of the gods, it seems that only the Hebraic myth gives them a clearly moral emphasis. This is absent from the early Greek accounts, which may reflect the influence of Babylon, where Enlil, the ruling deity, is merely disturbed by the noise made by men; and the

Egyptian tale does not go beyond an emphasis on the rebellious mutiny of man against Re (see Griffiths 1991, p. 14).

Other Solar Myths. The falcon god Horus, whose name probably means "he who is on high," is naturally, as a god of heaven, intimately connected with solar manifestations. In the earliest corpus of literary import, the Pyramid Texts, the legend of his feud with his brother Seth is given primary force; although incorporated into the Osiris myth, it is of earlier origin. In the feud Seth is said to have injured and removed one of the eyes of Horus; in reply, Horus deprives Seth of his testicles. The intervention of Thoth leads to the restoration of the mutilated parts and to a reconciliation of the warring brothers. In the integrated Osiris myth, Seth becomes the slayer of his brother Osiris, and as a result Horus becomes, by adjustment, the nephew of Seth and also the avenger of Osiris. A trial at Heliopolis is also portrayed, but in two forms: one relates to Horus and Seth concerning the eye that was stolen; the other shows Seth being tried for his violence to Osiris. In each case Seth is defeated, and it becomes clear that the real issue is the inheritance of Geb—that is, the sovereignty of Egypt. Re is often the judge, or Geb himself. The theme persists in an extensive literature that includes the Memphite Theology (where the first verdict is a division between the two, but then the whole kingdom to Horus), the *Contendings of Horus and Seth,* and several texts in the Ptolemaic temples. There are suggestions in many texts that the eyes of Horus were associated with the crowns, as symbols of sovereignty (Griffiths 1960, pp. 120–122). That Seth was yet regarded in the early dynasties as sharing in a pan-Egyptian sovereignty is evident in the first dynasty queen's title, "She who Sees Horus and Seth," found with other early queens. It is reasonable to see here clear evidence of the evolution of a united nation and kingdom. The theology of kingship is a vital element here, the living king often being identified with Horus and also called "the son of Re." A statue of King Khafre in the fourth dynasty shows the Horus falcon spreading his wings behind the pharaoh's head, suggesting close protection if not identity. Note the suggestion of Z. Hawass that the Sphinx of Giza "represents Khafre, as Horus" giving offerings to Khufu "as the sun-god" (1995, p. 227).

Various astral elements enter into the exegesis of the myth, especially in late texts that explain the right eye of Horus as being the Sun and his left eye as the Moon. Other cosmic aspects can be rightly evoked. Seth is often portrayed as a storm god, or as a deity connected with the desert or with foreign lands. The *Contendings of Horus and Seth* ends with his defeat by Horus in regard to the succession; yet he is allowed to go free and join the sun god in the sky to renew his thundering. If the court has decreed that Horus is to succeed Osiris, yet a perennial

cosmic role is conceded to Seth, suggesting the doctrine that "opposing forces were in equilibrium in the universe" (Frankfort 1948, p. 129). Admittedly, this is from a text tinted with a touch of the burlesque. The opposing forces ranged in the myth are differently defined in an impressive study by Herman te Velde, *Seth, God of Confusion* (1967; 2nd ed., 1977). He discounts the impress of the early historical and political background and locates the essence of the myth in the opposing forces of light (Horus) and sexuality (Seth). The universal antonym of light is of course darkness, but an opposition found in sexuality is supplied by a parallel in Tibet discovered in a work by Mircea Eliade (te Velde, p. 51). In support of this unexpected outcome, we find much emphasis on the homosexual episode in the myth, with Seth as the aggressive partner, although Horus in fact shares that role.

Egypt's solar cult reached its acme, in one sense, when Akhenaten elevated the sun disk, the Aten, to be the sole and sovereign object of worship. From the point of view of mythology, however, it was not an acme but a nadir: the solar myths were abandoned, as indeed was the mythology of other cults, including that of Osiris. Theologically, the status of "King" borrows from tradition: he is the son of the Aten, just as the pharaoh was from early times the son of Re. A triad of the Aten, King Akhenaten, and Queen Nefertiti suggests a claim that worship should include the king and his queen (see Griffiths 1996, pp. 57–59). Yet the Aten's primacy is beyond question. He is the creator and sustainer of the whole earth, including Syria and Kush; an imposing universalism is presented and also a compassionate ethic, symbolized by sun-rays seen as helping hands; but mythic details about the process of creation are missing (see Redford 1984, pp. 169, 177f.).

A feature of texts from the Greco-Roman era is their expansive treatment of mythological themes. Two solar myths are here conspicuous. One concerns the fiery raging eye of Re, identified with his daughter Tefnut or Hathor-Tefnut, who went to Nubia in the form of a lioness; the sun god sent Thoth to mollify her wrath, inducing her to return to Egypt by telling her a number of animal fables. The *Legend of the Winged Disk* and the *Triumph of Horus* come from the temple of Edfu, and their main protagonist is Re or Re-Harakhty. Although he is assisted by three Horuses—Horus of Beḥdet, Horus the son of Isis, and Horus the Elder—Re himself is the theological mainspring and the leader of massive campaigns against Seth and his followers. If the general impression is given of a rehash of the Horus-Seth myth, important differences emerge. The status of Seth is much degraded as compared with the parity often granted to him in the early myth. He is now denigrated within Egypt by a series of attacks on the crocodiles and hippopotami associated with him, often culminating in a vengeful sacrificial meal. In these sections, the essence of the struggle is a cult feud in de-fined localities. In other sections, a wider political conflict is denoted, which seems to reflect the expulsion of the Hyksos. Seth is now the foreigner who must be driven from Egypt into the sea; the struggle between Re and Seth echoes the tension relating to the Hyksos as people who "ruled without Re." The emblematic great Winged Disk is the sun disk fitted with a falcon's wings; it is the form assumed by Horus of Beḥdet in the bark of Re.

[*See also* Aten; Atum; Hathor; Horus; Hymns, *article on* Solar Hymns; *and* Re and ReHorakhty.]

BIBLIOGRAPHY

Allen, James P. "The Cosmology of the Pyramid Texts." In *Religion and Philosophy in Ancient Egypt*, edited by W. K. Simpson. Yale Egyptological Studies, 3. New Haven, 1989. The celestial framework is ably analyzed.

Andrews, Carol. *Amulets of Ancient Egypt*. London, 1994. A comprehensive survey which includes solar affiliations and their doctrinal meaning, as on p. 89, suggesting a popular funerary belief that a solar amulet furthered beneficent unity with the sun god.

Assmann, Jan. *Ägypten: Theologie und Frömmigkeit einer frühen Hochkultur*. Stuttgart, 1984. A study enriched with an abundance of quoted source material. The myth of the Celestial Cow is perceptively dealt with on pp. 138–141. The following works by Assmann treat solar myths and their liturgical implications, as well as related theological tensions, especially in the aftermath of the Amarna period.

Assmann, Jan. *Der König als Sonnenpriester*. Glückstadt, 1970.

Assmann, Jan. *Liturgische Lieder an den Sonnengott*. Berlin, 1969.

Assmann, Jan. *Re und Amun*. Freiburg, 1983.

Bradshaw, Joseph. *The Imperishable Stars of the Northern Sky in the Pyramid Texts*. London, 1990.

Bradshaw, Joseph. *The Night Sky in Egyptian Mythology*. London, 1997.

Fairman, H. W. *The Triumph of Horus*. London, 1974. A valued guide to texts from Edfu.

Frankfort, Henri. *Ancient Egyptian Religion*. New York, 1948.

Griffiths, J. Gwyn. *The Conflict of Horus and Seth*. Cardiff, 1960.

Griffiths, J. Gwyn. *The Divine Verdict*. Leiden, 1991.

Griffiths, J. Gwyn. *Triads and Trinity*. Cardiff, 1996.

Hawass, Z. "On Royal Funerary Complexes of the Fourth Dynasty." In *Ancient Egyptian Kingship*, edited by D. O'Connor and D. P. Silverman, pp. 221–262. Leiden, 1995.

Hornung, Erik. *Ägyptische Unterweltsbücher*. 2d ed. Zürich and Munich, 1984. This and the following are three magisterial studies of the solar mythology, especially of the sun's nocturnal voyage in the underworld.

Hornung, Erik. *Das Amduat*. 3 vols. Wiesbaden, 1963–1967.

Hornung, Erik, et al. *Der Ägyptische Mythos von der Himmelskuh*. Freiburg, 1982. Includes the hieroglyphic text, translation, and commentary.

Jenkins, Nancy. *The Boat beneath the Pyramid: King Cheops' Royal Ship*. London, 1980. Discusses use of boats in burials, citing the views of Černý and A. Youssef Moustafa.

Jones, Dilwyn. *Boats*. London, 1995. Boats in burials are discussed on pp. 12–15 and 76–78.

Lesko, Leonard H. "Ancient Egyptian Cosmogonies and Cosmology." In *Religion in Ancient Egypt*, edited by Byron E. Shafer, pp. 88–122. Ithaca, 1991. Offers pertinent remarks on the cosmogonies of Heliopolis, Hermopolis, and the Memphite Theology.

O'Connor, D. "Boat Graves and Pyramid Origins." *Expedition* 33 (1991), 5–17.

Redford, Donald B. *Akhenaten, the Heretic King*. Princeton, 1984; reprinted, 1987. Although the developed creed at Tell el-Amarna abandoned the solar mythology, the valid critical analysis of the process is helpful.

Silverman, David P. "Divinity and Deities in Ancient Egypt." In *Religion in Ancient Egypt*, edited by Byron E. Shafer, pp. 7–87. Ithaca, N. Y., 1991. Solar themes are well related to their wider contexts in this profusely illustrated essay.

Silverman, David P. "The Nature of Kingship." In *Ancient Egyptian Kingship*, edited by D. O'Connor and D. P. Silverman, pp. 48–92. Leiden, 1995.

Sternberg, Heike. *Mythische Motive und Mythenbildung in den ägyptischen Tempeln und Papyri der griechisch-römischen Zeit*. Wiesbaden, 1985. A comprehensive treatment of mythological texts from the temples of Edfu (the Winged Disk), Esna, and Kom Ombo; also from Papyrus Boulaq No. 2 and P. Jumilhac; with translations and commentaries.

Velde, Herman te. *Seth, God of Confusion*. Leiden, 1967; reprint, revised, 1977. Despite its unbalanced title, this book is an imposingly thorough study that does not neglect the beneficent role of Seth as defender of the sun god Re.

J. GWYN GRIFFITHS

Lunar Cycle

The Moon was considered by the Egyptians to be the nightly replacement of the Sun, yet its mythology was never as important as that involving the Sun. In the known creation accounts, the role of the Sun is always paramount. The relationship between the Moon and the stars is more important, because the lunar god can be designated as "ruler of the stars."

The Sun and Moon were commonly referred to together by Egyptians as "the two lights." The weaker light of the Moon is compared to the evening Sun. The most common theological interpretation of the lights declares them to be the eyes of Re or of the sky god Horus, whose left eye was the Moon and whose right eye was the Sun; the left eye was weaker than the right because it had been damaged. This myth was elaborated in many religious centers, giving rise to specialized forms of Horus such as Khenty-Khety of Letopolis and the later Hor-Merty of Horbeit. The mythology surrounding the eyes of the sky god was extensive, and variants abounded. Four different myths may be distinguished surrounding the divine eyes: that of the eyes of the sky god; the injured eye of Horus; the solar eye; and the distant goddess who is brought back. Often, elements of these different myths are found mixed or interchanged.

The Moon is most often depicted as a combination of the full-moon disk with the crescent moon. The lunar gods nearly always have this symbol on their heads. The full-moon disk may have the *wedjat* (*wḏ3t*) eye inside it—either the left or the right eye—or the image of a lunar divinity. The Moon, like the Sun and the stars, is represented traversing the sky in a boat. The most complete extant depiction of the entire lunar cycle is found inside the *pronaos* of the Edfu temple.

The starting point of the lunar cycle is the new moon, and its culminating point is the moment of full moon. The Moon thus becomes visible only on the second day of the lunar month. The lunar cycle is represented either as a six-day evolution up to the sixth day, or as a fifteen-day evolution up to the ideal day of full moon. The importance of the sixth day is probably explained by the increasing intensity of moonlight at this stage of the cycle. Sometimes, the seventh day is mentioned in its stead.

A Symbol of Renewal. The moon became used as a symbol of rejuvenation; in late texts it is called "the one that repeats its form." Lunar gods may be represented as youths, while the entire lunar cycle may be compared to the life cycle of a man, with the moon being the "old man who becomes a child." A New Kingdom pharaoh may be declared "young as the moon," and Amenhotpe III identifies himself fully with the moon in his temple at Soleb.

An important political application of lunar mythology followed from the identification of the moon with the god Horus. The birth of Horus (or Harsiese) was celebrated on the second lunar day in the month Pharmuthi. The full moon could then be equated with the adult Horus as in Edfu: "When he completes the half month, he assumes control of the sky rejuvenated." At the moment of full moon, Horus was declared "true of voice" and "joyful," because of his victory over Seth in the divine tribunal of Heliopolis. The lunar cycle was linked to the renewal of royal powers, and temple rituals based on this theme are known from Karnak.

Likewise, in mortuary beliefs the lunar cycle was a beloved image of cyclical renewal. The feast of the sixth day counted as the day of the victory of Osiris, and even though the moment of full moon could have the same significance, the sixth day became of particular importance in funerary rituals. Already in the Pyramid Texts, the deceased is sometimes identified with the moon. According to evidence from Middle Kingdom coffins, the funerary religion was particularly concerned with the night sky. Nevertheless, lunar associations were not common in the Middle Kingdom, but the Coffin Texts from Deir el-Bersheh accord an equal place in the afterworld to the lunar god Thoth, next to Osiris and Re. In the New Kingdom and later, the role of the moon in the afterlife remains minimal, but it is found, for instance, in chapter 131 of the *Book of Going Forth by Day*.

A Symbol of Fecundity. The moon is compared to a bull on account of the similarity in shape of the crescent moon and a bull's horns. Lunar gods may be characterized as "with sharp horns." In texts from the Ptolemaic period in Edfu and Karnak, this metaphor is developed in calling the crescent moon the "rutting bull" and the waning moon the "ox." The moon is "the rutting bull who inseminates the cows," but it is also said: "You unite with young women, you are an inseminating bull who fertilizes the girls" (Edfu VII, 116, 2–3), indicating a perceived relationship between female fertility and the moon.

The Egyptians understood that a relationship existed between the Moon and the growth of plants and that sowing was best done at the time of a full moon. Similarly, the minerals in the desert were thought to come into being under the Moon's influence.

Interruptions in the usual cycle were feared. A lunar eclipse was considered a bad omen, as is evident from some Late period texts describing the sky swallowing the moon. It was also felt to influence daily life, and the Egyptians dedicated stelae to it at Deir el-Medina, and formed personal names with the element *i'ḥ* ("moon"). On the stelae, the moon god *I'ḥ*-Thoth may be called "the merciful," which may refer to another aspect of the lunar god, "reckoner of the lifespan."

Myth of Horus and Seth. By far the predominant myth concerning the moon relates its cycle to the battle between Horus and Seth. During this famous battle over the inheritance of Osiris, Seth steals the eye of Horus, damages it, and divides it into six parts. Thoth later restores it "with his fingers," or by spitting on it. In the temple of Kom Ombo (scene 950) a series of medical instruments is depicted being used in the healing of the eye by the god Haroeris. The restored eye is called *wedjat* (*wḏ3t*) from the New Kingdom onward, but the myth in question is much older and was found in the Coffin Texts, as in Spell 335. Onuris, Thoth, or Osiris as moon returns the complete eye to Horus. Thoth may also be said to catch the lunar eye in a net, acting together with the god Shu.

"Filling the *wedjat* eye," "entering into the left eye," or "joining the left eye" also means restoring the eye. It was performed on the sixth lunar day. The eye is said to be filled with specific minerals and plants. Thoth, together with a specific group of fourteen gods principally performed this act. In Greco-Roman temple reliefs from the region between Dendera and Esna, this group is the Ennead of Hermopolis. Together with Thoth, these gods represent the fifteen days leading up to the full moon, and again the days of the waning moon. As representing the latter, they are said to exit from the eye. In Edfu and Philae, the gods Tanenent and Iunyt of the Hermopolitan Ennead are replaced by the pair Hekes and Hepuy.

An iconographic variant of this theme occurs in the temples at Edfu and Dendera in the form of a staircase with fourteen steps that support the fourteen gods of the waxing moon. Reliefs in Edfu, Dendera, and Ismant el-Kharab (Dakhleh oasis) list a different group of thirty mostly male deities associated with the days of the lunar month. In the legends inscribed with these gods at Ismant el-Kharab, the first fifteen are said to fill the *wedjat* eye with a fraction each day, after which the moon's reduction is recorded up to the twenty-fourth day, when the intensity of the moonlight has all but disappeared.

Other Myths. The opposition of Sun and Moon in the sky on the fifteenth or sixteenth day of the month was the most important moment of the lunar cycle. Its importance appears from inscriptions at temples in Edfu, Dendera, and Karnak. This moment was designated as *snsn kȝwy*, "the uniting of the two bulls," and a description of this moment was known from the New Kingdom Osireion at Abydos. In the later temples, this moment could be ritually celebrated by the offering of two mirrors, symbolizing the two lights, at this precise moment. In Thebes and in the Dakhleh oasis, the moment symbolized the rejuvenation of the sun god Amun-Re, when his son and successor, the moon god Khonsu, received his heritage of cosmic rule.

Osiris was an important lunar god. Griffiths (1969, pp. 239–240) has argued that Osiris became identified with the moon only in the New Kingdom (*The Origins of Osiris*, Münchner Ägyptologische Studien 9 Munich 1969, 239–40). At an uncertain time, the murder of the god and his resurrection were recognized in the lunar cycle, and the body of Osiris was equated with the moon. Seth cut his body into fourteen parts, which were later reassembled and restored to life. The number of parts corresponds to the days of the waning or waxing moon.

Elsewhere, the entire life cycle of Osiris related to the lunar cycle, with the god's conception on the first day and his birth on the second lunar day. The temple of Opet in Karnak was dedicated to this event. Osiris' murder and subsequent dismemberment were associated with the time following the full moon. The second day of the month then saw the reassembly of the god's members and his "entering into the moon" on the sixth day. The rejuvenation and the defeat of the god's enemies were placed on the day of full moon, when Osiris was declared victorious in the tribunal, and when Horus was awarded his heritage.

The name of the lunar god Khonsu relates to the verb "moving in various directions," which characterizes the lunar orbit. Especially in the earlier sources, Khonsu is ascribed an aggressive nature. According to later Theban sources, Khonsu traveled every day from the east (his temple at Karnak) to the west (the temple of Djeme) to revitalize his deceased father, Amun. It is especially the Theban theology that declares the moon god to be the son of the sun god.

Apart from Thoth, there were a few more gods with specific links to the moon, such as Min and the Hellenistic form of Isis. In general, goddesses were associated with the moon only when they were identified with the eye of Re, as were Tefnut and Hathor. The annual journey from Dendera to Edfu by Hathor was timed in accordance with the phases of the Moon.

[*See also* Khonsu.]

BIBLIOGRAPHY

Aufrère, S. "De l'influence des Luminaires sur la croissance des vegetaux." *Memnonia* 6 (1995), 113–121.

Bonnet, H., *Reallexikon der ägyptischen Religionsgeschichte*. Berlin, 1952. See the entries on Horusauge, Mond, Mondauge, and Sonnenauge.

Caminos, R. *The Chronicle of Prince Osorkon*. Rome, 1958. On lunar eclipse, pp. 88–89.

Derchain, P. "Mythes et dieux lunaires en Egypte." In *Sources Orientales 5: La lune, mythes et rites*, pp. 17–68. Paris, 1962. The most comprehensive discussion of the ancient lunar mythology.

Derchain, P. "La pêche de l'oeil et les mystères d'Osiris à Dendara." *Revue d'Égyptologie* 15 (1963), 11–25. Study of the temple scenes of fishing of the lunar eye by Thoth and Shu in late temples, and of the lunar staircases in the late temples.

Griffiths, J. G. *The Origins of Osiris*. Münchner Ägyptologische Studien, 9. Munich, 1969.

Griffiths, J. G. "Remarks on the Mythology of the Eyes of Horus." *Chronique d'Égypte* 33 (1958), 182–193. Sheds doubt on the generally assumed early origins of the concept of the moon as equivalent of the *wedjat* eye of the sky god.

Helck, W. "Mond." In *Lexikon der Ägyptologie*, 4: 192–196. Wiesbaden, 1980.

Herbin, F. "Un hymne à la lune croissante." *Bulletin de l'Institut français d'archéologie orientale* 82 (1982), 237–282. This important article presents and discusses a lunar hymn which has been preserved in several copies dating from the Third Intermediate Period onward.

Junker, H. *Der sehende und blinde Gott (Mhntj-irtj und Mhntj-n-irtj)*. Munich, 1942. On mythological references regarding the eyes of the sky god.

Junker, H. *Die Onurislegende*. Vienna, 1917; reprinted 1988. A comprehensive account of the myths of the returning of the eye to its divine owner.

Kaper, O. "The Astronomical Ceiling of Deir el-Haggar in the Dakhleh Oasis." *Journal of Egyptian Archaeology* 81 (1995): 191–192.

Otto, E. "Augensagen." In *Lexikon der Ägyptologie*, 1: 562–567. Wiesbaden, 1974.

Willems, H. *The Coffin of Heqata*. Louvain, 1996. Connection of funerary practice to the night sky, pp. 361–362.

OLAF E. KAPER

N

NAGA ED-DEIR, "Village of the Monastery," a site located on the eastern bank of the Nile River in Upper Egypt (26°22′N, 31°54′E). The site stretches for approximately 2 kilometers (1.5 miles) along the gebel (mountains) from the Coptic monastery *(deir* in Arabic) and modern village, after which the site is named, to the area known as Sheikh Farag after the tomb of a local Islamic holy man. The site primarily consists of a series of cemeteries that contain thousands of burials dating from early Predynastic (c.3800 BCE) to Coptic times (after 400 CE). Inscriptions from dynastic-era tombs associate individuals buried at Naga ed-Deir with the ancient town of Thinis (also Tjeni or This), the most important town of the eighth Upper Egyptian nome.

Archaeological work began at the site with the 1901–1904 excavations of the Phoebe A. Hearst Egyptian Expedition of the University of California, under the direction of the American Egyptologist George A. Reisner. Albert Lythgoe, Arthur C. Mace, and Frederick W. Green worked with Reisner at that time. The Hearst expedition numbered cemeteries 100 to 3500 between wadis 1 and 3 at the southern end of the site, cemeteries 9000 and 10,000 to the north, and the Coptic *deir* to the south. For a few seasons after 1910, and again in 1923, Reisner or his associates returned to the site, this time under the auspices of the joint Museum of Fine Arts, Boston–Harvard University Expedition. At that time, Reisner was assisted by Alan Rowe, Clarence S. Fisher, and Dows Dunham. The MFA–Harvard expedition worked in some of the same areas as the Hearst expedition and also identified cemeteries in the area of Sheikh Farag. Since that time, Naga ed-Deir has been visited briefly by various archaeologists and others, but no major excavations have occurred at the site. Artifacts from the site are found in museums throughout the world, but the largest collections outside of Egypt are at the Museum of Fine Arts, Boston, and the University of California at Berkeley. Egyptologists and anthropologists continue to work on the Naga ed-Deir material.

Naga ed-Deir is best known for remains dating to the Predynastic (c.3800–3200 BCE), the late Old Kingdom, and the First Intermediate Period (c.2300–2061 BCE), although the full time span for the recovered materials is much broader. The preservation of perishable materials in Predynastic cemetery 7000 was remarkably good, so cloth-ing, wood, and basketry, as well as human hair, skin, and even internal organs were recovered. Examination of the best-preserved bodies by anatomist Grafton Elliot Smith revealed no trace of the practice of clitoridectomy (female circumcision) during this period, although evidence of male circumcision was documented. The transitional late Old Kingdom/First Intermediate Period at Naga ed-Deir, particularly at cemetery 3500, has become famous for the large series of painted limestone stelae (grave stones) of local dignitaries, both male and female.

Other remains date from the Early Dynastic period and the Old Kingdom. Early Dynastic finds (c.3050–2700 BCE), primarily from cemeteries 1500 and 3500, included large flint knives, metal tools and weapons, cylinder seals, and gold jewelry. The published Old Kingdom (c.2687–2206 BCE) remains from cemeteries 500–900 included mud-brick *mastaba* tombs, some of large size, as well as tombs of more ordinary people. Reisner excavated mud-brick beehive tombs at Naga ed-Deir that were similar to those found in the Old Kingdom workmen's cemeteries near the Giza pyramids.

Large portions of the remains recovered from Naga ed-Deir are unpublished. With the exception of some rare papyri, which document construction and dockside activities, Middle Kingdom (c.2061–1665 BCE) materials, including coffins, jewelry, stone vessels, ceramics, and funerary masks from cemeteries 400, 1500, 200, SF 500, and elsewhere at the site remain virtually unknown. Although less numerous than graves of the earlier periods, burials of the Second Intermediate Period and the New Kingdom (c.1569–1081 BCE), which contained pottery, coffins, furniture, scribal palettes, uninscribed funerary cones, and more, were recovered. Burials from the Third Intermediate Period, the Late period, and from Greco-Roman times (c.1081 BCE–400 CE) were uncommon at Naga ed-Deir. Those found contained mostly ceramics, were not grouped but scattered throughout the site, and had often reused earlier tombs. Large numbers of Coptic burials, some that were dated into recent times, were also found throughout the site. They illustrate the changing burial customs of the local Christians.

Naga ed-Deir is important today not only for its artifactual, architectural, and human remains, which span more than six thousand years, but also for the quality of the documentation produced early in the twentieth century, the time of its excavation. Reisner was a pioneer in the use of photography in archaeology (more than seven thousand Hearst photographs of the site exist), and he, along with his assistants, took notes and made sketches of almost every tomb encountered. The existence of this documentation almost one hundred years after the excavations makes it possible to study the cemeteries, which today have been seriously affected by local population growth and development. The books, scholarly theses, and articles written about Naga ed-Deir have focused on only a portion of the material obtained from this site.

BIBLIOGRAPHY

Dunham, Dows. *Naga-ed-Dêr Stelae of the First Intermediate Period.* Boston, 1937. Illustrated compendium of known stela from Naga ed-Deir; includes translations of text and other information.

Lythgoe, Albert M. Edited by Dows Dunham. *The Predynastic Cemetery N 7000. Naga-ed Dêr, Part IV.* University of California Publications, Egyptian Archaeology, 7. Berkeley, 1965. Illustrated publication of Lythgoe's field notes and Elliot Smith's anatomical comments.

Mace, Arthur C. *The Early Dynastic Cemeteries of Naga-ed Dêr, Part II.* University of California Publications, Egyptian Archaeology, 3. Leipzig, 1909. Illustrated publication of the Early Dynastic tombs from cemeteries 3000 and 3500; a few First Intermediate Period materials are also illustrated; includes some analysis and discussion of the significance and historic context of the remains.

Podzorski, Patricia V. *Their Bones Shall Not Perish: An Examination of Predynastic Skeletal Remains from Naga-ed-Dêr in Egypt.* New Malden, England, 1990. Compilation and analysis of information available from the specimens, field notes, and photographs, as well as other published and unpublished sources on the human remains from cemetery 7000. Includes a discussion of topics, such as Predynastic health, mortality, and skeletal pathologies. Hard to find outside of the British Museum, London.

Reisner, George A. *A Provincial Cemetery of the Pyramid Age. Naga-ed-Dêr Part III.* University of California Publications, Egyptian Archaeology, 6. Oxford, 1932. Illustrated publication of the Old Kingdom tombs from cemeteries 500 to 900; includes analysis and some discussion of the significance of the materials and historic context.

Reisner, George A. *The Early Dynastic Cemeteries of Naga-ed-Dêr, Part I.* University of California Publications, Egyptian Archaeology, 2. Leipzig, 1908. Illustrated publication of the Early Dynastic tombs from cemetery 1500, with some analysis and discussion of significance and historic context.

Simpson, William K. *Papyrus Reisner I: The Records of a Building Project in the Reign of Sesostris I.* Boston, 1963. Transliteration and translation of this Middle Kingdom (Dynasty 12) papyrus from Naga ed-Deir tomb 408; includes commentaries on grammar, syntax, and meaning, as well as photographs of the text.

Simpson, William K. *Papyrus Reisner II: Accounts of the Dockyard Workshop at This in the Reign of Sesostrisr I.* Boston, 1965. Similar in format to volume 1, with additional materials presented.

PATRICIA V. PODZORSKI

NAG HAMMADI.

Five hundred kilometers (320 miles) upriver from Cairo on the western bank of the Nile is the city of Nag Hammadi (26°,3′N, 32°,15′E). An industrial and agricultural center (aluminum, sugar cane production), Nag Hammadi also possesses one of the few bridges across the Nile. Three major archaeological complexes are associated with its name.

In 1843, Richard Lepsius from Berlin surveyed the sixth dynasty tombs situated across the river from Nag Hammadi in the cliff face of Gebel el-Tarif. Earlier, Wilkenson had noted both these tombs and the ancient city site of Hou, just 5 kilometers (3.2 miles) south of present-day Nag Hammadi on the river's western bank. Sixty years later (1898–1899) W. M. Flinders Petrie excavated both a Roman temple at Hou and a nearby Predynastic cemetery. In 1945, thirteen leather-bound codices containing Gnostic and Orthodox Christian tractates, in Coptic, were discovered by local fertilizer miners on the east side of the Nile near the village of Faw Qibli; the name of Nag Hammadi was given to this manuscript find. A brief but inconclusive excavation was conducted by Debono (early 1950s) of the supposed Pachomian monastery remains in Faw Qibli (ancient Pbow), but only with the publication of the manuscript finds, beginning in the 1950s, did work begin both at the discovery site itself and also directly in Faw Qibli. James M. Robinson, organizer of the manuscript publication team, sought to clarify the origin of the manuscripts through archaeological investigation of the find site and in Faw Qibli. Beginning in 1975, six seasons of work have been conducted in the village. Directors have included James M. Robinson, Torgny Säve Söderbergh, Bastiaan van Elderen (all sponsored by the Claremont Institute for Antiquity and Christianity), and Peter Grossmann (from the German Archaeological Institute, Cairo).

There is no doubt that the village of Faw Qibli is to be identified with ancient Pbow, headquarters of the fourth-century system of monasteries founded by Pachomius (c.297–346 CE). Over the six seasons of excavations, the outside walls and inner stylobates (low interior walls on which columns supporting the roof were mounted) of the basilica (dedicated in the year 459 CE) were recovered, along with the remains of earlier ecclesiastical structures. The final season (1989) succeeded in establishing the ground plans of an intermediate church as well as the site's earliest church building. The three churches made extensive use of limestone blocks taken from earlier Roman structures in the immediate area; mud brick, both burned and unfired, was the main building material for the walls and stylobates. In size, each succeeding structure was half again as long as its predecessor: the fifth-century basilica was about 78 meters (250 feet) in length, the intermediate church 56 meters (180 feet) long, and the earliest church building only 40 meters (130 feet) in extent.

These buildings are both historically and architecturally important. All the churches, beginning with the earliest one, were of five-aisled design with a narrow nave, and all apparently featured column-bearing stylobates, or low interior walls. Dating these buildings, and thus clarifying the chronology of Pachomius and the emergence of Egyptian monasticism, has proven difficult. Although the latest building, the so-called basilica, is firmly anchored by its dedication in 459 CE, only imprecise dates can be given to the other churches. Preliminary ceramic analyses point to a date in the late fourth century or early fifth century for the intermediate structure. Extensive destruction and robbing have left almost no indicators for the earliest building, though it is possible that this structure is the initial church built (330–346 CE) by Pachomius. In addition, there are hints of even earlier construction on the site, with wall fragments emerging that cannot be linked to any of the church structures.

The end of the site's occupation was not marked by violent destruction: neither traces of fire nor indications of earthquake damage were detected. Presumably the site was abandoned before the Persian invasion of the 620s CE and the Muslim invasion of the 640s CE; even less likely is the legendary destruction attributed to el-Hakim in the eleventh century. By the end of the sixth century, therefore, it is likely that Christian monasticism had fallen on hard times in Upper Egypt. Even less clear is the connection between the monastic community at Faw Qibli and the famous Nag Hammadi Gnostic codices; about a possible relationship, the archaeological evidence is silent.

BIBLIOGRAPHY

Bacht, Heinrich. *Das Vermächtnis des Ursprungs: Pachomius—der Mann und sein Werk.* 2 vols. Würzburg, 1983. The most comprehensive collection of materials and analyses relating to Pachomius and his monastic movement in fourth-century Egypt.

Goehring, James. *Chalcedonian Power Politics and the Demise of Pachomian Monasticism.* Institute for Antiquity and Christianity, Occasional Paper 15. Claremont, Calif., 1989.

Habachi, Labib. "Sixth Dynasty Discoveries in the Jabal al-Tarif." *Biblical Archaeologist* 42 (1979), 237–238.

Lease, Gary. *Traces of Early Egyptian Monasticism: The Faw Qibli Excavations.* Institute for Antiquity and Christianity, Occasional Paper 22. Claremont, Calif., 1991. The most detailed description of the Faw Qibli excavations currently available, with summaries of all six seasons, site photos, ground plan drawings, and full bibliography.

Petrie, W. M. F. *Diospolis Parva, the Cemeteries of Abadiyeh and Hu, 1898–99.* London, 1901. Describes his excavations of the Roman temple and the predynastic cemetery at Hou.

Robinson, James M. "Introduction." In *The Nag Hammadi Library in English,* edited by James M. Robinson. New York, 1977. An authoritative description of the discovery of the Nag Hammadi codices and their later fate, by the scholar who organized their publication.

Salih, Abu. *The Churches and Monasteries of Egypt and Some Neighboring Countries.* Translated by B. T. A. Evetts. Oxford, 1895. A goldmine of information on the architectural remains of Egyptian monasticism, by an early Arab chronicler; much of the evidence has since disappeared, leaving him its only witness.

GARY LEASE

NAG HAMMADI CODICES AND RELATED TEXTS. A cache of twelve papyrus codices and pages from a thirteenth was discovered in late 1945 by villagers a few kilometers from the Upper Egyptian town of Nag Hammadi. The collection as a whole has usually been dated to the fourth century CE, since dates from this period are found on a few of the scrap documentary papyri used to stiffen some of the leather covers. The codices contain a total of fifty-two tractates written in Coptic, many or possibly all of which are translations from Greek. Most of the Greek originals would probably date from the second or third century CE, and in some instances conceivably earlier—though the only work whose original is without question earlier than the second century CE is a tractate consisting of a section from Plato's *Republic* (588a–589b).

The Nag Hammadi books have stirred enormous interest, especially among historians of ancient Christianity and related movements in the Late Antique period, primarily because the contents represent mostly heterodox forms of Christian religious expression. Several contain versions of myths or religious doctrines that were reported and condemned by ancient Christian heresiologists such as Irenaeus of Lyons, Hippolytus of Rome, or Epiphanius of Salamis. Texts from Nag Hammadi often provide a rare (in some instances, the only) glimpse we have of writings from advocates of these heterodox teachings.

Most of the mythology and doctrine in these codices has conventionally been categorized under the rubric of "Gnosticism," or, as some prefer, "Gnosis." The Greek term *gnosis* ("knowledge") in this case refers to special, redeeming revelation about the true nature of humanity's relation to the divine and to the material world. Most definitions of "Gnosticism" add more specific features, such as a virulent anticosmic attitude; a distinction between the creator of the cosmos and the true God; a rejection of conventional ethics; or a deterministic soteriology involving a special race of humans who alone possess the secret *gnosis*, and who are destined to be saved because of their divine ancestry. However, modern debate about an adequate definition of "Gnosticism" or "Gnosis" has been fueled precisely by ongoing study of texts such as those from Nag Hammadi, since even the supposedly "Gnostic" writings in the collection manifest remarkable diversity on some of the alleged characteristics just mentioned. Therefore, the problematic category "Gnosticism" is avoided here, though attention may be called to certain recurring features that presumably are among the elements in these codices that stirred the interest of their fourth-century owners.

Demiurgical Myths of Origin. At least half of the codices in the collection contain at least one tractate that consists primarily of a myth of origins, recounting a theogony or a cosmogony and anthropogony, or all of these. And well over half of the tractates in the collection include either mythology or allusion to mythology that we might label "demiurgical"—meaning simply that the responsibility for being the fashioner (Gr., *demiurgos*) of the material cosmos is removed from the most transcendent God and assigned to one or more lower beings. Indeed, while there are several "non-demiurgical" works within the collection, all the codices seem to contain at least one demiurgical tractate.

Although it is a matter of continuing debate, some researchers consider demiurgical traditions such as these to be the product of pre-Christian speculative myth among Jewish heterodox circles, with Egypt alleged to have been among the primary locales for such Jewish heterodoxy. In any event, Christian versions of demiurgical speculation are certainly attested in several regions of the Roman Empire at least as early as the first half of the second century CE. Famous examples in Egyptian Christianity from that period include the teachers Basilides and his son Isidore, and Valentinus, who is said to have moved from his native Egypt to Rome in about 140 CE. Demiurgical speculations in Christian circles were attacked by critics as the false teaching of pseudo-intellectuals, and as adulterations of the gospel with pagan myth that were a threat to monotheism. Nevertheless, such cosmologies were popular within certain philosophical currents in the Hellenistic-Roman period, especially among Pythagorean and Platonic circles. For many Christian converts, a demiurgical worldview must therefore have seemed the most natural intellectual framework within which to organize and make sense of theological and scriptural traditions. It is clear that some deemed demiurgical myth a solution to questions of theodicy that confronted a stricter monotheism, since demiurgical myths removed from the transcendent God any direct responsibility for physical and moral imperfections in the material realm.

It was already known from heresiological literature that there was great variety in the myths resulting from demiurgical speculation. A general idea of the range in character and variety among demiurgical cosmogonies in the Nag Hammadi collection can be illustrated by reference to four examples.

The myth in the *Paraphrase of Shem* depicts a cosmogonic process beginning with three primordial roots: the infinite Light; the Spirit, portrayed as an intermediate power; and evil, ignorant Darkness. Darkness possesses Mind, which in the course of the myth seems to belong more naturally to the realm of Spirit. How Mind had come to be entangled in Darkness is not actually explained, but in any event, evil is accounted for in this du-

alistic myth as belonging to the nature of one of the original powers. The cosmogonic activity is initiated by an arousal of Darkness that is willed by the infinite Light, with the benign purpose of separating Mind from Darkness. This separation process is a fundamental theme woven throughout the myth, and it seems to express the human experience of mind/spirit struggling with an awareness of a more transcendent order while burdened by existence in the realm of nature. On the one hand, the cosmogonic process in this very obscure narrative seems to include negative effects, in that in some sense it requires the descent of Light and Spirit into Darkness. Various elements of the material cosmos are portrayed as products of impurity—i.e., sexual acts within the realm of aroused Darkness, involving the Womb of Nature and the entities begotten from her. On the other hand, the ultimate result of the process is revelation, a clarification of the distinction between Darkness and the higher elements, and the eventual separation of these. Shem, the visionary who reports the revelation in the tractate, is presented as the mythical ancestor of those who rejoice in the thought of the Light, walk in Faith, and are separated from Darkness.

The lengthy, untitled treatise known today as the *Tripartite Tractate* offers a monistic demiurgical myth that differs fundamentally from the cosmogony in the *Paraphrase of Shem*. In the *Tripartite Tractate*, there is only one first principle, the absolutely incomprehensible Father, whose transcendence is stressed with an elaborate negative theology. Yet, paradoxically, the unknown Father wishes to be known, and the myth recounts this self-revelation by means of the gradual reification of aspects of the Father's self-knowledge or image. The divine attributes are depicted mythically as personal entities emanating from the Father—the population, as it were, of divine "perfection" (Gr., *pleroma*). Even though the Father's essence is unsearchable, he breathes a spirit into all things that creates in them the idea of searching after the unknowable, so that they are drawn to him as if by a sweet aroma. One of the entities, the *logos* (Gr., "reason," "word"), in the impossible attempt to comprehend the Father, produces only imperfect shadows and copies of divine perfection, and this becomes the origin of all material and moral imperfection in the universe. The *logos* immediately realizes this tragic and arrogant fruit of what had been a benign and even divinely willed intent. Converted to proper humility, the *logos* is restored to perfection by divine grace and revelation. The escalating defects spawned by the original mistake must then be brought under control through the fashioning of the ordered cosmos, and a lower being—a demiurge, the Creator—is used by the *logos* for this purpose. The remainder of the myth describes the creation, constitution, and salvation of humanity. The diverse levels of perfection or imperfection in human moral character, including patterns of acceptance or rejection of divine revelation, are accounted for as products mirroring the earlier acts of the *logos*. The paradoxical tension between the incomprehensibility of the Father and the Father's desire to be known is integral to the theodicy of the myth, since the dynamics of the myth render precisely the highest values—love for and knowledge of God—as the inadvertent catalysts of evil.

The demiurgical cosmogony in the *Apocryphon of John* is similarly monistic in its depiction of an ineffable Monad or Spirit from whom all subsequent multiplicity has emanated, beginning with the unfolding of the realm of divine perfection. The mythic drama reveals a rather different cast of specific characters, though some of the plot is parallel. Instead of the *logos*, the *Apocryphon of John* has a similarly ambiguous character, Wisdom, whose presumptuous behavior results in the production of an imperfect image of divinity, a beastlike ruler or archon named Ialdabaoth. Unlike the rather sympathetically portrayed demiurge in the *Tripartite Tractate*, who serves as instrument of the *logos*, Ialdabaoth in the *Apocryphon of John* is a rebellious, foolish, and despicable figure. He creates the material cosmos with its various heavens unaware that he has done so in subconscious imitation of a higher, truly divine realm. He populates the heavens with subordinate powers who are his offspring. In his arrogance and ignorance he boasts that he is the highest God, but he is corrected by a revelation from above of the image of perfect divinity. The creation of Adam by Ialdabaoth and his powers is a failed attempt to imitate, capture, and control this image. This myth explains both beauty and imperfection in the material order, while distancing true divinity from any direct responsibility for what is evil. There is also an interest, more direct and detailed than in the *Paraphrase of Shem* and the *Tripartite Tractate*, to rewrite elements of the Genesis narrative, so that shifting the reference to Ialdabaoth removes difficulties otherwise arising from scripture's occasional anthropomorphic depictions of God (as vengeful, jealous, changeable, etc.). According to the *Apocryphon of John*, divine providence has seen to it that humanity carries the spiritual image of the divine, which can be awakened by revelation and restored to perfection.

Finally, one may compare the demiurgical myth in another untitled work from Nag Hammadi, often referred to today with the title *On the Origin of the World*. This lengthy and complex work contains many similarities to the cosmogonic myth in the *Apocryphon of John*, with a cast including some of the same mythic characters, such as Wisdom, Ialdabaoth, and some of the other cosmic archons. There is also an extensive rewriting of narrative episodes and elements from the early chapters of Genesis. But there are also numerous differences from the *Apocryphon of John* in details and in the structure of the cosmogony. Among the most interesting is that in *On the Origin of the World* there is a striking rupture within the ranks of the archons. One of Ialdabaoth's offspring, Sabaoth, responds positively to divine revelation, condemns his father, and is rewarded by being enthroned in a heaven superior to Ialdabaoth. This conveys a more complicated interpretation of the relation between true divinity and the creator God of more orthodox Judaism and Christianity. Not all of the demiurgical powers are completely ignorant and hostile to truth, and in this way the myth accounts for the mixture of justice and injustice in human experience, and of truth and error in religious traditions.

Prehistory and Destinies of Souls/Spirits. The soteriology of several forms of ancient Christianity and Judaism included the theme of the restoration of a primordial condition possessed by the ancestral first humans, or the attainment of an even more perfect state. Most Christian teaching came to express this by reference to a future resurrection of the body. By contrast, the more common theme among the Nag Hammadi tractates is a return of souls or spirits to a primordial state, or to a place from whence they came, or were sown, into the world to dwell in the body. Several variations are represented, including the notion of multiple reincarnations of souls until they have a chance to accept or reject the revealed truth, as is found in the *Apocryphon of John*. Often these works refer to spiritual humanity as a "seed" sown into the material realm from the divine realm—for example, by the Father, or Christ, or the Spirit, or by the primordial divine Adam belonging to the immaterial realm of perfection. In the latter instances the perfect Adam, and his offspring Seth, are imagined as spiritual entities in the image of the true God, the prototype imitated by the demiurgical powers in their creation of material humanity.

It is typical of most of these texts that the salvation brought by the restoration of the spiritual seed to perfection is achieved by only a portion of humanity. Human society is frequently referred to as consisting of different categories of persons: the spiritual versus the fleshly or material, with the psychical or "soulish" sometimes mentioned as an intermediate category. Many interpreters, both ancient heresiologists and modern scholars, have viewed these as anthropologies entailing deterministic theories of salvation. This may have been true in some cases, but it is not clear that the language was intended deterministically by all or even most of these authors. In any event, the nature and mechanisms involved in the "sowing" of the spiritual seed are understood in diverse ways. For example, there are writings in which this appears to refer to a spiritual rebirth effected by rituals such as baptism or chrism. In other works, it would seem that the "seed" is viewed as a potential that is present in all humanity at birth but comes to maturation only in some individuals, depending on their response to revelation.

Notions of the preexistence of the soul, its fall into the body, and its hope for ascent are found even in some of the tractates that are not demiurgical by the definition mentioned earlier—for example, *Authoritative Teaching* and *Exegesis on the Soul,* both of which are extended treatments of the theme of the soul's descent into the material world and her eventual ascent and restoration. This kind of anthropology and soteriology would have seemed more natural than the idea of a resurrection of the body to many in the Greco-Roman world, especially among circles influenced by philosophical traditions such as Platonism.

Literary Genres and Revelation. It is notable that most of the literary genres represented among the Nag Hammadi writings imply a claim to some special revelatory authority. There are several exceptions to this—for example, in writings such as the *Tripartite Tractate* and *On the Origin of the World* that have the more straightforward form of theological treatises or discussions. However, the majority of the Nag Hammadi tractates are in other forms: a long discourse allegedly delivered by a divine revealer or teacher (e.g., Christ, Seth); a dialogue between such a revealer and a special individual or group (e.g., Christ and John); an account of a heavenly ascent or vision experienced either by an ancient worthy (e.g., Adam, Shem, Melchizedek) or by an apostolic authority figure (e.g., Paul, James, Peter); a revelation supposed to have been written down in an earlier generation (e.g., by Adam, by Seth) to be kept secret from the unworthy; or some genre that contains more than one of the above features.

The implications of these literary genres for corresponding social history are not entirely clear. From the presence of themes of special revelation and secrecy, it might be inferred that this literature was typically the product of exclusive, intensely secretive conventicles. However, many of the secrecy motifs have to do with a truth imagined to have been secret in the *past,* but now revealed for anyone willing to accept it. Such genres may often be an indication less of social concealment of information than of literary strategies for legitimizing religious innovations.

Religious Innovation and Religious Movements. The Nag Hammadi collection is made up of remnants from a lively history of multiple religious innovations in late antiquity. It is not always certain whether a given text expresses the eccentric speculations of an individual innovator, or summarizes the doctrine of a distinct social group or new religious movement. It is possible to classify portions of the Nag Hammadi collection according to common traditions. In some instances, such traditions apparently corresponded to identifiable social groups or movements, even though current evidence hardly permits reconstruction of a true social history of these groups.

The clearest case can be made that certain tractates belong to the Valentinian Christian tradition, as in the instance of the *Tripartite Tractate.* More than a half-dozen tractates from Nag Hammadi contain mythic themes and terminology that seem to derive from circles associated with the name of Valentinus. The precise contours of his own teaching remain rather obscure, but the mythological speculations of teachers allegedly influenced by him are elaborated by the ancient heresiologists. According to the latter, Valentinian tradition was not uniform, but rather inclined to lively innovation and variety, and the Valentinian evidence from Nag Hammadi supports that impression.

Another possible grouping within the collection involves a dozen or so writings sometimes termed "Sethian" by modern researchers. The precise label is less important than the fact that these works manifest numerous overlapping relationships in their mythic patterns, names of mythic characters, and other special terminology. For example, several, like the *Apocryphon of John,* portray a lower creator named Ialdabaoth. There must have been social connections and shared histories of some sort accounting for the similarities. However, there are also dramatic variations among the "Sethian" texts. While the *Apocryphon of John* is a heterodox Christian text in the form of a post-Resurrection dialogue between Christ and the apostle John, other writings with "Sethian" mythic themes or jargon contain no features that are clearly Christian. One such subgroup of "Sethian" texts is closely related to philosophical speculation known to have been in fashion in the third century CE among acquaintances of the Neoplatonic philosopher Plotinus, after the latter had moved from Egypt to Rome, and the tractate titles (e.g., *Zostrianos, Allogenes*) even match some of those reported by Plotinus's student and biographer Porphyry to have been the focus of debate and criticism in Plotinian circles.

Another case of texts that represent an identifiable tradition involves a group of three tractates (all in one codex) belonging to the non-Christian Hermetic tradition. But more than a third of the writings in the Nag Hammadi collection are not easily classified with any special tradition or attested sectarian movement.

Provenance. If the Nag Hammadi manuscripts mostly date from about the mid-fourth century CE, it remains a matter of conjecture and debate who produced and owned the codices, and why they were eventually buried. Some scholars have believed that the codices bear witness to a period of pre-orthodox diversity in ascetic communities in Upper Egypt that were associated with the fourth-century monastic founder Pachomius. Wording in some of the colophons, references to monks in some of the scrap papyri from the bindings, and the prominence of ascetic themes in many tractates are among the evidence invoked in support of the hypothesis that the codices were part of the library of some sort of heterodox Christian monastic group, Pachomian or not. Several factors (multiple copies of certain tractates, paleographic and codicological evidence) indicate that the surviving collection is secondary, built out of earlier subcollections that may have been combined as new members joined a monastic commune and brought their books with them. The books may have been buried during the fourth or fifth century (or later?) to protect them from destruction during efforts to purge monastic and other libraries of heterodox materials.

Related Works. The Coptic papyrus Codex Berolinensis 8502 (c. fifth century CE) contains copies of two works also in the Nag Hammadi collection: the *Apocryphon of John* and the *Wisdom of Jesus Christ*. These tractates are bracketed by two others, an opening revelation dialogue, the *Gospel of Mary*, and the *Act of Peter*, a tale that extols the value of virginity. The Coptic parchment Codex Askewianus (fourth or fifth century) is commonly referred to by the title *Pistis Sophia* ("Faith Wisdom"). Most of its content is in the form of post-Resurrection dialogues between Jesus and the disciples, and entails revelation about the fate of souls, of whom fallen and repentant Wisdom is portrayed as the Mother/prototype, and about cosmic powers. Codex Brucianus is a designation given to what seem to be the remains of at least two independent Coptic papyrus codices of uncertain date. One of these is an untitled treatise whose mythology is akin to the so-called "Sethian" mythology among the Nag Hammadi collection. The remaining leaves of Codex Brucianus are conventionally referred to as the *Books of Jeu*. A revelation dialogue between the resurrected Jesus and his disciples presents a complex myth, complete with diagrams, about the origin and structure of the transcendent world, and the disciples are initiated into the ritual mysteries, allowing their souls to ascend through these realms.

Though they probably represent the tastes of very small minorities, the Nag Hammadi collection and related manuscripts such as those just mentioned attest to a perduring influence and evolution of heterodox mythologies that had been part of the fabric of Egyptian Christianity since at least the early second century CE.

BIBLIOGRAPHY

The Facsimile Edition of the Nag Hammadi Codices. Published under the Auspices of the Department of Antiquities of the Arab Republic of Egypt in conjunction with the United Nations Educational, Scientific and Cultural Organizations. 12 vols. Leiden, 1972–1984. The standard facsimile edition of the Nag Hammadi manuscripts.

Layton, Bentley. *The Gnostic Scriptures: A New Translation with Annotations and Introductions.* Garden City, 1987. Excellent annotated translations of selected Nag Hammadi writings, and sources from Christian heresiologists.

Layton, Bentley, ed. *The Rediscovery of Gnosticism.* 2 vols. Supplements to *Numen*, 41. Leiden, 1980–1981. Papers from a seminal conference, including seminars focused specifically on Valentinian and "Sethian" traditions.

Ménard, Jacques-É., Paul-Hubert Poirier, and Michel Roberge, eds. *Bibliothèque Copte de Nag Hammadi. Section "Textes"; Section "Études"; Section "Concordances."* Québec and Louvain-Paris, 1977– . Appearing in this important series are editions of Nag Hammadi and many related texts, with French translation and commentary; and an invaluable Coptic concordance of the Nag Hammadi codices.

Pearson, Birger A. *Gnosticism, Judaism, and Egyptian Christianity.* Studies in Antiquity and Christianity. Minneapolis, 1990. An important collection of essays with special interest in the relevance of Nag Hammadi materials for the history of Judaism and Christianity in Egypt.

Pearson, Birger A., and James E. Goehring, eds. *The Roots of Egyptian Christianity.* Studies in Antiquity and Christianity. Philadelphia, 1992. Crucial reading for any study of early Egyptian Christianity and the interrelated traditions from which it developed.

Robinson, James M., and Richard Smith, eds. *The Nag Hammadi Library in English.* 3d ed. San Francisco and Leiden, 1988. A one-volume English translation of the Nag Hammadi collection, and the *Gospel of Mary* and the *Act of Peter* from Codex Berolinensis 8502.

Rudolph, Kurt. *Gnosis: The Nature and History of Gnosticism.* Translated by R. McL. Wilson. San Francisco and Edinburgh, 1983. Combines a phenomenological discussion of the nature of "Gnosis" with a historical treatment of various sectarian forms.

Schmidt, Carl, and Violet MacDermot eds. *The Books of Jeu and the Untitled Text in the Bruce Codex.* Nag Hammadi Studies 13. Leiden, 1978. Coptic text and English translation of Codex Brucianus. The major English critical editions/translations of Nag Hammadi tractates have also been appearing in the series Nag Hammadi Studies (or more recently, Nag Hammadi and Manichaean Studies).

Schmidt, Carl, and Violet MacDermot eds. *Pistis Sophia.* Nag Hammadi Studies 9. Leiden, 1978. Coptic text and English translation of Codex Askewianus.

Scholer, David M., ed. *Nag Hammadi Bibliography 1948–69.* Nag Hammadi Studies 1. Leiden, 1971.

Scholer, David M., ed. *Nag Hammadi Bibliography 1970–94.* Nag Hammadi and Manichaean Studies 32. Leiden, 1997. The two volumes by Scholer are the most comprehensive bibliographies on this subject area. Includes sections on "Gnosticism" in general, individual traditions, each codex in the Nag Hammadi collection, and the Berlin 8502, Askew, and Bruce codices. Continuing updates are published annually in the journal *Novum Testamentum*.

Tardieu, Michel, ed. *Écrits gnostiques: Codex du Berlin.* Source Gnostiques et Manichéennes 1. Paris, 1984. An important introduction, translation, and extensive commentary on the Berlin 8502 codex.

Tardieu, Michel, and Jean-Daniel Dubois. *Introduction à la littérature gnostique I: Histoire du mot "gnostique"; Instruments de travail; Col-*

lections retrouvées avant 1945. Invitations au christianisme ancien. Paris, 1986. A valuable discussion of relevant manuscript and patristic sources available prior to the Nag Hammadi discovery.

Till, Walter, ed. *Die gnostischen Schriften des koptischen Papyrus Berolinensis 8502.* 2d ed. by Hans-Martin Schenke. Texte und Untersuchungen zur Geschichte der altchristlichen Literatur 60. Berlin, 1972. A revised edition of the *editio princeps* of Codex Berolensis 8502. The principal German editions of Nag Hammadi tractates, with translations and commentary, have also been appearing in the Texte und Untersuchungen series.

Williams, Michael Allen. *Rethinking "Gnosticism".* Princeton, 1996. Argues that the category "gnosticism" has become an obstacle, because of prevalent stereotypes and misconceptions, to an adequate understanding of texts and traditions such as those evidenced by Nag Hammadi.

MICHAEL A. WILLIAMS

NAMES. To the ancient Egyptians, names were considered ritually and magically potent, a vital part of the individual. A person could therefore have multiple names expressing different aspects of his or her personality. Kings had at least five names, corresponding to the five-part titulary, and are known to have changed their names to suit changes in their religious or administrative policies. Gods frequently had many names designating their different manifestations, and major gods and goddesses had secret names that were unknown even to other deities. Chapter 142 of the *Book of Going Forth by Day* (*Book of the Dead*), "the spell for knowing the names of Osiris," lists more than one hundred names of Osiris. Likewise, a well-known New Kingdom story describes a successful attempt by Isis to learn the secret name of Re.

Survival after death depended in part on having one's name remembered and repeated, and funerary texts ask visitors to speak the name of the deceased. When inscribing funerary monuments for relatives, people credit themselves with "causing his/her name to live." Enemies, on the other hand, were designated primarily through derogatory epithets, causing their names to remain unspoken. The destruction of a name could deprive its holder of both power and eternal existence. Unpopular or controversial rulers could therefore suffer the deliberate defacement of their monuments or the omission of their names from king lists. The names of enemies, dangerous animals, and foreigners were written on figurines and other symbolic objects that were ritually destroyed in order to render the named entities powerless.

Composition of Names. Egyptian names could be composed of single words, phrases, or complete sentences, all of which had meanings independent of their use as names. The largest category of names, called theophoric names, includes those describing attributes or characteristics of deities (e.g., Amenhotpe, "Amun is content," or Djehutynakht, "Thoth is powerful"), or establishing the relationship between a deity and the holder of the name (e.g., Sobekemsaf, "Sobek is his protection"; Meryre, "Beloved of Re"; or Ankhesenpaaten, "she lives for the Aten"). A second popular category, basilophoric names, describes attributes of the king, often in the form of a complete sentence. While private people were rarely named directly after gods, it was not unusual for them to be named after kings, especially in periods of strong central authority. Prophetic names could relate to the circumstances of the bearer's birth or express wishes for health and well-being. Other names mention characteristics of the child, the deity responsible for facilitating the birth, or the time of year in which it occurred. Names could describe ideal personal attributes, such as Meru, "beloved," Nakht, "strong," and Nofret, "beautiful." In some cases, such as when a blind man is named "the seer," names appear to have been chosen deliberately to contradict a physical abnormality. Often, children were named after family members, so that the same names remained in families for generations.

History of Names. Because their composition varied over time, names show distinct forms in each major period of Egyptian history. Herman Ranke traces this development in *Die ägyptischen Personennamen* (Glückstadt, 1935–1977). Evidence for the Early Dynastic period suggests that theophoric names in the form of sentences and phrases (such as Iri-netjer, "one whom the god created," or Ankh-netjer, "may the god live") were particularly common. Early Dynastic names repeatedly include the generic designation "the god" (*ntr*), along with a variety of local gods, as well as the *ka.* Neith is especially popular. Re first appears in royal names of the second dynasty, after which he enters the repertory of private names.

Theophoric names remain popular in the Old Kingdom, a period in which many preserved names invoke Ptah of Memphis. Other regional gods and goddesses also appear, as well as the *ka,* although funerary deities are largely absent. Personal names describe the gods with such adjectives as "great" (*'3, wr*) and "powerful" (*wr*), or express the relationship between the individual and the gods. Basilophoric names are also numerous, incorporating many of the same phrases used in theophoric names. In contrast to the Early Dynastic period, the Old Kingdom witnesses an increase in purely secular names referring to attributes of the child, such as hair color, birth order, and personality traits. Old Kingdom names, reflecting the grammar of the period, tend to omit the first-person pronoun, as in Mereruka, "[my] *ka* is beloved."

From the early Old Kingdom, private individuals are often designated by a pair of names: the major name (the *rn '3*), which is typically theophoric or basilophoric, and a shorter name (the *rn nḏs*), often an abbreviation of the longer one. Later, the *rn nḏs* is replaced by what was known as the "good name" (*rn nfr*), which seems originally to have been acquired some time after birth; it expresses the characteristics and status of the name-holder. It appears to have lost this meaning by the end of the Old Kingdom, however, and largely drops out of use altogether in the Middle Kingdom.

The Middle Kingdom is characterized by a great number and variety of names, many newly introduced. While theophoric names remain extremely common, significant changes in their composition occur, and Amun begins to play a dominant role. Previously, only kings could be named "son of" a deity, but private citizens begin adopting such names during the First Intermediate Period. Meanwhile, the Old Kingdom designation "belonging to" a god or goddess becomes rare. Private people are named "son" or "daughter" of kings and nomarchs as well. Names of the form "beloved of" a god, introduced in the sixth dynasty, increase in frequency dramatically. Basilophoric names are popular, especially during the period of strong royal authority in the twelfth dynasty, when private citizens are named after deceased and ruling kings; the names Montuhotep, Antef, Amenemhet, and Senwosret occur repeatedly. Names of purely secular content reach their peak in the Middle Kingdom. New categories of names refer to birthplace, lineage, and ancestry. Particularly common are those in which parents and other relatives are said to be revived in the newborn. For the first time, names such as "the Near Eastern" (*ʿ3m*) designate their holders as foreign.

No dramatic break in the composition of names occurs at the beginning of the New Kingdom—changes are not clearly discernible until the late eighteenth dynasty. With the appearance of nonliterary Late Egyptian in official inscriptions after the Amarna period, the definite articles occur regularly within names such as Paenamun, "The one belonging to Amun." Personal piety is very apparent, especially during the Ramessid period, and a wealth of new theophoric names is found, often incorporating the name of the state god Amun. While children continue to be named "son" or "daughter" of a deity—now *šri(t)*, "child," as opposed to the earlier *s3(t)*—they are also more likely to be called the god's *b3k(t)*, "servant." Various theophoric names describe the gods themselves, while others invoke their beneficence toward the newborn. Particularly popular are variations of "born of" a deity, such as Thutmose ("born of Thoth") and Ramose ("born of Re"). Similar names refer to the king, and now the queen as well. With Egypt's military expansion, new forms of names focus on the king's strength (*nḫt*) and other warlike attributes. Secular names fade from popularity after the eighteenth dynasty but never disappear altogether. Several new types are created, including names referring to the attractive appearance of the child (e.g., Nefertiti, "the

beautiful one has come") and even the profession of the father (e.g., Satepehu, "son of the overseer of oxen").

In the Third Intermediate and Late periods, many familiar names disappear. The majority of names are theophoric, designating the child as "given by" or "belonging to" a deity (e.g., Padiamun, "the one whom Amun has given," or Paenamun, "the one belonging to Amun"). Names referring to the individual as the "son," "daughter," or "servant" of a god or goddess continue into the Greco-Roman period. Complex new names in the form of sentences also occur, referring to both personal piety and mythological subjects, and often attributing the birth of a child to divine oracles (e.g., Djedamuniwefankh, "Amun decrees that he shall live"). Basilophoric names often refer to earlier kings such as Amenemhet III and Ramesses II. Such names, which may praise the king or state that the child belongs to the king, are particularly popular during the twenty-sixth dynasty. Several new secular names also appear.

Relatively few new name types appear during the Greco-Roman period. Theophoric names continue to follow established patterns, referring most often to Horus, although many of the most common names (such as Petosiris) invoke Osiris. As in the Late period, children are often named directly after deities. The names of foreign rulers are not used in personal names, but kings from the powerful twenty-sixth dynasty and even earlier are sometimes mentioned. Some new forms of secular names appear, referring to personal characteristics, but there is less variety than in earlier periods.

[*See also* Titulary.]

BIBLIOGRAPHY

Baines, John. "Society, Morality, and Religious Practice." In *Ancient Egyptian Religion: Gods, Myths and Personal Practice*, edited by Byron E. Shafer, pp. 176–178. Ithaca, 1991. Discusses theophoric names, their meaning, and their relationship to personal religion and piety.

Beckerath, Jürgen von. *Handbuch der ägyptischen Königsnamen*. Berlin, 1984. Handbook of royal names and titles from Early Dynastic through Roman times.

Beckerath, Jürgen von. "Königsnamen und -titel." In *Lexikon der Ägyptologie*, 3: 540–556. Wiesbaden, 1980. Analysis and list of royal names associated with the five-part titulary.

Hornung, Erik. *Conceptions of God in Ancient Egypt: The One and the Many*. Translated by John Baines. Ithaca, 1982. Analyzes theophoric names of the Early Dynastic period and their meaning.

Lüddeckens, Erich, et al. *Demotisches Namenbuch*. Wiesbaden, 1980. Major collection and analysis of Demotic names.

Posener, Georges. "Sur l'attribution d'un nom à un enfant." *Revue d'Égyptologie* 22 (1977), 204–205. Discusses the theory that the child's name was uttered by the parents at the time of his or her birth.

Ranke, Herman. *Die ägyptischen Personennamen*. 3 vols. Glückstadt, 1935–1977. The major work on ancient Egyptian names, including a comprehensive list of names, thematic groups of names, and analysis.

Silverman, David. P., ed. *Ancient Egypt*. New York, 1997.
Vernus, Pascal. "Name," "Namengebung," "Namensbildung," and "Namenstilgung." In *Lexikon der Ägyptologie*, 4: 320–341. Wiesbaden, 1982. Thorough encyclopedic treatment of Egyptian names, with relevant bibliography.

DENISE M. DOXEY

NAPATA (Old Egyptian, *Npt, Npy*; Meroitic, *Napa*; Greek, *ta Napata*), an important ancient city in Upper Nubia (Kush), 960 kilometers (600 miles) up the Nile River from Aswan and 20 kilometers (12.5 miles) downstream from the Fourth Cataract, near present-day Karima, Sudan (18°32′N, 31°49′E). Napata's chief landmark is the 102-meter- (335-foot-) high sandstone butte known today as Gebel Barkal. Napata was the prime river crossing on the direct overland trade route that connected the regions of the Fifth Cataract and the Third. During the New Kingdom, Napata was the uppermost permanent settlement in the Egyptian Nubian empire, lying in the southernmost district, called Karoy *(Kȝry)*, and it became the chief Nubian seat of the Egyptian state god Amun. Later, during and after the twenty-fifth dynasty, it became the cult center and sometime capital of the Egyptianized kingdom of Kush.

The Egyptians had first occupied Napata during the eighteenth dynasty reign of Thutmose III (r. 1504–1452 BCE), probably following the final overthrow of the Kushite monarchy at Kerma. According to his Barkal stela, Thutmose established his frontier there, built a fortress called "Repelling the Foreigners," and identified Gebel Barkal as a residence of Amun. The stela, addressed to the local inhabitants, implies a preexisting town, which had possibly been an outpost of the Kerma kingdom. Kerma sherds have been found at the site in unstratified conditions; and Neolithic and Protohistoric ("Pre-Kerma") sherds indicate even earlier settlements. Napata is the first named on the Amada Stela of Amenhotpe II (r. 1454–1419 BCE), who claims to have hung a slain Syrian prince from its walls.

The Egyptians called Gebel Barkal alternately *Pȝ Ḏw-wʿb* ("The Pure Mountain") and *Nswt* (or *Nst)-Tȝwy* ("Thrones [or "Throne"] of the Two Lands"), thus identifying it as the source of Amun's most ancient epithet "Lord of the Thrones of the Two Lands." They attached cosmogonic significance to the mountain because of its freestanding, 74 meters (250-foot) high pinnacle, which appeared to them variously as an erect phallus and as a royal *uraeus* (the rearing cobra). The mountain, thus, was seen both as a home of the creator god and as a primary source of kingship. The pharaohs of both the eighteenth dynasty and the nineteenth claimed to derive a part of their royal authority from this Amun; by the eighth cen-

tury BCE, the kings of the neo-Kushite state at Napata would justify their rule over Egypt by the claimed primacy of the kingship given to them by this god.

The Barkal sanctuary was developed in the fifteenth century BCE, under Thutmose III and IV, possibly over a preexisting Kerma sanctuary, but under Akhenaten (r. 1372–1355 BCE), efforts were made to destroy it and the cult. It was rebuilt under Tutankhamun and/or Horemheb in the later fourteenth century BCE, massively enlarged by Sety I and Ramesses II at the turn of the thirteenth century BCE. Subsequently, all evidence for Egyptian activity ceases at Napata, and in the twentieth dynasty, the Egyptians apparently abandoned the site. No trace of the New Kingdom town has been found, but the ledges at nearby Hillet el-Arab are honeycombed with plain rock tombs of probable New Kingdom date.

Napata was revived in the mid-eighth century BCE by the Nubian chiefs buried at nearby el-Kurru. Alara and Kashta built a temple and a palace of mud brick. With the late eighth-century BCE conquest of Upper Egypt by Piya, the city briefly became an imperial capital, and the great Amun temple of the New Kingdom (B 500) was fully restored, in stone. The king's son and third successor, Taharqa, added some new temples (B 200, 300) and developed, on the opposite bank, the important suburbs of Sanam Abu Dom and Nuri. At Nuri, Taharqa built his own pyramid and established a royal cemetery that would be used by nineteen of his successors and their queens until the fourth century BCE.

After the twenty-fifth dynasty's ouster from Egypt by Assyria in 663 BCE, it continued *in absentia* to claim rule over Egypt by the authority of the Napatan god. Thus in 593 BCE, Napata was attacked and ravaged by the Egyptian army of Psamtik II, which forced the move of the Kushite court to Meroë, some 250 kilometers (160 miles) to the southeast.

The Barkal sanctuary was maintained throughout Napatan and Meroitic times. During the third and first centuries BCE, the area west of the mountain was developed as a royal cemetery; in the early first century CE, the sanctuary underwent its last major restoration and enlargement. This activity was doubtless prompted by the second destruction of Napata, in 24 BCE, by the Roman general Petronius. The only urban remains of Napata yet recovered belong to this period. Throughout the history of Kush, Napata remained an important cult center and site for both coronations and royal burials.

BIBLIOGRAPHY

Dunham, Daws. *The Barkal Temples*. Boston, 1970.
Kendall, Timothy. "Kings of the Sacred Mountain: Napata and the Kushite Twenty-fifth Dynasty of Egypt." In *Sudan: Ancient Kingdoms of the Nile*, edited by Dietrich Wildung, pp. 161–171. Paris and New York, 1997.

Reisner, George A. "The Barkal Temples in 1916." *Journal of Egyptian Archaeology* 4 (1917), 213–227.

Reisner, George A. "The Barkal Temples in 1916 (Continued)." *Journal of Egyptian Archaeology* 5 (1918), 99–112.

Reisner, George A. "The Barkal Temples in 1916 (Continued)." *Journal of Egyptian Archaeology* 6 (1920), 247–264.

Reisner, George A., and M. B. Reisner. "Inscribed Monuments from Gebel Barkal." *Zeitschrift für die Altestementliche Wissenschaft* 66 (1931), 76–100.

TIMOTHY KENDALL

NAQADA (also Nagada in local dialect), a modern town 27 kilometers (18 miles) north of Luxor on the western bank of the Nile River, midway between Qurna and Dendara, and opposite Qena. Site surveys near this town during the last decade of the nineteenth century by Jacques J. M. de Morgan, W. M. Flinders Petrie, and J. E. Quibell led to the discovery of several sites. They were from the time that predated the emergence of the first Egyptian dynasties, near a first dynasty *mastaba*, a small pyramid, two *tumuli*, and a number of Predynastic cemeteries. The region also included some twelfth dynasty tombs and the Nubt temple.

The large *mastaba* (54 × 27 meters/165 × 85 feet) is 2.4 kilometers (1.5 miles) south of Naqada, on the edge of the desert. It has a niched, palace-façade and includes many subsidiary rooms with numerous grave offerings. Small ivory and wood labels, as well as seal impressions, bear the names of Hor-Aha and Queen Neithhotep. This first dynasty *mastaba* is associated with a cemetery of the same period; however, the majority of the nearby cemeteries in an area that extends from Danfiq in the south to Ballas in the north belong to the Predynastic period. Various types of pottery from those cemeteries were identified on the basis of surface finish, form, and decoration (e.g., rough, polished red, black-topped red, white cross-lined, wavy-handled, decorated). Petrie developed an ingenious scheme, called seriation, to arrange the tombs in chronological order (by sequence dating). His approach was then widely employed by archaeologists for the relative dating of ceramics. In seriation, Petrie used a sequence of pottery types to establish two ceramic assemblage zones (which are often referred to as "cultures"). The earliest culture, called Naqada I (the Amratian) generally lacks wavy handled and decorated pottery but has a high frequency of black-topped red ware with characteristic white cross-lined bodies. This culture was succeeded by Naqada II (the Gerzean), which has a relatively high rate of rough pottery, but is marked by the presence of decorated and wavy-handled pots. A third culture (Naqada III), with characteristic "Late" pottery (a melange of pottery types that includes hard "orange," buff, or pink ware) was also recognized in the region. The sequence, modified by Wer-

ner Kaiser and others, is still widely used. Radiocarbon age determinations have shown that Naqada I ceramics from settlement sites in the region date from 3800 to 3650 BCE. Naqada II followed with a time span from 3600 to 3300 BCE. Elsewhere in the Nile Valley, Naqada III ceramics dated from 3300 to 3000 BCE. Near Assyut, north of Qena, sites associated with a ceramic assemblage zone called the Badarian revealed the presence of much earlier Predynastic sites, which dated to c.4400 or 4200 BCE. At Naqada, some Badarian potsherds were included in an early occupation of the Naqada I zone, confirming continuities with the earlier Badarian style.

In addition to cemeteries, in the nineteenth century de Morgan examined the remains of Predynastic settlements at Tukh (north of Naqada), which he referred to as kitchen middens. A new survey of the region has revealed numerous settlements, some with clearly stratified sequences. Excavations of settlement areas by Hassan (1984, 1985) provided not only the first coherent radiocarbon chronology of the Naqada cultures but also systematic information on settlement patterns, lithic artifacts, ceramics, and, most significantly, the subsistence and economy of Predynastic times.

The majority of Predynastic sites in the Naqada region belong to Naqada I. The sites range in area from a few thousand square meters to 3 hectares. They represent the overlapping occupations of scores of huts in small villages and hamlets lining the edge of the former floodplain. The settlements probably housed between 50 and 250 persons. Small postholes and the wooden stub of a post suggested flimsy wickerwork around a frame of wooden posts. The abundance of rubble and mud clumps indicated that many dwellings were constructed from the local Nile mud and desert surface rubble. The houses contained hearths and storage pits. In some cases, graves were dug into the floor of houses. Trash areas were interspersed with domestic dwellings. The houses included animal enclosures (*zeribas*), as was indicated by thick layers of dung. The faunal remains, studied by Achilles Gautier, indicated that the Naqadans herded and ate cattle, sheep/goats, and pigs. By Naqada I, hunting had become a minor subsistence activity; however, fishing and fowling, which were previously practiced in the Nile Valley, were still important. The meat supplemented a cereal diet that was based on the cultivation of barley and wheat, as was revealed by the paleobotanical investigations of Wilma Wetterstrom. The lithic artifacts from Early Naqada sites, studied by Diane Holmes, showed a high frequency of burins, scrapers, notchers, and some perforators. They also included *grand perçoirs*, planes, bifacial tools, concave-based projectiles, and axes. The axes are distinctive.

Naqada II ceramics were found in only two sites: South Town and North Town. The ceramic assemblage zone Naqada mostly belonged to Kaiser's (1957) Naqada IIcd. With the exception of sickle blades, the lithic assemblage was very similar to that of the earlier Naqada sites. The pottery, however, was markedly different. South Town and North Town also showed a high density of artifacts that indicated very small early towns. A systemic survey of South Town, which contained evidence of rectangular mud-brick houses and fortifications, as identified by Petrie and Quibell, revealed that the settlement began closer to the edge of the desert, in the southwestern corner of the site, and that Nile floods destroyed the eastern sector of the site that overlooked the floodplain. North Town also grew from an initial small settlement—first to the south and then to the north—where Naqada III ceramics were recognized. The rarity of Naqada II sites, as compared with the earlier sites, may be related to a shift of settlement location away from the desert margin, where the early Nagada sites were located, and closer to the inner part of the Nile floodplain. The reasons for that shift were presumably due to the decline in Nile flood levels at that time.

The Predynastic peoples of the Naqada region buried their dead in cemeteries in the low desert, adjacent to their settlements. Mortuary analyses showed evidence of a gradual, increasing social hierarchy and a shift in sociopolitical organization from a "chiefdom" to a provincial state society. The tombs yielded a rich variety of grave goods, including copper objects, flint knives, amulets, stone vessels, pendants, hairpins, combs, and slate palettes. Only a few graves contained large numbers of special goods, suggesting a segment of a rising elite (administrative/religious). By Naqada II, the elite were buried in a separate cemetery. The frequency of grave goods also suggested a group of well-to-do townspeople. As revealed by seal impressions from an Early Dynastic cemetery, a part of the prosperity of Naqada was perhaps due to trade in gold, a material recovered from the mines of the Wadi Hamammat across the river.

The rise of the local Naqada elite was associated with the emergence of a religious ideology linked with mortuary rituals, as was indicated by the standard placement of the dead; they were buried with their heads to the south, facing west. The iconography of the Gerzean pottery (Naqada II) and a variety of figurines from mud and vegetable substances suggested that the incipient ideology included notions of female-male duality, associated with concepts of life, death, and resurrection.

BIBLIOGRAPHY

Adams, B. *Predynastic Egypt.* London, 1988.
Bard, K. "The Evolution of Social Complexity in Predynastic Egypt: An Analysis of the Naqada Cemeteries." *Journal of Mediterranean Archaeology* 2 (1989), 223–248.
Baumgartel, Elise J. *Petrie's Naqada Excavations, A Supplement.* London, 1970.
Castillos, J. J. "An Analysis of the Tombs in the Predynastic Cemeteries at Naqada." *Journal of the Society for the Study of Egyptian Antiquities* 11 (1981), 97–106.
de Morgan, Jacques J. M. *Recherches sur les origines de l'Egypte.* Paris, 1897.
Emery, Walter B. *Archaic Egypt.* Harmondsworth, 1961.
Hassan, F. A. "Radiocarbon Chronology of Predynastic Nagada Settlements." *Current Anthropology* 25 (1984), 681–683.
Hassan, F. A. "Radiocarbon Chronology of Neolithic and Predynastic Sites in Upper Egypt and the Delta." *The African Archaeological Review* 3 (1985), 95–116.
Hassan, F. A. "The Predynastic of Egypt." *Journal of World Prehistory* 2.2 (1988), 135–185.
Kaiser, W. "Zur inneren Chronologie der Nagadakultur." *Archaeologia Geographica* 6 (1957), 69–77.

FEKRI HASSAN

NAQADA I. *See* Predynastic Period.

NAQADA II. *See* Predynastic Period.

NAQADA III. *See* Predynastic Period.

NARMER (c. 3150 BCE–?) first king of the first dynasty, Early Dynastic period. This is the conventional rendering of the name of this king, which is written as an apparent rebus composed of a catfish (thought to be read as *n'r*) and a chisel (thought to be read *mr*). It has been argued that Narmer belonged to the period immediately preceding the first dynasty, but his position now seems assured by his leading appearance on seal impressions from the tombs of Den and Ka at Abydos. Whether by coincidence or not, the Ka impression puts Narmer at the head of a sequence of eight kings, precisely as given by Manetho for the first dynasty.

Narmer is best known for the great Narmer Palette, discovered in Quibell's 1897–1898 excavation season at Hierakonpolis (Kom el-Ahmar). The obverse of the palette is divided into three registers, the uppermost of which gives Narmer's name placed in a *serekh*, flanked by human-faced bovines. The second register dominates the obverse: Narmer, wearing the White Crown of Upper Egypt, smites an enemy in a posture that was to become emblematic of pharaonic power to the end of Egypt's pre-Christian civilization. The third register shows dead, nude enemies. On the reverse of the palette, the upper register of the obverse is duplicated. The second register shows Narmer wearing the Red Crown of Lower Egypt, inspecting rows of nude, decapitated enemies. The third register shows a man mastering serpent-necked lions, and the fourth register shows a bull destroying a town and trampling a dead enemy.

NARMER. *Restored first dynasty calcite vase inscribed with the name of Narmer, from Abydos.* (University of Pennsylvania Museum, Philadelphia. Neg. # S8–31480)

The earliest interpretation of this palette was to view it as a genuine historical document, with Narmer seen in the act of conquering Lower Egypt on the palette's obverse, and on the reverse as having successfully extended Upper Egyptian hegemony to the north. How far the palette should in fact be read in this way is open to question, but based on the Den and Ka necropolis sealings already mentioned, it seems certain that Narmer was viewed as the dynasty's foundational king by his immediate successors. Similarly, Egyptian sherds inscribed with the name of Narmer have been found in Lower Egypt (e.g., Minshat Abu Omar and Tarkhan) and in southern Palestine (e.g., Tel Erani and Tel Arad). The precise historical import of these facts is difficult to establish, but at a minimum, Narmer's presence was felt to some extent throughout Egypt and even into Palestine.

Narmer appears to have been buried in the Umm el-Qaab cemetery at Abydos. The double tomb B17/18 has been attributed to him, although whether this really was his tomb has been questioned.

[*See also* Menes.]

BIBLIOGRAPHY

Hoffmann, M. *Egypt before the Pharaohs.* London, 1980.
Wilkinson, T. A. H. *Early Dynastic Egypt.* London, 1999.

STEVE VINSON

NARRATIVES, the recounting of events, in Egyptian literature, have consisted primarily of the telling of myths and stories. Narrative can be said to occur first in the late Old Kingdom—not as a separate literary kind or genre, but embedded in tomb inscriptions. One notes particularly those of Weni or Harkhuf of the sixth dynasty, where the narrative form is used in the recollection and commemoration of a life, usually in terms of public service and the king's favor. Narrative also appears occasionally in the Old Kingdom in what has come to be called the "Catalog of Virtues," as in the sixth dynasty tomb of Nefer-seshem-re:

> I came forth from the city,
> I descended from the nome;
> I did justice for its lord,
> I pleased him in whatever he desired.

Here is the beginning of the connected telling of events that becomes elaborated in the tomb autobiography and in the historical or commemorative inscription. [*See* Biographies.]

Early Narratives. Extended narratives as self-contained "fictions" or stories first appear in the record during the Middle Kingdom. Their sophistication and the skill with which many of them are told testify to a long tradition of such narrative expression, now lost through the vagaries of preservation. Three Middle Kingdom tales survive at present: the *Story of Sinuhe*, the *Shipwrecked Sailor*, and the *Westcar Tales*.

Story of Sinuhe. This narrative is preserved entirely or in part on both papyri and ostraca, so that a complete eclectic text of good quality can be recovered. Of the papyri, Berlin 3022 (*B*) and Berlin 10499 (*R*) are the major copies and date from the Middle Kingdom; there are other, fragmentary papyri. Of the ostraca, the major pieces are Ostracon Ashmolean (1945.40, in Oxford) and the Cairo Ostracon (CG 25216); there are about twenty more ostraca.

The tale is widely considered to be the gem of ancient Egyptian literary narrative. It is cast in the form of an autobiography recounting the life of a courtier, Sinuhe, who served in the harem of Queen Neferu and was active during the reigns of Amenemhet I and Senwosret I. Whether the account is based on a historical character is currently unknown. The narrative opens with the death of King Amenemhet and finds Crown Prince Senwosret leading the army in the field in the western Delta. Sinuhe is a member of the expedition and overhears an apparently treasonous conversation, which points to an attempted coup back at the capital. He flees into Syria-Palestine, into the area of Upper Retenu, where he is received by the local king, Amunenshi. After hymning the praises of Senwosret, Sinuhe is welcomed to the court, married to Amunenshi's daughter, and settled on his own land. There he happily spends decades as his children appear and grow up, serving as a vassal to Amunenshi and acting as his military leader. When Asiatics encroach on the little kingdom, Sinuhe neutralizes them; and when the surrounding local tribes are stirred up through envy of Sinuhe's favored status, he defeats their champion in single combat. He is now at the height of his power and

reputation. But he begins to long for home. He sends a letter to King Senwosret, asking to return, and is overjoyed at the king's reply, which absolves him of any wrongdoing and urges him to return to Egypt. The tale concludes with Sinuhe's return, with the royal reception he is given, and finally with his death and burial as a favored courtier.

With the inclusion of a variety of literary kinds—lyric, epistle, encomium—all embedded in the underlying narrative structure, the tale nevertheless is cast in verse and structured by the "thought couplet," though not all scholars would agree with this assertion. *Sinuhe* reflects many of the values of ancient Egyptian civilization. The first of these is loyalty to the king. This is particularly seen in Sinuhe's praise of Senwosret when the fugitive first arrives at Amunenshi's court. The eulogy testifies to his loyalty to the throne; at this stage in his story, Sinuhe does not know that Senwosret survived the plotted attempt on his life and kingship. The portrait the author draws of the king shows him as a benign as well as powerful monarch. He is forgiving and understanding of Sinuhe's situation (Sinuhe had thought of himself as a traitor, though he was not); he fully reinstates Sinuhe at the court (with the help of a plea of intercession by the royal princesses); and he awards Sinuhe a tomb within the walls of the royal pyramid complex. Loyalty to this king is richly rewarded.

Sinuhe's longing for home and his return embody the Egyptian's valuation of his civilization. One must not be buried abroad, in Asia, in a sheepskin. Rather, the rites of burial in Egypt must be performed for the soul to rest easy in the next world. And there are other touches: the affection shown by the royal family, the awe toward royalty Sinuhe exhibits when he faints in the presence of the king, and the king's high regard abroad shown by Amunenshi. In sum, the tale fundamentally is about the proper relationship between a sovereign and a valued courtier, all brought to a head when the courtier momentarily loses faith and then spends a lifetime regaining his self-respect while in exile.

Shipwrecked Sailor. The *Story of the Shipwrecked Sailor* is preserved on a single manuscript, Papyrus Leningrad 1115, dating to the earlier Middle Kingdom. The story is complete, but there are hints that it is part of a larger work, perhaps consisting of several stories. Unlike the *Story of Sinuhe*, which purports to be an actual autobiography, the *Shipwrecked Sailor* introduces the world of the exotic and marvelous. Where the former strives for verisimilitude and a realistic presentation of the events surrounding its main character, the *Sailor* is a comic story (though with a serious background), full of exaggerations, tall tales, and a never-never land setting. The tale opens with the safe return of an expedition to Nubia. But the expedition has apparently been unsuccessful, because the sailor is attempting to cheer its commander as the latter goes to face his sovereign. He narrates his own earlier experience of shipwreck and being washed ashore on a magic island ruled by a huge talking serpent, who turns out to be friendly and kindly, listening to the sailor's account of his misfortune and, in turn, narrating his own story of the destruction of all his friends and relatives by a falling star. The serpent can forecast the future and tells the sailor that a ship will come from Egypt to rescue him, and he loads the sailor with an abundance of goods from the exotic island (which will disappear as soon as the sailor leaves). The sailor returns home, has his audience with the king, and is heaped with honors and wealth.

The comic irony of all this is that the sailor's own tale is totally inappropriate to his commander's situation—the sailor prospered, while his commander seems to be returning to his king with empty hands. The sailor himself is a comic character—blustery, stretching the truth, a little dim-witted, making inappropriate moves in his desire to look good. Devices like comedy and irony are difficult to detect in narratives so ancient (witness the lack of "satire" in the so-called *Satire on the Trades*); but in this tale there seem to be enough instances of inappropriate language or action for the modern reader to see the entire tale as light-hearted, with the comedy directed by the unknown author at the figure of the sailor himself.

Westcar Tales. The *Westcar Tales* are preserved in a single copy on papyrus, now in Berlin (Papyrus Berlin 3033). The story was evidently composed in the twelfth dynasty, but this papyrus is from the Hyksos period.

This little collection of interrelated tales is also known by the title *King Khufu and the Magicians.* It is set in the reign of Khufu. The sons of the king—Khafre, Baefre, and Hordjedef are known, while the first teller's name is lost in a lacuna—each tells a tale of a marvel performed by a magician in a past reign. The first tale is lost. The second treats of the infidelities of a magician-priest's wife and of the priest's fashioning a wax crocodile which becomes alive, seizes the lover, and carries him to the depths of a nearby lake; the wife is burned, though the point of the story lies in the magical power of the priest. The third tale concerns a boating party for the amusement of the king, set in the time of Sneferu. The crews consist of young women dressed in nets, one of whom loses a piece of her jewelry. The king's magician parts the waters of the lake, piling one side upon the other, in order to recover the piece. The fourth tale is set in the fictional present, with Hordjedef acquainting Khufu with a living magician who is also a prophet. The man, Djedi, is brought to court, where he refastens the severed heads of several animals to their bodies and tells Khufu the place of certain hidden chambers the king had been seeking. He then turns to prophecy: Khufu will be succeeded by his son and grand-

son, but then a new line of kings will come to the throne of Egypt—sons at that very moment being born to Redjedet, wife of a priest of Re. These children will belong to the fifth dynasty. The final tale is actually a continuation of the Hordjedef situation; but the court fades out and the narrator turns to the actual birth of Redjedet's three sons, assisted by Isis, Nephthys, Meshkhenet, and Heket, in the guise of singing-girls, along with their "servant" Khnum. Shortly after the births, the papyrus breaks off.

New Kingdom Narratives. Several literary narratives also survive from the New Kingdom. The most significant of these, all preserved in their entirety, are the *Contendings of Horus and Seth,* the *Story of the Two Brothers,* and the *Battle of Kadesh.*

Contendings of Horus and Seth. This tale is preserved on a single papyrus (Papyrus Chester Beatty I, now in Dublin), which also contains love songs, hymns, and other writings. It dates to the later Ramessid period. The tale consists of a series of quarrels between the gods Horus and Seth over the throne of Egypt. According to Egyptian tradition and myth, Horus, as son of the murdered Osiris, succeeded to the kingship. In this tale Seth repeatedly refuses to accept the decision of the Ennead; and in this version he is unaccountably abetted by Re-Horakhty, king of the gods. The Ennead are continually confused by Seth's rebellion and do not know how to bring the quarrel to a conclusion. One authority after another is invoked—Neith, Atum, Osiris—until finally Osiris, who of course favors Horus, threatens to unleash otherworld demons upon the All-Lord and the Ennead. They give in, and Horus is awarded Egypt while Seth is adopted by Re-Horakhty.

The story is simple—even simple-minded. Events follow one another without clear causation (other than to perpetuate the quarrel for the delight of the audience); and the conclusion occurs without a climax. The humor is sometimes broad and even coarse: the All-Lord tells Horus his breath smells bad; Baba tells the All-Lord his shrine is empty, and there are sexual jokes involving the disrobing of Hathor before Re to entice him to return to the conclave after he leaves with hurt feelings, or the attempted sodomizing of Horus by Seth. The story is apparently meant to be humorous, and certainly the conduct of the gods is indecorous—they are portrayed as silly, indecisive, and quarrelsome. All these things point to the humble milieu and origins of the story.

Story of the Two Brothers. This story is preserved in a single manuscript (Papyrus British Museum 10183, also known as Papyrus D'Orbiney) dating to the twentieth dynasty. The brothers of this story are Anubis and Bata, the first married and the second living with his elder brother and his wife. Life is harmonious, with the two men working in the fields and the wife at home, until one day Anubis's wife attempts to seduce Bata (the later Potiphar's Wife motif). When Anubis returns, his wife says that Bata attempted to rape her; Anubis lies in wait to kill Bata, but Bata's cattle, who can speak, warn him of his brother's plans. Bata runs off, tells his brother his own version of the incident, emasculates himself, and leaves for the Valley of the Pine. There Bata prospers, and a beautiful wife is fashioned for him by Khnum at the behest of the Ennead. A lock of her hair, taken by the sea, is washed up among pharaoh's washermen, and the perfume from it captivates the king. He brings her back to Egypt as his consort, while Anubis searches for Bata, who has placed his heart on the pine tree. After several transformations of Bata, involving the faithlessness of his wife, he is restored to life and prosperity by pharaoh; his wife is executed, he is reunited with his brother, and first he and then his brother become kings of Egypt.

The *Story of the Two Brothers* is a folktale moving in a realm of events more symbolic and metaphorical than realistic. Marvels occur one after the other, and their significance is not always apparent. Yet the incidents are vividly presented. Certainly the two wives are drawn in dark shades—their actions bring misery and estrangement to the brothers and also result in their own deaths. This world is one of mysterious turns of event, where normal causation does not operate, and where, despite death and estrangement, there is a happy ending for the central characters.

Battle of Kadesh. This complex piece has three parts that all commemorate the same event: there are the "Bulletin," the "Poem," and the wall reliefs. The event is commemorated in the temples of Karnak, Luxor, Abydos, and Abu Simbel, and above all in the Ramesseum. It also appears on three papyri. For present purposes, only the "Poem" will be considered as a piece intended as literature.

The *Battle of Kadesh* is especially interesting because it is a narrative of events, as witness the beginning and end of the poem. Yet the piece is so centered on the valor of King Ramesses II in battle that the narrative of external events is overwhelmed by the thoughts, attitude, and actions of the king himself during one crucial incident during the battle, when he stands alone to fight off hordes of enemy chariotry—and wins. The poem is a psychological narrative or a dramatic monologue by the main character of the drama, though neither characterization fits the ancient narrative exactly. There is a narrator who briefly describes the enemy facing Ramesses and continues with a laudatory description of the king as a surpassing warrior. This is followed by a description of the situation as Ramesses takes the field. At this point, the third-person narration changes to first-person, with Ramesses himself describing the desertion of his troops, praying to his fa-

ther Amon, and attacking the enemy. He also describes the second day of battle, when he defeats the Hittite coalition. Then the narration returns to the third person to describe the prince of Khatti suing for peace, as well as the return of Ramesses' army to Egypt.

The tone of the unknown author in the poem is probably intended to be "high style" or heroic, as, for example, in the later epics of Greece. This accounts for what to the modern reader are the exaggerations and boasts of both the third-person account and its main character. But this poem—in tone, in situation, and in the portrayal of Ramesses—is proto-epic, and the main character is drawn as a hero. The point to be made here is that the poem is a piece of literature, not merely a historical document, and the exaggerations contribute to the heightened style.

Wenamun. This piece is preserved on a single papyrus (Papyrus Moscow 120), originally from el-Hibe and dated to the twenty-second dynasty. It is uncertain whether this narration is intended as a piece of literature (fiction) or as a report (and thus a historical document). The narration is set in the declining phase of the late New Kingdom when Egypt is but a shadow of its former power and wealth. Wenamun, a priest of Amun, is sent to the Syrian coast to obtain timber to refurbish the bark of Amun. The narration describes Wenamun's difficulties with Prince Beder and the Tjeker ships—his goods are stolen and Beder procrastinates, refusing to help him. A picture is painted of an Egypt weakened and earning little respect from former vassals and allies. Wenamun finally leaves with a partial shipment of wood for the royal bark and sails to Cyprus, where he meets with more difficulties from the queen of Cyprus. At this point the narration breaks off.

Shorter narratives. Other New Kingdom narratives exist, but they are shorter pieces and for the most part fragmentary.

The *Destruction of Mankind* is written in Middle Egyptian and thus may go back to the Middle Kingdom. It is a myth comprising the first portion of the *Book of the Heavenly Cow* (copied on the walls of several New Kingdom royal tombs), in which an aging Re convokes the Ennead and Nun to discuss the rebellion of mankind. They determine to send the Eye of Re as Hathor to destroy them. She partly accomplishes this but is deterred from completing her task. In the second portion of the book, Re, tired of governing the world, withdraws to the sky, leaving the other gods to rule.

The *Doomed Prince*, preserved on Papyrus Harris 500, is a fragmentary tale in which a newborn prince is fated to die by a crocodile, a snake, or a dog. When the boy grows up, he set off for Naharin, where he wins and marries a princess. She tries to protect him from his fate, but he is seized by a crocodile—at which point the story breaks off.

Truth and Falsehood, preserved on Papyrus Chester Beatty II (Papyrus British Museum 10682) is an allegorical tale of two brothers and a marvelous dagger which the jealous younger brother claims the elder brother has taken and failed to return. Falsehood has Truth blinded, and even attempts to kill him; but he survives in the humble position of a gate attendant. A noble lady sees him and conceives a son by him, who in time rescues his father and brings Falsehood to justice, whereupon the latter is blinded, receiving the same punishment he falsely had visited upon Truth.

The *Taking of Joppa,* also preserved in Papyrus Harris 500, is the fragmentary end of a battle narrative in which the Egyptian general devises a stratagem to gain his troops entry into a city. They are sewn into sacks and carried within the gates, then freed. The piece is a precursor to the Trojan Horse motif.

Other tales exist—*Apophis and Sekenenre, General Sisenet, The Pleasures of Fishing and Fowling, The Sporting King, A Mythological Story,* a tale of a king and a goddess, another of a shepherd and a goddess, still another concerning Astarte, and a ghost story, among others—but they are in very fragmentary form and their purport is all but impossible to determine.

Narrative Characteristics. Half a dozen more or less complete tales, along with another dozen fragments of narrative, surviving from more than a thousand years of ancient Egyptian literary history, does not make for confidence in attempting generalizations or drawing conclusions about the nature of the narrative genre. The following observations, therefore, are tentative.

First of all, the surviving tales seem to fall into two groups. On the one hand, we have artfully worked narration which is the result of consciously used artistic devices by an experienced literary craftsman (*Sinuhe, Shipwrecked Sailor, Battle of Kadesh,* and *Wenamun,* if the last is indeed fiction). On the other, there is the folktale with its more easygoing narrative, frequent repetitions, marvels, and general artlessness, which may well go back to an oral tradition preceding the surviving written form (*Westcar Tales, Horus and Seth,* and *Two Brothers*).

Judging from the surviving tales—and drawing most on those that are most complete—the ancient Egyptian literary narrative was primarily a story of adventure, often accompanied with marvels and/or divine appearances. There are exceptions (cf. the locale of the *Westcar Tales,* or what can be deduced from the several very fragmentary New Kingdom examples); but, by and large, the events of the tale take place outside Egypt. Sinuhe narrates his experiences after living in exile and away from the court which he sadly misses; the shipwrecked sailor is thrown up on the shore of a mysterious island, where he meets a mysterious talking serpent—all this taking place down the Red Sea coast of Africa somewhere near the land of Punt; the two brothers, Anubis and Bata, begin their adventures (or misadventures) in a domestic context, but soon the younger flees to the Valley of the Pine; the Battle of Kadesh is fought in Syria-Palestine; Wenamun, in a later age, voyages to the same area for timber, only to end up in what is probably Cyprus as the manuscript breaks off. Of the complete or nearly complete tales, only the *Westcar Tales* are set in Egypt, though backdated to a romanticized fourth dynasty in the time of Khufu, and *Horus and Seth* is set in the realm of the gods.

Similarly, the kinds of events that happen to the characters, even in the fairly straightforward narratives, partake of the adventurous, the daring, the hazardous, and even the heroic. Sinuhe flees in fear of his life, nearly dying of thirst; he faces the hero of Retenu in single combat; and he serves as commander of Amunenshi's military forces. Ramesses II in the Battle for Kadesh is deserted by his infantry and chariotry; with the help of Amun, he singlehandedly routs the enemy through his personal heroism. The magician Djedi is able to restore the severed heads of various creatures and bring them back to life in the court of Khufu. That is, the things that happen to the characters, and their careers, are out of the ordinary.

Thus, one can say that for the Egyptian tale realism and verisimilitude are not primary criteria. Of the narratives where the purport of the story is clear, perhaps only *Sinuhe* and *Wenamun* (again, if it is fiction) present events in a realistic manner; and one notes that both pieces are sometimes claimed to be nonfiction, the one an autobiography and the other a travel report, largely because of this quality of verisimilitude. The marvelous events—miracles, epiphanies, and supernatural occurrences—are too common in most of the tales to mention in detail. But we can note the Island of the Ka in the *Shipwrecked Sailor,* which will disappear after the sailor leaves; or the serpent himself, some 15 meters (50 feet) long and rearing like a royal cobra. In *Horus and Seth,* Isis transforms herself into a beautiful young woman to seduce Seth; Horus becomes angry with Isis and cuts off her head; the semen of Horus is born out of Seth; and the two contestants have a naval battle in ships made of stone. In *The Two Brothers,* speaking cattle save Bata's life; Bata emasculates himself; he removes his own heart and places it in a blossom of the pine tree. In some of the fragments a deity appears to a person, whether king or a shepherd.

In terms of the kinds of characters presented, the Middle Kingdom literary narratives offer the first examples in Egyptian literature of human characters. Earlier pieces, like the Pyramid Texts, had dealt with the king and the gods, and the hymns and prayers had similarly addressed either royalty or deity. The one exception to this lies in the genre of wisdom literature like the *Instructions of Ptahhotep*, where, in a very limited and specific context, a father passes on the wisdom of his years in public office to a son; both are human characters, but ancillary to the wisdom being promulgated.

Even so, most of the narratives still deal either with the gods (*Horus and Seth*, the *Destruction of Mankind*) or with the divine king and the royal court (*Kadesh, Westcar Tales,* or even the *Doomed Prince*). And of these characters, most are rather one-dimensional; that is, the emphasis of the story is not so much on their thoughts, feelings, and attitudes as on what happens to them. The two brothers, Anubis and Bata, despite the folkloric interest of the story as well as its several marvels, are counters moved about—after the initial abortive domestic situation—by the author's sense of adventure and the sense of the symbols he uses. As in many of the surviving stories, whether of kings, courts, or deities, they are presented not for who they are but for what happens to them. Emphasis is placed rather more on events rather than on character.

A few of the human characters are more complex—not, perhaps, the princes and magicians of the *Westcar Tales,* who, though certainly human, are seen more as a framework for the marvelous tales of the magicians. Yet if one looks, for instance, at the *Battle of Kadesh,* Ramesses II is the focal point of the narrative; and in fact his personal account of his situation, prayer, and personal victory all but overwhelm the narrative that encloses the speech of the king. Nevertheless, Ramesses is given the traits of courage, valor, and piety, which characterize him as a heroic person. Of course, he is a divine king of Egypt, son of Amun, and thus is presumed to have these traits, as well as the lust for battle, victory, and invincibility. But the author endows him with the qualities of a hero and has him act the part of the god-king, which Egyptian tradition had assigned to the pharaoh.

A character who is all too human (as opposed to gods and kings) is Sinuhe. His story is one of flight, exile, and ultimate return to the king and culture that had formed him. But there is a more complex dimension to the tale, and in it one finds the beginnings of literary characterization in the Egyptian narrative tradition. Perhaps the form of the autobiography was the proper genre for the Egyptian author to tell his tale, because such first-person presentation of a life would be the most likely place for "character" to develop, idealized or not. In Sinuhe himself, we find one who was a member of the innermost circle of the court, who panics and flees in a moment of crisis, and who then spends a lifetime in exile regaining his self-confidence and self-esteem. He had seen himself as a coward and a traitor to his king and country. But his song in praise of Senwosret early in the tale demonstrates his loyalty, and the single combat with the hero of Retenu

similarly demonstrates his courage. It is then that he thinks back on life in the palace. The point of this is that the unknown author seems to have intended these moments of characterization: there are crises surmounted by Sinuhe that reveal his character and the nature of the man. And the conquest of adversity—which Sinuhe himself caused by running away—earns him the right to return to his country and be forgiven for a lapse which the king graciously says never occurred.

Perhaps the finest surviving example of characterization is that of the shipwrecked sailor. Whereas Sinuhe is an essentially noble person who has a momentary lapse which costs him a lifetime of atonement, the sailor is a mere crew member of a ship returning from an unsuccessful expedition into Nubia. We admire Sinuhe, but the author has us smile, if gently, at the sailor. The tale, of course, is a sailor's yarn, a tall tale exaggerated by the marvelous, reminding one of the later *Sindbad*. But the comedy that the reader or hearer understands is directed at the sailor himself. The author makes him a figure of fun—not denigrating him or cutting him down, as would be the case in satire, but rather pointing up his foibles, pretensions, and downright stretching of the truth. Perhaps the most revealing of these comic authorial touches lies in the inappropriateness of the story the sailor chooses to relate to his downcast commander. Elsewhere, the sailor brags of the crew who sailed with him on the earlier voyage, how brave they were, what experts they all were at seamanship; in the next line of the story, a storm wrecks them and drowns them all except the main character. Also, the sailor claims he never stretches truth; and then he narrates a yarn about a magic island and a huge talking serpent, complete with relatives, friends, and a little daughter. The sailor is brash and egotistical without being at all aware of himself; and it is this treatment of his character—the comic gap between his idea of himself and the reality—that makes the tale a joy to read. Along with *Sinuhe*, it is the culmination of surviving ancient Egyptian literary narrative.

[See also Battle of Kadesh: Sources; Contendings of Horus and Seth; Destruction of Mankind; Doomed Prince; Papyrus Westcar; Shipwrecked Sailor; Sinuhe; Taking of Joppa; Two Brothers; *and* Wenamun.]

BIBLIOGRAPHY

Foster, John L. *Echoes of Egyptian Voices.* Norman, Okla., 1992.

Lichtheim, Miriam. *Ancient Egyptian Literature.* 2 vols. Los Angeles, 1973, 1978.

Loprieno, Antonio, ed. *Ancient Egyptian Literature.* Leiden, 1996. Includes an excellent, extensive, and up-to-date general bibliography.

Parkinson, R. B. *The Tale of Sinuhe and Other Ancient Egyptian Poems. 1940–1640 BC.* Oxford, 1997.

Simpson, William Kelly, ed. *The Literature of Ancient Egypt.* New Haven, 1973.

JOHN L. FOSTER

NATRON. *See* Lakes; *and* Mummification.

NATRUN, WADI. *See* Lakes.

NATURAL RESOURCES. Before agriculture, in the Nile Valley the peoples of prehistoric Egypt subsisted on what they gathered along the banks of the river and in the adjacent desert. For example, the plants identified at Wadi Kubanniya, a prehistoric site near Aswan, included nut-grass tubers, club-rush tubers, and dom-palm fruits—cat's tail (or reed-mace), bullrushes, and papyrus would have been gathered. Young reed and rush rhizomes may be baked, steamed, or roasted, and commonly used would be the rhizomes of the waterlily (*Polyganum*), as well as sedge nutlets, acacia seeds, wild palm dates, capers (*Capparis*), the fruits of *Zizyphus* and *Citrullus*, and *Rumex*, *Chenopodium*, and wild millet (*Panicum*).

The Nile provided abundant fish and other aquatic resources, the most important being catfish (*Clarias*), but *Tilapia* and *Lates* were also caught. Catfish were caught in shallow, muddy water, but *Lates* require deep-water fishing. Turtles and mussels were also taken. One of the prized Nile catches was the hippopotamus, but prehistoric hunting was mostly focused on the pursuit of wild cattle (*Bos primigenius*) and hartebeest in the floodplain, and gazelles, wild ass, and hares from the edge of the desert. Geese, ducks, and coots wintering in Egypt from October to March were taken when the tubers and waterlilies matured. From spring to high summer (before the floods inundated the valley), hunting, fishing, and foraging for root foods under the floodplain muds, as well as the consumption of acacia seeds, provided a variety of food resources. Beginning in early July and reaching its peak in mid-August, rising Nile water inundated the floodplain; during peak flood, water occasionally extended into the adjoining dry wadis that cross the low desert bordering the floodplain. Plants and animals of the floodplain were restricted to the higher grounds and to the edge of the floodplain. As floodwater receded, catfish were stranded in abundance in pools; the seeds of grasses and other plants that grew in the wake of the flood also provided a rich food resource.

The Nile's channel is bordered by natural levées at the concave sides of its meanders and by sand bars along the convex sides. Sand islands have formed within the channel. The surface of the floodplain has become high close to the channel, because of the great deposition rate of muds during the flood season. Depressions in the floodplain, called flood basins, retain water after the flood and thus sustain the growth of plants. At the outer edge of the floodplain, low areas receive seepage water, which supports an outer fringe of wetlands and ponds, a favorite place for migratory fowl. In addition to food resources, the Nile provided fuel, from the *Acacia* and *Tamarix* trees; their wood could also have been used for digging sticks and other implements. The reed *Phragmites* was used for arrows, and the *Papyrus* sedge, as well as *Cladium*, *Juncus*, and the palm and dom palm were used in basketry and matting.

For stone tools, prehistoric Egyptians utilized the chert bands and nodules found in the limestone outcrops, as well as the quartz pebbles and cobbles in the Nubia sandstone. Grinding stones were mostly manufactured from quartzite, from the Nubia formation, or from silicified or dolomitic limestone. Clay was taken from local Nile muds or made from shales and marls from the geologic formations in the hills adjacent to the Nile Valley. Reeds, tree branches, animals hides, and mud provided the basic materials for dwellings. The utilization of those resources continued after the agricultural villages were settled in and near the Nile Valley; but hunting for food had almost vanished by the Middle Predynastic (c.3800 BCE), because of the depletion of wildlife in the vicinity of the villages and the emergence of an agricultural ethos centered on cultivation and herding. In later periods, wild animals, fowl, and fish were hunted by the elite for sport, and the ponds, marshes, and swamps bordering the Nile became a recreational resource.

The principal natural resources of pharaonic times were the fertile floodplain and the Nile waters. Flood basins, irrigated by the annual inundation, were ideal for growing barley, wheat, and flax. The cultivation of cereals conflicted with the herding of cattle and sheep on the floodplain. Because cereal cultivation is more productive than herding per unit area, cattle herding was favored in both the Delta marshlands and the uncultivated marshy areas of the floodplain, while sheep and goats were raised on the edge of the floodplain and allowed to graze in the fields after the harvest. The river continued to provide ample fish resources.

The fertile plain of the Nile Valley primarily results from the annual accumulation of silt deposited by floodwater. The annual load of silt is variable. (It ranged, for example, in recent times from 59 million tons in 1943 to a maximum of 228 million tons in 1936.) The additions of silt to the floodplain are not uniform and vary both laterally away from the channel and in the different parts of the Valley and the Delta. The rates of deposition are also influenced by changes in the volume of Nile flood discharge. The natural levées that border parts of the channel are topped by high Nile floods, and may also be breached, thus altering the preexisting depositional regimes. The position of the channel has also shifted in places. The dramatic changes in floodplain geomorphology is provided by the changes in the Cairo area from 942 to 1281 CE, which were coincident with two major episodes of low Nile floods (930–1070 CE and 1180–1350 CE). Near Memphis, the Nile channel shifted in pharaonic times to the east from its original position near the Old Kingdom capital. After the mid-seventh-century Arab conquest of Egypt, the Nile channel also shifted—this time to the west—from Fustat, north of Memphis. Such changes would have influenced not only the water supply and the agricultural hinterland of urban settlements but also direct access to the channel for transport by boats.

The configuration and distribution of the optimal land for ancient Egypt's farming has thus varied though time. Protection from the Nile floods necessitated the construction of dikes. Canals were dug to provide water for areas deprived of floodwater (because of diversions of the channel or a change in the geomorphic setting) or to irrigate areas rarely reached by flooding. The Nile's channel (6.75–8.52 meters/21–26 feet deep) was also subject to silting in—the accumulation of bottom deposits. The height of water necessary to irrigate the ancient fields was therefore a function of the volume of Nile flood discharge, the shape and depth of the channel, and the height of the floodplain relative to the depth of the channel. When the volume of flood discharge was low or when the floodplain rose faster than the channel, it was necessary to deepen, or dig, new canals that delivered water to outlying fields. From south to north, the gradient of the river (from about 1:10,000 to 1:15,000) controls the flow of floodwater over the floodplain. In historical times, the flooding required a coordination of activities among communities to control the flow downstream; they built artificial dikes that had gates, which could be opened to release floodwater downstream.

Because of the differences in the width of the floodplain—which varied from 2 kilometers (1.5 miles) at Aswan to 17.6 kilometers (11 miles) at Minia in Middle Egypt—the agricultural potential of different districts along the Nile Valley was not uniform. The area of the floodplain ranged from 72 square kilometers for Elephantine to 650 square kilometers for El-Ashmunein. The total area of the floodplain is estimated at being about 8,000 square kilometers during the New Kingdom. The productivity of the land depended on the height of the Nile floods, which varied considerably, both episodically and annually. For example, in recent times, Nile water discharge during the flood peak ranged from 474 million cubic meters per day in 1941 to 935 million cubic meters per day in 1938. There were also major variations in pharaonic and later historical times that drastically influenced land productivity. Accordingly, the variations in Nile flood discharge, the amount of silt carried by the floods, the episodic climatic events, the concomitant changes in both geometry and channel depth, the topography, and the relative height of the floodplain, were all inherent elements of the ancient Nile landscape. The agricultural resources of the Nile Valley were thus subject to significant and at times abrupt fluctuations, which must have played a role in social and political affairs.

The Nile also served as a major transport artery; it flowed from south to north, with an average speed of 4 knots (about 7.4 kilometers/4.5 miles per hour) during the season of inundation. Day travel was favored because shallow sand islands were not easily avoided at night. During the low flood season, the speed of the current was only about 1 knot, and the river was extremely shallow (2–5.3 meters/6–16 feet). Nile traffic was therefore slowed considerably. The trip from Thebes to Cairo, a distance of 900 kilometers (550 miles) by the Nile could have been accomplished in two weeks during the flood season, but it would have required as long as two months during the drought season. In general, the trip from north to south—against the current—would have been extremely slow until sails were developed, to take advantage of the northerly and northwesterly winds blowing off the Mediterranean. The bend near Qena, where the Nile flows from east to west and then back from west to east, slows riverine travel considerably. Changes in the position of the channel, as well as the topography of its floor, influenced navigation and landing sites, which necessitated the deepening of access to ports, the digging of canals, or the repositioning of some riverine installations.

The emergence of social stratification in Egypt (which began well before the unification of Egypt into a nation state) created a demand for a variety of resources. This demand accelerated as the upper strata of society increased in number and influence. A variety of resources were particularly required for the funerary cults, the royal tombs, and the temples, shrines, and palaces. Stones and minerals from the Eastern Desert were quarried or mined and transported by donkey caravans and then by boats and barges to their final destinations. In Predynastic times, stone for vases and plates was taken from the hills surrounding the Nile Valley; it included limestone, sandstone, gypsum, and calcite (Egyptian alabaster). From the Eastern Desert came volcanic porphyry as well as marble, greywacke, quartz, schist, serpentine, and talc. Slate was used for cosmetic and ceremonial palettes; a variety of quartz minerals—agate, jasper, and amethyst—as well as garnet and green microcline were used for beads; gold nuggets were obtained from placer deposits in the wadis of the Eastern Desert. From the Red Sea lead ores, galena was used for kohl eyeliner. Copper ores came from both the Eastern Desert and the Sinai; green copper minerals such as malachite and atacamite were used for cosmetic pigments. Calcite (Egyptian alabaster) was obtained from the Wadi Garawi, south of Helwan and opposite Memphis, but the most important calcite quarries were at Hatnub, southeast of Tell el-Amarna. Quartzite (a naturally cemented sandstone) was available near Cairo, at Al-Gebel Al-Ahmar, and in association with the Nubian sandstones south of Edfu. Basalt, used as a special building material because of its black color, occurred in many parts of Egypt; sources close to the Nile and building sites include Abu Rowash and Gebel Qatrani (Widan el-Faras), north of the Faiyum Depression, since the Faiyum was the main source of the basalt used in ancient Egypt. Greywacke (a dark, varicolored, attractive stone) was obtained from the Wadi Hammamat between Luxor (Thebes) and Qusseir. Anorthositic gneiss (the so-called Khephren diorite) was quarried from a restricted area in the desert west of Abu Simbel. Granite was one of the favorite building and ornamental stones and is widespread in the Eastern Desert and the Sinai; there are also outcrops near Aswan. As indicated by the causeway inscriptions of King Unas, granite was quarried, shaped into objects, and then polished before transport by boats down the Nile. Talc and serpentine, softer and easier to work than granite, were used for a variety of objects, including weights, spinning wheels, and beads; both were common in the Eastern Desert region east of Edfu.

For common use, salt was obtained from the shores of the Mediterranean and from Red Sea lagoons and sabkhas. Natron, used with other substances for dyes and for mummification, was obtained from the Wadi Natrun. During the Old Kingdom, gypsum was ground into pastes and used for plaster and for the production of a variety of objects. Both gypsum and ground limestone were used for white pigments; malachite provided green pigment; red and yellow ochers supplemented the color palette. The oases of the Western Desert contained abundant ocher deposits. Colors were important in Egyptian ideology, and the use of paint pigments and colored minerals was therefore common. Gold (yellow), turquoise, and lapis lazuli (blue) as well as red agate and red-brown carnelian were highly desirable and were obtained from a variety of sources. Amethyst was obtained from the Wadi el-Hudi, some 35 kilometers (22 miles) southeast of Aswan, and it was greatly prized during the Middle Kingdom. During the Greco-Roman period, emerald was mined from Zabara, Um Kabo, and Sekkait and from Nugrus in the Eastern Desert; peridot was then obtained from the Zabargad Island in the Red Sea.

In ancient Egypt, gold was obtained from at least ninety gold mines in the Eastern Desert (between 22°E, and 27°50′N); gold is associated with quartz veins in basement rocks. Copper minerals, including turquoise, were obtained from the Sinai and the Eastern Desert, the main source being at Serabit el-Khadim and Mughara in the Sinai. Nile Valley copper ores for the production of copper metal were limited in comparison to those in the northeast, at Wadi Araba (located between Jordan and Palestine), but copper ores came from Attawi, Gebel Dara, Dingash, Hamash (together with gold), Abu Sayal, Um Samiuki, and Abu Ghousoun in the Eastern Desert, and Wadi Nasseib in the Sinai, and several other locations. Although iron ores are known from Egypt, near Aswan, the technology of iron smelting seems not to have been developed there even as late as the New Kingdom.

The stone and mineral resources of Egypt expanded during the Greco-Roman period to include granite from Mons Claudianus, which is pale in color with small dark spots of iron-rich minerals. A variety of porphyritic rocks, including "Imperial Porphyry," were obtained from Gebel el-Dokhan, Gebel Abu Harba, and Gebel Gattar—from west of Hurghada in the Red Sea Hills. The Romans also exploited the greywacke and green breccia of the Wadi Hammamat.

Sandstone in the South and limestone in the North had always been used for building purposes. A mixture of sand, shale, and limestone rubble (available from lenses or beds interlayered with sandstone and limestone formations) provided a durable mortar. Nile muds were used, and gypsum was used as mortar and filler. The limestone varied in quality, with the best limestone quarried at Tura and M'asara, opposite Memphis. These quarries go back to the third dynasty. The bulk of the limestone used for the Giza pyramids was obtained from nearby quarries, with the superior Tura limestone reserved for the outer casing. Limestone outcrops continue from Tura to beyond Thebes. Although sandstone became the predominant cliff-forming stone from Esna to Aswan, it was not widely used until the New Kingdom; the most important quarry for sandstone was Gebel es-Silsila, located between Kom Ombo and Edfu. Limestone and sandstone for palaces, temples, tombs, and statues overshadow the most common building resources in Egypt—namely, the Nile muds and sands from the older Nile formations—which were exposed in the low desert, adjacent to the floodplain. They were used to make mud bricks (both unfired and fired); local woods and reeds were also used for common construction.

Egypt's wood resources were limited and of poor quality in comparison to the woods imported from the Levant. Wood was used for boats, needed to transport food and other resources on the Nile and in the Red Sea and the Mediterranean. Wood was also used for funerary purposes and for the transport of the king and his noble entourage. Papyrus was used to craft small boats and rafts. Local woods—the acacia, sycamore fig, and the tamarisk—were mainly used for domestic furniture and some tools. The Egyptians also exploited certain plants and trees for their resins and for the production of perfumes, which were both luxury items and used for religious purposes. One of the key resources for ancient Egypt was the papyrus plant, a sedge that grew in the Nile marshes, used for boat-building, basketry, and food; it became the fundamental raw material for Egypt's paper industry, which was important until the Arabs in the seventh century CE introduced paper-making, based on a Chinese technology.

Ceramics and the use of pottery in the Nile Valley are associated with the beginnings of Egyptian agricultural villages. Initially, Nile mud (silt mixed with sand) tempered with dung, straw, or grog was used to produce domestic vessels (fired in kilns). In late Predynastic times, marl and shale from the hills adjacent to the Nile Valley were used in the manufacture of hard pottery wares. In Predynastic times, the Egyptians also developed faience—a vitreous ceramic—from copper minerals, quartzose sand, limestone, and natron salts. Subsequently, pigments were added to mud pastes to produce colored and glazed ceramic objects.

The geological setting of Egypt favored it with the fertile Nile floodplain and the rock and mineral resources of the surrounding hills. In prehistoric times, the wild food resources of the Valley and the adjacent deserts provided sufficient subsistence resources for its sparse inhabitants. Stone for tools was also available. With the establishment of agricultural villages, the floodplain supported farmers who not only changed its ecology but also fashioned a social organization and an ideology that required the economic integration of the resources of the adjacent deserts. Internal and external trade encouraged the building of boats, for use on the Nile, the Mediterranean, and the Red Sea. Today, Egypt still focuses on the Nile for its livelihood, but the growth of population well beyond the feeding capacity of the floodplain has necessitated farming outside the Nile Valley, utilizing groundwater resources and the cultivable land of ancient dry lakebeds; urbanization is still reducing the areas devoted to agriculture, and industrialization is adding a new element to Egypt's ecology. Egypt has begun to exploit its geopolitical position, its oil deposits, and its cultural heritage—as well as the sunshine, desert allure, and fine beaches—in an effort to secure a prosperous and peaceful future.

[See also Fauna; Flora; Geology; Gold; Minerals; Nile; and Quarries and Mines.]

BIBLIOGRAPHY

Brewer, D. J., D. B. Redford, and S. Redford. *Domestic Plants and Animals: The Egyptian Origins*. Warminster, 1995.

Houlihan, P. F. *The Birds of Ancient Egypt*. Cairo, 1988. A fully illustrated source book on the birds of ancient Egypt.

Husseein, Abdel Aziz. "Mineral Deposits." In *The Geology of Egypt*, edited by Rushdi Said. Rotterdam, 1990.

Kees, Herman. *Ancient Egypt: A Cultural Topography*. Chicago, 1961. An essential account of the historical and cultural geography of Egypt, with a detailed treatment of the environmental elements of the countryside, cities, and districts of ancient Egypt.

Lucas, A. *Ancient Egyptian Materials and Industries*. 4th ed. London, 1962.

Said, R. *The River Nile: Geology, Hydrology, and Utilization*. Oxford, 1993.

Wetterstrom, W. "Foraging and Farming in Egypt: The Transition from Hunting and Gathering to Horticulture in the Nile Valley." In *The Archaeology of Africa: Food, Metals and Towns*, edited by T. Shaw, P. Sinclair, B. Andah, and A. Okpoko, pp. 165–226. London, 1996. A comprehensive summary of plant-food resources.

FEKRI HASSAN

NAVY. *See* Military, *overview article*.

NECHO I (Eg., *N(y)-kȝw;* Gk., *Nekos;* Assy., *Ni-ku-u*), Egyptian dynast, ruler of Sais and Memphis, who was killed in 664 BCE. The most important sources for Necho's career are the annals of the Assyrian kings Esarhaddon (680–669 BCE) and Assurbanipal (668–633 BCE), which give a detailed narrative of events, though very much from an Assyrian perspective. There is also supplementary material in Egyptian texts and the work of the fifth-century BCE Greek historian Herodotus.

Necho's career was played out against the backdrop of conflict between the Assyrians and the Nubian rulers of the twenty-fifth dynasty to decide control of Egypt. Within Egypt, political power at a local level lay largely with semi-autonomous dynasts, of whom Necho of Sais was apparently the most powerful. When Esarhaddon expelled the Nubian Taharqa from Egypt in 671 BCE, he retained this system of local administration. During Assurbanipal's invasion of Egypt in 667–666 BCE, in response to a successful attempt by Taharqa to regain control of the country, these dynasts, including Necho, remained loyal to the Assyrians. Subsequently, however, nervous at Assyrian intentions, they entered into a conspiracy with Taharqa; the plot was revealed, and the rebel dynasts were arrested. The inhabitants of all rebel cities, including Necho's Sais, were massacred and flayed and had their skins draped on their city walls. All the rebel kings were executed, with the exception of Necho, who presumably convinced the Assyrians that he had participated unwillingly in the insurrection. Shown great favor, he was restored to his kingdom, but under close Assyrian supervision to guarantee his loyalty. At the same time, Necho's son Nabushezibanni (the later Psamtik I?) was appointed to rule Athribis. On the death of Taharqa, Tanutamun reasserted Nubian control of Egypt and defeated the Assyrians at Memphis in 664 BCE. In these operations Necho, who had remained loyal to the Assyrians, was killed.

BIBLIOGRAPHY

James, T. G. H. *The Assyrian and Babylonian Empires and Other States of the Near East from the Eighth to the Sixth Centuries B.C.* In *Cambridge Ancient History*, edited by J. Boardman, vol. 3, part 2. 2d ed. Cambridge, 1991. An excellent survey.

Kitchen, K. A. *The Third Intermediate Period in Egypt (1100–650 B.C.)*. Warminster, 1973. A masterly analysis of the many historical problems of this period.

Lloyd, Alan B. *Herodotus Book II*. Etudes préliminaires aux religions orientales dans l'empire romain, 43. 3 vols. Leiden, 1975–1993. Includes discussion of the Herodotean data on Necho in the light of other evidence.

Pritchard, J. B. *Ancient Near Eastern Texts Relating to the Old Testament*. 3d ed. Princeton, 1969. Provides a key to the detailed Assyrian evidence on this ruler.

ALAN B. LLOYD

NECHO II (r. 610–595 BCE), second king of the twenty-sixth Saite dynasty, Late period. A son of Psamtik I, he was one of the most vigorous and far-sighted of Late period rulers. Sources on Necho are dominated by his foreign policy, where the major issue was the threat of Chaldean expansion. He relied heavily on Greek and Carian mercenaries, who were permanently based in Egypt. This situation is reflected in his calculated policy of donations to major shrines in eastern Greece, which included dedications to Athena Polias at Ialysus on the island of Rhodes and the major Ionian oracular shrine at Branchidae. His military resources on land were supplemented by a force of ramming warships, which may have been triremes (a galley having three tiers of oars on each side). This fleet was intended to counter any attempt to mount a two-pronged attack by land and water on Egypt and also to support the western flank of Necho's forces in the Near East.

His campaign in Syria-Palestine was initially designed to assist the Assyrians in forcing out the Chaldeans, and Necho enjoyed some early success. He defeated Josiah, King of Judah, at Megiddo in 609 BCE, thus guaranteeing

NECHO II. *Bronze statuette of Necho II kneeling in worship, from the twenty-sixth dynasty.* (University of Pennsylvania Museum, Philadelphia. Neg. # S8–31605)

his freedom of movement up the grand trunk road to Mesopotamia, and he established a base at Carchemish, which he held until his catastrophic defeat there in 605 BCE. The Chaldeans subsequently pushed the Egyptians south to the eastern frontier of the Delta, but the Egyptians held there. Necho's operations in this area were reflected in Herodotus' fifth-century BCE account of his successes against Migdol and Gaza in 601–600 BCE. Necho also focused his foreign policy efforts on the Red Sea, in which the Egyptians had longstanding commercial interests, and he began the construction of a canal through the Wadi Tumilat to join it to the Nile. He also based a force of warships there, presumably to guarantee safe passage for his ships in the face of threats from Edomite or Sabean raiders.

Research in the latter twentieth century indicates that Necho also dispatched a military force into Nubia, where the Saites were more deeply involved than previous scholarship indicated.

BIBLIOGRAPHY

The Cambridge Ancient History. 2d ed. Cambridge, 1991. Includes an excellent survey of the twenty-sixth dynasty, with much on Necho.

Lloyd, Alan B. "Triremes and the Saite Navy." *Journal of Egyptian Archaeology* 58 (1972), 268–279. A discussion of the development of the Saite navy and the part that Greeks may have played in it.

Lloyd, Alan B. *Herodotus Book II*. Etudes préliminaires aux religions orientales dans l'empire romain, 43. 3 vols. Leiden, 1975–1993. A discussion of the Herodotean data on Necho II in the light of all other evidence.

Lloyd, Alan B. "Necho and the Red Sea: Some Considerations." *Journal of Egyptian Archaeology* 63 (1977), p. 142–155. The evidence for the circumnavigation of Africa allegedly instigated by Necho is analyzed in detail with skeptical results.

Lloyd, Alan B. "The Late Period, 664–323 BC." In *Ancient Egypt: a Social History*. Cambridge, 1983. Necho placed firmly within the history of twenty-sixth dynasty.

ALAN B. LLOYD

NECROPOLIS. As early as the Neolithic period, the ancient Egyptians buried their dead in cemeteries, and eventually an elaborate funerary cult developed around the tombs. Necropolises therefore emerged as privileged areas of monumental and artistic display, and consequently they are among the most prominent, archaeological sites of pharaonic Egypt.

Role in Archaeological Research. Attracted by the richness of these sites, Egyptological research has tended to concentrate on tombs and cemeteries, while neglecting other aspects of the archaeological record, the settlements in particular. The deficits in our knowledge that resulted from this attitude are being felt more and more acutely, and it is certainly advisable to strive for a more balanced appreciation of the available evidence. The prominence of the funerary sector, however, is an inherent trait of pharaonic culture.

The prosopographical and historical information derived from inscriptions in the tombs of kings and the elite is crucial to an understanding of the composition of the aristocracy, the organization of the administration, and many other aspects of the workings of society. The buildings and their decoration stand out as the finest examples of pharaonic art, scenes of daily activities on the walls provide lively (though heavily biased) views of life in ancient Egypt. Recovering and recording these monuments was always a priority of archaeology in Egypt. The necropolises of the elite are vast sites, and individual tombs are often quite complex, so their exploration is still far from complete. Even the site of Giza, which was excavated systematically during the early decades of the twentieth century, is still far from exhausted. Sites like Saqqara or the Theban necropolis are even less systematically explored.

The cemeteries of the ordinary people held rather less appeal to artistically and epigraphically minded archaeologists. Their scientific potential became evident when the whole epoch of Egyptian prehistory became known through W. M. Flinders Petrie's 1895 excavations in the cemeteries of Naqada and Ballas, and when George Reisner's 1910 excavations in the cemeteries of Shellal near Aswan revealed the existence of several indigenous Nubian cultures. In fact, the material from cemeteries is particularly suited to define archaeological cultures and their chronological subphases. The principle of chronological seriation, ingeniously discovered by Petrie, provided the methodological key to make the best use of this potential. Petrie also realized that it was no less necessary to describe the material culture of the historical phases of pharaonic Egypt, and the excavation of cemeteries was the ideal way to fill in the corpora of artifact types that were to embody his fascinating vision of a "systematic archaeology" of ancient Egypt. Consequently Petrie and his coworkers spent considerable effort on systematically exploring the cemeteries situated on the desert margins during the decades before World War II. Brunton's extensive work in the area between Qau and Matmar south of Asyut (1922–1931), where he uncovered more than five thousand burials ranging from the early Neolithic until Coptic times, marks the climax of this strain in Egyptian archaeology. Deriving the definition of archaeological phases from cemetery data has come under criticism in recent years. This seems only partly justified, however. In fact, the information derived from the excavation of cemeteries is still fundamental to our knowledge of the material culture of ancient Egypt. The appreciation of many of these excavations, however, is seriously hampered by incomplete publication; in many cases, it would be both

NECROPOLIS. *Representation of tombs in a necropolis, from a stele at Giza.*

possible and worthwhile to supplement the printed volumes on the basis of the original documentation and the finds kept in museum collections.

Although a great deal of archaeological work has been done on ancient Egyptian cemetery sites, most of this work focused on individual tombs or on classes of objects and their chronology. It has been less common to study cemeteries as coherent entities playing a part in the cultural life of a community, and to address their significance within an anthropological framework. Reisner, however, grasped the importance of this aspect already in his pioneering analysis of an Old Kingdom cemetery at Naga ed-Deir (opposite Abydos), excavated in 1901–1902. In his publication, Reisner attempts to reconstruct the social composition of a provincial community on the basis of its cemetery, contrasting the cultural situation at this remote site in Upper Egypt with the contemporary necropolises of the elite. This great work well exemplifies the potential of cemetery data to elucidate the internal differentiation of pharaonic culture along both social and geographical lines. More recent studies address their value for the reconstruction of settlement patterns and demographic development as well. This new anthropological perspective can be applied to the analysis of the great wealth of cemetery data which are already available, and it should influence the research design of new excavations. A site should be excavated completely enough to enable population estimates; the excavated human remains should be analyzed by an expert biologist; close attention should be given to complex patterns of use and reuse and of cult activities; and an attempt should be made to establish the relationship between a cemetery and the settlement to which it belongs.

Necropolises and Settlements. Egyptian cemeteries lie outside the settlements they served. Only burials of babies and very small children (often deposited in large jars) are regularly encountered within settlements, and special beliefs were probably associated with this custom; W. Blackman in *The Fellahin of Upper Egypt* (London, 1927, p. 101) reports that babies were buried within houses in modern Egypt to make sure that the mother would have another child. Otherwise, burial within the settlement is irregular; rarely, bodies of low-ranking persons are found interred in abandoned building plots. Burials in the Neolithic settlement of Merimda Beni Salama, which gave rise to the interpretation that house burial was a regular trait of the prehistoric cultures of Lower Egypt, have been shown by subsequent excavations not to have been strictly contemporary with the settlement remains. The custom of house burial, securely attested at Tell ed-Dabʿa during the Second Intermediate Period, resulted from the influence of the Syrian-Palestinian Middle Bronze II culture in the eastern Delta during that time.

The Egyptian ideal held that a cemetery should be situated on the Western Desert margin, and terms like "The Beautiful West" are used frequently as synonyms for "necropolis." Many necropolises—and, in fact, all royal necropolises—conform to this ideal, but just as many do not. Cemeteries are found on the eastern and western banks of the valley, naturally confined to sites not reached by the annual inundation. Cemeteries were preferably located immediately outside or rather close to a settlement. A greater distance between settlement and necropolis (up to a few kilometers) was accepted only if the site had to satisfy specific technical or locational demands. For the rock-cut tombs of the elite from the late Old Kingdom onward, for example, sites in the flanks of the desert mountains had to be chosen, preferably at places that overlooked the territory formerly governed by the tomb-owner. For the pyramid cemeteries of the Old Kingdom, sites were selected that afforded easy access to quarries and occupied commanding positions, like the desert plateaus of Giza or Abu Rowash. Such cemeteries were at a considerable distance from residences, and therefore settlements were founded to house the people associated with the necropolis in an administrative, construction, or maintenance capacity.

The distribution pattern of cemeteries in the country, as revealed by archaeological excavation, is severely distorted by unequal preservation. Because of the rise of the alluvial land over the course of time, most of the cemeteries that originally lay in the plain of the valley and in the

Delta are now buried under several meters of Nile mud, creating the false impression that cemeteries lay exclusively on the desert margins. Even here, however, preservation is rather unequal in the different sections of the valley. In Middle Egypt, for instance, the western desert margin, which was very low, was also covered by the rise of the alluvium. If the hazards of preservation and recovery are carefully taken into account, cemeteries provide the most valuable information on the structure of settlement available from ancient Egypt, and in particular on the distribution of social groups across the country.

The close relationship between settlement and cemetery does not imply, however, that the group buried in a cemetery is identical with the population of a nearby settlement. Rather, it is obvious that access to a cemetery could depend on status and social affiliation. Cemeteries of the elite were normally inaccessible to burials of ordinary people; on the other hand, there are cemeteries where only children were interred. The unequal representation of the sexes, a very common feature in Egyptian cemeteries, equally attests to selective processes.

Types and Layouts. Ancient Egyptian cemeteries were not fenced in, and there was no communal cult site nor, as a rule, a temple attached to them. From an archaeological point of view, cemetery sites may be classified according to their geographical situation and according to the types of tombs that occupy them. In addition, the size of the group buried in a cemetery and its social structure are to be considered.

In prehistoric times, cemeteries were laid out on flat ground where strata of soft rock, compacted gravel, or sand offered little resistance to the excavation of graves. The tombs are scattered informally over the available space and were probably marked on the surface by small tumuli. Today, however, most of the surface layer has been eroded away.

A special type of elite cemetery appeared in the second half of the fourth millennium BCE near emerging Upper Egyptian cities such as Hierakonpolis, Naqada, and Abydos. These cemeteries were reserved for members of the uppermost level of local society. The first dynasty royal cemetery at Abydos also belongs to this class of necropolis.

During the Old Kingdom and in subsequent periods, the layout pattern of village cemeteries remained basically similar (though all other aspects of funerary culture underwent profound changes). Tomb shafts became deeper, and the tombs were covered by small *mastaba*s. The cemeteries of important provincial towns are considerably larger, and the presence of a local elite makes itself felt. In the Old Kingdom, these people were buried in large *mastaba* tombs, and places like Edfu, Naga ed-Deir, and Qau illustrate well how these important buildings prefera-

bly formed a continuous row occupying the most conspicuous part of the cemetery, while the lesser tombs were scattered in front of or behind this line. The layout of these cemeteries served to emphasize the dominant role of the elite within local society.

A specific type of necropolis developed during the Old Kingdom in the cemeteries of the royal court near the capital. Here the tombs of the most important officials were concentrated, and these sites abound in monuments of high artistic and epigraphic importance. Court cemeteries in the strict sense appear at the beginning of the fourth dynasty at Meidum, Dahshur, and Giza, where the royal mortuary complexes—the tombs of the members of the royal family and the important officials—were laid out (at least in part) according to a common master plan. The individual *mastaba*s were arranged on a regular grid and built in standard sizes and shapes. The general principle of uniting the ruling elite in a monumental necropolis centered around the mortuary complex of the reigning king remained in effect throughout pharaonic history and characterizes, to a greater or lesser degree, the structure of the cemeteries of the Egyptian capitals.

The invention of rock-cut tombs during the latter part of the fourth dynasty had a considerable impact on the appearance of Egyptian necropolises. Already during the fifth dynasty, a type of tomb adapted to the geological conditions of Upper Egypt was developed, and it rapidly established itself there as the standard model for monumental tombs. The forecourts and the façades of these tombs are cut into the slope of the hillside, while the chapels and the burial apartments are excavated from the living rock. From this time, the flanks of the desert mountains approaching the Nile Valley became the preferred sites for the tombs of the provincial elite, which are usually laid out in several horizontal rows halfway up the hillside, so as to overlook the valley. Depending on the conditions at an individual site, cemeteries of shaft tombs of the lesser inhabitants of the town may be excavated on the hill slope or on the plain below the file of rock-cut tombs.

During the Middle Kingdom, the layouts developed during the late Old Kingdom largely remained in effect throughout Upper Egypt. Here the archaeological record is characterized by rock-cut tomb necropolises of the local elite near important provincial towns, and by cemeteries of simple shaft tombs, originally covered by small chapels, for the ordinary inhabitants. The court cemeteries near the royal residence reverted to Old Kingdom patterns as well, though on a less grandiose scale. Here the most important officials of the administration were buried in tombs, often archaistic *mastaba*s, attached to the pyramid complexes of the kings. A special role was played by the necropolis of Abydos during the Middle Kingdom. Its importance as the principal center of the cult of Osiris attracted many people who were eager to participate in its festivals. Numerous mortuary chapels, including cenotaphs, therefore cluster near the processional routes used during these occasions.

During the New Kingdom, the Theban necropolis gained supreme importance. Starting in the early eighteenth dynasty, the kings and their family members were buried in the Valley of the Kings and Valley of the Queens, two strictly exclusive areas, sheltered from sight from the valley by the first range of the desert mountains. Lined up along the margin of the valley, the mortuary temples of the kings were, at the same time, shrines devoted to the cult of the god Amun, and they played an important part in the festivals of the Theban necropolis. The sites of these temples and the processional routes used during these festivals had an important impact on the location of the tombs of private individuals in the necropolis. These were mainly rock-cut tombs, some of them decorated with the finest paintings that have survived from ancient Egypt. In their location, a ranking according to status can often be discerned.

A necropolis duplicating the basic layout of that at Thebes was begun at Tell el-Amarna during the reign of Akhenaten. A second important necropolis, mainly of the later New Kingdom, is situated at Saqqara, where the officials associated with Egypt's northern capital at Memphis were buried in sumptuous tombs of temple-like appearance. In Upper Egypt, small groups of decorated rock-cut tombs have been found at a few sites. In addition, there is a series of town cemeteries in Egypt, and, in particular, in Nubia. At these sites, the tombs of lesser provincial officials and townspeople are well attested.

During the Late period, the necropolises of the important political centers of the country, Thebes and the Memphite region, continue to flourish. Cemeteries of ordinary people as well as individual decorated tombs are attested throughout the country. Very exceptional as a type of cemetery, however, are the burials of members of the ruling house within temple precincts during the Third Intermediate Period and the Late period. Archaeologically attested examples of this custom are the burials of the kings of the twenty-first to twenty-third dynasties at Tanis, and the Third Intermediate Period and Late period tombs in front of the temple of Medinet Habu in Western Thebes—in particular, those of the "divine consorts of Amun," dating from the twenty-fifth and twenty-sixth dynasties. Similarly, the scions of the twenty-ninth dynasty are buried within the great Temenos of Ba-neb-djed at Mendes. A similar situation is described by Herodotus for the temple of Sais.

Patterns of Use through Time. Necropolises were often used for a considerable span of time, especially if they served large, permanent communities and if important elite tombs were present on the site. Because of the accumulation of tombs over the course of time, the center of occupation often shifted gradually from one location to another. Sometimes clear patterns of growth emerge from this process and can provide important information for establishing the archaeological chronology of a cemetery. Yet it can sometimes be shown that family members wished to be buried in close proximity to their ancestors; there are several cases in which sons had their tombs built next to those of their fathers or even chose to be buried in their fathers' tombs; in a few cases, groups of tombs spanning several generations of a single family can be discerned. Reisner grounded his interpretation of the structure of the fourth dynasty cemetery at Giza and of an Old Kingdom provincial cemetery at Naga ed-Deir mainly on hypothetical family groups, but he overemphasized the importance of this principle. In fact, there are no cemeteries that show an overall segmentary structure which could reflect long-term family groups among the occupants.

The gradual shift of a cemetery from one site to another is often associated with a shift in the social level of its occupants. Areas that had been reserved for elite tombs came to be occupied by lesser burials after the cult activities at the large tombs had ceased. Then the spaces available between the earlier buildings, in their courts and even in their chapels, were densely filled in with small tombs; in rock-cut tombs, intrusive shafts were added to receive humble burials. This sequence of reuse often followed the original occupation directly, and the personnel associated with the cults of the larger tombs even played an important part in it.

Necropolises in Social Life. Ancient Egyptian necropolises were complex social institutions, but evidence to elucidate this is sparse and unevenly distributed. The extant documents refer mainly to the elite level of society and to the necropolises of important centers. Any attempt to generalize from this evidence should take into account the differences among individual places and among social strata.

The right to receive a burial and a mortuary cult depended, in theory, on the king. In practice, however, this claim represented a reality, to a certain degree, only for the elite and the necropolises of the royal residence; after all, the sixth dynasty nomarch Djau at Deir el-Gebrawi refers in his inscriptions to a document testifying to his right to build a tomb for himself. In general, however, both burial and mortuary cult depended on the status and means of the deceased and their families.

The texts state that tombs should be built in "a pure place in which no tomb had been before." In fact, archaeological observations tend to confirm that people were careful, as far as possible, not to infringe on earlier tombs, at least not on those still in use for burials. From the late

Old Kingdom onward it became more and more the rule that a single tomb served for burials of the members of an extended family over several generations, and ownership of the tomb was passed on through inheritance. There is one instance on record in which a tomb in the Theban necropolis that had become vacant was assigned to a new owner by a state official at the end of the eighteenth dynasty.

Sometimes elite tombs were built by the king and assigned to his officials, or individual items of the furnishings of the tomb—like false door stelae or costly sarcophagi—were presented by the king to his followers. Similarly, great officials sometimes cared for the burials of their attendants. In most cases, however, tombs were built from private means, and, during the Old Kingdom, tomb inscriptions frequently assert that the tomb was built from the rightful possessions of the tomb-owner and that the craftsmen who built and decorated it had received fair payment.

Apart from building the tomb, steps to secure its mortuary cult had to be taken. The cult at the tomb usually depended on the family of the deceased, ideally the eldest son. In the elite level of society, however, it was common to set up a special foundation to guarantee regular offerings in the future. A certain amount of property was set apart and assigned, on a hereditary basis, to a group of mortuary priests who in return were to conduct the cult for the deceased. Among Old Kingdom tomb inscriptions there are several documents concerned with regulations of this type. A series of contracts in the tomb of the twelfth Dynasty nomarch Djefaihapy at Asyut attest to complex legal arrangements regarding his mortuary cult between the tomb-owner, the priesthoods of the temples of Asyut, and several necropolis officials.

Both through the resources regularly spent on tomb construction and through the endowments for the mortuary cults, considerable wealth was concentrated in the necropolis, providing a living for a considerable number of people. First, specialist workmen were needed to excavate and eventually decorate tombs on demand, as well as workshops to provide stelae, coffins, and other tomb equipment. A special class of stonemasons even took their title from this business. During the Middle Kingdom in particular there is a series of titles attesting to a complex organization of these gangs. During the New Kingdom, they are also found to be associated with various temples and the state administration. In fact, necropolis workmen are also listed as members of expeditions to quarries, and their title was understood to denote their special range of skills. Nevertheless, necropolis workmen are regularly found in various forms of employment in necropolises. The best-known community of workmen attached to a necropolis is the village of Deir el-Medina in western Thebes

during the New Kingdom. Their main task was to excavate and decorate the royal tombs in the Valley of the Kings and the Valley of the Queens, but it is well attested that they also manufactured tomb furnishings on demand. Although this special group of workmen was housed in a separate village in the Theban cemetery, other necropolis workers, as well as the priests serving the mortuary cults, probably lived in the villages or towns near the necopolises, or, in the case of the royal necropolises of the Old and Middle Kingdoms, in the pyramid towns.

The necropolises were under the civil administration. The Theban necropolis was supervised during the New Kingdom by a "mayor for the western side of Thebes" who was also the chief of the necropolis police. In the Middle Kingdom contracts of Djefaihapy, mentioned above, there is a possible reference to an "overseer of the necropolis," and, in the same texts, an "officer of the desert" (i.e., of the necropolis) is mentioned. This person was probably in charge of security in the necropolis; during the Middle Kingdom, the title "Guard of the Necropolis" is attested as well.

In the performance of the mortuary cult, festivals were of particular importance. During the Old Kingdom (and, in a modified form, also in later periods) a standard list of festivals is attested, which features, among others, New Year's Day, various dates in the lunar month, and the festivals of the gods Thoth, Sokar, and Min. With the probable exception of the *wag*-festival, these occasions were not festivals for the dead in a restricted sense. Rather, the mortuary cults were eager to participate in these wider communal celebrations.

From the Middle Kingdom onward it is evident from the documents that mortuary cults became linked more and more with the cults and festivals of local gods and their temples. Statues for private individuals were set up in the temples to participate ideally in the daily offerings of the gods. From the contracts for the mortuary cult of Djefaihapy, it emerges that offerings were to be presented to his statues during the processional festivals of Wepwawet and Anubis, the local gods of his hometown, Asyut.

Among the known "festivals of the necropolis," the most comprehensive documentation is available for the Valley Festival, which was celebrated in the Theban necropolis at least from the twelfth dynasty onward. Its ceremonies are depicted in the wall decorations of Theban tombs, especially during the eighteenth dynasty. During this festival, the image of the god Amun from the Karnak temple was carried in festive procession to the west bank to visit the gods of the Theban necropolis and the mortuary temples of the kings. On this occasion, cultic activities at the tombs reached their climax; families gathered at the tombs of their ancestors to celebrate the festival with joyful banquets.

Linking the cult of the dead to the great festivals of a town did not merely take advantage of the stability of the cults of the gods. Rather, it was central to the symbolic meaning of these festivals to display the sense of community and collective identity uniting the population of a town or a region. Therefore, it was perfectly logical to express the community between the dead and the living within the same symbolic framework.

A consideration of events in a necropolis cannot overlook tomb robbery and the destruction of tombs. The liveliest relevant account is provided by a series of official documents from the twentieth dynasty which pertain to investigations into several cases of royal tombs reported to have been violated by thieves. It emerges clearly from these texts that tomb robbery was a common feature in the necropolis of western Thebes at this time. Archaeological data confirm that this was not at all unusual; in many cemeteries, most tombs had been violated, in particular the better equipped ones. It seems significant that in most cases the robbers were evidently well informed about the layout and content of the burials. Evidently most tomb robberies took place not long after the original burial. In a few cases, there is even clear evidence that a burial was partly robbed before it was complete. There are also many cases in which, after a few generations, later tombs intruded on earlier ones, obstructing their cult places and even damaging them severely.

From the available documentation, it emerges that tomb robbery, while clearly considered a criminal act, was in fact a regular phenomenon, and so it seems that religious fears did not trouble the minds of the ancient Egyptians as overwhelmingly as is sometimes supposed. On the other hand, it appears that the protection of the tombs depended mainly on the continuing interest of the living in their cults and on the continuity of the surviving group's claim to ownership. As soon as a tomb dropped out of the network of social processes within the community, it was bound to face rapid destruction.

The Necropolis in Egyptian Thought. The principal Egyptian word for "necropolis" is *ḥr.t-nṯr* ("the property of the god"). The word "god" in this term probably referred originally to the king who bestowed the right of burial on members of the elite. Later, however, it was probably understood with reference to other gods who were regarded as "lords of the necropolis," like Osiris. As synonyms, "the West," "the Beautiful West," and "the Western Desert" are particularly common. In addition, there exists a great wealth of expressions used for the necropolises of individual places or those bound to specific contexts, like *t3-ḏsr* ("the sacred [secluded] land"), the domain of the god Anubis, or *r3-sṯ3.w* ("the beginning of the corridors"), associated in particular with the god Sokar and the Memphis necropolis.

The necropolis is the place in the real world where the tombs are. At the same time, however, the necropolis is the metaphysical realm where the destiny of the dead is carried out. Both aspects are inseparable in Egyptian thought. Necropolises as sites and as social institutions were the places at which the imaginary concepts of funerary religion were anchored to physical and social reality. The necropolis forms part of a tripartite model of a world that comprises heaven, earth, and necropolis; in its sense of "netherworld" and "hereafter," it is contrasted to the realm of the living (*t3-pn* "this land"; *tp-t3* "[being] upon earth"). The necropolis is the realm where the dead "live" (as a class of beings, along with gods and men). In that sense, the cemetery (as a site) is just the entrance to a netherworld realm of cosmic dimensions.

The dead do not pass the threshold to the netherworld once and for all. In some sense, they continue to dwell in the tomb as the living dwell in their houses. Therefore, the dead can be approached ritually at their tombs. Yet mobility is a prime concern to the spirits of the dead: they wish to move about freely in the netherworld, and they wish to be able to exit from it to see the light of the sun and to revisit the "places of yesterday." The necropolis is thus a place of transition in both directions and of continuous contact between this world and the world beyond.

The living and the dead are engaged in a network of mutual relationships which were conceptualized in highly ambivalent, even contradictory terms. For the dead, death could be a state of ultimate weakness. The dead depended on being cared for by the surviving group, both through ritually correct burial and through regular offerings. Otherwise, they would not be able to face the many hazards of their netherworld existence. The dead therefore need to muster the solidarity of the living, and they need to be remembered. One important argument in this context is to recall the moral integrity and the achievements of the deceased person during life, which entitles her or him to claim the support of her or his group in return. The same idea is expressed in a mythological guise in the concept of a universal judgment of the dead by the divine court of Osiris. At the same time, however, the dead could be powerful beings. For the surviving group, the dead did not lose their identity nor their status as social persons. Having access to the world of gods and spirits, they could lend magical support to their families. If offended by impious behavior, the spirits of the dead could prove fearful enemies; in fact, they are cited as a frequent cause of illness. For the living, interaction with the dead therefore could be risky and highly ambivalent. The necropolis was a place to seek support from them, to conciliate them, and even to combat them with magical means.

Very much as a necropolis appears, to the archaeologist, as the counterpart to a settlement, the community of the dead appeared, in Egyptian thought, as a counterpart to the society of the living, mirroring both its structure and its norms, raised to a metaphysical level.

[*See also entries on the individual sites mentioned in this article;* Tomb Robbery Papyri; *and the composite article on* Tombs.]

BIBLIOGRAPHY

Breasted, James H. *Ancient Records of Egypt,* vol. 1. Chicago, 1906. A handy collection of English translations of Egyptian documents, including several contracts referring to the establishment of mortuary cults.

Brunton, Guy. *Qau and Badari I-III, British School of Archaeology in Egypt 44-45 and 50.* London, 1927-1930; *Mostagedda and the Tasian Culture.* London, 1937; *Matmar.* London, 1948. Brunton's volumes on his excavations in the cemeteries between Qau and Matmar illustrate best the traditional approach of Egyptian archaeology to provincial cemeteries.

Černý, Jaroslav. *A Community of Workmen at Thebes in the Ramesside Period.* Bibliothèque d'Études, 50. Cairo, 1973. Study of the organization of necropolis workmen at Thebes.

Gomaa, Farouk, Jaromir Malek, and Dieter Kessler. "Nekropolen." In *Lexikon der Ägyptologie,* 4: 395-449. Wiesbaden, 1982. Catalog listing the known necropolises for the major divisions of Egyptian history.

Kampp, Friederike. *Die thebanische Nekropole: Zum Wandel des Grabgedankens von der 18. bis zur 20. Dynastie. Theben 13.* Mainz, 1996. Comprehensive survey of the history of the tombs of private individuals in the Theban necropolis.

Kemp, Barry J. "Dating Pharaonic Cemeteries, I: Non-mechanical Approaches to Seriation." *Mitteilungen des Deutschen Archäologischen Instituts Kairo* 31 (1975), 259-292.

Kemp, Barry J. "Automatic Analysis of Predynastic Cemeteries: A New Method for an Old Problem." *Journal of Egyptian Archaeology* 68 (1982), 5-15. Kemp's two articles provide an introduction to the methodological issues of the chronological analysis of cemetery data.

O'Connor, David. "A Regional Population in Egypt to ca. 400 B.C." In: *Population Growth,* edited by B. Spular, pp. 78-100. New York, 1972.

O'Connor, David. "Political Systems and Archaeological Data in Egypt 2600-1780 B.C." *World Archaeology* 6 (1974/75), 15-38. O'Connor's two articles are excellent examples of the interpretation of cemetery data within an anthropological and historical framework.

Peet, Thomas E. *The Great Tomb-Robberies of the Twentieth Egyptian Dynasty.* Oxford, 1930. Translation and analysis of documents referring to the plundering of royal tombs in western Thebes.

Petrie, W. M. Flinders, and James E. Quibell. *Naqada and Ballas, 1895.* British School of Archaeology in Egypt, 1. London, 1896. Report on the excavation of the first prehistoric cemeteries discovered in Egypt.

Reeves, Carl N. *Valley of the Kings: The Decline of a Royal Necropolis.* London, 1990.

Reisner, George A. *The Archaeological Survey of Nubia. Report for 1907-1908.* Cairo, 1910. Report on the first cemeteries of indigenous Nubian cultures to be excavated.

Reisner, George A. *A Provincial Cemetery of the Pyramid Age, Naga-ed-Dêr III.* Oxford, 1932. Report on the excavation of an Old Kingdom provincial cemetery, reconstructing the social organization of the community from the cemetery data and comparing the provincial material with contemporary Memphite monuments.

Reisner, George A. *A History of the Giza Necropolis.* Cambridge, Mass., 1942.

Seidlmayer, Stephan J. "Wirtschaftliche und gesellschaftliche Entwicklung im Übergang vom Alten zum Mittleren Reich." In *Problems and Priorities in Egyptian Archaeology,* edited by Jan Assmann et al., pp. 175-218. London, 1987. An attempt to assess economic and social developments on the basis of cemetery data.

Valbelle, Dominique. *"Les ouvriers de la tombe": Deir el-Médineh à l'époque ramesside.* Bibliothèque d'Études, 96. Cairo, 1985. Comprehensive account of the organization of the workmens' village of Deir el-Medina and of the life of its inhabitants.

STEPHAN J. SEIDLMAYER

NEFERTI. Attested in twenty-two New Kingdom copies, the *Prophecy of Neferti* is an example of the literary genre of political lamentation characteristic of the preceding Middle Kingdom. Paralleling the frame story of Papyrus Westcar, the *Prophecy* is set in the yet earlier Old Kingdom court of Pharaoh Sneferu (c.2649-2609 BCE), who seeks distraction by "fine words and choice phrases." At the recommendation of his courtiers, Sneferu summons the priest and sage Neferti, who offers to regale the monarch with tales of the past or future. Dismissing the past as irrelevant, the king takes writing equipment in hand and personally records the inspired prophecy that comprises the remainder of the tale. This striking role reversal, in which the king acts as scribe for a commoner, is in keeping with the informal and human portrayal of Sneferu in Egyptian popular sources.

Despite this Old Kingdom setting, however, the true date of the composition is evident not only from its classical grammar, but also from the contents of the prophecy itself. Adopting many of the clichés of Middle Kingdom lamentations, Neferti's prophecy bemoans a land in distress from political and cosmological upheaval. Great families no longer rule; the sun refuses to shine; the Nile evaporates and the winds are at war. Paradox is rampant. Though the land withers, the rulers proliferate; harvest is low, yet taxes increase; nobles are reduced to robbing while beggars and slaves become wealthy; the dead multiply, but mourning is supplanted by indifference. In these literary reminiscences of the turbulent First Intermediate Period (c.2206-2041 BCE), Neferti's text assigns particular blame to roaming Near Eastern Bedouin, described as "strange birds" infesting the northern Delta, harassing the harvest, and plundering the wealth of the Nile. If the north is the source of Egypt's weakness, its salvation will derive from a "man of the south." Hailing from the region of Aswan, a king named Ameny will assume the crown and reunite the kingdom, erecting a strong border fortress to halt the Near Eastern infiltration. Chaos will yield to order and misery to joy.

The Ameny of the text is readily identifiable as Amenemhet I (c.1991-1962 BCE), founder of the prosperous twelfth dynasty, and it is to the early years of his reign that one may assign the composition of this propagandistic narrative disguised as ancient prophecy. The optimism of the piece is in stark contrast to the *Instructions of Amenemhet*, written at the conclusion of the reign, when court intrigue rather than Asiatics threatened the stability of the reinvigorated nation. Composed in a mixture of prose and poetry, the prophecy employs the standard literary device of thematic couplets, in which parallel clauses form the structure of the verse.

The primary manuscript is Papyrus Petersburg (Leningrad) 1165B, dating to the eighteenth dynasty (reign of Amenhotpe II, c.1454–1419 BCE). It is supplemented by two contemporary writing tablets (Cairo 25224 and British Museum 5647) and nineteen Ramessid school ostraca from Deir el-Medina. The continued popularity of the text in the New Kingdom may reflect a perceived relevance of its concerns for the later Near Eastern (Hyksos) infiltration of the Delta in the Second Intermediate Period, which was ended by yet another southern Ameny, Amenhotpe I.

BIBLIOGRAPHY

Blumenthal, Elke. "Neferti, Prophezeiung des." In *Lexikon der Ägyptologie*, 4: 380–381. Wiesbaden, 1982.

Helck, Wolfgang. *Die Prophezeiung des Nfr.tj*. Kleine ägyptische Texte, 2d rev. ed. Wiesbaden, 1992 (1970). The standard text edition.

Lichtheim, Miriam. *Ancient Egyptian Literature*. Berkeley, 1973. See pages 139–145.

Parkinson, Richard B. *Voices from Ancient Egypt*, Norman, Okla., Selections appear on pages 34–36.

Parkinson, Richard B. *The Tale of Sinuhe and Other Ancient Egyptian Poems 1940–1640 BC*. Oxford, 1997. For the *Prophecy*, see pages 131–143.

Simpson, William K., ed. *The Literature of Ancient Egypt*. 2d rev. ed. New Hanen, 1973. See pages 234–240 by Raymond O. Faulkner.

ROBERT K. RITNER

NEFERTITI, the principal queen of Amenhotpe IV (Akhenaten) of the eighteenth dynasty, New Kingdom (r. 1372–1355 BCE), and mother of six of his daughters. Nothing definitive is known about Nefertiti's parentage,

NEFERTITI. *The queen stands before an offering table, with her eldest daughter behind her.* (Courtesy Donald B. Redford)

but there is no reason to doubt that she was born into a high-ranking Egyptian family with a close connection to the royal court.

The earliest attestations of Nefertiti's existence show her accompanying her husband as he performed both official and religious duties. She bore the epithet "Nefer-neferuaten," which associated her with the sun god Aten, whose cult was at the center of Akhenaten's "revolution." She played an unprecedented role in the decorative program of the temples built by Akhenaten for Aten's worship at Karnak during the earlier Theban phase of his reign. The reliefs and statuary of that period, executed in a radical, "expressionistic" style, did not distinguish Nefertiti's physiognomy from the king's. A personal, official likeness of the queen was created only after Akhenaten moved the court to his new capital city, Akhetaten, where a moderated style was evolved. The queen's economic institutions and cult installations were well documented archaeologically at Akhetaten (the site of Tell el-Amarna), where Nefertiti made her home with her husband and their daughters.

Nefertiti's preeminent status in Akhenaten's harem was signaled not only by a series of titles and epithets that are exclusively hers but also by other royal markers. Among his wives, only Nefertiti wore crowns and only she was entitled to have a *uraeus* at her brow. Aten, too, was known to be partial to Nefertiti; she is the only person, other than Akhenaten, who received life from the god and who was fondled by Aten's hands. In return, she was often shown actively worshiping the sun disk.

Some depictions of Nefertiti show her with attributes and in contexts normally associated only with the ruler, which has led to scholarly questions about her role in the politics of the period. (Unlike Akhenaten's mother Tiye, she was, however, not mentioned in the Amarna Letters.) There is no unequivocal evidence in support of the theory that she was Akhenaten's coregent at the end of his reign. Whether she acceded to the kingship, however briefly, following his death remains an open question. When she died is not known.

In the proclamation issued when Akhenaten founded his new capital, he expressed the intention that Nefertiti be buried there, like him and their eldest daughter. Whether he ordered a separate tomb for her or planned that she be interred in a suite of rooms in his own tomb is moot. A single *shawabti* is all that remains of any funerary equipment that might have been prepared for Nefertiti.

In the post-Amarna period, figures of Nefertiti and texts naming her were attacked, perhaps not to destroy her image but concomitantly with the persecution of Akhenaten's memory. Those in ancient times who wanted to eradicate the Amarna episode from history would be disconcerted to discover that today the well-known painted bust of Nefertiti has made the queen one of the most widely recognized symbols of ancient Egypt.

BIBLIOGRAPHY

Allen, James P. "Nefertiti and Smenkh-ka-re." *Göttinger Miszellen* 141 (1994), 7–17. Advocates the identification of Nefertiti as Akhenaten's coregent and successor (a view not shared by this author).

Arnold, Dorothea. *The Royal Women of Amarna: Images of Beauty from Ancient Egypt.* New York, 1996. Exhibition catalog, with extensive bibliography; includes a thorough discussion of Nefertiti's statuary and the representations of her in reliefs.

Krauss, Rolf. "1913–1988: 75 Jahre büste der NofretEte/Nefret-iti in Berlin." *Jahrbuch Preussischer Kulturbesitz* 24 (1987), 87–124; 28 (1991), 123–57. Two-part article that recounts the history of the well-known painted bust of Nefertiti (Berlin Egyptian Museum 21300) since its discovery.

Krauss, Rolf. "Nefretitis Ende." *Mitteilungen des Deutschen Archäologischen Instituts Kairo* 53 (1997), 209–213. Publication and analysis of Hieratic dockets from Amarna, with clues to Nefertiti's status and the date of her death.

Smith, Ray Winfield, and Donald B. Redford. *Akhenaten Temple Project 1: Initial Discoveries.* Warminster, 1976. Deals with Nefertiti's role during the Theban phase of Akhenaten's reign.

Vergnieux, Robert. *Recherches sur les monuments thébains d'Amenhotep IV à l'aide d'outils informatiques.* Cahiers de la Société d'Égyptologie, 4. Geneva, in press. Considers Nefertiti's status as reflected in her representations and inscriptions on blocks from Karnak temple.

MARIANNE EATON-KRAUSS

NEFERTUM. The god Nefertum was primarily a solar deity who was linked to several Egyptian creation myths. His name, *Nfr-tm*, means "Amun is good" or "he who has newly appeared is perfect," and his primary symbol was the blue lotus blossom. He is most often depicted in Egyptian art as a human male wearing a headdress composed of a lotus blossom flanked by two tall plumes. Many times, the symbols are accompanied by *menat*-necklace counterpoises, emphasizing his youthful nature. He also carries a sickle-shaped object in his left hand.

Nefertum's connection to the solar realm is made known in Spell 266 of the Pyramid Texts, in which he is referred to as "the lotus blossom at the nose" of the sun god Re. He eventually unites with Re to form a single deity. One of his other representations is a man with a lion's head or a man standing on the back of a lion, a solar animal. His appearance in the Pyramid Texts also illustrates his connection with the Egyptian kingship; in Spell 249, he is described as "the king as a flower in the hand of the sun god."

In the Coffin Texts, Nefertum is described as a child-god. He is the son of the leonine goddess, Sekhmet, and, beginning in the New Kingdom, he fills a new role as the child-member of the Memphite triad, along with his mother, Sekhmet, and the Memphite creator god, Ptah.

NEFERTUM. *Statue of Nefertum at the Brooklyn Museum of Art.* (Courtesy Stephen Phillips)

Because of the close connection between the aggressive lioness goddess, Sekhmet, and her more peaceful feline counterpart, Bastet, Nefertum is sometimes described as the child of Bastet. As the son of the fierce goddess, Sekhmet, Nefertum sometimes takes on a warlike role and, in that form, he can be associated with other warlike gods such as Montu, Sopdu, and Hormenty, as well as with several other leonine goddesses in whose cults he was thought to participate. Nefertum also acts together with his mother, Sekhmet, as an apotropaic deity who could be called upon for protection from illness and plague. There is a chapel of Nefertum in the temple of Sety I at Abydos, where he is accompanied by Ptah-Sokar and other Memphite deities.

Nefertum plays a role in one of the ancient Egyptian creation myths. It was believed that the lotus blossom was the first living thing to appear out of the water of chaos at the beginning of time. When the petals of this blue lotus opened, the sun god appeared for the first time. This creation image is nicely illustrated in a wooden statue of King Tutankhamun that shows the head of the youthful king appearing atop a lotus blossom.

Nefertum is also associated with funerary religion in his form as the deity Sokar-Henu-Nefertum. He appears in the *Book of Going Forth by Day* (*Book of the Dead*) as the one who brings the unfortunate evildoers to the slaughter block and as a member of the council of gods who judge the dead (chapter 125 of the *Book of Going Forth by Day*).

Because of his associations with the fragrant blue lotus flower, Nefertum is also thought of as a god of perfume.

Some of his divine epithets include "Protector of the Two Lands" and "Lord of Provisions."

BIBLIOGRAPHY

David, A. Rosalie. *Religious Ritual at Abydos (c. 1300 BC)*. Warminster, 1973.

Lurker, Manfred. *The Gods and Symbols of Ancient Egypt*. Translated by Barbara Cummings. New York, 1980.

Schlögl, Hermann. "Nefertem." In *Lexikon der Ägyptologie*, 4:378–380. Wiesbaden, 1980.

JENNIFER HOUSER-WEGNER

NEGATIVE CONFESSION. *See* Ethics and Morality.

NEITH. The goddess Neith, who occupies an important place in the Egyptian pantheon, served in a number of different capacities. She was the fierce goddess of war and hunting. Her symbols, known as early as the first dynasty in a tomb in Abydos, are a shield and two crossed arrows. The deity is frequently depicted holding these weapons; she is also crowned with these attributes.

Neith has certain domestic characteristics. She is the patron of weaving. The hieroglyph for her name is a loom, which is sometimes illustrated above her head. In addition, she is involved in funerary rituals: with Isis and other deities, she watches over the coffin of Osiris; as the goddess of weaving, she bestows mummy shrouds upon the deceased.

Neith is associated with Lower Egypt. She is worshiped as the goddess of this region, and in some of her representations she wears the Red Crown. In fact, one of her names is "she of the Lower Egyptian crown."

She is identified as the mother of all, "creating the seed of gods and men." During the New Kingdom, she is known as the mother of the sun god, Re. At this time, she is also regarded as the primeval goddess who produced the world. Neith also gave birth to Sobek, the crocodile god of Lower Egypt, who became a popular figure during the twelfth dynasty, when the rulers enjoyed hunting in the marshes.

Neith plays a pivotal role in Egyptian myth. When Osiris is murdered by Seth and a successor must be found, it is the wise and powerful Neith to whom the other deities turn for guidance. In a letter that she writes to the gods, she states authoritatively, "Give the office of Osiris to his son Horus! Do not go on committing these great wrongs, which are not in place, or I will get angry and the sky will topple to the ground. But also tell the Lord of All, the Bull who lives in Heliopolis, to double Seth's property. Give him Anathe and Astarte, your two daughters, and put Horus in the place of his father."

Neith's roots are very ancient; in the earliest dynasties, several queens bore her name. However, it was in the Late period that she gained the greatest prominence. She was venerated by the twenty-sixth dynasty pharaohs at their capital, Sais, in the Nile Delta, where she served as protector for the fifth nome of Lower Egypt. It has been suggested that Neith was of Libyan descent; this may in part explain the Saite rulers' fondness for her, because they too were of Libyan ancestry.

A great temple was built in Neith's name at Sais. According to Plutarch, an inscription in this impressive structure read: "I am all that has been, that is, and that will be. No mortal has yet been able to lift the veil that covers me."

BIBLIOGRAPHY

Ames, Delano. *Egyptian Mythology*. London, 1965.

Clark, R. T. Rundle. *Myth and Symbol in Ancient Egypt*. London, 1991.

David, A. Rosalie. *The Ancient Egyptians*. London, 1982.

Gardiner, Alan. *Egypt of the Pharaohs*. Oxford, 1961.

James, T. G. H. *Myths and Legends of Ancient Egypt*. London, 1969.

Lurker, Manfred. *The Gods and Symbols of Ancient Egypt*. New York, 1974.

Patrick, Richard. *Egyptian Mythology*. London, 1972.

Quirke, Stephen. *Ancient Egyptian Religion*. London, 1992.

Schlichting, R. "Neit." In *Lexikon der Ägyptologie*, 4:392–394. Wiesbaden, 1980.

Watterson, Barbara. *Gods of Ancient Egypt*. Gloucestershire, 1996.

CATHERINE SIMON

NEITHHOTEP. Neithhotep (or Hetep-neith) may have been the wife or the mother of King Aha of the first dynasty; if she was his mother, then she probably was the spouse of King Narmer. The differing opinions stem in part from the fact that she is never designated as "mother" or "wife." Like those of other important royal women of the Early Dynastic period (Merneith, Herneith), her name is compounded with that of the goddess Neith, whose main cult center was at Sais in the Nile Delta.

Her name appears on some two dozen objects—clay sealings, ivory tags and cosmetic items, and stone vessels—the majority of which were discovered at Naqada and Abydos. The pieces from Naqada were found in the so-called Great Tomb excavated by Jacques de Morgan in 1897 and by John Garstang in 1904. This tomb also contained objects inscribed for Aha. This massive mud-brick *mastaba* (approximately 54 × 27 meters/177 × 88 feet), situated about 3 kilometers (2 miles) northwest of the town of Naqada and some 7 kilometers (4.2 miles) south of the main Predynastic cemetery, had a well-preserved superstructure decorated with a continuous palace façade. It has been attributed to Neithhotep herself, but the original tomb owner is likely to have been a man whose name was written with three bird hieroglyphs (reading uncertain). Judging from the size of the tomb and the types of grave goods, he was surely the local ruler of the province. The placement of Neithhotep's objects in the tomb suggests that she was related to him and thus may have belonged to an important Upper Egyptian family. She was probably buried at Abydos.

One seal documented by several ancient impressions from the Naqada Great Tomb depicts her name with crossed arrows—the sign for the goddess Neith—placed on top of the palace façade *(srḫ)* instead of the Horus falcon, the signal for the king's Horus name, a royal prerogative. This so-called palace seal has been used as evidence that Neithhotep may have served as a queen regent. A fragmentary ivory label from a grave at Helwan preserves the head of a female figure beside the name Neithhotep.

BIBLIOGRAPHY

Bryan, Betsy M. *Mistress of the House, Mistress of Heaven: Women in Ancient Egypt*, edited by Anne K. Capel and Glenn E. Markoe, pp. 27–28. New York, 1997. Bryan ascribes the Naqada Great Tomb to Neithotep (the traditional view) and notes that she was probably the wife of Aha and regent for his successor Djer.

Emery, W. B. *Archaic Egypt*. Harmondsworth, 1961. Emery believed that Neithhotep was married to Narmer and that it was a diplomatic marriage that joined North and South.

Helck, Wolfgang. "Neith-hotep." In *Lexikon der Ägyptologie*, 4:394–395. Wiesbaden, 1980. Succinct presentation, including possibility that she was queen regent for an ephemeral successor of Aha.

Hoffman, Michael. *Egypt before the Pharaohs*. New York, 1979. One of the best English sources for a description of the Naqada Great Tomb and for puzzling out the confusion of Neithhotep's genealogy as the wife of either Narmer or Aha (see especially pp. 280, 322).

Kaplony, Peter. *Die Inschriften der Ägyptischen Frühzeit*. 3 vols. Ägyptologische Abhandlungen 8. Wiesbaden, 1963. Most scholarly discussions about Neithhotep refer to Kaplony's commentary and the list of objects inscribed with her name; also provides the original publication information (vol. 1, pp. 588–592).

Saad, Zaki Y. *The Excavations at Helwan: Art and Civilization in the First and Second Dynasties*. Norman, Okla., 1969. The ivory label depicting Neithhotep's name and the upper part of a female figure are illustrated in figure 14 and plate 93.

Seipel, Wilfried. "Untersuchungen zu den ägyptischen Königinnen der Frühzeit und des Alten Reiches: Quellen und historische Einordung." Ph.D. diss., University of Hamburg, 1980. This study of early queens in Egypt has a very useful assessment of the evidence about her (listed under *Ḥtp.wj-Nt*).

Troy, Lana. *Patterns of Queenship in Ancient Egyptian Myth and History*. BOREAS: Uppsala Studies in Ancient Mediterranean and Near Eastern Civilizations, 14. Uppsala, 1986. Troy suggests (pp. 106, 152, 183) that an ivory lid from Abydos (now in the British Museum [BM 35512]) has a title for Neithhotep, which she interprets as "consort" *(smȝyt nbwy*, "the one is united with the Two Lords"). Other scholars, such as Kaplony, read it differently, as a personal name, not a title.

BARBARA A. PORTER

NEKHEN. *See* Hierakonpolis.

NEKTANEBO, the name of two kings of the thirtieth dynasty, Late period. Nektanebo I (r. 380–363 BCE) founded the dynasty and Nektanebo II (r. 360–343 BCE), is usually considered to be its final ruler and the last native king of Egypt, despite the possibility that a man named Khababash may have succeeded as king (see Spalinger 1978). Tachos (Teos II), son of Nektanebo I and an uncle of Nektanebo II, ruled briefly between the reigns of the Nektanebos. Little is known about Tachos and he built few, if any, monuments. There is some uncertainty about the regnal years of these kings, and the dates listed above may be plus or minus at least one year.

Nektanebo I, from the central Nile Delta city of Sebennytos, was born into a military family, the son of a man named Djedhor. Soon after the death of Hakoris (r. 392–380 BCE), the penultimate king of the twenty-ninth dynasty, Nektanebo seized power. The brief reign of Nepherites II (a son of Hakoris) was disrupted by a period of unrest that resulted in a revolt that unseated him, leaving Nektanebo I to rule. The first seven years of his rule were peaceful, this interlude ending with an invasion by the Persian king, Artaxerxes II. Nektanebo I repulsed the attack, then entered into an alliance with Sparta and Athens. Although his capital was Mendes in Lower Egypt, his monuments have survived from the Mediterranean Sea to the Nubian border. He built a large number of temples—probably more than any of the other pharaohs who ruled after the New Kingdom. If that vast amount of construction is an accurate indicator, his rule was economically extremely successful.

Apart from numerous highly idealized relief representations of Nektanebo I on temple walls, three inscribed statues, or statue fragments, of him are extant. An over life-size limestone portrait (now standing outside the Egyptian Museum in Cairo) is the best known—intact except for its nose and feet. The Mansoura storage magazine in the Delta contains the upper part of a graywacke statue, which skillfully and carefully imitates the style of the late twenty-sixth dynasty, and was probably carved near the beginning of Nektanebo I's reign. A granite head in Paris at the Musée du Louvre is in the later style of the Cairo portrayal. There are undoubtedly other portraits of him not bearing a name (see Josephson 1997). Nektanebo I was venerated long after his death, with cults dedicated to him enduring at least into the middle years of the Ptolemaic (Hellenistic) domination of Egypt.

Nektanebo II ascended the throne as a result of the duplicity of his father, Tjahepimu, a brother of Tachos, who was left in charge of Egypt when Tachos, accompanied by Greek mercenaries and the Egyptian army, journeyed to Phoenicia to battle the Persians who had invaded North Africa. The mercenaries, acting under instructions from Sparta, supported Nektanebo II, and Tachos fled to the

Persian court. Upon returning to Egypt, the new pharaoh, Nektanebo II, defeated the prince of Mendes, his only opposition, then turned his attention to the construction and restoration of temples throughout Egypt, an undertaking that enriched the powerful priesthood and ensured their endorsement of his kingship. Coincidentally, the Persians were also preoccupied with problems of succession, so Egypt had a respite from interference by that powerful empire. This state of affairs lasted until 351–350 BCE, when Artaxerxes III, then in full control of his realm, led an invasion force into Egypt. Nektanebo II's troops defeated that formidable foe, who retreated northward, abandoning much of the conquered territory that bordered the Mediterranean Sea.

Emboldened by his military success, Nektanebo II did not conclude treaties with the Greeks and other Mediterranean powers, although together, they might have presented a strong enough alliance to discourage Artaxerxes from attempting to reconquer the wealthy states of Phoenicia and Egypt. In 343 BCE, Persia reinvaded Egypt and prevailed against the isolated Egyptian pharaoh; Artaxerxes had craftily insured success by recruiting two extraordinary generals, Bagoas and Mentor of Rhodes, as well as a substantial force of Greek soldiers. Nektanebo II fled from the Persians, presumably south to Nubia, and never returned to Egypt. Whether Khababash succeeded him is conjectural; if he did, it was in name only.

Although the reign of Nektanebo II ended ignominiously, it was, for the most part, replete with achievements and lasted a considerable period of years, marked by great turbulence in the region. His memory was honored by the Hellenic conquerors of the Persians, led by Alexander the Great. (The so-called Alexander Romance intimates that Nektanebo II fathered Alexander.) As with Nektanebo I, cults were established for his worship during the Ptolemaic period. Some representations of Nektanebo II survive as the pharaoh standing under the protecting Horus in the form of a hawk, which made a rebus of his name, *Nect-hor-heb*. Other noninscribed heads of Nektanebo II have also been identified on the basis of their style (see Josephson 1997).

Sadly, and unfairly, Nektanebo II is best remembered as the pharaoh whose reign ended almost three thousand years of mostly native rule in an unparalleled civilization. Often forgotten is that those final years included an extraordinary rebirth of artistic and literary creativity. When Alexander the Great conquered Egypt, only eleven years after Artaxerxes III had established his primacy there, the Hellenistic period began for Egypt.

BIBLIOGRAPHY

De Meulenaere, Herman. "Nektanebo I." In *Lexikon der Ägyptologie*, 4: 450–453. Wiesbaden, 1982.

Grimal, Nicholas. *A History of Ancient Egypt,* translated by Ian Shaw. Oxford, 1992.
Josephson, J. *Egyptian Royal Sculpture of the Late Period, 400–246 B.C.* Mainz, 1997.
Kienitz, F. *Die politische Geschichte Ägyptens*, vol. 7. Berlin, 1953.
Spalinger, Anthony. "Reign of King Chabbash." *Zeitschrift für Ägyptische Sprache und Altertumskunde* 105 (1978), 142–154.

JACK A. JOSEPHSON

NEPHTHYS. Although she appears frequently in Egyptian sources, the deity Nephthys apparently did not have her own body of myth independent of the Osiris legend. Her role is primarily funerary, as the counterpart of her sister Isis, in mourning and protecting the dead. Nephthys is usually portrayed as a woman with her name, *Nb-ḥwt*, "mistress of the mansion," on her head. Sometimes she is shown with outstretched wings; more rarely she is depicted in the form of a bird.

Nephthys' character was established by the time of the Pyramid Texts (c.2400 BCE). According to the texts, she is one of the Ennead of Heliopolis, the daughter of Geb and Nut, and the sister of Osiris, Isis and Seth. Although she is Seth's consort, she supports Osiris, and is closely associated with Isis. When Osiris dies, Isis and Nephthys transform themselves into kites, lament his death, and restore his body, thus protecting it from decay. Together, they guard the young Horus and the deceased king. Isis and Nephthys are typically paired, and while both are essentially beneficent, Nephthys can be associated with darkness, as when Isis represents the ascending day bark and Nephthys the descending night bark.

The Pyramid Texts refer to Nephthys as the mother and nurse of the king, suggesting an association with divine birth, and the Westcar Papyrus portrays her aiding the birth of future kings. In solar religion, Isis and Nephthys assist Re, indicating a possible origin as sky goddesses.

Most representations of Nephthys occur in funerary contexts. She protects the canopic jars; her association is with Hapy as the guardian of the lungs. Isis and Nephthys are depicted behind the throne of Osiris in the *Book of Going Forth by Day (Book of the Dead)*, occupying the solar bark in the *Book of Gates*, and beside the tomb of Osiris in the *Book of That Which Is in the Underworld (Amduat)*. They adorn the exteriors of New Kingdom royal sarcophagi; the feather patterns on Theban *rishi*-coffins represent their outstretched wings, and they figure prominently in the vignettes on cartonnage coffins of the New Kingdom and later. Funerary scenes in nineteenth dynasty private tombs show Nephthys at the head of the coffin, Isis at the foot, and Anubis administering to the deceased.

From the fifth dynasty onward, female *dryt* mourners are shown portraying Isis and Nephthys in funerary scenes. Two Graco-Roman versions of the *Lamentations of Isis and Nephthys* were intended to be performed by women impersonating the goddesses in temples and funerals respectively. There is little evidence for an individual cult of Nephthys, although three twentieth dynasty priests of her cult, and one from the Late Period, are attested. The birthday of Nephthys was celebrated on the last epagomenal day.

Nephthys is usually portrayed as childless, although in some Greco-Roman versions of the Osiris legend, Anubis is the child of Nephthys by Osiris. Other sources list her as the mother of a son by Re and a daughter by Hemen. Although rarely associated with deities other than Isis, she is occasionally identified with Seshat or Anuket. In the Ptolemaic period, Nephthys attends the Apis bull, and the Greeks sometimes identified her with Aphrodite or Nike.

BIBLIOGRAPHY

Armour, Robert A. *Gods and Myths of Ancient Egypt*. Cairo, 1986. Brief discussion of Nephthys and her role in the Osiris legend.

Bonnet, Hans. *Reallexikon der ägyptischen Religionsgeschichte*. Berlin, 1952. Encyclopedic treatment of source material for the history of Egyptian religion, with details of textual evidence for the cult of Nephthys and associated deities.

Fischer, Henry George. "Representations of Dryt–mourners in the Old Kingdom." *Egyptian Studies I: Varia*. pp. 39–50. New York, 1976. Presents additional evidence for female mourners who impersonate Isis and Nephthys, supplementing Wilson's earlier study.

Griffiths, John Gwynn. *Plutarch's De Iside et Osiride*. Cardiff, 1970. Edited text of the Graco-Roman account of the Osiris legend, with introduction, translation, and commentary.

Hart, George. *A Dictionary of Egyptian Gods and Goddesses*. London, 1986. Brief, popular description of Nephthys and her portrayal in art.

Quirke, Stephen. *Ancient Egyptian Religion*. London, 1992. A recent study of Egyptian religion for the general reader, emphasizing art historical evidence from the British Museum.

Wilson, John A. "Funeral Services of the Old Kingdom." *Journal of Near Eastern Studies* 3 (1944), 201–208. A discussion of female mourners in the guise of Isis and Nephthys.

DENISE M. DOXEY

NEW KINGDOM. [*This article surveys the New Kingdom of ancient Egypt, with reference to that period's major kings, main historical events, and significant cultural and social developments. It comprises five articles:*

An Overview
Eighteenth Dynasty to the Amarna Period
Amarna Period and the End of the Eighteenth Dynasty
Nineteenth Dynasty
Twentieth Dynasty

For related discussions, see articles on specific New Kingdom kings.]

An Overview

The third major era of Egyptian history (c.1569–1076 BCE) is called the New Kingdom. Although periodization has been criticized as reflecting the categories, outmoded or gratuitous, of Western historiography (e.g., Redford 1979, pp. 16–18), there is some justification for this period in ancient records. In an episode of the feast of the god Min from Ramesses II's memorial temple on the western bank of the Nile at Thebes (published by the University of Chicago Epigraphic Survey, *Medinet Habu*, 1930–1970, vol. 4, pl. 213), the rites are witnessed by a selection of royal ancestors, each represented by a statue; most of these are the current ruler's official forebears and are traced back to Ahmose, whose victory over the Near Eastern Hyksos regime had earned him recognition as the "founder" of the eighteenth dynasty. Earlier periods are represented in a more cursory fashion by only two figures: Nebhepetre Montuhotep I (eleventh dynasty), who reunited Egypt about 2040 by putting an end to the rival tenth dynasty at Herakleopolis; and Menes, the semi-mythical founder of the united monarchy of Upper and Lower Egypt. Underlying this arrangement is a conception of Egyptian history defined by three periods of national unity—a combined "Early Dynastic period/Old Kingdom," followed by a "Middle Kingdom," and finally by the third, then current, "New Kingdom" era consisting of the eighteenth (c.1569–1315 BCE) and nineteenth (c.1315–1201 BCE) dynasties, to which would be added the twentieth dynasty (c.1200–1081 BCE).

Imperialism is the hallmark of New Kingdom statecraft. While earlier pharaohs had felt free to chastise troublemakers beyond their borders, no one had ever sought to end such disturbances through the mechanisms of permanent control. The virtual hegemony Egypt had exercised over the Sinai and parts of Nubia during earlier periods had been intermittent, enforced whenever Egyptians needed the products of those areas by expeditionary forces deployed against feeble opponents. Even those foreign princes who had recognized the pharaoh as their overlord were independent and sovereign rulers, deferring only in the few areas—such as state trade and the occasional recruitment of mercenaries or local labor—that impinged directly on their suzerain's interests. Egyptian outposts on foreign territory (such as the string of forts built during the Middle Kingdom at the Second Cataract in Nubia) marked a functional extension of the Egyptian border rather than an attempt to occupy hostile powers, most of which still lay beyond the range of Egyptian control. Before the New Kingdom, it might be said that Egypt's foreign policy focused on obtaining what it needed from the outside world, which otherwise it kept comfortably at arm's length.

The bitter experience of the Second Intermediate Period, when a rump pharaonic state in Upper Egypt had been hemmed in by its Hyksos overlord in the north and the kingdom of Kush to the south (c.1664–1545 BCE), must have influenced the more aggressive tack that Egyptian policy subsequently took toward its neighbors. The approach was consistent in neither substance nor pace. Change came soonest, and most boldly, in Nubia, which was assuming the character of a separate province in the earliest eighteenth dynasty, even before Egyptian conquests there had reached their fullest extent. Under Kamose (reckoned as the last king of the seventeenth dynasty), Egypt had repossessed the Second Cataract forts that had been abandoned during the late Middle Kingdom and then occupied by forces of the "ruler of Kush"; and in the time of Ahmose, Kamose's brother and successor, comes the first mention of the viceroy who would govern the rapidly growing territory. To be sure, the tight control Egypt asserted so swiftly in Nubia may reflect its anxiety to avert further danger from the upper Nile Valley; but security concerns at home may also have played a part. Certainly it seems odd that Ahmose, a full-blooded scion of the Theban royal family, faced no fewer than two rebellions in Upper Egypt; the first was led by one Aata, perhaps a Nubian, "who came on behalf of (?) the south" (as a contemporary says) before he was subdued by the gods of Upper Egypt; the other was led by an Egyptian named Tetian. Although a challenge to the reigning dynasty has been read into the second uprising, both may reflect discontent among Ahmose's subjects. Some were surely affected by the new and intolerant nationalism that arose from the regime's drive against its foreign enemies: no longer could Thebans trade with the Hyksos and their Egyptian allies to the north; and in Upper Egypt, where Kushite rulers had recruited mercenaries to staff the border forts, the restrictive new order probably strained loyalties all the more. Under these circumstances, it would hardly be surprising that repressing dissidence at home coincided with extending the borders of Egypt in the southern Nile Valley.

In any case, the conquest of Nubia continued steadily until it had pushed beyond the Fourth Cataract under Thutmose I. This king's crude rock stela at Kurgus, not far south of the second great bend in the Nile at Abu Hamed, marks the southernmost limit of Egypt's conquests in Africa. Though the new province was not thoroughly pacified for another two generations, when Thutmose III added his own commemorative text at the southern border beside his grandfather's, the pattern of local government was already developed by then. A daring innovation, considering the trouble that ambitious officials had given the central government in earlier times, was the appointment of a viceroy to govern this vast province, which combined the Nubian regions of Kush and Wawat with the southern districts of Upper Egypt, up to Elkab. The extent of the viceroy's power was reflected in his title, "king's son," apparently reflecting an earlier method of delegating royal authority by conferring princely status on high-ranking appointees who did not actually belong to the royal family. Subordinates of this "king's son of Kush," as he came to be known, held military titles (such as "troop commander") that more clearly reveal this government to be one of armed occupation. A few elite Nubians were still recognized as magnates in their home territories, but theirs were empty titles, since they served merely as intermediaries between their "subjects" and the ruling pharaonic power. Economic life in Nubia was dominated by Egyptians, with the "king's house" and temples in the northern Nile Valley controlling extensive land holdings there. Culturally, too, Egypt sought to absorb the deep South. Local Nubian deities in Egyptian "dress" (gods in the form of Horus, goddesses at Hathor) became part of official cults, which also embraced the worship not only of historic pharaohs (such as Senwosret III) but even of contemporary monarchs (most notably, Amenhotpe III and Ramesses II). Towns that grew up around state temples at places such as Gebel Barkal also played a part in mediating between Egypt's administration and a Nubian population that had no choice but to become ever more Egyptianized, though the native identity was never completely submerged.

The new dynasty's foreign policy was more conservative in other areas. Libya required little attention; and though representations of northerners in Egyptian tombs mirror the shift from Minoan to Mycenaean predominance that was taking place in the eastern Mediterranean during this period, nothing beyond commercial relations between those powers and the Nile Valley can be assumed at this time. In the Levant, where Ahmose had subdued the last outposts of Hyksos power, a potential new foe was rising in the Hurrian kingdom of Mitanni. Egypt's response was the strike that Thutmose I led deep into northern Syria; but although a number of Asiatic city-states became tributary to Egypt as a result, the system had yet to consolidate the fruits of a foreign policy that was still in essence reactive. Firmer mechanisms of imperial control would only emerge two generations later, once other storms had been weathered at home.

The "Thutmosid succession" was the regime's first major domestic crisis. The royal family (which descended directly from the ruling house of the late seventeenth dynasty) was heavily inbred. Although consequences are difficult to prove, the family's main line ended with Amenhotpe I: his successor, Thutmose I, came from a different stock, at most a collateral branch of the old royal family, and he may not have been related to it at all. It has long been believed that Thutmose I began the practice of maintaining the new family's connection with the dynasty's founding line by marriage to an "heiress," while his son and grandson, the future kings, were begotten on non-royal women. Evidence for this presumed link with Ahmose's family is fragile, although it is hard otherwise to explain why three generations of queens (Ahmose, Nefertari, Hatshepsut, and Nefrure) formed a female "dynasty" through their husbands, Thutmose I, II, and III. Most scholars today hesitate to read into their prominence any tendency toward matriarchy, although the unusual career of Hatshepsut has influenced (or distorted) our interpretation of events: from a position of exceptional power as consort to her half-brother, Thutmose II, she became regent for her infant stepson and nephew, Thutmose III, and finally his coregent (r. 1502–1482 BCE) after being declared the pharaoh by an oracle of the god Amun-Re at Thebes. Resentment at Hatshepsut's usurpation has been adduced from Thutmose III's subsequent attack on her memory, when her monuments were altered to absorb her reign into those of her father, brother, and stepson. This persecution came late in Thutmose III's reign, however, long after Hatshepsut's death, and it is likelier to have been a calculated political move—perhaps a nervous overreaction designed to shore up the legitimacy of Thutmose III's heir, Amenhotpe II, who would have been the first of his line to have no connection whatever with the eighteenth dynasty's founding family.

The reign of Thutmose III (c.1504–1452 BCE) is also a watershed in Egypt's progress toward empire. In no fewer than fourteen campaigns, starting about 1482, he broke up a potentially threatening coalition of Syrian-Palestinian city-states and successfully resisted encroachments into Egypt's new sphere of influence by the rival kingdom of Mitanni. Even more significant, Thutmose III was the first king of Egypt to forge a continuous relationship with conquered city-states in Asia: their rulers were now the pharaoh's vassals, formally installed by him, serving at his pleasure and, like the subject Nubians, sending their sons to be educated (in gilded captivity) at the Egyptian court. Competition between Egypt and Mitanni, who were both defining their imperial orbits at this time, ebbed and flowed through succeeding reigns until it became clear that neither side could achieve all it wanted. True peace, and an *entente cordiale* between the two superpowers, finally came when Thutmose IV (r. 1419–1410 BCE) married the first of three generations of Mitannian princesses who symbolized the pharaoh's "brotherhood" with the Hurrian king.

Although the mid-eighteenth dynasty is rich in monuments, few of its domestic events are known. Uncertainties about the reign of Thutmose IV in particular have given rise to conflicting estimates of its length and conse-

quent differing reconstructions of the dynasty's absolute and relative chronology. These questions remain unresolved, with one "long" chronology (Wente and Van Siclen 1976) and a representative "short" scheme (Kitchen 1987)—being typical both for the problems and attempts to settle them.

The long reign of Amenhotpe III (c.1410–1372 BCE) found imperial Egypt at the height of its power. At home, the king cultivated the traditional images of sportsman and builder before stressing, especially in the last decade of his reign, a heightened divine identity to match his supreme status in society. A vast building program was expedited by the king's favorite, Amenhotep, son of Hapu, a man whose great ability matched the extravagant honors he was allowed to assume, perhaps by some political design of his master: in death he was eventually deified, and his cult survived into the last centuries of paganism. Thanks to the military and diplomatic achievements of his predecessors, moreover, Amenhotpe III was preeminent among the "great kings" in the Near East; princesses from both Mitanni and Babylon (as well as from less important allied and vassal states) graced his harem, though all were outranked by Tiye, his Egyptian chief queen; and—as the pharaoh reminded his brother-in-law, the king of Babylon—"From time immemorial no daughter of the king of Egypt is given to anyone" (EA 4: 4–10 in William L. Moran, *The Amarna Letters* [Baltimore, 1992], p. 8). Agreement among the superpowers, along with the absence of effective challengers, allowed trade to flourish, with gold and exotica from southern Africa being Egyptian specialties. Settled conditions in the Near East also gave Egypt the luxury of ruling its empire with a light hand. Troops and senior administrators were kept in only a few areas that, usually, were under direct Egyptian control. Garrisons were only sporadically present elsewhere and seem to have been rotated as needed. Even so, "the mighty arm of pharaoh" coerced vassals from afar into reporting pertinent news and cooperating with Egyptian commissioners and armies on the march. Amounts of "tribute" and the regularity of its collection are obscure, owing not least to the elasticity of Egyptian terms in such matters (although see Edward Bleiberg, *The Official Gift in Ancient Egypt* [Norman, 1996], pp. 114–125). It is clear, though, that vassals not only traded with their overlord but were even allowed (in some well-documented cases) to attack and even conquer one another: the pharaoh tolerated such rearrangements within his empire so long as the victors remembered their obligations to him. By the age of Amenhotpe III, then, the mechanisms of conquest had given way to those of imperial maintenance: instead of the regular campaigning that once had kept vassals in line, Egypt was now running its empire through intermediaries, intervening in force only under the strongest provocation. This policy, while suitable to an age of general peace, would prove costly in later, less settled times.

No one could have predicted that Egypt would be wracked by both foreign and domestic crises in the generation that followed Amenhotpe III. From the very beginning of his reign (c.1372–1355 BCE), Amenhotpe IV showed a preference for a new conception of the sun god, embodied in the solar orb ("Aten" in Egyptian), and this soon surpassed his devotion to the other gods whose cults were traditionally in the king's care. At first the pharaoh merely raised a new "one" above Egypt's many gods; but in word and deed he showed himself so hostile to the established cults that a breach soon followed. Withdrawing royal patronage from Thebes, the "city of Amun," the king changed his name to Akhenaten ("effective on behalf of the orb") and moved his capital to a new cult center for the Aten, freshly built on virgin territory at Tell el-Amarna in Middle Egypt, which he named Akhetaten ("horizon of the orb"). Despite the conspicuous public role of Akhenaten, along with his queen Nefertiti and their six daughters, little is known about events in Egypt during the so-called Amarna period. Clearly, though, the king's new order (which included the attempted banishment of the old gods by erasing their names and images from all earlier monuments) was unpopular. It was being abandoned by his ephemeral successor(s)—perhaps a female pharaoh identifiable with Nefertiti or (less probably) with her daughter Meritaten, and subsequently (?) the latter's husband, Smenkhkare—even before the orthodox religion was fully restored under Tutankhamun (r. 1355–1346 BCE). In political terms, Akhenaten's most significant accomplishment was to weaken the royal family: apart from the uncertain effects the "troubles" had on the heretic and other members of his house, it seems clear that the most enduring successor of his line, Tutankhamun, merely reigned while real power was held by others, notably the chief courtier Ay and his rival, the general Horemheb. When Tutankhamun died suddenly, the throne passed in succession to these two nonroyal magnates before it fell to the family of another military man, Ramesses I (r. 1315–1314 BCE), who began the nineteenth dynasty.

Not the least of Akhenaten's misfortunes was that his religious revolution coincided with a dramatic shift in the balance of power throughout the Near East. First came the Hittite kingdom's victory over Mitanni, which quickly caused the latter to disintegrate. With Mitanni's collapse came the emergence of Assyria, after centuries of impotence under Hurrian and Babylonian suzerainty, as a regional power in northern Mesopotamia. With one out of three fixtures of the old "great powers club" eliminated and the others at risk from two new contenders, there began a protracted period of adjustment. Most immediately affected was Egypt: it was the pharaoh's empire that now faced the destabilizing effects of the Hittite victory in northern Syria, where vassal states on all sides wavered between a cautious Egypt and the unpredictable new colossus. The loss of Egyptian vassals such as Ugarit and Kadesh, captured or enticed away under military pressure by Hatti, might have been tolerated; but when the king of Kadesh began to act aggressively as a Hittite recruiter, the pharaoh's patience wore out. What ensued was not all-out war between the two principals, but rather a carefully limited contest in which Egypt tried, unsuccessfully, to recover Kadesh and was then punished by Hittite raids on one of its border territories. (These failures, duly noted by Akhenaten's enemies at home, were interpreted as signs of divine anger at his revolution.) When Tutankhamun died, a faction in Egypt tried to normalize relations between the superpowers by offering his widow, and the throne of Egypt, to a Hittite prince; but the young man's death on the way (murdered, as the Hittites believed) finally unleashed the war both sides had been avoiding, putting off a settlement in western Asia for more than two generations to come.

The period of the nineteenth and twentieth dynasties is referred to as the Ramessid age because two of its most important pharaohs, along with most of the less significant rulers, bore the personal name Ramesses. The earlier nineteenth dynasty continued to be dominated by reactions to the events of the Amarna period: damage inflicted on the orthodox temples by Akhenaten's iconoclasts was still being repaired under Sety I and Ramesses II; and the alternating pattern of hot and cold war with the Hittites continued. Although defections from the Egyptian empire are now seen as less extensive than was earlier believed—being confined to the northern Syrian territories of Ugarit, Amurru, and Kadesh—imperial government in Asia was firmer and less tolerant than before. Warfare between vassals seems to have been discouraged, and new "governors' residencies" sprang up to serve as local headquarters for troops and depots for supplies. It might be said, with only slight exaggeration, that Egypt had implemented a policy of armed occupation in Asia, by contrast with the lighter governance up to the Amarna period. Egypt held its own by such measures, but it could not improve its position by much or for long. Sety I's temporary success in recovering Kadesh and Amurru was negated by the fresh loss of these provinces (and, briefly, more land in southern Syria) under Ramesses II, although the latter's confrontation with the Hittites at Kadesh was portrayed as a qualified victory in a widely circulated "official version" that was also displayed on the walls of temples in Egypt and Nubia. [*See* Battle of Kadesh.] Ramesses' stubbornness, as well as pressure on Hatti—from both civil strife and trouble with its increasingly active neighbor, Assyria—helped Egypt hold its own and eventually led to negotiations and a peace treaty. Neither side could claim total victory: Egypt had to accept the loss of its northern frontier provinces, and the Hittite regime tacitly acknowledged its dependence on Ramesses' good will, inasmuch as a deposed king of Hatti (who had fled to Egypt some years earlier) continued to live with his family at the pharaoh's court. More important, though, the treaty laid foundations for cooperation that had not existed since the *entente cordiale* between Egypt and Mitanni. The process of normalization was completed with the arrival in Egypt of the first of two Hittite princesses who would marry Ramesses II during his long reign.

Although the reign of Ramesses II would become a byword for splendor and stability at home, his successors had to face the problems their great ancestor avoided or finessed. His son Merneptah had to cope, almost simultaneously, with a rebellion in Nubia and invasion from the west, where a coalition of Libyans and Mediterranean marauders (generally termed the Sea Peoples) joined in a hard-fought but unsuccessful attack on the Egyptian Delta. Merneptah's son, Sety II, faced a more formidable challenge from a usurper named Amenmesse (probably representing a rival branch of the royal family) who reigned for several years before being dislodged. The succession question was far from settled, though. When Sety II died he was succeeded not by a son of his own, but by a crippled youth named Siptah (perhaps Amenmesse's son) who was controlled by his sponsor, a royal cupbearer of Near Eastern descent named Bay: this man is probably the Near Easterner called Irsu, "(He) Who Made Himself," in the historical summary of the period recorded in the Harris Papyrus I. When Siptah died he was briefly succeeded by a woman, Tawosret (r. 1209–1201 BCE), who had been Sety II's chief queen. The dynasty ended in renewed civil war, with many in the country's higher administrators (including Siptah's vizier and viceroy of Kush) aligning themselves with a pretender, Sethnakht, whose opposition was supported by Asiatic mercenaries. Sethnakht's victory in his second year on the throne brought an end to this time of troubles and to the nineteenth dynasty.

The problems of the new twentieth dynasty continued into the reign of Sethnakht's son, Ramesses III (r. 1198–1166 BCE). The earliest dangers were from abroad, including fresh fighting in Nubia, two invasions from Libya, and a massive new assault by the Sea Peoples. The last were mostly different groups from those Merneptah had faced thirty years earlier, and the threat they represented was more formidable than before: the collapse of the Hittite empire had left a political vacuum in the Levant that Assyria, Hatti's eastern neighbor (and the only credible contender for supremacy in the area), was not yet ready to fill, leaving a clear path for the invaders. The most obvious of these foreign perils were seemingly quelled by the victories won in the first third of Ramesses III's reign. Even so, while the pharaoh might pose as a new Ramesses II,

not a few unresolved issues stirred beneath his grandiloquent image. To begin with, the break-up of the "great powers" system in the Near East seems to have weakened Egyptian policy-makers' commitment to maintaining the empire in the Near East. A pharaonic presence there is last attested in the reign of Ramesses VI (c.1156–1149 BCE), and by the end of the twelfth century, Egyptian hegemony was barely a memory, as other peoples (including such Sea Peoples as the Tchekker and Philistines, as well as the Phoenicians and Aramaeans farther north) formed small states in the areas formerly divided between the Egyptian and Hittite empires. The "Libyan problem," too, was far from settled. For all their victories in set battles, neither Ramesses III nor Merenptah had been able to cut off the flow of Libyans who kept trickling into the Delta. Moreover, when Ramesses III pressed captured Libyans into his army and settled them in northern fortress-towns, he unwittingly gave them an identity within Egyptian society and a structure through which to interact with it: from these beginnings would come the Egyptian-Libyan military elites that would play a major role in the Nile Valley during the Third Intermediate and Late periods.

Conditions at home also belied pretenses of Ramessid splendor during the twentieth dynasty. Starting in Year 29 of Ramesses III, a series of "strikes" by the craftsmen who worked on royal and elite tombs at Thebes hint at "cash flow" difficulties (perhaps temporary) that inhibited the state's ability to cover all its obligations. Moreover, although Ramesses III was the first king since Ramesses II to celebrate a jubilee, his death shortly afterward (c.1166 BCE) was clouded by a conspiracy against the heir apparent that involved not only dissidents from the royal family but also high officials at court and in the military establishment. No such disturbances seem to have marred the next seven reigns (since scholars no longer believe in hostilities between Ramesses VI and his two predecessors), but serious economic problems did. Notable was an increase in the price of grain, which rose to four times its earlier normal price before it stabilized, late in the period, at roughly twice its earlier cost. The causes of this inflation (which seems to have affected no other commodity prices) are elusive, though climatic change resulting in lower Nile flood levels may be involved. Hard times are often blamed for the startlingly high incidence of corruption and other law-breaking attested during the twentieth dynasty. Anecdotal evidence includes the pilfering of large amounts of grain and other property belonging to the temple of Khnum at Elephantine (Turin Indictment Papyrus, reigns of Ramesses IV and V), and trials for robbery of royal tombs under Ramesses IX and Ramesses XI. Widespread criminality in this period is patent, but the fundamental reasons for it remain unclear.

Civic peace was disrupted even more seriously under the dynasty's last ruler, Ramesses XI (c.1111–1081 BCE), by what contemporaries called "the war of the high priest" Amenhotep. Though some scholars (most notably Janssen-Winkeln 1992) continue to believe this was a rebellion instigated by the head of the Theban clergy in a bid for independence, it seems likelier that Amenhotep was the victim and languished in captivity for more than eight months before he was restored to office by loyalist troops commanded by the viceroy of Kush (see Wente 1966). Certainly by Ramesses XI's Year 12, the effective governor of Thebes was Panehsy, the viceroy of Nubia; but seven years later he had been replaced by another military man, Herihor, who also professed loyalty to Ramesses XI. The pharaoh still reigned, but he was now merely a shadow-king: while the new era Herihor started at Thebes (dubbed "Renaissance" or "Repeating of Births") acknowledged Ramesses XI's kingship, it also accentuated Herihor's independence—especially when the latter made himself high priest of Amun and, after Year 5 of the "Renaissance," nominal pharaoh with a throne name, "High Priest of Amun," that proclaimed a divine basis for Herihor's titular kingship. Even in the North, Ramesses XI became invisible in his last years, when power devolved onto a magnate named Smendes, ruling from Tanis (c.1081–1055 BCE), whose family ties linked him with the Theban pontiffs. It was this man who would become the king of record, and founder of the twenty-first dynasty, when Ramesses XI finally died.

The end of the era is more indicative of where Egypt was going than of where it had been. For nearly five centuries the center had held firm in Egypt; but where the nascent eighteenth dynasty had reunified the country, the troubles of the late twentieth are a prelude to national disintegration. What happened is easier to document than to explain. Final appearances to the contrary, secular authority seems not to have succumbed to priestly power in the South: during the later New Kingdom, we find the upper clergy of Amun functioning increasingly as the pharaoh's chief administrators in Upper Egypt, but no high priest of Amun before Herihor can be convincingly taxed with aggrandizing himself at the crown's expense. Assuming that the leader of the Theban hierarchy was in fact rescued by representatives of the central government in the "war of the high priest," nothing is certain either about the nature of the opposition or its aims. With the root causes of the unrest still unclear, and local separatism not traceable to developments within the clergy of Amun during the mid-twentieth dynasty, it may be that the breakup of the kingdom under Ramesses XI came primarily through the political maneuvering of the principals—army leaders and local "strong men" who took advantage of the pharaoh's weakness in troubled times to press their own claims to power. Herihor's regime in Upper Egypt only masqueraded under the legitimizing façade of priestly power, a practice later taken up by kings

of the twenty-first dynasty, who would also ground their right to rule in the authority of the "true" pharaoh, the god Amun-Re. Such ploys, however, do not explain the manifest decline that set in during the twentieth dynasty, and to that extent the end of the New Kingdom remains an enigma.

The inglorious end of the twentieth dynasty was also Egypt's demise as an imperial power. Although the viceroy Panehsy lost Upper Egypt to Herihor, he was able to take the Nubian province permanently out of the orbit of the northern Nile Valley. This loss, which accompanied the first splintering of the state, hardly proves that national identity and empire were one, because although imperialism is characteristic of the New Kingdom, it does not fully explain its success or failure. The regime's inner cohesion had not depended on the empire: the assumptions of pharaonic triumphalism were sustainable without actually being proved; and in the Near East, at least, Egypt's record of half-measures and its apparent haste in winding up its affairs suggest discomfort with the responsibilities of running an empire outside the Nile Valley. Arguably, the pharaohs' interest in outside areas always depended on how they affected Egypt. The shock of Hyksos and Kushite successes during the Second Intermediate Period had stimulated an unprecedentedly active foreign policy early in the eighteenth dynasty, leading to the conquest of Nubia and a widening involvement in the Near East that reached its peak during the nineteenth dynasty. Need, cost, and feasibility had played parts in shaping the foreign policy that had maintained the empire during the New Kingdom. These same factors may well be behind the seeming retreat from that policy, when Egypt abandoned its Near Eastern empire late in the twentieth dynasty and did not pursue the reconquest of Nubia. Egypt's fate—when it succumbed in succession to Nubia, Assyria, Persia, Macedon, and Rome—demonstrates its folly: not in failing to keep its empire but in playing, even as an imperialist, a minimal and essentially isolationist role, as if it could continue indefinitely to hold the outside world at arm's length.

BIBLIOGRAPHY

Adams, William Y. *Nubia: Corridor to Africa.* Princeton, 1977. Chapters on New Kingdom relations with Nubia offer good if rather generalized coverage.

Aldred, Cyril. *Akhenaten, King of Egypt.* New York, 1988. This revised edition does a fine job of surveying the heretic king's reign and the main problems in the period, although many of the author's ideas (on the vexed issue of the heretic's alleged coregency with his father, or on the genealogy of royal females) are debatable.

Assmann, Jan. *Egyptian Solar Religion in the New Kingdom: Re and Amun.* Translated from the German by Anthony Alcock. London and New York, 1995. A densely written but stimulating examination of New Kingdom religious thought, particularly significant for monotheistic tendencies, translated and updated from the original German edition.

Edgerton, William F. *The Thutmoside Succession.* Studies in Ancient Oriental Civilization, 8. Chicago, 1933. Classic study that establishes the sequence of events surrounding the reign of the female pharaoh Hatshepsut and her persecution by Thutmose III.

Edwards, I. E. S. ed. *The Cambridge Ancient History: History of the Middle East and the Aegean Region c.1800–1000 B.C.* vol. 2, 3d ed. Cambridge, 1973–1975. Chapters by various specialists present detailed surveys, with extensive bibliographies, that reflect scholarship current in the late 1960s.

Frandsen, Paul J. "Egyptian Imperialism." In *Power and Propaganda: A Symposium on Ancient Empires,* edited by M. T. Larsen, pp. 167–190. Mesopotamia, 7. Copenhagen, 1979.

Gardiner, Alan H. *Egypt of the Pharaohs: An Introduction.* Oxford, 1961. Although somewhat out of date and focused on the written sources at the expense of archaeological or art-historical evidence, this survey of ancient Egyptian history offers lay readers a good introduction to both the subject and the bases for modern interpretations.

Grimal, Nicolas. *A History of Ancient Egypt.* Translated from the French by Ian Shaw. Oxford and Cambridge, Mass., 1992. More up-to-date and balanced in its use of source materials than Gardiner's book, but also less detailed, and including some controversial conclusions.

Habachi, Labib. *Sixteen Studies on Lower Nubia.* Cairo, 1981. Discusses facets and patterns of New Kingdom government in Nubia.

Janssen-Winkeln, Karl. "Das Ende des Neuen Reiches." *Zeitschrift für Ägyptische Sprache* 119 (1992), 22–37.

Kemp, Barry J. "Imperialism and Empire in New Kingdom Egypt." In *Imperialism in the Ancient World: The Cambridge University Research Seminar in Ancient History,* edited by P. D. A. Garnsey and C. Whittaker, pp. 7–58, 284–297. Cambridge, 1978.

Kemp, Barry J. *Ancient Egypt: Anatomy of a Civilization.* London and New York, 1989. An unusually stimulating survey, ending with the later New Kingdom, by a scholar who is equally at home with archaeological and written evidence.

Kitchen, Kenneth A. "The Basics of Egyptian Chronology in Relation to the Bronze Age." In *High, Middle or Low,* edited by Paul Astrom, vol. 1, pp. 37–55. Gothenburg, 1987.

Kitchen, Kenneth A. *Pharaoh Triumphant: The Life and Times of Ramesses II.* Warminster, 1982.

Liverani, Mario. *Prestige and Interest: International Relations in the Near East ca. 1600–1100 B.C.* Padua, 1990. Superb in its comparative study of world views and their consequences for Egypt and its major neighbors in the Near East, although not all readers will share the author's pessimism on the way ideologies compromise the historical reliability of ancient documents.

Liverani, Mario. *Three Amarna Essays.* Monographs on the Ancient Near East, 1.5. Malibu, 1979. Several important studies of international relations in the Amarna age translated into English.

Murnane, William J. *The Road to Kadesh: A Historical Interpretation of the Battle Reliefs of King Sety I at Karnak.* 2d rev. ed. Studies in Ancient Oriental Civilization, 42. Chicago, 1990. Examines the military and diplomatic background of Egyptian foreign policy in western Asia from the later eighteenth into the earlier nineteenth dynasty.

O'Connor, David. "New Kingdom and Third Intermediate Period, 1152–664 BC." In *Ancient Egypt: A Social History,* Bruce Trigger, et al., pp. 183–278. Cambridge, 1983. This survey, with its own bibliography, was originally published in volume 1 of *The Cambridge History of Africa* (New York, 1975) and is especially valuable for its focus on institutions in New Kingdom Egypt.

Redford, Donald B. "The Historiography of Ancient Egypt." In *Egyptology and the Social Sciences,* edited by Kent R. Weeks, pp. 3–20. Cairo, 1979.

Redford, Donald B. *History and Chronology of the Eighteenth Dynasty of Egypt: Seven Studies.* Toronto, 1967. Though written for specialists, these seven studies are a pleasure to read; and while they have become dated in certain respects, most of them are still models in demonstrating how historical materials may be hammered into history.

Redford, Donald B. *Pharaonic King-Lists, Annals and Daybooks: A Contribution to the Study of Egyptian History.* Mississauga, 1986. A fundamental study of the materials for ancient Egyptian historiography, particularly in the New Kingdom.

Redford, Donald B. *Egypt, Canaan and Israel in Ancient Times.* Princeton, 1992. This well-written survey, addressed to a popular audience, ably summarizes the course of Egypt's involvement in the Middle East from earliest times down to later antiquity.

Säve-Söderbergh, Torgny. "The Tomb of the Prince of Teh-khet, Amenemhet." *Kush* 11 (1963), 159–174. Reflects the survival of some native princes in New Kingdom Nubia.

Schulman, Alan R. "Diplomatic Marriage in New Kingdom Egypt." *Journal of Near Eastern Studies* 38 (1979), 177–193.

Simpson, William Kelly. *Heka-Nefer and the Dynastic Material from Tashka and Arminna.* New Haven, 1963. Includes discussion of the career of a native Nubian prince who was contemporary with Tutankhamun.

Vandersleyen, Claude. *Les guerres d'Amosis, fondateur de la XVIII dynastie.* Monographies Reine Elisabeth, 1. Brussels, 1971. A detailed and tightly argued study of the achievements of the founder of the eighteenth dynasty, notable for its methodological rigor.

Vandersleyen, Claude. *L'Égypte et al vallée du Nil,* vol. 2, *De la fin de l'Ancien Empire à la fin du Nouvel Empire.* Paris, 1995. This excellent survey is especially valuable for its detailed coverage of major controversies, though the author's insistence on some strongly held views (most notably on the identification of some ancient place names) is more tendentious than useful.

Vernus, Pascal. *Affaires et scandales sous les Ramsès: La Crise des valeurs dons l'Égypte du Nouvel Empire.* Paris, 1993. Though aimed at a popular audience, this is a solidly documented book that attempts to interpret the high incidence of corruption in the late New Kingdom as a crisis of social values.

Weinstein, James. "The Egyptian Empire in Palestine: A Reassessment." *Bulletin of the American Schools of Oriental Research* 241 (1982), 1–28.

Wente, E. F. "The Suppression of the High Priest Amenhotep." *Journal of Near Eastern Studies* 25 (1996), 73–87.

Wente, E. F., and C. C. Van Siclen III. "A Chronology of the New Kingdom." In *Studies in Honor of George H. Hughes,* pp. 217–261. Chicago, 1976.

WILLIAM J. MURNANE

Eighteenth Dynasty to the Amarna Period

The eighteenth dynasty marks the beginning of a new period in Egyptian history. For over a century, control over Egypt had been divided between the Hyksos in the North and the Thebans in the South. Reunification under the Theban rule and the spread of Egyptian interests north to the Euphrates and south to the Fourth Cataract characterize this period, with the creation of an empire that embodied the political, economic, and ideological power of a united Egypt.

Reestablishment of a United Egypt (c.1569–1525 BCE). Nebpehtyre Ahmose (r. 1569–1545 BCE) was the son of the seventeenth dynasty king Senakhtenre Ta'o II and his sister-wife Ahhotep. Ahmose's immediate predecessor, Kamose, had dealt a decisive blow to the Hyksos rulers, delimiting but not destroying the political power of the Northern dynasty. The task of Egyptian reunification fell to the young king Ahmose. He mounted a campaign that led to the capture of the Hyksos palace city of Avaris in the eastern Delta, as well as the liberation of the ancient capital Memphis. Hyksos influence was rooted out with the three-year siege of the southwestern Palestinian fortress town of Sharuhen, opening the way for the northeastern expansion of Egyptian political influence.

The autobiographies of two professional soldiers—Ahmose, son of Ibana, an admiral in the Egyptian navy, and Ahmose Pen-nekhbet—provide information concerning military expeditions up to the time of Thutmose II. Both men list the expeditions in which they participated and the rewards they received from different kings. Ahmose son of Ibana accompanied the king on the expedition to Lower Nubia that secured Egyptian dominion over that region. The territory between the First and Third Cataracts had been under the kingdom of Kush, with its capital Kerma at the Third Cataract. Although Kamose may have precipitated the reconquest of this territory with an earlier expedition, it was Ahmose who reincorporated Lower Nubia into the economic structure of the Egyptian state. An administrative center was established at the Second Cataract fort at Buhen, and a new post, viceroy of Nubia, was created (his title was "King's Son of the Southern Lands"). The last years of Ahmose's reign saw Egypt reassume control over the trade routes that had traditionally moved luxury goods between Asia and Africa.

The administrative structure was reformed to suit the growing complexity of the Egyptian state. The New Kingdom model accommodated functional rather than regional needs. Two viceroys, one for Upper Egypt and the other for Lower Egypt, were in charge of the domestic economy. The military administration was separate from that of temple personnel and property, and from that which governed Lower Nubia.

Monumental stone construction had been limited during the seventeenth dynasty by lack of access to the regional quarries. The reopening of the limestone quarry at Tura in the area near Memphis in Year 22 of Ahmose's reign marks the beginning of an acceleration in monumental construction throughout the country.

Three palaces are known for Ahmose. A Theban residence is documented in the texts. The archaeological remains of a palace city in Middle Egypt at Deir el-Ballas are also associated with this king. In addition, recent excavations at the site of Avaris (Tell ed-Dab'a) have revealed a citadel, confirming a reoccupation of the site after the defeat of the Hyksos that lasted into the reign of Am-

enhotpe II. Remains of fresco decoration display bull-leaping motifs similar to those of Crete, indicating a close relationship with this Aegean culture.

Ahmose's young son and successor, Djeserkare Amenhotpe I (r. 1545–1525 BCE), inherited a united Egypt, strong and at peace. The southern border for Egyptian authority had moved south to Sais, halfway between the Second and Third Cataracts, and the oases had been included in the Egyptian political sphere. Records from the reign of Amenhotpe I also provide an important astronomical fixed point in Egyptian chronology with a notation of the heliacal rising of the star Sirius for Year 9 of the reign.

Both Ahmose's mother and grandmother were alive when he ascended the throne. His grandmother, Tetisheri, was the daughter of a high official and shared a cult with her grandson at Abydos. His mother, Ahhotep, sister of her husband Senakhtenre Ta'o II, is praised in a hymn found at Karnak, describing her special care for the army. A period of regency, possibly entailing military command, has been hypothesized for this queen. Ahhotep survived into the reign of her grandson Amenhotpe I. A stela from Edfu records a cult commemorating the queen-mother Ahhotep, along with the seventeenth dynasty royal wife Sobekemsaf and the wife of Thutmose I. Ahmose's consort was his sister Ahmose Nefertari. The position of second priest of Amun was conferred on her; this title became transmuted to "God's Wife of Amun," a position which not only carried great religious and even political prestige but also brought personal wealth in the form of an estate, household goods, and a staff. Ahmose Nefertari and her son Amenhotpe I were worshiped as the patrons of the Theban necropolis. Ahmose Nefertari survived her son, living into the reign of his successor. The wife of Amenhotpe I, his sister Meritamun, also carried the title "God's Wife of Amun," inherited from her mother. Ahhotep, Ahmose Nefertari, and Meritamun were remembered in the cult of Amenhotpe I into the twenty-first dynasty. An unusual focus is placed on the royal women of this period; there is no evidence, however, to substantiate the oft-repeated assertion that the successor to the king was chosen according to the status of his mother.

Beginning of Empire (c.1525–1482 BCE). With no surviving children, Amenhotpe I was succeeded by a Aa-kheperkare Thutmose I (r. 1525–1516 BCE). The connection of this king to the previous royal family is unknown, although it is often hypothesized that his wife Ahmose, in spite of lacking the title "Daughter of the King," was the sister of Amenhotpe I.

The coronation of Thutmose I is recorded on two known stelae, on which the king is seen accompanied by his wife Ahmose and the dowager queen, Ahmose Nefertari. The conquest of Nubia was completed early in his reign, moving the border of Egyptian influence south to the Third Cataract, where Kerma, the capital of Kush, had been destroyed by Thutmose's forces. The administration of Nubia was restructured to include the participation of native princes, a step which furthered the Egyptianization of Nubia. Another expedition took Thutmose I as far northeast as the Carchemesh region, near the Euphrates, where a stela was erected. It was there that Egypt met its first conflict with the Hurrian power of Mitanni, with its center in northern Mesopotamia.

Just as the military expeditions of Thutmose I inaugurated a period of political expansion, an increasingly ambitious building program suggests expanding economic resources. This reign provided the first major renovation of the Middle Kingdom temple at Karnak, including the erection of two obelisks. An additional royal residence at Memphis, occupied by the crown prince Amenmese is also documented. During the reign of Thutmose I, the tomb and the funerary temple were separated for the first time, creating a division between the tombs of the Valley of the Kings and the funerary temples, which were placed just beyond cultivated ground on the western bank of the Nile River. The establishment of the royal necropolis required the foundation of the workers' village at Deir el-Medina.

Crown Prince Amenmese predeceased the king, and the throne passed to Aa-kheperenre Thutmose II (r. 1516–1504 BCE), son of a secondary wife, Mutnefert. He undertook only one major military expedition, in his first year, to quell a minor uprising in Lower Nubia. The autobiography of the architect and official Ineni tells of construction projects under Amenhotpe I and Thutmose I. It also records the death of Thutmose II and the coronation of Men-kheperre Thutmose III (r. 1504–1452 BCE), son of a minor wife named Isis. The royal sister and wife Hatshepsut, the regent for the boy-king, ascended the throne as coregent under the name Maatkare Khenemamun Hatshepsut (r. 1502–1482 BCE) no later than Year 7 of the reign of Thutmose III.

Hatshepsut's prestige had been established during the reign of her father Thutmose I, when she succeeded to the position of "God's Wife of Amun" after the sister-wife of Amenhotpe I. The overseer of the estate of the "God's Wife" and overseer of construction, Senmut, became a central figure in her reign, documented by numerous statues and two tombs. Thutmose III acted, however, in civil matters in his own name during this period. On Hatshepsut's ascent to the throne, the office of "God's Wife" was passed on to her daughter Neferure.

A journey to Punt to acquire exotic goods, such as myrrh, for the temple of Amun at Karnak is recorded in Hatshepsut's funerary temple at Deir el-Bahri, where an illustrated text was found telling of Hatshepsut's birth as the natural child of the Theban god Amun. The reliefs of Deir el-Bahri were defaced by Thutmose III, as were the other monuments of this queen. Occurring late in his reign, this usurpation appears to be less an act of hatred than of political expediency, with the intention of reinforcing the claims of his own lineage.

Expansion into the Levant (1482–1419 BCE). At the death of Hatshepsut, Thutmose III embarked on a military career that has earned him the reputation of an Egyptian emperor. A narrative inscribed around the bark chapel of Karnak describes sixteen campaigns during his regnal Years 22 to 42. An Egyptian presence had been established in southern Palestine during the early part of the dynasty, but through the years, internal alliances with ties to the northern Mesopotamian power Mitanni had challenged Egypt's hold over this area. The expeditions of Thutmose III were focused on three goals: first, it was important to bring the strategically significant Levant back into the Egyptian political and economic sphere; second, Egyptian access to the coast and its ports was to be secured; and finally, the influence of Mitanni was to be curtailed.

The first stage included the Battle of Megiddo, described in the texts with emphasis on the strategic brilliance of the king. By the sixth campaign, Thutmose had access to a Syrian port and was able to arrive by sea. At the end of this expedition, he returned to Egypt with thirty-six sons of local rulers, who were to be brought up at court. Direct confrontation with Mitanni is recorded from Year 33, when Egyptian forces crossed the Euphrates by using specially constructed riverboats hauled overland. Pillaging the area south of Carchemesh, Thutmose III set up a stela alongside that of his grandfather and then returned south, hunting elephants at Niy, as had Thutmose I. His remaining expeditions, undertaken between Years 34 and 42, were attempts to maintain the political and territorial gains made earlier in the reign. Rebellions were repeatedly put down as the Levantine city-states sought renewed alliance with Mitanni. It is at this time that a formalization of Egyptian political control can be discerned, with the establishment of garrisons, regulated tax collection, and local rulers functioning as Egyptian vassals. For Egypt, the economic rewards of political control included a levy on the population that could take the form of significant amounts of silver, lapis lazuli, a bronze alloy called "Asiatic copper," opium, wine, and ornamental metalwork, as well as the requisite timber for boat-building.

Although Nubia no longer required military attention, the inauguration of a cult of Amun at Gebel Barkal, at the Fourth Cataract, during the last years of this reign emphasized the ongoing acculturation of Nubia. Thutmose III was succeeded by his son and coregent, Aa-kheperure

Amenhotpe II (r. 1454–1419 BCE). Son of the royal consort Merytre Hatshepsut, Amenhotpe may have been born in Memphis; one inscription records his early years there and praises his skill with horses.

Amenhotep II inherited a vacillating dominion over Syria-Palestine. His first campaign involved a clash with Mitanni at Kadesh, one of the most powerful city-states of the central Levant, resulting in the capture and later execution of seven local rulers. Facing insurrection and disloyalty throughout the territory, Amenhotpe mounted another campaign four years later which ended in a massive deportation of the population, with the Egyptians using terror tactics to maintain rule. At that point, the burgeoning Hittite coalition began to negotiate alliances with Mitannian vassal states. The political competition from the Hittites appears to have encouraged a peace settlement between Mitanni and Egypt. A treaty came into effect sometime after Amenhotpe II's Year 9, when a Mitanni emissary arrived in Egypt with tribute.

Amenhotpe II was buried in the Valley of the Kings, like his father, grandfather, and great-grandfather. His tomb was later used as a cachette for royal mummies (which were discovered there in the nineteenth century).

The royal women of the families of the Thutmose III and Amenhotep II are not as visible in the historical record as their predecessors. The title "God's Wife of Amun" was initially passed on, according to custom, to the daughter of Thutmose III, Meritamun. Later in his reign, however, it was borne by his mother, Isis. Two successive royal mothers—Meritre Hatsheput (mother of Amenhotpe II) and Tia (mother of Thutmose IV)—succeeded to the title, which then disappears from the documentation, not to recur until the nineteenth dynasty. Both these women had nonroyal backgrounds and are better known as king's mothers than as royal wives. One tomb was found with the burials of three otherwise undocumented wives of Thutmose III; their names suggest foreign origin.

Peace and Prosperity (c.1419–1372 BCE). Amenhotpe II was succeeded by Men-kheprure Thutmose IV (r. 1419–1410 BCE), son of the royal wife Tia. In the inscription on the Sphinx Stela, Thutmose tells of a dream in which the sphinx, manifest as the sun god Re-Horakhty, appeared to the young prince and asked him to clear away the sand covering the monument. Having done this, the prince was rewarded with the kingship. The evidence for Thutmose IV's involvement in the Near East suggests military activity directed against Mitanni vassals. This appears to have led to the renewal of the treaty made under Amenhotpe II.

Nebmaatre Amenhotpe III (r. 1410–1372 BCE) was the son of his predecessor and a minor royal wife, Mutemwia. During the first years of his reign he married Tiye, the daughter of an important chariot officer, Yuya, and his

wife Tuya. This couple is known to have had family ties, as well as extensive holdings, in the region of Akhurim. Their rich burial in the Valley of the Kings is evidence of the extensive influence of their daughter Tiye. The marriage between Tiye and Amenhotpe is recorded on one of the five commemorative scarabs issued to celebrate outstanding events of the reign.

Egypt was at the peak of its power under Amenhotpe III, with little evidence of conflict either to the north or the south. International contacts spread the name of this king as far away as Mycenae, Yemen, and Assur. The Akkadian diplomatic correspondence discovered at Amarna reveals the close ties between this king and his former Mitanni foes. The king married two Mittanni princesses, Giluhepa and Taduhepa, the former commemorated with a scarab inscription. Amenhotpe III was not the first king, however, to wed a royal woman from Mittanni; the correspondence speaks of the marriage of an earlier Egyptian king, generally identified as Thutmose IV, to a princess of that nation.

This period of peace and prosperity encouraged extensive construction. At Thebes, Luxor was expanded with a colonnade and hypostyle hall. A copy of the divine-birth legend, found earlier for Hatshepsut at Deir el-Bahri, was reworked for Amenhotpe III in this temple. The Mut temple at Karnak was furnished with about six hundred statues of Sakhmet, possibly erected in an attempt to alleviate the ill health of the king. A palace of enormous proportions was built on the western bank of the Nile, at a site known as Malqata, as was the largest of the funerary temples, of which only the two so-called Colossi of Memnon still stand.

The construction work of this king was led by a man known as Amenhotep, son of Hapu, who, like Senmut before him, was the overseer of the estate of a royal daughter. Later deified, Amenhotep, son of Hapu, gained a reputation as one of the sages of ancient Egypt and was the object of a cult that lasted long into the Greco-Roman period.

Tia, "God's Wife of Amun" and mother of Thutmose IV, was the most important woman of that reign. Several wives are known for Thutmose IV—Iaret, Nefertiry, and Mutemwia; in addition, there is evidence that he married a princess of Mitanni. Of these women only one, Iaret, was of royal birth. Titled both "Daughter" and "Sister" of the king, she may have been the daughter of Amenhotpe II or, less likely, of Thutmose himself. Nefertiry appears to have been the senior wife of this king.

The mother of Amenhotpe III, Mutemwia, does not appear in monuments from the reign of her husband and thus should be regarded a minor wife. The major female figure of this reign is undoubtedly the great royal wife Tiye. Closely linked to her husband and later to her son

NEW KINGDOM: EIGHTEENTH DYNASTY TO THE AMARNA PERIOD. *Relief of Thutmose IV, from his festival hall at Karnak.* (Courtesy Donald B. Redford)

Amenhotpe IV (Akhenaten), Tiye is given unprecedented prominence in the monuments, appearing in one tomb representation as the manifestation of the goddess of truth Maat. Amenhotpe III also had several daughters; two of them, Satamun and Isis, were titled "Royal Wife" during his reign, which might indicate that they were married to their father.

Overview. The political configuration of Egypt was transformed during this time—from one in which regional loyalties were decisive to one focused on the separate hierarchies of the domestic government, the military organization, and the temple administration. The national economy was managed by the two viziers, who ranked directly under the king. The spoils of war, marginally exploited as payment for the army, benefited the tem-

ples in the form of royal offerings, consisting of prisoners of war, livestock, and precious objects. In addition, a significant portion of the arable land was passing into the administrative system of the temples. This land, worked by tenant farmers, provided the base of the temple economy. The extent to which the economic input from Nubia, primarily in the form of gold, was recycled in local administrative costs or fed into the national economy, is a subject of some debate. This distribution of the control of wealth created the predisposition for alternative sources of political power, found during this period and later in the army and the temple, as well as in the national government.

Thebes, as the city of origin of the dynasty, and the site of the expanding cult of Amun, was a natural center of political influence and economic wealth. Memphis, however, with its ancient cult of Ptah and its strategically important military harbor and arms manufacture, continued to function as the Northern residence, evidenced early in the dynasty by the presence of the crown prince. Heliopolis, the traditional theological center of Egypt, was also an important recipient of donations from the king, although it never became a political center.

The Egypt of the late eighteenth dynasty incorporated into its political and economic sphere the now Egyptianized Nubia, extending to the Fourth Cataract, as well as the conglomerate of the Levantine city-states. This extension of Egyptian influence not only facilitated the export of Egyptian culture but also opened the country up to the outside. Nubians had resided in Egypt since the Old Kingdom and had been traditionally employed in the Egyptian army as mercenaries. The cultural border between Egypt and Palestine—in the area of the eastern Delta and southern Palestine—had always allowed cross-cultural contact, but with the eighteenth dynasty this intensified. The most immediate point of contact was the military, resulting in the incorporation of a significant West Semitic military vocabulary into ancient Egyptian. Innovations in warfare, such as the chariot and the composite bow, had already been adopted by the Egyptian military from the Hyksos forces.

A Canaanite population entered Egypt as prisoners of war and later as refugees. Large numbers of these became agricultural workers. Their descendants, however, were able to rise in the hierarchy and later attained high-ranking positions. Intermarriage was common, with Hurrian and Canaanite names occurring in Egyptian genealogies. A northern suburb of Memphis was the site of a Canaanite community, established around temples of Ba'al and Astarte. Canaanite merchants were also trading along the Nile.

Near Eastern gods entered the Egyptian pantheon at this time; besides Ba'al and Astarte, Anat and Reshef took on Egyptian identities. A statue of Ishtar was requested by Amenhotpe III from his Mitannian brother-in-law, in hopes of affecting a cure for an unspecified illness.

The wealth imported into Egypt facilitated advances in art and architecture. The expansion of the temple of Karnak, initiated by Thutmose I and carried on throughout the dynasty, the creation of a temple at Luxor by Amenhotpe III, and the planning of the royal tombs and western bank temples are examples of both an economic and an ideological flowering that centered on the close association of the king with a solar creator. In literature, the king is presented as a model of wisdom, strength, and courage, in a form of historical narrative termed *Königsnovelle*.

This period is also known for the decoration of the private tombs of the Theban necropolis. Although their scenes are stereotypic ones of agriculture, manufacture, banquets, and so forth, they represent a high point in Egyptian painting and relief carving. In addition, the textual descriptions of the owners contribute information concerning the structure of the government. The tomb of Rekhmire, vizier under Thutmose III, preserves a classic text describing the appointment and duties of that office.

The status of women, royal and aristocratic, is also reflected in the documentation. The royal women were incorporated into the ideological imagery of the kingship, particularly as it was linked to the cult of Amun. As "God's Wife of Amun," the royal daughter-wife of the early part of the dynasty acquired an independent platform that may have provided the foundation for Hatshepsut's political success. This was countermanded during the reign of Thutmose III, when the title was passed on to his mother, whose status was dependent on that of her son. By the end of the dynasty, a greater emphasis on solar theology intensified the iconographic identification between the royal women and the goddess Hathor. This development is contemporary with evidence for father-daughter marriages, which may have been motivated by the father-daughter relationship between the sun god Re and Hathor.

The royal women owned estates, which provided a source of income. A special residence for royal women and their households was founded by Thutmose III in the Faiyum at Medinet el-Ghurab. Functioning as a self-contained settlement, the residence is known to have specialized in the production of cloth. A number of finds relating to the royal women, such as the well-known head of Tiye (now in Berlin), come from this site, which has been described in relationship to the cortège of 317 attendants whom the Mitannian princess Giluhepa brought with her. Indeed, some scholars see the elaborate harem settlement of the eighteenth dynasty as the result of the influence of royal wives from the Near East.

The women of the aristocracy were commonly titled "Mistress of the House," sometimes with the addition of a title indicating a relationship to the royal family, such as "Royal Nurse." The area of activity for these women had diminished in comparison to their Middle Kingdom counterparts, who could be actively involved in the temple cults as priestesses. The temple activity of the women of New Kingdom nobility was confined to the role of singer in the temple, suggesting a life that was more restricted than earlier in Egyptian history.

[See also Ahmose; Ahmose Nefertari; Amenhotpe I; Amenhotpe II; Amenhotpe III; Hatshepsut; Thutmose I; Thutmose III; and Thutmose IV.]

BIBLIOGRAPHY

Bietak, Manfred. *"Avaris," the Capital of the Hyksos: Recent Excavations at Tell ed-Dab'a.* London, 1996. A review of the results of the excavation of this site and a discussion of their significance.
Bryan, Betsy M. *The Reign of Thutmose IV.* Baltimore and London,

1991. A commentary and interpretation of the sources from his reign.

Dorman, Peter F. *The Monuments of Senenmut*. London, 1988. A collection of the monuments of the overseer of the estates of Hatshepsut; includes a historical commentary.

Grimal, Nicolas. *A History of Ancient Egypt*. Translated by Ian Shaw, Oxford, 1992.

Kozloff, Arielle P., and Betsy M. Bryan, *Egypt's Dazzling Sun: Amenhotep III and His World*. Cleveland, 1992. A collection of essays on different topics relating to this reign, accompanying a catalogue of an exhibit at the Cleveland Museum of Art.

Lacovara, Peter. *The New Kingdom Royal City*. Studies in Egyptology. London, 1997. Treats the domestic architecture of the palace city and discusses the architecture of the harem town.

Redford, Donald B. "The Concept of Kingship during the Eighteenth Dynasty." In *Ancient Egyptian Kingship*, edited by David O'Connor and David P. Silverman, pp. 157–184. Leiden, 1995.

Redford, Donald B. *Egypt, Canaan, and Israel in Ancient Times*. Princeton, 1992.

Redford, Donald B. *History and Chronology of the Eighteenth Dynasty of Egypt: Seven Studies*. Toronto, 1967.

Robins, Gay. "The God's Wife of Amun in the 18th Dynasty in Egypt." In *Images of Women in Antiquity*, edited by A. Cameron and A. Kuhrt, pp. 65–78. London and Canberra, 1983.

Robins, Gay. *Women in Ancient Egypt*. London, 1993. A good review of the role of women.

Smith, Stuart Tyson. *Askut in Nubia: The Economics and Ideology of Egyptian Imperialism in the Second Millenium B.C.* Studies in Egyptology. London, 1995. Interprets the excavation results from the Second Cataract fort and relates it to different models for imperialism.

Tyldesley, Joyce. *Hatchepsut: The Female Pharaoh*. London, 1996. A review of the sources and speculations concerning this female pharaoh.

LANA TROY

Amarna Period and the End of the Eighteenth Dynasty

The death of Amenhotpe III in his regnal Year 39 (c. 1372 BCE) ushered in a brief but remarkable era in Egyptian history, now named after the modern designation (Tell el-Amarna) for the site of the new capital built by Amenhotpe's son and successor, the so-called heretic pharaoh, Akhenaten. The details of this period are still much debated among Egyptologists, partly because the quantity and character of the evidence prompt many more questions than can be answered with confidence, if at all, and partly because the enigmatic figure who stands at the center of this epoch has elicited such an extraordinary range of characterizations—ranging from the first monotheist, or even the first individual, in history, to religious reformer, to ruthless, determined, narrow-minded despot. Complicating the historian's work still further is the fact that the rulers of the early nineteenth dynasty relegated all of the Amarna rulers between Amenhotpe III and Horemheb to historical oblivion, leaving only whispers in the later record.

Amenhotpe IV (r. 1372–1355 BCE) was the eldest surviving son of Amenhotpe III, his elder brother Thutmose having predeceased their father. Some scholars have argued for a co-regency between father and son, ranging anywhere from a few months to as long as twelve years, but the evidence is not persuasive. A letter from King Tushratta of Mitanni, a frequent correspondent with and ally of the Egyptian royal family, certainly views Amenhotpe IV as having ascended the throne at his father's demise. As is not unusual for the eighteenth dynasty, there is only one record of this Prince Amenhotpe during his father's lifetime. Nor would his actions at the outset of his reign have given much indication of the radical departures that lay ahead. At his accession, he adopted as his throne-name Nefer-kheperure ("perfect are the forms of Re"), with the additional epithet Waenre ("The Chosen One of Re"). Moreover, he participated in the cults of such traditional deities as the state/imperial god Amun-Re and the hawk-headed solar deity Re-Horakhty ("Re-Horus of the horizon"), as well as continuing his father's various building projects, notably at Karnak, the cult center of Amun-Re. Things soon began to change, however.

As early as his second regnal year, Amenhotpe IV decided, for reasons that remain unclear, to celebrate the *sed*-festival, a royal reinvigoration ceremony more typically undertaken after thirty years on the throne and every three years or so thereafter. Amenhotpe III had celebrated it three times and was gearing up for yet another when death intervened. It may be that Amenhotpe IV saw this as a way of emphasizing that he was the divine continuation of his equally divine parent, but the matter remains obscure. Apparently in connection with the *sed*-festival, the new king ordered the construction of a complex of four temples on the east side of Karnak dedicated to a solar deity called "the Aten" (or simply "Aten"), the solar disk (or, as it is sometimes depicted in relief, the solar orb). These structures were put up rapidly with sandstone building blocks (modern *talatat*) cut to a size that could be easily carried on the shoulder of a laborer. (They proved just as easily dismantled when Horemheb reused them in a nearby monument of his own; fortunately, some forty-five thousand of these blocks survive and have been used to reconstruct the decorations of the Gem-pa-Aten temple and its associated shrines.) Other temples to the Aten were begun elsewhere in Egypt and in Nubia. Remarkably, the reconstructed scenes indicate that in one of the Aten-temples, Amenhotpe's chief wife, Nefertiti, is the sole officiant before the god, signaling her prominence in the king's innovations.

At some point during his fourth regnal year, Amenhotpe began construction of a new capital and cult center exclusively for the Aten at a tract of about 21 square miles along the eastern bank of the Nile in Middle Egypt. Work began the following year, and the king visited the site at least once to inspect the progress. In Year 6, at about the same time as the king, the royal family, and court moved to the still unfinished city, named Akhetaten ("horizon of the Aten"), the monarch changed his birth name, Amenhotpe ("may Amun be content") to Akhenaten ("one who is serviceable to the Aten"). The boundary stelae carved at the new capital state that the Aten had chosen the site, the place of his first dawning, a place untouched by any other cult. Before leaving to take up permanent residence in Akhetaten, the king took the radical step of proscribing the worship of Amun, a prohibition that was soon extended to all of the traditional gods and goddesses of Egypt. In due course, the old temples were closed, their income and properties likely reassigned. Henceforth there were to be no other gods worshiped in Egypt apart from the solar disk and his son, Akhenaten. So determined was the king to eliminate every vestige of the older gods that he assigned workmen to carve out their names—even from his own father's birth-name—wherever they found them inscribed; in addition, words or concepts, such as "mother" or *maat* ("order, justice, truth"), had to be written phonetically rather than with hieroglyphics that might suggest the name of some deity. Akhenaten seems rarely if ever to have left the confines of the new capital thereafter. The balance of his seventeen-year reign was devoted to elaborating the theology and practices of the cult of the Aten and to the reaffirming the central role of the pharaoh.

In establishing the exclusive worship of the Aten, Akhenaten built on older forms and recently emergent developments. From an early point in the eighteenth dynasty, the growing dominance of the various aspects of the sun god is evident. The Upper Egyptian fertility god Amun ("the Hidden One") was linked more and more with the solar god Re, yielding in time Amun-Re, a solar deity whose universality lent itself to the imperial expansion under the Thutmosids. The conqueror-pharaohs—Thutmose I, Thutmose III, and Amenhotpe II—gave great donations to the temples out of the proceeds of empire-building in gratitude for the empire that extended from Upper Nubia in the south well into north-central Syria. In the process, the priesthood of Amun-Re in particular gained a great deal of wealth and influence. Though they never actually controlled the monarchy, the priests gained influence over the succession to the throne and therefore the legitimization of kings. They also gained a good deal of authority over the temples of all the other deities. Akhenaten thus attempted to redirect the flow of power.

When Akhenaten had fully articulated his vision, he had become a king, supported by the military caste and a host of parvenus, before whom all bowed and scraped and on whom all attention was focused. Akhenaten presented himself as the son of the Aten; this was not entirely novel, because every king since the mid-fourth dynasty had been styled "Son of Re." But there was a major difference here:

Akhenaten and his queen worshiped the Aten, and the rest of Egypt had to come to the father by way of the son. Akhenaten, the androgynous father and mother of all mankind, was the highest priest of the solar disk and was himself the center of the cult for all Egyptians; there was a high priest of Nefer-kheperure—the chief priest of the cult of the living king. Nefertiti was clearly part of this monarchical focus, for we find her name in a cartouche, reminiscent of the king's throne name: Nefer-neferuaten ("perfect is the beauty of the Aten").

Akhenaten intensified his focus on the monarchy by conceiving of the Aten as a king. This too was not exactly new; Amun-Re had long been called "the king of the gods." But now the Aten was a god who celebrated *sed*-festivals. Moreover, Akhenaten devised for his god a new "didactic" name cast within two cartouches. Early in the reign, this name was "(1) The Living One, Re-Horus of the Horizon, Who Rejoices in the Horizon (2) in His Name 'Light Which Is from the Disk.'" Re and Horus, both closely associated with the solar and royal traditions, and Shu, a god of air and light, remained acceptable for the moment. In his regnal Year 9, Akhenaten altered the god's name to read "(1) The Living One, Ruler of the Horizons, who Rejoices in the Horizon (2) in his Name 'Re, the Father who Comes (Forth) from the Disk,'" thus eliminating even Horus and Shu.

The Aten was not an invention of Akhenaten. The name is known quite early in Egyptian religious history, although it had always taken a minor place in the pantheon. For reasons that remain unclear, Akhenaten's grandfather, Thutmose IV, had given some special attention to this deity, and Amenhotpe III had done likewise, going so far as to call himself "the Dazzling Sun Disk." Despite considerable speculation, it is not known how or why Akhenaten came to regard the Aten as the only god. That he refers to the Aten as "the Sole One" or "the Unique One" is not new either; in the previous reign, such epithets had been applied to Amun-Re, without any connotation of exclusivity. A major innovation, in terms of the classical Egyptian representations of the gods, is the rapid transformation of the image of the Aten as a hawk-headed deity with a human body to the dominating image of the Aten as the solar disk (or orb) from which rays emanate. The only concession to lingering anthropomorphic notions is the hands at the ends of those rays which hold the sign of life (*ankh*) to the nostrils of the king, his wife, and their children. In the great hymn to the Aten preserved in the Amarna tomb intended for Ay, the deity is far away, yet felt by humans as the author of all things in this world, providing his bounty for all, regardless of region, skin color, or language. But the only one who truly "knows" the Aten is his son, Akhenaten. Scholars have applied a number of terms to Akhenaten's religion—henotheism, monotheism, monolatry, etc.—but none quite gets at the essence of this dyarchy of heavenly and earthly god-rulers, lacking a mythology and the traditional Egyptian view of the afterlife. Akhenaten emphasized *maat*, calling himself "One who Lives on *Maat*," thus linking his kingship and that of the Aten in terms of cosmic, political, and social order.

One of the radical departures in Akhenaten's religion comes in the design of the temples for the Aten, notably but not exclusively "the House of the Aten in Akhetaten." The main area for cultic activities—the centerpiece being huge piles of offerings on a multitude of subsidiary altars—was a large court open to the sky, reminiscent of the main feature of the solar temples built by several kings of the fifth dynasty. The king and his entourage spent a great deal of time on these practices. Indeed, a surviving letter from the king of Assyria reproaches Akhenaten for requiring the Assyrian ambassadors to stand out in the broiling sun during the seemingly endless rites; that might be fine for the king of Egypt and his people, but not for mere mortals like the Assyrian ambassadors.

Little can be said about the domestic features of Akhenaten's reign. His authority probably carried throughout the country, although there may well have been some private resistance. The day-to-day operation of the country outside the somewhat rarefied atmosphere of Akhetaten probably continued along traditional bureaucratic lines, although the details are mostly missing. We know a number of his officials, many of whom appear to be new to royal administration. Most of the officials seem to be native Egyptians, but there are some foreigners, notably the vizier (chief minister) for the northern part of the country, a certain Aper-El, with a Semitic-sounding name, whose tomb has been discovered at Saqqara. His colleague in the vizierate was Nakht, who had a fine villa and tomb at Amarna. Of considerable influence was Ay, who may have been Akhenaten's maternal uncle. The military commanders Maya and Ramose stand out, as does the chief of police, Mahu. Among the most important individuals at Amarna, of course, were the various priests who assisted Akhenaten in the year-round celebrations of the cult.

Because of a cache of cuneiform diplomatic correspondence found at Amarna (known as the Amarna Letters), the outline of Egypt's relations with its foreign satellites and neighbors in southwestern Asia can be discerned. It is often asserted that Akhenaten neglected, and thereby seriously weakened, the Egyptian Empire and its prestige. This is probably an overstatement. In fact, the aggressive policies of the earlier eighteenth dynasty had largely ended with Amenhotpe II. Nubia was a somewhat different matter, and when needed, force was applied, even under Akhenaten. Until the early fourteenth century BCE, the major power in southwestern Asia was the Hurrian/Indo-European kingdom of Mitanni, situated in northwestern Mesopotamia and northeastern Syria. Thutmose III and Amenhotpe II had successfully contested northern Syria with the Mitanni, but neither Thutmose IV nor Amenhotpe III engaged in any extensive military campaigning there, both preferring an Asian policy based on diplomacy—notably, diplomatic marriages and judicious applications of gold—and, as far as the Syrian vassals were concerned, a cautious policy of setting one against the other was followed, thereby weakening any potential for dangerous alliances. By the time that Akhenaten had ascended the Egyptian throne, however, the situation in northern Syria was beginning to change. A new king, Shuppiluliumas I, had managed to bring coherence back to the Hittite state and had ambitions in Syria. He defeated and effectively neutralized the Mitanni kingdom—something later Hittite kings would have reason to regret—and became a force to reckon with in Syria. Some of Egypt's more northerly vassals allied themselves with Shuppiluliumas, concluding that the closer power was the more dangerous one. Akhenaten appears to have been angered by this turn of events, but he was apparently not prepared to employ anything stronger than words. The Hittite power was extended to central Syria, but not beyond. A serious plague had hit the Near East and may well have made further aggression out of the question for all concerned, at least temporarily.

In the last years before Akhenaten's death in his regnal Year 17, there were some shifts in alignment within the royal family. The Great King's Wife, Nefer-neferwaten Nefertiti, who had produced six daughters and had been a major force in Akhenaten's reign, may have served as a coregent with the king, although some have detected a waning of her influence and presence. Her throne name appears in conjunction with a relief showing Akhenaten and another king. Akhenaten had other favorite wives, notably the somewhat mysterious Kiya, who appears to have predeceased him. It also seems that in this last period the king's eldest daughter, Merytaten, had taken over as the primary female figure in Akhetaten. She had married a certain Smenkhkare, and it is likely that he served, if briefly, as a coregent with Akhenaten. Whether he survived the king and had an independent reign of about three years defies demonstration. His parentage is not known, but there has been scholarly speculation that he was Akhenaten's elder son by Kiya. There is now some reason to suppose that he was the brother of his successor, Tutankhamun.

The eight- or nine-year-old successor to Akhenaten, and/or Smenkhkare, originally had been named Tutankhaten ("living image of the Aten"); he was married—when is not clear—to the third daughter of Akhenaten and Nefertiti, Ankhesenpaaten ("she lives for the Aten"). Exactly who was in charge at this critical point is unknown, but it seems likely that Ay played the dominant role. For perhaps as long as three years, Tutankhaten reigned from Akhetaten, but it is clear that negotiations were already under way—perhaps already begun by Smenkhkare and Merytaten—to return to Thebes and reestablish the traditional divinities and their temples. The new king's name was changed to Tutankhamun ("living image of Amun"), and that of his wife to Ankhesenamun ("she lives for Amun"). The power brokers formulated in the king's name a stela breaking with the Amarna "heresy" and restoring traditional religious observances. The text portrays an Egypt before Tutankhamun that had fallen into ruin, the temples desolate, and the armies unsuccessful in Syria—a place the gods ignored. All of that was now reversed by the acts of the new king. Unexpectedly, Tutankhamun died after a reign of approximately ten years, leaving no heir. He was buried in a rather small tomb in the Valley of the Kings, perhaps not intended for him originally. Its discovery with most of its treasures intact, by Howard Carter in 1922, caused a sensation.

An astonishing letter has survived from Ankhesenamun to Shuppiluliumas, soliciting a husband for the queen from among the Hittite princes. Understandably surprised and not a little suspicious of the Egyptians' game, Shuppiluliumas sent agents to discover whether or not Egypt was without a king; convinced finally that this new power amalgam was possible, he sent one of his sons, who appears to have been murdered (by persons unknown) on the way, leading to a long chain of hostility between Egypt and Hatti. The events that brought the elderly Ay to the throne cannot be reconstructed, but clearly there was a powerful alliance between this long-time supporter of the royal family and General Horemheb. Ay (throne-name, Kheper-kheperure, "the forms of Re have come into being") reigned for only about three years. He was succeeded on the throne by Horemheb (throne-name, Djeser-kheperure, "sacred are the forms of Re"), who had the support of both the army and the priesthood of Amun.

Horemheb's reign of about twenty-seven years allowed for a considerable period in which to institutionalize the restoration of the traditional order. He had risen to the top of the military under Tutankhamun, without connections to Akhenaten, although at some point he was married to a woman named Mutnodjmet, who may have been Nefertiti's sister. The primary emphasis of his reign was the restoration of order and the curtailing of corruption, to which ends he set up a new judicial apparatus. Although he seems to have been unable to alter the boundary between the Egyptian and Hittite spheres of influence, it remained comparatively steady during his reign. Horemheb reorganized the army to enhance its effectiveness. In keeping with his support of Amun and the old order,

he became a prolific builder of temples, especially at Karnak; he built new structures, usurped some of Tutankhamun's monuments, and almost totally dismantled Akhenaten's Theban temples. Seeing that he was going to die without an heir, Horemheb sought to maintain the stability and military dominance he had established by naming as his successor a general from the Nile Delta, a certain Piramessu, who became Ramesses I, the first king of the nineteenth dynasty. When Horemheb died, he was buried in the Valley of the Kings (tomb 57). So effective were his efforts that his nineteenth dynasty successors regarded him as the first legitimate ruler after Amenhotpe III. Their own place in the sun, of course, they owed to him as well.

[*See also* Akhenaten; Amarna Letters; Amarna, Tell el-; Aten; Ay; Horemheb; Monotheism; Nefertiti; *and* Tutankhamun.]

BIBLIOGRAPHY

Aldred, Cyril. *Akhenaten: King of Egypt.* London, 1988.
Assmann, Jan. *Egyptian Solar Religion in the New Kingdom: Re, Amun, and the Crisis of Polytheism.* Translated by A. Alcock. London, 1995.
Assmann, Jan. *Monotheismus und Kosmotheismus: Ägyptische Formen eines "Denken des Einen" und ihre europäische Rezeptionsgeschichte.* Heidelberg, 1993.
Breasted, James H. *The Development of Religion and Thought in Ancient Egypt.* New York, 1912.
Hornung, Erik. *Conceptions of God in Ancient Egypt.* Translated by J. Baines. Ithaca, 1982.
Kemp, Barry J. *Amarna Reports.* 6 vols. London, 1984–1997.
Kemp, Barry J. *Ancient Egypt: Anatomy of a Civilization.* London and New York, 1989.
Krauss, Rolf. *Das Ende der Amarnazeit.* Hildesheimer Ägyptologische Beiträge, 7. Hildesheim, 1978.
Martin, G. T. *A Bibliography of the Amarna Period and Its Aftermath.* London and New York, 1991. The most important bibliographical source for the Amarna period.
Martin, Geoffrey T. *The Royal Tomb at el-Amarna.* 2 vols. London, 1974–1989.
Moran, William L., ed. and trans. *The Amarna Letters.* Baltimore, 1992.
Murnane, William J. *Texts from the Amarna Period in Egypt.* Writings from the Ancient World, 5. Atlanta, 1995.
Murnane, William J., and C. C. van Siclen III. *The Boundary Stelae of Akhenaten.* London and New York, 1993.
O'Connor, David and E. H. Cline, eds. *Amenhotep III: Perspectives on His Reign.* Ann Arbor, 1998.
Redford, Donald B. *Akhenaten: The Heretic King.* Princeton, 1984.
Redford, Donald B. *The Akhenaten Temple Project,* vol. 2. Toronto, 1988.
Redford, Donald B., and R. W. Smith. *The Akhenaten Temple Project,* vol. 1. Warminster, 1976.
Reeves, Nicholas. *The Complete Tutankhamun.* London, 1990.
Tyldesley, Joyce. *Nefertiti: Egypt's Sun Queen.* New York, 1998.

GERALD E. KADISH

Nineteenth Dynasty

This dynasty comprised eight rulers of Egypt (seven kings and one queen-regnant). It stemmed from a military family that appears to have originated from the eastern Nile Delta at Avaris, city of the god Seth. Avaris had previously reached prominence in the Middle Kingdom as a summer capital (called Ro-waty) for the twelfth and thirteenth dynasties (twentieth to sixteenth centuries BCE) and later, as Avaris, for the foreign Hyksos kings of the fifteenth dynasty.

At the end of the eighteenth dynasty, King Horemheb had no son and heir to succeed him on the Egyptian throne; but through the years he came to value the abilities of a close military colleague, Piramesse, the son of a troop-commander Sety, from the district of Avaris. Under his patronage, Piramesse rose to the highest offices in Egypt (e.g., vizier) before finally being declared his deputy and heir by Horemheb. This no doubt led Horemheb to have new work done at the temple of Seth at Avaris (cf. Bietak 1986, p. 270 and pl. 38a), and to favor his close colleague with a pair of statues in the Karnak temple of Amun in Thebes (the inscriptions are translated in Davies 1995, pp. 89–90).

At Horemheb's death, Piramesse duly took the throne as king Menpehtyre Ramesses (I), deliberately modeling his royal style on that of Nebpehtyre Ahmose I, as if he were to be the founder of a new eighteenth dynasty, a practice initially followed by his son and grandson (Kitchen 1979, pp. 383–384). His son and heir, Sety, lost no time in leading Egypt's troops into Canaan, but little else had been achieved when Ramesses I died in his second year, after perhaps only sixteen months' reign. It was his energetic son, Sety I, who threw himself unreservedly into the task of restoring the glory of Egypt at home and abroad, seeking even to surpass the deeds and works of the formidable eighteenth dynasty in both war and peace.

In war, Sety I sought to impose his authority on the Levant without delay. Year 1 (as depicted in scenes at Karnak) saw him sweeping along the Sinai coast road to Gaza, destroying Shasu dissidents on the way and near Gaza. It is clear that he went through Canaan all the way to Galilee: a stela of his Year 1 at Beth-Shan reports his quelling rebels there and at Hammath and nearby Yenoam. Being late in the year, this probably happened on Sety's return from the north, most likely from Phoenicia. The capture of Yenoam is shown in the Karnak scenes (middle register, east side) that culminate in the submission of "the chiefs of Lebanon," so it is tempting to link this register with the events of Year 1 of the Beth-Shan stela. At Tyre was found part of a stela of Sety I, indicating the Egyptian presence there in Year 1 or later. East of Lake Galilee, another stela of Sety I from Tell es-Shihab indicates a move to secure the inland routes up to Egypt's province of Upe in southern Syria, including Damascus.

Having set his existing Levantine territories in order, Sety then moved (in Year 2 or possibly later) to recover the area lost to the Hittites by Akhenaten some sixty years before. He subdued the mountainous kingdom of Amurru (just behind the Phoenician coast) and marched inland to seize Kadesh, where he set up a victory stela. However, since the Hittites would not be prepared to give these up, we may infer that the Hittite king Muwatallis II marched south next season to recover control of Amurru and Kadesh. By now (if we read the west-side registers at Karnak from top to bottom), probably in Year 3 or later, Sety had to deal with a new threat to Egypt: from Libya on her west flank, for the first time in two hundred years. That done, he then returned north (Year 4 or later) to contest the control of central Syria with the Hittites. Significantly, his Karnak war scenes for this conflict include no specific conquests whatsoever—no names of towns conquered. From a later allusion in the Hittite treaty of Ramesses II, it is clear that both sides recognized that neither could oust the other, so a treaty was signed between the two powers: the Hittites would keep Amurru and Kadesh, while the Egyptian interests along the Phoenician coast would be respected. In distant Nubia, in about Year 8, a rebellion in Irem was quickly crushed. So, in Africa, the new dynasty ruled as widely as its model, the eighteenth dynasty; but in the Near East, the formidable power of Hatti could not be pushed back, and Sety I was realistic enough to understand this.

In peace, Sety I's priorities were twofold: first, to please the traditional gods as spectacularly as possible, to gain their support and Egypt's well-being; and second, on the mundane level, to achieve an honest and efficient administration. Thus, he embarked on a magnificent building program for the four most important gods in Egypt: for the three state gods, Amun, Re, and Ptah in this life, and for Osiris, god of the afterlife. In Thebes, the immense hypostyle hall at Karnak was well begun; for his own permanent cult as a manifestation of Amun, he built a substantial memorial temple (Qurnah) on the western bank. It is highly probable that he had also planned and begun the great pylon and forecourt at Luxor temple, because Ramesses II brought it to rapid completion in the first three years of his reign. At Heliopolis, the sun god Re was to benefit from a pylon, forecourt, and obelisks (a "working model" appears in Badawy 1973); of all this, little more survives than the Flaminian Obelisk in Rome. At Memphis, the venerable creator god Ptah was to have a great hall fronting his temple, from which only part of a foundation deposit survives (Kitchen, *Translations*, 1993, p. 105; see Kitchen, *Notes*, 1993, pp. 100–101). At Abydos, a vast temple was at once a "pantheon" of Egypt's chief gods, a memorial temple of the king as Osiris, and a new sanctuary of Osiris alongside his traditional temple. Behind it, Sety I built a subterranean cenotaph (the Osireion) for the rites of Osiris and himself.

In administration, Sety I had a keen appreciation of character, choosing able men for high office, such as the vizier Paser and the cup-bearer and "troubleshooter" Asha-hebsed. Attempts were made to root out corruption and abuse, as the Nauri decree for the great Abydos temple makes evident. The work force for royal tombs in Western Thebes had been reorganized; they cut an immense tunnel-tomb for Sety I. In Year 11 at the earliest up to a theoretical Year 14 at the latest, Sety I suddenly passed to rest in that tomb, leaving a flourishing empire to his son Ramesses II, who had already served a few years of apprenticeship with him as prince regent with full royal trappings (excluding only his own regnal year-count).

Ramesses II was young and ambitious, even over-ambitious. Again, he achieved more in peace than by war. In Year 4, while confirming his hold on Phoenicia, he overwhelmed the Hittite vassal Amurru, in breach of his father's treaty with Muwatallis. His next objective was to recapture Kadesh, as a gateway to the rest of Syria once held by the previous dynasty. However, Muwatallis decided to put a brutal end to the young king's ambitions. When Ramesses II came north (by the inland route) to Kadesh in Year 5, he walked straight into a trap, from which he escaped only by personal bravery and the prearranged arrival on time of his second force, fresh from traversing the coast route: this was the notorious Battle of Kadesh. A second day's conflict achieved nothing, and Ramesses II refused Muwatallis's offer of a *status quo* agreement, returning to Egypt. The Hittite followed him down the Beqa Valley, but not over the Lebanese mountains, whence Ramesses gained the safety of the coast. The Hittites temporarily occupied the Egyptian zone of Upe in southern Syria. Thus Ramesses won, but Egypt lost. Year 7 may have seen a minor campaign in Moab and Edom. In Year 8, Ramesses fought to crush a rebellion in Galilee and to recover southern Syria; he then moved up the coast and inland past Kadesh to raid deep into Hittite Syria. Once he had gone back, the Hittites simply reoccupied the area. In Year 10, Ramesses repeated his exploit, but again he could not retain such distant territory. At last he had to realize that he could not push back the Hittite power, any more than his father had done. Thus, after a brief crisis in Year 18 (Beth-Shan stela) over the flight into Egypt of the Hittite ex-king Urhi-Tesup, Ramesses II was ready to respond to overtures by the hard-pressed Hattusil III, ending with a great state treaty in Year 21. This brought internal peace to the Levant and was confirmed through Ramesses' marriage to two successive Hittite princesses in Year 34 and later. Relations became close; the Hittite court eagerly sought Egyptian physicians.

In peace, Ramesses II pushed his father's great temples to completion, often in his own name (as at Karnak, Memphis, and in part Heliopolis). At Avaris, Sety I had a summer palace; Ramesses II built an entire eastern Delta capital, Piramesse ("Domain of Ramesses," the biblical Raamses of *Exodus* 1:11), with its own great temples, barracks, docks, city, and vineyards. During his sixty-six years, he built in varying measure in the Levant and throughout Egypt and Nubia. Suffice it to mention only the West Hall at Memphis, his own memorial temples at Abydos and in Thebes (the Ramesseum), his own tomb plus a mausoleum for his offspring in the Valley of the Kings and tombs for several queens in the Valley of the Queens in Western Thebes, and a chain of temples in Nubia—often rock-cut (Beit el-Wali, Derr, two at Abu Simbel), partly so (Gerf Husein, Wadi es-Sebua), or stone-built (Aksha, Amarah West, Napata). Nonreligious works included a chain of forts along the Libyan coast route.

Prominent at Ramesses' court were his mother, Tuya, and his own queens, especially Nefertari, Istnofret, and the princess-queens; the Hittite queens made spectacular arrivals before simply becoming part of his harem. Several of his sons fought in his wars; Khaemwaset became a distinguished priestly scholar, investigating the ancient pyramids and inaugurating the Serapeum tunnel-tombs for the Apis bulls. Ramesses outlived at least three successive crown princes, until Merenptah finally succeeded him. His government included the veteran vizier Paser, and such viceroys of Nubia as Huy—who had escorted the first Hittite princess to Egypt—and Setau, who taxed the Nubians hard and superintended the building of Ramesses' later temples there.

At the aged king's death, when the invigoration of fourteen successive jubilee rituals (*sed*-festivals) could sustain him no more, his thirteenth son, Merenptah, succeeded him. Despite his years, the new king reacted vigorously to rising threats to Egypt and her domains. He promptly quelled unrest in Canaan (in his Year 1 or 2?), sending his son, the crown prince Sety, to crush revolt in Ascalon, Gezer, and Yenoam, and to chastise a "new" tribal group, Israel, in the hills, where a strategic well station was established near Jerusalem. Called the "Well of Merenptah," this was later reinterpreted in Semitic as "Wellspring of the waters of Naftoah." Thus, in Year 3, normal communications in the Egyptian-ruled Levant could continue unhindered, as a postal register shows. In Year 5 came a double threat. With a population augmented by Sea People immigrants from across the Mediterranean and food resources consequently scarcer, the Libyans attempted an invasion of the Egyptian Delta, having persuaded the Nubians to raise a diversionary revolt to the south of Egypt. However, Merenptah got wind of these intentions and mobilized swiftly to move first, while the Nubians delayed so long that Merenptah could decisively defeat the Libyans in the northwest while his viceroy crushed the Nubians in the south. Egypt could breathe again.

Already old, Merenptah could not rival his father's vast building projects; however, he carried out an inspection and refurbishment of Egypt's temples (Years 1 and 2), thus justifying adding his names to many standing monuments as his visiting card to the gods. His memorial temple in Western Thebes had to be built as quickly as possible, and so much stone for it was taken from older buildings. It was a little more than half the size of his father's Ramesseum, a fact cleverly disguised by fronting it with a pylon designed to be almost as large as that of the Ramesseum.

After Merenptah, the succession is clouded in obscurity. The general view of scholars has been that Amenmesse managed to usurp the throne for three years at Merenptah's death, so that the crown prince, Sety, had to oust him to ascend the throne as Sety II. This is still the simplest (and perhaps best) view of the matter, despite able advocacy of the theory that Sety II followed his father Merenptah directly on the throne, only for Amenmesse to arise in Nubia and Upper Egypt as a rival king for three years until Sety II managed to suppress him. The question must remain open at present. In any case, Sety II was succeeded by a young prince who reigned originally as Ramesses Siptah, later changing his throne name to Merenptah-Siptah. The powers behind his throne were the dowager queen Twosret (widow of Sety II) and a powerful courtier, the chancellor Bay, who was perhaps instrumental in placing Siptah on the throne. At the young king's death (Year 6), Twosret took over as female pharaoh with full titles, continuing his regnal years through to Year 8. She then disappeared (either by natural death or a coup d'état), and out of the following brief confusion—when Bay may have sought the supreme role—a new strong man, Sethnakhte, took over to found the twentieth dynasty.

The nineteenth dynasty was a transitional period in Egypt's political fortunes: from now on, Egypt could no longer guarantee to vanquish every foe in war. In other respects, there was innovation in several fields. Following Akhenaten's attempt at monotheism (centered on the sun god), Egypt's godhead was centered on the trio of Amun of Thebes, Re of Heliopolis, and Ptah of Memphis, whom one or two theological thinkers even considered to be aspects of one deity; but this was an elite concept, not much affecting the polytheism of ordinary folk. The Memphite Theology, cut on a basalt slab under Shabaqa (c.700 BCE) from a decaying papyrus, was probably a Ramessid product; in it, Ptah fashions all by his creative word (cf. the Greek *logos*). More prosaically, Ramesses II encouraged statue-cults of himself, embodying various aspects of the kingship, as foci of popular devotion. He built an unprecedented number of temples hewn in the living rock, especially in Nubia. Mausoleums for his sons (in the Valley of the Kings, Western Thebes) and for successive genera-

tions of sacred Apis bulls (buried at Saqqara, by Memphis) were a new concept in funerary usage. In education, the scribal curriculum was revised; alongside the old Middle Kingdom classics, works in the current (Late Egyptian) idiom were introduced, and with a practical bent. Such is the "Satirical Letter," which teaches Levantine geography through one scribe appearing to taunt another over his incompetence. In art, fine sculpture and painting continued, though often lapsing into formalized mass production. Experiments included attempts at shading in facial color, as in Queen Nefertari's tomb. Foreigners featured in Egyptian society at all levels, from royal cup-bearers to whom the kings increasingly entrusted government missions, through most layers of officialdom all the way down to prisoners of war and hapless slaves toiling as cultivators on great estates of temple and state, or as laborers on building projects, making bricks or hauling stone blocks. In Thebes, the chief draftsman of Amun, Didia, could trace his ancestors (Semites and Hurrians) back through seven generations, with their often foreign wives. The Hurrian-named general Urhi-Tesup served under Sety I, while his son Yupa (a Canaanite name) had a distinguished career under Ramesses II, beginning as a stablemaster, overseeing brick-making, and then following his father up through the army before becoming high steward of the Ramesseum and having the honor of proclaiming Ramesses II's ninth jubilee. Foreign merchants offered their varied wares. This was perhaps the most cosmopolitan epoch in Egypt's long history.

[*See also* Battle of Kadesh; Merenptah; Piramesse; Ramesses I; Ramesses II; Sety I; *and* Sety II.]

BIBLIOGRAPHY

Badawy, Alexander. *A History of Egyptian Architecture: The Empire (the New Kingdom)*. Berkeley and Los Angeles, 1968. Gives a convenient account of towns, houses, palaces, administrative buildings, military works, temples, and tombs for the New Kingdom, including the nineteenth dynasty.

Badawy, Alexander. *A Monumental Gateway for a Temple of Sety I*. Brooklyn, 1973.

Beckman, Gary. *Hittite Diplomatic Texts*. Atlanta, 1996. Contains modern English translations of almost all treaties made by the Hittite great kings, including that with Ramesses II of Egypt.

Bietak, M. *Avaris and Piramesse*. 2d ed. London, 1986.

Bleiberg, Edward, Rita Freed, and Anna Kay Walker. *Fragments of a Shattered Visage: The Proceedings of the International Symposium of Ramesses the Great*. Memphis, Tenn., 1991. A series of scholarly but readable studies on several different aspects of nineteenth dynasty Egypt.

Caminos, Ricardo A. *Late-Egyptian Miscellanies*, London, 1954. Annotated translations of a series of papyri (copied out by ancient students) that contain varied background information on life in the nineteenth and early twentieth dynasties.

Davies, Benjamin G. *Egyptian Historical Records of the Later Eighteenth Dynasty*. Fascicle 6. Warminster, 1995.

Epigraphic Survey. *The Battle Reliefs of King Sety I*. Chicago, 1986. Full and definitive copies of the great series of war scenes of Sety on the Great Hall at Karnak, together with translations and notes.

Freed, Rita E. *Ramesses the Great.* Memphis, Tenn., 1987. A lavishly illustrated exhibition catalogue on the world of Ramesses II and the nineteenth dynasty, with good general introduction.

Hayes, William C. *The Scepter of Egypt.* Part 2, *The Hyksos Period and the New Kingdom (1675–1080 B.C.).* Cambridge, Mass., 1959. Based on the Metropolitan Museum of Art Egyptian collection, a superb handbook on the material culture and artifacts of the New Kingdom, including the nineteenth dynasty.

Kitchen, K. A. *Pharaoh Triumphant: The Life and Times of Ramesses II King of Egypt.* Warminster, 1982. Popular account of the epoch of Ramesses II, with source references.

Kitchen, K. A. *Ramesside Inscriptions Translated and Annotated: Translations.* 2 vols. Oxford, 1993, 1996. Full English translations of all the principal historically relevant inscriptions of Ramesses I and Sety I (vol. 1), and of the official inscriptions of Ramesses II (vol. 2).

Kitchen, K. A. *Ramesside Inscriptions Translated and Annotated: Notes and Comments.* 2 vols. Oxford, 1993, 1998. Basic bibliography, introductions, background, and specialized notes (plus maps) to accompany the previous entry.

McDonald, John K. *House of Eternity: The Tomb of Nefertari.* London, 1996. A vividly illustrated, compact and readable book on Ramesses II's favorite queen, her splendidly decorated tomb, the tomb-builders, and the relevant Egyptian religious beliefs about the afterlife.

Redford, Donald B. *Egypt, Canaan and Israel in Ancient Times.* Princeton, 1992. Part 2 of this book (pp. 125–237) gives a well-documented survey of the interrelationships of Egypt with the Levant in the New Kingdom, including the nineteenth dynasty.

Ruffle, John, G. A. Gaballa, and K. A. Kitchen, eds. *Orbis Aegyptiorum Speculum: Glimpses of Ancient Egypt, Studies in Honour of H. W. Fairman.* Warminster, 1979. The essays by Gaballa, Lowle, Ruffle, and Kitchen deal with significant nineteenth dynasty private monuments, including foreigners in Egypt (Urhiya, etc.).

Smith, William Stevenson. *Interconnections in the Ancient Near East: A Study of the Relationships between the Arts of Egypt, the Aegean, and Western Asia.* New Haven and London, 1965. Excellent background work on the mutual stimulus in the arts between Egypt and her neighbors.

KENNETH A. KITCHEN

Twentieth Dynasty

The twentieth dynasty (1200–1081 BCE) was the second dynasty of the Ramessid period, and the last of the New Kingdom. It comprised ten kings: Sethnakht and nine kings named Ramesses, whom modern scholarship knows as Ramesses III to XI, but whom their contemporaries distinguished by a praenomen, or coronation name, and by a surname.

The founder of the dynasty, Sethnakht (r. 1200–1198 BCE), like the founders of the preceding dynasty, was probably a general of the troops garrisoned in the eastern Nile Delta. He had no known relationship to the royal family of the nineteenth dynasty. He became king on the death without posterity of Queen Twosret, that dynasty's last ruler. There is no solid proof of his having been particularly hostile to her, as is sometimes surmised, nor of a civil war having led to his coronation. A historical stela from his second year, discovered in Elephantine, seems to imply that his seizure of power, probably agreed on previously by his peers, the leaders of the priesthood, army, and administration, was implemented by an oracle of Seth in this god's temple in Piramesse. Already an elderly man, he reigned only about two years, with his son Ramesses, shortly to become Ramesses III, acting as his deputy and second-in-command. A brief campaign of pacification was necessary to quell domestic unrest, probably bequeathed by the conflict between two lines of descent from Merenptah, which best explains the political troubles at the end of the nineteenth dynasty.

Ramesses III (r. 1198–1166 BCE), son of Sethnakht and of his wife, Queen Tiy-Merenese, ruled Egypt for thirty-one years, and his figure dominates the whole period. Born before his father's accession to the throne, he was probably another military man. He had at least ten sons, by two main queens: Isis, daughter of Hemdjeret, and an anonymous lady. A secondary wife, Tiy, bore him a son, Pentawere, who would stand as a pretender to the throne against the legitimate heir, Ramesses IV, at the end of the reign. Three of these sons would reign after him: Ramesses IV, VI, and VIII. The intervening Ramesses V and VII were his grandsons, who died without living posterity, so that each time the crown reverted to a surviving uncle. After the death of Ramesses VIII, the crown went to the latter's nephew Ramesses IX, and then to this king's son and grandson, Ramesses X and XI. There is some speculation that two daughters of Ramesses XI, Tentamun and Henuttawy, married respectively Smendes I, the first king of the twenty-first dynasty, and the high priest of Amun, Pinodjem I, father of its third king, for purposes of legitimation, so that some of the early rulers of the Third Intermediate Period descended from Ramesses III on the maternal side.

The record of Ramesses III's reign is impressive. Between his Years 5 and 12, he built his famous funerary temple at Medinet Habu in Western Thebes, the last great architectural achievement of the New Kingdom. Meanwhile, he had to fight three major wars: in Years 5 and 11, at the Delta's western border, he conducted two campaigns against two successive groups of invading Libyan tribes, led respectively by the Libu and Meshwesh peoples; and in Year 8, in Palestine, there was a campaign against the migrating Sea Peoples, who on their way from the Aegean had destroyed all the states of the ancient Near East—even powerful Hatti. They were stopped by Ramesses III in Palestine on land and sea, but the king did not prevent them from settling in that country, especially on the coast (Dor, Akko, Tel Qasile), where they were later known as the biblical Philistines.

In the wake of these wars, from Year 15 on, Ramesses

III implemented a systematic restoration and reorganization of all the temples of Egypt, lavishing on them a wealth of gifts brought as booty or as the product of expeditions abroad. Despite these achievements, strikes broke out in Deir el-Medina in Year 29, prompted by the inability of the administration to pay the workers their wages in grain. Traditionally viewed as a symptom of a general disorganization of the country's economy, these strikes seem better explained by a more conjectural factor: the impending celebration of the king's jubilee, which would require the collection of enormous quantities of food and goods, and which was held in Memphis on the thirtieth anniversary of his coronation.

At the end of the reign, prompted by Ramesses III's impending death, some discontented officials conspired with queen Tiy to deprive the legitimate heir Ramesses of the crown and give it to her son Pentawere. This so-called Harem Conspiracy sheds an interesting light on the existence of internal conflicts, which probably raged more or less permanently inside the leadership, behind the mask of unanimity conveyed by the official documents. The plot's exposure brought a bloody and ruthless repression, heralded by official texts such as the Judicial Papyrus of Turin, and the compilation for propaganda purposes of an official history of the reign, preserved as Papyrus Harris I.

After the death of Ramesses III, the history of the twentieth dynasty is one of the swift decline of Egypt, in less than a century, from the position of an aggressive international power, ruling territories in Asia and Nubia, to that of a second-rate, self-centered, impoverished country, racked with internal troubles. This decline was the result of a complex interaction of internal and external causes, of which three seem the most important. One was probably the repeated changes of line of descent among the successors of Ramesses III, which frequently raised to the throne kings unprepared for their tasks, thus preventing the emergence of a strong and able political leadership. Meanwhile, officialdom and local nobility showed more continuity than the central power, a sign that had always portended periods of political troubles in Egypt.

A second probable factor in Egypt's decline during the period was that, from the days of Ramesses III on, Middle and Upper Egypt, especially the Thebaid, experienced a growing state of public insecurity brought about by bands of roving Libyans who repeatedly raided the valley. The powerlessness of the administration to cope with the problem created a highly unfavorable context for the enforcement of law because it brought about a loss of confidence in the traditional institutions.

Third and most important, Egypt lost control during this period of all its external territories. In the Near East, the settlement of the Philistines on the Palestinian coast at last achieved what Egyptian policy and the contradictory ambitions of local rulers had conspired to avoid for so long: the progressive unification of the peoples of the country into a single independent political entity—later to become the Israelite kingdom—which had no reason to continue to contribute gratuitously to Egypt's standing. Meanwhile, by the end of the dynasty, the establishment of an independent princedom in Nubia deprived Egypt of its free access to the gold mines of the Wadi Allaqi. This stifled Egypt's redistributive economy, which needed more income than it produced, and relied accordingly on the appropriation of foreign goods. Because the legitimacy of the Egyptian ruler was founded largely on his ability to ensure by this appropriation the welfare of his people, the resulting penury weakened the primacy of the ruling house and its administration. People had to seek other means of income for themselves, and they found them in the tombs of their fathers and the temples of their gods.

By the death of Ramesses III, however, Egypt was still far from this sorry state. Ramesses IV (r. 1166–1160 BCE) was obviously eager to follow in his father's steps. During his first three years of reign, he instituted new offerings for Amun at Karnak, ordered his cartouches and titulature to be engraved wherever possible, began the wall decoration of his father's Khonsu temple at Karnak, and sent four expeditions to the Wadi Hammamat. The last one, which comprised nine thousand people (including a whole division of the army), brought back a sufficient quantity of graywacke stone, favored for statuary, to last until the end of the dynasty.

After an unusually late beginning (more than one year after his coronation), the work on Ramesses IV's tomb in the Valley of the Kings (tomb 2, of which a papyrus in Turin preserves a map), proceeded rapidly, aided by a doubling of Deir el-Medina's work force from 60 to 120 men. Meanwhile, the king made two successive plans for the construction of a great mortuary temple in the Asasif section of the Theban necropolis.

In his fourth year, Ramesses IV erected at Abydos two great stelae for Osiris and the local gods, stressing his legitimacy and showing them his piety, as exemplified by his works. He asked them, as a reward, to be granted a reign of double the sixty-seven years of rule of Ramesses II, but his prayer went unheeded: all his architectural projects as well as his political ones, if any, were cut short by his death after about six years of reign. Even the building of his mortuary temple was hardly begun by his death, so that his funerary cult would finally be enacted in a very small chapel adjoining the temple of the deified architect of the eighteenth dynasty, Amenhotep, son of Hapu, to the north of Medinet Habu. The brevity of this king's reign is in contrast with the tenure of office of the vizier Neferrenpet, active until Ramesses VI, and of the high priest of Amun Ramessesnakht, who was appointed to this post in the first year of Ramesses IV and who held it until his death under Ramesses IX, more than thirty years later.

Uneventful as it was, the reign of Ramesses IV still seems imposing in comparison with the colorless rule of the following kings, whose greatest achievements were the realization of their tombs in the Valley of the Kings and the usurpation of the names of their predecessors on existing monuments, while all signs of Egyptian control over Palestine disappear from the record. Ramesses V (r. 1160–1156 BCE) was the son of Ramesses IV by his queen, Tentopet. A young man, he died after only about three years of reign, a victim of an infectious disease, probably smallpox. Besides some minor works, he tried without success to complete for himself his father's projected mortuary temple in the Asasif. The brevity of his reign did not allow him even to complete his tomb in the Valley of the Kings (tomb 9), which was to serve as the sepulcher of his successor Ramesses VI. He was the last Egyptian king to use the copper mines of Timna, north of Elath.

As a kind of compensation for its lack of sources on political history, the reign of Ramesses V produced three papyri that are exceptionally interesting for our knowledge of the society and its institutions: the Wilbour Papyrus, about 10 meters (32 feet) long, which is a detailed agricultural survey of the region between the Faiyum and Minia; the Turin Indictment Papyrus (Papyrus Turin 1887), which lists offenses of all sorts committed between the reigns of Ramesses III and V by a priest of Khnum of Elephantine, Penanqet, against this god's estate; and the complicated last will of the Lady Naunakhte, of Deir el-Medina.

The next king, Ramesses VI (r. 1156–1149 BCE), was an uncle of Ramesses V and ascended the throne on his nephew's death without posterity. His reign of seven years has not left us much more than his cartouches engraved over his predecessors' on existing monuments. He tried, with no more success than Ramesses V, to build the projected funerary temple of Ramesses IV in the Asasif, which was afterward abandoned. He presented his mother, Isis, widow of Ramesses III, with a tomb in the Valley of the Queens (tomb 51), and completed for himself, in the Valley of the Kings, the tomb that his predecessor had barely begun. This predecessor's body he did not allow to be buried for sixteen months after death, a fact that has elicited much speculation and no satisfactory explanation. About the same time, the workforce of Deir el-Medina, doubled by Ramesses IV, was reduced to its initial size of sixty. Abroad, Ramesses VI is the last pharaoh whose name is attested in the Sinai. In Nubia, the reign produced in Aniba the fine tomb of Penne, the viceroy of Kush's deputy for Wawat. It is also the last reign of the dynasty to produce significant statuary. Ramesses VI's

Karnak statue (Cairo 42152), showing him as he leads a Libyan captive by the hair to Amun, as well as a triumphal scene in the temple, attests at least some campaigning against Egypt's western neighbors.

Of Ramesses VII (r. 1149–1141 BCE), son of Ramesses VI, very little is known, despite a reign of seven years. Five grandiloquent hymns in his honor, preserved in Turin papyri, stand in ironic contrast to the scarcity of his achievements: like his predecessors, his main activities were adding his cartouches to previously existing monuments, the excavation of his tomb in the Valley of the Kings (tomb 1), and the burial of the sacred Mnevis bull in Heliopolis. In his two first years, we know of small expeditions being periodically sent to the Eastern Desert by the temple of Amun in quest for gold and galena. In Year 7, the log of a ship of the high priest of Amun shows that this institution was able to trade goods along the Nile. During the reign, the exchange value of grain seems to have risen steeply at Deir el-Medina. The scarcity of data prevents any generalization to the whole of Egypt of this growing "inflation," for which no satisfactory explanation has been yet given.

Ramesses VII was predeceased by his son and heir Ramesses, so that for the second time in the dynasty the crown reverted to a king's uncle. The new ruler, Ramesses VIII (r. 1140–1139 BCE), who was probably the last surviving son of Ramesses III, is totally obscure. He was probably very old, and he reigned no longer than a year, so that he was not even able to make himself a tomb in the Valley of the Kings. Because he left no surviving son, the crown went to his nephew, Ramesses IX, the son of one of his elder brothers, Montuherkhopshef, who was long dead and had not himself been king.

In spite of a reign of eighteen years, Ramesses IX (r. 1139–1120 BCE) left no significant monuments. He built some minor works in Karnak, in the court between the third and fourth pylons, where he erected a stela to Amun. He also excavated two tombs in the Valley of the Kings: his own (tomb 6), and that of his prematurely deceased son Montuherkhopshef (tomb 19), hastily completed for this prince's burial. Outside Thebes, the funerary chapel of another of his sons, Nebmare, high priest of Re, has been preserved in Heliopolis. There was still some activity under this reign in Nubia, where three viceroys of Kush are known to have ruled the province, in succession from father to son.

In the second year of the reign, the high priest of Amun, Ramessesnakht, carrying out the king's order to procure galena, a lead ore used as eye paint, sent expeditions to Muqed, the desert hinterland of the Red Sea shore, where the coveted mineral was known to abound. For this he hired a little private army of Nubian Nehesy people to "pacify" the dangerous local Shosu bedouin. Ramessesnakht had been high priest of Amun since the first year of Ramesses IV, almost thirty years before. When he died, he was succeeded first by his son Nesamun, who died before Year 10, and then by his another son, Amenhotep, who would be high priest until the reign of Ramesses IX.

In Thebes, between Years 8 and 13 and probably before, the western bank of the Nile was rendered more and more insecure by repeated Libyan raids. The temple of Medinet Habu, whose exterior walls were those of a real fortress, became on these occasions a refuge for the local population, especially the workmen of Deir el-Medina, and was the seat of their institutions. From Year 13 on, in the lonely northern part of the Theban necropolis, and probably making use of these opportunities, a gang led by one Amunpanefer, coppersmith of the temple of Amun, began to rob the private tombs of their valuables. Some time later, encouraged by a feeling of total impunity (their chief demonstrated on two occasions that he knew how to bribe his way out of jail), they plundered the tomb of King Sobekemsaf II, of the seventeenth dynasty. This trespass against royalty roused from its lethargy an administration indifferent to the fate of the private sepulchers. The culprits were quickly arrested, tried by the Southern vizier Khaemwese, and put to death.

During his trial, Amunpanefer warned that his gang had not been alone in the plunder of the Theban necropolis. He had even hinted that the whole population of the western bank had been doing the same. One year later, his warning proved true when a group of eight workmen from Deir el-Medina, led by one Amenwau, son of Hori, plundered a tomb in the Valley of the Queens—probably the tomb of Queen Isis, the wife of Ramesses III. Even this relatively modest tomb yielded to its violators about 50 kilograms of gold and silver. How could the people dwelling in Western Thebes, in the context of Libyan raids and powerless institutions, have resisted the attraction of vast quantities of precious metals, relatively easy to get and useful in procuring any official complicity they needed? Tomb robberies continued well into the two next reigns.

Ramesses X (r. 1120–1111 BCE) was the son and successor of the preceding king. Of his reign we know next to nothing, which makes it likely that it lasted three years rather than the nine that are conventionally assumed. His wife was probably Queen Tity, who was presented with a tomb in the Valley of the Queens (tomb 52). The king's own tomb in the Valley of the Kings was never completed (tomb 18).

The last king of the dynasty, Ramesses XI (r. 1111–1081 BCE), ruled Egypt for at least twenty-seven years. This long reign—the longest since Ramesses III—falls into two parts, divided at the beginning of his Year 19. During the first half, Upper Egypt knew serious troubles,

about which we are ill informed, although all written sources for the reign come from this part of the country. In the king's Year 9, an investigation revealed that a party of priests and temple employees, mainly from Medinet Habu, having secured the complicity of various craftsmen, had entirely stripped the Ramesseum of the enormous quantities of gold that decorated its walls and furniture, and then organized the demolition of its shrines of precious wood to sell them as planks. All this had apparently been done in a smooth, businesslike way, with no more trouble than buying the silence of some officials with a small share of plunder. It seems obvious that the reason why the Ramesseum was such easy prey was that it was by then totally abandoned and standing in an area largely deserted, owing to fear of raiding Libyans. This view is confirmed by a papyrus from Year 12 listing the houses on the Theban western bank. Of a total of 182, only 10 are listed between the temple of Sety I in Qurna and the Ramesseum, and 14 between the Ramesseum and Medinet Habu, against 155 around Medinet Habu.

These troubles demonstrated the failure of the civil power to enforce law and order, and so the king commissioned the nearest leader of troops, the viceroy of Kush, Panehsy, to rule Upper Egypt under martial law. His name is cited in this capacity not improbably as early as Year 9, and certainly between Years 12 and 17. In Year 12, besides his military titles, he bears that of "Director of the Royal Granaries," charged with supervising the collection of grain around Thebes for the subsistence of the city, including Deir el-Medina.

Sometime in Year 17 or 18, for unknown reasons (some have proposed a conflict of power), Panehsy unlawfully ousted from office the high priest of Amun, Amenhotep, who had held the post since Ramesses VII. As Amenhotep fled to the king's court in Piramesse, Panehsy declared rebellion against the pharaoh and drew north with his army, into which Thebans—including former tomb-robbers—had been drafted. Taking everyone by surprise, he probably reached Lower Egypt before meeting serious resistance; however, he was soon forced to retreat to Upper Egypt, then to Nubia, his troops leaving behind them a trail of destruction. The Middle Egyptian town of Hardai was severely sacked, and Cyril Aldred (1979) has argued with some ground that Panehsy's Nubians were the ones mainly responsible for the plundering of the Valley of the Kings, an act of depredation requiring much manpower. Eloquently, some Thebans later remembered these events as the "year of the hyenas, when one was hungry." It must be noted that the sequence of these events and the parts played by their protagonists has been much debated. There are some grounds, however, for rejecting the former dating of the "war of the high priest," as it was sometimes called, prior to Year 8, as well as the theory that Panehsy first came into Upper Egypt to help Amenhotep, who would then have been deprived of his office by other, unknown enemies.

As Panehsy fled back to Nubia, Ramesses XI came to Thebes with his troops to inspect the disaster, and proclaimed his nineteenth year to begin a new era, the *wḥm msw.t*, or Renaissance (lit. "repeating of births"), by which Theban documents are usually dated until the end of his reign. Significantly, this era was inaugurated by the appointment of the pharaoh's leading general, Herihor, a man of probable Libyan descent, to the combined governorship of Upper Egypt and viceroyalty of Kush—the latter being, however, more nominal than effective, since Panehsy was able to maintain himself in his original fiefdom as an independent ruler. Herihor was soon granted permission to add the high priesthood of Amun to his civil and military titles, since Amenhotep died shortly after having been restored to office. There is reason to assume that Herihor's appointment by Ramesses XI to the position of sole ruler of Upper Egypt was paralleled in the northern half of the country by the appointment to similar powers of another general, Smendes, who would become the first king of the twenty-first dynasty.

Herihor inaugurated his tenure by implementing a series of trials against the tomb robbers and temple robbers of the preceding period. These trials were far-reaching, as if intended to break the feeling of impunity the robbers had enjoyed for so long. In Year 6 of the Renaissance, he ordered the reburial of Ramesses II and Sety I, whose tombs had been violated during the preceding troubles. Meanwhile, in his role of high priest of Amun, he made some restorations in the temple of Karnak, and he finalized the decoration of the Khonsu temple, begun almost a century earlier. On this temple's inscriptions, he assigned himself a complete but fictive (ritual) royal titulature, while in his court he erected a stela, whose text is so damaged that it is impossible to determine the significance of its mention of an oracle of Amun having allotted him twenty, then thirty years either of tenure or of life. On the same temple's walls there is a representation of the procession of an Opet festival, for which he claims to have constructed a new bark for Amun. Dated in Year 5 of the Renaissance, the *Story of Wenamun* narrates the tribulations of the priest of this name sent to Byblos to buy the wood for this bark. The text is obviously fictional, although some scholars consider it an administrative report.

By Year 7 of the Renaissance, Herihor had been succeeded by another general, like him of probable Libyan descent: Piankh, who assumed all his titles, including high priest of Amun. Piankh's relationship to Herihor is unknown; there is no proof that he was his son, as was formerly accepted, nor that he preceded Herihor, as has

recently been proposed. He settled three of his sons as second prophet of Amun (the future high priest, Pinodjem I), steward of Amun, and high priest of Medinet Habu, thus setting a definitive end to the local dynasty of Meribastet, which had ruled Amun's estate since the beginning of Ramesses III's reign. His priestly duties did not prevent Piankh from campaigning in Nubia against Panehsy, as late as Year 10, as recorded in his correspondence with Djehutymose and Butehamun, the last scribes of Deir el-Medina. However, his hopes to reclaim Nubia (and its gold mines) were frustrated, as proven by Panehsy's later burial in the tomb he had prepared for himself in Aniba. A tough military man, Piankh is known to have curtly ordered in one of his letters that two trespassing Theban policemen be placed in caskets and drowned by night. A cynic and a realist, he is also known for his famous reply, in the same letter: "Of whom is Pharaoh, l.p.h., superior still?"

Shortly after Piankh's disappearance of the scene, the dynasty came to an end. Ironically, one of the last acts of Ramesses XI was to send a crocodile and a monkey to the king of Assyria, Assur bel Kala, in a pathetic imitation of the exchange of diplomatic gifts in the days of Egypt's splendor. Because the intended Theban tomb of the king lay unfinished, it is possible that he was buried in his northern residence, which was still at Piramesse. At Thebes, the long process had begun which would transfer some of his ancestors' bodies to the Deir el-Bahri cachette (Ramesses III and IX) and the cachette of the tomb of Amenhotep II in the Valley of the Kings (Ramesses IV to VI). Shortly after the last Ramesses' death, almost as a symbol of the end of their rule, the silting up of the pelusiac branch of the Nile, on which Piramesse was situated, prompted the beginning of the transfer of the royal residence to the new site of Tanis, 25 kilometers (16 miles) to the north, and the complete devastation of its ancient counterpart.

[*See also* Ramesses III; Ramesses IV; Ramesses VI; Ramesses IX; *and* Ramesses XI.]

BIBLIOGRAPHY

History

Aldred, Cyril. "More Light on the Ramesside Tomb Robberies." In *Orbis Ægyptiorum Speculum: Glimpses of Ancient Egypt, Studies in Honour of H. W. Fairman* edited by J. Ruffle et al., pp. 92–99. Warminster, 1979. See also below, under "Tomb and Temple Robberies."

Bierbrier, Morris L. *The Late New Kingdom in Egypt.* Warminster, 1975. For the family of Meribastet, see pp. 10–13.

Černý, J. "Egypt: From the Death of Ramesses III to the End of the Twenty-First Dynasty." In *Cambridge Ancient History*, 3d ed., pp. 606–657. Cambridge, 1975. A statement of the traditional, "standard" view of the period's history.

Grandet, Pierre. *Ramsès III: Histoire d'un règne.* Paris, 1993.

Jansen-Winkeln, Karl. "Das Ende des Neuen Reiches." *Zeitschrift für ägyptischen Sprache und Altertumskunde Ägyptens* 119 (1992), 22–37. Advocates the order of succession Piankh—Herihor, which was not followed here, and the order of events which was.

Jansen-Winkeln, Kark. "Die Plünderung der Königsgräber des Neuen Reiches." *Zeitschrift für ägyptischen Sprache und Altertumskunde Ägyptens* 122 (1995), 62–78. An attempt to prove that Piankh himself robbed tombs to finance his Nubian campaign; seductive but without serious proof.

Kitchen, Kenneth A. "Ramses V–XI." In *Lexikon der Ägyptologie*, 5:124–128. Wiesbaden, 1982.

Kitchen, Kenneth A. *The Third Intermediate Period in Egypt (1100–650 BC).* 2d edn. with supplement. Warminster, 1986. Reprinted, 1995, with a new preface, pp. xi–xlvi, reviewing recent contributions, especially those of Jansen-Winkeln listed above.

Kitchen, Kenneth A. "The Twentieth Dynasty Revisited." *Journal of Egyptian Archaeology* 68 (1982), 116–125. Fundamental work on the genealogy of the dynasty and its main source, the "Lists of Princes of Medinet Habu."

Peden, Alexander J. *The Reign of Ramesses IV.* Warminster, 1994.

Sources

Černý, Jaroslav. *Late Ramesside Letters.* Bibliotheca Aegyptiaca, 9. Brussels, 1939. Hieroglyphic text of the letters to and from Piankh, translated in Wente's book.

Epigraphic Survey. *The Temple of Khonsu.* 2 vols. Oriental Institute of the University of Chicago. Oriental Institute Publications, 100, 103. Chicago, 1979, 1981. The official publication of the temple of Khonsu at Karnak.

Kitchen, Kenneth A. *Ramesside Inscriptions: Historical and Biographical.* Oxford, 1975–1990. See vol. 5 (reigns of Sethnakht and Ramesses III), 6 (reigns of Ramesses IV to XI), and 7 (addenda to the preceding volumes). The authoritative collection of all sources in their original hieroglyphic script; a translation is forthcoming.

Peden, Alexander J. *Egyptian Historical Inscriptions of the Twentieth Dynasty.* Documenta Mundi: Egyptiaca, 3. Jonsered, 1994. An anthology of various sources in translation.

Seidlmayer, Stephan J. "Epigraphische Bemerkungen zur Stele des Sethnachte aus Elephantine." In *Stationen, Beiträge zur Kulturgeschichte Ägyptens, Rainer Stadelmann gewidmet,* edited by H. Guksch et al., pp. 363–386. Mainz, 1998. Plates 20–21, Beilage 3a, are the latest publication of the Elephantine Stela of Sethnakht.

Wente, Edward F. *Late Ramesside Letters.* Oriental Institute of the University of Chicago, Studies in Ancient Oriental Civilization, 33. Chicago, 1967. A translation of the texts published by Černý (1939).

Tomb and Temple Robberies

Goelet, Ogden, Jr. "A New 'Robbery' Papyrus: Rochester MAG 51.346.1." *Journal of Egyptian Archaeology* 82 (1996), 107–127, pl. IX–X. A new papyrus to add to the documents in Peet's publication.

Peet, Thomas E. *The Great Tomb-Robberies of the Twentieth Egyptian Dynasty.* 2 vols. Oxford, 1930. The classic publication of the original documents relative to the tomb and temple robberies under Ramesses IX and XI.

PIERRE GRANDET

NILE. The river Nile flows about 6,800 kilometers (4,200 miles) from equatorial Africa to the Mediterranean Sea, across thirty-five degrees of latitude. In the far south, several large East African lakes temporarily collect and store runoff and direct precipitation from the early summer and autumn rainy seasons, discharge that is then delayed several months as it slowly moves through the Sudd swamps. Relatively impoverished in sediment and nutrients, these White Nile waters pass the central Sudan after the peak discharge of the summer monsoon over Ethiopia. It is the runoff from Ethiopia, mainly the Blue Nile system, that determines the duration and level of the annual flood in Egypt, and that contributes its increment of silt and nutrients. The blending of these two distinct sources of water during the span of the hydrological year provides a comparatively reliable river that has served as a lifeline for Egypt, allowing the emergence of stable adaptations in late prehistoric times.

The strong seasonal flux of water volume is fundamental to the spilling of water out of the channel and onto the flood and delta plains late each summer. The annual fusing of staggered rainfall maxima and the temporary storage of water volume along this longitudinal waterway, in turn, prolong peak discharge. The Nile, therefore, guarantees a substantial energy pulse, but one that is beneficial and not destructive. Temporary storage in Ethiopia, and especially East Africa, also moderates year-to-year fluctuations of rainfall, while a primary catchment greater than 1.5 million square kilometers (930 thousand square miles) averages out at least some of the interannual deviations of rainfall among the many contributing watersheds.

Nonetheless, there are and always have been substantial positive or negative trends in the composite volume of water passing through Egypt. For example, the mean for 1870–1898 was 16 percent higher than for 1899–1971, a trend spanning a century. For shorter time spans, the discharge for 1954–1967 was 11 percent above, but for 1972–1986 almost 13 percent below the mean for 1899–1971; these represent irregular cycles with a wavelength of nine to seventeen years, each characterized by different amplitudes and year-to-year variability. Efforts to explain such fluctuations using modern records since the 1870s, or flawed notations since 622 CE, have included solar output (sunspot) cycles, lunar tidal forcing, and ENSO (El Niño), but all have been inconclusive. Each of these quasiperiodic factors may well have played a part in a multicausal spectrum effecting short-term variation, but each such anomaly during the twentieth century seems to play out differently among the many tropical watersheds, and correlation of rainfall trends over Ethiopia with the equatorial lake regions is in fact random. For longer-term trends, of a century or more, there can be little more than speculation, and for changes spanning centuries to millennia, systemic interactions among atmosphere, oceans, land surfaces, and biota must assume a much greater role.

Whatever their explanations, and the uncertain progression of change in different segments of the tropical

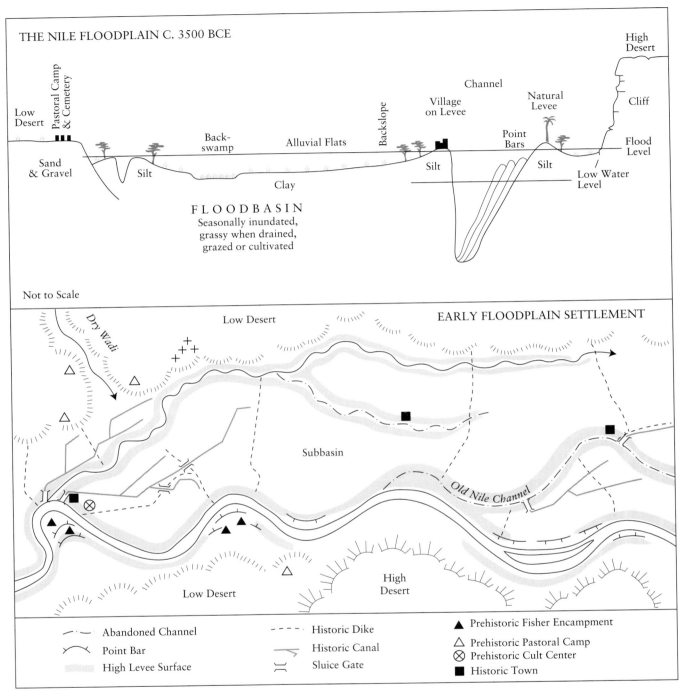

THE NILE FLOODPLAIN C. 3500 BCE

High Desert

Low Desert

Pastoral Camp & Cemetery

Sand & Gravel

Silt

Back-swamp

Alluvial Flats

Backslope

Channel

Village on Levee

Point Bars

Silt

Natural Levee

Silt

Cliff

Flood Level

Low Water Level

Clay

FLOODBASIN
Seasonally inundated,
grassy when drained,
grazed or cultivated

Not to Scale

EARLY FLOODPLAIN SETTLEMENT

Dry Wadi

Low Desert

Subbasin

Old Nile Channel

Low Desert

High Desert

—·— Abandoned Channel
⌢⌣ Point Bar
▨ High Levee Surface

- - - - Historic Dike
╲╲ Historic Canal
⊐⊏ Sluice Gate

▲ Prehistoric Fisher Encampment
△ Prehistoric Pastoral Camp
⊗ Prehistoric Cult Center
■ Historic Town

NILE. *Diagram of the Nile floodplain, c.3500 BCE, and a plan of an early floodplain settlement.*
(Courtesy Karl W. Butzer)

watershed, the variations of the Nile flood volume over decades, centuries, or millennia have had economic, biotic, and even physical repercussions or impacts in Egypt. Such changes in equilibrium or vulnerability are outlined below, beginning with the evolution of the flood and delta plain environments, and concluding with questions of eco-

nomic and possibly social implications in the course of Egyptian history.

Geological and Archaeological Records prior to the Predynastic. Most major rivers have long geological histories, and the Nile is no exception. Even its existing valley within Egypt had been cut down to well below modern sea level by five million years ago, and its delta also had begun to subside tectonically. In part this was a response to the drying out of the Mediterranean Sea about seven to five million years ago (late Miocene). Subsequently, this deep canyon was submerged when the sea rose again (Pliocene), flooding its northern end and filling in the overdeepened valley with lagoonal, lake, and stream deposits. During the two million years of Pleistocene time, the axis of the river was already well defined, as it underwent repeated cycles of river cutting and filling that nonetheless left much of the Pliocene sequence of sediments in place, in part near the modern valley margins, but mainly buried underneath thick bodies of sands and gravels. Minerals of both clay and sand size leave no doubt that Ethiopian floodwaters were flowing to the sea throughout this time, but the geological record is dominated by coarse sweeps of material derived from Saharan tributaries that responded to episodic heavy winter rains in an environment periodically less arid than today.

In most parts of Africa, this time range would have seen Acheulian occupation on at least a sporadic basis. Yet in or on the Nile "terrace" deposits of one million to 150,000 years ago, Acheulian materials are only locally common, and such occurrences date mainly to the later part of the time interval. From late during this time range, there also are geological deposits in which Nilotic flood silts, of Ethiopian flood origin, are interbedded with thick sandy gravels carried into the Nile Valley by then-active desert watercourses in the form of alluvial fans. This documents a transition of the Nile to a river resembling that of today. The braiding and unstable channels of the mid–Pleistocene probably were less productive or dependable than the Saharan spring-fed oases, some of which were attractive to early prehistoric settlement; in fact, Mousterian sites of perhaps 150,000 to 40,000 years ago are better documented in Saharan oases than in the Nile Valley.

About 25,000 years ago, the transition to a silt floodplain was completed, when summer flood silts accumulated in and around the valley—no longer to be eroded or overwhelmed during the cooler half year by torrential, tributary runoff. Although minor moist intervals in the Egyptian deserts and Sahara promoted some wadi activity or higher water tables in the oases, the climate of Egypt has been too dry during the last 50,000 years or more to dominate the geomorphic processes of the Nile Valley. The Nile had become an exotic river, supplied by a distant watershed, and responding mainly to environmental changes in Ethiopia and East Africa.

By 20,000 years ago, Late Paleolithic peoples were continually settled along the shifting banks of the Nile, even as the river dwindled c.17,000–15,000 BCE, or as it swelled during a period of exceptionally high floods, the "Wild Nile" of 11,500–11,000 BCE. The basic continuity of site location, economic utilization, and stone tool assem-

blages across at least eight millennia implies a fairly stable adaptation to this "tropical" river regime: riverine food resources were exploited during an annual cycle of flood, post-flood abundance, and pre-flood shortage.

The picture was different in the Nile Delta, reflecting the changing level of the Mediterranean Sea. While ocean waters were bound in the great continental glaciers during the ice ages, the world sea level was much lower than now—as much as 100 meters (325 feet). Thus, in about 33,000–14,000 BCE, the coastline was located far out on the modern continental shelf, so that the several branches of the Nile responded by cutting deeper channels into the older delta surface, eventually eroding a fairly level topography—which is now buried under 30 to 50 meters (100 to 165 feet) of younger deposits. When the sea level once again rose rapidly after 14,000 BCE, seasonal flood deposits began to accumulate rapidly across the exposed delta surface. About 9000–5000 BCE, the sea returned to near its present level, flooding the edge of a long-exposed plain, consisting of multiple, sandy channels, with zones of (summer) flood silts in between. The distinctive marine sands and muds of this transgression in the northernmost Nile Delta form a critical marker horizon. This shows that the Nile branches had already been actively building up sediment for many millennia, and it explains the development of poorly drained tracts near the shore that supported lagoons or marshland. Such organic beds are dated as early as 6500 BCE, and were most extensive about 2,500 years later, at about 3750 BCE.

Although the basic configuration of the modern Delta landscape was falling into place during the time range of the Levantine Neolithic, whatever late Paleolithic or Neolithic record there was within the immediate Delta is now buried under many meters of sediment. Visible or accessible are only those sites, such as Merimde and Maadi, that were at the edge of the desert, or those occupation traces of the fourth millennium BCE recovered underneath younger settlements.

A part of the missing occupation sequence in Lower Egypt is recorded in the Faiyum Depression, connected to the Nile Valley across a buried threshold at 10 meters (33 feet) below sea level. This medium-sized basin was fed by overflow from the Nile whenever the floodplain was higher than this bedrock sill, bringing in silt and supporting a non-outlet lake. But it was dry and subject to wind erosion until about 8500 BCE, evidence that the lowermost Nile was also undercut in response to the sea level regression that affected the Delta. At that point the Faiyum was abruptly flooded, and within a millennium it was settled by Epipaleolithic people who exploited the aquatic resources of the lakeshores. About 5500 BCE, other Neolithic people, practicing a little agriculture, replaced the fishers and gatherers already around the lake.

This late appearance of farming is similar to the archaeological record of the Nile Valley farther south. There, a major period of river adjustment led to some five hundred years of floodplain entrenchment (about 9500 BCE), during which resources appear to have been unusually scarce. When the floodplain began to build up and again to expand laterally, there were far fewer sites in the valley, implying a strong reduction of population. The stone tool industries had also changed, and there was a new emphasis on fishing, in addition to hunting and gathering. That suggests a turnover in social identity, accompanying a shift in economic and ecological adaptation. Evidence for farming and herding in the main valley of Egypt begins only during the fifth millennium BCE, assuming importance after 4000 BCE. With the archaeological bias of a record based on sites limited to the floodplain-desert margin, and heavily represented by cemeteries rather than habitation sites, it is still uncertain whether, in addition to residual fisher and gathering groups, there may also have been distinct groups favoring farming activities or pastoralism.

In both the Faiyum and Nile Valley, therefore, it is plausible that there was no "Neolithic Revolution." Instead, it is possible that several groups of people with different ecological adaptations utilized the larger system represented by the Egyptian Nile, emphasizing complementary or only partially overlapping econiches. Alternatively, their economies may have been uncharacteristically flexible and fluid—from season to season, year to year, or place to place—in response to fluctuating and variable resource types. That is what may well emerge from contemporaneous archaeological residues in the Saharan oases or in the central Nile reaches of Sudan. In any event, there is growing reason to suspect that the long prehistoric millennia preceding full-fledged farming, pastoralism, or metallurgy in Africa were a great deal more fluid and complex than the conventional archaeological sequence of the Near East or southern Europe.

An Environmental Model for the Late Prehistoric Nile. A river floodplain is primarily a zone of sediment accumulation rather than erosion. The subtle but significant surface features are determined by the prevailing processes of alluviation. These reflect the turbulence of flow in the channel during times of peak discharge, and the concentration of suspended sediment in the floodwaters.

A turbulent stream, with a dominant "bed load" of sand and gravel, tends to have a broad, shallow channel; the rapid accumulation of channel bars forces the weaving stream axis to shift repeatedly, so that the floodplain is built up of lenticles of sand and gravel. As the river tops its low banks during the flood peak, a gentler flow deposits a thin mantle of overbank silt and clay across the flat floodplain. This cover of overbank sediments tends to be

ephemeral, much of it swept away the next time flood waters spill over; when they abate, they deposit fresh or reworked overbank silts. This pattern is typical of arid zone watercourses and can be observed in some wadis of the Eastern Desert.

On the other extreme, a major river with abundant suspended sediment has little channel turbulence and moves only finer grades of sand. The channel is deep and comparatively narrow, flowing through fairly stable banks of silt and sand, so that the excess water and energy is dispersed across the floodplain, rather than being concentrated on temporarily deepening and then refilling a channel. Sediment builds up fastest on the inside bends (point bars) of the river, and directly where water spills out of the channel during flood stage. This is where energy is greatest. As a result the perimeters of the channel—the levees—tend to rise up to a meter or two above the alluvial flats, where flood energy is rapidly reduced and particle sizes in transport are much smaller. Here, the annual increments of silt and clay build up somewhat more slowly, but provide the most fertile soils. Because the perimeter of the channel is slightly higher than the seasonally flooded plain, this landform complex is known as a convex floodplain. The Nile and Mississippi are two of the best known examples of the kind, but the floodplains of the middle Niger in Africa, or the Ganges and Mekong in Asia, are very similar.

On convex floodplains, settlements are preferably located on the levees that form higher ground near the channel. The levee crests do not flood regularly, but only during the highest flood events and, since mud-brick structures rise through countless collapses and rebuilding, villages and towns grow above the levees on which they are situated. A second feature of convex floodplains occurs when a period of waxing floods may carry enough water through levee breaches to create diverging, secondary channels, such as the Bahr Jussef on the western side of the floodplain in Middle Egypt. Although smaller and lower, the levees of such branches will eventually offer advantageous settlement sites, with permanent water and navigability. Finally, whereas the river channels of convex floodplains do not migrate rapidly, as those of flat floodplains do, increasingly convoluted meanders eventually become unstable. At that point, an exceptionally strong flood may cut off a meander loop or even bypass a longer channel stretch. This "jumping" of the main channel, known as an avulsion, will leave a cut-off lake or even a stretch of river in a state of atrophy, but the levees remain, so that there now will be several ridges of higher ground within the floodplain.

In these various ways, a convex floodplain creates multiple, linear environments of elevated ground, suitable for settlement location, and that outline distinct flood basins, which will eventually lend themselves to compartmentalized irrigation. That is the environmental model for the prehistoric Nile and for dynastic Egypt. It presupposes that convex floodplains can be settled permanently with minimal technological application, by either fisher-hunter-foragers or farmer-herders. The floodplain will be underwater for four to six weeks annually, even as the majority of levee-top sites remain dry in most years. Livestock, like the native fauna, move to higher ground or the desert edge while the water is up, and then return to the emerging pastures when the waters drain back into the main channels, as the flood recedes. Since the floodwaters rise and move slowly, there are few losses among such animals, and even so, water depths are mainly in the range of only 1.0 to 1.5 meters (3 to 5 feet). For agriculture, the natural hydraulic system is even more advantageous, since seed can be broadcast on the wet increment of overbank silt as the waters recede; furthermore, the clayey soil retains abundant moisture that, in damper areas, is adequate to the maturation of a crop.

The features describe a model of a Nile floodplain where the raised river banks and old levee ridges have always been favored as settlement sites, even as the flood-basins fill and empty when the annual flood rises and recedes. It is a free draining, not a marshy floodplain, and one that invites riverine settlement. The model is supported by settlement patterns and ethnographic data from other convex floodplains on several continents. Most compellingly, however, it can be tested archaeologically.

Late Prehistoric Settlement Mosaics. Egyptological archaeologists and historians tend to be occupied with reconstructing the evolution of a stratified society in the Nile Valley, the unification of Upper and Lower Egypt, and the emergence of the Egyptian state—primarily in the context of other complex societies in the Near East. Africanist archaeologists, on the other hand, prefer to examine a broader, African canvas, to identify prehistoric processes in the deserts, as well as in the Nile Valley. They seek to understand how that long transition—from hunting, gathering, and fishing, to food production and, ultimately, a complex society—played out, when, and where. Such research clusters are not monolithic, and the dichotomy is overdrawn, but it draws attention to different questions, methodologies, and conceptual modes. Largely as a result of overemphasis on Predynastic social evolution and state formation, some significant implications of the Paleolithic and Neolithic records have been overlooked.

The great majority of Late Paleolithic sites in Southern Egypt, dating c.19,000–11,000 BCE, were situated on point bars and levees of the Late Pleistocene Nile, for example, on the Kom Ombo Plain. Some of these sites extend for hundreds of meters along the former riverbank, and sea-

sonality studies suggest that they were occupied as soon as the floodwaters began to recede until well into the post-flood season, or beyond. Others were located around ponds fed by flood seepage into depressions between levees and dune ridges, or within a dune field, such as between Esna and Edfu, or in the embouchure of Wadi Kubanniya. The faunas represent a riparian ecotone: wild cattle (favoring brush or woodland), hartebeest (requiring a grassy groundcover), gazelles (adapted to semidesert settings), an occasional hippo (aquatic), a variety and abundance of fish remains (some of which spawn on flooded surfaces), occasional river clams, and a good range of waterfowl. The hartebeest and fish remains are the most common and ubiquitous. Fishing was apparently done with fish-gorges, baskets, and nets. Study of plant remains has begun, and indicate the presence of aquatic plants (*Cyperus* and *Scirpus*), ferns, dom palm, and tamarisk at a limited number of sites. But the residues indicate food processing of aquatic tubers, perhaps during the pre-flood season.

Such Late Paleolithic sites extend in large numbers from Qena to Wadi Halfa, a 650-kilometer (403-mile) stretch where fluvial deposits of the period are exposed above the modern floodplain along the desert edge. Hunter-gatherers are mobile, of course, so that such sites would not be permanent. But key base-camps were reutilized indefinitely, and the tentative bioarcheological inference is that they were occupied for one or more seasons, perhaps even most of the year. That is supported by the apparent absence of sites on the former desert margins: all are water-edge locations, regardless of differences in stone tool assemblages.

Similar riparian adaptations are evident after the floodplain had readjusted to deep entrenchment of the river, but there are far fewer sites pertaining to Epipaleolithic industries such as the Shamarkian and Elkabian, which span the interval from 10,500 to about 6000 BCE. The faunal palimpsests are sparse but indicate a consistent dependence on hartebeest or wild cattle, as well as fish. Such sites are also found on former riverbank locations. A special case is the Faiyum, where Qarunian sites (c.7300–6200 BCE) are situated along the former fluctuating lake shores. By weight, the Qarunian fauna consists overwhelmingly of fish bone, with subsidiary wild cattle and hartebeest; bone points and harpoons underscore the aquatic adaptation.

Insufficient attention has been paid to the Epipaleolithic sites, but the key problem is visibility. In the Nile Valley, contemporary sediment exposures are limited to the reach south of Esna, and the deposits are commonly thin or somewhat eroded. Except for a desert pediment west of Luxor, where similar stone artifacts (Tarifian) are found at the surface, no sites younger than 6000 BCE have been identified. After a sharp recession of the Faiyum lake, that area was recolonized by settlers with a Neolithic tool inventory, and who practiced some cultivation of grains and herding of animals, primarily sheep or goat. But most of the food remains are fish and soft-shelled turtle, and the seasonality of fishing activities was unchanged from the Qarunian. Nonetheless, there is only minimal evidence of big-game hunting. Known as the Faiyum A (or Faiyumian), this occupation of c.5500–4400 BCE was not associated with permanent settlements. A few large sites were repeatedly reoccupied as base-camps, above the fluctuating shoreline, but consist primarily of large, superimposed hearths and storage pits for grain. More common are intermediate-sized occupation areas, with large concentrations of stone artifacts and potsherds, repeatedly used on a perhaps seasonal basis on tracts that were periodically flooded. Other sites are small and were only occasionally used in the course of seasonal rounds. The implied mobility patterns are those of hunter-gatherers, rather than farmers.

The Faiyum A was succeeded by what is now called the Moerian (c.4400–3800 BCE). This has been labeled Neolithic by virtue of bifacial and blade tools, as well as pottery, in an otherwise Epipaleolithic artifact assemblage. Fish bone is abundant, but domesticates are not evident. A Predynastic occurrence, based on its pottery, is found in the same setting, but it, too, is a fishing site.

The Faiyum settlements are highly informative for several reasons: (1) They show that similar economic adaptations could be pursued by social groups with different material cultures. Designations such as Neolithic, based on a handful of diagnostic artifacts, do not necessarily identify land use or settlement type. (2) The Moerian indicates persistence of a food-collecting social group, possibly in the process of assimilation, within the lower Nile ecosystem until the early fifth millennium BCE. That raises the reasonable hypothesis that two or more interrested socio-cultural groups occupied the Nile Valley during the previous millennium; these probably exploited complementary ecological niches, but with diverging spatial expression. (3) Economic modes in the Nile ecosystem, from the Faiyum to the Central Sudan, were in a state of flux during the fifth, and perhaps even the fourth millennium BCE. The Faiyum A suggests that opportunistic exploitation of highly productive natural resources was as important as available agro-pastoral experience, which would then affect site location and mobility patterns.

Merimde, situated on the southwestern edge of the Delta, was a very different matter. Five periods of occupation are identified, spanning perhaps five hundred years (c.4750–4250 BCE), the last two covering an area of 25 hectares (62 acres). There is good evidence of house structures, and the economy was predominately agro-pastoral.

But it was located directly above the bank of a minor Nile channel, and fish, as well as other aquatic resources, were intensively used. In the southern suburbs of Cairo, Omari (c.4600–4400 BCE) was situated on the banks of a wadi, next to the edge of the floodplain. Initially a fishing encampment, Omari developed into a small farming village, in which living areas continued to shift. Although pig, cattle, and some sheep/goat were kept, most of the excavated bone belongs to fish. The small settlement sites near Badari (c.4500–4000 BCE) were not much different—on the desert edge but close to a Nile branch, so that fish were a prominent economic element. These late fifth millennium BCE sites were effectively riverine sites, even if on the desert margin, and they combined older gathering pursuits with agro-pastoral activities. In the case of Merimde and the Badarian sites, there also were floodplain and desert game animals, suggesting that the wildlife was not yet hunted to extinction, or that the adjacent deserts still supported some game, or both.

The fourth millennium BCE saw an ecological shift. Near Cairo, the desert edge site of Maadi (c.3900–3500 BCE) has minimal evidence for fish and game, as do the early Predynastic sites of Armant and Hu. The desert edge settlement of Hierakonpolis (c.3700–3400 BCE) however, has considerable fish bone and a stronger herding component. Its counterparts at Nagada (c.3600–3300 BCE) and the slightly younger Delta site of Tell Ibrahim Awad also have abundant fish bone. Yet none of these has evidence for more than incidental game. They were preeminently agro-pastoral sites, some of which had convenient access to water bodies, others not.

Paleobotanical studies at Nagada and Ibrahim Awad, as well as at the Old Kingdom delta site of Kom el-Hisn, focused on animal dung, mainly of small livestock (sheep/goat). They reveal that mostly wetland plants were fed to the animals, presumably kept in enclosures. That shows that there was no desert pasturage, and that pastoralism did not extend into the desert in any significant way. The inference is that domesticated stock were grazed in the floodplain during the post- and pre-flood seasons, but that they were removed to higher ground during the flood months, to be fed with cut vegetation from wetlands, presumably gathered previously. In other words, fourth millennium small-stock pastoralism was not only fairly intensive, but it was very much tied to the floodplain. Whatever the importance of cattle, they were managed differently, in keeping with their different ecology. In East Africa cattle can be observed to their dewlaps in water, consuming emergent aquatic plants, and much the same can be seen on Old Kingdom tomb reliefs. Presumably Egyptian cattle in the Valley and the Delta remained in the shallower fringes of the floodbasins during the annual inundation.

NILE. *The Nile at Philae, before the inundation.* (Courtesy David P. Silverman)

This confirms that Predynastic (and probably earlier) pastoralism in the lower Nile ecosystem was essentially limited to riverine pasturage. The desert edge was used like the levee environments, to keep small stock during the flood season, with the help of cut feed. There were no desert pastoralists, even if pastoralism had once been introduced from the desert oases. Whatever desert game may have been available during the fifth millennium BCE had disappeared by Predynastic times.

That supports the geoarchaeological model of an "accessible" floodplain mosaic described above. The agro-pastoral economy of the Egyptian Nile ecosystem, even during its initial stages of complementary or supplementary fishing and hunting, was focused on one and the same riverine environment. When the desert edge settlements disappear during late Predynastic times, that does not indicate a settlement shift "into" the floodplain, but rather a further intensification of subsistence activities with respect to the linear distribution of higher ground, provided by active or abandoned levees within the floodplain and Delta.

Nile Flood History. The changing behavior of the Nile River becomes tangible from the geological record in southern Egypt after about 19,000 BCE, when high-level flood silts interfinger with mobile dunes on the Western

Desert edge. About 16,000 BCE, flood volume declined and the river incised its channel, before achieving a more vigorous flow about a millennium later. Increased turbulance allowed the transport of pebbles in the stream bed over great distances, with some channel erosion into the hard rocks of the cataracts. In wide floodplain sectors, such as at Kom Ombo, the Nile formed multiple, shifting channels, and flood waters seeped into old dune fields to the west of the valley. About 11,500 BCE, the river entered a "Wild Nile" stage, with repeated "catastrophic" floods to 5 or even 10 meters (16 to 33 feet) above the floodplain, which signalled a major change of climate in East Africa. By 11,000 BCE, the floods dwindled rapidly, causing the channel to downcut its bed by as much as 25 meters (82 feet). At that time, only a very narrow floodplain remained inundated, and the number and size of population groups was greatly diminished.

A flood regime, broadly similar to that of today but a little more vigorous, resumed about 10,500–6000 BCE, interrupted by two or more intervals of weaker floods. This is the time of dispersed fisher-hunter-gatherer settlements (Epipaleolithic), and evidence for Nile behavior increasingly comes from the Faiyum and the Delta. About 6000–5800 BCE there was another hydrological readjustment, possibly marked by repeated failures of the Blue Nile floods, that left the shores of the Faiyum lake dry. Epipaleolithic sites seem to disappear, but the Faiyum A Neolithic appears shortly thereafter, to be followed by the Neolithic of Merimde and Omari, the Badarian, and the enigmatic Moerian of the Faiyum. The next Nile "crisis" is dated about 4000 BCE, and again lasted perhaps two centuries. The Faiyum lake level fell abruptly and in the Delta, peat formation was possibly interrupted and channels deepened, perhaps in response to erratic low and very high floods, as the White Nile failed repeatedly for much of the fourth millennium BCE. But the Blue Nile and Atbara floods appear to have been strong during most of the Predynastic period, which would imply greater amplitude between high and low water, a stressful pattern for agricultural land use.

A more equitable picture is suggested for the time of the first dynasty, but during the second dynasty sporadic historical observations point to a 1 meter (3 foot) decline in flood height and a 25 to 30 percent decrease in Ethiopian discharge. Toward 2800 BCE, there was recurrent flood failure, but the geochemical record suggests that it was the White Nile discharge that was reduced throughout the Old Kingdom period. If there was a failure of the Nile floods during the sixth dynasty, it was very brief, and by 2150 BCE, the Blue and White Niles were both strong. By 2050 BCE, the lower valley was experiencing a repetition of the "Wild Nile," with four periods of very high flooding in the Faiyum. In the Delta, the surge of flood waters required the river to cut deeper channels to accommodate the phenomenal discharges. Indeed, such flood episodes are verified by more than twenty high-water marks, dating about 1840–1770 BCE in the Semna cataracts. They would indicate that two years out of every five would create flood levels 4 to 7 meters (13 to 23 feet) higher than those of the late nineteenth century at Aswan, and 3 to 5 meters (10 to 16 feet) higher across the broader floodplain near Cairo.

These flood perturbations of the Middle Kingdom now are well documented by convergent lines of evidence, and spanned up to 350 years. Their implications for Egyptian agriculture would be negative, since such catastrophic floods would wash out dikes, endanger settlements, and rapidly silt up irrigation canals. In addition to repeatedly destroying Egypt's infrastructure, very high floods imply a much longer flood season, so that crops could only be planted many weeks later, maturing early in the season of hot khamsin winds, with increasing drought stress. Long-term waterlogging of soils also increases soil parasites and endangers crops through rot, vernim, and blight. The Middle Kingdom was, in other words, a period of great environmental stress.

In Ramessid times, the Blue Nile floods began to fail, and much of the floodplain in Nubia was no longer inun-

dated. Under Ramesses III (1198–1166 BCE), the Egyptian records first inform us about food shortfalls on a serious scale. Wildly fluctuating food prices (relative to other prices) argue that shortfalls or famines were common in about 1170–1100 BCE. They probably contributed to the destabilization of the New Kingdom.

The floods appear to have regained a more "normal" level during the tenth century BCE, and were comparatively high at the time of Herodotus's visit (c.450 BCE), judging by water levels in the Faiyum. The divergence of the Nile over five or more tributaries in the Delta, according to Strabo (c.25 BCE) and Ptolemy (c.160 BCE), also suggests a "strong" Nile, but in Nubia flood levels only returned to those of 1250 BCE during the period of about 600–1000 CE. By the time of Idrisi (1154 CE) however, the Delta tributaries were reduced to two, with the failure of the western and easternmost Canopic and Pelusiac branches. This suggests a lower discharge norm, comparable with that of the twentieth century.

Egyptian Names and Symbols. Egyptologists have adopted an Egyptocentric nomenclature for the cataracts that occur along the Nile's course, so that numbering begins with the First Cataract at Aswan and proceeds south to the Sixth Cataract not far north of Khartoum. The First Cataract had to be periodically cleared of rocks that impeded its navigability; the Second Cataract (the Batn el-Hagar, "Belly of Stone") was navigable only by very small boats, making it necessary to portage around it. It was there that the twelfth dynasty kings established a line of fortresses to keep Nubians from penetrating farther north.

During those times of the year when the Nile was not in flood, the Egyptians called the river "Iteru" (*itrw*), the term's origin is unclear, but it has been suggested that it means "the Seasonal One." The Nile in inundation was designated as Hap or Happy (*Hʿpy*), and was thus deified as the god of the Nile and father of all beings (not to be confused with Hapy, one of the Four sons of Horus). The form of this hypostasis of the Nile's fertilizing bounty of water and silt was represented most commonly by an androgynous figure: bearded, with pendulous breasts and prominent belly, but with no visible genitalia. In some representations, the body is covered with wavy blue lines evoking the river's waters. Frequently, the Hapy figures are seen in pairs flanking the emblem for the unification of Egypt (*smȝ tȝwy*), signifying the Nile as a basic unifying feature of Egypt. In other representations, processions of Hapy figures bear on their heads the names of the nomes (the districts of Egypt) or depictions of the characteristic riverine plants, the papyrus and lotus. They are often shown bearing offering jars for libations, plants, trays of offerings, or simply the hieroglyph for offering. The south-to-north flow of the Nile formed the basic idea of a river for the Egyptians, so that the rivers of the Near East, notably the Euphrates, were puzzling; they referred to the latter as "the river that goes backwards."

[*See also* Hymns, *article on* Nile Hymns; *and* Irrigation.]

BIBLIOGRAPHY

Andres, W., and J. Wunderlich. "Late Pleistocene and Holocene Evolution in the Eastern Nile Delta and Comparisons with the Western Delta." In *From the North Sea to the Indian Ocean*, edited by H. Brückner and U. Radtke, pp. 120–130. Stuttgart, 1991. Synthesizes important observations on buried sites and their environmental context.

Bell, Barbara. "The Oldest Records of the Nile Floods." *Geographical Journal* 136 (1970), 569–573. Plots the surviving flood records from the first to fifth dynasties.

Bell, Barbara. "Climate and the History of Egypt: The Middle Kingdom." *American Journal of Archaeology* 79 (1975), 223–269. Analyzes the exceptionally high flood levels recorded at Semna.

Brewer, Douglas J. *Fishermen, Hunters and Herders: Zooarchaeology in the Fayum, Egypt (ca. 8,200–5,000 B.P.)* Oxford, 1989. A key resource on the fishing economy of the prehistoric Faiyum.

Butzer, Karl W. *Recent History of an Ethiopian Delta: The Omo Delta and the Level of Lake Rudolf.* Chicago, 1971. Documents a modern delta and floodplain, with its settlement patterns, including aerial photographs of characteristic features.

Butzer, Karl W. *Early Hydraulic Civilization in Egypt: A Study in Cultural Ecology.* Chicago, 1976. Examines the implications of the floodplain environment and its changes for the evolution of irrigation. In part, now dated.

Butzer, Karl W. "Long-term Nile Flood Variation and Political Discontinuities in Pharaonic Egypt." In *From Hunters to Farmers: Causes and Consequences of Food Production in Africa*, edited by J. D. Clark and S. A. Brandt, pp. 102–112. Berkeley, 1984.

Butzer, Karl W. "Sociopolitical Discontinuity in the Near East c 2200 B.C.E.: Scenarios from Palestine and Egypt." In *Third Millennium B.C. Climate Change and Old World Collapse*, edited by H. N. Dalfes et al., pp. 245–296. Berlin, 1997. Reexamines and rejects the First Intermediate Period "low Nile" as a factor in Old Kingdom collapse.

Butzer, Karl W. "Late Quaternary Problems of the Egyptian Nile: Stratigraphy, Environments, Prehistory." *Paleorient* 23/2 (1998), 151–173. Revises the history of the Nile floods and floodplain from 20,000 BP to the end of the Old Kingdom, based in good part on recent evidence from the Faiyum and Delta, with critical overview of the literature.

Gautier, Achilles, and Willem van Neer. "Animal Remains from the Late Paleolithic Sequence at Wadi Kubbaniya." In *The Prehistory of Wadi Kubbaniya*, edited by F. Wendorf and R. Schild, vol. 2, pp. 119–151. Dallas, 1989. The most comprehensive examination of animal remains available.

Krzyzaniak, Lech, M. Kobusiewicz, and J. Alexander, eds. *Environmental Change and Human Culture in the Nile Basin and Northern Africa until the Second Millennium B.C.* Poznan, 1993.

Krzyzaniak, Lech, and M. Kobusiewicz, eds. *Late Prehistory of the Nile Basin and the Sahara.* Poznan, 1989. Like its 1993 counterpart, and van den Brink's edited volume, a rich repository of current research relevant to this article.

Shahin, Mohammed. *Hydrology of the Nile Basin.* Amsterdam, 1985. A fine, reasonably up-to-date guide.

van den Brink, Edward, ed. *The Nile Delta in Transition.* Amsterdam, 1993.

Wetterstrom, Wilma. "Foraging and Farming in Egypt: The Transition from Hunting and Gathering to Horticulture in the Nile Valley."

In *The Archaeology of Africa: Food, Metals, and Towns*, edited by T. Shaw et al., pp. 165–226. London, 1993. A fresh and revolutionary monographic treatment of the paleobotanical record, in an excellent volume presenting the Africanist perspective.

KARL W. BUTZER

NINE BOWS. *See* Insignias.

NINETEENTH DYNASTY. *See* New Kingdom, *article on* Nineteenth Dynasty.

NITOKRIS. *See* Queens.

NOMARCH. *See* Administration, *article on* Provincial Administration; *and* Officials.

NOME. *See* Administration, *article on* Provincial Administration; *and* Geography.

NUBIA, part of the Nile Valley occupied by Nubian speakers, encompassing the region from Aswan, in the north, upstream to ed-Debba. Nubia is subdivided into Lower Nubia, from the First to the Second Cataracts of the Nile River, and Upper Nubia. As used by archaeologists and historians, Nubia is frequently extended into central Sudan, to include those areas that were under the control of the Kushite state, based on Napata and Meroë, during the first millennia BCE and CE, and of the southernmost of the three medieval kingdoms, the kingdom of Alodia (Ar., Alwa). A clear border did not always exist between Egypt and Nubia. For the earliest phases, and as late as the C-Group, Nubian cultural assemblages have been found as far north as Kubaniyya, 18 kilometers (about 11 miles) downstream of Aswan, and there was clearly a zone of contact. The strategic importance of the settlement at Elephantine, on a island at the downstream end of the First Cataract, and of its successor Aswan, on the right bank, have however made this the de facto border point.

The ancient Egyptians designated the regions south of Aswan by a variety of toponyms. During the Old Kingdom, Wawat, Irtjet, Setju, Yam, and others were frequently mentioned. At a later date, Shaat and Kush dominated the scene. Although precise locations are not known, they are all within the broadest modern definitions of Nubia. The term Aethiopia was applied by the Greeks, Macedonians

NUBIA. *Sword from Buhen.* (University of Pennsylvania Museum, Philadelphia. Neg. # S4–141841)

(Ptolemies), and Romans to a much wider region, which was not clearly defined but extended well beyond the Nile Valley.

Climate and Geomorphology. Nubia, taking here the broadest definition, is confined to the Nile Valley and its immediate hinterland. From Sennar on the Blue Nile and Kosti on the White Nile downstream to Aswan, the river traverses a wide range of climatic zones, passing through the savannah deep into the Sahara, from regions of considerable rainfall to regions where rain seldom occurs. Throughout these regions, however, the Nile provides an oasis, a focus for sedentary human activity; the river be-

comes progressively more important as it enters the arid zones. The climate of this region has become dry during the post-Pleistocene, particularly with the onset of the present arid phase. Northern Nubia, today a harsh desert environment, was much wetter and greener in pharaonic times, offering a wide range of possibilities for human activities. Although the general trend has been toward greater aridity during the last several thousand years, there have been some short, wetter periods. [*See* Desert Environment.]

The Nile Valley provides a route across the desert from central Africa to the Mediterranean, but in Nubia the sinuous course of the river and a series of rapids, called cataracts, makes travel alongside the river or on the river far from ideal. Many of the old trade routes avoided parts of the Nile Valley, with people preferring to risk cross-desert journeys. The geomorphology and geography of the Nile Valley have therefore tended to favor a measure of isolation between one reach of the river and another—hence the existence of wide-ranging polities have been the exception rather than the rule.

Archaeology in Nubia. Nubia was first opened to scholars on the conquest of the valley south of Aswan by the armies of Moḥammed Ali in 1820. A number of nineteenth-century European antiquaries and travelers, among them Linant de Bellefonds, Frederick Cailliaud, and Richard Lepsius, recorded many of the ancient monuments. Archaeological investigations using "modern" techniques began in the first decade of the twentieth century, when the initial heightening of the Aswan Dam resulted in an archaeological survey; it was conducted initially by George Reisner and later by Colin Firth, to record the monuments that were to be flooded. This was followed by a second rescue project from 1929 to 1934, and it culminated in a survey necessitated by the construction of the Sadd el-Ali in the 1960s, which flooded more than 500 kilometers (312 miles) of the Nile Valley, from the First to the Dal Cataracts. As a result of these activities, Lower Nubia is archaeologically one of the best-known areas in the world, although a considerable amount of work has been, and is continuing to be, undertaken farther to the south, as far upstream as Khartoum and beyond. [*See* Aswan.]

Egyptian Interest in Nubia. Egyptian interest in Nubia is as old as dynastic Egypt itself. Although originally sharing many features in common, the post-Neolithic development of the cultures to the north and south of the First Cataract diverged markedly. By about 3000 BCE, a powerful centralized state had developed in Egypt, whereas the inhabitants of Lower Nubia, the A-Group, in a much less fertile region and, therefore, with a considerably weaker power base, enjoyed a much less developed political system. Egyptian interest in Nubia was twofold: Egypt sought to exploit the mineral wealth of the region, especially its reserves of gold and fine-grained stone and sought to gain access to the regions farther to its south, to exert a measure of control on the lucrative trade from the Upper Nile Valley and its hinterland. The level of Egyptian control over Nubia was determined on the one hand by the ability of the pharaohs to maintain political control and on the other by the ability of the Nubians to assert their independence. The wealth generated from the trade with Egypt fostered the development of powerful states in Nubia, which in turn served to frighten the Egyptian authorities, thus stimulating bouts of conquest. By the New Kingdom, as far as we are aware, the Egyptians had succeeded in removing all the major middlemen in the Nile trade and in advancing close to the major sources of the trade goods, which had, by that stage, become an important feature in the maintenance of the pharaoh's prestige. Among the trade goods, as well as agricultural produce and livestock, were ivory, ebony, gold, and slaves. [*See* A-Group.]

One of the earliest Egyptian monuments known from Nubia is a rock inscription from the Second Cataract that appears to be a record of a campaign by a first dynasty pharaoh, perhaps Djer, against the Nehesyw, as the region's inhabitants were generally known to the Egyptians. By the fourth dynasty, under the pharaoh Khafre (ruled c.2575–2550 BCE), diorite for monumental statuary was being quarried in the desert 65 kilometers (about 40 miles) to the west of Toshka and a small settlement that has evidence for copper working was located at Buhen. Written during the sixth dynasty, the Annals of Harkhuf by a merchant who made four journeys into the lands south of Aswan, give a detailed picture both of Egyptian contacts with the Nehesyw, equated at this period with the archaeologically attested C-Group culture, and of the political situation among them at a time when they enjoyed independence from Egypt. Later in the sixth dynasty, the situation changed and direct military intervention was recorded under Pepy II, which resulted in two of the local rulers, of Wawat and Irtjet, traveling to Memphis to pay homage to the pharaoh. Egyptian references, probably of this time, refer to expeditions being sent "to hack up Wawat." [*See* C-Group.]

Egyptian weakness during the First Intermediate Period allowed the Nehesyw to regain their independence, but this was short-lived. Renewed Egyptian interference was instigated by the pharaoh Amenemhet I (r. 1991–1962 BCE) and concluded by Senwosret I (r. 1971–1928 BCE), culminating in the conquest of the whole of Lower Nubia and the establishment of a frontier at the upstream end of the Second Cataract at Semna, perhaps with an outpost at Sai 100 kilometers (about 65 miles) to the south. The area was rigidly controlled, with a large number of massive fortresses being constructed in the Second Cataract zone and also at strategic locations along the valley to the north. These valley fortresses served both to overawe the local population and to guard the major routes from the valley to the gold-bearing regions in the eastern desert. The massive nature of these fortresses served to highlight the potential military strength of the Nehesyw, who, for centuries, had provided valued troops for the Egyptian armies.

Egypt and Kerma. Sai appears to have been the actual frontier between the Egyptians and their trading partner to the south, the kingdom of Kush. The arrangement reflects a *modus operandi* between the two major powers, based on an appreciation of their relative military strengths and on the mutual benefits, at least to the rulers, of peace and trade. This kingdom of Kush is equated with the archaeologically attested Kerma culture, named after its capital, Kerma, in the northern Dongola Reach. At Kerma has been found the earliest evidence for urbanism in Africa outside of Egypt. By the time of the Middle Kingdom, Kerma was a walled city of some 16 hectares, set in a rich and densely populated hinterland. Its territory extended from the major settlement toward the southern end of Sai Island, as far upstream as Gebel Barkal. [*See* Kerma.]

During the Second Intermediate Period, when the unified Egyptian state disintegrated in the face of onslaughts from the Hyksos, the Kushite kings occupied the political and military vacuum left by the Egyptians in Lower Nubia, advanced to the First Cataract, and opened diplomatic relations with the Hyksos. This prompted the seventeenth dynasty pharaoh Kamose (r. 1571–1569 BCE) to bemoan "to what end am I aware of . . . this power of mine, when a chieftain is in Avaris, and another in Kush, and I sit in league with an Asiatic and a African, every man holding his slice of Egypt?" At this time, the importance of the kingdom of Kush should not be underestimated. Of the three states on the Nile, it was by far the largest in territorial extent and was a true rival to Egypt. The Kushites soon occupied the Egyptian fortresses and employed a number of the Egyptian officials who remained within them. An inscription from Buhen recorded that an Egyptian, then in the employ of the king of Kush, built a temple in honor of the god Horus on behalf of the Kushite ruler. At this time, both the Kushite and the Egyptian armies made use of mercenary troops who have been identified as the Medjay of the Egyptian texts, originating in the Eastern Desert. Archaeologically, they are recognized by their distinctive circular graves, which have given their culture its name, the Pan-Grave Culture. Although their culture has much in common with the contemporary C-Group and Kerma cultures, they appear to be a separate Nubian group. [*See* Pan-Grave People.]

The Second Intermediate Period was the apogee of the power of the Kushite monarchy, and the wealth of the rulers is reflected in the grandiose tomb monuments they constructed at Kerma. Tumulus K X, which was one of the largest, was more than 80 meters (250 feet) in diameter and contained not only the burial of the ruler but also 322 (possibly originally 400) retainers or sacrificial victims who accompanied him to his death. Placed among the sacrificial victims in Tumulus K III were the statues of the twelfth dynasty Egyptian prince Hepzefa and his wife Sennuwy, included there perhaps to symbolize the dominance of Kush over Egypt. The town at Kerma, lying 4 kilometers (about 2.5 miles) to the west of the cemetery, had outgrown its earlier defences, and a new palace with its associated storerooms had been built over the western ditch. It was dominated by a massive temple, in its latest phase a mud-brick structure, which still survives to a height of 18 meters (about 55 feet). The discovery of seals and sealings indicates that a complex administrative organization was in place. Although the influence of Egypt may be clearly recognized there, much owes its origins to African traditions. It is in the context of the rich culture of Kerma, amply attested by archaeological discoveries, that Egyptian references to "miserable Kush" and "vile Kush" must be understood. Clearly such epithets are biased, but they are interesting in an assessment of Pharaonic propaganda if not in a consideration of the history of Nubia.

Nubia During the New Kingdom. With the defeat of the Hyksos in the north, the revival of the fortunes of Egypt opened the way for an advance against the Kushites. The Kushites were the victim of their own success; they were much too powerful for the Egyptians to tolerate as a neighbor athwart the trade routes from the south. Hostilities began under Ahmose in the mid-sixteenth century BCE. Thutmose I (c.1525–1516 BCE) penetrated through the Third Cataract in the second year of his reign and proclaimed that [he] "penetrated valleys which the royal ancestors knew not, which the wearers of the double diadem had not seen." The Kushites were defeated and their capital was taken, the Egyptians advancing to the limit of the Kushite state at Gebel Barkal. At Kurgus, 200 kilometers (some 125 miles) upstream of Barkal, are two inscriptions of Thutmose I and III, and close by the remains of a fortress of that period may also exist. Whether these forces advanced to Kurgus along the Nile or across the desert from Korosko is not clear. However the Egyptian forces reached this point, this is the farthest upstream that an army from Egypt is known to have penetrated until 1819. Although, presumably, the Egyptians interacted with the peoples to the south in central Sudan, there is very little evidence for this, and the Neolithic cultures of that region continued their independent development into the first millennium BCE.

The area around Gebel Barkal, known as Napata, marked the border of Egyptian territory, and a fortress called "Slayer of the Foreigners" was constructed there by Thutmose III. From the walls of this fortress, Amenhotpe II hung the body of one of his Asian prisoners. A shrine was built to Amun, and the prominent flat-topped gebel, known to the Egyptians as "The Pure Mountain," was credited as one of the two ancestral homes of the state god Amun.

The fortresses in Lower Nubia and at the Second Cataract remained in use, and a number were extensively rebuilt. In Upper Nubia, between the Dal and the Third Cataracts, fortified towns were constructed at Soleb, Sedeinga, Sai, and under Amenhotpe IV at Sesebi. Of them, Sesebi is the best known, having been extensively excavated in 1937 by the Egypt Excavation Society; it consisted of a rectangular enclosure defended by a mud-brick wall with projecting rectangular towers, within which lay a temple, magazines, and dwellings. The administrative capital of the region was at Soleb, where a massive temple was constructed by Amenhotpe III, who also built a temple to his queen, Tiye, at the nearby town of Sedeinga. Under Sety I, a new town was built at Amara West, and this replaced Soleb as the administrative center of Kush.

Upstream of the Third Cataract, occupation continued at the old Kushite capital of Kerma, although the settlement shifted a little to the north. Finds of inscribed blocks recording several of the pharaohs of the eighteenth and nineteenth dynasties indicate that the Kushite settlement at Tabo, on Argo Island, remained in use. Some 40 kilometers (25 miles) upstream, the town at Kawa was probably also constructed on the site of an earlier Kushite settlement. The name of this town, *Gem-Aten* (*Gm-itn*), meaning "the Aten is perceived," suggests that it was founded by Amenhotpe IV if not by his father Amenhotpe III. Between Kawa and Napata, a distance of 185 kilometers (about 115 miles) along the river, no Egyptian sites are yet known, prompting the suggestion that this region may have been under the control of local dynasts who swore allegiance to the pharaoh. Farther downstream, the local rulers, Amenemhat and Djehuty-Hotep, the "Princes of Tekhet," assisted the conquerors in governing the region. Another of these collaborators was the local chief Heka-Nefer, from Aniba in Lower Nubia. They were buried in Egyptian-style tombs with all the trappings of Egyptian civilization.

Ramesses II was the greatest builder of the nineteenth dynasty, and he constructed a considerable number of temples in Nubia, the most famous being the rock-cut temple at Abu Simbel, dedicated to himself and the other gods, Re-Horakhty and Amun. At Napata, on the limits of his empire he completed the construction of a temple begun either by Horemheb (r. 1343–1315 BCE) or Sety I (r. 1314–1304 BCE).

NUBIA. *Wood box with ivory inlay, from a grave at Karanog, Meroitic period (300 BCE–100 BCE).* (University of Pennsylvania Museum, Philadelphia. Neg. # S8–32166)

Less than two centuries after the death of Ramesses II, Egyptian control of Nubia had ceased. At Amara West, the town appears to have been abandoned during the twentieth dynasty, the temple fittings and regalia being removed in an orderly manner. A similar fate seems to have befallen all the other Egyptian settlements, and the temple of Amun at Gebel Barkal fell into ruins. This Egyptian withdrawal was caused by unsettled conditions in Egypt, where rival dynasts fought for the Throne of the Two Lands. One of the main players came from south of Aswan, Panehsy, the viceroy of Kush, who advanced into Egypt but was defeated by Herihor and forced to withdraw. Herihor's son, Piya (Piankhy), was given the title "King's Son of Kush," but he was presumably unable to establish direct control south of Aswan.

The Kushite State of Napata and Meroë. For several centuries thereafter, we have only glimpses of what was happening in Nubia. At Qasr Ibrim, a mud-brick fortification was constructed during the tenth century BCE, but by whom we are not certain. Egyptian sources refer to invasions of the area by pharaohs of the twenty-second dynasty, but the extent of those activities and against whom they were directed is unclear. Archaeologically, the population of Lower Nubia at this time appears to have

been very sparse and probably remained so into the mid-first millennium CE. During this phase, a new center of power was developing a little downstream of Gebel Barkal. From the ninth century BCE onward, and some scholars maintain from as early as the eleventh century BCE, important individuals were buried at el-Kurru, initially in simple pit and side-niche graves marked by tumuli, but progressively in more elaborate tombs marked by rectilinear *mastabas* and finally by pyramids. These rulers rapidly came to dominate Nubia and, by the later years of the eighth century BCE, ruled the largest ancient state on the Nile, stretching from central Sudan to the southern border of Palestine. Their involvement in Egypt began under Kashta, who may have advanced as far as Thebes, but it was his successor Piya who undertook the conquest of the whole country, as is recorded in great detail on a stela he set up at Napata in the twenty-first year of his reign, around 714 BCE.

In Egypt, these rulers came to be known as the twenty-fifth dynasty, but this should not disguise their totally non-Egyptian origins. Although they were worshipers of the state god of Egypt, Amun, and assumed many of the trappings of Egyptian civilization, they were a distinct people and their culture, although much influenced by

NUBIA. *Engraving (c.1890) of the First Cataract of the Nile, between Aswan and Philae, in the borderland between Egypt and Nubia.*

that of Egypt, maintained a complexion of its own for more than a millennium. Their culture is today divided into two phases, that of Napata and that of Meroë, named after the two principal centers of the state. Their history was a continuum, although there were clearly many changes with time, some brought about by the new influences filtering down from Egypt, whose Pharaonic culture was itself dramatically altered first by Persian, then by Macedonian (Ptolemaic) and Roman culture.

The focus of the state known as the kingdom of Kush, like its predecessor based at Kerma, was early moved from el-Kurru to the Napata region at Gebel Barkal, although the rulers continued to be buried at the ancestral burial ground until the mid-seventh century BCE. They refurbished and greatly expanded the temples at the foot of Gebel Barkal; by assuming the worship of Amun and by capitalizing both on the myth of Barkal as one of the ancestral homes of the god and on the troubled situation in Egypt, they were able to pose as the champions of the Egyptian and Kushite state god. Their involvement with Egypt dragged them into Near Eastern power politics, and in so doing they came into contact with the aggressive Assyrians, in the face of whose military prowess they

were ousted from the regions north of Aswan by 663 BCE. Although thereafter confined to the regions upstream of the First Cataract, their power appears undiminished. To the south, they expanded their empire at least as far as Sennar on the Blue Nile, 250 kilometers (about 160 miles) upstream of Khartoum. Periodic invasions from the north, by Psamtik II, Cambyses, the Ptolemies, and the Romans under Gaius Petronius, some of which were credited with marching as far upstream as Napata, seem to have had no long-term effect on the prosperity of the state.

Like the earlier states on the Middle Nile, Kushite rulers presumably derived much wealth as middlemen in the African trade. The extremely fine objects of Mediterranean manufacture found in their elite burials testify to this wealth and to the importance the Mediterranean powers saw in cultivating good relations with them. As at earlier periods, the staple of the economy would have been agriculture and pastoralism, so life for the inhabitants of the Kushite empire may have been little changed from that enjoyed by their Kerma, C-Group, and New Kingdom predecessors.

Although Gebel Barkal may have remained the major

Kushite religious center, as early as the reign of Aspelta there was a royal presence at Meroë. The rulers continued to be buried at Nuri, 7 kilometers (about 4.2 miles) upstream from Barkal, into the late fourth century BCE. Soon afterward, royal burials begin at Meroë, first in a cemetery that had been in use for several centuries and, thereafter, across the Wadi Tarabil in what is known as the North Cemetery. With only a few exceptions, all subsequent rulers were buried there until the collapse of the state in the fourth century CE.

During the third century CE, the dominant power in the Mediterranean, the Roman empire, was undergoing catastrophic financial crises in the face of almost continual external and civil wars; this must have had repercussions beyond their Egyptian frontier as it did elsewhere. The diminished wealth of the Roman world would reduce its demand for luxury goods from Africa. This reduced demand coincided with a shift in the trade routes from the Nile Valley east to the Red Sea, where trade was in the hands of the Axumites. With these crises, and with the increasing threat from the peoples living to the east and west of the Nile—the Blemmyes and Nobatae in the north, the Noba and perhaps also the Axumites in the south—the Kushite state fragmented. Within the old Kushite state were probably a number of small chiefdoms, perhaps under the general suzerainty of a few powerful rulers; one was certainly based in the region around Abu Simbel and its rulers were buried under massive tumuli at Ballana and Qustul. To the south, a "royal" burial ground has recently been investigated at el-Hobagi, and other rich burials are known from Gamai, Firka, Kosha, Wawa, ez-Zuma, Tanqasi, Khuzeinah, Hagar el-Beida, and Sururab. These new overlords appear to have seen themselves as successors to the old Kushite monarchy, and they continued to use many of the Kushite symbols of power and funerary rituals.

Although Christianity had taken a firm hold in Egypt for several centuries, there is no hint either of its penetration into the Kushite empire or of its acceptance by the rulers of what has been called the Ballana, X-Group, and post-Meroitic periods. By the sixth century CE, the political situation had stabilized with the creation of three kingdoms dominating Nubia—Nobatia with its capital at Faras in the north, Makuria centered on Old Dongola, and Alodia (Alwa) with its capital on the Blue Nile at Soba East. The conversion to Christianity of the rulers of these states, and progressively of their subjects, during the sixth and seventh centuries, marked a monumentous cultural change. It was the death knell for the pharaonic civilization and beliefs that had flourished in the Nile Valley for well over three thousand years.

[*See also* Abu Simbel; Aniba; Buhen; Foreign Incursions; Imperialism; Kawa; Kerma; Kush; Meroë; Napata; *and* Third Intermediate Period.]

BIBLIOGRAPHY

Archéologie du Nil Moyen 1986–present. Lille, France. A journal appearing most years which contains a wide range of articles relating to the archaeology of Sudan.

Adams, William Y. *Nubia: Corridor to Africa.* Princeton, 1977. The most comprehensive account of Nubia's archaeology and history, it is now somewhat out of date, particularly the section on the Kerma culture.

Bonnet, Charles. *Kerma: Royaume de Nubie.* Geneva, 1990. An exhibition catalog with excellent introductory chapters by several scholars on the Kerma culture.

Davies, W. Vivian, ed. *Egypt and Africa: Nubia from Prehistory to Islam.* London, 1991. A collection of papers by leading scholars on many aspects of Nubian archaeology.

Emery, Walter B. *Egypt in Nubia.* London, 1965.

Hochfield, Sylvia, and Elizabeth Riefstahl, eds. *Africa in Antiquity I. The Essays.* Brooklyn, 1978. Published to coincide with a major exhibition in New York, Seattle, New Orleans, and The Hague, it provides a general introduction to Nubian culture by several leading specialists. For the companion volume, see Wenig 1979.

Kendall, Timothy. *Kush: Lost Kingdom of the Nile.* Brockton, Mass., 1982.

Kush. The Journal of the Sudan Antiquities Service Khartoum, 1953–present. This journal, which appeared annually from 1953 to 1968, and intermittently thereafter, contains a wealth of articles and preliminary reports on all aspects of Sudan's archaeology.

O'Connor, David. *Nubia: Egypt's Rival in Africa.* Philadelphia, 1993. A stimulating account focusing particularly on the Lower Nubian site of Karanog. Includes an exhibition catalogue.

Priese, Karl-Heinz. *The Gold of Meroe.* New York, 1993. A catalog for the exhibition on the gold and other jewelry found by Ferlini in the pyramid of the Kushite queen Amanishakheto at Meroë.

Shinnie, Peter L. *Meroe. A Civilisation of the Sudan.* London, 1967.

Shinnie, Peter L. *Ancient Nubia.* London and New York, 1996.

Török, László. *The Kingdom of Kush: Handbook of the Napatan/Meroitic Civilisation.* Leiden, 1997.

Trigger, Bruce G. *Nubia under the Pharaohs.* London, 1976.

Welsby, Derek A. *The Kingdom of Kush: The Napatan and Meroitic Empires.* London, 1996. An up-to-date account of the Kushite state, which partly replaces Shinnie's 1967 book.

Wenig, Steffen. *Africa in Antiquity. II. The Catalogue.* Brooklyn, 1979. Catalog of a major exhibition in New York, Seattle, New Orleans, and The Hague.

Wildung, Dietrich, ed. *Sudan: Ancient Kingdoms of the Nile.* Translated from the German by Peter Der Manuelin. Paris and New York, 1997. Introductory essays and a catalogue of a large exhibition that toured Europe from 1996 to 1998, which assembled many of the finest pieces of Nubian art from the Neolithic to the post-Meroitic periods.

DEREK A. WELSBY

NUN. For the ancient Egyptian, the sphere of life floated as a bubble, surrounded by the limitless dark waters of the inert god Nun. This oceanic abyss, while giving rise to and sustaining the cosmogony, also concealed the threat of disorder in its chaotic depths. It is the supreme mystery in the Egyptian cosmology.

The concept of the primeval waters is common to all Egyptian creation models. When the king sets sail into the realm of the afterlife, it is to Nun that he appeals. When the Egyptians dug down for water, it was in search of Nun. This presence was actively sought in temple and field as the basis for life, religious and secular. Nun, as a principle of the void mysteriously merging towards creation, is the progenitor of all differentiation, divine and earthly, and the image of water, manifesting both form and formlessness simultaneously, perfectly contains this idea in itself. One can see a poetic and sensuous appreciation of this in a text from the time of Amenhotpe III (c.1410–1372 BCE) near Luxor. "How beautiful is Nun in his pool in every season, more is he like wine than water, a full Nile, born of the Lord of Eternity."

The typical Egyptian Ennead (group of nine gods) reveals Nun as a sort of translucent entity at the point of origin alongside the actual creator-god Atum.

NUN

ATUM

SHU——TEFNUT

GEB——NUT

OSIRIS——ISIS   SETH——NEPHTHYS

Nun is ubiquitous in all phases of Egyptian religious history; indeed, he is depicted on the walls of all the Ptolemaic temples in the Greco-Roman period in his usual form, and is well represented in the larger Ptolemaic temples of the South, often presented in fusion with Ptah (Kalabasha, Philae, Edfu), Sobek (Kom Ombo), Hapy (Opet temple, Karnak), Horus (Opet temple, Dendera), and Khnum-Amun (Esna).

From the Middle Kingdom onward, Nun is described as "the Father of the Gods," and this is perhaps his enduring legacy. That the Greeks derived this idea from the Egyptians is likely, and philosophy, proper, has had recourse to deal with the perennial issue of form appearing out of formlessness. One can see the conundrums of Nun permeating the writings of the third-century CE Neoplatonist Plotinus, for example, the seventeenth-century mystic Jakob Böhme, and the nineteenth-century F. W. Schelling's "will of the depths," as well as, perhaps, Arthur Schopenhauer's writings on "the will."

In Coptic Christian writings, Nun (ⲛ̄ⲟ̄ⲛ̄, in Coptic) came to the mean "abyss of hell." The debasement of this once-majestic creator-god was facilitated by the ambiguity of the word as it was used in Gnostic and magical texts, although the Gnostics continued to view Nun as the very wellspring of divinity. In any event, the association of the word with a pagan deity and developing heresies were the determining factors in the eventual demise of Nun. Although venerated for millennia, Nun eventually came to be exclusively associated with chaos and disorder, forces that were conceptually, as well as politically, set loose upon occupied Egypt in the Late period.

BIBLIOGRAPHY

Barta, Winfried. *Untersuchen zum Götterkreis der Neunheit.* Munich, 1973.

Barta, Winfried. "Die Bedeutung der Personifikation Huh im Unterscheid zu den Personifikation Hah und Nun." *Göttinger Miszellen* 127 (1992), 7–12.

Hornung, Erik. "Chaotische Bereiche in der geordneten Welt." *Zeitschrift für Ägyptische Sprache und Altertumskunde* 81 (1956), 28–32.

Hornung, Erik. *Der Ägyptische Mythos von der Himmelskuh.* Freiberg, 1982.

te Velde, H. "Relations and Conflicts between Egyptian Gods, Particularly in the Divine Ennead of Heliopolis." In *Struggles of Gods: Papers of the Groningen Work Group for the Study of the History of Religions,* edited by H. G. Kippenberg. New York, 1984.

Westendorf, Wolfhart. "Zweitheit, Dreiheit, und Einheit in der altägyptichen Theologie." *Zeitschrift für Ägyptische Sprache und Altertumskunde* 100 (1974), 136–141.

Zandee, Jan. "Der Androgyne Gott in Ägypten ein Erscheinungsbild des Weltschöpfers." In his *Religion im Erbe Ägyptens: Beitrage zur spätantiken Religiongeschichte zu Ehren von Alexander Böhlig.* Wiesbaden, 1988.

DANIEL R. MCBRIDE

NURSES. *See* Childhood.

NUT. The sky goddess Nut was probably one of the oldest deities in the Egyptian pantheon. She was incorporated into the Heliopolitan Ennead in the Old Kingdom Pyramid Texts, the earliest surviving corpus of religious texts. In this source she is a central figure as the granddaughter of the creator god Atum, the daughter of Shu and Tefnut (air and moisture), the sister and wife of Geb (earth), the mother of Osiris, Isis, Seth, and Nephthys, and the grandmother of Horus. In Spell 548 of the Pyramid Texts, Nut the Great is described as a long-horned celestial cow who suckles the king and takes him to herself in the sky. This imagery recurs much later in the shrines of Tutankhamun (r. 1355–1346 BCE), where it is greatly elaborated, and again in the Ptolemaic period (305–31 BCE) in association with the goddess Hathor at her temple in Dendera.

In the Pyramid Texts and Coffin Texts there are series of Nut spells. On the sarcophagus of Teti (first king of the sixth dynasty, ruled c.2374–2354) there are a number of recitations by Nut (Spells 1 ff.), and in the later sixth dynasty pyramids there are a number of addresses (Spells 427 ff.) asking the sky goddess to conceal her son Osiris from Seth, to take possession of the earth, and to install every god who has a bark as an imperishable star in the starry sky—that is, in Nut herself.

In the Middle Kingdom Coffin Texts, Spell 77 describes Nut as "she who bore the gods," and Spell 864 calls her "mother of the gods." She enfolds and protects the sun god Re, as well as re-creating him daily. Although she is given the epithet "Mother of Seth" numerous times in the Ramessid story of the *Contendings of Horus and Seth,* her role as mother of Osiris, and by extension of Horus, is much more significant in the New Kingdom.

Unlike many other great deities, Nut had no particular cult center. This situation may have resulted from her originally chthonic rather than anthropomorphic nature. In spite of the fact that in some texts of all periods she is associated with the cow goddess, she was also depicted very early in the history of the pantheon as a human female figure whose nude body arched over the earth, sustained the stars, gave birth to the sun every day, and swallowed it at dusk so that it could pass through her body. In Spell 306 of the Coffin Texts, Nut performs the same remaking for the deceased, identified with Re. This rebirth of the sun god, together with the resurrection of her son, Osiris, gave her a very important role in the two major Egyptian cults centered on the afterlife. Coffins and burial chambers of tombs are both personified as Nut, who is frequently depicted on their lids and ceilings, for example, in the beautiful representation found in the tomb of Sety I in the Valley of the Kings.

In the Ptolemaic temples at the great cult sites of Edfu and Esna, there are separate chapels to Nut near their main sanctuaries, which depict her body bent around the chapel ceilings. At Dendera, the ceiling of the first hypostyle hall prominently features the goddess Nut in what must be one of the largest representations of any deity in Egypt.

BIBLIOGRAPHY

Hollis, Susan T. "Women of Ancient Egypt and the Sky Goddess Nut." *Journal of American Folklore* 100 (1987), 497.

Hollis, Susan T. "Five Egyptian Goddesses in the Third Millennium B.C." *KMT: A Modern Journal of Ancient Egypt* 5.4 (1994), 48–49.

Hornung, Erik. *The Valley of the Kings: Horizon of Eternity.* Translated by David Warburton. New York, 1990.

Lesko, Barbara S. *The Great Goddesses of Egypt* (forthcoming).

Thompson, Stephen E. "A Study of the Pyramid Texts Occurring on Middle Kingdom Saqqara Coffins." M. A. thesis, Brown University, 1986.

LEONARD H. LESKO

O

OASES. *See* Western Desert.

OBELISK, a tall, narrow, four-sided single shaft of stone surmounted by a small pyramid (or pyramidion); the sides of the obelisk taper slightly as they rise. The modern term derives from Greek *obeliskos,* meaning "little spit"—a reference to its shape. The primary ancient Egyptian term was *thn;* often written in the dual, *thn.wy,* since obelisks mostly occurred in pairs. The pyramidion on top was referred to as *bnbnt.*

Stone obelisks occur in two architectural contexts in ancient Egypt: in temples and before tomb-chapels (although offering loaves in the shape of obelisks are also known). In both contexts, the religious meaning of the obelisk is related to solar cults—in particular that of the sun god Re at Heliopolis—who dates back to the beginning of pharaonic history. He had as his fetish a pyramidion (called *bn* or *bnbn*), which was found in his temple. At the same time, the pyramidion was also related to the *bnw*-bird, or phoenix, who also dwelt upon the great *bnbn* at Heliopolis.

During the fifth dynasty, two sun temples were raised at Abusir by the pharaohs Userkaf and Newoserre Any. These temples had as their focal points very large obelisk-like structures that were built of separate blocks and sheathed in white limestone. The proportions of these primitive obelisks differed from those of the later, true obelisk. Contemporary with the sun temples, there began the practice of putting pairs of small obelisks at the entrance to private tombs. These funerary obelisks were usually inscribed on one side only with the name and titles of the tomb owners. The practice of using funerary obelisks continued sporadically through most of pharaonic times.

The story of true obelisks used in temples is more complex. The oldest known true obelisk survives from Heliopolis; it bears the name of Teti, the first king of the sixth dynasty, Old Kingdom. There are references to other sixth dynasty obelisks but none is known. A text within the pyramid of Pepy I refers to the "obelisks of Re," and an inscription from Aswan made by Sabni, a local governor under Pepy II, refers to the safe delivery of two large obelisks to Heliopolis. No obelisks were made during the First Intermediate Period. The production of obelisks was re-

sumed during the Middle Kingdom, when Sesostris I raised a pair at Heliopolis—one of which still stands, more than 20 meters (62 feet) high. He may also have sponsored the single obelisk dedicated to Horus that was later usurped by Ramesses II (and found at Tanis). Sesostris I was also responsible for a tall obelisk-like stela raised at Abgig in the Faiyum. No other great Middle Kingdom pharaohs raised any obelisks, and only a few minor ones are known from the Second Intermediate Period.

The great age of obelisks began during the New Kingdom, in the eighteenth dynasty, when Thutmose I raised a pair at Karnak. His successors Thutmose II, Hatshepsut, Thutmose III, Amenhotpe II, Thutmose IV, Amenhotpe III, Amenhotpe IV/Akhenaten, and Horemheb all continued those efforts, primarily at Karnak and Heliopolis, but in other places as well. The practice of raising obelisks continued into the nineteenth dynasty under Ramesses I, Sety I, Ramesses II, Merenptah, and Sety II. A single small obelisk of Ramesses IV is known from the twentieth dynasty. During the later pharaonic periods, again the production of obelisks became sporadic. The Kushite king Atlanersa (c.650 BCE) raised an obelisk in Nubia, although he held no power in Egypt proper. During the twenty-sixth and thirtieth dynasties, obelisks were again made for Psamtik II, Apries, Amasis, and Nektanebo II. Obelisks are also known from the reigns of Ptolemy III and Ptolemy IX, and production was resumed during the early Roman occupation of Egypt. A number of uninscribed obelisks quarried in Egypt, but destined for Rome are attributed to Augustus, and another is dated to the emperor Domitian. The last obelisk with an original hieroglyphic inscription seems to be dated to the emperor Hadrian, about 130 CE. It was raised, probably, in Antinoöpolis for the cult of the emperor's dead friend Antinous, who drowned in the Nile.

Although obelisks were made from a variety of stones—quartzite, sandstone, calcite (Egyptian alabaster), and schist—the most common material used was granite, generally of a reddish hue. The granite came from quarries at Aswan. The Lateran obelisk of Thutmose III is the tallest known, at just over 32 meters (97 feet) in height, and the New Kingdom obelisks are between 20 and 30 meters (62 and 92 feet). An unfinished obelisk in the Aswan quarry was intended to be over 40 meters (122 feet) high. Owing

OBELISK. *Pink granite obelisk at Heliopolis, twelfth dynasty.* This obelisk is from the reign of Senwosret I. (Courtesy Donald B. Redford)

to flaws in the stone, it was left finished, but its present state tells much about the quarrying process. After selecting a likely piece of stone in the quarry, the surface was leveled, using alternating heat and cold. The outline of the obelisk was marked, and side trenches were dug down using dolerite pounders. Once the sides were detached, the pounders were again used to break the obelisk free from the quarry floor. (Chisels and wooden wedges were not generally used to remove stones in pharaonic times.) According to an inscription of Hatshepsut at Karnak, the quarrying of a large obelisk could be completed in a mere seven months. The rough obelisk would be levered out of the quarry, perhaps fixed to a sled and set upon rollers, then dragged to the river bank. The obelisk was placed on a barge—how is not known—to be towed on the river to

the site where it would be erected. A scene in the temple of Hatshepsut at Deir el-Bahri shows a barge with a pair of her obelisks being towed by a fleet of nine towboats.

Evidence from two obelisks in Rome (the Lateran and Popolo obelisks) suggests that three sides of an obelisk were dressed and decorated while it lay on the ground, while the forth side was decorated only after the obelisk was erected. The smooth surface of the granite was achieved by pounding with diorite balls. The hieroglyphs and figures were cut into the stone using emery powder, perhaps in conjunction with copper or bronze tools, but the emery was the primary agent. On occasion, gold plating could be affixed to the upper parts of the obelisk. In some cases, a separate pyramidion was attached at the top.

Most obelisks were raised in pairs at the entrance to

a temple, on either side of a primary axis. Their decoration reflects such positioning. Several single obelisks are known, but their existence may merely reflect the inability of successfully extracting or raising a pair. There is much debate as to how obelisks were actually erected. The difficulty lies in their great weight and slender form. It seems reasonable that some system was used that included an artificial hill of sand on which the obelisk could be raised and set onto its base. The base had a groove to catch and position the edge of the obelisk. Having an edge resting on the base, the obelisk would then have been pulled upright by many workers pulling on ropes affixed around the obelisk's girth.

In Egypt, obelisks are found at sites where they were first erected or where they were transported, either by the Egyptians or by the Greeks or Romans. A pair of sandstone obelisks was found in the solar chapel in front of the temple of Ramesses II at Abu Simbel, and a variety of granite obelisks of different dates were found at Elephantine and Philae. Most of the obelisks in Upper Egypt were raised at Karnak (seven pairs plus a single one) and Luxor (one pair), in conjunction with the solar aspect of the god Amun-Re. The major center of obelisks in Lower Egypt was the great temple of the sun god at Heliopolis. Only the single Middle Kingdom obelisk of Sesostris I still stands at the site, but there is literary evidence concerning its mate, and fragments of other obelisks have been discovered there. A number of the obelisks from Heliopolis had been moved to other sites, primarily the Mediterranean port of Alexandria, where five such obelisks can be attested. In Ramesses II's city of Piramesse, there were a large number of obelisks, some original and some usurped. Many were also transported to the Delta city of Tanis in late pharaonic times.

During the Roman and early Byzantine periods, many of Egypt's ancient obelisks were moved abroad and new obelisks were also made for export. Written accounts of these moves survive, as does some of the physical evidence of their removal from Karnak. At least fifteen obelisks were transferred to Rome, although only thirteen now remain there. In size, these obelisks range in height from less than 3 meters to more than 32 meters (10 feet to 100 feet). Of the thirteen still in Rome, as many as five were brought there uninscribed. Sometime toward the end of the fourth century CE, under Emperor Theodosius, an obelisk of Thutmose III from Karnak was transferred to Constantinople (now Istanbul), to adorn the center of the Great Hippodrome; a part of it stands there to this day. Remains of the scaffolding used to remove it are visible at Karnak.

In the nineteenth century, three of Egypt's remaining obelisks were taken abroad to Paris, London, and New York. The Paris obelisk was first raised by Ramesses II in front of the western tower of the Pylon of the Great Temple at Luxor. In 1830, after much diplomatic maneuvering, the obelisk was presented to France by Mohammed Ali, then ruler of Egypt. With great difficulty, the obelisk was taken down, shipped, and re-erected, this time in the Place de la Concorde in Paris. The obelisks sent to London and New York were originally made for Thutmose III, for the temple of the sun at Heliopolis. They were transferred to Alexandria, under Augustus, to stand before the temple of the deified Julius Caesar. Ironically, they are referred to as "Cleopatra's Needles," although they were not brought to Alexandria until twenty years after that queen's death. In 1301 CE, the obelisk now in London fell, while the other remained standing until its removal to New York. After a sea voyage that involved the loss (and subsequent recovery) of the barge holding the London obelisk in the Bay of Biscay, it was set up along the Thames River in late 1878. By comparison, the transport of the New York obelisk was uneventful, and it was re-erected in New York's Central Park in early 1881.

Renaissance Europeans and, in particular, the inhabitants of Rome rediscovered the obelisk as an architectural form. The ancient obelisks of Rome were set up in plazas—often with fountains—throughout the city. At the same time, new obelisks of various sizes were also made to commemorate events or people. Small obelisks continued as a decorative motive in European art and are sold to this day. With the reopening of Egypt by the Napoleonic Expedition of 1798, Europe and the newly formed United States experienced an Egyptian revival. Many buildings were constructed in the Egyptian fashion, and obelisks continued to be used as an appropriate funerary or civic monument. The Washington Monument in Washington, D.C., is in the form an obelisk, although it is constructed, not made from a single stone in the Egyptian fashion.

BIBLIOGRAPHY

Arnold, Dieter. *Building in Egypt: Pharaonic Stone Masonry.* New York, 1991. Up-to-date study on building with stone in ancient Egypt.

Boatwright, Mary Taliaferro. *Hadrian and the City of Rome.* Princeton, 1987. A useful discussion of the problems of the last Egyptian obelisk.

Budge, E. A. Wallis. *Cleopatra's Needles and Other Egyptian Obelisks.* London, 1926. A somewhat dated but readily available account of the obelisks and their removal from Egypt.

Carrott, Richard G. *The Egyptian Revival: Its Sources, Monuments, and Meaning, 1808–1858.* Berkeley, 1978. A general discussion of Egyptianized monuments, especially with relation to American monuments.

Clarke, Somers, and R. Engelbach. *Ancient Egyptian Masonry: The Building Craft.* London, 1930. The first thorough study of Egyptian stoneworking.

Curl, James Stevens. *The Egyptian Revival.* London, 1982. A study of Egyptianizing trends, mainly from the European perspective.

Dibner, Bern. *Moving the Obelisks.* Cambridge, Mass., 1970. A detailed account of the erection of the Vatican obelisk.

Engelbach, Reginald. *The Aswan Obelisk.* Cairo, 1922. A detailed study of the unfinished obelisk at Aswan.

Engelbach, Reginald. *The Problem of Obelisks.* New York, 1923. The first major technical study of obelisks manufacture; still unsurpassed.

Gorringe, Henry H. *Egyptian Obelisks.* New York, 1882. A detailed account of the transport of the Central Park obelisk to New York.

Habachi, Labib. *The Obelisks of Egypt: Skyscrapers of the Past.* New York, 1977. A study of obelisks; designed for the lay reader, but with material useful to the specialist.

Hayward, R. *Cleopatra's Needles.* Buxton, 1978. A discussion of the London obelisk.

Iversen, Erik. *Obelisks in Exile.* 2 vols. Copenhagen, 1968–1972. The most important and best documented work on the removal of obelisks from Egypt; includes Rome, New York, London, and Paris.

Iversen, Erik. *The Myth of Egypt and Its Hieroglyphs in European Tradition.* Princeton, 1993. A general study on Egyptianizing trends in Europe.

Thompson, Peter. *The Magic of Obelisks.* New York, 1981. Discusses much of the lore of obelisks, including a brief account of their removal; also discusses arcane topics modernly connected to obelisks.

CHARLES C. VAN SICLEN

OFFERINGS. [*This entry surveys offerings in ancient Egypt, with reference to their theological significance and chronological development. It discusses the various types of offerings and the personnel and accessories related to them. It comprises three articles:*

An Overview
Offering Formulas and Lists
Offering Tables

For a related discussion, see the composite entry on Cults.]

An Overview

Offerings to the dead have become known from prehistoric times through finds in ancient Egyptian graves. Special offering places have also been found in relation to graves throughout Egypt's historical period; the earliest were placed outside the superstructures of the tombs and the later inside. Most likely, offerings were also made in the shrines depicted on prehistoric material, since offerings were part of temple rituals; they are well documented in textual material and, from the New Kingdom onward, also in temple reliefs.

The Ideology of Offerings. Two concepts are linked to the notion of offerings that cover all kinds of offerings and explain the meaning of offerings in the Egyptian worldview. One concept is "the Eye of Horus" (*irt Ḥr*), one of the most important symbols of ancient Egypt and used about all kinds of gifts. The other concept is *maat,* which means "order, structure, justice, truth, and harmony."

Horus, the god who represented all that is good and all

constructive forces in the universe, was once, according to a myth, deprived of one of his eyes while fighting with his eternal enemy Seth, the god of confusion, of violence, and of all destructive forces of the cosmos. Seth managed to capture the eye of Horus, demolished it, and threw it away. Thoth, the god of knowledge and magic skill, found the parts and put them together so that the injured eye was healed again. The healed eye was then called the *wedjat*-eye (*wḏ3t*), the "sound eye," and it became the symbol for the reestablishment of ordered conditions after disturbance. The eye is important in the myths, as for example in the myth of Osiris. Horus is said to have brought his eye to his dead father Osiris who devoured it as an offering meal and by means of it was recalled to life; it thus became the guarantee of life and of the regeneration of life. The fact that offerings are called "the Eye of Horus" indicates that they are considered participants in the preservation of life. This designation also characterizes the offerings as divine substance and even allows for discussions about the transsubstantiation of the materia of the offerings. The Eye of Horus is the greatest gift of all, and it constitutes the quintessence of gifts.

The concept of *maat,* also used to designate offerings of all kinds, supports the idea that the gifts to the gods were meant to strengthen the established order and to help preserve it. The goddess Maat, the daughter of the creator, represented the order and structure of the creation on all levels: on the cosmic level, in the form of the right and orderly rising and setting of the Sun, Moon, and stars; on the earth, in the form of the right and just functioning of society, its laws and rules; and in the personal human sphere, in the form of righteous and truthful lives. Maat, like the Eye of Horus, represented what was sound and perfect.

Offerings were, above all, a means to maintain the order of the world so that evil forces were checked and not allowed to prevail. They were a way to show that people put all their efforts on the side of good. Further, they were a symbol of gratitude offered by those living on earth to the divine, given in the hope of gifts in return, indicating an exchange of gifts to maintain the order of the world. At the same time they were a means of communication between the two worlds—the everyday world and the supreme reality beyond the everyday world.

The temple offerings to the gods intended for the preservation of life were actually of two different kinds. First, the offerings consisted of "all good and pure things on which the god lives." The recipient was regarded as the father or the lord of the offerings, as was often attested in the texts "to give X to its father or its lord," and supposedly the things brought back to their rightful owner were considered to strengthen the recipient so that he was able and willing to give in his turn. That process of offering was *do ut des,* which means "I give in order that you give." Second, there were offerings that represented the destructive forces, such as animals attached to the god of confusion, Seth—the ass, hippopotamus, crocodile, gazelle, and geese. They symbolize the chaotic forces threatening the created ordered cosmos.

The offerings to the dead were intended for the restoration of life. The dead were momentarily in an inert state, according to the Egyptian way of thinking, and to bring them out of that state and back to life they were given "all good and pure things on which the god lives," which was the appropriate offering for those who entered the divine world.

The Daily Temple Cult. Offerings were given to the gods during the daily temple cult. The daily ritual is known from several sources that were dated from the New Kingdom to Greco-Roman times. There are papyri, now in Berlin, dating from the twenty-second dynasty, that describe sixty-six scenes of the ritual for Amun and Mut in Karnak. Scenes of the daily cult were also depicted on temple walls, where single scenes often represented the whole ritual. The most comprehensive were found in the temple of Sety I at Abydos (thirty-six scenes), in the Edfu temple (nineteen scenes), and in the temple of Dendera (six scenes). The king was the "Lord of ritual" (*nb irt ḫt*). In all reliefs, the reigning king was always depicted officiating before a statue of god, although the duty was, in reality, delegated to the head priest of each temple.

The morning cult was the most important; the offerings were prepared in the offering room, consecrated through libations and censing, then brought into the sanctuary to be presented to the statue of the god. At noon and in the evening, a shorter ritual took place. Possibly, during some periods and in certain temples, Edfu for example, an hourly ritual was celebrated throughout the day and night.

Although many depictions and descriptions of the daily cult are known, there is no consensus about its ritual order. The cult seems to be based on human morning ritual: washing, dressing, and eating. Since the status of the cult statue was one of a mighty god, it was treated like a king and offered royal insignia. All the ritual acts were accompanied by libations and censing.

The cult was a means of entering into contact with the powers that governed the world, as well as a means of maintaining communication with the divine world. In pictured scenes, there are indications of what is being recited during the rites—what the priest says and what the god answers. Giving implied a gift in return; inherent in the nature of a gift. The very acts of the cult were, in themselves, offerings to the gods. As the priest approached the sanctuary with the intention of executing the cult ritual and bringing the offerings, the flow of gifts started in re-

OFFERINGS: AN OVERVIEW. *King Horemheb making an offering to the gods.* This eighteenth dynasty wall painting is from Horemheb's tomb in the Valley of the Kings. (SEF / Art Resource, NY)

turn. In response to the cult actions and the material offerings—such as food, clothes, and other objects—the god bestowed life on the king-priest who acted as a mediator, allowing all the country and its inhabitants to benefit. Linked with the gift of life were the gifts of stability, prosperity, and other beneficial states, such as health and joy. With reciprocal giving, the god also bestowed power on the king-priest to maintain the realm and to be victorious over the country's foes. The divine gifts were also intended to confirm the king's divine status; thus he was offered the rank and function of the great gods like Atum and Geb as well as the kingship of the gods Re and Horus.

Festival Cults. Numerous festivals marked the annual seasons and months. Each temple had its own calendar of festivals, which were celebrated with cultic activities within the temples and processions outside them. The daily cult as well as the festival activities within the temple were enacted in the privacy of the sanctuary, without the participation of the public. Only the processions took place in public. The lists of food deliveries for the festivals show that large amounts were brought in for those occasions and offered to the gods. During the processions, there were music, dancing, and singing; according to the Wisdom Literature (Ani), the gods also considered such activities as offerings.

The Offering Cult for the Dead. The dead were given offerings on the occasion of the burial, and their offerings were to be renewed forever, on principle, at certain named festivals during the year: the new year festival, the Thoth festival, the Wag festival, the Sokar festival, and others, according to a lengthy list. In reality there were probably not so many days celebrated with a meal at the tomb, during which members of the family came together (as was the custom in Thebes, for example, at the Valley Festival, from the Middle Kingdom to Greco-Roman times).

Food offerings had been given to the dead in prehistoric times, and this custom continued throughout historical times. As early as the first dynasties, the deceased was depicted before an offering table, beside which there was an inscription enumerating all that was offered. In the tombs in the Theban necropolis in the latter part of the eighteenth dynasty, this rather simple though copious meal was changed into a scene of a banquet with many participants, servants, and entertaining musicians, which resembled the family meal in front of the tomb during the Valley Festival.

The king presented the offerings to the gods in the temples, and the idea of the king as the giver of offerings was also maintained in the tombs. The offering formula used in the tombs says "an offering that the king gives"; this was actually true, owing to a peculiarity of the Egyptian offering system called reversion of offerings.

Reverted Offerings. The reversion of offerings implied that offerings went from the temple out to the necropolis. Offerings presented to the main god of the temple were carried out of the sanctuary, were presented to gods having subsidiary cults in the temple, then to statues of kings and private persons placed in the temple courts, and finally to the necropolis. After all those symbolic presentations, the offerings were distributed to the priests and all the staff involved in the rituals as a reward, or salary, for their work. This custom of reverted offerings was established as early as the Old Kingdom and was continued.

The custom of reverted offerings was not only a salary system for priests and temple staff in a non-monetary society, it also offered a possibility for old age insurance and tax planning, since fewer taxes were paid for fields belonging to the temples than for privately owned fields. From the Ramessid era onward, it was customary for higher officials to donate a statue of the king to the king and the temple, as well as the means to furnish it with offerings (i.e., fields). The king then put the donator in charge of the statue with the usufruct of the attached income. When the official retired, and thus lost the income of his former office, he kept charge of the statue and the usufruct of its income. The gifts to the gods thus had economic as well as religious implications.

Contracts of Offering. Tomb owners and the priesthood of their hometown temple contracted to ensure future offerings during the generations to come. The most well known are the ten contracts of Hapidjefa at Asyut, an important official of the Middle Kingdom; they were established between him and the *wab*-priests, the hour-priests, and some specialist priests of both Wepwat and Anubis, as well as with the overseer of the necropolis and his staff. Hapidjefa stipulated what was going to be offered to him: bread and beer, on some occasions in very large quantities: twenty-two jars of beer and 2,255 pieces of bread of two different types, a roast of meat, wicks for the torches used during nocturnal processions, and the participation of some priests in those processions. In return for such services, bread, beer, land, and part of the temple income were given to them. On the occasion of the Wag festival, he gave in return exactly the same large amount as they offered to him on that day—an example of reverted offerings. Most of what Hapidjefa gave away came from his own inherited property ("of the house of his father," according to the Egyptian term) or property from his own special funerary foundation. He also stipulated rewards originating from income that came from his office as a nomarch, which, however, was a less secure asset (the succeeding nomarch might disapprove of the arrangement and cancel it). His stipulations primarily concerned two important moments of the year: (1) the end of the year—the first epagomenal day and the fifth—which equals new year's eve and new year's day; (2) the Wag festival, eighteen days later. The end of the year was equated with death and burial, and the new year was equated with resurrection. The Wag festival was the great festival of the dead. On those occasions, ceremonies and processions took place in the temples and in the necropolis. It was important that Hapidjefa's statue was present, as it was for all dead persons.

Ancient Egyptian Terms for Offerings. The specialized words for the verb "to offer" expressed, through their associative field, the different aspects of offerings. The word most frequently used was *hotep* (*ḥtp*), written with the hieroglyph representing the offering slab (a loaf of bread), and it has also been determined with the offering table. *Ḥtp* was the word used in the offering formula, "an offering that the king gives" (*ḥtp di nsw*). *Ḥtp* also has the following meanings "to be pleased, happy, gracious"; "to be peaceful"; "to become calm"; "to satisfy"; "to pacify"; and their corresponding nouns. *Ḥtp* had to do with gifts in a holistic perspective of communication between the worlds, given in gratitude, received in happiness and grace, and leading to contentment, graciousness, mercy, and peace.

"To present" and "to hand over" the offerings were expressed by *ḥnk*; in hieroglyphic script, it is followed by the determinative of an outstretched arm holding a small offering bowl.

When the offerings had been carried in they had to be consecrated, and several words were used in that context. There is *kherep* (*ḥrp*), which has to do with the provenence of the offerings and which covers a large associative field. The offerings came from special districts and estates (*ḥrp*) that were administered (*ḥrp*) by the temples, and they had to pay taxes (*ḥrpwt*) in the form of their produce to the temple to which they belonged. So they brought in (*ḥrp*) their produce and provided (*ḥrp*) the temple with the necessities "to make offerings" (*ḥrp*). The products then had to be consecrated (*ḥrp*) and dedicated (*ḥrp*) to the gods. The word *ḥrp* has as its determinating sign an arm that holds a baton of office—very appropriate for all those different meanings. A similar determining sign, an arm with a stick, is also used in *drp*, with the meaning "to offer," or "to present and make offerings." So the word *drp* might also have to do with the consecration. That was probably also the case with *skr*, determined with a mace and with the general meaning of "to strike," but it was also used in the sense of "to offer" and "to present offerings."

Other words for "to offer" are linked to the things offered and to their treatment. Animals and birds were often offered, but first they had to be slaughtered. There is the word *i₃m*, "to offer," written with the baton of office; it also meant "to bind the sacrifice," then written with a rope as the determinating sign or with a knife to indicate the next step of the process. As to birds, they were killed by wringing the neck, *wšn*, which besides this meaning also meant "to make an offering." Another word for "to offer" and "offering" is *wdn*, which has a flower on a long stalk as a determining sign. Since flowers and vegetables were an important part of the offerings, this word is probably related to such offerings.

During the offering ritual, the offering had to be purified. A purified offering was called *wdḥw*. The word is determined by the sign of water flowing out of a recipient, as well as with the signs of bread and beer. It is related to a word of the same stem with the meaning "to pour out" and to one of the words for "offering table."

A word that has to do with offerings and at the same time with purification and purity is *abu* (*ʿbw*). What is offered to the gods must first be pure and sanctified, and that was done by a libation poured out from special liba-

tion vessels. *Abu* also means "impurity," thus including the two opposites of the notion of cleanliness; so the word comprises the meaning of the impurity that has to be eliminated to make the gift suitable for the gods. The removal of what is impure and evil leads us to the word *sfḫ*, which means "lose," "loosen," "release," "purify," "remove evil," "to separate fighting animals," "offer to god," and "offerings." So an offering is likened to the parting of fighting animals and removing evil, thus releasing forces, or freeing from bonding. It was not only what was good and pure that was offered to god but also what was bad that had been removed and laid aside, so that energies that were blocked by evil and by fighting were released and got a chance. Among the offering animals were also animals that symbolized the bad, the Seth side of existence. Those were offered so that the bad could not spread and defile the totality. In Ptolemaic times, bound victims were occasionally seen on the offering tables, symbolizing the menacing disordered forces that had to be defeated.

Types of Offerings. In prehistoric and in early dynastic times, the offerings to the dead mostly consisted of vessels, incense, oil, cosmetics, fruit, and meat. At first, there were real food and drink offerings. Next, the real offerings were supplemented with a list of the items and the amount of each offering, as were found on early dynastic stelae. Eventually, the offering lists and an offering formula could replace the gift of the material offering.

According to Winfried Barta in *Die altägyptische Opferliste* (Berlin, 1963), at first no established custom existed as to what offerings should be presented nor was there an order for appearance in the lists. The early period enumerations included both the offerings of objects that were part of the tomb equipment plus all that was needed for the burial, the commemorative ritual, and the meal. During the Old Kingdom, those two types of offerings were gradually separated into different lists. From the fifth dynasty onward, there are great offering lists of as many as ninety items for the ritual meal.

As for the temple offerings, the temple reliefs abound in offering scenes that refer to the daily temple cult. All over the walls, the richly furnished offering tables are laden with choice meat, fruit, vegetables, and so on. The scenes are often accompanied by offering lists that enumerate the items brought to the gods; such lists contain up to forty entries: bread of different kinds, several qualities of beer with different strengths; meat from cattle and wild desert animals, such as oxen and cows, sheep and goats, gazelles and antelopes; birds of different species, such as geese and water fowl; fruits, such as dates, grapes, figs, and pomegranates; vegetables, especially onions, garlic, and leek; honey; milk and wine; grease, oil, perfumes, and incense; lamps and wicks; wax; salt; natron; cloth; jewelry; and royal insignia.

According to Barta, the offering lists for the deceased and for the gods should be distinguished from the various other offering lists, those related to the festivals and to supplying the statues and the other foundations (which had the secular aim of nourishing the priests and attending staffs and probably also festival participants). The temple and tomb offerings had, rather, a sacred function, to contribute primarily to the preservation and restoration of life; although they, too, through the practice of reversion, secondarily entered the secular domain. Thus offerings were intended for the maintenance of life and of the living. Whether offerings were burned in a regular manner remains an open question. New Kingdom scenes sometimes show offerings surrounded by flames, and these have been interpreted as gifts to a god that no one else was to share. In the Late period, the destruction of offerings by fire came to symbolize offerings that represented hostile powers needing annihilation.

Human sacrifices were not part of ancient Egyptian religious rites (yet a few prehistoric and early dynastic finds have been interpreted in that way by some scholars).

Substitute Offerings. Despite the superabundance of offerings, the material offering was not the essential thing. The act of devotion was more important than the material gift, as was attested by substitute offerings. Reciting the offering formula was an adequate substitute for the actual offering. This is particularly well attested where tomb owners address themselves to passers-by, demanding that the offering formula be read on their behalf. It takes no effort to read it, and it does not take long, they say, but for the grave owner, it is of great importance. As the owner's name is mentioned in the formula, reading it out makes the owner live on, in the memory of posterity. Further evidence for substitutes of the actual offerings are the figures of wax or incense and the replicas made of cake that replace material offerings.

Sculptural Offerings. As mentioned above, the offering of a sculpture with attached fields for sustenance was a means to secure an income after retiring from official service, and it belongs to the secular sphere. There were also sculptural offerings belonging to the sacral sphere. Among them were the offering of a statuette of Maat. Well aware of how fragile is the state of equilibrium and harmony, Egyptians saw it as the main task of the pharaoh to strengthen that state, to work for *maat*. That is why the king-priest is often shown offering a small statue of Maat. In so doing, he shows that he acknowledges the principle of *maat* and tries to keep the world in the order in which it was at its creation.

A variant of the *maat* offering is found in cases where the king, as the officiating priest, offers his name to the god. This variant is particularly found with names of Ramessid kings that contain the word *maat*. Ramses II is

on many occasions seen offering his name Weser-Maat-Re to Amun, to Re-Horakhty, or to some other god, a name that means "Re's *maat*-order is powerful" or "may Re's *maat*-order be powerful." There is also the possibility of interpreting the gift of the name as an offering of the self, the name being one of the expressions of the individual.

Another gift that might be interpreted as a gift of the self is a statue of the offering king—kneeling, prostrated, or in some other posture—presented to the god by the offering king himself. It could mean that the king offers himself, his action, and his power for the maintenance of life and order. Yet there are texts, such as the Harris Papyrus, which concern such statuettes and indicate that they are made and placed in the temple "in order to give thee [the god in question] daily offerings." That is, they are meant to make the king and his gift a permanent presense in the temple. Not only the living king but also dead kings were thus permanently present in the temples by means of such statuettes piously preserved.

Priestly Personnel Connected with Offerings. Given the extensive offerings in temples and tombs, many people were involved in the handling of the offering material and of the connected rituals.

In tomb service. Usually the oldest son took the responsibility for the care of the burial, the offerings, and the subsequent rituals, but this charge could also, if necessary, be given to another individual. In the Old Kingdom, the priest in charge of the private tomb had the titles *sekhen-akh* (*sḥn-3ḫ*), *hem-sekhen-akh* (*ḥ-sḥn-3ḫ*), or *hem-sekhen-per-djet* (*ḥm-sḥn-pr-ḏt*). *Sḥn* means either "embrace," "seek," or "meet," and *akh* (*3ḫ*) is the designation of the deceased, so the title indicates the one who is in contact with the deceased. The word *ḥm* means "servant" and *pr-ḏt* is the designation of the foundation furnishing the funeral offerings of food, which the priest will eventually receive in return for his services. In the Middle Kingdom, a new title appeared, *ḥm-k3*, which means "the servant of the Ka," with the Ka being one of the designations of the immaterial, psycho-spiritual aspects of a human being. From the New Kingdom onward, the most frequent title was *w3ḥ-mw*, meaning "the offerer of the water," who, however, also took care of the food offerings.

In temples. The person responsible for the offerings and the reversion of offerings was entitled "Overseer of the god's offerings" (*imy-r ḥtpt-nṯr*) or "Scribe of the god's offerings" (*sš ḥtpt-nṯr*). These were the main officials but, given the enormous responsibilities, there were many other titles for those who handled specialized tasks.

Offerings According to the Egyptian Worldview. How did the ancient Egyptians look upon such extensive offerings? It seems that the material offerings were not the most important, and there are a few indications of this in texts from differents periods. In the *Instructions for Merikare* (lines 128–129) it is said "the good qualities of the straightforward person are preferred to the ox of the evil-doer." The same attitude toward substantial gifts was also reflected in the story of "The Shipwrecked Sailor" (line 159). When the shipwrecked Egyptian was going back home to Egypt, he took leave of the owner of the island, the divine serpent, who was a representation of the creator god, and he offered to send all the riches of Egypt to the serpent once he had reached home. The divine serpent, however, laughed at him and at his proposals and said that he had plenty of all that, since he was the rightful owner of all good things and there was nothing that did not exist in excess on his island. There was, however, one thing that he wished, that the sailor should make his name renowned in his home town. "Lo, that is my due from you." So the inner attitude of thankfulness, remembrance, and testimony about the divine were more important than the actual gifts. Most important of all was *maat*, the righteousness, justice, truth, harmony, and balance as a gift in the temples, as that which accompanies the deceased into the netherworld.

According to Marcel Mauss in his *Essai sur le don. Forme et raison de l'échange dans les sociétés archaïques* (Année Sociologique, II série, I, 1923–24, pp. 30–186), gifts are charged with the essence of the giver and imply that the receiver is obliged to give a gift in return. This is exactly what happened in the Egyptian offerings system. Humanity made offerings to the gods in order to urge the gods to give in turn. What was given was what had been received. Offerings were part of a continuous exchange of energies that corresponded to the Egyptian holistic worldview—where everything in the universe was ecologically linked in a network of energies. The human being had to take an active part in this network and contribute to its perfect functioning, so it is with this perspective that the offerings are to be understood.

[*See also the composite article on* Cults; Funerary Ritual; *and Priesthood.*]

BIBLIOGRAPHY

David, A. Rosalie. *Religious Ritual at Abydos (c. 1300 B.C.).* Warminster, 1973. Describes the offering scenes in the temple of Sety I, with an account of the interpretations of the order of the scenes, as given by various scholars.

Englund, Gertie. "Gifts to the Gods—A Necessity, for the Preservation of Cosmos and Life. Theory and Praxis." In *Gifts to the Gods: Proceedings of the Uppsala Symposium 1985,* edited by T. Linders and G. Nordquist, pp. 57–66. Uppsala, 1987. Comprises the collected papers presented at a symposium on offerings, particularly in the ancient Mediterranean civilizations but also some on Scandinavian traditions.

Frandsen, Paul John. "Trade and Cult." In *The Religion of the Ancient Egyptians: Cognitive Structures and Popular Expressions,* edited by G. Englund, pp. 95–108. Uppsala, 1989. Lectures given at two symposia on Egyptian religion, with the article discussing various opinions on offerings that are held by Egyptologists.

Meeks, Dimitri, and Christine Favard-Meeks. *Daily Life of the Egyptian Gods.* Translated from the French by G. M. Goshgarian. London, 1997. A good description of gods, temples, and cults in ancient Egypt.

Spencer, A. J. *Death in Ancient Egypt.* London, 1982. The third chapter, entitled "Providing for the Dead," gives a detailed description of offerings and gifts for the dead.

GERTIE ENGLUND

Offering Formulas and Lists

One of the most ubiquitous classes of texts found in ancient Egypt, offering formulas have their origins in the cult of the dead. Since to ancient Egyptians death was simply a continuation—albeit on a different plane—of the life they had known, shelter and material goods were considered necessary for the deceased's well-being. A tomb equipped with clothing and everyday utensils supplied their needs, along with the appropriate food and drink. Nourishment was supplied through an elaborate set of legal transactions between an individual and the funerary priests, whereby the priests contracted to furnish a specified amount of sustenance to the individual's *ka* after that person had died. The food was brought into the tomb-chapel, where it was offered to the deceased at his false door, from which his *ka* would emerge to partake of the items spiritually. To safeguard against the cessation of sustenance within the tomb, the magical power of the written and spoken word was employed, to ensure a continual supply of offerings. This took the form of an offering formula, a genre first known from the fourth dynasty. On the false door inside the tomb-chapel a prayer was carved, requesting that offerings be given to the deceased. If the actual food offerings stopped, the offering formula would magically guarantee an eternal supply of food and enable the deceased to dispense with the assistance of the funerary priests for his continued sustenance.

The offering formula operated on another symbolic level, which related to the role of the king in granting offerings. This aspect of the offering formula had its origins in the daily offerings in the divine temples, where the king ensured the well-being of the country by presenting offerings to the gods. The essential role of the king as intermediary between the gods and mankind was central to the phrasing of the offering formula. Just as the king had struck a bargain with the gods, whereby he offered goods to them in exchange for prosperity and harmony in the land, so would the king intercede on behalf of the dead to ensure them a prosperous afterlife. On a more practical level, the offering formula grew out of the fact that the divine offerings—the actual foods—were distributed to the temple employees after the gods had spiritually satisfied themselves. Egyptologists refer to this practice as "the reversion of offerings." In this way, what the king offered to the gods could subsequently be enjoyed by the population.

Given the importance of the offering formula, it is not surprising to see it on so many objects from ancient Egypt. First appearing on the architrave of the false door, the formula was also used as a descriptive title accompanying funerary scenes. It was later written on offering tables, coffins, and statues, and eventually became the standard inscription engraved on funerary and commemorative stelae.

Composition. A typical offering formula from the Middle Kingdom demonstrates the sentiments expressed in the prayer. "An offering that the king gives (to) Osiris, lord of Busiris, the great god and lord of Abydos, that he [i.e., Osiris] may give invocation offerings consisting of bread and beer, (cuts of) oxen and fowl, alabaster ([calcite] vessels) and clothing, (in fact) all good and pure things on which a god lives, for the *ka*-spirit of N."

The offering formula always begins with the phrase "An offering that the king gives" (*ḥtp-di-nsw* in ancient Egyptian). The word "offering" here was mostly meant to signify food offerings, such as the bread, beer, meat, and poultry mentioned in the prayer, but other boons were also prayed for that would guarantee success in this life and the next. Although the word *ḥtp* is rendered generically as "offering" in this phrase, the basic root meaning of the noun is "satisfaction" or "contentment," which refers to the feelings of the deceased upon the presentation of the offerings. The fact that the king (*nsw*) himself is said to "give" (*di*) the offerings shows not only the symbolic role of the king, but also the fact that the king was regarded as the source of all goods in ancient Egypt. The source of the offerings was always understood to be the "reversion of offerings" as shown by one of the items requested; this was said to be "food-offerings that have gone up before the great god."

The "great god" mentioned in the example is Osiris, the preeminent god of the dead in ancient Egypt. Osiris was the god most often invoked in the offering formulas throughout the length of Egyptian history, although other divinities could be mentioned. In the Old Kingdom, for example, the god Anubis is found in all examples that predate the fifth dynasty, at which time Osiris and Geb first appear. It is noteworthy that the god Amun-Re is first mentioned sporadically in offering formulas of the twelfth dynasty but becomes popular in the eighteenth dynasty, reflecting the historical development of this divinity. Short epithets describing the god's nature and attributes were added after the divine name (" . . . Osiris, lord of Busiris, the great god and lord of Abydos").

The next expression in the prayer, "invocation-offer-ings" (*prt-ḥrw*), literally means "the going forth of the voice" and shows the importance of the oral component of the ritual. That the offering formula was meant to be recited out loud by the dedicant is shown by the phrase itself as well as by representations that accompanied the formula. Such scenes occasionally have a caption, "Performing (the ritual of) an Offering-that-the-king-gives," and show the officiant standing with one arm raised in a gesture of invocation, reciting the offering formula aloud.

Offerings of food are the most common requests in prayer, but additional phrases such as "that which heaven gives, the earth creates, and the Nile brings" can be added before "all things good and pure on which a god lives." Lists of funerary and calendrical festivals, specifying the time at which the offerings were meant to be given, sometimes followed this request. The requests in offering formulas are too numerous to detail here, but these can be grouped into a few categories. One set deals with wishes for a prosperous career during the owner's life. This includes petitions for a long life, especially the traditional wish for a lifetime of 110 years, as well as honor and respect in one's lifetime, participation in various religious festivals, and so forth. A second group consists of requests for a successful transitional period between life and death. The most common of these is a plea for a "fine burial in the necropolis of the Western Desert," but they also include wishes for the performance of the proper rites at the tomb, the reassurance of an unimpeded way to the tomb, and the proper placement of the mummy in the grave. The third group is concerned with wishes for a happy sojourn in the hereafter. These deal with matters as disparate as the preservation of the body, the granting of proper funerary gifts for eternity, and requests for a successful outcome of the final judgment, for freedom of movement in the underworld, and so forth. Wishes for the hereafter are noteworthy, especially when found in inscriptions from the Old Kingdom. These texts contradict an older theory that only royalty could achieve a beatific state in the hereafter during the Old Kingdom, because the only sizable body of funerary literature from that period—the Pyramid Texts—was reserved for the use of kings and queens. In fact, many of the wishes for the hereafter encountered in the offering formulas from the Old Kingdom were repeated in later funerary collections such as the Coffin Texts and the *Book of the Going Forth by Day* (*Book of the Dead*), which date to the Middle and New Kingdoms respectively. The offering formula shows that all people had access to a felicitous hereafter from the beginning of Egyptian history.

Appeal to the Living. The paramount importance given to the oral component of ritual in ancient Egypt, where the spoken word was charged with such potency, is emphasized by a development in the offering formula

OFFERINGS: OFFERING FORMULAS AND LISTS. *Nineteenth dynasty offering list from the temple of Ramesses II at Abydos.* (Courtesy David P. Silverman)

known as the "Appeal to the Living." If actual offerings were not forthcoming, the deceased could appeal to passersby to recite the formula for him. A typical example of such an appeal reads: "O you who (still) live upon the earth, who shall pass by this tomb of mine, whether going northward or southward, who love life and hate death, and who shall say 'A thousand loaves of bread and jugs of beer for the owner of this tomb,' I shall watch over them in the necropolis, for I am an excellent equipped *akh*-spirit."

A further development of the Appeal to the Living is the "Breath of the Mouth" formula. In this formula, the deceased assures the living that nothing more than a spoken prayer is requested of them, and that giving is better than receiving. After the initial phrases of the Appeal to the Living, a typical example of this new formula adds: "Please offer to me from what is in your hands. But if (perchance) there is nothing in your hands, you need only say with your mouths. 'A thousand of bread and beer, of oxen and fowl, of alabaster (calcite vessels) and linen, (in fact) a thousand of all pure things for the owner of this tomb.' It is (after all) only the breath of the mouth. This is not something of which one ever wearies, and is more profitable to the one who does it than to the one who receives it." Such eloquent pleas on the part of the deceased

show the need for continued sustenance and the fear of not receiving it.

Offering List. On the walls of Old Kingdom tomb chapels, in close connection with the false door, the offering formula is often accompanied by a fuller menu of the items requested by the deceased, the offering list. With its origins in the royal offering lists found in the Pyramid Texts (for example, Spells 23 to 57 and 72 to 171), the full offering list, as it had developed by the time of the fifth dynasty, consisted of more than ninety items, engraved within little rectangles neatly laid out in rows and columns, with each rectangle giving the name and a pictorial representation of the article desired, as well as the stipulated amount to be offered. A typical examples lists "Water libation, (pour) one; Incense, (burn) one; green eye-paint, one (bag); cloth, two (strips)."

Most of the items in the list are food or drink, from the standard bread and beer to cool water and five varieties of wine, and from cuts of meat to various kinds of pastries and cakes. Also mentioned are cultic items, such as pellets of natron and incense and the traditional seven sacred oils. The list usually ends with a series of ritual acts such as "assigning the offering," "presenting cool water," "breaking the red pottery," "purification," "hand-washing," and so forth. This bill of fare is sometimes accompanied by a scene of priests performing the offering ritual before the deceased, who is seated before a table laden with the traditional half-loaves of bread and reaches with one hand for the loaves. Like the offering formula, the offering list was meant to be read out loud, with the recitation enabling the items magically to come alive for the deceased.

Changes in the Offering Formula. Although there is scholarly debate over the interpretation of the offering formula, the fact that the writing of this prayer—in terms of paleographic variations and the actual words used—changed from one period to another suggests that, over time, some innovations occurred in its interpretation. For example, the opening phrases of a typical offering formula from the Old Kingdom read, "An offering that the king gives, (and) an offering that Osiris gives, (namely) invocation-offerings consisting of bread and beer, etc.," with the word "offering" repeated. This parallel construction introduces the king and the god as equal donors of the offering. By the First Intermediate Period, this introductory phrase has been reformulated with the god introduced by a preposition, although this preposition is not always written. The formula now reads, "An offering that the king gives (to) Osiris." This change suggests that the king was still considered the original donor of the offerings, but that he now gave them to the god, who then passed the offerings on to the recipient. To clarify this new interpretation, the theologians of the twelfth dynasty added the phrase "that he may give" before the expression "invocation-offerings." That "he" in the phrase refers to the divinity and not the king is substantiated by the fact that when a goddess is mentioned—for example, Maat or Hathor—the feminine form "she" is used. Thus, the beginning of a traditional offering formula from the Middle Kingdom reads: "An offering that the king gives (to) Osiris, lord of Busiris, that he [i.e. Osiris] may, in turn, give invocation-offerings."

In the system of writing devised by the ancient Egyptians, honorific consideration made it necessary to write the word "king" before the noun "offering" and the verb "to give" (*nsw-ḥtp-di*) in the writing of the introductory phrase "An offering that the king gives," even though the syntactic relationship among the three words should have demanded that "king" be written last (*ḥtp-di-nsw*). This satisfied a calligraphic rule that divine or royal names, as well as the word for "king" and "god," should precede any other word in the sentence, regardless of their syntactic function. The beginning of the Second Intermediate Period in the late thirteenth dynasty saw a change in the order of these words (although a few earlier examples are known). From the earlier *nsw-ḥtp-di*, the order was now *nsw-di-ḥtp*, a rewriting influenced by a less formal tradition of writing, such as the bureaucracy's. Although a definitive explanation of this calligraphic change eludes us,

the actual interpretation of the prayer was not changed, as far as can be ascertained. Other significant changes in the offering formula from the New Kingdom onward were the use of new divinities invoked and a proliferation of wishes.

Such variations in the offering formula are useful to modern scholars as dating criteria, since they help to determine fairly precise dates for many monuments found outside their original context. Other variations in the prayer, such as the addition during the Middle Kingdom of the "Abydos Formula," which requests participation in the great festival of the god Osiris at the city of Abydos, also help to date and localize certain types of objects, such as commemorative stelae.

BIBLIOGRAPHY

Barta, Winfried. *Aufbau und Bedeutung der altägyptischen Opferformel.* Glückstadt, 1968. Although not readily available in even the best libraries, this is still the only major scholarly study of the offering formula; note that the author does not believe the formula changed over time.

Davies, Norman de G., and Alan H. Gardiner. *The Tomb of Amenemhēt (no. 82).* Theban Tomb Series, 1. London, 1915. Not readily available, but Gardiner's excursus on the offering formula, pp. 79–93, remains a classic study of the formula.

Gardiner, Alan H. *Egyptian Grammar.* 3d rev. ed. Oxford, 1957. Excursus B, pp. 170–173, is an excellent introduction to the offering formula and the changes in the writing as they occurred between the Old and Middle Kingdoms.

Hassan, Selim. *Excavations at Giza,* vol. 6: *The Offering List in the Old Kingdom.* Cairo, 1948. This remains one of the only full scholarly treatments of the offering list in English.

Lichtheim, Miriam. *Ancient Egyptian Autobiographies Chiefly of the Middle Kingdom: A Study and an Anthology.* Freiburg, 1988. Translations of a great number of texts that contain the Offering Formula as well as a discussion of the "Abydos Formula."

Spanel, Donald B. "Palaeographic and Epigraphic Distinctions between Texts of the So-called First Intermediate Period and the Early Twelfth Dynasty." In *Studies in Honor of William Kelly Simpson,* edited by P. Der Manuelian, pp. 765–786. Boston, 1996. An excellent example of a study using the changes in the writing of the offering formula to assist in dating museum pieces.

RONALD J. LEPROHON

Offering Tables

The bringing of offerings was the focal element of ancient Egyptian tomb and temple cults; thus, the offering table was one of the main features of cult monuments. As yet, Egyptologists have formulated no satisfactory definition of "offering tables." This term may designate any object on which offerings were placed, regardless of its place within a tomb, even though there are obvious functional dissimilarities between cult rooms and burial chambers and their respective equipment. At the same time, although temple offering tables are typologically very similar to those in tombs, they are often called "altars," which

OFFERINGS: OFFERING TABLES. *Second dynasty offering table, in the Egyptian Museum, Cairo.* (Courtesy David P. Silverman)

is confusing from the standpoint of nomenclature. Strictly speaking, only objects from cult chambers that are equipment for the perpetual cult should be regarded as offering tables; artifacts from burial chambers must be otherwise designated.

In Predynastic times, bread was put on a mat spread in front of the grave; the memory of this most ancient offering furniture survived in the shape of the hieroglyph *ḥtp,* used to spell the words belonging to the root with the general meaning "to be satiated," which becomes "to be satisfied, peaceful, etc."; hence *ḥtp* denotes "offering" (the interpretation in Mostafa 1982, pp. 81–91 is hardly plausible).

All the basic types of offering stones had assumed their forms during the Old Kingdom, although afterward they changed noticeably. They were placed in front of the tomb's false door; inscriptions and representations on them were usually oriented in a manner to make it convenient for the tomb owner, who was meant to face out toward the opening of the tomb, or, as Egyptian texts say, "going forth."

As far back as the Predynastic period, there appeared a type of little one-legged round table *(ḥȝw.t),* commonly made of calcite (alabaster) or limestone, or rarely of harder stone. Its leg is often separate from the top, suggesting that it originated from a plate on a stand. The tomb owner is represented at such a gueridon in endless table scenes, from the mid-first dynasty. Judging from these scenes, the *ḥȝw.t* was used in life and was included among the tomb furniture as an article of daily necessity.

The earliest *ḫꜣw.wt* belonged to the goods of the burial chamber, and as such they were meant to be used by the deceased; in one case, real food was found on the table, but models were also provided. These *ḫꜣw.wt* cannot be considered offering tables because they had nothing to do with the funerary cult. However, during the fourth dynasty they were also placed in front of the false doors and for some time even became the commonest type of offering stone. Thus, in different contexts, the same object could have different functions, the meaning of the artifact being obscure if isolated from its context.

The tables with thin pedestal legs were too unsubstantial and vulnerable to serve as the main site for cult offerings. Eventually this form was replaced by a round slab without protruding parts. Such round offering tables imitating *ḫꜣw.t* (e.g., GC 1304, 57037; see Bibliography below) are not among the most widespread types. Much more common were offering tables with one, two, or several rectangular depressions for libations of water, beer, or wine. These basins could be stepped, with one or several steps. Some of them had a spout to let water spurt out, but these were rare in the Old Kingdom. The original name of this type of offering stone was *š*, a word that could designate any reservoir, lake, or pond; in the Middle Kingdom it was replaced by the rather indefinite terms *mꜥḥꜥ.t* and *jꜥ*.

The most important type of offering table prevailing after the middle of the Old Kingdom imitates in stone the ancient mat for a loaf. In its simplest form, this is a rectangular slab with the *ḥtp* sign occupying its entire upper surface. The name for these offering tables was also *ḥtp*. Rarer are large *mastaba*-shaped structures, usually monolithic. Because of their considerable size (primarily their height), they could not stand in front of the false doors, and so they were placed to the side (e.g., in the Saqqara chapel of Khentika Ikhekhi). To all appearances, they were used to put out food and equipment before priestly services, and thus they cannot be considered offering tables proper. Four-legged tables (*wdḥw*) are known principally as models found in burial chambers. They were manufactured of copper or later also of bronze, or of wood. They were so light and perishable that no trace of them remains in the chapels. It is interesting that later the hieroglyph depicting *wdḥw* became a common determinative to various words for offering tables (e.g., *ḥtp*).

All the above types are extremely rare in their pure form; much more often, heterogeneous elements are combined in a single object. The upper surface may bear both the *ḥtp* sign with one or several libation basins or basins together with a circle representing the *ḫꜣw.t*. Often we also see a ewer in high relief, with its spout turned to the basin, which increases the number of possible combinations. Circular offering stones may also bear the *ḥtp* sign and/or basin and ewer. The top of the *wdḥw* table may be

shaped like the *ḥtp*, while the *mastaba*-form tables may have low legs, thus merging with the *wdḥw*. Numerous offering tables are covered with representations of food.

The earliest temple offering tables come from Old Kingdom pyramid complexes (starting with Djoser) and from solar temples of the fifth dynasty. These may be either monolithic or brick, and they differ from the private ones in their monumentality. Another contrasting characteristic is a generalization of form and an austerity in decoration.

At the early stage of development, offering tables may seem to have been regarded solely as receptacles for real food and drink, which would conform well to Old Kingdom realism in all spheres of ideology; however, this statement would be wide of the truth. The presence of pictorial decoration means that besides their functions in the ritual feeding of the deceased, the offering tables had to generate eternally the *ka*-doubles of the depicted food. Moreover, the imitation ewers prove that the offering stones were used also in rituals of purification. Even more telling are the steps in the basins, which show that the latter were associated with sacred lakes that had the same stepped sides (the earliest known example is in the valley temple of Menkaure). Most interesting in this regard is offering table CG 1330, on which each of the three steps of the basin bears a low, mean, and high water mark, referring to the respective seasons. Thus, the basin represents a reservoir filled with the Nile flood. Representations of boats with the tomb owner are seen on the sides of one offering table (Louvre E.25369), while on CG 1353, the same boats are arranged around the basin; in accordance with Egyptian artistic conventions, this means that they are shown navigating on it.

The Middle Kingdom followed some of the old traditions (see, e.g., the *ḥtp*-shaped offering table CG 23008), but serious changes are also obvious. The most significant innovation is the spread of offering tables with numerous basins arranged at different levels and joined by channels. Liquid poured into the upper basin, flowed down to the lower levels, and often drained from the offering stone through a spout. Usually very shallow basins occupy the whole surface of the offering table. At the same time, the number of representations of food increases; they often cover the bottom of the largest flat basin, so that water was poured onto them. Thus, the function of the offering tables shifted from the Old Kingdom practice, and henceforth they were used mainly for libations and purification rites.

Widespread are offering tables with two symmetrical deep basins which are also frequent from Old Kingdom tombs. Middle Kingdom materials explicate the meaning of this form. Often two deep grooves go out to the basins and join before the spout. Sometimes the basins are replaced by representations of two libation vessels that may

OFFERINGS: OFFERING TABLES. *Limestone offering table from Meidum, dating from the Greco-Roman period or later.* (University of Pennsylvania Museum, Philadelphia. Neg. # S5–36560)

have water emerging, the spurts crossing as the grooves do. These two givers of water may be identified with the two sources of the Nile, very important in the Egyptian mythological picture of the world.

The New Kingdom did not contribute greatly to the development of offering tables. Its innovations include cartouche-shaped basins, appearing as a result of the proliferation of ritual libation vessels, and pictorial compositions with two vessels flanking the *ḥꜣw.t* table and effusing water both onto the table and into the spout.

Most unusual among New Kingdom offering tables are those from the Amarna temples. For the first time since the solar temples of the fifth dynasty, the cult was transferred from dark sanctuaries to open courts, where it was celebrated on a scale incomparable with anything else in the history of Egypt. The temple courts are packed with rows of hundreds of similar brick offering tables; the most important of them, probably the place where the king served, is distinguished only by its size. Murals depicting the temples of Akhetaten (Tell-el-Amarna) with these countless offering tables are known in the Amarna tombs of Meryre I and Panehsy.

The archaizing tendencies of the Saite period, which followed the Old Kingdom tradition, affected offering tables as well as other items of tomb and temple furniture. In some cases, this resulted only in a general simplification in appearance, but careful reproductions were made of Old Kingdom forms. Archaization can be observed in some later monuments as well. [*See* Archaism.]

In the final stages of Egyptian history, the repertory of representations extended, especially as concerns the mythological significance of the offering tables. Of special note are images of the *ba* drinking water and of the owner receiving water from the goddess of the tree. Also widespread are symbols with generally positive connotations—'*nh* hieroglyphs, lotus flowers, and so on. Coexisting with this tendency is one toward simplification in the form and decoration of the offering tables. Basins become optional, and the offering table often becomes only a flat slab with representations of two vessels and food. In Roman times, the exact meaning of the decoration of the offering tables was lost, and although traditional motifs survived, they no longer formed meaningful compositions; then offering tables with purely ornamental decoration were used.

BIBLIOGRAPHY

Abou-Ghazi, D. *Denkmäler des Alten Reiches*, vol. 3: *Altars and Offering-Tables (CG 57024–57049)*. Cairo, 1980. Catalog of the foremost museum collection; in default of general studies, this and the other museum catalogs cited here are the best sources.
Borchardt, Ludwig. *Denkmäler des Alten Reich (ausser den Statuen) im Museum von Kairo*, vol. 1: *(CG 1295–1541)*. Cairo, 1937.
Gessler-Lohr, Beatrix. *Die Heiligen Seen ägyptischer Tempel: Ein Beitrag zur Deutung sakraler Baukunst im alten Ägypten*. Hildesheimer ägyptologische Beiträge 21. Hildesheim, 1983. Discusses sacred temple lakes and libation basins as their imitations.
Habachi, Labib. *Catalogo del Museo Egizio di Torino*, vol. 2: *Tavole d'offertà, are e bacili da libagione, n. 22001–22067*. Turin, 1977.
Hassan, Selim. *Excavations at Giza, V (1933–1934)*. Cairo, 1944. Contains a brief but thorough review on pp. 180–189.
Kamal, Ahmed. *Tables d'offrandes I–II (CG 22001–23256)*. Cairo, 1904–1905. An early catalog of the Cairo Museum collection.
Mostafa, Maha M. F. *Untersuchungen zu Opfertafeln im Alten Reich*. Hildesheimer ägyptologische Beiträge, 17. Hildesheim, 1982. An attempt at constructing a typology of Old Kingdom offering tables; though unsatisfactory in many respects, it at least gives an idea of the main types.
Radwan, Ali. *Die Kupfer- und Bronzegefässe Ägyptens*. Munich, 1983. Includes some metal offering tables.

ANDREY O. BOLSHAKOV

OFFICIALS. In principle, throughout the Bronze Age, Egyptian society was ruled by a hereditary aristocracy of officials. The origins of the bureaucracy lay in the necessity of organizing the palace during the Early Dynastic period. Then and later, provincial notables strove for royal recognition of their own local powers as "officials." Given the importance of the bureaucracy for the Egyptian state, the royal and provincial families were ultimately dependent upon the bureaucrats, and vice versa.

The earliest officials must have emerged from several groups: retainers and relatives of the king, and powerful provincial families. Gradual increases in the power and wealth of the state apparatus led to the emergence of a hierarchy of officials, which may be termed an administration or a government. Advancement depended upon capability and royal whims. It is customary to think in terms of an administration, but it is probably more useful to consider the Egyptian state as having been guided by royal intentions executed by officials. It is nearly impossible to distinguish the ruling class from the bureaucratic meritocracy.

In the Egyptian social structure, the greatest divide was between the literate and the illiterate. The literate class was effectively the ruling class, or at least so they thought of themselves. The literate were only a small fraction of the population, but they and their social values determined not only the character of Egyptian society, but also what we know of ancient Egypt. Scribes were effectively the bureaucrats of ancient Egypt, although in the sense of officeholders rather than office workers: they are frequently depicted supervising work in the fields, and their graffiti adorn desolate mountains in the wastes of the Sinai and the Eastern Desert as well as the quarries at the cataracts of the Nile.

They were usually dispatched to these wastes by the king. Throughout those periods of Egyptian history when the land was unified, officials were answerable to the king, and ultimately confirmed in their posts by him (or her). Many offices were legitimately hereditary, but nevertheless required royal approval, whether tacit, real, or pro forma. Both curse formulas and the "Appeal to the Living" imply that officials hope to have their children follow in their footsteps. Some officials emphasize, however, that they owed their advancement to royal recognition of their "excellence."

Lower officials may have been beyond royal reach, but kings could either promote or dismiss high officials. They could promote the competent or their favorites by pushing individuals up through the ranks, either by giving them positions of responsibility, awarding them special privileges, or redefining responsibilities. Teti awarded high offices to his personal barber. Amenophis II seems to have placed comrades in high office, at the expense of established families. Hatshepsut bartered royal privileges to officials in place, in exchange for support, and she also increased a favorite's power by increasing the scope of his responsibilities, rather than giving him high office. Akhenaten dispatched the high priest of Amun on a mission into the desert to get him out of the way. Individuals were frequently more significant than the offices they happened to hold. The king therefore determined the scope of bureaucratic power, but successful administration was ultimately dependent upon the same small pool of literate aristocrats, without whom the king could not govern.

As royal power grew (first through third dynasties) at the expense of the provinces, the state was increasingly centralized and dictated terms to the provinces. From the third dynasty, the royal family usurped bureaucratic prerogatives and bureaucrats usurped royal titles. It is not certain which of the highest officials were actually relatives of the king and which merely appropriated the title of "king's son." During the fourth dynasty, power may briefly have been concentrated in the hands of a small elite, but the argument is based on the credibility of the title "king's son." Even if royal usurpation of the bureaucracy is credible in the fourth dynasty, it diffused rapidly thereafter, and the power of bureaucrats at the center and the periphery increased in equal measure. In the subsequent collapse of the centralized state (eighth through eleventh dynasties), the provincial aristocracy recovered autonomy and the central bureaucrats lost all significance, turning to poetry rather than bookkeeping. The rebirth of the centralized state (dynasties eleven and twelve) had to contend with diffused power. The Theban kings of the eleventh and twelfth dynasties recognized independent provincial officials (nomarchs) who recognized them, while removing those who had unsuccessfully opposed them. The kings then tried to incorporate the provincial officials into the central government, and central power increased accordingly, but the centralized bureaucracy then appropriated power from the dynasty (thirteenth dynasty) before the administration failed and the land divided again (thirteenth through seventeenth dynasties). The birth of the New Kingdom was accompanied by the rapid assertion of central power throughout the land (eighteenth dynasty), and this hold was maintained, even after the kings themselves had abandoned all hope of power (end of the twentieth dynasty).

Understanding this bureaucracy is difficult for several reasons. One is that it involved overlapping responsibilities in domains that would be classified as religious, military, judicial, and financial in modern terminology. It has been noted that individual high officials not only held several positions in different hierarchies, but also—simultaneously—several positions at different levels of the same hierarchy as well. Some titles are known to have designated the same office, for example, the "Servants in the Place of Truth" were the same as the "Necropolis Workmen." Other titles may have been acquired ad hoc, such as an "Overseer of Royal Works" who built for the king in Karnak and became an "Overseer of Works of Amun." Terms like "King's Son" became titles of rank, and thus even straightforward designations can be misleading or useless. Other titles were ex officio offices held by the vizier, such as those pertaining to documents in the Old Kingdom and the priesthoods in the New Kingdom. Other titles, such as the "Guardian of Nekhen," cannot be understood today.

Because titles are our main source of information, another obstacle to our understanding is the fact that there are very few means of establishing the actual responsibilities of any given official. The significance of the titles is frequently open to quite divergent interpretations. As these interpretations themselves depend upon the interpretation of the character, origins, and development of the state, the logic is circular.

During periods of strong state rule (in the Old, Middle, and New Kingdoms), everyone in Egypt identified himself through a relation to the state. Our reconstruction of the social hierarchy of ancient Egyptian society is therefore based on a system of titles, including both secular and sacral offices. Everyone who was anybody in ancient Egypt had a title, usually interpreted as reflecting some kind of position in the apparatus of the state. Almost every official was a scribe (*sš*, *sḫ3*) who held an office (*i3w.t*). These titles usually reflect the owner's most prestigious social position. The ideology of the Egyptian state encouraged people to proclaim social elevation in terms of the state. Title and office were not identical, however, and both titles and offices changed over time. Not every officeholder was an official: water carriers, herdsmen, and cultivators can clearly be dismissed, but they would have been under the authority of overseers, who would have been officials.

Those who worked their way through the meritocracy of the Egyptian bureaucracy usually acquired a long string of titles. In official documents, they may have used a single title or several, but in their tombs, every title—including purely honorific titles—that they had ever held in their lives may have been recorded somewhere. Long chains of titles suggest that the owner was in fact an official, even if some of the titles were effectively fictitious. Many titles of lesser individuals may not have been official titles, but mere designations, and others will have been purely honorific, without a corresponding office, or without demonstrating that the owner actually fulfilled the duties of that office. Individuals with only a single title can only be identified as officials where that title is clearly bureaucratic.

Offices and Responsibilities. The top secular officials in ancient Egypt were the "vizier," the "chief of works," and various "treasurers." The top sacral officials were the high priests of the most important gods; Re and Ptah throughout Egyptian history, Amun from the New Kingdom on. During the New Kingdom at least, the vizier was, however, nominally in command of the priests of all the gods. These highest officials stood at the apex of the bureaucracy.

During the middle of the eighteenth dynasty, the king was responsible for warfare, but military authority was delegated to a crown prince, who stood at the top of a hierarchy including military officers and military officials. After the eighteenth dynasty, the military officers became increasingly involved in affairs of state and less concerned with military activity. During earlier periods of Egyptian history, the military had been controlled by the king and his officials, like the rest of the state.

Justice was the responsibility of the king, and the vizier was the final arbiter in most judicial issues. Magistrates, justices, and judges would appear to have been appointed to examine specific cases, ex officio on an ad hoc basis. Their authority came not so much from their role as judges as such, but from their prestige derived from positions in the state hierarchy.

The bureaucrats wielded administrative power; the royal family political power. Occasionally political and administrative power was combined in the hands of the royal family. During the fourth dynasty, the viziers, chiefs of works, and high priests all claimed to be close relatives of the king. This need not imply that they actually were, and certainly does not suggest that earlier officials were close relatives either. But it does suggest the appearance of a "family firm." Neither before nor after the fourth dynasty were viziers members of the royal family. Regardless of their political position however, the administration was in the hands of the literate scribes, and administrative power was the most important power in Egypt.

During the New Kingdom, there were overseers of the treasury, cattle, domains, granaries, fields, etc. Each administrative unit had its own hierarchy with its own overseer, such as the "Overseer of the Granary of the Estate of Amun," which was administratively different from the "Overseer of the Granary of the Lord of the Two Lands," although both offices could be held by the same official. The officials at the peak of the state administration usually held several (sometimes dozens of) offices, being responsible for both sacral and secular offices. By the end of the New Kingdom, a "Scribe of the Necropolis" found himself collecting taxes and a general became the high priest of Amun.

The distribution of responsibilities, therefore, did not correspond to the titles. Powerful men could presumably hide behind innocuous titles, while the powerless might sport impressive ones. During the late Old Kingdom, even high officials used antique titles while their provincial subordinates styled themselves as "viziers." Equally incongruously, the sources of wealth and income need not correspond to the titles: during the Roman period, businessmen farmers were councilors at Alexandria. Wealthy landowners doubtless formed the backbone of the Egyptian bureaucracy, since power and prestige came from office rather than wealth alone. Wealth could, however,

doubtless be increased by exploiting the possibilities of the office.

On the other hand, a valued "official" could be entrusted with military and judicial tasks aside from purely administrative responsibilities: office and responsibility were not the same. Regardless of titles and bureaucratic positions, skill and royal confidence determined advancement. At the behest of sixth dynasty kings, Weni carried out the highest judicial and military responsibilities, although he emphasizes that this was not officially his job. This case suggests that the creation of additional titles during the fifth dynasty did not really rationalize or streamline the bureaucracy, although the contemporary proliferation of titles suggests that this may have been the object. The sheer number of private tombs and their geographical distribution in provincial cemeteries (from Aswan/Elephantine to the Dakhla Oasis as well as cities along the Nile and in the Delta) is complemented by the increasing size of the private tombs of the highest officials in the Memphite necropolis, suggesting that the number, power, and wealth of the bureaucrats increased substantially during the fifth and sixth dynasties. It would appear that during the reign of Teti, the Memphite viziers actually held a number of other departments, and thus concentrated administrative power in their hands rather than delegating it. This suggests not that the bureaucracy functioned as its royal masters may have envisioned (if they had such a vision), but merely that the bureaucracy became an end in itself, which dispersed the power of the center and ultimately brought about havoc rather than order in the state.

The tendency in the Middle Kingdom was the mirror image of that during the Old Kingdom. At the reunification of Egypt during the eleventh dynasty, power was fragmented and nomarchs acting as local chiefs governed their own territories. The kings could not rely on an all-powerful centralized bureaucracy, and built diminutive pyramids as a result. The nomarchs maintained their power for some time (into the reigns of Amenemhet II or Senwosret III, depending upon the region), but eventually the provincial cemeteries were abandoned and the official cemetery at el-Lisht grew. Royal statuary increased in size during the twelfth dynasty, but the balance of power remained precarious.

During the New Kingdom, the bureaucracy was responsible for the temples and the military as well, with specific offices associated with specific tasks. During the late Old Kingdom and the first millennium BCE titles were commonly nominal and honorific rather than administrative, and the individuals themselves mattered more. During the New Kingdom, titles and officials may have been more balanced than at other times, but even then title inflation was common and responsibilities not invariably clear cut.

Officials of the State Administration

Vizier. The apex of the bureaucracy was the (*t3ty*) *tjaty*, now translated as "vizier," the Turkish word (from the Arabic) for the chief minister of state, the highest official of the land. The full title was *t3ty t3ty (n) s3b*, suggesting a combination of administrative and judicial titles. The title had existed since at least the beginning of the fourth dynasty. It is probably derived from an office (or possibly a personal name) dating to the Predynastic or Early Dynastic period, but the officeholder need not have been the paramount official, as later viziers were; the size of the incipient archaic bureaucracy was quite restricted and thus made an official second to the king superfluous. By the third dynasty, without holding the title, individual officials may have carried out the function later associated with the office during the fourth dynasty.

The fourth dynasty viziers were the paramount officials, and all claimed to be close relatives of the king. During the fifth dynasty, the nonroyal bureaucratic viziers headed a growing number of subordinates responsible for specific departments (which were then recovered by the viziers of the early sixth dynasty). The Old Kingdom viziers shared power with the overseers of works and the treasurers. By the end of the Old Kingdom, the vizier's title became an honorific assumed by numerous officials, although only one official at the capital in Memphis bore the full responsibility of the office. Viziers were highly respected. Wisdom texts have been ascribed to the viziers Ptahhotep and Kagemni. The vizier would appear to be among the few who generally worked out of an office, although treasurers probably enjoyed the same luxury.

Opinions differ on the character of the eighteenth dynasty texts relating to the office of the vizier: some maintain that the texts are contemporary, and some that they are older. Regardless, the New Kingdom texts concerning the installation and duties of the vizier suggest the breadth of his responsibilities: the vizier was effectively the administrative deputy of the king. The king was responsible for guaranteeing the cosmic order, or *maat*. Therefore, according to Egyptian judicial concepts, the vizier's highest responsibility was to ensure that justice prevailed. He was at once the official responsible for legal justice and also the official entrusted with the management of the land, and in both capacities he was obliged to be just "to the one whom he knew and the one whom he knew not." During the eighteenth dynasty, administratively, he was ultimately responsible for settling legal appeals and land disputes, managing the royal estate, supervising finances, heading the civil administration; the archives; royal and public security; and irrigation.

Although the office was hereditary for several generations during the early eighteenth dynasty, viziers were officially appointed by the king and could be dismissed by him. Kings could evidently negotiate with viziers.

Probably in return for political support, Hatshepsut allowed the vizier Weser-Amun to copy royal texts of the netherworld (the *Book of That Which Is In The Underworld* [Amduat] and *Litany of Re*) in his private tomb away from the Valley of the Kings. Conversely, Amenhotpe II evidently dismissed Rekhmire, replacing him with an old friend.

Since the beginning of the New Kingdom, the office was divided, with one vizier responsible for the Delta and another for the Valley. The division of the office may have resulted from the division of the country during the Second Intermediate Period, or it may date to an earlier period. With separate governments functioning simultaneously in the North and South, there must have been two bureaucracies with two chief ministers. After the reconquest of the North, the Thebans may simply have retained the administrative division (perhaps recalling the fate of Montuhotep IV, who seems to have been the victim of a coup d'état carried out by his vizier Amenemhet, who may have made himself the first king of the twelfth dynasty). During the first part of the thirteenth dynasty, this office was in the hands of a single family which provided the viziers Weser-Amun and Rekhmire. By the end of the New Kingdom, the vizier's powers were largely lost to the high priest of Amun.

Viceroy of Kush. The first viceroy of Kush belonged to the same family as the southern viziers of the early eighteenth dynasty. The title itself dates to the late seventeenth dynasty, and disappeared at the end of the twentieth dynasty (with a single exception). During the New Kingdom, the king's chief legate in Nubia was the "King's Son of Kush," now rendered "Viceroy of Kush." Initially the office was a military one, whereby the first viceroy, Turi, merely bore the title "King's son" (without Kush) and was also commandant of the fortress at Buhen. His successors under the early kings of the eighteenth dynasty styled themselves "King's Son of Kush" adopting, as had Turi, the title "Overseer[s] of the Southern Foreign Countries" as well, but surrendering their military role as commander of the fortress to another official. Subsequently, the position was separated from that of the fortress commander, and the administrative office moved north to Aniba. All were directly responsible to the king rather than to the vizier.

During the New Kingdom, these officials were doubtless among the highest in Egypt, along with the vizier and the High Priest of Amun. The officeholders were generally drawn from the administration of the stables, chariotry, or local administration and not from the cream of Egyptian society. The office is thus conterminous with Egyptian direct rule in Nubia. In contrast to the title, and in contrast to the viziers (who were possibly royal offspring during the fourth dynasty), the viceroy's office was swiftly opened up to the ambitious, if indeed it was ever held by an actual son of the king. Even during the New Kingdom, viziers rarely carved images of themselves on temple walls in Egypt. The viceroys in Nubia did, however, depict themselves worshipping gods at the temple in Buhen.

Overseer of works. Tombs and temples were important in ancient Egypt, and therefore throughout Egyptian history the overseers of works were among the most important officials. The usual title was that of the overseer of "all the works of the king," but major New Kingdom temples also had their own overseers (in Senmut's case, the same person with different titles). During the Old Kingdom, the office was frequently held by viziers. During the New Kingdom, the office was split off, and viziers were no longer directly responsible for construction. At all times, overseers of works were personally accountable to the king, who was responsible for all major construction projects.

Treasurer. There are several titles relating to the treasury. The treasury itself was the House of Silver, or Double House of Silver of the Lord of the Two Lands (*pr-ḥd*, or *pr.wy-ḥd*). During the Old Kingdom and the New Kingdom, it was supervised by an overseer, one of the highest officials in the land. Overseers of the Treasury (*imy-r pr-ḥd*) were responsible for finances, and in the hierarchy were below the vizier. During the intermediate periods and the Middle Kingdom, an "Overseer of the Secure Room" (*imy-r ḥtmy*) was paramount, and equal to the vizier in rank, while the heads of the treasury were subordinate officials. The New Kingdom treasury kept stocks of precious metals, semiprecious stones, ivory, and wood—seemingly everything that was received as taxes and official trade with foreign countries.

Overseer of the granaries. State policy was dependent upon grain reserves to supply the palace and the workers employed by the state. Most of the state income was not in precious metals but in grain, and virtually all wage expenses were paid in grain, so the granaries played a central role in Egyptian fiscal policy. The largest temples had their own granaries, as did cities and private individuals, and the king and his dependents. During the Old Kingdom, the vizier assumed the office of overseer of granaries ex officio, but did not emerge from the granary administration to the vizerate. The New Kingdom viziers likewise assumed responsibility for the granaries, but did not learn administration there. Although there were individual titles for the various granaries in the different parts of the administration, individual officials frequently held several of them.

Overseer of fields. Grain income was secured from the agricultural land of Egypt as production from state-run fields, as rent from state-owned fields, and also as taxes from privately owned fields. Officials, soldiers, and other state dependents were assigned fields to provide grain for their income. Together with ordinary peasants and other landholders, they had to till the fields and deliver grain or other taxes or rents to the state administration. The boundary stelae demarcating the fields determined harvest and taxation; assessments determined state income. These could be shifted by the waters of the inundation or by dishonest peasants, and therefore required verification. Lands reassigned to new tenants or owners likewise required documentation. The vizier was ultimately responsible for the income, the fields, and the boundary stelae. During the Bronze Age, the "Overseers of the Fields" and their scribes were local officials. Their main duty consisted of checking boundaries and taxes due, and they were therefore ultimately responsible for rent and tax payments. Patterns of landownership changed around the end of the New Kingdom, and this had an enormous impact on the role of the overseers of fields. Toward the end of the Ramessid period, taxation was driving small holders into tenancy status, while landownership was increasingly concentrated in the hands of large landowners and institutions, particularly the temple of Amun-Re. The overseers of fields were thus extremely important officials during the first millennium BCE, in contrast to their relative insignificance during the Bronze Age.

Chief royal archivist. The written word was among the most important elements in Egyptian society, and records were kept of laws, property, and taxes. The state kept its records in secure offices (*ḫnrt* is translated "prison" during the New Kingdom). During both the Old Kingdom and the New Kingdom, the official documents were kept centrally. The "Overseer of the Scribes of the King's Documents" was among the titles borne by Old Kingdom viziers, and the New Kingdom viziers were responsible for the archives.

General. Security, expeditions, commerce, and conquest all contributed to the emergence of the armed forces as a separate branch of government. During the Old Kingdom, administrators (including judges and "chamberlains") or "expedition leaders" could be dispatched to foreign parts with the dual goals of acquiring booty and securing the borders of Egypt. The army must have been basically a provincial militia system during the Old Kingdom and the Middle Kingdom. This ad hoc system proved insufficient by the time of the New Kingdom, when a state army was created to support the growing empire. The empire was the creation of the kings, and initially the officer corps consisted merely of administrators. The crown prince was awarded the title of Great General (*imy-r mš' wr*) and given responsibility for military affairs, much as the viziers had been given responsibility for civil affairs during the Old Kingdom.

During the thirteenth dynasty, chariotry officers gained in administrative and social significance, eventually seiz-

OFFICIALS. *Sennefer, the Mayor of Thebes, and his wife being sprinkled with holy water by a priest.* This eighteenth dynasty wall painting is from Sennefer's tomb at Qurna. (Scala/Art Resource, NY)

ing the throne at the end of the Amarna period. General Horemheb evidently enjoyed either as much or more prestige than did King Tutankhamun, and in any case became the last legitimate king of the dynasty. The army administration was entrusted to military officials at all periods of Egyptian history, but military officers came to political and military power only during the New Kingdom.

Fortress commander. The Egyptian boundaries were marked with forts at the Second Cataract of the Nile, the Mediterranean coast, and the fringes of the Delta. The fortifications were entrusted to officials (*imy-r ḫtm*) with some military but mostly administrative responsibilities, such as the collection of customs duties and the conduct of official trade. These fortresses were effectively strong-houses intended to keep the wealth secure rather than to militarily secure the boundaries as trade increased the quantities of portable wealth, usually in the form of precious metal and semiprecious stones. During the New Kingdom, fortress commanders in Libya, the Delta, and Nubia were important parts of the state treasury organization.

Justice. Many officials doubled as judges, members of courts, or magistrates. Judgeships were not therefore of-

fices as such, but offices held by officials as needed. The responsibility for dispensing justice lay with the king and the vizier in the final instance. The decisions of the judges could thus be overturned on appeal. Responsibility for the judicial system lay in the maintenance of the written records. Legal documents were maintained in archives specifically associated with the judicial system during all periods, but the titles of the departments changed, and rarely disclosed their importance. Scribes were thus responsible for justice, as were clerks and judges, depending on their role.

Chamberlains and butlers. Literally, the title translated as "Chamberlain" was the "Overseer of the Audience Hall" (*imy-r ꜥ-ḫnwty*). The short form is probably an abbreviation for the various extended forms, which append specific offices, e.g., "of the king's apartments," or "of the overseer of the treasury." The title was borne by high officials and was common—it was possibly honorary. An individual with this title is specifically placed beside the vizier in the *Instructions for the Vizier*, so it bore responsibilities. It has been suggested that these were primarily related to palace protocol, but bearers were also involved in both construction and military activity, aside from quarrying and mining. The title is probably an honorary title allowing for increased scope of authority rather than an office. A high official or a favorite would thus have become a "chamberlain," rather than a chamberlain being important as such. The "butlers" (*wdpw*) of the New Kingdom probably had a similar position.

Stewards. Wealthy families and institutions alike required managers for their fields and other property. Tiy acquired such responsibilities during the Old Kingdom, and Hatshepsut's favorite, Senmut, rose to power through the administration of the properties, without climbing either the ladder of the priesthood or the vizierate. Kheruef and others prospered in the same fashion. It was not ordinarily a route to power, but certainly one to wealth.

Governor of Upper Egypt. The title "Overseer of Upper Egypt" appears near the end of the fifth dynasty, and the officials bearing it were ultimately buried in Abydos. Although the title appears later, the office may have existed since the third dynasty. During the New Kingdom, the office was clearly part of the central state government, designed to maintain control of the provinces. It probably served the same function in the Old Kingdom. The officeholders were responsible to the vizier and the king.

Provincial Administration Officials. The state administration represented by the viziers, archivists, judges, and treasury officials stood at the apex of a pyramid controlling the state. They were dependent upon the king at all times, and their powers evaporated during periods of weak kingship or internal division; at times of state weakness, the provincial authorities became prominent.

From the time of the first unification, there must have been a central administration that dealt directly with the provinces. Individuals may have been local nobles, either unrepresented in the records, or preserved as officials responsible for state organized tasks and income. It is possible that the emergence of the state created a class of official dependent upon the court, drawn mainly from the conquered Delta, while a provincial nobility with close personal ties to the court prospered in Upper Egypt. The character of this provincial system and possible tensions between the provinces and the center must remain largely a matter of speculation, and the very character of the relationship suggested is purely hypothetical.

The twelfth dynasty's pragmatic recognition of the nomarchs reveals that when the rule of the central state tightened, provincial nobles found it expedient to allow the state to co-opt them. The centrifugal tendencies at the end of the Old Kingdom indicate that the autonomy of state officials in distant regions increased substantially when the central power weakened.

Nomarchs and mayors. By the end of the Old Kingdom, political power had fragmented, and a decentralized system emerged, which prevailed during the First Inter-

mediate Period. The reestablishment of central power was a long process, lasting well into the twelfth dynasty. During the First Intermediate Period and the early twelfth dynasty, power fell into the hands of local rulers. Originally, nomarchs (*ḥḳȝ spȝ.t*) had been administrators of the central government assigned to work in the provinces. Centrally appointed, they could be and were shifted from one nome to another. Although first documented in the third dynasty, the system of delegating central administrators to provincial seats may go back to the Early Dynastic period. The principle endured until the fifth dynasty, from which time the provincial seats became hereditary power centers in their own right, and the power of the nomarchs extended to control over the local cults, cementing the principle of decentralization. The collapse of central power ensured that political authority fell into the hands of the nomarchs (henceforth called *ḥry-tp ʿȝ* of the tenth nome), who assumed full control. The resurgence of central power under the Theban dynasties eleven and twelve was unable to eliminate the provincial powers, and even the powerful kings of the twelfth dynasty were obliged to recognize the sovereignty of the nomarchs in Middle Egypt, so that the nomarchs only ceased to exist in the reign of Senwosret III. At their peak, the Middle Egyptian nomarchs dated events according to their own reigns, only avoiding the usurpation of the kingship itself. Those allied with the northern kingdom were ejected and replaced immediately, but the process of negotiating the remaining nomarchs out was gradual, progressing reign by reign through the Middle Kingdom. When provincial power bases ceased to exist by the end of the Middle Kingdom, power was divided between cities and territories. Local power thus fell to the mayors of major towns. Although translatable as "canal digger" (or the like), the title *ʿḏ-mr* is associated with deserts as early as the first dynasty, and thus it is probably not related to irrigation. A translation as "boundary adjuster" might be nearer the mark, but desert boundaries are equally problematic. It appears to be the Lower Egyptian equivalent of "nomarch," but soon became a strictly honorary title without meaning.

Expedition leader. A characteristic feature of Old Kingdom diplomacy and trade was the "expedition" leader. The most prominent are those dispatched on commercial missions from Elephantine to Nubia, but expeditions were required as well for virtually any mining or quarrying project. Ordinarily, high officials would be appointed to carry out the task, but the officials in Elephantine designated specialists for it.

Temple Administration Officials. There was no single uniform organization for the cults of all of the gods. During the Bronze Age, state and local cults existed in parallel. By the New Kingdom, pharaoh was recognized as the ultimate high priest of all the gods, but services were executed in temples throughout the land by priests and officials acting in his name. The progressive royal usurpation of priestly authority probably proceeded in parallel with the growth of the state from the third dynasty, and must have accelerated during the fifth, twelfth, and thirteenth dynasties. The heads of the earliest cults bore archaic titles, and thus the high priest of Ptah at Memphis was the "Greatest of the Controllers of the Craftsmen" (*wr ḥrp.w ḥm.wt*), and the high priest of Re at Heliopolis was the "Greatest of Seers" (*wr mꜣꜣ.w*). Coming much later, the high priest of Amun was simply the prosaic "First Prophet of Amun" (*ḥm-nṯr tp.y n Imn*). Below them were prophets (*ḥm-nṯr*) and priests (*wꜥb*), supervised by overseers and inspectors.

Even the local cults probably had several layers of hierarchical organization, but only the highest offices were held by "officials," the high priests and overseers who were probably all appointed or recognized by the king. Only with increasing autonomy in the fifth dynasty did the nomarchs usurp responsibility for local cults. Central administrative responsibility for the local gods was thus only achieved during the New Kingdom, when mayors responsible to the central government were responsible for all local cults, and themselves subordinated to the vizier, who was responsible for all the cults of the land.

[*See also* Military; Priesthood; Scribes; State; Taxation; *and the composite article on* Administration.]

BIBLIOGRAPHY

Baines, J., and C. J. Eyre. "Four Notes on Literacy." *Göttinger Miszellen* 61 (1983), 65–96. An extensive bibliography follows remarks on social classes.

Boorn, G. F. van den. *The Duties of the Vizier: Civil Administration in the Early New Kingdom.* London, 1988. The authoritative discussion.

Cruze-Uribe, E. "A Model for the Political Structure of Ancient Egypt." In *For His Ka Essays Offered in Memory of Klaus Baer*, edited by D. Silverman, pp. 45–53. Chicago, 1994. A very different approach from that of Baines and Eyre.

Donadoni, S., ed. *The Egyptians.* Chicago, 1997. Chapters discuss "scribes," "bureaucrats," "priests," etc.

Fisher, H. G. *Egyptian Titles of the Middle Kingdom: A Supplement to Wm. Ward's Index.* 2d ed. New York, 1997. Essential.

Gauthier, H. "Le titre (*imi-ra âkhnouti*) et ses acceptions diverses." *Bulletin de l'Institut Français dé l'Archéologie Orientale* 15 (1918), 169–206.

Helck, W. *Zur Verwaltung des Mittleren und Neuen Reichs.* Leiden, 1958. The standard work on the subject. Unfortunately, out of date and based on speculative interpretations about the character of the Egyptian state and the degree to which conclusions can be drawn from titles.

Helck, W. *Untersuchungen zur Thinitenzeit.* Wiesbaden, 1987.

Helck, W., E. Otto, and W. Westendorf, eds. *Lexikon der Ägyptologie.* 7 vols. Wiesbaden, 1975ff. Numerous articles on "Beamtentum," "Landesverwaltung," "Gaufürst," etc.

Kanawati, N. *Governmental Reforms in Old Kingdom Egypt.* Warminster, 1980.

Martin-Pardey, E. *Untersuchungen zur ägyptischen Provinzialverwaltung bis zum Ende des Alten Reiches.* Hildesheim, 1976.

McDowell, A. G. *Jurisdiction in the Workmen's Community of Deir el-Medina.* Leiden, 1990. Detailed discussion of complex issues.

Römer, M. *Zum Problem von Titulatur und Herkunft bei den Ägyptischen "Königssöhnen" des Alten Reiches.* Berlin, 1977.

Schmitz, B. *Untersuchungen zum Titel Sꜣ-njswt "Königssohn."* Bonn, 1976.

Schulman, A. R. *Military Rank, Title, and Organization in the Egyptian New Kingdom.* Berlin, 1964.

Strudwick, N. *The Administration of Egypt in the Old Kingdom.* London, 1985. Balanced and careful.

Ward, W. A. *Index of Egyptian Administrative and Religious Titles of the Middle Kingdom.* Beirut, 1982.

DAVID A. WARBURTON

OGDOADS. *See* Myths, *article on* Creation Myths.

OILS AND FATS. As natural products, oils and fats were used at all levels of Egyptian society: they were employed as illuminants, lubricants, and emollients and had culinary and medicinal purposes. Mixed with components such as flowers, herbs, and/or resins, oils and fats formed the matrix of a variety of scented unguents, used not only for daily life but for funerary and religious rituals.

The extraction of oils and fats was begun in ancient Egypt by the Early Dynastic period. Seeds, nuts, or tubers were ground, pressed, or boiled to separate oils from pulp; fats were removed from wild and domesticated animals. Chemical analysis confirms their presence in jars dating to the first dynasty, but the identification of specific plant or animal sources by scientific means is problematic. Thus, the lists of potential oil sources, such as that proposed by A. Lucas, in Lucas and Harris, *Ancient Egyptian Materials and Industries* (London, 1962), have not been verified. Many oil-producing plants are multipurpose, and lexicographical problems exist for interpreters. Therefore, proposed introductions of certain foreign oils to Egypt, based purely on linguistic grounds, remain unconfirmed. Translations of *bꜣk*, a Middle Kingdom term for either "moringa" or "olive," and *nḥḥ*, a word that first occurred in New Kingdom texts from the mid-eighteenth dynasty as "sesame" or "olive," deserve caution.

Taking into account regional botanical studies and archaeobotanical remains, from Predynastic times onward, available oil sources included oilseeds from castor (*Ricinus communis*), colocynth (*Citrullus colocynthus*), and linseed (*Linum usitatissimum*), as well as nuts from balanos trees (*Balanites aegyptiaca*) and tubers from tigernuts (*Cyperus esculentus*). Moringa nuts (*Moringa aptera*) are another presumed early source, although botanical remains are absent until Ptolemaic times. Among some

OILS AND FATS. *A woman wearing a fat cone on her head.* These cones were often worn at banquets; as they melted, they anointed the bearer with perfumes or insect-repelling substances that were blended into the fat.

later Near Eastern introductions, safflower *(Carthamus tinctorius)* did not reach Egypt until the Middle Kingdom and then, perhaps, primarily as a dye plant. Kernels from imported Aegean or Western Asiatic almond trees *(Prunus dulcis)* first occurred in the mid-eighteenth dynasty. Oil from the seeds of the opium poppy *(Papaver somniferum)* was transported, at the earliest, to Egypt via the Aegean during the New Kingdom. Lettuce and radish oils were noted by Lucas and Harris, but if artistic representations of lettuce occurred from Old Kingdom times, archaeobotanical remains of both were missing until the Greco-Roman period. More controversial still is the date of introduction of sesame *(Sesamum indicum)*. Although possible finds from Predynastic-era Naqada and Tutankhamun's tomb have been noted, most archaeobotanists would not place the introduction of sesame (probably originally from the Indus Valley) into the Near East any sooner than the first millennium BCE and then, subsequently, into Egypt.

Olives *(Olea europaea)* were exploited for their oil in Palestine by Chalcolithic times. Their inception in Egypt has been dated to the Middle Kingdom, but olives were probably not cultivated there until New Kingdom times, if not later, and then only in a limited way. Therefore, olive oil may have been one of the first imports to Egypt. Lucas and Harris also mentioned oil of cinnamon from India, although this was unlikely to have been accessible until the Greco-Roman period and was probably a product of the distillation of the leaves and bark, rather than a fixed oil.

With regard to animal fats, many sources existed in Egypt, from Predynastic times onward, probably as a by-product of butchery practices. Substantial deposits of fat

were available in many common domesticates—cow (genus *Bos*), pig (genus *Sus*), sheep (genus *Ovis*), and others—as well as fish oil or fats from a range of wild birds and other animals. Animal fats might be rendered (melted down) or stored and used in solid form; in addition, butter and fat-rich dairy products were made from the milk of various animals.

Most oils could have been used for diverse purposes; however, the toxic properties of castor oil would have restricted its culinary use, and animal fats used in food would need to be extracted soon after slaughter to retard rancidity. Similarly, linseed oil is prone to rancidity. Moringa and balanos have little odor or taste, making them especially suitable as a base for scented ointments.

One group of unguents of particular significance, recognized today as the *Seven Sacred Oils*, were known to the Egyptians simply as *mrht*, a generic word for any type of vegetable oil or animal fat. Their lack of distinction is understandable, since oils and fats are chemically similar, and both are fluid when heated. In fact, a number of words believed to refer generally to oils or fats, such as *nwd*, *sgnn*, and *mrht*, are also used to describe scented ointments. Thus, the title translated as "oil boiler" might apply to an individual involved in the production of raw oils and fats and/or scented admixtures, making it difficult for Egyptologists to distinguish between these two industries.

Tomb reliefs indicate that scented ointments were prepared by grinding the aromatic components, steeping them in heated oils or fats, and wringing them out in a sack press, which was identical to that used for expressing wine. Although comparable representations of oil manufacture are lacking and no archaeological evidence of presses or oil/fat processing workshops have been identified from pharaonic sites, it seems feasible that oil processing was carried out in an analogous manner. Alternatively, ground or mashed pulp might have been heated or brought to a boil in water, just as the title oil boiler suggests. Since oil floats on water, it can be separated and skimmed into containers. Fatty animal deposits could have been treated in much the same fashion, the fluid fat skimmed from the surface as it floated above the water, then stored in containers.

The production of fats and oils may have been carried out to some degree as a "cottage industry," but texts make it clear that oil boilers were attached to major temples. Processing areas were part of the workshops in temple and palace precincts, and oils and fats were stored in containers in their treasuries. Both commodities were clearly part of the redistributive temple economy. They would be handed out as wages to workmen, and they were important for illumination while working in the tombs. Elaborate stone vessels were often used for the storage of valuable ointments, but pottery amphorae known as *mn* jars were used, as for most fluids, for bulk storage and transport. Their capacity, given in fluid *hin* measures (roughly half a liter/quart), generally ranged from 20 to 40 liters/ quarts. The transport of oil from Syria/Palestine in imported Canaanite amphorae, also known as *mn* jars, was recorded in documents such as the Annals of Thutmose III, where hundreds of oil jars were received in a single year, implying the importance of these products on both the domestic and the international level.

[*See also* Toiletries and Cosmetics.]

BIBLIOGRAPHY

Chassinat, Émile. "Le mot *mrḥt* dans les textes médicaux." In *Recueil d'études égyptologiques dédiées à la mémoire de Jean-François Champollion*, Bibliothèque de l'École des Haute Études, pp. 447–465. Paris, 1922. Discusses the lexicography of oil and fat sources.

Germer, Renate. *Flora des Pharaonischen Ägypten*. Mainz am Rhein, 1985. Provides information of the botanical sources of vegetable oils in ancient Egypt.

Janssen, Jac. J. *Commodity Prices from the Ramessid Period*. Leiden, 1975. Details on the use of oils in payments to workmen during the New Kingdom.

Lucas, A., and J. R. Harris, ed. *Ancient Egyptian Materials and Industries*. 4th rev. ed. London, 1962. The chapter "Oils, Fats and Waxes" has been the standard reference work for decades but is now largely superseded by more recent research.

Sandy, D. Brent. *The Production and Use of Vegetable Oils in Ptolemaic Egypt*. Atlanta, 1989. Also provides information on oilseed crops.

Serpico, Margaret, and Raymond White. "Oil, Fat and Wax." In *Ancient Egyptian Materials and Technologies*, edited by P. Nicholson and I. Shaw, Cambridge, forthcoming. General background on all aspects of the use and production of oils and fats.

Serpico, Margaret, and Raymond White. "A Report on the Analysis of the Contents of a Cache of Jars from the Tomb of Djer." In *Aspects of Early Egypt*, edited by J. Spencer, pp. 128–139. London, 1996. Scientific evidence of oils and fats in Early Dynastic times and a general overview of their sources.

Stager, Lawrence E. "The Firstfruits of Civilization." In *Palestine in the Bronze and Iron Ages: Studies in Honour of Olga Tufnell*, edited by J. N. Tubb, pp. 172–188. London, 1985. Commentary on olives in the Near East and Egypt, including lexicography.

Zohary, Daniel, and Maria Hopf. *Domestication of Plants in the Old World*, 2d. rev. ed. Oxford, 1993. Provides valuable and current botanical and archaeobotanical background on most oilseed crops; although the entire Old World is covered, occurrences in Egypt are discussed.

MARGARET T. SERPICO

OLD KINGDOM. [*This entry surveys the Old Kingdom, with reference to that period's major kings, main historical events, and significant cultural and social developments. It comprises five articles:*

An Overview
Third Dynasty
Fourth Dynasty
Fifth Dynasty
Sixth Dynasty

For related discussions, see articles on individual Old Kingdom kings.]

An Overview

The Old Kingdom is the name usually given to ancient Egypt's third dynasty (c.2687 BCE) to the end of the sixth (c.2190 BCE), although some Egyptologists apply it through the end of the eighth dynasty. The key role in the transition from the second to the third dynasty was probably played by Queen Nimaathep. According to one theory, she was a secondary wife of the last second dynasty king, Khasekhemwy, and secured a leading position for herself and her children, the first two rulers of the third dynasty, after the chief queen failed to produce an heir to the throne. According to another theory, Nimaathep was Khasekhemwy's daughter and a wife of the first third dynasty pharaoh, Nebka, and mother of Netjerikhet Djoser, its most powerful ruler. A find at Abydos indicates that King Djoser arranged the funeral of Nimaathep. The beginning of the third dynasty has therefore become the subject of renewed discussion, which so far remains inconclusive.

Third Dynasty. The real founder of the third dynasty was Netjerikhet, better known under the name Djoser (r. 2687–2668 BCE). His fame has been ensured down the centuries by the glory of his post mortem residence: the Step Pyramid at Saqqara, and the complex of burial and cult buildings surrounding it. This is the oldest of all Egyptian pyramids, and its design was evidently connected with the beginning of the solar cult. Imhotep, probably Djoser's son, is considered to have been its architect. It is believed that the complex was built on the model of Djoser's earthly residence, but while this had been constructed out of perishable materials (mud brick, timber, reeds, and matting), the burial complex was supposed to last forever and was therefore built of stone, principally limestone. The change of medium, however, was too sudden for the established forms of architecture to be fully adapted to the properties of the new material. The result, the oldest work of monumental stone architecture in the world, is both massive and in many respects bizarre. It is also proof of the unprecedented economic and political flowering that Egypt enjoyed under Djoser's reign of perhaps twenty years, and of the accompanying successes in astronomy, surveying, mathematics, crafts, and the organization of labor forces. Egyptian expeditions were dispatched to the Sinai and its deposits of malachite, turquoise, and copper ore. Djoser also left a relief similar to that of Sanakht on the rocks of the Wadi Mughara.

Djoser's successor, Sekhemkhet, ruled for only a short time. He started to build himself a tomb complex similar to that of Djoser in the vicinity of the Step Pyramid, but he never completed it. A sealed calcite (Egyptian alabaster) sarcophagus was found in the underground burial chamber under the unfinished pyramid. Still lying on the sarcophagus was the withered funeral bouquet, but the sarcophagus itself was empty. The find poses yet another of the many unanswered questions of Egyptian archaeology. Among the few antiquities that survive from the time of Sekhemkhet is the rock inscription that he, too, had cut in the Wadi Mughara.

The remainder of the third dynasty is somewhat obscure. Apparently there was a distinct weakening in the ruling line. Several rulers were crowned in quick succession. If we omit Sanakht, who has not been securely dated, then two of these—Khaba and Huny—emerge more clearly. It is to Khaba that an unfinished pyramid (known as the Layer Pyramid) in Zawiyet el-Aryan, a few kilometers north of Saqqara, has been attributed.

The third dynasty ended with the reign of Huny (r. 2673–2649 BCE). It was probably this period that saw the founding of the fortress on Elephantine, a small island at the First Cataract of the Nile by Aswan, on Egypt's southern frontier. Huny was the first (if we except a somewhat obscure fragment of a cartouche from Beit Khallaf) to write one of his names—the so-called throne name—in a cartouche, an oval symbolizing the eternal and boundless authority of the ancient Egyptian ruler, the pharaoh.

The tomb of the high state official Metjen at Saqqara has been dated to the reign of Huny. Biographical inscriptions on its walls include information on the material circumstances of the tomb's owner, which provide evidence of the deep economic and social changes that occurred in Egypt during the third dynasty. At its onset, the pharaoh was the sole proprietor of the entire country, owning all fields and gardens, waters, mines, quarries, and livestock, as well as exercising unlimited power over the whole population. Metjen's inscription shows, however, that at the end of the third dynasty a commoner could own a large amount of property and could even acquire it by purchase.

Fourth Dynasty. The rulers of the fourth dynasty developed to its highest point the state dogma of ancient Egypt: the idea of the divine monarch, who is the guarantor of the stability and prosperity of the country. They created a strictly centrist state in a form that none of their successors was to achieve again. At the summit of a social order, which has itself been likened to a pyramid, was the pharaoh, a living god, source of all power in the state and the guarantor of the prosperity of the entire Egyptian population. He entrusted the highest offices both in state administration and in religious cults to his nearest relatives, and this small ruling group ran the state through an ever more numerous lower bureaucracy. Trade and crafts were in state ownership. The most numerous and lowest social group, the rural agricultural population, had the status of serfs.

According to later tradition, Huny's immediate heir, Sneferu (r. 2649–2609 BCE), was a great and beneficent ruler. Such a reputation might have been reinforced by his name, which contains the word "good," and also by the unusual architectural monuments that he left. In addition to a pyramid in Meidum, the site of Sneferu's original residence of Djedsneferu, he was also responsible for the two large pyramids at Dahshur known as the Bent Pyramid and Red Pyramid. The reasons behind his abandonment of Meidum and establishment of a new royal residence at Dahshur are not entirely clear. It is possible that they were related to an attempt to move closer to the capital city Inebuhedj (later Memphis), or perhaps they were of a family nature. Members of the so-called first generation of Sneferu's family would have been buried at Meidum, and those of the following generation in Dahshur. During the building of the Bent Pyramid, the construction was threatened by the instability of the geological foundation and the building plan was changed, giving the pyramid its peculiar shape. Although this pyramid was completed, Sneferu had another built, in which he was buried. The most recent archaeological research has shown that Sneferu was responsible for yet another pyramid, albeit small. It stands on a rocky hillock in Sila, on the eastern edge of the Faiyum Oasis, and probably has a purely state-symbolic significance. Sneferu's four pyramids contained an aggregate volume of roughly 3.7 million cubic meters of stone, making him the most prolific builder of pyramids in the history of Egypt.

The construction of the pyramids was merely the external expression of the consolidation of internal political affairs—after the weakening of the state that had occurred during the second half of the third dynasty—and also of the economic upswing that occurred under Sneferu's government. Written records of the mining of raw materials, even in distant and relatively inaccessible areas of Nubia and Sinai, and of trading contacts with parts of the Levant (from which Egypt obtained, among other commodities, high-quality timber) are consonant with this picture of prosperity.

Khnemkhufu, the younger son of Sneferu and his chief wife, Queen Hetepheres I, is better known as king under the shorter version of his name, Khufu (r. 2609–2584 BCE). He evidently came to power because the heir to the throne had died prematurely. Khufu transferred the royal residence even farther north, to present-day Giza, and there, on a rocky promontory of the Libyan desert plateau, he established a new royal cemetery. He continued Sneferu's policy of consolidating central power and building a strong state. Rich booty flowed into the state treasury from his military campaigns in Nubia and Libya. One remarkable building of the period is the Sadd el-Kafara, the oldest archaeologically attested ancient Egyptian dam, which is situated in the Wadi Gerawi in the mountains east of Helwan.

Khufu is best known, however, as the builder of the Great Pyramid at Giza. His pyramid inspires admiration not only for its size but also for the complexity and originality of its system of chambers and passages, partly underground and partly within the pyramid itself. The Great Gallery and the King's Chamber, in particular, are masterpieces of ancient Egyptian architecture. A whole complex of other buildings adjoined the pyramid, including a valley temple, a causeway, a mortuary temple at the eastern foot of the pyramid, and five large funerary boats placed in pits in front of the eastern and southern sides of the Great Pyramid. Three small pyramids belonging to Khufu's mother and wives are included in the complex; the northernmost probably belonged to Khufu's mother Hetepheres I, the middle to Meretites, perhaps the oldest of Khufu's wives, and the southernmost has been attributed to Queen Henutsen.

East of the Great Pyramid, a cemetery was established for members of the royal family and high state officials. These persons had no greater wish than to continue, after death, to dwell in the shadow of the pharaoh whom they had served in life. Another large cemetery, west of the pyramid, was the burial place of the pyramid's builders and managers of works, mortuary priests, and important officials. The craftsmen and artists who shared in the building established a cemetery for themselves not far away, on the southeastern edge of Giza and near the site of a big bakery, food store, and other facilities that had provided sustenance for the large number of people employed in the construction of the pyramid.

The long-term support of a mortuary cult depended on income earmarked from what were known as mortuary estates. The ruler would bestow such income on the owner of a tomb as an expression of his favor. The building of the tomb depended on the pharaoh's favor, beginning with the allocation of a site in the cemetery and ending with royal assent to the use of stone from the sovereign's quarries.

The construction of huge pyramids and large neighboring cemeteries, together with the establishment of mortuary cults, was a serious drain on Egypt's material and labor resources. This ultimately became one cause of the growing economic and social difficulties that emerged just as the greatness and glory of the land seemed at its height. The unexpected death of Crown Prince Kawab, the eldest of Khufu's sons, probably led to a split in the royal family, which also contributed to the gradual decline and the demise of the fourth dynasty.

Khufu was followed by Djedefre (r. 2584–2576 BCE), who probably did not come to power by direct legitimate succession. Djedefre probably favored the solar cult that was spreading at the time. He built his pyramid not at Giza but several kilometers to the north near the present-

OLD KINGDOM: AN OVERVIEW. *Group statuette of the fifth dynasty steward Memi and his wife Sabu, from Giza.* This statuette is of white limestone and was originally painted. (The Metropolitan Museum of Art, Rogers Fund, 1948. [48.111])

day village of Abu Rowash. Earlier it was believed that the pyramid had never been completed, but now the evidence suggests that it has simply been particularly badly devastated. The apparently deliberate damage inflicted on Djedefre's burial complex, which was supposed to have occurred in the reign of Khufu's younger son Khafre (r. 2576–2551 BCE), was once considered evidence of conflict inside the royal family. Today, however, it is believed that the devastation of the complex occurred only much later, primarily in the Roman period. It is not clear whether Djedefre's wife Khentetenka was buried at Abu Rowash. Another of the ruler's wives was evidently Hetepheres II. The celebrated sculptures of Djedefre that are today kept mostly in the Louvre were discovered at Abu Rowash.

Before his ascent to the throne, Khafre was probably called Khufukhaf, and one of the large tombs in front of the Great Pyramid in Giza had been prepared for him. It appears that in Khafre the main branch of the royal line returned to power, but the influence of the solar cult continued to grow. Khafre too had a pyramid complex built at Giza. Fragments of the casing have survived to the present day at the top of the pyramid, which was almost as high as Khufu's. The architecture of the mortuary and valley temples is distinguished by its severe, geometric, but nonetheless effective style. The valley temple is the site of the discovery of the famous diorite sculpture (now in the Egyptian Museum in Cairo) of Khafre seated on his throne, with his head protected from behind by the unfurled wings of the falcon god Horus. The Great Sphinx and the temple lying before its front paws are also parts of the complex (although some attribute the Sphinx to the earlier Khufu).

Probably the last legitimate ruler of the dynasty established by Sneferu, and also the last to have his pyramid built at Giza, was Khafre's son, Menkaure (r. 2551–2523 BCE). His pyramid is the smallest of the three royal pyramids at Giza, and some parts of the tomb complex were hurriedly completed by his successor. Archaeological excavations in the valley temple discovered the celebrated "Menkaure triad," representing the pharaoh accompanied by the goddess Hathor and the leading deities of several Egyptian nomes.

The death of Menkaure was followed by a serious dynastic crisis, probably connected with the premature death of his son Khuenre, the legitimate heir to the throne. Menkaure was succeeded by Shepseskaf (r. 2523–2519 BCE), possibly his son by a secondary wife. Shepseskaf completed the construction of his predecessor's pyramid complex, but he built his own tomb at a remote site at South Saqqara. Today it is known by its Arabic name, Mastabat Faraun ("the Pharaoh's bench"), because it is in the form of a large *mastaba* or, more likely, a sarcophagus. The shape of the tomb has sometimes been erroneously regarded as an expression of Shepseskaf's opposition to the growing political power of the solar priesthood, with which the pyramid form was supposed to be closely connected. The relatively small dimensions of Shepseskaf's tomb provide, however, further evidence of the gradual decline of the economic and political power of pharaohs at the end of the fourth dynasty.

The extinction of the fourth dynasty and the rise of the fifth constitute one of the most tangled genealogical and historical problems of the entire Old Kingdom. At this still obscure period, an important role was played by Queen Khentkawes I, probably Menkaure's daughter, whose isolated two-step tomb lies near Menkaure's valley temple in Giza. There are many indications that when the main branch of the royal line became extinct on the male side, it was this queen, the royal mother, who became the link between the old line of Sneferu and the new line of the "sun kings," as the pharaohs of the fifth dynasty are sometimes called today. The queen was the bearer of a title that is unique in the history of ancient Egypt. It can be translated in two ways, both grammatically correct but entirely different in meaning: "Mother of the Two Kings of Upper and Lower Egypt," or "King of Upper and Lower Egypt and Mother of the King of Upper and Lower Egypt."

Fifth Dynasty. Userkaf, the first pharaoh of the fifth dynasty (r. 2513–2506 BCE), may have been another of Menkaure's sons by a secondary queen—even, perhaps, Shepseskaf's brother. The solar cult evidently reached its zenith during his reign, and it was at this time that the title "Son of Re" became an inseparable part of royal titulary. Userkaf also established the first sun temple, in the Memphite necropolis near the present-day village of Abusir. Five succeeding pharaohs of the fifth dynasty were to build similar temples, which became important elements not only of the solar cult but also of the royal mortuary cult. As yet, however, only two of these—those of Userkaf and Newoserre Any—have been discovered.

During a reign of perhaps eight years, Userkaf also undertook a military expedition into Nubia, and the find of a stone vessel with his name on the island of Kythera in the Aegean Sea testifies to existence of commercial contacts between Egypt and this distant region. Perhaps in an attempt to bolster the legitimacy of his ascent to the throne by closely identifying himself with the symbols of Egyptian statehood—Djoser and his Step Pyramid—Userkaf chose a site near the northeastern corner of Djoser's complex in Saqqara for his own modestly proportioned pyramid and the even smaller pyramid of his wife.

Userkaf's successor and perhaps also son, Sahure (r. 2506–2492 BCE), reigned for a longer period, but he continued along the lines of his predecessor in both domestic and foreign policy. Surviving written records show that during his reign copper ore was mined in the Wadi Mughara in Sinai and diorite in quarries near Abu Simbel; cedarwood was imported from the Levant via Byblos, and an expedition to obtain exotic southern goods was sent to the mysterious land of Punt, which was probably on the coast of present-day Somalia.

Sahure had his tomb built in the vicinity of Userkaf's solar temple at Abusir and founded a new royal necropolis there. His pyramid complex is a milestone in the development of the ancient Egyptian royal tomb. No longer was priority given to huge size and volume; instead, the emphasis was on balanced proportions, the color harmony of various types of stone, and brilliant relief decoration, all of which created an extraordinarily effective whole.

It was not Sahure's eldest son and legitimate heir, Netjerirenre, who succeeded him, but Neferirkare Kakai (r. 2492–2482 BCE), whose origin is unclear. Several modifications made to reliefs from Sahure's mortuary temple may suggest that the two rulers were brothers. If so, then an uncle usurped the throne at the expense of a crown prince who was not yet of age. Neferirkare's wife, Khentkawes II, mother of the pharaohs Raneferef (Neferefre) and Newoserre Any bore the same unusual title as Khentkawes I.

The reign of Neferirkare Kakai saw a continuing rise in the numbers of the bureaucracy and priesthood and gradual weakening in the power of the ruler, even though he remained a god on earth. He had his own pyramid, and a smaller one for his wife, built at Abusir. At the time of his death, however, both were still unfinished; they were completed (in the case of the pharaoh's complex, only partially) by his successors. Papyrus fragments from the archive of his pyramid temple, the oldest archive of its type yet discovered in Egypt, were found by tomb robbers at the end of the nineteenth century. These records provide insights into the organization of royal mortuary cults and the complex economic, administrative, and religious conditions of the period. It seems that the king managed to complete his solar temple, which has not yet been discovered, but which, according to contemporary written sources, was the largest of all the solar temples built by pharaohs of the fifth dynasty.

Raneferef (Neferefre), the eldest son of Neferirkare and Khentkawes II, ruled only very briefly (2475–2474 BCE) and scarcely had time to begin the construction of his pyramid at Abusir. Together with his mortuary temple, and changed from the original design into a square-shaped *mastaba*, the pyramid was completed by his successor, Newoserre Any (r. 2474–2444 BCE), who was probably his younger brother. Many important antiquities have been found in Neferefre Kakai's brick mortuary temple, among them another papyrus archive and a set of stone statues of the pharaoh. Although the existence of Neferefre Ka-

kai's solar temple, "Re's Offering Table," is recorded in an inscription from the Tomb of Ti, an important official of the time, efforts to locate it have not yet succeeded.

There are many indications that after Neferefre Kakai's death disputes once again broke out between the two discordant branches of the royal family. (It is probably to this period, rather than before Neferefre Kakai, that we should date the short reign of Shepseskare, the pharaoh of obscure origin.) The situation began to stabilize only after Neferirkare Kakai's younger son Newoserre Any assumed power. The legitimacy of his ascent to the throne was evidently secured by the royal mother, Khentkawes II. This remarkable historical situation, now occurring for a second time, was to fascinate ancient Egyptians for many centuries to come. A queen who appears to combine in her person features of both Khentkawes I and II ultimately entered their literature as the heroine of a tale about the divine birth of the kings of the fifth dynasty, as recorded in the Westcar Papyrus and dated a thousand years later than the time in which it is set. Newoserre's path to power was apparently smoothed by several important officials and courtiers, among them Ptahshepses, who was the vizier, Newoserre Any's son-in-law, and the owner of a monumental *mastaba* in Abusir—the largest tomb of its kind yet known from the Old Kingdom.

Newoserre Any also had his pyramid complex built at Abusir, as well as fulfilling his obligation to finish the three incomplete complexes belonging to his father, mother, and elder brother. There was already a shortage of space for his own pyramid, and so the site and peculiar plan of the entire pyramid complex represent the best compromise that the circumstances would permit. Newoserre Any's solar temple lies in Abu Ghurob at the northern edge of the Abusir necropolis.

The reign of Newoserre Any's successor, Menkauhor, was short (r. 2444–2436 BCE). This pharaoh, whose origins are obscure, left a rock inscription in the Wadi Mughara and was the last of the kings of the fifth dynasty to build a solar temple. Neither the temple nor Menkauhor's pyramid have been discovered.

Djedkare, also known as Izezi, ruled for more than thirty years (r. 2436–2404 BCE). In an attempt to strengthen royal power and improve the administration of the country, he established the office of "Governor of Upper Egypt," with a seat in Abydos. He also carried out the reorganization of the royal mortuary cults at the Abusir necropolis, but he decided to build his own pyramid in South Saqqara, together with a smaller one for his wife.

The reign of Djedkare saw important changes in the sphere of religion and the mortuary cult. The solar religion was evidently declining in importance, and the cult of Osiris, god of the dead and symbol of the eternal natural cycle of life and death, was coming to the fore. The mortuary cult was also becoming increasingly popular, and religious privileges once reserved for the ruler and the highest state dignitaries were being appropriated and adapted by the lower ranks of society. Perhaps as a result of changes in religious beliefs, and possibly also for economic reasons, Djedkare abandoned the practice of building solar temples, and his successors did not resume it.

Under Djedkare's rule, trading expeditions were sent to Byblos, Punt, Nubia, and other countries. These were not purely commercial in character, as is shown by a scene of the siege of a Near Eastern fortress preserved in the tomb of the magnate Inty in Deshasheh in Middle Egypt. The important literary work known as the *Instructions of Ptahhotep* possibly dates from this period; it is a didactic work probably written by the pharaoh's vizier, Ptahhotep.

The three decades of the reign of Djedkare's successor, Unas (r. 2404–2374 BCE), had a deepening of the long-term trends toward lessened power for the ruler, growth in the numbers of officials and priests, and deterioration in the national economic situation. Growing unrest on the southern frontier can be indirectly deduced from written sources that record a journey to Elephantine that Unas undertook in order to meet with Nubian chieftains. The important religious work known as the Memphite Theology, a syncretistic doctrine of the creation of the world by the god Ptah, which has survived only in a later transcript, is often dated to the reign of Unas.

Although the pyramid of Unas, built in Saqqara between the complexes of Djoser and Sekhemkhet, is the smallest of the fifth dynasty pyramids, it is nevertheless an important milestone in Egyptian history, because it is the earliest pyramid in which the religious texts relating to the ruler's life in the afterlife—known as the Pyramid Texts—appear on the walls of the underground chambers. From this time until the eighth dynasty, such texts appear in the pyramids of the pharaohs and certain of their queens.

Sixth Dynasty. During the reign of Unas there were no events important enough to have justified a change of dynasty. The explanation for the establishment of a new dynasty, therefore, may simply be that its founder, Teti (r. 2374–2354 BCE), was Unas's son-in-law rather than his son. Teti's Horus name, "he who reconciles the Two Lands," indirectly suggests, however, that the situation in the country had not entirely stabilized. Teti built his pyramid complex in North Saqqara. The tombs of his two wives, Iput I and Khuit, are nearby.

According to a later legend, Teti perished by violence as a victim of assassination. The role played at this time by the next pharaoh, Weserkare, who reigned only briefly, has yet to be fully explained. In the end, however, Teti's son Pepy I came to power (r. 2354–2310 BCE), perhaps with the help of the royal mother, Iput I. Pepy I tried to

prevent further weakening of the royal power by establishing personal relations with the provincial nobility, who were acquiring an ever more independent status. He contracted successive marriages with the two daughters (Ankhesenmerire I and II) of the influential magnate Khuy of Abydos. In order to secure the continuity of the succession to the throne, he may have appointed his eldest son Merenre Antyemsaf as coregent (r. 2310–2300 BCE) within his own lifetime (this is the earliest, if not conclusively proven, recorded example of coregency in Egyptian history). An unsuccessful conspiracy against the pharaoh plotted by one of his numerous wives indirectly supports the idea that political conditions were unstable. The pyramid complex of Pepy I was called Menneferpepy ("The Beauty of Pepy Endures") and gave a new name to the capital city originally called Inebuhedj ("White Walls"). The Greek name for the town, Memphis, evolved out of the abbreviated form, Mennefer.

Pepy's son Merenre Antyemsaf died very young, and real power after his death lay in the hands of Ankhesenmerire II, mother of Pepy II, another son of Pepy I who was not yet of age. Pepy II ultimately ruled for a very long period (c.2300–2206 BCE), longer than any other Egyptian pharaoh. One opinion holds that he reigned for ninety-four years, and another that he ruled for a mere sixty-four years.

Neither the expeditions of the Elephantine nomarchs (governors) to Nubia nor a number of other foreign political initiatives and administrative steps taken by Pepy II, managed to halt the accelerating decline of central power in the state. It is possible that the long reign and advancing age of the pharaoh even contributed to the decline. The pyramid complex of Pepy II in South Saqqara, which includes the three small pyramids of the ruler's wives—Neith, Iput II, and Wedjebten—is the last great royal tomb of the Old Kingdom. After the death of Pepy II there were probably disputes over the throne. The legitimate heir may have died before his father (since the latter was so long-lived), and it was ultimately a woman, Nitokerty (or Nitocris), who ascended the throne (r. 2205–2200 BCE), evidently because there was no male candidate who was acceptable to all or who was able to enforce his claim.

The disintegration of the state caused by the collapse of central government was the culmination of a long-drawn-out crisis. One of its causes was the long-term exploitation of great material resources and human potential. The redistribution system, which had originally consisted in the concentration of power and resources at a single center around the pharaoh, had gradually succumbed to a paralysis induced by its own mechanisms. The pharaoh, ideologically and legally the owner of all resources including the labor of the inhabitants, was forced to expend or release ever greater amounts of his property not only for the development of the country's economy and administration, but also for the construction of huge pyramids and, initially, private tombs, as well as for the maintenance of costly mortuary cults. The central power in the country was also weakened by the granting to temples of privileges in the form of exemptions from taxes and corvée labor. That typical feature of any strictly centralized state—excessive growth in the bureaucracy leading to decreasing efficiency—was another factor contributing to the disintegration of the system.

The weakening of the center of power was accompanied by the opposite development in the provinces. Here administrative, economic and even military power was being concentrated in the hands of the regional governors, the nomarchs. Among the circumstances that they were able to exploit as they consolidated their power was the fact that at this period Egypt still had no standing army under the command of the pharaoh or crown prince. When necessary, local forces would be gathered, led by officers mainly appointed by the regional governors.

Another factor contributing to the economic difficulties of the Egyptian state at the end of the Old Kingdom was a deterioration in climatic conditions that occurred roughly in the middle of the third millennium BCE. This was associated with the end of the wet phase known as the Neolithic Subpluvial, which had had long-term favorable effects on the natural environment throughout northeastern Africa, and the rapid onset of a hot, dry climate which changed pastureland into desert and forced the inhabitants of Egypt to withdraw closer to their main water source, the Nile.

[See also Pyramid.]

BIBLIOGRAPHY

Callender, G. *Egypt in the Old Kingdom.* Melbourne, 1998.

Grimal, N. *A History of Ancient Egypt.* Oxford, 1992.

Guillemette, Andrew. *Egypt in the Age of the Pyramids.* Translated by D. Lorton. Ithaca and London, 1997.

Hayes, W. C. *The Scepter of Egypt.* Part 1. 5th rev. ed. New York, 1990.

Smith, W. S. "The Old Kingdom in Egypt and the Beginning of the First Intermediate Period." In *Cambridge Ancient History,* 3d ed. Cambridge, 1971.

Trigger, B. G., B. J. Kemp, D. O'Connor, and A. B. Lloyd. *Ancient Egypt: A Social History.* Cambridge, 1983.

Vercoutter, J. *L'Égypte et la vallée du Nil.* Vol. 1. Paris, 1992.

Ziegler, C., ed. *L'art égyptien au temps des pyramides.* Paris, 1999.

MIROSLAV VERNER

Third Dynasty

Encompassing a period of approximately fifty-five years (2687–2632 BCE), the third dynasty's exact chronology is not yet available. Owing to the paucity of chronologically relevant material, the dynastic sequence of the kings is also not quite clear. To complicate matters, in period documents, the kings were predominantly mentioned with their Horus-names, scarcely ever with their throne names, and never with their birth names. Later generations, however, remembered them in king lists, quoting their throne names or birth names. Added to these variations, there were not only different names but also different numbers of kings mentioned in the later records: there were five in the Royal Canon of Turin; four, in the Saqqara list of the chief lector Tjuloy; five, in the Abydos lists of Sety I and Ramesses II; and eight and nine names in different versions of Manetho's lists from the third century BCE. (The latter, however, seems to be an artificial expansion under the influence of the ideal number "9" as an "Ahnendynastie.") Therefore, an absolute identification of the various kings is not possible (for the discussion of the dynastic succession, see Nabil Swelim, *Some Problems on the History of the Third Dynasty* [Alexandria, 1983], pp. 5–11; Jürgen von Beckerath, *Handbuch der ägyptischen Königsnamen* [Munich, 1984], pp. 40–42, 50–52, and 176–177).

Kings. Some of the later lists (e.g., the Abydos lists, the Royal Canon of Turin) mention a king named Nebka as the founder of the third dynasty; however, he does not seem to be documented by contemporary inscriptions, and there are only posthumous mentions of his name. The most important king of the third dynasty was Horus Netjerikhet (Gold name: Nebu; Nebti name: Netjerikhet Nebti). He can be equated to King Djoser of the later king lists, who reigned, according to the Royal Canon of Turin, for nineteen years (c.2687–2668 BCE). He was more than likely the first king of the third dynasty, as attested in contemporary inscriptions. His wife, his mother, or his mother-in-law was Nimaathep, who had some connection with Khasekhem(wy), the last king of the second dynasty. Today Djoser's restored and reconstructed funerary complex in North Saqqara is very well known because of the famous Step Pyramid; with other ritual buildings (e.g., the *heb-sed* courtyard, the southern tomb, a funerary temple), it was enclosed by a niche-panelled wall of 277 meters × 544 meters (about 900 feet × 1,800 feet). Architectural structures that would have been made of organic materials, such as wood or bundles of reed, in earlier buildings were completely translated into stone in his funerary complex. Remains of Djoser's burial were found in a room situated under the Step Pyramid, including his skull (now lost) and other parts of his skeleton. In underground galleries, also beneath the Step Pyramid, about 40,000 ceramic and stone vessels were discovered, dating from the reigns of his predecessors. In carved reliefs with Djoser were the princesses Hetephernebty and Intkaes, and their names were inscribed on the numerous boundary stelae of the Step Pyramid enclosure.

Horus Sekhemkhet, the successor of Djoser, had also planned to build his tomb as a step pyramid. Situated to the southwest of Djoser's Step Pyramid, the funerary complex of Sekhemkhet was intended to be of greater dimensions than that of his predecessor, but it was never finished. In a rough-cut subterranean chamber, a sarcophagus was found made from calcite (Egyptian alabaster); although closed and decorated with flowers, it was empty and proved never to have been used. The southern tomb of his funerary complex contained the burial of a young male child; that tomb had been violated shortly after the burial.

Presumably, Horus Sanacht was Sekhemkhet's successor. Sanacht was mentioned in inscriptions at Elephantine, Beit Khallaf, Saqqara, and Wadi Mughara in Sinai. His tomb has not as yet been located.

Horus Khaba (Gold name: Netjer-Nebu) is not well known. The Layer Pyramid at Zawiyet el-Aryan has been attributed to him, but no remains of a burial were found in it. The adjacent, so-called, *mastaba* 500 is supposed to be its funerary temple. The otherwise unknown Horus Qahedjet was attested by a limestone stela that depicted him embracing the god Horus. He can be regarded as identical to Huny, King of Upper and Lower Egypt (ruled c.2673–2649 BCE), who was attested only by a single contemporary inscription, from Elephantine.

Development. During the third dynasty, some of the typical features of the Egyptian state were created and established. The funerary complex of Djoser, for example, documented rapid progress in building techniques. That was the first time a building was completely constructed of dressed limestone; before, dressed stone was used only sporadically. Djoser's pyramid also denoted the outset of the pyramid age. The sculpture and bas reliefs of the third dynasty have marked an important turning point in the evolution of Egyptian art. Only the royal sculptures of Djoser have been preserved (for example, the *serdab* statue of his funerary complex), but about fifteen seated or standing stone statues of princesses, higher officials, and their wives have become known. In Djoser's reign the writing system was reformed, and for the first time a continuous text was written, in hieroglyphs. A specialization of the administration also occurred during the third dynasty (see Jochem Kahl, *Das System der ägyptischen Hieroglyphenschrift in der 0.–3. Dynastie* [Wiesbaden, 1994], pp. 162–163 [indicia for a writing reform] and pp. 833–835 [specialized titles of scribes]). The possibly oldest dam in the world, the Sadd el-Kafara near Helwan, was planned and begun at the end of the third dynasty (see G. Garbrecht and H.-U. Bertram, *Der Sadd-el-Kafara. Die älteste Talsperre der Welt, 2600 v. Chr.* [Braunschweig, 1983]).

Archaeological Sites. There is a lack of archaeological sources from the third dynasty. With the exception of the

main necropolis, located in North Saqqara (the Step Pyramid enclosure of Djoser and Sekhemkhet; private tombs) and modern-day, southern Abusir, only a few major sites with third dynasty remains are known: (1) Beit Khallaf, with tombs of higher officials (see J. Garstang, *Mahâsna and Bêt Khallâf* [London, 1902]; Garstang wrongly assumed some of these tombs to be royal); (2) Elephantine, with the temple of Satet (see Günter Dreyer, *Elephantine VIII: Der Tempel der Satet. Die Funde der Frühzeit und des Alten Reiches* [Mainz, 1986]), an administrative building complex, and a small step pyramid; (3) Wadi Mughara (Sinai), with rock inscriptions carved during expeditions undertaken to exploit copper, turquoise, and malachite; and (4) Heliopolis, with the remains of a shrine or a temple probably devoted to the Ennead (for the problematics of temples, see David O'Connor, "The Status of Early Egyptian Temples: An Alternative Theory," in *The Followers of Horus: Studies Dedicated to Michael Allen Hoffman*, edited by R. Friedman and B. Adams, pp. 83–98 [Oxford, 1992]).

Across Egypt, seven small step pyramids are known; six of them (near or at Elephantine, Edfu, Hierakonpolis, Naqada, Abydos, and Zawjet el-Mejtin) were erected in the reign of Huny and one (Seila) in the reign of Sneferu (fourth dynasty). Since all of them lack burial apartments, they cannot have been tombs. Probably they "marked the locations of an official cult centered around the person of the king" (see Stephan Johannes Seidlmayer, "Town and State in the Early Old Kingdom: A View from Elephantine," in *Aspects of Early Egypt*, edited by J. Spencer, p. 122 [London, 1996]).

Remembrance of Persons in Later Times. From the third dynasty, four kings were remembered by later generations: Djoser (Netjerikhet), Nebka, Sekhemkhet (Djoser-Tety), and Huny. The following examples are especially worth mentioning: In the Prisse Papyrus, the *Instructions of Kagemni* was framed by a story mentioning King Huny's death; the Westcar Papyrus (written in classical Middle Egyptian and dated to the Second Intermediate Period) contains tales that, among others, relate events from the time of Nebka and Djoser. Graffiti left by pilgrims in the funerary complex of Djoser date from the eighteenth dynasty to the twenty-sixth and prove the remembrance of that king in later times. The Famine Stela on Sehel Island, a decree issued by Ptolemy V, referred to Djoser and Imhotep; the latter was the most famous person from third dynasty times for later generations. As inscriptions make plausible, Imhotep was the supervisor of the pyramid-building projects during the reigns of Djoser and Sekhemkhet. The only known monuments that mentioned Imhotep's name during his lifetime are the pedestal (Cairo JE 49889) of one of Djoser's statues (stating both Imhotep's name and titles) and a graffito on the wall surrounding Sekhemkhet's step-pyramid enclosure. Imhotep's tomb—probably in North Saqqara—has not yet been found.

During the New Kingdom, Imhotep became a demigod and was venerated as both patron of the scribes and as a wise man. Since the twenty-sixth dynasty, and especially in the Ptolemaic period, he became deified and was considered to be a god of writing, architecture, wisdom, and medicine (see W. G. Waddell, *Manetho* [London, 1948], pp. 40–45); the main centers of his overregional cult were Memphis, Saqqara, and Thebes.

Important Nonroyal Persons. Besides Imhotep, a further important high-ranking official was Hesyra, "overseer of the royal scribes, greatest of physicians and dentists." His tomb at Saqqara is number 2405, and it contained wall paintings and wooden reliefs of the highest quality (see J. E. Quibell, *The Tomb of Hesy* [Cairo, 1913] and Wendy Wood, "A Reconstruction of the Reliefs of Hesy-re," in *Journal of the American Research Center in Egypt* 15 [1978], pp. 9–24). There was also Ankh, who seems to have been concerned with the administration of Upper Egypt, and two statues of him (Leiden D 93 and Louvre A 39) and a seal impression that mentions him are known. Aa-Achti was "God's-servant of the temple of King Nebka," and reused blocks from his and his wife's tomb were found at Abusir; originally his tomb had been built at Saqqara. Kha-Bau-Seker was "controller of the craftsmen of the workshop" and was buried at Saqqara in tomb number 3073, with his wife Nefer-Hetep-Hathor (see Margaret A. Murray, *Saqqara Mastabas I*, reprint [London, 1989], pp. 2–4, pl. 1–2).

[*See also* Imhotep; Pyramid; *and* Saqqara.]

BIBLIOGRAPHY

Dreyer, Günter, and Werner Kaiser. "Zu den kleinen Stufenpyramiden Ober- und Mittelägyptens." *Mitteilungen des Deutschen Archäologischen Instituts, Abteilung Kairo* 36 (1980), 43–59. A discussion of the small step pyramids and their interpretation.

Dreyer, Günter, "Der erste König der 3. Dynastie." In *Stationen: Beiträge zur Kulturgeschichte Ägyptens, Rainer Stadelmann gewidmet*, edited by Heike Guksch and Daniel Polz pp. 31–34. Mainz, 1998. Deals with the succession of the kings.

Eaton-Krauss, Marianne. "Two Masterpieces of Early Egyptian Statuary." *Oudheidkundige Mededelingen uit het Rijksmuseum van Oudheden te Leuven* 77 (1997), 7–21. Deals with the private sculpture of the third dynasty.

Firth, Cecil M., and J. E. Quibell. *The Step Pyramid.* 2 vols. Cairo, 1935. Reports on the excavation of Djoser's Step Pyramid at Saqqara; also see below, Lauer (1936–1939).

Goneim, M. Zakaria. *Horus Sekhem-khet, The Unfinished Pyramid at Saqqara.* Cairo, 1957. Reports on the excavation of Sekhemkhet's step pyramid at Saqqara.

Helck, Wolfgang. *Untersuchungen zur Thinitenzeit.* Ägyptologische Abhandlungen, 45. Wiesbaden, 1987. Concerns aspects of Egyptian history through the end of the third dynasty.

Kahl, Jochem, Nicole Kloth, and Ursula Zimmermann. *Die Inschriften der 3. Dynastie: eine Bestandsaufnahme.* Ägyptologische Abhandlungen, 56. Wiesbaden, 1995. A compilation of all published inscriptions of the third dynasty.

Lauer, Jean-Philippe. *La pyramide à degrés.* 3 vols. Cairo, 1936–1939. Presents an ample description of the architecture of the Step Pyramid.

Lauer, Jean-Philippe. *Saqqara: The Royal Cemetery of Memphis*, pp. 90–140. London, 1976. Conveys an outline of the funerary complexes of Djoser and Sekhemkhet.

Smith, W. Stevenson. *The Art and Architecture of Ancient Egypt.* 2d ed., rev. and enl. by W. K. Simpson, pp. 53–69. New York, 1981. Gives a brief summary of the major achievements in art and architecture during the third dynasty.

Sourouzian, Hourig. "L'iconographie du roi dans la statuaire des trois premières dynasties." In *Kunst des Alten Reiches: Symposium im Deutschen Archäologischen Institut Kairo, on 29 und 30 Oktober 1991*, pp. 143–154. Sonderschrift des Deutschen Archäologisches Institut, Abteilung Kairo, 7. Mainz, 1995. Discusses royal sculpture (with plates).

Stadelmann, Rainer. *Die Ägyptischen Pyramiden: vom Ziegelbau zum Weltwunder.* 2d rev. ed. Mainz, 1991. Deals with royal architecture and building technique.

Vercoutter, Jean. *L'Égypte et la vallée du Nil. Tome 1: Des origines à la fin de l'Ancien Empire, 12000–2000*, pp. 245–263. Paris, 1992. Gives a summary of the history of the third dynasty and discusses the kings' names.

Wildung, Dietrich. *Egyptian Saints: Deification in Pharaonic Egypt*, pp. 31–81. New York, 1977. Describes how the cult of Imhotep developed.

Wildung, Dietrich. *Die Rolle ägyptischer Könige im Bewußtsein ihrer Nachwelt, Teil I: Posthume Quellen über die Könige der ersten vier Dynastien.* Münchner Ägyptologische Studien, 17. Berlin, 1969. A compilation of later documents mentioning kings of the third dynasty.

JOCHEM KAHL

Fourth Dynasty

Egyptian historians did not use a term meaning "dynasty" until the third-century BCE historian Manetho introduced the Greek word during the Ptolemaic era. The Egyptians would have used the word *pr* ("house") in the sense of "family." The fourth dynasty was the family of Sneferu, its first, long-reigning king and progenitor of seven kings who reigned over nearly one and a half centuries. Sneferu probably descended from his predecessor, Huny, but during the Old Kingdom the royal father of a king is never explicitly named as such, nor a crown prince during the reign of his father, so there is no sure evidence. He was probably the son of a minor queen, Meresankh, who is called "mother of Sneferu" on the Palermo Stone and was venerated together with him at Meidum.

Sneferu's reign (c.2649–2609 BCE) can be divided into three periods according to his building activities and places of residence. He built his first royal residence and a pyramid complex with a high step pyramid at Meidum within the first fourteen or fifteen years of his reign. He then moved his residence to Dahshur, where during the next fifteen years he engaged in the construction of a towering true pyramid at Dahshur South. This, the so-called Bent Pyramid, could not be completed as planned because of faulty construction and a sagging foundation. He then began a third pyramid in his regnal Year 29, the Northern or Red Pyramid, which he finally completed in about Year 45, shortly before his death. These years are well attested in contemporary graffiti and quarry marks on the stones of his pyramids, especially on those of the Northern Pyramid. There, the year of the fifteenth counting (Year 29 of his reign) is mentioned on the cornerstone of the southwest corner of the pyramid; several times the years of counting 15, 16, and 24 (twice)—corresponding to regnal Years 29/30, 32/33, and 45/46—are recorded. (Thus, the twenty-four years that the Turin Canon assigns to Sneferu is surely not correct and may be a misunderstanding of the year of counting 24.) Some events of Sneferu's reign are recorded on the Palermo Stone: the building of large fleets of ships, including seagoing ships of cedarwood from Lebanon; a raid in Nubia from which Sneferu brought thousands of people and cattle to be settled in Egypt; the establishment of fortified settlements; and the construction of a new palace, probably that of Dahshur. With such a long reign, it is not surprising that we find several family branches; an older one is attested at Meidum, with the princes Nefermaat and Rahotep and their respective wives, Atet and Nofret. Nefermaat, according to his titles, may have built the Meidum pyramid. A son of his, Hemiunu, became the chief architect of his uncle Khufu at Giza. Rahotep, whose splendid statue, together with that of his wife, Nofret, was found embedded in his *mastaba* at Meidum (without, however, any burial), may have followed his father to Dahshur and constructed the ill-fated Bent Pyramid. Near the stepped pyramid of Meidum, a queen's tomb was recorded. This may have been the first main consort of Sneferu, who had died at Meidum. A large *mastaba* (M 17) to the east of the stepped pyramid contained a burial of a prince, perhaps a prematurely deceased crown prince.

At Dahshur South, some of the large *mastaba* tombs in front of the Bent Pyramid can be ascribed to king's sons, like that of Ii-nofer, and others to high courtiers, like the "maitre de plaisir" and musician Ipi. Most of the tomb-owners remain to be identified. About 400 meters (a quarter mile) east of the Northern Pyramid are four rows of large *mastaba*s that can be assigned to the royal family of the later period of Sneferu's reign. So far, two king's sons can be identified, Prince Netjeraperef and Prince Kanofer. A large *mastaba* in the first row might have been intended for Queen Hetepheres, who outlived her husband Sneferu and followed her son Khufu to his new residence at Giza, where she was buried in the northernmost small pyramid (G1a). Crown Prince Khufu is not attested at Dahshur, and he had no *mastaba* tomb in his father's necropolis because he was supposed to construct his own pyramid.

Khufu's full name is Khuefuwi-Khnum ("the god Khnum protects me"), and he is widely known by the Greek version, Cheops (r. 2609–2584 BCE). He moved his court and residence far to the north near modern Giza, where he started to build his pyramid. Abandoning Dahshur was by no means a hostile act against his father Sneferu, whose burial ceremonies he performed and whose funerary cult he supported. Rather, he sought an appropriate place for his own pyramid, projected to be the largest and tallest monument ever built. It seems that it was a custom in the Old Kingdom for a new king to abandon the residence and necropolis of his father in order to construct his own pyramid precinct. Thus, Sneferu had abandoned the residence and necropolis of his predecessor Huny at Saqqara and chosen first Meidum and then Dahshur. Khufu's son Djedefre moved even farther north, to Abu Rowash. The next king, Khafre, returned to central Giza; his putative successor Baka or Bikheris again chose Saqqara. Menkaure came back to the south of Giza, and the last king of the fourth dynasty, Shepseskaf, went to Saqqara South to build his tomb monument. The older residences and pyramid towns of the previous kings were, however, never abandoned; they continued to flourish throughout the Old Kingdom, especially the pyramid town Akhet-Khufu and its necropolis at Giza, which was a center of royal aristocracy, pyramid-builders, and artists until the end of the Old Kingdom.

When Khufu transferred his court to his new residence, Akhet-Khufu at Giza, he certainly took along the core of the trained pyramid-builders, including the architects and engineers. Remarkably, none of his brothers, were attached to his court or had tombs at Giza; they had their responsibilities and tombs at Dahshur, but no position or function in the new court. His mother Hetepheres, however, joined his new court and was buried there. As the head of construction for his pyramid he appointed his nephew Hemiunu, son of an older brother, Nefermaat. Hemiunu may have acquired knowledge and experience during the construction of the two Dahshur pyramids.

Very few contemporary facts about Khufu and his great construction are known. Some graffiti in and around the pyramid indicate the progress of the work: for example, in the fourth year the eastern boat shafts were excavated. Those on the southern side of the pyramid, where in 1954 the famous large bark of Khufu was discovered, had graffiti of the twenty-second year, when the beams were prepared and put into the shaft. The Year 17 in a graffito on a block in one of the so-called relief chambers above the burial chamber is by no means certain. The Turin Canon assigns Khufu a reign of twenty-three years, which is not sufficient for the construction of the Great Pyramid, with its mass of 2.7 million cubic meters, or more than 2.3 million blocks of limestone, weighing on average 2.5 tons, along with a causeway more than 1200

OLD KINGDOM: FOURTH DYNASTY. *Two great monuments from the fourth dynasty: the Pyramid of Khafre and the Great Sphinx, at Giza.* (Courtesy David P. Silverman)

meters (3,900 feet) long, three queens' pyramids, and more than fifty large *mastaba*s for princes and high officials. The number "23" (regnal years) may be an inverted writing of "32," which would be more probable. The Turin Canon, which was composed twelve hundred years later and is clearly in error in many details of Old Kingdom chronology, is certainly less reliable than contemporary sources, especially considering the time necessary for the construction of the pyramids.

Almost nothing is known about Khufu as a person. Later traditions characterizing him as a cruel tyrant are undoubtedly wrong and influenced by the Greek viewpoint, which would see in the towering pyramid only the idea of human hubris. The Egyptian view was mixed. During the Old Kingdom, Khufu was venerated as a sun god by his own descendants, who thus traced their origin through him back to divinity. Khufu's sons were the first to bear the new royal title *s₃-R'w* ("Son of Re"). In the First Intermediate Period, the building of pyramids was dismissed as vain and futile, and the builders scornfully contrasted with poor men who had just died beside a canal. This disapproval did not last long. Until the Late period, Khufu and his pyramid complex remained highly venerated, and people of all social ranks wanted to be buried near his pyramid, or at least in sight of it. Of Khufu, only one certain depiction is known, an ivory statuette

from Abydos just 7.5 centimeters (3 inches) high. This is the smallest piece of Egyptian royal sculpture, but it is a masterpiece, showing the aging king with individualized features that can also be recognized in the majestic face of the Great Sphinx of Giza, the living effigy of the sun god.

The king's mother, Hetepheres, and his two principal queens, Meritites and Henutsen, the mothers of Khufu's sons and successors, Djedefre and Khafre, were buried in smaller pyramids to the east of the king's pyramid. These were the first queens' pyramids. Khufu's sons and daughters received enormous solid stone double *mastaba*s to the east, apportioned strictly according to age. The most famous of these persons was Hordjedef, a philosopher-prince and author of a much-copied *Instruction*. The queens Meresankh, Hetepheres, and Meritites had important roles in the family. Sneferu's mother, Meresankh, was associated with the divine cult of her son at Meidum; his consort Hetepheres I, mother of Khufu, received a royal burial at Giza. Intrafamily marriages between the sons and daughters of Khufu seem to have been the rule, perhaps to preserve the pure, divine blood of the sun king. Princess Hetepheres II was first married to her brother, Prince Kawab, who was not the royal heir; after his death, she married her brother, King Djedefre. Her daughter Meresankh III, from her marriage with Kawab, later married her uncle Khafre. Neither of these ladies, however, became the mother of a future king, so these marriages may have been only honorary. There is, however, no evidence of a family feud among the children of Khufu. On the contrary, there exist donation decrees and offerings by descendants of Khafre to the cult of Djedefre at Abu Rowash.

Never in Egyptian history were the claims of divine kingship so strictly conceived and applied. Khufu intervened even in the planning and decoration of the tomb-chapels, which uniformly contained only the most important offering scenes. In his reign, large-scale sculptures of notables were deliberately restricted to a few exceptional individuals, such as the powerful overseer of building works, Prince Hemiunu. His remarkable, dynamic tomb statue shows us an image of the men who constructed the great pyramids. Even the highest dignitaries had to be content with portrait heads—the reserve heads—in their burial chambers. Only the sons and daughters of Khufu had the privilege of decorated chapels and statues; Prince Kawab had more than ten statues in his chapel. Still, one can observe a remarkable revolution during the reign of Khufu regarding the status of these princes. Whereas the sons of Sneferu had important titles and real functions, serving as directors of works and leaders of troops and expeditions, the sons of Khufu bore purely honorific or juridical titles and had strictly priestly functions in the cult of their father. This suggests that the direct offspring of the divine blood were not allowed to execute profane responsibilities. The real administration of the state had already passed into the hands of a new class of qualified people: master builders, engineers, architects, and able administrators, from the new class of "scribes." These were academics who had learned to master everything, from transportation to construction, from prospecting in distant deserts to quarrying in hard stone and carving marvelous works of art, including the most eminent of statues—the Great Sphinx.

The successor of Khufu was his son Djedefre (r. 2584–2576 BCE), who transferred his court and pyramid precinct 8 kilometers (5 miles) farther north, to Abu Rowash. For Djedefre, no tomb was planned in his father's necropolis; he was therefore already the designated crown prince at the early stages of construction work at Giza. His royal cartouche is found on the large beams that cover the southern bark pit of Khufu, so he must have overseen and conducted his father's funeral. He was the first king to bear the new royal title "Son of Re," a pious reference to Khufu, who had become the living sun god in his pyramid precinct. During Djedefre's reign of only eight years, he could not complete his pyramid, but his funeral temple was adorned with a variety of beautiful statues, including sphinxes and family groups with his queen, sons, and daughters. His fine portraits are individualized representations reflecting physiognomic study, perhaps under the

influence of the reserve heads. Despite a certain melancholy, they radiate youth and humanity.

After Djedefre's death, another son of Khufu, Khaefkhufu, ascended to the throne, modifying his name into Khafre (r. 2576–2551 BCE). It seems immediate descent from the sun king Khufu carried more weight than a father-to-son succession. This principle was again evident in the beginning of the fifth dynasty, when three brothers succeeded one another because they were supposed to be the children of the sun god. Another of Khafre's brothers, Prince Ankh-khaf—whose marvelous bust offers us a realistic portrait of a person of the pyramid age—assisted him as vizier and may have been the architect of his pyramid.

Khafre returned to Giza, choosing for his pyramid a slightly higher site to the southwest of Khufu's in order to equal his father's pyramid, even naming his own "Khafre's Pyramid is the Greatest." Nothing new and exciting is reported from his reign, which may have lasted as much as thirty years, the time needed to build the pyramid and its temples. The Greeks accorded him the same bad character as his father Khufu because of his ambitious monument. The design of the funerary apartments inside the pyramid is very simple, but this is compensated for by the extensive, lavishly constructed funerary temple. The valley temple is well preserved and hosted at least twenty-three seated statues, the best preserved being the famous diorite statue with the Horus-falcon protecting the king.

Khafre was succeeded by a poorly documented king, Baka or Bicheris, probably a son of Djedefre, who reigned only four years. This king began an ambitious project farther south at Zawiet el-Aryan, excavating a wide, deep pit for a large pyramid. Only the pit and the foundations of the funerary apartment, completely furnished with dark granite, were complete when Baka died, and the pyramid precinct was abandoned.

Then, a son of Khafre, Menkaure (Gr., Mycerinos) succeeded to the throne (r. 2551–2528). The biographies in the tombs of contemporary high officials in Giza and Saqqara do not report any disqualification from office or fall in disgrace in the period from Khafre's reign to that of Menkaure and even into the fifth dynasty, so a power struggle cannot be assumed within the reigning family. Admittedly, the procedure for appointment or election to the throne in the Old Kingdom is not known and must therefore accept an apparently peaceful transition between members of different family branches. Menkaure's pyramid is considerably smaller than those of his predecessors but remains partially cased with granite from Aswan. The funerary apartments inside it are characterized by an extraordinary succession of rooms, staircases, and a vaulted hall, a masterpiece of engineering comparable only to Khufu's pyramid. His superb sarcophagus of dark granite, the first royal sarcophagus to be decorated with a palace façade, was lost in the Mediterranean Sea in 1838, on its way to England.

It is unwise to conclude that political or religious disturbances prevented Menkaure or his successors from continuing the construction of tall pyramids. This was due, rather, to a remarkable shift in the cultic concept, and a transfer of the cult from the pyramid as the center of appearance to the mortuary temple as the center of ritual. The Greek tradition regards Menkaure as a pious ruler. His statuary display new proportions—a rather athletic ideal with a comparatively small head on broad, strong shoulders, but with well-modeled, almost soft features, presaging the royal images of the early fifth dynasty.

The end of the fourth dynasty is obscure. Shepseskaf (r. 2523–2519 BCE), the last king attested on monuments, was probably not the son of Menkaure but rather his brother. An advanced age at accession would explain his short reign of four years. Shepseskaf transferred his residence to the far south of Saqqara, where he constructed his tomb in the form of a monumental *mastaba*, a revival of a traditional tomb form of the first and second dynasties at Saqqara. This was done not out of antagonism toward the pyramid-builders, but rather in search of a form more appropriate to a royal tomb. Shepseskaf might also have been prompted by his anxiety to complete a monumental royal tomb in time. This form was copied by his successor, Queen Khentkawes, at Giza. She was the mother of the first two or even three kings—Userkaf, Sahure, and perhaps Neferirkare—who passed the divine blood of the descendants of the sun god to the new dynasty. Whether or not she was a daughter of Shepseskaf, or married to him (or to an otherwise unknown and undocumented King Thamphtis, perhaps Djedef-Ptah) is uncertain.

To summarize, the fourth dynasty was the zenith of the Pyramid Age, an epoch in which great and magnificent monuments were constructed, and in which the Egyptian arts of relief sculpture and painting reached their highest development. In the natural sciences and medicine, the foundations of a wide knowledge and practice were explored and developed, and the results would remain accepted for centuries in eastern Mediterranean culture, into the Greek era. The cultural evolution of the state and society was greatly inspired by the ascent of the universal sun god Re, creator of all things, who from this time dominated the religion, ethics, and ideas of the state in Egypt.

[See also Abu Rowash; Dahshur; Giza; Khafre; Khufu; Menkaure; Pyramid; *and* Sneferu.]

BIBLIOGRAPHY
Callender, G. *Egypt in the Old Kingdom.* Melbourne, 1998.
Goedicke, H. *Königliche Dokumente aus dem Alten Reich.* Wiesbaden, 1967.
Grimal, N. *A History of Ancient Egypt.* Oxford, 1992.
Hart, G. *Pharaohs and Pyramids.* London, 1991.
Malek, J. *In the Shadow of the Pyramids: Egypt during the Old Kingdom.* London, 1986.

RAINER STADELMANN

Fifth Dynasty

The total number of years for the fifth dynasty is not preserved in the Turin Canon. The third-century BCE historian Manetho reports 248 years, but its actual duration is probably more realistically estimated at approximately 150 years. Its kings, in order of reign, are Userkaf, Sahure, Neferirkare Kakai, Shepseskare, Raneferef, Newoserre Any, Menkauhor, Djedkare, and Unas. The period from the reign of the fourth dynasty King Menkaure to Newoserre Any of the fifth dynasty spans approximately one generation, as deduced from the biography of the high official Ptahshepses in Saqqara.

The transition from the fourth to the fifth dynasty was probably peaceful. It is unclear whether the first kings of the fifth dynasty were descendants of King Menkaure by two different wives, as Málek (1997, p. 15) suggests. Such a situation might explain why the first three kings are described as brothers in the Westcar Papyrus from the Middle Kingdom.

The most important events of the fifth dynasty are recorded in the annals of the Old Kingdom, which have been partially preserved on the Palermo Stone. Since this record ends with the reign of Neferirkare Kakai, other sources must be consulted. Among these are the royal and private monuments, mostly from the necropolises of Giza and Saqqara, as well as administrative records from the funerary temples of Neferirkare and Neferefre, and inscriptions left by expeditions to the north (the Sinai), the Eastern Desert (the Wadi Hammamat), and the south (Aswan, Nubia).

With regard to domestic politics, the fifth dynasty was a time of change. Under the leadership of its kings, the centralized state of the god-kingship was transformed into a bureaucratic state. The highest offices—e.g., vizier and expedition overseer—were no longer held exclusively by princes. A new rising class of officials emerged. From the middle of the fifth dynasty onward, the nomes were administered by officials who no longer lived in the royal residence (i.e., capitol) but in the districts they oversaw. The services of these administrators were remunerated in land and people. At first, the goods and people were directly linked to the office and remained the property of the king. As the offices became inheritable however, the lands and people given as payment became private property. Thus a decentralized upper class was created. The nomarchs (provincial governors) arranged for their own burials in their provinces, instead of at the capital. This gradual distancing from court promoted the decentralization of the administration and created a provincial nobility. The tombs of the high officials became more monumental as their wealth increased. The cult rooms were decorated with colorful reliefs; statues were placed, often hidden, in the interior of the cult rooms. Artworks of great quality were created for private commissions, comparable to the work done on royal commissions. The statues of Ranefer, a high priest of Ptah at the beginning of the fifth dynasty, and the statue of the high official Ti from the end of the dynasty are accomplished sculpture.

For the first time, biographical data for officials were published. Thus, it is learned, Nesytpunetjer, buried at Giza, lived from the reign of Djedefre until the time of Sahure; Prince Sekhemkare, a son of Khafre, died under Sahure after having been vizier under Userkaf and Sahure; and the high priest of Memphis, Ptahshepses, from Saqqara, indicates that his life spanned the period from Menkaure to Newoserre.

In religion, the conception of Osiris experienced its first great upswing. The figure of Osiris sprang from an idea of the period with regard to the fate of the dead king in the underworld. In death, the king became an Osiris. The royal tomb was redesigned under the influence of the dichotomy between the solar cult and the emerging Osiris cult. Sun temples were founded that stand as autonomous complexes near to the pyramid installations.

Userkaf (c.2513–2506 BCE). The first king of the fifth dynasty, Userkaf ("powerful is his *Ka*"; Horus-name Iry-Ma'at, "performer of Maat") is thought to have reigned seven years. His pyramid at Saqqara, called "Pure Are the Places of Userkaf," is smaller than those of the fourth dynasty rulers. He founded the tradition of sun temples; the first of its kind, is at Abusir and is called "Residence [or "Stronghold"] of Re." The complex, situated in the necropolis area, comprises a valley temple, a causeway, and an upper temple. In place of the pyramid-tomb, however, it features an open courtyard with a freestanding obelisk.

Little is known about this king's activities. Userkaf commissioned the construction of a temple in Upper Egypt (at Tod), of which some ruins remain. Offering endowments named in the annals of the Old Kingdom may have been intended for further building projects carried out in his Years 2 and 6 for the gods of Heliopolis, and in Year 6 for the gods of Buto. The tribute presented to the king, probably from the Eastern Desert, in the second year of his reign may have been connected to military campaigns. Under Userkaf, many officials continued to build their tombs in Giza—for example, the vizier Seshathotep or Heti (tomb 5150).

Sahure (c.2506–2492 BCE). Userkaf was succeeded by his half-brother, Sahure. The Turin Canon records a duration of twelve years for the king's reign. On the Palermo Stone the last is given as a "year after the seventh occasion of the count," which would correspond to a four-

teenth year. The king would therefore have reigned for thirteen full years.

The name of Sahure's pyramid is "The *Ba* of Sahure Appears"; his solar temple, not yet found, bore the name "Field of Re." The funerary temple of the king is the first for which remains worth mentioning exist. Important new discoveries of the causeway to the pyramid, whose details have yet to be published, complete our knowledge of the decoration of this burial monument. The historical depictions in the funerary temple document an expedition by sea to the Lebanese coast (at Byblos) and a victory over nomadic Libyan tribes (the Tjemehu). The historical veracity of these depictions is, however, questionable; it is more likely that not all these cases refer to actual historical events but rather, are representations that serve to exalt the monarchy.

The annals of the Old Kingdom on the Palermo Stone document a number of offerings and donations of land to various temples in Lower Egypt. These were most likely in connection with specific building projects. One such project in Upper Egypt may be the source of a statue depicting the king and the district god of Coptos. This group figure is, however, not an original piece of Sahure's, but more likely one of Khafre, from the fourth dynasty.

For the last years of Sahure, the annals mention an expedition into the Sinai and one to Punt. Royal inscriptions in the Wadi Mughara in the Sinai provide indirect confirmation; similar evidence exists for the Punt expedition, witnessed by a graffito in the Eastern Desert. Extensive trade relations existed with Nubia, where the name of Sahure is attested on seals from Buhen, and possibly also in the Near East, where an inscribed object bearing Sahure's name was discovered at Dorak. The vizier under Sahure was Werbauba, depicted in the funerary temple of the king, as is a famous physician of the time, Niankhsekhmet, whose tomb in Saqqara was fitted with a false door by Sahure.

Neferirkare Kakai (c.2492–2482 BCE). The king succeeding Sahure was his brother, Neferirkare, surnamed Kakai. The duration of his reign is indicated as slightly over ten years in the Turin Canon, and in Manetho as twenty years. A realistic estimate would be thirteen years. The later King Shepseskare was probably a descendant of Neferirkare and his first wife. His second wife was Khentkawes II, whose funerary temple was discovered in Abusir; she bore his son, the future King Raneferef (or Neferefre).

The royal pyramid, called "Neferkirare Takes Form," is situated in Abusir. The site of his sun temple, called "Site of the Heart of Re," has not been archaeologically identified; it was probably in the vicinity of the pyramid. The pyramid is approximately the same size as that of Menkaure. The projected funerary temple is executed in mud

OLD KINGDOM: FIFTH DYNASTY. *Head of a fifth dynasty statuette of a man.* The head is painted limestone and is from Giza. (The Metropolitan Museum of Art, Dodge Fund, 1947. [47.105.1])

brick. The valley temple was never completed and was later taken over and expanded by Newoserre. The Abusir papyri furnish vital information about the cult traditions of the funerary temple of Neferirkare. In the main, these papyri date from the end of the fifth dynasty. (Djedkare, Years 15 to 41; Unas, Years 6 to 15), but continue into the sixth dynasty (Teti, Pepy II). They refer to the administration of the funerary temple and provide good insight into the economic significance of the sun temples of the fifth dynasty. An exemption decree for a temple in Abydos is an indication of that city's growing importance during the period of Neferirkare. The cult center of Khentyamentiu may have been favored with endowments.

We have no knowledge of Neferkirare's relations with neighboring countries, with the exception of trade relations with Nubia. Under him, officials began to inscribe detailed biographies in their tombs, which would develop into the traditional biography of officials; for the first time, details from the lives of those individuals are described. Among the most interesting biographies of this period are those of the vizier Ptahwash and of the court official Rawer. Ptahwash (or Isi), who served as vizier under Sahure and Neferirkare, fell ill under Neferirkare and died suddenly. Of the court official Rawer, the biography tells us that he was accidentally hit by the king's scepter during a ceremony and that his life was saved by the immediate intervention of the king.

Shepseskare (c.2482–2475 BCE). Shepseskare was probably a son of Neferirkare. The location and name of his pyramid and sun temple are not known. His position as successor to Neferirkare is documented in the list of kings in Saqqara and in Manetho. There are, however, no monuments of this king, with the exception of one scarab. He is assigned a reign of seven years in the Turin Canon and in Manetho.

Raneferef (c.2475–2474 BCE). Raneferef (or Neferefre), whose personal name is Isi, was also a son of Neferirkare and probably a descendant of Khentkawes II. In Manetho he is assigned a reign of twenty years, but his actual reign is likely to have been no more than two years. His funeral monument did not take the form of a pyramid, but of a *mastaba*. Its name is "The *Ba*s of Raneferef Are Divine." In the severely damaged funerary temple, several royal statues and numerous statues of prisoners (Nubians and Near Easterners) were found, as well as remnants of papyri from the temple archives. The papyri are comparable to those of the funerary temple of Neferirkare and a further parallel is evident in the papyri from the funerary temple of Queen Khentkawes II. The king's sun temple, called "Re Is Content," has not yet been located; it was most likely in the vicinity of the funerary temple.

Newoserre Any (c.2470–2440). He was probably a son of Raneferef, and the length of his reign is incomplete in the Turin Canon. Based on his celebration of a *sed*-festival, it must have been at least thirty years long. In Manetho's history, he is assigned forty-four years. Newoserre was married to Reputnub, whose three daughters were all buried near the pyramid. One of these daughters, Khamerernebty, was married to the vizier Ptahshepses.

The name of the king's pyramid is "The Places of Newoserre Endure." The decoration of the funerary temple is preserved only in part. The remains are better in the sun temple, called "Joy of the Heart of Re," near Abu Ghurob to the north of Abusir; this is the largest and best preserved temple of its kind. In the numerous sections of wall relief, we find illustrations of the king's *sed*-festival and images of the effects of the sun god in nature. The images in the so-called World Chamber illustrate seasonal events (inundation; summer). In this context they also show themes that are in evidence in the great pictorial cycles in private tombs from the same period (e.g., fishing and fowling scenes; hunting scenes).

Little is known of Newoserre's foreign relations. His name is inscribed in the Wadi Mughara in the Sinai, an indication of an expedition into the mining area. Under Newoserre we also find extensive evidence of building activities by officials and administrators. The *mastaba* of the vizier Ptahshepses in Abusir is of great importance; its architecture and decorative detail incorporate royal elements (e.g., sun barks and monumental figures), possibly because Ptahsepses was a son-in-law of the king. Other viziers during the long reign of the king were Kay and Pehenuka, whose tombs are preserved in Saqqara, and perhaps Minufer. Officials under Newoserre commissioned elaborate tomb complexes, mostly in Saqqara. Among the best preserved of this period are the tomb of the twins Niankhkhnum and Khnumhotep, who served as manicurists under Newoserre, and that of the "First Royal Hairdresser," Ti.

Menkauhor (c.2444–2436 BCE). The personal name of Menkauhor is Hor-ikau or Ikau. The duration of his reign is given as eight years in the Turin Canon, and as nine in Manetho; eight is more likely. His pyramid is named "The Places of Menkauhor Are Divine"; his yet-undiscovered sun temple was called "Field of Horus."

Little is known about this king. A *sed*-festival statue of him (Cairo CG 40) is probably unrelated to an actual historic event, since Menkauhor was unlikely to have celebrated a *sed*-festival. A monument of Menkauhor has been discovered in the Near East, in Dorak, an indication of possibly far-reaching trade contacts.

Djedkare Izezi (c.2436–2304 BCE). For Djedkare, personal name Izezi, the Turin Canon documents a reign of twenty-eight years; Manetho, however, indicates forty-four years. The Abusir papyri from the funerary temple of Neferirkare record a twenty-first year of the taxation estimate. In consideration of the fact that under Djedkare we find evidence of the tax evaluation taking place every second year, we perhaps ought to estimate his reign at a minimum of forty-one to forty-two years. Such a long reign is further corroborated by the fact that Djedkare celebrated a *sed*-festival, commemorated in the inscription on a vessel now in the Louvre (E. 5323). We have very little information about the queens of Djedkare: Meresankh IV was probably one of them; and another, as yet anonymous queen, buried to the northeast of Djedkare's pyramid is likely the mother of the later king Unas. The pyramid and funerary temple of the king, called "Djedkare Is Perfect" are in Saqqara. Under his reign, the construction of sun temples was discontinued.

The various campaigns and expeditions of Djedkare reached Nubia and Punt, from which a dancing dwarf was brought to Egypt. Under his long reign the administration expanded. The provincial officials gained greater autonomy from the central government, leading to a weakening of the central administration. To redress the balance, the office of "Overseer of Upper Egypt," answering directly to the central administration, was created with its seat in Abydos. The tendency to pass on offices to family members grew, especially evident in the case of viziers. The viziers of the Ptahhotep family have tombs in Saqqara. One of these viziers was believed in later periods to have been author of instructions for officials. Other viziers of Djedkare's reign established their tombs in Giza,

including Seshemnefer III (tomb 5170) and Senedjemib Inti (tomb 2370). This is another example of an office being handed from father to son, here Senedjemib Mehi (tomb 2378). The close relationship of the viziers Senedjemib Inti and Rashepses with their king is shown in the so-called royal letters that were inscribed in their *mastaba*s.

Officials were increasingly able to afford large *mastaba*s decorated with elaborate pictorial cycles. Even craftsmen commissioned large funerary complexes; the career of a goldsmith from Djedkare's period, contained in the biography of Semenkhuiptah Itwesh from Saqqara, is evidence of the new wealth of craftsmen and artisans. The great number of commissions led to a higher profile for the royal workshops and greater perfection in the craftsmen's work.

Unas (c.2404–2374 BCE). As successor to Djedkare, his son Unas ascended to the throne. With him, the fifth dynasty came to an end. His reign is given as thirty years in the Turin Canon and as thirty-three by Manetho; thirty is likely. His queens were Chenut and Nebet.

The pyramid of Unas lies in Saqqara at a site where more ancient royal tombs had already been erected; these were leveled by Unas. Its name is "The Places of Unas Are Perfection." It is the first pyramid of the Old Kingdom whose subterranean burial chambers are inscribed with Pyramid Texts, writings intended to ensure the continued life of the king in the afterworld. Their location in the interior of the pyramid is to safeguard the king's path into the heavenly world beyond, even if his mortuary cult should come to an end. The pyramid temple is largely destroyed. Nevertheless, we can see that in addition to different religious scenes, *sed*-festival scenes were also incorporated into the decorative program of the temple. "Historical images" of the earlier period—for example, the famine reliefs of Sahure—are incorporated into the areas linked to the funerary temple, but without any historical basis.

Few concrete historical documents remain of Unas. It is nevertheless evident that during his reign, the administration was once more capable of great achievements. Expeditions to Elephantine to gather building materials for the pyramid and the funerary temple are illustrated along the causeway to the pyramid and are confirmed by inscriptions at Elephantine.

Several viziers held office under Unas, and large funerary complexes were erected for them. The tombs of the viziers Akhtihotep and Ptahhotep II in Saqqara, and that of the vizier and architectural overseer Senedjemib Mehi in Giza (tomb 2378), count among the foremost tombs of this period. Others were created along the Unas causeway, among the tombs of Prince Unasankh and of the viziers Iinefret Shanef, Ihy, and Akhtihotep Hemi. A vizier called

Nefersehemseshat is depicted on the causeway to the pyramid temple.

Although sun monuments and temples were no longer constructed during this period, the all-encompassing sun god remained the highest of all deities. As ruler of the dead and judge in the underworld, Osiris now took on a higher profile. Abydos, the funerary site of rulers of the early period, became the main cult site of Osiris. The cult of Osiris brought about a revolutionary change in afterlife beliefs; instead of the king, the god is now the guarantor of continued life after death. Existence in the afterlife no longer depends on the relationship between the individual mortal and the king or the individual's social status; instead, it is linked to his ethical position in direct relation to Osiris. The idealized biography took over from the reality-based biography of earlier times.

[*See also* Pyramid.]

BIBLIOGRAPHY

Kaiser, Werner. "Zu den Sonnenheiligtümern der 5. Dynastie." *Mitteilungen des Deutschen Archäologischen Instituts, Abteilung Kairo* 14 (1956), 104–116.

Málek, Jaromir. "La division de l'histoire d'Égypte et l'Égyptologie moderne." *Bulletin de la Société Française d'Égyptologie* 138 (1997), 6–17.

Munro, Peter. *Der Unas-Friedhof Nord-West I.* Mainz, 1993.

Roccati, Alessandro. *La littérature historique sous l'Ancien Empire égyptien.* Paris, 1982.

Seipel, Wilfried. *Untersuchngen zu den ägyptischen Königinnen der Frühzeit und des Alten Reiches.* Hamburg, 1980.

Spalinger, Anthony. "Dated Texts of the Old Kingdom." *Studien zur Altägyptischen Kultur* 21 (1994), 275–319.

Stadelmann, Rainer. *Die ägyptischen Pyramiden: Vom Ziegelbau zum Weltwunder.* Mainz, 1985.

Verner, Miroslav. *Abusir III: The Pyramid Complex of Khentkaus.* Prague, 1995.

Verner, Miroslav. *Lost Pyramids, Lost Pharaohs: Abusir.* Prague, 1994.

Winter, Erich. "Zur Deutung der Sonnenheiligtümer der 5. Dynastie." *Wiener Zeitschrift für die Kunde des Morgenlands* 54 (1957), 222–233.

HARTWIG ALTENMÜLLER
Translated from German by Elizabeth Schwaiger
and Jane McGary

Sixth Dynasty

In the third-century BCE king lists of Manetho, those from Teti to Nitokerty (Gr., Nitocris) comprise the sixth dynasty; this ascribed a total of 203 years. The Turin Canon calculates 181 years, but adds three kings, concluding with Aba; this slightly shorter time period is more compatible with the documented dates. If Aba belongs to the eighth dynasty, as stated in Manetho, then the kings of the eighth dynasty reigned for approximately 26 years, so approximately 155 years can be calculated for the sixth dynasty.

The political history of the sixth dynasty (c.2374–2200 BCE) is defined by its kings: Teti, Userkare, Pepy I, Merenre Antyemsaf, Pepy II, Merenre [Antyemsaf] II, and Nitokerty. The end of the dynasty was followed by a quick succession of ephemeral rulers (c.2200–2165), among them Aba. The dissolution of Egyptian state administration occurred during the reign of these last kings.

The history of the sixth dynasty is recorded, as in the earlier period, in the form of annals. One has recently been discovered as a palimpsest from the period of Pepy II on the lid of Queen Ankhnespepy's (III) sarcophagus. The events depicted there encompass the reigns of Teti, Userkare, and Pepy I. Since the recovered annals are very fragmentary and cover only the period up to Pepy I, other sources must be consulted for a more complete historical picture. Most useful are the royal and private monuments, mainly in the necropolises of Giza and Saqqara, along with royal decrees from Abydos, Dahshur, and Coptos. The question remains unsolved as to why the ancient tradition begins the sixth dynasty with Teti, placing a break between him and Unas of the fifth dynasty. It is possible that Teti ascended to the throne not as a prince, but as Unas's son-in-law.

The beginning of the sixth dynasty is characterized by powerful and long-reigning rulers (Teti, Pepy I). Pepy I, one of Egypt's great pharaohs, reformed the administration toward the middle of the dynasty. This reform led to a decentralization of the administration, which in turn started the dissolution of the state during the long reign of Pepy II. During this dynasty, a large part of state property became private or temple property. Administrative reforms which gave more rights to the individual resulted in a decentralized state. The central administration was undermined, and provincial administrations gained in autonomy. Numerous surviving royal decrees document the developments connected to this reform; most of them focus on exemptions from taxes, corvée labor, and donations to the king.

The nomarchs—a hereditary office of provincial governors from the middle of the sixth dynasty onward—built their tombs close to their official residences in Middle and Upper Egypt and erected large rock-cut tombs or large *mastabas*, depending on the nature of the landscape. In the oases, too, were found cemeteries for oasis administrators of this period. A growing number of titles were bestowed on officials. By the end of the sixth dynasty, viziers found themselves without any real administrative authority because the high officials were able to bypass them by means of their own rank and titles.

The dissolution of the state and of central administration was further hastened by striving for independence on the part of the provincial nomarchs. In the final phase of the Old Kingdom, the nomarchs united in their own persons both temple administration and state offices. The balance between the previously equal and independent administrative spheres of province and temple was disrupted. The nomarchs gained ever greater independence from the king. They made themselves the center of small court-like states, whose members were interred near or even in the tombs of their patrons.

Concurrent with this development, there emerged a democratization of beliefs about the afterlife among officials. Magical strategies originally available only to the king—ritual spells in the pyramids, or deification of the dead as "Osiris" through transfiguration—now became accessible to the officials. At the end of the sixth dynasty, the first instances of nonroyal dead assume the title of Osiris—a privilege formerly reserved for the king. Tombs in the royal residence and in the provinces grew smaller and are sometimes devoid of elaborate decoration. The dimensions of private sculptures and carvings lessened. Increasingly we see the use of softer materials (limestone, calcite [Egyptian alabaster], wood) instead of the previously treasured hard stones.

The complete collapse of the Old Kingdom, which occurred in the interior of the country in the years following Pepy II, was the most profound—and, for the political and spiritual development of the country, the most significant—turning point in Egyptian history. The people witnessed the failure of all the powers of the state. The order of the universe, hitherto regarded as eternal, became subject to doubt. The literature of the Old Kingdom laments the loss of values. A comparison of past and present sparked questions about the meaning of life. In the Wisdom Literature, the very existence of gods is open to debate.

Teti (c.2374–2354 BCE). There is no consensus as to the length of Teti's reign. The dates given in the Turin Canon have been destroyed; the versions of Manetho mention thirty (Syncellus) and thirty-three years (Eratosthenes) respectively. Records from Teti's period give as the highest date a "sixth year after the count," which corresponds to year 12 or 13. A reign of twenty-three years may be a realistic estimate.

Teti's mother, Seshseshet, was probably of nonroyal descent. His wives Khuit (II) and Iput (I) were probably daughters of King Unas. The descent of a queen named Khenti + [. . .] during Teti's reign is unknown. The pyramid of Teti is named "Enduring Are the Sites of Teti."

Teti's building and offering activities encompass the most important sacred sites of the land: in Bubastis, a *ka*-house was erected for him, and in Heliopolis, a quartzite obelisk was raised with his name. Offerings were consecrated in the temple of Hathor at Dendera, among them a sistrum with Teti's name. The Khentyamentiu temple in Abydos was exempted from tribute through a protective decree. There exists documented evidence of an expedi-

tion to the calcite quarries in Hatnub, dated to Year 12 or 13.

The government could rely on trustworthy officials from the fifth dynasty. Teti's viziers Mehu and Kagemni both began their careers under Djedkare Izezi and Unas. Isi of Edfu followed a similar career path, serving as a residence official under Izezi and Unas and subsequently given the office of "Overseer of the Province" of Edfu under Teti. The significance of these three officials may be measured by the adoration as gods bestowed on them after death. Like Ptahhotep, who had been vizier under Djedkare Izezi, Kagemni was posthumously recognized as the author of instructions for officials. Nikau-Isesi, the "vizier of Upper Egypt" whose seat was in Abydos, had also held high office under Unas. Another significant official from the Teti period is the vizier Mereruka, who may have taken on the viziership as Teti's son-in-law toward the end of the reign.

Under Teti, the development of the Egyptian state unfolded peacefully. This makes more shocking the report by Manetho that King Teti was the victim of assassination, something that cannot be verified from contemporary sources.

Userkare (c.2358?–2354 BCE). King Userkare can be placed between Teti and Pepy I. His reign of two to six years is recorded in the annals of the sixth dynasty, but specific events during this period are not known. The name of Userkare is included in the official list of Sety I of Abydos, and also in the Turin Canon. Still, he is barely attested on contemporary monuments (a copper blade and two seal cylinders), and his name is completely absent in the funerary complexes of the officials of his time.

The kingship of Userkare is altogether mysterious. It is unclear whether he was a son of Teti and Khuit (II), and whether he should be connected to the assassination of Teti as recorded in Manetho.

Pepy I (c.2354–2310 BCE). Pepy I was a son of Teti and Queen Iput (I). He may have succeeded to the throne as a minor, so that a regency by his mother is not to be excluded. As king, his throne name was initially Nefersahor; from his Year 10 at the latest, he was named Meryre. His reign is recorded in the Turin Canon as having lasted twenty years, but the annals of the sixth dynasty record at least a twenty-fifth occasion of the count for Pepy I, which corresponds to Year 49 or 50 of reign. Manetho (version of Africanus) assigns a reign of fifty-three years, which may be realistic, given the information from recently discovered annals.

Pepy I had five wives. The first queen was removed after a harem conspiracy, following a thorough judicial investigation led by the high official Weni. In a subsequent marriage, Pepy I united with the noble family of Khui at Abydos, whose two daughters he married in the last years of his reign. The elder of the two, Ankhnesmeryre (I), was the mother of King Merenre and of Queen Neith; the younger, Ankhnesmeryre (II), was still alive during the reign of her son, Pepy II. The pyramids of two other queens of Pepy I, Nubunet and Inenek Inti, have also been discovered.

The pyramid of the king bears the name MenneferPepy Meryre ("The Perfection of Pepy Endures"). The later designation of the city of Memphis is derived from "Mennefer."

Although records pertaining to the reign of Pepy I were largely destroyed in the annals of the sixth dynasty, other sources indicate that he celebrated, "in the year following the eighteenth count" (i.e., in Year 36/37 of his reign), a first, somewhat belated *sed*-festival. Several monuments exist, created for this occasion, above all statues (e.g., Brooklyn 39.120) and vases. The date is inscribed repeatedly in the Sinai and in the Wadi Hammamat of the Eastern Desert. In the calcite quarries of Hatnub, it is mentioned again as late as Year 49/50 of the king's reign. Problematic is the question of whether the biennial counts had by this time become annual designations.

The country's predominant political and cultural focus on the royal residence was abandoned during the long reign of Pepy I. The cults of local deities were promoted through protective decrees, construction, and dedications. Pepy I especially favored the cult of Hathor in Dendera with several endowments, including statues. Other cults for which he instituted endowments were those of Satet of Elephantine, for which a granite shrine was created, Min at Koptos, Horus at Hierakonpolis, Osiris at Abydos, and Bastet at Bubastis. The endowments promoted the division of property, in the form of land and people, that originally belonged to the king. The exemption decree for the pyramid city of Sneferu in Dahshur, issued in the "year of the twenty-first count" (Year 41/42 of the king), belongs in the same context; it mentions several eminent contemporaries of the king, among them Merptahankhmeryre Nekhebu and Weni.

To counteract the fragmentation of state power, royal *ka*-chapels were built on many sites throughout the land to symbolize the constant presence of the king. Such a *ka*-chapel has been discovered in Bubastis. Further *ka*-chapels were erected in the Nile Delta under the leadership of the architect Merptahankhmeryre Nekhebu. Nekhebu was also given a royal commission to dig a canal in the Nile Delta and another in Cusae, both likely intended for transportation rather than irrigation.

Expeditions during Pepy's reign led into the Sinai, to Middle Egypt to the calcite quarries of Hatnub, into the Eastern Desert to the Wadi Hammamat, and south to Nubia, where gold and hard stone could be obtained. A lively trade existed with neighboring countries to the south and the north. Incense was imported from Punt on the shore of the Red Sea. Tribute was delivered by foreign delegations to the residence—whether as gifts in the aftermath of warlike confrontations or merely to honor the pharaoh cannot be determined.

The biography of Weni from Abydos reports a punitive expedition to suppress nomads in Palestine. The account indicates that the army was composed of recruits from various districts of Egypt, as well as contingents of tribute-owing Nubian tribes. This leads us to assume that during the reign of Pepy I there was as yet no standing army.

Among the significant artifacts of Pepy I is a copper statue showing the king with Merenre, the heir to the throne, as a child (Cairo JE 33034–33035). The majority of other royal sculptures from this period are small in scale.

Merenre Antyemsaf I (c.2310–2300 BCE). This king was a son of Pepy I and his wife Ankhnesmeryre I. He ascended the throne as a young man and died after an estimated six-year reign. The Turin Canon calculates six years; Manetho indicates seven. The latest documented date of the king is, however, indicated as one "year after the year of the fifth count," which would correspond to a tenth year. Since his half-brother Pepy II ascended the throne at age six, Merenre's reign could not have lasted more than six years. Under Merenre, the count must have been taken several times in successive years, which would explain the "fifth time of the count."

The pyramid of the king, named "The Perfection of Merenre Rises," is in Saqqara. Weni, who had already served under Teti and Pepy I, and was elevated by Merenre to "Overseer of Upper Egypt," tells in his biography of acquiring building materials and a pyramidion, and of equipping a funerary monument with a sarcophagus, a false door, and an offering tablet. Weni led several expeditions to Elephantine, where he was active in canal construction, and to Hatnub. Together with Merptahankhmeryre Nekhebu, he is counted among the most important personages of the time.

Under Merenre, contacts with Nubia were intensified by the nomarch and caravan-leader Herkhuef, whose tomb is at Aswan. Herkhuef was commissioned by the king to lead three expeditions to Upper Nubia into the land of Yam, which is presumed to have been in the Dongola region. Yam was a transfer point for trade with the Sudan, a source of tropical precious woods and ivory. The first of the three trade expeditions led by Herkhuef lasted seven months; the second required eight. During the third expedition he found the prince of Yam engaged in a military campaign against the prince of Tjemehu (a Libyan group). Herkhuef joined the fight on the side of the Yam, who richly rewarded him for his efforts. From Herkhuef's inscription we know further that during the period of Merenre the tribes of Lower Nubia, from the regions of Satju, Irtjet, and Wawat, combined into a single state.

In the year following the fifth count—the last year of Merenre's reign—the king traveled to Elephantine to the seat of the governor of Upper Egypt. There he received the homage of the Nubian chiefs. It is possible that he combined this journey with a visit to the temple of Satet in Elephantine to renew the granite shrine erected by Pepy I.

Pepy II (c.2300–2206 BCE). Pepy II, whose throne name is Neferkare, was a son of Pepy I and his wife Ankhnesmeryre (II), and therefore a younger half-brother of Merenre. He ascended the throne as a child, with his mother acting as regent. According to the otherwise reliable Turin Canon, Pepy II is supposed to have reigned more than ninety years; Manetho assigns exactly ninety-four years. The high numbers are surely a miswriting of a lower number (perhaps sixty-four years). There is proof of a year of the second count, a thirty-first count, a year following that, and, as the latest date, a year of the thirty-third count. Assuming that the count was taken every second year, this could amount to a sixty-fifth year.

Pepy II had four royal wives, all buried near his pyramid in Saqqara South, which was named "The Life of Neferkare/Pepy II Endures." The queens were his two half-sisters, Neith and Iput (II), and Udjebten and Ankhnespepy (III), the latter two most likely of nonroyal descent. The lid of Ankhnespepy's sarcophagus is made of a stone that contains the annals of the sixth dynasty. Neith, whose first husband may have been Merenre I, seems to have been the mother of Pepy II's successor, Merenre Nemtymsaf (or Antyemsaf) II.

The long reign of Pepy II witnessed the final fall of the Old Kingdom and the dissolution of the state. The only trace of a state presence in Upper Egypt is found in the royal decrees for the protection of offering-endowments at Abydos and Coptos.

Expedition inscriptions occur in great numbers in the Sinai, Hatnub, the Eastern Desert, Upper Egypt, and Nubia at the beginning of the reign. The overseers of expeditions on the Nubian border also left behind extensive inscriptions. In the "year of the second count," Herkhuef undertook his last campaign into Nubia, from which he returned with a pygmy, anxiously awaited by the child-king. Mekhu and Sabni succeeded Herkhuef in Elephantine. Sabni's achievements are documented in a detailed biographical inscription at the entrance to his tomb on the Qubbet el-Hawa near Aswan. Aside from several successfully executed trade expeditions into Nubia, Sabni is notable for having transported back to Egypt the corpse of his father Mekhu, who had died on a trade expedition in Nubia.

Pepynakht, called Hekaib, whose tomb is also on the Qubbet el-Hawa and who was deified in the Middle Kingdom, guided several expeditions abroad as a royal residence administrator, commissioned by the king. In his autobiography, he tells of two expeditions to Nubia and a third to the Red Sea, from which he returned with the corpses of two civil servants who had been killed during the construction of Byblos ships for a journey to Punt. His son Sabni was commissioned by Pepy II to transport two "large obelisks" from Elephantine to Heliopolis and built two large transport vessels for this purpose.

Toward the end of the sixth dynasty, the far-reaching collapse of the administration threatened the food supply of the country, which was wholly dependent on agriculture. After Pepy II's death and the short reign of his son, the land fell into chaos. For a short period Queen Nitokerty (c.2205–2200 BCE) reigned, a period that was followed by an interregnum.

Eighth Dynasty (c.2190–2165 BCE). The eighth dynasty is characterized by fierce struggles over the throne. In only six years, eleven kings succeeded, followed by six short-lived rulers (although it is sometimes called the "eighteen kings"). Nevertheless, the political unity of Egypt at first remained intact under its nominal leadership. A small pyramid of the fourteenth ruler, Aba, is preserved at Saqqara. The names of the last three rulers (Neferkaure, Neferkauhor, and Neferirkare) are known to us through edicts issued by them to the benefit of their brothers-in-law, the princes of Coptos. Upper Egypt was governed by local rulers, relying on the local citizen armies and on Nubian archers. Prince Ankhtifi, son of a prince of Elkab, went to war with the princes of Coptos and Thebes. The biographical inscription in his tomb is evidence in form and content of the chaotic nature of this period.

[*See also* Pepy I; Pepy II; Pyramid; *and* Teti.]

BIBLIOGRAPHY

Baud, Michel, and Vassil Dobrev. "De nouvelles annales de l'Ancien Empire égyptien: Une Pierre de Palerme pour la VIᵉ dynastie." *Bulletin de l'Institut Français d'Archéologie Orientale* 95 (1995), 23–92. Report of the recently discovered annals from the sarcophagus of Queen Ankhnespepy III.

Eichler, Eckhard. *Untersuchungen zum Expeditionswesen des ägyptischen Alten Reiches.* Göttinger Orientforschungen, 4.26. Wiesbaden, 1993. A study of expeditions.

Goedicke, Hans. *Königliche Dokumente aus dem Alten Reich.* Ägyptologische Abhandlungen, 14. Wiesbaden, 1967.

Kanawati, Naguib. *Governmental Reforms in the Old Kingdom.* Warminster, 1981.

Lichtheim, M. *Ancient Egyptian Literature.* Vol. 1. Berkeley, 1973.

Martin-Pardey, Eva. *Untersuchungen zur ägyptischen Provinzialverwaltung bis zum Ende des Alten Reiches.* Hildesheimer Ägyptologsiche Beiträge, 1. Hildesheim, 1976. On the internal political development of the state during the sixth dynasty.

Müller-Wollermann, Renate. *Krisenfaktoren im ägyptischen Staat des ausgehenden Alten Reiches.* Tübingen, 1986. On the decline of the Old Kingdom and its causes.

Roccati, Alessandro. *La littérature historique sous l'Ancien Empire égyptien.* Paris, 1982.

Seidlmayer, Stephan Johannes. *Gräberfelder aus dem Übergang vom Alten zum Mittleren Reich: Studien zur Archäologie der Ersten Zwischenzeit.* Studien zur Archäologie und Geschichte Altägyptens, 1. Heidelberg, 1990.

Seipel, Wilfried. *Untersuchungen zu den ägyptischen Königinnen der Frühzeit und des Alten Reiches.* Hamburg, 1980. Discussion of sixth dynasty queens.

Spalinger, Anthony. "Dated Texts of the Old Kingdom." *Studien zur Altägyptischen Kultur* 21 (1994), 275–319. Up-to-date discussion of chronology of the sixth dynasty.

HARTWIG ALTENMÜLLER
Translated from German by Elizabeth Schwaiger
and Jane McGary

ONOMASTICA are word lists, essentially catalogs of the universe, grouped by the major items in heaven, earth, and the waters. The earliest Egyptian onomasticon is the fragmentary Ramesseum Onomasticon (Berlin Papyrus 10495), dated to the late Middle Kingdom, and from a find that contained several important manuscripts and a collection of objects, perhaps the property of a magician and storyteller. The list of words originally contained more than three hundred entries. The beginning is unfortunately lost, but the list continues with plant names, liquids, birds, fish, quadrupeds, southern fortresses, twenty-nine towns, cakes, loaves and biscuits, cereals, parts of the human body, salt, natron, and the markings and body parts of cattle.

The most important word list is the Onomasticon of Amenemope, dating probably to the end of the twentieth dynasty and known from at least ten copies or fragmentary versions on papyrus, a writing board, a strip of leather, and several potsherds. Gardiner (1947) characterized the heading as bombastic:

Beginning of the teaching for clearing the mind, for instruction of the ignorant and for learning all things that exist: what Ptah created, what Thoth copied down, heaven with its affairs, earth and what is in it, what the mountains belch forth, what is watered by the flood, all things upon which Re has shone, all that is grown on the back of earth, excogitated by the scribe of the sacred books in the House of Life, Amenemope son of Amenemope, he said.

This is followed by the list. Note that the text is characterized as an instruction or teaching and is thus assigned to that genre; it also explains its function.

Gardiner's commentary on all the terms is widely consulted, and its excellence has in some ways discouraged other scholars from studying the onomastica as such. The main text is that of the Golenischeff Papyrus in Moscow,

which was discovered at el-Hiba along with the papyri containing the *Misadventures of Wenamun* and the *Story of Woe.* The Golenischeff Papyrus has as many as 610 items listed, until it breaks off at the end of its seventh page.

As Gardiner indicated, the ancient Egyptian author had not only the principles of enumeration but also classification in mind; in addition, it is "a first rate authority for the topography of the Nile Valley." The classification consists of nine sections: (1) introductory heading; (2) sky, water, and earth; (3) persons, court, offices, and occupations; (4) classes, tribes, and types of human beings; (5) the towns of Egypt; (6) buildings, parts of buildings, and types of land; (7) agricultural land, cereals, and their products; (8) beverages; (9) parts of an ox and kinds of meat. The order is generally hierarchical, from highest to lowest, as particularly noted in the third section: god, goddess, male *ȝḫt*-spirit, female *ȝḫt*-spirit, king, queen, king's wife (the usual term for "queen"), king's mother, king's offspring, crown prince, vizier, sole companion, eldest king's son, great overseer of the army, and so forth. Although there is no commentary or explanation of each term, the idea of such word lists as a teaching device for scribes is obvious, particularly the unfamiliar designations of foreign places. The Miscellany Literature similarly has instructional elements, such as the list of the parts of a chariot.

[*See also* Vocabulary.]

BIBLIOGRAPHY

Gardiner, Alan H. *Ancient Egyptian Onomastica.* 2 vols. and plate vol. Oxford, 1947. The major source for these lists, with abundant commentary.

Herbin, François-René. "Une version inachevée de l'onomasticon d'Aménémopé (P. BM 10474 vo.)." *Bulletin de l'Institut français d'archéologie orientale* 86 (1986), 187–199.

Nims, Charles F. "Egyptian Catalogues of Things." *Journal of Near Eastern Studies* 9 (1950), 253–262. A substantial review article on Gardiner's edition.

Osing, Jürgen. "Onomasktika." In *Lexikon der Ägyptologie,* 4: 572. Wiesbaden, 1981.

WILLIAM KELLY SIMPSON

OPENING OF THE MOUTH. The Opening of the Mouth ceremony is arguably the most important ancient Egyptian ritual. It was performed on cult statues of gods, kings, and private individuals, as well as on the mummies of humans and Apis bulls; it could even be performed on entire temples. The effect of the ritual was to animate its recipient, or, in the case of the dead, to reanimate it. It allowed the mummy, statue, or temple to eat, breathe, see, hear, and otherwise enjoy the provisions offered by the cult. (It was sometimes accompanied by secondary ritual gestures said to open the eyes.) The ritual could be performed with various implements (most commonly a wood-carving adze), which were touched to the lips by a cult functionary.

The Egyptian terms for the ritual are *wpt-r* and *wn-r*, both of which translate literally as "opening of the mouth." The verb *wpi* seems to predominate, although *wn* often occurs in parallel with it. The two verbs are not exact synonyms. The verb *wpi* seems to connote an opening that entails splitting, dividing, or separating; it can be used, for example, to describe the separation of two combatants, the dividing of time, or even an analysis or determination of the truth. The verb *wn* seems to give more emphasis to accessibility and exposure and is used in contexts such as *wn-ḥr*, literally "open the face," but in fact meaning "see or be seen." It has been suggested that the use of the verb *wpi* points to the ritual's origin in statue carving, because the woodcarver's adze is more likely to split than to open up, and because the verb implies greater force. However, other uses of *wpi* are nonviolent, and the adze is normally used not to cleave but to shave wood. *Wpi* is more probably favored because the opening of the mouth entails the parting of the lips.

The ritual clearly changed and evolved over the centuries of its use. The principal study on the subject is that of Otto (1960), who published an extensive translation, commentary, and analysis of the New Kingdom version of the ritual. He argues that the Opening of the Mouth was a confused amalgamation of many different rituals, some originally unrelated, and that the cult functionaries who performed it were often entirely ignorant of the origins and meanings of the implements and words they employed. In the New Kingdom redaction of the ritual, he sees traces of a statue ritual, an offering ritual, an embalming ritual, a burial ritual, a butchering ritual, and a temple ritual. Because of the centrality of the adze in the New Kingdom depictions of the ritual, he argues that the preparation of cult statues was the earliest context in which the ritual was used, and in which it developed.

A different reconstruction of the ritual's origins has been proposed by Roth (1993), based on her analysis of its Old Kingdom version. She argues that it was not until the sixth dynasty that the statue ritual was incorporated into an Opening of the Mouth ceremony that had already developed independently as part of the funerary ritual. Based on the fact that the earliest funerary implements seem to have been the little fingers of the priest (later supplanted by finger-shaped blades of meteoric iron), and on the context in which the earliest redaction of the Opening of the Mouth occurs, she proposes that the funerary ritual was a metaphorical reenactment of the clearing of a baby's mouth at birth, and that the statue ritual may have developed independently from the same metaphor. She

concludes that the New Kingdom redaction was an intentionally complex and redundant combination of new forms with the old.

Old Kingdom. The earliest Old Kingdom textual references to the Opening of the Mouth (*pace* Brovarski, *Serapis* 4[1977–1978], 1–2) date to the early fourth dynasty, when references to the statue ritual can be found both in the Palermo stone and in the decoration of the tomb of the royal official Metjen. The Palermo stone tells us that the ritual takes place in the *ḥwt nbw*, the quarter of the goldsmiths (or possibly the similarly written quarry of Hatnub). The Palermo stone and similar historical notations use the formula [*god X*] *mst wpt-r m ḥwt-nbw*, "the fashioning (literally, the birth) and opening of the mouth of (a statue of) god X in the goldsmiths' quarter/Hatnub." Examples of this formula prior to the fourth dynasty use only the form [*god X*] *mst*, "the fashioning of god X," which suggests that the opening of the mouths of statues was introduced only in the fourth dynasty. The captions of the Metjen scenes mention that the ritual is performed four times, and a fourfold repetition may also be mentioned in a fragment from the mortuary temple of Sneferu. Metjen's Opening of the Mouth ritual occurs in conjunction with censing and the ritual of transforming the deceased into a *ꜣḥ* (or *sꜣḥt*). In none of these references to the ritual is the ritual action represented.

The next clear textual mention of the ritual is in the Pyramid Texts of Unas, dating to the end of the fifth dynasty. On the north wall of Unas's burial chamber is inscribed an offering ritual in which two blades of meteoric iron, called the *nṯrwy*, are said to open the mouth (Spell 30b). One blade is described as Lower Egyptian and the other as Upper Egyptian. Van Walsem (1978) argues that the ritual sequence preserved in this part of the offering ritual was already badly confused, and in fact represented a ritual of embalming entirely unrelated to the ritual of the Opening of the Mouth. Opposing this, Roth (1993) observes that this entire ritual sequence mimics the birth and maturation of a child, and that the *nṯrwy* blades represent the pair of little fingers that would have cleared a newborn baby's mouth. In later collections of Pyramid Texts, there are references to Horus's opening the mouth of Osiris with his little fingers (in Spells 1329–1330) and to the sons of Horus opening the mouth with little fingers of meteoric iron (in Spells 1983). Other elements in the sequence following the *nṯrwy* blades are milk jars (one empty, one holding milk), described as the breasts of Isis and Horus, and five cloves of garlic described as teeth. The implement preceding the *nṯrwy* blades was the *pšs-kf* knife, which Roth believes was used to cut the umbilical cord.

Actual *nṯrwy* blades are not preserved archaeologically; however, models are occasionally found in "*pšs-kf* sets," limestone platters with recesses that hold (usually) the two *nṯrwy* blades, a blunt *psš-kf* knife, two tiny bottles, and four tiny cups. The bottles and cups are half of light-colored stone and half of black stone. These implements represent all the nonperishable requirements for the first row of the offering ritual given in the Pyramid Texts of Unas, and are therefore also known as "Opening of the Mouth sets." The same set of implements is listed together in the inventories of temple equipment found at the mortuary temple of Neferirkare at Abusir.

This ritual may be older than its earliest surviving appearance, at the end of the fifth dynasty. Elements of the same sequence of implements and offerings listed in the Pyramid Texts occur in royal offering lists as early as the reign of Sahure, the second king of the fifth dynasty. The *psš-kf* knife is attested archaeologically even earlier; it was buried in prehistoric tombs as early as the Naqada I period. Since this knife is otherwise known only in connection with the Opening of the Mouth ritual, its presence suggests that some form of the ritual dates back to prehistoric times.

Only in the sixth dynasty was a second new sequence added to the beginning of the Pyramid Text ritual (Spells 11–15). These new spells describe the Opening of the Mouth using the foreleg of a bull and an iron woodworking adze, both of which can be related to the constellation Ursa Major. These spells are clearly related to the statue ritual, since the foreleg is said to be offered four times. In addition to the little fingers and the little fingers of meteoric iron, the other implements mentioned in these later Pyramid Texts include the *dwȝ-wr*, probably a chisel (Spell 1329c), and the *sšȝ*, a mysterious implement not attested elsewhere (Spell 1329b). The rite with the *dwȝ-wr* was again said to occur in the *ḥwt-nbw*, so it is clearly part of the statue ritual. That these are later additions to the mortuary ritual can also be demonstrated by the fact that no adzes or chisels seem to be mentioned in the inventories of temple equipment from the mortuary temple of Neferirkare at Abusir.

Middle Kingdom. The implements used in both the original and the later redactions of the Opening of the Mouth ritual in the Pyramid Texts continue to appear in private tombs of the Middle Kingdom, in both offering lists and friezes of objects. A rather different version of the ritual also appears in the Coffin Texts (*CT I,65*), in which Horus and Ptah open the mouth of the deceased, Ptah and Thoth do the ritual of transfiguration, and Thoth replaces the heart in the body "so that you remember what you have forgotten, and can eat bread as you desire." The importance of Ptah and Thoth points to new developments, since neither is mentioned in earlier versions; however, there is little further evidence for the development of the ritual during the Middle Kingdom period.

New Kingdom. The New Kingdom Opening of the Mouth ritual shows two different traditions. The tradition of the Coffin Text spell has developed into chapter 23 of the *Book of Going Forth by Day* (the *Book of the Dead*). In this chapter, the mouth is opened by Ptah and the local god of the deceased, while Thoth stands by, equipped with magic. The bonds that had been obstructing the mouth and preventing it from functioning are associated with the god Seth. The mouth is also said to be opened by the god Shu with a harpoon of iron, and the deceased is identified with the goddess Sakhmet and the constellation Orion. The conclusion of the spell invokes the entire Ennead of gods to protect the deceased from any negative spell.

This tradition is clearly different from the conception of the Opening of the Mouth developed in the Pyramid Texts ritual and the related offering list sequence. Not only are different gods involved (Ptah is mentioned in only three spells altogether in the Pyramid Texts, none of them connected with opening the mouth); in addition, the protective purpose seems entirely different. The identification of Seth with the bonds restricting the mouth is in direct contradiction to Pyramid Texts Spell 14, in which the iron of the adze that opens the mouth is said to have come forth from Seth. The second New Kingdom version of the opening of the mouth is, however, clearly descended from the Old Kingdom version. The adze, the *dwȝ-wr*, the fingers, and the *psš-kf* are all included, together with several other elements.

Otto (1960) distinguishes seventy-five scenes in the New Kingdom version of the ritual. In most cases the ritual is given a title, normally "the Performance of the Opening of the Mouth for the Statue in the *Ḥwt-nbw*." In the first scene, the mummy is placed on the sand, naked, with his face to the south, his clothes (wrappings?) behind him. In scenes 2 through 7, he is purified with poured libations, incense, and natron. These scenes are reminiscent of the first spells in the earliest Pyramid Text sequence (Spells 16–29). The similarities include not only the offerings but also the repetition of purification spells four times—once for each of four gods (Horus, Seth, Thoth, and Dewen-ʿanwy), each of whom represents one of the cardinal directions.

Scenes 8 through 22 are the scenes that are most clearly associated with the statue ritual, involving as they do craftsmen as well as priests. In scene 8, the lector-priest and the *imy-ḫnt*-priests go to the workshop (*is*); in scene 9 they wake the *stm*-priest, who is sleeping there; and in scene 10 they converse with him about a dream or vision he has had regarding the statue. The *stm*-priest dresses (scene 11) and instructs the craftsmen about the statue (scene 12), with special instructions for the specialized workers (scene 13). In scene 14, however, the mouth of the statue is opened with the little fingers by the *stm*-priest, who identifies himself as Horus. This use of the fingers, rather than the more usual wood-carving tool, may be intended to emphasize the humanity of the statue. In scene 15 the workers are instructed to continue their work, while in scene 16 the priest denies Seth's ability to whiten the head of the statue. Scenes 17 and 18 are interpreted by Otto as the completion and delivery of the statue. The texts make reference to Horus's search for his father. In scenes 19 through 21, the apparel of the *stm*-priest is augmented, and scene 22 is a procession of priests to the next group of rituals.

Scenes 23 through 27 involve the butchering of a bull and the presentation of its heart and foreleg, followed by Opening of the Mouth rituals using other implements—in scene 26, the *ntrty*, here pictured as an adze. In scene 27, another adze called the *wr-ḥk3w* ("great of magic") opens the eyes, and the statue is delivered to the *iry-pʿt* in scene 28. Scenes 29 and 30 are repetitions of scenes 17 and 16 from the statue ritual, with some variations in the latter.

Scene 31 introduces the "son whom he loves," a priest who will carry out the next series of mouth-opening rituals. This series again includes several elements of the Old Kingdom sequence, interspersed with newer implements. In scene 32 the "son whom he loves" opens the mouth with the ebony *mddft*-tool and a finger of gold, while in scene 33 the little finger is again used. In scene 34 the *nms* is offered in a jar, and in scenes 35 and 36 the four *ʿbt* are offered; neither of these offerings has been identified. Scene 37 shows the offering of the *psš-kf*, with the same accompanying speech that was used in the Pyramid Texts. In scene 38 grapes are offered, and in scene 39, an ostrich feather. Scene 39 is derived from Pyramid Texts Spell 32b, where an empty *mns3* jar is offered; the feather used to write *šw*, "empty," has mistakenly been read as a separate offering. Scene 40 is a repetition of scenes 20/21 and scene 36. In scene 41 a basin of water is offered, and in scene 42 the "son whom he loves" departs, marking the end of the sequence.

Scenes 43, 44, and 45 repeat the butchering of a bull and the offering of its heart and foreleg. In scene 45, the mouth is opened with a chisel, and in scene 46, incense is burnt. In scenes 48 through 54, a sequence of cloth strips and clothing is presented (perhaps derived from the cloth offerings in Pyramid Texts Spells 60–61 and 81). Scene 55 depicts the anointing of the statue, in some examples with the seven sacred oils known from the Old Kingdom ritual (Spells 72–78), where they appear immediately after the "B sequence." As in the Pyramid Texts (Spells 79–80), the anointing is directly followed by the offering of green and black eye paint in scene 56. Scene 57 shows the presenta-

tion of scepters (perhaps a distillation of the weapons and scepters presented in Pyramid Texts Spells 57–59 and 62–71), while scenes 58 through 61 describe censing the statue in various ways.

Scene 62 begins a sequence that may have had its origin in temple rituals. It depicts an act of homage with *nmst* jars. It is followed by libation (scene 63) and censing (scene 64). Scenes 65–72 deal with the preparation and presentation of the food offering, interspersed with censing and libation. The *ḥtp-di-nswt* offering formula is recited and the footprints of the priests are wiped away in scene 70. After an offering of incense to Re-Harakhti (scene 71), the offering concludes (scene 72).

The last three scenes deal with the final placement of the statue or the mummy, and the conclusion of the ceremony. While it is clear that many elements have been added to the Old Kingdom version of the ritual as given in the Pyramid Texts of Unas and later kings, many of the basic elements remain, in an order surprisingly close to the original sequence.

Late Period. The Late period redactions of the Opening of the Mouth ritual continue the traditions of the earlier periods. A group of mortuary rituals in this tradition from as late as the first century CE are known (Smith 1993). These late rituals retain many elements of the New Kingdom ritual, including the variety of officiants. The later texts, however, are specifically said to allow the dead person to breathe, and as such they seem to have taken on some of the characteristics of the "letters of breathing" known from this period. In addition to being performed as part of the funeral, it is possible that, like the letters of breathing, they were placed in the tomb for the use of the deceased. This development illustrates again the tendency of this ritual to incorporate new elements with the passage of time.

Peculiar to this period is the depiction of the ritual in temple dedication ceremonies. (The rituals may have been performed on temples from a much earlier period, of course.) The dedication ceremonies at the Ptolemaic temple of Edfu seem to combine elements of the tradition from the Coffin Texts and the *Book of Going Forth by Day* with the separate New Kingdom ritual derived from the Pyramid Texts. As summarized by Blackman (1946), the ritual contains many elements of the New Kingdom mortuary rite—for example, the use of multiple tools (an adze, a chisel, and a finger of gold) and the butchering of offerings. Yet several of the acts are said to be performed by Ptah, and Thoth is also involved; such an involvement of the gods is more typical of the Coffin Texts tradition. Like the mortuary tradition, the temple ritual would have been a complex series of actions selected from several different traditions.

BIBLIOGRAPHY

Blackman, A. M., and H. W. Fairman. "The Consecration of an Egyptian Temple According to the Use of Edfu," *Journal of Egyptian Archaeology* 32 (1946), 75–91. Gives a translation of the temple ceremony at Edfu and attempts to relate it to episodes of the New Kingdom rite.

Budge, E. A. W. *The Book of the Opening of the Mouth.* London, 1909. Long out of date, this was one of the earliest attempts to analyze the ritual.

Otto, Eberhard. *Das Ägyptische Mundöffnungsritual.* Ägyptologische Abhandlungen, 3. Wiesbaden, 1960. The basic edition and translation of the New Kingdom ritual, with full commentary.

Roth, Ann Macy. "Fingers, Stars, and the Opening of the Mouth: The Nature and Function of the *Nṯrwj* Blades." *Journal of Egyptian Archaeology* 79 (1993), 57–79. An argument for the origin of the ritual as an imitation of a child's birth and maturation.

Smith, Mark. *The Liturgy of Opening the Mouth for Breathing.* Oxford, 1993. Publication of several Demotic versions of the ritual.

van Walsem, Rene. "The *Psš-kf*: An investigation of an ancient Egyptian funerary instrument." *Oudheidkundige Mededelingen uit het Rijksmuseum van Oudheden te Leiden* 59 (1978), 193–249. Argues that the *psš-kf* knife and the *nṯrwy* blades, usually taken as early elements of the ritual, were instead part of a ritual of mummification.

ANN MACY ROTH

OPET FESTIVAL. *See* Festivals.

ORACLES. To distinguish them from individual magical practices, such as oneiromancy or recourse to seers, the Egyptian consultation of oracles may be described as requesting a deity to answer some practical question through the agency of its public image. The evidence for such oracles before the Ptolemaic period comprises four sources: the many oracular decrees, either engraved on the outer walls of temples or delivered on papyrus to private persons to use as amulets; references to particular oracular processes found in administrative or private records; a few original petitions on papyrus or ostraca laid before the god; and statues and reliefs clearly associated with oracles.

Origins and Development. A few three-dimensional artifacts have been thought to constitute archeological evidence of early oracles, but, for lack of any explicit text that supports this opinion, it is impossible to decide whether the "rocking" falcon of Predynastic date in the Brooklyn Museum was a cult statue of Horus capable of delivering oracles by nodding, or a simple ex-voto.

Actual documents concerning oracles do not predate the New Kingdom, and most come from the Ramessid or Third Intermediate Period. Recently, however, *biꜣyt* (strictly speaking, "omen"), translated as "oracle," has been documented in the king's address engraved in the tombs of some early eighteenth dynasty viziers, in a provision pertaining to disputes about field boundaries and forbidding the settlement of such problems through "any *biꜣt*." The date of composition of this text is much debated, however. According to van den Boorn, it is not earlier than the second part of Ahmose's reign; but the more traditional late Middle Kingdom date may be better, since titles attested before the seventeenth dynasty and already out of use at the very beginning of the eighteenth occur in it (BiOr, 48, 5/6, 821–831).

Such an early date is not surprising, since Egyptian oracles probably developed from the use of processional statues during the yearly festivals. Before Amenhotpe I, there is no figure of the dummy bark of Amun and its booth enclosing the oracular image of the god of Karnak, but the existence of this most often reproduced of all oracular statues can easily be traced much earlier through appearances of its name in texts. In New Kingdom dedications of temples visited by processions as well as in oracular documents, the idiom referring to the portable statues that were to utter public oracular sentences was "this august god." Obviously a colloquial expression, this phrase is to be distinguished from "image," the term used for the hidden cult statues. The processional Amun of Karnak, carried in his bark during the Opet and Valley festivals, was the most prominent of all such oracular gods from the Theban area. "Lord of Gods" (*Nb-nṯrw*) his epithet in documents, stresses his supremacy over his many lesser oracular gods of the region, such as those listed in Papyrus BM 10335 dating from the reign of Ramesses IV ("Amun of Pe Khenty," "Amun of Te Shenyt," "Amun of Bukenen"). The term "Lord of Gods" for a portable image is encountered as early as the beginning of the twelfth dynasty (Stela Louvre C 200, graffito from Deir el-Bahri), suggesting that processions around Thebes were a well-established practice by then. This would explain the provision not much later in the *Duties of the Vizier* to prevent people from interrogating the portable gods about such important matters as field boundaries.

Nonetheless, we have to wait until the time of Thutmose III for details about the oracular process. In a biographical inscription engraved at Karnak, the king tells how he was chosen as the next pharaoh. During the morning, the god in his bark "perambulated" the northern hypostyle hall and, before the eyes of the gathered courtiers, eventually "settled" in front of the young prince. Thutmose III prostrated himself on the ground, and the god led him to the place reserved for the king (a procedure that was repeated by the *Nb-nṯrw* to "enthrone" Ramesses IV some 330 years later, according to Papyrus Turin 1882). Other instances of "advice" asked by pharaohs of the "Lord of Gods" are reported during the eighteenth dynasty. To know the best route to Punt, Queen Hatshepsut herself questioned the *Nb-nṯrw*. This oracle was not sought during a procession, when the statue could move as a way to answer questions; rather, she "heard" the divine "order" "at the Lord of Gods' stairway"—a reference to his bark shrine at Karnak, where the bark rested on its altar. This may hint at a speaking oracle, or at a revelation obtained while sleeping inside this "Great Seat."

During the Ramessid period, evidence about oracles grows more abundant. Many ostraca and papyri have been found at Deir el-Medina, where the development of the judicial powers of oracles came as a response to the collapse of the pharaonic court system (a fact emphasized by the literary topic of Amun "the vizier of the feeble," met from Merenptah on). Thus, we have information about lesser oracles of the Theban area, particularly those involving the processional statues of the deified Amenhotpe I, worshipped by the workmen of the necropolis. Through many short and often elliptical questions on ostraca found in the garbage pit near their village, we get a glimpse of what the workmen used to ask their gods: whether they would retrieve something lost or stolen; whether the object was in the hands of a neighbor; whether the questioner would be promoted. All these questions could be answered by nodding. Ramessid oracles on papyrus or stelae gives a more accurate picture of the practical way the "god" transmitted his advice to the gathered people.

Oracular Proceedings. Oracles could be uttered by any processional image. This is the reason that so many oracular gods are attested, not only at Thebes but all through the country: Horus of the Camp and Horus-khau at el-Hiba, Sutekh at Dakhla, Isis at Coptos, the deified Ahmose at Abydos, and others. The statues were either hidden in a tabernacle, fastened to a portable bark or mounted directly on poles, or they were unveiled and visible to the public. Thus, the statue of the deified Amenhotpe I of the west bank sat in an open palanquin. The Lord of Gods, however, always remained inside the booth of his bark, except in an oracle scene dating from 651 BCE that represents him in a portable shrine (Papyrus Brooklyn 47–218–3). Oracles took place during a public appearance of the statue carried on its priests' shoulders. The "putting down" of the tabernacle on its "Great Seat" (a station built on the processional way or a temple bark shrine, such as the granite sanctuary of Karnak) signified the end of the oracular session: from that point on, the god could no longer be approached by anyone except his priests (Papyrus Nevill, late twentieth dynasty).

Barks, shrines, or palanquins were carried around by *wʿb*-priests, as opposed to the higher-ranking "prophets," who were the only ones admitted into the presence of the nonremovable cult statues. Of course, the Egyptians were aware that the porters, especially those who led the march, could interfere in the oracular process. That is probably why the "*wʿb* of the front (of the bark)" and "procession master" of the Lord of Gods Pameshemu was forbidden to introduce his own petition during the oracles held under Pinudjem II to punish the scribes of the temple found guilty of embezzlement (inscription of the steward of Amun Thutmose, near the tenth pylon of Karnak).

In theory, to be successful, the oracular process had to be carried out without any influence along the route. Therefore, the path had to be carefully prepared and protected, so as to be pure. Some of the precautions include the arrangement of processional sphinx-lined avenues to connect Karnak and Luxor; the use, during the twenty-first dynasty, of a "soil of silver" (owing to its color, the purest existing material), where oracles of the Lord-of-Gods could be held safely; fan-bearers and censer-bearers all around the tabernacle to ward off flies; and the fixing of the time of the session (during the "morning," whenever stated). In all likelihood, the oracular process itself, or at least the procession during which it took place, began with an Opening of the Mouth rite carried out on the god as well as on the prow and stern figureheads of his bark, since "prophets" garbed in the leopardskin of the funerary priest associated with this ritual are always figured walking alongside the tabernacle.

Perambulating and nodding. Oracles could identify an evildoer as well as an individual worthy of appointment to an office (not just kingship). The bark was carried around before the likely persons; then it "stopped" supposedly of its own accord, in front of the appropriate person. In this way, a "chief of *mḏзy*-policemen" was appointed by the bark of Isis at Abydos under Ramesses II (Stela Oxford 1894/106), and the evil scribes of Amun were identified under Pinudjem II. When it was impossible to summon all the candidates, their names could be read aloud, and the "god" likewise "stopped" at one of them. Such were the cases of the cultivator Pethauemdiamun, who stole garments (Papyrus BM 10335), or of the official Nesamun, who was promoted to the rank of "scribe of the storehouse" instead of his father (Karnak, relief dating from Ramesses XI). Usually, however, the god was only asked an oral question by the "prophet" who led the session. The god answered by "nodding" in approval or by "walking backward" as a way to say no (tomb of Amenmose, the "first prophet" of Amenhotpe of the Forecourt under Ramesses II; Ostraca Petrie 21, Year 27 of Ramesses III; etc.).

Drawing from a pair of petitions. Sometimes, a set of two documents, one with a statement and the other with its contrary, was put before the portable statue, and the god "took" one of them. That *ṯзy* meant in practice some process of drawing lots is clear in Ostr. Gardiner 103

(Ramesses III's reign). According to this report of a dispute over inheritance, the contradictory documents put before the deified Amenhotpe I were "cast" twice. The most complete account of this procedure is found in the aforementioned inscription of Thutmose. These documents were also put before the god twice, and the Lord-of-Gods "took" twice the one that said "one says that there is nothing to investigate against Thutmose," discarding that which said "one says that there is something to investigate against Thutmose."

Only one original pair of documents has survived: Papyrus Boston a+b, a petition relating to a dispute over a cow dating from the early twenty-first dynasty; it is addressed to Horus of the Camp, the god of el-Hiba. But we possess examples of the documents "taken" by the god written in Demotic, Greek, or Coptic from Oxyrhynchus, Tebtunis, and Antinoe. These examples are good evidence that the oracular process by drawing of lots continued to be used well into the Greco-Roman and even Islamic period, in spite of the disappearance of the old gods.

Speaking statues and other procedures. In many cases, however, the mechanical process employed to obtain oracular utterances remains obscure. All the amuletic decrees on papyrus protecting the carrier against a long list of diseases and dangers, delivered during the twenty-first to twenty-third dynasties, begin with the word "said" written in a darker ink before the name of the oracular god. Such an opening, also met in the Stela of Apanage from the twenty-second dynasty, does not help us to understand how these oracles were pronounced. It is likely that in addition to the moving of the statue or the drawing of lots used during the New Kingdom, other methods developed until the Late period, and that these involved some device to let people hear the voice of the god. Such speaking oracles took place in a special room, before a statue of the god or in front of a relief representing his bark facing and resting on a pedestal (Coptite chapel of Cleopatra VII). At Kom el-Wist in the Delta, a bronze tube concealed in the pedestal of a Ptolemaic statue of a bull and connected to a small chamber where a priest could be hidden was discovered in 1941. It is recorded that Hatshepsut was told the route to Punt, and Alexander the Great was spoken to by Zeus-Ammon when alone in the temple of Siwah. This development may explain Herodotus's statement (400 BCE) that the way of issuing oracles varied from temple to temple.

Theban Theocracy and *Nb-nṯrw*. Most of the Theban oracular decrees from Ramesses VI onward were issued by "this august god Lord of Gods Amun-Re," often also referred to as "the great god first to come into existence," an epithet stressing the demiurgic powers originally held by the *Nb-nṯrw*, which was later taken over by lesser processional images. Many of these texts, sometimes accompanied by reliefs of the oracular setting, are engraved along the processional route of the bark, leading from the tenth pylon to the granite sanctuary, where the *Nb-nṯrw*, "who pronounces oracles" and "announces what comes before it exists" (Taharka's hymn to the Lord of gods), was stored between festivals. It is likely that this area also held the "soil of silver" of Karnak mentioned by the inscriptions of Henttawy and Thutmose as the place of the "god's approach." Such "beautiful feasts(s) of the *pḥ-nṯr*" were sophisticated forms of oracular sessions, which could be held alongside the yearly festivals. They often included other processional images—Mut, Khons-Neferhotpe, Mentu-Re, or Thoth—with the Lord of Gods as a way of strengthening his decisions. As an image that issued decrees about such important matters as the endowment of high-ranking persons and shrines or the recall of exiles from the oases, the *Nb-nṯrw* became a powerful political weapon through which his clergy ruled Upper Egypt; there are decrees concerning the properties of Henttawy, Maatkare, and the chief of Ma-tribes Nimlot, an inscription reporting the acquittal of the steward Thutmose, a stela from Akoris recording a donation to a temple, the so-called Stele de l'apanage and the Stele du Bannissement.

This fact perhaps explains the steady decrease in the power of the Lord of Gods after the twenty-first dynasty, when more efficient kings put an end to the independence of the Theban clergy. But in their distant capitals, the Napatan and Meroitic priests went on pulling the strings of their puppet-pharaohs through similar devices (cf. Coronation Stela of Aspelta), until their ruthless suppression by the skeptic Ergamenes around 200 BCE.

BIBLIOGRAPHY

Baines, John. "Magic and Divination." In *Religion in Ancient Egypt*, edited by B. E. Shaefer, pp. 164–172. London, 1991. A few interesting remarks on the links between individual magical practices and oracles.

Baines, John. "Practical Religion and Piety." *Journal of Egyptian Archaeology* 73 (1987), 79–98. Discusses possible examples of oracles, or at least divinatory practices, before the New Kingdom.

Barns, John. "The Nevill Papyrus: A Late Ramesside Letter to an Oracle." *Journal of Egyptian Archaeology* 35 (1949), 69–71.

Blackman, Aylward M. "Oracles in Ancient Egypt." *Journal of Egyptian Archaeology* 11 (1925), 249–255. Translation and commentary of Papyrus BM 10335.

Blackman, Aylward M. "The Stela of Shoshenḳ, Great Chief of the Meshwesh." *Journal of Egyptian Archaeology* 27 (1941), 83–95.

Brunton, Guy. "The Oracle of Kôm el-Wist." *Annales du Service des Antiquités de l'Égypte* 47 (1947), 293ff.

Edwards, I. E. S. *Hieratic Papyri in the British Museum, IVth Series, Oracular Amuletic Decrees of the Late New Kingdom*, London, 1960.

Gardiner, Alan H. "The Dakhleh Stela." *Journal of Egyptian Archaeology* 19 (1933), 19–30.

Gardiner, Alan H. "The Gods of Thebes as Guarantors of Personal Property." *Journal of Egyptian Archaeology* 48 (1962), 57–69. Translation and commentary of the Lord of Gods' decrees concerning the princesses Henttawy and Maatkare.

Kákosy, L. "Orakel." In *Lexikon der Ägyptologie* 4:600–604. Wiesbaden, 1982.

Kees, Hermann. "Wêbpriester der 18. Dynastie im Trägerdienst bei Prozessionen." *Zeitschrift für ägyptische Sprache* 85 (1960), 45–56. Data about the people who carried—and therefore probably manipulated—the oracular statues.

McDowell, A. G. *Jurisdiction in the Workmen's Community of Deir el-Medineh.* Leiden, 1990. The most up-to-date and comprehensive study of the oracles of the deified Amenhotpe I in the settlement of the necropolis workmen (pp. 107–141), with useful indexes.

Nims, C. F. "An Oracle Dated in the 'Repeating of Births.'" *Journal of Near Eastern Studies* 7 (1948), 157–162.

Parker, Richard A. *A Saite Oracle Papyrus from Thebes in the Brooklyn Museum.* Providence, 1962. Translation and commentary of Papyrus Brooklyn 47–218–3, with a chapter on "Egyptian Oracles" by Jaroslav Černý, containing many quotations from Egyptian sources (pp. 35–48).

Ryholt, Kim. "A Pair of Oracle Petitions Addressed to Horus-of-the-Camp." *Journal of Egyptian Archaeology* 79 (1993), 189–198.

Skeat, T. C., and E. G. Turner. "An Oracle of Hermes Trismegistos at Saqqara." *Journal of Egyptian Archaeology* 54 (1968), 199–208.

Welsby, Derek A. *The Kingdom of Kush: The Napatan and Meroitic Empires.* London, 1996. For the circumstances surrounding the accession of some kings to the throne and the important role of the priesthood of Amun, see pp. 19–32.

JEAN-MARIE KRUCHTEN

ORAL TRADITION. A number of recent commentators on Egyptian literature have suggested that its origins lie in oral tradition. The challenge is to define the material's characteristics that betray this origin. Some assistance in the task comes from the work done on orality, oral tradition, and performance in other cultures from the ancient world, like Greece and Israel, as well as from discussions of modern oral cultures.

By definition, *orality* and *oral* mean "spoken," and they assume *aurality* and *aural*, or "heard." The latter implies the presence of an audience that hears the speaking, whether the speaking is simple narration, instruction, rhetoric, ritual invocation, or song of some kind—in other words, performance. Because performance occurs in a time and place, the concept of orality also incorporates an ephemerality, at least for the individual act. With regard to the specific oral performance, such ephemerality is absolute; but with the inclusion of tradition, as in the traditional content of performance, a sense of stability comes into play.

Tradition includes the transmission of any kind of cultural communication, spoken or otherwise, from generation to generation. The idea thus embodies the sense of an unbroken line with the past which projects into the future by means of the heirs of the present-day carrier of the tradition. One must understand tradition as a document belonging to the time of its bearer, however, as well as containing the past. For example, the Pyramid Texts were the prerogative of Old Kingdom royalty, whereas during the Middle Kingdom, nobles and officials used variants of many of them on their coffins; during the New Kingdom, other variants of these same texts appeared as parts of the *Book of Going Forth by Day* (*Book of the Dead*), commonly considered available to any who could afford them. Even more dramatic is the use of parts of the Underworld Books from New Kingdom royal tombs in the mythological papyri of the Third Intermediate Period by those who could afford them. Tradition, then, is not the rote transmission of the past but, rather, the past in the context of the present and thus affected by that context to a greater or lesser extent. One must therefore approach tradition as dynamic, not static, noting that it includes conservation of the past while reflecting the effects of the present. Thus, when one finds written material from an oral narrative—for example, a recorded folktale—what is present represents one instance of performance for one particular audience. This performance brings to this audience the story as told many times before by many different narrators, but it also presents the story in response to this particular audience in this particular time and place.

Performance also includes what the audience brings to it. The language and words used resonate with the audience as they actively involve themselves in the performance. This involvement may be evident in overt actions of the audience, such as accompanying a singer with song, clapping, appreciative sounds, and the like; more significant, however, are the values, traditional understanding, and knowledge that the performer activates in the audience through words and actions. In a way, the performance itself is incomplete if viewed simply in terms of the performer; only the audience can complete it.

Much of the study of oral tradition in written form has revolved around the identification of formulas and themes that recur within a given traditional genre, such as epic or folktale. Since we lack a significant corpus of any given genre, or even a clear identification of what the genre identification is, of many Egyptian materials, we must look for alternative kinds of markers of oral tradition in order to ascertain the presence and extent of such a tradition in ancient Egypt. One of these markers appears in the ancient Egyptians' sense of the power inherent in a name. Arguably the best narrative example comes from the tale in which Isis tricks Re into revealing his name. The fact that in this revelation, only she (and, through her, Horus) learns the name—the audience gets no clue—delineates the ancient Egyptians' concept of the power of the name: if one knows an individual's name, one has power over that person. The name of a person designates that individual's essence. Consequently, a person is called into life by name and, correspondingly, can be annihilated by the loss of his or her name. The Egyptians' use of theophoric names—personal names incorporating the name of a deity—also speaks to the power of the name, in this case relating the person to the god.

Written materials often betray their roots in oral traditional culture in the appearance and treatment of the actual writing. An example is the attenuation or "cutting" of parts of various Egyptian hieroglyphs, such as the talons of an owl or the mouth of a wild dog, in order to eliminate the danger that the animation of the animal or bird represents. Writing was thus perceived as more than representation: it was active magic, a characteristic understanding of people who live in an orally based culture. Similarly, the gestures visible in many hieroglyphs related to humans and gods reveal the somatic nature of oral tradition translated into writing, while the actual written form of the texts in writing also speaks to an oral tradition underlying ancient Egyptian culture. Especially in the earlier writings, there is no distinctive separation between adjacent words, sentences, or thoughts. In later texts, rubrics written in red and red dots in the text may be present to provide such differentiation, but even then, the presence of such helps is inconsistent. This lack further characterizes writing in an oral culture.

The absence of abstract thinking in ancient Egypt, so often observed by Egyptologists and others, comprises yet another marker of Egypt as a culture based on oral tradition. The goddess Maat provides perhaps the best example of this idea: she represents order, sometimes seen as truth, justice, or balance, but she appears in very concrete form, even being presented by the king to the gods. Similar deities include Hu, divine utterance, Sia, divine knowledge, and Heka, magic.

The presence of word play, or paronomasia, in ancient Egyptian writings provides more evidence of the oral nature of their world. Word play is an aural feature; by definition, one does not see it in writing but hears it in speech. In reading such word play, one can totally bypass the fun the narrator is providing; in hearing the same words, it is virtually impossible to miss. A well-known example is the Egyptians' word for themselves, *rmt*, which they often juxtaposed with the word for "tears," *rmt*, in telling about the creation of the Egyptians from the tears of a god.

The dialogic nature of some texts similarly suggests roots in oral tradition; here, Coffin Text Spell 335 and the related chapter 17 of the *Book of Going Forth by Day* come to mind. Even if one considers these two corpora of texts as largely written, it is hard to escape the conclusion that the question-and-answer form of these two spells goes back to an oral model. One might even suggest the same for various literary texts, such as *A Man's Dispute with His Soul* and *The Eloquent Peasant*, both readily imagined in performance.

Another piece of evidence attesting to the presence of oral tradition in the ancient Egyptian culture, even concomitant with the written word, is the formulaic and repetitive nature of much textual material. The Pyramid Texts show much repetition and parallelism, along with an additive progression of ideas and a lack of enjambment—that is, the carryover of an idea from one line to the next. When found together, these characteristics provide good evidence of the oral basis of the material under examination. The so-called Cannibal Speech, Pyramid Utterance 273–274, provides some excellent examples:

> The sky is overcast,
> The stars are darkened,
> The bows of heaven quiver,
> The bones of the earth-gods shake,
> They cease from moving,
> For they have seen the King appearing in power,
> A god who lives on his fathers
> And feeds on his mothers;
>
> . . .
>
> It is the King who lives on their magic
> And swallows their spirits,
> Their big ones are for his morning meal,
> Their middle-sized ones are for his evening meal,
> Their little ones are for his night meal.

From this evidence one surmises that initially the spells were orally presented rituals, known to those carrying them out. Placing the ritual texts on the walls of the pyramid's burial chamber permitted the ritual to be spoken on behalf of the inhabitant throughout eternity, further attesting to the Egyptians' sense of the magical nature of the word.

Ancient Egyptian materials provide various other clues which point to their oral origins, among which is the use of orally related words in their writing. For example, text after text from the pyramids begins with direct address ("O Atum"), a command ("O Osiris the king, dance"), or the king's introduction of himself ("O Geb, Bull of the sky, I am Horus . . . ,"). All these conventions suggest an oral basis. In a similar fashion, ancient Egyptian magical spells attest to an oral tradition with their frequent concluding words, such as "to be said . . . ," followed by explicit instructions about how and over what, and the number of repetitions required to be effective. These spells, which generally exist in single copies and mostly date in written form from the Middle Kingdom and later, also provide us with the earliest comprehensive mythic narratives, excellent evidence of the oral tradition that underlies many Egyptian written texts. Although the mortuary texts hint at the content of a particular myth, such as the fight between Horus and Seth, they do not relate the details, suggesting common and oral knowledge of these narratives. These allusions also suggest a performance venue, possibly ritual, for which the writing might have served as a mnemonic device. Correspondingly, the brief allusions, notwithstanding the elusive factor of decorum, likely represent the whole, under the magical *pars pro toto* principle.

Many other kinds of material reveal the presence of an oral tradition in ancient Egypt, among them the so-called Wisdom Literature or Instructional texts, to which parallels exist in neighboring cultures. There appears to be no doubt that the ancient Egyptians contributed to and drew on a widespread body of material concerned with the management of a "wise" life—one in which a person was successful according to contemporary standards in relation to peers, superiors, inferiors, and the deity or deities of the culture. The similarities among Egyptian materials, and similarities between them and some from Hebrew scriptures, suggest oral transmission. In addition, the nature of these materials, with their short, pithy couplets and verses, parallel lines, and vivid depictions which are easily recalled, suggests an oral basis that reminds one of modern proverbs, which, though found in writing, are usually learned orally. Similarly, one can imagine the oral transmission to apprentices of medical remedies and diagnoses of the kind found in the Ebers Papyrus or the Edwin Smith Papyrus. Although experienced medical practitioners were quite likely literate, the logistical problems of working with material written on a roll of papyrus—owing both to its bulk and to difficulty in locating the needed reference—suggest an oral tradition for medical practitioners. Furthermore, some contents of these papyri anticipate the common oral remedies, diagnoses, and cures found in oral traditions of modern times. One might place in a similar category the so-called dream books, which purport to analyze a person's night-time sleep activity.

Among other types of Egyptian writings deriving from an oral basis, one must include tales of heroic kings. For example, the poem about Ramesses II's Battle of Kadesh quite plausibly could have been part of a court singer's repertory. Even more certainly, hymns, both divine and royal, form part of Egyptian oral tradition, since music, including singing, was one of the traditional skills transmitted through apprenticeship; love songs, too, fall into this category. Also to be included here are the autobiographies found in private tombs from the Old Kingdom and appearing as *Königsnovellen* in later royal writings. At the core of the autobiography lies a praise song, quite likely with oral antecedents; like various mortuary texts, such songs attest to the power of the word as the deceased asserts that he practiced ethical behavior during life in order to gain entrance to the otherworld. Prayers, too, were of an oral nature, and their committal to writing, or even to the notable "hearing ear" stelae, suggests an attempt to make permanent the transitoriness of the spoken word, thus betraying an active oral tradition in the sense of the magic of the word.

The oral background of ancient Egyptian narratives appears clearly exemplified in Papyrus Westcar's cycle of stories, reminiscent of the frame narrative beloved in oral tradition everywhere. Embedded in the tale are constant reminders of the oral basis of the written material. For example, the narrative of Djedi the magician opens with the words: "The king's son Hardedef stood up to speak [*mdt*], and he said [*dd.f*]." Virtually the entire episode is narration, thin on description and heavy on action—both prominent characteristics of oral composition. The *Story of Sinuhe*, relating the self-exile of a member of the royal court, is similarly characterized by easily recalled short episodes, the presence of hymnic and poetic material, and action rather than extended thought. As a concrete, situational story, it exalts Senwosret I while presenting basic ideas of Egyptian thinking: the lands outside Egypt are living death; the king and queen can be gracious and forgiving; the king is a god; and the hero prevails. In sum, it contains all the components of a good story, welcome to its audience.

Several New Kingdom tales resonate with the folktale genre of oral tradition. One of the best examples appears in the *Story of Two Brothers*, in which the audience finds not only formulaic phrases such as "now when the land was light" and "now many days after this," but also speaking animals, extraordinary outside help, life without a soul (heart), omens of trouble, revival of the apparently dead, lack of character development, and intensification and building tension—all characteristic of typical orally based folktales. One can imagine a performer telling this tale, embellishing it here and elaborating it there, depending on the audience, each time it was told.

The ability to deduce that an active oral tradition existed in ancient Egypt, even in the presence of writing, is owed to that scribal tradition, paradoxical as that may seem. Only from the work of largely anonymous scribes can we know what little we do of Egyptian literary materials.

[*See also* Literacy.]

BIBLIOGRAPHY

Primary Sources
Borghouts, J. F. *Ancient Egyptian Magical Texts*. Leiden, 1978. An excellent collection of magical texts, providing many mythic details unavailable elsewhere and also showing their active oral nature through directions for their use.
Foster, J. L., trans. *Hymns, Prayers, and Songs: An Anthology of Ancient Egyptian Lyric Poetry*, edited by Susan Tower Hollis. Atlanta, 1995. A readily available collection of materials from various time periods, translated with poetic sensibility and attention to the thought couplets characteristic of oral traditional forms.
Lichtheim, M. *Ancient Egyptian Literature: A Book of Readings*, vol. 1: *The Old and Middle Kingdoms*; vol. 2: *The New Kingdom*; vol. 3: *The Late Period*. Berkeley, 1973–1980. Standard translations of ancient Egyptian texts from all periods.
Parkinson, R. B. *Voices from Ancient Egypt: An Anthology of Middle*

Kingdom Writings. Norman, Okla., 1991. A broad variety of texts from, or thought to date to, the Middle Kingdom, the so-called classical period of Egyptian writing. Includes an excellent discussion of Egyptian genres, with short, helpful introductions to each text and an emphasis on the oral basis of many Egyptian writings.

Simpson, W. K., ed. *The Literature of Ancient Egypt: An Anthology of Stories, Instructions, and Poetry.* New Haven, 1973. Standard one-volume collection of materials from all periods, with short introductions for each text.

Secondary Discussions

Dijk, J. van. "Myth and Mythmaking in Ancient Egypt." In *Civilizations in the Ancient Near East,* edited by J. Sasson, vol. 3, pp. 1697–1709. New York, 1995. Short overview with a current bibliography of primary sources and secondary discussions.

Foley, J. M. *The Theory of Oral Composition: History and Methodology.* Bloomington and Indianapolis, 1988. A classic in the field.

Foley, J. M. "Word-Power, Performance, and Tradition." *Journal of American Folklore* 105 (1992), 275–301. Brings together different strands of discussion of oral tradition.

Hollis, S. T. *The Ancient Egyptian "Tale of Two Brothers": The Oldest Fairy Tale in the World.* Norman, Okla., 1990. A "thick description" of the New Kingdom tale in its Egyptian and ancient Near Eastern context, suggesting the kinds of thinking an audience might have brought to a performance of the tale.

Lord, A. B. *The Singer of Tales.* Cambridge, Mass., 1960. The classic work on oral composition that forms the basis for any discussion of the topic.

Lord, A. B. *Epic Singers and Oral Tradition.* Ithaca, 1991. Collection of Lord's papers, some refining the work presented in 1960. The opening essay, "Words Heard and Words Seen," is particularly relevant to the present discussion.

Muhawi, I., and S. Kanaana. *Speak, Bird, Speak Again: Palestinian Arab Folktales.* Berkeley, 1989. Examples of contemporary oral folktales collected from illiterate and semiliterate narrators, accompanied by an excellent discussion explaining and setting the tales in their contemporary context.

Niditch, S. *Oral World and Written Word: Ancient Israelite Literature.* Louisville, 1996. Excellent discussion of biblical materials as originating in an oral culture.

Ong, W. J. *Orality and Literacy: The Technologizing of the Word.* London and New York, 1982. Discussion of the psychodynamics of orality, and theory about the impact of writing and eventual literacy on oral cultures.

Redford, Donald B. "Ancient Egyptian Literature: An Overview." In *Civilizations of the Ancient Near East,* edited by J. Sasson, vol. 4, pp. 2223–2241. New York, 1995. Fine overview with a short introductory section paying special attention to oral composition and transmission.

Vansina, J. *Oral Tradition as History.* Madison, Wis., 1985. A classic in the field.

SUSAN TOWER HOLLIS

OSIRIS. In origin a royal mortuary god, Osiris exemplified a cult that was begun in a fairly restricted context, but one which achieved wide popularity and a notable expansion of functions. The exclusive link with royalty was abandoned just prior to the Middle Kingdom; the funerary aspect, however, always persisted, and Osiris was always shown in mummy wrappings. While the funerary aspect was primarily based on the experience of death, it enabled believers, through the force of myth and ritual, to accept the conviction that life after death was warranted.

Form and Name. The representation of Osiris in its developed form shows him wearing the White Crown of Upper Egypt and carrying the crook and the flail. Elsewhere, the White Crown often became the *atef*-crown through the addition of feathers, and there were various complex versions of it. The preponderance of the White Crown in the earlier versions of Osiris suggests an Upper Egyptian origin for the god. As for the crook and the flail, they both raise questions of political and sociological import. The crook suggests a shepherd god, and Wolfgang Helck (1962) has argued that the Syrian Adonis provides the closest contemporary analogy. Marked differences existed, however, in both myths and cults; and, in fact, the concept of a sovereign god as shepherd of his people was shared by other religious ideologies of the ancient Near East, expressed both in art and literature. The function and origin of the flail are more enigmatic. Perhaps it is a fly-whisk or a shepherd's whip. It is shown sometimes with other deities, such as Min. Both flail and crook, however, appear with the god Andjety of the ninth Lower Egyptian nome, which suggests a possible source.

The constant feature of the figure of Osiris was its mummified form, with a close linkage of the legs. The funerary import was thus stressed. Whereas the Old Kingdom, by and large, has yielded no iconographic evidence, a relief on a block from the pyramid temple of the king Djedkare Izezi of the fifth dynasty presents a figure bearing the name of Osiris; it belongs to a row of divine figures, today partly damaged, and it has been dated to the closing years of that dynasty (c.2405 BCE). The lower part of the Osiris figure is missing, but the left arm hangs freely, suggesting that here the figure was not mummiform. Absent also are the flail and the crook, although the missing right arm might be grasping something; on the head is a long wig. Since the form is that of a standing anthropomorphic figure, with none of the distinctive Osirian attributes, discussion and debate about it have emerged (see Griffiths 1980; Lorton 1985; and Eaton-Krauss 1987). Rival gods at that time were Anubis, Khentamenthiw, and Wepwawet, and all three had jackal forms; that Osiris, too, was originally imagined as a jackal has been suggested by words in the pyramid of Neferkare, which say of the dead king, "thy face is [that of] a jackal, like Osiris." Osiris' ensuing human form clearly became a vital feature of his appeal, and his identity with the dead king contributed to his popularity.

The god's name *Wsir* (in Coptic, *Oycipe* or *Oycipi*) was written at first with the sign for a throne, followed by the sign for an eye; later the order was inverted. Among the many meanings suggested is one cognate with *Ashur,* implying a Syrian origin; but also "he who takes his seat or throne"; "she or that which has sovereign power and is

OSIRIS. *Bronze statuette of Osiris, from the Ptolemaic period.* (University of Pennsylvania Museum, Philadelphia. Neg. # S8–31580)

creative"; "the place of creation"; "seat of the Eye," with the Eye explained as the Sun; "the seat that creates"; and "the Mighty One," deriving from *wsr* ("mighty"). Since the throne sign occurs also with the deity Isis, Wolfhart Westendorf tried to relate the two names, but he ended by positing an originally female Osiris, although the deity's male potency was so often emphasized. No consensus has been reached on the basic and original meaning of the name. Perhaps we must be content with the popular etymology offered in the Pyramid Texts, 2054 (PN): "The king makes his seat like Osiris"; there, elements of the name were deployed but without a valid order (Erman 1909).

Myth and Kingship. Although the Pyramid Texts do not provide a consecutive account of the Osiris myth, they abundantly supply in scattered allusions the principal details about his fate and especially about his relationship to the deceased pharaoh. He was presented as the brother and husband of Isis and as a member of the Great Ennead of Heliopolis; and in that group, Geb and Nut were named (clearly as parents) before Osiris, Isis, Seth, and Nephthys. Osiris' brother Seth was said to have caused his death and yet there is a lack of explicit statements about the death of Osiris. Not that the death of gods was unmentionable to the Egyptian mind—even the sun god Re was depicted as suffering old age and death.

In the case of Osiris, however, despite the absence of a firm dictum that he died, a cluster of details have allowed that conclusion to be held. Above all, he was constantly represented as mummified. He was smitten by his brother Seth in a place called Nedyet or Gehestey. With that account should perhaps be connected the tradition, found in the Memphite Theology (late eighth century BCE) and elsewhere, that Osiris was drowned—a tradition that resulted in the ancient Egyptian idea that being drowned in the Nile River was a blessed death. Yet doubt has been cast on the validity of that tradition in an important study by Pascal Vernus (1991), in which he examines numerous allusions to the god's death; he concludes that the myth represents Osiris as being dead when he was hurled into the water, that it never tells of his being drowned.

In the Memphite Theology, Horus commanded Isis and Nephthys to grasp Osiris so that they might protect him from the action of *mḥii*. They had been shocked when they saw him, but then they brought him to land, and the sequel implied a glorious burial in Memphis. In Egyptian, the verb *mḥi* can mean "drown," but also "swim" or "drift, float," and Vernus (1991) opted for the last meaning in that and other contexts, including three references in the Pyramid Texts to "the place where you (Osiris-King) were drowned." There, "the place where you have drifted [or floated]" is not convincing, since a corpse that is drifting in the river can scarcely be attached long to a defined place. It should be added that the idea of an Osirian apo-

OSIRIS. *Three Osiris-figures, probably from the Late period.* The mummified penis of the defunct was kept in a small opening in the base. Sometimes the opening was used to store a papyrus roll bearing the text of the *Book of Going Forth by Day (Book of the Dead)*. On the right is a figurine of a *ba*-bird. All the figures are of painted wood, now in the Agyptisches Museum in Berlin. (© Photograph by Erich Lessing / Art Resource, NY)

theosis by drowning has been well attested for the New Kingdom and later, when special honors in burial were accorded to the drowned.

In the earliest evidence, Osiris was given the role of sovereign ruler of the realm of the dead, and the deceased pharaoh was equated with him. Utterance 219 is the oldest Osiris-litany in the Pyramid Texts, and it affirms that "he [Osiris] lives, this king lives; he [Osiris] is not dead, this king is not dead." That claim was made to Atum, then to several other deities: an analogy between Osiris and the dead king was being urged, and the claim that the king was still alive was based on the continued life of Osiris.

The argument might be made that there is a suggestion of Osiris himself being in origin a king who had died, as was the view of Plutarch and of a few modern scholars. The Turin Canon and Manetho's dynasties name several gods, with Osiris among them, as early rulers of Egypt. Yet no one has suggested that those gods—such as Re, Geb, and Horus—were originally human kings; that would imply a form of Euhemerism, with its belief that all deities were at first outstanding human beings. In the case of Osiris, it was his identification with the deceased pharaoh that furthered the idea of his historical origin as

a real king. Sometimes it was by analogy (as in the example quoted above) that this equating was promoted; or a categorical claim was made, as in the Pyramid Texts (1657 a MN) "this king is Osiris." Far more often, the juxtaposition of the names occurs, as in Osiris-Unas, which means, in effect, "Unas who has now become Osiris." In the Coffin Texts, where the exclusive Osirian royal identity was relaxed, the deceased's *ba* is said to be the *ba* of Osiris; but the method of simple juxtaposition was regularly followed.

From the end of the fifth dynasty, references to Osiris occurred in private tombs, mostly in offering formulas (Begelsbacher-Fischer 1981, pp. 124–125), but with no suggestion of a special relationship to the god. A much wider area was covered by the Coffin Texts, when the "democratization of royal prerogatives" meant a more varied choice of religious themes (Silverman 1989, p. 36). Yet a steady increase in the range and appeal of Osiris was plainly attested; one reason for that was the stability of his concern with death and its sequel—his *Sitz im Tod*, if one can thus describe it. The living Horus-King, in spite of his divine theological import, has been shown of late to be subject, in facets of Egyptian literature, to the foibles of humanity. In constrast, the dead Osiris-King has escaped all that, mainly because he is rooted in the experience of death; and the same inviolate sanctity attends his identity with the multitude of nonroyal believers.

Cult Centers and Ideology. Some early sources connect Osiris with the towns of Heliopolis and Busiris, both in Lower Egypt; but others connect him with Upper Egypt, especially with the town of Abydos and its nome (province), where kings of the first two dynasties were buried. Moreover, Osiris often wore the crown of Upper Egypt. Some texts link the god with both Busiris and Abydos, and David Lorton has suggested that a court at Memphis might well have planned the double emphasis, with a pan-Egyptian political purpose.

The early ritual of royal burial points to Osiris as the central ideological figure. Mummification was the basic rite, and the deity Anubis, guide to the underworld, was considered the embalmer who rendered that service to the deceased king, just as he did to Osiris. The rites of mourning and of "Opening the Mouth" led to the idea of the mummy being endowed with renewed life. A concomitant idea was the defeat of the deity Seth, Osiris' brother and the perpetrator of his death. That was prominent in the Osirian rites portrayed in the Stela of Ikhernofret, from the twelfth dynasty: there, Sethian enemies were said to attack the *Nšmt*-bark of Osiris, but they were repulsed, after which Osiris was glorified in Abydos.

The burial rites, including mummification, had an earlier origin than did Osiris; and probably the deity Anubis should be credited as the divine originator of the process of embalming. Perhaps Khentamentiu, the "first of the Westerners" and another jackal god at Abydos, whose identity was merged into that of Osiris, was involved. The revivified corpse, which received offerings, became the basis of belief in an afterlife; and Osiris, as the initial paradigm, received the epithet *Wn-nfr* (Gr., *Onnophris*), "He Who Is Permanently Benign and Youthful."

As the ruler of the realm of the dead, Osiris was physically associated with the earth, which embraces the dead. Yet his chthonic aspect never excluded him from generous access to the celestial world, of which the sun god Re was the chief deity. In that astral world, Osiris was especially associated with the circumpolar stars, with the constellation of Orion and with the brightest star in the sky, Sirius. During the Ramessid era, he was shown as a composite figure, united with the sun god Re, as in the tomb of Nefertiri; this striking figure was unusual, and it did not affect the figure of the god as it was regularly shown throughout most of the pharaonic era and beyond (with the exception of part of the Amarna age). Akhenaten, when king, clearly rejected Osirian myth and doctrine, promoting a form of monotheism based on Aten.

Although the mortuary role of Osiris could arouse fear and dread, his benign promise of renewed life came to be expressed through the appeal of new life, in the cycle of nature's fertility, especially with water and vegetation. Initially it was the water used in the libations for the dead, but through links with Orion, Sirius, and the new year, Osiris was associated with the Nile and its annual inundation. He was also equated with Neper, the prehistoric harvest god, and he was credited with the creation of wheat and barley. In association with this were the funerary practices of the Grain-Osiris and Osiris-Bed; for the Festival of Khoiak, a mold in the form of Osiris was filled with sprouting plants.

In the Greco-Roman era, the human appeal of the Osiris cult—which was spread to other countries—achieved emotional intensity; this direction is especially evident in the works of the ancient writers Diodorus, Plutarch, and Apuleius, who bear witness, also, to the force of Greek religion, particularly from the deities Demeter and Dionysus, and from the Eleusinian Mysteries. Isis then assumed a more prominent role and, to some extent, Osiris was replaced by the god Sarapis, also of Egyptian origin, in a combined form of Osiris and Apis. The basic elements of the myth and cult remained Egyptian.

An idea that was wrongly inferred from some of the classical and other sources was that parts of the body of Osiris were worshiped as relics in various regions. Yet the true Egyptian belief was that parts of his body were explicitly equated with the nomes of Egypt, often in relation to their standards and symbols, so that Osiris was thus identified with the whole of Egypt, but without specific cults.

The rule of Osiris over the realm of the dead led to his most important role—that of supreme arbiter in the judgment of the dead. The general concept of such a judgment appeared in the early Old Kingdom sources, but in the New Kingdom it was elaborately developed, both textually and pictorially, the *locus classicus* being Spell 125 of the *Book of Going Forth by Day* (*Book of the Dead*). There, the weighing of the heart before Osiris as the presiding judge depicts many supporting divine functionaries; among them is Thoth as "Recorder," Anubis as "Lord of the Balance," aided by Horus, and the figure of the goddess Maat, who is conceptually dominant. Magic doubtless entered into the popular idea of such a scene; a copy of the *Book of Going Forth by Day* pushed into a tomb provided all the questions and the ready-made answers (but the moral criteria expressed in the "Declarations of Innocence" point to a deep concern with humanity's final destiny). In the Roman era, an urge to intensify the deceaseds' identity with Osiris is seen in representations of the deceased in the form of the god, with private persons accoutred with his royal crown. The judgment before Osiris had a strong impact on other religions, particularly on the eschatology of Judaism and then Christianity—with the development of Judgment Day and the Last Judgment.

Punishments and rewards were conspicuous elements in the Egyptian doctrine, and the punishments were most often portrayed in iconography. In the Ptolemaic era, at Alexandria, Osiris was sometimes identified with Aion, the snake-clad god of time, who was much honored in Mithraism. Aion was seen as a peaceful deity, beyond the force of change; so was Osiris, "Lord of Eternity," for the most part, but it has been shown by Lázló Kákosy (1977) that Osiris displayed an aggressive and warlike aspect in the mythic matter relating to his feud with Seth.

[*See also* Hymns, *article on* Osiris Hymns; *and* Myths, *article on the* Osiris Cycle.]

BIBLIOGRAPHY

Assmann, Jan. *Ma'at: Gerechtigkeit und Unsterblichkeit im Alten Ägypten.* Munich, 1990. Essential reading for serious students of ancient Egypt's religion; chapter 5 deals with the Osirian judgment of the dead.

Begelsbacher-Fischer, Barbara. *Untersuchungen zur Götterwelt des Alten Reiches im Spiegel der Privatgräber der IV, und V. Dynastie.* Orbis biblicus orientalis, 37. Freiburg, 1981. A careful survey of the evidence from private tombs of the fourth and fifth dynasties.

Beinlich, Horst. "Zur Deutung der Sogenannten Osirisreliquien." *Göttinger Miszellen* 54 (1982), 17–29.

Beinlich, Horst. "Osiris in Byblos." *Die Welt des Orients* 14 (1983), 63–66.

Beinlich, Horst. *Die 'Osirisreliquien': Zum Motiv der Körperzergliederung in der altägyptischen Religion.* Ägyptologische Abhandlungen, 42. Wiesbaden, 1984.

Beinlich, Horst. "Reliquie." In *Lexikon der Ägyptologie,* 5: 230–231. Wiesbaden, 1984.

Brunner, Hellmut. "Osiris in Byblos." *Revue de l'Égyptologie* 27 (1975), 37–40. Argues for the antiquity of Plutarch's episode on the arrival in Byblos of the chest with the dead body of Osiris.

Brunner-Traut, Emma. *Gelebte Mythen.* 3d ed., rev. & enl. Darmstadt, 1988. Varied and selected essays; outstanding is the fourth, comparing Egyptian and Christian ideas on heaven and hell, judgment, and resurrection.

David, Rosalie A. *A Guide to Religious Ritual at Abydos.* rev. ed. Warminster, 1981. See chapter 6, "The Osiris Complex."

Duquesne, Terence. *At the Court of Osiris: Book of the Dead, Spell 194: A Rare Egyptian Judgement Text.* Oxfordshire Communications in Egyptology, 4. London, 1994. Mainly concerned with the judicial role of Anubis.

Eaton-Krauss, Marianne. "The Earliest Representation of Osiris." *Varia Aegyptiaca* 3 (1987), 233–236.

Erman, Adolf. "Zum Namen des Osiris," *Zeitschrift für Ägyptische Sprache und Altertumskunde* 46 (1909), 92–95.

Griffiths, John Gwyn. "Osiris and the Moon in Iconography." *Journal of Egyptian Archaeology* 62 (1976), 153–159.

Griffiths, John Gwyn. *The Origins of Osiris and His Cult.* Studies in the History of Religions, 40. Leiden, 1980.

Griffiths, John Gwyn. "Osiris." In *Lexikon der Ägyptologie,* 4: 623–633. Wiesbaden, 1982.

Griffiths, John Gwyn. *The Divine Verdict: A Study of Divine Judgement in the Ancient Religions.* Studies in the History of Religions, 52. Leiden, 1991. Offers a study of divine judgment in the ancient religions, with particular attention to Egypt, Israel, Iran; and Christianity, including their possible interactions.

Griffiths, John Gwyn. *Triads and Trinity.* Cardiff, 1996.

Heerma van Voss, Matthieu. *Anoebis en de Demonen.* Leiden, 1978. A perceptive study of part of a papyrus in Leiden that contains a twenty-first dynasty version of extracts from the *Book of Going Forth by Day.*

Helck, Wolfgang. "Osiris." *Paulys Realencyclopädie der Classischen Altertumswissenschaften,* edited by George Wissowa, suppl. 9: 469–514. Stuttgart, 1962.

Helck, Wolfgang. "Zu Klaus Kuhlmann, Zur Etymologie des Götternamens Osiris." *Studien zur Altägyptischen Kultur* 4 (1976), 121–124.

Hornung, Erik. *Conceptions of God in Ancient Egypt.* Translated from the German by John Baines. London, 1983.

Kákosy, Lázló. "Osiris-Aion." *Oriens Antiquus* 3 (1964), 15–25.

Kákosy, Lázló. "Osiris als Gott des Kampfes und der Rache." In *Fragen an die altägyptische Literatur: Studien zum Gedenken an Eberhard Otto,* edited by Jan Assmann, et al., pp. 285–288. Wiesbaden, 1977.

Kákosy, Lázló. "Probleme der Ägyptischen Jenseitsvorstellungen in der Ptolemäer und Kaiserzeit." In *Selected Papers (1956–1973),* pp. 195–205. Studia Aegyptiaca, 7. Budapest, 1981. Analysis of the changing trends in the Greco-Roman era, with astral immortality taking priority and Osiris-Orion aiding the ascent of the soul through the heavenly spheres.

Kákosy, Lázló. *Selected Papers (1956–1973).* Studia Aegyptiaca, 7. Budapest, 1981.

Kákosy, Lázló. "Selige und Verdammte in der spätägyptischen Religion." In *Selected Papers (1956–1973),* pp. 227–237. Studia Aegyptiaca, 7. Budapest, 1981.

Leclant, Jean, and Gisèle Clerc. *Inventaire bibliographique des Isaica.* 4 vols. Etudes préliminaires aux religions orientales dans l'Empire Romain, 18. Leiden, 1972–1991.

Lloyd, Alan B. *Herodotus, Book II.* 3 vols. Etudes préliminaires aux religions orientales dans l'Empire Romain, 43. Leiden, 1975–1988.

Lorton, David. "Considerations on the Origin and Name of Osiris." *Varia Aegyptiaca* 1 (1985), 113–126.

Meeks, Dimitri, and Christine Favard-Meeks. *Daily Life of the Egyptian Gods.* Translated from the French by G. M. Goshgarian. London, 1997. A lively and engaging study.

Morenz, Siegfried. "Das Problem des Werdens zu Osiris in der griechisch-römischen Zeit Ägyptens." In *Religions en Égypte hellénistique et romaine,* colloque de Strasbourg, 16–18 May 1967, pp. 75–91. Paris, 1969. He wisely avoids the idea of an *unio mystica.*

Otto, Eberhard. *Egyptian Art and the Cults of Osiris and Amon.* Translated from the German by Kate Bosse-Griffiths. London, 1968. An admirable study of the cults at Abydos and Thebes. Osiris is said to embody the "chthonic power of fertility" in the forms of a "male being" (p. 24).

Redford, Donald B. *Akhenaton, the Heretic King.* Princeton, 1984; reprint 1987. Incisively emphasizes the rejection of Osirianism by this religious revolutionary.

Redford, Donald B. *Egypt, Canaan, and Israel in Ancient Times.* Princeton, 1992.

Silverman, David P. "Textual Criticism in the Coffin Texts." In *Religion and Philosophy in Ancient Egypt,* by James Allen, et al., pp. 29–53. Yale Egyptological Studies, 3. New Haven, 1989. Ably encompasses wider themes than that of the title.

Silverman, David P. "Divinity and Deities in Ancient Egypt." In *Religion in Ancient Egypt,* edited by Byron E. Shafer, pp. 7–87. London, 1991.

Tooley, Angela M. J. "Osiris Bricks." *Journal of Egyptian Archaeology* 82 (1996), 167–179.

Vernus, Pascal. "Le Mythe d'une Mythe: le prétendue noyade d'Osiris." *Studi di Egittologia e di antichità Puniche* 9 (1991), 19–32.

J. GWYN GRIFFITHS

OSORKON, a name of Libyan origin given to five kings of ancient Egypt and several high dignitaries.

Osorkon the Elder (r. 990–984 BCE) was the fifth king of the twenty-first dynasty known by Manetho's reference to a king as Osochor. He was son of the Libyan chief of the Meshwesh, Sheshonq A, by Lady Mehtenweskhet A, and hence uncle to the future Sheshonq I, founder of the fully Libyan twenty-second dynasty. Only one damaged text, from the Karnak temple at Thebes, has been found from Osorkon/Osochor's reign.

Osorkon I, born of Karamat A to Sheshonq I, was the second king of the twenty-second dynasty; he reigned from 924 to 889 BCE, based on the existence of tabs on a mummy that mention Years 33 (Osorkon I?) and 3 (Sheshonq II or Takeloth I?). His family relationships, the sequences of generations of Theban priests within his reign, and the probability of his having celebrated two jubilees (normally held in a king's thirtieth and thirty-third regnal years) tabulate as a reign of thirty-five years rather than the fifteen years ascribed by Manetho. In Thebes, Osorkon I appointed his own eldest son, Sheshonq (II), as high priest of Amun and as military governor of Upper Egypt. Osorkon I added a court and pillared hall to the goddess Bastet's temple in Bubastis, as well as a new temple for Atum, with a long inscription celebrating in detail the enormous gifts (over 370 tons of silver and gold) given to the deities of Egypt in his first four years of reign. He built at Memphis, Atfih, and El-Hibeh, and he continued work on his father's forecourt at Karnak in Thebes. He also founded a fortress at the entry to the Faiyum. He maintained relations with Byblos, whose king, Elibaal, added his own inscription to a statue sent by Osorkon.

Osorkon II, born of Kapes to Takeloth I, reigned as fifth king of the twenty-second dynasty. He added a forecourt to the temple of Amun at Tanis, and a small temple behind it. At Bubastis, he later added a festival gateway in honor of the royal jubilee festival of the twenty-fourth year of his reign. Other traces of his activities occur at Memphis and at the Karnak temple in Thebes, where he appointed a high priest, Harsiese A, who took royal titles. Abroad, Osorkon II sent a statue to Byblos in Phoenicia; he also made an alliance with Levantine states (including Israel, judging from a vase found at Samaria) to ward off Assyria, sending one thousand troops to the Battle of Qarqar in 853 BCE.

Osorkon III, born of Kama(ma) F, was the second king of the twenty-third dynasty. He reigned for thirty-eight years (783–745 BCE); his son Takeloth III was co-regent for five years (c.764–759 BCE). His mother may have been Queen Kama(ma), who was buried at Tell Moqdam (Leontopolis). His daughter, Shepenupet I, became God's Wife of Amun in Thebes.

Osorkon IV, born of Tadibast, was the last king of the twenty-third dynasty and was based in Bubastis and the Tanis district. He submitted to the Kushite conqueror Piankhy around 728 BCE. He was probably the "So, king of Egypt" from whom the Israelite king Hoshea sought help against Assyria in 726–725 BCE (*2 Kings* 17.4); some would read this passage "to Sais, [city], [to] the king of Egypt," but this involves emending the text. In 720 BCE, Osorkon IV probably sent the commander Re'e to help Hanun of Gaza against Sargon II of Assyria, who defeated them. Thus, in 716 BCE, when Sargon penetrated the northern Sinai, Osorkon (named as "(U)shikanni") quickly sent him a propitiatory present.

The name Osorkon also occurs in the historical record as that of elite persons who were not kings, as follows:

Osorkon A, high priest of Ptah at Memphis, c.895–870 BCE; last of nine generations.

Osorkon B, or Prince Osorkon, son and heir of Takeloth II, held (or later, claimed) office as high priest of Amun of Thebes from year 11 of Takeloth II to year 39 of Sheshonq III, c. 840–787 BCE, a total of at least fifty-three years. From year 15 of Takeloth II, the Thebans rebelled, appointing their own high priests; Prince Osorkon also lost the throne to Sheshonq III.

Osorkon C, Libyan "chief of the Meshwesh" at Sais in the Delta, c. 750 BCE, probably the direct predecessor of Tefnakht; he held much of the western Delta.

Osorkon D, ordinary priest of Amun, c. 900 BCE, son of the high priest Sheshonq (II).

Osorkon E, a priest of Ptah in Memphis, c. 830 BCE, grandson of Osorkon A.

Osorkon, F, son of Takeloth III and high priest of Amun in Thebes, c. 754–734 BCE.

Osorkon [G], seventeenth son of the Theban high priest Herihor, c. 1080 BCE.

BIBLIOGRAPHY

Caminos, Ricardo A. *The Chronicle of Prince Osorkon*. Rome, 1958.

Kitchen, Kenneth A. *The Third Intermediate Period in Egypt (1100–650 BC)*. 2d ed. with suppl. Warminster, 1996. Includes all the Osorkons with data, and the course of scholars' discussions about them to 1995.

Young, Eric E. *Journal of the American Research Center in Egypt* 2 (1963), 100–101. Identifies the only certain inscription so far known of Osorkon/Osochor.

Yoyotte, Jean. "Le talisman de la victoire d'Osorkon, Prince de Saïs et autres lieux." *Bulletin de la Société Française d'Égyptologie* 31 (1960), 13–22.

Yoyotte, Jean. "Les principautés du Delta au temps de l'anarchie libyenne." In *Mélanges Maspero*, vol. 1: *Orient Ancient*, pp. 121–181. Memoires publies par les membres d'l'Institut Français d'archéologie orientale du Caire, 66. Cairo, 1961.

KENNETH A. KITCHEN

OSTRACA. The plural in English usage of the ancient Greek word *ostracon* (οστρακον), which means "an earthen vessel, a fragment of such a vessel, a potsherd." The Greek use of ostraca, or potsherds, in casting ballots for banishment or exile provides the basis for the derivation of the English word "ostracize." In the specialized terminology used by Egyptologists, the words "ostracon" and "ostraca" refer not only to potsherds but also, by extension, to chips of limestone used as surfaces on which to write or draw. The employment of such materials by scribes and artists grew out of the natural desire to economize on more costly papyrus for certain forms of documentation that were considered of lesser importance. For the scribe and the artist, the substitution of broken pottery fragments or flakes of limestone was an obvious choice, since both were available in great abundance in ancient Egypt. The pottery fragments were the result of normal breakage, and the limestone fragments were a by-product of building operations, particularly the excavation of tombs in the cliffs near Thebes. Both materials seem unlikely choices, but the usual curve of the pottery fragment does not appear to have been a hindrance to its use as a writing surface, and the limestone often flakes into regular, flat planes. Since both materials are relatively resistant to destruction, a considerable amount of documentary evidence for the history of Egypt and Egyptian art has come down to us in the form of ostraca.

The reed pen was generally employed as a writing instrument, with an ink made of carbon or lampblack and red ocher for the two principle colors of red and black. The form of writing used on ostraca was either Hieratic or Demotic Egyptian, two cursive forms of hieroglyphic script that were employed for almost all uses except formal inscriptions. Hieratic, or "priestly," script appears as early as the Old Kingdom; it is an adaptation of hieroglyphs to the more natural forms created by the reed pen. Demotic, or "popular," writing came into use in the Late period as a more rapidly written form of Hieratic; in the Ptolemaic and Roman periods, it was the form of writing in common use. Coptic, the last developed form of the ancient Egyptian language, was written with the Greek alphabet plus seven additional characters used to express sounds not found in Greek. Texts in both Greek and Coptic appear on ostraca in later times.

Ostraca in the form of potsherds should not be confused with documents that are identified in the literature as "jar dockets." Often a description or label of the contents of a jar was inscribed in ink on the exterior, usually on the shoulder. These can sometimes be useful for the archaeologist and historian because they may also include a date, particularly a regnal date associated with a particular ruler. These are not ostraca in the strict sense,

but chance fragments of labels found on surviving parts of the original containers. Examples of jar dockets found on complete vessels include the descriptive labels on a number of wine jars discovered in the tomb of Tutankhamun, which give information on the vineyard and the vintage year, much like modern wine labels. Even if these had been found on pottery fragments rather than on the complete vessels, they would still have been recognized as not being "ostraca" in the strict Egyptological sense of the word.

Literary Texts. An important part of the education of student scribes was the imitation of classic literary examples. They gained skill and learned their trade by copying excerpts from texts in accepted literary styles or of acknowledged importance and traditional value. Ostraca provided a cheap, abundant, and easily accessible material for the student, and as a result, a number of literary texts, either whole or in part, have been preserved through student copies in this form. Although most of the preserved examples are excerpts, which number in the hundreds, one of the longest of these documents is an almost complete text of the Middle Kingdom *Story of Sinuhe*, written on a single large ostracon (now in the collection of the Ashmolean Museum at Oxford). Even student exercise pieces that contain only a portion of a copied literary text can prove valuable. They may furnish alternative versions, or provide some elements or parts of a text that can be used to fill in gaps in other examples that have suffered loss or damage. This is particularly true when other surviving examples of literary texts are written on fragile papyri, always subject to deterioration and particularly to the loss of the beginning or end of a scroll.

Archival Documents. A great deal of information and evidence for the details of daily life in ancient Egypt has come down to us in the form of ostraca. The use of ostraca for documents of various kinds is amply attested by the numerous finds of such material in several workers' villages, particularly the one at Deir el-Medina in the foothills of Western Thebes. Preserved examples from this site include correspondence, official reports, lists that detail the composition of work gangs, work schedules, pay rosters, and lists of food rations. Legal documents such as memoranda, contracts of various kinds—including marriage agreements, deeds, and wills—are also preserved in this form. Such day-to-day documentation provides invaluable evidence for a social history of the laborers, craftsmen, and supervisors who excavated and decorated the royal tombs in the Valley of the Kings. By extension, this "archive" of material, exhaustively preserved from one village, can be used to postulate the structure of similar societal situations.

Ritual Objects. Actual ritual or devotional objects are occasionally preserved on ostraca, particularly on larger limestone chips. These include crude dedicatory stelae, letters to the dead, and offering lists or prayers. These may not be preparatory studies or drafts for a more finished or complete object but, rather, evidence of a pious act or wish of a draftsman or other craftsman. They are finished in ink and rarely carved, and are meant to be complete in themselves.

Figural Ostraca. The abundant figural ostraca found at Deir el-Medina and in the Valley of the Kings give considerable insight into the working methods of the artist-craftsmen employed in the preparation of tomb decoration. Often a single piece may have the same design element repeated several times, suggesting an attempt to perfect the rendering of a hieroglyph or part of a figure. This is particularly true of elements considered difficult to draw, such as the quail chick with its subtle contour or the owl with its frontal face, both complex hieroglyphs to capture accurately. Some drawings have a squared grid imposed on the design, indicating that they were meant to be enlarged as a part of a wall decoration. Others include some standard element, such as the open hand or closed fist, to indicate the standard measurement of a part. Still others suggest a kind of *aide-mémoire* for the delineation of an element that would have been repeated in a wall decoration, such as the ruler's profile, the arrangement of the signs in a cartouche, or some decorative device.

The training of the artist is presumed to have been based on a workshop and apprenticeship system. No manuals or books of instruction have been preserved, probably because it was not considered necessary to commit to writing the information that was passed on orally from master to student. Because of the relatively indestructible nature of the material, many ostraca preserve important evidence for the understanding of artistic training and methods that would otherwise be unknown to us. These include examples of trials, sketches, and practice pieces, as well as layout drawings that were meant to be expanded and duplicated on a larger scale. From an examination of a number of the figured ostraca, it can be demonstrated that the beginning draftsman studied and copied the work of a master. Annotations or corrections can be seen to have been made at times by a more experienced hand, probably in the process of teaching, just as instructors in draftsmanship have always corrected the work of students through history.

Architectural elevations and plans are not preserved in great number, but some exist on ostraca to supplement the few that have been found on papyrus. One large stone chip in the Cairo Museum bears the layout of an identifiable royal tomb. Other architectural drawings are of details, such as single columns or the façade of a shrine; in one instance, an arch with written measurements of its arc attests to the calculation involved. Some layout drawings for the ground plans of houses and gardens have also been preserved. As sketchy as some of these appear, the drawings, with occasional notations of measurement, still give some indication of the working methods of Egyptian architects and builders.

A distinct class of figural ostraca illustrates fable-like situations in which unlikely combinations of humans and animals appear in curious contexts. The cat may act as the herdsman for geese, or as nursemaid for a baby mouse, or human children may be punished by animals who conduct themselves as overseers. These so-called satirical drawings are in all probability the illustrations for moral tales, either totally lost to history or never committed to writing and transmitted by the Egyptians orally. There are also a limited number of caricatures and erotic illustrations, but these are very much in the minority, probably because they were less often preserved.

To the casual modern viewer who has experienced only the most formal of Egyptian art forms, Egyptian art may seem a static and lifeless artistic expression. The immediacy of the ancient drawings preserved on ostraca exerts a tremendous appeal on the viewer who is given, through this medium, a brief glimpse into the creative act that was a part of an otherwise highly stylized and proscribed structure. Since all forms of Egyptian art were based in linear abstraction, the insights to be gained through a study of the art of drawing are even more valuable because they provide us with many of the preparatory stages in the development of finished objects in every medium.

BIBLIOGRAPHY

Barnes, J. W. *The Ashmolean Ostraca of Sinuhe.* Oxford, 1952.

Brunner-Traut, E. *Egyptian Artists' Sketches: Figured Ostraca From the Gayer-Anderson Collection at the Fitzwilliam Museum.* Cambridge, 1979.

Carter, H. and A. H. Gardiner. "The Tomb of Ramesses IV and the Turin Plan of a Royal Tomb." *Journal of Egyptian Archaeology* 4 (1917), 130–158.

Černý, Jaroslav. *Catalogue des ostraca hiératiques non littéraires de Deir el-Medineh.* 7 vols. Cairo, 1935–1970.

Daressy, G. *Ostraca, Catalogue général des antiquites egyptiennes du musée du Caire: no. 25001–25385.* Cairo, 1901.

Peck, W. H. *Drawings from Ancient Egypt.* London, 1978.

Posener, G. *Catalogue des ostraca hiératiques littéraires de Deir el-Medineh.* Cairo, 1972.

Vandier d'Abbadie, J. *Catalogue des ostraca figurés de Deir el-Medineh.* 4 vols. Cairo, 1937–1946.

WILLIAM H. PECK

OVERSEER OF PRIESTS. *See* Administration, *article on* Temple Administration.

OXYRHYNCHUS, a town in Middle Egypt, on the western bank of the Bahr Yusuf (28°32'N, 30°40'E). Oxyrhynchus was called *Pr-mḏd* in ancient Egyptian; in Coptic, Pemdje; and in Arabic, al-Bahnasa. It has become best known for the extensive papyrus finds from the Greco-Roman period. First attested in the New Kingdom, little is known about this town until the later Third Intermediate Period and the Saite dynasty, when it was described as the capital of the nineteenth Upper Egyptian nome. In the Late period, both the town and its district came to be identified with the fish of the genus *Oxyrhynchus*, which was revered there. The town increased in importance as an administrative and cultural center during the Greco-Roman period, eventually becoming the capital of the late Roman province of Arcadia; it was, for a time after the division of the empire, known as Justinianopolis, after Justinian (483–565 CE), the Byzantine emperor. The activities of the population of Roman and late antique Oxyrhynchus have become known from the thousands of papyri found at the site. Oxyrhynchus continued to exist well after the Muslim conquest of the seventh century CE, had already begun to decline by then, and the site was abandoned by the Mamluk period.

Although Oxyrhynchus was an important city and a district capital, little of the town itself has survived. Papyri attest to many features of the layout and topography of Oxyrhynchus: public buildings, gymnasia, the theater, temples (and later churches), baths, and residential structures are frequently mentioned, and individual quarters and even streets are named. Little of this information can be matched, however, with the archaeological remains. When formal excavation of the site began at the end of the nineteenth century, most of the stone buildings had long since been plundered for reuse, while the activities of *sebakh*-diggers and antiquities hunters had turned the extensive quarters of mud-brick structures into a confused mound of rubble. Excavators concentrated primarily on the recovery of papyri from the rubbish dumps and debris of the site. The earliest excavations were carried out in 1897 by Bernard P. Grenfell and Arthur S. Hunt for the Greco-Roman Branch of the Egypt Exploration Fund (now Society) in London; this first season led to the discovery of thousands of papyri, and Grenfell and Hunt continued their excavations at Oxyrhynchus from 1903 through 1907. Oxyrhynchus was subsequently excavated by Guilio Farina for the Società per la Ricerca dei Papiri, from 1910 to 1913, and later by Evaristo Breccia from 1927 through 1934 for the same institution, resulting in additional papyrus finds. William Matthew Flinders Petrie worked at the site in 1922, in the Late Roman-era cemeteries and in the Roman theater. Both British and Italian excavators at Oxyrhynchus made notes on surviving archaeological remains, but much of their work has re-

mained unpublished. Extensive digging at the site by local inhabitants, however, has yielded papyri and other artifacts, including the series of life-size funerary statues of the late Roman period now in the Rijksmusem van Oudheden, in Leiden, the Netherlands. Although active excavation is no longer being carried out on the site, the Greco-Roman Branch of the Egypt Exploration Society has continued to publish papyri from its excavations, and plans are underway for a special publication to mark the hundredth anniversary of British work at Oxyrhynchus.

In terms of textual evidence, Oxyrhynchus is perhaps the best-documented site of Greco-Roman Egypt, because of the enormous numbers of papyri excavated there. British and Italian excavations at Oxyrhynchus unearthed several thousand papyri (as well as texts on other mediums), mostly written in Greek, but also in Latin, Coptic, Demotic, and Arabic. The Oxyrhynchus papyri range in date from the Ptolemaic through Early Islamic periods, but the majority come from the Roman period and present an unusually complete record of the culture, society, and economy of the town. The archaeological contexts of the Oxyrhynchus papyri are known in a general way: most of the papyri from the British excavations were found in ancient rubbish dumps, while papyri from the Italian excavations came from the town itself. The papyri have been the object of extensive publication efforts: Greek and Latin texts from the British excavations have regularly appeared in the series *The Oxyrhynchus Papyri*, from 1898 to the present; papyri from the Italian excavations were published in fifteen volumes as *Papiri greci e latini*, from 1912 to 1979. In addition, hundreds of Oxyrhynchus papyri in Greek have been published individually in monographs and journal articles; the Demotic, Coptic, and Arabic papyri found during the British and Italian excavations, however, remain largely unpublished.

The contents of the Oxyrhynchus papyri span an enormous range of literary and nonliterary texts. The British excavations initially concentrated on the discovery of Greek literary papyri; in addition to known Greek literature, the Oxyrhynchus papyri have yielded hundreds of fragments of "new" Greek texts by known authors, along with anonymous poems, plays, orations, grammars, and scholia. They also included, in Greek, fragments of numerous philosophical, rhetorical, and historical compositions; there were as well scientific, astronomical, astrological, mathematical, medical, and magical texts. In Greek, with a smaller (but significant) number in Latin, documentary texts included official documents, legal contracts, wills, accounts, lists, private letters; the majority of these were of Roman date. Papyri from the Roman period also documented the importance of both Egyptian and Hellenistic cults at Oxyrhynchus, and they attested to a significant Jewish presence. Many important early Christian texts came from Oxyrhynchus, including fragments of biblical manuscripts, hymns, and documentary texts. Documentary texts from the later periods have attested to a localized system of dating—the so-called eras of Oxyrhynchus. An important archive of Byzantine period papyri from Oxyrhynchus are the papers of the Apion family, documents pertaining to the running of a large estate in late antique Egypt. Demotic, Coptic, and Arabic papyri from Oxyrhynchus include documentary, literary, and magical texts.

BIBLIOGRAPHY

Grenfell, Bernard P., and Arthur S. Hunt et al., eds. *The Oxyrhynchus Papyri. Graeco-Roman Memoirs.* London, 1898- present. Ongoing series (65 volumes to date) of Greek and Latin papyri from the British excavations; descriptions, text, and critical apparatus provided for most papyri, as well as an English translation.

Krüger, Julian. *Oxyrhynchos in der Kaiserzeit: Studien zur Topographie und Literaturrezeption.* Frankfurt a. M., 1990. Two unrelated studies of the topography of Roman Oxyrhynchus and the role of literature in the intellectual life there; useful but incomplete and with little synthesis of the extensive material for both subjects.

Montserrat, Dominic. "Oxyrhynchus." In *The Dictionary of Art,* edited by Jane Turner, vol. 23, pp. 692–693. New York, 1996. Useful summary with bibliography.

Petrie, W. M. Flinders. *The Tombs of the Courtiers and Oxyrhynkos.* London, 1925. Publication of Flinders Petrie's work at the site.

Rowlandson, Jane. *Landowners and Tenants in Roman Egypt: The Social Relations of Agriculture in the Oxyrhynchite Nome.* Oxford, 1996. Study of agriculture and social relations in Oxyrhynchus and environs; important work for agriculture of Roman Egypt in general.

Schneider, Hans D. *Beelden van Behnasa: Egyptische kunst uit de Romeinse keisertijd 1e-3e eeuw na Chr.* Zutphen, 1982. Publication of the funerary sculptures from the Oxyrhynchus cemeteries; also contains archival views of the site.

Turner, Eric. "The Graeco-Roman Branch." In *Excavating in Egypt: The Egypt Exploration Society, 1882–1982,* edited by T. G. H. James, pp. 160–178. Chicago, 1982. Detailed survey of the British activities at Oxyrhynchus.

Turner, Eric. "Roman Oxyrhynchus." *Journal of Egyptian Archaeology* 38 (1952), 78–93. Excellent survey of what was known in 1952 of the layout of Oxyrhynchus and its intellectual life; still extremely useful and interesting reading.

TERRY G. WILFONG

EGYPTIAN KING LIST

Mesolithic Period (8500–5500 BCE)

PREDYNASTIC PERIOD

Neolithic Period (5500–3100 BCE)

Badarian	5500–4000 BCE
Amratian (Naqada I)	4000–3500 BCE
Gerzean (Naqada II)	3500–3150 BCE

Dynasty "0"

["Uj" occupant]	c.3150 BCE
Iry-Hor (?)	
Ka	c.3100–3050
"Scorpion"	

EARLY DYNASTIC PERIOD

First Dynasty (Thinite)

Narmer; Aha; Djer; Wadji;	c.3050–2850
Den; Enedjib; Semsem; Ka'a	

Second Dynasty (Thinite)

Hotepsekhemwy	c.2850–2820
Ranebi	c.2820–2790
Ninuter	c.2790–2754
Wadjnas	c.2754–2734
Senedy	
Peribsen	c.2734–2714
Khasekhemwy	c.2714–2687

OLD KINGDOM

Third Dynasty

Djoser	c.2687–2668
Nebka	c.2688–2682
Sekhemkhet	?
Khaba	?
Neferkare	c.2679–2673
Huny (?)	c.2673–2649

Fourth Dynasty

Sneferu	c.2649–2609
Khufu	c.2609–2584
Djedefre	c.2584–2576
Khafre	c.2576–2551
Menkaure	c.2551–2523
Shepseskaf	c.2523–2519
[2 unknown kings]	c.2519–2513

Fifth Dynasty

Userkaf	c.2513–2506
Sahure	c.2506–2492
Neferirkare Kakai	c.2492–2482
Shepseskare	c.2482–2475
Raneferef	c.2475–2474
Newoserre Any	c.2474–2444
Menkauhor	c.2444–2436
Djedkare Izezi	c.2436–2404
Unas	c.2404–2374

Sixth Dynasty

Teti	c.2374–2354
Userkare	?
Pepy I	c.2354–2310
Merenre Antyemsaf	c.2310–2300
Neferkare Pepy II	c.2300–2206
[Antyemsaf] II	c.2206
Nitokerty (Nitocris)	c.2205–2200
Neferka the child	[c.2200–2199]

Nefer	c.2199–2197
Aba	c.2197–2193
[. . .]	c. 2193–2191
[. . .]	c.2191

FIRST INTERMEDIATE PERIOD

Seventh Dynasty

Numerous ephemeral kings

Eighth Dynasty

"18 kings"		c.2190–2165
Merenre Anty-emsaf II (sic)	Ny-kare	
	Neferkare Terer	
Neterkare	Neferkahor	
Menkare	Neferkare	
Neferkare	Pepysonby	
Neferkare Neby	Sneferka-'anu	
Djedkare Shemay	Kakaure	
Neferkare Khenedy	Neferkaure	
Merenhor	Neferkauhor	
Sneferka	Neferirkare II	

Ninth and Tenth Dynasties (Herakleopolitan)

"18 kings"		c.2165–2040
Akhtoy I	Shed[. . .]	
. . .	Hu-[. . .]	
Neferkare	[6 kings]	
Akhtoy II	Akhtoy III	
Seneni (?)	Merikare	
. . .	. . .	
Mer[. . .]		

Early Eleventh Dynasty (Theban)

Antef I	2134–2118
Antef II	2118–2068
Antef III	2068–2061

MIDDLE KINGDOM

Late Eleventh Dynasty (All Egypt)

Nebhepetre Montuhotep I Se'ankhibtowy	2061–2011
Montuhotep II	2011–2000
Nebtowyre Montuhotep III	2000–1998
(Civil Strife 1998–1991)	

Twelfth Dynasty

Amenemhet I	1991–1962
Senwosret I	1971–1928
Amenemhet II	1929–1895
Senwosret II	1897–1877
Senwosret III	1878–1843
Amenemhet III	1843–1797
Amenemhet IV	1798–1790
Sobekneferu	1790–1786

Thirteenth and Fourteenth Dynasties

Khutowyre Sobekhotpe I	1786–1763
Sekhemkare Amenemhet-sonbef	1783–1780
(13 kings)	1780–1760
[. . .]	
Sekhemkare Amenemhet	
Sehtepibre	
Afni	
Seonkhibre Ameny-intef-Amenemhat	
Smenkare	

Sehtepibre Qemau si-Harendotes	
Sewadj-kare	
Nodjemibre	
Sobekhotep I	
Rensonbe	
Awibre Hor	
Sedjefakare Qay-Amenemhat	
Sobekhotpe II	1750–1756
Khendjer	1756–1751
(3 kings) [. . .]	1751–1749
Sekhemkare Sobekhotpe III	1749–1747
Khasekhemre Neferhotpe I	1747–1736
Sihathor	1735
Khaneferre Sobekhotpe IV	1734–1725
Khahetepre Sobekhotpe V	1725–1721
Wahibre Ya'ib	1721–1712
Merneferre Aya	1712–1700
Merhotepre An	1700–1698
Se'ankhenre Sewadjtu	1698–1695
Mersekhemre Neferhotpe	1695–1692
Sewadjkare Hori	1691
Merkare Sobekhotpe VI	1690–1688
(14 kings)	1688–c.1665
Merkheperre	Djedkherure
[3 or 4 kings]	Seonkhibre
Nehesy	Nefertumre
Khatire	Sekhem[. . .]re
Nebawre	Ka[. . .]re Kem
Sehebre	Neferibre
Merdjefare	[. . .]
Sewadjkare	Kha[. . .]re
Nebjefare	Akare
Webenre	Semen[. . .]re
[3 kings]	Djed[. . .]re
Awibre	[6 kings]
Heribre	Seneferre
Nebseure	Men[. . .]re
[. . .]	Djed[. . .]
Sekheperenre	

SECOND INTERMEDIATE PERIOD

Fifteenth Dynasty (Hyksos)

Maa-ibre Sheshy	c.1664–1662
Mer-userre Ya'akob-har	c.1662–1653
Seuserenre Khayan	c.1653–1614
[. . .] Yansas-adoen	c.1614–1605
Aa-woserre Apophis	c.1605–1565
[. . .] Hamudi	c.1565–1555

Early Sixteenth Dynasty (Hyksos)

22 kings+ 65+ years	c.1665–1600

Late Seventeenth Dynasty (Theban)

Sekenenre Ta'o	c.1600–1571
Senakhtenre Ta'o	
Kamose	c.1571–1569

NEW KINGDOM

Eighteenth Dynasty

Ahmose	c.1569–1545
Amenhotpe I	c.1545–1525
Thutmose I	c.1525–1516
Thutmose II	c.1516–1504
Thutmose III	1504–1452
Hatshepsut	1502–1482
Amenhotpe II	1454–1419
Thutmose IV	1419–1410